# ESSENTIAL FAMILY PRACTICE 2002

# ESSENTIAL FAMILY PRACTICE 2002

## VOLUME 1
## FINANCE


*Consulting Editor*
**Mr Justice Peter Singer**

*General Editors*
**Stephen Wildblood** QC
**Deborah Eaton** Barrister

*Contributors*
**Tim Amos** Barrister
**Nicholas Anderson** Barrister
**Nicholas Cusworth** Barrister
**David Davidson** Solicitor
**Charles Hyde** Barrister
**Daniel Leafe** Barrister
**Richard Todd** Barrister
**Stephen Trowell** Barrister
**Claire Wills-Goldingham** Barrister

**Butterworths**
London, Dublin and Edinburgh
2002

| | |
|---|---|
| United Kingdom | Butterworths, a Division of Reed Elsevier (UK) Ltd, Halsbury House, 35 Chancery Lane, LONDON WC2A 1EL and 4 Hill Street, EDINBURGH EH2 3JZ |
| Australia | Butterworths, a Division of Reed International Books Australia Pty Ltd, CHATSWOOD, New South Wales |
| Canada | Butterworths Canada Ltd, MARKHAM, Ontario |
| Hong Kong | Butterworths Asia (Hong Kong), HONG KONG |
| India | Butterworths India, NEW DELHI |
| Ireland | Butterworth (Ireland) Ltd, DUBLIN |
| Malaysia | Malayan Law Journal Sdn Bhd, KUALA LUMPUR |
| New Zealand | Butterworths of New Zealand Ltd, WELLINGTON |
| Singapore | Butterworths Asia, SINGAPORE |
| South Africa | Butterworths Publishers (Pty) Ltd, DURBAN |
| USA | Lexis Law Publishing, CHARLOTTESVILLE, Virginia |



A CIP Catalogue record for this book is available from the British Library.

**VOLUME 1**

ISBN 0-406-95690-1

9 780406 956903

**SET**

ISBN 0-406-95689-8

9 780406 956897

Typeset by Thomson Litho Ltd, East Kilbride, Scotland
Printed by The Bath Press, Bath

# FOREWORD TO EFP 2002

If I wish to remind myself that I am growing old, I remember that it is now 40 years since I was the new tenant in One Mitre Court Buildings. The young barristers' library in those days was in one sense narrow: for practice in the Probate, Divorce and Admiralty Division there was a choice between *Rayden* and *Latey on Divorce*. Neither was probably affordable. That hardly mattered since to survive to practice in the Division the young tenant spent years of apprenticeship in other fields where *Stone's Justices' Manual* and the *Green Book* answered all questions likely to be encountered. Such family work as came his way would be before the justices, who tried out issues of marital misconduct and fixed rates of maintenance for dependants.

How different is the life of the young tenant today. Specialist chambers, and specialist sections within chambers, abound. There is now the prospect of developing a specialist practice from the outset. But there is a bewildering choice in creating a specialist library. There are two series of specialist law reports. *Latey* has gone but the monumental, comprehensive and ever-dependable *Rayden* remains to beg or borrow if not to buy. Then there is a galaxy of titles tackling particular topics within the wider field. Why then should he or she choose *Essential Family Practice*? Because it is a succinct and portable guide, practically divided into two separate volumes. Furthermore, it is cross-referenced to ensure that where profounder research is required, its user is sign-posted on to the relevant section or paragraph in *Rayden*. Thus it justifies its title.

*The Rt Hon Lord Justice Thorpe*
21 March 2002

# FOREWORD TO EFP 2000

A family practitioner might be forgiven for asking—why publish another book on family law designed for practitioners and judges when the family law shelf already has several publications?

The answer is simple, as is the layout of this new venture. *Essential Family Practice* is designed to be user-friendly for those going to court on family cases as well as for those in court or in the office. It is in two volumes, one devoted to finance and the other to children. The enormous advantage is that each volume is eminently portable. Another advantage is the updating supplement that will be issued between the annual editions. The layout is innovative with the relevant statutory material easily identifiable, and the notes are helpful and commendably brief. It contains the case law, relevant directions and in the finance volume useful precedents. It is, as its title explains, intended to provide essential information for immediate reference and does not aspire to be encyclopaedic. It has distinguished consulting editors and a formidable team of contributors.

These volumes are in my view an essential part of the family law library and room for them ought to be found on the shelves of all family practitioners and judges who wish to keep up-to-date on finance and children.

*Elizabeth Butler-Sloss*
23 March 2000

# PREFACE

What does a practitioner need in court? Where should a practitioner turn when put on the spot by a client, an opponent or the judge? These were the questions we had in mind when devising this book and its companion volume on children.

The selection of our editorial and writing team was designed to ensure that these questions were considered from all angles: from the academic analysis to the humbler concept of making the work light in weight but not in content.

Whilst it was not possible to emblazon on the front cover, in large friendly letters, the words 'Don't Panic', as on the *Hitchhiker's Guide to the Galaxy*—a book which tells you everything you want to know about anything whilst travelling through the Universe—our aim is to attempt to offer the same service to practitioners in the family courts. We believe we have achieved this.

In the finance volume the text of the relevant statutes, rules and regulations is interspersed with explanatory notes as to both law and practice. Introductory chapters new to the 2002 edition are 'Injunctions in Financial Proceedings' and 'Cohabitees – Property Rights'. We have also made this edition even easier to navigate, enabling you to find the essential information you need in an instant. We trust that practitioners will find that all the materials they will need are thus presented in a thoughtful and imaginative way.

Our team of editors and contributors has made a commitment to updating this work on a regular basis. The annual editions will be complemented by a supplement distributed half way through each year revising the text in a succinct form. Thus we plan to achieve the most comprehensive and up-to-date exposition of the subject matter.

We are very grateful to District Judge Philip Waller, to the authors of *Clarke Hall & Morrison on Children* and to the editors of *Rayden and Jackson on Divorce and Family Matters* (17th edn) for their helpful advice and constructive criticism during the preparation of this work.

The law is stated as at 1 April 2002.

*Mr Justice Singer*
*Judith Parker QC*
*Stephen Wildblood QC*
*Deborah Eaton*
*Stephen Cobb*

# CONTENTS



**Volume 1**

**FINANCE**

**PART 1 – Introductory Chapters**



**PART 2 – Statutes**

# TABLE OF ABBREVIATIONS

| Abbreviation | Full Title |
| --- | --- |
| AA 1955 | Army Act 1955 |
| AA 1958 | Adoption Act 1958 |
| AA 1976 | Adoption Act 1976 |
| AEA 1925 | Administration of Estates Act 1925 |
| AFA 1955 | Air Force Act 1955 |
| A(IA)A 1999 | Adoption (Intercountry Aspects) Act 1999 |
| AJA 1876 | Appellate Jurisdiction Act 1876 |
| AJA 1920 | Administration of Justice Act 1920 |
| AJA 1960 | Administration of Justice Act 1960 |
| AJA 1969 | Administration of Justice Act 1969 |
| AJA 1970 | Administration of Justice Act 1970 |
| AJA 1982 | Administration of Justice Act 1982 |
| AJA 1999 | Access to Justice Act 1999 |
| A(S)A 1978 | Adoption (Scotland) Act 1978 |
| AtEA 1971 | Attachment of Earnings Act 1971 |
| BA 1990 | Broadcasting Act 1990 |
| BNA 1981 | British Nationality Act 1981 |
| CA 1989 | Companies Act 1989 |
| CAA 1984 | Child Abduction Act 1984 |
| CACA 1985 | Child Abduction and Custody Act 1985 |
| CCA 1981 | Contempt of Court Act 1981 |
| CCA 1984 | County Courts Act 1984 |
| CEA 1968 | Civil Evidence Act 1968 |
| CEA 1972 | Civil Evidence Act 1972 |
| CEA 1995 | Civil Evidence Act 1995 |
| ChA 1989 | Children Act 1989 |
| CJA 1982 | Criminal Justice Act 1982 |
| CJA 1991 | Criminal Justice Act 1991 |
| CJA 1994 | Criminal Justice Act 1994 |
| CJCSA 2000 | Criminal Justice and Court Services Act 2000 |
| CJJA 1982 | Civil Jurisdiction and Judgments Act 1982 |
| CLSA 1990 | Courts and Legal Services Act 1990 |
| COA 1979 | Charging Orders Act 1979 |
| CPA 1947 | Crown Proceedings Act 1947 |
| CPA 1997 | Civil Procedure Act 1997 |
| CSA 1991 | Child Support Act 1991 |
| CSA 1995 | Child Support Act 1995 |
| CSPSSA 2000 | Child Support, Pensions and Social Security Act 2000 |
| CYPA 1933 | Children and Young Persons Act 1933 |
| CYPA 1963 | Children and Young Persons Act 1963 |
| CYPA 1969 | Children and Young Persons Act 1969 |
| DA 1869 | Debtors Act 1869 |
| DAP(RP)A 1968 | Domestic and Appellate Proceedings (Restriction of Publicity) Act 1968 |
| DMPA 1973 | Domicile and Matrimonial Proceedings Act 1973 |
| DPA 1964 | Diplomatic Privileges Act 1964 |
| DPMCA 1978 | Domestic Proceedings and Magistrates' Courts Act 1978 |
| DVMPA 1976 | Domestic Violence and Matrimonial Proceedings Act 1976 |

EA 1996 ........ Education Act 1996
FA 1986 ........ Finance Act 1986
FA 1989 ........ Finance Act 1989
FJ(RE)A 1933 ........ Foreign Judgments (Reciprocal Enforcement) Act 1933
FLA 1986 ........ Family Law Act 1986
FLA 1996 ........ Family Law Act 1996
FLRA 1969 ........ Family Law Reform Act 1969
FLRA 1987 ........ Family Law Reform Act 1987
FL(S)A 1985 ........ Family Law (Scotland) Act 1985
FoA 1982 ........ Forfeiture Act 1982
HA 1985 ........ Housing Act 1985
HA 1988 ........ Housing Act 1988
HA 1996 ........ Housing Act 1996
HFEA 1990 ........ Human Fertilisation and Embryology Act 1990
HRA 1998 ........ Human Rights Act 1998
IA 1978 ........ Interpretation Act 1978
IA 1986 ........ Insolvency Act 1986
ICTA 1970 ........ Income and Corporation Taxes Act 1970
I(FP)A 1938 ........ Inheritance (Family Provision) Act 1938
I(PFD)A 1975 ........ Inheritance (Provision for Family and Dependants) Act 1975
ITA 1984 ........ Inheritance Tax Act 1984
JP(RR)A 1926 ........ Judicial Proceedings (Regulation of Reports) Act 1926
LA 1976 ........ Legitimacy Act 1976
LAA 1988 ........ Legal Aid Act 1988
LASSA 1970 ........ Local Authority Social Services Act 1970
LCA 1925 ........ Land Charges Act 1925
LCA 1972 ........ Land Charges Act 1972
LRA 1925 ........ Land Registration Act 1925
LPA 1925 ........ Law of Property Act 1925
LP(MP)A 1989 ........ Law of Property (Miscellaneous Provisions) Act 1989
LR(MP)A 1970 ........ Law Reform (Miscellaneous Provisions) Act 1970
LR(S)A 1995 ........ Law Reform (Succession) Act 1995
LTA 1954 ........ Landlord and Tenant Act 1954
MA 1949 ........ Marriage Act 1949
MCA 1965 ........ Matrimonial Causes Act 1965
MCA 1973 ........ Matrimonial Causes Act 1973
MCA 1980 ........ Magistrates' Courts Act 1980
MC(PM)A 1958 ........ Matrimonial Causes (Property and Maintenance) Act 1958
MEA 1991 ........ Maintenance Enforcement Act 1991
MeHA 1983 ........ Mental Health Act 1983
MFPA 1984 ........ Matrimonial and Family Proceedings Act 1984
MHA 1967 ........ Matrimonial Homes Act 1967
MOA 1950 ........ Maintenance Orders Act 1950
MOA 1958 ........ Maintenance Orders Act 1958
MO(FE)A 1920 ........ Maintenance Orders (Facilities for Enforcement) Act 1920
MO(RE)A 1972 ........ Maintenance Orders (Reciprocal Enforcement) Act 1972
MP(MC)A 1960 ........ Matrimonial Proceedings (Magistrates' Courts) Act 1960
MPPA 1970 ........ Matrimonial Proceedings and Property Act 1970
MWPA 1882 ........ Married Women's Property Act 1882
NAA 1948 ........ National Assistance Act 1948
NMPPA 1865 ........ Naval and Marine Pay and Pensions Act 1865
NDA 1957 ........ Naval Discipline Act 1957
NF(EML)A 1957 ........ Naval Forces (Enforcement of Maintenance Liabilities) Act 1957
PA 1995 ........ Pensions Act 1995
PACE 1984 ........ Police and Criminal Evidence Act 1984
PCA 1999 ........ Protection of Children Act 1999

PHA 1997 .................... Protection from Harassment Act 1997
POA 1999 .................... Protection of Offenders Act 1999
PSA 1993 .................... Pension Schemes Act 1993
RA 1977 .................... Rent Act 1977
R(A)A 1976 .................... Rent (Agriculture) Act 1976
RRA .................... Race Relations Act 1976
SAA 1985 .................... Surrogacy Arrangements Act 1985
SCA 1981 .................... Supreme Court Act 1981
SOA 1997 .................... Sexual Offenders Act 1997
TA 1968 .................... Theft Act 1968
TA 2000 .................... Terrorism Act 2000
TCGA 1992 .................... Taxation of Chargeable Gains Act 1992
TLATA 1996 .................... Trusts of Land and Appointment of Trustees Act 1996
WA 1837 .................... Wills Act 1837
WRPA 1999 .................... Welfare Reform and Pensions Act 1999

# TABLE OF CASES

## 1

PARA

### A

## B

## C

## D

## E

PARA

## F



## G

## H

## I



## J

## K

## L

## M

## N

PARA

## O



## P

PARA



## S

## X

PARA

## Y



## Z

# TABLE OF STATUTES

Paragraph references printed in bold type indicate where an Act is set out in part or in full.

## F

## M

# TABLE OF STATUTORY INSTRUMENTS

Paragraph references printed in **bold** type indicate where a provision is set out in part or in full.

## H



## I



## L

# PART 1

# Introductory Chapters

## 1. Costs

Contents



## Civil Procedure Rules 1998

### [1.1]

In Family Proceedings generally the Civil Procedure Rules 1998 (CPR 1998), Pts 43, 44 (subject to one minor and one major exception), 47 and 48 and the *Practice Directions* supplementing those Parts introduce a new regime which applies to family cases. The former Rules, the Family Proceedings (Costs) Rules 1991, SI 1991/1832, are revoked.

For a discussion of this topic, see generally *Rayden and Jackson on Divorce and Family Matters* (17th edn, 1997), vol 1, paras 3.18 and 23.32, chaps 53 and 54 and the Noter-up thereto.

### [1.1A]

CPR 1998, Pt 45, which deals with fixed costs, does not apply to family proceedings[1]. Where fixed costs would be applicable in the other Divisions, for example on an application for a charging order[2], the court's general discretion in relation to costs is preserved if the application is made within family proceedings.

1 See the Family Proceedings (Miscellaneous Amendments) Rules 1999, SI 1999/1012, r 4(1).
2 RSC Ord 50, r 1.

### [1.2]

The major difference between costs under the CPR 1998 generally and costs in family cases is that the rule in civil proceedings that the unsuccessful party will be ordered to pay the costs of the successful party ('costs follow the event', provided for in CPR 1998, Pt 44.3(2)(a)) is specifically disapplied in relation to family proceedings. CPR 1998, Pt 44.3 lists a number of factors to which the court should have regard when considering the exercise of its discretion in relation to costs. These do apply to family proceedings.

**[1.3]**

The starting point for the consideration of costs in family proceedings, subject to CPR 1998, Pt 44.3, is the decision of the Court of Appeal in *Gojkovic v Gojkovic (No 2)*[1]. In this case Russell and Butler-Sloss LJJ held that in the consideration of costs in the Family Division, in particular in relation to financial disputes, the starting point is that costs prima facie should follow the event. This presumption is much more readily and easily displaced than in the other divisions of the High Court but the general position is that the applicant in financial proceedings is entitled to, and is likely to obtain, an order for costs against the respondent. There is a recognition in the Family Division that there is greater flexibility and judges are astute to see whether the circumstances justify a decision that the prima facie position should not be followed[2].

1 [1992] Fam 40, [1991] 2 FLR 233, CA.
2 See *T v T (Joinder of Third Parties)* [1996] 2 FLR 357 at 366G per Wilson J, FD.

**[1.4]**

The circumstances which would justify the departure from the normal position include the inequitable behaviour of one party (although there is a difference between inequitable conduct during the marriage – which may be reflected in the ancillary relief order under the MCA 1973, s 25(2)(g) – and during the conduct of the litigation – which may only be reflected in costs), whether one or both parties has the benefit of public funding, the available assets and offers to settle which have preceded the hearing. The effect of offers to settle is provided for in r 2.69B and r 2.69C of the FPR 1991[1].

1 See paras **[3.456]** and **[3.457]** below.

**[1.5]**

Following *Gojkovic* it is now clear that there is a positive duty upon the parties to negotiate towards settlement. Once full and frank disclosure has been made by the parties the respondent to the application must make a 'serious' offer in settlement. When such an offer has been made the onus is upon the applicant to accept or reject the offer. If the applicant rejects the offer he or she must then put forward a counter offer in settlement. Failure to do so can be penalised in costs at the hearing[1]. There is also a duty to include within any *Calderbank* offer a proposal in relation to costs. The applicant, however, need not wait for an offer to be made by the respondent. It is open to either party to the application at any time to make a written offer to the other party which is expressed to be 'without prejudice except as to costs'[2].

1 See, for example *Butcher v Wolfe* [1999] 2 FCR 165, [1999] 1 FLR 334, CA.
2 See FPR 1991, r 2.69(1) at para **[3.454]** below.

**[1.6]**

In the proceedings the court should, where appropriate, deal with the costs incurred in the following way. The judge should add back into the assets of each party the costs which have already been paid less those costs which would never be recoverable (ie the difference between solicitor/client costs and party and party costs) and future liability for costs should be disregarded. To make allowances for costs paid or future costs would be to anticipate an order for costs upon which the judge has heard no argument and is not in a position to make any orders without reference to offers which may have preceded the hearing[1].

1 See *Leadbeater v Leadbeater* [1985] FLR 789, FD; but cf *H v H (Financial Relief: Costs)* [1998] 2 FCR 27, [1997] 2 FLR 57, FD.

### [1.6A]

In an application for maintenance pending suit the judge cannot order the payment of a lump sum in respect of the applicant's costs[1]. However, as part of the applicant's reasonable maintenance requirements under the MCA 1973, s 22[2] the judge can order regular payments to be made in respect of past and future legal expenses if to decline to do so would deprive the applicant of his or her representation[3].

1 *Wicks v Wicks* [1999] Fam 65, [1998] 1 FCR 465, CA.
2 Set out at para **[2.116]** below.
3 *A v A (maintenance pending suit: provision for legal costs)* [2001] 1 FCR 226, [2001] 1 FLR 377.

### [1.7]

Failure to make full disclosure and the incurring of excessive costs by a party or a legal representative can be penalised in costs. Only those costs which are proportionate to the matters in issue will be allowed as reasonable on assessment (formerly taxation). The client must be kept informed of the level of current and potential future costs at all stages in proceedings regardless of whether they are privately or publicly funded.

## Assessment of costs

### [1.8]

In matters proceeding under the ancillary relief rules[1] at every court hearing or appointment all parties must produce to the court an estimate in Form H of the costs incurred by him up to the date of that hearing or appointment[2]. If the case is outside the ancillary relief rules a privately funded litigant seeking to claim the costs of any hearing, including the final hearing, from any other party must provide the court with a schedule in Form 1 of the costs claimed[3]. Failure to comply with these rules can result in costs sanctions, including a wasted costs order on the basis of the solicitor's misconduct[4].

1 See para **[3.433]** et seq below.
2 See FPR 1991, r 2.61F at para **[3.447]** below.
3 CPR 1998, *Practice Direction* relating to Pt 44.7, paras 4.3 and 4.4.
4 See CPR 1998, Pt 44.14.

### [1.9]

The court will make a summary assessment of costs in any hearing lasting less than one day unless there is a good reason not to do so or at least one party is publicly funded. A party must comply with an order for costs (whether following a detailed or summary assessment) within 14 days of the order[1]. If the paying party fails to make payment within this time the court has the power to stay the proceedings.

1 See CPR 1998, Pts 44.7 and 44.8.

### [1.10]

CPR 1998, Pt 47 lays down a new procedure for the final assessment of costs which must be followed in family cases. It is still possible to appeal against an *order* for costs although leave is required to appeal to the Court of Appeal under RSC Ord 59, r 1B. This should be contrasted with an appeal by the legal representative or by the party against the *amount* allowed on assessment provision for which is made by CPR 1998, Pt 47.20.

### [1.10A]

If costs are awarded against a publicly funded party the court may assess the person's ability to meet the costs order under s 10(1) of the Access to Justice Act 1999[1]. If the publicly funded party cannot meet the costs in full the other party may apply for his costs to be met by the Legal Services Commission under reg 10 of the Community Legal Service (Costs) Regulations 2000[2] if he can show that he would suffer 'severe financial hardship' if an order is not made[3].

1 Set out at para **[2.500]** below.
2 SI 2000/441; set out at para **[3.561A]** et seq below.
3 See reg 5 of the Community Legal Service (Cost Protection) Regulations 2000, SI 2000/824.

## Wasted costs

### [1.11]

The CPR 1998 provide a new procedure for claiming costs from a legal representative personally (wasted costs). It is anticipated that courts will be much more willing to make use of these powers[1]. The rules governing when a wasted costs order should be made are still contained in s 51(6) and (7) of the SCA 1981. The rules relating to wasted costs are not affected by the AJA 1999.

1 See CPR 1998, Pt 48.7.

## Community Legal Service Funding

### [1.11A]

If the costs of a publicly funded party (known as 'a client'[1]) are to be paid by another party to the proceedings or prospective proceedings then the client's costs shall be assessed on the same basis as they would be if the costs were to be paid to a person who had not received CLS funding. There is no rule that the costs which the client can claim from the paying party are limited to the amount or rates which he is liable to pay to his legal representatives[2].

1 See reg 2 of the Community Legal Service (Costs) Regulations 2000, SI 2000/441 at para **[3.561B]** below.
2 See reg 15 of SI 2000/441 at para **[3.561O]** below.

### [1.11B]

Any money awarded to a client other than periodical payments of maintenance[1] must be paid to the client's solicitor. The solicitor must inform the CLS Regional Director who may direct the solicitor to pay to the Legal Services Commission such sums as may be necessary to safeguard the interests of the Commission and release the balance to the client[2].

1 See reg 18(2)(a) of the Community Legal Service (Costs) Regulations 2000, SI 2000/441 at para **[3.561R]** below.
2 See regs 18 to 20 of SI 2000/441 at paras **[3.561R]** to **[3.561T]** below.

## Property and costs recovered by a publicly funded party

### [1.12]

Unless the costs of the client are paid in full, a first charge ('the statutory charge') attaches to any property recovered or preserved within the proceedings covered by CLS funding under s 10(7) of the AJA 1999[1]. The only property which is exempt from the statutory charge is periodical payments of maintenance, clothes, furniture and the tools of the client's trade, sums awarded under s 5 of the I(PFD)A 1975[2] or Pt IV of the FLA 1996 and the first £2,500 of money or property awarded under the MCA 1973[3]. For all other purposes the nature and location of the property is immaterial for the purposes of the operation of the statutory charge.

1 Set out at para **[2.500]** below.
2 Set out at para **[2.246]** below.
3 See reg 44 of the Community Legal Service (Financial) Regulations 2000, SI 2000/516 at para **[3.561AA]** below.

### [1.13]

In practice in family cases the Statutory Charge will often attach to an interest which is recovered or preserved in the former matrimonial home. Under the Community Legal Service (Costs) Regulations 2000, reg 21[1] and the Community Legal Service (Financial) Regulations 2000, regs 51 and 52[2] if the property recovered or preserved is, under an order or with the agreement of the court, to be used as home for the client or his dependants or if money recovered is to be used to purchase such a home the enforcement statutory charge can be postponed.

1 Set out at para **[3.561U]** below.
2 Set out at paras **[3.561HH]** and **[3.561II]** below.

### [1.14]

Under reg 51 of the Community Legal Service (Financial) Regulations 2000[1] whether a family home is recovered or preserved or money recovered is used to purchase such a home the order must specify that the property preserved or to be purchased (as the case may be) is to be used as a home by the client or his dependants. Under the regulation the Commission may agree to defer enforcing the charge provided that it is satisfied that the home will provide adequate security for the amount to be secured under the statutory charge. A charge will then be registered against the home under the Land Charges Act 1925. Interest will accrue at the rate of 8% per annum from the date of registration of the charge.

1 Set out at para **[3.561HH]** below.

### [1.15]

Where a property is subject to the statutory charge and the assisted person wishes to purchase a new property in substitution for the charged property the Commission may agree to release the charge. In such a case the client must consent to a charge being entered against the new property, which will attract interest at the rate of 8% per annum[1].

1 See regs 52(2) and 53(2) of the Community Legal Service (Financial) Regulations 2000, SI 2000/516 at paras **[3.561II]** and **[3.561JJ]** below.

## The Ancillary Relief Rules

### [1.16]–[1.17]

The ancillary relief rules (FPR 1991, rr 2.51A to 2.70) apply to all applications for ancillary relief[1]. The rules are set out in full at para **[3.433]** et seq below. Various of the rules have an effect on costs. The rules expect the parties, their advisers and the court to be more aware of the costs of the proceedings. The overriding objective of the rules includes the provision that the court should seek to 'save expense'[1]. The two objectives of the first appointment are 'defining the issues and saving costs'[2].

1 See FPR 1991, r 2.51B(2)(b) at para **[3.434]** below.
2 See FPR 1991, r 2.61D(1) at para **[3.445]** below.

### [1.18]–[1.19]

Under r 2.61F of the FPR 1991, at every hearing or appointment the parties are under an obligation to produce to the court an estimate in Form H of the costs incurred by him up to the date of that hearing or appointment regardless of whether the party is privately paying or funded by the Community Legal Service.

### [1.20]

The procedure for making offers 'without prejudice save as to costs' is provided in r 2.69[1]. The parties may at any time make a written offer relating to any issue in the proceedings. Such an offer must not be communicated to the court other than at an FDR appointment until the question of costs falls to be decided.

1 See para **[3.454]** below.

### [1.21]

Where the judgement or order in favour of the applicant or the respondent is more advantageous to him than an offer made under r 2.69 the court *must* order the other party to pay his costs from 28 days after the offer unless it considers it unjust to do so[1].

1 See FPR 1991, r 2.69B at para **[3.456]** below.

### [1.22]

Where both parties have made offers under r 2.69 of the FPR 1991 and the judgment or order in favour of the applicant or the respondent is more advantageous to him than any of the offers the court may, if it considers it just, order interest on the whole or part of any money awarded at a rate not exceeding 10% above the base rate. The court may also order that the successful party is entitled to his costs on an indemnity basis and to interest on those costs at a rate not exceeding 10% above the base rate[1].

1 See FPR 1991, r 2.69C at para **[3.457]** below.

### [1.23]

The factors which the court must take into account when considering whether to exercise any of these powers are set out in r 2.69D of the FPR 1991. The court is specifically directed to considering the conduct of the parties with regard to the giving or refusing to give information for the purposes of enabling an offer to be made or evaluated[1].

1 See FPR 1991, r 2.69D(1)(d) at para **[3.458]** below.

## Appeals on costs

### [1.23A]

It is possible to appeal solely against the order for costs in an ancillary relief case. On appeal the judge must exercise his own discretion, giving such weight as he thinks fit to the way the district judge exercised his discretion. The judge need not conclude that the district judge was 'plainly wrong' as a preliminary point. He can interfere on the simple basis that he would have reached a different conclusion[1]. The notice of appeal must be lodged within 14 days[2]. The notice of appeal does not operate as a stay against the costs order[3].

1 See *A v A (Costs Appeal)* [1996] 1 FCR 186, [1996] 1 FLR 14.
2 See CCR Ord 37, r 6 at para **[1.57]** below.
3 See FPR 1991, r 8.1(6) at para **[1.55]** below.

## Costs Tables

### [1.24]
**General Principles**

| | |
|---|---|
| **Name** | *Calderbank v Calderbank* [1976] Fam 93, [1975] 3 WLR 586, [1975] 3 All ER 333, CA |
| **Subject** | **Calderbank offers in settlement** |
| **Outcome** | In ancillary relief proceedings either party may make an offer in settlement of the case without prejudice to their open position or to their position at the hearing but reserving their right to refer to the offer on the consideration of costs. |

| | |
|---|---|
| **Name** | *Leadbeater v Leadbeater* [1985] FLR 789, FD |
| **Subject** | **Treatment of costs in the substantive proceedings** |
| **Outcome** | In the substantive proceedings the judge should add back into the assets of each party the costs which have already been paid less those costs which would never be recoverable (ie the difference between solicitor/client costs and party and party costs). Similarly, future liability for costs should also be omitted on the basis that to make allowances for costs paid or future costs would be to anticipate an order for costs upon which the judge has heard no argument and is not in a position to make any orders without reference to offers which may have preceded the hearing. |

| | |
|---|---|
| **Name** | *Collins v Collins* [1987] 1 FLR 226, CA |
| **Subject** | **A lump sum order in ancillary relief proceedings cannot be increased because of the Legal Aid Statutory Charge** |
| **Outcome** | The wife was legally aided and the judge made no order as to costs but awarded the wife an increased lump sum to take into account the fact that her costs would be recouped under the statutory charge. The Court of Appeal held that this was not the correct approach and reduced the award by the amount which the judge had allowed to cover the statutory charge. The substantive order could only be made on the basis of s 25 of the MCA 1973. |

| | |
|---|---|
| **Name** | *Gojkovic v Gojkovic (No 2)* [1992] Fam 40, [1991] 2 FLR 233, CA |
| **Subject** | **General principles in respect of costs** |
| **Outcome** | (1) The starting point in the Family Division is that costs follow the event. The applicant in a financial dispute should receive their costs where possible but the court must take all factors into account when considering the exercise of its discretion.<br>(2) This presumption is much more easily displaced than in other Divisions of the High Court, particularly in relation to children cases.<br>(3) The behaviour of a party within the litigation, such as in the relation to material non-disclosure, can affect the court's discretion to make a costs order.<br>(4) The incidence of legal aid and the inadequacy of the total assets available may affect the order for costs.<br>(5) Once both parties have made full disclosure the Respondent to a financial application must make a serious offer in settlement this should include provision for costs; once he does so the Applicant must make a counter offer; the absence of an offer or counter offer may well be reflected in costs. |

| | |
|---|---|
| **Name** | *H v H (Clean Break: Non-disclosure: Costs)* [1994] 2 FLR 309, FD |
| **Subject** | **Costs should not generally be awarded on an indemnity basis** |
| **Outcome** | The wife did better than her *Calderbank* offer and was awarded her costs. The wife argued that the husband's non-disclosure should be penalised by an order for costs on the indemnity basis. The court held that such an order would be unduly draconian and that the husband's litigation misconduct was reflected in the costs order. |

| | |
|---|---|
| **Name** | *M v M (Financial Provision: Party Incurring Excessive Costs)* [1995] 3 FCR 321, FD |
| **Subject** | **Litigation misconduct can be reflected both in the substantive award and in costs in an exceptional case** |
| **Outcome** | In a case where the husband was described by Thorpe J as being 'obsessed' with the litigation and where his conduct of the case was 'so gross and so extreme that it would be inequitable to disregard it' the judge quantified the wife's share of the matrimonial assets on the basis of what would have remained had the husband's 'policy of waste and destruction' not been pursued. In addition (although both parties were legally aided) the husband was ordered to pay the wife's costs in full notwithstanding that after payment of both parties' costs his share of the assets would be virtually nil. |

| | |
|---|---|
| **Name** | *T v T (Interception of Documents)* [1995] 2 FCR 745, [1994] 2 FLR 1083 |
| **Subject** | **Effect of non disclosure on costs** |
| **Outcome** | Where the husband was dishonest in relation to the disclosure of his financial position the court was entitled to infer that his resources were greater than he had disclosed and to order him to pay the costs of the proceedings to reflect his misconduct within the litigation. |

| | |
|---|---|
| **Name** | *A v A (Costs Appeal)* [1996] 1 FCR 186, [1996] 1 FLR 14, FD |
| **Subject** | **Duty to negotiate: 21 days is a reasonable time in which to respond substantively to an offer** |
| **Outcome** | A *Calderbank* offer was made by the wife and no counter proposal was put forward by the husband for two years. A response made one working day before the trial was made far too late. Since the wife bettered her *Calderbank* position at trial she was entitled to her costs in full from 21 days following the date of her offer regardless of the effect of such an order upon the husband's financial position. |

| | |
|---|---|
| **Name** | *T v T (Joinder of Third Parties)* [1997] 1 FCR 98, [1996] 2 FLR 357, FD |
| **Subject** | **Displacing the presumption that costs follow the event** |
| **Outcome** | Although the prima facie position is that costs should follow the event Family Division judges are 'particularly astute to see whether there are circumstances which should displace that prima facie result, so that there is a greater flexibility about costs perhaps than in the other two Divisions' – [1996] 2 FLR 357 at 366G per Wilson J, FD. |

| | |
|---|---|
| **Name** | *Dart v Dart* [1997] 1 FCR 21, [1996] 2 FLR 286, CA |
| **Subject** | **The court cannot increase the level of a lump sum to make provision for a costs order** |
| **Outcome** | The judge should not anticipate what order he might make in relation to costs since he would not know what negotiations have taken place or what other arguments may be advanced in relation to the issue. A lump sum should not be increased to take into account a costs liability: 'the court's power to control [costs abuses] would be emasculated if the applicant could include a cost liability, actual or potential, as a factor to be reflected in the lump sum award.' – [1996] 2 FLR 286 at 300G per Thorpe LJ. |

| | |
|---|---|
| **Name** | *Dart v Dart* [1997] 1 FCR 21, [1996] 2 FLR 286, CA |
| **Subject** | **A costs award can reflect litigation misconduct** |
| **Outcome** | The judge made a costs award against the wife who received a lump sum of £9 million out of total assets of £400 million on the basis that the award did not better her *Calderbank* offer. He also ordered the wife to pay the pre-*Calderbank* costs in condemnation of her unjustifiable insistence on superfluous detailed disclosure in a case where the husband ran the Millionaires' defence. This was upheld by the Court of Appeal on the basis of the wife's 'prodigal' conduct of the litigation. |

| | |
|---|---|
| **Name** | *H v H (Financial Relief: Costs)* [1998] 2 FCR 27, [1997] 2 FLR 57, FD |
| **Subject** | **The impact of an adverse costs order cannot be taken into account in the substantive proceedings** |
| **Outcome** | Holman J declined to follow the approach in *Leadbeater v Leadbeater* [1985] FLR 789, FD on the basis that 'that is merely to treat as an asset something which in truth the family has no longer got' (at 60H). Instead he came to his decision on the basis of the parties' financial position after the payments on account to solicitors had been paid. The judge refused to earmark a proportion of the total assets for the payment of the husband's own costs as that would give priority to his legal adviser's over the wife's claim. The husband suggested that the impact of the substantive order and the liability for both parties' costs would drive him to bankruptcy. Notwithstanding this the judge concluded that since the negotiations had been reasonable costs should follow the event and the husband was ordered to meet the wife's costs. |

| | |
|---|---|
| **Name** | *Young v Young* [1999] 3 FCR 36, [1998] 2 FLR 1131, CA |
| **Subject** | **Misconduct within the marriage is not to be reflected in costs** |
| **Outcome** | Where the conduct by a party within the marriage has been taken into account on the calculation of the ancillary relief order under the MCA 1973, s 25(2)(g) this misconduct cannot be reflected again on the consideration of costs. Only misconduct within the litigation will be reflected in costs: see, for example, *Dart v Dart* [1996] 2 FLR 286, CA; and *M v M (Financial Provision: Party Incurring Excessive Costs)* [1995] 3 FCR 321, FD. |

| | |
|---|---|
| **Name** | *Butcher v Wolfe* [1999] 2 FCR 165, [1999] 1 FLR 334, CA |
| **Subject** | **Duty to negotiate applies not just to proceedings covered by the Family Proceedings Rules 1991; failure to negotiate can be reflected in the successful party's costs** |
| **Outcome** | In an action relating to a farming partnership Simon Brown LJ rejected the submission that the duty upon parties to negotiate imposed by *Gojkivic* was restricted to proceedings governed by the FPR 1991. This would involve 'too narrow and inflexible an approach to this valuable means of protecting parties to litigation against unreasonable opponents'. A party who beats a *Calderbank* award will not necessarily be protected from being penalised in costs. If there is a point blank refusal of the offer coupled with a failure to negotiate this can be reflected in the costs award. |

| | |
|---|---|
| **Name** | *A v A (maintenance pending suit: provision for legal costs)* [2001] 1 FCR 226, [2001] 1 FLR 377 |
| **Subject** | **Maintenance pending suit can include a costs element** |
| **Outcome** | On an application for maintenance pending suit the judge can order regular payments to be made in respect of the applicant's past and future costs if to decline to do so would deprive the applicant of his or her representation. |

## [1.25] Security for Costs

| | |
|---|---|
| **Name** | *Penny v Penny* [1997] 1 FCR 126, [1996] 1 FLR 646, CA |
| **Subject** | **Security for costs can be ordered in the Family Division** |
| **Outcome** | An application for security for costs under RSC Ord 23 (which survives the CPR by virtue of the transitional provisions contained in CPR 1998, Pt 55) can be made by a Respondent to proceedings in the Family Division to cover the costs of pending litigation. Unless the applicant gives the security there will be a stay of the proceedings. No such order can be made to guard against costs which have already been incurred. |

## [1.26] Wasted Costs

| | |
|---|---|
| **Name** | *Re a Barrister (Wasted Costs Order) (No 1 of 1991)* [1993] QB 293, CA |
| **Subject** | **Three-stage test** |
| **Outcome** | On consideration of a wasted costs order the court should consider the following three-stage test:<br>(1) Has the legal representative acted improperly, unreasonably or negligently [the words used in s 51(7) of the SCA 1981 which gives the court the power to order wasted costs]?<br>(2) If so, did the conduct cause unnecessary costs to be incurred?<br>(3) If so, is it just in all the circumstances to order the legal representative to pay all or part of the costs? |

| | |
|---|---|
| **Name** | *Re A Solicitor (Wasted Costs Order)* [1993] 2 FLR 959, CA |
| **Subject** | **Conduct must amount to a dereliction of the solicitor's duty to the court to justify a wasted costs order** |
| **Outcome** | Conduct must be worse than an error of judgement in order to justify a wasted costs order. Conduct which is improper, unreasonable or negligent will involve a dereliction of a solicitor's duty to the court. |

| | |
|---|---|
| **Name** | *Ridehalgh v Horsefield* [1994] Ch 205, [1994] 3 All ER 848, [1994] 2 FLR 194, CA |
| **Subject** | **Improper, unreasonable or negligent conduct** |
| **Outcome** | The words 'improper, unreasonable or negligent' bear their established meaning. 'Improper' includes conduct which would be regarded as improper by a consensus of professional opinion regardless of whether it violated a professional code; 'unreasonable' means conduct without a reasonable explanation and conduct which is vexatious rather than intended to resolve the disputes in a case; 'negligent' means a failure to act with the competence reasonably to be expected of ordinary members of the profession. |

| | |
|---|---|
| **Name** | *Filmlab Systems International Ltd v Pennington* [1994] 4 All ER 673, [1995] 1 WLR 673, CA |
| **Subject** | **An error of judgement cannot justify a wasted costs order against counsel** |
| **Outcome** | Conduct which amounts to an error of judgement with the benefit of hindsight cannot support a wasted costs order. The conduct must be such that no reasonably well informed and competent barrister would make the error. |

| | |
|---|---|
| **Name** | *Re Freudiana Holdings Ltd* (1995) Times, 4 December, CA |
| **Subject** | **Preventing 'satellite litigation'** |
| **Outcome** | A judge has a discretion to refuse to hear an application for wasted costs if it would necessitate a substantial rehearing of the issues in the original trial. |

| | |
|---|---|
| **Name** | *Re Sasea Finance Ltd (in liquidation)* [1998] 1 BCLC 559, Ch D |
| **Subject** | **Inaccurate time estimates can be penalised by limiting costs** |
| **Outcome** | If time estimates are 'wholly unrealistic' a possible sanction is to limit the recovery of costs to the estimated length of the hearing, per Sir Richard Scott V-C. |

| | |
|---|---|
| **Name** | *General Mediterranean Holdings SA v Patel* [1999] 3 All ER 673, [2000] 1 WLR 272, QBD |
| **Subject** | **Disclosure on a wasted costs application under CPR 1998, Pt 48.7(3)** |
| **Outcome** | CPR 1998, Pt 48.7(3) which provides that the court may direct the disclosure of privileged documents both to the court and to the other party to a wasted costs application is ultra vires. Documents which are protected by legal professional privilege may not be disclosed without the consent of the client. Toulson J acknowledged the difficulty faced by a legal adviser who is unable to refer to privileged documents without the consent of the client in a wasted costs application. The lawyer is protected by the fact that a judge hearing the wasted costs application should make full allowance for the inability of the lawyer fully to put forward his case. |

| | |
|---|---|
| **Name** | *Re G, S and M (Wasted Costs)* [2000] 1 FLR 52, FD |
| **Subject** | **Wasted costs against counsel where experts not kept up-to-date** |
| **Outcome** | Where witnesses have not been kept up to date and had not read the evidence in the case (such as witness statements or medical notes) prior to giving oral evidence counsel had committed two elementary breaches of established good practice in the Family Division. The judge was entitled to commence an inquiry to establish whether counsel should pay the costs wasted as a result of the expert being recalled on a second day. The fact that the 'costs of the inquiry' exceeded the costs potentially in issue was irrelevant on the basis that the judge did not propose to allow the 'costs of the inquiry' to be recovered by any party. |

| | |
|---|---|
| **Name** | *Re CH (A Minor)* [2000] 2 FCR 193, FD |
| **Subject** | **Wasted costs where Practice Direction not complied with** |
| **Outcome** | Where the parties had not complied with the President's *Practice Direction (Family Proceedings: Court Bundles)* [2000] 1 FLR 536 (set out at para **[4.27]** below), with the result that the case took four times as long as it should have done in court Wall J disallowed one half of the fees of the solicitors and counsel concerned. He also indicated that in future any practitioners against whom such orders were made should be identified. |

## [1.27]
## Costs against third parties

- See also CPR 1998, Pt 48.2

| | |
|---|---|
| **Name** | *Northampton Health Authority v Official Solicitor and Governors of St Andrews Hospital* [1994] 2 FCR 206, [1994] 1 FLR 162, CA |
| **Subject** | **Costs against a non-party** |
| **Outcome** | Where a judge makes a costs order against a non-party he should only do so where the non-party payer, although not a party to the proceedings, 'is so closely connected with, or responsible for, the proceedings as to make it just to saddle him with liability for the costs' – [1994] 1 FLR 162 at 170E per Sir Thomas Bingham MR, CA. |

| | |
|---|---|
| **Name** | *T v T (Joinder of Third Parties)* [1997] 1 FCR 98, [1996] 2 FLR 357, FD |
| **Subject** | **Costs orders can be made against third parties in ancillary relief applications** |
| **Outcome** | Where the trustees of a Jersey trust fund contested an application for them to be joined as a party to an ancillary relief action and lost they should be liable for the costs of the application. |

| | |
|---|---|
| **Name** | *Hurley v Hurley (David Intervening)* [1998] 2 FCR 14, [1998] 1 FLR 213, CA |
| **Subject** | **Costs orders can be in favour of a third party even though no substantive order was made in their favour** |
| **Outcome** | An intervener secured for herself the right to remain in the former matrimonial home for life but no substantive order was made in her favour. She had succeeded in the proceedings and was awarded her costs. Where an intervention was reasonable and the intervener's conduct of the proceedings was also reasonable there were no grounds from departing from the prima facie position that a successful party is awarded costs. |

| | |
|---|---|
| **Name** | *Dennis v Dennis* [2000] 2 FLR 231, FD |
| **Subject** | **Costs against the Lord Chancellor's Department** |
| **Outcome** | Where an administrative error by a member of the court staff leads to a party sustaining increased costs the court may order the additional costs to be paid by the Lord Chancellor's Department. The proper procedure is to adjourn the proceedings to enable a settlement to be reached, in default of which the Lord Chancellor's Department should be given notice of a further hearing in order that it may seek to be represented.<br>If the additional costs arose as a result of a judicial act then the court has no power to make such costs orders. |

### [1.28]
### Costs appeals

| | |
|---|---|
| **Name** | *McDonnell v McDonnell* [1977] 1 All ER 766, CA |
| **Subject** | **Costs on appeal; applicability of *Calderbank* principles on appeal** |
| **Outcome** | Ormrod LJ recognised that the Family Division was less rigid in the application of the principle that costs follow the event than the other Divisions. On appeal, however, 'costs usually follow the result of the appeal even in family matters, although some flexibility is retained' – [1977] 1 All ER 766 at 769e. Where a *Calderbank* offer has been made between the first instance hearing and the appeal the Court of Appeal should take it into account and make the order for costs accordingly. |

| | |
|---|---|
| **Name** | *Wilkinson v Kenny* [1993] 1 WLR 963, CA |
| **Subject** | **Appeals to the Court of Appeal as to costs only: costs orders not to be overturned lightly** |
| **Outcome** | An order for costs is in the discretion of the trial judge. The order should not be overturned on appeal to the Court of Appeal unless the judge fails to exercise his discretion or exercises the discretion unjudicially. |

| | |
|---|---|
| **Name** | *A v A (Costs Appeal)* [1996] 1 FCR 186, [1996] 1 FLR 14 |
| **Subject** | **Appeals against a District Judge's order as to costs** |
| **Outcome** | On an appeal as to costs alone the judge can exercise his discretion afresh. It is not necessary to show that there had been a wrongful exercise of discretion at first instance. This is to be contrasted with an appeal to the Court of Appeal on costs alone – see *Wilkinson v Kenny* [1993] 1 WLR 963, CA. |

| | |
|---|---|
| **Name** | *Piglowska v Piglowski* [1999] 2 FLR 763, CA and HL |
| **Subject** | **When should leave to appeal be granted** |
| **Outcome** | Lord Hoffman expressed the view that 'to allow successive appeals in the hope of producing an answer which accords with perfect justice is to kill the parties with kindness…even if a case does raise an important point of practice or principle, the Court of Appeal should consider carefully whether it is fair to have it decided at the expense of parties with very limited resources or whether it should wait for a more suitable vehicle' – [1999] 2 FLR 763 at 785F and 785H–786A. |

### [1.29]
### Proportionality

| | |
|---|---|
| **Name** | *Piglowska v Piglowski* [1999] 2 FLR 763, CA and HL |
| **Subject** | **The concept of proportionality will be applied to costs in the Family Division** |
| **Outcome** | The total assets in dispute were approximately £127,400 and legal costs exceeded £128,000. This was described as a 'disaster' by Lord Hoffman who approved the principle that there should be proportionality between the amount at stake and the total costs incurred in resolving the dispute (see also the overriding objective of the ancillary relief rules: FPR 1991, r 2.51B at para **[3.434]** below). |

## [1.30]
## The Community Legal Service Statutory Charge

| | |
|---|---|
| **Name** | Access to Justice Act 1999, s 10 (set out at para **[2.500]** below) |
| **Subject** | **Order for costs against a publicly funded party** |
| **Outcome** | The court must order costs against a publicly funded party exceeding an amount which it is reasonable for him to pay having regard to the financial resources of all the parties to the proceedings and the conduct of all parties in connection with the case. |

| | |
|---|---|
| **Name** | Community Legal Service (Financial) Regulations 2000, SI 2000/516, reg 52 (set out at para **[3.561II]** below) |
| **Subject** | **Deferring the enforcement of the statutory charge over property or money recovered or preserved** |
| **Outcome** | Where in matrimonial proceedings property or money is recovered or preserved which by order or by agreement is to be used as a home for the client or his dependants or to pay for such a home the Legal Services Commission may postpone the enforcement of the statutory charge provided that:<br>(a) the assisted person agrees to allow the Commission to execute a charge over the property and such a charge is in fact registered pursuant to the Land Registration Act 1925;<br>(b) the charge will accrue simple interest at the rate of 8% per annum; and<br>(c) the Commission is satisfied that the property will provide adequate security for the amount of the statutory charge. |

| | |
|---|---|
| **Name** | Community Legal Service (Financial) Regulations 2000, SI 2000/516, reg 52(2) (set out at para **[3.561II]** below) |
| **Subject** | **Substituting one charged property for another** |
| **Outcome** | Where a property is subject to a deferred charge created pursuant to reg 52 and the client wishes to purchase a new property in substitution for the charged property the Commission may agree to release the charge provided that:<br>(a) the client agrees to allow the Commission to execute a charge over the new property;<br>(b) simple interest will continue to accrue on the same amounts and at the same rate as applied to the old property; and<br>(c) the Commission is satisfied that the property to be purchased will provide adequate security for the charge. |

| | |
|---|---|
| **Name** | *Cooke v Head (No 2)* [1974] 1 WLR 972, CA |
| **Subject** | **The extent of the Statutory Charge** |
| **Outcome** | Where both parties are legally aided and an order is made that the husband should pay the wife's costs this should be complied with first. The Statutory Charge in respect of his costs will take effect on the balance ie the property which he recovered or preserved less the amount which he pays in respect of his wife's costs. |

| | |
|---|---|
| **Name** | *Airey v Ireland* (1979) 2 EHRR 305, ECtHR |
| **Subject** | **Duty upon signatory countries under the European Convention on Human Rights to provide parties with legal representatives in certain types of case** |
| **Outcome** | Article 6(1) of the European Convention on Human Rights guarantees to litigants an effective right of access to the courts for the determination of their 'civil rights and obligations'. In Judicial Separation proceedings before the Irish High Court which were described as 'complex … involving complicated points of law' and the examination of witnesses there was a breach of Art 6(1) because the Irish government refused to provide free legal aid. The court rejected as 'improbable' the submission by the government that the wife could effectively present her own case. The court recognised, however, that this decision does not imply that the State must provide free legal aid for every dispute relating to a 'civil right'. |

| | |
|---|---|
| **Name** | *Hanlon v Law Society* [1981] AC 124, HL |
| **Subject** | **Property recovered or preserved** |
| **Outcome** | Property which has been the subject of a property adjustment application under the MCA 1973, s 24(1)(a) has been recovered or preserved and is subject to the Statutory Charge if its ownership has in fact been in dispute during the proceedings. |

| | |
|---|---|
| **Name** | *Re Solicitors, Re Taxation of Costs* [1982] 2 All ER 683, Ch D |
| **Subject** | **Duty upon solicitors to obtain client's approval before taking an unusually expensive step under a legal aid certificate** |
| **Outcome** | In a legally aided case, as in a private case, the solicitor must obtain specific instructions from the client. The client may, on being informed of the probable increase in costs and the effect of the Statutory Charge, wish to avoid the step, such as briefing a leader, no matter how firmly the solicitor and junior counsel advise that the step ought to be taken. |

| | |
|---|---|
| **Name** | *Stewart v Law Society* [1987] 1 FLR 223, FD |
| **Subject** | **Capitalised maintenance is subject to the Statutory Charge** |
| **Outcome** | Periodical payments of maintenance are exempt from the Statutory Charge under reg 94(c) of the Civil Legal Aid (General) Regulations 1989, SI 1989/339. If maintenance is capitalised to effect a clean break settlement this is a capital payment and will be subject to the Statutory Charge. |

| | |
|---|---|
| **Name** | *Collins v Collins* [1987] 1 FLR 226, CA |
| **Subject** | **A lump sum order in ancillary relief proceedings cannot be increased because of the Legal Aid Statutory Charge** |
| **Outcome** | The wife was legally aided and the judge made no order as to costs but awarded the wife an increased lump sum to take into account the fact that her costs would be recouped under the statutory charge. The Court of Appeal held that this was not the correct approach and reduced the award by the amount which the judge had allowed to cover the statutory charge. The substantive order could only be made on the basis of s 25 of the MCA 1973. |

| | |
|---|---|
| **Name** | *Evans v Evans* [1990] 2 All ER 147, [1990] 1 FLR 319, FD |
| **Subject** | **Duty to keep legally aided client informed as to the impact of costs** |
| **Outcome** | 'Solicitors and counsel should keep their clients informed of the costs at all stages of the proceedings and, where appropriate, should ensure that they understand the implications of the legal aid charge.' – [1990] 2 All ER 147 at 149c per Booth J. |

| | |
|---|---|
| **Name** | *Watkinson v Legal Aid Board* [1991] FCR 775, [1991] 2 FLR 26, CA |
| **Subject** | **Statutory Charge applies to all proceedings under a certificate** |
| **Outcome** | Where proceedings result in an increase of periodical payments the Statutory Charge cannot apply since no capital has been recovered or preserved. If the same certificate is then used in proceedings which result in a capitalisation of the periodical payments the Statutory Charge will apply both to these proceedings and to the earlier variation action. Solicitors should seek to avoid this by discharging a certificate once the work has been completed and applying for a new certificate where appropriate. |

| | |
|---|---|
| **Name** | *Chaggar v Chaggar* [1997] 2 FCR 486, [1997] 1 FLR 566, CA |
| **Subject** | **Proceeds of sale of a property can be used to meet the Statutory Charge** |
| **Outcome** | The Legal Aid Act 1988 has the effect that a party who succeeds against a legally aided person has to pay his own costs from the results of his success except in exceptional circumstances. Although this may be seen as unfair it is a result built into the Act. Under s 17 of the Legal Aid Act 1988 the court cannot take into account an assisted person's dwelling-house in deciding what contributions he should make towards the successful party's costs. However if the dwelling-house is sold, the proceeds of sale form part of the assisted person's disposable capital. If this money is not needed for the purchase of a new property it can be used to pay the successful party's costs. |

| | |
|---|---|
| **Name** | *Piglowska v Piglowski* [1999] 2 FLR 763, CA and HL |
| **Subject** | **Anticipation of the effect of the Statutory Charge should not result in an award to a party which is substantially more than the court would otherwise have made** |
| **Outcome** | The Court of Appeal made an order providing the husband with sufficient capital to enable him to purchase a property in order to delay the impact of the Statutory Charge which would otherwise attach to the property recovered or preserved within the proceedings. This is not acceptable: 'I would certainly accept … that the effect of the Legal Aid Board's charge and its possible postponement is a vital matter to be taken into account in making a transfer of property order. The judge needs to know what the actual effect of the order will be. But I would not agree that a court should award a husband substantially more than it would otherwise have thought proper, at the expense of the wife, on the ground that it would enable the husband to postpone the charge … the question for the court was simply whether it was fair and just, having regard to all the matters listed in s 25(2) [of the MCA 1973] and all the circumstances of the case to award him such a sum.' – [1999] 2 FLR 763 at 781B–D per Lord Hoffman. |

# 2. Appeals and Setting Aside Orders

Contents

---

**[1.31]**
**Which remedy?**

*Question 1*

- **Is it an appeal or an application to set aside?**[1]

*Answer*

- **An application to set aside** (go to Section (1) at para **[1.35]** below).
- **An appeal** (see *Question 2* below).

*Question 2*

- **Is it an appeal to the Court of Appeal?**

*Answer*

- **Yes** (use the procedure and forms referred to in Section (2) at para **[1.36]** below).
- **No** (see *Question 3* below).

*Question 3*

- **Is it an appeal in respect of a family law matter or a civil matter?**[2]

*Answer*

- **Civil matter** (use the procedure and forms referred to in Section (2) at para **[1.36]** below).
- **Family law matter** (use the procedure and form referred to in Section (3) at para **[1.54]** below[3]).

1 For a definition of applications to set aside as opposed to appeals see para **[1.32]** below.
2 For a definition as to which applications are family and which are not see para **[1.34]** below.

3 Note however that the FPR 1991 proscribe different time limits for ChA 1989 appeals (see Pt 4 of the of the FPR 1991) to financial/domestic violence appeals (see Pt 8 of the FPR 1991). Children appeals are dealt with in Vol 2 of *Essential Family Practice*.

## [1.32]
## An appeal or an application to set aside?

There are three ways to attack an order made by a court of first instance:

(1) **Appeal against the order**
(Appeals from district judges of the Principal Registry are usually listed before a High Court Judge). The time limit for such an appeal is 14 days. However, the court should grant an extension where the 14 day time limit is exceeded and good reasons are given[1]. Such appeals will be regulated by FPR 1991, r 8.1[2] which for most financial appeals in turn utilises CCR Ord 37, r 6[3].

Leave is not required provided the appeal is made in time.

(2) **To apply to set aside the order pursuant to CCR Ord 37, r 1**
Leave is not required provided the application is made in time. CCR Ord 37, r 1 survives the new CPR 1998, Pt 52 for both civil and family matters.

(3) **To bring a fresh action; such as for mutual mistake or fraud**. This latter form of action is likely to prove more expensive than either (1) or (2) above. Second, it is likely to be simply a duplication of an appeal or an application to set aside. Its sole real practical applications are:
(a) where damages are sought which cannot be recovered in (1) or (2) above; or
(b) fraud.

In fraud cases there is no time limit. Thus where an appeal or an application to set aside is very much out of time the threat of an action for fraud (which cannot be out of time) may persuade a potential Respondent to consent to the necessary extension of time.

As applications under this third heading will be so rare, it is not addressed further in this book; practitioners are referred to *Rayden and Jackson on Divorce and Family Matters* (17th edn, 1997) and the *Civil Court Practice*.

The test of whether an application to set aside or an appeal should be brought is whether an error of the court is complained of as opposed to the behaviour of one (or both) of the parties. If an error of the court is alleged then the order should be appealed. If not then the application should be made back to the original court for the order to be set aside.

1 See *Johnson v Johnson* (1980) 1 FLR 331, CA but also note *Harris (formerly Manahan) v Manahan* [1996] 4 All ER 454, CA.
2 See para **[1.55]** below.
3 See para **[1.57]** below.

## [1.33]
## Error of the court

The test applied by Lord Merriman P in *Peek v Peek*[1] was:

> 'Is the allegation which is made against the decision an allegation that the court went wrong on the materials before it, or is it an allegation that the court went wrong because evidence on a vital matter was concealed from the court?'

In the latter case a rehearing can be ordered, in the former an appeal is the appropriate remedy.

An application under the rule is required to be made to the judge by whom the proceedings were tried, unless the court otherwise orders (eg because the trial judge is no longer available or because the application is to be consolidated with an appeal).

An application for rehearing is to be made on notice, which must be filed and served on the opposite party not more than 14 days after the day of the trial and not less than seven days before the hearing of the application. These time periods may be extended in the circumstances set out below.

Examples of where an application to set aside is more appropriate than an appeal are where there has been material non-disclosure, where there has been a vitiating factor which has undermined the basis of the order and mistake. Examples of where an appeal would be the appropriate remedy would be where the judge exercised his discretion wrongly (or not at all) or misled himself on a point of law.

### [1.34]
### Which cases are treated as family law cases as opposed to civil matters?

'Family proceedings' is defined by reference to s 61(1), (3) of, and Sch 1 to, the Supreme Court Act 1981:

- (a) all matrimonial causes and matters (whether at first instance or on appeal) ie prayers for divorce, nullity or judicial separation and any ancillary relief enquiries;
- (b) all causes and matters (whether at first instance or on appeal) relating to–
  - (i) legitimacy;
  - (ii) the exercise of the inherent jurisdiction of the High Court with respect to minors, the maintenance of minors and any proceedings under the Children Act 1989, except proceedings solely for the appointment of a guardian of a minor's estate;
  - (iii) adoption;
  - (iv) non-contentious or common form probate business;
- (c) applications for consent to the marriage of a minor;
- (d) proceedings on appeal under section 13 of the Administration of Justice Act 1960 from an order or decision made under section 63(3) of the Magistrates' Courts Act 1980 to enforce an order of a magistrates' court made in matrimonial proceedings [or proceedings under Part IV of the Family Law Act 1996] or with respect to the guardianship of a minor;
- (e) proceedings under the Children Act 1989;
- (f) all proceedings under–
  - (i) Part IV of the Family Law Act 1996;
  - (ii) the Child Abduction and Custody Act 1985;
  - (iii) the Family Law Act 1986;
  - (iv) section 30 of the Human Fertilisation and Embryology Act 1990; and
- (g) all proceedings for the purpose of enforcing an order made in any proceedings of a type described in this paragraph.
- (h) all proceedings under the Child Support Act 1991.

If a matter is not included on the above list (and is not one of the other exceptions under CPR 1998, Pt 2.1(2)) then it is regulated by CPR 1998, Pt 52. Enforcement of family proceedings is found in (g) above and so is regulated under the old RSC and CCR. However, applications for a Freezing Order and a Search Order are not enforcement and so will be civil (in any event the bases of jurisdiction in those cases are the High Court's inherent jurisdiction and s 37 of the Supreme Court Act 1981; neither of which are included in the above list).

References in the above list to appeals should not be taken as extending to the Court of Appeal as this is now expressly dealt with by CPR 1998, PD2.2 which provides that such appeals shall be regulated by CPR 1998, Pt 52.

Conspicuous by their absence from the above list are the matters under the TLATA 1996, the I(PFD)A 1975 and (surprisingly as it features in the FPR 1991) the MWPA 1882. The appeal route for these 'civil' matters should be that laid down by the CPR 1998.

1 [1948] P 46 at 48, affd by the Court of Appeal [1948] 2 All ER 297.

## (1)
## APPLICATIONS TO SET ASIDE

### [1.35]

**CCR Ord 37, r 1 Rehearing**

(1) In any proceedings tried without a jury the judge shall have power on application to order a rehearing where no error of the court at the hearing is alleged.

(2) Unless the court otherwise orders, any application under paragraph (1) shall be made to the judge by whom the proceedings were tried.

(3) A rehearing may be ordered on any question without interfering with the finding or decision on any other question.

(4) Where the proceedings were tried by the district judge, the powers conferred on the judge by paragraphs (1) and (3) shall be exercisable by the district judge and paragraph (2) shall not apply.

(5) Any application for a rehearing under this rule shall be made on notice stating the grounds of the application and the notice shall be served on the opposite party not more than 14 days after the day of the trial and not less than 7 days before the day fixed for the hearing of the application.

(6) On receipt of the notice, the court officer shall, unless the court otherwise orders, retain any money in court until the application has been heard.

### [1.35.1]
**Keypoints**

- Jurisdiction
- Error of the court
- Where the Respondent is absent
- Default or misconduct of opposite party
- Perjury or mistake of a witness
- Mistake by counsel
- Change of circumstances which has undermined the basis of the order
- Leave to apply to set aside an order out of time

### [1.35.2]
**Jurisdiction**

This remedy is available in respect of both determinations by district judges and county court judges. There is no corresponding provision in the High Court but arguably it is a power which the court has as part of its inherent jurisdiction.

### [1.35.3]
**Error of the court**

The test applied by Lord Merriman P in *Peek v Peek*[1] is set out above at para **[1.33]** above.

1 [1948] P 46 at 48, affd by the Court of Appeal [1948] 2 All ER 297.

### [1.35.4]
**Where the Respondent is absent**

If there is no appearance by or on behalf of the defendant at the hearing, judgment given against him may be set aside under CPR 1998, Pt 39.3 if the case is governed by the CPR 1998 or under CCR Ord 37, r 2 under the old rules.

## [1.35.5]
## Default or misconduct of opposite party

If one side is taken by surprise by a fraudulent trick on the part of the other side, a rehearing will be granted[1].

1 *Anderson v George* (1757) 1 Burr 353.

## [1.35.6]
## Perjury or mistake of a witness

A conviction for perjury of witnesses on whose evidence the verdict was obtained was held a ground for a new trial[1]. It is also at least arguable that where a witness has made a mistake and that undermines the basis of the court's exercise of discretion then there should be a rehearing. Also a rehearing may be justified where there has been a misunderstanding at first instance[2].

1 *Benfield v Petrie* (1781) 3 Doug KB 24.
2 *Beale v Taylor* [1967] 3 All ER 253, [1967] 1 WLR 1193.

## [1.35.7]
## Mistake by counsel

Mistake by counsel in presenting his case will rarely justify the grant of a retrial if this will cause injustice to the other party[1].

1 *Morris-Thomas v Petticoat Lane Rentals Ltd* (1986) 53 P & CR 238.

## [1.35.8]
## Change or circumstances which has undermined the basis of the order

Perhaps the most common basis for making an application to set aside an order is that there has been some change of circumstances which has undermined the basis of the order. Often this will require an application to be made very considerably out of time. If a supervening event has occurred which has undermined the basis of an order then that event and the application should happen within one year of the original order[1].

Where the complaint is of some material non-disclosure then time should not be treated as running; material non-disclosure is usually fraudulent[2].

Often there will be both an appeal and an application to set aside. Alternatively the application to set aside will contain quasi-fraud allegations; as a matter of practice, the district judge should transfer the application to a High Court judge for hearing[3].

1 See *Barder v Caluori* [1988] AC 20, [1987] 2 All ER 440, HL (Consent order made in divorce proceedings, five weeks later wife killed the two children of the marriage and committed suicide: judge entitled to grant husband leave to appeal out of time and to allow the appeal on the ground that it had been based on the assumption that the wife and children would require a suitable home for a substantial period).
2 See *Livesey (formerly Jenkins) v Jenkins* [1985] AC 424, [1985] 1 All ER 106, HL.
3 See *Re C (financial provision: leave to appeal)* [1994] 1 FCR 33, [1993] 2 FLR 799; and *C v C (financial provision: non-disclosure)* [1995] 1 FCR 75, [1994] 2 FLR 272.

## [1.35.9]
## Leave to apply to set aside an order out of time

A district judge has jurisdiction to hear an application for leave to appeal out of time[1].

In *Barder v Barder (Caluori intervening)*[2] it was held the court can grant leave to appeal out of time (and by implication leave to apply to set aside) against an order for financial provision or property adjustment where (inter alia) new events had occurred within a relatively short time (months not years) after the making of the order which invalidated the basis upon which it had been made. Such applications had to be made promptly and must not prejudice third parties who had acquired in good faith, and for valuable consideration, an interest in the property which was the subject matter of the order[3].

1 *Ritchie v Ritchie* [1996] 3 FCR 609, [1996] 1 FLR 898, CA.
2 [1988] AC 20, [1987] 2 All ER 440, HL.
3 See also *Hope-Smith v Hope-Smith* [1989] FCR 785, [1989] 2 FLR 56, CA.

## (2)
## ALL APPEALS TO THE COURT OF APPEAL AND APPEALS IN ALL NON-FAMILY PROCEEDINGS' CASES

### [1.36]
### CPR 1998, Pt 52

The scheme of CPR 1998, Pt 52 is:

- the time for all appeals is now 14 days;
- there will be a uniform system of appeals in civil cases (one can expect the system to be extended to family cases in due course);
- a number of appeals from the county court previously made to the Court of Appeal will, in future, be made to a single High Court judge;
- in civil cases appeals from a district judge to a circuit judge will require permission and the appeal will not take the form of a complete rehearing but will be in the nature of a review of the decision under appeal;
- the court will, without a hearing, have the power to strike out an appeal 'for a compelling reason';
- all appeals to the Court of Appeal will require permission except appeals in relation to the liberty of the citizen (an order for committal, applications of habeas corpus and an order in relation to secure accommodation under the ChA 1989);
- TLATA 1996 and I(PFD)A 1975 cases will still be by way of appeal from the district judge (or Master) to a High Court judge. This is because these proceedings are treated as multi-track and/or they are specialist proceedings pursuant to CPR 1998, Pt 49.2;
- appeals are made in the new Form N161. Responses to appeals are made in Form N162;
- skeleton arguments should be in Form N163. They will ordinarily be served with the appropriate notices[1];
- 'family proceedings' defined above, are excluded by CPR 1998, Pt 52, save for appeals to the Court of Appeal.

The new CPR 1998, Pt 52 is supplemented by an extensive Practice Direction which is set out in **Part 4 – Practice Directions** at para **[4.38]** below. For appeals to the Court of Appeal, see generally *Rayden and Jackson on Divorce and Family Matters* (17th edn), vol 1, chap 50 and the Noter-up thereto.

1 See para 5.9 of the *Practice Direction* at para **[4.38]** below.

### [1.37]

PART 52
APPEALS

*I General Rules about Appeals*

#### 52.1 Scope and interpretation

(1) The rules in this Part apply to appeals to—
(a) the civil division of the Court of Appeal;
(b) the High Court; and
(c) a county court.

(2) This Part does not apply to an appeal in detailed assessment proceedings against a decision of an authorised court officer.

…

(Rules 47.21 to 47.26 deal with appeals against a decision of an authorised court officer in detailed assessment proceedings)

(3) In this Part—

(a) 'appeal' includes an appeal by way of case stated;

(b) 'appeal court' means the court to which an appeal is made;

(c) 'lower court' means the court, tribunal or other person or body from whose decision an appeal is brought;

(d) 'appellant' means a person who brings or seeks to bring an appeal;

(e) 'respondent' means—

(i) a person other than the appellant who was a party to the proceedings in the lower court and who is affected by the appeal; and

(ii) a person who is permitted by the appeal court to be a party to the appeal; and

(f) 'appeal notice' means an appellant's or respondent's notice.

(4) This Part is subject to any rule, enactment or practice direction which sets out special provisions with regard to any particular category of appeal.

**Amendment**

Inserted by SI 2000/221, r 19, Sch 5. Date in force: 2 May 2000 (except where a person seeks to appeal a judgment or order made before that date): see SI 2000/221, rr 1(b), 39(a). Para (2): SI 2000/2092, rr 20, 21. Date in force: 2 October 2000: see SI 2000/2092, r 1.

## [1.38]

### 52.2 Parties to comply with the practice direction

All parties to an appeal must comply with the relevant practice direction.

**Amendment**

Inserted by SI 2000/221, r 19, Sch 5. Date in force: 2 May 2000 (except where a person seeks to appeal a judgment or order made before that date): see SI 2000/221, rr 1(b), 39(a).

## [1.38.1]
**Keypoint**

- Practice Direction

## [1.38.2]
**Practice Direction**

See the *Practice Direction* that supplements CPR 1998, Pt 52 which is set out at para **[4.38]** below.

## [1.39]

### 52.3 Permission

(1) An appellant or respondent requires permission to appeal—

(a) where the appeal is from a decision of a judge in a county court or the High Court, except where the appeal is against—

(i) a committal order;

(ii) a refusal to grant habeas corpus; or

(iii) a secure accommodation order made under section 25 of the Children Act 1989; or

(b) as provided by the relevant practice direction.

(Other enactments may provide that permission is required for particular appeals)

(2) An application for permission to appeal may be made—

(a) to the lower court at the hearing at which the decision to be appealed was made; or

(b) to the appeal court in an appeal notice.

(Rule 52.4 sets out the time limits for filing an appellant's notice at the appeal court. Rule 52.5 sets out the time limits for filing a respondent's notice at the appeal court. Any application for permission to appeal to the appeal court must be made in the appeal notice (see rules 52.4(1) and 52.5(3))

(Rule 52.13(1) provides that permission is required from the Court of Appeal for all appeals to that court from a decision of a county court or the High Court which was itself made on appeal)

(3) Where the lower court refuses an application for permission to appeal, a further application for permission to appeal may be made to the appeal court.

(4) Where the appeal court, without a hearing, refuses permission to appeal, the person seeking permission may request the decision to be reconsidered at a hearing.

(5) A request under paragraph (4) must be filed within seven days after service of the notice that permission has been refused.

(6) Permission to appeal will only be given where—

(a) the court considers that the appeal would have a real prospect of success; or

(b) there is some other compelling reason why the appeal should be heard.

(7) An order giving permission may—

(a) limit the issues to be heard; and

(b) be made subject to conditions.

(Rule 3.1(3) also provides that the court may make an order subject to conditions)

(Rule 25.15 provides for the court to order security for costs of an appeal)

**Amendment**

Inserted by SI 2000/221, r 19, Sch 5. Date in force: 2 May 2000 (except where a person seeks to appeal a judgment or order made before that date): see SI 2000/221, rr 1(b), 39(a).

## [1.39.1]
### Keypoints

- Practice Direction
- Second appeals
- Case management decisions

## [1.39.2]
### Practice Direction

See CPR 1998, PD52, paras 4.1 to 4.19 at para **[4.38]** below.

## [1.39.3]
### Second appeals

A stricter test is imposed in second appeals (examples include where one party has appealed from the district judge to the judge and is now appealing to the Court of Appeal). Section 55 of the AJA 1999[1] provides that no appeal may be made to the Court of Appeal in a second appeal unless the Court of Appeal considers that the appeal raises an important point of principle or practice or there is some other compelling reason for the Court of Appeal to hear it.

1 See para **[2.525]** below.

## [1.39.4]
### Case management decisions

Additional considerations may be taken into account where an appellant seeks permission to appeal a case management decision, such as whether the issue is of sufficient significance to justify the costs of appeal[1].

1 See CPR 1998, PD52, para 4.5 at para **[4.32]** below.

## [1.40]

### 52.4 Appellant's notice

(1) Where the appellant seeks permission from the appeal court it must be requested in the appellant's notice.

(2) The appellant must file the appellant's notice at the appeal court within—

(a) such period as may be directed by the lower court; or

(b) where the court makes no such direction, 14 days after the date of the decision of the lower court that the appellant wishes to appeal.

(3) Unless the appeal court orders otherwise, an appeal notice must be served on each respondent—

(a) as soon as practicable; and

(b) in any event not later than 7 days,

after it is filed.

**Amendment**

Inserted by SI 2000/221, r 19, Sch 5. Date in force: 2 May 2000 (except where a person seeks to appeal a judgment or order made before that date): see SI 2000/221, rr 1(b), 39(a).

## [1.40.1]
### Keypoints

- Practice Direction
- Service of appellant's notice
- Documentation
- Form

## [1.40.2]
### Practice Direction

See CPR 1998, PD52, paras 5.1 to 5.25[1]. Note that the much-reduced time limit (14 days) for filing an appellant's notice provided by CPR 1998, Pt 52.4(2). See CPR 1998, PD52, paras 5.2 to 5.4 if an extension of time is needed.

1 Set out at para **[4.38]** below.

## [1.40.3]
### Service of appellant's notice

In an appeal from a county court, service on the district judge of an appellant's notice is no longer necessary (except where the appeal is from the grant of a decree nisi of divorce or nullity[1].

1 See CPR 1998, PD52, para 21.1(3), set out at para **[4.38]** below.

## [1.40.4]
### Documentation

The appellant is expected to file with his notice the documents required by para 5.6 of the *Practice Direction*[1]. In particular solicitors are reminded of their duty to obtain a transcript.

1 See para **[4.38]** below.

## [1.40.5]
### Form

The appeal should be made in Form N161.

## [1.41]

### 52.5 Respondent's notice

(1) A respondent may file and serve a respondent's notice.

(2) A respondent who—

(a) is seeking permission to appeal from the appeal court; or

(b) wishes to ask the appeal court to uphold the order of the lower court for reasons different from or additional to those given by the lower court,

must file a respondent's notice.

(3) Where the respondent seeks permission from the appeal court it must be requested in the respondent's notice.

(4) A respondent's notice must be filed within—

(a) such period as may be directed by the lower court; or

(b) where the court makes no such direction, 14 days after the date in paragraph (5).

(5) The date referred to in paragraph (4) is—

(a) the date the respondent is served with the appellant's notice where—

(i) permission to appeal was given by the lower court; or

(ii) permission to appeal is not required;

(b) the date the respondent is served with notification that the appeal court has given the appellant permission to appeal; or

(c) the date the respondent is served with notification that the application for permission to appeal and the appeal itself are to be heard together.

(6) Unless the appeal court orders otherwise a respondent's notice must be served on the appellant and any other respondent—

(a) as soon as practicable; and

(b) in any event not later than 7 days,

after it is filed.

**Amendment**

Inserted by SI 2000/221, r 19, Sch 5. Date in force: 2 May 2000 (except where a person seeks to appeal a judgment or order made before that date): see SI 2000/221, rr 1(b), 39(a).

## [1.41.1]
### Keypoints

- Practice Direction
- Form

## [1.41.2]
### Practice Direction

See CPR 1998, PD52, paras 7.1 to 7.13[1].

1 Set out at para **[4.38]** below.

## [1.41.3]
### Form

The response should be made in Form N162.

## [1.42]

### 52.6 Variation of time

(1) An application to vary the time limit for filing an appeal notice must be made to the appeal court.

(2) The parties may not agree to extend any date or time limit set by—

(a) these Rules;

(b) the relevant practice direction; or

(c) an order of the appeal court or the lower court.

(Rule 3.1(2)(a) provides that the court may extend or shorten the time for compliance with any rule, practice direction or court order (even if an application for extension is made after the time for compliance has expired))

(Rule 3.1(2)(b) provides that the court may adjourn or bring forward a hearing)

**Amendment**

Inserted by SI 2000/221, r 19, Sch 5. Date in force: 2 May 2000 (except where a person seeks to appeal a judgment or order made before that date): see SI 2000/221, rr 1(b), 39(a).

## [1.43]

### 52.7 Stay

Unless—

(a) the appeal court or the lower court orders otherwise; or

(b) the appeal is from the Immigration Appeal Tribunal,

an appeal shall not operate as a stay of any order or decision of the lower court.

**Amendment**

Inserted by SI 2000/221, r 19, Sch 5. Date in force: 2 May 2000 (except where a person seeks to appeal a judgment or order made before that date): see SI 2000/221, rr 1(b), 39(a).

## [1.43.1]
**Keypoint**

- Stay of execution

## [1.43.2]
**Stay of execution**

An appeal does not operate as a stay of execution and a separate application for a stay should be made or included in an application for permission to appeal. Applications made after the filing of an appeal notice are made in accordance with CPR 1998, Pt 23. The law in this area is unchanged.

## [1.44]

### 52.8 Amendment of appeal notice

An appeal notice may not be amended without the permission of the appeal court.

**Amendment**

Inserted by SI 2000/221, r 19, Sch 5. Date in force: 2 May 2000 (except where a person seeks to appeal a judgment or order made before that date): see SI 2000/221, rr 1(b), 39(a).

## [1.44.1]
**Keypoint**

- Amendment of appeal notice

## [1.44.2]
**Amendment of appeal notice**

See para 5.25 of CPR 1998, PD52 at para [4.38] below where an appellant wishes to pursue grounds for which permission to appeal has not been granted.

## [1.45]

### 52.9 Striking out appeal notices and setting aside or imposing conditions on permission to appeal

(1) The appeal court may—

(a) strike out the whole or part of an appeal notice;

(b) set aside permission to appeal in whole or in part;

(c) impose or vary conditions upon which an appeal may be brought.

(2) The court will only exercise its powers under paragraph (1) where there is a compelling reason for doing so.

(3) Where a party was present at the hearing at which permission was given he may not subsequently apply for an order that the court exercise its powers under sub-paragraphs (1)(b) or (1)(c).

**Amendment**

Inserted by SI 2000/221, r 19, Sch 5. Date in force: 2 May 2000 (except where a person seeks to appeal a judgment or order made before that date): see SI 2000/221, rr 1(b), 39(a).

## [1.45.1]

**Keypoint**

- Security for costs of an appeal

## [1.45.2]

**Security for costs of an appeal**

See CPR 1998, Pt 25.15 (set out at para **[1.313]** below).

## [1.46]

### 52.10 Appeal court's powers

(1) In relation to an appeal the appeal court has all the powers of the lower court.

(Rule 52.1(4) provides that this Part is subject to any enactment that sets out special provisions with regard to any particular category of appeal—where such an enactment gives a statutory power to a tribunal, person or other body it may be the case that the appeal court may not exercise that power on an appeal)

(2) The appeal court has power to—

(a) affirm, set aside or vary any order or judgment made or given by the lower court;

(b) refer any claim or issue for determination by the lower court;

(c) order a new trial or hearing;

(d) make orders for the payment of interest;

(e) make a costs order.

(3) In an appeal from a claim tried with a jury the Court of Appeal may, instead of ordering a new trial—

(a) make an order for damages; or

(b) vary an award of damages made by the jury.

(4) The appeal court may exercise its powers in relation to the whole or part of an order of the lower court.

(Part 3 contains general rules about the court's case management powers)

**Amendment**

Inserted by SI 2000/221, r 19, Sch 5. Date in force: 2 May 2000 (except where a person seeks to appeal a judgment or order made before that date): see SI 2000/221, rr 1(b), 39(a).

## [1.47]

### 52.11 Hearing of appeals

(1) Every appeal will be limited to a review of the decision of the lower court unless—

(a) a practice direction makes different provision for a particular category of appeal; or

(b) the court considers that in the circumstances of an individual appeal it would be in the interests of justice to hold a re-hearing.

(2) Unless it orders otherwise, the appeal court will not receive—

(a) oral evidence; or

(b) evidence which was not before the lower court.

(3) The appeal court will allow an appeal where the decision of the lower court was—

(a) wrong; or

(b) unjust because of a serious procedural or other irregularity in the proceedings in the lower court.

(4) The appeal court may draw any inference of fact which it considers justified on the evidence.

(5) At the hearing of the appeal a party may not rely on a matter not contained in his appeal notice unless the appeal court gives permission.

**Amendment**

Inserted by SI 2000/221, r 19, Sch 5. Date in force: 2 May 2000 (except where a person seeks to appeal a judgment or order made before that date): see SI 2000/221, rr 1(b), 39(a).

## [1.47.1]
### Keypoints

- Appeal hearings
- Fresh evidence
- *Marsh v Marsh*
- Disposing of applications and appeals by consent

## [1.47.2]
### Appeal hearings

CPR 1998, Pt 52.11 is a new provision. However, previous authorities concerning the circumstances in which the Court of Appeal would entertain an appeal will remain relevant.

*Appeals against finding of facts*

Great weight is given by the Court of Appeal to any finding of fact made by the judge in the court below on the basis of his view of the credibility and reliability of witnesses seen and heard by him, arising from their demeanour and manner. It is unusual for the Court of Appeal to differ from the judge where such an assessment is the whole basis of the decision and it will do so only in exceptional circumstances[1]. On the other hand, where there is conflicting evidence, the court is free to weigh it and draw its own conclusions. There is a distinction to be drawn between:

- the primary facts found by a judge or not in dispute; and
- the inferences to be drawn from them.

The Court of Appeal is quite willing to differ from the judge as to such inference[2].

*Appeals from the exercise of a judge's discretion*

The Court of Appeal is reluctant to interfere with the exercise of a judge's discretion but will certainly do so if it can be shown that the judge had:

- misunderstood the facts,
- taken account of irrelevant matters,
- in fact failed to exercise the discretion, or

- made a decision that no reasonable judge could have made or one which there was no material before him to justify,

in other words, the judge was plainly wrong since the conclusion reached was 'outside the generous ambit within which a reasonable disagreement is possible'[3].

*Appeals on points of law*

If a judge is wrong on a matter of law crucial to his decision, then an appeal will succeed unless his decision can be upheld by some alternative and sound proposition of law. An appeal on the grounds that there is no evidence to support a finding is an appeal on a point of law, but it is insufficient to show that there was little evidence. The *Practice Direction* to RSC Ord 59 provided (at para 2.9.1) that permission to appeal should not be granted unless the judge considered that there was a realistic prospect of the Court of Appeal coming to a different conclusion on a point of law which would materially affect the outcome of the case.

1 See *Arkerhielm v De Mare* [1959] AC 789, [1959] 3 All ER 485, PC.
2 See *Benmax v Austin Motor Co Ltd* [1955] AC 370, [1955] 1 All ER 326, HL.
3 See *G v G* [1985] 2 All ER 225, [1985] 1 WLR 647, HL.

## [1.47.3]
### *Marsh v Marsh*

The long established case of *Marsh v Marsh*[1] appears to adopt a different test in financial/domestic violence appeals from District Judges to Circuit Judges. This approach has been attacked by the President in *Cordle v Cordle*[2] and she suggests that CPR 1998, Pt 52.11 should be applied.

1 [1993] 2 All ER 794, [1993] 1 WLR 744, CA.
2 [2001] EWCA Civ 1791, [2002] 1 FCR 97.

## [1.47.4]
### Disposing of applications and appeals by consent

See CPR 1998, PD52, paras 12.1 to 13.5 at para **[4.38]** below.

## [1.48]

### 52.12 Non-disclosure of Part 36 offers and payments

(1) The fact that a Part 36 offer or Part 36 payment has been made must not be disclosed to any judge of the appeal court who is to hear and finally determine an appeal until all questions (other than costs) have been determined.

(2) Paragraph (1) does not apply if the Part 36 offer or Part 36 payment is relevant to the substance of the appeal.

(3) Paragraph (1) does not prevent disclosure in any application in the appeal proceedings if disclosure of the fact that a Part 36 offer or Part 36 payment has been made is properly relevant to the matter to be decided.

**Amendment**

Inserted by SI 2000/221, r 19, Sch 5. Date in force: 2 May 2000 (except where a person seeks to appeal a judgment or order made before that date): see SI 2000/221, rr 1(b), 39(a).

## [1.49]

*II Special Provisions Applying to the Court of Appeal*

### 52.13 Second appeals to the court

(1) Permission is required from the Court of Appeal for any appeal to that court from a decision of a county court or the High Court which was itself made on appeal.

(2) The Court of Appeal will not give permission unless it considers that—
(a) the appeal would raise an important point of principle or practice; or
(b) there is some other compelling reason for the Court of Appeal to hear it.

**Amendment**

Inserted by SI 2000/221, r 19, Sch 5. Date in force: 2 May 2000 (except where a person seeks to appeal a judgment or order made before that date): see SI 2000/221, rr 1(b), 39(a).

**[1.50]**

### 52.14 Assignment of appeals to the Court of Appeal

(1) Where the court from or to which an appeal is made or from which permission to appeal is sought ('the relevant court') considers that—
(a) an appeal which is to be heard by a county court or the High Court would raise an important point of principle or practice; or
(b) there is some other compelling reason for the Court of Appeal to hear it,
the relevant court may order the appeal to be transferred to the Court of Appeal.

(The Master of the Rolls has the power to direct that an appeal which would be heard by a county court or the High Court should be heard instead by the Court of Appeal—see section 57 of the Access to Justice Act 1999)

(2) The Master of the Rolls or the Court of Appeal may remit an appeal to the court in which the original appeal was or would have been brought.

**Amendment**

Inserted by SI 2000/221, r 19, Sch 5. Date in force: 2 May 2000 (except where a person seeks to appeal a judgment or order made before that date): see SI 2000/221, rr 1(b), 39(a).

**[1.51]**

### 52.15 Judicial review appeals

(1) Where permission to apply for judicial review has been refused at a hearing in the High Court, the person seeking that permission may apply to the Court of Appeal for permission to appeal.

(2) An application in accordance with paragraph (1) must be made within 7 days of the decision of the High Court to refuse to give permission to apply for judicial review.

(3) On an application under paragraph (1), the Court of Appeal may, instead of giving permission to appeal, give permission to apply for judicial review.

(4) Where the Court of Appeal gives permission to apply for judicial review in accordance with paragraph (3), the case will proceed in the High Court unless the Court of Appeal orders otherwise.

**Amendment**

Inserted by SI 2000/221, r 19, Sch 5. Date in force: 2 May 2000 (except where a person seeks to appeal a judgment or order made before that date): see SI 2000/221, rr 1(b), 39(a).

**[1.52]**

### 52.16 Who may exercise the powers of the Court of Appeal

(1) A court officer assigned to the Civil Appeals Office who is—
(a) a barrister; or
(b) a solicitor
may exercise the jurisdiction of the Court of Appeal with regard to the matters set out in paragraph (2) with the consent of the Master of the Rolls.

(2) The matters referred to in paragraph (1) are—
(a) any matter incidental to any proceedings in the Court of Appeal;

(b) any other matter where there is no substantial dispute between the parties; and
(c) the dismissal of an appeal or application where a party has failed to comply with any order, rule or practice direction.

(3) A court officer may not decide an application for—

(a) permission to appeal;
(b) bail pending an appeal;
(c) an injunction;
(d) a stay of any proceedings, other than a temporary stay of any order or decision of the lower court over a period when the Court of Appeal is not sitting or cannot conveniently be convened.

(4) Decisions of a court officer may be made without a hearing.

(5) A party may request any decision of a court officer to be reviewed by the Court of Appeal.

(6) At the request of a party, a hearing will be held to reconsider a decision of—

(a) a single judge; or
(b) a court officer,

made without a hearing.

(7) A single judge may refer any matter for a decision by a court consisting of two or more judges.

(Section 54(6) of the Supreme Court Act 1981 provides that there is no appeal from the decision of a single judge on an application for permission to appeal)

(Section 58(2) of the Supreme Court Act 1981 provides that there is no appeal to the House of Lords from decisions of the Court of Appeal that—

(a) are taken by a single judge or any officer or member of staff of that court in proceedings incidental to any cause or matter pending before the civil division of that court; and
(b) do not involve the determination of an appeal or of an application for permission to appeal,

and which may be called into question by rules of court. Rules 52.16(5) and (6) provide the procedure for the calling into question of such decisions)]

**Amendment**

Inserted by SI 2000/221, r 19, Sch 5. Date in force: 2 May 2000 (except where a person seeks to appeal a judgment or order made before that date): see SI 2000/221, rr 1(b), 39(a).

### [1.53]
### Practice Direction

CPR 1998, PD52 (Appeals) is set out in **Part 4 – Practice Directions** at para **[4.38]** below.

## (3)
## FAMILY APPEALS

### [1.54]
### Family appeals[1]

For a definition of 'family proceedings' see para **[1.34]** above.

Note CCR Ord 37, r 6[2] remains in force for family proceedings even though it is abolished in civil proceedings.

In practice this Section of the text will only apply to appeals from district judges

1 In practice this Section of the text will only apply to appeals from district judges. Appeals from circuit judges and High Court judges, in both cases to the Court of Appeal, will be regulated by CPR 1998, Pt 52.

2 See para **[1.57]** below.

**[1.55]**

### FPR 1991, r 8.1 Appeals from district judges

(1) Except where paragraph (2) applies, any party may appeal from an order or decision made or given by the district judge in family proceedings in a county court to a judge on notice; and in such a case—

(a) CCR Order 13, rule 1(10) (which enables the judge to vary or rescind an order made by the district judge in the course of proceedings), and

(b) CCR Order 37, rule 6 (which gives a right of appeal to the judge from a judgment or final decision of the district judge),

shall not apply to the order or decision.

(2) Any order or decision granting or varying an order (or refusing to do so)—

(a) on an application for ancillary relief, or

(b) in proceedings to which rules 3.1, 3.2, 3.3 [or 3.6] apply,

shall be treated as a final order for the purposes of CCR Order 37, rule 6.

(3) On hearing an appeal to which paragraph (2) above applies, the judge may exercise his own discretion in substitution for that of the district judge.

(4) Unless the court otherwise orders, any notice under this rule must be issued within 14 days of the order or decision appealed against and served not less than 14 days before the day fixed for the hearing of the appeal.

(5) Appeals under this rule shall be heard in chambers unless the judge otherwise directs.

(6) Unless the court otherwise orders, an appeal under this rule shall not operate as a stay of proceedings on the order or decision appealed against.

**Amendment**

Para (2): in sub-para (b) words 'or 3.6' in square brackets substituted, in relation to proceedings commenced after 1 October 1997, by SI 1997/1893, rr 6, 9.

**[1.55.1]**
**Keypoint**

- Appeals under FPR 1991, r 8.1 and those under CCR Ord 37, r 1

**[1.55.2]**
**Appeals under FPR 1991, r 8.1 and those under CCR Ord 37, r 1**

The following should follow the CCR Ord 37, r 6 route to appeal; ancillary reliefs (para 2(a)), applications in case of failure to maintain (FPR 1991, r 3.1), alteration of maintenance agreements during life (FPR 1991, r 3.2) or death (FPR 1991, r 3.3) and the MWPA 1882 (FPR 1991, r 3.6). The reference to MWPA 1882 proceedings only relates to such proceedings commenced after 1 October 1997 (see SI 1997/1893, rr 6, 9). All other Family Division (non-children) appeals are dealt with by FPR 1991, rr 8.1 or 8.1A.

In *Marsh v Marsh*[1] the Court of Appeal stated that full meaning and effect must be accorded to r 8.1(3) of the FPR 1991 and that the judge should exercise his own discretion but may give such weight as he thinks fit to the manner in which the district judge exercised his discretion. This decision has been questioned in *Cordle v Cordle*[2] where Thorpe LJ felt that the harmonisation of the law following *White v White*[3], means that now:

- '… any appeal from a decision of a District Judge in ancillary relief shall only be allowed by the Circuit Judge if it is demonstrated that there has been some procedural irregularity or that in conducting the necessary balancing exercise the District Judge has taken into account matters which were irrelevant, or ignored matters which were relevant, or has otherwise arrived at a conclusion that is plainly wrong';
- '… equally it seems to me that a Circuit Judge hearing an appeal from a District Judge should not admit fresh evidence, unless there is a need to do so on the application of the more liberal rules for the admission of fresh evidence that are recognised as necessary in family proceedings'.

The President suggested that CPR 1998, Pt 52.11 would apply.

These observations need to be made:

- as currently expressed, the Court of Appeal's views do not appear to extend to an appeal from a District Judge to a High Court Judge;
- the basis of the Court of Appeal's judgments is controversial; they purport to overturn a very strong unanimous three Judge Court of Appeal which had the benefit of argument from leading (now Wall J) and junior counsel on one side and junior counsel on the other side. Mr Cordle appeared in person. The *Bristol Aeroplanes* test is not referred to.

1 [1993] 2 All ER 794, [1993] 1 WLR 744, CA. See also commentary to CCR Ord 37, r 6 at para **[1.57.1]** below.

2 [2001] EWCA Civ 1791, [2002] 1 FCR 97.

3 [2001] 1 AC 596, [2000] 3 FCR 555, HL.

**[1.56]**

## FPR 1991, r 8.1A Appeals from orders made under Part IV of the Family Law Act 1996

[(1) This rule applies to all appeals from orders made under Part IV of the Family Law Act 1996 and on such an appeal—

(a) paragraphs (2), (3), (4), (5), (7) and (8) of rule 4.22,

(b) paragraphs (5) and (6) of rule 8.1, and

(c) paragraphs (4)(e) and (6) of rule 8.2,

shall apply subject to the following provisions of this rule and with the necessary modifications.

(2) The justices' chief executive for the magistrates' court from which an appeal is brought shall be served with the documents mentioned in rule 4.22(2).

(3) Where an appeal lies to the High Court, the documents required to be filed by rule 4.22(2) shall be filed in the registry of the High Court which is nearest to the magistrates' court from which the appeal is brought.

(4) Where the appeal is brought against the making of a hospital order or a guardianship order under the Mental Health Act 1983, a copy of any written evidence considered by the magistrates' court under section 37(1)(a) of the 1983 Act shall be sent by the justices' chief executive to the registry of the High Court in which the documents relating to the appeal are filed in accordance with paragraph (3).

(5) A district judge may dismiss an appeal to which this rule applies for want of prosecution and may deal with any question of costs arising out of the dismissal or withdrawal of an appeal.

(6) Any order or decision granting or varying an order (or refusing to do so) in proceedings in which an application is made in accordance with rule 3.8 for—

(a) an occupation order as described in section 33(4) of the Family Law Act 1996,

(b) an occupation order containing any of the provisions specified in section 33(3) where the applicant or the respondent has matrimonial home rights, or

(c) a transfer of tenancy,

shall be treated as a final order for the purposes of CCR Order 37, rule 6 and, on an appeal from such an order, the judge may exercise his own discretion in substitution for that of the district judge and the provisions of CCR Order 37, rule 6 shall apply.]

**Amendment**

Inserted, in relation to proceedings commenced after 1 October 1997, by SI 1997/1893, rr 7, 9. Amended by SI 2001/821.

## [1.57]

### CCR Ord 37, r 6 Appeal from district judge

(1) Any party affected by a judgment or final order of the district judge may, except where he has consented to the terms of the order, appeal from the judgment or order to the judge, who may, upon such terms as he thinks fit—

(a) set aside or vary the judgment or order or any part of it;

(b) give any other judgment or make any other order in substitution for the judgment or order appealed from;

(c) remit the claim or any question in the claim to the district judge for rehearing or further consideration; or

(d) order a new trial to take place before himself or another judge of the court on a day to be fixed.

(2) The appeal shall be made on notice, which shall state the grounds of the appeal and be served within 14 days after the day on which judgment or order appealed from was given or made.

## [1.57.1]
### Keypoints

- Right of appeal
- Appealing consent orders
- Appealing judge's refusal to extend time for appealing from district judge
- New evidence
- CPR

## [1.57.2]
### Right of appeal

An appeal from a district judge lies to the judge. The position in relation to ancillary relief in family proceedings is governed by r 8.1(2) of the FPR 1991, so that, in such cases, the county court judge is entitled to admit fresh evidence and, if appropriate, to substitute his discretion for that of the district judge[1].

1 See *Marsh v Marsh* [1993] 2 All ER 794, [1993] 1 WLR 744, CA.

## [1.57.3]
### Appealing consent orders

Consent orders are excluded from CCR Ord 37, r 6. Despite this provision, it appears that an appeal does lie and that appeal does not require leave. In *Harris (formerly Manahan) v Manahan*[1] Ward LJ concluded that it was at least arguable that an appeal lies as of right and without leave against a consent order made by a district judge and therefore if the appeal is entered in time the judge is bound to approach the matter de novo by virtue of FPR 1991, r 8.1(3)[2].

1 [1996] 4 All ER 454, CA.
2 See also *Benson v Benson* [1996] 3 FCR 590, [1996] 1 FLR 692.

## [1.57.4]
### Appealing judge's refusal to extend time for appealing from district judge

There is an appeal to the Court of Appeal from a judge's refusal to extend the time for appealing from a district judge's order[1].

1 See *Rickards v Rickards* [1990] Fam 194, [1989] 3 All ER 193, CA.

### [1.57.5]
### New evidence

As the judge is entitled to substitute his exercise of discretion for that of the district judge it is right that he should also have an unfettered discretion as to the admission of evidence (including new evidence). In *Marsh v Marsh*[1] Sir Stephen Brown P held that no party shall be entitled as of right to adduce further evidence or oral evidence but the judge may in his discretion admit such further or oral evidence as he thinks relevant and just upon such terms as he thinks fit. Such a judge is not strictly bound by the rules as expressed in *Ladd v Marshall*[2].

1 [1993] 2 All ER 794, [1993] 1 WLR 744, CA.
2 [1954] 3 All ER 745, [1954] 1 WLR 148.

### [1.57.6]
### CPR

This rule is abolished in civil proceedings but survives in family proceedings.

### [1.58]

**CCR Ord 37, r 8 Imposition of terms and stay of execution**

(1) An application to the judge or district judge under any of the foregoing rules may be granted on such terms as he thinks reasonable.

(2) Notice of any such application shall not of itself operate as a stay of execution on the judgment or order to which it relates but the court may order a stay of execution pending the hearing of the application or any rehearing or new trial ordered on the application.

(3) If a judgment or order is set aside under any of the foregoing rules, any execution issued on the judgment or order shall cease to have effect unless the court otherwise orders.

### [1.58.1]
### Keypoint

- Terms

### [1.58.2]
### Terms

The court has a discretion as to imposing terms. It may, though it is not bound to do so, make the payment of the costs of the first trial a condition precedent to a fresh trial[1].

1 See *May v Lee* (1898) 104 LT Jo 357.

## (4)
## APPEALS FROM MAGISTRATES' COURTS

## A
## APPEALS

### [1.59]
### Note

This chapter does not deal with appeals under s 94 of the ChA 1989 (see Vol 2, Pt 2, para **[2.1382]**). Appeals to the Crown Court and against fines for contempt of court are so rare that they fall outside of the scope of this book. For appeals from magistrates' courts other than under s 94 of the ChA 1989, see *Rayden and Jackson on Divorce and Family Matters* (17th edn, 1997), vol 1, chap 50.

**[1.60]**

*Provisions relating to the High Court and county court*

### 27 Refusal or order in case more suitable for High Court

Where on hearing an application for an order under section 2 of this Act a magistrates' court is of the opinion that any of the matters in question between the parties would be more conveniently dealt with by the High Court, the magistrates' court shall refuse to make any order on the application, and no appeal shall lie from that refusal; but if in any proceedings in the High Court relating to or comprising the same subject matter as that application the High Court so orders, the application shall be reheard and determined by a magistrates' court acting for the same petty sessions area as the first mentioned court.

**Appointment**
Commencement order: SI 1980/1478.

**[1.61]**

### 29 Appeals

(1) Subject to section 27 of this Act, where a magistrates' court makes or refuses to make, varies or refuses to vary, revokes or refuses to revoke an order (other than an interim maintenance order) under this Part of this Act, an appeal shall lie to the High Court.

(2) On an appeal under this section the High Court shall have power to make such orders as may be necessary to give effect to its determination of the appeal, including such incidental or consequential orders as appear to the court to be just, and, in the case of an appeal from a decision of a magistrates' court made on an application for or in respect of an order for the making of periodical payments, the High Court shall have power to order that its determination of the appeal shall have effect from such date as the court thinks fit, not being earlier than the date of the making of the application to the magistrates' court [or, in a case where there was made to the magistrates' court an application for an order under section 2 and an application under section 6 and the term of the periodical payments was or might have been ordered to begin on the date of the making of the application for an order under section 2, the date of the making of that application].

(3) Without prejudice to the generality of subsection (2) above, where, on an appeal under this section in respect of an order of a magistrates' court requiring any person to make periodical payments, the High Court reduces the amount of those payments or discharges the order, the High Court shall have power to order the person entitled to payments under the order of the magistrates' court to pay to the person liable to make payments under that order such sum in respect of payments already made in compliance with the order as the court thinks fit and, if any arrears are due under the order of the magistrates' court, the High Court shall have power to remit the payment of those arrears or any part thereof.

(4) …

(5) Any order of the High Court made on an appeal under this section (other than an order directing that an application shall be reheard by a magistrates' court) shall for the purposes of the enforcement of the order and for the purposes of [section 20] of this Act be treated as if it were an order of the magistrates' court from which the appeal was brought and not of the High Court.

**Appointment**
Commencement orders: SI 1979/731, 1980 No 1478.

**Amendment**
Sub-s (2): words in square brackets inserted by the MFPA 1984, s 46(1), Sch 1. Sub-s (4): repealed by the ChA 1989, s 108(7), Sch 15. Sub-s (5): words in square brackets substituted by the ChA 1989, s 108(5), Sch 13, para 42.

**[1.62]**

### FPR 1991, r 8.2 Appeals under Domestic Proceedings and Magistrates Courts' Act 1978

(1) Subject to paragraph (9) below, every appeal to the High Court under the Domestic Proceedings and Magistrates' Courts Act 1978 shall be heard by a Divisional Court of the Family Division and shall be entered by lodging three copies of the notice of motion in the principal registry.

(2) The notice must be served, and the appeal entered, within 6 weeks after the date of the order appealed against.

(3) Notice of the motion may be served in accordance with RSC Order 65, rule 5.

(4) On entering the appeal, or as soon as practicable thereafter, the appellant shall, unless otherwise directed, lodge in the principal registry—

- (a) three certified copies of the summons and of the order appealed against, and of any order staying its execution,
- (b) three copies of the clerk's notes of the evidence,
- (c) three copies of the justices' reasons for their decision,
- (d) a certificate that notice of the motion has been duly served on the clerk and on every party affected by the appeal, and
- (e) where the notice of the motion includes an application to extend the time for bringing the appeal, a certificate (and a copy thereof by the appellant's solicitor, or the appellant if he is acting in person, setting out the reasons for the delay and the relevant dates.

(5) If the clerk's notes of the evidence are not produced, the court may hear and determine the appeal on any other evidence or statement of what occurred in the proceedings before the magistrates' court as appears to the court to be sufficient.

(6) The court shall not be bound to allow the appeal on the ground merely of misdirection or improper reception or rejection of evidence unless, in the opinion of the court, substantial wrong or miscarriage of justice has been thereby occasioned.

(7) A district judge may dismiss an appeal to which this rule applies for want of prosecution or, with the consent of the parties, may dismiss the appeal or give leave for it to be withdrawn, and may deal with any question of costs arising out of the dismissal or withdrawal.

(8) Any interlocutory application in connection with or for the purpose of any appeal to which this rule applies may be heard and disposed of before a single judge.

(9) Where an appeal to which this rule applies relates only to the amount of any periodical or lump sum payment ordered to be made, it shall, unless the President otherwise directs, be heard and determined by a single judge, and in that case—

- (a) for the references in paragraphs (1) and (4)(a), (b) and (c) to three copies of the documents therein mentioned there shall be substituted references to one copy;
- (b) the parties may agree in writing or the President may direct that the appeal be heard and determined at a divorce town.

**[1.62.1]**
**Keypoints**
- Appeal
- Procedure
- Time for appeal and stay

- Venue
- Notes of evidence
- Reasons
- Findings of fact
- Divisional Court

### [1.62.2]
### Appeal

No appeal lies from the refusal of a magistrates' court to make an order where it is of the opinion that the question between the parties would be more conveniently dealt with by the High Court. The procedure for appeals under the DPMCA 1978 is now governed by r 8.2 of the FPR 1991. In all cases the appeal may be heard by a single judge of the Family Division or, if the court so directs, by the Divisional Court of the Family Division.

### [1.62.3]
### Procedure

An appeal by notice of motion should be in the form set out in the *Practice Direction* of 11 May 1977. It must be served on every party affected by the appeal and on the justices' clerk of the court from which the appeal is brought.

### [1.62.4]
### Time for appeal and stay

The notice of motion must be served, and the appeal entered, within six weeks, from the date of the judgment or order or the date on which the decision was given. The Divisional Court has power to extend the time for appealing.

The bringing of an appeal by notice of motion does not operate as a stay.

### [1.62.5]
### Venue

The parties may consent to the appeal being heard at a place other than the Royal Courts of Justice and any such request, together with the consent of all the parties, should be filed at the outset to prevent delay: the President may direct that the appeal be heard and determined at a divorce town.

### [1.62.6]
### Notes of evidence

It is the duty of the clerk to the court to take a full note of the evidence given at the hearing. Either party is entitled to be furnished with a copy of the note[1]. The clerk's note will be treated as the best evidence of what has occurred in the court below; but the court may allow the note to be supplemented by an affidavit sworn by someone present at the hearing below.

1 See *Barker v Barker* (1905) 74 LJP 74.

### [1.62.7]
### Reasons

When making an order or when refusing an application under Pt I of the DPMCA 1978, the court, or one of the justices constituting the court by which the decision is made, must state any findings of fact and the reasons for the court's decision.

### [1.62.8]
### Findings of fact

The Divisional Court will not reverse any finding of fact by the magistrates' court, unless it appears that such finding is clearly wrong[1]. Only in very rare instances will any fresh evidence be received by the Divisional Court[2].

1 See *Pheasey v Pheasey* (1932) 96 JP 93.
2 See *Pearce v Pearce* (1929) 93 JP 64.

### [1.62.9]
### Divisional Court

The court is not bound to allow an appeal on the ground merely of misdirection or improper reception or rejection of evidence unless, in the opinion of the court, substantial wrong or miscarriage has been thereby occasioned.

## B
## APPEALS BY WAY OF CASE STATED: JUDICIAL REVIEW

## MAGISTRATES' COURTS ACT 1980

### [1.63]

#### 111 Statement of case by magistrates' court

(1) Any person who was a party to any proceeding before a magistrates' court or is aggrieved by the conviction, order, determination or other proceeding of the court may question the proceeding on the ground that it is wrong in law or is in excess of jurisdiction by applying to the justices composing the court to state a case for the opinion of the High Court on the question of law or jurisdiction involved; but a person shall not make an application under this section in respect of a decision against which he has a right of appeal to the High Court or which by virtue of any enactment passed after 31st December 1879 is final.

(2) An application under subsection (1) above shall be made within 21 days after the day on which the decision of the magistrates' court was given.

(3) For the purpose of subsection (2) above, the day on which the decision of the magistrates' court is given shall, where the court has adjourned the trial of an information after conviction, be the day on which the court sentences or otherwise deals with the offender.

(4) On the making of an application under this section in respect of a decision any right of the applicant to appeal against the decision to the Crown Court shall cease.

(5) If the justices are of opinion that an application under this section is frivolous, they may refuse to state a case, and, if the applicant so requires, shall give him a certificate stating that the application has been refused; but the justices shall not refuse to state a case if the application is made by or under the direction of the Attorney General.

(6) Where justices refuse to state a case, the High Court may, on the application of the person who applied for the case to be stated, make an order of mandamus requiring the justices to state a case.

**Appointment**
Commencement order: SI 1981/457.

### [1.64]

#### 112 Effect of decision of High Court on case stated by magistrates' court

Any conviction, order, determination or other proceeding of a magistrates' court varied by the High Court on an appeal by case stated, and any judgment or order of the High

Court on such an appeal, may be enforced as if it were a decision of the magistrates' court from which the appeal was brought.

**Appointment**
Commencement order: SI 1981/457.

### [1.64.1]
### Keypoints

- Case stated or appeal?
- Procedure
- Judicial review

### [1.64.2]
### Case stated or appeal?

Appeals against any order or determination by justices in regard to the enforcement of an order:

(i) for payment of money made by virtue of the DPMCA 1978, or
(ii) for the payment of money to a wife for her maintenance or for the maintenance of herself and of any child or children of hers, registered in a court in England or Wales under Pt II of the MOA 1950 or under the MO(FE)A 1920 (repealed by the MO(RE)A 1972) or under the 1972 Act[1], or
(iii) confirmed under the MOA 1950 or the MO(RE)A 1972,
(iv) the enforcement of an order for periodical or other payments made or having effect as if made under Pt II of the MCA 1973 which has been registered in a magistrates' court under the MOA 1958 (but variations are by notice of motion, above)

are by way of case stated to a single judge.

Where it is alleged that the magistrates had reached a decision without any or sufficient evidence to support it, the proper course is to proceed by way of case stated rather than judicial review. (Judicial review should be used for administrative decisions not judicial ones)[1].

1 See *Southwark London Borough Council v H* [1985] 2 All ER 657, [1985] 1 WLR 861, DC; and *R v Cardiff Justices, ex p Salter* [1986] 1 FLR 162.

### [1.64.3]
### Procedure

Where the appeal is by way of case stated it must be made within 21 days after the day on which the magistrates' court decision was given. There is no provision for extending that period. The application must identify the question or questions of law or jurisdiction on which the High Court's opinion is sought; and if one of those questions is whether there was evidence on which the court could come to its decision the particular finding of fact challenged must be specified.

The clerk must within 21 days after receipt of the application send a draft case to the parties or their solicitors. The case should state the facts found by the court and the question or questions of law or jurisdiction on which the High Court's opinion is sought. (For cases where the magistrates refuse to state their reasons see *Rayden and Jackson on Divorce and Family Matters* (17th edn, 1997).)

### [1.64.4]–[1.89]
### Judicial review

It will be rare for judicial review to challenge a matrimonial finance order made by the Magistrates. Their function in these cases is essentially judicial and not administrative, therefore appeals by way of notice of motion or case stated would usually be used. In view of the rarity of Judicial Review in these cases the subject is not dealt with in this book and practitioners are referred to the *Civil Court Practice* and the CPR 1998 contained therein.

# 3. Pensions

Contents

## Background

### [1.90]

Pension schemes have come to form an increasingly important part of the average family's assets[1]. Occupational pension schemes received an impetus from tax reliefs introduced in 1921 and have grown hugely. Self-employed pension policies were initiated following the Millard Tucker Report in 1956. Thus the whole spectrum of the working population that is now reaching retirement has been able to avail itself of one sort of scheme or the other. Capping regulations introduced in the Finance Act 1989 are still too recent to have affected a substantial percentage of the age group of divorcing couples whose pensions rights are a really material asset.

1 For the treatment of pensions in divorce, see generally *Rayden and Jackson on Divorce and Family Matters* (17th edn, 1997), vol 1, chap 22 and the Noter-up thereto.

## The position prior to 1 July 1996

### [1.91]

The court had a duty to consider the effect of loss of pension rights under s 25(2)(h) of the MCA 1973, which remains unamended and reads:

> 'in the case of proceedings for divorce or nullity of marriage, the value to each of the parties to the marriage of any benefit ... which, by reason of the dissolution or annulment of the marriage, that party will lose the chance of acquiring'.

### [1.92]

More generally, s 25(2)(a) and (b) of the MCA 1973[1] have always required the court to have regard to 'the income, earning capacity, property and other financial resources which each of the parties to the marriage has or is likely to have in the foreseeable future ...' and 'the financial needs ... which each of the parties to the marriage has or is likely to have in the foreseeable future'.

1 See para **[2.120]** below.

### [1.93]

The courts were hampered, and remained so hampered in general terms until after 1 December 2000, by their inability to invade pension funds and adjust pension rights between spouses. There was the further problem that in the case of some pension schemes, the pension deed contained a protective trust which effectively forfeited any pension payments if an order had been made against the pension fund itself. This was illustrated by the case of *Edmonds v Edmonds*[1].

1 [1965] 1 All ER 379n.

### [1.94]

Another aspect of the problem was that pensions as a resource had to pass the test of foreseeability under s 25(2)(a) of the MCA 1973[1]. This could be particularly relevant to the question of deciding whether or not to make an order that a husband pay a wife a lump sum when he was able to draw pension benefits, part of which would be his commutation lump sum. The order could not be specifically directed at the commutation lump sum but merely have the effect of ensuring in practice that that was a resource used by the husband. That was the approach resorted to in the cases of *Milne v Milne*[2] and *Priest v Priest*[3]. In each of these Court of Appeal decisions, the orders provided that a percentage of the capital payable at retirement was ordered as a lump sum to the wife. The prospective date of retirement was respectively ten years and five years, a matter which had troubled the court at first instance as to the foreseeability of the capital being paid.

1 See para **[2.120]** below.
2 (1981) 2 FLR 286.
3 (1978) 1 FLR 189.

### [1.95]

In more general terms, where pension benefits were a material part of the family assets, the courts resorted to offsetting, the process by which it adjusts upwards a lump sum payable by the spouse with pension rights (usually the husband) to the spouse without such rights (usually the wife) to achieve a just division of the family capital.

## Loss of widows pension as a defence to divorce

### [1.96]

Under s 5(1) of the MCA 1973[1]:

> 'the Respondent to a Petition for divorce in which the Petitioner alleges five years separation, may oppose the grant of a Decree on the grounds that the dissolution of the marriage will result in grave financial or other hardship to him and that it would in all circumstances be wrong to dissolve the marriage'.

It is a two stage test. The Respondent, usually the wife, must prove grave financial hardship. The court then exercises its discretion based on the circumstances of the case[2].

1 See para **[2.113]** below.
2 See *Jackson v Jackson* [1993] 2 FLR 848 per Bulter-Sloss LJ.

### [1.97]

In practice, loss of widows pension rights has seldom proved a bar to a husband obtaining a decree because, frequently, he has been able to make up that loss by other means, such as the purchase of a deferred annuity[1]. In both *Jackson v Jackson*[2] and *Reiterbund v Reiterbund*[3] the court found that there was no grave financial hardship because the wife was able to make up in state benefits what she lost by way of widow's pension.

1 See *Parker v Parker* [1972] Fam 116.
2 [1994] 2 FCR 393, [1993] 2 FLR 848, CA.
3 [1975] Fam 99, CA.

### [1.98]

The case of *K v K*[1] gives an interesting instance of where the court adjourned the case to give the husband time to come up with a solution sufficient to remove the element of grave financial hardship. In that case, the husband's advisers had not read the terms of the pension scheme properly. Under those terms he was able to allocate a sum towards a pension after his death to someone who would not otherwise be entitled, ie a dependent ex-wife. That allocation would be irrevocable in the event of the ex-wife predeceasing but it was the obvious way of affording the necessary financial protection to the ex-wife so as to enable a decree to be pronounced. The outline financial facts were that the husband's net income was just under £20,000 per annum; the wife's net income was just under half that amount. The wife was legally aided and her costs were about £9,000 and any lump sum she received would be subject to the statutory charge. The husband could retire in 1998 with an index linked pension of £15,674 or a capital sum of £57,877 and a reduced pension of £11,755. He was likely to carry on working until 2003. The widow's pension that the wife would lose was half his gross pension. The wife's own pension at 65 would be at most £3,388 a year, plus her state pension.

It was held that the wife was exactly the kind of person for whom the protection of the statute was devised.

1 [1997] 1 FLR 35.

## Section 10 of the MCA 1973

### [1.99]

Under s 10 of the MCA 1973[1] the Respondent to a Petition alleging either two years separation with the Respondent's consent or five years separation can apply to the court for it to consider what his or her financial position will be after the decree and to stay the Decree Absolute until that has occurred. The court must consider all the circumstances, including 'the financial position of the Respondent … should the Petitioner die first', which clearly includes the loss of pension rights. Under s 10(3) of the MCA 1973 the court must not make the Decree Absolute:

> 'unless it is satisfied:
> (a) that the Petitioner should not be required to make any financial provision for the Respondent or
> (b) that the financial provision made by the Petitioner for the Respondent is reasonable and fair or the best that can be made in the circumstances'.

Under s 10(4):

> 'the Court may if it thinks fit make the Decree Absolute notwithstanding the requirements of subsection (3) above if:
> (a) it appears that there are circumstances making it desirable that the Decree should be made Absolute without delay and
> (b) the Court has obtained a satisfactory undertaking from the Petitioner that he will make such financial provision for the Respondent as the Court may approve'.

1 See para **[2.114]** below.

### [1.100]

The distinction between s 5 and s 10 is well stated by Ormrod LJ in the case of *Le Marchant v Le Marchant*[1] when he said:

> '… Section 10 offers … an unreliable protection to a wife … the marriage would have been dissolved by the Decree Nisi, there would have been therefore a finding of fact that she has not suffered grave financial hardship in consequence of the Decree and she would then have to do the best she could under Section 10'.

1 [1977] 3 All ER 610 at 612.

## Variation of settlement applications under s 24(1)(c) of the MCA 1973

### [1.101]

It was very late in the day before Martin Pointer QC's ingenuity led to the court's finding that in certain circumstances a pension fund could be a nuptial settlement capable of variation under s 24(1)(c) of the MCA 1973[1]. The basic guidelines that emerged from the judgments of the Court of Appeal and the House of Lords were that whatever a pension scheme member had power to do himself under the rules (eg nominate, allocate or commute), the court had power to do by variation of settlement order provided third party rights were unaffected and the revenue approval for the scheme in question would not be sacrificed.

1 See *Brooks v Brooks* [1995] Fam 70, [1994] 4 All ER 1065 (in the Court of Appeal), [1996] AC 375, [1995] 3 All ER 257 (in the House of Lords). Section 24 of the MCA 1973 is set out at para **[2.118]** below.

## [1.102]

The requirements of s 24(1)(c) of the MCA 1973[1] are:

(a) that there should be a settlement post-marriage (it is almost inevitable that the variation of settlement jurisdiction has been invoked vis a vis a pension scheme because there is a post-nuptial, rather than a pre-nuptial, settlement); and
(b) that there should be (in the words of the authorities) a 'nuptial element'.

This in practice means that:

(a) the pension scheme should be set up post-marriage; and
(b) that the scheme should include provision for a widow.

The word 'settlement' under s 24 of the MCA 1973 is interpreted broadly and may cover any sort of continuing financial arrangement for both or either of the parties to the marriage.

The spouse seeking to benefit need not be named and a subsequent spouse can be capable of benefiting under the settlement as framed.

It does not matter that the interest under the settlement may be contingent.

1 See para **[2.118]** below.

## [1.103]

Non funded schemes (civil servants' pension schemes are the prime example) will not be amenable to the court's jurisdiction because there is no underlying fund.

Money purchase schemes, earnings related/final salary schemes, private retirement annuity contracts and personal pension plans are all potentially amenable to this jurisdiction. If any one of those schemes has only one member, namely the husband, it is potentially possible for the court to vary its terms so as to prescribe a guaranteed contingent dependant's pension for the wife. This would, of course, require that the wife was actually a dependant, by receipt of maintenance, on the death of the husband.

## [1.104]

In the case of an occupational scheme where the wife is also an employee of the scheme employer, the court can also diminish the husband's fund to create a separate fund for the wife as an employee so as to give her a retirement pension not exceeding the Inland Revenue maximum applicable to her.

## [1.105]

In *W and W*[1] Connell J made a variation of settlement order against a particularly obstructive husband, varying the terms of a managed pension contract with the Equitable Life.

1 [1996] 2 FLR 480.

## [1.106]

Applications for a variation of settlement order in respect of a pension scheme will continue to be relevant in respect of all original ancillary relief applications made in proceedings, which are begun before 1 December 2000 or on a variation application under s 31(7B) of the MCA 1973[1], if the marriage was dissolved by a decree in proceedings begun before that date[2].

1 See para **[2.129]** below.
2 See the WRPA 1999, s 85(4).

**[1.107]**

In practice it is difficult to see how a court would use the variation of settlement jurisdiction to effect a 'clean break' on a s 31(7B) variation of maintenance application brought in respect of a case to which s 85(4) of the WRPA 1999 does apply, as the most obvious use of that jurisdiction is to ensure that a husband gives up a part of his pension to provide a dependant's pension for an ex-spouse. The ex-spouse, in order to satisfy Revenue rules as to entitlement, must be dependent on him under a periodical payments order of the court at the time of his death, ie there would therefore be a continuing maintenance order and no 'clean break'.

## Changes made to the MCA 1973 by the Pensions Act 1995

**[1.108]**

These changes apply to all proceedings commenced by a Petition presented on or after 1 July 1996 where a Notice of Intention to Proceed has been filed on or after 1 August 1996.

**[1.109]**

The changes in the MCA 1973 specify more fully the court's duty to take into account pension rights:

(a) The Pensions Act 1995 emphasises that pensions are '... property or other financial resources' under s 25(2)(a) of the MCA 1973, and not merely a benefit lost by reason of the divorce under paragraph (h);

(b) It removes the reference to 'foreseeable future' in s 25(2) of the MCA 1973 so far as pension benefits are concerned. Other future resources must still fulfil the foreseeability test.

**[1.110]**

It is doubtful whether this change of emphasis was in any way dramatic. Practitioners dealing with a couple in their 30s or early 40s where one or both had already acquired substantial accrued pension rights, would not have ignored the existence of that fund before this legislative change and taken no account of it in performing the balancing exercise under s 25 of the MCA 1973[1] in advising their client. The point that has always been of overriding relevance is that, although pension benefits may be possessed by one or both relatively young spouses, they are not going to enjoy them until their retirement years. Inevitably pension funds assume greater significance in cases concerning spouses in their late 40s and beyond.

1 See para **[2.120]** below.

## The attachment provisions

**[1.111]**

The Pensions Act 1995 imported three new sections after s 25A of the MCA 1973, namely ss 25B to 25D[1], placing a mandatory duty on the court to consider whether 'an attachment order' should be made in cases where one of the parties has or will have benefits under a 'pension arrangement'. These are the attachment provisions enacted by s 166(1) of the Pensions Act 1995.

1 See paras **[2.122]** to **[2.124]** below.

**[1.112]**

Section 25B(4) of the MCA 1973[1] gives the court power on making an attachment order to require the person responsible for the pension arrangement:

> 'if at any time any payment in respect of any benefits under the scheme becomes due to the party with pension rights, to make a payment for the benefit of the other party'.

1 See para **[2.122]** below.

**[1.113]**

Section 25B(6) of the MCA 1973 makes it clear that any such payment by the person responsible for the pension arrangement discharges their liability to the party with pension rights 'as corresponds to the amount of the payment', and that it will be treated 'as a payment made by the party with pension rights in or towards the discharge of his liability under the Order'.

**[1.114]**

Section 25B(7) of the MCA 1973 gives the court power to order the party with pension rights to exercise the whole or part of his/her commutation rights and thereby to attach the commutation lump sum.

**[1.115]**

So, in summary, s 25B of the MCA 1973 gives the court power to attach a pension annuity when it comes into payment by way of a periodical payments order and the commutation lump sum by way of either a lump sum order or a secured provision order.

**[1.116]**

Section 25C of the MCA 1973[1] gives the court power to attach any lump sum payable in respect of the death of a spouse who is a member of a pension arrangement.

This can apply to the lump sum payable, for example, in an occupational scheme on death in service, and to a lump sum payable on death before drawing benefits under, for example, a personal pension scheme or a retirement annuity contract. It can also apply to the whole or part of any lump sum payable under the provisions of some pension schemes where the death of the member spouse occurs within ten years of retirement. Such a lump sum usually equates to the balance of the pension that would have been payable had the member spouse survived to the tenth anniversary of his retirement.

1 See para **[2.123]** below.

**[1.117]**

Section 25C(2) of the MCA 1973 contains three subsections aimed at different types of death benefits:

- **s 25C(2)(a)** – applies to those very common death in service lump sum provisions where the person responsible for the pension arrangement retains discretion as to whom the lump sum death benefit will be paid.
- **s 25C(2)(b)** – applies to those rare cases where the member spouse's nomination as to whom the lump sum death benefit will be paid is binding on the person responsible for the pension arrangement.
- **s 25C(2)(c)** – overrides the provisions of a trust of the lump sum death benefit established by the policy holder of, for example, a personal pension plan.

The wording of s 25C(1) of the MCA 1973 makes it quite clear that an order under that section in respect of lump sum death benefits is specifically categorised as a 'lump sum' order, although it is far more characteristic of a 'secured provision' order. Consequently, if the court has made a lump sum order or lump sum claims have been dismissed and you keep alive the non-member spouse's claims for secured provision, those claims cannot include an order under s 25C of the MCA 1973 in respect of lump sum death benefit.

## Which schemes are covered?

**[1.118]**

Attachment orders can only be made in respect of benefits under a 'pension arrangement'. Section 25D(3) of the MCA 1973[1] defines a pension arrangement as an occupational pension scheme, a personal pension scheme, a retirement annuity contract, annuities or insurance policies purchased or transferred to give effect to rights under an occupational or personal pension scheme and annuities purchased or entered into to discharge liability for pension credits created pursuant to pension sharing orders.

1 See para [2.124] below.

### [1.119]

In effect attachment orders can attach to benefits under an occupational pension scheme, a personal scheme and a public service pension scheme, but not to state pensions or to state earnings related pensions. Attachment covers all types of pension arrangements in the first three categories, including unapproved benefits.

## Summary of characteristics of attachment order

### [1.120]

It is important to appreciate that attachment orders are made under s 23 of the MCA 1973[1] and are financial provision orders. They are not property adjustment orders under s 24 of the MCA 1973[2].

Thus, when making an order under the attachment provisions the court may specify one of the following, either:

(a) periodical payments;
(b) secured periodical payments; or
(c) lump sum or sums,

in each case either immediate or deferred.

1 See para [2.117] below.
2 See para [2.118] below.

### [1.121]

Each of these orders is, of course, directed at the Respondent to the application and the involvement of the person responsible for the pension arrangement is ancillary and consequential. Attachment does not give the court original jurisdiction to rewrite pension schemes except to the extent that the trustees' discretion in respect of death in service lump sums can be overridden by the court order. The trustees, abiding by the direction of the court, assist the Respondent in fulfilling the terms of the order.

### [1.122]

The court is given additional powers to ensure compliance with its orders by the party with pension rights. It may, for example:

- require him to commute his pension up to allowable limits (s 25B(7) of the MCA 1973[1]) and to pay all or part of the tax free sum to the other party. This was new. Previously the court could only do that indirectly, by making a lump sum order which would necessitate some form of payment out of the commutation;
- in the case, at least, of an occupational pension, make an attachment of earnings order (s 91(4)(a) of the Pensions Act 1995). Normally, of course, this would be unnecessary where the person responsible is being directed to divert the payments under s 25B(4) of the MCA 1973.

1 See para [2.122] below.

## Defects of the attachment provisions

### [1.123]

Although under these attachment provisions the court can order one spouse to commute, it cannot oblige him/her to retire and/or take benefits at any particular time. Thus, he/she may be able to bring forward or delay retirement, either of which may have a direct impact on the other spouse's receipt of a share in the lump sum.

**[1.124]**

An order to pay all or some of the pension (rather than the lump sum) will not survive the death of either of the parties or the remarriage of the payee spouse. The payee spouse therefore needs to consider insuring the member against him/her predeceasing the payee, since the pension payments will cease on the member's death. In fact, if he/she dies too early they may never begin.

**[1.125]**

If the pension arrangement is a contributory scheme, particularly a personal pension scheme or retirement annuity contract, the member spouse can switch payments to another pension arrangement so that future contributions go to a personal pension plan that is unaffected by the order.

**[1.126]**

The obvious shortcomings with these provisions are that there can be no continuing provision for the the dependent former spouse after the member's death, and that the arrangement detracts from the clean break principle.

## Supplementary provisions

**[1.127]**

### Section 25D of the MCA 1973

Section 25D(1) of the MCA 1973[1] enables the court to impose 'following' orders where a person moves all his/her rights from one arrangement to another. Provided notice is given in a prescribed form to the new trustees or managers, they will become bound as if named in the original order. This subsection as originally drafted was defective, but its defects have been made good by an amendment brought in by the Welfare Reform and Pensions Act 1999.

1 See para **[2.124]** below.

**[1.128]**

Section 25D(2)(c) of the MCA 1973[1] makes provision for regulations as to valuations of pension rights. The Divorce etc (Pensions) Regulations 1996[2] prescribe that a scheme member will only be required to provide a cash equivalent transfer value (CETV). New regulations, namely the Divorce etc (Pensions) Regulations 2000[3], have replaced the 1996 regulations in any proceedings for divorce, judicial separation or nullity commenced on or after 1 December 2000 but it is still CETV which will be required. There are defects in using the CETV but, in practice, they have not proved to have been of importance in implementing the attachment legislation.

1 See para **[2.124]** below.
2 SI 1996/1676.
3 SI 2000/1123. Set out at para **[3.642]** et seq below.

**[1.129]**

Section 25D(2)(b) of the MCA 1973[1] requires notification of changes of circumstances such as the fact that a member of a scheme is made redundant or changes his/her job, or a change of address by the party without pension rights. Indeed failure by the party without pension rights to notify the scheme trustees or managers of a change of address may result in him/her losing the benefits payable under an attachment order.

1 See para **[2.124]** below.

## [1.130]
## Children

As stated above, s 25B of the MCA 1973[1] gives a court power to make one or more financial provision orders under s 23 of the MCA 1973[2] in a pensions case. Financial provision orders include orders in favour of a child but Parliament has clearly decided by the drafting of the legislation that attachment orders cannot be made in favour of children.

1 See para **[2.122]** below.
2 See para **[2.117]** below.

## [1.131]
## Variation

The Pensions Act 1995 amendment of the MCA 1973, by way of introduction of s 31(2)(dd)[1], enacted for the first time that a lump sum order is variable as to any part of the order including quantum when it is made by the court exercising its attachment jurisdiction under s 25B(4) (commutation of lump sums)[2] or s 25C (lump sums payable on death)[3]. Previously, only the instalments of a lump sum order were variable[4].

1 See para **[2.129]** below.
2 See para **[2.122]** below.
3 See para **[2.123]** below.
4 See the MCA 1973, s 31(2)(d). See also the judgment of Bodey J in the Court of Appeal in *Westbury v Sampson* [2001] EWCA Civ 407 [2001] 2 FCR 210 at 219 in which he held that the quantum of lump sum orders by instalments should only be varied under s 31 'when the anticipated circumstances have changed very significantly, and/or cogent reasons' exist why it would be unjust or impracticable to hold the payer 'to the overall quantum of the order originally made'. Quaere the applicability of this judgment to the issue of variation of lump sum orders under ss 25B and 25C of the MCA 1973.

## [1.132]

The following examples can be given of why this widening of the court's previously limited power to vary lump sum orders has been enacted.

## [1.133]

Lump sum attachment orders will be made in cases where there is a deferred clean break, or, particularly with regard to s 25C orders, where there is no clean break. In these circumstances in years subsequent to the order the spouse in whose favour the order is made may undergo a change of circumstances such that, particularly, a s 25C order will no longer be needed.

## [1.134]

The power is needed where the member spouse effects a partial transfer of rights from one scheme to another. In that event the 'following order' provisions of s 25D(1)(a) of the MCA 1973[1] will not apply as that subsection only covers cases involving a transfer of 'all' rights under a scheme.

1 See para **[2.124]** below.

## [1.135]

The non-member spouse may remarry. A lump sum order is unaffected by remarriage. Particularly in the case of s 25C orders, remarriage will end the payee's right to periodical payments and dependency, thus removing the need for the non-member payee to be compensated for that loss in the event of the member spouse's subsequent death from the death in service lump sum.

**[1.136]**

It is most important to note s 31(2B) of the MCA 1973[1] whereby a s 25C order redirecting the whole or part of the lump sum death in service benefit ceases to be variable on the death of either spouse. If the member spouse has died the order comes into effect. If the non-member spouse dies, the member spouse will not be able to vary the order so that if he/she then dies before retirement, the lump sum due under the order will be paid to the non-member spouse's estate. For that reason it is essential to draft all orders under s 25C so that they are prefaced with the words:

> 'save in the event that the [non-member spouse] predeceases the [member spouse] …'

1 See para **[2.129]** below.

## Case law

**[1.137]**

***T v T* [1998] 1 FLR 1072**

This was the first contested attachment case to come before a High Court Judge. The parties had been married 17 years and by the time of the marriage each had already been employed for 10 years by Bank A. W remained so employed for half the effective duration of the marriage until the parties separated. H switched employers one year before the end of the marriage. They had cohabited for 14 years. H was aged 47 and W was aged 46.

**[1.138]**

W asserted that she should be compensated for pension loss. Singer J rejected W's counsel's argument that the new attachment provisions in the legislation manifested:

> 'an intention on the part of the legislature to require, not just to enable, a spouse in the position of this wife to be compensated for her actual or potential loss of pension benefits.'

He held that:

> 'the 1973 Act did not require the court to compensate for pension loss. It obliged the court first to consider whether an order for periodical payments, secured provision or a lump sum was appropriate, and second to consider how pension considerations should affect the terms of any such order. The answer to that second question might be "not at all"'.

He did note though that there may be cases where the concept of compensation 'would dominate and outweigh other factors such, for instance, as whether needs had already reasonably been met'.

**[1.139]**

W sought a deferred attachment maintenance order against H's pension once in payment with Bank A and an attachment order against the lump sum he could commute under Bank A's pension scheme. She also sought an order attaching H's death in service lump sum benefit with his new employers, Bank B, amounting to £336,000.

**[1.140]**

Singer J held that:

> 'there was no advantage in this case in directing an order at the pension providers for deferred periodical payments, or a lump sum … Orders which earmarked sums so far into the future would not provide the wife with any particular certainty, subject as they would be to further variation, even in the case of a deferred lump sum order. If earmarking the pension proved to be necessary, the court would be in a much better position to make an order once the husband had retired, by which time a number of the variables would be less uncertain. If the wife were still dependent on the husband at his post-retirement death, her income would be protected in part by her right as a dependant to raise claims against his estate.'

### [1.141]

Singer J did accede to the request to attach part of the lump sum death in service benefit under Bank B's scheme by requiring the trustees to pay W a sum equal to ten times the annual maintenance order in force at H's death in service. The reasoning was that without an order the trustees would not be obliged to direct any part of the death in service payments to W, even if H nominated her.

### [1.142]

An important feature of this case was the amount of actuarial evidence produced as to notional capital values relating to each party's 'shares' in the future stream of pension income after retirement, plus a notional present capital value for loss of widower's and widow's pension after the death of each party.

### [1.143]

As an important matter of practice it is clear that Singer J did not obtain any assistance from this evidence. He said:

> '… I should … emphasise that these values are at best a guide, and that their apparent precision (down to the nearest pound) is illusory, and the product of mathematical rather than predictive accuracy'.

### [1.144]

Before comparing this judgment with that of the subsequent case of *Burrow* decided by Cazalet J and drawing conclusions from the two judgments, it is instructive to see what other resources there were and how Singer J dealt with them.

### [1.145]

The joint assets were a house with an equity of £150,000 and a joint bank account with £36,000 in it. The husband had in his sole name £40,000 to £48,000 in the bank, £33,000 in the surrender value of policies and £17,500 of shares. It was never disputed that W could not expect the outcome to leave her in long term residence in the former matrimonial home. H's income was currently £109,000 per annum, W currently had no income but it was found that she could earn £5,000 per annum.

### [1.146]

Singer J held that it was reasonable for W to aspire to a house costing £175,000, inclusive of costs of purchase and refurbishment. He therefore ordered that she should have £175,000 and retain her £18,000 share of the joint account. The result was that W came out with £193,000 and H only £87,000 (taking a mid-figure of the fluctuating bank accounts). These figures ignored costs liabilities and resulted in 'a substantial imbalance in favour of W'. Singer J made an order for periodical payments at the rate of £22,000 per annum until mid-1999 and from 1 July 1999 onwards during joint lives until W remarried or further order at the rate of £17,000 per annum. He felt that by then W should be earning £5,000 per annum.

### [1.147]
### *Burrow v Burrow* [1999] 1 FLR 508

This was an appeal from District Judge Bowman to Cazalet J. W was aged 50 and H was aged 48. They had married in 1978. H was director of a family building company and there were two children aged 17 and 12. H was living with another woman who had two of her four children living with her. There had been sixteen years plus of cohabitation in the marriage. There was a trust for the children's education.

The proceeds of sale of the matrimonial home net of mortgage produced around £400,000.

**[1.148]**

To all intents and purposes H accepted that the building company was his alter ego. He owned almost 100% of it. 51% was derived from inheritance and the remaining shares had been acquired at various times, some with the assistance of W. The value of the shares was £275,000.

**[1.149]**

There was a jointly owned Welsh cottage worth £50,000 derived from H. W had an interest in her mother's property of £34,750 and her mother was still alive. H had an Abbey Life Policy with a surrender value of £9,400 and Legal & General policies worth £31,000.

H had £2,000 in Building Societies and W £2,600 in such Societies.

**[1.150]**

H's pension fund was worth £267,712 and one quarter could be commuted on benefits being taken.

**[1.151]**

By the time the appeal came on, H's father had died which had some effect in freeing up income from the building company.

**[1.152]**

Cazalet J found that the capital split ordered by District Judge Bowman, including an award of £349,500 of the proceeds of sale of the matrimonial home to W, resulted in a nearly 50/50 split of capital excluding the pension fund, with a slight excess in favour of W.

He said that the 'District Judge formed the view that this had been a marriage which had operated as "a joint enterprise of sharing and equality"'.

**[1.153]**

Cazalet J referred extensively to Singer J's judgment in *T v T*.

**[1.154]**

W sought a deferred periodical payments order attaching part of H's pension annuity once it came into payment. Cazalet J commented:

> 'I bear in mind very much the points which Singer J made in regard to the disadvantages that can arise when earmarking orders are made against an annuity fund well before any sums can expect to become payable under it'.

He referred to the possibility of a variation application at some point in the future which would fix the appropriate level of periodical payments, possibly before or at the time the pension came into payment. He said that if W had not remarried, the pension annuity would be a factor in assessing her periodical payments then.

**[1.155]**

Cazalet J rejected W's counsel's argument that she had an accrued right against the pension fund. He found that the district judge was not justified in making the attachment order against what he called the 'annuity fund', ie the pension annuity once it came into payment.

**[1.156]**

However, he held that different considerations applied to the capital fund. He upheld the district judge's order attaching 50% of the capital fund as, 'on the particular facts of this case an order awarding the wife 50% of the capital fund appropriately reflected the contributions of each party…'

### [1.157]
**Conclusions to be drawn from the two judgments**

The fact that the commutation lump sum was attached in one case and not in the other is largely explained by the division of the other capital on the facts of the two cases. Mr T had, of necessity, received very much less of the other capital, so that it would have been inequitable to have further reduced his capital resources by letting Mrs T have a share of the commutation fund.

### [1.158]

Mr Burrow was receiving nearly 50% of the other capital and so equity decreed that when the existing capital commutation became available, that too should be shared. In both cases the wives had the potential to receive a proportion of the pension annuity, if the facts of their circumstances at the appropriate time justified a continuing maintenance order when their respective husbands took their pension annuities.

### [1.159]

In *Burrow* the issue of the husband's death in service was not relevant as there was other provision for the wife in the event of that happening.

### [1.160]

The ages of the parties in the two cases are not dissimilar and it can be concluded that the courts are going to be slow to attach pension annuities when the date of retirement is some years off, and ready to attach death in service lump sums where such protection is necessary for a periodical payments order. They will also consider attaching the commutation lump sum where it reflects an asset as a joint venture of the marriage and a marriage of some duration, or it is desirable to do so so as to produce a fair capital distribution between the parties

## Changes introduced by the Welfare Reform and Pensions Act 1999

### [1.161]

The Welfare Reform and Pensions Act 1999 is a far more significant piece of legislation than the amendments to the MCA 1973 introduced by the Pensions Act 1995. It introduced the concept of and the power for the court to make pension sharing orders. Such orders can only be made in proceedings for divorce or nullity begun on or after 1 December 2000[1]. Pension sharing orders cannot be made in judicial separation proceedings.

1 WRPA 1999, s 85(3). In an unreported case, *S v S* (21 December 2001), Singer J granted an application to rescind a decree nisi brought with the consent of both parties for the purpose of clearing the way for fresh divorce proceedings in which a pension sharing order would be sought.

### [1.162]

The legislation enables the court to invade pension arrangements and make a debit to the member spouse's rights and provide a corresponding credit in the form of a right against the person responsible for the pension arrangement for the non-member spouse[1]. This power applies to occupational pension schemes, personal pension schemes and retirement annuity contracts, self-administered schemes, unapproved schemes such as FURBS/UURBS, the state earnings related pension scheme (SERPS) and the new stakeholder pensions. It does not apply to schemes or arrangements operated outside the jurisdiction nor to the basic state retirement pension scheme but does apply to the additional pension element of category A retirement pension which is only payable to employees who have contributed to SERPS in any tax year[2].

1 See the WRPA 1999, s 29 at para **[2.551]** below.
2 See the WRPA 1999, ss 27 and 47 at paras **[2.549]** and **[2.569]** below.

**[1.163]**

The amendments to the MCA 1973 are introduced by s 19 of, and Sch 3 to, the WRPA 1999. Sch 3, para 2 inserts a new s 21A into the MCA 1973 which introduces pension sharing orders, that will constitute a quite separate category of order from a financial provision order or a property adjustment order, and that will therefore need specific dismissal to achieve any 'clean break' settlement.

**[1.164]**

Schedule 3, para 4 of the WRPA 1999 inserts a new s 24B into the MCA 1973 which specifies in sub-para (1) that one or more pension sharing orders may be made in relation to the marriage on granting a decree of divorce or of nullity of marriage 'or at any time thereafter (whether before or after the decree is made absolute)'.

**[1.165]**

The WRPA 1999 does nothing to alter the broad discretionary principles under which the court must exercise its powers to make financial provision, property adjustment or pension sharing orders under s 25 of the MCA 1973.

**[1.166]**

Save in the case of unfunded public service pension schemes, the persons responsible for the pension arrangement can discharge their liability for the pension credit either:

(i) by creating rights for the former non-member spouse within the scheme itself; or

(ii) by making a transfer payment to another suitable pension scheme or arrangement approved by the Statute or by regulations made by the Secretary of State[1].

1 See the WRPA 1999, Sch 5, paras 1, 3 and 4; set out at para **[2.574]** below.

**[1.167]**

The latter option will not be available where the pension sharing order is made against a member of a non-funded public service pension scheme. In such a case a non-member spouse will simply acquire credits in the unfunded public service scheme or, if that scheme is closed to new members, in another appropriate public service scheme[1]. Such rights in public service schemes will be fully protected against inflation by indexation in the same way as the rights of other members of the scheme.

1 See the WRPA 1999, Sch 5, para 2; set out at para **[2.574]** below.

**[1.168]**

Schedule 6 to the WRPA 1999[1] deals with state scheme pension debits and credits. Spouses who are entitled to a pension credit in respect of SERPS or the additional pension element of category A retirement pension will not be entitled to a transfer payment.

1 Set out at para **[2.575]** below.

**[1.169]**

The amount of the pension debit and credit will not be expressed in cash terms but as a percentage of the member spouse's cash equivalent transfer value[1]. It can be any percentage up to 100%, depending on the circumstances of the case.

1 See the WRPA 1999, s 29 (set out at para **[2.551]** below) and Sch 3, para 2.

**[1.170]**

It will be possible to make a pension sharing order both in respect of rights that are accruing as well as pensions that are in payment. In the latter case the cash equivalent transfer value method of valuation will also be used[1].

1 See the WRPA 1999, s 27 (see para **[2.549]**) and, for state scheme rights, s 47 (see para **[2.569]**).

### [1.171]

The spouse against whom a pension sharing order is made will not recover the pension debit suffered if the ex-spouse predeceases him or her. The value of the pension credit will be payable to the ex-spouse's estate.

## What can a transferee spouse do with their pension credit?

### [1.172]

The Welfare Reform and Pensions Act 1999 has amended the Pension Schemes Act 1993 so that:

- The rights in an occupational pension scheme that derive from a pension credit following a pension sharing order are to be treated in a way broadly similar to those of deferred members, ie members who have before retirement age left the employment of the company whose scheme it is;
- If the transferee of the pension credit ('former spouse member') becomes in consequence a member of a funded occupational pension scheme or personal pension scheme, as stated above, they can transfer their rights to another pension scheme or arrangement or purchase an insurance policy or annuity contract with an appropriate insurance company or friendly society approved by the Statute or regulations thereunder made by the Secretary of State;
- A former spouse member will not be able to transfer a pension credit from a funded occupational pension scheme if their ex-spouse's pension is already payable or there is less than a year to go until the ex-spouse reaches normal benefit age[1];
- The right of a former spouse member to request a transfer from a salary related occupational pension scheme must be exercised by written request within three months of receiving from the trustees or managers the statement of entitlement of the amount of cash equivalent of his/her pension credit benefit[2];
- As no new retirement annuity contracts can be created under the Taxes Act 1988, s 618, pension credits carved out of such contracts will be secured by a transfer either to a personal pension scheme, or to an occupational pension scheme of which the ex-spouse is already a member.

1 See the WRPA 1999, s 37 (set out at para **[2.559]** below); PSA 1993, s 101G.
2 See the PSA 1993, s 101G, as amended by the WRPA 1999, s 37.

## The effect of pension sharing on the transferor and transferee

### [1.173]
**The transferor**

In all cases save those concerning active members of occupational pension schemes, the pension debit will be a once and for all reduction of the percentage of the accrued value of the fund. Each qualifying benefit (eg each benefit included in the cash equivalent calculation) must be reduced in the same proportion[1]. A more complex calculation arises in the case of an active member of an occupational pension scheme. This is intended to prevent schemes from enjoying a windfall at the expense of a member.

1 See the WRPA 1999, s 31 at para **[2.553]** below.

### [1.174]
**The transferee**

It is important to remember in advising wives that, due to the different actuarial assumptions applied to the longevity of men and women, a wife who receives a pension credit of, say, 50% of her ex-husband's pension arrangement will not receive a pension equal to his at the same age.

**[1.175]**

The same scheme regulations as to taking a pension benefit will apply to the transferee spouse who has received a pension credit under a pension sharing order as to the transferor spouse who has suffered a pension debit. For example:

- It will not be possible to commute more than a certain percentage, usually circa 25%, of the value of the fund on reaching retirement age;
- Retirement age or the age for drawing benefits will be as set out in the revenue rules for the relevant scheme, ie 50 years of age for personal pension policy-holders, and 60 years of age, subject to certain exceptions, for members of most other schemes.

**[1.176]**

Advice as to whether or not the transferee of a pension credit should transfer the credit to another scheme and, if so, what type of scheme, can only be given by authorised independent financial advisers and cannot be given by solicitors.

## Pension rights that can be either attached or shared but not both

**[1.177]**

| | |
|---|---|
| 1 | Rights in the same pension arrangement[1]; |
| 2 | Rights under a pension arrangement that are the subject of an attachment order following a previous marriage[2]; |
| 3 | It is not possible to have a sharing order made on a variation application under s 31(7B) of the MCA 1973[3] where the pension rights are already subject to an attachment order[4]; |
| 4 | It is not possible to attach lump sum death benefits in schemes that are the subject of a pension sharing order, despite the fact that in the case of final salary related occupational schemes the lump sum death benefit is not part of the CETV of the pension rights; |
| 5 | Any pension rights not already the subject of a sharing or attachment order. |

1 See the WRPA 1999, Sch 3, para 4(5) and Sch 4, para 1(9).
2 See the WRPA 1999, Sch 3, para 4; and the MCA 1973, s 24B(5) (set out at para **[2.119A]** below).
3 See para **[2.129]** below.
4 See the WRPA 1999, Sch 3, para 7(6)

## Pension rights which can be attached or shared even though the subject of a previous order or acquired through a previous order

**[1.178]**

| | |
|---|---|
| 1 | Pension rights which have already been the subject of a pension sharing order made against the scheme member as a result of a previous marriage[1]; |
| 2 | Pension rights acquired by one spouse as a result of a pension sharing order can be the subject of attachment or sharing orders on a divorce following a subsequent re-marriage[2]; |
| 3 | An annuity purchased, or entered into, for the purpose of discharging liability in respect of a pension credit in one marriage can be shared or attached if that spouse re-marries and then divorces[3]. |

1 See the WRPA 1999, Sch 3, para 4 and Sch 4, para 1; and the MCA 1973, ss 24B(3), (4) and 25B(7B) (set out at paras **[2.119A]** and **[2.122]** below).
2 See the WRPA 1999, s 26(1)(e) and Sch 4, para 3(5).
3 See the WRPA 1999, s 26(1) and Sch 4, para 3(5); and the MCA 1973, s 25D(3) (set out at para **[2.124]** below).

### [1.179]

By way of general note it is important to remember that many people, particularly the self-employed, have more than one pension arrangement or policy, so it will be possible in cases involving a deferred clean break to have attachment of lump sum death benefits under some of the member spouse's policies to cover the eventuality of him/her dying during the duration of a maintenance order and to have a pension sharing order made against other of his/her policies.

## Variations

### [1.180]

If the decree has not been made absolute so that the pension sharing order has not, therefore, taken effect, a pension sharing order is now within the category of orders capable of variation[1]. It cannot be varied after the decree has been made absolute.

1 See the WRPA 1999, Sch 3, para 7; and the MCA 1973, s 31(2)(g) and (4A) (set out at para **[2.129]** below).

### [1.181]

An application for a variation prevents the pension sharing order from taking effect before the application has been dealt with. Obviously the actual application must be made before the order has taken effect and before the decree has been made absolute[1]. On the variation application a pension sharing order cannot be made so as to take effect before decree absolute[2].

1 See the WRPA 1999, Sch 3, para 7; and the MCA 1973, s 31(4A) (set out at para **[2.129]** below).
2 See the WRPA 1999, Sch 3, para 7; and the MCA 1973, s 31(4B).

### [1.182]

It will be possible to make a pension sharing order on a variation of maintenance application with a view to capitalising the maintenance, ie achieving a clean break, relating to a maintenance order made pursuant to a divorce or a nullity petition filed on or after 1 December 2000[1], subject to the same restrictions as apply to pension sharing orders generally.

1 See the WRPA 1999, Sch 3, para 7(5); and the MCA 1973, s 31(7B)(ba) (set out at para **[2.129]** below).

## Avoidance of transactions intended to prevent or reduce financial relief for spouse

### [1.183]

The Welfare Reform and Pensions Act 1999, Sch 3, para 9 amends s 37 of the MCA 1973[1] so as to give the court power on application to restrain or set aside dispositions relating to rights under a pension scheme. The classic example would be one spouse arranging for his/her pension fund to be transferred to an offshore trust company where it would be beyond the reach of the English court. An alternative example would arise if a spouse in receipt of maintenance were applying for a clean break pension sharing order on a variation application under s 31(7B)(ba) of the MCA 1973[2] and the other spouse sought to transfer pension rights into a scheme that was the subject of an attachment order made at the time of the original divorce.

1 See para **[2.136]** below.
2 See para **[2.129]** below.

## Appeals

### [1.184]

The procedure for an appeal will depend upon whether or not the pension sharing order has taken effect. Regulation 9 of the Divorce etc (Pensions) Regulations 2000[1] provides that a pension sharing order will not take effect earlier than seven days after the end of the period for filing notice of appeal against the order. The order continues to be stayed until the disposal of the appeal.

1 SI 2000/1123; set out at para **[3.650]** below.

### [1.185]

Problems will arise where the order has already taken effect. The appeal will be out of time. Generally speaking, if a would-be appellant is out of time by a short period, and the delay is explicable and the merits justify hearing of an appeal, the court will allow an appeal to go ahead provided the delay does not cause prejudice. In more extreme cases, where the delay is greater, the court would consider the question of whether or not to grant leave on the principles applied by the case of *Barder v Caluori*[1].

1 [1988] AC 20, [1987] 2 FLR 480, HL.

### [1.186]

Paragraph 10 of Sch 3 to the WRPA 1999 inserts a new s 40A into the MCA 1973[1] which governs appeals relating to pension sharing orders which have taken effect.

1 See para **[2.139A]** below.

### [1.187]

Any practitioners thinking that the death of the transferee of the pension credit before or shortly after implementation will be a ground of appeal, should appreciate that the relevant civil service consultation group has indicated that it is the policy underlying the WRPA 1999 and the regulations that such a death will not be a ground for setting aside a pension sharing order on appeal[1].

1 See also the WRPA 1999, s 35 at para **[2.557]** below; and reg 6 of the Pension Sharing (Implementation and Discharge of Liability) Regulations 2000, SI 2000/1053 (set out at para **[3.594]** below) which makes provision for discharge of liability Re a pension credit following the death of the person entitled to it.

### [1.188]

Accordingly, it may be appropriate to incorporate into a consent order a provision that should the transferee, as opposed to the transferor, die before the pension sharing order is implemented, the order shall not be carried into effect.

## Implementation and valuation

### [1.188A]

The implementation period for a pension sharing order is four months beginning from the latter of:

- the day on which the relevant order or provision takes effect; and
- the first day on which the person responsible for the pension arrangement has received the relevant documents and information[1].

The valuation for the purposes of the pension credit will be the figure calculated on the valuation day, ie such day within the implementation period as the person responsible for the relevant arrangement specifies by notice in writing to the transferor and transferee[2].

1 See the WRPA 1999, s 34 at para **[2.556]** below.
2 See the WRPA 1999, s 29(7) at para **[2.551]** below.

## The Statutory Charge

### [1.188B]

It is unclear to what extent the statutory charge in favour of the Legal Services Commission applies to sums recovered or preserved by legally assisted parties under pension attachment or pension sharing orders. The Legal Services Commission has issued a Guidance Note which (in the view of the author) may well be erroneous in part once tested in the courts.

It is clear that periodical payments recovered under a pension attachment order are exempt.

An assisted person who recovers either a lump sum commutation under s 25B of the MCA 1973 or a death in service lump sum under s 25C of the MCA 1973 will find that the statutory charge applies, subject to the £3,000 exemption[1]. If the original pension member is also an assisted party such part of his lump sum pension commutation as he preserves from an attachment order may well be well be subject to the charge, a factor which could influence a party in such a position not to commute.

It seems the statutory charge will apply to a pension fund created by a pension sharing order in favour of a legally assisted person. Likewise, it will apply to the pension fund of a legally assisted party that is preserved from a pension sharing order where such an application has been made. A consequence of this is that (uniquely in respect of the operation of the statutory charge) the income element of such a pension fund recovered or preserved could be subject to the statutory charge. Contrast this with the fact that periodical payments, including periodical payments received under a pension attachment order, have never been subject to a statutory charge.

It also appears possible that interest on the charge could, under the present state of the regulations, run from the date the order is made, as it may be some years before the pension benefits are drawn, with potentially profound consequences.

For contrasting views compare the Legal Services Commission Guidance Note and the helpful article by Christopher Wagstaffe in August [2001] Family Law at p 623.

In the writer's view there is an urgent need for legislative and regulatory amendment to achieve clarity and a fair and sensible operation of the charge.

1 The exemption increased from 3 December 2001 from £2,500 to £3,000: see Community Legal Service (Financial) (Amendment No 3) Regulations 2001, SI 2001/3663, reg 22.

## Rules and Regulations

### [1.189]

This section deals with selected elements of the regulations that are most likely to be encountered by practitioners. The provisions themselves are printed in full in **Part 3 – Subordinate Legislation**.

### [1.190]

#### Family Proceedings (Amendment) Rules 2000, SI 2000/2267

Note that r 2.61(1)(dd) of the FPR 1991[1] provides that where a consent order is to be made incorporating a pension attachment and/or pension sharing order, the draft order must be served on the person responsible for the pension arrangement and they must have 14 days to make objection to such an order.

These rules[2], inter alia, insert a new r 2.70[3] providing a new procedural code for applications for pension sharing and an amended code for attachment orders. The new r 2.70 applies (in respect of pension sharing applications) to proceedings for divorce or nullity commenced on or after 1 December 2000 and (in relation to attachment applications) in respect of applications for ancillary relief or notices of intention to proceed with an application for an order under ss 25B or 25C of the MCA 1973[4] commenced on or after 1 December 2000.

1 Set out at para **[3.441]** below.
2 Set out at para **[3.652]** below.
3 Set out at para **[3.461]** below.
4 See paras **[2.122]** and **[2.123]** below.

### [1.191]

It is important to note that r 2.70 applies to all cases where 'the applicant or respondent has or is likely to have any benefits under a pension arrangement'[1].

1 See r 2.70(1) of the FPR 1991 at para **[3.461]** below.

### [1.192]

Rule 2.70(2) imposes an obligation on the party with pension rights to request the relevant information required under the Pensions on Divorce etc (Provision of Information) Regulations 2000[1] from the persons responsible for his/her pension arrangements within seven days of receiving notice of the First Appointment. See also reg 2(5) of the Pensions on Divorce etc (Provision of Information) Regulations 2000 for the time in which the person responsible must provide the information.

1 SI 2000/1048; set out at para **[3.562]** below.

### [1.193]

Rule 2.70(3) requires that party then to send on that information within seven days of receipt of it to the other party together with the name and address of each pension arrangement.

### [1.194]

The obligation to request this information does not apply if the party with pension rights has a relevant valuation as at a date not more than 12 months earlier than the first appointment[1].

1 See r 2.70(4) and (5) at para **[3.461]** below.

### [1.195]

As one would expect applicants for pension sharing orders have to serve the person responsible for the relevant pension arrangement[1].

1 See r 2.70(6) at para **[3.461]** below.

### [1.196]

There are detailed provisions in respect of attachment applications. Rule 2.70(7) deals with the details that have to be provided on service of the application on the pension arrangement[1]. Rule 2.70(8) entitles the person responsible to require the applicant to send him a copy of section 2.16 of his/her Form E and r 2.70(9) enables the person responsible to serve on both parties and the court a statement in answer. Rule 2.70(10) requires the court, within four days of receipt of such a statement in answer, to give the person responsible notice of the date of the first appointment so that he can be represented at it.

1 Set out at para **[3.461]** below.

### [1.197]

Rule 2.70(11) deals with the requirements for service of consent attachment orders on the person responsible and r 2.70(12) states categorically that no consent order shall be made unless the person responsible has not made any objection within 21 days of service or the court has considered the objection. Curiously, this is a different time limit from that set out in r 2.61(1)(dd) of the FPR 1991[1], which also applies to consent sharing orders as well as attachment orders.

1 Set out at para **[3.441]** below.

**[1.198]**

Rule 2.70(13) makes it clear that all orders will state in the body of the order that, if applicable, there is provision by way of pension sharing or attachment in an annex(es) to the order and be accompanied by one annex for each pension sharing arrangement.

**[1.199]**

Rule 2.70(14) sets out in great detail what an annex making a pension sharing order must contain.

**[1.200]**

Rule 2.70(15) sets out in similar detail what an annex making an attachment order shall state. This rule will apply to all attachment orders made in ancillary relief proceedings commenced on or after 1 December 2000.

**[1.201]**

Rule 2.70(16) and (17) impose an obligation on a court making, varying or discharging a pension sharing or attachment order to send certain documents to the person responsible for the pension arrangement.

**[1.202]**

### Divorce etc (Pensions) Regulations 2000, SI 2000/1123

These Regulations[1] replace the identically named 1996 Regulations and apply to all proceedings for divorce, judicial separation and nullity commenced on or after 1 December 2000. They apply to pension sharing and attachment, hence the inclusion of judicial separation proceedings.

1 Set out at para **[3.642]** below.

**[1.203]**

Regulation 3[1] governs valuations and cross-refers to the Pensions on Divorce etc (Provision of Information) Regulations 2000[2], thus maintaining the CETV as the basis of valuation. Importantly it states that pension 'benefits shall be valued as at a date to be specified by the court (being not earlier than one year before the date of the petition and not later than the date on which the court is exercising its power)'.

1 Set out at para **[3.644]** below.
2 SI 2000/1048.

**[1.204]**

Regulation 4[1] deals with the requirements for notices when an attachment order has to 'follow' a transfer of all of someone's rights from one scheme to another under the MCA 1973, s 25D(1)(a)[2].

1 See para **[3.645]** below.
2 See para **[2.124]** below.

**[1.205]**

Regulation 5[1] deals with the requirements for notices when a scheme member suffers a partial reduction of benefits, particularly where there is a transfer of some of his benefits. The person responsible for the original pension arrangement must give notice within 14 days of the transfer of the name and address of the person responsible for the new arrangement.

1 See para **[3.646]** below.

**[1.206]**

Regulation 6[1] deals with changes of circumstances and is particularly applicable where the payee under an attachment order changes address.

1 See para **[3.647]** below.

**[1.207]**

Regulation 9[1], as stated at para **[1.165]** above, states that a pension sharing order shall not take effect earlier than seven days after the end of the period for filing a notice of appeal against the order.

1 Set out at para **[3.650]** below.

**[1.208]**

**Pensions on Divorce etc (Provision of Information) Regulations 2000, SI 2000/1048**

These Regulations came into force on 1 December 2000 and are set out in full at para **[3.562]** below.

**[1.209]**

Regulation 2 deals with the requirements for provision of information imposed on a person responsible for a pension arrangement under the WRPA 1999, s 23. Different rules apply according to whether the information is required by a member, his spouse or a court order.

Inter alia:

- Regulation 2(3)(d) and (e)[1] requires the scheme to indicate whether or not the transferee of a pension credit will be offered membership of the same scheme;
- Regulation 2(3)(f) requires information to be given as to charges to be levied;
- Regulation 2(5) states that the date for the provision of information/ a valuation to a member or by order of the court must be—
  - (i) within three months of the receipt of the request or the order; or
  - (ii) within six weeks if notice has been given that the information/valuation is required for proceedings specified under the WRPA 1999, s 23(1)(a); or
  - (iii) within such shorter period for a valuation as a court order may specify;
- Regulation 2(6) abbreviates the period for providing information to one month if a valuation is not required.

  Similar time limits apply to the Secretary of State in respect of information about a spouse's shareable state scheme rights in the Sharing of State Scheme Rights (Provision of Information and Valuation) (No 2) Regulations 2000[2].

See the FPR 1991, r 2.70(2)[3] as to when the party with pension rights must request the information.

1 Set out at para **[3.563]** below.
2 SI 2000/2914.
3 SI 1991/1247, as amended by SI 2000/2267; r 2.70 is set out at para **[3.461]** below.

**[1.210]**

Regulation 3 deals with the bases of valuation and, broadly, requires CETVs to be supplied[1].

1 Reg 3 is set out at para **[3.564]** below.

**[1.211]**

Regulation 4 requires a person responsible for a pension arrangement to give the name and address of the arrangement to which any order should be sent and certain information within 21 days of receiving notice a pension sharing order may be made[1]. The information to be given includes whether or not details can be requested about the member's state of health and whether the transferee can nominate someone to receive the pension credit benefit, including any lump sum which may be payable, if the transferee dies before the liability in respect of pension credit benefit has been discharged.

1 Reg 4 is set out at para **[3.565]** below.

### [1.212]

Regulation 5 deals with the information the person responsible for a pension arrangement may request before the implementation period of a pension sharing order begins to run[1].

1 Reg 5 is set out at para **[3.566]** below.

### [1.213]

Regulation 6 deals with the situation where the transferee has died before the order has been implemented[1]. The wording implies the pension credit benefit will go to the transferee's nominee.

1 Reg 6 is set out at para **[3.567]** below.

### [1.214]

Regulation 7 imposes a 21 day time limit from receipt of a pension sharing order on the person responsible for the pension arrangement to provide information, including notice of implementation of the order or why the order has not been implemented, eg because their charges have not been paid[1].

1 Reg 7 is set out at para **[3.568]** below.

### [1.215]

Regulation 8 states that within 21 days of discharging liability under a pension sharing order the person responsible must issue a notice of discharge of liability giving certain information[1].

1 Reg 8 is set out at para **[3.569]** below.

### [1.216]

Regulation 10 states that a person responsible for a pension arrangement must, within 21 days of receipt of an attachment order, provide information, in particular, a list of the changes of circumstances of which either party must give notice and details of unpaid charges[1].

1 Reg 10 is set out at para **[3.571]** below.

### [1.217]
### Pensions on Divorce etc (Charging) Regulations 2000, SI 2000/1049

These Regulations came into force on 1 December 2000 and are set out in full at para **[3.572]** below.

- Regulation 2 specifies the requirements that must be met by persons responsible for pension arrangements before they may recover charges[1]. In particular they must notify the parties of the details of the charges, including any periodic charges that may be made where the transferee is to become a member of the same pension arrangement, before the pension sharing order is made.
- Regulation 2(8) provides no charge may be made for information/valuations unless the information/valuation has already been provided within the previous 12 months or the request or court order for the information/valuation is made within 12 months of the member spouse reaching normal pension age or he/she has reached the normal pension age.

- Regulation 4 says that where persons responsible are entitled to charge for information they can insist on payment by the member spouse before providing it[2].
- Regulation 6 enables persons responsible to levy additional charges where more than 12 months have elapsed between supplying information/valuations and the taking effect of an order[3].
- Regulation 7 specifies that if the person responsible is entitled to charge, then on giving appropriate notice, he can insist on payment before implementing the order[4].
- Regulation 8 states that a payment of charges by one party to a pension sharing order on behalf of the other party is recoverable as a debt[5].

1 Reg 2 is set out at para **[3.573]** below.
2 Reg 4 is set out at para **[3.575]** below.
3 Reg 6 is set out at para **[3.577]** below.
4 Reg 7 is set out at para **[3.578]** below.
5 Reg 8 is set out at para **[3.579]** below.

## [1.218]
## Pension Sharing (Valuation) Regulations 2000, SI 2000/1052

These Regulations came into force on 1 December 2000 and are set out in full at para **[3.582]** below.

Inter alia these specify that rights in respect of which a person is in receipt of a pension or income withdrawal by virtue of being a widow, widower or dependant are not shareable. They also make provision for the calculation and verification of cash equivalents for the purpose of creating pension credits and debits, ie implementing pension sharing orders. See also s 29(7) of the WRPA 1999[1] which specifies the valuation day for the creation of the pension credit is a day chosen by the person responsible for the pension arrangement in the implementation period.

1 Set out at para **[2.551]** below.

## [1.219]
## Pension Sharing (Implementation and Discharge of Liability) Regulations 2000, SI 2000/1053

These Regulations came into force on 1 December 2000 and are set out in full at para **[3.589]** below.

- Regulation 3 specifies the circumstances in which persons responsible can apply for an extension of the implementation period and they include the failure of the parties to provide information or a dispute over the cash equivalent[1].
- Regulation 4 deals with postponement or cessation of the implementation period when an application is made for leave to appeal out of time[2].
- Regulation 6 deals with the death of a person entitled to a pension credit before liability for it is discharged[3].

1 Reg 3 is set out at para **[3.591]** below.
2 Reg 4 is set out at para **[3.592]** below.
3 Reg 6 is set out at para **[3.594]** below.

## [1.220]
## Pension Sharing (Pension Credit Benefit) Regulations 2000, SI 2000/1054

These Regulations came into force on 1 December 2000 and are set out in full at para **[3.607]** below.

These Regulations are lengthy and deal with a mass of technical issues such as transfers of pension credits between schemes, the age at which a transferee can take benefits, securing pension credit benefit by insurance policies and the limited circumstances in which transfers can be made to overseas schemes.

## Timetable when application is made for Pension Sharing (MCA 1973, s 24B) and Pension Attachment (MCA 1973, ss 25B and 25C) orders

**[1.220A]**

| | |
|---|---|
| 1 | • Form A seeking s 24B order must be served on person responsible for pension sharing arrangement ('PRPA')<br>• Form A seeking s 25B and 25C order must also be so served together with details set out in FPR 1991, r 2.70(7)[1] |
| 2 | • Within seven days of receipt of notice of First Appointment, party with pension rights requests information for each pension arrangement under which he/she has benefits to provide information referred to in FPR 1991, r 2.70(2) |
| | • PRPA to provide information within six weeks if notified it is required for s 24B, s 25B or s 25C proceedings[2]<br>• If party with pension rights has relevant valuation (or has requested one) as defined under FPR 1991, r 2.70(5), he/she need not request information under FPR 1991, r 2.70(2)[3] |
| 3 | • Within seven days of receiving information the party with pension rights shall send copy to other party together with name and address of the person responsible for each pension arrangement[4]. No such obligation imposed on party who already has information to serve it, as he/she will provide that information with Form E |
| 4 | • A PRPA shall within 21 days of notification s 24B order may be made, provide information to the member spouse, for example prior s 25B or s 25C order, a bankruptcy order, details of charges if not supplied, whether PRPA can enquire regarding member's health etc[5] |
| 5 | • A PRPA served with a Form A seeking order under s 25B or s 25C may request section 2.16 of Form E within 21 days[6] |
| 6 | • Applicant must provide PRPA with section 2.16 by date for filing Form E or 21 days after request, if later |
| 7 | • PRPA may within 21 days of receipt of section 2.16, send court and both parties' statement in answer[7] |
| 8 | • Court must give PRPA notice of date of First Appointment within four days of filing of statement in answer[8] |
| 9 | **Consent order**<br>• Serve PRPA with notice of application, draft order etc and give court statement no objection raised by PRPA within 14 days of service[9] |
| 10 | • Court must within seven days of making s 24B, s 25B or s 25C order or of making Decree Absolute of divorce or nullity or decree of judicial separation, whichever is later, send PRPA:<br>– copy of relevant decree<br>– in case of divorce or nullity a copy of Decree Absolute<br>– a copy of the financial order and annex relating to that PRPA only[10] |
| 11 | **Implementation**<br>• Pension sharing order does not take effect earlier than seven days after end of period of filing of Notice of Appeal[11]<br>• PRPA has four months from the date order takes effect, or, if later, date when they received information under the Pensions on Divorce etc (Provision of Information) Regulations 2000, reg 5[12] |

- Pensions on Divorce etc (Provision of Information) Regulations 2000, reg 5 sets out the information PRPA can request before implementation period begins to run
- Pensions on Divorce etc (Provision of Information) Regulations 2000, reg 7 states PRPA must provide Notice of Implementation or why order not implemented within 21 days of receipt of order[13]
- Pensions on Divorce etc (Provision of Information) Regulations 2000, reg 8 states that within 21 days of discharging liability under s 24B order PRPA must issue Notices of Discharge of Liability[14]
- Pensions on Divorce etc (Provision of Information) Regulations 2000, reg 10 states PRPA must within 21 days of receipt of s 25B or s 25C order provide certain information[15]

1 See para **[3.461]** below.
2 See reg 2(5)(b) of the Pensions on Divorce etc (Provision of Information) Regulations 2000, SI 2000/1048 at para **[3.563]** below.
3 See FPR 1991, r 2.70(4) at para **[3.461]** below.
4 See FPR 1991, r 2.70(3).
5 See reg 4 of the Pensions on Divorce etc (Provision of Information) Regulations 2000, SI 2000/1048 at para **[3.565]** below.
6 See FPR 1991, r 2.70(8).
7 See FPR 1991, r 2.70(9).
8 See FPR 1991, r 2.70(10).
9 See FPR 1991, rr 2.61(1)(dd) and 2.70(11), (12) at paras **[3.441]** and **[3.461]** below.
10 See FPR 1991, r 2.70(16) and (17).
11 See reg 9 of the Divorce etc (Pensions) Regulations 2000, SI 2000/1123 at para **[3.650]** below.
12 SI 2000/1048; set out at para **[3.566]** below.
13 SI 2000/1048. Reg 7 is set out at para **[3.568]** below.
14 SI 2000/1048. Reg 8 is set out at para **[3.569]** below.
15 SI 2000/1048. Reg 10 is set out at para **[3.571]** below.

## No 'Brooks' property adjustment applications in respect of divorce or nullity proceedings commenced on or after 1 December 2000

### [1.221]–[1.222]

The WRPA 1999, Sch 3, para 3 amends the MCA 1973, s 24[1] so that it will not be possible to make a property adjustment application or for the court to make a property adjustment order in respect of a pension arrangement in proceedings for divorce or nullity commenced on or after 1 December 2000.

1 Set out at para **[2.118]** below.

## Important amendments of the earmarking provisions of the Matrimonial Causes Act 1973 by the Welfare Reform and Pensions Act 1999

### [1.223]

All attachment orders made under s 25B(4) of the MCA 1973 pursuant to a Form A filed on or after 1 December 2000 must be expressed as a percentage of the payment which becomes due to the party with pension rights[1].

1 See the WRPA 1999, Sch 4, para 1(6); the MCA 1973, s 25B(5) (set out at para **[2.122]** below); and the Family Proceedings (Amendment) Rules 2000, SI 2000/2267, reg 2(2) and (3) (set out at para **[3.653]** below).

**[1.224]**

Section 25B(7) of the MCA 1973[1] has been amended by the WRPA 1999, Sch 4, para 1(8) so that, where there is a right of commutation under a pension arrangement, the order may require the person benefiting from the arrangement to exercise the right of commutation 'to any extent'. That means it can order him/her not to exercise it at all so that any attached periodical payments order that it is making simultaneously against the pension in payment will be effective against a larger pension.

1 See para **[2.122]** below.

**[1.225]**

The WRPA 1999, Sch 4, para 2(3) deletes the largely meaningless subsection (2) of s 25B of the MCA 1973.

It also makes a general amendment to ss 25B and 25C of the MCA 1973 so that wherever the words 'Trustees or managers of' appear there are substituted the words 'person responsible for' and wherever the word 'scheme' appears, there is substituted the word 'arrangement'.

Schedule 4 to the WRPA 1999 also widens the definition of pension arrangements that can be attached to include:

> 'an annuity purchased, or entered into, for the purpose of discharging liability in respect of a pension credit under section 29(1)(b) of the Welfare Reform and Pensions Act 1999…'[1].

1 See the WRPA 1999, Sch 4, para 3(5); and the MCA 1973, s 25D(3) (set out at para **[2.124]** below).

## Pension sharing and attachment after an overseas divorce

**[1.226]**

The WRPA 1999 amends Pt III of the MFPA 1984 so that attachment and pension sharing orders can be made in applications commenced on or after 1 December 2000 for financial relief after an overseas divorce[1].

1 See the WRPA 1999, s 22 and Sch 12, paras 2 to 4.

## Valuation

**[1.227]**

Given that the CETV will be the standard basis of valuation in respect of pension rights and that that is not always the appropriate basis of valuation in determining the true value of a spouse's pension rights, it remains to be seen to what extent the courts will pay attention, in suitable cases, to other methods of valuation, eg to substantiate a claim for a larger percentage order. Practitioners must bear in mind the rules relating to expert evidence contained in Pt 35 of the CPR 1998 now incorporated into the FPR 1991.

The type of evidence and information that practitioners and the courts will want to know is the quantum of pension annuity/commutation lump sum that different percentages of the CETV will purchase for either party at a specified retirement age or ages, assuming industry standard rates of growth between the date of the hearing and the date of the respective retirements.

**[1.228]**

**Offsetting**

Where offsetting is used to achieve a solution rather than pension sharing, it is important to remember that two different bases of valuation need to be borne in mind in orders involving continuing periodical payments and in clean break orders.

## Orders involving continuing periodical payments

**[1.229]**

The valuation of the member spouse's pension rights/fund, encompasses a total fund, the majority of which will be subject to tax in his/her hands on his/her retirement when he/she draws it as an annuity. The only part that will not be taxable will be the maximum commutable by way of lump sum. If there is going to be a continuing periodical payments order for the non-member spouse, you are envisaging that the member spouse may be paying a part of that taxable annuity to the non-member. It is therefore wrong to bring into account the gross value for the non-commutable element of the pension fund. You should make a broad estimate of the post-retirement tax rate and apply it to the non-commutable elements. For example, a husband aged 50 has a pension fund of £300,000. On his retirement, say, £75,000 can be commuted tax-free. £225,000 will be available to purchase a taxable annuity. At a broad estimate, his average tax rate may be about 20% and so about £45,000 should be deducted from the value of the non-commutable element.

## Clean Break orders

**[1.230]**

The gross value of the member's pension fund should be brought into account in performing the balancing exercise when calculating an appropriate clean break order. If the fund forms a substantial element of the resources that are being divided to achieve the clean break, then the provision made may include an appropriate pension sharing order. If the fund is not so significant a part of the overall resources so that there is no need for a pension sharing order to effect a clean break, then it must still be appropriate to take its gross value into account. The court is looking at the capital and other resources that each spouse will have to generate an income that will enable them both to stand on their own two feet. After deducting liabilities, it only nets down those resources to allow for capital gains tax on their realisation, so as to compare the gross income that each party can generate. To value the member's spouses pension annuity fund net of tax (a calculation which of itself gives rise to argument as to the appropriate marginal tax rate) would be to treat it differently from all other capital resources that the spouses have.

## Other valuation considerations

**[1.231]**

The need for a discount for accelerated payment and for risks such as the likelihood of death of the non-member spouse before the member spouse must be taken into account in valuing the widow's/widower's pension.

**[1.232]**

The test applied by Singer J in *T v T* was[1]:

> '... there are three stages to arriving at this "offset" value for a spouse's loss through divorce. First must be determined the quantum of benefit which the loser would have enjoyed but for the ending of the marriage; next must be applied a discount to reflect present payment as compensation for future loss; and finally must be included a contingency factor to reflect the probabilities of survival at the various points in the future of both the husband and the wife'.

1 [1998] 1 FLR 1072 at 1077H.

## *H v H* [1993] 2 FLR 335

**[1.233]**

This decision of Thorpe J (as he then was) may yet come to have important ramifications upon how the courts approach issues relating to attachment and pension sharing. H was 39 and W was 42. It had been a 12-year marriage with three children where the doctor husband came of an affluent family from whom he received considerable financial benefit. W was qualified as a teacher and a nurse but on marriage had no actual or prospective capital. She received a nominal periodical payments order, so there was no clean break. The parties had separated in April 1987 so H must presumably have been about 34 and W about 37 at that time. H had pension rights in the National Health Service.

### [1.234]

Thorpe J said:

> 'I think that in deciding what weight to attach to pension rights, it is more important in this case to look to the value of what has been earned during cohabitation and then to look to the prospective value of what may be earned over the course of the 25 to 30 years between separation and retirement age. Of course, I bear in mind that in the future accumulation of pension rights, the husband has very great advantages. He has already an established position in the National Health Service which is likely to develop to consultancy status in approximately three years time. Although the wife is well qualified, she is three years older than the husband and even when she returns to employment it is likely to be on a part-time basis until the children are considerably older. But I do not think that this disparity in their ability to accumulate pension rights over decades post-separation should be given undue weight in the performance of the balancing exercise'.

### [1.235]

The passage seems a very useful exercise in how to consider pension rights in respect of couples in their thirties or early forties. The thrust of the observation about the weight to be given to the remarks about the disparity in their ability to accumulate pension rights over time post-separation obviously diminishes the older the spouses in question are and the closer they are to retirement. In the light of the House of Lords' decision in *White v White*[1], one can see a court taking a different view of the value of a pension fund that had accrued prior to a second marriage, from the value that had been built up in the duration of that second marriage, particularly in cases where financial resources exceed financial needs.

1 [2000] 3 FCR 555, [2000] 2 FLR 981, HL.

### [1.235A]

***Maskell v Maskell* [2001] EWCA Civ 858, [2001] 3 FCR 296**

In this case Thorpe LJ cautioned against comparing the transfer value of a pension which represents a future annuity stream and a portion of future capital on a 'like for like' basis with currently available capital.

## MCA 1973, s 5 in the light of pension sharing

### [1.236]

Obviously loss of pension rights will no longer found a defence to a petition under s 1(2)(e) of the MCA 1973 on the grounds of grave financial hardship unless the scheme in question is an overseas one and thus beyond the jurisdiction of the court.

# 4. Council Regulation (EC) No 1347/2000 of 29 May 2000 on the jurisdiction and the recognition and enforcement of judgments in matrimonial matters and in matters of parental responsibility for children of both spouses

Contents



## 'Brussels II': an overview

### [1.237]

Council Regulation (EC) No 1347/2000 of 29 May 2000 on the jurisdiction and the recognition and enforcement of judgments in matrimonial matters and in matters of parental responsibility for children of both spouses[1] is directly effective in the United Kingdom and other Member States of the European Union from 1 March 2001. The content of the Council Regulation is substantially derived from the Convention on Jurisdiction and the Recognition and Enforcement of Judgments in Matrimonial Matters of 28 May 1998 (Brussels II)[2]. The text of the Council Regulation is set out below at para **[3.656A]**.

The Council Regulation applies to civil proceedings relating to divorce, legal separation or marriage annulment and to civil proceedings relating to parental responsibility for the children of both spouses on the occasion of those matrimonial procedings[3]. The preamble to the Regulation states (inter alia) that the recognition of divorce and annulment rulings affects only the dissolution of matrimonial ties; despite the fact that they may be interrelated, the Regulation does not affect issues such as the fault of the spouses, property consequences of the marriage, the maintenance obligation or any other ancillary measures. The grounds of jurisdiction are based on the rule that there must be a real link between the party concerned and the Member State exercising jurisdiction; the decision to include certain grounds corresponds to the fact that they exist in different national legal systems and are accepted by the other Member States. The lawful habitual residence of a child is maintained as the ground of jurisdiction in cases of child abduction. The Council Regulation does not prevent the courts of a Member State from taking provisional, including protective, measures, in urgent cases, with regard to persons or property situated in that State.

The Council Regulation is binding in its entirety and directly applicable in the following Member States of the European Union: Belgium, Germany, Greece, Spain, France, Ireland, Italy, Luxembourg, the Netherlands, Austria, Portugal, Finland, Sweden and the United Kingdom, and any State which subsequently adopts the Council Regulation. Denmark has not participated in the adoption of the Regulation and is not bound by nor subject to its application.

Amendments have been made to the Domicile and Matrimonial Proceedings Act 1973, the CACA 1985 and the FLA 1986 in order to avoid inconsistent provisions of national law[4]. The amendments to the Domicile and Matrimonial Proceedings Act 1973 do not apply in respect of proceedings commenced before 1 March 2001. The Council Regulation takes precedence over some Conventions[5].

The FPR 1991 are amended with effect from 1 April 2001 to provide for the procedure for consideration of jurisdiction under Arts 9, 10 and 11 of the Council Regulation[6] and for the registration, enforcement and recognition of judgments under the Regulation[7].

The application of the Council Regulation is to be reviewed every five years[8].

For the jurisdiction of the court in family matters, including matrimonial proceedings, see generally *Rayden and Jackson on Divorce and Family Matters* (17th edn, 1997), vol 1, chap 2 and the Noter-up thereto.

1 [2000] OJ L160/19, 30.6.2000; the full text of the Council Regulation is set out at para **[3.656A]** below.
2 [1998] OJ C221/1, 16.7.1998.
3 Art 1.
4 The European Communities (Matrimonial Jurisdiction and Judgments) Regulations SI 2001/310, made under s 2(2) of the European Communities Act 1972.
5 Art 37.
6 FPR 1991, r 2.27A, inserted with effect from 1 April 2001 by the Family Proceedings (Amendment) Rules 2001, SI 2001/821; amendments to App 2 to the FPR 1991 and to forms M5 and M6 (requiring certain additional information for the purpose of determining jurisdiction) take effect from 3 September 2001 (see para **[1.244A]** below).
7 FPR 1991, rr 7.40 to 7.50, inserted with effect from 1 April 2001 by the Family Proceedings (Amendment) Rules 2001, SI 2001/821.
8 Art 43.

## The court's jurisdiction under the Council Regulation

### [1.238]

In matters relating to divorce, judicial separation or nullity of marriage, jurisdiction shall lie[1] with the courts of the Member State:

(a) in whose territory:

- the spouses are habitually resident, or
- the spouses were last habitually resident, in so far as one of them still resides there, or
- the respondent is habitually resident, or

- in the event of a joint application, either of the spouses is habitually resident, or
- the applicant is habitually resident if he or she resided there for at least a year immediately before the application was made, or
- the applicant is habitually resident if he or she resided there for at least six months immediately before the application was made and is either a national of the Member State in question or, in the case of the United Kingdom and Ireland, has his 'domicile' there;

(b) of the nationality of both spouses or, in the case of the United Kingdom and Ireland, of the 'domicile'[2] of both spouses.

Without prejudice to the above, a court of a Member State which has given a judgment[3] on a legal separation shall also have jurisdiction for converting that judgment into a divorce, if the law of that Member State so provides[4]. The court in which proceedings are pending shall also have jurisdiction to examine a counterclaim[5].

1 Art 2(1).
2 'Domicile' shall have the same meaning as it has under the legal systems of the United Kingdom and Ireland: Art 2(2).
3 For meaning of 'judgment' see Art 13; it includes a decree, order or decision.
4 Art 6.
5 Art 5.

## Jurisdiction of the courts of England and Wales to entertain proceedings for divorce or judicial separation

### [1.239]

As from 1 March 2001, the court[1] shall have jurisdiction to entertain proceedings for divorce or judicial separation if (and only if):

(a) the court has jurisdiction under the Council Regulation; or
(b) no Court of a Contracting State has jurisdiction under the Council Regulation and either of the parties to the marriage is domiciled in England and Wales on the date when the proceedings are begun[2].

These provisions do not give the court jurisdiction to entertain proceedings in contravention of Art 7 of the Convention[3].

1 'The court' means the High Court and a divorce county court within the meaning of Pt V of the Matrimonial and Family Proceedings Act 1984: Domicile and Matrimonial Proceedings Act 1973, s 5(1A), inserted by the European Communities (Matrimonial Jurisdiction and Judgments) Regulations, SI 2001/310, with effect from 1 March 2001.
2 Section 5(2) of the Domicile and Matrimonial Proceedings Act 1973, as amended by SI 2001/310, with effect from 1 March 2001.
3 Section 5(3A) of the Domicile and Matrimonial Proceedings Act 1973, inserted by SI 2001/310 with effect from 1 March 2001. For Art 7 and the exclusive nature of jurisdiction under Arts 2 to 6 see below.

## Jurisdiction of the courts of England and Wales to entertain proceedings for nullity of marriage

### [1.240]

As from 1 March 2001, the court shall have jurisdiction to entertain proceedings for nullity of marriage if (and only if):

(a) the court has jurisdiction under the Council Regulation; or
(b) no Court of a Contracting State has jurisdiction under the Council Regulation and either of the parties to the marriage—
  (i) is domiciled in England and Wales on the date when the proceedings are begun; or

(ii) died before that date and either was at death domiciled in England and Wales or had been habitually resident in England and Wales throughout the period of one year ending with the date of death[1].

Again, these provisions do not give the court jurisdiction to entertain proceedings in contravention of Art 7 of the Convention[2].

1 Section 5(3) of the Domicile and Matrimonial Proceedings Act 1973, as amended by the European Communities (Matrimonial Jurisdiction and Judgments) Regulations, SI 2001/310, with effect from 1 March 2001.

2 Section 5(3A) of the Domicile and Matrimonial Proceedings Act 1973, inserted by SI 2001/310, with effect from 1 march 2001. For Art 7 and the exclusive nature of jurisdiction under Arts 2 to 6 see below.

## Jurisdiction of the courts of England and Wales in matters of parental responsibility for children of both spouses

### [1.241]

The Courts of a Member State exercising jurisdiction by virtue of Art 2 on an application for divorce, legal separation or marriage annulment shall have jurisdiction in a matter relating to parental responsibility over a child of both spouses where the child is habitually resident in that Member State[1]. Where the child is not habitually resident in that Member State, the courts of that State shall have jurisdiction in such a matter if the child is habitually resident in one of the Member States and:

(a) at least one of the spouses has parental responsibility in relation to the child;and

(b) the jurisdiction of the courts has been accepted by the spouses and is in the best interests of the child[2].

The jurisdiction conferred by the above provisions ceases as soon as the judgment allowing or refusing the application for divorce, legal separation or marriage annulment has become final or, in those cases where proceedings in relation to parental responsibility are then pending, a judgment in these proceedings has become final, or, in either case, the proceedings have come to an end for another reason[3].

The FLA 1986 is amended with effect from 1 March 2001 to permit a court in England and Wales to make orders under s 8 of the ChA 1989 in or in connection with matrimonial proceedings in England and Wales where:

(a) the child concerned is a child of both parties to the matrimonial proceedings and the court has jurisdiction to entertain those proceedings by virtue of the Council Regulation; or

(b) the condition in s 2A of the 1986 Act is satisfied[4].

1 Art 3(1).

2 Art 3(2).

3 Art 3(3).

4 Family Law Act 1986, s 2(1), as amended by the European Communities (Matrimonial Jurisdiction and Judgments) Regulations, SI 2001/310, with effect from 1 March 2001.

## Child abduction

### [1.242]

The courts with jurisdiction in relation to a child under Art 3 of the Council Regulation are to exercise their jurisdiction in conformity with the Hague Convention on the Civil Aspects of International Child Abduction and in particular Arts 3 and 16 of that Convention[1]. The Council Regulation takes precedence over the European Convention on Recognition and Enforcement of Decisions concerning Custody of Children and on Restoration of Custody of Children[2], and the CACA 1985 has been amended to reflect this[3].

1 Art 4.
2 Art 37.
3 CACA 1985, s 12(3), inserted by the European Communities (Matrimonial Jurisdiction and Judgments) Regulations, SI 2001/310, with effect from 1 March 2001.

## Exclusive and residual jurisdiction

### [1.243]

A spouse who: (a) is habitually resident in the territory of a Member State, or (b) is a national of a Member State, or, in the case of the United Kingdom and Ireland, has his or her 'domicile' in the territory of one of the latter Member States, may be sued in another Member State only in accordance with Arts 2 to 6 of the Council Regulation[1].

Where no court of a Member State has jurisdiction pursuant to Arts 2 to 6, jurisdiction shall be determined, in each Member State, by the laws of that State. As against a respondent who is not habitually resident and is not either a national of a Member State or, in the case of the United Kingdom and Ireland, does not have his 'domicile' within the territory of one of the latter Member States, any national of a Member State who is habitually resident within the territory of another Member State may, like the nationals of that State, avail himself of the rules of jurisdiction applicable in that State[2].

1 Art 7.
2 Art 8(1). This provision is reflected in s 5(2) and (3) of the Domicile and Matrimonial Proceedings Act 1973, as amended by the European Communities (Matrimonial Jurisdiction and Judgments) Regulations, SI 2001/310, with effect from 1 March 2001; note however that s 5(2) and (3) do not give the court jurisdiction to entertain proceedings in contravention of Art 7: Domicile and Matrimonial Proceedings Act 1973, s 5(3A), inserted by SI 2001/310.

## Examination as to jurisdiction and admissibility

### [1.244]

Where a court of a Member State is seised of a case over which it has no jurisdiction under the Council Regulation and over which a court of another Member State has jurisdiction by virtue of the Council Regulation, it shall declare of its own motion that it has no jurisdiction[1]. Where a respondent habitually resident in a State other than the Member State where the action was brought does not enter an appearance, the court with jurisdiction shall stay the proceedings so long as it is not shown that the respondent has been able to receive[2] the document instituting the proceedings or an equivalent document in sufficient time to enable him to arrange for his defence, or that all necessary steps have been taken to this end[3].

The FPR 1991 are amended with effect from 1 April 2001 to make provision for the examination of jurisdiction under Arts 9, 10 and 11 of the Council Regulation[4]. Where at any time after the presentation of a petition, it appears to the court that, under Arts 9, 10 or 11, it does not have jurisdiction to hear the petition and is or may be required to stay the proceedings, the court shall stay the proceedings and fix a hearing to determine the question of jurisdiction and whether there should be a stay or other order[5]. Notice of the hearing is to be served on the parties; the court may, if the parties agree, deal with any question about jurisdiction without a hearing[6]. The court must give reasons for its decision under Arts 9, 10 or 11, stating any findings of fact[7]; any order under Art 9 that the court does not have jurisdiction must be recorded in writing[8].

1 Art 9.
2 For provisions dealing with service in a Member State, see Art 10(2); and for provisions dealing with service in State other than a Member State see Art 10(3).
3 Art 10(1).

4 FPR 1991, r 2.27A, inserted with effect from 1 April 2001 by the Family Proceedings (Amendment) Rules 2001, SI 2001/821.
5 FPR 1991, r 2.27A(2).
6 FPR 1991, r 2.27A(2) and (5).
7 FPR 1991, r 2.27A(3).
8 FPR 1991 r 2.27A(4).

## Establishing jurisdiction: pleadings

### [1.244A]

In proceedings for divorce, nullity or judicial separation in England and Wales, the FPR 1991 require information to be given in the petition and acknowledgement of service as to the basis of jurisdiction and the existence of any other proceedings. Where it is alleged that the court has jurisdiction under the Council Regulation, the petition must state the grounds of jurisdiction under Art 2(1) of the Regulation[1]; where it is alleged that the court has jurisdiction, other than under the Regulation, on the basis of domicile or habitual residence the petition must give details of the domicile or habitual residence of the petitioner or, where the domicile or habitual residence of the respondent is relied on, of the respondent[2]. The petition must also state whether there are or have been any proceedings in England and Wales or elsewhere with reference to the marriage or to any child of the family or between the parties with reference to their property, or are any proceedings continuing in any country outside England and Wales which relate to the marriage or are capable of affecting its validity or subsistence and must give details of any such proceedings[3].

The form of Acknowledgement of Service[4] now includes additional questions (1A, 1B, 1C) asking the respondent to give information about his or her habitual residence and domicile/nationality and the existence of other proceedings and the Notice of Proceedings[5] gives guidance on answering these questions and on the effect of the Regulation.

1 FPR 1991, App 2, para 1(bb), inserted by SI 2001/821 as from 3 September 2001.
2 FPR 1991, App 2, paras 1(c) and (d), as amended by SI 2001/821 as from 3 September 2001.
3 FPR 1991, App 2, paras 1(i) and (j).
4 FPR 1991, App 1, Form M6, as amended by SI 2001/821 as from 3 September 2001.
5 FPR 1991, App 1, Form M5, as amended by SI 2001/821 as from 3 September 2001.

## Concurrent proceedings in different Member States; exclusive jurisdiction of the court first seised; mandatory stays

### [1.245]

Where proceedings between the same parties, either involving the same cause of action, or, divorce, legal separation or marriage annulment not involving the same cause of action, are brought before courts of different Member States, the court second seised shall of its own motion stay its proceedings until such time as the jurisdiction of the court first seised is established[1]. Where the jurisdiction of the court first seised is established, the court second seised shall decline jurisdiction in favour of that court[2]. In that case, the party who brought the relevant action before the court second seised may bring that action before the court first seised. There is no power to decline jurisdiction in favour of a more appropriate forum[3].

A court shall be deemed to be seised[4]: (a) at the time when the document instituting the proceedings or an equivalent document is lodged with the court, provided that the applicant has not subsequently failed to take the steps he was required to take to have service effected on the respondent, or (b) if the document has to be served before being lodged with the court, at the time when it is received by the authority responsible for service, provided that the applicant has not subsequently failed to take the steps he was required to take to have the document lodged with the court. There is no provision which permits the parties to agree to oust the jurisdiction of the court of the Member State with exclusive jurisdiction in favour of the court of another Member State.

1 Art 11(1) and (2). An application for a stay under Art 11 is to be made to a district judge, who may determine the application or refer it to a judge for decision: FPR 1991, r 2.27A(1), inserted with effect from 1 April 2001 by the Family Proceedings (Amendment) Rules 2001, SI 2001/821.
2 Art 11(3).
3 The provisions of s 5(6) and para 9(1) of Sch 1 to the Domicile and Matrimonial Proceedings Act 1973, as amended by the European Communities (Matrimonial Jurisdiction and Judgments) Regulations SI 2001/310, only apply to matrimonial proceedings other than proceedings governed by the Council Regulation. For stays, see generally *Rayden and Jackson on Divorce and Family Matters* (17th edn, 1997), vol 1, chap 9 and the Noter-up thereto.
4 Art 11(4). See also *Canada Trust Co v Stolzenberg (No 2)* [2002] 1 AC 1, [2000] 4 All ER 481, HL (for the purpose of Arts 2 and 6 of the Lugano Convention (which is in identical terms as the Brussels Convention 1968 (Brussels I)) the English Court took jurisdiction over a defendant on the date that the writ was issued, not on the date that it was served on the defendant).

## Protective measures; injunctions

### [1.246]

In urgent cases, even if the court of another Member State has exclusive jurisdiction as to the substance of the matter, that shall not prevent the courts of another Member State from taking such provisional, including protective, measures in respect of persons or assets in that State as may be available under the law of that Member State[1].

1 Art 12.

## Recognition of a judgment

### [1.247]

The recognition of a judgment[1] relating to a divorce, legal separation or a marriage annulment may not be refused because the law of the Member State in which such recognition is sought would not allow divorce, legal separation or marriage annulment on the same facts[2]. A judgment given in a Member State shall be recognised in the other Member States without any special procedure being required[3]. Any interested party may, in accordance with the procedures provided for in the Council Regulation, apply for a decision that the judgment be or not be recognised[4]. Where the recognition of a judgment is raised as an incidental question in a court of a Member State, that court may determine that issue[5]. Recognition proceedings may be stayed if the judgment is under appeal or, in the case of a judgment given in the United Kingdom or Ireland enforcement is suspended by reason of an appeal[6].

1 For meaning of 'judgment' see Art 13(1); it includes a decree, order or decision.
2 Art 18.
3 Art 14(1).
4 Art 14(3). For the procedure on an application for recognition in England and Wales of a judgment given in another Member state, see FPR 1991, r 7.48, inserted with effect from 1 April 2001 by the Family Proceedings (Amendment) Rules 2001, SI 2001/821; an application for registration must be made in the High Court and filed in the Principal Registry; Art 22 and FPR 1991, r 7.41; registration of a judgment under the provisions of the FPR 1991 shall serve for the purposes of Art 14(3) as a decision that the judgment is recognised: FPR 1991, r 7.48(1).
5 Art 14(4).
6 Art 20.

## Grounds of non-recognition of a judgment

**[1.248]**

A judgment relating to a divorce, legal separation or marriage annulment shall not be recognised[1]:

(a) if such recognition is manifestly contrary to the public policy of the Member State in which recognition is sought[2];

(b) where it was given in default of appearance, if the respondent was not served with the document which instituted the proceedings or with an equivalent document in sufficient time and in such a way as to enable the respondent to arrange for his or her defence unless it is determined that the respondent has accepted the judgment unequivocally;

(c) if it is irreconcilable with a judgment given in proceedings between the same parties in the Member State in which recognition is sought; or

(d) if it is irreconcilable with an earlier judgment given in another Member State or in a non-member State between the same parties, provided that the earlier judgment fulfils the conditions necessary for its recognition in the Member State in which recognition is sought.

A court of a Member State may, on the basis of an agreement on the recognition and enforcement of judgments, not recognise a judgment given in another Member State[3]. Under no circumstances may a judgment be reviewed as to its substance[4].

1 Art 15(1).
2 See however the prohibition in Art 17: the jurisdiction of the court of the Member State of origin may not be reviewed and the test of public policy referred to in Art 15(1)(a) may not be applied to the rules relating to jurisdiction set out in Arts 2 to 8.
3 Art 16.
4 Art 19.

## Registration and enforcement: general provisions

**[1.249]**

A judgment on the exercise of parental responsibility[1] in respect of a child of both parties given in a Member State which is enforceable in that Member State and has been served shall be enforced in another Member State when, on the application of any interested party, it has been declared enforceable there[2]. In the case of the United Kingdom, such a judgment shall be enforced in England and Wales, in Scotland or in Northern Ireland if it has been registered for enforcement in that part of the UK[3].

The local jurisdiction for the purpose of making an application for a declaration of enforceability or for registration is determined by reference to the habitual residence of the person against whom enforcement is sought or of any child to whom the application relates; if neither of these is found in the Member State where enforcement is sought, the local jurisdiction is to be determined by reference to the place of enforcement[4].

1 For meaning of 'judgment' see Art 13(1); this provision encompasses an order made under s 8 of the ChA 1989 in or in connection with matrimonial proceedings, since such orders relate to the exercise of parental responsibility.
2 Art 21(1).
3 Art 21(2).
4 Art 22; the court to which application is to be made in any given Member State is specified in Annex 1 to the Regulation and the courts to which appeals are to be made are specified in Annex 2.

## Registration and enforcement: procedure

### [1.250]

An application under Art 21(2) to register in England and Wales a judgment given in another Member State must be made to the High Court[1] and must be filed with the Principal Registry[2]. The application must be accompanied by a statement sworn to be true or an affidavit, exhibiting the judgment relied on and certain other documents and giving prescribed information[3]. Notice of the application is not served on any other party[4]. The court to which the application is made shall give its decision without delay and the person against whom enforcement is sought is not entitled at that stage to make any representations[5]. The application may be refused only for one of the reasons set out in Arts 15, 16 and 17, but under no circumstances may a judgment be reviewed as to its substance[6]. The court shall notify the applicant of the decision without delay[7] and, where an order is made giving permission to register a judgment, an order is to be drawn which must state the period within which an appeal against the order must be made and must contain a notice that the court will not enforce the judgment until after the expiry of that period[8]. That notification does not prevent an application for protective measures under Art 12 pending final determination of any issue relating to enforcement of the judgment[9]. A register of judgments ordered to be registered under Art 21(2) is kept in the Principal Registry[10].

Notice of the registration of a judgment must be served on the person against whom the judgment was given by delivering it to him personally or by sending it to his usual or last known address or place of business, or otherwise as directed by the court[11] and any person wishing to apply to enforce the judgment must produce to the court a sworn statement or affidavit of service of the notice and of any order made in relation to the judgment[12]. The notice must state full particulars of the judgment and of the order for registration, the name of the person making the application and his address for service and the right to appeal against the order and the period within which such an appeal may be made[13].

A judgment registered under Art 21(2) may not be enforced until after the expiration of the period specified for making an appeal, but again this does not prevent an application for protective measures under Art 12 pending final determination of any issue relating to enforcement of the judgment[14].

A decision on an application for registration or for a declaration of enforceability may be appealed by either party. In England and Wales an appeal lies to the High Court[15]. An appeal against an order registering a judgment or against a declaration of enforceability must be lodged within one month of service the order or, if the party against whom enforcement is sought is habitually resident in a Member State other than that in which the declaration of enforceability was given, two months from the date of service[16]. If the applicant for registration appeals against a refusal, the other party shall be summoned to appear before the appellate court; the Regulation does not prescribe any period for the lodging of such an appeal[17].

A judgment given on appeal may only be contested in accordance with Art 27 of and Annex 3 to the Regulation; in the United Kingdom a party is limited to a single further appeal on a point of law.

An applicant who, in the Member State of origin, has benefited from complete or partial legal aid or exemption from costs or expenses shall be entitled, in the procedures provided for in Arts 22 to 25, to benefit from the most favourable legal aid or the most extensive exemption from costs and expenses provided for by the law of the Member State addressed[18].

1 Art 22(1) and Annex 1. For the procedure see generally FPR 1991, Chap 5 (rr 7.40 to 7.50), inserted with effect from 1 April 2001 by the Family Proceedings (Amendment) Rules 2001, SI 2001/821.
2 FPR 1991, r 7.41.
3 FPR 1991, r 7.43.
4 FPR 1991, r 7.42.
5 Art 24(1).
6 Art 24(2) and (3).

7 Art 25.
8 FPR 1991, r 7.44(1) and (2).
9 FPR 1991, r 7.44(3).
10 FPR 1991, r 7.45.
11 FPR 1991, r 7.46(1).
12 FPR 1991, r 7.47(2).
13 FPR 1991, r 7.46(2).
14 FPR 1991, r 7.47(1) and (3).
15 Art 26(1) and (2) and Annex 2.
16 Art 26(5).
17 Art 26(4).
18 Art 30.

## Enforcement in another Member State of a judgement in England and Wales

### [1.251]

A party applying for a declaration of enforceability or applying for or contesting recognition of a judgment must produce a duly authenticated copy of the judgment and a certificate giving prescribed information about the judgment[1]. Where the judgment was given in England and Wales, an application for a certified copy of the judgment must be made to the court in which the order was made, by lodging a witness statement or affidavit and without notice to the other party[2]. The witness statement or affidavit must contain prescribed information about the judgment, including confirmation that it has been served on the other party and whether any notice of appeal against the judgment has been given[3]. The certified copy of the judgment will be an office copy sealed with the seal of the court and signed by the district judge and will be accompanied by a certified copy of any order which has varied the original order[4].

1 Art 32; for the form of certificate see Art 33 and Annexes 4 and 5.
2 FPR 1991, r 7.49(1), inserted with effect from 1 April 2001 by the Family Proceedings (Amendment) Rules 2001, SI 2001/821.
3 FPR 1991, r 7.49(2).
4 FPR 1991, r 7.49(3).

## Transitional provisions

### [1.252]

The provisions of the Regulation apply only to legal proceedings instituted, to documents formally drawn up or registered as authentic instruments and to settlements which have been approved by a court in the course of proceedings after its entry into force. Judgments given after the date of entry into force of this Regulation in proceedings instituted before that date shall be recognised and enforced in accordance with the provisions of Chapter III (Arts 13 to 35) if jurisdiction was founded on rules which accorded with those provided for either in Arts 2 to 12 of the Regulation or in a convention concluded between the Member State of origin and the Member State addressed which was in force when the proceedings were instituted[1].

1 Art 42.

# 5. Injunctions in Financial Proceedings

Contents

## Introduction

### [1.253]

This Introductory Chapter will consider:

- Injunctions under s 37 of the MCA 1973;
- Injunctions under the inherent jurisdiction;
- Freezing (formerly *Mareva*) and Search (formerly *Anton Piller*) orders.

## Section 37 of the MCA 1973

### [1.254]

Section 37 of the MCA 1973[1] provides for the making of injunctions where an application for financial relief has been brought.

1 Set out at para **[2.136]** below. See generally *Rayden and Jackson on Divorce and Family Matters* (17th edn, 1997), vol 1, chap 20 and the Noter-up thereto.

### [1.255]

Financial relief means any relief under the following sections of the MCA 1973:

- s 22[1];
- s 23[2];
- s 24[3];
- s 24B[4];
- s 27[5];
- s 31[6] (except sub-s (6)); and
- s 35[7].

Different types of relief are available under s 37 of the MCA 1973:

- orders to prevent a party who intends to defeat an applicant's claim from dealing with property[8];
- orders setting aside[9] a reviewable disposition which has been made with the intention of defeating the applicant's claim and which would result in different financial relief being afforded to the applicant[10];
- orders setting aside a reviewable disposition that has been made with the intention of defeating the enforcement of a financial order that has been made[11].

1 Set out at para **[2.116]** below.
2 Set out at para **[2.117]** below.
3 Set out at para **[2.118]** below.
4 Set out at para **[2.119A]** below.
5 Set out at para **[2.125]** below.
6 Set out at para **[2.129]** below.
7 Set out at para **[2.134]** below. See also s 37 of the MCA 1973 at para **[2.136]** below.
8 See s 37(2)(a) of the MCA 1973, the full text of which reads: 'Where proceedings for financial relief are brought by one person against another, the court may, on the application of the first-mentioned person … if it is satisfied that the other party to the proceedings is, with the intention of defeating the claim for financial relief, about to make any disposition or to transfer out of the jurisdiction or otherwise deal with any property, make such order as it thinks fit for restraining the other party from so doing or otherwise for protecting the claim'.
9 Where the court sets aside a disposition under this subsection or the next (ie under s 37(2)(b) or (c) it may give such consequential directions as it thinks fit for giving effect to the order (including directions requiring the making of any payments or the disposal of any property: see s 37(3) of the MCA 1973.
10 See s 37(2)(b) of the MCA 1973, the full text of which reads: 'Where proceedings for financial relief are brought by one person against another, the court may, on the application of the first-mentioned person … if it is satisfied that the other party has, with that intention, made a reviewable disposition and that if the disposition were set aside financial relief or different financial relief would be granted to the applicant, make an order setting aside the disposition'. The application for the injunction must be brought within the ancillary relief proceedings: see the last clause in s 37(2).
11 See s 37(2)(c) of the MCA 1973, the full text of which reads: 'Where proceedings for financial relief are brought by one person against another, the court may, on the application of the first-mentioned person … if it is satisfied, in a case where an order has been obtained under any of the provisions mentioned in subsection (1) above by the applicant against the other party, that the other party has, with that intention, made a reviewable disposition, make an order setting aside the disposition'.

### [1.256]
### Defeating the claim

The reference to defeating a person's claim for financial relief is a reference to preventing financial relief from being granted to that person, or to that person for the benefit of a child of the family, or reducing the amount of any financial relief which might be so granted, or frustrating or impeding the enforcement of any order which might be or has been made at the applicant's instance[1].

1 See s 37(1) of the MCA 1973 at para **[2.136]** below.

### [1.257]
### Disposition

Section 37(6) and (7) of the MCA 1973 state that 'disposition' does not include any provision contained in a will or codicil but, with that exception, includes any conveyance, assurance, gift of property of any description, whether made by an instrument or otherwise after 1 January 1968.

### [1.258]

The remedies under the section are directed to dispositions by a party to the proceedings. Thus where a party makes a disposition of property but the recipient then makes a further disposition of the property, the court will not have jurisdiction under the section to set aside the further disposition[1].

1 *Green v Green (Barclays Bank, third party)* [1981] 1 All ER 97, [1981] 1 WLR 391.

### [1.259]

A notice of termination of a tenancy is not a disposition for the purposes of s 37 of the MCA 1973 and, therefore a court has no jurisdiction to set it aside or otherwise to revive the tenancy after the expiration of the notice to terminate[1]. In *Harrow London Borough Council v Johnstone*[2] and *Newlon Housing Association v Alsulaimen*[3] Lord Hoffmann left open the question of whether the court would have the jurisdiction under s 37(2)(a) of the MCA 1973 to restrain a spouse from giving notice to terminate. In the case of *Bater and Bater v Greenwich London Borough Council*[4] Thorpe LJ considered that the court did have such power (although Lord Lloyd, giving the third judgment in the case of *Bater*, expressly stated that he did not wish to pronounce upon the point left open by Lord Hoffman). Thorpe LJ suggested that, where the act of one party might destroy the tenancy of a property that is likely to be in issue in ancillary relief proceedings, a written undertaking should be sought from the other party that no steps will be taken to defeat the tenancy prior to the ancillary relief hearing. If given, the undertaking should be served on the landlord. If not given, the party who sought the undertaking should apply to the court for an order under s 37(2)(a) to prevent the other party giving notice to the landlord of the termination of the tenancy.

1 See *Newlon Housing Trust v Alsulaimen* [1999] 1 AC 313 at 319, [1998] 3 FCR 183 at 188.
2 [1997] 1 All ER 929 at 940–941, [1997] 2 FCR 225 at 239, HL.
3 [1999] 1 AC 313, [1998] 3 FCR 183, HL.
4 [1999] 3 FCR 254, [1999] 2 FLR 993.

### [1.260]
### Reviewable disposition

For the purposes of the above, a reviewable disposition is any disposition made by the other party to the proceedings for financial relief in question (whether before or after the commencement of those proceedings) unless it was made for valuable consideration (other than marriage) to a person who, at the time of the disposition, acted in relation to it in good faith and without notice of any intention on the part of the other party to defeat the applicant's claim for financial relief.

## [1.261]

Constructive notice of the intention to defeat the applicant's claim will be sufficient[1].

1 See *Kemmis v Kemmis (Welland intervening)* [1988] 1 WLR 1307, [1988] 2 FLR 223, CA; and *B v B (P Ltd intervening) (No 2)* [1995] 2 FCR 670, [1995] 1 FLR 374, CA.

## [1.262]

### Proof

The standard of proof is that the judge must be 'satisfied' that the requirements of the relevant subsection are fulfilled[1]. An intention to defeat the claim for ancillary relief does not have to be the sole or even dominant intention, so long as it plays a substantial part in the intentions of the respondent to the application[2]. The court will accept the normal inference that a man knows the consequences of his own actions[3].

1 See *K v K (avoidance of reviewable disposition)* (1982) 4 FLR 31, CA.
2 See *Kemmis v Kemmis (intervening)* [1988] 1 WLR 1307, [1988] 2 FLR 223, CA.
3 See *Sherry v Sherry* [1991] 1 FLR 250, FD.

## [1.263]

The granting of an injunction is a discretionary remedy and the court may have to balance the hardship that would be caused by the grant of the injunction against the hardship that would arise if it were refused[1].

1 See *Sherry v Sherry* [1991] 1 FLR 307, CA.

## [1.264]

Where an application is made with respect to a disposition which took place less than three years before the date of the application, or with respect to a disposition or other dealing with property which is about to take place and the court is satisfied—

(a) in a case falling within s 37(2)(a) or (b), that the disposition or other dealing would (apart from this section) have the consequence, or

(b) in a case falling within s 37(2)(c), that the disposition has had the consequence,

of defeating the applicant's claim for financial relief, it shall be presumed, unless the contrary is shown, that the person who disposed of or is about to dispose of or deal with the property did so or, as the case may be, is about to do so, with the intention of defeating the applicant's claim for financial relief. The court may infer that a reviewable disposition is about to take place as a result of earlier conduct of a party[1].

1 See *Quartermain v Quartermain* (1974) 4 Fam Law 156, FD.

## [1.265]

### Property

The court may make an order under s 37 of the MCA 1973 in relation to property that is situated abroad. Although the court may, in its discretion, refuse such an order where enforcement would not be possible[1], injunctions are enforceable in personam (ie against the person of the party against whom they are directed) and, therefore enforcement will usually be possible[2].

1 See *Hamlin v Hamlin* [1986] Fam 11, [1985] 2 All ER 1037, CA; *Razelos v Razelos (No 2)* [1970] 1 All ER 386n, [1970] 1 WLR 392; and *Bheekhun v Williams* [1999] 2 FLR 229, CA.
2 See eg *Murbarak v Murbarak* [2001] All ER (D) 2302, [2001] 1 FCR 193, [2001] 1 FLR 698, CA in which the following is said at para 67 of the judgment: 'We know from the answer given by the solicitors on behalf of the husband that he has a substantial interest under a trust. What that is precisely we do not know, nor do we know the details of the trust; but almost certainly all those details are extractable, if necessary by court orders. There is no reason, as far as I can see, why some sort of remedy against the husband's interest in that trust is not directly obtainable. The fact that the trust is abroad, the fact that many of the assets of the trust are also abroad, is neither here nor there. He is here and any order made will be in personam and enforceable against him'.

### [1.266]

Where a company is the alter ego of one of the parties, the court may make orders that pierce the corporate veil and treat the company as if it were the property of that party[1].

1 See eg *Nicholas v Nicholas* [1984] FLR 285, CA, followed by Connell J in *Green v Green* [1993] 1 FLR 326 (but cf *Crittenden v Crittenden* [1991] FCR 70, [1990] 2 FLR 361, CA). As to piercing the corporate veil in a non-family case, see *Trustor AB v Smallbone (No 2)* [2001] 3 All ER 987, [2001] 1 WLR 1177, Ch D per Morritt VC. In the family case of *Murbarak v Murbarak* [2001] All ER (D) 2302, [2001] 1 FCR 193, [2001] 1 FLR 698, CA the husband conceded in ancillary relief proceedings that a company's assets could be treated as being his property, it was held that orders could only be made against the company's assets where:
(a) The party making the concession owned and controlled the company; and
(b) Prejudice would not be caused to third parties (such as those who held true minority interests, creditors and directors).

In the case of *McGladdery v McGladdery* [2000] 1 FCR 315, [1999] 2 FLR 1102, CA the court refused to pierce the corporate veil, holding: 'a consideration of the terms of s 37, in particular sub-s (4), shows the application to be misconceived. By that subsection only transfers by the other spouse are reviewable. The transfer of which complaint is made was effected by Rapid Gen which, as conceded, is not to be regarded as the alter ego of either spouse. The fact that it was made to the other spouse or her alter ego is immaterial. If the husband has no claim as a spouse then it is clear that his claim as a minority shareholder can only be pursued in the Chancery Division.'

### [1.267]

Before making an application to set aside a disposition, consideration should be given to the effect of the disposition in question. Money transferred by a party to a third party may in fact be held by the third party as a bare trustee of the transferring party (therefore the court will be able to treat it as the property of the transferor without needing to have recourse to s 37 of the MCA 1973)[1].

1 See *Purba v Purba* [2000] 1 FCR 652, [2000] 1 FLR 444, CA.

### [1.268]
### Orders

Under s 37(2)(a) of the MCA 1973 the court may make 'such order as it thinks fit for restraining the other party from [making the disposition] or otherwise for protecting the claim'. As well as making orders that prohibit the respondent from making the disposition, the court may make other protective orders. These include, for instance, ordering that money is paid into court or that money is paid to a party's solicitor[1]. It has been held that, where an order is made directing that money be held by a party's solicitor, the applicant for the order is put into the more advantageous position of a secured creditor in the event that the respondent is subsequently made bankrupt[2].

1 See *Graham v Graham* (1987) unreported; and *Re Mordant* [1997] 2 FCR 378, [1996] 1 FLR 334.
2 See *Re Mordant* [1997] 2 FCR 378, [1996] 1 FLR 334.

### [1.269]
### Procedure

The following points are of relevance to the procedure under this section:

(i) It is necessary for the ancillary relief proceedings to be in existence before the court can make an order (due to the words at the start of s 37(2): 'Where proceedings for financial relief are brought ...'). Where it is not possible to bring proceedings for ancillary relief, it may be possible to pursue the application under the court's inherent jurisdiction.
(ii) An application under s 37(2)(a) does not fall within the definition of 'ancillary' under r 1.2 of the FPR 1991[1]. Therefore, the rules that apply only to applications for ancillary relief do not govern such applications (save as specifically extended by r 2.68 of the FPR 1991[2]). Thus, unlike applications under s 37(2)(b) and (c), applications under s 37(2)(a) are not made in Form A. They are made by notice of application within the ancillary relief proceedings, supported by affidavit.

(iii) By contrast, applications under s 37(2)(b) and (c) do fall within the definition of ancillary relief. They are made by notice of application within the ancillary relief proceedings, supported by affidavit. Applications under s 37(2)(b) and (c) are made in Form A[3].
(iv) The application may be heard by a district judge[4].
(v) An application for an avoidance of disposition order should, if practicable, be heard at the same time as any related application for ancillary relief[5].
(vi) It is essential for an injunction to be expressly continued, if that is what is intended; the failure to do so cannot be corrected retrospectively under the slip rule[6].
(vii) An undertaking as to damages will not usually be included in an order unless specifically required by the court and expressly offered[7]. This has to be compared with the general rule, for instance in relation to freezing orders in civil litigation, where an undertaking as to damages will be required[8].

1 Set out at para **[3.402]** below.
2 Set out at para **[3.453]** below. Under r 2.68(2), rr 2.65 (reference of application by district judge to judge) and 2.66 (arrangements for hearing of application by judge following reference to judge by district judge).
3 See r 2.53 of the FPR 1991; set out at para **[3.436]** below.
4 Rule 2.68(1) of the FPR 1991 provides that an application under s 37(2)(a) of the MCA 1973 may be heard by a district judge. Applications under s 37(2)(b) and (c) will usually be herd by a district judge, just as any other application for ancillary relief would be.
5 See r 2.62(2) of the FPR 1991; set out at para **[3.448]** below.
6 See *Langley v Langley* [1994] 2 FCR 294, [1994] 1 FLR 383, CA.
7 See *Practice Direction (undertaking as to damages)* [1974] 2 All ER 400, [1974] 1 WLR 576; and *W v H (Family Division: without notice orders)* [2001] 1 All ER 300, sub nom *W v H (ex parte injunctions)* [2000] 3 FCR 481, [2000] 2 FLR 927. In the latter case Munby J said: 'I can well see that it will often not be appropriate – indeed, I would go so far as to say that typically it will be inappropriate – to exact an undertaking or cross-undertaking in damages, even if the matter does concern property matters, where the person sought to be injuncted is the other party to the marriage. This is because in such cases the court will typically be able by the exercise of its statutory discretionary powers to achieve that appropriate justice between the parties, and to protect the person injuncted from that risk of injustice identified by Lord Diplock in *Hoffmann-La Roche (F) & Co v Secretary of State for Trade and Industry* [1975] AC 295 at 360–361, [1974] 2 All ER 1128 at 1150, HL, which, in the absence of such powers, can otherwise be achieved only by exacting an undertaking or cross-undertaking in damages. That is, no doubt, why the *Practice Direction* draws a distinction between what it calls cases "when the claim is to protect rights" – cases where it contemplates that an undertaking may be exacted – and cases where the applicant is invoking the court's discretionary powers – cases where it contemplates that an undertaking is unlikely to be exacted. I should add that I have deliberately used the words "often" and "typically" to indicate that there will, of course, be cases even of the type which I have just mentioned where it will or may be appropriate to exact an undertaking or cross-undertaking in damages. In this area of practice, particularly I might add in the Family Division, there can be no rigid rules. Circumstances alter cases and, in the final analysis, every case must be considered on its own facts.'
8 See CPR 1998, Pt 25, PD5.1(1).

## Inherent jurisdiction of the court

### [1.270]

Circumstances may arise where the precise wording of s 37 of the MCA 1973 cannot be satisfied but where injunctive relief should be obtained in order to preserve assets pending the determination of the ancillary relief application (eg where the necessary proof of an intention to defeat the ancillary relief claim cannot be proved)[1]. In that event recourse may be had to the inherent jurisdiction of the court. In the High Court this arises under s 37 of the SCA 1981. In the county court it arises under s 38 of the CCA 1984. The continuing existence of the inherent jurisdiction to grant injunctions in family proceedings has been recognised by Lord Mustill in the House of Lords in the case of *Harrow London Borough Council v Johnstone*[2] and by the Court of Appeal in *Khreino v Khreino (No 2) (court's power to grant injunctions)*[3].

1 See eg *Shipman v Shipman* [1991] FCR 628, [1991] 1 FLR 250, FD; and *Roche v Roche* (1981) 11 Fam Law 243, CA.
2 [1997] 1 All ER 929 at 936, [1997] 2 FCR 225 at 234, HL.
3 [2000] 1 FCR 80, CA.

### [1.271]

Two particular types of injunction are freezing (formerly *Mareva*) and search (formerly *Anton Piller*) orders.

### [1.272]

Other examples are orders preventing a person from leaving the jurisdiction (A 'writ ne exeat regno'). Such orders may be made in support of freezing or search orders[1]. However, such orders cannot be made not as a free-standing means of enforcement[2].

1 See *Al Nakhel for Contracting and Trading Ltd v Lowe* [1986] 1 QB 235, [1986] 1 All ER 729; and *Bayer AG v Winter* [1986] 1 WLR 497.
2 See *B v B (Restraint on Leaving Jurisdiction)* [1997] 2 FLR 148. In that case Wilson J said (at p 154): 'It is clear from the above that there are a number of circumstances in which under s 37(1) it is possible to restrain a party from leaving the jurisdiction and to make a consequential order for the surrender of his or her passport. The jurisdiction exists where the other party has established a right to interlocutory relief (such as an *Anton Piller* order), which would otherwise be rendered nugatory. It exists where a hearing is shortly to take place, the efficacy of which would be frustrated by his absence. In my view it exists in principle in aid of all the court's procedures leading to the disposal of the proceedings.

I consider that the jurisdiction is also available in some circumstances after judgment. To be specific, it can be invoked to aid the court's established procedures for enforcement of the judgment. In *Thaha v Thaha* [1987] 2 FLR 142, Wood J issued a writ ne exeat regno so as to detain a husband within England for a few days until the hearing of a judgment summons which was to be issued against him for alleged arrears under orders for maintenance. Although, with respect, the use of the writ was inapt at a stage after the orders for maintenance had been made, it seems to me that the judge's order was entirely permissible under s 37(1). Equally, I consider, contrary to the submissions of Lord Phillimore, that in the present case Bennett J had the power to make the order which obliged the husband to remain within the jurisdiction for 26 days pending his oral examination under RSC Ord 48. A judgment summons and an oral examination are both established procedures for enforcement and they should not be permitted to be frustrated by the debtor's departure from the jurisdiction.

Where I part company with Mr Mostyn is upon his submission that s 37(1) enables a debtor to be restrained from leaving the jurisdiction not simply as an aid to the court's established procedures for enforcement of a judgment but as a free-standing enforcement procedure in its own right. He asks that this husband be kept in England and Wales indefinitely until the costs are paid. He defies the emphasis in the reported cases upon the short-term nature of the restraint.'

## Freezing orders

### [1.273]

A freezing order is defined in the CPR 1998[1] as one 'restraining a party from removing from the jurisdiction assets located there; or restraining a party from dealing with any assets whether located within the jurisdiction or not'. The orders used to be called *Mareva* injunctions[2].

1 CPR 1998, Pt 25.1(1)(f).
2 After the case of *Mareva Compania Naviera SA v International Bulkcarriers SA ('The Mareva')* [1980] 1 All ER 213n, CA.

### [1.274]

An application for an order must be ancillary to proceedings that are either continuing in this country or elsewhere. Prior to the amendment of s 25 of the CJJA 1982 in 1997, orders could only be made in support of proceedings in this country or in a country that is a signatory to the Brussels Convention 1968 or the Lugano Convention on Jurisdiction and Judgments 1991[1]. However, s 25 has been extended to non-Convention countries and to proceedings that fall outside of the Conventions[2]. Consequently, the High Court may now make interim orders in support of proceedings elsewhere.

1 See s 25 of the CJJA 1982; and eg *The Siskina* [1979] AC 210, HL.
2 See the Civil Jurisdiction and Judgments Act 1982 (Interim Relief) Order 1997, SI 1997/302 which came into force on 1 April 1997.

## [1.275]

Orders may be made in support of proceedings in a foreign country but that jurisdiction should be issued with extreme care and only in exceptional circumstances[1].

1 See *Rosseel NV v Oriental Commercial Shipping (UK) Ltd* [1990] 3 All ER 545, [1990] 1 WLR 1387, CA; and *Republic of Haiti v Duvalier* [1990] 1 QB 202, [1989] 1 All ER 456, CA. It will be necessary to show that the order can be properly served on the respondent: *Mercedes Benz AG v Leiduck* [1996] AC 284, [1995] 3 All ER 929, PC.

## [1.276]

Orders may be made freezing assets worldwide but that power should also be exercised with extreme caution[1]. Normally, the order should be limited to assets within the jurisdiction[2]. In most circumstances the most appropriate court to deal with assets is the court of the State in which the assets are situated[3] Where an order is made in relation to foreign assets, the applicant will be required to give an undertaking that he will not seek to enforce the order in a foreign country and will not bring proceedings against the respondent abroad[4].

1 See *Derby & Co Ltd v Weldon (Nos 3 and 4)* [1990] Ch 65, sub nom *Derby & Co Ltd v Weldon (No 2)* [1989] 1 All ER 1002, CA; and *Babanaft International Co SA v Bassatne* [1989] 1 All ER 433.
2 See *Allied Arab Bank Ltd v Hajjar* [1988] QB 787, [1987] 3 All ER 739.
3 See the decision of the European Court of Justice in Case 125/79: *Denilauler v SNC Counchet Fréres* [1980] ECR 1553.
4 See *Derby & Co Ltd v Weldon (No 1)* [1990] Ch 48, [1989] 1 All ER 469, CA.

## [1.277]
## Jurisdiction of the High Court and county court

Orders may be made in the High Court as a result of s 37 of the SCA 1981. That section provides that:

> '(1) The High court may by order (whether interlocutory or final) grant an injunction … in all cases in which it appears to the court to be just and convenient to do so …
>
> (3) The power of the High Court under subsection (1) to grant an interlocutory injunction restraining a party to any proceedings from removing from the jurisdiction of the High Court, or otherwise dealing with any assets located within that jurisdiction shall be exercisable in cases where that party is, as well as in cases where he is not domiciled, resident or present within that jurisdiction'.

## [1.278]

A county court, when exercising its jurisdiction in family proceedings within the meaning of Pt V of the MFPA 1984 and for the purpose of making an order for the preservation, custody or detention of property which forms or may form the subject matter of proceedings, may make a freezing order unless the nature of the issues of fact or law raised in the case make it more suitable to be heard in the High Court[1]. In most instances, applications for freezing orders are more appropriately dealt with in the High Court. The judge hearing the application must be 'duly authorised'[2].

1 County Court Remedies Regulations 1991, SI 1991/1222.
2 See CPR 1998, Pt 25, PD25, para 1.1.

## [1.279]
## Civil Procedure Rules 1998

The CPR 1998 do not strictly apply to freezing orders made in family proceedings (as a result of r 2.1(1)(a) of the CPR 1998). However, in practice the procedure under Pt 25 of the CPR 1998 (and the *Practice Direction* annexed to that rule) governs the making of the application for such an order[1]. The rule provides standard forms that are to be used in connection with the applications[2].

1 See para **[1.284]** below.
2 See CPR 1998, Pt 25, PD25, para 6.

## [1.280]
## Discretionary factors

Injunctions are discretionary. In deciding whether to grant a freezing order the court will consider whether the applicant has shown that he has a good arguable case and that there is a real risk of injustice if the court rejects the application[1]. If the court concludes that there is inadequate evidence to show that the respondent will dispose of anything, it may, in its discretion, reject the application[2]. Further, the court may need to balance the competing hardship that would be caused by the order as against that which would result from a refusal to make it[3]. The court should not be required to decide complex issues of law or fact on an application for a freezing order[4].

1 See *Ninemia Corpn v Trave Schiffahrtsgesellschaft mbH & Co KG* [1984] 1 All ER 398, [1983] 1 WLR 1412; *Aiglon Ltd v Gau Shan Co Ltd* [1993] 1 Lloyd's Rep 164; and *W v H (Family Division: without notice orders)* [2001] 1 All ER 300, sub nom *W v H (ex parte injunctions)* [2000] 3 FCR 481.
2 See eg *Araghchinchi v Araghchinchi* [1997] 3 FCR 567, [1997] 2 FLR 142, CA.
3 See *Nikitenko v Lebeouf Lamb Greene & Macrae (A firm)* [1000] TLR 61.
4 See *Derby & Co Ltd v Weldon (No 1)* [1999] Ch 48, [1989] 1 All ER 469, CA.

## [1.281]

Orders may be made to preserve assets that are not yet under the control of the respondent but which are likely to do so[1].

1 Eg an impending award of damages for personal injuries: *Roche v Roche* (1981) 11 Fam Law 243.

## [1.282]

The inherent jurisdiction may be used to freeze the property of someone who is not a party to the proceedings where, ultimately, those assets may be transferred or made available for the benefit of the applicant spouse[1].

1 See *Khreino v Khreino (No 2) (court's power to grant injunctions)* [2000] 1 FCR 80, CA in which Thorpe LJ says (at p 84): 'It is simply fanciful to suggest that in a cosmopolitan case such as this the husband could emasculate the Family Division judge by saying: "Oh, I have put the home into a British Virgin Island company. It is a bearer share company and my brother holds the shares …"'.

## [1.283]
## Duty on applicant

In making the application, the applicant must:

- Give full and frank disclosure of facts that are material and discoverable by him on reasonable enquiry[1].
- File an application notice which must state the order sought and the date, time and place of the hearing[2].
- Where the court is to serve the application notice and evidence, provide sufficient copies of the application notice and evidence in support for the court and for each respondent (where notice is to be given, the application notice and evidence in support must be served as soon as possible after issue and in any event not less than three days before the court is due to hear the application)[3].

- If possible, file a draft of the order sought together with a copy of the draft order on a disk (using WordPerfect 5.1)[4].
- Support the application with evidence on affidavit[5].
- In an appropriate case, give an undertaking as to damages[6]. An undertaking as to damages will not usually be included in an order made in family proceedings unless specifically required by the court and expressly offered[7]. This has to be compared with the general rule, for instance in relation to freezing orders in civil litigation, where an undertaking as to damages will be required[8]. However, where the order is directed against third parties, an undertaking as to damages is likely to be appropriate even in financial proceedings in the Family Division.

1 See CPR 1998, Pt 25, PD25, para 3.3; and *Brinks–MAT Ltd v Elcombe* [1988] 3 All ER 188, [1988] 1 WLR 1350, CA.
2 See CPR 1998, Pt 25, PD25, para 2.1.
3 See CPR 1998, Pt 25, PD25, paras 2.3 and 2.2.
4 See CPR 1998, Pt 25, PD25, para 2.3.
5 See CPR 1998, Pt 25, PD25, para 3.1.
6 See CPR 1998, Pt 25, PD25, para 5.1(1).
7 See para **[1.269]**, sub-para (vii) above and, in particular, the case of *W v H (Family Division: without notice orders)* [2001] 1 All ER 300, sub nom *W v H (ex parte injunctions)* [2000] 3 FCR 481, [2000] 2 FLR 927.
8 See CPR 1998, Pt 25, PD5.1(1).

**[1.284]**

Where the application is made without notice, the following additional requirements apply:

(i) The evidence must also set out why notice was not given[1].
(ii) The order should contain an undertaking by the applicant to the court to serve on the respondent the application notice, evidence in support and any order made as soon as possible[2].
(iii) The order should contain a return date for a further hearing when the other party can be present[3].
(iv) Where the application is made after the issue of a claim form (in ancillary relief this will be the application for ancillary relief by analogy):
  (a) the application notice, evidence in support and a draft order should be filed with the court two hours before the hearing wherever possible;
  (b) if an application is made before the application notice has been issued, a draft order should be provided at the hearing, and the application notice and evidence in support must be filed with the court on the same or next working day or as ordered by the court;
  (c) except in cases where secrecy is essential, the applicant should take steps to notify the respondent informally of the application[4].
(v) Where the application is made before the issue of the claim form (eg for ancillary relief), in addition to the matters set out in CPR 1998, Pt 25, PD25, para 4.3 (see sub-para (ii) above) there are the following additional requirements:
  (a) unless the court orders otherwise, either the applicant must undertake to the court to issue a claim form immediately or the court will give directions for the commencement of the claim;
  (b) where possible, the claim form should be served with the order for the injunction;
  (c) an order made before the issue of a claim form should state in the title after the names of the applicant and respondent 'the Claimant and Defendant in an Intended Action'[5];
  (d) the order should contain an undertaking to issue the claim and pay the appropriate fee on the same or next working day or should contain directions for the commencement of the claim[6]. If the application has been made before the application notice has been filed, an undertaking by the applicant should be recorded in the order to file the notice and pay the appropriate fee on the same or next working day[7].

1 See CPR 1998, Pt 25, PD25, para 3.4.
2 See CPR 1998, Pt 25, PD25, para 5.1(2).
3 See CPR 1998, Pt 25, PD25, para 5.1(3).
4 See CPR 1998, Pt 25, PD25, para 4.3.
5 See CPR 1998, Pt 25, PD25, para 4.4.
6 See CPR 1998, Pt 25, PD25, para 5.1(5).
7 See CPR 1998, Pt 25, PD25, para 5.1(4).

### [1.285]
### Telephone application

Where applications are to be made by telephone:

(i) Where it is not possible to arrange a hearing, applications can be made between 10.00am and 5.00pm weekdays by telephoning the Royal Courts of Justice on 020-7947-6000 and asking to be put in contact with a High Court Judge of the appropriate Division available to deal with an emergency application in a High Court matter. The appropriate District Registry may also be contacted by telephone. In county court proceedings, the appropriate county court should be contacted.

(ii) Where an application is made outside those hours, the applicant should either:

(a) telephone the Royal Courts of Justice on 020-7947-6000 where he will be put in contact with the clerk to the appropriate duty judge in the High Court (or the appropriate area Circuit Judge where known); or

(b) the Urgent Business Officer of the appropriate circuit who will contact the local duty judge.

(iii) Where the facility is available, it is likely that the judge will require a draft order to be faxed to him.

(iv) The application notice and evidence in support must be filed with the court on the same or next working day or as ordered, together with two copies of the order for sealing.

(v) Injunctions will only be heard by telephone where the applicant is acting by counsel or solicitors[1].

1 See CPR 1998, Pt 25, PD25, para 4.5.

### [1.286]
### The order

The order must state clearly what the respondent must and must not do[1]. In addition:

(i) The value of the assets that are frozen should not exceed the maximum amount that the applicant might receive within the proceedings.

(ii) The respondent should not be prevented from meeting his normal living expenses (including his legal costs) or from carrying on his business[2].

(iii) The order should normally be served on third parties who hold funds on behalf of the respondent (since this will then fix them with notice of the order).

(iv) The order will usually require the respondent to file an affidavit of his means, giving the location, value and other details in relation to his assets. The respondent may be cross-examined on the affidavit in an appropriate case, although his privilege against self-incrimination should not be infringed[3].

1 See CPR 1998, Pt 25, PD25, para 5.3.
2 See *Ghoth v Ghoth* [1992] 2 All ER 920, [1993] 1 FCR 177, CA; and *Polly Peck International plc v Nadir (No 2)* [1992] 4 All ER 769, CA.
3 See *Memory Corpn plc v Sidhu* [2000] Ch 645, [2000] 1 All ER 434.

## Search orders

### [1.287]

These orders were originally called *Anton Piller* orders after the case of *Anton Piller KG v Manufacturing Processes Ltd*[1]. The order permits the representative of the applicant to enter the premises of the respondent in order to inspect the premises and remove documents. Due to the extreme nature of the application an order will only be made in exceptional circumstances[2]. It is the responsibility of the applicant to give full disclosure in support of the application; a failure to do so may lead to the order being discharged[3].

1 [1976] Ch 55, [1976] 1 All ER 779, CA.
2 See eg *Araghchinchi v Araghchinchi* [1997] 3 FCR 567, [1997] 2 FLR 142, CA.
3 See *Dormeuil Frères SA v Nicolian International (Textiles) Ltd* [1988] 3 All ER 197, [1988] 1 WLR 1362.

**[1.288]**

The orders have their statutory origin in s 7 of the Civil Procedure Act 1997, which provides:

'(1) The court may make an order under this section for the purpose of securing, in the case of any existing or proposed proceedings in the court—

(a) the preservation of evidence which is or may be relevant; or

(b) the preservation of property which is or may be the subject-matter of the proceedings or as to which any question arises or may arise in the proceedings.

(2) A person who is, or appears to the court likely to be, a party to proceedings in the court may make an application for such an order.

(3) Such an order may direct any person to permit any person described in the order, or secure that any person so described is permitted—

(a) to enter premises in England and Wales; and

(b) while on the premises, to take in accordance with the terms of the order any of the following steps.

(4) Those steps are—

(a) to carry out a search for or inspection of anything described in the order; and

(b) to make or obtain a copy, photograph, sample or other record of anything so described.

(5) The order may also direct the person concerned—

(a) to provide any person described in the order, or secure that any person so described is provided, with any information or article described in the order; and

(b) to allow any person described in the order, or secure that any person so described is allowed, to retain for safe keeping anything described in the order.

(6) An order under this section is to have effect subject to such conditions as are specified in the order.

(7) This section does not affect any right of a person to refuse to do anything on the ground that to do so might tend to expose him or his spouse to proceedings for an offence or for the recovery of a penalty.

(8) In this section—

'court' means the High Court, and

'premises' includes any vehicle,

and an order under this section may describe anything generally, whether by reference to a class or otherwise.'

**[1.289]**

In the case of *Anton Piller* itself, Ormrod LJ identified the following requirements before an order will be made:

(i) there must be an extremely strong prima facie case;

(ii) the potential or actual damage must be very serious for the applicant;

(iii) evidence must demonstrate clearly that the respondents possess incriminating material; and

(iv) there must be a real possibility that the respondents may destroy that material before a hearing on notice can take place.

**[1.290]**

Examples of applications for search orders in ancillary relief proceedings have been:

- *Kepa v Kepa*[1];
- *Emmanuel v Emmanuel*[2]; and
- *Burgess v Burgess*[3].

1 (1982) 4 FLR 515 – husband failed to give proper disclosure of assets. Wife's evidence of husband's hidden wealth. Order made as aid to discovery.
2 [1982] 2 All ER 342, [1982] 3 FLR 319 – husband ignored undertaking and court orders and there was strong evidence that he had given a false presentation of his means. Order made in wife's application to set aside financial order.
3 [1997] 1 FCR 89, [1996] 2 FLR 34, CA – husband made inappropriate application for search order. Judge ordered indemnity costs against him. Husband's appeal dismissed.

**[1.291]**

It has been held by the House of Lords that a defendant to an order might refuse to comply with it where there was a realistic possibility that compliance would lead to the bringing of criminal charges against him[1] (in reliance upon the privilege against self-incrimination). There are certain statutory exceptions to this privilege[2].

1 See *Rank Film Distributors Ltd v Video Information Centre* [1982] AC 380, [1981] 2 All ER 76, HL. In the case of *Emmanuel v Emmanuel* [1982] 2 All ER 342, [1982] 3 FLR 319, Wood J had before him an application for a search order made without notice to the husband; the judge said (at p 327): 'In the present case there was prima-facie evidence before me that it might be alleged that the respondent husband had committed perjury. I, therefore, had to consider whether some provision should be made in the order to protect him against self-incrimination. I was referred to *Rice v Gordon* (1843) 13 Sim 580. The report of this case is very short and I set it out in full: "In this case an indictment was pending, against the defendant, for perjury committed in the Cause; and, on Mr Cole for the plaintiff moving for the production of documents which the defendant had admitted in his answer to be in his custody Mr Chandless contended that he was not bound to produce them because they tended to support the indictment; and cited *Paxton v Douglas* (1809) 16 Ves 239. The Vice-Chancellor said that, in the case cited, the offence was committed prior to the institution of the suit; but, in the present case, it was committed in the very cause in which the motion was made; and that, if he were to refuse the motion, he should be holding out an inducement to a defendant to commit perjury in an early stage of the cause, in order to prevent the court from administering justice in the suit. The motion was granted."
That case was cited without criticism by Templeman LJ in *Rank Film Ltd v Video Information Centre* [1980] 2 All ER 273 at p 290. In the present case the only possible criminal offence that is disclosed is the prima-facie evidence of perjury, and in the circumstances I did not require any special clause to be inserted in the order to encourage the respondent husband to invoke the principle of privilege against self-incrimination.'
2 Eg in relation to intellectual property (s 72 of the SCA 1981) and where an offence under the Theft Act 1968 is alleged (see s 31(1) of that Act).

**[1.292]**

As with freezing orders in family proceedings, the CPR 1998 do not strictly apply (as a result of r 2.1(1)(a) of the CPR 1998). However, in practice the procedure under Pt 25 of the CPR 1998 (and the *Practice Direction* annexed to that rule) governs the making of the application for a search order[1]. The rule provides standard forms that are to be used in connection with such applications[2].

1 See para **[1.294]** below.
2 See CPR 1998, Pt 25, PD25, para 8.6.

**[1.293]**

Search orders may be made by High Court Judges or 'any other Judge duly authorised'[1].

1 See CPR 1998, Pt 25, PD25A, para 1.1.

## [1.294]

The application for a search order is governed by CPR 1998, Pt 25 and the *Practice Direction* annexed to it. The procedural provisions set out above in relation to freezing orders apply also to search orders. In addition, however:

(i) The supervising solicitor must be experienced in the operation of search orders. A supervising solicitor may be contacted through the Law Society or, in the London area, through the London Solicitors Litigation Association[1].

(ii) The affidavit must state the name, firm and its address, and experience of the supervising solicitor, also the address of the premises and whether it is a private or business address[2].

(iii) The affidavit must disclose very fully the reason why the order is sought, including the probability that relevant material will disappear if the order is not made[3].

1 See CPR 1998, Pt 25, PD25, para 7.2.
2 See CPR 1998, Pt 25, PD25, para 7.3(2).
3 See CPR 1998, Pt 25, PD25, para 7.3(3).

## [1.295]

In relation to the order itself, the CPR 1998 provide[1]:

(i) the order must be served personally by the Supervising Solicitor, unless the court otherwise orders, and must be accompanied by the evidence in support and any documents capable of being copied;

(ii) confidential exhibits need not be served but they must be made available for inspection by the respondent in the presence of the applicant's solicitors while the order is carried out and afterwards be retained by the respondent's solicitors on their undertaking not to permit the respondent –

(a) to see them or copies of them except in their presence, and

(b) to make or take away any note or record of them;

(iii) the Supervising Solicitor may be accompanied only by the persons mentioned in the order;

(iv) the Supervising Solicitor must explain the terms and effect of the order to the respondent in every day language and advise him of his right to –

(a) legal advice[2], and

(b) apply to vary or discharge the order;

(v) where the Supervising Solicitor is a man and the respondent is likely to be an unaccompanied woman, at least one other person named in the order must be a woman and must accompany the Supervising Solicitor; and

(vi) the order may only be served between 9.30 am and 5.30 pm Monday to Friday unless the court otherwise orders.

1 See CPR 1998, Pt 25, PD25, para 7.4.
2 The respondent should have a reasonable time to obtain legal advice before permitting the search to occur although he must seek that advice diligently. If he decides to apply to discharge the order before permitting the search to take place he runs the risk of being found to be in contempt of the order: *Bhimji v Chatwani* [1991] 1 All ER 705, [1991] 1 WLR 989.

## [1.296]

Further provision is made in relation to the search in CPR 1998, Pt 25, PD25, para 8 as follows:

(1) the Supervising Solicitor must not be an employee or member of the applicant's firm of solicitors;

(2) if the court orders that the order need not be served by the Supervising Solicitor, the reason for so ordering must be set out in the order;

(3) the search order must not be carried out at the same time as a police search warrant;

(4) there is no privilege against self incrimination in Intellectual Property cases (see the SCA 1981, s 72) therefore in those cases, paragraph (4) of the respondent's entitlements and any other references to incrimination in the Search order, should be removed;

(5) applications in intellectual property cases should be made in the Chancery Division[1].

1 It has to be doubted whether this would be appropriate in a family case.

**[1.297]**

The Practice Direction annexed to Pt 25 of the CPR 1998 makes specific provision about the conduct of the search and the custody of materials[1] in the following terms:

'(1) no material may be removed unless clearly covered by the terms of the order;

(2) the premises must not be searched and no items shall be removed from them except in the presence of the respondent or a person who appears to be a responsible employee of the respondent;

(3) where copies of documents are sought, the documents should be retained for no more than two days before return to the owner;

(4) where material in dispute is removed pending trial, the applicant's solicitors should place it in the custody of the respondent's solicitors on their undertaking to retain it in safekeeping and to produce it to the court when required;

(5) in appropriate cases the applicant should insure the material retained in the respondent's solicitors' custody;

(6) the Supervising Solicitor must make a list of all material removed from the premises and supply a copy of the list to the respondent;

(7) no material may be removed from the premises until the respondent has had reasonable time to check the list;

(8) if any of the listed items exists only in computer readable form, the respondent must immediately give the applicant's solicitors effective access to the computers, with all necessary passwords, to enable them to be searched, and cause the listed items to be printed out;

(9) the applicant must take all reasonable steps to ensure that no damage is done to any computer or data;

(10) the applicant and his representatives may not themselves search the respondent's computers unless they have sufficient expertise to do so without damaging the respondent's system;

(11) the Supervising Solicitor must provide a report on the carrying out of the order to the applicant's solicitors;

(12) as soon as the report is received the applicant's solicitors must –
  (a) serve a copy of it on the respondent, and
  (b) file a copy of it with the court; and

(13) where the Supervising Solicitor is satisfied that full compliance with paragraph 7.5(7) and (8) above is impracticable, he may permit the search to proceed and items to be removed without compliance with the impracticable requirements.'

1 See CPR 1998, Pt 25, PD25, para 7.5.

## CPR 1998, Pt 25

**[1.298]**

### CPR 1998, Pt 25 and *Practice Directions*

Part 25 of the CPR 1998 is set out below. The *Practice Directions* supplementing CPR 1998, Pt 25 are:

- PD25A – Interim Injuctions (set out at para **[4.34]** below);
- PD25B – Interim Payments (set out at para **[4.35]** below); and
- PD25C – Accounts and Inquiries (set out at para **[4.36]** below).

**[1.299]**

## PART 25
## INTERIM REMEDIES AND SECURITY FOR COSTS

### *I Interim Remedies*

### 25.1 Orders for interim remedies

(1) The court may grant the following interim remedies—
- (a) an interim injunction;
- (b) an interim declaration;
- (c) an order—
  - (i) for the detention, custody or preservation of relevant property;
  - (ii) for the inspection of relevant property;
  - (iii) for the taking of a sample of relevant property;
  - (iv) for the carrying out of an experiment on or with relevant property;
  - (v) for the sale of relevant property which is of a perishable nature or which for any other good reason it is desirable to sell quickly; and
  - (vi) for the payment of income from relevant property until a claim is decided;
- (d) an order authorising a person to enter any land or building in the possession of a party to the proceedings for the purposes of carrying out an order under sub-paragraph (c);
- (e) an order under section 4 of the Torts (Interference with Goods) Act 1977 to deliver up goods;
- (f) an order (referred to as a 'freezing injunction')—
  - (i) restraining a party from removing from the jurisdiction assets located there; or
  - (ii) restraining a party from dealing with any assets whether located within the jurisdiction or not;
- (g) an order directing a party to provide information about the location of relevant property or assets or to provide information about relevant property or assets which are or may be the subject of an application for a freezing injunction;
- (h) an order (referred to as a 'search order') under section 7 of the Civil Procedure Act 1997 (order requiring a party to admit another party to premises for the purpose of preserving evidence etc);
- (i) an order under section 33 of the Supreme Court Act 1981 or section 52 of the County Courts Act 1984 (order for disclosure of documents or inspection of property before a claim has been made);
- (j) an order under section 34 of the Supreme Court Act 1981 or section 53 of the County Courts Act 1984 (order in certain proceedings for disclosure of documents or inspection of property against a non-party);
- (k) an order (referred to as an order for interim payment) under rule 25.6 for payment by a defendant on account of any damages, debt or other sum (except costs) which the court may hold the defendant liable to pay;
- (l) an order for a specified fund to be paid into court or otherwise secured, where there is a dispute over a party's right to the fund;
- (m) an order permitting a party seeking to recover personal property to pay money into court pending the outcome of the proceedings and directing that, if he does so, the property shall be given up to him; and
- (n) an order directing a party to prepare and file accounts relating to the dispute.

(Rule 34.2 provides for the court to issue a witness summons requiring a witness to produce documents to the court at the hearing or on such date as the court may direct)

(2) In paragraph (1)(c) and (g), 'relevant property' means property (including land) which is the subject of a claim or as to which any question may arise on a claim.

(3) The fact that a particular kind of interim remedy is not listed in paragraph (1) does not affect any power that the court may have to grant that remedy.
(4) The court may grant an interim remedy whether or not there has been a claim for a final remedy of that kind.

**[1.300]**

### 25.2 Time when an order for an interim remedy may be made

(1) An order for an interim remedy may be made at any time, including—
- (a) before proceedings are started; and
- (b) after judgment has been given.

(Rule 7.2 provides that proceedings are started when the court issues a claim form)
(2) However—
- (a) paragraph (1) is subject to any rule, practice direction or other enactment which provides otherwise;
- (b) the court may grant an interim remedy before a claim has been made only if—
  - (i) the matter is urgent; or
  - (ii) it is otherwise desirable to do so in the interests of justice; and
- (c) unless the court otherwise orders, a defendant may not apply for any of the orders listed in rule 25.1 (1) before he has filed either an acknowledgement of service or a defence.

(Part 10 provides for filing an acknowledgment of service and Part 15 for filing a defence)
(3) Where the court grants an interim remedy before a claim has been commenced, it may give directions requiring a claim to be commenced.
(4) In particular, the court need not direct that a claim be commenced where the application is made under section 33 of the Supreme Court Act 1981 or section 52 of the County Courts Act 1984 (order for disclosure, inspection etc. before commencement of a claim).

**[1.301]**

### 25.3 How to apply for an interim remedy

(1) The court may grant an interim remedy on an application made without notice if it appears to the court that there are good reasons for not giving notice.
(2) An application for an interim remedy must be supported by evidence, unless the court orders otherwise.
(3) If the applicant makes an application without giving notice, the evidence in support of the application must state the reasons why notice has not been given.
(Part 3 lists general powers of the court)
(Part 23 contains general rules about making an application)

**[1.302]**

### 25.4 Application for an interim remedy where there is no related claim

(1) This rule applies where a party wishes to apply for an interim remedy but—
- (a) the remedy is sought in relation to proceedings which are taking place, or will take place, outside the jurisdiction; or
- (b) the application is made under section 33 of the Supreme Court Act 1981 or section 52 of the County Courts Act 1984 (order for disclosure, inspection etc before commencement) before a claim has been commenced.

(2) An application under this rules must be made in accordance with the general rules about applications contained in Part 23.

(The following provisions are also relevant—
Rule 25.5 (inspection of property before commencement or against a non-party)
Rule 31.16 (orders for disclosure of documents before proceedings start)
Rule 31.17 (orders for disclosure of documents against a person not a party))

**[1.303]**

### 25.5 Inspection of property before commencement or against a non-party

(1) This rule applies where a person makes an application under—
- (a) section 33 (1) of the Supreme Court Act 1981 or section 52 (1) of the County Courts Act 1984 (inspection etc of property before commencement);
- (b) section 34 (3) of the Supreme Court Act 1981 or section 53 (3) of the County Courts Act 1984 (inspection etc of property against a non-party).

(2) The evidence in support of such an application must show, if practicable by reference to any statement of case prepared in relation to the proceedings or anticipated proceedings, that the property—
- (a) is or may become the subject matter of such proceedings; or
- (b) is relevant to the issues that will arise in relation to such proceedings.

(3) A copy of the application notice and a copy of the evidence in support must be served on —
- (a) the person against whom the order is sought; and
- (b) in relation to an application under section 34 (3) of the Supreme Court Act 1981 or section 53 (3) of the County Courts Act 1984, every party to the proceedings other than the applicant.

**[1.304]**

### 25.6 Interim payments—general procedure

(1) The claimant may not apply for an order for an interim payment before the end of the period for filing an acknowledgement of service applicable to the defendant against whom the application is made.
(Rule 10.3 sets out the period for filing an acknowledgment of service)
(Rule 25.1 (1)(k) defines an interim payment)

(2) The claimant may make more than one application for an order for an interim payment.

(3) A copy of an application notice for an order for an interim payment must—
- (a) be served at least 14 days before the hearing of the application; and
- (b) be supported by evidence.

(4) If the respondent to an application for an order for an interim payment wishes to rely on written evidence at the hearing, he must—
- (a) file the written evidence; and
- (b) serve copies on every other party to the application,

at least 7 days before the hearing of the application.

(5) If the applicant wishes to rely on written evidence in reply, he must—
- (a) file the written evidence; and
- (b) serve a copy on the respondent,

at least 3 days before the hearing of the application.

(6) This rule does not require written evidence—
- (a) to be filed if it has already been filed; or
- (b) to be served on a party on whom it has already been served.

(7) The court may order an interim payment in one sum or in instalments.
(Part 23 contains general rules about applications)

[1.305]

### 25.7 Interim payments—conditions to be satisfied and matters to be taken into account

(1) The court may make an order for an interim payment only if—

- (a) the defendant against whom the order is sought has admitted liability to pay damages or some other sum of money to the claimant;
- (b) the claimant has obtained judgment against that defendant for damages to be assessed or for a sum of money (other than costs) to be assessed;
- (c) except where paragraph (3) applies, it is satisfied that, if the claim went to trial, the claimant would obtain judgment for a substantial amount of money (other than costs) against the defendant from whom he is seeking an order for an interim payment; or
- (d) the following conditions are satisfied—
  - (i) the claimant is seeking an order for possession of land (whether or not any other order is also sought); and
  - (ii) the court is satisfied that, if the case went to trial, the defendant would be held liable (even if the claim for possession fails) to pay the claimant a sum of money for the defendant's occupation and use of the land while the claim for possession was pending.

(2) In addition, in a claim for personal injuries the court may make an order for an interim payment of damages only if—

- (a) the defendant is insured in respect of the claim;
- (b) the defendant's liability will be met by—
  - (i) an insurer under section 151 of the Road Traffic Act 1988; or
  - (ii) an insurer acting under the Motor Insurers Bureau Agreement, or the Motor Insurers Bureau where it is acting itself; or
- (c) the defendant is a public body.

(3) In a claim for personal injuries where there are two or more defendants, the court may make an order for the interim payment of damages against any defendant if—

- (a) it is satisfied that, if the claim went to trial, the claimant would obtain judgment for substantial damages against at least one of the defendants (even if the court has not yet determined which of them is liable); and
- (b) paragraph (2) is satisfied in relation to each of the defendants.

(4) The court must not order an interim payment of more than a reasonable proportion of the likely amount of the final judgment.

(5) The court must take into account—

- (a) contributory negligence; and
- (b) any relevant set-off or counterclaim.

[1.306]

### 25.8 Powers of court where it has made an order for interim payment

(1) Where a defendant has been ordered to make an interim payment, or has in fact made an interim payment (whether voluntarily or under an order), the court may make an order to adjust the interim payment.

(2) The court may in particular—

- (a) order all or part of the interim payment to be repaid;
- (b) vary or discharge the order for the interim payment;
- (c) order a defendant to reimburse, either wholly or partly, another defendant who has made an interim payment.

(3) The court may make an order under paragraph (2)(c) only if—

- (a) the defendant to be reimbursed made the interim payment in relation to a claim in respect of which he has made a claim against the other defendant for a contribution, indemnity or other remedy; and

(b) where the claim or part to which the interim payment relates has not been discontinued or disposed of, the circumstances are such that the court could make an order for interim payment under rule 25.7.

(4) The court may make an order under this rule without an application by any party if it makes the order when it disposes of the claim or any part of it.

(5) Where—

(a) a defendant has made an interim payment; and

(b) the amount of the payment is more than his total liability under the final judgment or order,

the court may award him interest on the overpaid amount from the date when he made the interim payment.

**[1.307]**

### 25.9 Restriction on disclosure of an interim payment

The fact that a defendant has made an interim payment, whether voluntarily or by court order, shall not be disclosed to the trial judge until all questions of liability and the amount of money to be awarded have been decided unless the defendant agrees.

**[1.308]**

### 25.10 Interim injunction to cease if claim is stayed

If—

(a) the court has granted an interim injunction [other than a freezing injunction]; and

(b) the claim is stayed other than by agreement between the parties,

the interim injunction shall be set aside unless the court orders that it should continue to have effect even though the claim is stayed.

**[1.309]**

### 25.11 Interim injunction to cease after 14 days if claim struck out

(1) If—

(a) the court has granted an interim injunction ; and

(b) the claim is struck out under rule 3.7 (sanction for non-payment of certain fees),

the interim injunction shall cease to have effect 14 days after the date that the claim is struck out unless paragraph 2 applies.

(2) If the claimant applies to reinstate the claim before the interim injunction ceases to have effect under paragraph (1), the injunction shall continue until the hearing of the application unless the court orders otherwise.

**[1.310]**

## *II Security for Costs*

### 25.12 Security for costs

(1) A defendant to any claim may apply under this Section of this Part for security for his costs of the proceedings.

(Part 3 provides for the court to order payment of sums into court in other circumstances. Rule 20.3 provides for this Section of this Part to apply to Part 20 claims).

(2) An application for security for costs must be supported by written evidence.

(3) Where the court makes an order for security for costs, it will—
- (a) determine the amount of security; and
- (b) direct—
  - (i) the manner in which; and
  - (ii) the time within which

the security must be given.

**[1.311]**

### 25.13 Conditions to be satisfied

(1) The court may make an order for security for costs under rule 25.12 if—
- (a) it is satisfied, having regard to all the circumstances of the case, that it is just to make such an order; and
- (b)
  - (i) one or more of the conditions in paragraph (2) applies, or
  - (ii) an enactment permits the court to require security for costs.

(2) The conditions are—
- (a) the claimant is an individual—
  - (i) who is ordinarily resident out of the jurisdiction; and
  - (ii) is not a person against whom a claim can be enforced under the Brussels Conventions or the Lugano Convention [or the Regulation], as defined by section 1(1) of the Civil Jurisdiction and Judgments Act 1982;
- (b) the claimant is a company or other incorporated body—
  - (i) which is ordinarily resident out of the jurisdiction; and
  - (ii) is not a body against whom a claim can be enforced under the Brussels Conventions or the Lugano Convention [or the Regulation];
- (c) the claimant is a company or other body (whether incorporated inside or outside Great Britain) and there is reason to believe that it will be unable to pay the defendant's costs if ordered to do so;
- (d) the claimant has changed his address since the claim was commenced with a view to evading the consequences of the litigation;
- (e) the claimant failed to give his address in the claim form, or gave an incorrect address in that form;
- (f) the claimant is acting as a nominal claimant, other than as a representative claimant under Part 19, and there is reason to believe that he will be unable to pay the defendant's costs if ordered to do so;
- (g) the claimant has taken steps in relation to his assets that would make it difficult to enforce an order for costs against him.

(Rule 3.4 allows the court to strike out a statement of case and Part 24 for it to give summary judgment)

**[1.312]**

### 25.14 Security for costs other than from the claimant

(1) The defendant may seek an order against someone other than the claimant, and the court may make an order for security for costs against that person if—
- (a) it is satisfied, having regard to all the circumstances of the case, that it is just to make such an order; and
- (b) one or more of the conditions in paragraph (2) applies.

(2) The conditions are that the person—
- (a) has assigned the right to the claim to the claimant with a view to avoiding the possibility of a costs order being made against him; or

(b) has contributed or agreed to contribute to the claimant's costs in return for a share of any money or property which the claimant may recover in the proceedings; and

is a person against whom a costs order may be made.

(Rule 48.2 makes provision for costs orders against non-parties).

**[1.313]**

### 25.15 Security for costs of an appeal

(1) The court may order security for costs of an appeal against—

(a) an appellant;

(b) a respondent who also appeals,

on the same grounds as it may order security for costs against a claimant under this Part.

(2) The court may also make an order under paragraph (1) where the appellant, or the respondent who also appeals, is a limited company and there is reason to believe it will be unable to pay the costs of the other parties to the appeal should its appeal be unsuccessful.

# 6. Cohabitees – Property Rights

**Contents**



## Introduction

**[1.314]**

This chapter examines the issues that may arise between cohabitees in relation to the ownership of property. To a significant extent, those issues still fall to be determined in accordance with the rules of equity. Statutes have made some inroads into equity's rules[1], but much of the statutory intervention has been procedural only[2]. The Law Commission has considered these rules and has concluded that they 'are uncertain and difficult to apply and can lead to serious injustice'[3]. In the case of *Hammond v Mitchell*[4], Waite J described the process of determining the beneficial interests between parties in this way:

> 'In general, their financial rights have to be worked out according to their strict entitlements in equity, a process which is anything but forward looking and involves, on the contrary, a painfully detailed retrospect.'

1 Eg under the MPPA 1970, s 37 where parties were married or engaged.
2 Eg the MWPA 1882.
3 See sixth programme of Law Reform (Law Com no 234), item 8.
4 [1992] 1 FLR 229 at 231.

**[1.315]**

Many of the older reported cases arose at a time when the court's statutory discretion in divorce proceedings was more constrained than under present law (ie prior to the introduction of the MPPA 1970, s 5 which was the forerunner of the MCA 1973, s 25). Although many of those older cases may refer to 'the matrimonial home' and to 'spouses', the rules of equity are not dependent upon the nature of the relationship between the parties. However in some circumstances the nature of the relationship may assist the court in determining the inferences that can be drawn from the conduct of the parties. In the case of *Bernard v Josephs*[1], Griffiths LJ said:

> 'The legal principles to be applied are the same whether the dispute is between married or unmarried couples, but the nature of the relationship between the parties is a very important factor when considering what inferences should be drawn from the way they conducted their affairs. There are many reasons why a man and a woman may have decided to live together without marrying, and one of them is that each values his independence and does not wish to make the commitment of marriage; in such a case it will be misleading to make the assumption and to draw inferences from their behaviour as in the case of a married couple. The judge must look most carefully at the nature of the relationship, and only if satisfied that it was intended to involve the same degree of commitment as marriage will it be legitimate to regard them as different from a married couple.'

1 [1982] Ch 391 at 402, [1982] 3 All ER 162 at 169, CA. See also *Mortgage Corpn v Lewis Silkin, Mortgage Corpn v Shaire* [2000] 2 FCR 222 at 228.

### [1.316]

The most significant statutory intervention in this field during recent years has emanated from the TLATA 1996. That Act has changed the nature of the trusts that will arise where there is shared ownership of property and has introduced changes in the substantive and procedural law relating to applications for orders of the court relating to property that is in shared ownership[1].

1 Ie through the introduction of the concept of the trust of land and, in relation to orders of the court, under the TLATA 1996, ss 13, 14 and 15.

### [1.317]

In the case of *Mortgage Corpn v Lewis Silkin, Mortgage Corpn v Shaire*[1] Neuberger J considered the effect of s 15 of the TLATA 1996 in the following terms:

> 'To my mind, for a number of reasons … s 15 has changed the law.
>
> Firstly, there is the rather trite point that if there was no intention to change the law, it is hard to see why Parliament has set out in s 15(2) and, indeed, on one view, s 15(3), the factors which have to be taken into account specifically, albeit not exclusively, when the court is asked to exercise its jurisdiction to order a sale.
>
> Secondly, it is hard to reconcile the contention that Parliament intended to confirm the law as laid down in Byrne with the fact that, while the interest of a chargee is one of the four specified factors to be taken into account in s 15(1)(*d*), there is no suggestion that it is to be given any more importance than the interests of the children residing in the house (see s 15(1)(*c*)). As is clear from the passage I have quoted from the judgment of Nourse LJ in *Citro* as applied to a case such as this in light of *Byrne*, that would appear to represent a change in the law.
>
> Thirdly, the very name "trust for sale" and the law as it has been developed by the courts suggests that under the old law, in the absence of a strong reason to the contrary, the court should order sale. Nothing in the language of the new code as found in the 1996 Act supports that approach.
>
> Fourthly, it is clear from the reasons in *Byrne* and indeed the later two first instance cases to which I have referred, that the law, as developed under s 30 of the Law of Property Act 1925, was that the court should adopt precisely the same approach in a case where one of the co-owners was bankrupt (*Citro*) and a case where one of the co-owners had charged his interest (*Byrne*). It is quite clear that Parliament now considers that a different approach is appropriate in the two cases – compare ss 15(2) and 15(3) of the 1996 Act with s 15(4) and the new s 335A of the Insolvency Act 1986.

Fifthly, an indication from the Court of Appeal that the 1996 Act was intended to change the law is to be found in (an albeit plainly obiter) sentence in the judgment of Peter Gibson LJ in *Banker's Trust Co v Namdar* [1997] CA Transcript 349. Having come to the conclusion that the wife's appeal against an order for sale had to be refused in light of the reasoning in *Citro* and *Byrne*, Peter Gibson LJ said:

"It is unfortunate for Mrs Namdar, that the very recent Trusts of Land and Appointment of Trustees Act 1996 was not in force at the relevant time [ie at the time of the hearing at first instance] …"

Of course it would be dangerous to build too much on that observation, but it is an indication from the Court of Appeal and indeed from a former chairman of the Law Commission, as to the perceived effect of the 1996 Act.

Sixthly, the leading textbooks support the view that I have reached. In *Megarry & Wade* one finds this (para 9-064, p 510):

"Although the authorities on the law prior to 1997 will therefore continue to provide guidance, the outcome will not in all cases be the same as it would have been under the previous law. This is because the legislature was much more specific as to the matters which a court is required to take into account."

*Emmet on Title* (19th edn, January 1999 release), contains this (para 22-035):

"Cases decided on pre-1997 law may be disregarded as of little, if any, assistance because their starting point was necessarily a trust for sale implied or expressed as a conveyancing device enabling the convenient co-ownership of the property …"

Seventhly, the Law Commission report which gave rise to the 1996 Act, Transfer of Land, Trusts of Land (Law Com No 181), 8 June 1989, tends to support this view as well. It is fair to say that the Law Commission did not propose a new section in a new Act such as s 15 of the 1996 Act, but a new s 30 of the Law of Property Act 1925. It is also fair to say that the terms of the proposed new s 30 were slightly different from those of s 15. However, in my judgment, the way in which the terms of the 1996 Act, and in particular s 15, have been drafted suggests that the Law Commission's proposals were very much in the mind of, and were substantially adopted by, the legislature. In para 12.9 of the report the Law Commission describe the aim as being to "consolidate and rationalise"(emphasis added) the current approach. When commenting on the proposed equivalents of what are now ss 15(2) and 15(3), the Law Commission said (note 143):

"Clearly, the terms of these guidelines may influence the exercise of the discretion in some way. For example, it may be that the courts' approach to creditors' interests will be altered by the framing of the guideline as to the welfare of children. If the welfare of children is seen as a factor to be considered independently of the beneficiaries' holdings, the court may be less ready to order the sale of the home than they are at present."

Finally, the Law Commission said (para 13.6):

"Within the new system, beneficiaries will be in a comparatively better position than beneficiaries of current trusts of land. For example, given that the terms governing applications under section 30 will be less restrictive than they are at present, beneficiaries will have greater scope to challenge the decisions of the trustees and generally influence the management of the trust land."

Eighthly, to put it at its lowest, it does not seem to me unlikely that the legislature intended to relax the fetters on the way in which the court exercised its discretion in cases such as *Citro* and *Byrne*, and so as to tip the balance somewhat more in favour of families and against banks and other chargees. Although the law under s 30 was clear following *Citro* and *Byrne*, there were indications of judicial dissatisfaction with the state of the law at that time. Although Bingham LJ agreed with Nourse LJ in *Citro*, he expressed unhappiness with the result ([1991] Ch 142 at 161, [1990] 3 All ER 952 at 965), and Sir George Waller's dissatisfaction went so far as led him to dissent (see his judgment ([1991] Ch 142 at 161–163,[1990] 3 All ER 952 at 965–966)). Furthermore, there is a decision of the Court of Appeal in *Abbey National plc v Moss* [1994] 2 FCR 587, which suggests a desire for a new approach.

All these factors, to my mind, when taken together point very strongly to the conclusion that s 15 has changed the law. As a result of s 15, the court has greater flexibility than heretofore, as to how it exercises its jurisdiction on an application for an order for sale on facts such as those in *Citro* and *Byrne*. There are certain factors which must be taken into account (see s 15(1) and, subject to the next point, s 15(3)). There may be other factors in a particular case which the court can, indeed should, take into account. Once the relevant factors to be taken into account have been identified, it is a matter for the court as to what weight to give to each factor in a particular case.

The only indication the other way is a decision of Judge Wroath in the Newport, Isle of Wight County Court in *TSB plc v Marshall* [1998] 2 FLR 769 at 771–772, where he said this, having referred to *Byrne*, *Moss*, and *Hendricks*:

"Those three cases were all decided where the applications to the court were under s 30 of the Law of Property Act. However, it has been submitted that the principles established are applicable to an application under s 14, and I accept that submission."

It does not appear clear to what extent the matter was argued before him, or, indeed, whether it was argued before him. With all due respect to Judge Wroath, I disagree with his conclusion.

A difficult question, having arrived at this conclusion, is the extent to which the old authorities are of assistance, and it is no surprise to find differing views expressed in the two textbooks from which I have quoted. On the one hand, to throw over all the wealth of learning and thought given by so many eminent judges to the problem which is raised on an application for sale of a house where competing interests exist seems somewhat arrogant and possibly rash. On the other hand, where one has concluded that the law has changed in a significant respect so that the court's discretion is significantly less fettered than it was, there are obvious dangers in relying on authorities which proceeded on the basis that the court's discretion was more fettered than it now is. I think it would be wrong to throw over all the earlier cases without paying them any regard. However, they have to be treated with caution, in light of the change in the law, and in many cases they are unlikely to be of great, let alone decisive, assistance.'

1 [2000] 2 FCR 222 at 228.

### [1.318]

This part of the chapter will therefore consider the rules of law and equity by which it may be established that property is jointly owned – ie the general law of trusts and estoppel[1].

1 See generally *Rayden and Jackson on Divorce and Family Matters* (17th edn, 1997), vol 1, chaps 29 and 30.

## The documents of title

### [1.319]

In the case of *Pettitt v Pettitt*[1] Lord Upjohn said:

'In the first place, the beneficial ownership of the property in question must depend upon the agreement of the parties determined at the time of its acquisition. If the property in question is land, there must be some lease or conveyance which shows how it was acquired. If that document declares not merely in whom the legal title is to vest but in whom the beneficial title is to vest, that necessarily concludes the question of title as between spouses for all time, and in the absence of fraud or mistake at the time of the transaction the parties cannot go behind it at any time thereafter even on death or the break up of the marriage.'

1 [1970] AC 777 at 813.

### [1.320]

The documents of title are clearly of fundamental importance as has been stressed in many subsequent cases[1]. Claims to rectification or rescission of the documents of title are rare[2]. In the case of *Roy v Roy*[3], it was held that a party who sought the rectification of a transfer (on the basis that, by mistake, it did not reflect the parties' intentions) had to prove that the intention of the parties was as he asserted.

1 Eg *Bernard v Josephs* [1982] Ch 391, [1982] All ER 162.
2 For an example of a case where a transfer was rectified on the grounds of mistake, see *Thames Guaranty Ltd v Campbell* [1985] QB 585.
3 [1996] 1 FLR 541.

**[1.321]**

The documents of title have to be read in the light of the provisions of the LPA 1925, s 53, which are as follows:

> '(1) Subject to the provisions hereinafter contained with respect to the creation of interests in land by parole—
> (a) no interest in land can be created or disposed of except by writing signed by the person creating or conveying the same, or by his agent thereunto lawfully authorised in writing, or by will, or by operation of law;
> (b) a declaration of trust respecting any land or any interest therein must be manifested and proved by some writing signed by some person who is able to declare such trust or by his will;
> (c) a disposition of an equitable interest or trust subsisting at the time of the disposition, must be in writing signed by the person disposing of the same, or by his agent thereunto lawfully authorised in writing or by will.
> (2) This section does not affect the creation or operation of resulting, implied or constructive trusts.'

**[1.322]**

In the case of *Roy v Roy*[1] it was held that s 53(1) of the LPA 1925 is irrelevant where a trust for sale arose only as result of a joint tenancy (since s 53(1) is concerned only with a declaration of trust). Fox LJ said[2]:

> 'I do not think that s 53(1) is material here. What we are concerned with is a transfer on sale by an absolute owner. She conveyed the land to the plaintiff and the defendant (as purchasers) to hold as joint tenants in law and equity. It is true that s 36(1) of the Law of Property Act 1925 superimposes upon that (principally for the purposes of making title free from equities) the mechanism of a trust for sale. But that is simply the consequences of the joint tenancy. The crucial fact is that the property had actually been conveyed by the owner to the plaintiff and the defendant as joint tenants. This is not a case of a plaintiff claiming that the person in whom the land is vested holds it under a declaration of trust for the benefit of such plaintiff. The present plaintiff simply asserts the transfer to him and the defendant jointly.'

1 [1996] 1 FLR 541.
2 [1996] 1 FLR 541 at 545.

**[1.323]**

Section 53 may need to be considered in conjunction with the Law of Property (Miscellaneous Provisions) Act 1989, s 2 which provides as follows:

> '(1) A contract for the sale or other disposition of an interest in land can only be made in writing and only by incorporating all the terms which the parties have expressly agreed in one document or, where contracts are exchanged, in each.
> (2) The terms may be incorporated in a document either by being set out in it or by reference to some other document.
> (3) The document incorporating the terms or, where contracts are exchanged, one of the documents incorporating them (but not necessarily the same one) must be signed by or on behalf of each party to the contract.
> (4) Where a contract for the sale or other disposition of an interest in land satisfies the conditions of this section by reason only of the rectification of one or more documents in pursuance of an order of a court, the contract shall come into being, or be deemed to have come into being, at such time as may be specified in the order.

(5) This section does not apply in relation to—
(a) a contract to grant such a lease as is mentioned in section 54(2) of the Law Property Act 1925 (short leases);
(b) a contract made in the course of a public auction; or
(c) a contract regulated under the Financial Services Act 1986;
and nothing in this section affects the creation or operation of resulting, implied or constructive trusts.

(6) In this section—
'disposition' has the same meaning as in the Law of Property Act 1925;
'interest in land' means any estate, interest or charge in or over land.

(7) Nothing in this section shall apply in relation to contracts made before this section comes into force.'

## [1.324]

In the case of *Yaxley v Gotts and Gotts*[1] the proceedings at first instance omitted any reference to s 2 of the 1989 Act. In the Court of Appeal consideration was given to the section. It was contended by the appellants that, as a result of that section, an oral agreement that the plaintiff would own the ground floor of premises (and upon which the plaintiff had relied) was void. The Court of Appeal held that the oral agreement was sufficient to found a constructive trust given the reliance that was placed upon it by the plaintiff (Beldam LJ holding that the plaintiff's claim could equally well have been based on equitable estoppel).

1 [1999] 2 FLR 541, CA.

## [1.325]

In the light of the importance that is attached to the documents of title, a solicitor acting on a joint purchase should investigate with the proposed purchasers the intended beneficial interests in the property and ensure that any intended beneficial interests are declared in the documents of title. It has been said that solicitors acting for joint purchasers should discover the intentions of the clients as to the beneficial ownership of property and should ensure that the documents of title reflect those intentions. A failure to do so may give rise to a claim in negligence or breach of contract for any loss that is suffered as a result of a solicitor's failure to do so[1].

1 See *Cowcher v Cowcher* [1972] 1 All ER 943; and *Bernard v Josephs* [1982] Ch 391, [1982] All ER 162.

## [1.326]

In any claim to negligence or breach of contract, it would be necessary to prove that loss had been suffered as a result of the failure of the solicitor to record the beneficial ownership within the documents of title (or as a result of the failure to advise that the beneficial interests should be so recorded). The loss might be represented by one or more of the following:

(i) the value of the lost beneficial interest[1];
(ii) the amount of the beneficial interest awarded by the court (in a negligence claim by the respondent to the equitable claim);
(iii) the unrecovered costs of pursuing or defending the equitable claims.

When considering such a claim for negligence or breach of contract, the practitioner needs to keep a firm eye on the issues of limitation.

1 See *Taylor v Harman* [1982] LS Gaz 29, June 26.

## [1.327]

The main points that the solicitor acting for purchasers will have to consider with them are as follows:

- **Do they understand the difference between joint tenancy and tenancy in common?**
  When explaining the joint tenancy, it is not sufficient to explain the position that would arise in the event of the death of one of the joint tenants (ie it is not enough to explain the rights of survivorship). It is also necessary to explain that a joint tenancy may be severed and that, in the event of severance, the purchasers will hold as beneficial tenants in common in equal shares[1].
- **Do they understand the importance of the documents of title?**
  In particular, do they understand that, whilst they remain unmarried, the documents of title will determine their respective interests in the property, irrespective of the duration of the relationship, or the number of children that they have (subject to the provisions of the ChA 1989, Sch 1, whereby the court may make limited property adjustment orders for the benefit of children).
- **Do they need to have separate advice as to their rights?**
  Although many people embarking on a relationship may be reluctant to pursue matters with such a degree of formality that they seek separate representation, the practitioner may need to canvass this with them, stressing the sense in ensuring that things are right from the start.
- **Do they wish to write a will, in order to ensure that any property held on a tenancy in common passes to the intended testamentary beneficiary?**

1 See *Goodman v Gallant* [1986] Fam 106, [1986] 1 All ER 311, CA.

## [1.328]

In unregistered land the document of title will be the conveyance (in rare cases there may also be a separate document which expressly declares the trusts affecting the property). Where there is an express declaration of trust in the conveyance or in a separate document, the beneficial interest will usually be plain (eg the conveyance may say that the parties purchase the property 'to hold unto the purchasers as beneficial tenants in common in equal shares'). The fact that the parties hold the legal title as joint tenants plainly does not mean that the beneficial interest are held as joint tenants also (the legal title will always be held as joint tenants where there is shared ownership of the legal title[1]). In the case of *Roy v Roy*[2], it was held that the fact that the purchasers did not sign the transfer did not of itself prevent the transfer being an effective disposition which accurately gave effect to the intentions of the purchasers.

1 See the LPA 1925, s 36.
2 [1996] 1 FLR 541 at 547.

## [1.329]

Where the title to land is registered, the main document of title will often be the transfer. In relation to registered land, the standard form of transfer will often be used to vest title in the purchaser. Where the standard form of transfer contains a declaration that 'the survivor of them can give a valid receipt for capital money arising on the disposition of the land' that declaration alone is not sufficient to constitute a declaration of the parties' beneficial interests in the property. This has been decided as a result of the following cases:

- ***Huntingford v Hobbs***[1]
  Where it was said that 'in deciding whether or not the declaration in the transfer constituted a declaration of trust, the meaning of the words used was alone material, and since the words used, though entirely consistent with the existence of a beneficial joint tenancy, are no less consistent with the parties holding the property as trustees for a third party, it follows that it is impossible to read the declaration as constituting a declaration of beneficial interest'. The court therefore went on to consider the parties' respective beneficial interests on other grounds, having decided that the transfer did not record a declaration of trust.

- ***Harwood v Harwood*[2]**
  Which came to the same conclusions on this issue as those reached by the subsequent case of *Huntingford v Hobbs*.

1 [1993] 1 FCR 45, [1993] 1 FLR 736, CA.
2 [1992] 1 FCR 1, [1991] 2 FLR 274, CA.

**[1.330]**

Different wording in a transfer fell to be considered in the case of *Re Gorman*[1]. In *Re Gorman*, the transfer contained a declaration stating that the transferees were 'entitled to the land for their own benefit and that the survivor of them could give a valid receipt for capital moneys arising on the disposition of the land'. That wording was sufficient to amount to a declaration that the parties held as beneficial joint tenants. *Re Gorman* was distinguished in the later cases of *Harwood v Harwood* and *Huntingford v Hobbs* on the grounds that in *Re Gorman* there was a specific declaration that the parties were 'entitled to the land for their own use'(and therefore the possibility that the trustees might hold the land for third parties was ruled out).

1 [1990] 1 All ER 717, [1990] 2 FLR 284.

**[1.331]**

From the above it will be plain that inspection of the office copy entries on the register will not be sufficient. It is usually necessary to inspect the whole 'conveyancing' file where there is a dispute about the beneficial ownership of a property. The file needs to be requested at an early stage, so that any subsequent enquiries can be pursued.

**[1.332]**

Where the documents of title do not contain a declaration of trust, they may contain evidence of the parties intentions as to the beneficial interests in the property[1].

1 See *Re Gorman* [1990] 1 All ER 717, [1990] 2 FLR 284; and *Roy v Roy* [1996] 1 FLR 541, CA.

**[1.333]**
**Severance of the joint tenancy**

A beneficial joint tenancy may be severed in accordance with the LPA 1925, s 36(2) (as amended by the TLATA 1996)[1]. Plainly, if a severance is intended, it should be effected by express notice wherever possible. It has been held that the mere issue of a divorce petition which includes a prayer for a property adjustment order is not sufficient to effect a severance of a beneficial joint tenancy[2], whereas the issue of a summons under the MWPA 1882, s 17 has been held to be sufficient to create a severance[3]. Where one joint tenant becomes bankrupt and his interest is vested in the trustee in bankruptcy the joint tenancy will be severed by operation of law[4]. In the case of *Kinch v Bullard*[5] it was held that good service may be effected of a notice of severance if it can be proved that it was left at the last known address of the intended recipient (even if the intended recipient did not receive it). In *Grindal v Hooper*[6] it was held that a notice of severance was effective between co-owners in circumstances where:

(a) it was a requirement of the conveyance that the notice of severance should be endorsed on the conveyance (in order that subsequent purchasers might acquire good title), but where
(b) the notice of severance was not endorsed on the conveyance at the time of service.

1 The relevant part of the LPA, s 36(2) reads as follows: 'Where a legal estate (not being settled land) is vested in joint tenants beneficially, and any tenant desires to sever the joint tenancy in equity, he shall give to the other joint tenants a notice in writing of such desire or do such other acts or things as would, in the case of personal estate, have been effectual to sever the tenancy in equity, and thereupon the land shall be held in trust on terms which would have been requisite for giving effect to the beneficial interests if there had been an actual severance ... Nothing in this Act affects the right of a survivor of joint tenants, who is solely and beneficially interested, to deal with his legal estate as if it were not held in trust.'
2 See *Harris v Goddard* [1983] 3 All ER 242, [1983] 1 WLR 1203, CA.
3 See *Re Draper's Conveyance* [1969] 1 Ch 486, [1967] 3 All ER 853.
4 See *Re Gorman* [1990] 1 All ER 717, [1990] 1 WLR 616.
5 [1998] 4 All ER 650, [1999] 1 WLR 423.
6 [1999] EGCS 150.

**[1.334]**
Where there is a declared beneficial joint tenancy within the documents of title, the parties will hold the property on trust for themselves as beneficial tenants in common in equal shares following any severance of the beneficial joint tenancy (in the absence of any claim for rectification or rescission)[1].

1 See *Goodman v Gallant* [1986] Fam 106, [1986] 1 All ER 311, in which it was said: 'In the absence of any claim for rectification or rescission, the provision in a conveyance of an express declaration of trust conclusively defines the parties' respective beneficial interests; accordingly, the provision that the plaintiff and the defendant hold the property in trust for themselves as joint tenants entitles them on severance to the proceeds of sale in equal shares.'

**[1.335]**
When acting for a person who has a beneficial joint tenancy, it should not always be assumed that the beneficial joint tenancy should be severed on a breakdown of the relationship. The severance of the joint tenancy would bring the right of survivorship to an end. The question of whether to serve a notice of severance is something that should be specifically considered with the client.

## Where the documents of title are silent about beneficial ownership – A Checklist

**[1.336]**
The following checklist may assist when first approaching a case where there is a claim to a beneficial interest in a property which is not supported by express declarations within the documents of title.

- Bring all outstanding claims before the court by way of a consolidated action at the same time.
- Determine the nature of the claim. Is it a claim where there is a resulting trust, a constructive trust or a claim to some other form of equitable relief?
- Discover who paid what towards the purchase.
- Consider what express agreements, arrangements or understandings were made at the time of purchase.
- Decide whether there is basis for inferring a common intention that the claimant should have a beneficial interest.
- Consider who carried out what improvements to the property and the basis upon which the improvements were carried out.
- Consider any issues relating to estoppel and the 'equity of exoneration'.
- Ascertain the size of the share claimed in the property
- Consider the date for the valuation of that share.
- Consider the question of sale.
- Consider any issues relating to chattels or other items of property.

### [1.337]

In the case of *Mortgage Corpn v Shaire*[1], Neuberger J gave the following summary of the principles that the court applies when determining the beneficial interest of people who live together:

'(1) Where parties have expressly agreed the shares in which they hold, that is normally conclusive: see *Lloyds Bank plc v Rosset* [1991] 1 AC 107, 163F, [1990] 2 FLR 155, 163F respectively, and *Goodman v Gallant* [1986] Fam 106, [1986] 1 FLR 513.

(2) Such an agreement can be in writing or oral: see *Rosset* at 132F and 163F respectively.

(3) Where the parties have reached such an agreement, it is open to the court to depart from that agreement only if there is very good reason for doing so, for instance, a subsequent renegotiation or subsequent actions which are so inconsistent with what was agreed as to lead to the conclusion that there must have been a variation or cancellation of the agreement.

(4) Where there is no express agreement the court must rely on the contemporary and subsequent conduct of the parties: see *Rosset* at 132H and 163F respectively, and *Midland Bank plc v Cooke* [1995] 2 FLR 915.

(5) In this connection one is not confined to the conduct of the parties at the time of the acquisition or the time of the alleged creation of the alleged interest. The court can look at subsequent actions: see *Stokes v Anderson* [1991] 1 FLR 391, 399G.

(6) The extent of the respective financial contributions can be, and normally is, a relevant factor although it is by no means decisive: see for instance in *Cooke* where the wife's contribution was 7% and yet she was held to have a 50% interest[2].

(7) Further, the extent of the financial contribution is perhaps not as important an aspect as it was once thought to be. It may well carry more weight in a case where the parties are unmarried than when they were married: see *Cooke* at 928F and the closing part of *Stokes* at 401.

(8) Nonetheless, subject to other factors, relevant payments of money should, or at least can, be "treated as illuminating the common intention as to the extent of the beneficial interest" per Nourse LJ in *Stokes* at 400B.

(9) As the same case demonstrates at 400C, where there is no evidence of a specific agreement "the court must supply the common intention by reference to that which all the material circumstances show to be fair".

(10) Only at the last resort should the court resort to the maxim that equality is equity: see *Cooke* at 926G.

(11) It may well be of significance whether the property is in joint names or in the name of one party, as in *Rosset* and *Cooke*, and as appears to have been in *Stokes*: see at 394D and E. In this connection see the discussion in *Rosset* at 128D and 159F respectively, and 133C–H and 164C–H respectively, which is not directly in point but tends to support that view.'

1 [2000] 1 FLR 973.

2 This has to be contrasted with the opinion of Lord Bridge in the case of *Lloyds Bank v Rosset* [1991] 1 AC 107 at 133, in which he thought that it was "extremely doubtful" that, where there was no express common intention to share the beneficial interest and no direct contribution to the purchase by the claimant (through the payment of the deposit or the mortgage), the court could infer that there was a common intention to create a constructive trust: see further, [2000] 2 FCR at 229.

## Bringing outstanding claims together

### [1.338]

In the case of *Hammond v Mitchell*[1] Waite J said:

'Whatever form the proceedings take in cases of this kind and whatever the High Court Division or the County Court in which the process is initiated, it must be a matter of prime concern to the parties' advisers and to the District Judge or Magistrate before whom they come in the first instance to see that all possible issues, including those of maintenance, are raised at the earliest stage so that an informed judgement can be made as to the form and the procedure which will provide the quickest and most effective means of resolving them'.

1 [1991] 1 WLR 1127, [1992] 2 FLR 229 at 1138.

### [1.339]

It is most likely that the practitioner will have to give consideration to some or all of the following:

- seeking declaratory relief in respect of property ownership[1];
- seeking orders for sale in respect of jointly owned property[2];
- seeking orders in respect of chattels[3];
- seeking orders for financial provision in respect of children under the ChA 1989, Sch 1;
- seeking any other necessary financial orders (for instance, relating to a jointly owned endowment policy).

1 Under the MWPA 1882, s 17 (set out at para **[2.11]** below) or under the court's general equitable jurisdiction or under the TLATA 1996, s 14 (set out at para **[2.465]** below).
2 Under the TLATA 1996, s 14 (or the MWPA 1882, s 17, as extended by the Matrimonial Causes (Property and Maintenance) Act 1958, s 7(7)).
3 Either under the court's general equitable jurisdiction or under the LPA 1925, s 188 (that section provides that, where any chattels belong to persons in undivided shares, persons interested in a moiety or upwards may apply to the court for an order for the division of the chattels or any of them, according to a valuation or otherwise).

## The difference between resulting and constructive trusts

### [1.340]

Where the documents of title are silent about the beneficial ownership of the property, it will be necessary to consider whether there is a basis for a claim that the claimant has a beneficial interest in the property under a resulting or constructive trust. This involves distinguishing between the two types of trust.

### [1.341]

The resulting trust arises from a contribution to the purchase of a property on the principle that the trust reverts to the person who pays the purchase price[1]. A constructive trust is one that is based on the common intention of the parties. In the case of *Drake v Whipp*, the following was said[2]:

> 'All that is required for the creation of a constructive trust is that there should be a common intention that the party who is not the legal owner should have a beneficial interest and that that party should act to his or her detriment in reliance thereon.'

Thus, the constructive trust depends on two things for its existence:

(i) the existence of a common intention (either express or inferred) that the claimant should have a beneficial interest;
(ii) detrimental act or acts by the claimant in reliance on that intention.

1 See eg *Dyer v Dyer* (1788) 2 Cox Eq Case 92.
2 [1996] 1 FLR 826 at 830 per Gibson LJ.

### [1.342]

Although the distinction between the two forms of trust can be clearly seen when comparing the case of an express common intention (ie constructive trust) with the resulting trust (eg where the claim is based on paying one half of the purchase price), the distinction becomes much less clear when comparing the case of an inferred common intention (where the inference of a constructive trust may arise from direct contributions to the purchase of the property) and the resulting trust.

## The resulting trust

### [1.343]

The case of *Drake v Whipp* is an example of where the court held that it was material to distinguish between the constructive and resulting trust. In that case the following was said:

> 'Given the view which I and, I understand, my Lords have formed that the case is one of a constructive trust and that [the] concession that there was no common intention was wrongly made, it would in my judgement be artificial in the extreme to proceed to decide this appeal on the false footing that the parties' shares are to be determined in accordance with the law on resulting trusts'[1].

Thus the primary focus in that case should have been on the common intention of the parties and the issue of constructive trusts.

1 [1996] 1 FLR 826 at 830C.

### [1.344]

It is well established that, in the absence of any express declaration or of a common intention as to beneficial interests, the parties' contributions to the purchase price will determine their share in the equity unless the contribution was by way of gift or loan[1]. Where part of the purchase price for the property is made up by a council house discount, that council house discount is likely to be treated as a contribution to the purchase price by the person to whom the discount was afforded[2]. Where part of the purchase price was paid as a result of a gift from a third party, it is necessary to determine to whom the gift was made in order to ascertain the identity of the person who contributed the money from the gift to the purchase of the property[3]. In the case of *Lowson v Coombes*[4] a property had been placed in the name of the defendant in order to defeat any claim by the plaintiff's wife within the divorce proceedings. As such, the placing of the property in the defendant's name was illegal, in the sense that it was avoidable under s 37 of the MCA 1973. The judge at first instance held that the plaintiff could not rely on his own illegality in order to justify his claim for a declaration that he had a beneficial interest in the property[5]. The Court of Appeal held that, rather than relying on any illegality, the plaintiff could rely on a claim based upon a resulting trust arising from his contributions to the purchase of the property.

1 See *Bernard v Joseph* [1982] Ch 391, [1982] 4 FLR 178; *Crisp v Mullings* [1976] 239 EG 119; and *Walker v Hall* [1984] FLR 126.
2 See *Springette v Defoe* [1992] 2 FCR 561, [1992] 2 FLR 388, CA; and *Evans v Hayward* [1995] 2 FCR 313, [1995] 2 FLR 511, CA.
3 See, for instance, *McHardy and Sons v Warren* [1994] 2 FLR 338 in which the Court of Appeal was prepared to assume that a wedding present made by one spouse's parents was in fact a gift to both contribution by the spouses to the purchase price. This case was followed in the Court of Appeal decision in *Halifax Building Society v Brown* [1995] 3 FCR 110, [1996] 1 FLR 103. There is, however, some authority for the suggestion that gifts from the relatives of one spouse are to be presumed to be gifts only to that spouse and not to both (see *Samson v Samson* [1960] 1 All ER 653, [1960] 1 WLR 190, CA).
4 [1999] Ch 373, [1999] 1 FLR 799, CA.
5 Relying on *Tinker v Tinker* [1970] P 136, [1970] 1 All ER 540, CA.

### [1.345]

In considering whether a contribution to the purchase of a property was by way of gift, equity developed 'the presumption of advancement'. By that presumption it was assumed that the payment by certain classes of people towards the purchase of property by another was by way of gift rather than by way of investment. It is doubtful whether that presumption will bear much weight in modern litigation. The presumption was said to arise where:

(i) a husband buys a property with his own money and puts the property into the name of his wife. Equity will presume that his intention is to fulfil his duty to maintain her and to make a gift of the property to her[1]. However, if the husband buys a property with his wife's money, the presumption will not apply and he will be presumed to hold the property on trust for her[2];
(ii) a man buys a property in the name of his fiancée[3].

1 See *Re Eykin's Trusts* (1877) 6 Ch D 115.
2 See *Mercier v Mercier* [1903] 2 Ch 98.
3 See *Moate v Moate* [1948] 2 All ER 486.

## [1.346]

The presumption of advancement would not apply if the parties were not married, because the man would not be under any duty to maintain the woman[1]. Further, the presumption could be rebutted by evidence of a contrary intention. In the case of *Pettitt v Pettitt*[2], the House of Lords expressed the opinion that the presumptions are much less strong 'today' (ie in 1969) than previously because evidence of the parties intentions will usually be available; their Lordships doubted whether the presumption has any application given that the principles behind the presumption were stated at a time when social and economic conditions were vastly different[3]. In *Gissing v Gissing*[4], Lord Diplock added to these doubts about the relevance of the presumption by saying:

> 'If the land is conveyed into the name of a spouse who has not provided the whole of the purchase price, the sum contributed by the other spouse may be explicable as having been intended by both of them either as a gift or as a loan of money to the spouse to whom the land is conveyed or as consideration for a share in the beneficial interest in the land. In a dispute between living spouses the evidence will probably point to one of these explanations as being more probable than the others, but if the rest of the evidence is neutral the prima facie inference is that their common intention was that the contributing spouse should acquire a share in the beneficial interest in the land in the same proportion as the sum contributed bears to the total purchase price. This prima facie inference is more easily rebutted in favour of a gift where the land is conveyed into the name of the wife; but as I understand the speeches in *Pettitt v Pettitt* four of the members of your Lordships' House who were parties to that decision took the view that even if the 'presumption of advancement' as between husband and wife still survived today, it could seldom have any decisive part to play in disputes between living spouses in which some evidence would be available in addition to the mere fact that the husband had provided part of the purchase price of property conveyed into the name of the wife.'

1 See *Soar v Foster* (1858) 4 K & J 152 (void marriage—no presumption); and *Lowson v Coombes* [1999] Ch 373, [1999] 1 FLR 799, CA.
2 [1970] AC 777 at 793, 811 and 824, [1969] 2 All ER 385, HL at 389, 404, 406–407 and 414.
3 [1970] AC 777 at 823–824, [1969] 2 All ER 385, HL at 414.
4 [1970] 2 All ER 780 at 790.

## [1.347]
### Mortgages – the two approaches

In the case of *Marsh v Von Sternberg*[1] Bush J identified that the Court of Appeal had adopted two different approaches to the issue of the creation of a beneficial interest arising out of mortgage arrangements. Those two approaches are:

(i) a person's mortgage liability is treated as a contribution to the purchase of a property thereby conferring a beneficial interest by reason of a resulting trust;

(ii) a person's contributions to the mortgage payments form the basis of the inference that the beneficial ownership is jointly held.

1 [1986] 1 FLR 526.

## [1.348]
### *(1) The liability approach*

An example of this approach would be as follows:

(i) Hopeless Hall was bought in 1985 for £100,000 in the joint names of Mr Rich and Miss Poor (there was no express declaration of trust and no express agreement as to the beneficial interest).

(ii) Mr Rich paid £50,000 in cash towards the purchase. The balance of £50,000 was paid by a mortgage in the joint names of Mr Rich and Miss Poor.

(iii) At the time of purchase, therefore, Mr Rich contributed 75% of the gross purchase price and Miss Poor contributed 25%.

(iv) Hopeless Hall sells in 1994 for £175,000 (after solicitors' and estate agents' fees). The mortgage is still £50,000.

(v) The share of Miss Poor is 25% × £175,000 = £43,750. However, she is responsible for one half of the mortgage debt, ie one half of £50,000 = £25,000. She, therefore, receives £43,750 – £25,000 = £18,750.

(vi) Mr Rich receives 75% × £175,000 = £131,250. However, he is also responsible for one half of the mortgage. He therefore receives £131,250 – £25,000 = £106,250.

This approach was adopted in cases such as *Marsh v Von Sternberg*[1] and *Huntingford v Hobb*[2]. It is entirely consistent with the approach that a person's beneficial interest in a property will be determined by the amount the person contributes to the purchase price (in the absence of express declaration or agreement). It can only be of relevance where the claimant has assumed a liability for the mortgage (and not where the claimant has made payments towards someone else's liability).

1 [1986] 1 FLR 526.
2 [1993] 1 FCR 45, [1993] 1 FLR 736, CA.

### [1.349]

*(2) Inferred interest from mortgage payments*

The alternative approach to mortgages is that it will be inferred that, where a person pays or contributes to the mortgage on another's property, the payer of the mortgage has a beneficial interest under a constructive trust. These issues are considered in more detail below[1]. However, the advantage in framing a claim primarily as one where a constructive trust should be inferred may well be that the court has a wider discretion to determine the size of the beneficial interest in that type of case than in a case which is based on a claim that a resulting trust exists[2].

1 See para **[1.351]** below.
2 See *Drake v Whipp* [1996] 2 FCR 296, [1996] 1 FLR 826, CA; and *Midland Bank plc v Cooke* [1995] 4 All ER 562, [1995] 2 FLR 915.

### [1.350]

**Quantifying the interest – resulting trusts**

The size of the share will be determined by the extent of the contribution towards the purchase price[1] (save in the case where the contribution to the purchase price forms the basis of an inferred constructive trust – as to which see the passages below relating to constructive trusts).

1 See, for instance, *Fibrance v Fibrance* [1957] 1 All ER 357, [1957] 1 WLR 384, CA; and *Lowson v Coombes* [1999] Ch 373, [1999] 1 FLR 799, CA.

## Constructive trusts – common intention

### [1.351]

The common intention that may lead to the finding that a constructive trust exists may either be express or implied.

The identification of the parties' common intention in relation to the purchase of a property sets the court a difficult task, particularly where the court is examining events leading up to purchase that took place many years ago. The task is made all the more difficult where the court is asked to infer the common intention. In *Hammond v Mitchell* Waite J described that task in this way[1]:

> 'The investigation of … events has to take the form of an inferential analysis involving a scrutiny of all events potentially capable of throwing evidential light on the question whether, in the absence of express discussion, a presumed intention can be spelt out of the parties' past course of dealing. This operation was vividly described by Dixon J in Canada as "the judicial quest for the fugitive or phantom common intention" (*Pettkus v*

*Barker* (1980) 117 DLR (3d) 257), and by Nourse LJ in England as "a climb up the familiar ground which slopes down from the twin peaks of *Pettitt v Pettitt* and *Gissing v Gissing*. The process is detailed, time consuming and laborious."'

1 See [1992] 1 FLR 229 at 231f–h.

## [1.352] Express common intention

The principles arising under this area were enunciated by Lord Bridge in the case of *Lloyds Bank plc v Rosset*[1] in which he said at p 132:

> 'The first and fundamental question which must always be resolved is whether, independently of any inference to be drawn from the conduct of the parties in the course of sharing the house as their home and managing their joint affairs, there has at any time prior to acquisition or exceptionally at some later date, been any agreement, arrangement or understanding reached between them that the property is to be shared beneficially. The finding of an agreement or arrangement to share in this sense can only, I think, be based on evidence of express discussion between the partners, however imperfectly remembered and however imprecise their terms may have been. Once a finding to this effect is made, it will only be necessary for the partner asserting a claim to a beneficial interest against a partner entitled to the legal estate to show that he or she had acted to his or her detriment or significantly altered his or her position in reliance on the agreement, in order to give rise to a constructive trust or a proprietary estoppel.'

A similar passage is to be found in the opinion of Lord Diplock in the case of *Gissing v Gissing*[2].

1 [1991] 1 AC 107, [1990] 1 All ER 1111, HL.
2 See [1970] 2 All ER 780 at 790c–d.

## [1.353]

In order to substantiate a claim to a beneficial interest relying upon this principle, the relevant intention of the parties must be a shared intention that was expressly communicated between them. It cannot mean an intention which either happened to have in his or her own mind but had never communicated to the other[1].

1 See *Springette v Defoe* [1992] 2 FCR 561 at 567.

## [1.354]

In pleading a case where this principle is relied upon, the express discussions to which the court's initial enquiries will be addressed should be set out in the greatest detail, both as to language and to circumstances. This therefore means that the practitioner must take detailed and careful instructions at the outset in respect of what was said between the parties[1].

1 See *Hammond v Mitchell* [1991] 1 WLR 1127, [1992] 1 FLR 229.

## [1.355]

Examples of cases where there has been a finding of such an intention are:

- ***Drake v Whipp***[1]
  In that case the judge found that it was 'their joint decision to purchase with contributions from each'. He recited Mrs Drake's evidence of the purchase: 'I thought it was joint otherwise I would not have put my money into it. He said he would put my name on it in about a month's time. I trusted him completely.' He also recounted that later she had asked Mr Whipp about it a number of times and that he usually said he was busy. The judge recounted Mr Whipp's evidence that he was always willing that Mrs Drake should have a 'fair proportion of the value of the house according to what she had contributed'[2].

- ***Hammond v Mitchell***[3]
  In that case the man told the woman that it would be better for tax and divorce reasons that the bungalow should be in his sole name. However, he also said: 'Don't worry about the future, because when we are married it will be half yours anyway, and I will always look after you and our child'[4].
- ***Risch v McFee***[5] and ***Stokes v Anderson***[6]
  Promises were made that the claimant's name would be put on the title deeds to the property.

1 [1996] 2 FCR 296, [1996] 1 FLR 826, CA.
2 See [1996] 1 FLR 826 at 829B–E.
3 [1991] 1 WLR 1127, [1992] 1 FLR 229.
4 See [1992] 1 FLR 229 at 233B–D.
5 [1991] FCR 168, [1991] 1 FLR 105, CA.
6 [1991] FCR 539, [1991] 1 FLR 391, CA.

## [1.356]

It may often be difficult to extract from a client the full extent of the exchanges that took place at the time of the purchase of the property, particularly where that purchase was a long time ago. Further, most clients will come to solicitors at a time when they are feeling the full effect of the fraught circumstances that arise at the time that a relationship is ending. It is therefore wise for the practitioner to allow the client sufficient time to give full instructions on the intention that existed at the time of purchase, before committing the case to pleading or affidavit. A pleading that is defective or inadequate may cause considerable damage to a claim. It is better to wait for a short period in order to ensure that the client has given full instructions for the preparation of the pleadings. It is also necessary to examine the full range of things that have been said between the couple and to plead them all. The eye of the practitioner has to be on the facts necessary to show the common intention – for instance, would an assertion that 'this is as much your home as mine' be sufficient to represent an agreement that the beneficial interests are shared or would it simply mean that this was the home in which they were both to live (just as a child may refer to 'my home' without making a claim to ownership)[1].

1 See *Ungarian v Lesnoff* [1990] Ch 206, where there was an understanding that the plaintiff would provide a home for the defendant.

## [1.357]
### Implied common intention

A fundamental statement of principle on this issue came from the opinion of Lord Diplock in *Gissing v Gissing*[1] where he said:

> 'A resulting, implied or constructive trust – and it is unnecessary for present purposes to distinguish between these three classes of trust – is created by a transaction between the trustee and the cestui que trust in connection with the acquisition by the trustee of a legal estate in land, whenever the trustee has so conducted himself that it would be inequitable to allow him to deny to the cestui que trust a beneficial interest in the land acquired. And he will be held so to have conducted himself if his words or conduct he has induced the cestui que trust to act to his own detriment in the reasonable belief that by so acting he was acquiring a beneficial interest in the land … parties to a transaction in connection with the acquisition of land may well have formed a common intention that the beneficial interest in the land shall be vested in them jointly without having used express words to communicate this intention to one another; or their recollections of the words used may be imperfect or conflicting by the time any dispute arises. In such a case – a common one where the parties are spouses whose marriage has broken down – it may be possible to infer their common intention from their conduct'[2].

1 [1971] AC 886, [1970] 2 All ER 780, HL.
2 [1970] 2 All ER 780 at 790a–g.

**[1.358]**

In considering whether there is an implied constructive trust the following principles apply:

(1) There is no special class of family assets which falls to be treated under the law of trusts in some way differently from other assets[1].

(2) The court applies an objective test when considering the inferences that should be drawn from conduct[2].

(3) Where a property was bought in joint names the court will usually have little difficulty in finding that there was a common intention that both parties should have a beneficial interest in it[3].

(4) In deciding whether there was a common intention to share the beneficial interests in the property, primary regard is paid to the events leading up to the acquisition. As to events after the acquisition, Lord Diplock said the following in the case of *Gissing*:'Unless it is alleged that there was some subsequent fresh agreement, acted on by the parties, to vary the original beneficial interests created when the matrimonial home was acquired, what they said and did after the acquisition was completed is relevant if it is explicable only on the basis of their having manifested to one another at the time of the acquisition some particular common intention as to how the beneficial interests should be held'[4]. A clear example of relevant post acquisition conduct must be the payment of the mortgage. In advising clients and in settling pleadings or affidavits it is essential to have primary regard to the events leading up to the purchase of the property. Clients may often not understand this and may inundate the lawyer with information that post-dates the purchase (since this may be the most clearly recollected information).

(5) Direct contributions to the purchase of a property will usually justify the inference of a shared beneficial ownership in the absence of a suggestion of a loan or gift to other party[5]. However, although this is cited as an example of the court drawing inferences, it is suggested that it would normally be regarded as a simple example of a resulting trust rather than a constructive trust[6]. The benefit to the claimant in bringing such a claim within the umbrella of the constructive trust might be that there would appear to be a greater flexibility and discretion in the determination of the size of the beneficial interest in cases of constructive trusts rather than resulting trusts[7].

(6) A common intention may be inferred from direct contributions to the mortgage payments[8].

(7) The payment of other household bills will not usually justify the finding of a beneficial interest, save to extent considered below in relation to indirect contributions to the purchase of the property[9].

1 See the opinion of Viscount Dilhorne in *Gissing v Gissing* [1971] AC 886, [1970] 2 All ER 780; see also *Pettitt v Pettitt* [1970] AC 777 at 817.

2 See *Midland Bank plc v Cooke* [1995] 4 All ER 562, [1995] 2 FLR 915; *Drake v Whipp* [1996] 1 FLR 826 at 830; and *Gissing v Gissing* [1970] 2 All ER 780 at 790j–791a.

3 See *Walker v Hall* [1984] FLR 126.

4 See *Gissing v Gissing* [1971] AC 886, [1970] 2 All ER 780 at 791b.

5 See *Gissing v Gissing* [1971] AC 886, [1970] 2 All ER 780 at 791f.

6 The analysis of this type of case as being more usually that of a resulting trust can be seen in the judgment of Lord MacDermott CJ in the Northern Ireland appeal case of *McFarlane v MacFarlane* [1972] NI 59, cited by the Court of Appeal in *Ivin v Blake* [1994] 2 FCR 504, [1995] 1 FLR 70.

7 See *Midland Bank plc v Cooke* [1995] 4 All ER 562, [1995] 2 FLR 915.

8 See *Gissing v Gissing* [1971] AC 886, [1970] 2 All ER 780 at 792e–f.

9 See *Gissing v Gissing* [1971] AC 886, [1970] 2 All ER 780 at 793f–j; and *Burns v Burns* [1984] Ch 317, [1984] 1 All ER 244, CA.

**[1.359]**

### Indirect mortgage contributions

In the case of *Lloyds Bank plc v Rosset*[1], Lord Bridge thought that it was 'extremely doubtful' that, where there was no express common intention to share the beneficial interest and no direct contribution to the purchase by the claimant (through the payment of the deposit or the mortgage), the court could infer that there was a common intention to create a constructive trust[2]. However, in the case of *Mortgage Corpn v Lewis Silkin, Mortgage Corpn v Shaire*[3], Neuberger J expressed broader principles, stating:

> 'The extent of the respective financial contributions can be, and normally is, a relevant factor although it is by no means decisive: see for instance in *Cooke* where the wife's contribution was 7% and yet she was held to have a 50% interest. Further, the extent of the financial contribution is perhaps not as important an aspect as it was once thought to be. It may well carry more weight in a case where the parties are unmarried than when they were married: see *Cooke* at 928F and the closing part of *Stokes* at 401. Nonetheless, subject to other factors, relevant payments of money should, or at least can, be "treated as illuminating the common intention as to the extent of the beneficial interest" per Nourse LJ in *Stokes* at 400B.'

1 [1991] 1 AC 107, HL.
2 [1991] 1 AC 107 at 133.
3 [2000] 2 FCR 222 at 229.

## [1.360]

Where two people live together in a property that is being bought on mortgage, it may be that one party will pay the mortgage leaving the other to meet a disproportionately high share of the other bills. In those circumstances it may be unbalanced to regard the party from whose funds the mortgage was paid as being the sole contributor of the mortgage payments (for the other party may have bought the food that he ate and paid the other bills thereby allowing the mortgage payer to pay the mortgage). A strong body of authority recognises that contributions to the other household bills may amount to an indirect contribution to the mortgage and, therefore, be sufficient to establish a constructive trust[1]. An example of dicta supporting this proposition is the following said by Lord Pearson in *Gissing v Gissing*[2]:

> 'Contributions are not limited to those made directly in part payment of the price of the property or to those made at the time when the property is conveyed into the name of one of the spouses. For instance there can be a contribution if by arrangement between the spouses one of them by payment of the household expenses enables the other to pay the mortgage instalments.'

1 See *Gissing v Gissing* [1971] AC 886, [1970] 2 All ER 780 at 793h; *Burns v Burns* [1984] Ch 317, [1984] FLR 216 at 226; and *Bernard v Josephs* [1982] Ch 391, [1982] 4 FLR 178.
2 [1971] AC 886, [1970] 2 All ER 780 at 787.

## [1.361]

In *Bernard v Joseph*[1] the following was said:

> 'If the house has been bought on a mortgage, the inquiry is more difficult. The fact that one party paid the mortgage may indicate that it was recognised by the couple that that party was solely responsible for providing the purchase price and therefore to be regarded as the sole beneficial owner. But often where a couple are living together and both are working and pooling their resources, which one of them pays the mortgage may be no more than a matter of internal accounting between them. In such a case the judge must look at the contributions of each to the "family" finances and determine as best he may what contribution each was making towards the purchase of the house.'

1 [1982] Ch 391, [1982] 4 FLR 178 at 187.

## [1.362]

This issue was further considered by the Court of Appeal in the case of *Ivin v Blake*[1] (which post dated *Lloyds Bank plc v Rosset*[2] and therefore considered the opinion of Lord Bridge in that case). The Court of Appeal placed considerable reliance on the decision of

Lord MacDermott CJ in the Northern Ireland case of *McFarlane v McFarlane*[3]. The Court of Appeal decided:

(i) that 'the principles set out in the speech of Lord Bridge in *Lloyds Bank plc v Rosset*, and in the judgments of the court in *McFarlane* … accurately state the law of England as well as of Northern Ireland'[4];

(ii) indirect contributions to the mortgage payment s may justify a finding that a constructive trust exists. Where one party has 'contributed to the purchase not directly by finding a part of the price, but indirectly and in a manner which has added to the resources out of which the property has been acquired as, for example, by work done or services rendered or by relieving the other spouse of some, at any rate, of his or her financial obligations'[5];

(iii) in order to justify such an inference, from indirect contributions there must have been an agreement or arrangement between the parties as to those contributions[6]. As to the nature of the agreement, Lord MacDermott said: 'Here I do not refer to a contractual relationship solely, but would include any understanding between the spouses which shows a mutual intention that the indirect contributions of one or other will go to create a beneficial proprietary interest in the contributor.'

1 [1994] 2 FCR 504, [1995] 1 FLR 70.
2 [1991] 1 AC 107, [1990] 1 All ER 1111, HL.
3 [1972] NI 59, CA.
4 See the judgment in the case of *Ivin v Blake* [1995] 1 FLR 70 at 83G.
5 See the passage from the *McFarlane* decision cited in *Ivin v Blake* [1995] 1 FLR 70 at 78F.
6 See the passage from the *McFarlane* decision cited in *Ivin v Blake* [1995] 1 FLR 70 at 79ff.

## [1.363]
## Inference from other conduct

There are passages within the authorities that suggest that there is a residual class of cases where the court may infer that a constructive trust exists from conduct other than the making of payments that are referable to the purchase of the property. Examples are:

- ***Savill v Goodall***[1]
  Nourse LJ refers to 'a second category such as *Gissing v Gissing* … where the necessary common intention can only be inferred from the conduct of the parties, *usually* from the expenditure incurred by them respectively'.
- ***Grant v Edwards***[2]
  In which Sir Nicholas Browne-Wilkinson VC said: 'Lord Diplock in *Gissing v Gissing* [1971] AC 886 points out that, even where parties have not used express words to communicate their intention and therefore there is no direct evidence), the court can infer from their actions an intention that they shall both have an interest in the house. This part of his speech concentrates on the types of evidence from which the courts are most often asked to infer such an intention, viz contributions (direct and indirect, the deposit, the mortgage instalments or general housekeeping expenses). In this section of his speech he analyses what types of expenditure are capable of constituting evidence of such common intention; he does not say that if the intention is proved in some other way such contributions are essential to establish a trust. In that case the court inferred that the property owner intended the claimant to have a share in the property because the owner had made an excuse for not putting it into joint names at the outset (he said that it would prejudice her in the divorce proceedings that were pending against her husband).
- ***Eves v Eves***[3]
  Although this case may be read as one in which there was an express agreement that Janet Eves should have a share in the property, the alternative reading is that it is one where the court inferred a common intention that she should have a share through the work that she carried out to the property.

- ***Mortgage Corpn v Lewis Silkin, Mortgage Corpn v Shaire***[4]
  In which Neuberger J said: 'The extent of the respective financial contributions can be, and normally is, a relevant factor although it is by no means decisive: see for instance in *Cooke* where the wife's contribution was 7% and yet she was held to have a 50% interest. Further, the extent of the financial contribution is perhaps not as important an aspect as it was once thought to be. It may well carry more weight in a case where the parties are unmarried than when they were married: see *Cooke* at 928F and the closing part of *Stokes* at 401. Nonetheless, subject to other factors, relevant payments of money should, or at least can, be "treated as illuminating the common intention as to the extent of the beneficial interest" per Nourse LJ in *Stokes* at 400B.'

1 [1994] 1 FCR 325, [1993] 1 FLR 755, CA.
2 [1986] Ch 638, [1986] 2 All ER 426, [1987] 1 FLR 87 at 97H.
3 [1975] 3 All ER 768, [1975] 1 WLR 1338.
4 [2000] 2 FCR 222 at 229.

### [1.364]
### Acts to detriment

Where the court finds that there is a common intention that the beneficial interests in property should be shared, it will need to consider whether the claimant has acted to her detriment in reliance upon that intention.

### [1.365]

It is not sufficient for the party claiming the benefit of a constructive trust to show that she (or he) has simply acted to her detriment: she must also prove that she did so on the basis of, or in reliance on, their common intention. This issue will usually be of particular importance where the court finds that there was an express common intention to share the beneficial ownership in a property. For where the finding of the common intention is based upon inferences drawn by the court, the facts that justified the inference (eg the payment of the mortgage) will usually amount to an act to the claimants detriment also – see *Grant v Edwards*[1].

1 [1986] Ch 638 at 648E per Nourse LJ.

### [1.366]

In the words of Nourse LJ in *Grant v Edwards*[1], generally speaking the detriment 'must be conduct on which the [claimant] could not reasonably have been expected to embark unless she was to have an interest in the house'. In that case the plaintiff had made a contribution to the general household expenses in excess of what would be regarded as normal and so enabled the defendant to keep up the mortgage repayments. She would not have been expected to provide these sums unless she was to take an interest in the property; consequently they established a constructive trust in her favour. On the other hand, the wife's using part of her earnings to purchase domestic equipment and to do some periodic decorating 'presumably … because she thought the expenditure appropriate' gave her no interest in a house bought by her husband in the absence of any agreement that this would give her a joint interest[2].

1 [1986] Ch 638 at 648, [1986] 2 All ER 426 at 439, CA. In the same case Sir Nicolas Browne-Wilkinson V-C considered that 'any act done by [the claimant] to her detriment relating to [the parties'] joint lives' would suffice, but Nourse LJ's views are more consonant with other cases.
2 See *Midland Bank plc v Dobson and Dobson* [1986] 1 FLR 171, CA.

### [1.367]

The act of setting up home together is unlikely on its own to be a sufficient act to the claimants detriment. In *Grant v Edwards*[1] Nourse LJ said:

'in the absence of evidence, the law is not so cynical as to infer that a woman will only go to live with a man to whom she is not married if she understands that she is to have an interest in the house'[2].

The detriment need not be financial: in both *Cooke v Head*[3] and *Eves v Eves*[4] the claimant's doing manual work on the property, which was to be their home, gave her an interest in it. It is unlikely that decorating the house will be sufficient on its own[5], although the payment of general household bills may be, where the payments are in excess of what would be expected as a normal contribution[6].

1 [1986] Ch 638, [1986] 2 All ER 426, CA.
2 [1986] Ch 638 at 648, [1986] 2 All ER 426 at 433 (Nourse LJ). See also Sir Nicolas Browne-Wilkinson V-C at 657 and 439 respectively.
3 [1972] 2 All ER 38, [1972] 1 WLR 38, CA. The work included demolishing a building, removing hard core and rubble, mixing cement, and painting.
4 [1975] 3 All ER 768, [1975] 1 WLR 1338, CA. In this case the work also included demolition and painting.
5 See *Midland Bank v Dobson and Dobson* [1986] 1 FLR 171, CA.
6 See *Grant v Edwards* [1986] Ch 638, [1986] 2 All ER 426.

## [1.368]
## Quantifying the interest in constructive trust cases

Prima facie, the court will declare that the parties have the shares in the property that they intended[1]. Notwithstanding the obvious sense in awarding the claimant the share that the parties intended, the court has demonstrated a flexibility in the quantification of the beneficial interests in the name of overall fairness[2].

1 See *Gissing v Gissing* [1970] 2 All ER 780 at 790; and *Savill v Goodall* [1994] 1 FCR 325. In the case of *Cheese v Thomas* [1994] 1 All ER 35, [1995] 1 FCR 162, the Court of Appeal had to decide how the loss that arose on the sale of the property should be apportioned between the parties that had contributed to its purchase. It was decided that the loss should be borne in the proportions in which the parties had contributed to its purchase.
2 See *Grant v Edwards* [1986] Ch 638 at 657G; *Eves v Eves* [1975] 1 WLR 1338, CA; and *Stokes v Anderson* [1991] 1 FCR 539, [1991] 1 FLR 391, CA.

## [1.369]

Even greater flexibility has been expressed in cases where the court determines the size of the share where a constructive trust arises as a result of an implied common intention. The court will survey the whole course of dealing between the parties in relation to their ownership and occupation of the home. That scrutiny is not confined to direct financial contributions to the purchase[1].

1 See *Midland Bank plc v Cooke* [1995] 4 All ER 562, [1996] 1 FCR 442; and *Drake v Whipp* [1996] 2 FCR 296, [1996] 1 FLR 826.

## [1.370]
## Improvements to property

Where parties were married or engaged, the Matrimonial Proceedings and Property Act 1970, s 37 will have to be considered. However, in the absence of available statutory provisions, it is settled law that the mere fact that A has expended money or labour on B's property does not entitle A to an interest in the property, in the absence of either an express agreement or of a common intention to be inferred from the conduct of the parties and of any question of estoppel[1].

1 See *Thomas v Fuller-Brown* [1988] 1 FLR 237, CA. In *Pettitt v Pettitt* [1970] AC 777, [1969] 2 All ER 385, HL it was held that in the absence of agreement and any question of estoppel, one spouse who does work or spends money on the property of the other has no claim whatever upon the property of the other; in that case the husband had carried out a number of 'DIY' jobs on the house.

### [1.371]

Work of improvement to a property may well represent an act to the claimant's detriment that enables her to complete a claim that there is an express agreement, arrangement or understanding that she should have a beneficial interest in the property.

### [1.372]

Where a claim to a beneficial interest is based upon improvements alone, it has been said that the beneficial share will be calculated on the basis of the cost of the improvements or the amount by which the value of the property increased as a result of those improvements, whichever is the less[1]. However, it is suggested that this need not always be the basis of the determination of the size of the share of a party who has improved a property and established a beneficial interest on the basis of the parties common intention (ie a constructive trust), the court has a wide discretion in that determination[2].

1 See *Re Pavlou* [1993] 3 All ER 955, [1993] 1 WLR 1046.
2 See eg *Grant v Edwards* [1986] Ch 638, [1987] 1 FLR 87; and *Eves v Eves* [1975] 3 All ER 768, [1975] 1 WLR 1338, CA.

### [1.373]

Where parties have been married or engaged, it will be possible to have recourse to the Matrimonial Proceedings and Property Act 1970, s 37. Section 37 provides:

> 'Where a husband or wife contributes in money or money's worth to the improvement of real or personal property in which or in the proceeds of sale of which either or both of them has or have a beneficial interest, the husband or wife so contributing shall, if the contribution is of a substantial nature and subject to any agreement to the contrary, express or implied, be treated as having then acquired by virtue of his or her contribution a share or an enlarged share as the case may be in that beneficial interest of such an extent as may have been agreed, or in default of such agreement, as may seem in all the circumstances just to any court before which the question of any existence or extent of the beneficial interest of the husband or wife arises (whether in proceedings between them or in any other proceedings).'

### [1.374]

The main points to note under the Matrimonial Proceedings and Property Act 1970, s 37 are:

- it relates to issues between spouses and formerly engaged couples (under the Law Reform (Miscellaneous Provisions) Act 1970, s 2);
- the contribution may be in money or money's worth (ie the claimant may have paid for the improvement or done it herself[1]);
- one or both of the parties must have a beneficial interest in the property in issue (thus this section cannot be used to claim a share in a property that is wholly owned by a third party);
- the contribution must be of a substantial nature[2];
- the claim may be defeated by a contrary agreement.

1 See *Harnett v Harnett* [1973] Fam 156 at 167.
2 See *Re Nicholson* [1974] 2 All ER 386, [1974] 1 WLR 476 (provision of a gas fire insufficient).

## Proprietary Estoppel

### [1.375]

The courts have recently drawn together the principles relating to constructive trusts and those relating to estoppel[1]. There is an obvious similarity between the principles that arise on a claim to a beneficial interest on the grounds of an express agreement, arrangement or understanding and those that arise on a claim based on proprietary estoppel. There remains, however, a line of authority whereby equitable rights have arisen through the application of the principles relating to estoppel.

1 See *Lloyds Bank v Rosset* [1991] 1 AC 107 at 132; and *Grant v Edwards* [1987] 1 FLR 87 at 99.

## [1.376]

In the past it has been said that the strict application of proprietary estoppel requires that five elements are shown:

(1) the claimant must have made a mistake as to his legal rights;
(2) the claimant must have expended some money or done some act on the faith of that mistaken belief;
(3) the defendant (eg the person with legal title to the property) must know of the existence of his own right which is inconsistent with the right claimed by the other party;
(4) the defendant must know of the claimant's mistaken belief in his right and
(5) the defendant must have encouraged the claimant in the expenditure of money, or in the other acts which he has done, either directly or by abstaining from asserting his legal right[1].

1 See *Crabb v Arun District Council* [1976] 1 Ch 179, [1975] 3 All ER 865, CA; and *Matharu v Matharu* [1994] 3 FCR 216, [1994] 2 FLR 597, CA.

## [1.377]

In the case of *Gillett v Holt*[1], the Court of Appeal carried out a thorough review of previous authorities relating to proprietary estoppel and adopted a broad interpretation of the doctrine. In particular the cases of *Re Basham*[2] and *Taylor v Dickens*[3] were considered. In the leading judgment in the case of *Gillett v Holt*, Robert Walker LJ said as follows[4]:

> 'The doctrine of proprietary estoppel cannot be treated as subdivided into three or four watertight compartments … the quality of the relevant assurances may influence the issue of reliance, that reliance and detriment are often intertwined, and that whether there is a distinct need for a "mutual understanding" may depend on how the other elements are formulated and understood. Moreover the fundamental principle that equity is concerned to prevent unconscionable conduct permeates all the elements of the doctrine. In the end the court must look at the matter in the round.'

1 [2001] Ch 210, [2000] 1 FCR 705, CA.
2 [1987] 1 All ER 405, [1987] 2 FLR 264.
3 [1998] 3 FCR 455, [1998] 1 FLR 806.
4 [2000] 1 FCR 705 at 718.

## [1.378]

In the case of *Re Basham*[1] the judge had said[2]:

> 'I turn to the law. The plaintiff relies on proprietary estoppel, the principle of which, in its broadest form, may be stated as follows: where one person, A, has acted to his detriment on the faith of a belief, which was known or encouraged by another person, B, that he either has or is going to be given a right in or over B's property, B cannot insist on his strict legal rights if to do so would be inconsistent with A's belief.'

In the case of *Taylor v Dickens*[3] the judge rejected the principles as stated in Re Basham being of the view that Re Basham interpreted the doctrine in terms that were too wide.

1 [1987] 2 FLR 264.
2 At p 269D.
3 [1998] 3 FCR 455, [1998] 1 FLR 806.

## [1.379]

The judgment of Robert Walker LJ also states the following:

(a) The criticisms of *Taylor v Dickens* were well-founded [at p 721];

(b) '*Re Basham* has been referred to at least twice in this court without its correctness being challenged. In *Jones v Watkins* [1987] CA Transcript 1200 Slade LJ referred to it as containing a helpful statement of the principle … in *Wayling v Jones* (1993) 69 P & CR 170 Balcombe LJ (at 172) cited Mr Nugee's statement of principle in *Re Basham (decd)* [1987] 1 All ER 405 at 410, [1986] 1 WLR 1498 at 1503, as having been accepted by the parties' [at p 720];

(c) Balcombe LJ (at 173) went on to state the relevant principles as to reliance and detriment:

'(1) There must be a sufficient link between the promises relied upon and the conduct which constitutes the detriment—see *Eves v Eves* ([1975] 3 All ER 768 at 774, [1975] 1 WLR 1338 at 1345), in particular *per* Brightman J *Grant v Edwards* ([1986] Ch 638 at 648–649, 655–657, 656, [1986] 2 All ER 426 at 432–433, 438–439, 439), *per* Nourse LJ and *per* Browne-Wilkinson V-C and in particular the passage where he equates the principles applicable in cases of constructive trust to those of proprietary estoppel.

(2) The promises relied upon do not have to be the sole inducement for the conduct: it is sufficient if they are an inducement—(*Amalgamated Investment and Property Co Ltd (in liq) v Texas Commerce International Bank Ltd* [1982] QB 84 at 104–105, [1981] 1 All ER 923 at 936).

(3) Once it has been established that promises were made, and that there has been conduct by the plaintiff of such a nature that inducement may be inferred then the burden of proof shifts to the defendants to establish that he did not rely on the promises—*Greasley v Cooke* ([1980] 3 All ER 710, [1980] 1 WLR 1306); *Grant v Edwards* ([1986] Ch 638 at 657, [1986] 2 All ER 426 at 439).'

### [1.380]

Where the claimant has adopted a course of conduct which is prejudicial or otherwise detrimental to her, there is at least a rebuttable presumption that she adopted that course of conduct in reliance on the assurances[1].

1 Compare *Coombes v Smith* [1986] 1 WLR 808 at P 821B-E with *Greasley v Cooke* [1980] 1 WLR 1306 at 1311H and 1313. If the presumption is rebutted no estoppel will arise: see *Wayling v Jones* [1996] 2 FCR 41, [1995] 2 FLR 1029.

### [1.381]

In *Coombes v Smith*[1], it was held that the plaintiff's conduct in leaving her husband and moving in with the defendant was insufficient to base a claim of estoppel.

1 [1986] 1 WLR 808, [1987] 1 FLR 352.

### [1.382]

The relief afforded by the courts will be the minimum equity to do justice to the parties; on the facts of the case of *Pascoe v Turner*[1], this was interpreted as meaning that the man must transfer the property to the woman (he had promised that the house would belong to her and she had made improvements to it).

1 [1979] 2 All ER 945, [1979] 1 WLR 431, CA.

## Equity of exoneration

### [1.383]

Where a property is jointly owned and it is charged to secure the debts of only one of the joint owners, the other owner is entitled to have that secured indebtedness discharged out of the debtor's interest in the property (in the absence of a contrary intention). In the case of *Re Pittortou*[1] the husband and wife owned a property in their joint names. A second mortgage was taken out to secure the husband's indebtedness to the bank; that indebtedness arose under a bank account that was used partly for his business and partly to meet household expenses. It was held that insofar as the husband's debts to the bank arose from his business, that indebtedness was to be met only from the husband's share in the property; however, the indebtedness arising from household expenditure was a debt that fell on the property as a whole.

1 [1985] 1 All ER 285, [1985] 1 WLR 58.

## The date for the quantification of shares

### [1.384]

As a result of a succession of cases it is now well established that the appropriate date for the valuation of parties' shares in property, in the absence of express contrary agreement as to the date of valuation, should be the date of sale of the property or realization of the shares[1].

1 See *Gordon v Douce* [1983] 2 All ER 228, [1983] 1WLR 563; *Turton v Turton* [1988] Ch 542, [1987] 2 All ER 641, CA; *Walker v Hall* [1984] FLR 126, CA; and *Passee v Passee* [1988] 1 FLR 263, CA.

## Agreement to vary beneficial interests

### [1.385]

The parties may always agree to vary the beneficial interests in the property. To be effective, however the variation would have to comply with the provisions of the LPA 1925, s 53 and the Law of Property (Miscellaneous Provisions) Act 1989, s 2[1] unless the variation was of itself sufficient to create a resulting or constructive trust.

1 See *United Bank of Kuwait plc v Sahib* [1997] Ch 107, [1996] 2 FCR 666, CA.

## The Married Women's Property Act 1882

### [1.386]

This Act (as amended) makes procedural provision for the determination of the property rights of married couples. The Act has been extended so that it applies:

- to people whose engagement has been terminated[1];
- to people whose marriage has been terminated[2];
- to claims where the husband, who had in his possession money or property in which the wife held a beneficial interest, has now ceased to be in possession or control of that money or property (or where the wife does not know whether the property or money is still in his possession)[3].

The procedure under the 1882 Act is laid down in r 3.6 of the FPR 1991[4].

1 Under and in accordance with the time constraints of ss 2 and 3 of the Law Reform (Miscellaneous Provisions) Act 1970.
2 Under and in accordance with the time constraints under s 39 of the Matrimonial Proceedings and Property Act 1970.
3 Under s 7 of the Matrimonial Causes (Property and Maintenance) Act 1958.
4 Set out at para **[3.467]** below. For the MWPA 1882, see generally *Rayden and Jackson on Divorce and Family Matters* (17th edn, 1997), vol 1, chap 29.

### [1.387]

Orders for sale of property held in beneficial joint names were previously dealt with under s 30 of the LPA 1925. As from 1 January 1997 they have been dealt with under the TLATA

1996. Under s 14 of that Act, 'any person who is a trustee of land or has an interest in a property subject to a trust of land may make an application to the court for an order under this section'. The Act states matters that the court must take into account when determining an application for an order under s 14; those factors include:

- the intentions of the person or persons (if any) who created the trust;
- the purposes for which the property subject to the trust is held;
- the welfare of any minor who occupies or might reasonably be expected to occupy any land subject to the trust as his home; and
- the interests of any secured creditor of any beneficiary.

**[1.388]**

An application under the TLATA 1996 must be brought under the procedure laid down by the CPR 1998, such applications are not 'family proceedings' under the MFPA 1984, s 32 (therefore the exclusion of family proceedings from the CPR 1998 under Pt 2 does not apply). If it is unlikely that there will be a significant dispute of fact, the application may be made under Pt 8 of the CPR 1998; otherwise the application will have to be brought under Pt 8. The application may be brought in either the High Court or the county court (although in most instances the county court will be the appropriate venue). District judges may hear applications under s 14 of the Act[1].

1 See *Practice Direction (Family Proceedings: Allocation and Costs)* [1999] 3 All ER 192, [1999] 1 WLR 1128.

# PART 2

# Statutes

# Debtors Act 1869



## Contents



*An Act for the Abolition of Imprisonment for Debt, for the punishment of fraudulent debtors, and for other purposes*

[9th August 1869]

**[2.1]**

### 1 Short title

This Act may be cited for all purposes as 'The Debtors Act 1869'.

**[2.2]**

### 2 Extent

This Act shall not extend to Scotland or Ireland.

**[2.3]**

### 3 Construction

… Words and expressions defined or explained in the Bankruptcy Act 1869 shall have the same meaning in this Act.

**Amendment**

Words omitted repealed by the Statute Law Revision (No 2) Act 1893.

**[2.4]**

### 4 Abolition of imprisonment for debt, with exceptions

With the exceptions herein-after mentioned, no person shall … be arrested or imprisoned for making default in payment of a sum of money.

There shall be excepted from the operation of the above enactment:

1. Default in payment of a penalty, or sum in the nature of a penalty, other than a penalty in respect of any contract:
2. Default in payment of any sum recoverable summarily before a justice or justices of the peace:
3. Default by a trustee or person acting in a fiduciary capacity and ordered to pay by a court of equity any sum in his possession or under his control:
4. Default by any attorney or solicitor in payment of costs when ordered to pay costs for misconduct as such, or in payment of a sum of money when ordered to pay the same in his character of an officer of the court making the order:
5. Default in payment for the benefit of creditors of any portion of a salary or other income in respect of the payment of which any court having jurisdiction in bankruptcy is authorised to make an order:
6. Default in payment of sums in respect of the payment of which orders are in this Act authorised to be made:

Provided, first, that no person shall be imprisoned in any case excepted from the operation of this section for a longer period than one year; and, secondly, that nothing in this section shall alter the effect of any judgment or order of any court for payment of money except as regards the arrest and imprisonment of the person making default in paying such money.

**Amendment**

Words omitted repealed by the Statute Law Revision (No 2) Act 1893.

## [2.4.1]
## Keypoint

- Purpose of section
- Maximum term of imprisonment

## [2.4.2]
## Purpose of section

This section abolishes imprisonment for debt, save in the exceptional circumstances listed. The exceptions most relevant to family law are those referred to under No 6, ie orders which are authorised to be made under this Act. Those orders are:

- committals for judgment debts[1];
- arrest on leaving jurisdiction[2]; and
- sequestration[3].

They do not include power to commit for failure to make payments relating to a property under the FLA 1996, s 40[4].

1 See DA 1869, s 5 at para **[2.5]** below.
2 See DA 1869, s 6 at para **[2.6]** below.
3 See DA 1869, s 8 at para **[2.7]** below.
4 See *Nwogbe v Nwogbe* [2000] 3 FCR 345, [2000] 2 FLR 744, CA.

## [2.4.3]
## Maximum term of imprisonment

Although s 4 provides that no person shall be imprisoned under this Act for longer than one year, the maximum sentence on committal for a judgment debt is six weeks[1], in contrast to the maximum two years available on committal for breach of other court orders. The maximum period of imprisonment on arrest under s 6 is six months[2].

1 See DA 1869, s 5 at para **[2.5]** below.
2 See para **[2.6]** below.

[2.5]

## 5 Saving of power of committal for small debts

Subject to the provisions herein-after mentioned, and to the prescribed rules, any court may commit to prison for a term not exceeding six weeks, or until payment of the sum due, any person who makes default in payment of any debt or instalment of any debt due from him in pursuance of any order or judgment of that or any other competent court.

Provided—(1) That the jurisdiction by this section given of committing a person to prison shall, in the case of any court other than the superior courts of law and equity, be exercised only subject to the following restrictions; that is to say,

(a) Be exercised only by a judge or his deputy, and by an order made in open court and showing on its face the ground on which it is issued:

(b) …

(c) Be exercised only as respects a judgment of a county court by a county court judge or his deputy.

(2) That such jurisdiction shall only be exercised where it is proved to the satisfaction of the court that the person making default either has or has had since the date of the order or judgment the means to pay the sum in respect of which he has made default, and has refused or neglected, or refuses or neglects, to pay the same.

Proof of the means of the person making default may be given in such manner as the court thinks just; and for the purposes of such proof the debtor and any witnesses may be summoned and examined on oath, according to the prescribed rules.

Any jurisdiction by this section given to the superior courts may be exercised by a judge sitting in chambers, or otherwise, in the prescribed manner.

For the purposes of this section any court may direct any debt due from any person in pursuance of any order or judgment of that or any other competent court to be paid by instalments, and may from time to time rescind or vary such order:

Persons committed under this section by a superior court may be committed to the prison in which they would have been confined if arrested on a writ of capias ad satisfaciendum, and every order of committal by any superior court shall, subject to the prescribed rules, be issued, obeyed, and executed in the like manner as such writ.

This section, so far as it relates to any county court, shall be deemed to be substituted for sections ninety-eight and ninety-nine of the County Courts Act 1846 and that Act and the Acts amending the same shall be construed accordingly, and shall extend to orders made by the county court with respect to sums due in pursuance of any order or judgment of any court other than a county court.

No imprisonment under this section shall operate as a satisfaction or extinguishment of any debt or demand or cause of action, or deprive any person of any right to take out execution against the lands, goods, or chattels of the person imprisoned, in the same manner as if such imprisonment had not taken place.

Any person imprisoned under this section shall be discharged out of custody upon a certificate signed in the prescribed manner to the effect that he has satisfied a debt or instalment of a debt in respect of which he was imprisoned, together with the prescribed costs (if any).

**Amendment**

Words omitted repealed by the Bankruptcy Act 1883, s 169(1), Sch 5.

PART 2
DA 1869

[2.5.1]
**Keypoints**

- Judgment summons can be used to enforce lump sums as well as periodical payments
- Evidential requirements and limited utility post-Human Rights Act 1998 and *Murbarak*

- Procedure
- Maximum term of imprisonment
- Priority of attachment of earnings orders

### [2.5.2]
### Judgment summons can be used to enforce lump sums as well as periodical payments

Although the section refers to default in payment of any debt, the term is in fact restricted to 'maintenance orders' and judgments to pay taxes and NI contributions[1]. However, maintenance orders are defined widely and include orders 'for periodical or other payments' as defined in Sch 8 to the Administration of Justice Act 1970. These include lump sums under the MCA 1973, Pt II; the DPMCA 1978, Pt I; the MFPA 1984, Pt III; and the ChA 1989.

The term 'maintenance orders' also includes orders for costs, and for payment-in pending the conclusion of ancillary relief proceedings (following *Re Mordant; Mordant v Halls*[2]). Further, the term includes an order to pay school fees direct to a school: see *L v L (Payment of School Fees)*[3]; and financial undertakings to pay eg school fees: *Symmons v Symmons*[4]; and to pay (as yet unascertained) CGT: *M v M (Enforcement: Judgment Summons)*[5].

For a discussion of this topic, see generally *Rayden and Jackson on Divorce and Family Matters* (17th edn, 1997), vol 1, para 34.7 et seq.

1 AJA 1970, s 11, Sch 4.
2 [1997] 1 FCR 378, [1996] 1 FLR 334.
3 [1997] 3 FCR 520, sub nom *L v L (School Fees: Maintenance)* [1997] 2 FLR 317, CA.
4 [1993] 1 FLR 317.
5 [1993] Fam Law 469.

### [2.5.3]
### Evidential requirements and limited utility post-Human Rights Act 1998 and *Murbarak*

Before a court can commit a person to prison on a judgment debt it must be satisfied that the judgment debtor has, or has had, the means to pay and that he has deliberately refused or neglected to pay[1]. The standard of proof is the criminal standard[2] and proceedings are criminal proceedings for the purpose of the ECHR[3]. In consequence, the case of *Murbarak v Murbarak*[4] and *Practice Direction: Committal Applications*[5] referred to in that case have the effect of making the judgment summons largely obsolete as a means of enforcement. The creditor has to prove ability to pay and, because of the quasi-criminal nature of the proceeding, also has to particularise the default so that the debtor can meet the charge[6]. As Thorpe LJ said in his judgment[7]:

> 'I suspect that the consequences of the re-evaluation of the … procedure in the light of the Human Rights Act will be that it will become a largely obsolete means of enforcement. I doubt whether experienced specialist practitioners will think that it has sufficient value for money to be worth its initiation. Certainly it seems to me that it will be more or less useless in cases involving fraudulent husbands seeking to conceal assets difficult or impossible to identify specifically.'

Brooke LJ added this warning[8]:

> 'In my judgment, it is essential for family law practitioners who are concerned with proceedings which may lead to committal to be fully acquainted with the requirements of article 6 of the [Human Rights] convention before they embark on any similar process in future.'

See also *Newman (t/a Mantella Publishing) v Modern Bookbinders Ltd*[9]; and more recently, *Quinn v Cuff*[10].

1 See the DA 1869, s 5(2).
2 *Woodley v Woodley* [1993] 1 FCR 701, [1992] 2 FLR 417, CA.
3 *Quiaa v Cuff* [2001] EWCA Civ 36, [2001] All ER (D) 29.

4 [2001] 1 FCR 193, [2001] All ER (D) 2302, CA, also reported as *Mubarak* at [2001] 1 FLR 673 (first-instance decision) and [2001] 1 FLR 698 (Court of Appeal).
5 [2001] 1 FLR 949. Set out at para **[4.30A]** below.
6 See Art 6(3) of the ECHR.
7 [2001] 1 FCR 193 at [41], CA.
8 [2001] 1 FCR 193 at [64], CA.
9 [2000] 2 All ER 814, [2000] 1 WLR 2559, CA.
10 [2001] EWCA Civ 36, [2001] All ER (D) 49.



## [2.5.4]
### Procedure

This is set out in detail in FPR 1991, rr 7.4 to 7.6[1]; but note the criticism of FPR 1991, r 7.4 and the Form M17 in the case of *Murbarak v Murbarak*[2] and the need to read the rule subject to *Practice Direction: Committal Applications* referred to in *Murbarak*. The application requires a request in Form M16 and a summons in Form M17, and is supported by affidavit. It must be personally served with 10 days' notice, and with conduct money for the judgment debtor to travel to and from court. Where there are a number of maintenance orders obtained in the same application (eg wife and children), a single judgment summons may be used to cover all maintenance orders in the original order[3].

At the hearing the judgment debtor is examined on oath[4] – ie cross-examined – with or without affidavit[5].

The court hearing the judgment summons has power to vary or rescind the original order[6], even if the judgment debtor himself does not request it[7]. See also below as to the court's powers in relation to attachment of earnings orders.

1 See paras **[3.479]** to **[3.481]** below.
2 [2001] 1 FCR 193, [2001] All ER (D) 2302, CA. *Practice Direction: Committal Applications* is set out below at para **[4.32]**.
3 FPR 1991, r 7.4(8).
4 See the DA 1869, s 5(2) at para **[2.5]** above.
5 See *B v B (Injunction: Restraint on Leaving Jurisdiction)* [1997] 2 FLR 148, and FPR 1991, rr 7.5 and 7.6.
6 See the DA 1869, s 5(2) at para **[2.5]** above.
7 See FPR 1991, r 7.4(9) at para **[3.479]** below.

## [2.5.5]
### Maximum term of imprisonment

The maximum sentence on committal for a judgment debt is six weeks, in contrast to the maximum two years available on committal for breach of other court orders and the maximum six months available on imprisonment on arrest under s 6 below.

## [2.5.6]
### Priority of attachment of earnings orders

Attachment of earnings takes priority over committal in two senses. First, the court has power to substitute attachment of earnings in place of committal – before or after the making of a committal order[1]. Second, where there is an attachment of earnings order in the county court, 'no warrant of commitment shall be issued in consequence of any proceedings for the enforcement of the debt begun before the making of the attachment of earnings order'[2].

1 See the AtEA 1971, s 3(4), (6) and (7) at para **[2.58]** below.
2 See the AtEA, s 8(2)(a) at para **[2.63]** below.

## [2.6]

### 6 Arrest of defendant about to quit England

... Where the plaintiff in any action in any of Her Majesty's superior courts of law at Westminster in which, if brought before the commencement of this Act, the defendant would have been liable to arrest, proves at any time before final judgment by evidence on oath, to the satisfaction of a judge of one of those courts, that the plaintiff has good cause of action against the defendant to the amount of fifty pounds or upwards, and that there is probable cause for believing that the defendant is about to quit England unless he be apprehended, and that the absence of the defendant from England will materially prejudice the plaintiff in the prosecution of his action, such judge may in the prescribed manner order such defendant to be arrested and imprisoned for a period not exceeding six months, unless and until he has sooner given the prescribed security, not exceeding the amount claimed in the action, that he will not go out of England without the leave of the court.

Where the action is for a penalty or sum in the nature of a penalty other than a penalty in respect of any contract, it shall not be necessary to prove that the absence of the defendant from England will materially prejudice the plaintiff in the prosecution of his action, and the security given (instead of being that the defendant will not go out of England) shall be to the effect that any sum recovered against the defendant in the action shall be paid, or that the defendant shall be rendered to prison.

**Amendment**

Words omitted repealed by the Statute Law Revision (No 2) Act 1893.

### [2.6.1]
### Keypoints

- Purpose of section
- Distinguish related powers/orders
- Requirement of a cause of action
- Means of security not enforcement
- Maximum term of imprisonment

### [2.6.2]
### Purpose of section

This section preserves the power of arrest and imprisonment as a means of security pending final judgment. It is not a means of enforcement of orders after judgment, although, by analogy, note the impact of the HRA 1998 on the judgment summons procedure[1].

1 See *Murbarak v Murbarak* [2001] 1 FCR 193, [2001] All ER (D) 2302, CA (Note that *Murbarak* is now also reported as *Mubarak* at [2001] 1 FLR 673 (first-instance decision) and [2001] 1 FLR 698 (Court of Appeal)); *Practice Direction: Committal Applications* [2001] 1 FLR 949 (set out at para **[4.32]** below); and *Newman (t/a Mantella Publishing) v Modern Bookbinders Ltd* [2000] 2 All ER 814, [2000] 1 WLR 2559, CA.

### [2.6.3]
### Distinguish related powers/orders

Arrest under s 6 should be distinguished from the writ/injunction ne exeat regno (which forbids a person to leave the jurisdiction, but by analogy has the same requirements as s 6)[1].

1 See *Felton v Callis* [1969] 1 QB 200, [1968] 3 All ER 673; and *Thaha v Thaha* [1987] 2 FLR 142; and also for the inherent jurisdiction (and the jurisdiction under the SCA 1981, s 37(1)) to order deposit of passport: *Re S (Financial Provision: Non-resident)* [1996] 1 FCR 148, CA; and *Re A-K (Minors) (Foreign Passport: Jurisdiction)* [1997] 2 FCR 563, [1997] 2 FLR 569, CA; and see generally *Rayden and Jackson on Divorce and Family Matters* (17th edn, 1997), vol 1, paras 32.77 and 32.78.

### [2.6.4]
### Requirement of a cause of action

The section requires that the applicant establish a good cause of action. A matrimonial cause is (because of its personal nature) probably not a cause of action[1]. In the Family Division the better course is to apply for deposit of passport[2].

1 *D'Este v D'Este* [1973] Fam 55; aliter where there is an order: *Thaha v Thaha* [1987] 2 FLR 142.
2 *Re S (Financial Provision: Non-resident)* [1996] 1 FCR 148.

**[2.6.5]**
**Means of security not enforcement**

The power to order arrest and imprisonment is a means of security before final judgment, not enforcement after final judgment[1]. The only exception to this is that the remedy is available pending a court hearing re enforcement (in order to secure the debtor's attendance at the hearing, not as a means of enforcement itself).

Under s 6 the power to imprison is only until the respondent has given such security as the court orders. In the Family Division there is in any event separate jurisdiction to make an interlocutory order for payment of money into court[2].

1 *B v B (Injunction: Restraint on Leaving Jurisdiction)* [1997] 2 FLR 148.
2 *Re Mordant, Mordant v Halls* [1997] 2 FCR 378, [1996] 1 FLR 334.



**[2.6.6]**
**Maximum term of imprisonment**

The maximum term under s 6 is six months, in contrast to the maximum six weeks sentence of committal on a judgement debt[1].

1 See the DA 1869, s 5 at para **[2.5]** above.

**[2.7]**

**8 Saving for sequestration against property**

Sequestration against the property of a debtor may … be issued by any court of equity in the same manner as if such debtor had been actually arrested.

**Amendment**
Words omitted repealed by the Statute Law Revision (No 2) Act 1893.

**[2.7.1]**
**Keypoints**

- Definition
- Availability
- Procedure
- Practice

**[2.7.2]**
**Definition**

Sequestration is an order of the court (by writ) to not less than four commissioners or sequestrators approved by the court. The commissioners/sequestrators have the duty to take possession of the property (real and personal) of the contemnor and to hold that property subject to directions by the Court as to its management, liquidation and distribution[1].

1 *Clark v Clark* [1989] FCR 101, [1989] 1 FLR 174.

**[2.7.3]**
**Availability**

Sequestration is primarily a process of contempt whereby the contemnor's property is detained until the contempt is purged. It requires the leave of the court to issue[1]. The remedy is available in children cases as well as in finance cases[2]. It is available to enforce payment of arrears of maintenance[3]; and exceptionally against a non-party deliberately frustrating the order of the court[4].

1 See para **[2.7.4]** below.
2 *Richardson v Richardson* [1989] Fam 95, [1990] 1 FLR 186.
3 See *Capron v Capron* [1927] P 243.
4 *Re S (Child Abduction: Sequestration)* [1995] 3 FCR 707, [1995] 1 FLR 858.

## [2.7.4]
### Procedure

The application is for leave to issue sequestration and is supported by affidavit, and is usually (but not necessarily) to a High Court Judge[1].

1 See CPR Procedural Guide No 40; RSC Ord 45, r 5(1) and RSC Ord 46, r 5.

## [2.7.5]
### Practice

Sequestration lies 'at the top scale of severity' as a means of enforcing the court's orders, and is (by its nature) very costly[1]. If a sequestration order is granted in relation to unregistered land, the writ of sequestration is registrable (for the purposes of protection and priority) under the register of writs and orders affecting land[2]. In the case of registered land it should be registered in accordance with the Land Registration Act 1925, s 59.

1 *Clark v Clark* [1989] FCR 101, [1989] 1 FLR 174.
2 See the LCA 1972, s 6 at para **[2.97]** below.

## [2.8]

### 10 Definition of 'prescribed'

In this part of this Act the term 'prescribed' means as follows:—

As respects the superior courts of common law, prescribed by general rules to be made in pursuance of the Common Law Procedure Act 1852;

As respects the superior courts of equity prescribed by general rules and orders to be made in pursuance of the Court of Chancery Act 1852;

As respects the county courts, prescribed by general rules to be made under the County Courts Act 1856; and

…

And general rules and orders may respectively be made by such authorities as aforesaid, for the purpose of carrying into effect this part of this Act.

**Amendment**

This section was repealed as respects courts of summary jurisdiction by the Justices of the Peace Act 1949, s 46(2), Sch 7, Pt II. Words omitted repealed by the Courts Act 1971, s 56(4), Sch 11, Pt IV.

# Married Women's Property Act 1882



Contents



*An Act to consolidate and amend the Acts relating to the Property of Married Women*

[18th August 1882]

**[2.9]**

### 10 Fraudulent investments with money of husband

If any investment in any such deposit or annuity as aforesaid, or in any of the public stocks or funds, or in any other stocks or funds transferable as aforesaid, or in any share, stock, debenture, or debenture stock of any corporation, company, or public body, municipal, commercial, or otherwise, or in any share, debenture, benefit, right, or claim whatsoever in, to, or upon the funds of any industrial, provident, friendly, benefit, building, or loan society, shall have been made by a married woman by means of moneys of her husband, without his consent, the Court may, upon an application under section seventeen of this Act, order such investment, and the dividends thereof, or any part thereof, to be transferred and paid respectively to the husband; and nothing in this Act contained shall give validity as against creditors of the husband, to any gift, by a husband to his wife, of any property, which, after such gift, shall continue to be in the order and disposition or reputed ownership of the husband, or to any deposit or other investment of moneys of the husband made by or in the name of his wife in fraud of his creditors; but any moneys so deposited or invested may be followed as if this Act had not passed.

**[2.10]**

### 11 Moneys payable under policy of assurance not to form part of estate of the insured

A married woman may … effect a policy upon her own life or the life of her husband for her [own benefit]; and the same and all benefit thereof shall enure accordingly.

A policy of assurance effected by any man on his own life, and expressed to be for the benefit of his wife, or of his children, or of his wife and children, or any of them, or by any woman on her own life, and expressed to be for the benefit of her husband, or of her children, or of her husband and children, or any of them, shall create a trust in favour of the objects therein named, and the moneys payable under any such policy shall not, so long as any object of the trust remains unperformed, form part of the estate of the insured, or be subject to his or her debts: Provided, that if it shall be proved that the policy was effected and the premiums paid with intent to defraud the creditors of the insured, they shall be entitled to receive, out of the moneys payable under the policy, a sum equal to the premiums so paid. The insured may by the policy, or by any memorandum under his or her hand, appoint a trustee or trustees of the moneys payable under the policy, and from time to time appoint a new trustee or new trustees thereof, and may make provision for the appointment of a new trustee or new trustees thereof, and for the investment of the moneys payable under such policy. In default of any such appointment of a trustee, such policy, immediately on its being effected, shall vest in the insured and his or her legal personal representatives, in trust for the purposes aforesaid … The receipt of a trustee or trustees duly appointed, or in default of any such appointment, or in default of notice to the insurance office, the receipt of the legal personal representative of the insured shall be a discharge to the office for the sum secured by the policy, or for the value thereof, in whole or in part.

**Amendment**

First words omitted repealed and words in square brackets substituted by the LR(MWT)A 1935, ss 5(1), (2), 8(2), Schs 1, 2; second words omitted repealed by the SL(R)A 1969.

**'Policy expressed to be for the benefit of …'**

For case law interpreting these provisions see *Griffiths v Fleming*[1]; *Re Equitable Life Assurance Society of US Policy v Mitchell*[2]; *Re Fleetwood's Policy*[3]; and *Re Browne's Policy*[4].

1 [1909] 1 KB 805.
2 (1911) 27 TLR 213.
3 [1926] Ch 48, [1925] All ER Rep 262.
4 [1903] 1 Ch 188.

## [2.11]

### 17 Questions between husband and wife as to property to be decided in a summary way

In any question between husband and wife as to the title to or possession of property, either party, … may apply by summons or otherwise in a summary way [to the High Court or such county court as may be prescribed and the court may, on such an application (which may be heard in private), make such order with respect to the property as it thinks fit.

In this section 'prescribed' means prescribed by rules of court and rules made for the purposes of this section may confer jurisdiction on county courts whatever the situation or value of the property in dispute.]

**Amendment**

Words omitted repealed by the SL(R)A 1969; words in square brackets substituted by the MFPA 1984, s 43.

## [2.11.1]

**Keypoints**

- Relief available
- Use of the MWPA 1882 where the MCA 1973 available
- Foreign property
- Post-divorce availability
- Formerly engaged couples
- Procedure
- Sale of the property

### [2.11.2]
### Relief available

This section is procedural and declaratory only. It does not permit the court to adjust property rights[1]. Thus on an application under this section, the issue is: '***To whom does this property belong***'; rather than: '***To whom in fairness should this property be awarded***'. Save to the limited degree by which this section is extended by statute (eg under s 37 of the MPPA 1970), this involves determining the parties' beneficial interests in property under the general trust and property law[2].

For a discussion of the scope, extent and application of this section, see generally *Rayden and Jackson on Divorce and Family Matters* (17th edn, 1997), vol 1, para 29.2 et seq.

1 See *Pettitt v Pettitt* [1970] AC 777, [1969] 2 All ER 385, HL; and *Burke v Burke* [1974] 2 All ER 944, CA.
2 As to which see *Gissing v Gissing* [1971] AC 886, [1970] 2 All ER 780, HL; and *Lloyds Bank plc v Rosset* [1991] 1 AC 107, [1990] 1 All ER 1111, HL.



### [2.11.3]
### Use of the MWPA 1882 where the MCA 1973 available

Where there are divorce, judicial separation or nullity proceedings, financial issues should be dealt with under the MCA 1973 unless there is a good reason for not doing so[1]. In ancillary relief proceedings it may be necessary in some circumstances to issue proceedings under the 1882 Act in order to declare the parties' beneficial interests in property (eg for the purposes of calculating their liabilities to capital gains tax[2] or where one of the parties is bankrupt).

1 *Suttill v Graham* [1977] 1 All ER 1117, [1977] 1 WLR 819, CA; *Kowalczuk v Kowalczuk* [1973] 2 All ER 1042, [1973] 1 WLR 930, CA; *Griffiths v Griffiths* [1974] 1 All ER 932, [1974] 1 WLR 1350; and *Fielding v Fielding* [1978] 1 All ER 267, [1977] 1 WLR 1146n.
2 See *B v B (Real Property: Assessment of Interests)* [1988] 2 FLR 490.

### [2.11.4]
### Foreign Property

Section 17 may be used to resolve disputes about property that is outside England and Wales. However, the court will not exercise its powers under this section in relation to such property if the order would be ineffective[1].

In considering enforceability a distinction has to be drawn between an order that is enforceable 'in personam' – ie against the person of the respondent and an order that is enforceable 'in rem' – ie against the 'thing' or property, itself. Since orders under the MWPA 1882 are enforceable against the person of the respondent, it may be easier to persuade a court that the order would be enforceable.

1 *Hamlin v Hamlin* [1986] Fam 11, [1985] 2 All ER 1037; and *Razelos v Razelos* [1969] 3 All ER 929, [1970] 1 WLR 390; and see generally *Rayden and Jackson on Divorce and Family Matters* (17th edn, 1997), vol 1, Noter-up and para 29.7.

### [2.11.5]
### Post-divorce availability

The section is available to parties who were formerly married provided the application is brought within three years from the date upon which the marriage was dissolved or annulled[1]. If that time limit is passed it will be necessary to apply under the general law that applies to people who have not married (eg under the TLATA 1996).

1 MPPA 1970, s 39 at para **[2.49]** below.

## [2.11.6]
### Formerly engaged couples

As a result of s 2 of the Law Reform (Miscellaneous Provisions) Act 1970[1] formerly engaged couples may apply under the MWPA 1882, subject to the time limit stated in that section of the 1970 Act.

1 As to which, see para **[2.52]** below.

## [2.11.7]
### Procedure

The procedure under this section is governed by rr 3.6 and 3.7 of the FPR 1991[1]. The jurisdiction of the county court is not limited by the value of the property in question.

1 See paras **[3.467]** and **[3.468]** below.

## [2.11.8]
### Sale of the property

An application for sale may be made under the MWPA 1882[1].

1 See the MC(PM)A 1958, s 7 at para **[2.45]** below.

## [2.12]

### 24 Interpretation of terms

… The word 'property' in this Act includes a thing in action.

**Amendment**
Words omitted repealed by the SL(R)A 1969 and the Statute Law Revision (Northern Ireland) Act 1976.

## [2.13]

### 26 Extent of Act

This Act shall not extend to Scotland.

# Administration of Justice Act 1920 (Pt II)



## Contents



### [2.14]
### Introduction

The text of the Administration of Justice Act 1920 (which is of very limited contemporary application) has been omitted because it is outside the scope of this book. The relevant provisions of the Act itself can be found in *Rayden and Jackson on Divorce and Family Matters* (17th edn, 1997), vol 2, p 2045 et seq.

### [2.15]
### Summary

In summary, the scheme of Pt II of the Act is to facilitate the reciprocal enforcement of civil money judgments of superior courts within what is now the British Commonwealth[1].

See also the Foreign Judgments (Reciprocal Enforcement) Act 1933 which has a similar (but not identical) jurisdiction and which to some extent was the successor to the AJA 1920.

1 See para **[2.17]** below.

### [2.16]
### Scheme of Act and Procedure

Under the AJA 1920 foreign money judgments (including lump sum orders and costs orders) which satisfy the requirements of s 9(2) may be registered in a UK High Court (or the Court of Session in Scotland), and, if so registered, can be enforced as if they were orders of the UK court. The application for registration must be made within 12 months of the judgment, unless the court extends this period, and the UK court has a discretion to refuse registration. There is a costs incentive to seek registration (rather than to seek recognition of the foreign judgment by other proceedings) in that no costs are recoverable in any UK proceedings which might have been registered, unless registration was previously applied for and refused (s 9(5)). The procedure for an application to register a foreign judgment, and if granted, thereafter to issue execution, is set out in RSC Ord 71 (CPR 1998 – Sch 1).

For outbound orders of the High Court the prerequisite to enforcement abroad is a certified copy of the judgment which it is desired to enforce abroad (s 10). The procedure for obtaining a certified copy of a judgment is set out in RSC Ord 71, r 13.

### [2.17]
### Territorial application

The Act applies to the following countries/territories:

Administration of Justice Act 1920 (Pt II)

- Akrotiri
- Anguila
- Antigua and Barbuda
- Bahamas
- Barbados
- Belize
- Bermuda
- Botswana
- British Indian Ocean Territory
- Cayman Islands
- Christmas Island
- Cocos Islands
- Cyprus
- Dhekelia
- Dominica
- Falkland Islands
- Fiji
- Gambia
- Ghana
- Grenada
- Guernsey
- Hong Kong
- India
- Jamaica
- Kenya
- Kiribati
- Lesotho
- Malawi
- Malaysia
- Malta and Gozo
- Mauritius
- Montserrat
- Newfoundland
- New South Wales
- New Zealand
- Nigeria
- Norfolk Island
- Northern Territory (Australia)
- Papua New Guinea
- Queensland
- St Christopher & Nevis
- St Helena
- St Lucia
- St Vincent & the Grenadines
- Seychelles
- Sierra Leone
- Singapore
- Solomon Islands
- South Australia
- Sri Lanka
- Swaziland
- Tanzania
- Tasmania
- Trinidad and Tobago
- Turks and Caicos Islands
- Tuvalu
- Uganda
- Western Australia
- Zambia
- Zanzibar
- Zimbabwe

# Maintenance Orders (Facilities for Enforcement) Act 1920

PART 2 MO(FE)A 1920

Contents



## [2.18]
### Introduction

The text of the Maintenance Orders (Facilities for Enforcement) Act 1920 (which is of very limited contemporary application) has been omitted because it is outside the scope of this book. The relevant provisions of the Act itself (and the regulations which govern its application in the magistrates' court[1]) can be found in *Rayden and Jackson on Divorce and Family Matters* (17th edn, 1997), Vol 1, paras 34.86 and 34.87; and vol 2, p 2035 et seq.

1 See para **[2.22]** below.

## [2.19]
### Summary

In summary, the scheme of the MO(FE)A 1920 is to facilitate enforcement of maintenance orders within what is now the British Commonwealth. It has to a very large extent been replaced by Maintenance Orders (Reciprocal Enforcement) Act 1972, but still applies to those countries ***not*** yet within Maintenance Orders (Reciprocal Enforcement Act 1972 (as amended)[1].

1 See further para **[2.21]** below.

## [2.20]
### Scheme of the Act

Maintenance orders, which for the purposes of the MO(FE)A 1920 are restrictively defined in s 10, are either provisional or final, and either inbound or outbound. An inbound order is one made in a reciprocating country/territory outside the United Kingdom which it is desired to enforce in England, Wales or Northern Ireland. An outbound order is one made in England which it is desired to enforce in a reciprocating country/territory outside the UK. A final order is one made whilst the payer is resident in the country/territory making the order. A provisional order is one made against a payer no longer resident in the country/territory making the order, but resident in a reciprocating country/territory. The Act covers the treatment of final orders (s 1 inbound, s 2 outbound), and provisional orders (s 3 outbound, s 4 inbound) but only from the perspective of England. It does not cover how the foreign court makes a provisional order, but sets out in detail (s 4) how a foreign provisional order may be confirmed in England. A final inbound order, certified by the governor of a foreign territory, is enforceable in England upon registration in accordance with s 1. A provisional order (whether inbound or outbound) cannot be enforced until it has been confirmed by a court in the country/territory where the payer is now resident. If a provisional order is confirmed (in accordance with s 4), it is enforceable (and variable) as if made in the court which confirms it; and the decision to confirm the provisional order is itself subject to appeal (see s 4(6A)). By contrast there is no appeal from the registration of a final order, nor any jurisdiction in the registering court to vary, revoke or discharge the original maintenance order[1]. For the equivalent jurisdiction in relation to the enforcement of lump sum money judgments and orders for costs see the Administration of Justice Act 1920.

1 *Pilcher v Pilcher* [1955] 2 All ER 644.

## [2.21]
## Territorial application

The Act applies to the following countries/territories:

- Antigua and Barbuda
- Bahamas
- Belize
- Botswana
- British Solomon Islands
- British Virgin Islands
- Brunei
- Cayman Islands
- Christmas Islands
- Cocos Islands
- Cyprus
- Dominica
- Gambia
- Gilbert and Ellice Islands
- Grenada
- Guernsey
- Guyana
- Jamaica
- Jersey
- Kiribati
- Lesotho
- Malawi
- Malaysia
- Mauritius
- Montserrat
- Newfoundland and Prince Edward Island
- Nigeria
- St Christopher and Nevis
- St Lucia
- St Vincent & the Grenadines
- Seychelles
- Sierra Leone
- Swaziland Protectorate
- Trinidad and Tobago
- Tuvalu
- Uganda
- Yukon Territory
- Zambia
- Zanzibar

## [2.22]
## Procedure

The procedure for registration and enforcement of orders under the MO(FE)A 1920 is governed by FPR 1991, r 7.17[1] and (in the magistrates' court) by the Maintenance Orders (Facilities for Enforcement) Rules 1922, SR & O 1922/1355.

1 Set out at para **[3.483]** below.

# Foreign Judgments (Reciprocal Enforcement) Act 1933

PART 2 FJ(RE)A 1933

Contents



## [2.23] Introduction

The text of this Act (which is of very limited contemporary application) has been omitted because it is outside the scope of this book. The relevant provisions of the Act itself can be found in *Rayden and Jackson on Divorce and Family Matters* (17th edn, 1997), vol 2, p 2077 et seq.

## [2.24] Summary

In summary, the scheme of the Foreign Judgments (Reciprocal Enforcement) Act 1933 is to facilitate the reciprocal enforcement of civil money judgments and certain criminal compensation orders[1].

See also the Administration of Justice Act 1920, which is still in force in territories other than those to which the FJ(RE)A 1933 applies, for the legislative forerunner to the 1933 Act. The equivalent early legislation for the reciprocal enforcement of maintenance orders (also still of limited application) was the Maintenance Orders (Facilities for Enforcement) Act 1920.

1 See para **[2.27]** below.

## [2.25] Scheme of the Act

Under the FJ(RE)A 1933 foreign money judgments (including lump sum orders, costs orders and orders for interest) can be registered in the High Court on application within six years of the judgment. If the foreign judgment satisfies the requirements of s 2 the court is obliged to register it. Once registered the sum for which a judgment is registered carries interest[1]. Non-money judgments which would be registrable if they were judgments for a sum of money, are also accorded recognition (irrespective of registration)[2].

Registration may be set aside if the registering court is subsequently satisfied that the judgment was not in fact one which was entitled to registration (s 4). As long as the registration remains in force the judgment is enforced as if originally given in the registering court[3].

By s 6 no proceedings for the recovery of a foreign money judgment capable of registration under the FJ(RE)A 1933 may be taken otherwise than under the Act.

1 See the FJ(RE)A 1933, s 2(2)(c).
2 See the FJ(RE)A 1933, s 8.
3 See the FJ(RE)A 1933, s 2(2).

## [2.26]
## Procedure

The procedure for inbound orders is set out in RSC Ord 71 (CPR 1998, Sch 1).

For outbound orders of the UK courts the prerequisite for enforcement abroad is a certified copy of the judgment which it is desired to enforce abroad[1]. The procedure for obtaining a certified copy of a judgment is set out in RSC Ord 71, r 13 (in the High Court) and CCR Ord 35 (for the county court).

1 See the FJ(RE)A 1933, s 10.

## [2.27]
## Territorial application

The Act applies to the following countries/territories:

- Australian Capital Territory
- Austria
- Canada (Federal Court, British Columbia, Manitoba, New Brunswick, Nova Scotia, Ontario, Prince Edward Island, Saskachewan, Yukon)
- Guernsey
- India
- Isle of Man
- Israel
- Italy
- Jamaica
- Jersey
- Norway
- Pakistan
- Surinam
- Tonga

# Maintenance Orders Act 1950

Contents





## [2.28]
## Introduction

The text of the Maintenance Orders Act 1950 has been omitted because the Act is outside the scope of this book. The relevant provisions of the Act itself (and the regulations which govern its application[1] can be found in *Rayden and Jackson on Divorce and Family Matters* (17th edn, 1997).

1 See para **[2.31]** below.

## [2.29]
## Summary

In summary, the scheme of the MOA 1950 is that maintenance orders made in one part of the UK may be registered for the purpose of enforcement in another part of the UK. Maintenance orders under the MOA 1950, as defined in s 16(2), include orders for, inter alia, lump sums.

## [2.30]
## Scheme of the Act

The basis of the application for registration is that the payer under a maintenance order is residing in another part of the UK. The application is made to the original court (or as otherwise provided by s 17) and, if granted, a certified copy of the original order is sent for registration to either the High Court (or equivalent), or the local magistrates' court, in that part of the UK where the payer is now resident. The court level of the court of registration depends on the level of the court which made the original order (see s 17(3)).

Once registered the order is enforced in all respects as if it had been made in the court of registration (s 18), subject in the case of arrears to s 20. An order registered in a superior court cannot be varied by the court of registration but only by the original court (s 21), although the registering court can assist in relation to a variation application by taking evidence for transmission to the original court in accordance with s 21(2) and (3). By contrast, in relation to an order registered in a summary court, the registering court does have jurisdiction to hear a variation application made by the payer (s 22).

Registration can be cancelled under s 24, either upon application by the payee or by the court of registration if it appears that the payer has ceased to reside the UK.

## [2.31]
## Procedure

The procedure for registration and enforcement (and, where possible, variation) of orders under the MOA 1950 is governed by FPR 1991, rr 7.18 to 7.21[1] and (in the magistrates' court) by the Maintenance Orders (Summary Jurisdiction) Rules 1950, SI 1950/2035.

1 See paras **[3.484]** to **[3.487]** below.

2020

# Maintenance Orders Act 1958

PART 2
MOA 1958

## Contents

*Section*



*An Act to make provision for the registration in the High Court or a magistrates' court of certain maintenance orders made by the other of those courts or a county court and with respect to the enforcement and variation of registered orders; to make provision for the attachment of sums falling to be paid by way of wages, salary or other earnings or by way of pension for the purpose of enforcing certain maintenance orders; to amend section seventy-four of the Magistrates' Courts Act 1952; to make provision for the review of committals to prison by magistrates' courts for failure to comply with maintenance orders; to enable Orders in Council under section twelve of the Maintenance Orders (Facilities for Enforcement) Act 1920 to be revoked or varied; and for purposes connected with the matters aforesaid*

[7th July 1958]

**[2.32]**

PART I
REGISTRATION, ENFORCEMENT AND VARIATION OF CERTAIN MAINTENANCE ORDERS

### 1 Application of Part I

(1) The provisions of this Part of this Act shall have effect for the purpose of enabling maintenance orders to which this Part of this Act applies to be registered—

(a) in the case of an order made by the High Court or a county court, in a magistrates' court; and

(b) in the case of an order made by a magistrates' court, in the High Court,

and, subject to those provisions, while so registered—

(i) to be enforced in like manner as an order made by the court of registration; and

(ii) in the case of an order registered in a magistrates' court, to be varied by a magistrates' court.

[(1A) In the following provisions of this Act 'maintenance order' means any order specified in Schedule 8 to the Administration of Justice Act 1970.]

[(2) For the purposes of subsection (1) above, a maintenance order made by a court in Scotland or Northern Ireland and registered in England under Part II of the Maintenance Orders Act 1950 shall be deemed to have been made by the court in England in which it is so registered.

(2A) This Part of this Act applies—

(a) to maintenance orders made by the High Court or a county court or a magistrates' court, other than orders registered in Scotland or Northern Ireland under Part II of the Maintenance Orders Act 1950, and

(b) to maintenance orders made by a court in Scotland or Northern Ireland and registered in England under Part II of the Maintenance Orders Act 1950.]

(3) Without prejudice to the provisions of section twenty-one of this Act, in this Part of this Act, unless the context otherwise requires, the following expressions have the following meanings—

'High Court order', 'county court order' and 'magistrates' court order' mean an order made by the High Court, a county court or a magistrates' court, as the case may be;

'order' means a maintenance order to which this Part of this Act applies;

'original court' and 'court of registration', in relation to an order, mean the court by which the order was made or, as the case may be, the court in which the order is registered;

'registered' means registered in accordance with the provisions of this Part of this Act, and 'registration' shall be construed accordingly;

and for the purposes of this Part of this Act an order for the payment by the defendant of any costs incurred in proceedings relating to a maintenance order, being an order for the payment of costs made while the maintenance order is not registered, shall be deemed to form part of that maintenance order.

[(4) For the purposes of this section a maintenance order [which is registered in a magistrates' court under Part I of the Maintenance Orders (Reciprocal Enforcement) Act 1972 or Part I of the Civil Jurisdiction and Judgments Act 1982] shall be deemed to be a maintenance order made by that court.]

**Appointment**

Commencement Order: SI 1958/2111.

**Amendment**

Sub-s (1A): inserted by the AJA 1970, s 27(3). Sub-ss (2), (2A): substituted by the AJA 1977, s 3, Sch 3, para 1. Sub-s (4): inserted by the MO(RE)A 1972, s 22(1), Schedule, para 4; words in square brackets substituted by the CJJA 1982, ss 15, 23, 36, Sch 12, Pt I.

**Definitions**

'Maintenance order' – see s 1(1A), and para **[2.32.3]** below.
'Registered' – see s 1(3), and para **[2.32.4]** below.
'Court of registration' – see s 1(3).

## [2.32.1]
## Keypoints

- Vertical transfer of maintenance orders between different court levels

- 'Maintenance orders' include lump sum orders
- The meaning of 'registered'
- Procedure

**[2.32.2]**
**Vertical transfer of maintenance orders between different court levels**

The scheme of the Act is to establish a system of vertical transfer of maintenance orders between different court levels, up and down. This is done by a process of registration of the original order in the transferee court (referred to in the Act as the 'court of registration'[1]). Although 'an order which is registered remains the order of the original court which made it'[2], for as long as the order remains registered the transferee court is treated for many purposes as if it had made the original order. In particular this is so as regards enforcement (subject to s 2A) and – to a lesser extent and subject to important qualifications in ss 4 and 4A – as regards variation. The scheme of the Act was most recently summarised in *K v M, M and L (Financial Relief: Foreign Orders)*[3].

The system operates only to enable orders made in the High Court or a county court to be transferred to a magistrates' court and orders made by a magistrates' court to be transferred to the High Court. It does not enable transfers between the High Court and the county court, which must be dealt with in the ordinary context of transfer of financial proceedings as a whole. Nor does it enable the transfer of a magistrates' court order to a county court.

The system of vertical transfer and registration of maintenance orders set out in the 1958 Act should be distinguished from the system of horizontal (geographic) transfer and registration of domestic (intra-national) UK maintenance orders (defined widely) under the MOA 1950, and from the registration of foreign (international) orders and transmission of UK orders under the MO(RE)A 1972. Note that orders registered under the MOA 1950 and/or the MO(RE)A 1972 are themselves capable of subsequent registration under the MOA 1958[4].

1 See the MOA 1958, s 1(3) at para **[2.32]** above.
2 Per Booth J in *Allen v Allen* [1985] FLR 107 at 113C, disapproved on a different point in *Berry v Berry* [1987] Fam 1, [1986] 2 All ER 948, CA.
3 [1998] 2 FLR 59 at 70C per Singer J; for the position of the Act see generally *Rayden and Jackson on Divorce and Family Matters* (17th edn, 1997), vol 1, paras 34.61 to 34.68.
4 See s 1(2), (2A) and (4) at para **[2.32]** above and para **[2.32.4]** below.

**[2.32.3]**
**'Maintenance orders' include lump sum orders**

In accordance with s 1(1A) the term 'maintenance order' includes orders 'for periodical or other payments' as defined in the Administration of Justice Act 1970, Sch 8. These include lump sums under the MCA 1973, Pt II; the DPMCA 1978, Pt I; the MFPA 1984, Pt III; and the ChA 1989.

The term also includes orders for costs, and for payment into court pending the conclusion of ancillary relief proceedings (following *Re Mordant; Mordant v Halls*[1]). Further, the term includes an order to pay school fees direct to a school[2]; and financial undertakings to pay, eg school fees[3]; and to pay (as yet unascertained) CGT[4].

1 [1997] 2 FCR 378, [1996] 1 FLR 334.
2 See *L v L (Payment of School Fees)* [1997] 3 FCR 520, sub nom *L v L (School Fees: Maintenance)* [1997] 2 FLR 252, CA.
3 *Symmons v Symmons* [1993] 1 FLR 317.
4 *M v M (Enforcement: Judgment Summons)* [1993] Fam Law 469.

**[2.32.4]**
**The meaning of 'registered'**

As defined in s 1(3) a 'registered' order means one registered under, and for the purposes of, MOA 1958. Note that the MO(RE)A 1972 provides a different scheme of registration, which applies to foreign orders, and that an order registered under the 1958 Act is not within the scheme of the 1972 Act[1]. An order registered under the MO(RE)A 1972 (or under the Civil Jurisdiction and Judgments Act 1982, which covers Brussels and Lugano Convention States) can subsequently be registered (ie transferred) also under the 1958 Act[2]. However, if an order is first registered under the 1958 Act and is then subsequently registered also under the 1972 Act, the registration under the 1958 Act must be cancelled in accordance with the MO(RE)A 1972, s 23(4). For provisions as to registration itself under the 1958 Act see s 2 (para **[2.33]** below), as to enforcement of registered orders see s 3 (para **[2.35]** below), as to variation see s 4 (para **[2.36]** below), and as to cancellation of registration see s 5 (para **[2.38]** below).

1 See the MO(RE)A 1972, ss 8(1) and 33(1).
2 See s 1(4) at para **[2.32]** above.

## [2.32.5]
### Procedure

The mechanics of the scheme are set out in ss 2 and 3 of the Act. The detailed procedure to be applied in the different respective court levels is set out in the FPR 1991, r 7.22 to 7.29[1] and the Magistrates' Courts (Maintenance Orders Act 1958) Rules 1959, SI 1959/3.

1 Set out at paras **[3.488]** to **[3.495]** below.

## [2.33]

### 2 Registration of orders

(1) A person entitled to receive payments under a High Court or county court order may apply for the registration of the order to the original court, and the court may, if it thinks fit, grant the application.

(2) Where an application for the registration of such an order is granted—

(a) no proceedings shall be begun, and no writ, warrant or other process shall be issued, for the enforcement of the order before the registration of the order or the expiration of the prescribed period from the grant of the application, whichever first occurs; and

(b) the original court shall, on being satisfied within the period aforesaid by the person who made the application that no such proceedings or process begun or issued before the grant of the application remain pending or in force, cause a certified copy of the order to be sent to the [justices' chief executive for] the magistrates' court acting for the petty sessions area in which the defendant appears to be;

but if at the expiration of the period aforesaid the original court has not been so satisfied, the grant of the application shall become void.

(3) A person entitled to receive payments under a magistrates' court order who considers that the order could be more effectively enforced if it were registered may apply for the registration of the order to the original court, and the court [may, if it thinks fit, grant the application].

[(3A) Without prejudice to subsection (3) of this section, where a magistrates' court order provides both for the payment of a lump sum and for the making of periodical payments, a person entitled to receive a lump sum under the order who considers that, so far as it relates to that sum, the order could be more effectively enforced if it were registered may apply to the original court for the registration of the order so far as it so relates, and the court may, if it thinks fit, grant the application.

(3B) Where an application under subsection (3A) of this section is granted in the case of a magistrates' court order, the provisions of this Part of this Act shall have effect in relation to that order as if so far as it relates to the payment of a lump sum it were a separate order.]

(4) Where an application for the registration of a magistrates' court order is granted—

(a) no proceedings for the enforcement of the order shall be begun before the registration takes place and no warrant or other process for the enforcement thereof shall be issued in consequence of any such proceedings begun before the grant of the application;

(b) … ; and

(c) the original court shall, on being satisfied in the prescribed manner that no process for the enforcement of the order issued before the grant of the application remains in force, cause a certified copy of the order to be sent to the prescribed officer of the High Court.

(5) The officer [of, or justices' chief executive for,] a court who receives a certified copy of an order sent to him under this section shall cause the order to be registered in that court.

[(6) Where a magistrates' court order is registered under this Part of this Act in the High Court, then—

(a) if payments under the magistrates' court order are required to be made (otherwise than to [a justices' chief executive]) by any method of payment falling within section 59(6) of the Magistrates' Courts Act 1980 (standing order, etc.), any order requiring payment by that method shall continue to have effect after registration;

(b) any order by virtue of which sums payable under the magistrates' court order are required to be paid to [a justices' chief executive] (whether or not by any method of payment falling within section 59(6) of that Act) on behalf of the person entitled thereto shall cease to have effect.

(6ZA) Where a High Court or county court order is registered under this Part of this Act in a magistrates' court, then—

(a) if a means of payment order (within the meaning of section 1(7) of the Maintenance Enforcement Act 1991) has effect in relation to the order in question, it shall continue to have effect after registration; and

(b) in any other case, the magistrates' court shall order that all payments to be made under the order in question (including any arrears accrued before registration) shall be made to [a justices' chief executive].

(6ZB) Any such order as to payment—

(a) as is referred to in paragraph (a) of subsection (6) of this section may be revoked, suspended, revived or varied by an exercise of the powers conferred by section 4A of this Act; and

(b) as is referred to in paragraph (a) or (b) of subsection (6ZA) of this section may be varied or revoked by an exercise of the powers conferred by section 3(2A) or (2B) or section 4(2A), (5A) or (5B) of this Act.

(6ZC) Where by virtue of the provisions of this section or any order under subsection (6ZA)(b) of this section payments under an order cease to be or become payable to [a justices' chief executive], the person liable to make the payments shall, until he is given the prescribed notice to that effect, be deemed to comply with the order if he makes payments in accordance with the order and any order under subsection (6ZA)(b) of this section of which he has received such notice.]

[(6A) In this section—

'High Court order' includes a maintenance order deemed to be made by the High Court by virtue of section 1(2) above, and

'magistrates' court order' includes a maintenance order deemed to be made by a magistrates' court by virtue of that subsection.]

(7) In this section 'certified copy' in relation to an order of a court means a copy certified by the proper officer of the court to be a true copy of the order or of the official record thereof.

**Appointment**

Commencement order: SI 1958/2111.

**Amendment**
Sub-ss (2), (4) to (6), (6ZA), (6ZC): AJA 1999, s 90(1), Sch 13. Sub-s (3): CJJA 1982, s 37, Sch 11. Sub-ss (3A), (3B): inserted by the CJJA 1982, s 37, Sch 11. Sub-ss (6), (6ZA) to (6ZC): substituted for sub-s (6) as originally enacted, by the MEA 1991, s 10, Sch 1.

**Definitions**
'Registration' – see s 1(3), and para **[2.32.4]** below.
'High Court order', 'magistrates' court order' – see s 2(6A).
'Prescribed period' in s 2(2)(a) – 14 days: FPR 1991, r 7.23 (at para **[3.489]** below).
'Original Court' – see s 1(3), and para **[2.32.1]** above.
'Certified copy' – as defined in s 2(7).
'Prescribed manner' in s 2(4)(c) – in accordance with Magistrates' Courts (Maintenance Orders Act 1958) Rules 1959, r 2(3) and (5).
'Prescribed officer of the High Court' in s24(c) – the Senior District Judge at the Principal Registry or such District Registrar as may be specified by the applicant: Magistrates' Courts (Maintenance Orders Act 1958) Rules 1959, rr 3, 25(4).
'Means of payment order' in s 2(6ZA) – standing order or other equivalent authority: MEA 1991, ss 4(a) and 5.
'Prescribed notice' in s 2(6ZC) – in Forms 8, 9 or 10 in the Schedule to the Magistrates' Courts (Maintenance Orders Act 1958) Rules 1959, r 5.

## [2.33.1]
## Keypoints

- Scheme of section
- Application for transfer (registration) to be made to original court
- Downward transfers
- Upward transfers
- Consequences of registration

## [2.33.2]
## Scheme of section

This section sets out the main structure for the system of registration: of High Court and county court orders (s 2(1) and (2)) and of magistrates' court orders (s 2(3) and (4)). In each case the application for registration is made to the original court and, if the application is granted, the original order is then transferred to, and registered in, the transferee court (s 2(5)). Consequential provisions for the different transferee courts are set out in s 2(6) (where a magistrates' court order is registered in the High Court) and s 2(6ZA) (where a High Court or county court order is registered in a magistrates' court).

For the procedure on an application for registration, see generally *Rayden and Jackson on Divorce and Family Matters* (17th edn, 1997), vol 1, para 34.63.

## [2.33.3]
## Application for transfer (registration) to be made to original court

The detailed procedure is set out in FPR 1991, r 7.22 to 7.26[1] (for the High Court and county court) and (for the magistrates' courts) in the Magistrates' Courts (Maintenance Orders Act 1958) Rules 1959. Note the Maintenance Orders Act 1950, s 18(3A):

> 'no court in England in which a maintenance order is registered under this Part of this Act shall enforce that order to the extent that it is for the time being registered in another court in England under Part 1 of the Maintenance Orders Act 1958.'

For a summary of the distinction between the MOA 1950 and the MOA 1958 see para **[2.32.1]** above.

The court hearing an application for registration under the MOA 1958 has a discretion whether or not to grant the application[2]. If the application is granted the court sends to the transferee court (the 'court of registration' as defined in s 1(3)) a certified copy of the original order.

1 Set out at paras **[3.488]** to **[3.492]** below.
2 See the MOA 1958, s 1(1) and (3) at para **[2.32]** above.

### [2.33.4]
### Downward transfers

On the grant of an application for registration of a High Court or a county court order in the magistrates' court, a certified copy of the original order must be sent for registration in the respondent's local magistrates' court[1].

Unless the original order is expressed to be payable by standing order (or an equivalent means of payment under the MEA 1991) the magistrates' court is obliged to order that payments shall be made through the court clerk[2]. The court has power to revoke or vary either form of order under s 2(6ZB)(b).

Note that on any subsequent cancellation of the registration under s 5, orders made under s 2(6ZA)(b) and means of payments orders cease to have effect[3]. Where a magistrates court makes a means of payment order under s 2(6ZA)(b) (or under similar provisions elsewhere in this Act) the clerk of the court is required to endorse on the maintenance order the means of payment ordered[4].

1 See the MOA 1958, s 2(2)(b) at para **[2.33]** above.
2 See the MOA 1958, s 2(6ZA)(b) at para **[2.33]** above.
3 See the MOA 1958, s 5(5) at para **[2.38]** below.
4 See the Magistrates' Courts (Maintenance Orders Act 1958) Rules 1959, SI 1959/3, r 5A.



### [2.33.5]
### Upward transfers

In contrast to the position as regards downward transfers, on the grant of an application for registration of a magistrates' court order in the High Court, a certified copy of the original order is sent to the High Court Registry of the applicant's choice[1]. Note that the applicant for registration of a magistrates' court order, being 'a person entitled … under a magistrates' court order' in s 2(3), may be the magistrates' court clerk, but only acting at the payee's request[2]. The payee is prima facie liable for any adverse award of costs[3].

Where a magistrates' court order makes both capital and maintenance provision, it is (at the payee's election) permissible to separate the maintenance and capital obligations for the purposes of registration, so that the part of the order which relates to maintenance continues to be payable (and enforceable) as a magistrates' court order but the part of the order which relates to capital is registered in the High Court and therefore enforceable as if made in the High Court[4].

1 See the MOA 1958, s 2(4)(c) at para **[2.33]** above.
2 See the MOA 1958, s 20(1) at para **[2.41]** below.
3 See the MOA 1958, s 20(1)(ii) at para **[2.42]** below.
4 See the MOA 1958, s 2(3A) and (3B) at para **[2.33]** above.

### [2.33.6]
### Consequences of registration

On the grant of an application (at any court-level) there is a temporary prohibition of any proceedings or process of enforcement in order to allow for the original order to be formally registered in the transferee court (ie the 'court of registration')[1]. However, it has been held that examination of a debtor under RSC Ord 48, r 1 (preserved in CPR 1998, Sch 1) does not amount to proceedings or process for the enforcement of the order[2].

Note also that, on the grant of an application for registration, any related attachment of earnings order made to secure maintenance payments ceases to have effect[3]. Further, an attachment of earnings order made to secure maintenance payments which has ceased to have effect by virtue of the AtEA 1971, s 11(1)(a) is not revived by the avoidance of the registration[4].

1 See the MOA 1958, s 2(2) and (4) at para **[2.33]** above.
2 *Fagot v Gaches* [1943] 1 KB 10, [1942] 2 All ER 476, CA.
3 See the AtEA 1971, s 11(1)(a) at para **[2.66]** below.
4 See the AtEA 1971, s 11(2) at para **[2.66]** below.

## [2.34]

### [2A Interest on sums recoverable under certain orders registered in the High Court]

[(1) Where, in connection with an application under section 2(3) of this Act for the registration of a magistrates' court order, the applicant shows in accordance with rules of court—

(a) that the order, though deemed for the purposes of section 1 of this Act to have been made by a magistrates' court in England, was in fact made in another part of the United Kingdom or in a county or territory outside the United Kingdom; and

(b) that, as regards any sum for whose payment the order provides, interest on that sum at a particular rate is, by the law of that part or of that country or territory, recoverable under the order from a particular date or time,

then, if the original court grants the application and causes a certified copy of the order to be sent to the prescribed officer of the High Court under section 2(4)(c) of this Act, it shall also cause to be sent to him a certificate in the prescribed form showing, as regards that sum, the rate of interest so recoverable and the date or time from which it is so recoverable.

(2) The officer of the court who receives a certificate sent to him under the preceding subsection shall cause the certificate to be registered in that court together with the order to which it relates.

(3) Where an order is registered together with a certificate under this section, then, subject to any provision made under the next following subsection, sums payable under the order shall carry interest at the rate specified in the certificate from the date or time so specified.

(4) Provision may be made by rules of court as to the manner in which and the periods by reference to which any interest payable by virtue of subsection (3) is to be calculated and paid, including provision for such interest to cease to accrue as from a prescribed date.

(5) Except as provided by this section sums payable under registered orders shall not carry interest.]

**Amendment**

Inserted by the CJJA 1982, s 37, Sch 11, Pt II.

**Definitions**

'Rules of Court' – Magistrates' Courts (Maintenance Orders Act 1958) Rules 1959, r 2.
'Certified copy' – as defined in s 2(7) at para **[2.33]** above.
'Prescribed officer of the High Court' – the Senior District Judge at the Principal Registry or such District Registrar as may be specified by the applicant: Magistrates' Courts (Maintenance Orders Act 1958) Rules 1959, rr 3, 25(4).
'Prescribed form' in sub-s (1) – in Form 4 in the Schedule to Magistrates' Courts (Maintenance Orders Act 1958) Rules 1959, r 5.
'Court of registration' – see s 1(3) at para **[2.32]** above.
'England' – includes Wales: see s 21(1) at para **[2.43]** below.
'Original court' – see s 1(3) at para **[2.32]** above.
'Registered' – as defined in s 1(3) at para **[2.32]** above.

## [2.34.1]
**Keypoint**

- Scheme of section

## [2.34.2]
**Scheme of section**

Because the MOA 1958 extends the scheme of registration also to UK maintenance orders made outside England and Wales[1], and to non-UK orders registered in the magistrates' court under the MO(RE)A 1972 (see s 1(4)), it is necessary to cover the situation where the 'foreign' law of the original order provides for interest not otherwise recognised in English law. This section prescribes the limits within which such orders may be registered and given effect under the MOA 1958, and provides that otherwise sums payable under registered orders shall not carry interest.

1 See the MOA 1958, s 1(2) and (2A) at para **[2.32]** above.



## [2.35]

### 3 Enforcement of registered orders

(1) Subject to the provisions of [section 2A of this Act and] this section, a registered order shall be enforceable in all respects as if it had been made by the court of registration and as if that court had had jurisdiction to make it; and proceedings for or with respect to the enforcement of a registered order may be taken accordingly.

[(2) [Subject to the provisions of subsections (2A) to (3) of this section], an order registered in a magistrates' court shall be enforceable as a magistrates' court maintenance order with the meaning of section 150(1) of the Magistrates' Courts Act 1980.]

[(2A) Where an order registered in a magistrates' court is an order other than one deemed to be made by the High Court by virtue of section 1(2) of this Act, section 76 of the Magistrates' Courts Act 1980 (enforcement of sums adjudged to be paid) shall have effect as if for subsections (4) to (6) there were substituted the following subsections—

> '(4) Where proceedings are brought for the enforcement of a magistrates' court maintenance order under this section, the court may vary the order by exercising one of its powers under paragraphs (a) to (d) of section 59(3) above.
>
> (5) In deciding which of the powers under paragraphs (a) to (d) of section 59(3) above it is to exercise, the court shall have regard to any representations made by the debtor and the creditor (which expressions have the same meaning as they have in section 59 above).
>
> (6) Subsection (4) of section 59 above shall apply for the purposes of subsection (4) above as it applies for the purposes of that section.'

(2B) Where an order registered in a magistrates' court is an order deemed to be made by the High Court by virtue of section 1(2) of this Act, sections 76 and 93 of the Magistrates' Courts Act 1980 (enforcement of sums adjudged to be paid and complaint for arrears) shall have effect subject to the modifications specified in subsections (2ZA) and (2ZB) of section 18 of the Maintenance Orders Act 1950 (enforcement of registered orders).]

(3) Where an order remains or becomes registered after the discharge of the order, no proceedings shall be taken by virtue of that registration except in respect of arrears which were due under the order at the time of the discharge and have not been remitted.

[(3A) Any person under an obligation to make payments under an order registered in a magistrates' court shall give notice of any change of address to the [justices' chief executive for] the court; and any person who without reasonable excuse fails to give such a notice shall be liable on summary conviction to a fine not exceeding level 2 on the standard scale ...]

(4) Except as provided by this section, no proceedings shall be taken for or with respect to the enforcement of a registered order.

**Appointment**
Commencement order: SI 1958/2111.

**Amendment**
Sub-s (1): CJJA 1982, s 37, Sch 11. Sub-s (2): substituted by the FLRA 1987, s 33(1), Sch 2, para 18. Sub-s (2): amended by the MEA 1991, s 10, Sch 1, para 8(1). Sub-ss (2A), (2B): inserted by the MEA 1991, s 10, Sch 1, para 8(2). Sub-s (3A): inserted by the MFPA 1984, s 46(1), Sch 1, para 4; amended by the AJA 1999, s 90(1), Sch 13. Sub-s (3A): amended by the SL(R)A 1993.

**Definitions**
'Registered' – see s 1(3) and para **[2.32.4]** above.
'Court of registration' – see s 1(3) at para **[2.32]** above.

### [2.35.1]
### Keypoints

- References to other Acts
- Appeals

### [2.35.2]
### References to other Acts

Paragraphs (a) to (d) of s 59(3) of the MCA 1980 (which include by reference also s 59(6)) empower the magistrates' courts to order that payment of periodical payments shall be made direct to the creditor, direct to the clerk, by standing order (or equivalent method requiring authority to pay a specific amount on specific dates), or by attachment of earnings.

The modifications in s 18(2ZA) of the MOA 1950 in relation to the MCA 1980, s 76 (enforcement of sums adjudged to be paid), are the provision of powers to direct payment to a magistrates' court clerk (not the creditor), by standing order (or equivalent method requiring authority to pay a specific amount on specific dates), or to make an attachment of earnings order. In relation to the MCA 1980, s 93 (complaint for arrears) the modifications in s 18(2ZB) of the MOA 1950, empower the court to direct payment to a magistrates' court clerk (not the creditor) by standing order (or equivalent method requiring authority to pay a specific amount on specific dates), or to make an attachment of earnings order, as preferred alternatives to imprisonment.

Where a magistrates' court makes a means of payment order under s 3(2A) or (2B) (or under similar provisions elsewhere in this Act) the clerk of the court is required to endorse on the maintenance order the means of payment ordered[1].

1 See the Magistrates' Courts (Maintenance Orders Act 1958) Rules 1959, r 5A

### [2.35.3]
### Appeals

As to appeal by way of case stated against any order or determination of justices with regard to the enforcement of an order registered in a magistrates' court, see the MCA 1980, s 111 and RSC Ord 56, r 5(2). The grounds for such an appeal are that the decision was wrong in law or in excess of jurisdiction. The time limit for applying for the case to be stated is 21 days after the day on which the decision was given. See also *Allen v Allen*[1], noted under s 4 (see para **[2.36]** below) and *Berry v Berry*[2] (which disapproved *Allen* in relation to appeals against a decision on the remission of arrears).

1 [1985] Fam 8, [1985] FLR 107.
2 [1987] Fam 1, [1986] 2 All ER 948, CA.

### [2.36]

**4 Variation of orders registered in magistrates' courts**

(1) The provisions of this section shall have effect with respect to the variation of orders registered in magistrates' courts, and references in this section to registered orders shall be construed accordingly.

(2) Subject to the following provisions of this section—

(a) the court of registration may exercise the same jurisdiction to vary any rate of payments specified by a registered order (other than jurisdiction in a case where a party to the order is not present in England when the application for variation is made) as is exercisable, apart from this subsection, by the original court; and

(b) a rate of payments specified by a registered order shall not be varied except by the court of registration or any other magistrates' court to which the jurisdiction conferred by the foregoing paragraph is extended by rules of court.



[(2A) The power of a magistrates' court to vary a registered order under subsection (2) of this section shall include power, if the court is satisfied that payment has not been made in accordance with the order, to vary the order by exercising one of its powers under paragraphs (a) to (d) of section 59(3) of the Magistrates' Courts Act 1980.

(2B) Subsection (4) of section 59 of that Act shall apply for the purposes of subsection (2A) of this section as it applies for the purposes of that section.

(2C) In deciding which of the powers under paragraphs (a) to (d) of section 59(3) of that Act it is to exercise, the court shall have regard to any representations made by the debtor and the creditor (which expressions have the same meaning as they have in section 59 of that Act).]

(3) …

(4) If it appears to the court to which an application is made by virtue of subsection (2) of this section for the variation of a rate of payments specified by a registered order [that it is for any reason] appropriate to remit the application to the original court, the first-mentioned court shall so remit the application, and the original court shall thereupon deal with the application as if the order were not registered.

(5) Nothing in subsection (2) of this section shall affect the jurisdiction of the original court to vary a rate of payments specified by a registered order if an application for the variation of that rate is made to that court—

(a) in proceedings for a variation of provisions of the order which do not specify a rate of payments; or

(b) at a time when a party to the order is not present in England.

[(5A) Subject to the following provisions of this section, subsections (4) to (11) of section 60 of the Magistrates' Courts Act 1980 (power of clerk and court to vary maintenance orders) shall apply in relation to a registered order (other than one deemed to be made by the High Court by virtue of section 1(2) of this Act) as they apply in relation to a maintenance order made by a magistrates' court (disregarding section 23(2) of the Domestic Proceedings and Magistrates' Courts Act 1978 and section 15(2) of the Children Act 1989) but—

(a) as if in subsection (8) after the words 'the court which may' there were inserted 'subject to subsection (10) below'; and

(b) as if for subsections (9) and (10) there were substituted the following subsections—

'(9) Subsection (4) of section 59 above shall apply for the purposes of subsection (8) above as it applies for the purposes of that section.

(10) In deciding which of the powers under paragraphs (a) to (d) of section 59(3) above it is to exercise, the court shall have regard to any representations made by the debtor and the creditor.'

(5B) Subject to the following provisions of this section, subsections (4) to (11) of section 60 of the Magistrates' Courts Act 1980 (power of clerk and court to vary maintenance orders) shall apply in relation to a registered order deemed to be made by the High Court by virtue of section 1(2) of this Act as they apply in relation to a maintenance order made by a magistrates' court (disregarding section 23(2) of the Domestic Proceedings and Magistrates' Courts Act 1978 and section 15(2) of the Children Act 1989) but—

(a) as if subsection (4) for paragraph (b) there were substituted—

'(b) payments under the order are required to be made to [a justices' chief executive] by any method of payment falling within section 59(6) above (standing order, etc)';

…

(b) as if in subsection (5) for the words 'to the [justices' chief executive for the court'] there were substituted 'in accordance with paragraph (a) of subsection (9) below';

(c) as if in subsection (7), paragraph (c) and the word 'and' immediately preceding it were omitted;

(d) as if in subsection (8) for the words 'paragraphs (a) to (d) of section 59(3) above' there were substituted 'subsection (9) below';

(e) as if for subsections (9) and (10) there were substituted the following subsections—

'(9) The powers of the court are—

(a) the power to order that payments under the order be made directly to [a justices' chief executive];

(b) the power to order that payments under the order be made to [a justices' chief executive] by such method of payment falling within section 59(6) above (standing order, etc) as may be specified;

(c) the power to make an attachment of earnings order under the Attachment of Earnings Act 1971 to secure payments under the order.

(10) In deciding which of the powers under subsection (9) above it is to exercise, the court shall have regard to any representations made by the debtor.

(10A) Subsection (4) of section 59 above (power of court to require debtor to open account) shall apply for the purposes of subsection (9) above as it applies for the purposes of that section but as if for paragraph (a) there were substituted—

'(a) the court proposes to exercise its power under paragraph (b) of section 60(9) below'.]

(6) No application for any variation of a registered order shall be made to any court while proceedings for any variation of the order are pending in any other court.

[(6A) [Except as provided by subsection (5B) of this section] no application for any variation in respect of a registered order shall be made to any court in respect of an order made by the Court of Session or the High Court in Northern Ireland and registered in that court in accordance with the provisions of this Part of this Act by virtue of section 1(2) above.]

[(6B) No application for any variation of a registered order shall be made to any court in respect of an order for periodical or other payments made under Part III of the Matrimonial and Family Proceedings Act 1984.]

(7) Where a magistrates' court, in exercise of the jurisdiction conferred by subsection (2) of this section, varies or refuses to vary a registered order, an appeal from the variation or refusal shall lie to the High Court; …

**Appointment**

Commencement order: SI 1958/2111.

**Amendment**

Sub-ss (2A) to (2C): inserted by the MEA 1991, s 10, Sch 1, para 9. Sub-s (3): repealed by the AJA 1970, ss 48(2), 54, Sch 11. Sub-s (4): AJA 1970, s 48(3). Sub-ss (5A), (5B): inserted by the MEA 1991, s 10, Sch 1, para 9. Sub-s (5B): amended by the AJA 1999, ss 90(1), 106, Sch 13. Sub-s (6A): inserted by the AJA 1977, s 3, Sch 3. Sub-s (6A): amended by the MEA 1991, s 10, Sch 1. Sub-s (6B): inserted by the MFPA 1984, s 46(1), Sch 1. Sub-s (7): AJA 1977, s 32, Sch 5.

**Definitions**

'Registered' – see s 1(3) and para **[2.32.4]** above.
'Court of registration' – see s 1(3) at para **[2.32]** above.
'England' – includes Wales: see s 21(1) at para **[2.43]** below.
'Original court' – see s 1(3) at para **[2.32]** above.

**[2.36.1]**

**Keypoints**

- Concurrent jurisdiction to vary orders registered in magistrates' court
- Same jurisdiction
- References to other Acts
- Application
- Appeals

**[2.36.2]**

**Concurrent jurisdiction to vary orders registered in magistrates' court**

There are three points to note. The first is that, in contrast to the position in relation to enforcement (see above), the original court (High Court or county court) retains its jurisdiction to vary the original order, and that that jurisdiction is exclusive where either the application for variation concerns provisions other than the rate of payment or one party is not present in England[1].

The second point is that the magistrates' court as the court of registration only has power to vary the rate of payments and the method of payments[2], not (for example) the term of an order.

Thirdly, a magistrates' court has the power to remit the application to the original court (High Court or county court) if, for any reason, it considers it appropriate to do so[3]. For circumstances in which a case should be remitted, see *Gsell v Gsell*[4] and (in relation to complexity and discovery) *Goodall v Jolly*[5].

For a discussion of this topic, see generally *Rayden and Jackson on Divorce and Family Matters* (17th edn, 1997), vol 1, para 34.66.

1 See MOA 1958, s 4(5) at para **[2.36]** above.
2 See MOA 1958, s 4(2A)–(2C) at para **[2.36]** above.
3 See MOA 1958, s 4(4) at para **[2.36]** above and the Magistrates' Courts (Maintenance Orders Act 1958) Rules 1959, r 6.
4 [1971] 1 All ER 559, [1971] 1 WLR 225n.
5 [1984] FLR 143.

**[2.36.3]**

**Same jurisdiction**

If the magistrates' court hears the application (as to which see above), it is obliged to exercise the same jurisdiction, that is 'act on the same principles and considerations'[1] as the original court[2]. The proper approach to be taken on such an application to vary was recently considered in *Hackshaw v Hackshaw*[3].

A variation may be back-dated at least to the date of the complaint[4]; and (at least in the High Court) potentially to the date of the original order[5].

1 Per Marshall J in *Miller v Miller* [1961] P 1, [1960] 3 All ER 115.
2 See MOA 1958, s 4(2)(a) at para **[2.36]** above. See also *Allen v Allen* [1985] Fam 8, [1985] FLR 107, but note that that case was disapproved (on a different point) in *Berry v Berry* [1987] Fam 1, [1986] 2 All ER 948, CA.
3 [1999] 2 FLR 876 per Wilson J at 879H.
4 *Moon v Moon* [1980] FLR 115.
5 *Morley-Clarke v Jones (HM Inspector of Taxes)* [1986] Ch 311, [1985] FLR 242.

**[2.36.4]**

**References to other Acts**

Paragraphs (a) to (d) of s 59(3) of the MCA 1980 (which include by reference also s 59(6)) empower the magistrates' courts to order that payment of periodical payments shall be made direct to the creditor, direct to the clerk, by standing order (or equivalent method requiring authority to pay a specific amount on specific dates), or by attachment of earnings. Section 59(4) gives the court power, where a person has unreasonably failed to open an account for the purpose of being able to satisfy a requirement to make payments by standing order, to order a person to open such an account.

Section 23(2) of the DPMCA 1978 and s 15(2) of the ChA 1989 both disapply the power of the court under MCA 1980, s 60 to vary, revoke and revive financial orders. Both provisions are specifically disregarded by s 4(5A) and (5B) of the MOA 1958.

Where a magistrates' court makes a means of payment order under the MOA 1958, s 4(2A), (5A) or (5B) (or under similar provisions elsewhere in this Act) the clerk of the court is required to endorse on the maintenance order the means of payment ordered[1].

1 See the Magistrates' Courts (Maintenance Orders Act 1958) Rules 1959, r 5A

## [2.36.5]
### Application

An application to a magistrates' court to vary an order registered in that court is by way of complaint[1].

1 See the MOA 1958, s 20(2) at para **[2.42]** below.

## [2.36.6]
### Appeals

Appeal against a magistrates' court variation or refusal to vary lies direct to the High Court[1]. It is heard by a Divisional Court of the Family Division[2]. The notice of appeal must be served, and the appeal entered, within six weeks after the date of the order appealed against. The appeal is not a hearing of the matter afresh[3].

An appeal against a refusal to remit arrears is not within s 4(7) of the MOA 1958[4]. Accordingly, in relation to a decision on the remission of arrears, the only appeal from a magistrates' court is by way of case stated under the MCA 1980, s 111 and RSC Ord 56, r 5(2). The grounds for such an appeal are that the decision was wrong in law or in excess of jurisdiction. The time limit for applying for the case to be stated is 21 days after the day on which the decision was given[5].

1 See the MOA 1958, s 4(7) at para **[2.36]** above.
2 FPR 1991, r 7.28 (applying also r 8.2); set out at para **[3.494]** below.
3 See *Hackshaw v Hackshaw* [1999] 2 FLR 876 per Wilson J at 879B.
4 See *Berry v Berry* [1987] Fam 1, [1987] 1 FLR 105 disapproving (on this point) *Allen v Allen* [1985] Fam 8, [1985] FLR 107. See also *K v M, M and L (Financial Relief: Foreign Orders)* [1998] 2 FLR 59 per Singer J at 66E/F.
5 See the analysis in *P v P (Periodical Payments: Appeals)* [1995] 1 FLR 563.

## [2.37]

### [4A Variation etc of orders registered in the High Court

[(1) The provisions of this section shall have effect with respect to orders registered in the High Court other than maintenance orders deemed to be made by a magistrates' court by virtue of section 1(4) of this Act, and the reference in subsection (2) of this section to a registered order shall be construed accordingly.

(2) The High Court may exercise the same powers in relation to a registered order as are exercisable by the High Court under section 1 of the Maintenance Enforcement Act 1991 in relation to a qualifying periodical maintenance order (within the meaning of that section) which has been made by the High Court, including the power under subsection (7) of that section to revoke, suspend, revive or vary—

(a) any such order as is referred to in paragraph (a) of section 2(6) of this Act which continues to have effect by virtue of that paragraph; and

(b) any means of payment order (within the meaning of section 1(7) of that Act of 1991) made by virtue of the provisions of this section.]

**Amendment**

Inserted by the MEA 1991, s 10, Sch 1, para 10.

**Definitions**

'Registered' – see s 1(3) at para **[2.32.4]** above.

**[2.37.1]**
**Keypoints**
- References to other Acts

**[2.37.2]**
**References to other Acts**

Section 1 of MEA 1991 mirrors s 59(6) of the MCA 1980 in terms of giving power to make means of payment orders (standing orders etc, see above) and also gives the court power to make attachment of earnings orders. By s 2(6)(a) of the MOA 1958 a means of payment order attached to the original order by a magistrates' court prior to registration continues to have effect notwithstanding registration in the High Court. By s 2(6ZB)(a) of the MOA 1958 such an order may be 'revoked, suspended, revived or varied by an exercise of the powers conferred' on the High Court by s 4A.

**[2.38]**

### 5 Cancellation of registration

(1) If a person entitled to receive payments under a registered order desires the registration to be cancelled, he may give notice under this section.

(2) Where the original court varies or discharges an order registered in a magistrates' court, the original court may, if it thinks fit, give notice under this section.

(3) Where [the original court] discharges an order registered in the High Court and it appears to [the original court] whether by reason of the remission of arrears by that court or otherwise, that no arrears under the order remain to be recovered, [the original court] shall be give notice under this section.

(4) Notice under this section shall be given to the court of registration; and where such notice is given—

- (a) no proceedings for the enforcement of the registered order shall be begun before the cancellation of the registration and no writ, warrant or other process for the enforcement thereof shall be issued in consequence of any such proceedings begun before the giving of the notice;
- (b) … ; and
- (c) the court of registration shall cancel the registration on being satisfied in the prescribed manner—
  - (i) that no process for the enforcement of the registered order issued before the giving of the notice remains in force; and
  - (ii) in the case of an order registered in a magistrates' court, that no proceedings for the variation of the order are pending in a magistrates' court.

[(4A) For the purposes of a notice under subsection (2) or (3) above—

'court of registration' includes any court in which an order is registered under Part II of the Maintenance Orders Act 1950, and

'registration' includes registration under that Act.]

[(5) On the cancellation of the registration of a High Court or county court order—

- (a) any order which requires payments under the order in question to be made (otherwise than to [a justices' chief executive]) by any method of payment falling within section 59(6) of the Magistrates' Courts Act 1980 or section 1(5) of the Maintenance Enforcement Act 1991 (standing order, etc) shall continue to have effect; and
- (b) any order made under section 2(6ZA)(b) of this Act or by virtue of the powers conferred by section 3(2A) or (2B) or section 4(2A), (5A) or (5B) of this Act and which requires payments under the order in question to be made to [a justices' chief executive] (whether or not by any method of payment falling within section 59(6) of the Magistrates' Courts Act 1980) shall cease to have effect;

but, in a case falling within paragraph (b) of this subsection, until the defendant receives the prescribed notice of the cancellation he shall be deemed to comply with the High Court or county court order if he makes payment in accordance with any such order as is referred to in paragraph (b) of this subsection which was in force immediately before the cancellation and of which he has notice.

(6) On the cancellation of the registration of a magistrates' court order—

(a) any order which requires payments under the magistrates' court order to be made by any method of payment falling within section 59(6) of the Magistrates' Courts Act 1980 or section 1(5) of the Maintenance Enforcement Act 1991 (standing order, etc) shall continue to have effect; and

(b) in any other case, payments shall become payable to the [justices' chief executive for] the original court;

but, in a case falling within paragraph (b) of this subsection, until the defendant receives the prescribed notice of the cancellation he shall be deemed to comply with the magistrates' court order if he makes payments in accordance with any order which was in force immediately before the cancellation and of which he has notice.

(7) In subsections (5) and (6) of this section 'High Court order' and 'magistrates' court order' shall be construed in accordance with section 2(6A) of this Act.]

**Appointment**

Commencement order: SI 1958/2111.

**Amendment**

Sub-s (3): AJA 1977, s 3, Sch 3. Sub-s (4): AJA 1999, ss 97(1), 106, Sch 15. Sub-s (4A): inserted by the AJA 1977, s 3, Sch 3. Sub-ss (5) to (7): substituted for sub-s (5) as originally enacted, by the MEA 1991, s 10, Sch 1. Sub-ss (5), (6): AJA 1999, s 90(1), Sch 13.

**Definitions**

'Person entitled' – see s 20(1) at para **[2.42]** below.
'Registered' – see s 1(3) at para **[2.32.4]** above, and s 5(4A).
'Original court' – s 1(3) at para **[2.32]** above.
'Court of registration' – see s 1(3) at para **[2.32]** above, and s 5(4A).
'Proceedings for enforcement' – see para **[2.33.1]** above.
'High Court order/magistrates court order' – see s 2(6A) at para **[2.33]** above.
'Defendant' – see s 21(1) at para **[2.43]** below.
'Prescribed notice' – in Form 10 of the Schedule to the Magistrates' Courts (Maintenance Orders Act 1958) Rules 1959, r 5(3).

## [2.38.1]
## Keypoints

- Consequences of cancellation

## [2.38.2]
## Consequences of cancellation

On the giving of notice under this section an attachment of earnings order to secure maintenance payments ceases to have effect[1]; compare the equivalent provisions on registration noted under s 2 above.

For a discussion of this topic, see generally *Rayden and Jackson on Divorce and Family Matters* (17th edn, 1997), vol 1, para 34.68.

1 See the AtEA 1971, s 11(1)(b) at para **[2.66]** below.

[2.39]

PART III
MISCELLANEOUS AND SUPPLEMENTAL

## 17 Prohibition of committal more than once in respect of same arrears

'Where a defendant has been imprisoned or otherwise detained under an order or warrant of commitment issued in respect of his failure to pay a sum due under a maintenance order, then, notwithstanding anything in this Act, no such order or warrant (other than a warrant of which the issue has been postponed under paragraph (ii) of subsection (5) of the next following section) shall thereafter be issued in respect of that sum or any part thereof.

**Appointment**
Commencement order: SI 1958/2111.

**Definitions**
'Defendant' – see s 21(1) at para **[2.43]** below.
'Maintenance order' – see s 1(1A) at para **[2.32]** above (and Keypoint at para **[2.32.2]**).

[2.40]

## 18 Powers of magistrates to review committals, etc

(1) Where, for the purpose of enforcing a maintenance order, a magistrates' court has exercised its power under [subsection 2 of section 77 of the Magistrates' Courts Act 1980], or this section to postpone the issue of a warrant of commitment and under the terms of the postponement the warrant falls to be issued, then—

(a) the warrant shall not be issued except in pursuance of subsection (2) or paragraph (a) of subsection (3) of this section; and
(b) the [justices' chief executive for] the court shall give notice to the defendant stating that if the defendant considers there are grounds for not issuing the warrant he may make an application to the court in the prescribed manner requesting that the warrant shall not be issued and stating those grounds.

(2) If no such application is received by the [justices' chief executive for] the court within the prescribed period, any justice of the peace acting for the same petty sessions area as the court may issue the warrant of commitment at any time after the expiration of that period; and if such an application is so received any such justice may, after considering the statements contained in the application—

(a) if he is of opinion that the application should be further considered, refer it to the court;
(b) if he is not of that opinion, issue the warrant forthwith;

and when an application is referred to the court under this subsection, the [justices' chief executive for] the court shall give to the defendant and the person in whose favour the maintenance order in question was made notice of the time and place appointed for the consideration of the application by the court.

(3) On considering an application referred to it under the last foregoing subsection the court shall, unless in pursuance of subsection (6) of this section it remits the whole of the sum in respect of which the warrant could otherwise be issued, either—

(a) issue the warrant; or
(b) further postpone the issue thereof until such time and on such conditions, if any, as the court thinks just; or
(c) if in consequence of any change in the circumstances of the defendant the court considers it appropriate so to do, order that the warrant shall not be issued in any event.

(4) A defendant who is for the time being imprisoned or otherwise detained under a warrant of commitment issued by a magistrates' court for the purpose of enforcing a maintenance order, and who is not detained otherwise than for the enforcement of such an order, may make an application to the court in the prescribed manner requesting that the warrant shall be cancelled and stating the grounds of the application; and thereupon any justice of the peace acting for the same petty sessions area as the court may, after considering the statements contained in the application—

(a) if he is of opinion that the application should be further considered, refer it to the court;

(b) if he is not of that opinion, refuse the application;

and when an application is referred to the court under this subsection, the [justices' chief executive for] the court shall give to the person in charge of the prison or other place in which the defendant is detained and the person in whose favour the maintenance order in question was made notice of the time and place appointed for the consideration of the application by the court.

(5) On considering an application referred to it under the last foregoing subsection, the court shall, unless in pursuance of the next following subsection it remits the whole of the sum in respect of which the warrant was issued or such part thereof as remains to be paid, either—

(a) refuse the application; or

(b) if the court is satisfied that the defendant is unable to pay, or to make any payment or further payment towards, the sum aforesaid and if it is of opinion that in all the circumstances of the case the defendant ought not to continue to be detained under the warrant, order that the warrant shall cease to have effect when the person in charge of the prison or other place aforesaid is informed of the making of the order;

and where the court makes an order under paragraph (b) of this subsection, it may if it thinks fit also—

(i) fix a term of imprisonment in respect of the sum aforesaid or such part thereof as remains to be paid, being a term not exceeding so much of the term of the previous warrant as, after taking into account any reduction thereof by virtue of the next following subsection, remained to be served at the date of the order; and

(ii) postpone the issue of a warrant for the commitment of the defendant for that term until such time and on such conditions, if any, as the court thinks just.

(6) On considering an application under this section in respect of a warrant or a postponed warrant, the court may, if the maintenance order in question is an affiliation order or an order enforceable as an affiliation order, remit the whole or any part of the sum due under the order; and where the court remits the sum or part of the sum in respect of which the warrant was issued or the postponed warrant could have been issued, [section 79 of the Magistrates' Courts Act 1980] (which provides that on payment of the sum for which imprisonment has been ordered by a magistrates' court the order shall cease to have effect and that on payment of part of that sum the period of detention shall be reduced proportionately) shall apply as if payment of that sum or part had been made as therein mentioned.

(7) Where notice of the time and place appointed for the consideration of an application is required by this section to be given to the defendant or the person in whose favour the maintenance order in question was made and the defendant or, as the case may be, that person does not appear at that time and place, the court may proceed with the consideration of the application in his absence.

(8) A notice required by this section to be given by the [justices' chief executive for] a magistrates' court to any person shall be deemed to be given to that person if it is sent by registered post addressed to him at his last known address, notwithstanding that the notice is returned as undelivered or is for any other reason not received by that person.

**Appointment**
Commencement order: SI 1958/2111.

**Amendment**
Sub-ss (1), (6): MCA 1980, s 154, Sch 7; AJA 1999, s 90(1), Sch 13. Sub-ss (2), (4), (8): AJA 1999, s 90(1), Sch 13.

**Definitions**
'Maintenance order' – see s 1(1A) at para **[2.32]** above (and Keypoint at para **[2.32.3]**).
'Notice' – see s 18(8): actual delivery is not required.
'Defendant' – see s 21(1) at para **[2.43]** below.
'Prescribed manner' – Magistrates' Courts (Maintenance Orders Act 1958) Rules 1959, r 22.
'Prescribed period' – eight days beginning with the day on which the clerk sends the notice: Magistrates' Courts (Maintenance Orders Act 1958) Rules 1959, r 22(3).



### [2.40.1]
### Keypoint

- Effect of section

### [2.40.2]
### Effect of section

This section provides for the review of committals, particularly in order to take account of changed circumstances[1].

See also *Murbarak v Murbarak*[2], also reported as *Mubarak v Mubarak*[3], noted at para **[2.5.3]** above, for the implications of the Human Rights Act 1998.

For a discussion of this topic, see generally *Rayden and Jackson on Divorce and Family Matters* (17th edn, 1997), vol 1, paras 49.71 and 49.72.

1 See *James v James* [1964] P 303, [1963] 2 All ER 465; and *Wood v Warley Justices* (1974) Fam Law 130.
2 [2001] 1 FCR 193, [2001] 1 FLR 698, CA.
3 [2001] 1 FLR 673.

### [2.41]

#### *19 Revocation and variation of Orders in Council under 10 & 11 Geo 5 c 33, s 12*

*Her Majesty may by Order in Council revoke or vary any Order in Council made under section twelve of the Maintenance Orders (Facilities for Enforcement) Act 1920 (which provides for the extension of that Act by Order in Council to certain oversea territories), and an Order under this section may contain such incidental, consequential and transitional provisions as Her Majesty considers expedient for the purposes of that Act.*

**Appointment**
Commencement order: SI 1958/2111.

**Amendment**
Prospectively repealed by the MO(RE)A 1972, s 22(2)(c), as from a day to be appointed.

### [2.42]

#### 20 Special provisions as to magistrates' courts

(1) Notwithstanding anything in this Act, [a justices' chief executive] who is entitled to receive payments under a maintenance order for transmission to another person shall not apply for the registration of the maintenance order under Part I of this Act or give

notice in relation to the order in pursuance of subsection (1) of section five thereof unless he is requested in writing to do so by a person entitled to receive the payments through him; and where [a justices' chief executive is] requested as aforesaid—

(i) he shall comply with the request unless it appears to him unreasonable in the circumstances to do so;

(ii) the person by whom the request was made shall have the same liabilities for all the costs properly incurred in or about any proceedings taken in pursuance of the request as if the proceedings had been taken by that person.

(2) An application to a magistrates' court by virtue of subsection (2) of section four of this Act for the variation of a maintenance order shall be made by complaint.

(3)–(7) …

(8) For the avoidance of doubt it is hereby declared that a complaint may be made to enforce payment of a sum due and unpaid under a maintenance order notwithstanding that a previous complaint has been made in respect of that sum or a part thereof and whether or not an order was made in pursuance of the previous complaint.

**Appointment**

Commencement order: SI 1958/2111.

**Amendment**

Sub-ss (1), (2), (8): AtEA 1971, ss 27, 29, Schs 5, 6. Sub-s (1): AJA 1999, s 90(1), Sch 13. Sub-ss (3) to (5), (7): repealed by the AtEA 1971, s 29(2), Sch 6. Sub-s (6): repealed by the MCA 1980, s 154, Sch 9.

**Definitions**

'Maintenance order' – see s 1(1A) at para **[2.32]** above (and Keypoint at para **[2.32.3]**).

## [2.42.1]
### Keypoint

- Limitation of clerk's powers

## [2.42.2]
### Limitation of clerk's powers

This section limits the powers of the clerk to act on behalf of the person in whose favour a maintenance order has been made. It also makes that person prima facie liable for the costs consequences of such actions.

## [2.43]

### 21 Interpretation etc

(1) In this Act, unless the context otherwise requires, the following expressions have the following meanings—

… 'magistrates' court' [has the meaning assigned to it by the Magistrates' Courts Act 1980 and] the reference to that Act in [subsection (2) of section 148 thereof] shall be construed as including a reference to this Act;

…

'defendant', in relation to a maintenance order or a related attachment of earnings order, means the person liable to make payments under the maintenance order;

…

'England' includes Wales;

…

'prescribed' means prescribed by rules of court;

…

'rules of court', in relation to a magistrates' court, means rules under section fifteen of the Justices of the Peace Act 1949.

(2) Any reference in this Act to a person entitled to receive payments under a maintenance order is a reference to a person entitled to receive such payments either directly or through another person or for transmission to another person.

(3) Any reference in this Act to proceedings relating to an order includes a reference to proceedings in which the order may be made.

(4) Any reference in this Act to costs incurred in proceedings relating to a maintenance order shall be construed, in the case of a maintenance order made by the High Court, as a reference to such costs as are included in an order for costs relating solely to that maintenance order.

(5) …

(6) Any reference in this Act to any enactment is a reference to that enactment as amended by or under any subsequent enactment.

**Appointment**

Commencement order: SI 1958/2111.

**Amendment**

Sub-s (1): AJA 1970, s 54, Sch 11; MCA 1980, s 154, Sch 7; FLRA 1987, s 33(4), Sch 4; AJA 1999, ss 76(2), 106, Schs 10, 15. Sub-s (5): repealed by the AJA 1970, s 54, Sch 11.

**Definitions**

'Maintenance order' – see s 1(1A) at para **[2.32]** above and Keypoint at para **[2.32.3]**.



**[2.44]**

## 23 Short title, extent, commencement and repeals

(1) This Act may be cited as the Maintenance Orders Act 1958.

[(2) The following provisions of this Act, namely—

section 2;

[section 2A]

section 5(2), (3), (4) and (4A);

extend to Scotland and Northern Ireland.

(2A) Section 20(3)(a) above extends to Northern Ireland.

(2B) Subject to subsections (2) and (2A) above, this Act extends only to England.]

(3) This Act shall come into operation on such date as the Secretary of State may by order made by statutory instrument, appoint; and different dates may be so appointed for the purposes of different provisions of this Act.

(4) Subsection (2) of section eight of the Guardianship of Infants Act 1925 and section ten of the Affiliation Proceedings Act 1957 are hereby repealed; but nothing in this subsection shall affect any order in force or deemed to be in force under either of those provisions at the commencement of this subsection, and any such order may be discharged or varied as if this subsection had not been passed.

**Appointment**

Commencement order: SI 1958/2111.

**Amendment**

Sub-s (2): substituted, together with sub-ss (2A), (2B) for sub-s (2) as originally enacted, by the AJA 1977, s 3, Sch 3, para 5, words in square brackets substituted by the CJJA 1982, ss 15, 23, 36, Sch 12, Pt III. Sub-ss (2A), (2B): substituted, together with sub-s (2) for sub-s (2) as originally enacted, by the AJA 1977, s 3, Sch 3, para 5.

**Definitions**

'England' – includes Wales: see s 21(1) at para **[2.43]** above.

'Order under this section' – Maintenance Orders Act 1958 (Commencement) Order 1958, SI 1958/2111, bringing this Act into operation on 16 February 1959.

# Matrimonial Causes (Property and Maintenance) Act 1958



Contents



*An Act to enable the power of the court in matrimonial proceedings to order alimony, maintenance or the securing of a sum of money to be exercised at any time after a decree; to provide for the setting aside of dispositions of property made for the purpose of reducing the assets available for satisfying such an order; to enable the court after the death of a party to a marriage which has been dissolved or annulled to make provision out of his estate in favour of the other party; and to extend the powers of the court under section seventeen of the Married Women's Property Act 1882*

[7th July 1958]

**[2.45]**

## 7 Extension of s 17 of Married Women's Property Act 1882

(1) Any right of a wife, under section seventeen of the Married Women's Property Act 1882 to apply to a judge of the High Court or of a county court, in any question between husband and wife as to the title to or possession of property, shall include the right to make such an application where it is claimed by the wife that her husband has had in his possession or under his control—

- (a) money to which, or to a share of which, she was beneficially entitled (whether by reason that it represented the proceeds of property to which, or to an interest in which, she was beneficially entitled, or for any other reason), or
- (b) property (other than money) to which, or to an interest in which, she was beneficially entitled,

and that either that money or other property has ceased to be in his possession or under his control or that she does not know whether it is still in his possession or under his control.

(2) Where, on an application made to a judge of the High Court or of a county court under the said section seventeen, as extended by the preceding subsection, the judge is satisfied—

- (a) that the husband has had in his possession or under his control money or other property as mentioned in paragraph (a) or paragraph (b) of the preceding subsection, and
- (b) that he has not made to the wife, in respect of that money or other property, such payment or disposition as would have been appropriate in the circumstances,

the power to make orders under that section shall be extended in accordance with the next following subsection.

(3) Where the last preceding subsection applies, the power to make orders under the said section seventeen shall include power for the judge to order the husband to pay to the wife—

(a) in a case falling within paragraph (a) of subsection (1) of this section, such sum in respect of the money to which the application relates, or the wife's share thereof, as the case may be, or

(b) in a case falling within paragraph (b) of the said subsection (1), such sum in respect of the value of the property to which the application relates, or the wife's interest therein, as the case may be,

as the judge may consider appropriate.

(4) Where on an application under the said section seventeen as extended by this section it appears to the judge that there is any property which—

(a) represents the whole or part of the money or property in question, and

(b) is property in respect of which an order could have been made under that section if an application had been made by the wife thereunder in a question as to the title to or possession of that property,

the judge (either in substitution for or in addition to the making of an order in accordance with the last preceding subsection) may make any order under that section in respect of that property which he could have made on such an application as is mentioned in paragraph (b) of this subsection.

(5) The preceding provisions of this section shall have effect in relation to a husband as they have effect in relation to a wife, as if any reference to the husband were a reference to the wife and any reference to the wife were a reference to the husband.

[(6) Any power of a judge which is exercisable on an application under the said section seventeen shall be exercisable in relation to an application made under that section as extended by this section.]

(7) For the avoidance of doubt it is hereby declared that any power conferred by the said section seventeen to make orders with respect to any property includes power to order a sale of the property.

**Appointment**

Commencement order: SI 1958/2080.

**Amendment**

Sub-s (6): substituted by the MFPA 1984, s 46(1), Sch 1.

## [2.45.1]
### Keypoints

- Power to order sale

## [2.45.2]
### Power to order sale

This section specifically provides that the court may order the sale of a property under s 17 of the MWPA 1882[1].

See generally *Rayden and Jackson on Divorce and Family Matters* (17th edn, 1997), vol 1, para 29.8.

1 See *Rawlings v Rawlings* [1964] P 398, [1964] 2 All ER 804, CA for a case where sale with vacant possession was ordered against the wishes of one co-owner.

## [2.46]

### 8 Interpretation

(1) In this Act, except in so far as the context otherwise requires, the following expressions have the meanings hereby assigned to them respectively, that is to say:—

'disposition' does not include any provision contained in a will, but, with that exception, includes any conveyance, assurance or gift of property of any description, whether made by an instrument or otherwise;

'property' means any real or personal property, any estate or interest in real or personal property, any money, any negotiable instrument, debt or other chose in action, and any other right or interest whether in possession or not;

'will' includes a codicil.

(2) Except in so far as the context otherwise requires, any reference in this Act to an enactment shall be construed as a reference to that enactment as amended by or under any other enactment.

**Appointment**
Commencement order: SI 1958/2080.



**[2.47]**

### 9 Short title, commencement and extent

(1) This Act may be cited as the Matrimonial Causes (Property and Maintenance) Act 1958.

(2) This Act shall come into operation on such day as may be appointed by the Lord Chancellor by an order made by statutory instrument.

(3) This Act shall not extend to Scotland or to Northern Ireland.

**Appointment**
Commencement order: SI 1958/2080.

# Matrimonial Proceedings and Property Act 1970



## Contents



*An Act to make fresh provision for empowering the court in matrimonial proceedings to make orders ordering either spouse to make financial provision for, or transfer property to, the other spouse or a child of the family, orders for the variation of ante-nuptial and post-nuptial settlements, orders for the custody and education of children and orders varying, discharging or suspending orders made in such proceedings; to make other amendments of the law relating to matrimonial proceedings; to abolish the right to claim restitution of conjugal rights; to declare what interest in property is acquired by a spouse who contributes to its improvement; to make provision as to a spouse's rights of occupation under section 1 of the Matrimonial Homes Act 1967 in certain cases; to extend section 17 of the Married Women's Property Act 1882 and section 7 of the Matrimonial Causes (Property and Maintenance) Act 1958; to amend the law about the property of a person whose marriage is the subject of a decree of judicial separation dying intestate; to abolish the agency of necessity of a wife; and for purposes connected with the matters aforesaid*

[29th May 1970]

**[2.48]**

### 37 Contributions by spouse in money or money's worth to the improvement of property

It is hereby declared that where a husband or wife contributes in money or money's worth to the improvement of real or personal property in which or in the proceeds of sale of which either or both of them has or have a beneficial interest, the husband or wife so contributing shall, if the contribution is of a substantial nature and subject to any agreement between them to the contrary express or implied, be treated as having then acquired by virtue of his or her contribution a share or an enlarged share, as the case may be, in that beneficial interest of such an extent as may have been then agreed or, in default of such agreement, as may seem in all the circumstances just to any court before which the question of the existence or extent of the beneficial interest of the husband or wife arises (whether in proceedings between them or in any other proceedings).

**[2.48.1]**
**Keypoint**

- Contributes in money or money's worth

## [2.48.2]
### Contributes in money or money's worth

The contribution may be in money or money's worth (ie the claimant may have paid for the improvement or done it herself[1]. The contribution must be of a substantial nature[2].

1 See *Harnett v Harnett* [1973] Fam 156, [1973] 2 All ER 593. See generally *Rayden and Jackson on Divorce and Family Matters* (17th edn, 1997), vol 1, chaps 29 and 30.
2 See *Re Nicholson* [1974] 2 All ER 386, [1974] 1 WLR 476 (provision of a gas fire insufficient).

## [2.49]

### 39 Extension of s 17 of Married Women's Property Act 1882

An application may be made to the High Court or a county court under section 17 of the Married Women's Property Act 1882 (powers of the court in disputes between husband and wife about property) (including that section as extended by section 7 of the Matrimonial Causes (Property and Maintenance) Act 1958) by either of the parties to a marriage notwithstanding that their marriage has been dissolved or annulled so long as the application is made within the period of three years beginning with the date on which the marriage was dissolved or annulled; and references in the said section 17 and the said section 7 to a husband or a wife shall be construed accordingly.

## [2.50]

### 43 Citation, commencement and extent

(1) This Act may be cited as the Matrimonial Proceedings and Property Act 1970.

(2) …

(3) Any reference in any provision of this Act, or in any enactment amended by a provision of this Act, to the commencement of this Act shall be construed as a reference to the date on which that provision comes into force.

(4) … this Act does not extend to Scotland or Northern Ireland.

**Amendment**

Sub-s (2): repealed by the MCA 1973, s 54, Sch 3. Sub-s (4): words omitted repealed by the MCA 1973, s 54, Sch 3 and the SL(R)A 1977.

# Law Reform (Miscellaneous Provisions) Act 1970

Contents



*An Act to abolish actions for breach of promise of marriage and make provision with respect to the property of, and gifts between, persons who have been engaged to marry; to abolish the right of a husband to claim damages for adultery with his wife; to abolish actions for the enticement or harbouring of a spouse, or for the enticement, seduction or harbouring of a child; to make provision with respect to the maintenance of survivors of void marriages; and for purposes connected with the matters aforesaid*

[29th May 1970]



**[2.51]**

### 1 Engagements to marry not enforceable at law

(1) An agreement between two persons to marry one another shall not under the law of England and Wales have effect as a contract giving rise to legal rights and no action shall lie in England and Wales for breach of such an agreement, whatever the law applicable to the agreement.

(2) This section shall have effect in relation to agreements entered into before it comes into force, except that it shall not affect any action commenced before it comes into force.

**[2.52]**

### 2 Property of engaged couples

(1) Where an agreement to marry is terminated, any rule of law relating to the rights of husbands and wives in relation to property in which either or both has or have a beneficial interest, including any such rule as explained by section 37 of the Matrimonial Proceedings and Property Act 1970, shall apply, in relation to any property in which either or both of the parties to the agreement had a beneficial interest while the agreement was in force, as it applies in relation to property in which a husband or wife has a beneficial interest.

(2) Where an agreement to marry is terminated, section 17 of the Married Women's Property Act 1882 and section 7 of the Matrimonial Causes (Property and Maintenance) Act 1958 (which sections confer power on a judge of the High Court or a county court to settle disputes between husband and wife about property) shall apply, as if the parties

were married, to any dispute between, or claim by, one of them in relation to property in which either or both had a beneficial interest while the agreement was in force; but an application made by virtue of this section to the judge under the said section 17, as originally enacted or as extended by the said section 7, shall be made within three years of the termination of the agreement.

### [2.52.1]
### Keypoints

- Need for there to have been an engagement
- MCA 1973 powers not available
- Time limit

### [2.52.2]
### Need for there to have been an engagement

Before this section can apply there must have been an engagement. In the case of *Shaw v Fitzgerald*[1] it was held that there could be an engagement for the purposes of s 2 of the LR(MP)A 1970 even if one party was already married to someone else.

For a discussion of this topic, see generally *Rayden and Jackson on Divorce and Family Matters* (17th edn, 1997), vol 1, para 29.11 and the Noter-up thereto.

1 [1992] 1 FCR 162, [1992] 1 FLR 357.

### [2.52.3]
### MCA 1973 powers not available

The above provisions do not mean that the court has powers under s 24 of the MCA 1973 where an agreement to marry is terminated[1].

1 See *Mossop v Mossop* [1989] Fam 77, [1988] 2 All ER 202, CA.

### [2.52.4]
### Time limit

Specific note should be taken of the time limit in s 2(2). Where it is exceeded it will be necessary to rely on the provisions available to parties who have not married or been engaged — eg under the TLATA 1996.

### [2.53]

**3 Gifts between engaged couples**

(1) A party to an agreement to marry who makes a gift of property to the other party to the agreement on the condition (express or implied) that it shall be returned if the agreement is terminated shall not be prevented from recovering the property by reason only of his having terminated the agreement.

(2) The gift of an engagement ring shall be presumed to be an absolute gift; this presumption may be rebutted by proving that the ring was given on the condition, express or implied, that it should be returned if the marriage did not take place for any reason.

### [2.54]

**5 Abolition of actions for enticement, seduction and harbouring of spouse or child**

No person shall be liable in tort under the law of England and Wales—

(a) to any other person on the ground only of his having induced the wife or husband of that other person to leave or remain apart from the other spouse;

(b) to a parent (or person standing in the place of a parent) on the ground only of his having deprived the parent (or other person) of the services of his or her child by raping, seducing or enticing that child; or

(c) to any other person for harbouring the wife or child of that other person,

except in the case of a cause of action accruing before this Act comes into force if an action in respect thereof has been begun before this Act comes into force.

[2.55]

### 7 Citation, repeal, commencement and extent

(1) This Act may be cited as the Law Reform (Miscellaneous Provisions) Act 1970.

(2) The enactments specified in the Schedule to this Act are hereby repealed to the extent specified in the third column of that Schedule, but the repeal of those enactments shall not affect any action commenced or petition presented before this Act comes into force or any claim made in any such action or on any such petition.

(3) This Act shall come into force on 1st January 1971.

(4) This Act does not extend to Scotland or Northern Ireland.

# Attachment of Earnings Act 1971



## Contents



*An Act to consolidate the enactments relating to the attachment of earnings as a means of enforcing the discharge of monetary obligations*

[12th May 1971]

## [2.56]

### 1 Courts with power to attach earnings

(1) The High Court may make an attachment of earnings order to secure payments under a High Court maintenance order.

(2) A county court may make an attachment of earnings order to secure—

(a) payments under a High Court or a county court maintenance order;

(b) the payment of a judgment debt, other than a debt of less than £5 or such other sum as may be prescribed by county court rules; or

(c) payments under an administration order.

(3) A magistrates' court may make an attachment of earnings order to secure—

(a) payments under a magistrates' court maintenance order;

(b) the payment of any sum adjudged to be paid by a conviction or treated (by any enactment relating to the collection and enforcement of fines, costs, compensation or forfeited recognisances) as so adjudged to be paid; or

(c) the payment of any sum required to be paid by a [order under section 17(2) of the Access to Justice Act 1999].

(4) The following provisions of this Act apply, except where otherwise stated, to attachment of earnings orders made, or to be made, by any court.

(5) Any power conferred by this Act to make an attachment of earnings order includes a power to make such an order to secure the discharge of liabilities arising before the coming into force of this Act.

**Amendment**

Sub-s (3): AJA 1999, s 24, Sch 4, para 8.

**Definitions**

'Maintenance order' – see s 2(a) at para **[2.57]** below; Sch 1 at para **[2.83]** below; 'Maintenance orders' at para **[2.56.3]** below.

'Earnings' – see s 24 at para **[2.79]** below.

'High Court maintenance order'; 'County court maintenance order'; 'Magistrates' court maintenance order' – see s 2(b) at para **[2.57]** below.

'Judgment debt' – see s 2(c) at para **[2.57]** below.

## [2.56.1]
## Keypoints

- Scheme of the Act
- 'Maintenance orders' include lump sum orders
- The meaning of 'earnings'
- Procedure

## [2.56.2]
## Scheme of the Act

As a means of enforcement attachment of earnings should be distinguished from Garnishee Orders (which attach debts other than earnings[1]) and from Deduction from Earnings Orders under the CSA 1991, ss 29 to 32.

The system of attachment of earnings orders, available in all courts, can be used to enforce inter alia maintenance and lump sums, but only against 'earnings' within s 24. Broadly this means that the remedy can only be used against employed persons and certain pensioners. See s 6 for the definition of what constitutes employment. The Act does not cover serving members of HM Armed Forces[2].

In relation to judgment debts the threshold exclusion referred to as 'other than a debt of less than £5'[3] is now £50[4].

Note that in relation to an attachment of earnings to enforce 'maintenance orders' (see below) there is no requirement to prove prior default[5]. An attachment of earnings can be used to enforce arrears as well as current/future payments due[6]. For variation, lapse and discharge of an attchment of earnings order see s 9[7].

In proceedings for committal or distress an attachment of earnings order can be made of the court's own motion and substituted for enforcement by committal or distress[8]. Attachment of earnings (if appropriate) takes precedence over committal[9].

The AtEA 1971 contains important disclosure powers against both respondents ***and*** employers[10].

1 See RSC Ord 49, r 1 and CCR Ord 30, r 1.
2 See the AtEA 1971, s 24(2) at para **[2.79]** below and notes thereto.
3 See the AtEA 1971, s 1(2)(b) at para **[2.56]** above.
4 See CCR Ord 27, r 7(9); CPR 1998, Pt 50 and Sch 2.
5 See the AtEA 1971, s 3(3A) at para **[2.58]** below.
6 See the AtEA 1971, s 6(b)(ii) at para **[2.61]** below.
7 See para **[2.64]** below.
8 See the AtEA 1971, s 3(4), (6) and (7) at para **[2.58]** below.
9 See the AtEA 1971, s 8 at para **[2.63]** below; and the MCA 1980, s 93(6).
10 See the AtEA 1971, s 14 at para **[2.69]** below.



### [2.56.3]
### 'Maintenance orders' include lump sum orders

In accordance with s 2(a) the term 'maintenance order' includes orders for maintenance and 'periodical or other payments' as defined in Sch 1. These include lump sums under the MCA 1973, Pt II; the DPMCA 1978, Pt I; and the ChA 1989.

The reference to 'payments under a magistrates' court maintenance order' includes an order under the MO(RE)A 1972, s 27A[1].

1 See the MO(RE)A 1972, s 27C(4)(c).

### [2.56.4]
### The meaning of 'earnings'

Earnings are defined widely, to include pensions (other than state pension)[1]. The court has power to determine whether payments are earnings[2].

1 See the AtEA 1971, s 24 at para **[2.79]** below.
2 See the AtEA 1971, s 16 at para **[2.71]** below.

### [2.56.5]
### Procedure

In the High Court: RSC Ord 105 (revoked 1991, since when the practice in the county court should be followed[1]). For the procedure in the county court see CCR Ord 27 (CPR 1998 Pt 50 and Sch 2). In the magistrates' court see s 19 below[2] and the Magistrates' Courts (Attachment of Earnings) Rules 1971, SI 1971/809.

For a discussion of the practice and procedure, see generally *Rayden and Jackson on Divorce and Family Matters* (17th edn, 1997), vol 1, para 34.21 et seq.

1 See the FPR 1991, r 7.1 at para **[3.476]** below.
2 See para **[2.74]** below.

### [2.57]

**2 Principal definitions**

In this Act—

(a) 'maintenance order' means any order specified in Schedule 1 to this Act and includes such an order which has been discharged if any arrears are recoverable thereunder;

(b) 'High Court maintenance order', 'county court maintenance order' and 'magistrates' court maintenance order' mean respectively a maintenance order enforceable by the High Court, a county court and a magistrates' court;
(c) 'judgment debt' means a sum payable under—
  (i) a judgment or order enforceable by a court in England and Wales (not being a magistrates' court);
  (ii) an order of a magistrates' court for the payment of money recoverable summarily as a civil debt; or
  (iii) an order of any court which is enforceable as if it were for the payment of money so recoverable,

but does not include any sum payable under a maintenance order or an administration order;
(d) 'the relevant adjudication', in relation to any payment secured or to be secured by an attachment of earnings order, means the conviction, judgment, order or other adjudication from which there arises the liability to make the payment; and
(e) 'the debtor', in relation to an attachment of earnings order, or to proceedings in which a court has power to make an attachment of earnings order, or to proceedings arising out of such an order, means the person by whom payment is required by the relevant adjudication to be made.

**[2.57.1]**
**Keypoint**
- Effect of section

**[2.57.2]**
**Effect of section**

This section sets out the principal definitions used in the Act. For other definitions see s 6(2) ('employer')[1], s 6(5) ('normal deduction rate' and 'protected earnings rate')[2], s 24 ('earnings')[3] and s 25 (other definitions, including, eg administration order)[4].

1 See para **[2.61]** below.
2 See para **[2.61]** below.
3 See para **[2.79]** below.
4 See para **[2.80]** below.

**[2.58]**

### 3 Application for order and conditions of court's power to make it

(1) The following persons may apply for an attachment of earnings order—
  (a) the person to whom payment under the relevant adjudication is required to be made (whether directly or through an officer of any court);
  (b) where the relevant adjudication is an administration order, any one of the creditors scheduled to the order;
  (c) without prejudice to paragraph (a) above, where the application is to a magistrates' court for an order to secure maintenance payments, and there is in force an order under [[section 59] of the Magistrates' Courts Act 1980] or section 19(2) of the Maintenance Orders Act 1950, that those payments be made to [a justices' chief executive, that justices' chief executive];
  (d) in the following cases the debtor—
    (i) where the application is to a magistrates' court; or
    (ii) where the application is to the High Court or a county court for an order to secure maintenance payments.

(2) …

(3) [Subject to subsection (3A) below] for an attachment of earnings order to be made on the application of any person other than the debtor it must appear to the court that the debtor has failed to make one or more payments required by the relevant adjudication.

[(3A) Subsection (3) above shall not apply where the relevant adjudication is a maintenance order.]

[(3B) Where—

(a) a magistrates' court imposes a fine on a person in respect of an offence, and

(b) that person consents to an order being made under this subsection,

the court may at the time it imposes the fine, and without the need for an application, make an attachment of earnings order to secure the payment of the fine.

(3C) Where—

(a) a magistrates' court makes in the case of a person convicted of an offence an order under section 130 of the Powers of Criminal Courts (Sentencing) Act 2000 (a compensation order) requiring him to pay compensation or to make other payments, and

(b) that person consents to an order being made under this subsection,

the court may at the time it makes the compensation order, and without the need for an application, make an attachment of earnings order to secure the payment of the compensation or other payments.]

(4) Where proceedings are brought—

(a) in the High Court or a county court for the enforcement of a maintenance order by committal under section 5 of the Debtors Act 1869; or

(b) in a magistrates' court for the enforcement of a maintenance order under [section 76 of the Magistrates' Courts Act 1980] (distress or committal),

then, … the court may make an attachment of earnings order to secure payments under the maintenance order, instead of dealing with the case under section 5 of the said Act of 1869 or, as the case may be, [section 76 of the said Act of 1980].

(5) …

(6) Where proceedings are brought in a county court for an order of committal under section 5 of the Debtors Act 1869 in respect of a judgment debt for any of the taxes, contributions or liabilities specified in Schedule 2 to this Act, the court may, in any circumstances in which it has power to make such an order, make instead an attachment of earnings order to secure the payment of the judgment debt.

(7) A county court shall not make an attachment of earnings order to secure the payment of a judgment debt if there is in force an order or warrant for the debtor's committal, under section 5 of the Debtors Act 1869, in respect of that debt; but in any such case the court may discharge the order or warrant with a view to making an attachment of earnings order instead.

**Amendment**

Sub-s (1): MCA 1980, s 154, Sch 7, para 97; MEA 1991, s 11(1), Sch 2; AJA 1999, s 90(1), Sch 13, paras 64, 65. Sub-ss (2), (5): repealed by the MEA 1991, s 11, Sch 2, para 1, Sch 3. Sub-s (3): MEA 1991, s 11(1), Sch 2, para 1. Sub-s (3A): inserted by the MEA 1991, s 11(1), Sch 2, para 1. Sub-ss (3B), (3C): inserted, in relation to offences committed, and compensation orders made on convictions for offences committed, on or after 1 October 1996, by the CPIA 1996, s 53. Sub-s (3C): PCC(S)A 2000, s 165(1). Sub-s (4): words in square brackets substituted by the MCA 1980, s 154, Sch 7, para 97; words omitted repealed by the MEA 1991, s 11, Sch 2, para 1, Sch 3.

**Definitions**

'Relevant adjudication' – see s 2(d) at para **[2.57]** above.
'Administration order' – s 25 at para **[2.80]** below.
'Debtor' – see s 2(e) at para **[2.57]** below.

## [2.58.1]
### Keypoints

- Requirement of prior default except in relation to 'maintenance orders'
- Precedence of attachment of earnings over committal
- Procedure

## [2.58.2]
### Requirement of prior default except in relation to 'maintenance orders'

Note that in relation to an attachment of earnings to enforce 'maintenance orders'[1] (see s 1 above) there is no requirement to prove prior default[2].

1 See the AtEA 1971, s 1 at para **[2.56]** above.
2 See the AtEA 1971, s 3(3A) at para **[2.58]** above.

## [2.58.3]
### Precedence of attachment of earnings over committal

In proceedings for committal or distress an attachment of earnings order can be made of the court's own motion and substituted for enforcement by committal or distress[1]. Attachment of earnings (if appropriate) takes precedence over committal[2].

1 See the AtEA 1971, s 3(4), (6) and (7) at para **[2.58]** above.
2 See the AtEA 1971, s 8 at para **[2.63]** below. See also the MCA 1980, s 93(6).

## [2.58.4]
### Procedure

In the High Court: RSC Ord 105 (revoked 1991), since when the practice in the county court should be followed[1]. For the procedure in the county court see CCR Ord 27 (CPR 1998, Pt 50 and Sch 2). In the magistrates' court see s 19 below[2] and the Magistrates' Courts (Attachment of Earnings) Rules 1971, SI 1971/809.

1 See the FPR 1991, r 7.1 at para **[3.476]** below.
2 See para **[2.74]** below.

## [2.59]

### 4 Extension of power to make administration order

(1) Where, on an application to a county court for an attachment of earnings order to secure the payment of a judgment debt, it appears to the court that the debtor also has other debts, the court—

(a) shall consider whether the case may be one in which all the debtor's liabilities should be dealt with together and that for that purpose [an administration order should be made]; and

(b) if of opinion that it may be such a case, shall have power (whether or not it makes the attachment of earnings order applied for), with a view to making an administration order, to order the debtor to furnish to the court a list of all his creditors and the amounts which he owes to them respectively.

(2) If, on receipt of the list referred to in subsection (1)(b) above, it appears to the court that the debtor's whole indebtedness amounts to not more than the amount [which for the time being is the county court limit for the purposes of section 112 of the County Courts Act 1984] (limit of total indebtedness governing county court's power to make administration order on application of debtor), the court may make such an order in respect of the debtor's estate.

[(2A) Subsection (2) above is subject to section 112(3) and (4) of the County Courts Act 1984 (which require that, before an administration order is made, notice is to be given to all the creditors and thereafter restricts the right of any creditor to institute bankruptcy proceedings).]

(3) …

(4) Nothing in this section is to be taken as prejudicing any right of a debtor to apply, under [section 112 of the County Courts Act 1984], for an administration order.

**Amendment**

Sub-s (1): words in square brackets substituted by the IA 1976, s 13(2). Sub-ss (2), (4): words in square brackets substituted by the CCA 1984, s 148(1), Sch 2, para 40. Sub-s (2A): substituted for second paragraph of sub-s (2) by the CCA 1984, s 148(1), Sch 2, para 40. Sub-s (3): repealed by the IA 1976, ss 13(1), 14(4), Sch 3.

**Definitions**

'Judgment debt' – see s 2(c) at para **[2.57]** above.
'Debtor' – see s 2(e) at para **[2.57]** above.
'Administration order' – see s 25 at para **[2.80]** below.
'County Court limit for the purposes of section 112 of the County Courts Act 1984' – is still £5,000.



**[2.59.1]**
**Keypoint**

- Effect of section

**[2.59.2]**
**Effect of section**

This section enables the court to make an adminstration order where the debtor has other debts. For priority as between more than one attachment of earnings order see Sch 3, Pt II below[1].

1 See para **[2.85]** below.

**[2.60]**

### 5 Attachment of earnings to secure payments under administration order

(1) Where a county court makes an administration order in respect of a debtor's estate, it may also make an attachment of earnings order to secure the payments required by the administration order.

(2) At any time when an administration order is in force a county court may (with or without an application) make an attachment of earnings order to secure the payments required by the administration order, if it appears to the court that the debtor has failed to make any such payment.

(3) The power of a county court under this section to make an attachment of earnings order to secure the payments required by an administration order shall, where the debtor is already subject to an attachment of earnings order to secure the payment of a judgment debt, include power to direct that the last-mentioned order shall take effect (with or without variation under section 9 of this Act) as an order to secure the payments required by the administration order.

**[2.61]**

### 6 Effect and contents of order

(1) An attachment of earnings order shall be an order directed to a person who appears to the court to have the debtor in his employment and shall operate as an instruction to that person—

(a) to make periodical deductions from the debtor's earnings in accordance with Part I of Schedule 3 to this Act; and

(b) at such times as the order may require, or as the court may allow, to pay the amounts deducted to the collecting officer of the court, as specified in the order.

(2) For the purposes of this Act, the relationship of employer and employee shall be treated as subsisting between two persons if one of them, as a principal and not as a servant or agent, pays to the other any sums defined as earnings by section 24 of this Act.

(3) An attachment of earnings order shall contain prescribed particulars enabling the debtor to be identified by the employer.

(4) Except where it is made to secure maintenance payments, the order shall specify the whole amount payable under the relevant adjudication (or so much of that amount as remains unpaid), including any relevant costs.

(5) The order shall specify—

(a) the normal deduction rate, that is to say, the rate (expressed as a sum of money per week, month or other period) at which the court thinks it reasonable for the debtor's earnings to be applied to meeting his liability under the relevant adjudication; and

(b) the protected earnings rate, that is to say the rate (so expressed) below which, having regard to the debtor's resources and needs, the court thinks it reasonable that the earnings actually paid to him should not be reduced.

(6) In the case of an order made to secure payments under a maintenance order (not being an order for the payment of a lump sum), the normal deduction rate—

(a) shall be determined after taking account of any right or liability of the debtor to deduct income tax when making the payments; and

(b) shall not exceed the rate which appears to the court necessary for the purpose of—

(i) securing payment of the sums falling due from time to time under the maintenance order, and

(ii) securing payment within a reasonable period of any sums already due and unpaid under the maintenance order.

(7) For the purposes of an attachment of earnings order, the collecting officer of the court shall be (subject to later variation of the order under section 9 of this Act)—

(a) in the case of an order made by the High Court, either—

(i) the proper officer of the High Court, or

(ii) the [appropriate officer] of such county court as the order may specify;

(b) in the case of an order made by a county court, the [appropriate officer] of that court; and

(c) in the case of an order made by a magistrates' court, the [justices' chief executive for that court or for] another magistrates' court specified in the order.

[(8) In subsection (7) above 'appropriate officer' means an officer designated by the Lord Chancellor.]

[(9) The Lord Chancellor may by order make such provision as he considers expedient (including transitional provision) with a view to providing for the payment of amounts deducted under attachment of earnings orders to be made to such officers as may be designated by the order rather than to collecting officers of the court.

(10) Any such order may make such amendments in this Act, in relation to functions exercised by or in relation to collecting officers of the court as he considers expedient in consequence of the provision made by virtue of subsection (9) above.

(11) The power to make such an order shall be exercisable by statutory instrument.

(12) Any such statutory instrument shall be subject to annulment in pursuance of a resolution of either House of Parliament.]

**Amendment**

Sub-s (7): AJA 1977, ss 19(5), 90(1), Sch 13. Sub-s (8): inserted by the AJA 1977, s 19(5). Sub-ss (9) to (12): prospectively inserted by the CLSA 1990, s 125(2), Sch 17, para 5, as from a day to be appointed.

**Definitions**

'Employment' – as defined in s 6(2).

'In accordance with Part I of Schedule 3' – ie in accordance with the calculation there set out.

'Prescribed particulars' – see CCR Ord 27 r 10(1) and the Magistrates' Courts (Attachment of Earnings Rules) 1971, SI 1971/809, r 7. Note power to order disclosure of employment particulars from respondent and/or putative employer: see s 14(1) at para **[2.69]** below; and also new employer's duty to notify court of new employment: see s 15 at para **[2.70]** below.

'Normal deduction rate'; 'The protected earnings rate' – see para **[2.61.2]** below.

'Earnings' – see s 24 at para **[2.79]** below.

'Debtor' – see s 2(e) at para **[2.57]** above.

'Debtor's resources and needs' – see s 25(3) at para **[2.80]** below.



## [2.61.1]
### Keypoint

- The meaning of 'normal deduction rate' and 'protected earnings rate'

## [2.61.2]
### The meaning of 'normal deduction rate' and 'protected earnings rate'

The normal deduction rate is the amount which the payee is to get (which is not necessarily the amount of the original order, but may include a payment towards any arrears[1]). The protected earnings rate means the minimum that the payer is to retain. Normally, but not necessarily, this should not be below the income support minimum[2]. See also s 9(3)(b) of the AtEA 1971 below for the power in the magistrates' court to make a temporary increase in the protected earnings rate. Note that a debtor's needs in s 6(5)(b) include 'the needs of any person for whom he must, or reasonably may, provide'[3].

1 See the AtEA 1971, s 6(b)(ii) at para **[2.61]** above.
2 See *Billington v Billington* [1974] Fam 24, [1974] 1 All ER 546.
3 See the AtEA 1971, s 25(3) at para **[2.80]** below.

## [2.62]

### 7 Compliance with order by employer

(1) Where an attachment of earnings order has been made, the employer shall, if he has been served with the order, comply with it; but he shall be under no liability for non-compliance before seven days have elapsed since the service.

(2) Where a person is served with an attachment of earnings order directed to him and he has not the debtor in his employment, or the debtor subsequently ceases to be in his employment, he shall (in either case), within ten days from the date of service or, as the case may be, the cesser, give notice of that fact to the court.

(3) Part II of Schedule 3 to this Act shall have effect with respect to the priority to be accorded as between two or more attachment of earnings orders directed to a person in respect of the same debtor.

(4) On any occasion when the employer makes, in compliance with the order, a deduction from the debtor's earnings—

(a) he shall be entitled to deduct, in addition, [£1.00], or such other sum as may be prescribed by order made by the Lord Chancellor, towards his clerical and administrative costs; and

(b) he shall give to the debtor a statement in writing of the total amount of the deduction.

(5) An order of the Lord Chancellor under subsection (4)(a) above—

(a) may prescribe different sums in relation to different classes of cases;

(b) may be varied or revoked by a subsequent order made under that paragraph; and

(c) shall be made by statutory instrument subject to annulment by resolution of either House of Parliament.

**Amendment**
Sub-s (4): sum in square brackets substituted by SI 1991/356, art 2.

**Definitions**
'Employer' – as defined in s 6(2) at para **[2.61]** above and s 25(1) at para **[2.80]** below.
'Debtor' – see s 2(e) at para **[2.57]** above.
'[£1.00], or such other sum as may be prescribed' – The current figure is £1: see the Attachment of Earnings (Employer's Deduction) Order 1991, SI 1991/356, made pursuant to s 7(5).

## [2.62.1]
### Keypoints
- Employer's obligations
- Priority of attachment orders

## [2.62.2]
### Employer's obligations
It is the employer's obligation to comply with an attachment of earnings order. Failure to comply is an offence[1]. Note the employer's duty also to keep the court notified if the employee leaves his employment[2], and the offence which the employer commits if he breaches the duty[3]. The making of false statements (whether knowingly or recklessly) is also an offence[4]. Compare the duty of a new employer to notify the court of new employment[5].

Note that under s 14(1)(b)[6] the employer can also be ordered to provide particulars of the debtor's earnings.

See s 12 below[7] for extent of employer's liability to debtor.

For a discussion of this topic, see generally *Rayden and Jackson on Divorce and Family Matters* (17th edn, 1997), vol 1, para 34.24.

1 See the AtEA 1971, s 23(2)(a) at para **[2.78]** below.
2 See the AtEA 1971, s 7(2) at para **[2.62]** above.
3 See the AtEA 1971, s 23(2)(b) at para **[2.78]** below.
4 See the AtEA 1971, s 23(2)(f) at para **[2.78]** below.
5 See the AtEA 1971, s 15 at para **[2.70]** below.
6 See para **[2.69]** below.
7 See para **[2.62]** below.

## [2.62.3]
### Priority of attachment orders
Maintenance orders (and other orders in the magistrates' court) take priority over judgment debts and administration orders, and (if there are more than one of either) priority is accorded in date order within each class, as set out in Sch 3, Pt II to the AtEA 1971 below[1].

1 See para **[2.85]** below.

## [2.63]

### 8 Interrelation with alternative remedies open to creditors

(1) Where an attachment of earnings order has been made to secure maintenance payments, no order or warrant of commitment shall be issued in consequence of any proceedings for the enforcement of the related maintenance order begun before the making of the attachment of earnings order.

(2) Where a county court has made an attachment of earnings order to secure the payment of a judgment debt—

(a) no order or warrant of commitment shall be issued in consequence of any proceedings for the enforcement of the debt begun before the making of the attachment of earnings order; and

(b) so long as the order is in force, no execution for the recovery of the debt shall issue against any property of the debtor without the leave of the county court.

(3) An attachment of earnings order made to secure maintenance payments shall cease to have effect upon the making of an order of commitment or the issue of a warrant of commitment for the enforcement of the related maintenance order, or upon the exercise for that purpose of the power conferred on a magistrates' court by [section 77(2) of the Magistrates' Courts Act 1980] to postpone the issue of such a warrant.

(4) An attachment of earnings order made to secure the payment of a judgment debt shall cease to have effect on the making of an order of commitment or the issue of a warrant of commitment for the enforcement of the debt.

(5) An attachment of earnings order made to secure any payment specified in section 1(3)(b) or (c) of this Act shall cease to have effect on the issue of a warrant committing the debtor to prison for default in making that payment.



**Amendment**

Sub-s (3): words in square brackets substituted by the MCA 1980, s 154, Sch 7, para 98.

**Definitions**

'Proceedings for enforcement' – see para **[2.63.2]** below.
'Judgment debt' – see s 2(c) at para **[2.57]** above.
'Execution for the recovery' – see para **[2.63.2]** below.
'Debtor' – see s 2(e) at para **[2.57]** above.

## [2.63.1]
## Keypoint

- Precedence of attachment of earnings

## [2.63.2]
## Precedence of attachment of earnings

The scheme is one of precedence based on the double jeopardy principle: an attachment of earnings in relation to a maintenance order supercedes and (in effect) stays a prior application for committal in respect of that maintenance order, in any court[1]. However, an application for committal which post-dates the attachment of earnings is not prohibited; but the attachment order will automatically cease to have effect if a committal order is made, or if a magistrates' court exercises its power under the MCA 1980, s 77(2) to postpone the issue of a warrant of distress (for the purpose of levying a sum adjudged to be paid by conviction or order)[2]. In the county court (only) an attachment of earnings in relation to a judgment debt supercedes a prior application for committal in respect of that judgment debt and also prevents the issue of execution (for the recovery of the debt) against any property[3]. Again however, an application for committal which post-dates the attachment of earnings is not prohibited; but the attachment order will automatically cease to have effect if a committal order is made[4]. Similarly an attachment order in the magistrates' court which is made respect of payment specified in s 1(3)(b) or (c) of the AtEA 1971 will automatically cease to have effect if a committal order is made[5]. Note also court's power to vary attachment order of its own motion[6].

It has been held that an examination of a debtor under RSC Ord 48, r 1 (preserved in CPR 1998, Sch 1) does not amount to proceedings for the enforcement of a debt[7].

1 See the AtEA 1971, s 8(1) at para **[2.63]** above.
2 See the AtEA 1971, s 8(3) at para **[2.63]** above.
3 See the AtEA 1971, s 8(2) at para **[2.63]** above.
4 See the AtEA 1971, s 8(4) at para **[2.63]** above.
5 See the AtEA 1971, s 8(5) at para **[2.63]** above.
6 See the AtEA 1971, s 9(3)(a) at para **[2.64]** below.
7 See the AtEA 1971, s 8(1) at para **[2.63]** above. See also *Fagot v Gaches* [1942] 1 KB 10, [1942] 2 All ER 476, CA.

## [2.64]

### 9 Variation, lapse and discharge of orders

(1) The court may make an order discharging or varying an attachment of earnings order.

(2) Where an order is varied, the employer shall, if he has been served with notice of the variation, comply with the order as varied; but he shall be under no liability for non-compliance before seven days have elapsed since the service.

(3) Rules of court may make provision—

(a) as to the circumstances in which an attachment of earnings order may be varied or discharged by the court of its own motion;

(b) in the case of an attachment of earnings order made by a magistrates' court, for enabling a single justice, on an application made by the debtor on the ground of a material change in his resources and needs since the order was made or last varied, to vary the order for a period of not more than four weeks by an increase of the protected earnings rate.

(4) Where an attachment of earnings order has been made and the person to whom it is directed ceases to have the debtor in his employment, the order shall lapse (except as respects deduction from earnings paid after the cesser and payment to the collecting officer of amounts deducted at any time) and be of no effect unless and until the court again directs it to a person (whether the same as before or another) who appears to the court to have the debtor in his employment.

(5) The lapse of an order under subsection (4) above shall not prevent its being treated as remaining in force for other purposes.

**Definitions**

'Employer' – as defined in s 6(2) at para **[2.61]** above and s 25(1) at para **[2.80]** below; see 'Employer's obligations' under s 7 at para **[2.62]** above.
'Rules of court' – under sub-s (3)(a): see CCR Ord 27, rr 13, 17(10) and the Magistrates' Courts (Attachment of Earnings) Rules 1971, SI 1971/809, rr 12, 13, 22(2)(d).
'Rules of court' – under sub-s (3)(b): see the Magistrates' Courts (Attachment of Earnings) Rules 1971, SI 1971/809, rr 14, 22(2)(e), 23(4), Schedule, Form 3.
'Single Justice' – ie a JP acting for the same petty sessions area: see s 25(1) at para **[2.80]** below; or, in this context, a justice's clerk: see the Magistrates' Court (Attachment of Earnings) Rules 1971, SI 1971/809, r 22(2)(e).
'Debtor' – see s 2(e) at para **[2.57]** above.
'Protected earnings rate' – see s 6(5) at para **[2.61]** above and notes thereto.
'Employment' – see s 6(2) at para **[2.61]** above.

## [2.64.1]
**Keypoint**

- Distinguish different forms of variation

## [2.64.2]
**Distinguish different forms of variation**

Variation or discharge under s 9(3)(a) of the AtEA 1971 should be distinguished from variation or discharge under s 9(1) which is on application/complaint in the usual way. Section 9(3)(a) is in effect an administrative provision, the court acting of its own motion: it covers cases eg where the 'employer' is not the employer, or where there is a new employer (and therefore different earnings), or where there is another attachment order with greater priority (under Sch 3, Pt II below[1]).

Variation of the protected earnings rate under s 9(3)(b) of the AtEA 1971 is only available in the magistrates' court and only on application by the debtor. Note that a debtor's needs include needs of any person for whom the debtor must, or reasonably may, provide[2].

1 See para **[2.85]** below.
2 See the AtEA 1971, s 25(3) at para **[2.80]** below.

**[2.65]**

## 10 Normal deduction rate to be reduced in certain cases

(1) The following provisions shall have effect, in the case of an attachment of earnings order made to secure maintenance payments, where it appears to the collecting officer of the court that—

(a) the aggregate of the payments made for the purposes of the related maintenance order by the debtor (whether under the attachment of earnings order or otherwise) exceeds the aggregate of the payments required up to that time by the maintenance order; and

(b) the normal deduction rate specified by the attachment of earnings order (or, where two or more such orders are in force in relation to the maintenance order, the aggregate of the normal deduction rates specified by those orders) exceeds the rate of payments required by the maintenance order; and

(c) no proceedings for the variation or discharge of the attachment of earnings order are pending.

(2) In the case of an order made by the High Court or a county court, the collecting officer shall give the prescribed notice to the person to whom he is required to pay sums received under the attachment of earnings order, and to the debtor; and the court shall make the appropriate variation order, unless the debtor requests it to discharge the attachment of earnings order, or to vary it in some other way, and the court thinks fit to comply with the request.

(3) In the case of an order made by a magistrates' court, the collecting officer shall apply to the court for the appropriate variation order; and the court shall grant the application unless the debtor appears at the hearing and requests the court to discharge the attachment of earnings order, or to vary it in some other way, and the court thinks fit to comply with the request.

(4) In this section, 'the appropriate variation order' means an order varying the attachment of earnings order in question by reducing the normal deduction rate specified thereby so as to secure that that rate (or, in the case mentioned in subsection (1)(b) above, the aggregate of the rates therein mentioned)—

(a) is the same as the rate of payments required by the maintenance order; or

(b) is such lower rate as the court thinks fit having regard to the amount of the excess mentioned in subsection (1)(a).

**Definitions**

'The collecting officer' – see s 6(7) at para **[2.61]** above.
'Debtor' – see s 2(e) at para **[2.57]** above.
'Normal deduction rate – see s 6(5)(a) at para **[2.61]** above.
'High Court or a county court' – see para **[2.56]** above.
'The prescribed notice' – see CCR Ord 27, r 17(9), Form N341.
'Appropriate variation order – see s 10(4).

**[2.65.1]**
**Keypoint**

- Effect of section

**[2.65.2]**
**Effect of section**

This section covers the situation where the payer appears (to the court) to have been paying too much and where there are no pending applications before the court. In this situation the collecting officer applies for a reduction and the application is deemed to be made on the request of the payee[1]. The payee is liable for any costs awarded[2]. The creditor has no right to object or to be heard. The debtor can be heard personally or by a legal representative[3].

1 See the AtEA 1971, s 18(3) at para **[2.73]** below.
2 See the AtEA 1971, s 18(2)(b) at para **[2.73]** below.
3 See the MCA 1980, s 122.

## [2.66]

### 11 Attachment order in respect of maintenance payments to cease to have effect on the occurrence of certain events

(1) An attachment of earnings order made to secure maintenance payments shall cease to have effect—

(a) upon the grant of an application for registration of the related maintenance order under section 2 of the Maintenance Orders Act 1958 (which provides for the registration in a magistrates' court of a High Court or county court maintenance order, and for registration in the High Court of a magistrates' court maintenance order);

(b) where the related maintenance order is registered under Part I of the said Act of 1958, upon the giving of notice with respect thereto under section 5 of that Act (notice with view to cancellation of registration);

(c) subject to subsection (3) below, upon the discharge of the related maintenance order while it is not registered under Part I of the said Act of 1958;

(d) upon the related maintenance order ceasing to be registered in a court in England or Wales, or becoming registered in a court in Scotland or Northern Ireland, under Part II of the Maintenance Orders Act 1950.

(2) Subsection (1)(a) above shall have effect, in the case of an application for registration under section 2(1) of the said Act of 1958, notwithstanding that the grant of the application may subsequently become void under subsection (2) of that section.

(3) Where the related maintenance order is discharged as mentioned in subsection (1)(c) above and it appears to the court discharging the order that arrears thereunder will remain to be recovered after the discharge, that court may, if it thinks fit, direct that subsection (1) shall not apply.

## [2.66.1]
### Keypoint

- Inter-relation with other Acts

## [2.66.2]
### Inter-relation with other Acts

The MOA 1958 provides for the vertical transfer and registration of High Court and county court maintenance orders (widely but not identically defined with maintenance orders under the AtEA 1971) to the respondent's local magistrates' court and similar registration of magistrates' courts orders in the High Court (in a registry of the applicant's choice).

The AtEA 1971, s 11(1)(a) provides that on the grant of the application to register the maintenance order under the MOA 1958 any related attachment of earnings order made to secure maintenance payments ceases to have effect; and s 11(2) provides that this is still the case even where the registration is subsequently avoided. The AtEA 1971, s 11(1)(b) provides for automatic cesser of the attachment of earnings order also upon the giving of notice with a view to cancellation of registration under the MOA 1958.

The reference in s 11(1)(c) of the AtEA 1971 to the discharge of the related maintenance order while it is not registered is a reference to a normal (ie un-registered) maintenance order. Note the discretion to disapply this subsection if there are still arrears outstanding under the discharged order[1].

The MOA 1950 provides for the horizontal (geographic) transfer and registration of domestic UK (ie including Scotland etc) maintenance orders (which are again widely but not identically defined).

1 See the AtEA 1971, s 11(3) at para **[2.66]** above.

[2.67]

## 12 Termination of employer's liability to make deductions

(1) Where an attachment of earnings order ceases to have effect under section or 11 of this Act, the proper officer of the prescribed court shall give notice of the cesser to the person to whom the order was directed.

(2) Where, in the case of an attachment of earnings order made otherwise than to secure maintenance payments, the whole amount payable under the relevant adjudication has been paid, and also any relevant costs, the court shall give notice to the employer that no further compliance with the order is required.

(3) Where an attachment of earnings order—

(a) ceases to have effect under section 8 or 11 of this Act; or

(b) is discharged under section 9,

the person to whom the order has been directed shall be under no liability in consequence of his treating the order as still in force at any time before the expiration of seven days from the date on which the notice required by subsection (1) above or, as the case may be, a copy of the discharging order is served on him.

**Definitions**

'Under section 8' – ie by operation of law discharging an attachment of earnings order upon the making of a committal order in respect of the same debt.

'Under section 11' – ie by operation of law discharging an attachment of earnings order upon the registration (or notice of cancellation of registration) of the related maintenance order under the MOA 1958, or upon the de-registration of the related order under the MOA 1950 or its registration outside England and Wales.

'Proper officer of the prescribed court' – see CCR Ord 27, r 12 and the Magistrates' Courts (Attachment of Earnings) Rules 1971, SI 1971/809, r 6.

'Person to whom the order was directed' – ie the employer at the time of the attachment of earnings order.

'Relevant costs' – see s 25(2) at para **[2.80]** below.

[2.68]

## 13 Application of sums received by collection officer

(1) Subject to subsection (3) below, the collecting officer to whom a person makes payments in compliance with an attachment of earnings order shall, after deducting such court fees, if any, in respect of proceedings for or arising out of the order, as are deductible from those payments, deal with the sums paid in the same way as he would if they had been paid by the debtor to satisfy the relevant adjudication.

(2) Any sums paid to the collecting officer under an attachment of earnings order made to secure maintenance payments shall, when paid to the person entitled to receive those payments, be deemed to be payments made by the debtor (with such deductions, if any, in respect of income tax as the debtor is entitled or required to make) so as to discharge—

(a) first, any sums for the time being due and unpaid under the related maintenance order (a sum due at an earlier date being discharged before a sum due at a later date); and

(b) secondly, any costs incurred in proceedings relating to the related maintenance order which were payable by the debtor when the attachment of earnings order was made or last varied.

(3) Where a county court makes an attachment of earnings order to secure the payment of a judgment debt and also, under section 4(1) of this Act, orders the debtor to furnish to the court a list of all his creditors, sums paid to the collecting officer in compliance with the attachment of earnings order shall not be dealt with by him as mentioned in subsection (1) above, but shall be retained by him pending the decision of

the court whether or not to make an administration order and shall then be dealt with by him as the court may direct.

**Definitions**

'The collecting officer' – see s 6(7) at para **[2.61]** above.
'Debtor' – see s 2(e) at para **[2.57]** above.
'Relevant adjudication' – see s 2(d) at para **[2.57]** above.
'Person entitled' – under the original maintenance order; there is no power to reopen the merits of the original order[1].

1 See *Sammy-Joe v GPO Mount Pleasant Post Office* [1966] 3 All ER 924, [1967] 1 WLR 370.

## [2.68.1]
## Keypoint

- Effect of section

## [2.68.2]
## Effect of section

This section covers how payments received under an attachment of earnings are applied, ie first to maintenance arrears (earliest first), then to costs. For priority as between more than one order see s 7(3) above[1] and Sch 3, Pt II below[2]. See s 17(3)(d)[3] for the application of payments made under consolidated orders.

1 See para **[2.62]** above.
2 See para **[2.85]** below.
3 See para **[2.72]** below.

## [2.69]

### 14 Power of court to obtain statement of earnings etc

(1) Where in any proceedings a court has power to make an attachment of earnings order, it may—

- (a) order the debtor to give to the court, within a specified period, a statement signed by him of—
  - (i) the name and address of any person by whom earnings are paid to him;
  - (ii) specified particulars as to his earnings and anticipated earnings, and as to his resources and needs; and
  - (iii) specified particulars for the purpose of enabling the debtor to be identified by any employer of his;
- (b) order any person appearing to the court to have the debtor in his employment to give to the court, within a specified period, a statement signed by him or on his behalf of specified particulars of the debtor's earnings and anticipated earnings.

(2) Where an attachment of earnings order has been made, the court may at any time thereafter while the order is in force

- [(a) make such an order as is described in subsection 1(a) or (b) above; and
- (b) order the debtor to attend before it on a day and at a time specified in the order to give the information described in subsection 1(a) above].

(3) In the case of an application to a magistrates' court for an attachment of earnings order, or for the variation or discharge of such an order, the power to make an order under subsection (1) or (2) above shall be exercisable also, before the hearing of the application, by a single justice.

(4) Without prejudice to subsections (1) to (3) above, rules of court may provide that where notice of an application for an attachment of earnings order is served on the

debtor, it shall include a requirement that he shall give to the court, within such period and in such manner as may be prescribed, a statement in writing of the matters specified in subsection (1)(a) above and of any other prescribed matters which are, or may be, relevant under section 6 of this Act to the determination of the normal deduction rate and the protected earnings rate to be specified in any order made on the application.

(5) In any proceedings in which a court has power to make an attachment of earnings order, and in any proceedings for the making, variation or discharge of such an order, a document purporting to be a statement given to the court in compliance with an order under subsection (1)(a) or (b) above, or with any such requirement of a notice of application for an attachment of earnings order as is mentioned in subsection (4) above, shall, in the absence of proof to the contrary, be deemed to be a statement so given and shall be evidence of the facts stated therein.



**Amendment**
Sub-s (2): words in square brackets substituted by the AJA 1982, s 53(1).

**Definitions**
'Name and address' – the name and address of business are sufficient: see *Simmons v Woodward* [1892] AC 100, HL; and *Edwards v Pharmaceutical Society of Great Britain* [1910] 2 KB 766.
'Earnings' – see s 24 at para **[2.79]** below.
'Resources and needs' – a debtor's needs include needs of any person for whom the debtor must, or reasonably may, provide: see s 25(3) at para **[2.80]** below.
'Employer'; 'employment' – see s 6(2) at para **[2.61]** above.
'Single Justice' – ie a JP acting for the same petty sessions area: see s 25(1) at para **[2.80]** below; or for these purposes by the justices' clerk instead: see the Magistrates' Courts (Attachment of Earnings) Order 1971, SI 809/1971, r 22(2)(a).
'Rules of court' – see CCR Ord 27 r 5 and 15: note that orders under s 14(1) must carry a penal notice.
'Such period and in such manner as may be presribed' – see CCR Ord 27, r 5.
'Normal deduction rate'; 'protected earnings rate' – see s 6(5)(a) and (b) respectively at para **[2.61]** above.
'Debtor' – see s 2(e) at para **[2.57]** above.

## [2.69.1]
## Keypoint

- General application

## [2.69.2]
## General application

This section provides disclosure powers in relation to the debtor's means and employment.

The reference to 'in any proceedings' in s 14(1) includes a free-standing application under s 1 above; or committal/distress proceedings[1]; or an application for a qualifying periodical maintenance order[2].

Note also that failure to comply with an order under s 14(1)(a) or (b) is an offence[3]; and that it is also an offence to make false statements (whether knowingly or recklessly)[4]. Failure to comply with an order under s 14(2)(b) is not an offence but leads to a further order to attend and thereafter, if the debtor fails to attend or refuses to give evidence, possible committal for up to 14 days[5].

As to timing and service of orders under s 14(1) see CCR Ord 27, rr 6 and 15 and the Magistrates' Courts (Attachment of Earnings) Order 1971, SI 1971/809, r 20.

1 See the AtEA 1971, s 3(4), (6) and (7) at para **[2.58]** above.
2 See the MEA 1991, s1.
3 See the AtEA 1971, s 23(2)(c) at para **[2.78]** below.
4 See the AtEA 1971, s 23(2)(f) at para **[2.78]** below.
5 See the AtEA 1971, s 23(1) at para **[2.78]** below.

**[2.70]**

## 15 Obligation of debtor and his employers to notify changes of employment and earnings

While an attachment of earnings order is in force—

(a) the debtor shall from time to time notify the court in writing of every occasion on which he leaves any employment, or becomes employed or re-employed, not later (in each case) than seven days from the date on which he did so;

(b) the debtor shall, on any occasion when he becomes employed or re-employed, include in his notification under paragraph (a) above particulars of his earnings and anticipated earnings from the relevant employment; and

(c) any person who becomes the debtor's employer and knows that the order is in force and by what court it was made shall, within seven days of his becoming the debtor's employer or of acquiring that knowledge (whichever is the later) notify that court in writing that he is the debtor's employer, and include in his notification a statement of the debtor's earnings and anticipated earnings.

### Definitions

'Debtor' – see s 2(e) at para **[2.57]** above.

'Employment'; 'employed'; 'employer' – see s 6(2) at para **[2.61]** above.

'Earnings' – see s 24 at para **[2.79]** below.

'Anticipated earnings' connotes a certain (albeit future) figure, ie anticipated actual earnings; as distinct from potential earnings which are uncertain and not taken into account[1]. However, the fact that earnings fluctuate is not a bar to making an attachment[2].

1 See *Pepper v Pepper* [1960] 1 All ER 529, [1960] 1 WLR 131.

2 See *R v York Magistrates' Court, ex p Grimes* (1997) 161 JP 550.

**[2.71]**

## 16 Power of court to determine whether particular payments are earnings

(1) Where an attachment of earnings order is in force, the court shall, on the application of a person specified in subsection (2) below, determine whether payments to the debtor of a particular class or description specified by the application are earnings for the purposes of the order; and the employer shall be entitled to give effect to any determination for the time being in force under this section.

(2) The persons referred to in subsection (1) above are—

(a) the employer;

(b) the debtor;

(c) the person to whom payment under the relevant adjudication is required to be made (whether directly or through an officer of any court); and

(d) without prejudice to paragraph (c) above, where the application is in respect of an attachment of earnings order made to secure payments under a magistrates' court maintenance order, the collecting officer.

(3) Where an application under this section is made by the employer, he shall not incur any liability for non-compliance with the order as respects any payments of the class or description specified by the application which are made by him to the debtor while the application, or any appeal in consequence thereof, is pending; but this subsection shall not, unless the court otherwise orders, apply as respects such payments if the employer subsequently withdraws the application or, as the case may be, abandons the appeal.

### Definitions

'Earnings' – see s 24 at para **[2.79]** below.

'Employer' – see s 6(2) at para **[2.61]** above.

'Collecting officer' – ie the magistrates' court clerk (s 6(7) at para **[2.61]** above), on behalf of the payee, but only at the payee's request: see s 18(1)(c) at para **[2.73]** below.

'Debtor' – see s 2(e) at para **[2.57]** above.

**[2.71.1]**
**Keypoint**
- Procedure

**[2.71.2]**
**Procedure**

The application is made (in the county court) in accordance with CCR Ord 27, r 11; and (in the magistrates' court) by complaint[1].

1 See the AtEA 1971, s 19(3) at para **[2.74]** below, with costs determined in accordance with the s 21 of the AtEA 1971 at para **[2.76]** below.



**[2.72]**

## 17 Consolidated attachment orders

(1) The powers of a county court under sections 1 and 3 of this Act shall include power to make an attachment of earnings order to secure the payment of any number of judgment debts; and the powers of a magistrates' court under those sections shall include power to make an attachment of earnings order to secure the discharge of any number of such liabilities as are specified in section 1(3).

(2) An attachment of earnings order made by virtue of this section shall be known as a consolidated attachment order.

(3) The power to make a consolidated attachment order shall be exercised subject to and in accordance with rules of court; and rules made for the purposes of this section may provide—

(a) for the transfer from one court to another—

(i) of an attachment of earnings order, or any proceedings for or arising out of such an order; and

(ii) of functions relating to the enforcement of any liability capable of being secured by attachment of earnings;

(b) for enabling a court to which any order, proceedings or functions have been transferred under the rules to vary or discharge an attachment of earnings order made by another court and to replace it (if the court thinks fit) with a consolidated attachment order;

(c) for the cases in which any power exercisable under this section or the rules may be exercised by a court of its own motion or on the application of a prescribed person;

(d) for requiring the [officer] of a court who receives payments made to him in compliance with an attachment of earnings order, instead of complying with section 13 of this Act, to deal with them as directed by the court or the rules; and

(e) for modifying or excluding provisions of this Act or [Part III of the Magistrates' Courts Act 1980], but only so far as may be necessary or expedient for securing conformity with the operation of rules made by virtue of paragraphs (a) to (d) of this subsection.

**Amendment**

Sub-s (3): AJA 1999, s 90(1), Sch 13; MCA 1980, s 154, Sch 7.

**Definitions**

'Judgment debts' – see s 2(c) at para **[2.57]** above.

'Rules of Court' – see CCR Ord 27, rr 18–22 and the Magistrates' Courts (Attachment of Earnings) Rules 1971, SI 1971/809, rr 15–17.

'Prescribed person' – see CCR Ord 27, r 19(1) and the Magistrates' Courts (Attachment of Earnings) Rules 1971, SI 1971/809, r 15(6).

**[2.73]**

### 18 Certain action not to be taken by collecting officer except on request

(1) [A justices' chief executive] who is entitled to receive payments under a maintenance order for transmission to another person shall not—

(a) apply for an attachment of earnings order to secure payments under the maintenance order; or

(b) except as provided by section 10(3) of this Act, apply for an order discharging or varying such an attachment of earnings order; or

(c) apply for a determination under section 16 of this Act,

unless he is requested in writing to do so by a person entitled to receive the payments through him.

(2) Where [a justices' chief executive] is so requested—

(a) he shall comply with the request unless it appears to him unreasonable in the circumstances to do so; and

(b) the person by whom the request was made shall have the same liabilities for all the costs properly incurred in or about any proceedings taken in pursuance of the request as if the proceedings had been taken by that person.

(3) For the purposes of subsection (2)(b) above, any application made by [a justices' chief executive] as required by section 10(3) of this Act shall be deemed to be made on the request of the person in whose favour the attachment of earnings order in question was made.

**Amendment**

Sub-ss (1) to (3): AJA 1999, s 90(1), Sch 13.

**Definitions**

'As provided by section 10(3)' – ie reduction of the normal deduction rate where the payer appears (to the court) to have been paying too much and where there are no pending applications before the court.

'Determination under section 16' – ie whether certain payments are 'earnings'.

**[2.74]**

### 19 Procedure on applications

(1) Subject to rules of court made by virtue of the following subsection, an application to a magistrates' court for an attachment of earnings order, or an order discharging or varying an attachment of earnings order, shall be made by complaint.

(2) Rules of court may make provision excluding subsection (1) in the case of such an application as is referred to in section 9(3)(b) of this Act.

(3) An application to a magistrates' court for a determination under section 16 of this Act shall be made by complaint.

(4) For the purposes of section [51 of the Magistrates' Courts Act 1980] (which provides for the issue of a summons directed to the person against whom an order may be made in pursuance of a complaint)—

(a) the power to make an order in pursuance of a complaint by the debtor for an attachment of earnings order, or the discharge or variation of such an order, shall be deemed to be a power to make an order against the person to whom payment under the relevant adjudication is required to be made (whether directly or through an officer of any court); and

(b) the power to make an attachment of earnings order, or an order discharging or varying an attachment of earnings order, in pursuance of a complaint by any other person (including a complaint in proceedings to which section 3(4)(b) of this Act applies) shall be deemed to be a power to make an order against the debtor.

(5) A complaint for an attachment of earnings order may be heard notwithstanding that it was made within the six months allowed by [section 127(1) of the Magistrates' Courts Act 1980].

**Amendment**

Sub-ss (4), (5): words in square brackets substituted by the MCA 1980, s 154, Sch 7, para 100.

**Definitions**

'Rules of Court' – see the Magistrates' Courts (Attachment of Earnings) Rules 1971, SI 809/1971.
'Complaint' – ie the equivalent of an information, but where the proceedings do not relate to an offence: see the MCA 1980, s 51. See also ss 19(4) and 19(5) at para **[2.74]** above. The court only has jurisdiction if the complaint is actually made: see *Trathan v Trathan* [1955] 2 All ER 701, [1955] 1 WLR 805.
'Section 9(3)(b)' – power of single justice/clerk to order temporary increase in protected earnings rate.
'Determination under section 16' – ie whether certain payments are 'earnings'.
'Section 3(4)(b)' – magistrates' power to substitute attachment of earnings for distress or committal.



**[2.75]**

## 20 Jurisdiction in respect of persons residing outside England and Wales

(1) It is hereby declared that a magistrates' court has jurisdiction to hear a complaint by or against a person residing outside England and Wales for the discharge or variation of an attachment of earnings order made by a magistrates' court to secure maintenance payments; and where such a complaint is made, the following provisions shall have effect.

(2) If the person resides in Scotland or Northern Ireland, section 15 of the Maintenance Orders Act 1950 (which relates to the service of process on persons residing in those countries) shall have effect in relation to the complaint as it has effect in relation to the proceedings therein mentioned.

(3) Subject to the following subsection, if the person resides outside the United Kingdom and does not appear at the time and place appointed for the hearing of the complaint, the court may, if it thinks it reasonable in all the circumstances to do so, proceed to hear and determine the complaint at the time and place appointed for the hearing, or for any adjourned hearing, in like manner as if the person had then appeared.

(4) Subsection (3) above shall apply only if it is proved to the satisfaction of the court, on oath or in such other manner as may be prescribed, that the complainant has taken such steps as may be prescribed to give to the said person notice of the complaint and of the time and place appointed for the hearing of it.

**Definitions**

'Complaint' – see s 19 at para **[2.74]** above.
'Appear' – appearance may be by a legal representative: see the MCA 1980, s 122.
'Prescribed' – see s 25(1) at para **[2.80]** below and the Magistrates' Courts (Attachment of Earnings) Rules 1971, SI 1971/809 rr 10, 11, and 22(2)(c).

**[2.75.1]**

### Keypoint

- The meaning of 'residing outside England and Wales'

**[2.75.2]**

### The meaning of 'residing outside England and Wales'

Residence is question of fact: 'to reside means simply to live'[1] (in the context of the MO(RE)A 1972, ss 10 and 32). The term implies a degree of permanence but a person may be resident in more than one place at once[2].

1 Per Singer J in *K v M, M and L (Financial Relief: Foreign Orders)* [1998] 2 FLR 59 at 75H.
2 See *Levene v IRC* [1928] AC 217, HL; and *Ikimi v Ikimi* [2001] EWCA Civ 873, [2002] Fam 72, [2001] 2 FCR 385, CA, dismissing the appeal from Coleridge J reported as *I v I (divorce: habitual residence)* [2001] 1 FLR 913 but disapproving the test formulated at first instance.

**[2.76]**

### 21 Costs on application under s 16

(1) On making a determination under section 16 of this Act, a magistrates' court may in its discretion make such order as it thinks just and reasonable for payment by any of the persons mentioned in subsection (2) of that section of the whole or any part of the costs of the determination (but subject to section 18(2)(b) of this Act).

(2) Costs ordered to be paid under this section shall—

- (a) in the case of costs to be paid by the debtor to the person in whose favour the attachment of earnings order in question was made, be deemed—
  - (i) if the attachment of earnings order was made to secure maintenance payments, to be a sum due under the related maintenance order, and
  - (ii) otherwise, to be a sum due to the [justices' chief executive for] the court; and
- (b) in any other case, be enforceable as a civil debt.

**Amendment**

Sub-s (2): AJA 1999, s 90(1), Sch 13.

**Definitions**

'Determination under section 16' – ie whether certain payments are 'earnings'.

'Section 18(2)(b) of this Act' – provides that the payee is prima facie liable for application made by clerk on payee's behalf.

'Debtor' – see s 2(e) at para **[2.57]** above.

'Deemed ... to be a sum due under the related maintenance order' – ie enforceable by warrant of distress or commitment: see the MCA 1980, ss 76, 77 and 92.

'Deemed ... to be a sum due to the clerk of the court' – ie deductible from payments received under the attachment: see s 13(1) at para **[2.68]** above.

'Enforceable as a civil debt' – ie enforceable by warrant of distress but not of commitment: see the MCA 1980, ss 76, 77 and 92.

**[2.77]**

### 22 Persons employed under the Crown

(1) The fact that an attachment of earnings order is made at the suit of the Crown shall not prevent its operation at any time when the debtor is in the employment of the Crown.

(2) Where a debtor is in the employment of the Crown and an attachment of earnings order is made in respect of him, then for the purposes of this Act—

- (a) the chief officer for the time being of the department, office or other body in which the debtor is employed shall be treated as having the debtor in his employment (any transfer of the debtor from one department, office or body to another being treated as a change of employment); and
- (b) any earnings paid by the Crown or a Minister of the Crown, or out of the public revenue of the United Kingdom, shall be treated as paid by the said chief officer.

(3) If any question arises, in proceedings for or arising out of an attachment of earnings order, as to what department, office or other body is concerned for the purposes of this section, or as to who for those purposes is the chief officer thereof, the question shall be referred to and determined by the Minister for the Civil Service; but that Minister shall not be under any obligation to consider a reference under this subsection unless it is made by the court.

(4) A document purporting to set out a determination of the said Minister under subsection (3) above and to be signed by an official of the [Office of Public Service …] shall, in any such proceedings as are mentioned in that subsection, be admissible in evidence and be deemed to contain an accurate statement of such a determination unless the contrary is shown.

(5) This Act shall have effect notwithstanding any enactment passed before 29th May 1970 and preventing or avoiding the attachment or diversion of sums due to a person in respect of service under the Crown, whether by way of remuneration, pension or otherwise.



**Amendment**

Sub-s (4): words in square brackets substituted by SI 1992/1296, art 6(1), Schedule, para 4, words omitted therein repealed by SI 1995/2985, art 5(1), Schedule, para 3.

**Definitions**

'Debtor' – see s 2(e) at para **[2.57]** above.
'Employment' – see s 6(2) at para **[2.61]** above: note continued exemption of service personnel pay: see s 24 at para **[2.79]** below.
'Earnings' – see s 24 at para **[2.79]** below.

**[2.78]**

### 23 Enforcement provisions

(1) If, after being served with notice of an application to a county court for an attachment of earnings order or for the variation of such an order [or with an order made under section 14(2)(b) above], the debtor fails to attend on the day and at the time specified for any hearing of the application [or specified in the order], the court may adjourn the hearing and order him to attend at a specified time on another day; and if the debtor—

(a) fails to attend at that time on that day; or
(b) attends, but refuses to be sworn or give evidence,

he may be ordered by the judge to be imprisoned for not more than fourteen days.

[(1A) In any case where the judge has power to make an order of imprisonment under subsection (1) for failure to attend, he may, in lieu of or in addition to making that order, order the debtor to be arrested and brought before the court either forthwith or at such time as the judge may direct.]

(2) Subject to this section, a person commits an offence if—

(a) being required by section 7(1) or 9(2) of this Act to comply with an attachment of earnings order, he fails to do so; or
(b) being required by section 7(2) of this Act to give a notice for the purposes of that subsection, he fails to give it, or fails to give it within the time required by that subsection; or
(c) he fails to comply with an order under section 14(1) of this Act or with any such requirement of a notice of application for an attachment of earnings order as is mentioned in section 14(4), or fails (in either case) to comply within the time required by the order or notice; or
(d) he fails to comply with section 15 of this Act; or
(e) he gives a notice for the purposes of section 7(2) of this Act, or a notification for the purposes of section 15, which he knows to be false in a material particular, or recklessly gives such a notice or notification which is false in a material particular; or
(f) in purported compliance with section 7(2) or 15 of this Act, or with an order under section 14(1), or with any such requirement of a notice of application for an attachment of earnings order as is mentioned in section 14(4), he makes any statement which he knows to be false in a material particular, or recklessly makes any statement which is false in a material particular.

(3) Where a person commits an offence under subsection (2) above in relation to proceedings in, or to an attachment of earnings order made by, the High Court or a county court, he shall be liable on summary conviction to a fine of not more than [level 2 on the standard scale] or he may be ordered by a judge of the High Court or the county court judge (as the case may be) to pay a fine of not more than [£250] or, in the case of an offence specified in subsection (4) below, to be imprisoned for not more than fourteen days; and where a person commits an offence under subsection (2) otherwise than as mentioned above in this subsection, he shall be liable on summary conviction to a fine of not more than [level 2 on the standard scale].

(4) The offences referred to above in the case of which a judge may impose imprisonment are—

(a) an offence under subsection (2)(c) or (d), if committed by the debtor; and
(b) an offence under subsection (2)(e) or (f), whether committed by the debtor or any other person.

(5) It shall be a defence—

(a) for a person charged with an offence under subsection (2)(a) above to prove that he took all reasonable steps to comply with the attachment of earnings order in question;
(b) for a person charged with an offence under subsection (2)(b) to prove that he did not know, and could not reasonably be expected to know, that the debtor was not in his employment, or (as the case may be) had ceased to be so, and that he gave the required notice as soon as reasonably practicable after the fact came to his knowledge.

(6) Where a person is convicted or dealt with for an offence under subsection (2)(a), the court may order him to pay, to whoever is the collecting officer of the court for the purposes of the attachment of earnings order in question, any sums deducted by that person from the debtor's earnings and not already paid to the collecting officer.

(7) Where under this section a person is ordered by a judge of the High Court or a county court judge to be imprisoned, the judge may at any time revoke the order and, if the person is already in custody, order his discharge.

(8) Any fine imposed by a judge of the High Court under subsection (3) above and any sums ordered by the High Court to be paid under subsection (6) above shall be recoverable in the same way as a fine imposed by that court in the exercise of its jurisdiction to punish for contempt of court; [section 129 of the County Courts Act 1984] (enforcement of fines) shall apply to payment of a fine imposed by a county court judge under subsection (3) and of any sums ordered by a county court judge to be paid under subsection (6); and any sum ordered by a magistrates' court to be paid under subsection (6) shall be recoverable as a sum adjudged to be paid on a conviction by that court.

(9) For the purposes of section 13 of the Administration of Justice Act 1960 (appeal in cases of contempt of court), subsection (3) above shall be treated as an enactment enabling the High Court or a county court to deal with an offence under subsection (2) above as if it were contempt of court.

(10) In this section references to proceedings in a court are to proceedings in which that court has power to make an attachment of earnings order or has made such an order.

[(11) A district judge, assistant district judge or deputy district judge shall have the same powers under this section as a judge of a county court.]

**Amendment**

Sub-s (1): words in square brackets inserted by the AJA 1982, s 53(2). Sub-s (1A): inserted by the CCA 1981, s 14(5), Sch 2, Pt III, para 6. Sub-s (3): maximum fines on summary conviction increased and converted to levels on the standard scale by the CJA 1982, ss 37, 38; sum in square brackets substituted by the CJA 1991, ss 17(3), 101(1), Sch 4, Pt I, Sch 12, para 6. Sub-s (8): words in square brackets substituted by the CCA 1984, s 148(1), Sch 2, para 41. Sub-s (11): inserted by the CLSA 1990, s 125(2), Sch 17, para 6.

**Definitions**
'Debtor' – see s 2(e) at para **[2.57]** above.
'Section 14(2)(b)' – an order to the debtor to attend court in order to give particulars of his employment and needs where attachment already made.
'Section 7(1) or 9(2)' – an employer's duty to comply with attachment/variation once he knows about it.
'Section 7(2)' – the obligation of an employer to notify the court if debtor not in his employment or ceases to be employed.
'Section 14(1)' – an order to the debtor to give particulars of his employment and needs, or to an employer to give particulars of the debtor's employment (prior to making attachment of earnings order).
'Section 14(4)' – the automatic requirement that the debtor give particulars of his employment and needs, contained in the notice of application for attachment of earnings order.
'Section 15' – the obligation of the debtor and the new employer to notify changes of employment and earnings.
'Level 2 on the standard scale' – now £500: see the MCA 1980, s 143 and the CJA 1982, s 37(2).



**[2.78.1]**
**Keypoint**
- Procedure

**[2.78.2]**
**Procedure**

For the procedure governing the issue of a summons in the county court in respect of offences see CCR Ord 27, r 16. Note the powers of district judge contained in s 23(11) of the AtEA 1971.

Section 13 of the Administration of Justice Act 1960 provides for appeal to the Court of Appeal in cases of contempt. Offences under the AtEA 1971 are deemed to be contempts for this purpose[1]. In the case of an appeal from the order of a district judge[2] there is also the usual route of appeal to the judge.

1 See the AtEA 1971, s 23(9) at para **[2.78]** above.
2 See the AtEA 1971, s 23(11) at para **[2.78]** above.

**[2.79]**

**24 Meaning of 'earnings'**

(1) For the purposes of this Act, but subject to the following subsection, 'earnings' are any sums payable to a person—

(a) by way of wages or salary (including any fees, bonus, commission, overtime pay or other emoluments payable in addition to wages or salary or payable under a contract of service);

(b) by way of pension (including an annuity in respect of past services, whether or not rendered to the person paying the annuity, and including periodical payments by way of compensation for the loss, abolition or relinquishment, or diminution in the emoluments, of any office or employment);

[(c) by way of statutory sick pay.]

(2) The following shall not be treated as earnings:—

(a) sums payable by any public department of the Government of Northern Ireland or of a territory outside the United Kingdom;

(b) pay or allowances payable to the debtor as a member of Her Majesty's forces [other than pay or allowances payable by his employer to him as a special member of a reserve force (within the meaning of the Reserve Forces Act 1996)];

(c) pension, allowances or benefit payable under any [enactment relating to social security];

(d) pension or allowances payable in respect of disablement or disability;

(e) [except in relation to a maintenance order] wages payable to a person as a seaman, other than wages payable to him as a seaman of a fishing boat;

[(f) guaranteed minimum pension within the meaning of the [Pension Schemes Act 1993]].

(3) In subsection (2)(e) above,

['fishing boat' means a vessel of whatever size, and in whatever way propelled, which is for the time being employed in sea fishing or in the sea-fishing service;

'seaman' includes every person (except masters and pilots) employed or engaged in any capacity on board any ship; and

'wages' includes emoluments.]

**Amendment**

Sub-s (1): para (c) inserted by the SSA 1985, s 21, Sch 4, para 1. Sub-s (2): in para (b) words from 'other than pay or allowances' to 'Reserve Forces Act 1996)' in square brackets inserted by SI 1998/3086, reg 6(1). Date in force: 1 January 1999: see SI 1998/3086, reg 1(2). Sub-s (2): in para (c) words 'enactment relating to social security' in square brackets substituted by the SSA 1986, s 86, Sch 10, para 102. Sub-s (2): in para (e) words 'except in relation to a maintenance order' in square brackets inserted by the MSA 1979, s 39(1). Sub-s (2): para (f) inserted by the SSPA 1975, s 65(1), Sch 4, para 15; words 'Pension Schemes Act 1993' in square brackets therein substituted by the PSA 1993, s 190, Sch 8, para 4. Sub-s (3): words from 'fishing boat' to 'emoluments.' in square brackets substituted by the MSA 1995, s 314(2), Sch 13, para 46.

**Definitions**

'Debtor' – see s 2(e) at para **[2.57]** above.

'Guaranteed minimum pension' – as defined by the PSA 1993, s 8(2).

### [2.79.1]
### Keypoint

- Further definition of 'earnings'

### [2.79.2]
### Further definition of 'earnings'

Earnings must be actual, not potential earnings[1]; but the fact that earnings fluctuate is not a bar to making an attachment[2]. Section 24(1)(a) also includes 'other emoluments': these must be of a financial nature[3].

The term 'pension' in s 24(1)(b) includes discretionary payments to a pensioner, but excludes payments made 'not to [the pensioner], but for his benefit' (eg discharging hotel bills)[4]. Note also that although payments under a pension may be attachable, the terms of the pension deed may provide that entitlement to payment ceases in the event, inter alia, of attachment, as happened in *Edmonds*[5].

For the purposes of s 24(1)(b), an employer's disability pension *is* paid in respect of past services (at least if calculated by reference to the length of service with employer)[6].

Sums payable by any public department of the Government of Northern Ireland or of a territory outside the United Kingdom are excluded under s 24(2)(a); it must follow that foreign earnings paid otherwise than by a public department are 'earnings' within the Act.

Although pay or allowances payable to the debtor as a member of Her Majesty's forces are excluded under the section, these should be distinguished from service pension, which is capable of attachment[7]. For attachment against serving members of armed services see the Army Act 1950, s 150; the Air Force Act 1950, s 150; and the Naval Forces (Enforcement of Maintenance Liabilities) Act 1957.

1 See *Pepper v Pepper* [1960] 1 All ER 529, [1960] 1 WLR 131.
2 See *R v York Magistrates' Court, ex p Grimes* (1997) 161 JP 550.
3 As to holiday pay credits, as distinct from holiday pay itself, see *LCC v Henry Boot & Sons Ltd* [1059] 1 WLR 1069.
4 See *Edmonds v Edmonds* [1965] 1 All ER 379n, [1965] 1 WLR 58.
5 See *Edmonds v Edmonds* [1965] 1 All ER 379n, [1965] 1 WLR 58.
6 See *Miles v Miles* [1979] 1 All ER 865, [1979] 1 WLR 371, CA.
7 See the AtEA 1971, s 22 (5) at para **[2.77]** above and s 24(1)(b) at para **[2.79]** above.

[2.80]

## 25 General interpretation

(1) In this Act, except where the context otherwise requires—

'administration order' means an order made under, and so referred to in, [Part VI of the County Courts Act 1984];

'the court', in relation to an attachment of earnings order, means the court which made the order, subject to rules of court as to the venue for, and the transfer of, proceedings in county courts and magistrates' courts;

'debtor' and 'relevant adjudication' have the meanings given by section 2 of this Act;

'the employer', in relation to an attachment of earnings order, means the person who is required by the order to make deductions from earnings paid by him to the debtor;

'judgment debt' has the meaning given by section 2 of this Act;

…

'maintenance order' has the meaning given by section 2 of this Act;

'maintenance payments' means payments required under a maintenance order;

'prescribed' means prescribed by rules of court; and

'rules of court', in relation to a magistrates' court, means rules under [section 144 of the Magistrates' Courts Act 1980];

…

(2) Any reference in this Act to sums payable under a judgment or order, or to the payment of such sums, includes a reference to costs and the payment of them; and the references in sections 6(4) and 12(2) to relevant costs are to any costs of the proceedings in which the attachment of earnings order in question was made, being costs which the debtor is liable to pay.

(3) References in sections 6(5)(b), 9(3)(b) and 14(1)(a) of this Act to the debtor's needs include references to the needs of any person for whom he must, or reasonably may, provide.

(4) …

(5) Any power to make rules which is conferred by this Act is without prejudice to any other power to make rules of court.

(6) This Act, so far as it relates to magistrates' courts, and [Part III of the Magistrates' Courts Act 1980] shall be construed as if this Act were contained in that Part.

(7) References in this Act to any enactment include references to that enactment as amended by or under any other enactment, including this Act.

**Amendment**

Sub-s (1): MCA 1980, s 154, Sch 7; CCA 1984, s 148(1), Sch 2; LAA 1988, s 45, Sch 5; AJA 1999, s 106, Sch 15. Sub-s (4): repealed by the DWA 1989, s 7(1), Sch 1. Sub-s (6): MCA 1980, s 154, Sch 7.

[2.81]

## 26 Transitional provision

(1) As from the appointed day, an attachment of earnings order made before that day under Part II of the Maintenance Orders Act 1958 (including an order made under that Part of that Act as applied by section 46 or 79 of the Criminal Justice Act 1967) shall take effect as an attachment of earnings order made under the corresponding power in this Act, and the provisions of this Act shall apply to it accordingly, so far as they are capable of doing so.

(2) Rules of court may make such provision as the rule-making authority considers requisite—

(a) for enabling an attachment of earnings order to which subsection (1) above applies to be varied so as to bring it into conformity, as from the appointed day, with the provisions of this Act, or to be replaced by an attachment of earnings order having effect as if made under the corresponding power in this Act;

(b) to secure that anything required or authorised by this Act to be done in relation to an attachment of earnings order made thereunder is required or, as the case may be, authorised to be done in relation to an attachment of earnings order to which the said subsection (1) applies.

(3) In this section, 'the appointed day' means the day appointed under section 54 of the Administration of Justice Act 1970 for the coming into force of Part II of that Act.

**Definitions**

'The appointed day' was 2 August 1971: see the Administration of Justice Act 1970 (Commencement No 4) Order 1971, SI 1971/834.
'Rules of Court' – see the Magistrates' Courts (Attachment of Earnings) Rules 1971, SI 1971/809, r 24, Schedule.

**[2.82]**

### 29 Citation, repeal, extent and commencement

(1) This Act may be cited as the Attachment of Earnings Act 1971.

(2) The enactments specified in Schedule 6 to this Act are hereby repealed to the extent specified in the third column of that Schedule.

(3) This Act, except section 20(2), does not extend to Scotland and, except sections 20(2) … does not extend to Northern Ireland.

(4) This Act shall come into force on the day appointed under section 54 of the Administration of Justice Act 1970 for the coming into force of Part II of that Act.

**Appointment**

2 August 1971: Administration of Justice Act 1970 (Commencement No 4) Order 1971, SI 1971/834.

**Amendment**

Sub-s (3): words omitted repealed by the NICA 1973, s 41(1), Sch 6, Pt I.

## SCHEDULE 1
## Maintenance orders to which this Act applies

(s 2)

**[2.83]**

**1**

An order for alimony, maintenance or other payments made, or having effect as if made, under Part II of the Matrimonial Causes Act 1965 (ancillary relief in actions for divorce etc).

**2**

An order for payments to or in respect of a child, being an order made, or having effect as if made, under Part III of the said Act of 1965 (maintenance of children following divorce, etc).

[3

An order for periodical or other payments made, or having effect as if made, under Part II of the Matrimonial Causes Act 1973.]

4

An order for maintenance or other payments to or in respect of a spouse or child, being an order made [under Part I of the Domestic Proceedings and Magistrates' Court Act 1978].

[5

An order for periodical or other payments made or having effect as if made under Schedule 1 to the Children Act 1989.]

6

...

7

An order under [paragraph 23 of Schedule 2 to the Children Act 1989] ... section 23 of the Ministry of the Social Security Act 1966 [... section 18 of the Supplementary Benefits Act 1976] [... section 24 of the Social Security Act 1986] [or section 106 of the Social Security Administration Act 1992] (various provisions for obtaining contributions from a person whose dependants are assisted or maintained out of public funds).

8

An order under section 43 of the National Assistance Act 1948 (recovery of costs of maintaining assisted person).

9

An order to which section 16 of the Maintenance Orders Act 1950 applies by virtue of subsection (2)(b) or (c) of that section (that is to say an order made by a court in Scotland or Northern Ireland and corresponding to one of those specified in the foregoing paragraphs) and which has been registered in a court in England and Wales under Part II of that Act.

10

A maintenance order within the meaning of the Maintenance Orders (Facilities for Enforcement) Act 1920 (Commonwealth orders enforceable in the United Kingdom) registered in, or confirmed by, a court in England and Wales under that Act.

[11

A maintenance order within the meaning of Part I of the Maintenance Order (Reciprocal Enforcement) Act 1972 registered in a magistrates' court under the said Part I.]

[12

An order under section 34(1)(b) of the Children Act 1975 (payments of maintenance in respect of a child to his custodian).]

[13

A maintenance order within the meaning of Part I of the Civil Jurisdiction and Judgments Act 1982 which is registered in a magistrates' court under that Part.]

[14

A maintenance judgment within the meaning of Council Regulation (EC) No 44/2001 of 22nd December 2000 on jurisdiction and the recognition and enforcement of judgments in civil and commercial matters, which is registered in a magistrates' court under that Regulation.]

**Amendment**

Para 3: substituted by the MCA 1973, s 53, Sch 2, para 13. Para 4: words in square brackets substituted by the DPMCA 1978, s 89(2)(a), Sch 2, para 32. Para 5: substituted by the CLSA 1990, s 116, Sch 16, para 38. Para 6: repealed by the FLRA 1987, s 33(1), Sch 2, para 44(b), Sch 4. Para 7: first words in square brackets substituted by the ChA 1989, s 108(5), (6), Sch 13, para 29, Sch 14, para 1; first word omitted repealed, and second words in square brackets inserted, by the SBA 1976, s 35(2), Sch 7, para 20; second word omitted repealed and third words in square brackets inserted by the SSA 1986, s 86, Sch 10, Pt II, para 43; final word omitted repealed and final words in square brackets inserted by the SS(CP)A 1992, s 4, Sch 2, para 7. Para 11: inserted by the MO(RE)A 1972, s 22(1), Schedule, para 7. Para 12: inserted by the CA 1975, s 108(1)(a), Sch 3, para 76. Para 13: inserted by the CJJA 1982, s 15(4), Sch 12, Pt I, para 6. Para 14: inserted by SI 2001/3929, art 5, Sch 3, para 9.

## SCHEDULE 2
### Taxes, Social Security Contributions etc relevant for Purposes of Section 3(6)

(s 3)

**[2.84]**

1

Income tax or any other tax or liability recoverable under section 65, 66 or 68 of the Taxes Management Act 1970.

2

. . .

[3

[Contributions equivalent premiums] under Part III of the [Pension Schemes Act 1993]].

[3A

Class 1, 2 and 4 contributions under Part I of the [Social Security Contributions and Benefits Act 1992].]

4

. . .

**Amendment**

Para 2: repealed by the SL(R)A 1989. Para 3: substituted by the SSPA 1975, s 65(1), Sch 4, para 16; words in square brackets substituted by the PA 1995, s 151, Sch 5, para 3; final words in square brackets substituted by the PSA 1993, s 190, Sch 8, para 4. Para 3A: inserted by the SS(CP)A 1975, s 1(3), Sch 2, para 42; words in square brackets substituted by the SS(CP)A 1992, s 4, Sch 3, para 6. Para 4: repealed by the SSA 1973, s 100, Sch 28, Pt I.

# SCHEDULE 3
Deductions by Employer under Attachment of Earnings Order

(ss 6, 7)

**[2.85]**

## PART I
SCHEME OF DEDUCTIONS

*Preliminary definitions*

**1**

The following three paragraphs have effect for defining and explaining, for purposes of this Schedule, expressions used therein.

**2**

'Pay-day', in relation to earnings paid to a debtor, means an occasion on which they are paid.

**3**

'Attachable earnings', in relation to a pay-day, are the earnings which remain payable to the debtor on that day after deduction by the employer of—

(a) income tax;

(b) …

[(bb) primary Class 1 contributions under Part I of the Social Security Act 1975].

[(c) amounts deductible under any enactment, or in pursuance of a request in writing by the debtor, for the purposes of a superannuation scheme, namely any enactment, rules, deed or other instrument providing for payment of annuities or lump sums—

(i) to the persons with respect to whom the instrument has effect on their retirement at a specified age or on becoming incapacitated at some earlier age, or

(ii) to the personal representatives or the widows, relatives or dependants of such persons on their death or otherwise,

whether with or without any further or other benefits.]

**[4**

(1) On any pay-day—

(a) 'the normal deduction' is arrived at by applying the normal deduction rate (as specified in the relevant attachment of earnings order) with respect to the relevant period; and

(b) 'the protected earnings' are arrived at by applying the protected earnings rate (as so specified) with respect to the relevant period.

(2) For the purposes of this paragraph the relevant period in relation to any pay-day is the period beginning—

(a) if it is the first pay-day of the debtor's employment with the employer, with the first day of the employment; or

(b) if on the last pay-day earnings were paid in respect of a period falling wholly or partly after that pay-day, with the first day after the end of that period; or

(c) in any other case, with the first day after the last pay-day, and ending—

(i) where earnings are paid in respect of a period falling wholly or partly after the pay-day, with the last day of that period; or

(ii) in any other case, with the pay-day.]

### *Employer's deduction (judgment debts and administration orders)*

**5**

In the case of an attachment of earnings order made to secure the payment of a judgment debt or payments under an administration order, the employer shall on any pay-day—

(a) if the attachable earnings exceed the protected earnings, deduct from the attachable earnings the amount of the excess or the normal deduction, whichever is the less;

(b) make no deduction if the attachable earnings are equal to, or less than, the protected earnings.

### *Employer's deduction (other cases)*

**6**

(1) The following provision shall have effect in the case of an attachment of earnings order to which paragraph 5 above does not apply.

(2) If on a pay-day the attachable earnings exceed the sum of—

(a) the protected earnings; and

(b) so much of any amount by which the attachable earnings on any previous pay-day fell short of the protected earnings as has not been made good by virtue of this sub-paragraph on another previous pay-day,

then, in so far as the excess allows, the employer shall deduct from the attachable earnings the amount specified in the following sub-paragraph.

(3) The said amount is the sum of—

(a) the normal deduction; and

(b) so much of the normal deduction on any previous pay-day as was not deducted on that day and has not been paid by virtue of this sub-paragraph on any other previous pay-day.

(4) No deduction shall be made on any pay-day when the attachable earnings are equal to, or less than, the protected earnings.

**Amendment**

Para 3: sub-para (b) repealed by the SSPA 1975, s 65(3), Sch 5; sub-para (bb) inserted by the SS(CP)A 1975, s 1(3), Sch 2, para 43; sub-para (c) substituted by the WA 1986, s 32(1), Sch 4, para 4, shall continue to have effect by virtue of the ERA 1996, s 240, Sch 1, para 3. Para 4: substituted by the AJA 1982, s 54.

**Definitions**

'Attachment of earnings order to which paragraph 5 does not apply' – The most significant orders to which para 5 does not apply are maintenance orders: see s 1(1) to (3) at para **[2.56]** above. As to priority between the different categories of attachment orders, see paras 7 and 8 below.

'So much of the … as was not deducted on that day and has not been paid by virtue of this sub-paragraph on any other previous pay-day' (sub-ss (2)(b) and (3)(b)) – means any previous shortfall/deficit in, respectively, the protected earnings and the normal deductions. The result is that not only is a shortfall in deductions carried forward but so too is any unused protected earnings relief. Where there are then sufficient earnings to allow it, arrears are recouped, but only after first allowing for any accumulated unused protected earnings relief and next deducting the current normal deduction.

## PART II
## PRIORITY AS BETWEEN ORDERS

**7**

Where the employer is required to comply with two or more attachment of earnings orders in respect of the same debtor, all or none of which orders are made to secure either the payment of judgment debts or payments under an administration order, then on any pay-day the employer shall, for the purpose of complying with Part I of this Schedule,—

(a) deal with the orders according to the respective dates on which they were made, disregarding any later order until an earlier one has been dealt with;
(b) deal with any later order as if the earnings to which it relates were the residue of the debtor's earnings after the making of any deduction to comply with any earlier order.



**8**

Where the employer is required to comply with two or more attachment of earnings orders, and one or more (but not all) of those orders are made to secure either the payment of judgment debts or payments under an administration order, then on any pay-day the employer shall, for the purpose of complying with Part I of this Schedule—

(a) deal first with any order which is not made to secure the payment of a judgment debt or payments under an administration order (complying with paragraph 7 above if there are two or more such orders); and
(b) deal thereafter with any order which is made to secure the payment of a judgment debt or payments under an administration order as if the earnings to which it relates were the residue of the debtor's earnings after the making of any deduction to comply with an order having priority by virtue of sub-paragraph (a) above; and
(c) if there are two or more orders to which sub-paragraph (b) above applies, comply with paragraph 7 above in respect of those orders.

**Definitions**

'Employer' – see s 6(2) at para **[2.61]** above.
'Debtor' – see s 2(e) at para **[2.57]** above.
'Judgment debts' – see s 2(1)(c) at para **[2.57]** above.
'Administration order' – see s 25 at para **[2.80]** above.
'Earnings' – see s 24 at para **[2.79]** above.

## [2.85.1]
## Keypoint

- Effect of Schedule

## [2.85.2]
## Effect of Schedule

Part II of Sch 3 provides the governing scheme for according priority as between more than one attachment of earnings referred to in s 7 above[1]. In summary a non-judgment debt/administration order attachment (primarily an attachment in respect of maintenance[2]) is dealt with in priority to a judgment debt/administration order attachment[3]. If there are more than one attachment of either category, then within each category the earliest in time has priority[4]. In addition, maintenance orders (and other non-Judgment debt/administration orders in the magistrates' court) are subject to the shortfall and carry-forward provisions set out in paragraph 6 above.

1 See para **[2.62]** above.
2 See the AtEA 1971, s 1(1) to (3) at para **[2.56]** above.
3 See the AtEA 1971, Sch 3, Pt II, para 8 above.
4 See the AtEA 1971, Sch 3, Pt II, para 7 above.

# Maintenance Orders (Reciprocal Enforcement) Acts 1972 and 1992



Contents



**[2.86]**
**Introduction**

The text of these Acts (and of the detailed rules and regulations ancillary to the MO(RE)A 1972) have been omitted because they are outside the scope of this book. The relevant statutory instruments are listed below. The text of both Acts and statutory instruments can be found in *Rayden and Jackson on Divorce and Family Matters* (17th edn, 1997). The MO(RE)A 1992 has no independent substance, having been enacted in order to amend the MO(RE)A 1972 and the Maintenance Orders (Facilities for Enforcement) Act 1920, and for connected purposes.

For the provisions of the 1972 Act, as amended by the 1992 Act, see *Rayden and Jackson on Divorce and Family Matters* (17th edn, 1997), vol 2, p 2399 et seq.

**[2.87]**
**Summary**

In summary, the purpose of the MO(RE)A 1972 (as amended) is to facilitate the reciprocal enforcement of maintenance orders and maintenance claims within a wide range of countries and states in what can broadly be categorised as Europe (in its expanded form), Israel, South and North America (but not all states of either continent), the Commonwealth and parts of Africa. It has to a very large extent replaced the Maintenance Orders (Facilities for Enforcement) Act 1920 (summarised at para **[2.18]** et seq above).

**[2.88]**
**Territorial application**

The Act has two main parts. Part I is concerned with the transmission and reciprocal enforcement of maintenance orders. Part II is concerned with the transmission and reciprocal enforcement of claims for maintenance (and also claims for variation of maintenance provision already made). Participating States are designated by Orders in Council.

States designated under Pt 1 are referred to in the Act as 'reciprocating countries', and Orders in Council so designating them (see below) are styled Reciprocal Enforcement of Maintenance Orders (Designation of Reciprocating Countries) Orders. States designated under Pt II are referred to as 'convention countries', after the United Nations Convention on the Recovery Abroad of Maintenance which was signed in New York in 1956. Orders in Council so designating Convention States are styled Recovery (Abroad) of Maintenance Orders (see below). There is also a Hague Convention of States (in Europe, including Poland, Estonia and now also Spain) designated as 'reciprocating countries' under Pt I.

A number of States are designated under both Pt I and Pt II, but equally a number of States have opted out of particular provisions of the Act and it is important always to check the particular case and the particular rules governing the designation of a particular State. The Act is expressly modified by particular statutory instruments in relation to particular States.

## [2.89]
## Scheme of the Maintenance Orders (Reciprocal Enforcement) Act 1972

Under both Pt I and Pt II of the MO(RE)A 1972 maintenance orders are defined widely to include orders 'for the payment of a lump sum or the making of periodical payments towards the maintenance of any person' or payments by a father of expenses incidental to the birth of a child (or, where the child has died, funeral expenses)[1].

The scheme of Pt I of the Act bears similarities to that of Maintenance Orders (Facilities for Enforcement) Act 1920 (see above) and rests on the concept of 'provisional' orders, as defined in s 21(1), and non-provisional (ie final) orders. Similarly, although they are not defined as such in either Act it is convenient to think of orders (whether provisional or final) as either inbound or outbound. An inbound order is one made in a reciprocating country outside the United Kingdom which it is desired to enforce in the UK. An outbound order is one made in the UK which it is desired to enforce in a reciprocating country outside the UK.

An existing UK maintenance order can be transmitted for enforcement in a reciprocating country in accordance with s 2. This is a non-provisional order. However in the absence of an existing order the Act also makes it possible to apply in England for a provisional order against a non-resident respondent living in a reciprocating country. Such applications are made to the magistrates' court (s 3) and, if an order is made, the resulting provisional order is transmitted to the reciprocating country for confirmation. Only when confirmed by the reciprocating country is the order capable of enforcement. The English court retains jurisdiction to enforce, vary, or revoke the original order (subject, in the case of variation of a provisional order, to confirmation in the reciprocating country of the order as varied)[2].

The equivalent scheme operates also for inbound orders. An existing foreign order (including a provisional order but only if it has been confirmed by another reciprocating country (s 6(1)), when transmitted to the UK in accordance with s 6, will be registered in the 'appropriate court' (s 21(1)), being the magistrates' court . Likewise a provisional foreign order may be transmitted to the UK in accordance with s 7, and, if confirmed, will be registered in the magistrates' court and enforced as if made by the registering court (s 8(1)). Confirmation is not a foregone conclusion. Until recently the confirming court has enjoyed a wide discretion either to confirm or to refuse to confirm or to vary and confirm a provisional order[3]. In relation to orders to and from Hague Convention Countries (see above under Territorial application) the discretion has now been removed by Reciprocal Enforcement of Maintenance Orders (Hague Convention Countries) (Variation) Order 1999, SI 1999/1318.

In relation to provisional orders, both outbound (s 3) and inbound (s 7), the basis of jurisdiction under Pt I is that the respondent resides in the reciprocating country (or appears to do so). Note that in relation to outbound existing orders (s 2) and non-provisional inbound orders (s 6) the jurisdiction of English courts is based on either the residence of the payer within the jurisdiction or the presence within the jurisdiction of assets belonging to him. Note also, however, that in the case of inbound orders from the Republic of Ireland and from Hague Convention countries the presence of assets belonging to the payer is not sufficient to found jurisdiction; residence is the sole ground[4].

The essential difference between Pt I and Pt II of the Act is that Pt II provides for the transmission of maintenance claims (as distinct from orders) to a convention country and that the claim is therefore judged and enforced in accordance with the law of the convention country. Because every application is a claim, not an order, there is no place for the final/provisional distinction discussed above in relation to Pt I. As under Pt I, all applications are dealt with by the magistrates' court and, in the case of outbound applications, the clerk is obliged to 'assist the applicant in completing an application which will comply with the requirements of the law applied in the convention country' (s 26(3)).

There is also an important difference between Pt I and Pt II in relation to the basis of jurisdiction. In contrast to Pt I (see above), under Pt II jurisdiction for an outbound application depends upon the respondent being 'for the time being subject to the jurisdiction of' the convention country (s 26 (1) and (2)); in the case of inbound applications jurisdiction is based solely upon the respondent's residence in England and Wales (s 27A). If the respondent is so resident the court treats the claim as an application for a maintenance order under the ChA 1989 (if the application is for maintenance for a child or children), or (in any other case) under the DPMCA 1978 (s 27A(2) to (4)). If a maintenance order is made it is the duty of the clerk to register it in accordance with s 27C(7).

Both Pt I and Pt II make provision for evidence to be obtained from, and in, reciprocating and convention countries. This includes in ss 14 and 38 provision for the taking of evidence in the UK for use in proceedings in reciprocating/convention countries.

The scheme of the Act was recently considered in *K v M, M and L (Financial Relief: Foreign Orders)*[5]. As to the meaning of residence as the basis of jurisdiction in this context see the judgment of Singer J in *K v M, M and L*[6]: 'to reside means simply to live'.

For a discussion of the 1972 Act and international enforcement generally, see *Rayden and Jackson on Divorce and Family Matters* (17th edn, 1997), vol 1, para 34.69 et seq.



1 See the MO(RE)A 1972, ss 21(1) and 39.
2 See the MO(RE)A 1972, ss 2(5), 3(6) and 5(3).
3 See *Horn v Horn* [1985] FLR 984.
4 See para **[2.90]** below.
5 [1998] 2 FLR 59.
6 [1998] 2 FLR 59 at 75E–H. See also *Ikimi v Ikimi* [2001] EWCA Civ 873, [2002] Fam 72, [2001] 2 FCR 385.

## [2.90]
## Orders in Council

- Reciprocal Enforcement of Maintenance Orders (Designation of Reciprocating Countries) Order 1974, SI 1974/556 (as amended);
- Recovery Abroad of Maintenance (Convention Countries) Order 1975, SI 1975/423 (as amended);
- Recovery of Maintenance (United States of America) Order 1993, SI 1993/591;
- Reciprocal Enforcement of Maintenance Orders (Hague Convention Countries) Order 1993, SI 1993/593 (as amended, including by, most recently, Reciprocal Enforcement of Maintenance Orders (Hague Convention Countries) (Variation) Order 1999, SI 1999/51318;
- Reciprocal Enforcement of Maintenance Orders (Republic of Ireland) Order 1993, SI 1993/594 (as amended); and
- Reciprocal Enforcement of Maintenance Orders (United States of America) Order 1995, SI 1995/2709.

## [2.91]
## Procedure

The majority of proceedings under the MO(RE)A 1972 take place in the magistrates' court where the procedure is governed by Magistrates' Courts (Reciprocal Enforcement of Maintenance Orders) Rules 1974 SI 1974/668 (as amended). See also:

- Magistrates' Courts (Reciprocal Enforcement of Maintenance Orders) (Republic of Ireland) Rules 1975, SI 1975/286 (as amended);
- Magistrates' Courts (Recovery Abroad of Maintenance) Rules 1975, SI 1975/488 (as amended), Magistrates' Courts (Reciprocal Enforcement of Maintenance Orders) (Hague Convention Countries) Rules 1980, SI 1980/108 (as amended, including by, most recently, Magistrates' Courts (Reciprocal Enforcement of Maintenance Orders) (Hague Convention Countries) Rules 1999, SI 1999/2002; and
- Magistrates' Courts (Reciprocal Enforcement of Maintenance Orders) (United States of America) Rules 1995, SI 1995/2802.

The procedure for cases in the High Court or county courts (especially in relation to transmission of outbound existing orders) is governed by FPR 1991, rr 7.30 to 7.38[1]. Note that the High Court is the prescribed court for the purposes of taking evidence pursuant to a request by a court in a reciprocating country under s 14 of the MO(RE)A 1972 where the request for evidence relates to a maintenance order made by a superior court in the UK and where the witness resides in England and Wales[2].

Appeals under Pt I are dealt with in s 12. In relation to Pt II an inbound claim for maintenance processed in England as a claim for maintenance is dealt with under the ordinary law subject to the modifications (to the ChA 1989 and the DPMCA 1978) for this purpose set out in ss 28, 28A and 28B.

1 See paras **[3.496]** to **[3.504]** below.
2 See the FPR 1991, r 7.34.

# Land Charges Act 1972



**Contents**



*An Act to consolidate certain enactments relating to the registration of land charges and other instruments and matters affecting land*

[9th August 1972]

**[2.92]**

### 1 The registers and the index

(1) The registrar shall continue to keep at the registry in the prescribed manner the following registers, namely—

(a) a register of land charges;

(b) a register of pending actions;

(c) a register of writs and orders affecting land;

(d) a register of deeds of arrangement affecting land;

(e) a register of annuities,

and shall also continue to keep there an index whereby all entries made in any of those registers can readily be traced.

(2) Every application to register shall be in the prescribed form and shall contain the prescribed particulars.

[(3) Where any charge or other matter is registrable in more than one of the registers kept under this Act, it shall be sufficient if it is registered in one such register, and if it is so registered the person entitled to the benefit of it shall not be prejudicially affected by any provision of this Act as to the effect of non-registration in any other such register.

(3A) Where any charge or other matter is registrable in a register kept under this Act and was also, before the commencement of the Local Land Charges Act 1975, registrable in a local land charges register, then, if before the commencement of the said Act it was registered in the appropriate local land charges register, it shall be treated for the purposes of the provisions of this Act as to the effect of non-registration as if it had been registered in the appropriate register under this Act; and any certificate setting out the result of an official search of the appropriate local land charges register shall, in relation to it, have effect as if it were a certificate setting out the result of an official search under this Act.]

(4) Schedule 1 to this Act shall have effect in relation to the register of annuities.

(5) An office copy of an entry in any register kept under this section shall be admissible in evidence in all proceedings and between all parties to the same extent as the original would be admissible.

(6) Subject to the provisions of this Act, registration may be vacated pursuant to an order of the court.

[(6A) The county courts have jurisdiction under subsection (6) above—

(a) in the case of a land charge of Class C(i), C(ii) or D(i), if the amount does not exceed £30,000;

(b) in the case of a land charge of Class C(iii), if it is for a specified capital sum of money not exceeding £30,000 or, where it is not for a specified capital sum, if the capital value of the land affected does not exceed £30,000;

(c) in the case of a land charge of Class A, Class B, Class C(iv), Class D(ii), Class D(iii) or Class E if the capital value of the land affected does not exceed £30,000;

(d) in the case of a land charge of Class F, if the land affected by it is the subject of an order made by the court under section 1 of the Matrimonial Homes Act 1983 [or section 33 of the Family Law Act 1996] or an application for an order under [either of those sections] relating to that land has been made to the court;

(e) in a case where an application under section 23 of the Deeds of Arrangement Act 1914 could be entertained by the court.]

[(6B) …]

(7) In this section 'index' includes any device or combination of devices serving the purpose of an index.

**Appointment**

Commencement order: SI 1972/2058.

**Amendment**

Sub-ss (3), (3A): substituted for existing sub-s (3) by the LLCA 1975, s 17(1)(a). Sub-s (6A): inserted by the CCA 1984, s 148(1), Sch 2, para 16. Sub-s (6A): substituted by SI 1991/724, art 2(6), (8), Schedule, Pt I. Sub-s (6A): in para (d) words 'or section 33 of the Family Law Act 1996' inserted by the FLA 1996, s 66(1), Sch 8, para 46. Date in force: 1 October 1997: see SI 1997/1892, art 3(1)(b). Sub-s (6A): in para (d) words 'either of those sections' in square brackets substituted by the FLA 1996, s 66(1), Sch 8, para 46. Date in force: 1 October 1997: see SI 1997/1892, art 3(1)(b). Sub-s (6B): repealed by SI 1991/724, art 2(6), (8), Schedule, Pt I. Sub-s (6B): inserted by the CCA 1984, s 148(1), Sch 2, para 16.

**Definitions**

'Prescribed' – see s 17(1) at para **[2.108]** below; and the Land Charges Rules 1974, 1974/1286, as amended by SI 1986/2001, 1990/485, 1995/1355.
'Land charge of Class F' – ie matrimonial home rights under the FLA 1996, ss 30 and 31.

### [2.92.1]
**Keypoints**

- Scope of section
- Relevance to family law practice

### [2.92.2]
**Scope of section**

This section, and this Act, deals exclusively with unregistered land[1].

1 See the LCA 1972, s 14 at para **[2.105]** below.



### [2.92.3]
**Relevance to family law practice**

The primary relevance of this Act to family lawyers is in relation to the priority of interests which are registered under it. This is so notwithstanding that the LCA 1972 applies only to unregistered land[1]. The registration of a land charge or other interest registrable under the LCA 1972 constitutes actual notice of the interest to a person who subsequently takes any interest in the land concerned[2].

The most common application of the Act is in relation to the Class F land charge (where land is held in the name of one spouse only). A Class F land charge is contained within the list of land charges to be kept on the register of land charges enumerated in s 2 and is defined at s 2(7)[3].

Of equal importance in some cases is the register of pending land actions[4], and the register of writs and orders affecting land[5]. In many cases a pending land action is referred to as a lis pendens. The two terms are synonymous. A pending land action is defined in s 17(1)[6].

An application for a property transfer order under MCA 1973, s 24, even where the interest claimed is not an existing one, is a pending land action[7]. This is so even where the application itself is subsequently dismissed (subject to the power of the court to vacate the register in accordance with s 5(10) below); and where the originating application (often the divorce petition) asks for a property transfer order only in generic terms without at that stage identifying the specific property[8]. In order to protect the priority of the applicant's interest against a subsequent dealing with the property the applicant's interest must be registered under the LCA 1972. This is of particular relevance in relation to applications under MCA 1973, s 37 to set aside subsequent charges registered against the property[9].

Likewise charging orders (and, where granted, writs of sequestration) are registrable under the register of writs and orders affecting land[10]. For the avoidance of argument a charging order is an order charging (and therefore affecting) the land, not merely the proceeds of sale of the land[11].

Note the expiry and powers of renewal in relation to registrations under s 5 (pending actions), s 6 (writs and orders) and s 7 (deeds of arrangement) which are contained in s 8. Note also the provision as to searches in ss 9 and 10, and the system of priority notices in s 11.

1 See the LCA 1972, s 14 at para **[2.105]** below.
2 See the LPA 1925, s 198.
3 See the FLA 1996, ss 30 and 31; and the LCA 1972, s 4(8) at para **[2.95]** below. See generally *Rayden and Jackson on Divorce and Family Matters* (17th edn, 1997), vol 1, para 32.6 et seq.
4 See the LCA 1972, s 5 at para **[2.96]** below.
5 See the LCA 1972, s 6 at para **[2.97]** below.
6 See para **[2.108]** below.
7 See *Whittingham v Whittingham* [1979] Fam 9; affd [1979] 19, CA.
8 See *Perez-Adamson v Perez-Rivas* [1987] Fam 89, [1987] 2 FLR 472, CA.
9 See para **[2.96.4]** below.
10 See the LCA 1972, s 6 at para **[2.97]** below.
11 See *Clark v Chief Land Registrar* [1994] Ch 370, [1995] 1 FLR 212, CA.

**[2.93]**

## 2 The register of land charges

(1) If a charge on or obligation affecting land falls into one of the classes described in this section, it may be registered in the register of land charges as a land charge of that class.

(2) A Class A land charge is—

(a) a rent or annuity or principal money payable by instalments or otherwise, with or without interest, which is not a charge created by deed but is a charge upon land (other than a rate) created pursuant to the application of some person under the provisions of any Act of Parliament, for securing to any person either the money spent by him or the costs, charges and expenses incurred by him under such Act, or the money advanced by him for repaying the money spent or the costs, charges and expenses incurred by another person under the authority of an Act of Parliament; or

(b) a rent or annuity or principal money payable as mentioned in paragraph (a) above which is not a charge created by deed but is a charge upon land (other than a rate) created pursuant to the application of some person under any of the enactments mentioned in Schedule 2 to this Act.

(3) A Class B land charge is a charge on land (not being a local land charge …) of any of the kinds described in paragraph (a) of subsection (2) above, created otherwise than pursuant to the application of any person.

(4) A Class C land charge is any of the following [(not being a local land charge)], namely—

(i) a puisne mortgage;
(ii) a limited owner's charge;
(iii) a general equitable charge;
(iv) an estate contract;

and for this purpose—

(i) a puisne mortgage is a legal mortgage which is not protected by a deposit of documents relating to the legal estate affected;

(ii) a limited owner's charge is an equitable charge acquired by a tenant for life or statutory owner under [[the Inheritance Tax Act 1984] or under] any other statute by reason of the discharge by him of any [inheritance tax] or other liabilities and to which special priority is given by the statute;

(iii) a general equitable charge is any equitable charge which—

(a) is not secured by a deposit of documents relating to the legal estate affected; and

(b) does not arise or affect an interest arising under a [trust of land] or a settlement; and

(c) is not a charge given by way of indemnity against rents equitably apportioned or charged exclusively on land in exoneration of other land and against the breach or non-observance of covenants or conditions; and

(d) is not included in any other class of land charge;

(iv) an estate contract is a contract by an estate owner or by a person entitled at the date of the contract to have a legal estate conveyed to him to convey or create a legal estate, including a contract conferring either expressly or by statutory implication a valid option to purchase, a right of pre-emption or any other like right.

(5) A Class D land charge is any of the following [(not being a local land charge)], namely—

(i) an Inland Revenue Charge;
(ii) a restrictive covenant;
(iii) an equitable easement;

and for this purpose—

(i) an Inland Revenue charge is a charge on land, being a charge acquired by the Board under [the Inheritance Tax Act 1984];

(ii) a restrictive covenant is a covenant or agreement (other than a covenant or agreement between a lessor and a lessee) restrictive of the user of land and entered into on or after 1st January 1926;

(iii) an equitable easement is an easement, right or privilege over or affecting land created or arising on or after 1st January 1926, and being merely an equitable interest.

(6) A Class E land charge is an annuity created before 1st January 1926 and not registered in the register of annuities.

(7) A Class F land charge is a charge affecting any land by virtue of the [Part IV of the Family Law Act 1996].

(8) A charge or obligation created before 1st January 1926 can only be registered as a Class B land charge or a Class C land charge if it is acquired under a conveyance made on or after that date.

(9) ...



**Appointment**
Commencement order: SI 1972/2058.

**Amendment**
Sub-s (3): words omitted repealed by the LLCA 1975, s 19, Sch 2. Sub-s (4): words '(not being a local land charge)' in square brackets inserted by the LLCA, s 17(1)(b). Sub-s (4): in second para (ii) first words in square brackets substituted by the FA 1975, s 52(1), Sch 12, paras 2, 18(1), (2). Sub-s (4): in second para (ii) words 'the Inheritance Tax Act 1984' in square brackets substituted by the ITA 1984, s 276, Sch 8, para 3(1)(a). Sub-s (4): in second para (ii) words 'inhertitance tax' in square brackets substituted by the FA 1975, s 52(1), Sch 12, paras 2, 18(1), (2). Sub-s (4): in second para (iii) words 'trust of land' in square brackets substituted by the TLATA 1996, s 25(1), Sch 3, para 12(2); for savings in relation to entailed interests created before the commencement of that Act, and savings consequential upon the abolition of the doctrine of conversion, see s 25(4), (5) thereof. Sub-s (5): words '(not being a local land charge)' in square brackets inserted by the LLCA, s 17(1)(b). Sub-s (5): words 'the Inheritance Tax Act 1984' in square brackets substituted by the ITA 1984, s 276, Sch 8, para 3(1)(b). Sub-s (7): words 'Part IV of the Family Law Act 1996' in square brackets substituted by the FLA 1996, s 66(1), Sch 8, para 47. Date in force: 1 October 1997: see SI 1997/1892, art 3(1)(b). Sub-s (9): repealed by the FA 1977, s 59, Sch 9.

**[2.93.1]**
**Keypoint**

- Inheritance Tax

**[2.93.2]**
**Inheritance Tax**

Inheritance tax – except in relation to a liability to tax arising before 25 July 1986 capital transfer tax shall be known as inheritance tax and the CTTA 1984 may be cited as the ITA 1984, by virtue of the FA 1986, s 100. Accordingly, references to capital transfer tax have been changed to references to inheritance tax.

**[2.94]**

### 3 Registration of land charges

(1) A land charge shall be registered in the name of the estate owner whose estate is intended to be affected.

[(1A) Where a person has died and a land charge created before his death would apart from his death have been registered in his name, it shall be so registered notwithstanding his death.]

(2) A land charge registered before 1st January 1926 under any enactment replaced by the Land Charges Act 1925 in the name of a person other than the estate owner may remain so registered until it is registered in the name of the estate owner in the prescribed manner.

(3) A puisne mortgage created before 1st January 1926 may be registered as a land charge before any transfer of the mortgage is made.

(4) The expenses incurred by the person entitled to the charge in registering a land charge of Class A, Class B or Class C (other than an estate contract) or by the Board in registering an Inland Revenue charge shall be deemed to form part of the land charge, and shall be recoverable accordingly on the day for payment of any part of the land charge next after such expenses are incurred.

(5) Where a land charge is not created by an instrument, short particulars of the effect of the charge shall be furnished with the application to register the charge.

(6) An application to register an Inland Revenue charge shall state the [tax] in respect of which the charge is claimed and, so far as possible, shall define the land affected, and such particulars shall be entered or referred to in the register.

(7) In the case of a land charge for securing money created by a company before 1st January 1970 or so created at any time as a floating charge, registration under *any of the enactments mentioned in subsection (8) below* [Part XII, or Chapter III of Part XXIII, of the Companies Act 1985 (or corresponding earlier enactments)] shall be sufficient in place of registration under this Act, and shall have effect as if the land charge had been registered under this Act.

(8) *The enactments* [The corresponding earlier enactments] referred to in subsection (7) above are section 93 of the Companies (Consolidation) Act 1908, section 79 of the Companies Act 1929 … section 95 of the Companies Act 1948 [and sections 395 to 398 of the Companies Act 1985] [as originally enacted].

**Appointment**

Commencement order: SI 1972/2058.

**Amendment**

Sub-s (1A): inserted by the LP(MP)A 1994, s 15(2). Sub-s (6): words in square brackets substituted by the FA 1975, s 52, Sch 12, paras 2, 18(1), (4). Sub-s (7): words in italics prospectively repealed and words in square brackets prospectively substituted by the Companies Act 1989, s 107, Sch 16, para 1(2), as from a day to be appointed. Sub-s (8): words in italics prospectively repealed, subsequent words in square brackets prospectively substituted, and final words in square brackets prospectively inserted, by the Companies Act 1989, s 107, Sch 16, para 1(3), as from a day to be appointed; word omitted repealed, and other words in square brackets substituted by the CC(CP)A 1985, s 30, Sch 2.

**[2.95]**

### 4 Effect of land charges and protection of purchasers

(1) A land charge of Class A (other than a land improvement charge registered after 31st December 1969) or of Class B shall, when registered, take effect as if it had been created by a deed of charge by way of legal mortgage, but without prejudice to the priority of the charge.

(2) A land charge of Class A created after 31st December 1888 shall be void as against a purchaser of the land charged with it or of any interest in such land, unless the land charge is registered in the register of land charges before the completion of the purchase.

(3) After the expiration of one year from the first conveyance occurring on or after 1st January 1889 of a land charge of Class A created before that date the person entitled to the land charge shall not be able to recover the land charge or any part of it as against a purchaser of the land charged with it or of any interest in the land, unless the land charge is registered in the register of land charges before the completion of the purchase.

(4) If a land improvement charge was registered as a land charge of Class A before 1st January 1970, any body corporate which, but for the charge, would have power to advance money on the security of the estate or interest affected by it shall have that power notwithstanding the charge.

(5) A land charge of Class B and a land charge of Class C (other than an estate contract) created or arising on or after 1st January 1926 shall be void as against a purchaser of the land charged with it, or of any interest in such land, unless the land charge is registered in the appropriate register before the completion of the purchase.

(6) An estate contract and a land charge of Class D created or entered into on or after 1st January 1926 shall be void as against a purchaser for money or money's worth [(or, in the case of an Inland Revenue charge, a purchaser within the meaning of [the Inheritance Tax Act 1984)]] of a legal estate in the land charged with it, unless the land charge is registered in the appropriate register before the completion of the purchase.

(7) After the expiration of one year from the first conveyance occurring on or after 1st January 1926 of a land charge of Class B or Class C created before that date the person entitled to the land charge shall not be able to enforce or recover the land charge or any part of it as against a purchaser of the land charged with it, or of any interest in the land, unless the land charge is registered in the appropriate register before the completion of the purchase.

(8) A land charge of Class F shall be void as against a purchaser of the land charged with it, or of any interest in such land, unless the land charge is registered in the appropriate register before the completion of the purchase.

**Appointment**

Commencement order: SI 1972/2058.

**Amendment**

Sub-s (6): first words in square brackets inserted by the FA 1975, s 52, Sch 12, paras 2, 18(1), (5); words in square brackets therein substituted by the ITA 1984, s 276, Sch 8, para 13.

**[2.95.1]**
**Keypoint**

- Inheritance Tax

**[2.95.2]**
**Inheritance Tax**

Inheritance tax – except in relation to a liability to tax arising before 25 July 1986 capital transfer tax shall be known as inheritance tax and the CTTA 1984 may be cited as the ITA 1984, by virtue of the FA 1986, s 100. Accordingly, references to capital transfer tax have been changed to references to inheritance tax.

**[2.96]**

## 5 The register of pending actions

(1) There may be registered in the register of pending actions—

(a) a pending land action;

(b) a petition in bankruptcy filed on or after 1st January 1926.

(2) Subject to general rules under section 16 of this Act, every application for registration under this section shall contain particulars of the title of the proceedings and the name, address and description of the estate owner or other person whose estate or interest is intended to be affected.

(3) An application for registration shall also state—

(a) if it relates to a pending land action, the court in which and the day on which the action was commenced; and

(b) if it relates to a petition in bankruptcy, the court in which and the day on which the petition was filed.

(4) The registrar shall forthwith enter the particulars in the register, in the name of the estate owner or other person whose estate or interest is intended to be affected.

[(4A) Where a person has died and a pending land action would apart from his death have been registered in his name, it shall be so registered notwithstanding his death.]

(5) An application to register a petition in bankruptcy against a firm shall state the names and addresses of the partners, and the registration shall be effected against each partner as well as against the firm.

(6) No fee shall be charged for the registration of a petition in bankruptcy if the application for registration is made by the registrar of the court in which the petition is filed.

(7) A pending land action shall not bind a purchaser without express notice of it unless it is for the time being registered under this section.

(8) A petition in bankruptcy shall not bind a purchaser of a legal estate in good faith, for money or money's worth, ... unless it is for the time being registered under this section.

(9) ...

(10) The court, if it thinks fit, may upon the determination of the proceedings, or during the pendency of the proceedings if satisfied that they are not prosecuted in good faith, make an order vacating a registration under this section, and direct the party on whose behalf it was made to pay all or any of the costs and expenses occasioned by the registration and by its vacation.

[(11) The county court has jurisdiction under subsection (10) of this section where the action was brought or the petition in bankruptcy was filed in that court.]

**Appointment**

Commencement order: SI 1972/2058.

**Amendment**

Sub-s (4A): inserted by the LP(MP)A 1994, s 15(3). Sub-s (8): words omitted repealed by the IA 1985, s 235, Sch 8, para 21, Sch 10, Pt III. Sub-s (9): repealed by the IA 1985, s 235, Sch 10, Pt III. Sub-s (11): inserted by the CCA 1984, s 148(1), Sch 2, para 17.

**Definitions**

'Pending land action' – see s 17(1) at para **[2.108]** below.
'Purchaser' – see s 17(1) at para **[2.108]** below.

## [2.96.1]
## Keypoints

- Effect of non-registration
- Limited validity and searches
- Inter-relation with MCA 1973, s 37

## [2.96.2]
## Effect of non-registration

Note s 5(7) above in relation to unregistered land a pending land action shall not bind a purchaser without express notice of it unless it is for the time being registered under this section[1]. In relation to unregistered land 'Purchaser' has the extended meaning set out in the LCA 1972, s 17(1)[2].

Note the distinction applied in *B v B (P Ltd Intervening)*[3] between 'notice' for the purposes of registration of interests in (registered) land, and 'notice' for the purposes of the MCA 1973, s 37(4) of an intention on the part of a spouse transferring an interest in land to defeat the claims of the other spouse[4].

1 For the position in relation to registered land, see LRA 1925, s 59(1): a pending land action may only be protected by caution.
2 See para **[2.108]** below: compare also the LPA 1925, s 205(1)(xxi).
3 [1994] 2 FLR 739.
4 See para **[2.96.4]** below.

### [2.96.3]
### Limited validity and searches

Note the expiry and powers of renewal in relation to registrations under s 5 (pending actions), s 6 (writs and orders) and s 7 (deeds of arrangement) which are contained in s 8[1].

Note also the provision as to searches in ss 9 and 10[2], and the system of priority notices in s 11[3].

1 See para **[2.99]** below.
2 See paras **[2.101]** below.
3 See para **[2.102]** below.



### [2.96.4]
### Inter-relation with MCA 1973, s 37

An application for a property transfer order under MCA 1973, s 24, even where the interest claimed is not an existing one, is a pending land action[1]. This is so even where the application itself is subsequently dismissed (subject to the power of the court to vacate the register in accordance with s 5(10)); and where the originating application (often the divorce petition) asks for a property transfer order only in generic terms without at that stage identifying the specific property[2]. In order to protect the priority of the applicant's interest against a subsequent dealing with the property the applicant's interest must be registered under the LCA 1972[3].

*Whittingham v Whittingham*[4] is authority for the proposition that 'a claim, if registrable, is not protected unless duly registered and the combined effect of s 5(7) of the LCA 1972 and s 199(1) of the LPA 1925 render unenforceable any matter capable of registration but not registered'[5].

Note the alternative route of protection offered by *B v B (P Ltd Intervening)*, albeit in a case relating to registered land; ie where the (subsequent) chargee has actual or constructive notice (under the MCA 1973, s 37) of an intention on the part of a spouse transferring an interest in land to defeat the claims of the other spouse. For these purposes there is a distinction between, on the one hand, the notice required for the purposes of the LRA 1925, s 59 (and, by analogy, it is suggested s 5(7) of the LCA 1972, 5(7)) and, on the other hand, the notice required for the purposes of the MCA 1973, s 37(4)[6].

1 See *Whittingham v Whittingham* [1979] Fam 9; affd [1979] Fam 19, CA.
2 See *Perez-Adamson v Perez-Rivas* [1987] 2 FLR 472.
3 See paras **[2.92.2]** and **[2.92.3]** above.
4 [1979] Fam 9; affd [1979] Fam 19, CA.
5 See *B v B (P Ltd Intervening)* [1994] 2 FLR 739 per Bracewell J at 746C.
6 See n 5 above at 749F. See also *Le Foe v Le Foe* [2001] 2 FLR 970.

### [2.97]

#### 6 The register of writs and orders affecting land

(1) There may be registered in the register of writs and orders affecting land—

(a) any writ or order affecting land issued or made by any court for the purpose of enforcing a judgment or recognisance;

(b) any order appointing a receiver or sequestrator of land;

[(c) any bankruptcy order, whether or not the bankrupt's estate is known to include land.]

[(d) any access order under the Access to Neighbouring Land Act 1992.]

[(1A) No writ or order affecting an interest under a trust of land may be registered under subsection (1) above.]

(2) Every entry made pursuant to this section shall be made in the name of the estate owner or other person whose land, if any, is affected by the writ or order registered.

[(2A) Where a person has died and any such writ or order as is mentioned in subsection (1)(a) or (b) above would apart from his death have been registered in his name, it shall be so registered notwithstanding his death.]

(3) No fee shall be charged for the registration of a [bankruptcy order] if the application for registration is made by an official receiver.

(4) Except as provided by subsection (5) below and by [section 37(5) of the Supreme Court Act 1981] and [section 107(3) of the County Courts Act 1984] (which make special provision as to receiving orders in respect of land of judgment debtors) every such writ and order as is mentioned in subsection (1) above, and every delivery in execution or other proceeding taken pursuant to any such writ or order, or in obedience to any such writ or order, shall be void as against a purchaser of the land unless the writ or order is for the time being registered under this section.

[(5) Subject to subsection (6) below, the title of a trustee in bankruptcy shall be void as against a purchaser of a legal estate in good faith for money or money's worth unless the bankruptcy order is for the time being registered under this section.]

(6) Where a petition in bankruptcy has been registered under section 5 above, the title of the trustee in bankruptcy shall be void as against a purchaser of a legal estate in good faith for money or money's worth ... claiming under a conveyance made after the date of registration, unless at the date of the conveyance either the registration of the petition is in force or a receiving order on the petition is registered under this section.

**Appointment**

Commencement order: SI 1972/2058.

**Amendment**

Sub-s (1): para (c) substituted by the IA 1985, s 235, Sch 8, para 21; para (d) inserted by the ANLA 1992, s 5(1). Sub-s (1A): inserted by the TLATA 1996, s 25(1), Sch 3, para 12(3); for savings in relation to entailed interests created before the commencement of that Act, and savings consequential upon the abolition of the doctrine of conversion, see s 25(4), (5) thereof. Sub-s (2A): inserted by the LP(MP)A 1994, s 15(4). Sub-s (3): words in square brackets substituted by the IA 1985, s 235, Sch 8, para 21. Sub-s (4): first words in square brackets substituted by the SCA 1981, s 152(1), Sch 5; second words in square brackets substituted by the CCA 1984, s 148(1), Sch 2, para 18. Sub-s (5): substituted by the IA 1985, s 235, Sch 8, para 21. Sub-s (6): words omitted repealed by the IA 1985, s 235, Sch 8, para 21, Sch 10, Part III.

**Definitions**

'Purchaser' – see s 17(1) at para **[2.108]** below.

## [2.97.1]
## Keypoints

- Registration of writs and orders
- Writs and orders affecting land
- Effect of non-registration
- Limited validity and searches

## [2.97.2]
## Registration of writs and orders

This section provides for the registration of writs and orders affecting unregistered land[1].

1 See further, the DTA 1994, s 28 in relation to charging orders made under the DTA 1994, s 27.

## [2.97.3]
## Writs and orders affecting land

Charging orders (and, where granted, writs of sequestration) are registrable under the register of writs and orders affecting land. For the avoidance of argument a charging order is an order charging (and therefore affecting) the land, not merely the proceeds of sale of the land[2].

1 See the LCA 1972, s 6 at para **[2.97]** above.
2 See *Clark v Chief Land Registrar* [1994] Ch 370, [1995] 1 FLR 212, CA.

## [2.97.4]
### Effect of non-registration

Note s 6(4) in relation to unregistered land writs and orders affecting land shall not (subject to limited statutory exceptions) bind a purchaser unless it is for the time being registered under this section. (Compare s 5(3)[1] in relation to the protection of pending actions which contains the additional exception of express notice.) In relation to unregistered land 'Purchaser' has the extended meaning set out in the LCA 1972, s 17(1)[2].

1 See para **[2.96]** above.
2 See para **[2.93]** below: compare the LPA 1925, s 205(1)(xxi).

## [2.97.5]
### Limited validity and searches

Note the expiry and powers of renewal in relation to registrations under s 5 (pending actions), s 6 (writs and orders) and s 7 (deeds of arrangement) which are contained in s 8[1].

Note also the provision as to searches in ss 9 and 10[2], and the system of priority notices in s 11[3].

1 See para **[2.99]** below.
2 See paras **[2.101]** below.
3 See para **[2.102]** below.



## [2.98]

### 7 The register of deeds of arrangement affecting land

(1) The deed of arrangement affecting land may be registered in the register of deeds of arrangement affecting land, in the name of the debtor, on the application of a trustee of the deed or a creditor assenting to or taking the benefit of the deed.

(2) Every deed of arrangement shall be void as against a purchaser of any land comprised in it or affected by it unless it is for the time being registered under this section.

**Appointment**
Commencement order: SI 1972/2058.

## [2.99]

### 8 Expiry and renewal of registrations

A registration under section 5, section 6 or section 7 of this Act shall cease to have effect at the end of the period of five years from the date on which it is made, but may be renewed from time to time and, if so renewed, shall have effect for five years from the date of renewal.

**Appointment**
Commencement order: SI 1972/2058.

## [2.100]

### 9 Searches

(1) Any person may search in any register kept under this Act on paying the prescribed fee.

(2) Without prejudice to subsection (1) above, the registrar may provide facilities for enabling persons entitled to search in any such register to see photographic or other images or copies of any portion of the register which they may wish to examine.

**Appointment**
Commencement order: SI 1972/2058.

**[2.101]**

## 10 Official searches

(1) Where any person requires search to be made at the registry for entries of any matters or documents, entries of which are required or allowed to be made in the registry by this Act, he may make a requisition in that behalf to the registrar, which may be either—

(a) a written requisition delivered at or sent by post to the registry; or

(b) a requisition communicated by teleprinter, telephone or other means in such manner as may be prescribed in relation to the means in question, in which case it shall be treated as made to the registrar if, but only if, he accepts it;

and the registrar shall not accept a requisition made in accordance with paragraph (b) above unless it is made by a person maintaining a credit account at the registry, and may at his discretion refuse to accept it notwithstanding that it is made by such a person.

(2) The prescribed fee shall be payable in respect of every requisition made under this section; and that fee—

(a) in the case of a requisition made in accordance with subsection (1)(a) above, shall be paid in such manner as may be prescribed for the purposes of this paragraph unless the requisition is made by a person maintaining a credit account at the registry and the fee is debited to that account;

(b) in the case of a requisition made in accordance with subsection (1)(b) above, shall be debited to the credit account of the person by whom the requisition is made.

(3) Where a requisition is made under subsection (1) above and the fee payable in respect of it is paid or debited in accordance with subsection (2) above, the registrar shall thereupon make the search required and—

(a) shall issue a certificate setting out the result of the search; and

(b) without prejudice to paragraph (a) above, may take such other steps as he considers appropriate to communicate that result to the person by whom the requisition was made.

(4) In favour of a purchaser or an intending purchaser, as against persons interested under or in respect of matters or documents entries of which are required or allowed as aforesaid, the certificate, according to its tenor, shall be conclusive, affirmatively or negatively, as the case may be.

(5) If any officer, clerk or person employed in the registry commits, or is party or privy to, any act of fraud or collusion, or is wilfully negligent, in the making of or otherwise in relation to any certificate under this section, he shall be guilty of an offence and shall be liable on conviction on indictment to imprisonment for a term not exceeding two years, or on summary conviction to imprisonment for a term not exceeding three months or to a fine not exceeding [the prescribed sum], or to both such imprisonment and fine.

(6) Without prejudice to subsection (5) above, no officer, clerk or person employed in the registry shall, in the absence of fraud on his part, be liable for any loss which may be suffered—

(a) by reason of any discrepancy between—

(i) the particulars which are shown in a certificate under this section as being the particulars in respect of which the search for entries was made, and

(ii) the particulars in respect of which a search for entries was required by the person who made the requisition; or

(b) by reason of any communication of the result of a search under this section made otherwise than by issuing a certificate under this section.

**Appointment**

Commencement order: SI 1972/2058.

**Amendment**

Sub-s (5): words in square brackets substituted by virtue of the MCA 1980, s 32(2).

[2.102]

## 11 Date of effective registration and priority notices

(1) Any person intending to make an application for the registration of any contemplated charge, instrument or other matter in pursuance of this Act or any rule made under this Act may give a priority notice in the prescribed form at least the relevant number of days before the registration is to take effect.

(2) Where a notice is given under subsection (1) above, it shall be entered in the register to which the intended application when made will relate.

(3) If the application is presented within the relevant number of days thereafter and refers in the prescribed manner to the notice, the registration shall take effect as if the registration had been made at the time when the charge, instrument or matter was created, entered into, made or arose, and the date at which the registration so takes effect shall be deemed to be the date of registration.

(4) Where—

(a) any two charges, instruments or matters are contemporaneous; and

(b) one of them (whether or not protected by a priority notice) is subject to or dependent on the other; and

(c) the latter is protected by a priority notice,

the subsequent or dependent charge, instrument or matter shall be deemed to have been created, entered into or made, or to have arisen, after the registration of the other.

(5) Where a purchaser has obtained a certificate under section 10 above, any entry which is made in the register after the date of the certificate and before the completion of the purchase, and is not made pursuant to a priority notice entered on the register on or before the date of the certificate, shall not affect the purchaser if the purchase is completed before the expiration of the relevant number of days after the date of the certificate.

(6) The relevant number of days is—

(a) for the purposes of subsections (1) and (5) above, fifteen;

(b) for the purposes of subsection (3) above, thirty;

or such other number as may be prescribed; but in reckoning the relevant number of days for any of the purposes of this section any days when the registry is not open to the public shall be excluded.

**Appointment**
Commencement order: SI 1972/2058.

**Definitions**
'Prescribed form' – s 1(1) and Land Charges Rules 1974, 1974/1286, as amended by SI 1986/2001, 1990/485, 1995/1355.

[2.103]

## 12 Protection of solicitors, trustees etc

A solicitor, or a trustee, personal representative, agent or other person in a fiduciary position, shall not be answerable—

(a) in respect of any loss occasioned by reliance on an office copy of an entry in any register kept under this Act;

(b) for any loss that may arise from error in a certificate under section 10 above obtained by him.

**Appointment**
Commencement order: SI 1972/2058.

[2.104]

## 13 Saving for overreaching powers

(1) The registration of any charge, annuity or other interest under this Act shall not prevent the charge, annuity or interest being overreached under any other Act, except where otherwise provided by that other Act.

(2) The registration as a land charge of a puisne mortgage or charge shall not operate to prevent that mortgage or charge being overreached in favour of a prior mortgagee or a person deriving title under him where, by reason of a sale or foreclosure, or otherwise, the right of the puisne mortgagee or subsequent chargee to redeem is barred.

**Appointment**

Commencement order: SI 1972/2058.

[2.105]

## 14 Exclusion of matters affecting registered land or created by instruments necessitating registration of land

(1) This Act shall not apply to instruments or matters required to be registered or re-registered on or after 1st January 1926, if and so far as they affect registered land, and can be protected under the Land Registration Act 1925 by lodging or registering a creditor's notice, restriction, caution, inhibition or other notice.

(2) Nothing in this Act imposes on the registrar any obligation to ascertain whether or not an instrument or matter affects registered land.

(3) Where an instrument executed on or after 27th July 1971 conveys, grants or assigns an estate in land and creates a land charge affecting that estate, this Act shall not apply to the land charge, so far as it affects that estate, if under [section 123A of the Land Registration Act 1925 (compulsory registration: effect of requirement to register)] the instrument will, unless the necessary application for registration under that Act is made within the time allowed by or under that section, become void so far as respects the conveyance, grant or assignment of that estate.

**Appointment**

Commencement order: SI 1972/2058.

**Amendment**

Sub-s (3): words from 'section 123A' to 'requirement to register)' in square brackets substituted by the LRA 1997, s 4(1), Sch 1, para 3. Date in force: 1 April 1998 (in relation to dispositions made on or after that date): see SI 1997/3036, arts 2(b), 3.

[2.106]

## 15 Application to the Crown

(1) This Act binds the Crown, but nothing in this Act shall be construed as rendering land owned by or occupied for the purposes of the Crown subject to any charge to which, independently of this Act, it would not be subject.

(2) References in this Act to restrictive covenants include references to any conditions, stipulations or restrictions imposed on or after 1st January 1926, by virtue of section 137 of the Law of Property Act 1922, for the protection of the amenities of royal parks, gardens and palaces.

**Appointment**

Commencement order: SI 1972/2058.

[2.107]

## 16 General rules

(1) The Lord Chancellor may, with the concurrence of the Treasury as to fees, make such general rules as may be required for carrying this Act into effect, and in particular—

(a) as to forms and contents of applications for registration, modes of identifying where practicable the land affected, requisitions for and certificates of official searches, and regulating the practice of the registry in connection therewith;

(b) for providing for the mode of registration of a land charge (and in the case of a puisne mortgage, general equitable charge, estate contract, restrictive covenant or equitable easement by reference to the instrument imposing or creating the charge, interest or restriction, or an extract from that instrument) and for the cancellation without an order of court of the registration of a land charge, on its cesser, or with the consent of the person entitled to it, or on sufficient evidence being furnished that the land charge has been overreached under the provisions of any Act or otherwise;

(c) for determining the date on which applications and notices shall be treated for the purposes of section 11 of this Act as having been made or given;

(d) for determining the times and order at and in which applications and priority notices are to be registered;

(e) for varying the relevant number of days for any of the purposes of section 11 of this Act;

(f) for enabling the registrar to provide credit accounting facilities in respect of fees payable by virtue of this Act;

(g) for treating the debiting of such a fee to a credit account maintained at the registry as being, for such purposes of this Act or of the rules as may be specified in the rules, payment of that fee;

(h) for the termination or general suspension of any credit accounting facilities provided under the rules or for their withdrawal or suspension in particular cases at the discretion of the registrar;

(j) for requiring the registrar to take steps in relation to any instrument or matter in respect of which compensation has been claimed under section 25 of the Law of Property Act 1969 which would be likely to bring that instrument or matter to the notice of any person who subsequently makes a search of the registers kept under section 1 of this Act or requires such a search to be made in relation to the estate or interest affected by the instrument or matter; and

(k) for authorising the use of the index kept under this Act in any manner which will serve that purpose, notwithstanding that its use in that manner is not otherwise authorised by or by virtue of this Act.

(2) The power of the Lord Chancellor, with the concurrence of the Secretary of State, to make [rules under section [412 of the Insolvency Act 1986]] shall include power to make rules as respects the registration and re-registration of a petition in bankruptcy under section 5 of this Act and [a bankruptcy order] under section 6 of this Act, as if the registration and re-registration were required [by [Parts VIII to XI] of that Act].

### Appointment

Commencement order: SI 1972/2058.

### Amendment

Sub-s (2): first, third and fourth words in square brackets substituted by the IA 1985, s 235, Sch 8, para 21; second and final words in square brackets substituted by the IA 1986, s 439(2), Sch 14.

### Definitions

'General rules' – see the Land Charges Rules 1974, 1974/1286, as amended by SI 1986/2001, 1990/485, 1995/1355.

**[2.108]**

## 17 Interpretation

(1) In this Act, unless the context otherwise requires,—

'annuity' means a rentcharge or an annuity for a life or lives or for any term of years or greater estate determinable on a life or on lives and created after 25th April 1855 and before 1st January 1926, but does not include an annuity created by a marriage settlement or will;

'the Board' means the Commissioners of Inland Revenue;

'conveyance' includes a mortgage, charge, lease, assent, vesting declaration, vesting instrument, release and every other assurance of property, or of an interest in property, by any instrument except a will, and 'convey' has a corresponding meaning;

'court' means the High Court, or the county court in a case where that court has jurisdiction;

'deed of arrangement' has the same meaning as in the Deeds of Arrangement Act 1914;

'estate owner', 'legal estate', 'equitable interest', … 'charge by way of legal mortgage', [and 'will'] have the same meanings as in the Law of Property Act 1925;

'judgment' includes any order or decree having the effect of a judgment;

'land' includes land of any tenure and mines and minerals, whether or not severed from the surface, buildings or parts of buildings (whether the division is horizontal, vertical or made in any other way) and other corporeal hereditaments, also a manor, an advowson and a rent and other incorporeal hereditaments, and an easement, right, privilege or benefit in, over or derived from land, but not an undivided share in land, and 'hereditament' means real property which, on an intestacy occurring before 1st January 1926, might have devolved on an heir;

'land improvement charge' means any charge under the Improvement of Land Act 1864 or under any special improvement Act within the meaning of the Improvement of Land Act 1899;

'pending land action' means any action or proceeding pending in court relating to land or any interest in or charge on land;

'prescribed' means prescribed by rules made pursuant to this Act;

'purchaser' means any person (including a mortgagee or lessee) who, for valuable consideration, takes any interest in land or in a charge on land, and 'purchase' has a corresponding meaning;

'registrar' means the Chief Land Registrar, 'registry' means Her Majesty's Land Registry, and 'registered land' has the same meaning as in the Land Registration Act 1925;

'tenant for life', 'statutory owner', 'vesting instrument' and 'settlement' have the same meanings as in the Settled Land Act 1925.

(2) For the purposes of any provision in this Act requiring or authorising anything to be done at or delivered or sent to the registry, any reference to the registry shall, if the registrar so directs, be read as a reference to such office of the registry (whether in London or elsewhere) as may be specified in the direction.

(3) Any reference in this Act to any enactment is a reference to it as amended by or under any other enactment, including this Act.

### Appointment

Commencement order: SI 1972/2058.

### Amendment

Sub-s (1): words omitted repealed by the TLATA 1996, s 25(2), Sch 4, for savings in relation to entailed interests created before the commencement of that Act, and savings consequential upon the abolition of the doctrine of conversion, see s 25(4), (5) thereof; words in square brackets substituted by the FA 1975, s 52(1), Sch 12, paras 2, 18(1), (6).

[2.109]

## 18 Consequential amendments, repeals, savings, etc

(1) Schedule 3 to this Act, which contains consequential amendments of other Acts, shall have effect.

(2) …

(3) The enactments specified in Schedule 5 to this Act are hereby repealed to the extent specified in the third column of that Schedule.

(4) …

(5) In so far as any entry in a register or instrument made or other thing whatsoever done under any enactment repealed by this Act could have been made or done under a corresponding provision in this Act, it shall have effect as if made or done under that corresponding provision; and for the purposes of this provision any entry in a register which under section 24 of the Land Charges Act 1925 had effect as if made under that Act shall, so far as may be necessary for the continuity of the law, be treated as made under this Act.

(6) Any enactment or other document referring to an enactment repealed by this Act or to an enactment repealed by the Land Charges Act 1925 shall, as far as may be necessary for preserving its effect, be construed as referring, or as including a reference, to the corresponding enactment in this Act.

(7) Nothing in the foregoing provisions of this section shall be taken as prejudicing the operation of section 38 of the Interpretation Act 1889 (which relates to the effect of repeals).

**Appointment**

Commencement order: SI 1972/2058.

**Amendment**

Sub-s (2): repealed by the LLCA 1975, s 19(1), Sch 2. Sub-s (4): revokes the Land Charges Rules 1972, SI 1972/50.

[2.110]

## 19 Short title, commencement and extent

(1) This Act may be cited as the Land Charges Act 1972.

(2) This Act shall come into force on such day as the Lord Chancellor may by order made by statutory instrument appoint; and different days may be so appointed for different purposes.

(3) This Act extends to England and Wales only.

**Appointment**

Commencement order: SI 1972/2058.

**Notes**

The Act was brought into force on 29 January 1973 by the Land Charges Act 1972 (Commencement) Order 1972, SI 1972/2058.

## SCHEDULE 1
Annuities

(s 1)

[2.111]

**1**

No further entries shall be made in the register of annuities.

**2**

An entry of an annuity made in the register of annuities before 1st January 1926 may be vacated in the prescribed manner on the prescribed evidence as to satisfaction, cesser or discharge being furnished.

**3**

The register shall be closed when all the entries in it have been vacated or the prescribed evidence of the satisfaction, cesser or discharge of all the annuities has been furnished.

**4**

An annuity which before 1st January 1926 was capable of being registered in the register of annuities shall be void as against a creditor or a purchaser of any interest in the land charged with the annuity unless the annuity is for the time being registered in the register of annuities or in the register of land charges.

**Appointment**

Commencement order: SI 1972/2058.

SCHEDULE 2
Class A Land Charges

(s 2)

**[2.112]**

**1**

Charges created pursuant to applications under the enactments mentioned in this Schedule may be registered as land charges of Class A by virtue of paragraph (b) of section 2(2) of this Act:—

| | |
|---|---|
| (a) The Tithe Act 1918 (8 & 9 Geo 5 c 54) | Sections 4(2) and 6(1) (charge of consideration money for redemption of tithe rentcharge). |
| (b) The Tithe Annuities Apportionment Act 1921 (11 & 12 Geo 5 c 20) | Section 1 (charge of apportioned part of tithe redemption annuity). |
| (c) The Landlord and Tenant Act 1927 (17 & 18 Geo 5 c 36) | Paragraph (7) of Schedule 1 (charge in respect of improvements to business premises). |
| (d) [The Land Drainage Act 1991 (c 59)] | [Section 34(2)] (charge in respect of sum paid in commutation of certain obligations to repair banks, water-courses etc.). |
| (e) The Tithe Act 1936 (26 Geo 5 & 1 Edw 8 c 43) | Section 30(1) (charge for redemption of corn rents etc.). |
| (f) The Civil Defence Act 1939 (2 & 3 Geo 6 c 31) | Sections 18(4) and 19(1) (charges in respect of civil defence works). |
| (g) The Agricultural Holdings Act 1948 (11 & 12 Geo 6 c 63) | [Section 74 (charge in respect of sums due to] occupier of agricultural holding). |
| . . . | |
| (h) The Corn Rents Act 1963 (1963 c 14) | Section 1(5) (charge under a scheme for the apportionment or redemption of corn rents or other payments in lieu of tithes). |
| [(i) The Agricultural Holdings Act 1986 | Section 85 (charges in respect of sums due to tenant of agricultural holding).<br>Section 86 (charges in favour of landlord of agricultural holding in respect of compensation for or cost of certain improvements).] |

**2**

The following provisions of paragraph 1 above shall cease to have effect upon the coming into operation of the first scheme under the Corn Rents Act 1963, that is to say:—

(a) in sub-paragraph (a), the words 'and 6(1)'; and
(b) sub-paragraph (e).

**3**

[The reference in paragraph 1(g) above to section 74 of the Agricultural Holdings Act 1948 and the references in paragraph 1(i) above to section 85 and 86 of the Agricultural Holdings Act 1986] include references to any previous similar enactment.

**Appointment**

Commencement order: SI 1972/2058.

**Amendment**

Para 1: first and second words in square brackets substituted by the WC(CP)A 1991, s 2, Sch 1, para 21; words omitted repealed and other words in square brackets substituted or inserted by the AHA 1986, ss 100, 101, Sch 14, para 51, Sch 15, Pt I. Para 3: words in square brackets substituted by the AHA 1986, s 100, Sch 14, para 51(4).

# Domicile and Matrimonial Proceedings Act 1973



## Contents

### PRE-1 MARCH 2001



### POST-1 MARCH 2001



*An Act to amend the law relating to the domicile of married women and persons not of full age, to matters connected with domicile and to jurisdiction in matrimonial proceedings including actions for reduction of consistorial decrees; to make further provision about the recognition of divorces and legal separations; and for purposes connected therewith*

[25th July 1973]

### PRE-1 MARCH 2001

**[2.112A]**

**5 Jurisdiction of High Court and county courts**

(1) Subsections (2) to (5) below shall have effect, *subject to section 6(3) and (4) of this Act,* with respect to the jurisdiction of the court to entertain—

(a) proceedings for *divorce, judicial separation or* nullity of marriage; and

(b) proceedings for death to be presumed and a marriage to be dissolved in pursuance of section 19 of the Matrimonial Causes Act 1973;

and in this Part of this Act 'the court' means the High Court and a divorce county court within the meaning of [Part V of the Matrimonial and Family Proceedings Act 1984].

*(2) The court shall have jurisdiction to entertain proceedings for divorce or judicial separation if (and only if) either of the parties to the marriage—*

*(a) is domiciled in England and Wales on the date when the proceedings are begun; or*

*(b) was habitually resident in England and Wales throughout the period of one year ending with that date.*

(3) The court shall have jurisdiction to entertain proceedings for nullity of marriage if (and only if) either of the parties to the marriage—

- (a) is domiciled in England and Wales on the date when the proceedings are begun; or
- (b) was habitually resident in England and Wales throughout the period of one year ending with that date; or
- (c) died before that date and either—
  - (i) was at death domiciled in England and Wales, or
  - (ii) had been habitually resident in England and Wales throughout the period of one year ending with the date of death.

(4) The court shall have jurisdiction to entertain proceedings for death to be presumed and a marriage to be dissolved if (and only if) the petitioner—

- (a) is domiciled in England and Wales on the date when the proceedings are begun; or
- (b) was habitually resident in England and Wales throughout the period of one year ending with that date.

*(5) The court shall, at any time when proceedings are pending in respect of which it has jurisdiction by virtue of subsection (2) or (3) above (or of this subsection), also have jurisdiction to entertain other proceedings, in respect of the same marriage, for divorce, judicial separation or nullity of marriage, notwithstanding that jurisdiction would not be exercisable under subsection (2) or (3).*

(6) Schedule 1 to this Act shall have effect as to the cases in which matrimonial proceedings in England and Wales are to be, or may be, stayed by the court where there are concurrent proceedings elsewhere in respect of the same marriage, and as to the other matters dealt with in that Schedule; but nothing in the Schedule—

- (a) requires or authorises a stay of proceedings which are pending when this section comes into force; or
- (b) prejudices any power to stay proceedings which is exercisable by the court apart from the Schedule.

**Amendment**

Sub-ss (1), (5): words in italics repealed with savings by the FLA 1996, s 66(3), Sch 10 as from a day to be appointed.

### [2.112A.1]
### Keypoints

- General
- Jurisdiction in divorce, judicial separation and nullity proceedings
- Jurisdiction in proceedings for death to be presumed
- Effect of Sch 1 to the DMPA 1973

### [2.112A.2]
### General

The above provisions apply only to the jurisdiction of the court with respect to proceedings commenced before 1 March 2001 (the commencement date of the amendments effected by the European Communities (Matrimonial Jurisdiction and Judgments) Regulations 2001, SI 2001/310.

### [2.112A.3]
### Jurisdiction in divorce, judicial separation and nullity proceedings

Only one type of the following proceedings – **nullity**, **divorce** or **judicial separation** – needs to have been commenced by that date for the court to have jurisdiction in respect of all three types of proceedings.

The tests set out are (former) domicile or habitual residence. In respect of which see *Ikimi v Ikimi*[1].

1 [2001] EWCA Civ 873, [2001] Fam 72, [2001] 2 FCR 385.

### [2.112A.4]
### Jurisdiction in proceedings for death to be presumed

The same tests apply to assuming jurisdiction in applications for death to be presumed.

### [2.112A.5]
### Effect of Sch 1 to the DMPA 1973

Stays may be obligatory or discretionary[1].

1 See Sch 1 at para **[2.112C]** below.



## POST-1 MARCH 2001

### [2.112B]

**5 Jurisdiction of High Court and county courts**

(1) Subsections (2) to (5) below shall have effect, *subject to section 6(3) and (4) of this Act*, with respect to the jurisdiction of the court to entertain—

(a) proceedings for *divorce, judicial separation or* nullity of marriage; and

(b) proceedings for death to be presumed and a marriage to be dissolved in pursuance of section 19 of the Matrimonial Causes Act 1973 …

[(1A) In this Part of this Act—

'the Council Regulation' means Council Regulation (EC) No 1347/2000 of 29th May 2000 on jurisdiction and the recognition and enforcement of judgments in matrimonial matters and in matters of parental responsibility for children of both spouses;

'Contracting State' means—

(a) one of the original parties to the Council Regulation, that is to say Belgium, Germany, Greece, Spain, France, Ireland, Italy, Luxembourg, the Netherlands, Austria, Portugal, Finland, Sweden and the United Kingdom, and

(b) a party which has subsequently adopted the Council Regulation; and

'the court' means the High Court and a divorce county court within the meaning of Part V of the Matrimonial and Family Proceedings Act 1984.]

[(2) The court shall have jurisdiction to entertain proceedings for divorce or judicial separation if (and only if)—

(a) the court has jurisdiction under the Council Regulation; or

(b) no court of a Contracting State has jurisdiction under the Council Regulation and either of the parties to the marriage is domiciled in England and Wales on the date when the proceedings are begun.]

[(3) The court shall have jurisdiction to entertain proceedings for nullity of marriage if (and only if)—

(a) the court has jurisdiction under the Council Regulation; or

(b) no court of a Contracting State has jurisdiction under the Council Regulation and either of the parties to the marriage—

(i) is domiciled in England and Wales on the date when the proceedings are begun; or

(ii) died before that date and either was at death domiciled in England and Wales or had been habitually resident in England and Wales throughout the period of one year ending with the date of death.]

[(3A) Subsections (2) and (3) above do not give the court jurisdiction to entertain proceedings in contravention of Article 7 of the Council Regulation.]

(4) The court shall have jurisdiction to entertain proceedings for death to be presumed and a marriage to be dissolved if (and only if) the petitioner—

(a) is domiciled in England and Wales on the date when the proceedings are begun; or

(b) was habitually resident in England and Wales throughout the period of one year ending with that date.

*(5) The court shall, at any time when proceedings are pending in respect of which it has jurisdiction by virtue of subsection (2) or (3) above (or of this subsection), also have jurisdiction to entertain other proceedings, in respect of the same marriage, for divorce, judicial separation or nullity of marriage, notwithstanding that jurisdiction would not be exercisable under subsection (2) or (3).*

(6) Schedule 1 to this Act shall have effect as to the cases in which matrimonial proceedings in England and Wales are to be, or may be, stayed by the court where there are concurrent proceedings elsewhere in respect of the same marriage, and as to the other matters dealt with in that Schedule; but nothing in the Schedule—

(a) requires or authorises a stay of proceedings which are pending when this section comes into force; or

(b) prejudices any power to stay proceedings which is exercisable by the court apart from the Schedule.

**Amendment**

Sub-s (1): words in italics repealed with savings by the FLA 1996, s 66(3), Sch 10 as from a day to be appointed; words omitted repealed by SI 2001/310, reg 3. Sub-s (1A): inserted by SI 2001/310, reg 3. Sub-ss (2), (3): substituted by SI 2001/310, reg 3. Sub-s (3A): inserted by SI 2001/310, reg 3. Sub-s (5): substituted with savings by the FLA 1996, s 66(1), Sch 8 as from a day to be appointed.

## [2.112B.1]
## Keypoints

- General
- Jurisdiction in divorce, judicial separation and nullity proceedings
- Jurisdiction in proceedings for death to be presumed
- Effect of Sch 1 to the DMPA 1973

## [2.112B.2]
## General

The above provisions apply only to the jurisdiction of the court with respect to proceedings commenced after 1 March 2001 with the coming into effect of the European Communities (Matrimonial Jurisdiction and Judgments) Regulations 2001, SI 2001/310.

## [2.112B.3]
## Jurisdiction in divorce, judicial separation and nullity proceedings

Only one type of proceedings – **nullity**, **divorce** or **judicial separation** – needs to have been commenced by that date for the court to have jurisdiction in respect of all three types of proceedings.

The tests set out are in compliance with Council Regulation (EC) No 1347/2000 of 29 May 2000 or in default thereof habitual residence. In respect of which see *Ikimi v Ikimi*[1].

1 [2001] EWCA Civ 873, [2001] Fam 72, [2001] 2 FCR 385.

## [2.112B.4]
## Jurisdiction in proceedings for death to be presumed

The same tests apply to assuming jurisdiction in applications for death to be presumed.

## [2.112B.5]
## Effect of Sch 1 to the DMPA 1973

Stays may be obligatory or discretionary[1].

1 See Sch 1 at para **[2.112C]** below. Note the amendment introduced into para 9(1) of Sch 1 below.

## SCHEDULE 1
## Staying of Matrimonial Proceedings (England and Wales)

(s 5(6))

**[2.112C]**

*Interpretation*

**1**

*The following five paragraphs* have effect for the interpretation of this Schedule.

**2**

*'Matrimonial proceedings' means any proceedings so far as they are one or more of the five following kinds, namely, proceedings for—*

*divorce,*
*judicial separation,*
*nullity of marriage,*
*a declaration as to the validity of a marriage of the petitioner, and*
*a declaration as to the subsistence of such a marriage.*

**3**

(1) 'Another jurisdiction' means any country outside England and Wales.

(2) 'Related jurisdiction' means any of the following countries, namely, Scotland, Northern Ireland, Jersey, Guernsey and the Isle of Man (the reference to Guernsey being treated as including Alderney and Sark).

**4**

(1) References to the trial or first trial in any proceedings do not include references to the separate trial of an issue as to jurisdiction only.

(2) For purposes of this Schedule, proceedings in the court are continuing if they are pending and not stayed.

**5**

Any reference in this Schedule to proceedings in another jurisdiction is to proceedings in a court of that jurisdiction, and to any other proceedings in that jurisdiction, which are of a description prescribed for the purposes of this paragraph; and provision may be made by rules of court as to when proceedings of any description in another jurisdiction are continuing for the purposes of this Schedule.

**6**

'Prescribed' means prescribed by rules of court.

*Duty to furnish particulars of concurrent proceedings in another jurisdiction*

**7**

*While matrimonial proceedings are pending in the court in respect of a marriage and the trial or first trial in those proceedings has not begun, it shall be the duty of any person who is a petitioner in the proceedings, or is a respondent and has in his answer included a prayer for relief to furnish, in such manner and to such persons and on such occasions as may be prescribed, such particulars as may be prescribed of any proceedings which—*

*(a) he knows to be continuing in another jurisdiction; and*
*(b) are in respect of that marriage or capable of affecting its validity or subsistence.*

*Obligatory stays*

**8**

*(1) Where before the beginning of the trial or first trial or first trial in any proceedings for divorce which are continuing in the court it appears to the court on the application of a party to the marriage—*

(a) that in respect of the same marriage proceedings for divorce or nullity of marriage are continuing in a related jurisdiction; and

(b) that the parties to the marriage have resided together after its celebration; and

(c) that the place where they resided together when the proceedings in the court were begun or, if they did not then reside together, where they last resided together before those proceedings were begun, is in that jurisdiction; and

(d) that either of the said parties was habitually resident in that jurisdiction throughout the year ending with the date on which they last resided together before the date on which the proceedings in the court were begun,

it shall be the duty of the court, subject to paragraph 10(2) below, to order that the *proceedings* in the court be stayed.

*(2) References in sub-paragraph (1) above to the proceedings in the court are, in the case of proceedings which are not only proceedings for divorce, to the proceedings so far as they are proceedings for divorce.*

**PRE-1 MARCH 2001**

*Discretionary stays*

**9**

*(1) Where before the beginning of the trial or first trial in any matrimonial proceedings which are continuing in the court it appears to the court—*

*(a) that any proceedings in respect of the marriage in question, or capable of affecting its validity or subsistence, are continuing in another jurisdiction; and*

*(b) that the balance of fairness (including convenience) as between the parties to the marriage is such that it is appropriate for the proceedings in that jurisdiction to be disposed of before further steps are taken in the proceedings in the court or in those proceedings so far as they consist of a particular kind of matrimonial proceedings,*

*the court may then, if it thinks fit, order that the proceedings in the court be stayed or, as the case may be, that those proceedings be stayed so far as they consist of proceedings of that kind.*

**POST-1 MARCH 2001**

*Discretionary stays*

**9**

*(1) Where before the beginning of the trial or first trial in any matrimonial proceedings[, other than proceedings governed by the Council Regulation,] which are continuing in the court it appears to the court—*

*(a) that any proceedings in respect of the marriage in question, or capable of affecting its validity or subsistence, are continuing in another jurisdiction; and*

*(b) that the balance of fairness (including convenience) as between the parties to the marriage is such that it is appropriate for the proceedings in that jurisdiction to be disposed of before further steps are taken in the proceedings in the court or in those proceedings so far as they consist of a particular kind of matrimonial proceedings,*

*the court may then, if it thinks fit, order that the proceedings in the court be stayed or, as the case may be, that those proceedings be stayed so far as they consist of proceedings of that kind.*

(2) In considering the balance of fairness and convenience for the purposes of sub-paragraph (1)(b) above, the court shall have regard to all factors appearing to be relevant, including the convenience of witnesses and any delay or expense which may result from the proceedings being stayed, or not being stayed.

*(3) In the case of any proceedings so far as they are proceedings for divorce, the court shall not exercise the power conferred on it by sub-paragraph (1) above while an application under paragraph 8 above in respect of the proceedings is pending.*

(4) If, at any time after the beginning of the trial or first trial in any matrimonial proceedings which are pending in the court, the court declares by order that it is satisfied that a person has failed to perform the duty imposed on him in respect of the proceedings by paragraph 7 above, sub-paragraph (1) above shall have effect in relation to those proceedings and, to the other proceedings by reference to which the declaration is made, as if the words 'before the beginning of the trial or first trial' were omitted; but no action shall lie in respect of the failure of a person to perform such a duty.

### *Supplementary*

**10**

(1) Where an order staying any proceedings is in force in pursuance of paragraph 8 or 9 above, the court may, if it thinks fit, on the application of a party to the proceedings, discharge the order if it appears to the court that the other proceedings by reference to which the order was made are stayed or concluded, or that a party to those other proceedings has delayed unreasonably in prosecuting them.

*(2) If the court discharges an order staying any proceedings and made in pursuance of paragraph 8 above, the court shall not again stay those proceedings in pursuance of that paragraph.*

**11**

*(1) The provisions of sub-paragraphs (2) and (3) below shall apply (subject to sub-paragraph (4)) where proceedings for divorce, judicial separation or nullity of marriage are stayed by reference to proceedings in a related jurisdiction for divorce, judicial separation of nullity of marriage; and in this paragraph—*

...

*'lump sum order' means such an order as is mentioned in paragraph (f) of section 23(1) of the Matrimonial Causes Act 1973 (lump sum payment for children), being an order made under section 23(1) or (2)(a) [or an order made in equivalent circumstances under Schedule 1 to the Children Act 1989 and of a kind mentioned in paragraph 1(2)(c) of that Schedule];*

*'the other proceedings', in relation to any stayed proceedings, means the proceedings in another jurisdiction by reference to which the stay was imposed;*

*'relevant order' means—*

- *(a) an order under section 22 of the Matrimonial Causes Act 1973 (maintenance for spouse pending suit),*
- *(b) such an order as is mentioned in paragraph (d) or (e) of section 23(1) of that Act (periodical payments for children) being an order made under section 23(1) or (2)(a) [or an order made in equivalent circumstances under Schedule 1 to the Children Act 1989 and of a kind mentioned in paragraph 1(2)(a) or (b) of that Schedule],*
- *(c) an order under section 42(1)(a) of that Act (orders for the custody and education of children) [or a section 8 order under the Children Act 1989], and*

*(d) except for the purposes of sub-paragraph (3) below, any order restraining a person from removing a child out of England and Wales or out of the [care] of another person; and*

*'stayed' means stayed in pursuance of this Schedule.*

(2) Where *any proceedings are stayed*, then, without prejudice to the effect of the stay apart from this paragraph—

(a) the court shall not have power to make a relevant order or a lump sum order *in connection with the stayed proceedings* except in pursuance of paragraph (c) below; and

(b) subject to paragraph (c) below, any relevant order *made in connection with the stayed proceedings* shall, unless the stay is previously removed or the order previously discharged, cease to have effect on the expiration of the period of three months beginning with the date on which the stay was imposed; but

(c) if the court considers that, for the purpose of dealing with circumstances needing to be dealt with urgently, it is necessary during or after that period to make a relevant order or a lump sum order *in connection with the stayed proceedings* or to extend or further extend the duration of a relevant order *made in connection with the stayed proceedings*, the court may do so and the order shall not cease to have effect by virtue of paragraph (b) above.

(3) Where *any proceedings are stayed* and at the time when the stay is imposed an order is in force, or at a subsequent time an order comes into force, which was made in connection with the other proceedings and provides for any of the … following matters, namely, periodical payments for a spouse of the marriage in question, periodical payments for a child, [or any provision which could be made by a section 8 order under the Children Act 1989] then, on the imposition of the stay in a case where the order is in force when the stay is imposed and on the coming into force of the order in any other case—

(a) any relevant order *made in connection with the stayed proceedings* shall cease to have effect in so far as it makes for a spouse or child any provision for any of those matters as respects which the same or different provision for that spouse or child is made by the other order;

(b) the court shall not have power *in connection with the stayed proceedings* to make a relevant order containing for a spouse or child provision for any of those matters as respects which any provision for that spouse or child is made by the other order; and

(c) if the other order contains provision for periodical payments for a child, the court shall not have power *in connection with the stayed proceedings* to make a lump sum order for that child.

[(3A) *Where any such order as is mentioned in paragraph (e) of section 23(1) of the Matrimonial Causes Act 1973, being an order made under section 23(1) or (2)(a) of that Act, ceases to have effect by virtue of sub-paragraph (2) or (3) above,* any order made under section 24A(1) of that Act which requires the proceeds of sale of property to be used for securing periodical payments under the first mentioned order shall also cease to have effect.]

*(4) If any proceedings are stayed so far as they consist of matrimonial proceedings of a particular kind but are not stayed so far as they consist of matrimonial proceedings of a different kind, sub-paragraphs (2) and (3) above shall not apply to the proceedings but, without prejudice to the effect of the stay apart from this paragraph, the court shall not have power to make a relevant order or a lump sum order in connection with the proceedings so far as they are stayed; and in this sub-paragraph references to matrimonial proceedings do not include proceedings for a declaration.*

(5) Nothing in this paragraph affects any power of the court—

(a) to vary or discharge a relevant order so far as the order is for the time being in force; or

(b) to enforce a relevant order as respects any period when it is or was in force; or

(c) to make a relevant order or a lump sum order *in connection with proceedings which were but are no longer stayed.*

**Amendment**

Paras 1, 8: words in italics prospectively repealed by the FLA 1996, s 19, Sch 3 as from a day to be appointed. Paras 2, 7: prospectively substituted with savings by the FLA 1996, s 19, Sch 3 as from a day to be appointed. Para 9(1): substituted with savings by the FLA 1996, s 19, Sch 3 as from a day to be appointed. Para 9(1): words in square brackets inserted by SI 2001/310, reg 4. Para 9(3): substituted with savings by the FLA 1996, s 19, Sch 3 as from a day to be appointed. Para 10(2): substituted by the FLA 1996, s 19, Sch 3 as from a day to be appointed. Para 11: words in italics prospectively repealed by the FLA 1996, s 19, Sch 3 as from a day to be appointed; amended by the ChA 1989, s 08, Schs 13, 15; and the MHPA 1981, s 8.



### [2.112C.1]
### Keypoints

- General
- 'Matrimonial proceedings'
- 'Trial of first trial'
- Concurrent proceedings
- Duty to provide particulars of concurrent proceedings
- Another/Related jurisdictions
- Obligatory and discretionary stays
- Effect of a stay

### [2.112C.2]
### General

Sch 1 to the DMPA 1973 sets out the proper approach of the court to proceedings occurring concurrently in two different courts and the obligation of the parties to provide information in relation to the same.

### [2.112C.3]
### 'Matrimonial proceedings'

Obligatory stays operate in relation to habitual residence, discretionary stays in relation to the balance of fairness.

### [2.112C.4]
### 'Trial of first trial'

The first trial does not include trial only of the issue of jurisdiction.

### [2.112C.5]
### Concurrent proceedings

Once the concurrent proceedings are concluded, or if there is unreasonable delay in their conclusion, the court may discharge the order staying the proceedings in this jurisdiction and may not stay the same again.

### [2.112C.6]
### Duty to provide particulars of concurrent proceedings

Both the petitioner and respondent can be under a duty to provide those details within their knowledge of concurrent proceedings in another jurisdiction.

### [2.112C.7]
### 'Another' / 'related' jurisdictions

'Another' jurisdiction is one other than England and Wales, 'related' jurisdictions to England and Wales are:

- Scotland;
- Northern Ireland;

- Jersey;
- Guernsey[1]; and
- Isle of Man.

1 The reference to Guernsey being treated as including Alderney and Sark.

## [2.112C.8]
### Obligatory and discretionary stays

Obligatory stays apply to proceedings in a related jurisdiction, discretionary stays to proceedings in another jurisdiction[1].

1 Note the amendment to para 9(1) of Sch 1 above, with effect from 1 March 2001.

## [2.112C.9]
### Effect of a stay

- Save in cases of urgency once the proceedings are stayed the court ceases to have the power to make a relevant[1] or lump sum orde and any such order already made ceases to have effect three months after the stay is imposed.
- Once proceedings are stayed orders for periodical payments for a spouse of the marriage in question, periodical payments for a child, are stayed in as far as and as soon as a concurrent order elsewhere provides for the same.

1 See s 11(1) of the DMPA 1973.

# Matrimonial Causes Act 1973

PART 2
MCA 1973

## Contents

*Section*

PART I
DIVORCE, NULLITY AND OTHER MATRIMONIAL SUITS



PART II
FINANCIAL RELIEF FOR PARTIES TO MARRIAGE AND CHILDREN OF FAMILY

---

*An Act to consolidate certain enactments relating to matrimonial proceedings, maintenance agreements, and declarations of legitimacy, validity of marriage and British nationality, with amendments to give effect to recommendations of the Law Commission*

[23rd May 1973]

**[2.113]**

PART I
DIVORCE, NULLITY AND OTHER MATRIMONIAL SUITS

### 5 Refusal of decree in five year separation cases on grounds of grave hardship to respondent

(1) The respondent to a petition for divorce in which the petitioner alleges five years' separation may oppose the grant of a decree on the ground that the dissolution of the marriage will result in grave financial or other hardship to him and that it would in all the circumstances be wrong to dissolve the marriage.

(2) Where the grant of a decree is opposed by virtue of this section, then—

(a) if the court finds that the petitioner is entitled to rely in support of his petition on the fact of five years' separation and makes no such finding as to any other fact mentioned in section 1(2) above, and

(b) if apart from this section the court would grant a decree on the petition,

the court shall consider all the circumstances, including the conduct of the parties to the marriage and the interests of those parties and of any children or other persons concerned, and if of opinion that the dissolution of the marriage will result in grave financial or other hardship to the respondent and that it would in all the circumstances be wrong to dissolve the marriage it shall dismiss the petition.

(3) For the purposes of this section hardship shall include the loss of the chance of acquiring any benefit which the respondent might acquire if the marriage were not dissolved.

**Appointment**
Commencement order: SI 1973/1972.

**Derivation**
This section derived from the DRA 1969, s 4.

## [2.113.1]
## Keypoints

- General
- Raising the defence
- The correct approach
- Grave financial or other hardship

## [2.113.2]
## General

Section 5 is intended to protect respondents to petitions under the MCA 1973, s 1(2)(e) (based on five year's separation) especially those who have reached middle age, from losing the financial security of being married, and the chance of acquiring those benefits (particularly pension rights) they would have acquired in the event that the other spouse predeceased them. See generally *Rayden and Jackson on Divorce and Family Matters* (17th edn, 1997), vol 1, para 8.60 and the Noter-up thereto.

Now that pension sharing and attachment orders are available, it is likely that s 5 will be of very limited application.

## [2.113.3]
## Raising the defence

A defence to a petition based on five year's separation under the MCA 1973, s 1(2)(e) on the grounds of 'grave financial or other hardship' must be raised in the answer to the petition[1]. The answer must contain details of the financial or other hardship the respondent will suffer and of the circumstances that make it wrong to dissolve the marriage. The cause will then proceed as a defended suit in the usual way[2].

A petitioner is estopped from raising grave financial or other hardship under the MCA 1973, s 5 if the respondent cross-petitions under the MCA 1973, s 1(2)(e) based on five year's separation[3].

A petition under the MCA 1973, s 1(2)(e) which is opposed under s 5 should be transferred to the High Court for hearing unless the issues of fact or law raised makes it more suitable for trial in the county court[4].

Failure to establish a defence under the MCA 1973, s 5 does not prevent the respondent from applying under the MCA 1973, s 10(2) to prevent a decree nisi being made absolute[5].

An application for maintenance pending suit under the MCA 1973, s 22 may be made pending determination of the suit in the usual way.

Upon dismissal of the petition under the MCA 1973, s 5(2)(b), in the event that the respondent fails to make proper financial provision for the petitioner or any child of the family, the court may make an order under the MCA 1973, s 27. Such an application may be consolidated with the petition for immediate consideration in the event that the petition is dismissed[6].

1 See FPR 1991, r 2.12(1)(c).
2 See FPR 1991, rr 2.24–25, 2.28–30.
3 See *Grenfell v Grenfell* [1978] Fam 128, [1978] 1 All ER 561.
4 See *Practice Direction (Family Division: Distribution of Business)* [1992] 1 WLR 586.
5 See *Wilson v Wilson* [1973] 2 All ER 17, CA per Stephenson LJ; and *Archer v Archer* [1999] 2 FCR 158, [1999] 1 FLR 327, CA.
6 RSC Ord 4, r 9; CCR Ord 13, r 9.

## [2.113.4]
## The correct approach

The court should adopt a two-stage test:

(1) it must first consider whether or not it has been established that the dissolution of the marriage would result in grave financial or other hardship to the respondent;
(2) it must then consider whether in all the circumstances of the case it would be wrong to dissolve the marriage[1].

If the court is not satisfied in respect of the first stage of the test (above), it is unnecessary to go on to consider whether the second stage is satisfied[2].

When considering the first stage, the court is concerned to inquire whether the respondent has made out a prima facie case of grave financial (or other) hardship. If the court is so satisfied, ordinarily the petition should be dismissed. However, it is generally appropriate to adjourn the case to give the petitioner an opportunity to put forward proposals to compensate for any loss to the respondent and which are sufficient to remove the element of grave financial hardship[3].

The court should (however) avoid entering into the bargaining process[4].

When considering the second stage of the test the court is concerned, inter alia, to balance the hardship likely to be caused to the respondent with the resultant harm to the petitioner in the court declining to dissolve the marriage.

However, the court is not concerned to have regard to which of the parties initiated the proceedings or to the grounds for bringing the proceedings[5].

So too, in deciding whether in all the circumstances it would be wrong to dissolve the marriage, the court should consider the broader aspect, namely whether a marriage which has so hopelessly broken down should be preserved or whether it is not right in the public interest to put an end to it[6].

1 See *Le Marchant v Le Marchant* [1977] 3 All ER 610, [1977] 1 WLR 559.
2 See *Jackson v Jackson* [1994] 2 FCR 393, [1993] 2 FLR 848, CA.
3 See *Parker v Parker* [1972] Fam 116, [1972] 1 All ER 410 approved in *Le Marchant v Le Marchant* [1977] 1 WLR 559 at 563 per Ormrod LJ.
4 See *K v K* [1997] 1 FLR 35, [1999] Fam Law 162.
5 See *Grenfell v Grenfell* [1978] Fam 128, [1978] 1 All ER 561.
6 See *Mathias v Mathias* [1972] Fam 287, [1972] 3 All ER 1, CA.

## [2.113.5]
### Grave financial or other hardship

The adjective 'grave' in the phrase 'grave financial or other hardship' applies not only to financial but also to other hardship[1].

The hardship relied on must be caused by the dissolution and not the breakdown of the marriage and is to be considered subjectively in relation to the particular marriage.

Most obviously the court will be concerned with financial hardship, and particularly with the loss of contingent pension rights in the event that the petitioner predeceases the respondent. The availability of pension sharing and attachment orders will mean that, in many cases, the court will be able to alleviate any potential hardship that would otherwise arise from loss of pension benefits.

Whilst it is unhelpful to substitute other expressions for that used in the MCA 1973, s 5 itself, it is generally accepted that to succeed the respondent must establish financial hardship that is 'really serious'[2].

So too it is not helpful to compare figures or percentages from one case with those relied on in another[3].

It is wrong to approach the case on the footing that the respondent is entitled to be compensated pound for pound for what will be lost in consequence of the divorce[4].

A material matter in considering the gravity, if any, of the financial hardship relied on is the age of the respondent. Although it is not impossible for a young and able-bodied respondent successfully to raise s 5 of the MCA 1973 as a defence, it will naturally be harder for him or her to do so[5].

It is not unreasonable where there are capital assets to expect those in their declining years to dip into capital to make up what is needed for ordinary living expenses[6].

Contrary to the approach adopted on an application for periodical payments, under the MCA 1973, s 5 the court is entitled (when looking at potential hardship on the hypothesis that the petitioner is dead) to take into account the availability of state benefits payable in lieu of any benefit (particularly a widow's pension) that would be lost on dissolution of the marriage[7].

Other hardship may comprise the respondent's disabilities or sickness, or the fact that he or she would be unable to manage.

The fact that the respondent would be exposed to shame, disgrace and degradation, as a social outcast in his or her community, is capable of forming a defence under the MCA 1973, s 5[8].

The Court of Appeal should be slow to interfere with a judge's finding as to whether resultant hardship would be grave or otherwise[9].

1 See *Rukat v Rukat* [1975] Fam 63, [1975] 1 All ER 343, CA.
2 See *Archer v Archer* [1999] 2 FCR 158, [1999] 1 FLR 327, CA.
3 See *Jackson v Jackson* [1994] 2 FCR 393, [1993] 2 FLR 848.
4 See *Le Marchant v Le Marchant* [1977] 1 WLR 559 at 562D per Ormrod LJ.
5 See *Mathias v Mathias* [1972] Fam 287, [1972] 3 All ER 1 (in which the court took account of the fact that the hardship relied on had been caused by the respondent's decision to abstain from working).
6 See *Archer v Archer* [1999] 1 FLR 327 at 331 per Butler-Sloss LJ.
7 See *Reiterbund v Reiterbund* [1975] Fam 99, [1975] 1 All ER 280; and *Jackson v Jackson* [1994] 2 FCR 393, [1993] 2 FLR 848, CA.
8 See *Banik v Banik* [1973] 3 All ER 45, [1973] 1 WLR 860, CA.
9 See *Jackson v Jackson* [1994] 2 FCR 393, [1993] 2 FLR 848 per Lloyd LJ.



**[2.114]**

### 10 Proceedings after decree nisi: special protection for respondent in separation cases

(1) Where in any case the court has granted a decree of divorce on the basis of a finding that the petitioner was entitled to rely in support of his petition on the fact of two years' separation coupled with the respondent's consent to a decree being granted and has made no such finding as to any other fact mentioned in section 1(2) above, the court may, on an application made by the respondent at any time before the decree is made absolute, rescind the decree if it is satisfied that the petitioner misled the respondent (whether intentionally or unintentionally) about any matter which the respondent took into account in deciding to give his consent.

(2) The following provisions of this section apply where—

(a) the respondent to a petition for divorce in which the petitioner alleged two years' or five years' separation coupled, in the former case, with the respondent's consent to a decree being granted, has applied to the court for consideration under subsection (3) below of his financial position after the divorce; and

(b) the court has granted a decree on the petition on the basis of a finding that the petitioner was entitled to rely in support of his petition on the fact of two years' or five years' separation (as the case may be) and has made no such finding as to any other fact mentioned in section 1(2) above.

(3) The court hearing an application by the respondent under subsection (2) above shall consider all the circumstances, including the age, health, conduct, earning capacity, financial resources and financial obligations of each of the parties, and the financial position of the respondent as, having regard to the divorce, it is likely to be after the death of the petitioner should the petitioner die first; and, subject to subsection (4) below, the court shall not make the decree absolute unless it is satisfied—

(a) that the petitioner should not be required to make any financial provision for the respondent, or

(b) that the financial provision made by the petitioner for the respondent is reasonable and fair or the best that can be made in the circumstances.

(4) The court may if it thinks fit make the decree absolute notwithstanding the requirements of subsection (3) above if—

(a) it appears that there are circumstances making it desirable that the decree should be made absolute without delay, and
(b) the court has obtained a satisfactory undertaking from the petitioner that he will make such financial provision for the respondent as the court may approve.

**Appointment**
Commencement order: SI 1973/1972.

**Derivation**
This section derived from the DRA 1969, ss 5, 6.

**Definitions**
'financial provision' – see s 21 at para **[2.115]** below.
'two years' separation' – see s 1(2)(d).
'five years' separation' – see s 1(2)(e).

## [2.114.1]
## Keypoints

- General
- Justifying an application
- Procedure
- Pursuing an application
- The petitioner's obligation
- Financial provision
- The best that can be made in the circumstances
- Satisfactory undertaking

## [2.114.2]
## General

Section 10(2) to (4) provides a respondent to a petition under the MCA 1973, s 1(2)(d) and (e) with a means of ensuring that the divorce is not made final until proper financial provision has been made, or clearly will be made, by the petitioner. The court is obliged to make an investigation into a number of relevant circumstances relating to the parties and to decide what financial provision ('reasonable and fair or the best that can be made in the circumstances') ought properly to be made for the respondent. In certain limited circumstances the court is able to make the decree absolute on the petitioner undertaking to make such financial provision as may be approved by the court.

See generally *Rayden and Jackson on Divorce and Family Matters* (17th edn, 1997), vol 1, paras 8.59 to 8.60 and the Noter-up thereto.

## [2.114.3]
## Justifying an application

It is not necessary to show that no other course is available to the respondent before an application is made under the MCA 1973, s 10(2)[1].

However, it is generally better if such applications are limited to those cases in which for some reason they are thought to have a special value[2]. It follows that the court will normally decline to exercise its jurisdiction under the MCA 1973, s 10(2) if the financial provision sought can and should be dealt with, both conveniently and appropriately, under an ordinary application for financial provision upon the making of the decree[3].

1 See *Garcia v Garcia* [1991] 3 All ER 451 at 458.
2 See *Cumbers v Cumbers* [1975] 1 All ER 1 at 4.
3 See *Garcia v Garcia* [1991] 3 All ER 451 at 460 per Ralph Gibson LJ.

### [2.114.4]
### Procedure

The application is made by filing Form B[1] either before or after decree nisi (but, obviously, before decree absolute). Thereafter, the general provisions relating to ancillary relief procedure apply to the application[2].

Prior to the availability of pension sharing and attachment orders, it was said that a solicitor should file an application under s 10(2) of the MCA 1973 where there are pension rights to be considered (and that it would probably be negligent of the solicitor not to do so in the absence of express instructions[3]). Now that such orders are available, the solicitor will have to consider whether that availability avoids the need to make an application under s 10(2), although an application under that section may still be a wise step to take in order to preserve a wife's potential status as a widow pending the final determination of the financial issues.

1 See FPR 1991, r 2.45 (as amended) at para **[3.406]** below.
2 See FPR 1991, r 2.45(7) (as amended) at para **[3.406]** below.
3 See *Griffiths v Dawson & Co* [1993] 2 FCR 515, [1993] 2 FLR 315.

### [2.114.5]
### Pursuing an application

The application proceeds as though an application for ancillary relief and the court has the usual powers to order discovery, etc[1]. The court will declare that it is or is not satisfied as to the matters mentioned in s 10(3) (namely: (a) that the petitioner should not be required to make any financial provision for the respondent; or (b) that the financial provision the petitioner has made is reasonable and fair or the best that can be made in the circumstances). In doing so the court is obliged to consider all the circumstances of the case, including those specific matters referred to in the MCA 1973, s 10(3). Additionally, the court must consider under the MCA 1973, s 10(4) whether it appears desirable in the light of the circumstances to make the decree final without delay on the petitioner undertaking to make such financial provision as the court may approve. Satisfaction as to these requirements are recorded in the court record[2].

It is desirable (in most cases) that any application under the MCA 1973, s 10(2) be heard together with any application for ancillary relief[3].

Failure to comply with the provisions of the MCA 1973, s 10(2) renders the decree absolute voidable and not void and the court retains a discretion to decide whether to declare that the decree should be void or valid. This discretion is only to be exercised after all the relevant circumstances have been considered, including the financial provision for the respondent which the court has power to order or which has been offered[4].

1 See FPR 1991, r 2.45(5) at para **[3.406]** below.
2 See FPR 1991, r 2.45(6).
3 See also *Registrar's Direction (Financial Protection of Respondent: Divorce on Proof of Separation)* 7 November 1973.
4 See *Wright v Wright* [1976] Fam 114, [1976] 1 All ER 796.

### [2.114.6]
### The petitioner's obligation

The making of proposals for financial provision for the respondent does not amount to the making of provision within the terms of the MCA 1973, s 10(3)(b) if it is open to a petitioner subsequently to resile from those proposals leaving the respondent without protection[1].

In an appropriate case financial provision will only have been made if the petitioner has actually made payment to the respondent[2].

More usually, before making the decree absolute, the court must approve the financial provision made by the petitioner (at least in outline) and then obtain an undertaking that those proposals would be given effect.

Such proposals need not however be in a completely concrete and detailed form[3].

Nor must the provision be 'specific in all its details, or necessarily specific as to amount'[4].

For an example of a case under the MCA 1973, s 10(3)(a) in which the petitioner was not expected to make any provision for the respondent see *Krystman v Krystman*[5].

1 See *Wilson v Wilson* [1973] 2 All ER 17, [1973] 1 WLR 555, CA.
2 See *Wilson v Wilson* [1973] 2 All ER 17 per Stephenson LJ.
3 See *Grigson v Grigson* [1974] 1 All ER 478, [1973] 1 WLR 228, CA.
4 See *Grigson v Grigson* [1974] 1 All ER 478 per Buckley LJ.
5 [1973] 3 All ER 247.

## [2.114.7]
### Financial provision

The phrase 'any financial provision' in the MCA 1973, s 10(3) is not confined to future financial provision but extends to all financial obligations including past obligations and those owed to a child of the family and it is open to the court to consider whether sums due under an earlier agreement should be paid before the decree is made absolute[1].

1 See *Garcia v Garcia* [1992] Fam 83, [1991] 3 All ER 451, CA.

## [2.114.8]
### The best that can be made in the circumstances

The words 'the best that can be made in the circumstances' in the MCA 1973, s 10(3)(b) are intended to deal with those cases where the petitioner's means are so slight that it is impracticable to make what would otherwise be a reasonable and fair order[1].

1 See *Lombardi v Lombardi* [1973] 3 All ER 625 at 629.

## [2.114.9]
### Satisfactory undertaking

'Satisfactory' refers to the nature and content of the undertaking.

It is not sufficient under the MCA 1973, s 10(4)(b) for the petitioner merely to give an undertaking that he will 'make such financial provision … as the Court may approve' at some unspecified date in the future: the undertaking must relate to some formulated proposal by the petitioner as to the kind and amount of financial provision to be made[1].

Further, the words 'may approve' in the MCA 1973, s 10(4)(b) refer to the moment at which the court is considering whether the undertaking is satisfactory[2].

1 See *Grigson v Grigson* [1974] 1 All ER 478, [1974] 1 WLR 228, CA.
2 See *Grigson v Grigson* [1974] 1 All ER 478 per Buckley LJ.

## [2.115]

PART II

FINANCIAL RELIEF FOR PARTIES TO MARRIAGE AND CHILDREN OF FAMILY

### 21 Financial provision and property adjustment orders

(1) The financial provision orders for the purposes of this Act are the orders for periodical or lump sum provision available (subject to the provisions of this Act) under section 23 below for the purpose of adjusting the financial position of the parties to a marriage and any children of the family in connection with proceedings for divorce, nullity of marriage or judicial separation and under section 27(6) below on proof of neglect by one party to a marriage to provide, or to make a proper contribution towards, reasonable maintenance for the other or a child of the family, that is to say—

(a) any order for periodical payments in favour of a party to a marriage under section 23(1)(a) or 27(6)(a) or in favour of a child of the family under section 23(1)(d), (2) or (4) or 27(6)(d);

(b) any order for secured periodical payments in favour of a party to a marriage under section 23(1)(b) or 27(6)(b) or in favour of a child of the family under section 23(1)(e), (2) or (4) or 27(6)(e); and

(c) any order for lump sum provision in favour of a party to a marriage under section 23(1)(c) or 27(6)(c) or in favour of a child of the family under section 23(1)(f), (2) or (4) or 27(6)(f);

and references in this Act (except in paragraphs 17(1) and 23 of Schedule 1 below) to periodical payments orders, secured periodical payments orders, and orders for the payment of a lump sum are references to all or some of the financial provision orders requiring the sort of financial provision in question according as the context of each reference may require.

(2) The property adjustment orders for the purposes of this Act are the orders dealing with property rights available (subject to the provisions of this Act) under section 24 below for the purpose of adjusting the financial position of the parties to a marriage and any children of the family on or after the grant of a decree of divorce, nullity of marriage or judicial separation, that is to say—

(a) any order under subsection (1)(a) of that section for a transfer of property;

(b) any order under subsection (1)(b) of that section for a settlement of property; and

(c) any order under subsection (1)(c) or (d) of that section for a variation of settlement.



**Appointment**

Commencement order: SI 1973/1972.

**Definitions**

'child of the family' – see s 52(1) at para **[2.140]** below.

## [2.115.1]

**Keypoint**

- General

## [2.115.2]

**General**

Section 21 defines the range of orders that can be made by the court under the MCA 1973, ss 23, 24 and 27(6) in terms of a financial provision order (providing for the payment of periodical or secured periodical payments and/or a lump sum) and a property adjustment order (providing for the transfer or settlement of property and/or the variation of a settlement).

A new s 21A of the MCA 1973 will enable the courts to make a pension sharing order enabling one party's shareable rights under a specified pension arrangement or shareable state scheme to be shared for the benefit of the other party. This is as a result of the Welfare Reform and Pensions Act 1999 (Commencement No 5) Order 2000[1].

1 SI 2000/1116.

## [2.115A]

### 21A Pension sharing orders

(1) For the purposes of this Act, a pension sharing order is an order which—

(a) provides that one party's—

(i) shareable rights under a specified pension arrangement, or

(ii) shareable state scheme rights,

be subject to pension sharing for the benefit of the other party, and

(b) specifies the percentage value to be transferred.

(2) In subsection (1) above—

(a) the reference to shareable rights under a pension arrangement is to rights in relation to which pension sharing is available under Chapter I of Part IV of the Welfare Reform and Pensions Act 1999, or under corresponding Northern Ireland legislation,

(b) the reference to shareable state scheme rights is to rights in relation to which pension sharing is available under Chapter II of Part IV of the Welfare Reform and Pensions Act 1999, or under corresponding Northern Ireland legislation, and

(c) 'party' means a party to a marriage.

**Amendment**

Inserted by the WRPA 1999, s 19. Date in force: 1 December 2000: see SI 2000/1116.

## [2.115A.1]
### Keypoints

- When in force
- Nature of orders
- Shareable rights

## [2.115A.2]
### When in force

This section was introduced by s 19, Sch 3, paras 1 and 2 of the Welfare Reform and Pensions Act 1999 (WRPA 1999). That Act came into force on 1 December 2000 and applies to petitions for divorce and nullity issued on or after that date[1]. The WRPA 1999 introduces pension sharing orders by amendment to the MCA 1973. The main amendments relating to pension sharing orders are:

| | |
|---|---|
| **Section** | **s 21A of the MCA 1973[2]** |
| **Effect** | Defines pension sharing orders |

| | |
|---|---|
| **Section** | **s 24B of the MCA 1973[3]** |
| **Effect** | Provides for the making of pension sharing orders on granting of a decree of divorce or a decree of nullity or at any time thereafter and limits the powers of the court where there has been no decree absolute or where there have been previous orders in relation to the pension |

| | |
|---|---|
| **Section** | **s 24C of the MCA 1973[4]** |
| **Effect** | Provides for the Lord Chancellor to make regulations in relation to when the pension sharing order comes into force |

| | |
|---|---|
| **Section** | **s 24D of the MCA 1973[5]** |
| **Effect** | Provides for the apportionment of charges between the parties that arise from pension sharing orders |

| | |
|---|---|
| **Section** | **ss 25, 25A, 31 (variation), 33A (consent orders) and 37 (avoidance of dispositions) of the MCA 1973[6]** |
| **Effect** | There are consequential amendments in relation to these provisions |

| | |
|---|---|
| **Section** | **s 40A of the MCA 1973[7]** |
| **Effect** | A new section is introduced concerning appeals relating to pension sharing orders |

1 In the case of *S v S (Rescission of decree nisi: pension sharing provision* [2002] 1 FCR 193, Singer J rescinded a decree nisi granted in proceedings commenced prior to 1 December 2000 to allow a new petition to be presented which would give the court power to make pension sharing orders. The application to rescind had the consent of both parties to the marriage and Singer J expressly states that this decision in not intended to effect the practice in relation to contested applications.
2 See para **[2.115A]** above.
3 See para **[2.119A]** below.
4 See para **[2.119B]** below.
5 See para **[2.119C]** below.
6 See paras **[2.120]**, **[2.121]**, **[2.129]**, **[2.132]** and **[2.136]** respectively below.
7 See para **[2.139A]** below.



## [2.115A.3]
### Nature of orders

Pension sharing orders are not hybrid forms of financial provision or property adjustment orders. They are a new form of order and must be specifically dealt with in ancillary relief orders. For instance, if a clean break is intended, there will need to be a specific dismissal of applications for pension sharing orders.

The orders take effect as a debit against the pension of the party that has the pension benefit and as a pension credit in favour of the other spouse – taking the husband as the spouse with the pension, the order therefore takes effect as a debit against his pension (eg 50% of the CETV of £200,000) and a credit in favour of the wife (ie for £100,000 of the husband's pension)[1]. The credit however, is a pension credit. It can only benefit the wife by creating or adding to a pension for her benefit and the income and/or lump sum which that credit will produce will depend upon the particular rules and circumstances of the pension scheme that receives the pension credit. Given the different life expectancy of men and women the same amount of pension credit will often give each spouse a different pension.

The date upon which the pension is to be valued by the pension managers or trustees is specified in ss 29(7) and 34(1) of the WRPA 1999. The pensions scheme managers or trustees can determine the date for valuation provided that it falls within the four month implementation period specified in s 34[2].

1 See s 29 of the WRPA 1999 at para **[2.551]** below.
2 See para **[2.556]** below.

## [2.115A.4]
### Shareable rights

In order to identify the pensions that may be subject to a pension sharing order one has to have recourse to ss 27 and 47 of the WRPA 1999. The relevant pensions will include:

- Occupational pensions;
- Personal pensions;
- Public service pensions (including the guaranteed minimum pension and protected rights which result from contracting out of SERPS);
- Retirement annuity contracts;
- Self-administered schemes;
- Unapproved schemes, such as FURBS and UURBS (Funded/unfunded unapproved retirement benefit schemes);
- The new stakeholder pensions.

The scheme of the WRPA 1999 only extends to pensions that are recognised as such within UK legislation. Foreign pensions (ie savings schemes that may be considered as pensions in other jurisdictions, but not in the UK, rather than pensions that hold assets in other jurisdictions) are not covered. The Act does not extend to the basic state retirement pension. Nor does it apply to pensions that are pensions of the Great Offices of State. For the treatment of pensions on divorce, see generally *Rayden and Jackson on Divorce and Family Matters* (17th edn, 1997), vol 1, chap 22 and the Noter-up thereto.

[2.116]

## 22 Maintenance pending suit

On a petition for divorce, nullity of marriage or judicial separation, the court may make an order for maintenance pending suit, that is to say, an order requiring either party to the marriage to make to the other such periodical payments for his or her maintenance and for such term, being a term beginning not earlier than the date of the presentation of the petition and ending with the date of the determination of the suit, as the court thinks reasonable.

**Appointment**

Commencement order: SI 1973/1972.

**Derivation**

This section derived from the MPPA 1970, s 1.

[2.116.1]
### Keypoints

- General
- Who may apply
- Making an application
- Maintenance and legal fees
- The correct approach
- Big money cases
- Appeals
- No interim lump sums
- Duration and variation

[2.116.2]
### General

Maintenance pending suit is the only form of financial provision that can make in favour of one of the parties until the court grants a decree nisi of divorce or nullity or a decree of judicial separation. Section 22 permits the court to make an order for periodical payments and there is no power to make an order for payment of an interim lump sum.

For a discussion of this topic, see generally *Rayden and Jackson on Divorce and Family Matters* (17th edn, 1997), vol 1, para 21.3 et seq and the Noter-up thereto.

[2.116.3]
### Who may apply

Either party to the marriage may apply under the MCA 1973, s 22 for an order against the other party or to ascertain the extent of his or her liability to maintain the other party[1].

1 See *Sherdley v Sherdley* [1988] AC 213, [1987] 2 All ER 54, HL; *Peacock v Peacock* [1984] FLR 263; *Simister v Simister* [1987] 1 FLR 189; and *Dart v Dart* [1997] 1 FCR 21, [1997] 2 FLR 286, CA.

[2.116.4]
### Making an application

An application for maintenance pending suit must be made in the petition or the answer, otherwise (unless the parties agree) the applicant will require the leave of the court[1].

The procedure governing applications for interim orders, including orders for maintenance pending suit, is set out in r 2.69F of the FPR 1991[2]. For procedure, see generally *Rayden and Jackson on Divorce and Family Matters* (17th edn, 1997), vol 1, ch 23 and the Noter-up thereto.

The court has a discretion to entertain an application for maintenance pending suit notwithstanding the fact that the other party questions whether the court has jurisdiction to entertain the suit[3].

So too the court can make an order under the MCA 1973, s 22 even if it is clear that the marriage founding the application is void[4].

The restriction contained in s 28(3) of the MCA 1973 upon applications made after remarriage applies equally to an application for maintenance pending suit under the MCA 1973, s 22. Moreover, no order for maintenance pending suit can be made after the grant of a decree absolute (or a decree in a case involving judicial separation) notwithstanding the fact that the application pre-dates the decree and has been pursued diligently[5]. The court is not constrained from making an order under the MCA 1973, s 22 simply because the parties have entered into a prior agreement or a deed of separation, although such an agreement may be an indication of what is a reasonable level of payment[6].



1 See FPR 1991, r 2.53 at para **[3.408]** below.
2 See para **[3.460]** below.
3 See *Cammell v Cammell* [1965] P 467, [1964] 3 All ER 255.
4 See *Foden v Foden* [1894] P 307; but see *Whiston v Whiston* [1998] 1 All ER 423, CA (the court declined to grant relief on grounds of public policy in a case involving a bigamous marriage).
5 *M v M* [1928] P 123.
6 See *T v T* [1990] FCR 169, sub nom *Re T (Divorce: Interim Maintenance: Discovery)* [1990] 1 FLR 1.

## [2.116.5]
## Maintenance and legal fees

The court may order maintenance pending suit to cover the legal fees of a party in divorce proceedings[1], particularly in a case where, in the absence of such an order, one party would be deprived of his or her representation.

1 *A v A (maintenance pending suit: provision for legal fees)* [2001] 1 WLR 605, [2001] 1 FCR 226, [2001] 1 FLR 377, [2001] Fam Law 96.

## [2.116.6]
## The correct approach

When considering an application under the MCA 1973, s 22 the court is given a wide and unfettered discretion to make such order 'as (it) thinks reasonable'.

This is the only test but what is 'reasonable' must be assessed in the light of the means and needs of the parties and upon consideration of any other relevant circumstances[1].

The court is not constrained under the MCA 1973, s 22 by the obligation imposed under the MCA 1973, s 25 to give first consideration to the welfare whilst a minor of any child of the family (although in practice regard will be had to such matters and in the short term they may well determine the outcome given the obvious need to meet interim housing needs).

In an ordinary case, a broad view should be taken of the means and income of the parties and the court will come to a fairly rough and ready conclusion given that it is not possible to go into all the detail the court will be required to investigate when dealing with the full hearing of the application for financial relief[2].

Whilst the court's discretion is not circumscribed by the matters set out in the MCA 1973, s 25, in an appropriate case, other relevant circumstances may include the conduct of the parties and the court might properly take account of the shortness of the marriage[3]. Whilst in the exercise of its general discretion the court may take account of the fact that the applicant is in receipt of supplementary benefit, the general rule (as when disposing of an application for periodical payments under the MCA 1973, s 23) is that the quantum of any order should be assessed upon consideration of what the other party can reasonably afford to pay, having regard to his or her needs and obligations[4].

Generally, the level at which maintenance pending suit is fixed by the court is not of itself significant in terms of the final outcome. If inadequate or excessive provision is made at the interim stage, there is normally an opportunity to make good the position later at the final hearing[5].

1 See *Offord v Offord* (1981) 3 FLR 309.
2 See *F v F* (1983) 4 FLR 382.
3 See n 2 above.
4 See *Peacock v Peacock* [1984] 1 All ER 1069, [1984] 1 WLR 532.
5 See *F v F (ancillary relief: substantial assets)* [1996] 2 FCR 397, [1995] 2 FLR 45.

### [2.116.7]
### Big money cases

In a case in which the assets are substantial and one party concedes an ability to meet any order the court might make, it is generally superfluous to conduct a detailed or large-scale investigation intended to determine the true extent of the other party's reasonable needs given that the true extent of those needs cannot properly be determined until there has been full discovery and the court has heard oral evidence.

Moreover, in a case in which large sums of money are involved, it is wrong in principle to impose a figure for maintenance pending suit simply because such a figure would seem generous by the standards of ordinary people. Nonetheless, even in a case in which the sums involved are substantial, it is wrong not to scrutinise the applicant's suggested budget to see if in fact it reflects the standard of living enjoyed by the parties prior to the breakdown of their relationship.

See generally *F v F (ancillary relief: substantial assets)*[1] in which the court took into account the fact that the wife and children had been significantly under-maintained since the parties had separated and noted that the wife should not be disadvantaged by the escalation of legal costs pending the final hearing.

1 [1996] 2 FCR 397, [1995] 2 FLR 45.

### [2.116.8]
### Appeals

Given the broad and unfettered nature of the discretion given to the court under the MCA 1973, s 22 it will be especially difficult to establish that the decision taken at first instance so exceeded the broad bracket of what might be thought reasonable such as to justify reconsideration on appeal[1].

However, given that under the MCA 1973, s 22 the court is generally concerned with an assessment of the actual cost of living expenses (in which a greater degree of accuracy is possible) the scope for interference on appeal is more obvious if it is established that the court has fallen into error[2].

1 See *Bellenden (formerly Satterthwaite) v Satterthwaite* [1948] 1 All ER 343, CA; and *G v G* [1985] 2 All ER 225.
2 See *Irvine v Irvine* (1963) 107 Sol Jo 213 per Donovan LJ.

### [2.116.9]
### No interim lump sums

Whilst at the substantive hearing the court has jurisdiction to make a lump sum order under the MCA 1973, s 23(1)(c) intended to meet liabilities and expenses incurred before the date of the application for ancillary relief[1], the court has no jurisdiction to order an interim lump sum[2]. Nor (it is now clear) does the court retain an administrative power of appropriation to allocate a particular asset to meet the interim needs (eg housing) of either party before the final hearing[3].

1 See the MCA 1973, s 23(3)(a) at para **[2.117]** below.
2 See *Bolsom v Bolsom* (1983) 4 FLR 21.
3 See *Wicks v Wicks* [1999] Fam 65, [1998] 1 FLR 470 (overruling: *Barry v Barry* [1992] Fam 140, [1992] 2 FLR 233; *Green v Green* [1993] 1 FLR 326; and *F v F (ancillary relief: substantial assets)* [1996] 2 FCR 397, [1995] 2 FLR 45).

### [2.116.10]
### Duration and variation

An order under s 22 of the MCA 1973 continues until decree absolute at which time the suit will no longer be 'pending'. An order for maintenance pending suit will often be expressed to continue after the date of the decree (until conclusion of the final hearing) as an order for interim periodical payments in the same amount.

On written application by the party in whose favour an order under the MCA 1973, s 22 has been made, the court has power after granting a decree to make a corresponding order for periodical payments at the same rate as that specified in the original order for maintenance pending suit. Neither party need attend on such an application if the other party (the maintenance payer) does not object[1]. Any order under the MCA 1973, s 22 will cease automatically upon the death of either of the parties to the marriage[2].

An order under the MCA 1973, s 22 may be suspended, varied or discharged under the MCA 1973, s 31 and arrears remitted in whole or in part under the MCA 1973, s 31(2A).

1 See FPR 1991, r 2.67 at para **[3.422]**.
2 *Barder v Caluori* [1988] AC 20, [1987] 2 All ER 440, HL.



### [2.117]

**23 Financial provision orders in connection with divorce proceedings, etc**

(1) On granting a decree of divorce, a decree of nullity of marriage or a decree of judicial separation or at any time thereafter (whether, in the case of a decree of divorce or of nullity of marriage, before or after the decree is made absolute), the court may make any one or more of the following orders, that is to say—

- (a) an order that either party to the marriage shall make to the other such periodical payments, for such term, as may be specified in the order;
- (b) an order that either party to the marriage shall secure to the other to the satisfaction of the court such periodical payments, for such term, as may be so specified;
- (c) an order that either party to the marriage shall pay to the other such lump sum or sums as may be so specified;
- (d) an order that a party to the marriage shall make to such person as may be specified in the order for the benefit of a child of the family, or to such a child, such periodical payments, for such term, as may be so specified;
- (e) an order that a party to the marriage shall secure to such person as may be so specified for the benefit of such a child, or to such a child, to the satisfaction of the court, such periodical payments, for such term, as may be so specified;
- (f) an order that a party to the marriage shall pay to such person as may be so specified for the benefit of such a child, or to such a child, such lump sum as may be so specified;

subject, however, in the case of an order under paragraph (d), (e) or (f) above, to the restrictions imposed by section 29(1) and (3) below on the making of financial provision orders in favour of children who have attained the age of eighteen.

(2) The court may also, subject to those restrictions, make any one or more of the orders mentioned in subsection (1)(d), (e) and (f) above—

- (a) in any proceedings for divorce, nullity of marriage or judicial separation, before granting a decree; and
- (b) where any such proceedings are dismissed after the beginning of the trial, either forthwith or within a reasonable period after the dismissal.

(3) Without prejudice to the generality of subsection (1)(c) or (f) above—

- (a) an order under this section that a party to a marriage shall pay a lump sum to the other party may be made for the purpose of enabling that other party to meet any liabilities or expenses reasonably incurred by him or her in maintaining himself or herself or any child of the family before making an application for an order under this section in his or her favour;

(b) an order under this section for the payment of a lump sum to or for the benefit of a child of the family may be made for the purpose of enabling any liabilities or expenses reasonably incurred by or for the benefit of that child before the making of an application for an order under this section in his favour to be met; and

(c) an order under this section for the payment of a lump sum may provide for the payment of that sum by instalments of such amount as may be specified in the order and may require the payment of the instalments to be secured to the satisfaction of the court.

(4) The power of the court under subsection (1) or (2)(a) above to make an order in favour of a child of the family shall be exercisable from time to time; and where the court makes an order in favour of a child under subsection (2)(b) above, it may from time to time, subject to the restrictions mentioned in subsection (1) above, make a further order in his favour of any of the kinds mentioned in subsection (1)(d), (e) or (f) above.

(5) Without prejudice to the power to give a direction under section 30 below for the settlement of an instrument by conveyancing counsel, where an order is made under subsection (1)(a), (b) or (c) above on or after granting a decree of divorce or nullity of marriage, neither the order nor any settlement made in pursuance of the order shall take effect unless the decree has been made absolute.

[(6) Where the court—

(a) makes an order under this section for the payment of a lump of sum; and

(b) directs—

(i) that payment of that sum or any part of it shall be deferred; or

(ii) that that sum or any part of it shall be paid by instalments,

the court may order that the amount deferred or the instalments shall carry interest at such rate as may be specified by the order from such date, not earlier than the date of the order, as may be so specified, until the date when payment of it is due.]

**Appointment**

Commencement order: SI 1973/1972.

**Definitions**

'child of the family' – see s 52(1) at para **[2.140]** below.

**Amendment**

sub-s (6): inserted by the AJA 1982, s 16.

## [2.117.1]
## Keypoints

- General
- Who may apply
- The range of orders available
- Procedural concerns
- Restrictions on applications by spouses
- Restrictions on applications for the benefit of children
- Date of the order
- Commencement and duration of orders for spouses
- Commencement and duration of orders for children
- Secured periodical payments
- Lump sum or sums
- *Duxbury*
- Interim periodical payments
- Interim lump sums
- Instalments and interest

### [2.117.2]
### General

Section 23 gives the court jurisdiction to make provision for periodical or secured periodical payments and an order for the payment of a lump sum either in favour of a party to the marriage or (subject to the restrictions contained in the Child Support Act 1991) in favour of a child of the family. This section must be read in the light of the restrictions contained in the MCA 1973, ss 25A, 28 and s 29.

For a discussion of this topic, see generally *Rayden and Jackson on Divorce and Family Matters* (17th edn, 1997), vol 1, para 21.79 et seq and the Noter-up thereto.



### [2.117.3]
### Who may apply

Either party to the marriage may apply under the MCA 1973, s 23 for an order against the other party or to ascertain the extent of his or her liability to the other party or to a child of the family[1].

1 See *Calderbank v Calderbank* [1976] Fam 93; *Sherdley v Sherdley* [1988] AC 213, [1987] 2 All ER 54, HL; *Simister v Simister* [1987] 1 FLR 189; and *Dart v Dart* [1997] 1 FCR 21, [1996] 2 FLR 286, CA.

### [2.117.4]
### The range of orders available

Under the MCA 1973, s 23 the court can make one or more of the following orders:

(1) periodical payments in favour of a party to the marriage or a child of the family (subject to the restrictions set out in the Child Support Act 1991)[1];
(2) secured periodical payments in favour of a party to the marriage or a child of the family (subject to the restrictions set out in the CSA 1991)[2];
(3) payment of a lump sum or sums in favour of a party to the marriage or a child of the family[3].

The court may in addition order any lump sum to be paid by instalments[4]. Practitioners should remember that a lump sum payable by instalments is variable[5].

A deferred lump sum or a lump sum payable by instalments may carry interest at such rate as may be specified[6].

Section 25B of the MCA 1973 sets out the court's additional jurisdiction to make orders in favour of a party to the marriage in respect of commuted capital lump sums and/or annuity income arising under a qualifying pension policy.

Section 25C of the MCA 1973 contains like powers in respect of 'death benefits' payable to a party to the marriage under such a policy.

Under the new s 21A(1) of the MCA 1973 following the introduction of the Welfare Reform and Pensions Act 1999 for all petitions for divorce or nullity issued after 1 December 2000 the court can make a pension sharing order enabling a spouse either to become a member of the other spouse's pension or to transfer a designated percentage of the other spouse's pension into their own pension scheme.

1 See the MCA 1973, s 23(1)(a) and (d) at para **[2.117]** above.
2 See the MCA 1973, s 23(1)(b) and (e) at para **[2.117]** above.
3 See the MCA 1973, s 23(1)(c) and (f) above.
4 See the MCA 1973, s 23(3)(c) above.
5 See the MCA 1973, s 31(2)(d) at para **[2.129]** below.
6 See the MCA 1973, s 23(6) above.

### [2.117.5]
### Procedural concerns

An application under the MCA 1973, s 23 must be made in the petition or the answer, otherwise (unless the parties agree) the applicant will require the leave of the court[1].

The procedure for ancillary relief application is laid down in rr 2.51A to 2.70 of the FPR 1991[2].

1 See the FPR 1991, r 2.53 at para **[3.408]** below.
2 See para **[3.433]** et seq below. For procedure, see generally *Rayden and Jackson on Divorce and Family Matters* (17th edn, 1997), vol 1, ch 23 and the Noter-up thereto.

## [2.117.6]
### Restrictions on applications by spouses

An order in favour of one of the parties to the marriage may be made at any time on or after grant of a decree nisi but does not take effect unless the decree is made absolute[1]. If no decree is granted and/or the petition is dismissed, an order for maintenance pending suit made under the MCA 1973, s 22 will lapse and the only relief available in the event of a continued failure by the other party to provide financial support is that available under the MCA 1973, s 27.

Subject only to a direction under the MCA 1973, s 25A(3) (below) that either party to the marriage may not make any further application for periodical or secured periodical payments in relation to the marriage, there is no limit to the number of applications that a party might make under the MCA 1973, s 23(1)(a) or (b).

Moreover, there is no limitation on the period during which an application must be made, although any delay may be taken into consideration when the court considers whether to exercise its discretion to make an order[2]. No application may be made for an order under the MCA 1973, s 23(1)(a), (b) or (c) after the applicant has remarried[3].

1 See the MCA 1973, s 23(5) at para **[2.117]** above.
2 See *Twiname v Twiname* [1992] 1 FCR 185, [1992] 1 FLR 29, CA (the court declined to strike out an application for a lump sum order made 17 years after an order for periodical payments had been made); and *Hill v Hill* [1997] 3 FCR 477, [1998] 1 FLR 198, CA.
3 See the MCA 1973, s 28(3) at para **[2.126]** below.

## [2.117.7]
### Restrictions on applications for the benefit of children

An order in favour of a child of the family for periodical and secured periodical payments or a lump sum may be made before the court grants a decree nisi or if the court dismisses the petition or declines to grant a decree either forthwith or within a reasonable time thereafter[1].

The restrictions contained in the MCA 1973, s 23(5) (stipulating that an order under the MCA 1973, s 23 in favour of a party to the marriage does not take effect until decree absolute) not to do not apply to orders made in favour of a child of the family and for this reason there is no additional power akin to that under the MCA 1973, s 22 to make orders for maintenance pending suit in favour of a child of the family.

Subject to the restrictions contained in the MCA 1973, s 29 the court's powers to make orders for periodical and secured payments and for lump sum provision in favour of a child of the family is exercisable from time to time[2]. In the absence of special circumstances or unless the child is (or would be) undergoing further education, no order for periodical or secured periodical payments may be made in favour of a child of the family who has reached the age of 18 years[3]. Moreover, the jurisdiction to make orders for periodical and secured periodical payments in favour of a child of the family under the MCA 1973, s 23(1)(d) and (e) is restricted by the terms of the Child Support Act 1991, inter alia, to the following situations:

- (i) when one or more of the absent parents, the person with care or the child itself is not habitually resident in the United Kingdom (s 44);
- (ii) when the parties seek an order by consent in the terms of a written agreement (s 8(5));
- (iii) when one party seeks a 'top up' order (s 8(6));
- (iv) when one party seeks a school fees order (s 8(7));
- (v) when the child is not a qualifying child (viz is married, over 19 years or over 16 years and not in further education) (s 55);

(vi) when one party seeks expenses for a disabled child (s 8(8)).

The CSA 1991 does not restrict the jurisdiction of the court to vary orders made before 5 April 1993[4] nor to make orders against a step-parent (when the special considerations set out in the MCA 1973, s 25(4) apply).

In practice the court has acceded to three situations in which the parties have sought to avoid the consequences of the CSA 1991:

(i) the filing of a written agreement providing only for a nominal periodical payments in favour of the child within the terms of the CSA 1991, s 8(5) immediately variable by the court under the MCA 1973, s 31 (but see the arguments put forward as to whether this is appropriate at [1998] Fam Law 510 and 701);

(ii) an application that the court make a global assessment of maintenance to provide both for the needs of the party to the marriage and the child with credit to be given and a deduction made for any assessment subsequently made upon application to the Child Support Agency[5];

(iii) an invitation by both parties to the court to indicate the annual maintenance figure the court would regard as reasonable for one party to make on the assumption that the parties are agreed an order should be made by consent to reflect that assessment[6].



1 See the MCA 1973 s 23(2).
2 See the MCA 1973 s 23(4).
3 See the MCA 1973, s 29(1) at para **[2.127]** below.
4 See the CSA 1991, ss 4(10) and 8(3A).
5 See *Dorney-Kingdom v Dorney-Kingdom* [2000] 3 FCR 20, [2000] 2 FLR 855, CA.
6 See *A v A* [1998] 3 FCR 421, [1998] 2 FLR 180.

## [2.117.8]
## Date of the order

If in breach of the restriction contained in the MCA 1973, s 23(1) an order is made in favour of one of the parties before grant of decree nisi the court has no inherent jurisdiction to validate the order, nor (subject to one exception) can the error be remedied:

- under the slip rule;
- by agreement between the parties; or
- by one party raising an estoppel against the other who seeks to avoid the effect of the order[1].

Notwithstanding the fact that an order made before decree nisi is made without jurisdiction, it cannot be ignored and remains valid unless and until set aside and is an effective bar to the court granting any further relief. Such an order will however be set aside as of right[2].

A simple clerical error (eg ascribing the wrong date to an order) does not invalidate the order and it can be corrected[3].

1 See *Munks v Munks* [1985] FLR 576; and *Board v Checkland* [1987] 2 FLR 257, CA.
2 See *Munks v Munks* [1985] FLR 576.
3 *Pounds v Pounds* [1994] 1 FLR 775 (in which the court indicated it was not inappropriate for the court to endorse the terms of a draft consent order under the MCA 1973, s 33A before granting a decree nisi on the basis that the order would come into being on the date set for pronouncement of the decree or on a fixed date thereafter).

## [2.117.9]
## Commencement and duration of maintenance orders for spouses

An order for periodical or secured periodical payments in favour of a party to the marriage may commence on the date on which the application was first made (eg in the prayer to the petition[1]) and may continue thereafter for such limited or unlimited period as the court thinks fit[2].

If the court orders that periodical or secured periodical payments should only continue for a fixed period it must in addition consider whether it is appropriate to give a direction under the MCA 1973, s 28(1A) preventing the party in whose favour the order is made from applying to extend the term specified in the order.

However, an order for periodical payments under the MCA 1973, s 23(1)(a) may not continue beyond the death of either of the parties or if earlier the remarriage of the party in whose favour the order is made[3].

An order for periodical payments will ordinarily be worded as follows: 'during the joint lives of the parties or until the **petitioner** shall remarry or until further order of the court'.

Any application to extend the term specified in an order for periodical or secured periodical payments must be made before expiry of the term specified[4].

When making an order for periodical or secured periodical payments in favour of a party to the marriage the court must consider whether it is appropriate to order those payments to be made or secured only for such period as would permit that party to adjust without undue hardship to the termination of his or her financial dependence on the other party[5].

1 See FPR 1991, r 2.53 at para **[3.408]**.
2 See the MCA 1973, s 23(1).
3 See the MCA 1973, s 28(1)(a) at para **[2.126]** below.
4 See *T v T (Financial Provision)* [1988] FCR 384, [1988] 1 FLR 480; and *Jones v Jones* [2001] Fam 96, [2000] 2 FCR 201, CA.
5 See the MCA 1973, s 25(2) at para **[2.120]** below.

## [2.117.10]
### Commencement and duration of maintenance orders for children

An order for periodical or secured periodical payments in favour of a child of the family may commence on the date on which the application was first made (eg in the prayer to the petition[1]) or such later date as the court may specify and (subject to what follows) shall not in the first instance extend beyond the age of 17 years (viz the birthday next following the upper age limit for compulsory school attendance specified in s 35 of the Education Act 1935)[2].

An order for periodical payments will cease to have effect automatically (save in respect of any arrears due) on the death of the party liable to make payment under the terms of the order[3].

Section 29(2)(b) of the MCA 1973 specifies that an order for periodical and secured periodical payments in favour of a child of the family shall not in any event extend beyond the age of 18 years unless:

- the child is (or would be) in receipt of further education or training for a trade or profession (whether or not also in gainful employment)[4];
- there are special circumstances justifying extension of the term beyond that date[5].

Dispute may arise as to whether an order in favour of a child who remains in further education should continue until the conclusion of secondary or tertiary education: an appropriate form of words would be 'until the said child attains the age of 17 years or ceases full-time *secondary/tertiary education (to the completion of a first degree)* whichever is the later or further order of the court'.

An application to extend the term of an order for periodical or secured periodical payments must be made before expiry of the term specified[6].

Special circumstances justifying continuation of the order beyond the age of 18 years may include physical or other handicap[7].

1 See FPR 1991, r 2.53 at para **[3.408]** below.
2 See the MCA 1973, s 29(2)(a) at para **[2.127]** below.
3 See the MCA 1973, s 29(4).
4 See the MCA 1973, s 29(3)(a).
5 See the MCA 1973, s 29(3)(b).
6 See *G v G* [1998] Fam 1, [1997] 1 FLR 368.
7 See *T v S (financial provision for children)* [1994] 1 FCR 743, [1994] 2 FLR 883; *C v F (disabled child: maintenance orders)* [1999] 1 FCR 39, [1998] 2 FLR 1, CA; and *V v V (child maintenance)* [2001] 2 FLR 799, [2001] Fam Law 649.

## [2.117.11]
### Secured periodical payments

An order for secured periodical payments under the MCA 1973, s 23(1)(b) may not continue beyond the death or (if earlier) the remarriage of the party in whose favour the order is made but may be expressed to continue beyond the death of the payer[1]. See generally, *Rayden and Jackson on Divorce and Family Matters* (17th edn, 1997), vol 1, para 21.92 et seq and the Noter-up thereto.

The obligation imposed on a party to make secured periodical payments is to secure the sum out of which payments will be made and not in fact to make periodical payments thereafter[2].

It is essentially a matter for the court to determine what amount of security should be provide and what proportion of the periodical payments need be secured[3].

It is not necessarily wrong to order security in a nominal sum on the basis that an application might be made at a later date under the MCA 1973, s 31 to vary the amount[4].

So too it is a matter for the court to decide over what assets to order security, but it is generally wrong to order a floating charge by way of security over all the assets in which the other party has an interest[5].

However, it is not necessarily wrong to order security over the sole asset in which the other party has an interest[6].

In practice having determined the appropriate level of security, the court will give the parties an opportunity to agree the precise nature of the assets to be charged[7].

An order for secured periodical payments is enforceable against the estate of the other party if (for example) the payer dies before execution of the security required to give effect to the order[8].

However, if not yet determined by the court, the mere fact that an application for secured provision has been made does not give rise to a cause of action against the estate of the other party under the I(PFD)A 1975[9].

1 See the MCA 1973, s 28(1)(b) at para **[2.126]** below.
2 See *Shearn v Shearn* [1931] P 1.
3 See *Chichester v Chichester* [1936] P 129, [1936] 1 All ER 271.
4 See *Foard v Foard* [1967] 2 All ER 660 (in which on appeal the court reduced the amount of security required from £1,000 to £10 to be secured against the husband's interest in a bungalow).
5 See *Barker v Barker* [1952] P 184, [1952] 1 All ER 1128, CA.
6 See *Aggett v Aggett* [1962] 1 All ER 190, [1962] 1 WLR 183, CA.
7 See *O'D v O'D* [1976] Fam 83, [1975] 2 All ER 993, CA.
8 See *Hyde v Hyde* [1948] P 198, [1948] 1 All ER 362
9 See *Dipple v Dipple* [1942] P 65, [1942] 1 All ER 234.

## [2.117.12]
### Lump sums or sums

Section 23(1)(c) of the MCA 1973 provides that the court may make 'an order' in favour of a party to the marriage. For a discussion of this topic, see generally *Rayden and Jackson on Divorce and Family Matters* (17th edn, 1997), vol 1, para 21.101 et seq and the Noter-up thereto.

The purpose of the words 'lump sum or sums' under the MCA 1973, s 23(1)(c) is to enable the court to provide for more than one lump sum payment in one order and the words do not confer on the court a power to make a plurality of lump sum orders[1].

It follows that whilst the court may only make a single order in favour of a party to the marriage, that order may provide for the payment of a single lump sum or for the payment of any number of lump sums.

The restrictions in the MCA 1973, s 23(1)(c) are now subject to the jurisdiction to make a further lump sum order under the MCA 1973, s 31(7B).

An order may provide for payment of different sums for different purposes, or for payment of a further lump sum contingently upon the happening of some future event (eg the falling in of a reversionary interest or the realisation of the proceeds of a policy on retirement)[2].

Previously there was a marked reluctance to adjourn an application for a lump sum too far into the future or unless there was a real prospect of future capital becoming available from an identified source in the near future[3]. However, post-*White* it seems that the courts will in certain circumstances adjourn lump sum generally[4].

Many of the problems previously encountered upon application for a lump sum will be avoided given the jurisdiction to make orders under the MCA 1973, s 25B (to 'earmark' capital available at some time in the future under a pension) and since 1 November 1998 under the MCA 1973, s 31(7B) to make, inter alia, a second lump sum order on the application of either party for an immediate or deferred clean break upon dismissal or restriction of the liability of one party to make ongoing periodical payments.

Before 1 November 1998, after an order had been made under the MCA 1973, s 23(1)(c), the only prospect of securing a further lump sum was with the agreement of the party obliged to make periodical payments on an undertaking to make further provision in a fixed amount upon dismissal of his or her liability to make ongoing payments[5].

1 See *Coleman v Coleman* [1973] Fam 10, [1972] 3 All ER 886; and *Banyard v Banyard* [1984] FLR 643, CA.

2 See *Minton v Minton* [1979] AC 593, HL; *Priest v Priest* (1980) 1 FLR 189, CA; and *de Lasala v de Lasala* [1980] AC 546 at 559–560 per Lord Scarman.

3 See eg *Michael v Michael* [1986] 2 FLR 389, CA (a mere expectancy of future capital); *Ranson v Ranson* [1988] 1 FLR 292, CA (a gratuity on retirement in seven years time); and *MT v MT (Financial Provision: Lump Sum)* [1991] FCR 649, [1992] 1 FLR 362.

4 *D v D (financial provision: lump sum order)* [2001] 1 FCR 561, [2001] 1 FLR 633.

5 See *S v S* [1986] Fam 189, [1986] 3 All ER 566; and *Boylan v Boylan* [1988] FCR 689, [1988] 1 FLR 282 (where the court rejected the undertaking offered by the husband and varied upwards the order for periodical payments).

## [2.117.13]

### *Duxbury*

Prior to the decision in *White*, courts in the bigger money cases would routinely consider *Duxbury* calculations as a potential ceiling to a wife's claim, representing the summit of her reasonable requirements. Now that that approach has been swept aside, the future uses of *Duxbury* will undoubtedly be restricted. Its limits were probably set by Lord Nicholls in the House of Lords in *White* when he said[1]:

> 'A *Duxbury* calculation is, no doubt, useful as a guide in assessing the amount of money required to provide for a person's financial needs. It is a means of capitalising an income requirement. But that is all …
>
> … [F]inancial needs are only one of the factors to be taken into account in arriving at the amount of an award. The amount of capital required to provide for an older wife's financial needs may well be less than the amount required to provide for a younger wife's financial needs. It by no means follows that, in a case where resources exceed the parties' financial needs, the older wife's award will be less than the younger wife's. Indeed the older wife's award may be substantially larger.'

*Duxbury* remains a method of calculation in the context of overall fairness of outcome for both parties when assessing the capital cost of an income requirement but nothing more[2]. It seems now to be accepted that in making an assessment of the future annual budgetary requirements of either party to the marriage some reduction should be made for a slow down in the rate of expenditure reasonably required in later years (generally after the applicant reaches 60 years):

- *F v F (Ancillary relief: Substantial Assets)* [1995] 2 FLR 45 (a reduction to 60% of current requirements and a presumed injection of additional capital upon realisation or downgrading of property);
- *A v A* [1998] 2 FLR 180 (a reduction to 80% of current requirement but not appropriate to presume additional capital upon downgrading in the future).

Where the assets are substantial in the exercise of its powers under the MCA 1973, s 25A the court may decide to meet future needs for income out of capital[3].

The '*Duxbury*' formula provides for the provision of a lump sum which, if invested on certain assumptions as to life expectancy, rates of inflation, return on investments, growth of capital and incidence of income tax, will produce enough to meet the recipient's needs for his or her presumed life span on the basis that withdrawals are made both from capital and interest until the entire fund is extinguished[4].

Notwithstanding the move in other jurisdictions to increase the rate of return presumed in any calculation based upon the investment and depletion of a capital sum during the remainder of the applicant's life span[5] there remains an accepted industry standard of return presumed in any calculation under the MCA 1973, s 23 of 4·25%[6].



1 [2000] 3 FCR 555 at 568.
2 See *Cowan v Cowan* [2001] EWCA Civ 679 [2001] 3 WLR 684, [2001] 2 FCR 331.
3 See *Duxbury v Duxbury (1985)* [1992] Fam 62n, [1990] 2 All ER 77; and *Preston v Preston* [1982] Fam 71, [1982] 1 All ER 41, CA.
4 See *B v B (Financial Provision)* [1990] FCR 105, [1990] 1 FLR 20 (where the court gave a helpful account of how the calculation works and of some of its limitations).
5 See *Wells v Wells* [1999] 1 AC 345, [1998] 3 All ER 481, HL.
6 See *F v F (Duxbury Calculation: Rate of Return)* [1996] 1 FLR 833 (and see the report of the self-proclaimed Duxbury Working Party in an article 'Duxbury: the Future' (1998) Fam Law 741).

## [2.117.14]
## Interim periodical payments

The court has an unlimited jurisdiction to make interim orders for periodical payments under the MCA 1973, s 23(1)(a) and (d) in favour of a party to the marriage or a child of the family if it is not otherwise in the position to determine a substantive application on its merits[1].

It should be noted that in limited circumstances (after making an occupation order under the FLA 1996, ss 33 to 35) the court has jurisdiction under the FLA 1996, s 40 to impose on either party an obligation:

(i) to maintain the matrimonial home (s 40(1)(a)(i));
(ii) to pay the rent, mortgage or other outgoings affecting the property (s 40(1)(a)(ii))[2].

In addition the court has jurisdiction to order the party who remains in occupation of the matrimonial home to make periodical payments to the other party if he or she would otherwise be entitled to occupy the property[3].

In deciding whether to exercise its powers under the FLA 1996, s 40 the court must have regard to the financial needs and resources of the parties and to their current and future financial obligations (including those to each other and to any relevant child[4]). Recent decisions have determined that the court has a jurisdiction in the appropriate case to award ongoing provision for legal fees as part of an order for maintenance pending suit[5], although the principle is currently understood to be the subject of an appeal.

1 See FPR 1991, r 2.64 at para **[3.419]** below.
2 However, note lack of enforcement power by way of committal to prison following such an order: *Nwogbe v Nwogbe* [2000] 3 FCR 345, [2000] 2 FLR 744, CA.
3 See the FLA 1996, s 40(1)(b).
4 See the FLA 1996, s 40(2).
5 See *A v A (maintenance pending suit: provision for legal fees)* [2001] 1 WLR 605, [2001] 1 FCR 226; *Gurtevoy v Gurtevoy* (forthcoming); and *Zand v Zand* (forthcoming).

## [2.117.15]
## Interim lump sums

The court has no jurisdiction to order an interim lump sum[1].

Nor does the court have an administrative power of appropriation to allocate a particular asset to meet the interim needs of either party before the final hearing[2].

The only course open to a party who wishes to secure a sale of the matrimonial home before final determination by the court is as follows:

(i) apply under the Married Women's Property Act 1882, s 17 (but note that RSC Ord 31, r 1 does not apply to applications under the 1882 Act and so vacant possession cannot be ordered on the grounds of expediency and an application would have to be made under FLA 1996, s 33 for vacant possession on or pending sale);

(ii) apply (if appropriate) under the TLATA 1996.

However, ordinarily it might be expected that any such application would be consolidated with any pending claims under MCA 1973 for determination at trial[3].

If it comes into force the FLA 1996, s 15, Sch 2, para 4 introduces a new s 22A(3) which will allow the court to make an interim lump sum order (or a series or such orders) if it is not otherwise in a position to make a financial provision order.

Notwithstanding the above, a lump sum order in favour of a party to the marriage or a child of the family made at the final hearing may take account of any liabilities incurred before an application was made to the court[4].

1 See *Bolsom v Bolsom* (1982) 4 FLR 21, 12 Fam Law 143, CA. For court power to adjourn a lump sum claim generally, see *D v D (financial provision: lump sum order)* [2001] 1 FCR 561, [2001] 1 FLR 633.

2 See *Wicks v Wicks* [1999] Fam 65, [1998] 1 FLR 470 (overruling: *Barry v Barry* [1992] Fam 140, [1992] 2 FLR 233, *Green v Green* [1993] 1 FLR 326; and *F v F (ancillary relief: substantial assets)* [1996] 2 FCR 397, [1995] 2 FLR 45).

3 See *Fielding v Fielding* [1978] 1 All ER 267, CA.

4 See the MCA 1973, s 23(3)(a) and (b).

## [2.117.16]
### Instalments and interest

An order for the payment of a lump sum or sums under the MCA 1973, s 23(1)(c) or (f) may require all or part of the amount payment to be made in instalments[1].

An order in favour of a party to the marriage for payment of a lump sum by instalments under the MCA 1973, s 23(1)(c) may be varied, discharged, or suspended under the MCA 1973, s 31 although it is doubted whether the court can increase the amount of any lump sum that has to be paid.

An order for payment of a lump sum at some time in the future (a deferred lump sum) or for payment by instalments may be ordered to carry interest from the date of the order and at such rate as the court may specify[2].

An order for the payment of interest must be made at the same time as the court makes the original order for the lump sum and the court does not have jurisdiction to make an order under the MCA 1973, s 23(6) at a later date[3].

1 See the MCA 1973, s 23(3)(c).

2 See the MCA 1973, s 23(6).

3 See *L v L* [1995] 1 FCR 60, [1994] 2 FLR 324.

## [2.118]

### 24 Property adjustment orders in connection with divorce proceedings, etc

(1) On granting a decree of divorce, a decree of nullity of marriage or a decree of judicial separation or at any time thereafter (whether, in the case of a decree of divorce or of nullity of marriage, before or after the decree is made absolute), the court may make any one or more of the following orders, that is to say—

(a) an order that a party to the marriage shall transfer to the other party, to any child of the family or to such person as may be specified in the order for the benefit of such a child such property as may be so specified, being property to which the first-mentioned party is entitled, either in possession or reversion;

(b) an order that a settlement of such property as may be so specified, being property to which a party to the marriage is so entitled, be made to the satisfaction of the court for the benefit of the other party to the marriage and of the children of the family or either or any of them;

(c) an order varying for the benefit of the parties to the marriage and of the children of the family or either or any of them any ante-nuptial or post-nuptial settlement (including such a settlement made by will or codicil) made on the parties to the marriage, other than one in the form of a pension arrangement (within the meaning of section 25D below);

(d) an order extinguishing or reducing the interest of either of the parties to the marriage under any such settlement, other than one in the form of a pension arrangement (within the meaning of section 25D below);

subject, however, in the case of an order under paragraph (a) above, to the restrictions imposed by section 29(1) and (3) below on the making of orders for a transfer of property in favour of children who have attained the age of eighteen.

(2) The court may make an order under subsection (1)(c) above notwithstanding that there are no children of the family.

(3) Without prejudice to the power to give a direction under section 30 below for the settlement of an instrument by conveyancing counsel, where an order is made under this section on or after granting a decree of divorce or nullity of marriage, neither the order nor any settlement made in pursuance of the order shall take effect unless the decree has been made absolute.

**Appointment**
Commencement order: SI 1973/1972.

**Amendment**
Sub-s (1): WRPA 1999, s 19. Date in force: 1 December 2000 (except in relation to proceedings in which the decree is granted were begun before that date): see SI 2000/1116 and the WRPA 1999, s 85(4).

**Derivation**
This section derived from the MPPA 1970, ss 4, 24(1)(b).

**Definitions:**
'child of the family' – see s 52(1) at para **[2.140]** below.

## [2.118.1]
## Keypoints

- General
- Who may apply
- The range of orders available
- Procedural concerns
- Property
- Third party interests
- Settlement of property
- Ante-nuptial or post-nuptial settlements
- Ownership of the matrimonial home
- Number of applications
- Restrictions on applications by spouses
- Restrictions on applications for the benefit of children
- Date of the order
- Interim orders

## [2.118.2]
## General

Section 24 gives the court jurisdiction to make property adjustment orders and to vary the terms of a settlement either in favour of a party to the marriage or in favour of a child of the family. This section must be read in the light of the restrictions contained in the MCA 1973, ss 25A, 28 (3) and s 29 and in conjunction with the MCA 1973, s 24A which gives the court jurisdiction to make orders for the sale of a property either at the time of making an order under s 24 or at any time thereafter.

For a discussion of this topic, see generally *Rayden and Jackson on Divorce and Family Matters* (17th edn, 1997), vol 1, para 21.120 et seq and the Noter-up thereto.

### [2.118.3]
### Who may apply

Either party to the marriage may apply under the MCA 1973, s 24 for an order against the other party or to ascertain the extent of his or her liability to the other party or to a child of the family[1].

1 See *Calderbank v Calderbank* [1976] Fam 93; *Sherdley v Sherdley* [1988] AC 213, [1987] 2 All ER 54, HL; and *Dart v Dart* [1997] 1 FCR 21, [1997] 2 FLR 286, CA.

### [2.118.4]
### The range of orders available

Under the MCA 1973, s 24 the court can make one or more of the following orders:

- (i) an order that one party transfer to the other or to (or for the benefit of) a child of the family any property in which that party has an interest[1];
- (ii) an order requiring one party to settle any property for the benefit of the other and/or for the benefit of any child of the family[2];
- (iii) an order varying any ante- or post-nuptial settlement for the benefit of the parties to the marriage and/or any child of the family[3];
- (iv) an order extinguishing or reducing the interest of either party under an ante- or post-nuptial settlement[4].

Section 24A of the MCA 1973 sets out the court's jurisdiction to order the sale of any property either at the time it makes an order under the MCA 1973, s 24 or at any time thereafter and to give such consequential directions as may be necessary to facilitate the sale (eg fixing the price at which the property must be sold and providing for the division of the net proceeds thereafter).

Any order for the sale of a property made after 1 October 1982 is now assumed to have been made under MCA 1973, s 24A[5].

1 See the MCA 1973, s 24(1)(a) above.
2 See the MCA 1973, s 24(1)(b).
3 See the MCA 1973, s 24(1)(c).
4 See the MCA 1973 s 24(1)(d).
5 See *Omielan v Omielan* [1996] 3 FCR 329, [1996] 2 FLR 306, CA; and *Re Harper (a bankrupt), Harper v O'Reilly* [1998] 2 FCR 475, [1997] 2 FLR 816.

### [2.118.5]
### Procedural concerns

An application under the MCA 1973, s 24 must be made in the petition or the answer, otherwise (unless the parties agree) the applicant will require the leave of the court[1]. For procedure, see generally *Rayden and Jackson on Divorce and Family Matters* (17th edn, 1997), vol 1, ch 23 and the Noter-up thereto.

A respondent who has filed no answer or who otherwise claims no substantive relief in the answer must apply in Form A.

An application under the MCA 1973, s 24 is governed by rr 2.51A to 2.70[2].

Particular regard should be had to the terms of FPR 1991, r 2.59(4) requiring a copy of any application for a property adjustment order under the MCA 1973, s 24 to be served on any mortgagee named in the application and to the terms of FPR 1991, r 2.59(3) that permit the district judge to order service on any other interested person (eg a third party who claims a legal or beneficial interest in the property).

In deciding whether to make an order the court must have regard to all the circumstances of the case (first consideration being given to the welfare of any child of the family whilst a minor)[3].

In respect of an order in favour of a party to the marriage, the court must have specific regard to those matters set out in the MCA 1973, s 25(2)(a) to (g).

In respect of a child of the family, the court must have regard to those matters set out in the MCA 1973, s 25(3)(a) to (e).

Unless there are special circumstances, it is generally inappropriate for property adjustment orders to be made which provide benefits for a child of the family after he or she has ceased full time education and has attained independence[4].

When making an order under the MCA 1973, s 24 the court should deal with all aspects of the parties' interests in the property (viz both legal and beneficial entitlement) and it is undesirable to leave them to litigate at a later stage to establish the precise extent of their entitlement[5].

Once the court's jurisdiction has been invoked under the MCA 1973, s 24, unless there are genuine issues as to the interests of third parties to be resolved it is generally inappropriate for the other party to issue an application under the TLATA 1996, s 14 in order to determine the strict property rights of the parties[6].



1 See FPR 1991, r 2.53 at para **[3.408]** below.
2 See para **[3.433]** et seq below.
3 See the MCA 1973, s 25(1).
4 See *A v A (A Minor: Financial Provision)* [1995] 1 FCR 309, [1994] 1 FLR 657; and *J v C (Child: Financial Provision)* [1998] 3 FCR 79, [1999] 1 FLR 152.
5 See *Rushton v Rushton* (1980) 1 FLR 195, CA (in which the court at first instance ordered a transfer into the joint names of the parties but failed to deal with their beneficial interests).
6 See *Fielding v Fielding* [1978] 1 All ER 267, CA; *Laird v Laird* [1999] 1 FLR 791, CA; and *Tee v Tee* [1999] 2 FLR 613, CA.

## [2.118.6]
## Property

All real and personal property is included within the category that may be the subject of an order under s 24 of the MCA 1973 and the only qualification is that either party must have an interest in or entitlement to it either in possession or in reversion. This can also include a company[1].

The mere fact that property is acquired after determination of the marriage does not mean it is excluded from consideration by the court[2].

Property includes the interest of either party under a periodic tenancy[3].

Property includes real property whether located within or outside the jurisdiction[4].

1 See *N v N (financial provision: sale of company)* [2001] 2 FLR 69, [2001] Fam Law 347.
2 See *Pearce v Pearce* (1980) 1 FLR 261; and *Schuller v Schuller* [1990] FCR 626, [1990] 2 FLR 193, CA (but see *Lombardi v Lombardi* [1973] 3 All ER 625, [1973] 1 WLR 1276, CA).
3 See *Hale v Hale* [1975] 2 All ER 1090, [1975] 1 WLR 931, CA; *Thompson v Thompson* [1976] Fam 25, [1975] 2 All ER 208, CA; and *Newlon Housing Trust v Alsulaimen* [1999] 1 AC 313, [1998] 3 FCR 183, HL.
4 See *Hamlin v Hamlin* [1986] Fam 11, [1986] 1 FLR 61, CA (in which the court considered an application restraining disposal of property located abroad under the MCA 1973, s 37).

## [2.118.7]
## Third party interests

On an application under the MCA 1973, s 24 for a property adjustment order the court has jurisdiction to determine not only the rights and interests of the parties to the marriage but also the rights and interests of third parties who have intervened in the application to claim an interest in the property[1].

The position in respect of property owned by a limited company in which one or both of the parties have an interest is less straightforward and the authorities are inconsistent:

- ***Nicholas v Nicholas* [1984] FLR 285** – the court will not make an order in respect of property owned by a company unless the company is the alter ego of one of the parties and any minority interest can be ignored;
- ***Crittenden v Crittenden* [1990] 2 FLR 361** – whilst the court has jurisdiction to make orders for the transfer of the shares held by either party in a company it does not have jurisdiction to deal with assets owned by the company itself;
- ***Green v Green*** [1993] **1 FLR 326** – the court has jurisdiction to order sale of land owned by a company when one party is the later ego of the company and has effective control over it or where any minority interests can be disregarded (overruled on other grounds in *Wicks v Wicks* [1998] 1 FLR 470);
- ***McGladdery v McGladdery* [1999] 2 FLR 1102** – the court does not have jurisdiction (under the MCA 1973, s 37) to set aside the disposal of assets by a company unless (it would appear) it is the alter ego of one of the parties;
- ***Mubarak v Mubarak* [2001] 1 FLR 673** – the court could only lift the corporate veil and make orders directly or indirectly regarding the company's assets where:
  (i) the spouse was owner and controller of the company concerned; and
  (ii) there were no adverse third party interests, even where a spouse conceded that the assets of a company could be treated as his own.

However, where one party to the marriage has access to property or other assets (even if no absolute entitlement to it), the court will not disregard the potential of those resources and may (subject to restrictions in respect of the interests of third parties) make orders with the intention of encouraging others to make those resources available to that party[2].

1 See *Tebbutt v Haynes* [1981] 2 All ER 238; and *Harwood v Harwood* [1992] 1 FCR 1, [1991] 2 FLR 274, CA (and in which the court held it could order the husband to transfer to the wife his interest under a partnership which included a share in the matrimonial home).

2 See *Thomas v Thomas* [1996] 2 FCR 544, [1995] 2 FLR 668, CA; and *Purba v Purba* [2000] 1 FCR 652, [2000] 1 FLR 444, CA.

## [2.118.8]
## Settlement of property

Care should be taken to distinguish between orders properly made under the MCA 1973, s 24(1)(b) providing for the settlement of property for the benefit of one or other of the parties to the marriage or a child of the family and those properly made under the MCA 1973, s 24(1)(c) or (d) varying the terms of an ante or post-nuptial settlement (most particularly the terms under which the parties will retain an interest in the jointly owned matrimonial home).

See generally, *Rayden and Jackson on Divorce and Family Matters* (17th edn, 1997), vol 1, para 21.142 et seq and the Noter-up thereto.

## [2.118.9]
## Ante-nuptial and post-nuptial settlements

The term 'any ante-nuptial or post-nuptial settlement' in the MCA 1973, s 24(1)(c) is to be given a wide meaning in the context of a section which gives the court jurisdiction to vary all property comprised in a settlement made on the parties to the marriage[1]. However, by the amendments to s 24(1)(c) and (d) that is effected by the WRPA 1999, the court is prevented from varying a pension arrangement by way of property adjustment order.

In order to establish whether a course of conduct or a particular transaction is a 'nuptial' settlement, the court will consider all the circumstances to establish the substance of the transaction involved[2].

Only a settlement made in relation to the marriage that is to be dissolved can be the subject of an application under the MCA 1973, s 24(1)(c) and whilst the marriage need not have been the sole cause for making the settlement it must be a fact of which the settlor took account in framing the settlement[3].

A settlement must be contrasted with an absolute gift between spouses not susceptible of variation under the MCA 1973, s 24(1)(c)[4].

The fact that a settlement is contingent or might be applicable for the benefit of a spouse by a subsequent marriage does not remove it from the category of settlements capable of variation under the MCA 1973, s 24(1)(c)[5].

However, care must be taken to ensure that the order extends only to property properly brought into the settlement[6].

Settled property includes income as well as capital and might properly extend to any obligation by one party to the marriage to make periodical payments to the other[7].

1 See *Brooks v Brooks* [1996] AC 375, [1995] 3 All ER 257, HL.
2 See *Parrington v Parrington* [1951] 2 All ER 916.
3 See *Joss v Joss* [1943] P 1, [1943] 1 All ER 102.
4 See *Prescott v Fellowes* [1958] P 260, [1958] 3 All ER 55, CA.
5 See *Lort-Williams v Lort-Williams* [1951] P 395, [1951] 2 All ER 241, CA.
6 See *Dormer v Ward* [1901] P 20, [1900–3] All ER Rep 363, CA.
7 See *Ponsonby v Ponsonby* [1884] 9 PD 58 (income derived under a trust); and *Brooks v Brooks* [1996] AC 375, [1995] 3 All ER 257 (a sole member pension scheme entered into by a husband with the intention of providing financial support for himself and his wife in his retirement).



## [2.118.10]
## Ownership of the matrimonial home

Orders transferring title to or varying the settlements under which a matrimonial property is held are capable of infinite variety, but generally fall into one of two basic types – that is, either:

(1) **Martin Order** – sale postponed or realisation of charge deferred until:
  - (i) the death of transferee;
  - (ii) the remarriage or cohabitation (for a defined period) of the transferee; or
  - (iii) voluntary removal from the property[1].

If included, a defined period of cohabitation as a trigger event to sale or realisation of the charge ought properly to be for a specified period[2]. Frequently, cohabitation will only trigger an express right to apply for a realisation of the charge, rather than an absolute entitlement to realisation.

(2) **Mesher Order** – sale postponed or realisation of charge deferred until:
  - (i) the death of the transferee;
  - (ii) the remarriage or cohabitation (for a defined period) of the transferee; or
  - (iii) the youngest child of the family reaches a certain age (17 years) or ceases full time education (whichever is later)[3].

There is no limit on the age at which a child of the family might be thought sufficiently independent to justify a sale[4].

It is to be noted that there is no assumption that the matrimonial home should be sold so soon as the children of the family cease full time education[5].

The inability of the court to extend the time limit after which a sale must take place or a charge must be realised underlines the draconian consequences of a 'Mesher type' order if events do not unravel as anticipated by the court[6].

Orders transferring or settling ownership of the matrimonial home on one of the parties to the marriage or providing for the variation or reduction of the interest of either party ought properly to contain provision to cater for an unexpected change in circumstances[7].

Such orders might also provide for restrictions upon the right of the other party to occupy the property, impose obligations on the party in occupation to meet the outgoings on the property and to maintain the fabric of the accommodation to a reasonable standard[8].

Sensibly such orders might properly permit sale of the property concerned and a deferral of any distribution between the parties of the net proceeds of sale upon reinvestment into a second property[9].

1 See *Martin v Martin* [1978] Fam 12.
2 See *Chadwick v Chadwick* [1985] FLR 606; and *Grimshaw v Grimshaw* (1980) 11 Fam Law 75. See also *Harvey v Harvey* [1982] Fam 83, [1982] 1 All ER 693; and *Tinsdale v Tinsdale* (1983) 4 FLR 641, CA (cohabits or becomes dependent on another man).

3 See *Mesher v Mesher and Hall* [1980] 1 All ER 126n, CA (followed in *Elliott v Elliott* [2001] 1 FCR 477, CA where *White v White* [2001] 1 AC 596, [2000] 3 FCR 555, HL applied).
4 See *Alonso v Alonso* (1974) 4 Fam Law 164 (child to be 21 years or ceased full time education); and *Harnett v Harnett* [1973] Fam 156, [1973] 2 All ER 593 (child to be 25 years or (if earlier) to have married).
5 See *Martin v Martin* [1978] Fam 12, [1977] 3 AllER 762, CA; and *Clutton v Clutton* [1991] FCR 265, [1991] 1 FLR 242, CA (if there is uncertainty about the custodial spouse's ability to re-house a 'Mesher type' order ought not to be made).
6 See *Thompson v Thompson* [1986] Fam 38, [1985] FLR 863, CA; and *Knibb v Knibb* [1987] 2 FLR 396.
7 See *Alonso v Alonso* (1974) 4 Fam Law 164 ('liberty to apply'); and *Thompson v Thompson* [1986] Fam 38, [1985] FLR 863, CA ('or further order').
8 See *Allen v Allen* [1974] 3 All ER 385, CA (exclusion of one party); *Hanlon v Hanlon* [1978] 2 All ER 889, CA (wife to assume responsibility for mortgage); and *Harvey v Harvey* [1982] Fam 83, [1982] 1 All ER 693, CA (payment of occupation rent after certain date).
9 See *T v T (Financial Provision)* [1990] FCR 169, sub nom *Re T* [1990] 1 FLR 1.

## [2.118.11]
## Number of applications

A property adjustment order under the MCA 1973, s 24 is a final order and is not susceptible of variation[1].

However, unless the court makes an order that is intended to be in full and final settlement of all claims that either party to the marriage may have against the other, the fact that an order has been made under one subsection of the MCA 1973, s 24 does not itself preclude a later application for an order under another subsection[2].

So too if an order made under the MCA 1973, s 24 is intended to deal only with the interest that either party to the marriage has in one particular property, a further application may be made for an order in respect of another property[3], though not in respect of that already the subject of an order.

It follows that care must be taken to ensure that it is clear from the terms of an order made under s 24 of the MCA 1973 whether it is intended to deal finally with all claims that either party could make for a property adjustment order or variation of settlement[4].

1 See *Carson v Carson* (1981) 2 FLR 352; and *Norman v Norman* (1983) 4 FLR 446.
2 See *Carson v Carson* (1981) 2 FLR 352 per Sheldon J.
3 See *Dinch v Dinch* [1987] 2 FLR 162 ('if what was intended was a final and conclusive once-for-all financial settlement, either overall or in relation to a particular property, then it must follow that that precludes any further claim to relief in relation to that property' – per Lord Oliver at 173).
4 See *Sandford v Sandford* [1986] 1 FLR 412, CA; and *Dinch v Dinch* [1987] 2 FLR 162 (mere silence will not necessarily be construed as amounting to a dismissal).

## [2.118.12]
## Restrictions on applications by spouses

An order in favour of one of the parties to the marriage may be made at any time on or after grant of a decree nisi but does not take effect unless the decree is made absolute[1].

There is no limitation on the period during which an application must be made, although any delay may be taken into consideration when the court considers whether to exercise its discretion to make an order[2].

No application may be made for an order under the MCA 1973, s 24 after the applicant has remarried[3].

1 See the MCA 1973, s 24(3) at para **[2.118]** above.
2 See *Twiname v Twiname* [1992] 1 FCR 185, [1992] 1 FLR 29, CA; and *Hill v Hill* [1997] 3 FCR 477, [1998] 1 FLR 198, CA.
3 See the MCA 1973, s 28(3) at para **[2.126]** below.

## [2.118.13]
### Restrictions on applications for the benefit of children

An order in favour of a child of the family may be made at any time on or after grant of a decree nisi but does not take effect unless the decree is made absolute[1].

Pursuant to s 29(1) of the MCA 1973 no transfer of property order under s 24(1)(a) may be made in favour of a child of the family who has reached the age of 18 years unless:

(i) the child is (or would be) in receipt of further education or training for a trade or profession (whether or not also in gainful employment)[2];

(ii) there are special circumstances justifying extension of the term beyond that date[3].

Special circumstances include physical or other handicap[4].

There is no comparable restriction upon the making of orders under the MCA 1973, s 24(1)(b) or (c) (creating or varying a settlement) in favour of a child of the family, but nor is there any presumption in favour of such a settlement being made merely because one party has the means to do so[5].

1 See the MCA 1973, s 24(3).
2 See the MCA 1973, s 29(3)(a).
3 See the MCA 1973, s 29(3)(b).
4 See *T v S (Financial Provision for Children)* [1994] 1 FCR 743, [1994] 2 FLR 883; and *C v F (Disabled Child: Maintenance Orders)* [1999] 1 FCR 39, [1998] 2 FLR 1, CA.
5 See *Lilford (Lord) v Glynn* [1979] 1 WLR 78.

## [2.118.14]
### Date of the order

If in breach of the restriction contained in the MCA 1973, s 24(1) an order is made in favour of one of the parties before grant of decree nisi the court has no inherent jurisdiction to validate the order, nor (subject to one exception) can the error be remedied:

(i) under the slip rule;

(ii) by agreement between the parties; or

(iii) by one party raising an estoppel against the other who seeks to avoid the effect of the order[1].

See the commentary to s 23 above[2] in respect of the approach adopted in the face of a simple clerical error and as to the endorsement of approval to agreements before the grant of decree nisi.

1 See *Munks v Munks* [1985] FLR 576, CA; and *Board v Checkland* [1987] 2 FLR 257, CA.
2 See para **[2.117.8]** above.

## [2.118.15]
### Interim orders

The court has no jurisdiction to make an interim property adjustment order under the MCA 1973, s 24[1].

Nor does the court have an administrative power of appropriation to allocate a particular asset to meet the interim needs of either party before the final hearing[2].

See the commentary to s 23 above[3] in respect of the potential applications open to a party who wishes to effect a redistribution of the parties' respective interests in the matrimonial home before the final hearing.

1 See *Bolsom v Bolsom* [1983] 4 FLR 21, CA.
2 See *Wicks v Wicks* [1999] Fam 65, [1998] 1 FLR 470, CA (overruling: *Barry v Barry* [1992] Fam 140, [1992] 2 FLR 233; *Green v Green* [1993] 1 FLR 326; and *F v F (ancillary relief: substantial assets)* [1996] 2 FCR 397, [1995] 2 FLR 45).
3 See para **[2.117.15]** above.

## [2.119]

### [24A Orders for sale of property]

[(1) Where the court makes under section 23 or 24 of this Act a secured periodical payments order, an order for the payment of a lump sum or a property adjustment order, then, on making that order or at any time thereafter, the court may make a further order for the sale of such property as may be specified in the order, being property in which or in the proceeds of sale of which either or both of the parties to the marriage has or have a beneficial interest, either in possession or reversion.

(2) Any order made under subsection (1) above may contain such consequential or supplementary provisions as the court thinks fit and, without prejudice to the generality of the foregoing provision, may include—

(a) provision requiring the making of a payment out of the proceeds of sale of the property to which the order relates, and

(b) provision requiring any such property to be offered for sale to a person, or class of persons, specified in the order.

(3) Where an order is made under subsection (1) above on or after the grant of a decree of divorce or nullity of marriage, the order shall not take effect unless the decree has been made absolute.

(4) Where an order is made under subsection (1) above, the court may direct that the order, or such provision thereof as the court may specify, shall not take effect until the occurrence of an event specified by the court or the expiration of a period so specified.

(5) Where an order under subsection (1) above contains a provision requiring the proceeds of sale of the property to which the order relates to be used to secure periodical payments to a party to the marriage, the order shall cease to have effect on the death or re-marriage of that person.

[(6) Where a party to a marriage has a beneficial interest in any property, or in the proceeds of sale thereof, and some other person who is not a party to the marriage also has a beneficial interest in that property or in the proceeds of sale thereof, then, before deciding whether to make an order under this section in relation to that property, it shall be the duty of the court to give that other person an opportunity to make representations with respect to the order; and any representations made by that other person shall be included among the circumstances to which the court is required to have regard under section 25(1) below.]]

#### Definitions

'lump sum order'; 'secured periodical payments order' – see s 21(1) at para **[2.115]** above; and s 23(1) at para **[2.117]** above.

'property adjustment order' – see s 21(2) at para **[2.115]** above; and s24(1) at para **[2.118]** above.

#### Amendment

Inserted by the MHPA 1981, s 7. Sub-s (6): inserted by the MFPA 1984, s 46(1), Sch 1.

## [2.119.1]
### Keypoints

- General
- Scope of the provision
- Procedural concerns
- Date of the order
- Property
- Third party interests
- Secured periodical payments
- Variation

### [2.119.2]
### General

Section 24A of the MCA 1973 contains the court's ancillary procedural power to order the sale of any property either at the time it makes certain specified orders under the MCA 1973, ss 23 and 24 or at any time thereafter and is limited to clarifying and expanding the court's power of implementation and enforcement[1].

1 See *Omielan v Omielan* [1996] 3 FCR 329, [1996] 2 FLR 306, CA.

### [2.119.3]
### Scope of the provision

Section 24A of the MCA 1973 sets out the court's jurisdiction to order the sale of any property either at the time it makes an order or at any time thereafter:

(i) for secured periodical payments or lump sum provision under the MCA 1973, s 23; or

(ii) for a property adjustment order under the MCA 1973, s 24 and to give such consequential directions as may be necessary to facilitate the sale (eg fixing the price at which the property must be sold and providing for the division of the net proceeds thereafter).

Whilst under the MCA 1973, s 24A the court might properly make provision for the payment of the marketing and legal costs of sale and direct payment to third parties which have a beneficial interest in the property or its proceeds of sale it has no jurisdiction under the MCA 1973, s 24A to order the payment pay of the debts of either party out of the proceeds of sale of the matrimonial home if those debts are unconnected to an interest in the property[1].

Any order for the sale of a property made after 1 October 1982 is now assumed to have been made under the MCA 1973, s 24A which is ancillary to the court's primary powers to transfer or settle property under the MCA 1973, s 24(1)(a) to (d)[2].

Consequently the rights of the parties pursuant to an order for sale of the matrimonial home and redistribution of the net proceeds vest at the time the order takes effect (upon decree absolute) and not only at the time the property is subsequently sold and the proceeds divided[3].

1 See *Burton v Burton* [1986] 2 FLR 419.
2 See *Omielan v Omielan* [1996] 3 FCR 329, [1996] 2 FLR 312, CA.
3 See *Harper v O'Reilly and Harper* [1998] 3 FCR 475, [1997] 2 FLR 816 (where the husband was made bankrupt after the date of the order but before the property was sold).

### [2.119.4]
### Procedural concerns

The definition of 'ancillary relief' contained in FPR 1991, r 1.2(1) does not include an order for sale under the MCA 1973, s 24A and consequently the provisions of FPR 1991, rr 2.51A to 2.66 (save for r 2.61, which relates to consent orders) do not apply. Most applications for an order under the MCA 1973, s 24A will be made at the same time as an application of a transfer or variation of settlement under the MCA 1973, s 24(1)(a) and (c) or (d) and will be regulated by procedure governing that application.

Logically the same procedure should be followed in respect of a separate application for an order under the MCA 1973, s 24A made some time *after* the court has already made an order under the MCA 1973, ss 23 and 24.

### [2.119.5]
### Date of the order

By implication, no order for sale under s 24A of the MCA 1973 can be made before the grant of decree nisi[1].

See the commentary to the MCA 1973, ss 23 and 24 above[2] for the consequences of failing to observe this restriction and the court's limited jurisdiction to correct any error.

An order for sale under s 24A of the MCA 1973 does not take effect until the decree is made absolute[3].

1 See the MCA 1973, ss 23(1) and 24(1).
2 See paras **[2.117.8]** and **[2.118.14]** above.
3 See the MCA 1973, s 24A(3).

## [2.119.6]
### Property

All real and personal property is included within the category that may be the subject of an order under the MCA 1973, s 24A and the only qualification is that either party must have a beneficial interest either in the property itself or in its proceeds of sale[1].

See the commentary to s 24 above[2] as to the range of real and personal property that may be the subject of an order under the MCA 1973, s 24A.

1 See the MCA 1973, s 24(1).
2 See para **[2.118.6]** above.

## [2.119.7]
### Third party interests

A third party who has an interest in any property (or in its proceeds of sale) in respect of which an application is made under the MCA 1973, s 24A must be given an opportunity to make representations and to be heard on the question of whether an order for sale should be made[1].

1 See the MCA 1973, s 24A(6).

## [2.119.8]
### Variation

Whilst there is express provision in the MCA 1973, s 31(2)(f) to vary an order made under the MCA 1973, s 24A, this must be interpreted in the light of the fact that s 24A is a procedural enactment and is ancillary to the court's primary jurisdiction contained in s 24(1) of the MCA 1973. It follows that any application to vary under the MCA 1973, s 31(1) might be concerned solely with questions of implementation and enforcement and not with altering substantive rights of the parties in the property[1].

It follows that the court does not have jurisdiction under s 31 of the MCA 1973 to extend the time specified under the MCA 1973, s 24A for a deferred sale[2].

However, the court does have jurisdiction (even in the face of opposition from the other party) to bring forward the date upon which a sale is due to take place, subject however to any variation giving effect to the spirit and construction of the original order[3].

1 See *Omielan v Omielan* [1996] 3 FCR 329, [1996] 2 FLR 306, CA.
2 See *Taylor v Taylor* [1987] 1 FLR 142, CA; and *Knibb v Knibb* [1987] 2 FLR 396, CA.
3 See *Thompson v Thompson* [1986] Fam 38, [1985] FLR 863, CA.

## [2.119A]

### 24B Pension sharing orders in connection with divorce proceedings etc

(1) On granting a decree of divorce or a decree of nullity of marriage or at any time thereafter (whether before or after the decree is made absolute), the court may, on an application made under this section, make one or more pension sharing orders in relation to the marriage.

(2) A pension sharing order under this section is not to take effect unless the decree on or after which it is made has been made absolute.

(3) A pension sharing order under this section may not be made in relation to a pension arrangement which—

(a) is the subject of a pension sharing order in relation to the marriage, or
(b) has been the subject of pension sharing between the parties to the marriage.

(4) A pension sharing order under this section may not be made in relation to shareable state scheme rights if—

(a) such rights are the subject of a pension sharing order in relation to the marriage, or
(b) such rights have been the subject of pension sharing between the parties to the marriage.

(5) A pension sharing order under this section may not be made in relation to the rights of a person under a pension arrangement if there is in force a requirement imposed by virtue of section 25B or 25C below which relates to benefits or future benefits to which he is entitled under the pension arrangement.

**Amendment**

Inserted by the WRPA 1999, s 19. Date in force: 1 December 2000 (except that a pension sharing order may not be made if the proceedings in which the decree is granted were begun before that date): see SI 2000/1116 and the WRPA 1999, s 85.

**Notes**

For commentary as to the effects of petitions pre- and post-1 December 2000 in particular, second petitions used to try and defeat first petition which pre-dated 1 December 2000, see [2001] Fam Law 691 referring to *S v S Dewsbury County Court* (26 April 2001) – second petition was held to be an abuse of process.



## [2.119A.1]
## Keypoints

- Proceedings in which orders may be made
- The need for an application
- Regulations
- Restrictions on the making of orders

## [2.119A.2]
## Proceedings in which orders may be made

Pension sharing orders are confined to divorce and nullity proceedings – they cannot be made in judicial separation proceedings.

## [2.119A.3]
## The need for an application

Section 24B(1) states that the court may make an order 'on an application made under this section, thus identifying the need for a party to formally apply for such orders. Form A should contain a claim for a pension sharing order, if such a claim is to be pursued. A summary of the main additional procedural points within the FPR 1991 is as follows:

| Rule<br>Procedure | **FPR 1991, r 2.61(1)(dd)** – set out at para **[3.441]** below<br>The person who arranges the pension must be served with a copy of any consent order and must not have objected to it |
|---|---|

| Rule<br>Procedure | **FPR 1991, r 2.70(2), (4)** and **(5)** – set out at para **[3.461]** below<br>The person with pension rights must request the information required under the Pensions on Divorce etc (Provision of Information) Regulations 2000, SI 2000/1048[1] from the pension provider. If the party with pension rights has relevant information as at a date not more than 12 months earlier than the first appointment, that information will be sufficient |
|---|---|

| Rule | FPR 1991, r 2.70(3) – set out at para [3.461] below |
|---|---|
| Procedure | The party with pension rights must pass on the pension information to the other party |

| Rule | FPR 1991, r 2.70(6) – set out at para [3.461] below |
|---|---|
| Procedure | If the Form A seeks pension sharing orders, it must be served on the pension provider by the applicant |

| Rule | FPR 1991, r 2.70(13)–(14) – set out at para [3.461] below |
|---|---|
| Procedure | The pension sharing order will be made as an annexe to the court's ancillary relief order and must contain prescribed information |

| Rule | FPR 1991, r 2.70(16)–(17) – set out at para [3.461] below |
|---|---|
| Procedure | A court that makes, varies or discharges a pension sharing order must send a copy of the following documents to the pension arranger: the decree of divorce or judicial separation upon which the order was made; and a copy of the relevant order |

1 See para [3.562] below.

**[2.119A.4]**
**Regulations**

The following regulations affect the making of pension sharing orders:

| Title | Pensions on Divorce etc (Provision of Information) Regulations 2000 |
|---|---|
| SI No | 2000/1048 |
| Purpose | **The supply of information to pension members and their spouses** |
| Cross-ref | See para [3.562] below |

| Title | Pensions on Divorce etc (Charging) Regulations 2000 |
|---|---|
| SI No | 2000/1049 |
| Purpose | **Recovery by pension arranger of costs of complying with the order, providing information and other 'pension sharing activity'** |
| Cross-ref | See para [3.572] below |

| Title | Pension Sharing (Valuation) Regulations 2000 |
|---|---|
| SI No | 2000/1052 |
| Purpose | **Pension rights that are not shareable and valuation of pension debits and credits** |
| Cross-ref | See para [3.582] below |

| Title | Pension Sharing (Implementation and Discharge of Liability) Regulations 2000 |
|---|---|
| SI No | 2000/1053 |
| Purpose | **Extension of the implementation period and how pension arranger may discharge his liability in respect of a pension credit** |
| Cross-ref | See para [3.589] below |

| | |
|---|---|
| **Title** | Pension Sharing (Pension Credit Benefit) Regulations 2000 |
| **SI No** | 2000/1054 |
| **Purpose** | **Requirements relating to and indexation of pension credit benefit. Also transfer values of pension credit benefit** |
| **Cross-ref** | See para **[3.607]** below |

| | |
|---|---|
| **Title** | Pension Sharing (Safeguarded Rights) Regulations 2000 |
| **SI No** | 2000/1055 |
| **Purpose** | **Treatment of safeguarded rights once pension has been shared** |
| **Cross-ref** | See para **[3.641A]** below |

| | |
|---|---|
| **Title** | Divorce etc (Pensions) Regulations 2000 |
| **SI No** | 2000/1123 |
| **Purpose** | **Valuation of pension, notices where pension attachment orders made, reduction in benefits where pension attachment orders made, changes of circumstances where pension attachment order made, transfer of rights where pension attachment order made, service of documents and time at which pension sharing order will take effect** |
| **Cross-ref** | See para **[3.642]** below |



## [2.119A.5]
### Restrictions on the making of orders

These are set out in s 24B(3) to (5). The effect of these provisions is:

(1) The court cannot make a pension sharing order in relation to a pension arrangement or a shareable state scheme where:
  (a) there is already a pension sharing order affecting the pension in relation to the marriage;
  (b) the pension has been subject to a pension sharing order between the parties to the marriage;
  (c) where the pension scheme comes within those exempted by the Pension Sharing (Exempted Schemes) Order 2001, SI 2001/358, namely the offices of the Prime Minister, Lord Chancellor and Speaker of the House of Commons.

(2) There cannot be a pension sharing order in relation to a pension over which a pension attachment (formerly called earmarking) order has been made.

There is nothing to prevent a pension sharing order being made in relation to a pension that has already been subjected to a pension sharing order in a marriage between one of the spouses and another previous spouse, however, a pension sharing order cannot be made in relation to a pension which is subject to a pension attachment order even if the attachment is made in relation to a different marriage.

## [2.119B]

### 24C Pension sharing orders: duty to stay

(1) No pension sharing order may be made so as to take effect before the end of such period after the making of the order as may be prescribed by regulations made by the Lord Chancellor.

(2) The power to make regulations under this section shall be exercisable by statutory instrument which shall be subject to annulment in pursuance of a resolution of either House of Parliament.

#### Amendment

Inserted by the WRPA 1999, s 19. Date in force (for the purpose only of the exercise of any power to make regulations): 11 November 1999: see the WRPA 1999, s 89. Date in force (for remaining purposes): 1 December 2000: see SI 2000/1116.

**[2.119B.1]**
**Keypoint**
- Regulations

**[2.119B.2]**
**Regulations**

Regulation 9 (Pension sharing order not to take effect pending appeal) of the Divorce etc (Pensions) Regulations 2000, SI 2000/1123 provides as follows:

> '(1) No pension sharing order under section 24B or variation of a pension sharing order under section 31 shall take effect earlier than 7 days after the end of the period for filing notice of appeal against the order.
> (2) The filing of a notice of appeal within the time allowed for doing so prevents the order taking effect before the appeal has been dealt with.'

**[2.119C]**

### 24D Pension sharing orders: apportionment of charges

If a pension sharing order relates to rights under a pension arrangement, the court may include in the order provision about the apportionment between the parties of any charge under section 41 of the Welfare Reform and Pensions Act 1999 (charges in respect of pension sharing costs), or under corresponding Northern Ireland legislation.

**Amendment**
Inserted by the WRPA 1999, s 19. Date in force: 1 December 2000: see SI 2000/1116.

**[2.119C.1]**
**Keypoint**
- Effect of section
- Section 41 of the Welfare Reform and Pensions Act 1999

**[2.119C.2]**
**Effect of section**

There will be charges made by those responsible for the pension arrangement for the costs incurred in sharing the pension. This section allows the court to apportion those charges.

**[2.119C.3]**
**Section 41 of the Welfare Reform and Pensions Act 1999**

Section 41 of the WRPA 1999[1] provides for the Secretary of State to make regulations dealing with the costs of pension sharing. The Regulations are the Pensions on Divorce etc (Charging) Regulations 2000, SI 2000/1049[2].

1 See para **[2.563]** below.
2 See para **[3.572]** below.

**[2.120]**

### [25 Matters to which court is to have regard in deciding how to exercise its powers under ss 23, 24 and 24A]

[(1) It shall be the duty of the court in deciding whether to exercise its powers under section 23, 24, 24A or 24B above and, if so, in what manner, to have regard to all the circumstances of the case, first consideration being given to the welfare while a minor of any child of the family who has not attained the age of eighteen.

(2) As regards the exercise of the powers of the court under section 23(1)(a), (b) or (c), 24, 24A or 24B above in relation to a party to the marriage, the court shall in particular have regard to the following matters—

(a) the income, earning capacity, property and other financial resources which each of the parties to the marriage has or is likely to have in the foreseeable future, including in the case of earning capacity any increase in that capacity which it would in the opinion of the court be reasonable to expect a party to the marriage to take steps to acquire;

(b) the financial needs, obligations and responsibilities which each of the parties to the marriage has or is likely to have in the foreseeable future;

(c) the standard of living enjoyed by the family before the breakdown of the marriage;

(d) the age of each party to the marriage and the duration of the marriage;

(e) any physical or mental disability of either of the parties to the marriage;

(f) the contributions which each of the parties has made or is likely in the foreseeable future to make to the welfare of the family, including any contribution by looking after the home or caring for the family;

(g) the conduct of each of the parties, if that conduct is such that it would in the opinion of the court be inequitable to disregard it;

(h) in the case of proceedings for divorce or nullity of marriage, the value to each of the parties to the marriage of any benefit *(for example, a pension)* which, by reason of the dissolution or annulment of the marriage, that party will lose the chance of acquiring.

(3) As regards the exercise of the powers of the court under section 23(1)(d), (e) or (f), (2) or (4), 24 or 24A above in relation to a child of the family, the court shall in particular have regard to the following matters—

(a) the financial needs of the child;

(b) the income, earning capacity (if any), property and other financial resources of the child;

(c) any physical or mental disability of the child;

(d) the manner in which he was being and in which the parties to the marriage expected him to be educated or trained;

(e) the considerations mentioned in relation to the parties to the marriage in paragraphs (a), (b), (c) and (e) of subsection (2) above.

(4) As regards the exercise of the powers of the court under section 23(1)(d), (e) or (f), (2) or (4), 24 or 24A above against a party to a marriage in favour of a child of the family who is not the child of that party, the court shall also have regard—

(a) to whether that party assumed any responsibility for the child's maintenance, and, if so, to the extent to which, and the basis upon which, that party assumed such responsibility and to the length of time for which that party discharged such responsibility;

(b) to whether in assuming and discharging such responsibility that party did so knowing that the child was not his or her own;

(c) to the liability of any other person to maintain the child.

**Derivation**

This section, as originally enacted, derived from the MPPA 1970, s 5.

**Definitions:**

'child'; 'child of the family' – see s 52(1) at para **[2.140]** below.

**Amendment**

Substituted by the MFPA 1984, s 3. Sub-s (1): WRPA 1999, s 19. Date in force: 1 December 2000: see SI 2000/1116. Sub-s (2): PA 1995, s 166(2) (for savings see SI 1996/1675, arts 4, 5); WRPA 1999, s 19.

**[2.120.1]**
**Keypoints**

- General – s 25(1)
- The s 25 exercise
- First consideration to the welfare of minors

Matrimonial Causes Act 1973

*Section 25(2)(a) – Income and earning capacity*
- Sources of income
- Current and future earning capacity

*Section 25(2)(a) – Property and resources*
- Property – general factors – definition – net assets and costs
- Property – big money
- Property – big money – old approach
- Property – big money – new approach
- Property – big money – millionaire's defence
- Property – businesses – valuations
- Property – businesses – forced collapse
- Property – piercing corporate veil
- Property – preservation of company
- Existing property rights
- Property – liquidity
- Inferring property
- Property 'in the foreseeable future' – inheritance prospects
- Property 'in the foreseeable future' – pensions
- Property 'in the foreseeable future' – adjournment
- Property – trusts
- Property – personal injury awards
- Property – tenancies
- Foreign property

*Section 25(2)(b) – Financial needs, obligations and responsibilities*
- Needs and minor children
- Needs and adult children
- Needs and debts
- Needs, subsistence level and the maintenance payer's standard of living
- Needs and expenditure
- Needs and housing
- Needs and *Martin/Martin* Orders
- Needs and reasonable requirements
- Needs – the *Besterman* cushion

*Section 25(2)(c) to (e) – Living standards, ages, duration and disability*
- Standard of living – s 25(2)(c)
- Ages of the parties – s 25(2)(d)
- Duration of the marriage
- Physical or mental disability – s 25(2)(e)

*Section 25(2)(f) – Contributions*
- Contributions – general
- Contributions – direct
- Contributions – entitlement
- Contributions – inheritance, gift, pre-marital ownership
- Contributions – indirect
- Contributions – short marriages
- Contributions – negative

*Section 25(2)(g) – Conduct*
- Conduct – general
- Conduct – reckless financial behaviour
- Conduct – adultery, bigamy and deception

- Conduct – violence
- Conduct – litigation misconduct

*Section 25(2)(h) – Lost Benefits*

- Value of any benefit (eg pension) which a party will lose the chance of acquiring
- Loss of widows pension

*Section 25(3) and (4) – Factors relating to children of the family*

- Section 25(3) – Matters for the courts regard in relation to a child of the family
- Who is a child of the family
- Factors to be taken into account
- Child's own assets
- Section 25(4) – Additional matters where a child of the family is not the child of a party
- Extent to which a child is treated as a child of the family
- Legal costs of a child seeking to enforce an order
- Lump sum and property adjustment orders which may be made in favour of a child
- Limit on applications by or on behalf of children
- Effect of orders for children on state benefits



**[2.120.2]**
**General – s 25(1)**

Section 25 of the MCA 1973 sets out those matters to which the court must have regard in deciding whether, and if so how, to exercise its powers under ss 23, 24 and 24A. The consideration of these matters as a part of the exercise of the court's discretion is frequently termed 'the s 25 exercise'. The generality of the court's discretion in this area is made clear by the duty in s 25(1) to have regard to 'all the circumstances of the case'.

**[2.120.3]**
**The s 25 exercise**

In order properly to exercise its discretion whether to make orders under the MCA 1973, ss 23, 24 and 24A the court must follow the directions set out in the section and should first consider all the circumstances of the case and in particular those matters set out in paras (a) to (g) of s 25(1) of the MCA 1973[1].

The ultimate object of s 25 of the MCA 1973 (although not defined in the section) has long been accepted as being to do what is fair, just and reasonable between the parties[2].

Save in respect of the welfare of any child of the family whilst still a minor, no emphasis has been placed in s 25 of the MCA 1973 on any of the factors listed in the MCA 1973, s 25(2) and consequently no priority should be given by the court to any one of them over another[3].

The approach that a court should adopt when conducting the s 25 exercise underwent a thorough overhaul by the House of Lords in the case of *White v White*[4]. The following are the main points emanating from that decision:

- implicitly, the objective must be to achieve a fair outcome[5];
- there should not be discrimination between spouses. If, in their different spheres, each contributed equally to the family, then in principle it matters not which of them earned the money and built up the assets. There should be no bias in favour of the money-earner and against the home-maker and the child-carer. There are cases, of which the Court of Appeal decision in *Page v Page*[6] is perhaps an instance, where the court may have lost sight of this principle'[7];
- there is no presumption of equality, given the court's statutory discretion. However, 'before reaching a firm conclusion … a judge would always be well advised to check his tentative views against the yard-stick of equality of division[8];

- needs 'even interpreted generously and called reasonable requirements' should not be assumed to be determinative, particularly where there is a surplus of resources'[9];
- the court should apply the statute – there is no hierarchy amongst the s 25 factors[10];
- the *Duxbury* approach 'may be a useful guide in assessing the amount of money required to provide for a person's financial needs. It is a means of capitalising an income requirement. But that is all';
- where the resources exceed need and the judge is considering the overall fairness of the case, he may attach such weight as he considers appropriate to a desire to leave money to children[11];
- the fact that money has been inherited or owned by one spouse before the marriage will be one of the circumstances of the case;
- although there is no hard and fast rule, the Court of Appeal in *White* could not be criticised for the use of net values when considering the assets[12].

See below for subsequent decisions of the court interpreting and applying *White*.

1 See *Preston v Preston* [1982] Fam 17, [1982] 1 All ER 41, CA; and *Dart v Dart* [1997] 1 FCR 21, [1996] 2 FLR 286, CA.
2 See *Page v Page* (1981) 2 FLR 198, CA; and *Gojkovic v Gojkovic* [1992] Fam 40, [1990] 2 All ER 84, CA.
3 See *Smith v Smith (Smith and Others Intervening)* [1991] 2 FLR 432 at 435–436 per Butler-Sloss LJ.
4 [2000] 3 FCR 555.
5 [2000] 3 FCR 555 at 563e.
6 (1981) 2 FLR 198, CA.
7 [2000] 3 FCR 555 at 563, 564c.
8 [2000] 3 FCR 555 at 564e per Lord Nicholls.
9 [2000] 3 FCR 555 at 567d–h.
10 [2000] 3 FCR 555 at 567f.
11 [2000] 3 FCR 555 at 569.
12 [2000] 3 FCR 555 at 572.

## [2.120.4]
### First consideration to the welfare of minors

The MCA 1973 requires first consideration to be given to the welfare (while a minor) of any child of the family who has not attained the age of 18[1].

A child remains a minor until he or she attains the age of 18 years, but in practice the court will give special consideration to the welfare of any child of the family until he or she ceases full-time (tertiary) education[2].

The welfare of minor children is the first but not the paramount consideration for the court in cases of ancillary relief[3].

However, the welfare of any minor child will be regarded as of first importance and all other factors set out in s 25(2) of the MCA 1973 must be assessed with this important factor kept in mind[4].

1 See the MCA 1973, s 25(1) at para **[2.120]** above.
2 See *Harvey v Harvey* [1982] Fam 83, [1982] 1 All ER 693, CA.
3 See *SRJ v DWJ (Financial Provision)* [1999] 3 FCR 153, [1999] 2 FLR 176, CA.
4 See *Suter v Suter and Jones* [1987] Fam 111, [1987] 2 All ER 336, CA; and *R v R* [1988] FCR 307, [1988] 1 FLR 89, CA.

## [2.120.5]

*Section 25(2)(a) – Income and earning capacity*

### Sources of income

The MCA 1973 requires regard to the income, earning capacity, property and other financial resources which each of the parties to the marriage has or is likely to have in the foreseeable future, including in the case of earning capacity any increase in that capacity which it would in the opinion of the court be reasonable to expect a party to the marriage to take steps to acquire[1].

Under s 25(2)(a) of the MCA 1973 the court must take account of the income of both parties from whatever source[1]. See generally, *Rayden and Jackson on Divorce and Family Matters* (17th edn, 1997), vol 1, para 21.34 et seq and the Noter-up thereto.

The court is concerned with 'net' income after deduction of income tax, national insurance and indispensable outgoings[2].

The court cannot make an order against the income of the new spouse or cohabitee of one of the parties to the marriage but limited account may be taken of such resources to the extent that they relieve the party to the marriage of the obligation to meet outgoings he otherwise would have to meet thereby freeing up income to meet the prospective claims for maintenance made by the other party to the marriage[3].

The fact that an order under the MCA 1973, s 23(1)(a) for periodical payments in favour of a party to the marriage would have the effect of reducing pro tanto the other party's entitlement to social security benefits is irrelevant to the assessment of what is the right level of maintenance[4].

The mere fact that one of the parties to the marriage is in receipt of income support does not mean that he or she could not be ordered to pay maintenance[5].

When assessing the extent and availability of income, the court may look, inter alia, to the standard of living enjoyed by one or both of the parties as indicative of the true level of resources available and then consider ways in which income might be made available to meet the needs of the other party[6].

Notwithstanding the availability of other resources the court should not act in direct invasion of the rights of third parties nor apply inappropriate pressure to force resources to be made available to one of the parties[7].

The burden of proving the availability of further undisclosed resources rests on the applicant to the usual civil standard of proof. However, the onus then shifts to the other party to explain the situation and any apparent inconsistency between what has been disclosed and the standard of lifestyle enjoyed by the parties[8].



1 See the MCA 1973, s 25(2)(a) at para **[2.120]** above.

1 See *Bonsor v Bonsor* [1897] P 77 (regular voluntary payments received from a relative); *Collins v Collins* [1943] P 106 (service allowance paid to one of the parties); *Howard v Howard* [1945] P 1; *Browne v Browne* [1989] 1 FLR 291 (income derived from a discretionary trust); *J-PC v J-AF* [1955] P 215 (borrowed money); *Rodewald v Rodewald* [1977] Fam 192; *Sibley v Sibley* (1979) 2 FLR 121 (perks from employment); *Klucinski v Klucinski* [1953] 1 All ER 683 (overtime from employment); *Claxton v Claxton* (1982) 3 FLR 415 (attendance allowance); *Slater v Slater* [1982] 3 FLR 363; *Stockford v Stockford* (1981) 3 FLR 58 (single parent allowance); *Griffiths v Griffiths* [1984] Fam 70; *Boylan v Boylan* [1988] FCR 689, [1988] 1 FLR 282; and *Whitfield v Whitfield* [1986] 1 FLR 99 (income derived from invested capital).

2 See *Furniss v Furniss* (1981) 3 FLR 46; *Stockford v Stockford* (1981) 3 FLR 58; *Peacock v Peacock* [1984] 1 All ER 1069; and *Allen v Allen* [1986] 2 FLR 265.

3 See *Macey v Macey* (1981) 3 FLR 7; *Grainger v Grainger* [1954] 2 All ER 665; *Foster v Foster* [1964] 3 All ER 541; *Sansom v Sansom* [1966] P 52; *Brown v Brown* (1981) 3 FLR 161; *Slater v Slater* (1982) 3 FLR 364; and *Furniss v Furniss* (1981) 3 FLR 46.

4 See *Ashley v Ashley* [1968] P 582, [1965] 3 All ER 554; *Fitzpatrick v Fitzpatrick* (1978) 9 Fam Law 16; *Stockford v Stockford* (1981) 3 FLR 58; *Peacock v Peacock* [1984] 1 All ER 1069; and *Foot v Foot* [1987] FCR 62.

5 See *Freeman v Swatridge* [1984] FLR 762; and *R v Cardiff Justices, ex p Salter* [1986] 1 FLR 162.

6 See *J-PC v J-AF* [1955] P 215 (borrowed money in expectation of future capital); *Robinson v Robinson* (1973) 2 FLR 1 (where the financial arrangements were complex but produced little income the court was entitled to look at the total resources and how they are organised); and *Thomas v Thomas* [1996] 2 FCR 544, [1995] 2 FLR 668 (income potentially available from family owned company).

7 See *Howard v Howard* [1945] P 1; *B v B* (1982) 3 FLR 298; *Browne v Browne* [1989] 1 FLR 291; *J v J (C intervening)* [1989] Fam 29, [1989] 1 All ER 1121; and *Thomas v Thomas* [1996] 2 FCR 544, [1995] 2 FLR 668.

8 See *Baker v Baker* [1996] 1 FCR 567, [1995] 2 FLR 829.

## [2.120.6]

### Current and future earning capacity

Under the MCA 1973, s 25(2)(a) account must be taken of any increase in the earning capacity of either party it would be reasonable to expect a party to the marriage to take steps to acquire.

It follows that the court is not only concerned with actual sources of income, but also with the ability of either party to generate an income[1].

However, whilst the court might properly take account of any unutilized capacity to generate income the court ought not to make an order not otherwise justified on the facts in an endeavour to force one party to embark upon a course of action that otherwise he or she has reasonably refused to do[2].

In an appropriate case, conduct on the part of one of the parties to the marriage, which frustrates an ability to pursue a more profitable earning capacity, might properly be reflected in a disparate division of the capital resources in favour of the other party[3].

So too conduct by one party to the marriage reducing the ability of the other party to exercise a greater future earning capacity may have an impact on an overall division of the available resources[4].

The court should exercise restraint and an element of caution when presuming to identify any ability to achieve self sufficiency within a finite period on the part of wives in middle age who have been out of employment for some years looking after the family[5].

However, young, healthy childless wives will almost certainly be presumed to have an earning capacity of some sort[6].

Where the assets are substantial it may not be appropriate to presume that one party should be obliged to exercise an actual or perceived earning capacity (at least not as a matter of economic necessity)[7].

See generally, *Rayden and Jackson on Divorce and Family Matters* (17th edn, 1997), vol 1, para 21.34 et seq and the Noter-up thereto.

1 See *J-PC v J-AF* [1955] P 215, [1955] 2 All ER 617.
2 See *Wakeford v Wakeford* [1953] 2 All ER 827; and *McEwan v McEwan* [1972] 1 WLR 1217.
3 See *Harwood v Harwood* [1991] 2 FLR 274, CA.
4 See *Jones v Jones* [1976] Fam 8; but see *A v A (Financial Provision: Conduct)* [1995] 2 FCR 137, [1995] 1 FLR 345.
5 See *Barrett v Barrett* [1988] FCR 707, [1988] 2 FLR 516; and *Flavell v Flavell* [1997] 1 FCR 332, [1997] 1 FLR 353, CA.
6 See *Mathias v Mathias* [1972] Fam 287; and *Frisbee v Frisbee* (1983) 14 Fam Law 19.
7 See *F v F (Duxbury Calculation: Rate of Return)* [1996] 1 FLR 833; *A v A (Financial Provision)* [1998] 3 FCR 421, [1998] 2 FLR 180; but see *P v P (Financial Relief: Non-disclosure)* [1994] 1 FCR 293, [1994] 2 FLR 381.

## [2.120.7]

*Section 25(2)(a) – Property and resources*

### Property – general factors – definition – net assets and costs

The word property is not defined in the MCA 1973. All property and financial resources of the parties have to be taken into account. The use of the phrase 'family asset' introduced through the case of *Wachtel v Wachtel*[1] has been rejected[2]. The courts will generally have regard to the net value of the assets after deduction of secured liabilities, costs of disposal and tax[3]; in the case of *White*[4] Lord Nicholls said that, although there is no hard and fast rule, the Court of Appeal in that case could not be criticised for the use of net values when considering the assets. The court should differentiate between hard and soft debts[5]. Costs that have been paid may be added back into the parties' resources[6].

1 [1973] Fam 72.
2 See eg *Daubney v Daubney* [1976] Fam 267. For a discussion of this topic, see generally *Rayden and Jackson on Divorce and Family Matters* (17th edn, 1997), vol 1, para 21.34 et seq and the Noter-up thereto.

3 See *O'D v O'D* [1976] Fam 83 ('puts him on the right scale of wealth').
4 [2000] 3 FCR 555 at 572.
5 See *M v B (Ancillary Proceedings: Lump sum)* [1998] 1 FCR 213, [1998] 1 FLR 53, CA.
6 See *Leadbeater v Leadbeater* [1985] FLR 789 per Balcombe J; followed in *A v A (Costs of Appeal)* [1996] 1 FCR 186, [1996] 1 FLR 14 per Singer J; but not followed by Holman J in *F v F (Duxbury Calculation: Rate of Return)* [1996] 1 FLR 833.



## [2.120.8]
### Property – big money

'Big money' cases can properly be defined as those where the parties have assets significantly in excess of those needed to provide for both parties' future requirements, including those of any children of the family[1]. See Connell J in *D v D*[1], a case where the assets barely exceeded £1million, but which he found justified the description 'big money' on the basis that 'the available assets certainly exceed the parties' financial needs for housing and income'[2].

It is in this class of case that the decision in *White* had had its real impact. In other cases, most District Judges would say that their approach has been little modified by recent jurisprudence.

1 [2001] 1 FLR 633.
2 [2001] 1 FLR 633 at 639.

## [2.120.9]
### Property – big money – old approach

Prior to the case of *White v White*[1], there were a number of cases where it was said that a wife's claims in ancillary relief proceedings levelled off at a point where her reasonable requirements were met[2], subject to a possible uplift as a result of her contributions[3]. The case of *White* gave rise to a thorough overhaul of this approach. The effect of that overhaul is summarised at para **[2.120.3]** above.

1 [2000] 3 FCR 555.
2 See eg, *Preston v Preston* [1982] Fam 17, [1982] 1 All ER 41, CA.
3 See eg, *Conran v Conran* [1998] 1 FCR 144, [1997] 2 FLR 615.

## [2.120.10]
### Property – big money – new approach

Following *White*, a number of recent decisions have emerged which have assessed and refined the court's approach to substantial asset cases:

- ***Dharamshi v Dharamshi* [2001] 1 FLR 736**
  The ceiling of reasonable requirements applied for nearly a generation had now been rejected, as had the previous distinction between the wife's work in a family business and her management of home and children. Giving the wife a substantial fraction of the assets not directly related to her reasonable needs was an approach fully vindicated by the Lords in *White*.
- ***N v N (Financial Provision: Sale of Company)* [2001] 2 FLR 69**
  The Lords in *White* did not intend that courts should cripple a family's financial edifice in order to achieve equality. The courts should be creative and sensitive to create an orderly redistribution of wealth – giving time to realise assets if necessary.
- ***S v S (Financial Provision: Departing from Equality)* [2001] 2 FLR 246**
  If an agreement was harder on one party than on the other, then there was good reason to depart from equality.
- ***Cowan v Cowan* [2001] EWCA Civ 679, [2001] 2 FLR 192**
  Fairness was the rule – the yardstick of equality was a cross-check against discrimination – the courts must apply the s 25 criteria. Acquisition of wealth by more than special skill and care was a reason for departure from equality. The traditional role of women was not to be valued at lower than the role of breadwinner.

## [2.120.11]
### Property – big money – millionaire's defence

It had been said that where a husband disclosed assets that were more than sufficient to meet a wife's justifiable claim, more detailed disclosure should not be ordered[1]. However, in order to comply with s 25 of the MCA 1973, the court does need a minimum of information – including an estimate of income and a summary of significant assets, including pension rights[2]. Following *White* the need for such information is all the more acute. It is unclear to what extent the earlier decisions limiting the obligation to provide detailed disclosure will be followed.

1 See *Thyssen-Bornemisza v Thyssen-Bornemisza (No 2)* [1985] FLR 1069, CA; and *Dart v Dart* [1997] 1 FCR 21. This is likely to remain good law in many cases notwithstanding the greater emphasis on equality that emanates from *White v White* [2000] 3 FCR 555, HL.
2 *Van G v Van G* [1995] 2 FCR 250, [1995] 1 FLR 328.

## [2.120.12]
### Property – businesses – valuations

Prior to the case of *White v White*[1] it had been repeatedly held to be inappropriate to attempt to achieve a precise valuation of a business in which one spouse had an interest, if the business is not to be sold[2]. In the pre-*White* cases it was held that the primary focus should generally be on the wife's reasonable requirements and the husband's ability to pay. Now, however, it is likely to be necessary for the judge to form a view about the value of a business in order to judge his intended award by reference to the yardstick of equality. Sale of the husband's business, albeit over time, may now be a real prospect on divorce. For a recent decision in which the correct approach to valuation and division of value in a business was considered, see *N v N (Financial Provision: Sale of Company)*[3].

1 [2000] 3 FCR 555, HL.
2 See eg, *Evans v Evans* [1990] FCR 498; and *Potter v Potter* (1982) 4 FLR 331.
3 [2001] 2 FLR 69.

## [2.120.13]
### Property – businesses – forced collapse

Where justice requires, the court has in the past forced the sale of a business (eg the farming cases of *Woods v Woods*[1] – sale the only way in which wife's justifiable claims could be met; *Moorish v Moorish*[2] – Farm being run unprofitably; and *Webber v Webber*[3] – charge over farm to take effect when husband 65, dies or sells/disposes of farm). Such decisions are now likely to be far more common, see eg *N v N (Financial Provision: Sale of Company)*[4] (a 14 year marriage with three children) per Coleridge J[5]:

Whilst–

> 'the theory behind *White* is one thing, the actual practicalities involved in valuing, dividing up and realising certain species of assets makes the attaining of the *White* objective sometimes either impossible or only achievable at a cost which may not overall be in the family's best interests ...'
>
> ' ... those old taboos against selling the goose that lays the golden egg have largely been laid to rest; some would say not before time. Nowadays the goose may well have to go to market for sale, but if it is necessary to sell her it is essential that her condition be such that her egg-laying abilities are damaged as little as possible in the process.'

The court should not accept on its face value a contention that a business will be forced into collapse[6].

1 (1982) 12 Fam Law 213, CA.
2 [1984] Fam Law 26, CA.
3 (1982) 12 Fam Law 179, CA.
4 [2001] 2 FLR 69.
5 [2001] 2 FLR 69 at 80.
6 See *O'D v O'D* [1976] Fam 83, CA.

**[2.120.14]**
**Property – piercing corporate veil**

The court can only make orders that fall within the ambit of the statutory provisions under which it is operating[1]. It must also frame its orders so as to recognise the legal nature of any relevant business. Even where a spouse conceded that the assets of a company could be treated as his own, the court could only lift the corporate veil and make orders directly or indirectly regarding the company's assets where:

(i) the spouse was owner and controller of the company concerned; and
(ii) there were no adverse third party interests[2].

However, where a company is the alter ego of a party and minority interest can be properly ignored, it has been said that the court can pierce the corporate veil and make orders that disregard the corporate identity[3].

1 See eg *Dinch v Dinch* [1987] 2 FLR 162, HL.
2 *Mubarak v Mubarak* [2001] 1 FLR 673 per Bodey J; revsd sub nom *Murburak v Murburak* [2001] 1 FCR 193, [2001] All ER (D) 2302, CA.
3 See *Nicholas v Nicholas* [1984] FLR 285, CA; and *Green v Green* [1993] 1 FLR 326, FD (but cf *Crittenden v Crittenden* [1991] FCR 70, [1990] 2FLR 361, CA).



**[2.120.15]**
**Property – preservation of company**

In the case of *Poon v Poon*[1] the court made orders to regulate the functioning of a company in which the parties were directors and shareholders, pending the hearing of the ancillary relief applications. Thorpe J held that it was not necessary for the issue to be litigated under company law and that the Family Division could regulate the company under its inherent jurisdiction[2].

1 [1994] 2 FCR 777, [1994] 2 FLR 857.
2 As to which see *Shipman v Shipman* [1991] FCR 628, [1991] 1 FLR 250.

**[2.120.16]**
**Existing property rights**

Section 25(2)(a) is only one of the factors under s 25. Therefore the fact that property may be vested in the sole or joint names of the parties may be a factor but will not generally dominate the position (see *Browne v Pritchard*[1] and *Walsh v Corcoran*[2] – both cases concerning short marriages where the former matrimonial home was in joint names).

The House of Lords has subsequently held that there is no hierarchy amongst the provisions of s 25(2)[3].

The House of Lords in *White v White*[4] emphasises the need to apply the statutory criteria in s 25.

1 [1975] 3 All ER 721, [1975] 1 WLR 1366, CA.
2 (1982) 4 FLR 59, CA.
3 See *Piglowska v Piglowski* [1999] 2 FCR 481, [1999] 2 FLR 763.
4 [2000] 3 FCR 555, HL.

**[2.120.17]**
**Property – liquidity**

In considering the extent of a party's resources the court will look at the reality of the position and will 'penetrate' the balance sheet of a business to establish the underlying reality of a party's financial position[1]. In doing so the court will not act in direct invasion of the rights or discretion of third parties[2]. A liquidity problem may nevertheless be an important reason advanced to justify departure from equality in any given case[3]. For an example of a situation where the problem proved illusory, see eg *Thomas v Thomas*[4] per Waite LJ:

> 'Certain principles emerge from the authorities. One is that the court is not obliged to limit its orders exclusively to resources of capital or income which are shown actually to exist. The availability of unidentified resources may, for example, be inferred from a spouse's expenditure or style of living, or from his inability or unwillingness to allow the complexity of his affairs to be penetrated with the precision necessary to ascertain his actual wealth or the degree of liquidity of his assets. Another is that where a spouse enjoys access to wealth but no absolute entitlement to it (as in the case, for example, of a beneficiary under a discretionary trust or someone who is dependent on the generosity of a relative), the court will not act in direct invasion of the rights of, or usurp the discretion exercisable by, a third party. Nor will it put upon a third party undue pressure to act in a way which will enhance the means of the maintaining spouse. This does not, however, mean that the court acts in total disregard of the potential availability of wealth from sources owned or administered by others. There will be occasions when it becomes permissible for a judge deliberately to frame his orders in a form which affords judicious encouragement to third parties to provide the maintaining spouse with the means to comply with the court's view of the justice of the case. There are bound to be instances where the boundary between improper pressure and judicious encouragement proves to be a fine one, and it will require attention to the particular circumstances of each case to see whether it has been crossed.'

1 See *O'D v O'D* [1976] Fam 83, CA.
2 See eg *Mubarak v Mubarak* [2001] 1 FLR 673.
3 But see the remarks of Coleridge J in *N v N (financial provision: sale of company)* [2001] 2 FLR 69, [2001] Fam Law 347.
4 [1995] 2 FLR 668 at 670, CA.

## [2.120.18]
## Inferring property

Where it is suggested that the court should infer that a party has property or resources greater than those disclosed the court applies the civil standard of proof[1]. For cases where the inference has been drawn see *F v F (Divorce Insolvency: Annulment Order)*[2]; *H v H (Financial Relief: Non-disclosure: Costs)*[3]; *C v C (Financial Provision: Non-disclosure)*[4]; and *T v T (Interception of Documents)*[5].

1 See *Baker v Baker* [1996] 1 FCR 567, [1995] 2 FLR 829, CA.
2 [1994] 2 FCR 689, [1994] 1 FLR 359.
3 [1994] 2 FCR 301, [1994] 2 FLR 94.
4 [1995] 1 FCR 75, [1994] 2 FLR 272.
5 [1995] 2 FCR 745, [1994] 2 FLR 1083.

## [2.120.19]
## Property 'in the foreseeable future' – inheritance prospects

In the case of *Michael v Michael*[1] it was held that the provisions of s 25(2)(a) could in certain circumstances extend to 'a mere expectancy or spes succession is, for example an interest which might be taken under the will of a living person' [at p 395]; however the circumstances where such a potential inheritances will be taken into account will be rare (see the case of *Calder v Calder*[2] where an interest in remainder under a trust was taken into account). In the case of *MT v MT*[3], the husband expected to inherit a large amount of money from his father, who was 83; Bracewell J adjourned the wife's ancillary relief claims since this was the only way in which justice might be afforded to the wife. However where there is a wide range of beneficiaries and a real prospect that the relevant sums may be appointed elsewhere, the court will be unlikely to take the potential inheritance into account[4].

1 [1986] 2 FLR 389, CA.
2 (1975) 6 Fam Law 242, CA.
3 [1991] FCR 649, [1992] 1 FLR 362.
4 See eg *H v H (Financial provision: Capital Allowance)* [1993] 2 FCR 308, [1993] 2 FLR 335, FD.

### [2.120.20]
### Property 'in the foreseeable future' – pensions

There was a succession of cases prior to the advent of ss 25B to 25D of the MCA 1973 in which the court considered whether pension benefits were resources that a party was likely to have in the foreseeable future. However, due to the provisions of s 25B(1) of the MCA 1973 the requirement of foreseeability is removed in relation to pensions.

### [2.120.21]
### Property 'in the foreseeable future' – adjournment

There is a general discretion to adjourn an application[1]. The court will order an adjournment where it is necessary to do so in order to do justice[2]. In the case of *Smith v Smith*[3] the wife sought an adjournment because the company in which the husband was concerned was trading badly at the time of the hearing; the court refused to adjourn the wife's claims and refused to make an order that the husband's shares in the company should stand charged to the wife's benefit[4]. See the recent case of *D v D (financial provision: lump sum order)*[5] – a court which decided to adjourn an application was doing no more than exercising the discretion vested in it, although it should only do so in the rare cases in which justice to both parties could only be done if there was an adjournment.

1 See *Gibson v Archibald* [1989] 1 WLR 123, HL.
2 See *MT v MT (Financial Provision: Lump sum)* [1991] FCR 649, [1992] 1 FLR 362; and *Davies v Davies* [1985] Fam 136, [1986] 1 FLR 152.
3 (1982) 4 FLR 154, CA.
4 See also *Scheeres v Scheeres* [1999] 2 FCR 476, [1999] 1 FLR 241.
5 [2001] 1 FCR 561, [2001] 1 FLR 633 per Connell J.

### [2.120.22]
### Property – trusts

Where a party has an interest under a trust the court is entitled to take that interest into account under s 25(2)(a) of the MCA 1973. Where the interest is under a discretionary trust the court will look at the reality of whether that interest is a resource in that party's hands[1]. Such interests must be disclosed by parties to an application in their statement in Form E.

1 See *Browne v Browne* [1989] 1 FLR 291, CA; *Thomas v Thomas* [1996] 2 FCR 544, [1995] 2 FLR 668, CA; and *H v H [Financial Provision: Capital Allowance)* [1993] 2 FCR 308, [1993] 2 FLR 335, FD.

### [2.120.23]
### Property – personal injury awards

Where a party has received damages as a result of personal injuries, those damages still represent a resource in the hands of the party receiving them. The court should not ignore them[1]. However the purpose of the personal injury award will often limit the extent to which the uninjured spouse will be able to have access to the funds created by the personal injury litigation. In the case of *Wagstaff,* Butler-Sloss LJ said [at p 337]:

> 'The reasons for the availability of the capital in the hands of one spouse, together with the size of the award, are relevant factors in all the circumstances of section 25. But the capital sum awarded is not sacrosanct, nor any part of it secured against the application of the other spouse. There may be instances where the sum awarded was small, and was specifically for pain and suffering, in which it would be unsuitable to order any of it to be paid to the other spouse. In some cases the needs of the disabled spouse may absorb all the available capital, such as the requirement of residential accommodation. In general, the reasons for the availability of the capital by way of damages must temper the extent of, and in some instances may exclude the sharing of, such capital with the other spouse'.

An example where the wife, who had been assaulted by the husband, needed the Criminal injuries Compensation award for herself is *H v H (Financial Provision: Conduct)*[2].

1 See *Daubney v Daubney* [1976] Fam 267, CA; *Wagstaff v Wagstaff* [1992] 1 FCR 305, [1992] 1 FLR 333, CA; and *C v C (Financial Provision)* [1996] 1 FCR 283, [1995] 2 FLR 171, FD.
2 [1994] 2 FLR 801.

## [2.120.24]
### Property – tenancies

A tenancy is property for the purposes of the MCA 1973[1]. Although in that case, it was held that the court should not interfere with the Local Authority's housing policy, the later case of *Jones v Jones*[2] describes the case of *Thompson* as being outmoded; the divorce court in ancillary relief proceedings has to make its decisions about the future occupation of a house by applying the provisions of s 25 of the MCA 1973. An expired assured tenancy would not be property[3].

1 See *Thompson v Thompson* [1976] Fam 25.
2 [1987] Fam 59, [1997] 1 FLR 27, CA.
3 *Newlon Housing Trust v Alsulaimen* [1999] 1 AC 313, [1998] 2 FLR 690, HL.

## [2.120.25]
### Foreign property

Ancillary relief orders take effect against the person of the spouse (in personam) rather than against the property itself (in rem). As such, if the court has jurisdiction in a case it may make orders against foreign properties in which one or both of the spouses has an interest. However, if an order in relation to that property would be unenforceable the court may, in its discretion, refuse to make an order in relation to it[1].

1 See *Hamlin v Hamlin* [1986] Fam 11, CA; and *Razelos v Razelos* [1969] 3 All ER 929.

## [2.120.26]

*Section 25(2)(b) – Financial needs, obligations and responsibilities*

### Needs and minor children

The MCA 1973, s 25(2)(b) requires the court to have regard to 'the financial needs obligations and responsibilities which each of the parties to the marriage has or is likely to have in the foreseeable future'. However, under s 25(1) of the MCA 1973, first consideration is given to the welfare of any child of the family who has not attained the age of 18; that provision will inevitably impact upon the approach to the needs of the family following separation. In the case of *R v R*[1] it was stated that there is a broad principle that a party should order his financial affairs in such a way as will reflect his responsibilities to children of the family. The housing of the children will be an important need for the court to consider; in the case of *Clutton v Clutton*[2] Ewbank J said:

> 'It is, of course, important to retain flexibility to meet the circumstances of individual cases and changes in social conditions. On the other hand, justice and the provisions of the statute, usually indicate that an asset which has been acquired by the joint efforts of the spouses should eventually be shared. Where the only asset is a jointly acquired home of modest value, it is often necessary to give its occupation to the parent with custody of children or to the spouse with the greater need.'

1 [1988] FCR 307, [1988] 1 FLR 89, CA. See generally, *Rayden and Jackson on Divorce and Family Matters* (17th edn, 1997), vol 1, para 21.31 and the Noter-up thereto.
2 [1991] 1 FLR 242 at 248.

### [2.120.27]
### Needs and adult children

In a succession of cases prior to the decision in *White v White*[1], it had been held that provision for adult children fell outside the legitimate ends that might be achieved under s 25[2]. However, in the case of *White*, Lord Nicholls said as follows[3]:

> 'In my view, in a case where resources exceed needs, the correct approach is as follows. The judge has regard to all the facts of the case and to the overall requirements of fairness. When doing so, the judge is entitled to have in mind the wish of a claimant wife that her award should not be confined to living accommodation and a vanishing fund of capital earmarked for living expenses which would leave nothing for her to pass on. The judge will give to that factor whatever weight, be it much or little or none at all, he considers appropriate in the circumstances of the particular case.'

1 [2000] 3 FCR 555.
2 See eg, *Preston v Preston* (1981) 2 FLR 331 at 336.
3 [2000] 3 FCR 555 at 568g–569d.



### [2.120.28]
### Needs and debts

The court in ancillary relief proceedings does not exercise a quasi bankruptcy jurisdiction and it is therefore wrong to prefer the claims of creditors over those of the wife and children[1]. There is no power to order one party to the pay unsecured debts[2]. Debts will be part of the needs of a party but the court should differentiate between hard debts (which have to be repaid on commercial terms) and soft debts (family loans), when approaching such needs[3].

1 See *Mullard v Mullard* (1982) 3 FLR 330, CA.
2 See *Burton v Burton* [1986] 2 FLR 419, CA.
3 See *M v B (Ancillary Proceedings: Lump sum)* [1998] 1 FCR 213, [1998] 1 FLR 53, CA.

### [2.120.29]
### Needs, subsistence level and the maintenance payer's standard of living

Although a husband may owe his primary obligations to his first family, the court will take into account obligations that he has to any new family[1]. A court should take into account the effect on a new family of any proposed order for ancillary relief[2]. Where a new partner has means of her own, those means will be relevant to the determination of what the husband can afford to pay, since the new partner may be able to relieve him of expenditure that he might otherwise have to bear[3]. The court should balance the needs of the first family against the needs of the new family and should not cripple the new family[4]. In *Delaney v Delaney*[5], Ward J said:

> 'In my judgment, the approach of this court in this case must be, first, to have regard to the need of the wife and the children for proper support. Having assessed that need, the court should then consider the ability of the husband to meet it. Whilst this court deprecates any notion that a former husband and extant father may slough off the tight skin of familial responsibility and may slither into and lose himself in the greener grass on the other side, none the less this court has proclaimed and will proclaim that it looks to the realities of the real world in which we live, and that among the realities of life is that there is a life after divorce. The respondent husband is entitled to order his life in such a way as will hold in reasonable balance the responsibilities to his existing family which he carries into his new life, as well as his proper aspirations for that new future …
>
> … the courts will balance the responsibility of the husband to the new family with the responsibility he bears to the old. Extravagance in his new family arrangements will not justify a diminution in his responsibilities to the first family.'

1 See *Stockford v Stockford* (1981) 3 FLR 58, CA.
2 See *Furniss v Furniss* (1981) 3 FLR 46.

3 See *Slater v Slater* (1981) 3 FLR 364, CA.
4 See *Delaney v Delaney* [1991] FCR 161, [1990] 2 FLR 457; and *E v C (Calculation of child maintenance)* [1996] 1 FCR 612, [1996] 1 FLR 472, FD.
5 [1991] FCR 161, [1990] 2 FLR 457 at 461.

## [2.120.30]
## Needs and expenditure

Lists of expenditure are required for the purposes of completing the Form E. However, the court does not adopt a 'budgetary approach' to a party's income needs[1]. Such lists will usually be trimmed by the court[2] and will often be no more than a starting point for the assessment of a party's needs[3].

For a discussion of this topic, see generally *Rayden and Jackson on Divorce and Family Matters* (17th edn, 1997), vol 1, para 21.48 et seq and the Noter-up thereto.

1 See *Cornick v Cornick (No 2)* [1995] 2 FLR 490, [1996] 1 FCR 179, CA.
2 See *B v B (Financial provision)* [1989] FCR 146, [1988] 1 FLR 119, FD.
3 See *F v F (Duxbury Calculation: rate of Return)* [1996] 1 FLR 833, FD.

## [2.120.31]
## Needs and housing

In the case of *Piglowska v Piglowski*[1] it was held that there is no presumption that both parties are entitled to purchased accommodation. However, in many cases an important consideration will be to ensure that both parties are rehoused[2]. Where one party has found secure alternative rented accommodation it may be wrong to force the other party to sell the former matrimonial home where to do so would leave him homeless[3]. It will often be in the interests of the children that the non-custodial parent should have a home in which to have contact with the children[4]. Where the former matrimonial home is a substantial property the court will carry out a balancing exercise in deciding whether it is appropriate for one party to remain in it[5]. However, a sentimental attachment to a property will not of itself justify a party remaining in it[6]. For the impact of *White* upon the consideration of the impact of needs, obligations and responsibilities with particular reference to housing, see now *S v S (financial provision: departing from equality)*[7].

1 [1999] 2 FCR 481, [1999] 2 FLR 763, HL.
2 See *M v B (Ancillary Proceedings: Lump sum)* [1998] 1 FCR 213, [1998] 1 FLR 53, CA; and *Browne v Pritchard* [1975] 1 WLR 1366, CA.
3 See *Brown v Brown* (1982) 3 FLR 161, CA.
4 See *Calderbank v Calderbank* [1976] Fam 93, CA; and *Delaney v Delaney* [1991] FCR 161, [1990] 2 FLR 457.
5 See *R v R (Financial Provision: Reasonable Needs)* [1994] 2 FLR 1044.
6 See *Crewe v Crewe* [1984] Fam Law 213, CA.
7 [2001] 3 FCR 316, [2001] 2 FLR 246.

## [2.120.32]
## Needs and *Mesher/Martin* Orders

A *Mesher* order is one that provides for the continued occupation by a spouse of a property until the death or remarriage of the occupying spouse, the youngest child attaining a certain age or the court making a further order; it is named after the case of *Mesher v Mesher and Hall*[1]. A *Martin* order provides for the continued occupation by a spouse of a property until the death or remarriage of the occupying spouse, or the court making a further order; it is named after the case of *Martin v Martin*[2]. *Mesher* orders can cause particular hardship to the custodial parent when the property is eventually sold, since she may well be left with insufficient money to rehouse herself – in the case of *Harvey v Harvey*[3] the making of a *Mesher* order was described as to 'simply postpone the evil day'[4]. However, where there will be sufficient for both parties to be rehoused, a *Mesher* order may be appropriate[5]; further, a *Mesher* order may be appropriate where there has been a short marriage and the husband has made the main financial contributions[6]. A *Martin* order may be appropriate where there is a real possibility of remarriage (ie as opposed to an outright transfer to the wife)[7]. For a consideration of the continuing importance of orders such as these, notwithstanding the impact of the clean break provisions, see *Clutton v Clutton*[8].

1 [1980] 1 All ER 126n, CA.
2 [1978] Fam 12.
3 [1982] Fam 83, 3 FLR 141, CA.
4 See also *Mortimer v de Mortimer-Griffin* [1986] 2 FLR 315, CA.
5 See *Mitchell v Mitchell* [1984] FLR 387, CA.
6 See *Drinkwater v Drinkwater* [1984] FLR 627, CA.
7 See *Tinsdale v Tinsdale* (1983) 4 FLR 641.
8 [1991] 1 FLR 242, CA per Ewbank J.



## [2.120.33]
### Needs and reasonable requirements

The concept of 'reasonable requirements' as an effective ceiling in big money cases has been removed by the decision of the House of Lords in *White*. Whilst the consideration of financial needs remains of importance, particularly in cases where less money is available, there is no longer a judicially imposed cap upon claimants once those needs have been comfortably met. Authorities prior to *White* where the consideration of 'reasonable requirements' played a central role must therefore now be treated with caution. Nevertheless, there will often in practice be cases where a consideration of the financial effect on a party of a proposed award will be necessary, by reference to the standard of living previously enjoyed in marriage[1].

1 See further the discussion of s 25(2)(c) at para **[2.120.35]** below

## [2.120.34]
### Needs – the *Besterman* cushion

The case of *Re Besterman*[1] was decided under the I(PFD)A 1975. The judge in that case held that the court could award an enhanced lump sum in order to take into account unforeseen contingencies ('the rainy day' payment). Prior to the decision in *White v White*[2] it had been held that, in ancillary relief proceedings an award of a rainy day cushion should not be made unless there was an evidential basis for it[3]. Following *White* the wife in a big money case is unlikely to need to seek to justify her award by reference to this authority.

1 [1984] Ch 458, [1984] FLR 503, CA.
2 [2000] 3 FCR 555.
3 See *O'Neill v O'Neill* [1993] 23 FCR 297, CA; *H v H (Financial Provision: Capital Allowance)* [1993] 2 FCR 308, [1993] 2 FLR 335, FD; and *Dart v Dart* [1997] 1 FCR 21, [1996] 2 FLR 286, CA.

## [2.120.35]

*Section 25(2)(c) to (e) – Living standards, ages, duration and disability*

### Standard of living – s 25(2)(c)

The MCA 1973 requires regard to 'the standard of living enjoyed by the family before the breakdown of the marriage'[1]. Whilst this factor would once have played a crucial role in the determination of so-called 'reasonable requirements' in the bigger money cases, it may now become more a matter of background detail in this class of case. In the majority of situations, however, it will remain as important as any of the other factors specified by the Act, especially as a guide to the level of resources actually available to the family during the time prior to the parties' separation. Indeed, the standard of living enjoyed prior to or after breakdown may of itself of course serve as evidence to assist the court in formulating a fuller view of the parties true resources[2].

Conversely, without 'ball-park' figures as to income and asset value, it may be difficult for the court to determine the standard of living which a particular party is able to enjoy[3].

Strict reliance on actual standards of living as opposed to what was actually available or affordable may lead to injustice, however:

- ***H v H (Clean break: Non-disclosure: Costs)*** – 'I must not penalise the wife, however, by providing less for her simply because she was frugal during the marriage. To do so would be to provide more for the extravagant wife than for the careful, thrifty wife'[4].

Furthermore, it may be reasonable to expect a future increase in standards of living if sacrifices to that end have been made during the marriage:

- ***Preston v Preston*** – 'it would be anomalous if (the standard of living) were taken as an indication for reducing the lump sum for a wife who has accepted a lower standard of living in the hope that she will benefit later'[5].

Inevitably it will often be the case that standards of living will drop when two households have to be created from the finances which previously supported only one – 'in the majority of cases the resources are not sufficient to enable both parties to be housed in accommodation of the standard to which they had previously been accustomed'[6].

Generally, the court will strive (especially where there are children involved) to create equivalent standards of living for both parties – 'in any case where there is, by stretch and a degree of risk- taking, the possibility of a division to enable both to rehouse themselves, that is an exceptionally important consideration and one which will almost invariably have a decisive impact on outcome'[7].

However, the reduction in living standards need not be apportioned equally, see for example *Blezard v. Blezard*[8], where Lawton LJ declined to reduce a wife and children's standard of living to the same level as that of the deserting husband.

1 See the MCA 1973, s 25(2)(c).
2 See eg *Hardy v Hardy* (1981) 2 FLR 321; *P v P* [1989] 2 FLR 241; and *Woodley v Woodley (No 2)* [1993] 2 FLR 477.
3 See *Van G v Van G (Financial Provision: Millionaire's Defence)* [1995] 2 FCR 250, [1995] 1 FLR 328.
4 [1994] 2 FLR 309 at 314 per R Hayward-Smith QC. See also *Boylan v Boylan* [1988] 1 FLR 282.
5 [1981] 2 FLR 331 at 336 per Ormrod LJ. See also *S v S* (1980) 10 Fam Law 240; and *A v A* [1998] 2 FLR 180.
6 *R v R (Financial Provision: Reasonable Needs)* [1994] 2 FLR 1044 per Sir Stephen Brown P.
7 *M v B (Ancillary Proceedings: Lump Sum)* [1998] 1 FLR 53 per Thorpe LJ.
8 (1978) 1 FLR 253.

## [2.120.36]
## Ages of the parties – s 25(2)(d)

The MCA 1973 requires regard to 'the age of each party to the marriage'[1]. Inevitably, age will have an important effect on a number of other factors within the s 25 exercise, such as financial needs or earning capacity. Pension considerations will be of lesser significance in cases where the parties are under 40.

> 'The younger the wife may be and the shorter the marriage (particularly if there are no children), the more difficult it will be for her to persuade the court that she is unable to earn her own living and to order her husband to make any substantial continuing provision for her'[2].

For the effect on *Duxbury* calculations when the wife is young, see Thorpe J in *F v F (Ancillary Relief: Substantial Assets)*[3]:

> 'The next statutory consideration is the age of the parties and the duration of the marriage. There is of course a gap of some 14 years in age between the husband and the wife. What is very significant in my judgment is that this is a marriage of only seven years duration and as at today the applicant wife is only 36. The simplistic application of a *Duxbury* calculation would manifestly not be appropriate in a case with these characteristics'[4].

For the older wife, see *White v White*[5] and para **[2.120.37]** below.

In the early 1980s, the courts made substantially smaller awards to older parties, on the basis of their reduced life expectancy[6].

In the majority of recent cases where life expectancy has been reduced, whether by age or illness, the courts have instead focused on contribution (as to which see below) in awarding a share which exceeded apparent need after a long marriage. The decisions following *White* have confirmed this approach as the correct one.

1 See the MCA 1973, s 25(2)(d) at para **[2.120]** above.
2 *Soni v Soni* [1984] FLR 294 at 297 per Sheldon J.
3 [1996] 2 FCR 397, [1995] 2 FLR 45.
4 [1995] 2 FLR 45 at 66C.
5 [2000] 3 FCR 555.
6 See eg *Page v Page* (1981) 2 FLR 198; and *Preston v Preston* [1982] Fam 17, (1981) 2 FLR 331.



## [2.120.37]
## Duration of the marriage

The MCA 1973 requires regard to 'the duration of the marriage'[1].

Inevitably, duration will often play a part in cases where age and contribution are also an issue. Whilst, for example, the fact of a child may go far to lessen the significance of a short marriage, provision may be far more limited where the parties have only been together for a short time.

The leading authority, other than in cases where both parties are very young remains the case of *S v S*[2]. The following passage from the judgment of Ormrod LJ has particular resonance:

> 'I think it is of importance, with these short marriages, particularly where the people concerned are not young, to look very closely to see what the effect of the marriage has been, mainly on the wife but of course also on the husband ... While there is no question of putting her back into the position I which she was before the marriage, or performing any hypothetical task of that kind, these are all factors which are to be born in mind in making an order which is just in all the circumstances of the case, which is the primary requirement of the 1973 Act ... So the court has to do the best it can to do broad justice between these two parties, bearing all the relevant circumstances in mind and trying not to take into account a lot of irrelevant matters which irritated the parties during the process of the hearings, the trial and so on, and try to look at the whole thing in a detached kind of way'[3].

See also, as an example of a pre-1984 short marriage case where ongoing maintenance was considered inappropriate, *Robertson v Robertson*[4].

> ' ... with a short marriage between mature people of this kind, the wife not having given up any job that she previously had and therefore not having lost her earnings potential simply because of the marriage, it would be inappropriate to make an order in her favour for periodical payments for the rest of her life'[5].

In *H v H (Financial Provision: Short Marriage)*[6], Balcombe J disregarded a six year period of cohabitation prior to a seven week marriage as 'lacking in any semblance of permanence'. He went on to say:

> 'In my judgment, where one has, as here, a very short marriage between two young persons, neither of whom have been adversely affected financially by the consequences of the marriage and each of whom is fully capable of earning his or her own living, the approach which the court should normally adopt is to allow for a short period of periodical payments to allow the party who is in the weaker financial position, (usually, as here, the wife) to adjust herself to the situation, and thereafter to achieve the wholly desirable result of a clean break, if necessary facilitated by a small lump sum payment'[7].

For examples of pre-marital cohabitation being taken into account as contribution to a short marriage, see *Foley v Foley*[8], and *Fournier v Fournier*[9]. See also para **[2.120.44]** below.

As to the effect of a child when considering the impact of a short marriage, see *C v C (Financial Relief: Short Marriage)*:

> '... although the marriage was indeed very short, it has had profound and continuing consequences for the earning capacity of the wife, certainly in the short to medium term, by virtue of her still demanding commitment to J, and of the impact on her health of the break up of the marriage ...'[10].

However, from the same passage:

> 'Even though it may be inappropriate in a short marriage case to limit support for the wife to a relatively short period for financial adjustment, the short duration of the marriage may nevertheless still be very relevant to the quantum of periodical payments which the court orders in favour of the wife on a continuing basis'[11].

For a case where the shortness of the marriage was insufficient to justify a clean break due to the wife's subsequent pregnancy by another, see *Fisher v Fisher*[12].

For a discussion of this topic, see generally *Rayden and Jackson on Divorce and Family Matters* (17th edn, 1997), vol 1, paras 21.55 to 21.56 and the Noter-up thereto.

1 See the MCA 1973, s 25(2)(d).
2 [1977] Fam 127, (1976) FLR Rep 640.
3 (1976) FLR Rep 640 at 645B.
4 (1982) 4 FLR 387.
5 (1982) 4 FLR 387 at 392F per Balcombe J.
6 (1981) 2 FLR 392.
7 (1981) 2 FLR 392 at 399G. See also *Attar v Attar (No 2)* [1985] FLR 653.
8 [1981] Fam 160, 2 FLR 215.
9 [1999] 2 FCR 20, 2 FLR 990.
10 [1997] 2 FLR 26 at 33D per Ward LJ.
11 [1997] 2 FLR 26 at 33E per Ward LJ
12 [1989] FCR 309, [1989] 1 FLR 423.

## [2.120.38]
## Physical or mental disability – s 25(2)(e)

The MCA 1973 requires regard to 'any physical or mental disability of either of the parties to the marriage'[1].

Plainly, any such disability will usually have a significant bearing upon other factors, such as a party's needs, requirements or earning capacity.

Many of the cases in this area have involved the treatment by the courts of personal injury awards received by one or other party, and the extent to which such awards should be taken into account in the discretionary exercise.

Where the injury giving rise to the award has actually been caused by the other party, this is very likely to be conduct that it would be inequitable for the court to disregard[2]. See para **[2.120.46]** et seq below.

Otherwise, the general principle is that such awards should be taken into account as a resource of the injured party, albeit to be set against their increased needs. Account of the specific purposes for which the award was made should be taken[3].

> 'The reasons for the availability of the capital in the hands of one spouse, together with the size of the award, are relevant factors in all the circumstances of section 25. But the capital sum awarded is not sacrosanct, nor any part of it secured against the application of the other spouse'[4].

Inevitably, each case in this category will depend upon its own facts, particularly in the case of structured damages awards[5].

Similarly, every case of chronic disability must be taken on its merits, with special allowance where appropriate being given to the needs of the disabled party. See, for example *B v B (Financial Provision)* (multiple sclerosis):

> 'The wife's needs require special consideration in this case owing to her medical condition, which means increasing disability and increasingly heavy financial expenditure for domestic assistance, and later nursing care and other expenses. Although she has a relatively large income ... she needs to preserve the greater part of her capital resources'[6].

Where the disability is (to some extent) self induced, the courts have tended to be less sympathetic – eg in the case of alcoholism. See *Seaton v Seaton*[7], and *K v K (Ancillary Relief)*[8], although in the latter case, the husband's housing needs did play a important role.

For other examples of cases where illness and disability have played an crucial part in argument over capital provision see *Chadwick v Chadwick*[9], *Sakkas v Sakkas*[10], and *Ashley v Blackman*[11].

Plainly, ongoing disability will often also be an important factor in quantifying (or discounting) earning capacity[12].

See generally, *Rayden and Jackson on Divorce and Family Matters* (17th edn, 1997), vol 1, para 21.57 and the Noter-up thereto.

1 See the MCA 1973, s 25(2)(e).
2 Cf *Jones (MA) v Jones (W)* [1976] Fam 8; and *H v H (Financial Provision: Conduct)* [1994] 2 FCR 1031, [1994] 2 FLR 801.
3 See eg *Daubney v Daubney* [1976] Fam 267; *Wagstaffe v Wagstaffe* [1992] 1 FCR 305, [1992] 1 FLR 333; *A v A (Financial Provision: Conduct)* [1995] 2 FCR 137, [1995] 1 FLR 345 (another husband assailant); and *C v C (Financial Provision: Personal Damages)* [1996] 1 FCR 283, [1995] 2 FLR 171.
4 *Wagstaffe v Wagstaffe* [1992] 1 FLR 333 at 337 per Butler-Sloss LJ.
5 *C v C (Financial Relief: Short Marriage)* [1997] 3 FCR 360, [1997] 2 FLR 26, CA.
6 (1982) 3 FLR 298 at 302 per Ormrod LJ.
7 [1986] 2 FLR 398.
8 [1990] FCR 372, [1990] 2 FLR 225.
9 [1985] FLR 606.
10 [1987] Fam Law 414.
11 [1988] Fam 85[1988] 2 FLR 278.
12 See *C v C (Financial Provision: Non-disclosure)* [1995] 1 FCR 75, [1994] 2 FLR 272; and *S v S (Financial Provision: Post-Divorce Cohabitation)* [1994] 2 FCR 1225, [1994] 2 FLR 228.

## [2.120.39]

*Section 25(2)(f) – Contributions*

### Contributions – general

The MCA 1973 requires regard to 'the contributions which each of the parties has made or is likely in the foreseeable future to make to the welfare of the family, including any contribution by looking after the home or caring for the family'[1].

> 'The reference in the subsection is to contributions "to the welfare of the family, including any contribution by looking after the home or caring for the family"; and it is well known that parliament favoured those words because it took the view that wives who had not made direct, financial contributions had been unfairly prejudiced under the previous law'[2].

There is no distinction between:

> 'those cases in which the wife makes an actual financial contribution to the assets of the family and those in which her contribution is indirect inasmuch as she supplies the infrastructure and support in the context of which the husband is able to work hard, prosper and accumulate his wealth'[3].

The House of Lords in *White* were clear on this point. Per Lord Nicholls[4]:

> ' … there is one principle of universal application which can be stated with confidence. In seeking to achieve a fair outcome, there is no place for discrimination between husband and wife and their respective roles. Typically, a husband and wife share the activities of earning money, running their home and caring for their children. Traditionally, the husband earned the money, and the wife looked after the home and the children. This traditional division of labour is no longer the order of the day. Frequently both parents work. Sometimes it is the wife who is the money-earner, and the husband runs the home and cares for the children during the day. But whatever the division of labour chosen by the husband and wife, or forced upon them by

> circumstances, fairness requires that this should not prejudice or advantage either party when considering para (f), relating to the parties' contributions. This is implicit in the very language of para (f): " ... the contribution which *each* has made or is likely ... to make to the *welfare of the family*, including any contribution by looking after the home or caring for the family". [See s 25(2)(f). Emphasis added.] If, in their different spheres, each contributed equally to the family, then in principle it matters not which of them earned the money and built up the assets. There should be no bias in favour of the money-earner and against the home-maker and the child-carer'.

Inevitably, advocates have long sought to use s 25(2)(f) in any number of ingenious ways to support their arguments in the larger ancillary relief claims. These had begun to become especially tortuous just prior to the decision in *White*[5]. It does now seem, following *White*, that contribution, balanced in this way, will still be one of the major features in the 'big money' cases, as advocates seek reasons to depart from or aspire to equality. A detailed examination of who put in what, and when, is likely to be urged on the court. It has already been successfully suggested that a 'stellar contribution' by an entrepreneurial husband may serve to depress a wife's award, notwithstanding her uncriticised efforts as a homemaker[6].

For the approach of the Court of Appeal post-*White* to the question of contribution generally, see now *Dharamshi v Dharamshi*[7] – the wife's contribution to the home and the children were just as valid as any active or productive work done by her in the business – the clear distinction previously made had been rejected; and *Cowan v Cowan*[8] where all three judges declined to generalise about the application of *White* to particular categories of big money case.

Specific examples of classes of contribution which have been considered are dealt with below.

1 See the MCA 1973, s 25(2)(f) at para **[2.120]** above.
2 See *Conran v Conran* [1997] 2 FLR 615 at 624 per Wilson J.
3 See *Vicary v Vicary* [1992] 2 FLR 271 at 289 per Purchas LJ.
4 [2000] 3 FCR 555 at 562–563.
5 [2001] 3 FCR 555; see also *Dart v Dart* [1997] 1 FCR 21; and *Conran v Conran* [1997] 2 FLR 615.
6 See *Cowan v Cowan* [2001] EWCA Civ 679, [2001] 2 FCR 331, [2001] 2 FLR 192.
7 [2001] 1 FCR 492, [2001] 1 FLR 736, CA.
8 [2001] EWCA Civ 679, [2001] 2 FCR 331, [2001] 2 FLR 192.

### [2.120.40]
### Contributions – direct

It might be thought that henceforth all contributions will be weighed equally by the courts. Per Lord Nicholls in *White v White*[1]:

> 'Today there is greater awareness of the value of non-financial contributions to the welfare of the family. There is greater awareness of the extent to which one spouse's business success, achieved by much sustained hard work over many years, may have been made possible or enhanced by the family contribution of the other spouse, a contribution which also required much sustained hard work over many years. There is increased recognition that, by being at home and having and looking after young children, a wife may lose for ever the opportunity to acquire and develop her own money-earning qualifications and skills'.

Notwithstanding the undoubted shift in emphasis wrought by the decision in *White*, there would nevertheless still appear to be value in the distinction between direct contribution to the family's financial position, as when for example an asset arrives in the family pot by way of gift to one party or the other, or by way of exceptional effort, and indirect, by provision of (perhaps) two decades of child care. The difference may be that now both parties are striving to demonstrate direct contribution over and above what might be expected during marital partnership, rather than merely the wife, as was formerly the case[2].

Indeed, in *White* itself the Court of Appeal justified the wife's reduction from a half-share to about 40% of the total assets by reference to financial help given by the husband's father at the outset of a 40-year marriage. Whilst the House of Lords doubted whether the contribution was sufficient to justify such a reduction, they appeared to accept that such a class of contribution was capable of justifying departure from equality. Similarly, in *Cowan v Cowan*[3], that the husband's 'stellar contribution' argument prevailed can only be ascribed to its presumed effect of direct enhancement of the family wealth at a greater rate than the indirect continuing contributions of the wife.

1 [2000] 3 FCR 555 at 563. See also *Dharamshi v Dharamshi* [2001] 1 FCR 492, [2001] 1 FLR 736, CA.
2 See *P v P (Financial Provision: Lump Sum)* [1978] 3 All ER 70, [1978] 1 WLR 483; and *Gojkovic v Gojkovic* [1992] Fam 40, [1990] 2 All ER 84, CA.
3 [2001] EWCA Civ 679, [2001] 2 FCR 331, [2001] 2 FLR 192.



## [2.120.41]
## Contributions – entitlement

Formerly, there were extreme cases where the courts would find that contribution over a lengthy marriage might entitle a wife to a greater share than her perceived need[1]. Generally, though, the courts were reluctant to find an entitlement on the part of a wife which entirely transcended the concept of 'requirements'[2]. Now, following the judgments in *White v White*[3], the courts may be more willing to start from a premise of entitlement to a substantial, if not an equal, share, where contributions on both sides have been full, before applying the various other factors in s 25(2).

For an example of a case where entitlement earned by contribution during a long marriage was subsequently outweighed by the impact of subsequent inheritance (as to which see below)[4].

1 See *Smith v Smith (Smith and Others Intervening)* [1991] FCR 791; and *Barber v Barber* [1993] 1 FCR 65.
2 As in *M v M (Property Adjustment: Impaired Life Expectancy)* [1994] 2 FCR 174, where the wife's entitled share was charged back to the husband in the light of her reduced life expectancy.
3 [2000] 3 FCR 555, HL.
4 See *Schuller v Schuller* [1990] FCR 626.

## [2.120.42]
## Contributions – inheritance, gift, pre-marital ownership

Plainly, where one party has received a significant inheritance, or alternatively an inter vivos family gift, this must be treated a relevant contribution by them to the assets of the family. Whilst it will not always serve to enhance their entitlement overall (see eg *Schuller* above) it will usually be an important factor for the court to consider. Just how important may depend upon the value of the available resources in the case, of course. Little weight was placed upon it in *Schuller v Schuller*[1], at least at first instance, because the husband's needs required that he retained the lion's share of the assets built up prior to the wife's inheritance. Much was said on this issue in the House of Lords in *White v White*[2]. It was pointed out that there exists in the codes of Scotland and New Zealand a distinction between inherited or pre-owned property and 'matrimonial property'[3]. However, per Lord Nicholls, when considering the correct approach to the disposal of such property:

> 'Plainly, when present, this factor is one of the circumstances of the case. It represents a contribution made to the welfare of the family by one of the parties to the marriage. The judge should take it into account. He should decide how important it is in the particular case. The nature and value of the property, and the time when and circumstances in which the property was acquired, are among the relevant matters to be considered. However, in the ordinary course, this factor can be expected to carry little weight, if any, in a case where the claimant's financial needs cannot be met without recourse to this property'[4].

Lord Cooke[5] quoted from the judgment of Lord Simon of Glaisdale in *Haldane v Haldane*[6], a New Zealand case heard in the Privy Council under now repealed legislation:

> 'Initially a gift or bequest to one spouse only is likely to fall outside the Act, because the other spouse will have made no contribution to it. But as time goes on, and depending on the nature of the property in question, the other spouse may well have made a direct or indirect contribution to its retention.'

He accepted that financial help given by the husband's father in the early stages of the marriage was a plausible reason for departing from equality, but also found that its significance diminished over the long marriage.

Inherited wealth has long been accepted to be squarely within the resources available to the court[7] and its treatment in the majority of cases is unlikely to show much change following the recent decisions. Where there are substantial assets, however, as a result solely of family gift or inheritance, that will be taken as a very significant contribution likely to move the courts firmly away from any notion of equal division. Earlier decisions, where the inheritance was on the wife's side and was taken significantly to enhance her contribution[8], are likely to be joined in the law reports by frequent similar pleas from husbands.

1 [1990] FCR 626.
2 [2000] 3 FCR 555.
3 [2000] 3 FCR 555 at 568.
4 See n 3 above.
5 [2000] 3 FCR 555 at 574.
6 [1977] AC 673 at 697.
7 See *Schuller v Schuller* [1990] FCR 626.
8 See *B v B* (1982) 3 FLR 298; and *H v H (Financial Provision: Capital Allowance)* [1993] 2 FCR 308.

## [2.120.43]
## Contributions – indirect

Usually to the home or to the bringing up of children, 'indirect' contribution is made expressly a principal focus by the wording of s 25(2)(f).

Whilst the distinction between the treatment of direct and indirect contributions should have been eroded significantly following the decision of the House of Lords in *White v White*[1], distinctions are still likely to be made in a number of ways (see para **[2.120.40]** above). Nevertheless, it is clear from *Dharamshi v Dharamshi*[2] that the guiding principle for the courts in this area will be that a wife's contribution to home and children is just as valuable as work done by her in a family business.

It remains to be seen how this principle will be applied to the wide variety of combination roles undertaken by women in modern society. Each case may be separately considered, but in other than short marriage cases, husbands seeking the lion's share will most likely have to look to their own circumstances to enhance their claim as against a fully contributing wife.

1 [2000] 3 FCR 555.
2 [2001] 1 FLR 736.

## [2.120.44]
## Contributions – short marriages

- ***Attar v Attar (No 2)***[1] – 'The question of contribution is irrelevant because there was no cohabitation which effectively required any contribution'. This in a marriage which effectively lasted only six months.

However, where a marriage has been short, contributions may often be of significance, as if for example there has bee significant pre-marital cohabitation, or where one party has provided all or much of the capital for the purchase of the matrimonial home. For example:

- ***Foley v Foley***[2] – 'in deciding these difficult financial problems there may be cases where the inability of the parties to sanctify and legitimize their relationship calls for a measure of sympathy which will enable the court to take what has happened during the period of cohabitation into account as a weighty factor'.
- ***B v B (Real Property: Assessment of Interests)***[3] – 'In so brief a marriage as this one it would be palpably unjust to resort either to a one half or even one third apportionment of the husband's total assets, or indeed any apportionment at all … An award should reflect the contribution made by the wife … and the reasonable requirements of the wife in her future life'.

1 [1985] FLR 653 per Booth J.
2 (1981) 2 FLR 215 at 219 per Eveleigh LJ. See also *Kokosinski* (1979) 1 FLR 205 (cohabitation as 'positive conduct'); and *Fournier v Fournier* [1999] 2 FCR 20, [1998] 2 FLR 990, CA.
3 [1988] 2 FLR 490 at 496 per Anthony Lincoln J.

## [2.120.45]
### Contributions – negative

In *E v E (Financial Provision)*[1], Ewbank J, rather than considering conduct as a separate item, dealt with it as an aspect of contribution and went on to find that the wife's contribution to the welfare of the family was both negative and minimal. Attempts to treat conduct as negative contribution since have been less successful[2].

Recently, Wilson J in *W v W*[3] has found the phrase 'negative contribution' an 'unhelpful oxymoron' to employ when considering each party's contributions under s 25(2)(f). He said that where a party had the material to allege that the other had made a nil-contribution to the welfare of the family, or that they had behaved in a way which would be inequitable to disregard, the allegation should be put in those terms.



1 [1990] 2 FLR 233.
2 See *A v A (Financial Provision)* [1998] 2 FLR 180 per Singer J.
3 [2001] Fam Law 656.

## [2.120.46]

*Section 25(2)(g) – Conduct*

### Conduct – general

The MCA 1973 requires regard to 'the conduct of each of the parties, if that conduct is such that it would in the opinion of the court be inequitable to disregard it'[1].

The court is entitled to take account of conduct whether it occurred during the time that the parties were married[2] or after it[3].

To have an impact upon a financial application the court will usually consider whether the conduct complained of has some impact on the parties' respective finances. Allegations of conduct may be raised as a positive factor to increase a claim[4] or (more usually) as a negative factor to reduce a claim.

Any case involving substantial allegations of conduct ought to be heard in the High Court see *Practice Direction (Family Division) (Family Proceedings: Distribution and Transfer)*[5]. The practice has developed in many registries that most cases involving contested issues of conduct will still be heard by the district judge.

The Form E makes provision for allegations of conduct to be raised where they are relevant. At a First Appointment the district judge will determine to what extent such issues are to be litigated and what evidence should be adduced – with the objective of defining the issues and saving costs.

1 See the MCA 1973, s 25(2)(g) at para **[2.120]** above.
2 See *Kokosinski v Kokosinski* [1980] Fam 72, [1980] 1 All ER 1106.
3 See *Kyte v Kyte* [1988] Fam 145, [1987] 3 All ER 1041; and *J(HD) v J(AM)* [1980] 1 All ER 156, [1980] 1 WLR 124.
4 See *Jones v Jones* [1976] Fam 8, [1975] 2 All ER 12, CA.
5 [1992] 3 All ER 151, [1992] 1 WLR 586.

## [2.120.47]
### Conduct – reckless financial behaviour

This head will always depend on a careful consideration of the extent to which a party should be held responsible for acts which may have lead to an overall reduction in the value of the family's assets.

Where a husband charges the matrimonial home without the wife's knowledge for his own purposes, this is very likely to be taken into account[1]. Addictions to alcohol[2] and gambling[3] which have lead to a significant deterioration in the family's financial situation have been penalised. So too has the management of an inherited farming business in an 'entirely wasteful way'[4], or failing to sell a failing farm after agreement with the wife that it should lead the husband to incur significant losses[5].

Conversely, where the court found that the husband's losses were as a result of ordinary business dealings[6], or by error of judgment leading to prison spell in Russia[7], the conduct was not taken into account. Neither was a wife criticised in a case with significant assets for selling property at an undervalue to her daughters, effectively advancing money to them[8].

1 See *Martin v Martin* [1976] Fam 335, [1976] 3 All ER 625, CA; and *Le Foe v Le Foe and Woolwich plc* [2002] 1 FCR 107, [2001] 2 FLR 970.
2 See *K v K (Conduct)* [1990] 2 FLR 225.
3 See *L v L (Financial Provision: Lump Sum)* [1994] 1 FCR 134, [1993] Fam Law 471.
4 See *Moorish v Moorish* [1984] Fam Law 26, CA.
5 See *Beach v Beach* [1995] 2 FCR 526, [1995] 2 FLR 160.
6 See *Dennis v Dennis* (1975) 6 Fam Law 54, CA; and *Daubney v Daubney* [1976] Fam 267, [1976] 2 All ER 453, CA.
7 See *Singer v Sharegin* [1984] FLR 114, CA.
8 See *Primavera v Primavera* [1992] 1 FCR 78, [1992] 1 FLR 16, CA.

## [2.120.48]
## Conduct – adultery, bigamy and deception

Simple adultery is rarely going to be conduct that the court will find it in equitable to disregard[1] especially if both have entered into adulterous relationships[2]. In *A v A (Financial Provision)*[3], Singer J confirmed that a wife's brief sexual relationship with another man did not detract from her contribution as mother, companion and homemaker. However, there are older cases in which certain aggravating circumstances have been found to render similar conduct relevant[4]. Whilst cohabitation with another is unlikely to be conduct without more, there have been circumstances where it has become relevant as conduct[5].

Culpable bigamy may be a bar in itself to any relief[6], but there is no rule to that effect. It is legitimate for the court to have regard to the nature of the crime and all the surrounding circumstances. In *Rampal v Rampal (No 2)*[7], it was held that while the gravity of the husband's offence was not such as to deny him his statutory rights on public policy grounds, his bigamy was conduct to be taken into account in the broad discretionary exercise.

Gross deception (for example about sexual identity) may also be sufficient to debar a claim[8]. At the other end of the spectrum, if not the scale, a failure to engage in the marriage and to live with the other party at all has been held to be conduct under the former 'gross and obvious' test[9]. Assisting the husband to attempt suicide whilst carrying on an affair, with the intention of gaining from his estate, has also been held to be conduct[10].

1 See *Harnet v Harnet* [1974] 1 All ER 764, [1974] 1 WLR 219, CA; and *W v W (Financial Provision: Lump Sum)* [1976] Fam 107, [1975] 3 All ER 970.
2 See *Campbell v Campbell* [1976] Fam 347, [1977] 1 All ER 1.
3 [1998] 2 FLR 180.
4 See *Cuzner v Underdown* [1974] 1 WLR 641; *Dixon v Dixon* (1974) 5 Fam Law 58; and *Backhouse v Backhouse* [1978] 1 All ER 1158, [1978] 1 WLR 243.
5 See *MH v MH* (1981) 3 FLR 429; *Suter v Suter and Jones* [1987] Fam 111, [1987] 2 All ER 336, CA; and *Atkinson v Atkinson* [1988] Fam 93, [1987] 3 All ER 849.
6 See *Whiston v Whiston* [1995] Fam 198, [1998] 1 All ER 423, CA.
7 [2001] EWCA Civ 989, [2002] Fam 85.
8 See *S-T (formerly J) v J (Transsexual: Void Marriage)* [1998] Fam 103.
9 See *West v West* [1978] Fam 1, [1977] 2 All ER 705, CA.
10 See *Kyte v Kyte* [1988] Fam 145, [1987] 3 All ER 1041, CA.

## [2.120.49]
## Conduct – violence

Serious sexual assaults upon the wife[1] or family[2] will usually be relevant conduct. Similarly, serious violent attacks will also be so considered[3].

Inciting others to murder the husband[4], or inflicting deep psychological damage as a result of a superficial wounding[5] are by no means too remote to be relevant. So too the killing of the children[6], or their kidnapping and permanent removal to Saudi Arabia[7].

Merely being callous and unkind will not however be sufficient[8].

1 See *H v H (Financial Provision: Conduct)* [1994] 2 FCR 1031, [1994] 2 FLR 801.
2 See *S v S* (1982) 12 Fam Law 183.
3 See *Jones v Jones* [1976] Fam 8, CA; *Armstrong v Armstrong* (1974) 4 Fam Law 156; *Hall v Hall* [1984] FLR 631, [1975] 2 All ER 12; and *Bateman v Bateman* [1979] Fam 25.
4 See *Evans v Evans* [1989] FCR 133, [1989] 1 FLR 351, CA.
5 See *M v M financial provision: party incurring excessive costs)* [1995] 3 FCR 321.
6 See *M v M (Financial Provision: Conduct)* (1981) 3 FLR 83.
7 See *W v H (No 2)* [2002] forthcoming.
8 See *Griffiths v Griffiths* [1974] 1 All ER 932, [1974] 1 WLR 1350, CA.



## [2.120.50]
## Conduct – litigation misconduct

This will often be visited in costs, as opposed to in the quantum of the award itself[1]. However, there are other instances where the misconduct has been sufficiently serious to affect the award itself – relating to non-disclosure[2], the incurring of costs in another action based upon a false assertion (of marriage)[3], or in the instant proceedings by issuing a series of extreme applications[4].

Similarly, inappropriate dealing with the available assets during the proceedings with a view to reducing the other party's award will often too justify a reduction in the eventual award, whether by positive action[5] or negative inaction[6].

Ultimately, the drawing of adverse inferences against a party guilty of litigation misconduct[7] may prove to be as effective a weapon in many cases as an attempt to allege conduct that it would be inequitable to disregard, although the two are by no means mutually exclusive.

1 See *T v T (Interception of Documents)* [1994] 2 FLR 1083; *P v P (Financial Relief: Non-disclosure)* [1994] 2 FLR 381; and *H v H (Clean Break: Non-disclosure: Costs)* [1994] 2 FLR 309.
2 See *Robinson v Robinson (No 2)* [1986] 1 FLR 37; and *B v B (Real Property: Assessment of Interests)* [1988] 2 FLR 490.
3 See *A v A (A Minor: Financial Provision)* [1994] 1 FLR 657.
4 See *M v M (Financial Provision: Party Incurring Excessive Costs)* [1995] 3 FCR 321.
5 See *H v H (Financial Relief: Conduct)* [1998] 1 FLR 971.
6 See *Hillard v Hillard* (1982) 12 Fam Law 176.
7 As in *C v C (Financial Provision: Non-disclosure)* [1994] 2 FLR 272.

## [2.120.51]

### *Section 25(2)(h) – Lost Benefits*

### Value of any benefit (eg pension) which a party will lose the chance of acquiring

The MCA 1973 requires regard, in the case of proceedings for divorce or nullity of marriage, to 'the value to each of the parties to the marriage of any benefit (for example, a pension) which, by reason of the dissolution or annulment of the marriage, that party will lose the chance of acquiring'[1].

This is conventionally taken as referring to loss of widow's pension rights and any other rights under pension schemes. However, the MCA 1973 does not limit the scope of this provision; it could thus be taken to include loss of an expectation of an inheritance or the loss of rights to share options.

1 See the MCA 1973, s 25(2)(h) at para **[2.120]** above.

## [2.120.52]
### Loss of widow's pension

This consideration does not apply in cases of judicial separation. At law the marriage still subsists and so therefore do the widow's pension rights.

In relation to petitions presented on or after 1 July 1996 the court is expressly required to have regard to any benefits under a pension scheme which, by reason of the dissolution or annulment a party will lose the chance of acquiring.

In *T v T (Financial Relief: Pensions)*[1] Singer J considered the powers of the court to deal with pension rights. He held that in considering this section the court was not under a duty to compensate the applicant spouse for loss of widow's pension rights. It was a factor to be considered; that was all. This view was endorsed by Cazalet J in *Burrow v Burrow*[2]. It will now be an unusual case where loss of widow's pension is compensated where that spouse will have an ongoing claim to periodical payments.

The court can take into account loss of widow's pension rights by either an enhanced lump sum payment (usually on a clean break) or by allowing an ongoing claim to periodical payments. When the pension is in payment the Applicant spouse would simply apply to vary that periodical payments order. Since the advent of attachment orders (formerly referred to as earmarking orders) and the availability of pension sharing orders, the court will usually be able to deal with pensions in a way that will avoid the impact on the wife of any loss of widow's pension.

1 [1998] 2 FCR 364, [1998] 1 FLR 1072, FD.
2 [1999] 2 FCR 549, [1999] 1 FLR 508.

## [2.120.53]

*Section 25(3) and (4) – Factors relating to children of the family*

### Section 25(3) – Matters for the courts regard in relation to a child of the family

The MCA 1973 requires regard, in relation to a child of the family, of the financial needs of the child; his income, earning capacity (if any), property and other financial resources; any physical or mental disability of the child; the manner in which he was being and in which the parties to the marriage expected him to be educated or trained; and the factors in s 25(2)(a) to (c) and (e) above[1]. For additional factors applying when a child of the family is not the child of one of the parties, see s 25(4).

1 See the MCA 1973, s 25(3) at para **[2.120]** above.

## [2.120.54]
### Who is a child of the family

A 'child', in relation to one or both of the parties to a marriage includes an illegitimate child of that party or, as the case may be, of both parties[1]. A child of the family in relation to the parties to a marriage, means:

(a) a child of both of the parties; and
(b) any other child (other than a foster child placed by a local authority or voluntary organisation), who has been treated by both of the parties as a child of their family[2]; and

A child who is born to a married woman as a consequence of AID is regarded as the child of her husband unless he can show that he did not consent to the artificial insemination[3] (even if he is shown not to have consented it is still possible for that child to be treated as a child of the family by virtue of the child's relationship to his mother).

In *Re A (Child of the Family)*[4], a child was found to be a child of the family of his grandparents. A child may be a 'child of the family' in relation to more than one marriage[5].

A child cannot be treated as a child of a family before he has been born[6].

If a respondent does not contest a divorce petition allegation that a child is a 'child of the family' and a finding is accordingly made to that effect, he is not estopped from contesting that fact later[7].

1 See the MCA 1973, s 52(1) at para **[2.140]** below.
2 See n 1 above.
3 See the HFEA 1990, s 28(2)(b).
4 [1998] 1 FCR 458, [1998] 1 FLR 347, CA.
5 See *Carron v Carron* [1984] FLR 805, CA.
6 See *A v A (Family: Unborn Child)* [1974] Fam 6, [1974] 1 All ER 755.
7 See *Rowe v Rowe* [1980] Fam 47, [1979] 2 All ER 1123, CA.



## [2.120.55]
### Factors to be taken into account

The court must have regard to all the circumstances of a case. It must give first consideration to the welfare, of any child of the family who has not attained the age of 18. In *R v R*[1], the mother was living with another man and the husband remarried a divorcee with a child from her first marriage. In deciding the appropriate rate of maintenance on a variation application, the judge compared the financial position of the two households and looked at the case 'from a family point of view'. The Court of Appeal held that that was a perfectly proper approach under 'all the circumstances of the case'.

1 [1988] FCR 307, [1988] 1 FLR 89, CA.

## [2.120.56]
### Child's own assets

These should be taken into account. However it is open to the court having taken these into account to decline to make an order on that basis. Thus in *J v J (C intervening)*[1] (children beneficiaries under a discretionary trust) the Court of Appeal said that the court 'had to perform a careful balancing exercise to ensure that the children's needs were met without requiring the father to pay more than he could properly afford while at the same time not placing improper pressure upon the trustees'. Contrast this with *H v H (financial provision: capital assets)*[2] where the judge declined to make an order on the basis of the considerable capital assets of the children.

1 [1989] Fam 29, [1989] 1 All ER 1121, CA.
2 [1993] 2 FLR 335 at 346.

## [2.120.56A]
### Section 25(4) – Additional matters where a child of the family is not the child of a party

The MCA 1973 requires regard (where a child of the family is not the child of one of the parties to the marriage), to whether that party assumed any responsibility for the child's maintenance, and, if so, to the extent to which, and the basis upon which, that party assumed such responsibility, and to the length of time for which that party discharged such responsibility; to whether in assuming and discharging such responsibility that party did so knowing that the child was not his or her own; and to the liability of any other person to maintain the child[1].

1 See the MCA 1973, s 25(4) at para **[2.120]** above.

## [2.120.57]
### Extent to which a child is treated as a child of the family

The court must have regard to the extent to which a child is treated as a child of the family. In *W v W (Child of the Family)*[1] the wife, to the husband's knowledge, was pregnant by another man at the time of the marriage. The parties only lived together for two weeks following the birth and during that time the husband treated the child as his own. The Court of Appeal upheld a finding that the child was a child of the family but set aside an order that the husband should pay periodical payments to the child. The court felt that the husband had assumed responsibility to the absolute minimum extent and that he should not have any continuing financial responsibility. Each case will turn on its own particular facts.

1 [1984] FLR 796, CA.

## [2.120.58]
### Legal costs of a child seeking to enforce an order

If it is sought to enforce an order in favour of a minor and legal aid is required for this purpose, it is the child who should obtain the legal aid, not the parent[1].

The decision in *Draskovic v Draskovic*[2] states that it is contrary to public interest for an order to be made in favour of a child designed to defeat the Legal Aid Board's statutory charge in relation to property recovered or preserved.

1 See *Shelley v Shelley* [1952] P 107, [1952] 1 All ER 70.
2 (1981) 11 Fam Law 87.

## [2.120.59]
### Lump sum and property adjustment orders which may be made in favour of a child

Lump sums and property adjustment orders. These are intended to provide for the child during his minority[1]. Although there is jurisdiction to make a lump sum and property adjustment order direct to the child it is only in the very rarest of cases that this will be done. See for example, Thorpe J in *A v A (Financial Provision)*[2]: 'the application of capital from a spouse to children is not a permissible objective of the statutory powers'. However, compare this with *H v H (Financial Relief: Conduct)*[3] and *Tavoulareas v Tavoulareas*[4].

Lump sums may be ordered where there is the likelihood that the non-residential parent will not pay child periodical payments[5].

It has been said that lump sums should not be used to correct absurd Child Support Agency assessments[6], but in the recent case of *V v V (child maintenance)*[7], Wilson J made lump sum orders in respect of two children to reflect their future maintenance needs after their father declined to consent at the end of a hearing to maintenance at the level that the judge had determined appropriate. Where the court had acceded to an application to determine the appropriate provision for children, but found its jurisdiction to reflect that provision in one form of order blocked, it should in principle (he found) seek to reflect the balance of the provision in a different form of order.

1 See *Chamberlain v Chamberlain* [1974] 1 All ER 33, [1973] 1 WLR 1557.
2 [1995] 1 FLR 345 at 348.
3 [1999] 1 FCR 225, [1998] 1 FLR 971.
4 [1999] 1 FCR 133, [1998] 2 FLR 418, CA.
5 *Griffiths v Griffiths* [1984] Fam 70, [1984] 2 All ER 626, CA (husband on supplementary benefit and unable to pay maintenance for the children: his share of proceeds of sale of matrimonial home amounting to £3,841: that amount preserved as a lump sum for the children).
6 See *Phillips v Peace* [1996] 2 FLR 230 (millionaire father assessed at minimal level for child support).
7 [2001] 2 FLR 799.

## [2.120.60]
### Limit on applications by or on behalf of children

Claims for capital sums should not be used as an opportunity to make a second ancillary relief application[1].

1 See *Kiely v Kiely* [1988] 1 FLR 248, CA (order made in divorce proceedings for transfer of house to wife with charge in favour of husband for 50%. Husband defaulted on his obligations to make child periodical payments. The trial judge made lump sum orders in favour of each of the children. Order discharged by the Court of Appeal).

## [2.120.61]
### Effect of orders for children on state benefits

Where an adult receives money under an order for periodical payments in favour of a child, those payments are taken into account as the adult's income for the purpose of calculating state benefits relating to the child.

## [2.121]

### [25A Exercise of court's powers in favour of party to marriage on decree of divorce or nullity of marriage]

[(1) Where on or after the grant of a decree of divorce or nullity of marriage the court decides to exercise its powers under section 23(1)(a), (b) or (c), 24, 24A or 24B above in favour of a party to the marriage, it shall be the duty of the court to consider whether it would be appropriate so to exercise those powers that the financial obligations of each party towards the other will be terminated as soon after the grant of the decree as the court considers just and reasonable.

(2) Where the court decides in such a case to make a periodical payments or secured periodical payments order in favour of a party to the marriage, the court shall in particular consider whether it would be appropriate to require those payments to be made or secured only for such term as would in the opinion of the court be sufficient to enable the party in whose favour the order is made to adjust without undue hardship to the termination of his or her financial dependence on the other party.

(3) Where on or after the grant of a decree of divorce or nullity of marriage an application is made by a party to the marriage for a periodical payments or secured periodical payments order in his or her favour, then, if the court considers that no continuing obligation should be imposed on either party to make or secure periodical payments in favour of the other, the court may dismiss the application with a direction that the applicant shall not be entitled to make any future application in relation to that marriage for an order under section 23(1)(a) or (b) above.

**Amendment**

Inserted by the MFPA 1984, s 3. Sub-s (1): WRPA 1999, s 19. Date in force: 1 December 2000: see SI 2000/1116.

## [2.121.1]
### Keypoints

- *Minton v Minton*
- Meaning of 'clean break'
- Duty to consider clean break
- No presumption of clean break
- Divorce or nullity – not judicial separation
- Deferred clean break and s 28(1A)
- Immediate clean break and s 25A(3)

## [2.121.2]

### *Minton v Minton*

In the *Minton*[1] case the House of Lords recognised the importance of achieving a clean break. Lord Scarman described this as being of equal importance to the principle that spouses should provide for their former spouses and children. However, in the case of *Dipper v Dipper*[2] it was held that the court could not dismiss an Applicant's claims to periodical payments without her consent; that position was changed in relation to divorce and nullity proceedings by the advent of s 25A of the MCA 1973 which was introduced by the MFPA 1984. In the case of *Whiting v Whiting*[3], Balcombe LJ quoted extensive passages from the Law Commission paper, 'The Financial Consequences of divorce', which considered the need for a statutory provision allowing the court to make non-consensual clean breaks.

1 Reported at [1979] AC 593, [1979] 1 All ER 79.
2 [1981] Fam 31, 1 FLR 286.
3 [1988] 2 All ER 275, [1988] 2 FLR 189, CA.

### [2.121.3]
### Meaning of 'clean break'

In the case of *Clutton v Clutton*[1], Ewbank J commented that the term 'clean break' was often used to cover a number of different financial arrangements. The term may be used in the following particular circumstances:

- where there is a 'capital clean break' – ie where capital issues are dealt with finally although income issues may remain outstanding;
- where there is a dismissal of claims for periodical payments and secured provision with an appropriate direction under s 25A(3) of the MCA 1973;
- where there is a deferred clean break. Such orders may include a provision against the extension of the term (ie under s 28(1A) of the MCA 1973) or may not. These orders are considered further below.

It is obviously important to establish how the term 'clean break is being used in any given circumstance. Here it is used to mean the conclusive dismissal of maintenance rights. A 'deferred clean break' is referred to as such.

1 [1991] 1 WLR 359, [1991] 1 FLR 242, CA.

### [2.121.4]
### Duty to consider clean break

The MCA 1973 imposes an obligation upon the court to consider a clean break when it exercises its powers of ancillary relief in divorce or nullity proceedings[1].

1 See *Suter v Suter and Jones* [1987] Fam 111, [1987] 2 All ER 336, [1987] 2 FLR 232, CA.

### [2.121.5]
### No presumption of clean break

There is, however, no presumption in favour of the court making a clean break[1]. Further, in the absence of an earning capacity or significant capital, a clean break will usually be inappropriate in a case of a woman in her mid-50's[2]. Although a clean break may be ordered where there are children[3] such orders will be rare[4]. Where a wife has an earning capacity or where other circumstances justify it, a deferred clean break may be ordered, even where there are children[5] although, in those circumstances, the inclusion within the order of a direction under s 28(1A) of the MCA 1973 will usually be inappropriate.

1 See *Barrett v Barrett* [1988] FCR 707, [1988] 2 FLR 516, CA (wife in 40's who had cared for children and had made unsuccessful efforts to find work).
2 See *Flavell v Flavell* [1997] 1 FCR 332, [1997] 1 FLR 353, CA. See also *SB v PB (Financial Provision)* [1995] 2 FCR 62, sub nom *B v B (Consent Order)* [1995] 1 FLR 9, FD.
3 See *Suter v Suter and Jones* [1987] Fam 111, [1987] 2 All ER 336, [1987] 2 FLR 232, CA.
4 See *N v N (Consent Order : Variation)* [1994] 2 FCR 275, [1993] 2 FLR 868, CA.
5 See *Waterman v Waterman* [1989] FCR 267, [1989] 1 FLR 380, CA; and *Mawson v Mawson* [1994] 2 FCR 852, [1994] 2 FLR 985.

### [2.121.6]
### Divorce or nullity – not judicial separation

The MCA 1973 provides that the court can exercise its powers to effect a non-consensual clean break in divorce or nullity proceedings, not proceedings for judicial separation.

### [2.121.7]
### Deferred clean break and s 28(1A)

The court may order periodical payments to be paid for a fixed period. Where it does so it may add to the order a provision under s 28(1A) of the MCA 1973 that the party in whose favour the order was made 'shall not be entitled to apply under section 31 below for the extension of the term specified in the order'. If it is intended to prevent the recipient spouse from extending the term of the order, it is vital to include the statutory wording of s 28(1A); the order should state that the prohibition against the extension of the term is being made pursuant to that subsection[1]. Where the order for periodical payments is for a limited period but does not include a provision under s 28(1A) of the MCA 1973, the recipient spouse will be able to apply for the extension of the term of the maintenance order; however the application to extend must be made before the term expires. In the case of *Jones v Jones*[2] it was held that, where an order for periodical payments was limited to a specific term but there was no bar against extension under s 28(1A) of the MCA 1973, the court could extend the term provided the application for the extension was made prior to the expiry of the term; it is not necessary for the application to be heard by the court before the term expires[3].

1 See *Richardson v Richardson* [1993] 4 All ER 673, [1994] 1 FLR 286; *Richardson v Richardson (No 2)* [1994] 2 FCR 826, [1994] 2 FLR 1051; *SB v PB (Financial Provision)* [1995] 2 FCR 62, sub nom *B v B (Consent Order: Variation)* [1995] 1 FLR 9.

2 [2000] 2 FCR 201, CA.

3 Therefore, the Court of Appeal in *Jones* disagreed with the provisional views expressed by Ward LJ in *G v G* [1997] 1 FLR 368 (in *G v G* Ward LJ had expressed the provisional view that the application to extend the term had to be *heard* before the expiry of the term).

### [2.121.8]
### Immediate clean break and s 25A(3)

Under s 25A(3) of the MCA 1973 the court can order a clean break in divorce and nullity proceedings; the Applicant's consent is not a prerequisite to such an order. Where it is intended to effect such an order, the wording of the subsection should be followed.

### [2.122]

**[25B Pensions]**

[(1) The matters to which the court is to have regard under section 25(2) above include—

(a) in the case of paragraph (a), any benefits under a pension arrangement which a party to the marriage has or is likely to have, and

(b) in the case of paragraph (h), any benefits under a pension arrangement which, by reason of the dissolution or annulment of the marriage, a party to the marriage will lose the chance of acquiring,

and, accordingly, in relation to benefits under a pension arrangement, section 25(2)(a) above shall have effect as if 'in the foreseeable future' were omitted.

(2) …

(3) The following provisions apply where, having regard to any benefits under a pension arrangement, the court determines to make an order under section 23 above.

(4) To the extent to which the order is made having regard to any benefits under a pension arrangement, the order may require the person responsible for the pension arrangement in question, if at any time any payment in respect of any benefits under the arrangement becomes due to the party with pension rights, to make a payment for the benefit of the other party.

(5) The order must express the amount of any payment required to be made by virtue of subsection (4) above as a percentage of the payment which becomes due to the party with pension rights.

(6) Any such payment by the person responsible for the arrangement—

(a) shall discharge so much of his liability to the party with pension rights as corresponds to the amount of the payment, and
(b) shall be treated for all purposes as a payment made by the party with pension rights in or towards the discharge of his liability under the order.

(7) Where the party with pension rights has a right of commutation under the arrangement, the order may require him to exercise it to any extent; and this section applies to any payment due in consequence of commutation in pursuance of the order as it applies to other payments in respect of benefits under the arrangement.

(7A) The power conferred by subsection (7) above may not be exercised for the purpose of commuting a benefit payable to the party with pension rights to a benefit payable to the other party.

(7B) The power conferred by subsection (4) to (7) above may not be exercised in relation to a pension arrangement which—
(a) is the subject of a pension sharing order in relation to the marriage, or
(b) has been the subject of pension sharing between the parties to the marriage.

(7C) In subsection (1) above, references to benefits under a pension arrangement include any benefits by way of pension, whether under a pension arrangement or not.

**Amendment**

Inserted with savings by the Pensions Act 1995, s 166(1); for savings see SI 1996/1675, regs 4, 5. Sub-ss (1) to (7): WRPA 1999, s 21. Date in force: 1 December 2000: see SI 2000/1116. Subs-ss (7A) to (7C): inserted by WRPA 1999, s 21. Date in force: 1 December 2000: see SI 2000/1116.

## [2.122.1]
## Keypoints

- Duty to consider
- Foreseeability
- Nature of orders under ss 25B to 25C
- Commencement and Procedure
- Order may be directed to pension managers or trustees
- Date for payment
- Attachment of pension income
- Pension lump sum and commutation
- Variation
- Armed forces pensions

## [2.122.2]
## Duty to consider

Under s 25B(1) of the MCA 1973 the court is required to have regard to pension benefits when applying the provisions of s 25(2). This does not mean that, in its discretion, the court must make orders in relation to pensions. There were two significant reported decisions in relation to the court's powers under ss 25B to 25D of the MCA 1973 prior to the shift in approach to ancillary relief in general following *White v White*[1] and the expansion of the court's powers following the introduction of pension sharing orders. They are both decisions of the High Court: *T v T (Financial Relief: Pensions)*[2] and *Burrow v Burrow*[3]. These cases do however now need to be seen in the light of *White*, the interpretation of that case by the Court of Appeal in *Cowan v Cowan*[4] and the expansion of the court's powers. In the recent case of *Maskell v Maskell*[5] Thorpe LJ cautioned against comparing the transfer value of a pension which represents a future annuity stream and a portion of future capital on a 'like for like' basis with currently available capital.

1 [2001] 1 AC 596, [2000] 3 FCR 555, HL.

2 [1998] 1 FLR 1072. For earlier cases, see generally *Rayden and Jackson on Divorce and Family Matters* (17th edn, 1997), vol 1, ch 22.
3 [1999] 1 FLR 508.
4 [2001] EWCA Civ 679, [2001] 2 FCR 331.
5 [2001] EWCA Civ 858, [2001] 3 FCR 296.



### [2.122.3]
### Foreseeability

The obscurity under the previous statutory provisions as to whether a pension would provide resources that a party was likely to have in the foreseeable future[1] is removed by s 25B(1) of the MCA 1973.

1 As to which, see eg *Priest v Priest* (1978) 1 FLR 189, CA.

### [2.122.4]
### Nature of orders under ss 25B to 25C

Sections 25B to 25C of the MCA 1973 provide that where the court makes an order for periodical payments or lump sum the order can be attached to a pension. These provisions are therefore orders for deferred, and in a sense secured, periodical payments and/or lump sum(s). These sections, unlike the pension sharing orders provided for in ss 21A, 24B, 24C and 24D do not provide a new breed of order[1]. Thus:

(1) if an order is made for a pension income to be attached–
 (a) it is not possible to make a binding order for an immediate clean break (since the income earmarking order is itself an order for periodical payments);
 (b) the order will cease to have effect on the death of either party or upon the remarriage of the applicant (due to the provisions of s 28 of the MCA 1973);
(2) most orders will be variable (see below).

1 See *T v T* [1998] 1 FLR 1072 at 1085E–G.

### [2.122.5]
### Commencement and Procedure

The provisions of ss 25B to 25D of the MCA 1973 were introduced by s 166 of the Pensions Act 1995. Relief is available where:

(i) the Petition was presented on or after the 1 July 1996 and the prescribed notice of application was filed on or after the 1 August 1996;
(ii) the Notice of Application specifically seeks relief under the relevant sections; and
(iii) the Application has been served on those responsible for the pension.

### [2.122.6]
### Order may be directed to those responsible for the pension

As a result of s 25B(4) to (6), orders may be directed to the pension managers or trustees. This avoids the risk of the party with the pension rights failing to make the payment due under the order. Lump sum orders that are directed to the pension managers or trustees will be variable, whereas lump sum orders directed to the paying spouse will usually not be variable (see para **[2.122.10]** below).

Where the person who has the pension rights has been made bankrupt the benefits under the pension scheme will vest in the Trustee in Bankruptcy[1]. The pension benefits on retirement are not discharged to the bankrupt but remain vested in the Trustee in Bankruptcy[2].

1 See the IA 1986, s 306 at para **[2.288]** below.
2 See *Re Landau (a bankrupt), Pointer v Landau* [1998] Ch 223, [1997] 3 All ER 322; *Jones v Patel and London Borough of Brent* [1999] BPIR 509; and *Krasner v Dennison; Lesser v Lawrence* [2001] Ch 76, [2000] 3 All ER 234, CA.

## [2.122.7]
### Date for payment

A party with pension rights cannot be ordered to take the pension benefits on a specific date[1].

1 See *T v T* [1998] 1 FLR 1072 at 1088B: 'the court has no power to direct when H is to draw his pension and thus cannot fix the date when he is to commute'.

## [2.122.8]
### Attachment of pension income

Since such orders are deferred periodical payment orders there will usually be little or no advantage in such an order over a straightforward order for periodical payments order. In the case of *T v T*[1], Singer J specifically declined to make an order earmarking the husband's pension income for the following reasons:

- it was virtually impossible to predict what the parties circumstances would be when the husband retired – not least because the husband could postpone his retirement until he was 75, if he chose;
- the order could be varied anyway;
- the court would have the jurisdiction to deal with periodical payments at the time of the husband's retirement (and could back up the order by an attachment of earnings order, since this was an occupational pension);
- to make an order now would lead the parties to controversy, since there would have to negotiations at the time of the retirement about the continuation or variation of the conventional maintenance order;
- there was no reason to suppose that the husband would or could defeat a conventional maintenance order at the time of his retirement.

1 [1998] 2 FCR 364, [1998] 1 FLR 1072. See also *SRJ v DWJ (financial provision)* [1999] 3 FCR 153, CA.

## [2.122.9]
### Pension lump sum and commutation

Section 25B(7) of the MCA 1973 permits the court to order the spouse with pension rights to commute the whole or part of the benefits under the pension that are capable of commutation. Taken together with s 25C this allows the court to require one spouse to commute part or whole of the lump sum payable under his pension and pay it to the other spouse. In the case of *Burrow*, the husband was ordered to pay to the wife a lump sum equal to one half of the maximum possible lump sum commutable under the pension.

## [2.122.10]
### Variation

Unless there is an express effective prohibition against variation (eg under s 28(1A) of the MCA 1973), an order for periodical payments is variable under s 31 of the MCA 1973. Further, s 31(1)(d)(ii) of the MCA 1973 states that the court may vary:

> 'any deferred order made by virtue of section 23(1)(c) (lump sums) which includes provision by virtue of–
>
> (i) section 25B(4), or
>
> (ii) section 25C.'

Under s 31(2B) of the MCA 1973 it is provided that:

> 'where the court has made an order referred to in section subsection 2(d)(ii) above, this section shall cease to apply to the order on the death of either of the parties'.

It has been said that s 31(1)(d)(i) means that all lump sum orders are fully variable. Indeed, Singer J said as follows in *T v T*[1]:

> ' … It is to be observed that the newly inserted paragraph represented by section 31(2)(dd) of the 1973 Act upon a variation application gives the court complete control over any deferred lump sum order that includes provision made by virtue of either

section 25B(4) or 25C. The obligation to pay a lump sum in future may therefore, before it takes effect, be varied in amount (obviously up as well as down), discharged or temporarily suspended. Thus the earmarking orders, both as to maintenance and capital (which W invites me to make to take effect so far into the future) because of their susceptibility to such variation will give her no real security'.

It is interesting to contrast these provisions with the very limited ability to vary a pension sharing order, which depends on whether the decree has been made absolute – if it has been and a further seven days have elapsed after the period for the filing of notice of appeal – then it is not possible to vary such an order.

1 [1998] 1 FLR 1072 at 1089G–H.



## [2.122.11]
## Armed forces pensions

Under the pre-Pensions Act law, there were restrictions to the court's ability to order that a former spouse should share in armed forces pension benefits[1].

Section 166(4) and (5) of the Pensions Act 1995 removed those restrictions. Those subsections state:

'(4) Nothing in the provisions mentioned in subsection (5) applies to a court exercising its powers under section 23 of the Matrimonial Causes Act 1973 … in respect of any benefits under a pension scheme (within the meaning of section 25B(1) of The Matrimonial Causes Act 1973) which a party to the marriage has or is likely to have.

(5) The provisions referred to in subsection (4) are –

(a) section 203(1) and (2) of the Army Act 1955, s 203(1) and (2) of the Air Force Act 1955, section 128G(1) and (20) of the Naval Discipline Act 1957 and (4A) of the Pension Scheme Act 1993 (which prevent assignment or orders being made restraining a person from receiving anything which he is prevented from assigning),

(b) section 91 of this Act [ie the Pensions Act 1995 which relates to the inalienability of occupational pensions generally];

(c) any provisions of any enactment (whether passed or made before or after this Act is passed) corresponding to any of the enactments mentioned in paragraphs (a), (b) and;

any provision of the scheme in question corresponding to any of those enactments.'

Pension sharing orders are available in respect of armed forces pension schemes.

1 See: ss 4 and 5 of the Naval and Marine Pay and Pensions Act 1865; s 203 of the Air Force Act 1955; s 203 of the Army Act 1955; and s 128G of the Naval Discipline Act 1957). The cases that considered these restrictions were *Cotgrave v Cotgrave* [1992] Fam 33, [1992] 1 FLR 10; *Happ v Happ* [1991] 4 All ER 527, [1990] 2 FLR 212; and *Legrove v Legrove* [1995] 1 FCR 102, [1994] 2 FLR 119, CA.

## [2.123]

### [25C Pensions: lump sums]

[(1) The power of the court under section 23 above to order a party to a marriage to pay a lump sum to the other party includes, where the benefits which the party with pension rights has or is likely to have under a pension arrangement include any lump sum payable in respect of his death, power to make any of the following provision by the order.

(2) The court may—

(a) if the person responsible for the pension arrangement in question has power to determine the person to whom the sum, or any part of it, is to be paid, require him to pay the whole or part of that sum, when it becomes due, to the other party,

(b) if the party with pension rights has power to nominate the person to whom the sum, or any part of it, is to be paid, require the party with pension rights to nominate the other party in respect of the whole or part of that sum,

(c) in any other case, require the person responsible for the pension arrangement in question to pay the whole or part of that sum, when it becomes due, for the benefit of the other party instead of to the person to whom, apart from the order, it would be paid.

(3) Any payment by the person responsible for the arrangement under an order made under section 23 above by virtue of this section shall discharge so much of his liability in respect of the party with pension rights as corresponds to the amount of the payment.

(4) The powers conferred by this section may not be exercised in relation to a pension arrangement which—

(a) is the subject of a pension sharing order in relation to the marriage, or

(b) has been the subject of pension sharing between the parties to the marriage.

**Amendment**

Inserted with savings by the Pensions Act 1995, s 166(1); for savings see SI 1996/1675, arts 4, 5. Sub-ss (1) to (3): WRPA 1999, s 21. Date in force: 1 December 2000: see SI 2000/1116. Sub-s (4): inserted by the WRPA 1999, s 21. Date in force: 1 December 2000: see SI 2000/1116.

### [2.123.1]
### Keypoints

- No power to order party to take out insurance
- Limitations on order that pension holder nominates the other spouse
- Proportion of benefits

### [2.123.2]
### No power to order party to take out insurance

There is no power to order a party to take out life insurance to the benefit of the other party[1]. Consequently the powers of the court under s 25C may be very important (although many pensions will only pay a lump sum on death during service and for a short period into retirement). The absence of life cover may render a dependant spouse particularly vulnerable when a maintenance paying husband dies. Although claims may be made by such a dependant spouse under the I(PFD)A 1975, that Act may provide only a limited remedy since:

- There may be no money in the estate;
- The dependant spouse may be reluctant to involve herself in litigation over the estate due to its inherent unpleasantness.

1 See *Milne v Milne* (1981) 2 FLR 286.

### [2.123.3]
### Limitations on order that pension holder nominates the other spouse

Under s 25C(2)(b) of the MCA 1973 the court may order the party with pension rights to nominate the other spouse to receive death lump sum benefits under the pension.

This power has two major drawbacks:

(i) The pension managers or trustees are likely to retain a discretion under the terms of the pension as to whether to respect the nomination. They could thus defeat the intention of the order[1];

(ii) If the party with pension rights does not make the nomination or rescinds it, contrary to the terms of the order, the beneficiary of the order may have difficulty enforcing it.

The proper course may be to apply for a pension sharing order provided the petition was issued on or after 1 December 2000. However, you cannot have an earmarking order and a pension sharing order in respect of the same pension scheme.

1 See *Wild v Pensions Ombudsman* [1997] 1 FCR 248, [1996] 2 FLR 680 which provides an interesting example of the scope of the jurisdiction of the Pension Ombudsman to overturn the exercise of the trustees' discretion. Competing claims may result in a dilution of the benefit payable to a former wife.

### [2.123.4]
### Proportion of benefits

The court has a wide discretion in deciding upon the extent of death benefits that should be received by the dependant spouse. In *T v T*[1], Singer J ordered that the wife should receive a lump sum equal to 10 times the annual maintenance payable at the time of the husband's death on the grounds that 'this solution is simple and should provide W between now and H's retirement with a significant degree of protection against the loss of her maintenance income'. The issue did not arise in the case of Burrow. Alternative approaches would be to order that the dependant spouse should receive a fraction or percentage of the benefits payable.

1 [1998] 2 FCR 364, [1998] 1 FLR 1072.



### [2.124]

#### 25D Pensions: supplementary

(1) Where—

(a) an order made under section 23 above by virtue of section 25B or 25C above imposes any requirement on the person responsible for a pension arrangement ('the first arrangement') and the party with pension rights acquires rights under another pension arrangement ('the new arrangement') which are derived (directly or indirectly) from the whole of his rights under the first arrangement, and

(b) the person responsible for the new arrangement has been given notice in accordance with regulations made by the Lord Chancellor,

the order shall have effect as if it had been made instead in respect of the person responsible for the new arrangement.

(2) The Lord Chancellor may by regulations—

(a) in relation to any provision of sections 25B or 25C above which authorises the court making an order under section 23 above to require the person responsible for a pension arrangement to make a payment for the benefit of the other party, make provision as to the person to whom, and the terms on which, the payment is to be made,

(ab) make, in relation to payment under a mistaken belief as to the continuation in force of a provision included by virtue of section 25B or 25C above in an order under section 23 above, provision about the rights or liabilities of the payer, the payee or the person to whom the payment was due,

(b) require notices to be given in respect of changes of circumstances relevant to such orders which include provision made by virtue of sections 25B and 25C above,

(ba) make provision for the person responsible for a pension arrangement to be discharged in prescribed circumstances from a requirement imposed by virtue of section 25B or 25C above,

(c) …

(d) …

(e) make provision about calculation and verification in relation to the valuation of—

(i) benefits under a pension arrangement, or

(ii) shareable state scheme rights,

for the purposes of the court's functions in connection with the exercise of any of its powers under this Part of this Act,

...

(2A) Regulations under subsection (2)(e) above may include—

(a) provision for calculation or verification in accordance with guidance from time to time prepared by a prescribed person, and

(b) provision by reference to regulations under section 30 or 49(4) of the Welfare Reform and Pensions Act 1999.

(2B) Regulations under subsection (2) above may make different provision for different cases.

(2C) Power to make regulations under this section shall be exercisable by statutory instrument which shall be subject to annulment in pursuance of a resolution of either House of Parliament.

(3) In this section and sections 25B and 25C above—

'occupational pension scheme' has the same meaning as in the Pension Schemes Act 1993;

'the party with pension rights' means the party to the marriage who has or is likely to have benefits under a pension arrangement and 'the other party' means the other party to the marriage;

'pension arrangement' means—

(a) an occupational pension scheme,

(b) a personal pension scheme,

(c) a retirement annuity contract,

(d) an annuity or insurance policy purchased, or transferred, for the purpose of giving effect to rights under an occupational pension scheme or a personal pension scheme, and

(e) an annuity purchased, or entered into, for the purpose of discharging liability in respect of a pension credit under section 29(1)(b) of the Welfare Reform and Pensions Act 1999 or under corresponding Northern Ireland legislation;

'personal pension scheme' has the same meaning as in the Pension Schemes Act 1993;

'prescribed' means prescribed by regulations;

'retirement annuity contract' means a contract or scheme approved under Chapter III of Part XIV of the Income and Corporation Taxes Act 1988;

'shareable state scheme rights' has the same meaning as in section 21A(1) above; and

'trustees or manager', in relation to an occupational pension scheme or a personal pension scheme, means—

(a) in the case of a scheme established under a trust, the trustees of the scheme, and

(b) in any other case, the managers of the scheme.

(4) In this section and sections 25B and 25C above, references to the person responsible for a pension arrangement are—

(a) in the case of an occupational pension scheme or a personal pension scheme, to the trustees or managers of the scheme,

(b) in the case of a retirement annuity contract or an annuity falling within paragraph (d) or (e) of the definition of 'pension arrangement' above, the provider of the annuity, and

(c) in the case of an insurance policy falling within paragraph (d) of the definition of that expression, the insurer.

**Amendment**

Inserted with savings by the Pensions Act 1995, s 166(1); for savings see SI 1996/1675, art 5. Sub-s (1): WRPA 1999, s 21. Date in force: 1 December 2000: see SI 2000/1116. Sub-s (2): WRPA 1999, s 21. Date in force: 11 November 1999: see the WRPA 1999, s 89. Sub-ss (2A) to (2C): inserted by the WRPA 1999, s 21. Date in force: 11 November 1999: see the WRPA 1999, s 89. Sub-ss (3), (4): substituted by the WRPA 1999, s 21. Date in force: 1 December 2000: see SI 2000/1116.

**[2.124.1]**
**Keypoints**
- Regulations
- Notices

**[2.124.2]**
**Regulations**

The principal regulations have been:

- The Occupational Pension Schemes (Disclosure of Information) Regulations 1996, SI 1996/1655. These relate to the disclosure of information relating to occupational pensions. Similar provisions relating to personal pensions are to be found in the Personal Pension Schemes (Disclosure of Information) Regulations 1987, SI 1987/1110;
- The Divorce etc (Pensions) Regulations 1996, SI 1996/1676. These relate to the valuation of pensions, the giving of information relating to pensions and the costs of doing so;
- The Pensions Act 1995 (Commencement) (No 5) Order 1996, SI 1996/1675 by which the provisions of the Act were brought into effect;
- The Pensions on Divorce etc (Provision of Information) Regulations 2000, SI 2000/1048 which came into force on 1 December 2000[1];
- The Divorce etc (Pensions) Regulations 2000, SI 2000/1123 which came into force on 1 December 2000[2];
- The Pensions on Divorce etc (Charging) Regulations 2000, SI 2000/1049 which came into force on 1 December 2000[3].

1 Set out in full at para **[3.562]** below.
2 Set out in full at para **[3.642]** below.
3 Set out in full at para **[3.572]** below.

**[2.124.3]**
**Notices**

- The Applicant for an order is required by r 2.70(4) of the FPR 1991 to notify the pension managers or trustees of:
  (a) an address to which any notice which the trustees or managers are required to serve under the Divorce etc (Pension) Regulations 1996, SI 1996/1676 is to be sent;
  (b) an address to which any payment which the trustees or managers are required to make to the applicant is to be sent; and
  (c) where the address in sub-paragraph (b) is that of a bank, a building society or the Department of National Savings, sufficient details to enable payment to be made into the account of the applicant.
- Further, by r 2.70 (9), upon the making, amendment or revocation of an order which by virtue of s 25B or s 25C of the MCA 1973 imposes any requirement on the trustees or managers of a pension scheme, the party in whose favour the order is or was made shall serve a copy of that order, or as the case may be of the order amending or revoking that order, upon the trustees or managers.
- Regulations 6 to 8A of the Divorce etc (Pensions) Regulations 1996, SI 1996/1676 specify the notices that must be given by the pension managers or trustees. Such notices may be given by ordinary first class post to the last known address of the intended recipient and ' shall be deemed to have been received on the seventh day following the date of posting' (reg 9). The Regulations provide that:
  (a) Where pension funds are transferred to a new scheme after an order has been made, reg 6 requires the pension managers or trustees to give notice to the party with the benefit of the order and to the new pension managers or trustees. The documents to accompany the notice are stated in reg 6(3);

(b) Where an event has occurred that is likely to reduce significantly the pension benefits, the pension managers or trustees must give notice to the party with the benefit of the order (reg 7);

(c) Where the party with the benefit of the order changes address or remarries (or any of the other particulars of which that party is required to give notice to the pension managers or trustees change) that party must give notice to that effect to the relevant pension managers or trustees. A failure to do so means that the pension managers or trustees may make payment to the party with pension rights and, thereby, discharge themselves from any liability under the order (regs 8 and 8A).

**[2.125]**

### 27 Financial provision orders, etc, in case of neglect by party to marriage to maintain other party or child of the family

[(1) Either party to a marriage may apply to the court for an order under this section on the ground that the other party to the marriage (in this section referred to as the respondent)—

(a) has failed to provide reasonable maintenance for the applicant, or

(b) has failed to provide, or to make a proper contribution towards, reasonable maintenance for any child of the family.]

(2) The court shall not entertain an application under this section [unless—

(a) the applicant or the respondent is domiciled in England and Wales on the date of the application; or

(b) the applicant has been habitually resident there throughout the period of one year ending with that date; or

(c) the respondent is resident there on that date].

[(3) Where an application under this section is made on the ground mentioned in subsection (1)(a) above, then, in deciding—

(a) whether the respondent has failed to provide reasonable maintenance for the applicant, and

(b) what order, if any, to make under this section in favour of the applicant,

the court shall have regard to all the circumstances of the case including the matters mentioned in section 25(2) above, and where an application is also made under this section in respect of a child of the family who has not attained the age of eighteen, first consideration shall be given to the welfare of the child while a minor.]

[(3A) Where an application under this section is made on the ground mentioned in subsection (1)(b) above then, in deciding—

(a) whether the respondent has failed to provide, or to make a proper contribution towards, reasonable maintenance for the child of the family to whom the application relates, and

(b) what order, if any, to make under this section in favour of the child,

the court shall have regard to all the circumstances of the case including the matters mentioned in [section 25(3)(a) to (e)] above, and where the child of the family to whom the application relates is not the child of the respondent, including also the matters mentioned in [section 25(4)] above.

(3B) In relation to an application under this section on the ground mentioned in subsection (1)(a) above, [section 25(2)(c) above] shall have effect as if for the reference therein to the breakdown of the marriage there were substituted a reference to the failure to provide reasonable maintenance for the applicant, and in relation to an application under this section on the ground mentioned in subsection (1)(b) above, [section 25(2)(c) above (as it applies by virtue of section 25(3)(e) above)] shall have effect as if for the reference therein to the breakdown of the marriage there were substituted a reference to the failure to provide, or to make a proper contribution towards, reasonable maintenance for the child of the family to whom the application relates.]

(5) Where on an application under this section it appears to the court that the applicant or any child of the family to whom the application relates is in immediate need of financial assistance, but it is not yet possible to determine what order, if any, should be made on the application, the court may make an interim order for maintenance, that is to say, an order requiring the respondent to make to the applicant until the determination of the application such periodical payments as the court thinks reasonable.

(6) Where on an application under this section the applicant satisfies the court of any ground mentioned in subsection (1) above, the court may make [any one or more of the following orders], that is to say—

(a) an order that the respondent shall make to the applicant such periodical payments, for such term, as may be specified in the order;

(b) an order that the respondent shall secure to the applicant, to the satisfaction of the court, such periodical payments, for such term, as may be so specified;

(c) an order that the respondent shall pay to the applicant such lump sum as may be so specified;

(d) an order that the respondent shall make to such person as may be specified in the order for the benefit of the child to whom the application relates, or to that child, such periodical payments, for such term, as may be so specified;

(e) an order that the respondent shall secure to such person as may be so specified for the benefit of that child, or to that child, to the satisfaction of the court, such periodical payments, for such term, as may be so specified;

(f) an order that the respondent shall pay to such person as may be so specified for the benefit of that child, or to that child, such lump sum as may be so specified;

subject, however, in the case of an order under paragraph (d), (e) or (f) above, to the restrictions imposed by section 29(1) and (3) below on the making of financial provision orders in favour of children who have attained the age of eighteen.

[(6A) An application for the variation under section 31 of this Act of a periodical payments order or secured periodical payments order made under this section in favour of a child may, if the child has attained the age of sixteen, be made by the child himself.

[(6B) Where a periodical payments order made in favour of a child under this section ceases to have effect on the date on which the child attains the age of sixteen or at any time after that date but before or on the date on which he attains the age of eighteen, then if, on an application made to the court for an order under this subsection, it appears to the court that—

(a) the child is, will be or (if an order were made under this subsection) would be receiving instruction at an educational establishment or undergoing training for a trade, profession or vocation, whether or not he also is, will be or would be in gainful employment; or

(b) there are special circumstances which justify the making of an order under this subsection,

the court shall have power by order to revive the first mentioned order from such date as the court may specify, not being earlier than the date of the making of the application, and to exercise its power under section 31 of this Act in relation to any order so revived.]

(7) Without prejudice to the generality of subsection (6)(c) or (f) above, an order under this section for the payment of a lump sum—

(a) may be made for the purpose of enabling any liabilities or expenses reasonably incurred in maintaining the applicant or any child of the family to whom the application relates before the making of the application to be met;

(b) may provide for the payment of that sum by instalments of such amount as may be specified in the order and may require the payment of the instalments to be secured to the satisfaction of the court.

(8) …

**Appointment**

Commencement order: SI 1973/1972.

**Derivation**

Sub-ss (1)–(7), as originally enacted, derived from the MPPA 1970, s 6; sub-s (8) as originally enacted derived from the MCA 1965, s 42(1), (3).

**Amendment**

Sub-s (1): substituted by the DPMCA 1978, s 63(1). Sub-s (2): words in square brackets substituted by the DMPA 1973, s 6(1). Sub-s (3): substituted by the MFPA 1984, s 4. Sub-ss (3A), (3B): substituted by the DPMCA 1978, s 63(2); words in square brackets substituted by theMFPA 1984, s 46(1), Sch 1, para 13. Sub-s (6): words in square brackets substituted by the DPMCA 1978, s 63(3). Sub-s (6A): inserted by the DPMCA 1978, s 63(4). Sub-s (6B): inserted by the DPMCA 1978, s 63(4); substituted by the FLRA 1987, s 33(1), Sch 2, para 52. Sub-s (8): repealed by the DPMCA 1978, s 63(5), 89(2)(b), Sch 3.

## [2.125.1]
## Keypoints

- Scope of section.
- Application for an order.
- Definitions

## [2.125.2]
## Scope of section

Section 27 of the MCA 1973 is designed to enable court to make orders against one part of the marriage in favour of the other or that of a child of the family.

For a discussion of this topic, see generally *Rayden and Jackson on Divorce and Family Matters* (17th edn, 1997), vol 1, para 21.160 et seq and the Noter-up thereto.

## [2.125.3]
## Application for an order

Once the applicant has established jurisdiction following the requirements set out under s 27(2), together with the fact that the other party has failed to provide reasonable maintenance, it allows the applicant to obtain an order for financial provision namely periodical payments, secured periodical payments, lump sum for him/herself and any children of the family without need for partitioning for a divorce. In essence this alters not only the mode of application but also the format for discovery and hearing of the matter. Applications are governed by the FPR 1991, rr 3.1 to 3.10 as amended by the Family Proceeding Rules (Amendment No 2) Rules 1999, SI 1999/3491, in particular rr 2.51A to 2.70.

These changes have substantially amended the procedure not only in respect of applications for financial relief but also governing the format of the proceedings themselves. However for s 27 applications, application is by way of originating application in Form M19 (r 3.1(1)), supported by an affidavit (r 3.1(2)). The contents of the affidavit are set out in r 3.1(3) to 3.1(4). Pursuant to r 3.1(10), rr 2.61 to 2.66 and r 10.10 apply. Thereafter the proceedings are governed by the FPR 1991 (as amended by SI 1999/3491). In particular: r 2.61B (procedure before first appointment), r 2.61D (the first appointment) and r 2.61E (the FPR appointment). Amendments have been made to the conducts of hearings itself, in particular r 2.62(4), (4A), (7), (8) and (9). The application is not by way of Form A[1].

1 See FPR 1991, r 2.71(3)(f) and SI 1997/1056.

## [2.125.4]
## Definitions

*'Failed'*

This must be past and present but cannot be future. If it is a complaint as to the current level of maintenance then it is that level of maintenance which is assessed rather than what the court might order looking at the matter afresh[1]. It therefore differs from applications made following the issue of a petition of divorce or judicial reparation.

*'Child'*

The welfare of the child remains the first consideration of the court if an application is made in relation to a child of the family (as amended by s 4 of the MFPA 1984).

*'Reasonable'*

As provided for in s 25(2) of the MCA 1973 (amended by the MFPA 1984, Sch 1, para 12) it is an objective test particular to the circumstances of each particular case[2]. If the application relates to a child who is not a child of the respondent and the court must have regard for facts of s 25(4) of the MCA 1973.

*'Jurisdiction'*

The applicant and/or the respondent must come within one of the categories as set out in s 27(2).

*'Orders which can be made under this section'*

Periodical payments[3], interim periodical payments, secured periodical payments and lump sums. However note only one lump sum order can be made and there is no provision for an interim lump sum order. The purposes for the lump sum order are for expenses incurred by the applicant or the child. A lump sum can be made by instalments (s 27(7)(5)). There is of course the availability of an application being made under Sch 1 to the ChA 1989 for the above orders. There are restrictions to these applications for example s 8 of the Child Support Act 1991 which sets out the jurisdiction of the Child Support Officer and furthermore note s 29(1) and (3) of the MCA 1973 in relation to orders in favour of a child over the age of 18. The duration of such orders are considered in ss 28 and 29 of the MCA 1973.

Any order made under s 27 is subject to the power of the court to vary under s 31 of the MCA 1973 and of course if the child is over the age of 16 years the child can apply himself (s 27(6)(A)) to vary subject to the FPR 1991, as amended by SI 1999/3491, r 2.57.

*'Revival'*

Section 27(6B) of the MCA 1973 – the court has power to revive an order if an application is made before the child attains the age of 18 years. The court will then exercise its powers derived from s 31 of the MCA 1973 whereby the order can be revived from a date earlier than the application for example the child's sixteenth birthday if that was one of the triggering events.

1 See *Scott v Scott* [1951] P 245, [1951] 1 All ER 216 (decided under Law Reform (Miscellaneous Provisions) Act 1999, s 1.
2 See *Dart v Dart* [1996] 2 FLR 286 at 296, CA.
3 See *Dorney-Kingdom v Dorney-Kingdom* [2000] 3 FCR 20, [2000] 2 FLR 855, CA where a global order was made for maintenance it is essential in order to preserve the legitimacy of the order that the order contains substantial ingredients of spouse's support. A *Segal* order is still appropriate.

**[2.126]**

### 28 Duration of continuing financial provision orders in favour of party to marriage, and effect of remarriage

(1) Subject in the case of an order made on or after the grant of a decree of a divorce or nullity of marriage to the provisions of sections 25A(2) above and 31(7) below, the term to be specified in a periodical payments or secured periodical payments order in favour of a party to a marriage shall be such term as the court thinks fit, except that the term shall not begin before or extend beyond the following limits, that is to say—

(a) in the case of a periodical payments order, the term shall begin not earlier than the date of the making of an application for the order, and shall be so defined as not to extend beyond the death of either of the parties to the marriage or, where the order is made on or after the grant of a decree of divorce or nullity of marriage, the remarriage of the party in whose favour the order is made; and

(b) in the case of a secured periodical payments order, the term shall begin not earlier than the date of the making of an application for the order, and shall be so defined as not to extend beyond the death or, where the order is made on or after the grant of such a decree, the remarriage of the party in whose favour the order is made.

(1A) Where a periodical payments or secured periodical payments order in favour of a party to a marriage is made on or after the grant of a decree of divorce or nullity of marriage the court may direct that that party shall not be entitled to apply under section 31 below for the extension of the term specified in the order.

(2) Where a periodical payments or secured periodical payments order in favour of a party to a marriage is made otherwise than on or after the grant of a decree of divorce or nullity of marriage and the marriage in question is subsequently dissolved or annulled but the order continues in force, the order shall, notwithstanding anything in it, cease to have effect on the remarriage of that party, except in relation to any arrears due under it on the date of the remarriage.

(3) If after the grant of a decree dissolving or annulling a marriage either party to that marriage remarries, whether before or after the commencement of this Act, that party shall not be entitled to apply, by reference to the grant of that decree, for a financial provision order in his or her favour, or for a property adjustment order, against the other party to that marriage.

**Appointment**

Commencement order: SI 1973/1972.

**Derivation**

This section derived from the MPPA 1970, s 7.

**Amendment**

Sub-s (1): first words in square brackets substituted by the MFPA 1984, s 5. Sub-s (1A): inserted by the MFPA 1984, s 5.

**[2.126.1]**
**Keypoints**

- MCA 1973, ss 25A(2) and 31(7)
- MCA 1973, s 28(1A)
- Remarriage

**[2.126.2]**
**MCA 1973, ss 25A(2) and 31(7)**

Under s 25A(2) of the MCA 1973, the court is obliged to consider in a case where an order for periodical payments is made, whether it would be appropriate to require those payments to be made or secured only for such term as would in the opinion of the court be sufficient to enable the party in whose favour the order was made to adjust without undue hardship to the termination of his or her financial dependence on the other party. Similarly, under s 31(7) of the MCA 1973, the court is required to consider the discharge of an order for periodical payments or secured periodical payments where it has before it an application to vary such an order. Provision now exists to capitalise an existing periodical payments order pursuant to s 31(7A) and (7B) of the MCA 1973 on an application. The factors to be considered are:

(a) the reasons for the original order;
(b) the reasons for any order varying the original order;
(c) the effect of maintenance orders for financial provision upon the position of the parties' respective lives;
(d) to recognise there is no power to vary any orders for payment of a lump sum; and
(e) the public and private interests in the finality of orders relating to the division of capital assets upon the termination of a marriage[1].

For a discussion of this topic, see generally *Rayden and Jackson on Divorce and Family Matters* (17th edn, 1997), vol 1, para 21.85 and the Noter-up thereto.



1 See *Cornick v Cornick (No 3)* [2001] 2 FLR 1240, [2001] Fam Law 871.

## [2.126.3]
## MCA 1973, s 28(1A)

The court may order periodical payments to be paid for a fixed period. Where it does so it may add to the order a provision under s 28(1A) of the MCA 1973 that the party in whose favour the order was made 'shall not be entitled to apply under section 31 below for the extension of the term specified in the order'. If it is intended to prevent the recipient spouse from extending the term of the order, it is vital to include the statutory wording of s 28(1A); the order should state that the prohibition against the extension of the term is being made pursuant to that subsection[1]. Where the order for periodical payments is for a limited period but does not include a provision under s 28(1A) of the MCA 1973, the recipient spouse will be able to apply for the extension of the term of the maintenance order; however the application to extend must be made before the term expires (and, probably, an order should be *obtained* extending the term of the order, prior to the expiry of the original order)[2]. Although a clean break may be ordered where there are children[3], such orders will be rare[4]. Where a wife has an earning capacity or where other circumstances justify it, a deferred clean break may be ordered, even where there are children[5] although, in those circumstances, the inclusion within the order of a direction under s 28(1A) of the MCA 1973 will usually be inappropriate[6].

1 See *Richardson v Richardson* [1993] 4 All ER 673, [1994] 1 FLR 286; *Richardson v Richardson (No 2)* [1994] 2 FCR 826, [1994] 2 FLR 1051; and *SB v PB (Financial Provision)* sub nom *B v B (Consent Order : Variation)* [1995] 1 FLR 9.
2 See *G v G* [1997] 1 FLR 368. See also *Jones v Jones* [2000] 3 WLR 1505, [2000] 2 FCR 201, CA where the court decided that provided the application to extend was made prior to the expiry of the term, then the court had jurisdiction to hear the matter even if that post-dated the expiry date of the original order. This is in contrast with the earlier view expressed by Ward LJ in *G v G*.
3 See *Suter v Suter* [1987] Fam 111, [1987] 2 FLR 232, CA.
4 See *N v N (Consent Order: Variation)* [1994] 2 FCR 275, [1993] 2 FLR 868, CA.
5 See *Waterman v Waterman* [1989] FCR 267, [1989] 1 FLR 380, CA; *and Mawson v Mawson* [1994] 2 FCR 852, [1994] 2 FLR 985.
6 See *N v N (Consent Order: Variation)* [1994] 2 FCR 275, [1993] 2 FLR 868, CA.

## [2.126.4]
## Remarriage

Under s 28(3) of the MCA 1973 a party who seeks ancillary relief must apply for that relief before remarriage. A party must make an application if he seeks an ancillary relief order in his favour[1]; it is not sufficient to rely on the fact that the other party has made such an application. An application made within the petition is sufficient to prevent the bar in s 28(3) of the MCA 1973 applying to the Petitioner[2]. An application seeking maintenance made prior to remarriage does not permit an application to be made for a lump sum after remarriage[3]. Similarly, an application for child periodical payments made before remarriage does not permit a subsequent lump sum application to be made[4]. However, it has been held that an application for a property transfer order does not prevent a party from amending the application after remarriage to include an application for a lump sum[5]. An indication of a party's intention to make an application for ancillary relief, given prior to remarriage in the acknowledgement of service of the petition, is insufficient[6].

1 See *Robin v Robin* (1983) 4 FLR 632, CA.
2 See *Jackson v Jackson* [1973] Fam 99.
3 See *Wilson v Wilson* [1976] Fam 142.
4 See *Nixon v Fox* [1978] Fam 173.
5 See *Doherty v Doherty* [1976] Fam 71.
6 See *Hargood v Jenkins* [1978] Fam 148.

**[2.127]**

### 29 Duration of continuing financial provision orders in favour of children, and age limit on making certain orders in their favour

(1) Subject to subsection (3) below, no financial provision order and no order for a transfer of property under section 24(1)(a) above shall be made in favour of a child who has attained the age of eighteen.

(2) The term to be specified in a periodical payments or secured periodical payments order in favour of a child may begin with the date of the making of an application for the order in question or any later date [or a date ascertained in accordance with subsection (5) or (6) below] but—

(a) shall not in the first instance extend beyond the date of the birthday of the child next following his attaining the upper limit of the compulsory school age [(construed in accordance with section 8 of the Education Act 1996)] [unless the court considers that in the circumstances of the case the welfare of the child requires that it should extend to a later date]; and

(b) shall not in any event, subject to subsection (3) below, extend beyond the date of the child's eighteenth birthday.

(3) Subsection (1) above, and paragraph (b) of subsection (2), shall not apply in the case of a child, if it appears to the court that—

(a) the child is, or will be, or if an order were made without complying with either or both of those provisions would be, receiving instruction at an educational establishment or undergoing training for a trade, profession or vocation, whether or not he is also, or will also be, in gainful employment; or

(b) there are special circumstances which justify the making of an order without complying with either or both of those provisions.

(4) Any periodical payments order in favour of a child shall, notwithstanding anything in the order, cease to have effect on the death of the person liable to make payments under the order, except in relation to any arrears due under the order on the date of the death.

[(5) Where—

(a) a maintenance assessment ('the current assessment') is in force with respect to a child; and

(b) an application is made under Part II of this Act for a periodical payments or secured periodical payments order in favour of that child—

(i) in accordance with section 8 of the Child Support Act 1991, and

(ii) before the end of the period of 6 months beginning with the making of the current assessment the term to be specified in any such order made on that application may be expressed to begin on, or at any time after, the earliest permitted date.

(6) For the purposes of subsection (5) above, 'the earliest permitted date' is whichever is the later of—

(a) the date 6 months before the application is made; or

(b) the date on which the current assessment took effect or, where successive maintenance assessments have been continuously in force with respect to a child, on which the first of those assessments took effect.

(7) Where—

(a) a maintenance assessment ceases to have effect or is cancelled by or under any provision of the Child Support Act 1991; and

(b) an application is made, before the end of the period of 6 months beginning with the relevant date, for a periodical payments or secured periodical payments order in favour of a child with respect to whom that maintenance assessment was in force immediately before it ceased to have effect or was cancelled,

the term to be specified in any such order made on that application may begin with the date on which that maintenance assessment ceased to have effect or, as the case may be, the date with effect from which it was cancelled, or any later date.

(8) In subsection (7)(b) above—

(a) where the maintenance assessment ceased to have effect, the relevant date is the date on which it so ceased; and

(b) where the maintenance assessment was cancelled, the relevant date is the later of—

(i) the date on which the person who cancelled it did so, and

(ii) the date from which the cancellation first had effect.]



**Appointment**

Commencement order: SI 1973/1972.

**Derivation**

This section derived from the MPPA 1970, s 8.

**Amendment**

Sub-s (2): first words in square brackets inserted by SI 1993/623, art 2, Sch 1, para1; in para (a) words in square brackets substituted by the EA 1996, s 582(1), Sch 37, para 136, final words in square brackets inserted by the MFPA 1984, s 5. Sub-ss (5) to (8): inserted by SI 1993/623, art 2, Sch 1, para 2.

**[2.128]**

## 30 Direction for settlement of instrument for securing payments or effecting property adjustment

Where the court decides to make a financial provision order requiring any payments to be secured or a property adjustment order—

(a) it may direct that the matter be referred to one of the conveyancing counsel of the court for him to settle a proper instrument to be executed by all necessary parties; and

(b) where the order is to be made in proceedings for divorce, nullity of marriage or judicial separation it may, if it thinks fit, defer the grant of the decree in question until the instrument has been duly executed.

**Appointment**

Commencement order: SI 1973/1972.

**Derivation**

This section derived from the MPPA 1970, s 25.

**[2.128.1]**
**Keypoints**

- General
- Enforcement where respondent refuses to execute a deed or transfer

**[2.128.2]**
**General**

Where the court decides to make a property adjustment order it may direct that the matter be referred to one of the conveyancing counsel of the court for him to settle a proper instrument to be executed by all the necessary parties. It may also defer the grant of 'the decree in question' until the instrument has been duly executed.

**[2.128.3]**
**Enforcement where respondent refuses to execute a deed or transfer**

If the respondent refuses or neglects to execute a deed transferring or settling property as ordered by the court, the court can order that it be executed by some other person (including the court). The court also has power to order a party to lodge documents necessary for the preparation of the transfer or settlement. These powers should be used in preference to committal for contempt[1].

1 See *Danchevsky v Danchevsky* [1975] Fam 17, [1974] 3 All ER 934, CA.

**[2.129]**

**31 Variation, discharge, etc, of certain orders for financial relief**

(1) Where the court has made an order to which this section applies, then, subject to the provisions of this section [and of section 28(1A) above], the court shall have power to vary or discharge the order or to suspend any provision thereof temporarily and to revive the operation of any provision so suspended.

(2) This section applies to the following orders, that is to say—

(a) any order for maintenance pending suit and any interim order for maintenance;

(b) any periodical payments order;

(c) any secured periodical payments order;

(d) any order made by virtue of section 23(3)(c) or 27(7)(b) above (provision for payment of a lump sum by instalments);

(dd) any deferred order made by virtue of section 23(1)(c) (lump sums) which includes provision made by virtue of—

(i) section 25B(4), or

(ii) section 25C,

(provision in respect of pension rights);

(e) any order for a settlement of property under section 24(1)(b) or for a variation of settlement under section 24(1)(c) or (d) above, being an order made on or after the grant of a decree of judicial separation;

(f) any order made under section 24A(1) above for the sale of property;

(g) a pension sharing order under section 24B above which is made at a time before the decree has been made absolute.

(2A) Where the court has made an order referred to in subsection (2)(a), (b) or (c) above, then, subject to the provisions of this section, the court shall have power to remit the payment of any arrears due under the order or of any part thereof.

(2B) Where the court has made an order referred to in subsection (2)(dd)(ii) above, this section shall cease to apply to the order on the death of either of the parties to the marriage.

(3) The powers exercisable by the court under this section in relation to an order shall be exercisable also in relation to any instrument executed in pursuance of the order.

(4) The court shall not exercise the powers conferred by this section in relation to an order for a settlement under section 24(1)(b) or for a variation of settlement under section 24(1)(c) or (d) above except on an application made in proceedings—

- (a) for the rescission of the decree of judicial separation by reference to which the order was made, or
- (b) for the dissolution of the marriage in question.

[(4A) In relation to an order which falls within paragraph (g) of subsection (2) above ('the subsection (2) order')—

- (a) the powers conferred by this section may be exercised—
  - (i) only on an application made before the subsection (2) order has or, but for paragraph (b) below, would have taken effect; and
  - (ii) only if, at the time when the application is made, the decree has not been made absolute; and
- (b) an application made in accordance with paragraph (a) above prevents the subsection (2) order from taking effect before the application has been dealt with.

(4B) No variation of a pension sharing order shall be made so as to take effect before the decree is made absolute.

(4C) The variation of a pension sharing order prevents the order taking effect before the end of such period after the making of the variation as may be prescribed by regulations made by the Lord Chancellor.]

(5) [Subject to subsections (7A) to [(7G)] below and without prejudice to any power exercisable by virtue of subsection (2)(d), (dd)[, (e) or (g)] above or otherwise than by virtue of this section,] no property adjustment order [or pension sharing order] shall be made on an application for the variation of a periodical payments or secured periodical payments order made (whether in favour of a party to a marriage or in favour of a child of the family) under *section 23* [section 22A or 23] above, and no order for the payment of a lump sum shall be made on an application for the variation of a periodical payments or secured periodical payments order in favour of a party to a marriage (whether made under *section 23* [section 22A or 23] or under section 27 above).

(5) Subject to subsections (7A) to (7G) below and without prejudice to any power exercisable by virtue of subsection (2)(d), (dd), (e) or (g) above or otherwise than by virtue of this section, no property adjustment order or pension sharing order shall be made on an application for the variation of a periodical payments or secured periodical payments order made (whether in favour of a party to a marriage or in favour of a child of the family) under section 23 above, and no order for the payment of a lump sum shall be made on an application for the variation of a periodical payments or secured periodical payments order in favour of a party to a marriage (whether made under section 23 or under section 27 above).

(6) Where the person liable to make payments under a secured periodical payments order has died, an application under this section relating to that order [(and to any order made under section 24A(1) above which requires the proceeds of sale of property to be used for securing those payments) may be made by the person entitled to payments under the periodical payments order] or by the personal representatives of the deceased person, but no such application shall, except with the permission of the court, be made after the end of the period of six months from the date on which representation in regard to the estate of that person is first taken out.

(7) In exercising the powers conferred by this section the court shall have regard to all the circumstances of the case, first consideration being given to the welfare while a minor of any child of the family who has not attained the age of eighteen, and the circumstances of the case shall include any change in any of the matters to which the court was required to have regard when making the order to which the application relates, and—

(a) in the case of a periodical payments or secured periodical payments order made on or after the grant of a decree of divorce or nullity of marriage, the court shall consider whether in all the circumstances and after having regard to any such change it would be appropriate to vary the order so that payments under the order are required to be made or secured only for such further period as will in the opinion of the court be sufficient [(in the light of any proposed exercise by the court, where the marriage has been dissolved, of its powers under subsection (7B) below)] to enable the party in whose favour the order was made to adjust without undue hardship to the termination of those payments;

(b) in a case where the party against whom the order was made has died, the circumstances of the case shall also include the changed circumstances resulting from his or her death.

(7A) Subsection (7B) below applies where, after the dissolution of a marriage, the court—

(a) discharges a periodical payments order or secured periodical payments order made in favour of a party to the marriage; or

(b) varies such an order so that payments under the order are required to be made or secured only for such further period as is determined by the court.

(7B) The court has power, in addition to any power it has apart from this subsection, to make supplemental provision consisting of any of—

(a) an order for the payment of a lump sum in favour of a party to the marriage;

(b) one or more property adjustment orders in favour of a party to the marriage;

(ba) one or more pension sharing orders;

(c) a direction that the party in whose favour the original order discharged or varied was made is not entitled to make any further application for—

(i) a periodical payments or secured periodical payments order, or

(ii) an extension of the period to which the original order is limited by any variation made by the court.

(7C) An order for the payment of a lump sum made under subsection (7B) above may—

(a) provide for the payment of that sum by instalments of such amount as may be specified in the order; and

(b) require the payment of the instalments to be secured to the satisfaction of the court.

(7D) [Section 23(6)] above apply where the court makes an order for the payment of a lump sum under subsection (7B) above as they apply where it makes such an order under [section 23] above.

(7E) If under subsection (7B) above the court makes more than one property adjustment order in favour of the same party to the marriage, each of those orders must fall within a different paragraph of section 21(2) above.

(7F) Sections 24A and 30 above apply where the court makes a property adjustment order under subsection (7B) above as they apply where it makes such an order under [section 24] above.

(7G) Subsections (3) to (5) of section 24B above apply in relation to a pension sharing order under subsection (7B) above as they apply in relation to a pension sharing order under that section.

(8) The personal representatives of a deceased person against whom a secured periodical payments order was made shall not be liable for having distributed any part of the estate of the deceased after the expiration of the period of six months referred to in subsection (6) above on the ground that they ought to have taken into account the possibility that the court might permit an application under this section to be made after that period by the person entitled to payments under the order; but this subsection shall not prejudice any power to recover any part of the estate so distributed arising by virtue of the making of an order in pursuance of this section.

(9) In considering for the purposes of subsection (6) above the question when representation was first taken out, a grant limited to settled land or to trust property shall be left out of account and a grant limited to real estate or to personal estate shall be left out of account unless a grant limited to the remainder of the estate has previously been made or is made at the same time.

[(10) Where the court, in exercise of its powers under this section, decides to vary or discharge a periodical payments or secured periodical payments order, then, subject to section 28(1) and (2) above, the court shall have power to direct that the variation or discharge shall not take effect until the expiration of such period as may be specified in the order.]

(11) Where—

(a) a periodical payments or secured periodical payments order in favour of more than one child ('the order') is in force;

(b) the order requires payments specified in it to be made to or for the benefit of more than one child without apportioning those payments between them;

(c) a maintenance assessment ('the assessment') is made with respect to one or more, but not all, of the children with respect to whom those payments are to be made; and

(d) an application is made, before the end of the period of 6 months beginning with the date on which the assessment was made, for the variation or discharge of the order,

the court may, in exercise of its powers under this section to vary or discharge the order, direct that the variation or discharge shall take effect from the date on which the assessment took effect or any later date.

(12) Where—

(a) an order ('the child order') of a kind prescribed for the purposes of section 10(1) of the Child Support Act 1991 is affected by a maintenance assessment;

(b) on the date on which the child order became so affected there was in force a periodical payments or secured periodical payments order ('the spousal order') in favour of a party to a marriage having the care of the child in whose favour the child order was made; and

(c) an application is made, before the end of the period of 6 months beginning with the date on which the maintenance assessment was made, for the spousal order to be varied or discharged,

the court may, in exercise of its powers under this section to vary or discharge the spousal order, direct that the variation or discharge shall take effect from the date on which the child order became so affected or any later date.

(13) For the purposes of subsection (12) above, an order is affected if it ceases to have effect or is modified by or under section 10 of the Child Support Act 1991.

(14) Subsections (11) and (12) above are without prejudice to any other power of the court to direct that the variation of discharge of an order under this section shall take effect from a date earlier than that on which the order for variation or discharge was made.

(15) The power to make regulations under subsection (4C) above shall be exercisable by statutory instrument which shall be subject to annulment in pursuance of a resolution of either House of Parliament.

**Appointment**

Commencement order: SI 1973/1972.

**Derivation**

This section, as originally enacted, derived from the MPPA 1970, s 9.

**Amendment**
Sub-s (1): MFPA 1984, s 6. Sub-s (2): PA 1995, s 166(3)(a); MHPA 1981, s 8(2)(a); WRPA 1999, s 19. Sub-s (2A): inserted by the AJA 1982, s 5. Sub-s (2B): inserted with savings by the PA 1995, s 166(3)(b). Sub-ss (4A) to (4C): inserted by the WRPA 1999, s 19, Sch 3. Sub-s (5): FLA 1996, s 66(1), Sch 8, para 16(5)(a); WRPA 1999, s 19. Sub-s (6): MHPA 1981, s 8(2)(b). Sub-s (7): substituted by the MFPA 1984, s 6; amended by the FLA 1996, s 66(1), Sch 8, para 16(6)(b). Sub-ss (7A) to (7F): inserted by the FLA 1996, s 66(1), Sch 8, para 16(7). Sub-s (7B): WRPA 1999, s 19. Date in force: 1 December 2000 (except that a pension sharing order may not be made if the marriage was dissolved by a decree granted in proceedings begun before that date): see SI 2000/116. Sub-s (7D): SI 1998/2572, art 4(a). Date in force: 19 October 1998 (this amendment has effect until such time as the FLA 1996, Sch 2 comes into force): (no specific commencement provision). Sub-s (7D): SI 1998/2572, art 4(a). Date in force: 19 October 1998 (this amendment has effect until such time as the FLA 1996, Sch 2 comes into force): (no specific commencement provision). Sub-s (7F): SI 1998/2572, art 4(b). Date in force: 19 October 1998 (this amendment has effect until such time as the FLA 1996, Sch 2 comes into force): (no specific commencement provision). Sub-s (7G): inserted by the WRPA 1999, s 19. Sub-s (10): inserted by the MFPA 1984, s 6. Sub-ss (11) to (14): inserted by SI 1993/623, art 2, Sch 1, para 3. Sub-s (15): inserted by the WRPA 1999, s 19.

## [2.129.1]
## Keypoints

- Scope of section
- Court's powers
- The exercise of the court's powers
- Lump sum
- Property adjustment orders
- The application of s 31(7A) and (7B)
- Principles applied – s 31(7)
- 'All the circumstances'
- Form of application

## [2.129.2]
## Scope of section

By s 31 of the MCA 1973, the court may exercise wide powers in relation to the following types of orders[1]:

- maintenance pending suit / interim periodical payments[2];
- periodical payments, whether or not secured (subject to any earlier direction under s 28(1A) of the MCA 1973))[3];
- lump sum orders by instalments[4], or deferred lump sums[5], including those made under the MCA 1973, ss 25B(4) or 25C;
- settlement or variation of settlement made in judicial separation proceedings[6] where there is a subsequent application for rescission of the decree or for divorce;
- orders for sale[7];
- a pension sharing order made prior to decree absolute[8].

Section 31 of the MCA 1973 also enables the court to deal with the situation following the death of the payer[9], as well as the situation concerning arrears[10]. For a discussion of this topic, see generally *Rayden and Jackson on Divorce and Family Matters* (17th edn, 1997), vol 1, chap 24 and the Noter-up thereto.

1 See the MCA 1973, s 31(2) above.
2 Under s 22 of the MCA 1973 (set out at para **[2.116]** above).
3 Under s 23(1)(a) or (b) of the MCA 1973 (set out at para **[2.117]** above).
4 Under ss 23(3)(c) or 27(7)(b) of the MCA 1973 (set out at paras **[2.117]** and **[2.125]** above).
5 Under s 23(1)(c) of the MCA 1973.
6 Under s 24(1)(b), (c) or (d) of the MCA 1973 (set out at para **[2.118]** above).
7 Under s 24A of the MCA 1973 (set out at para **[2.119]** above).
8 Under s 24B of the MCA 1973 (set out at para **[2.119A]** above). Note that as a pension sharing order can be varied only if there has been no decree absolute, steps may be needed to prevent the grant of a decree if variation may be sought.
9 Under s 31(8) of the MCA 1973.
10 Under s 31(2A) of the MCA 1973.

### [2.129.3]
### Court's powers

Where the court has made an order within the scope of s 31 of the MCA 1973, then the court has the following powers[1]:

- to vary the order;
- to discharge the order;
- to suspend any provision of the order;
- to revive the operation of any suspended provision.

Where the court discharges an order for periodical payments or secured periodical payments, or varies such an order so that payments under it are required only for a term the court additionally has power to make supplemental provision[2]. This may consist of any of:

- a lump sum order, including one by instalments which may be secured[3], and may carry interest[4];
- one or more property adjustment orders;
- one or more pension sharing orders;
- a direction that the applicant may not further apply for periodical payments, secured periodical payments or the extension of any term for such payments.

The powers of s 31(7B) of the MCA 1973 are retrospective in effect[5].

1 Under s 31(1) of the MCA 1973.
2 Under s 31(7B) of the MCA 1973.
3 See the MCA 1973, s 31(7C).
4 See the MCA 1973, s 31(7D).
5 See *Harris v Harris* [2001] 1 FCR 68, CA.

### [2.129.4]
### The exercise of the court's powers

Where an application has been made to vary the term of the order (periodical payments) the court considers the application de novo and must have regard to all the circumstances in the case. There is no burden on the party in whose favour the order has been made which is now subject to variation[1].

Although either party may apply to the court to vary[2], discharge, suspend temporarily etc. the existing order, if one of the parties is found to be in contempt of the court, the court can refuse to countenance such an application whilst that person remains in contempt[3].

The court has to consider all the factors in s 25 and should not just consider changes since the order was made[4].

There is no power to vary a maintenance order once that maintenance order has been dismissed[5]. A nominal order keeps a maintenance entitlement alive and so can be varied in the future for a substantive claim. A maintenance order once dismissed cannot be resurrected by way of variation pursuant to s 31 under the liberty to apply provisions[6].

The court on varying an order for periodical payments must consider whether a clean break would be appropriate[7], and may add an order pursuant to s 28(1A) of the MCA 1973[8]. Where an application is made to extend the term of an order for periodical payments, it must be made before the expiry of that term[9], although there is no need for an order to have been obtained on the application prior to the termination date[10].

Secured periodical payments can be varied after the payer's death, but the application must be made within six months of the grant of representation in regard to the estate, or leave will be required[11]. It should be noted that the right to apply for a first order for secured periodical payments does not survive against the deceased's estate[12]. Whilst recovery against the deceased's estate is permissible even after distribution, the personal representatives of the deceased are not liable for having effected that distribution once the six month period in s 31(6) of the MCA 1973 has expired[13].

1 See *Flavell v Flavell* [1997] 1 FCR 332, [1997] 1 FLR 353.
2 See *Dart v Dart* [1997] 1 FCR 21, [1996] 2 FLR 286, CA.
3 See *Baker v Baker (No 2)* [1997] 2 FCR 249, [1997] 1 FLR 148, CA which considers the criteria set out in *Hadkinson v Hadkinson* [1952] P 285, [1952] 2 All ER 567, CA.

4 See *Garner v Garner* [1992] 1 FCR 529, [1992] 1 FLR 573, CA.
5 See *L v L* [1962] P 101, [1961] 3 All ER 834, CA.
6 See *Thompson v Thompson* [1986] Fam 38, [1985] 2 All ER 243, CA. See also *Potter v Potter* [1990] FCR 704, [1992] FLR 27, CA on the issue of liberty to apply.
7 See the MCA 1973, s 31(7)(a).
8 See *Richardson v Richardson (No 2)* [1994] 2 FLR 1051.
9 See *G v G* [1998] Fam 1.
10 See *Jones v Jones* [2000] 2 FCR 201.
11 See the MCA 1973, s 31(6).
12 See *Dipple v Dipple* [1942] 1 All ER 234.
13 See the MCA 1973, s 31(8).

### [2.129.5]
### Lump sum

The court has power to defer payment and order payment by instalment[1]. However the court has no power to vary the amount or to order an interim lump sum payment[2].

1 See *Mansfield v Alexander (Lump Sum Order: Extension of Time)* [1995] 2 FCR 663, [1995] 1 FLR 100, CA.
2 See *Wicks v Wicks* [1999] Fam 65, [1998] 1 FLR 470, CA.

### [2.129.6]
### Property adjustment orders

The powers exercisable under section 31 do not extend to property which has been transferred[1]. Equally the court has no power to vary an order for sale, where the variation sought went to the core of the order[2]. Where, upon discharging or varying an order for periodical payments or secured periodical payments the court makes more than one property adjustment order under s 31(7B) of the MCA 1973, each of those orders must fall within a different paragraph of MCA 1973, s 21(2)[3], which provides that:

> '(2) The property adjustment orders for the purposes of this Act are the orders dealing with property rights available (subject to the provisions of this Act) under section 24 below for the purpose of adjusting the financial position of the parties to a marriage and any children of the family on or after the grant of a decree of divorce, nullity of marriage or judicial separation, that is to say–
>
> (a) any order under subsection (1)(a) of that section for a transfer of property;
> (b) any order under subsection (1)(b) of that section for a settlement of property; and
> (c) any order under subsection (1)(c) or (d) of that section for a variation of settlement'.

1 See *Dinch v Dinch* [1987] 1 All ER 818, [1987] 2 FLR 162, HL; *Peacock v Peacock* [1991] FCR 121, [1991] 1 FLR 324.
2 See *Omilean v Omilean* [1996] 3 FCR 329, [1996] 2 FLR 306, CA.
3 See the MCA 1973, s 31(7E) at para **[2.129]** above.

### [2.129.7]
### The application of s 31(7A) and (7B)

Under the provisions of the MCA 1973, s 31(7A), a court can order a capital sum instead of an existing periodical payment. There is nothing to suggest that the new provisions of s 31(7A) should not apply to any application built upon a sound financial foundation, brought under that new jurisdiction, and in those circumstances there is no limit to their retrospective effect[1]. In determining whether to capitalise periodical payments, the court has to have regard to all the circumstances of the case, including any change in any of the matters to which the court has had regard when making the original order, therefore giving a judge an almost unfettered discretion[2]. The power conferred by s 31(7A) of the MCA 1973 gives the court a wide choice and is in wide terms[3].

In *Cornick v Cornick (No 3)*[4], Charles J said that the earlier decision of the Court of Appeal in *Harris v Harris*[5] was not authority for the proposition that, in discharging an order for periodical payments and ordering a lump sum, the court is limited to taking an approach that first identifies the level of periodcial payments that would be appropriate and then capitalising it. However, this approach may be fair in many cases, and would in any event be a useful cross-check.

On an application under this subsection, a payee is not precluded from deriving benefit from an increase in the payers fortunes, even if this results in her enjoying a higher standard of living than she did during the marriage. Original direct and indirect contributions should not necessarily be left out of account, even where time has passed since the original order. However, any increase in a husband's wealth by dint of his subsequent business efforts may be too far removed from the marriage to justify quantifying any lump sum on a proportional basis[6].



1 See *Harris v Harris* [2001] 1 FCR 68, CA.
2 See *Harris v Harris* [2001] 1 FCR 68 at 73.
3 See *Cornick v Cornick (No 3)* [2001] 2 FLR 1240, [2001] Fam Law 871.
4 [2001] 2 FLR 1240.
5 [2001] 1 FCR 68, CA.
6 See n 3 above (per Charles J).

## [2.129.8]
## Principles applied – s 31(7)

The statutory criteria in relation to the exercising of the court's powers under s 31 of the MCA 1973 derive from s 31(7). In exercising the powers conferred by this section the court shall have regard to all the circumstances of the case, first consideration being given to the welfare while a minor of any child of the family who has not attained the age of 18, and the circumstances of the case shall include any change in any of the matters to which the court was required to have regard when making the order to which the application relates[1]. This has been held to give the trial judge almost unfettered discretion[2]. On an application to vary, all the factors set out in s 25 will be considered and not merely the changes since the order was made[3]. Each case will depend upon its own specific facts and not every change of circumstance will result in a variation. For example, where the wife's earning capacity is so small it was disregarded on an application to vary[4]. However, cohabitation may amount to a change of circumstances[5]. The test of 'adjust without undue hardship' depends on each particular case and is therefore subjective of the parties' respective means[6]. The frugal wife should not be penalised[7].

The amendments contained in s 31(7A) to (7C) have retrospective effect on orders which are subject to be varied[8].

1 See the MCA 1973, s 31(7) at para **[2.129]** above.
2 See *Harris v Harris* [2001] 1 FCR 68 at 73 per Thorpe LJ, CA.
3 See *Garner v Garner* [1992] 1 FCR 529, [1992] 1 FLR 573, CA.
4 See *SB v PB (Financial Provision)* [1995] 2 FCR 62, sub nom *B v B (Consent Order: Variation)* [1995] 1 FLR 9.
5 See *Atkinson v Atkinson* [1988] Fam 93, [1987] 2 All ER 849, CA.
6 See *Boylan v Boylan* [1988] FCR 689, [1988] 1 FLR 282, FD.
7 See *Boylan v Boylan* [1988] FCR 689, [1988] 1 FLR 282, FD.
8 See *Harris v Harris* [2001] 1 FCR 68, CA.

## [2.129.9]
## 'All the circumstances'

This will include updating an order to take into account inflation[1]. Equally the squandering of a large inheritance will be taken into account[2] as well as post-divorce conduct by the wife as a result of which the order was reduced[3].

1 See *McGrady v McGrady* (1977) 8 Fam Law 15.
2 See *Primavera v Primavera* [1992] 1 FCR 78, [1992] 1 FLR 16, CA.
3 See *J (HD) v J (AM) (Financial Provision: Variation)* [1980] 1 WLR 124.

**[2.129.10]**
**Form of application**

This application comes within the scope of applications for ancillary relief (FPR 1991, r 1.2(1)) and as such are governed by the FPR 1991, SI 1991/1247. See further para **[3.432.5]** below.

**[2.130]**

**32 Payment of certain arrears unenforceable without the leave of the court**

(1) A person shall not be entitled to enforce through the High Court or any county court the payment of any arrears due under an order for maintenance pending suit, an interim order for maintenance or any financial provision order without the leave of that court if those arrears became due more than twelve months before proceedings to enforce the payment of them are begun.

(2) The court hearing an application for the grant of leave under this section may refuse leave, or may grant leave subject to such restrictions and conditions (including conditions as to the allowing of time for payment or the making of payment by instalments) as that court thinks proper, or may remit the payment of the arrears or of any part thereof.

(3) An application for the grant of leave under this section shall be made in such manner as may be prescribed by rules of court.

**Appointment**

Commencement order: SI 1973/1972.

**Derivation**

This section derived from the MPPA 1970, s 10.

**[2.130.1]**
**Keypoints**

- Scope of section
- Leave
- Enforcement
- Form of application

**[2.130.2]**
**Scope of section**

Section 32 of the MCA 1973 provides that arrears which are more than one-year-old cannot be enforced without leave of the court.

See generally, *Rayden and Jackson on Divorce and Family Matters* (17th edn, 1997), vol 1, ch 24 and the Noter-up thereto.

**[2.130.3]**
**Leave**

Pursuant to s 32(2) of the MCA 1973 the court can on the hearing of an application for leave remit payment of the arrears or any part thereof or grant leave subject to restrictions and conditions including allowing time for payment or payment by instalments. Applications for leave are governed by FPR 1991, r 10.9 and CCR Ord 13, r 1. Unless special circumstances can be established arrears should be remitted[1].

1 See *R v Cardiff Magistrates Court, ex p Czech* [1999] 1 FCR 721, [1999] 1 FLR 95.

**[2.130.4]**
**Enforcement**

Enforcement can be by way of a variety of means, briefly these are:

*Attachment of earnings*

The court can order deductions to be made directly from the debtor's earnings. But once the order has been served on the debtor's employer the employer must comply and calculate the deduction in accordance with Sch 3 to the AtEA 1971. A failure to do so could result in a fine at level 2 or a fine pursuant to s 23(3) of the AtEA 1971. An attachment of earnings order can be varied.

*Judgment summons*

Maintenance orders can still be enforced in this way pursuant to the Administration of Justice Act 1970, s 11(a) and (b) together with s 5(2) of the Debtors Act 1869 and the FPR 1991, r 7.4(2). However the availability and appropriateness of judgment summonses to enforce orders in ancillary relief has been severely questioned in the light of the HRA 1998, Sch 1, Art 6[1]. In particular there is a query as to whether judgment summons should ever be used as a method of enforcing a 'substantial' debt[2]. A court has power to imprison for a period up to six weeks. The standard of proof is that of the criminal standard[3]. Imprisonment does not extinguish the debt and thus there can be a further application for a judgment summons in respect of the earlier judgment summons upon release from prison. However, leave would be required in this case as the debtor who would be in default under an existing committal order. The committal of the debtor can be suspended on terms such as payment by a specific date or payment by instalments together with the provision of costs of issuing the judgment summons[4]. Although additional time may be given to the judgment debtor to pay the sum ordered[5]. This may allow the debtor to apply to the court to vary the original order pursuant to s 31. Unless there is an application pursuant to s 31 of the MCA 1973 to vary the original order then the court on hearing a judgment summons cannot remit any of the arrears which have accrued under the existing order. The person seeking the judgment summons must comply with the requirements of service together with the provision of conduct money[6]. If the alleged debtor fails to appear the court can order a bench warrant.

*Garnishee proceedings*

Garnishee proceedings can be used for a sum in excess of £50[7]. This can be used not only to enforce arrears of maintenance but also capital sums. However it cannot be used to enforce regular maintenance payments themselves. It can however be used to enforce undertakings for payments of sums of money for example school fees[8]. However this is an equitable remedy and should only be used when other remedies have proved fruitless. The application is made ex parte unless the prospective garnishee is a deposit-taking institution and notice must be given.

1 See *Mubarak v Murbarak* [2001] 1 FLR 698 at 709 (para [40]), CA per Thorpe LJ.
2 See n 1 above per Jacob J at p 713 (para [66]).
3 See *Woodley v Woodley* [1993] 1 FCR 701, [1992] 2 FLR 417, CA.
4 See FPR 1991, r 7.4(10).
5 See FPR 1991, r 7.4(9).
6 See r 7.4 to r 7.6 of the FPR 1991 at para **[3.479]** et seq below.
7 See CCR Ord 30, r 1; and RSC Ord 49, r 1.
8 See *Gandolfo v Gandolfo (Standard Chartered Bank Garnishee)* [1981] QB 359, [1980] 1 All ER 833, CA.

**[2.130.5]**
**Form of application**

This depends upon the mode of enforcement sought. Attachment of earnings available in magistrates' courts, county courts and the High Court pursuant to the AtEA 1971, as amended by the MEA 1991. Note also CCR Ord 27 in Sch 1 to the AtEA 1971.

*Judgment summons*

Governed by the FPR 1991, r 7.4 and CCR Ord 28, r 3 in the county court and also applicable in the High Court. Furthermore, in the county court r 7.6 of the FPR 1991 applies.

In the High Court RSC Ord 38, r 2 and RSC Ord 62 applies together with r 7.5 of the FPR 1991.

*Garnishee proceedings*

Application by way of summons – applications are governed by CCR Ord 30, r 1 and RSC Ord 49, r 1.

In the magistrates' court it has power to enforce, revoke or discharge maintenance orders and can remit part or all of the arrears due pursuant to the Magistrates' Courts Act 1980, s 95.

See also *Practice Direction (family proceedings: committal applications)*[1].

1 [2001] 2 All ER 704, [2001] 1 WLR 1253.

**[2.131]**

## 33 Orders for repayment in certain cases of sums paid under certain orders

(1) Where on an application made under this section in relation to an order to which this section applies it appears to the court that by reason of—

(a) a change in the circumstances of the person entitled to, or liable to make, payments under the order since the order was made, or

(b) the changed circumstances resulting from the death of the person so liable,

the amount received by the person entitled to payments under the order in respect of a period after those circumstances changed or after the death of the person liable to make payments under the order, as the case may be, exceeds the amount which the person so liable or his or her personal representatives should have been required to pay, the court may order the respondent to the application to pay to the applicant such sum, not exceeding the amount of the excess, as the court thinks just.

(2) This section applies to the following orders, that is to say—

(a) any order for maintenance pending suit and any interim order for maintenance;

(b) any periodical payments order; and

(c) any secured periodical payments order.

(3) An application under this section may be made by the person liable to make payments under an order to which this section applies or his or her personal representatives and may be made against the person entitled to payments under the order or her or his personal representatives.

(4) An application under this section may be made in proceedings in the High Court or a county court for—

(a) the variation or discharge of the order to which this section applies, or

(b) leave to enforce, or the enforcement of, the payment of arrears under that order;

but when not made in such proceedings shall be made to a county court, and accordingly references in this section to the court are references to the High Court or a county court, as the circumstances require.

(5) The jurisdiction conferred on a county court by this section shall be exercisable notwithstanding that by reason of the amount claimed in the application the jurisdiction would not but for this subsection be exercisable by a county court.

(6) An order under this section for the payment of any sum may provide for the payment of that sum by instalments of such amount as may be specified in the order.

**Appointment**

Commencement order: SI 1973/1972.

**Derivation**

This section derived from the MPA 1970, ss 11, 34(1).

**[2.131.1]**
**Keypoints**

- Scope of section
- Applicable orders
- Form of application

**[2.131.2]**
**Scope of section**

Where there has been a change in circumstances of the payee or a change resulting from the death of the payer then there may be repayment of sums. There is no power to remit arrears under this section and the power to order repayment relates to the period before the order was varied (for example an application under s 31 of the MCA 1973).

See generally, *Rayden and Jackson on Divorce and Family Matters* (17th edn, 1997), vol 1, ch 24 and the Noter-up thereto.

**[2.131.3]**
**Applicable orders**

This relates to periodical payments as set out in s 2 of the MCA 1973. It does not apply to capital orders even if there has been a drastic change in circumstances such as the death of the payer[1]. The order can relate to either the payer or his personal representatives. The repayment can be by way of instalments (s 33(6) above).

1 See *Barder v Barder (Calouri intervening)* [1988] AC 20, [1987] 2 FLR 480.

**[2.131.4]**
**Form of application**

Specific reference is made to the form of the application in s 33(4) of the MCA 1973. It can clearly be made in the High Court or the county court where the jurisdiction of the latter is unlimited for the purposes of this application. There is no specific form of application laid down by the FPR 1991 in relation to an application under s 33 of the MCA 1973; however, if it is linked with an application under s 31 to discharge the order then it will be governed by rr 2.52 to 2.68 of the FPR 1991, as amended by the Family Proceedings Rules (Amendment No 2) Rules 1999, SI 1999/3491 with the addition of rr 2.51A and 2.51B, namely application commenced by Form A or B and the overriding objective in the FPR 1991, as amended.

**[2.132]**

**[33A Consent orders for financial provision on property adjustment]**

[(1) Notwithstanding anything in the preceding provisions of this Part of this Act, on an application for a consent order for financial relief the court may, unless it has reason to think that there are other circumstances into which it ought to inquire, make an order in the terms agreed on the basis only of the prescribed information furnished with the application.

(2) Subsection (1) above applies to an application for a consent order varying or discharging an order for financial relief as it applies to an application for an order for financial relief.

(3) In this section—

'consent order', in relation to an application for an order, means an order in the terms applied for to which the respondent agrees;

'order for financial relief' means an order under any of sections 23, 24, 24A, 24B or 27 above ; and

'prescribed' means prescribed by rules of court.]

**Amendment**

Inserted by the MFPA 1984, s 7. Sub-s (3): WRPA 1999, s 19. Date in force: 1 December 2000: see SI 2000/1116.

## [2.132.1]
### Keypoints

- Scope of section
- Prescribed information
- Mode of application

## [2.132.2]
### Scope of section

Section 33A of the MCA 1973 enables the court to make an order to which the parties consent without the necessity of a full investigation of the parties' finances by way of final hearing without oral evidence.

## [2.132.3]
### Prescribed information

This should contain such information as will enable the court to exercise its duty under ss 25 and 25A of the MCA 1973. The duty is on the litigants to make full and frank disclosure[1]. A failure to provide full disclosure may result in an application to set aside. However, note the duty on those negotiating as considered in *Xydhias v Xydhias*[2]. The court will not set aside a consent order on the basis of bad legal advice[3]. As far as representatives are concerned, solicitors owe clients a general duty of care[4] and the standard should be of a reasonably competent solicitor in that particular field of expertise[5]. The immunity from suit formerly enjoyed by advocates no longer exists in any proceedings[6].

Under s 33A(2) applies whether the parties are seeking to vary or discharge an order as well as an order for financial relief itself.

1 See *Jenkins v Livesey (formerly Jenkins)* [1985] AC 424, [1985] FLR 813, AC; *Pounds v Pounds* [1994] 1 WLR 1535, CA; *Dinch v Dinch* [1987] 1 All ER 818, [1987] 2 FLR 162, HL; and *Middleton v Middleton* [1999] 2 FCR 681, [1998] 2 FLR 821, CA.
2 [1999] 1 FLR 683, CA.
3 See *Harris v Manahan* [1996] 4 All ER 454 (must be finality to litigation).
4 See *Hedley Byrne & Co Ltd v Heller & Partners Ltd* [1964] AC 465.
5 See *Bolam v Friern Hospital Management Committee* [1957] 1 WLR 582; and *Smith v Smith* [2000] 3 FCR 374, CA – the judge has to make a proper evaluation of the claim considering all factors in s 25.
6 See Arthur JS *Hall & Co v Simons* [2000] 3 WLR 873, [1999] 2 FCR 193, CA.

## [2.132.4]
### Mode of application

Applications under s 33A of the MCA 1973 are governed by r 2.61 of the FPR 1991, as amended by SI 1999/3491, namely r 2.51A application for ancillary rules – application to commence by Form A or B for proceedings commenced on or after 5 June 2000 (and where the court considers it just and so directs, proceedings commenced before that date).

## [2.133]

### 34 Validity of maintenance agreements

(1) If a maintenance agreement includes a provision purporting to restrict any right to apply to a court for an order containing financial arrangements, then—

(a) that provision shall be void; but

(b) any other financial arrangements contained in the agreement shall not thereby be rendered void or unenforceable and shall, unless they are void or unenforceable for any other reason (and subject to sections 35 and 36 below), be binding on the parties to the agreement.

(2) In this section and in section 35 below—

'maintenance agreement' means any agreement in writing made, whether before or after the commencement of this Act, between the parties to a marriage, being—

(a) an agreement containing financial arrangements, whether made during the continuance or after the dissolution or annulment of the marriage; or

(b) a separation agreement which contains no financial arrangements in a case where no other agreement in writing between the same parties contains such arrangements;

'financial arrangements' means provisions governing the rights and liabilities towards one another when living separately of the parties to a marriage (including a marriage which has been dissolved or annulled) in respect of the making or securing of payments or the disposition or use of any property, including such rights and liabilities with respect to the maintenance or education of any child, whether or not a child of the family.

**Appointment**

Commencement order: SI 1973/1972.

**Derivation**

This section derived from the MPPA 1970, s 13.



## [2.133.1]
## Keypoints

- General
- Court's approach to agreements
- Any restriction on right to apply void
- 'Maintenance agreement'
- 'Financial arrangements'

## [2.133.2]
## General

Section 34 of the MCA 1973, with ss 35 and 36 below, sets out the powers of the court in relation to maintenance agreements. Section 34(1) deals with limitation to the validity of such agreements, whereas s 34(2) provides certain definitions.

For a discussion of this topic, see generally *Rayden and Jackson on Divorce and Family Matters* (17th edn, 1997), vol 1, ch 19 and the Noter-up thereto.

## [2.133.3]
## Court's approach to agreements

The court encourages parties to matrimonial disputes to settle their disputes amicably. Accordingly, separation agreements and financial agreements in anticipation of divorce or separation proceedings are of themselves perfectly lawful, unless they seek to oust the jurisdiction of the court or are unlawful or unenforceable for some other reason.

However, a truly 'clean break' whereby neither party has the right to apply to the court for further relief, can only be imposed by a court in proceedings for divorce or nullity of marriage and not purely by agreement between the parties without a court order[1].

An award of financial provision or property adjustment for a wife or child on a divorce is peculiarly a matter for the divorce courts; it is therefore a matter of public policy that the jurisdiction of the courts in regard to these matters is not to be ousted by the private agreement of the parties[2].

Where the parties to a marriage reach an agreement which is not incorporated into an order of the court but which effectively divides their assets in what is essentially a commercial settlement of matrimonial proceedings and one of them then dies, the agreement stands or falls at common law[3].

A wife who covenants by a deed of separation not to take proceedings for her maintenance beyond the provision made for her in the deed is not thereby precluded, when she obtains a divorce, from applying to the court for further provision[4].

However, the covenant in the deed is 'conduct' to be considered within the ambit of the MCA 1973, s 25(2)(g) and formal agreements are binding unless an injustice would be done by holding the parties to the terms of their agreement[5].

For examples of cases where earlier agreements have affected the exercise of the court's discretion on the hearing of an ancillary relief application, see *H v H (Financial Relief: Non-disclosure)*[6], *Smith v McInerney*[7] and *Beach v Beach*[8].

1 See eg *de Lasala v de Lasala* [1980] AC 546 at 559 per Lord Diplock, PC.
2 See eg *Sutton v Sutton* [1984] Ch 184.
3 See *Amey v Amey* [1992] 1 FCR 289, [1992] 2 FLR 89.
4 See eg *Hyman v Hyman* [1929] AC 601, HL; and *Minton v Minton* [1979] AC 593, [1979] 1 All ER 79, HL.
5 See *Edgar v Edgar* [1980] 3 All ER 887, CA; and *G v G (Financial Provision: Separation Agreement)* [2000] 2 FLR 18.
6 [1994] 2 FCR 301, [1994] 2 FLR 94.
7 [1994] 2 FCR 1086, [1994] 2 FLR 1077.
8 [1995] 2 FCR 526, [1995] 2 FLR 160.

## [2.133.4]
### Any restriction on right to apply void

By s 34(1)(a) of the MCA 1973 any provision included in a maintenance agreement purporting to restrict any right to apply shall be void.

By s 34(1)(b), other financial arrangements in any such agreement remain binding (if otherwise so), notwithstanding the fact of the void provision.

Although a party to such an agreement may apply, the fact of such an agreement, if properly entered into, may be crucial in determining the extent to which the court will make orders for additional financial provision beyond the terms so agreed[1].

1 See *Edgar v Edgar* [1980] 3 All ER 887, CA.

## [2.133.5]
### 'Maintenance agreement'

The term, as defined in s 34(2) of the MCA 1973, applies to agreements in writing between parties to a marriage. It applies regardless of its date, but must:

- contain financial arrangements made during or after the continuance of the marriage (see below), or
- be a separation agreement without financial arrangements (provided there is no other written agreement between the parties which does contain such arrangements).

## [2.133.6]
### 'Financial arrangements'

Also as defined in s 34(2) of the MCA 1973, these must relate to the parties to a marriage (whether or not extant) when living separately. They must govern those parties' rights and liabilities towards each other in respect of:

- making or securing payments, or
- the disposition or use of property, and
- including maintenance or education of any child, whether or not of the family.

## [2.134]

### 35 Alteration of agreements by court during lives of parties

(1) Where a maintenance agreement is for the time being subsisting and each of the parties to the agreement is for the time being either domiciled or resident in England and Wales, then, subject to subsection (3) below, either party may apply to the court or to a magistrates' court for an order under this section.

(2) If the court to which the application is made is satisfied either—

(a) that by reason of a change in the circumstances in the light of which any financial arrangements contained in the agreement were made or, as the case may be, financial arrangements were omitted from it (including a change foreseen by the parties when making the agreement), the agreement should be altered so as to make different, or, as the case may be, so as to contain, financial arrangements, or

(b) that the agreement does not contain proper financial arrangements with respect to any child of the family,

then subject to subsections (3), (4) and (5) below, that court may by order make such alterations in the agreement—

(i) by varying or revoking any financial arrangements contained in it, or

(ii) by inserting in it financial arrangements for the benefit of one of the parties to the agreement or of a child of the family,

as may appear to that court to be just having regard to all the circumstances, including, if relevant, the matters mentioned in [section 25(4)] above; and the agreement shall have effect thereafter as if any alteration made by the order had been made by agreement between the parties and for valuable consideration.

(3) A magistrates' court shall not entertain an application under subsection (1) above unless both the parties to the agreement are resident in England and Wales and at least one of the parties is resident [within the commission area … for which the court is appointed], and shall not have power to make any order on such an application except—

(a) in a case where the agreement includes no provision for periodical payments by either of the parties, an order inserting provision for the making by one of the parties of periodical payments for the maintenance of the other party or for the maintenance of any child of the family;

(b) in a case where the agreement includes provision for the making by one of the parties of periodical payments, an order increasing or reducing the rate of, or terminating, any of those payments.

(4) Where a court decides to alter, by order under this section, an agreement by inserting provision for the making or securing by one of the parties to the agreement of periodical payments for the maintenance of the other party or by increasing the rate of the periodical payments which the agreement provides shall be made by one of the parties for the maintenance of the other, the term for which the payments or, as the case may be, the additional payments attributable to the increase are to be made under the agreement as altered by the order shall be such term as the court may specify, subject to the following limits, that is to say—

(a) where the payments will not be secured, the term shall be so defined as not to extend beyond the death of either of the parties to the agreement or the remarriage of the party to whom the payments are to be made;

(b) where the payments will be secured, the term shall be so defined as not to extend beyond the death or remarriage of that party.

(5) Where a court decides to alter, by order under this section, an agreement by inserting provision for the making or securing by one of the parties to the agreement of periodical payments for the maintenance of a child of the family or by increasing the rate of the periodical payments which the agreement provides shall be made or secured by one of the parties for the maintenance of such a child, then, in deciding the term for which under the agreement as altered by the order the payments, or as the case may be, the additional payments attributable to the increase are to be made or secured for the benefit of the child, the court shall apply the provisions of section 29(2) and (3) above as to age limits as if the order in question were a periodical payments or secured periodical payments order in favour of the child.

(6) For the avoidance of doubt it is hereby declared that nothing in this section or in section 34 above affects any power of a court before which any proceedings between the parties to a maintenance agreement are brought under any other enactment (including a provision of this Act) to make an order containing financial arrangements or any right of either party to apply for such an order in such proceedings.

**Appointment**
Commencement order: SI 1973/1972.

**Derivation**
This section derived from the MPPA 1970, s 14.

**Amendment**
Sub-s (2): words in square brackets substituted by the MFPA 1984, s 46(1), Sch 1, para 13. Sub-s (3): words from 'within the commission' to 'court is appointed' in square brackets substituted by the MFPA 1984, s 46(1), Sch 1, para 13. Sub-s (3): words omitted repealed by the AJA 1999, s 106, Sch 15, Pt V, Table (1). Date in force: 27 September 1999: see the AJA 1999, s 108(3)(f).

## [2.134.1]
## Keypoints

- General
- Application for an order
- Jurisdiction
- Grounds for alteration
- Duration and effect of order

## [2.134.2]
## General

Section 35 of the MCA 1973 enables the court to alter a maintenance agreement during the lives of the parties to that agreement, in certain defined circumstances. This is the only section in Pt II of the MCA 1973 which vests jurisdiction additionally in the magistrates' courts.

See generally, *Rayden and Jackson on Divorce and Family Matters* (17th edn, 1997), vol 1, ch 19 and the Noter-up thereto.

## [2.134.3]
## Application for an order

Application is made by originating application containing, unless otherwise directed, the information required by Form M21[1].

That information includes the following:

- the names and addresses of the parties and the date of their marriage;
- the date of the maintenance agreement which it is sought to alter;
- the full names of any children of the family, and their dates of birth if under 18;
- whether any child over 16 is still receiving instruction or training;
- any other child who either was a child of the family but who has died, or who was not a child of the family but is provided for by the agreement;
- details of any previous proceedings with reference to the agreement or the marriage;
- the means of the applicant;
- the alteration sought;
- the facts relied on to justify the alteration.

The application may be made to any divorce county court and may be heard and determined by the district judge[2].

With the application must be filed an affidavit by the applicant exhibiting a copy of the agreement and verifying the statements in the application[3].

A copy of the affidavit and of the application should also be filed for service on the respondent[4]. Those copies are served together with a notice in Form M20 with Form M6 (acknowledgment) attached[5].

The respondent has eight days to acknowledge service (Form M20), and 14 days after the expiry of that time to file an affidavit in answer containing full particulars of his property and income. The court may order him to file such an affidavit if he fails to do so[6].

The respondent should also file a copy of his affidavit for service on the respondent[7].

The following rules apply with necessary modifications to an application under s 35 or s 36 of the MCA 1973, as if it were an application for ancillary relief[8].

Rule 2.66 of the FPR 1991 applies to an application under s 35 of the MCA 1973[9].

Subject to the provisions of rr 3.2 to 3.4 and 3.5(1), the FPR 1991 apply with the necessary modifications to an application under s 35 or s 36 of the MCA 1973, as if the application were a cause, the originating application or summons a petition, and the applicant the petitioner[10].

In magistrates' courts, application is made by way of complaint[11].



1 See the FPR 1991, r 3.2(1) at para **[3.463]** below.
2 See the FPR 1991, r 3.2(2)
3 See the FPR 1991, r 3.2(3).
4 See the FPR 1991, r 3.2(3).
5 See the FPR 1991, r 3.2(4).
6 See the FPR 1991, r 3.2(5).
7 See the FPR 1991, r 3.2(6).
8 See the FPR 1991, r 2.60, r 2.62(4), (5) and (6), r 2.63, r 2.64, r 2.65 and r 10.10. See also FPR 1991, r 3.5(1)(a).
9 See the FPR 1991, r 3.5(1)(b) at para **[3.466]** below.
10 See the FPR 1991, r 3.5(2).
11 See the Magistrates' Court Rules 1981, SI 1981/552, r 105.

## [2.134.4]
## Jurisdiction

A divorce county court or the Family Division of the High Court in an application transferred to it, has jurisdiction to alter a subsisting agreement to which the Act applies during the lifetime of both parties to the agreement, if each is for the time being either domiciled or resident in England and Wales (s 35(1)).

A magistrates' court has jurisdiction to alter an agreement during the lifetime of the parties, but not after the death of one of them. A magistrates' court cannot entertain an application unless both parties are resident in England and at least one of them is resident in the commission area (within the meaning of the Justices of the Peace Act 1979) for which the court is appointed (s 35(3)).

The magistrates' powers are further limited to making orders either:

- inserting orders for periodical payments by one party for the maintenance of the other or of any child of the family where the agreement includes no such provision (s 35(3)(a)), or
- increasing, reducing or terminating such payments where the agreement does include provision for periodical payments (s 35(3)(b)).

This jurisdiction does not affect any power of a court under any other enactment to make an order containing financial arrangements or any right of either party to the agreement to apply for such an order (s 35(6)). The court's powers and the parties' rights under other sections of the MCA 1973 and the DPMCA 1978 are therefore preserved.

Waite J stated as follows in *Simister v Simister (No 2)*[1]:

> 'the effect of s 35(6) is to ensure that s 35 remained subservient to other jurisdictions (in particular to that of granting ancillary relief in general terms) and that future variations of maintenance are more readily achieved under s 31.'

Remarriage by the applicant is a bar to seeking to add additional lump sum provision to a maintenance agreement[2].

1 [1987] 1 FLR 194 at 202–203. See also *Smith v Smith* [2000] 3 FCR 374, CA.
2 *Pace (formerly Doe) v Doe* [1977] Fam 18 at 24.

## [2.134.5]
## Grounds for alteration

The court may vary, revoke or insert financial arrangements for the benefit of one of the parties or a child of the family, provided it has been satisfied either:

(a) that there has been a relevant change of circumstances, or
(b) that the agreement does not contain proper financial arrangements for any child of the family (s 35(2)).

The court will exercise its powers as may appear just having regard to all the circumstances, which may include those matters mentioned in s 25(4) of the MCA 1973 above, that is (as against a party to a marriage in favour of a child of the family who is not the child of that party):

- whether that party assumed any responsibility for the child's maintenance, and, if so, to the extent to which, and the basis upon which, that party assumed such responsibility and to the length of time for which that party discharged such responsibility;
- whether in assuming and discharging such responsibility that party did so knowing that the child was not his or her own;
- the liability of any other person to maintain the child (s 35(2)).

Before the court can decide whether or not to vary an agreement, it must find that there has been a change of circumstances in the light of which the financial arrangements were made, whether or not foreseen at the time of the agreement. If it is then to go on and vary, it must be satisfied that the agreement has become unjust by reason of that change[1].

It is not possible to lay down as a matter of law what changes should or should not satisfy the court that an agreement should be altered; it is a question of fact and degree[2].

For the court's attitude where ancillary relief proceedings are instituted after a maintenance agreement has been made, see *Simister v Simister (No 2)*[3].

1 See *Gorman v Gorman* [1964] 3 All ER 739, [1964] 1 WLR 1440, CA.
2 See *K v K* [1961] 2 All ER 266.
3 [1987] 1 FLR 194. See also *G v G (Financial Provision: Separation Agreement)* [2000] 2 FLR 18.

## [2.134.6]
## Duration and effect of order

Upon alteration of an agreement by the court, the agreement thereafter has effect as if any alteration made had been made by agreement between the parties for valuable consideration (s 35(2)). It is not necessary that any further agreement be drawn up.

The variation may be retrospective[1].

The term for any amended or inserted provision for periodical payments shall be such term as the court may specify, subject to the following limits:

- the death of either party or the remarriage of the recipient where the payments will not be secured;
- the death or remarriage of the recipient where the payments will be secured (s 35(4)).

Where the alteration relates to or affects periodical payments for a child of a family, then the court applies the provisions of s 29 (2) and (3) of the MCA 1973 above as to age limits, that is:

- initially, unless the court thinks it right to specify a later date, it will not extend beyond the date of the child's seventeenth birthday;
- it will not extend beyond the age of 18 unless the child is, or if provision were made would be, receiving instruction or undergoing training; or there are special circumstances which justify the making of the provision (s 35(5)).

1 See *Warden v Warden* [1982] Fam 10, [1981] 3 All ER 193, CA.

## [2.135]

### 36 Alteration of agreements by court after death of one party

(1) Where a maintenance agreement within the meaning of section 34 above provides for the continuation of payments under the agreement after the death of one of the parties and that party dies domiciled in England and Wales, the surviving party or

the personal representatives of the deceased party may, subject to subsections (2) and (3) below, apply to the High Court or a county court for an order under section 35 above.

(2) An application under this section shall not, except with the permission of the High Court or a county court, be made after the end of the period of six months from the date on which representation in regard to the estate of the deceased is first taken out.

(3) A county court shall not entertain an application under this section, or an application for permission to make an application under this section, unless it would have jurisdiction by virtue of [section 22 of the Inheritance (Provision for Family and Dependants) Act 1975] (which confers jurisdiction on county courts in proceedings under [that Act if the value of the property mentioned in that section] does not exceed £5,000 or such larger sum as may be fixed by order of the Lord Chancellor) to hear and determine proceedings for an order under [section 2 of that Act] in relation to the deceased's estate.

(4) If a maintenance agreement is altered by a court on an application made in pursuance of subsection (1) above, the like consequences shall ensue as if the alteration had been made immediately before the death by agreement between the parties and for valuable consideration.

(5) The provisions of this section shall not render the personal representatives of the deceased liable for having distributed any part of the estate of the deceased after the expiration of the period of six months referred to in subsection (2) above on the ground that they ought to have taken into account the possibility that a court might permit an application by virtue of this section to be made by the surviving party after that period; but this subsection shall not prejudice any power to recover any part of the estate so distributed arising by virtue of the making of an order in pursuance of this section.

(6) Section 31(9) above shall apply for the purposes of subsection (2) above as it applies for the purposes of subsection (6) of section 31.

(7) Subsection (3) of [section 22 of the Inheritance (Provision for Family and Dependants) Act 1975 (which enables rules of court to provide for the transfer from a county court to the High Court or from the High court to a county court of proceedings for an order under section 2 of that Act) and paragraphs (a) and (b) of subsection (4)] of that section (provisions relating to proceedings commenced in county court before coming into force of order of the Lord Chancellor under that section ) shall apply in relation to proceedings consisting of any such application as is referred to in subsection (3) above as they apply in relation to [proceedings for an order under section 2 of that Act].

**Appointment**

Commencement order: SI 1973/1972.

**Derivation**

This section derived from the MPPA 1970, s 15.

**Amendment**

Sub-ss (3), (7): words in square brackets substituted by the I(PFD)A 1975, s 26(1).



**[2.135.1]**
**Keypoints**

- General
- Application for an order
- Time limits
- Jurisdiction
- Effect

### [2.135.2]
### General

Section 36 of the MCA 1973 enables the court to vary a maintenance agreement pursuant to the provisions of s 35 above, after the death of one of the parties, where that party has died domiciled in England and Wales.

### [2.135.3]
### Application for an order

An application under s 36 is made either: (a) in the High Court by originating summons out of the Principal Registry or any district registry; or (b) in a county court, by originating application, in Form M22[1].

Rule 3.3(2) of the FPR 1991 requires that an affidavit be filed by the applicant exhibiting a copy of the agreement, an official copy of the grant of representation to the deceased's estate, and of every testamentary document admitted to proof.

In addition the affidavit should state the following matters:

- whether the deceased died domiciled in England and Wales;
- the place and date of the parties' marriage and the name and status of the wife before the marriage;
- the name of every child of the family and of any other child for whom the agreement makes financial arrangements; and
  - (i) the date of birth of each such child who is still living (or, if it be the case, that he has attained 18) and the place where and the person with whom any such minor child is residing;
  - (ii) the date of death of any such child who has died since the agreement was made;
- whether there have been in any court any, previous proceedings with reference to the agreement or to the marriage or to the children of the family or any other children for whom the agreement makes financial arrangements, and the date and effect of any order or decree made in such proceedings;
- whether there have been in any court any proceedings by the applicant against the deceased's estate under the I(PFD)A 1975 and the date and effect of any order made in such proceedings;
- in the case of an application by the surviving party, the applicant's means;
- in the case of an application by the personal representatives of the deceased, the surviving party's means, so far as they are known to the applicant, and the information mentioned in sub-paragraphs (a),(b) and (c) of r 3.4(4) of the FPR 1991;
- the facts alleged by the applicant as justifying an alteration in the agreement and the nature of the alteration sought;
- if the application is made after the end of the period of six months from the date on which representation in regard to the deceased's estate was first taken out, the grounds on which the court's permission to entertain the application is sought[2].

The information mentioned in r 3.4(4) of the FPR 1991 is as follows:

(a) full particulars of the value of the deceased's estate for probate, after providing for the discharge of the funeral, testamentary and administration expenses, debts and liabilities, including the amount of the inheritance tax and interest thereon;

(b) the person or classes of persons beneficially interested in the estate (giving the names and addresses of all living beneficiaries) and the value of their interests so far as ascertained; and

(c) if such be the case, that any living beneficiary (naming him) is a minor or a patient within the meaning of FPR 1991, r.9.1 (a person who is incapable of managing and administering his property and affairs by reason of mental disorder within the meaning of the MeHA 1983).

CCR Ord 48, rr 3(1), 7 and 9 apply to an application under s 36 of the MCA 1973 as to an application under s 1 of the I(PFD)A 1975[3].

The district judge may at any stage of the proceedings direct that any person be added as a respondent to an application under r 3.3 of the FPR 1991, without prejudice to his powers under RSC Ord 15 (which deals with parties and other matters)[4].

A respondent who is a personal representative of the deceased must file an affidavit in answer within 14 days after the time limited for giving notice of intention to defend (eight days), stating the information mentioned in r 3.4(4) of the FPR 1991.

RSC Ord 15, r.13 applies to proceedings under r 3.3 of the FPR 1991 as if mentioned in that rule, with consequential amendments where the proceedings are in the county court as if reference were made to CCR Ord 5, r6[5].

If a respondent who is a personal representative of the deceased does not file an affidavit stating the matters mentioned in r 3.4(4) of the FPR 1991, the district judge may order him to do so[6].

A respondent who is not a personal representative of the deceased may, within 14 days after the time limited for giving notice of intention to defend, file an affidavit in answer to the application[7].

Every respondent who files an affidavit in answer to the application should at the same time lodge a copy, which will be served on the applicant[8].

By r 3.5(1)(a) of the FPR 1991, certain rules apply to applications under this section as to s 35 (see commentary to s 35 above).

Rule 2.66(1) and (2) of the FPR 1991 apply to applications under s 36 of the MCA 1973[9].

The FPR 1991 apply with the necessary modifications to an application under s 35 or s 36 of the MCA 1973, as if the application were a cause, the originating application or summons a petition, and the applicant the petitioner, subject to the exceptions noted under s 35 above[10].

'The deceased' in rr 3.3 and 3.4 of the FPR 1991 means the deceased party to the agreement to which the application relates[11].

1 See the FPR 1991, r 3.3(1) at para **[3.464]** below.
2 See the FPR 1991, r 3.3(2).
3 See the FPR 1991, r 3.3(3).
4 See the FPR 1991, r 3.4(1).
5 See the FPR 1991, r.3.4(2) and (3).
6 See the FPR 1991, r 3.4(5).
7 See the FPR 1991, r 3.4(6).
8 See the FPR 1991, r 3.4(7).
9 See the FPR 1991, r 3.5(1)(c).
10 See the FPR 1991, r 3.5(2).
11 See the FPR 1991, r 3.3(4).

## [2.135.4]
## Time limits

After six months from the date on which representation in regard to the estate of the deceased is first taken out, no application may be made under s 36 of the MCA 1973 except with the permission of the court (s 36(2)).

After that time, the personal representatives of the deceased will not be liable for any distribution of the estate on the ground that they ought to have taken into account the possibility of a court permitting a later application under s 36 (s 36(5)).

The above will not prejudice any power to recover any part of the estate so distributed (s 36(5)).

## [2.135.5]
## Jurisdiction

Section 36 of the MCA 1973 permits application for an order by the surviving party or the personal representatives of the deceased party under s 35 where:

- a qualifying maintenance agreement provides for the continuation of payments after the death of one of the parties; and
- that party dies domiciled in England and Wales (s 36(1)).

Notwithstanding s 36(3), county court jurisdiction is unlimited under s 36 of the MCA 1973, by virtue of art 2 of the High Court and County Courts Jurisdiction Order 1991, SI 1991/724.

Section 22 (3) and (4)(a) and (b) of the Inheritance (Provision for Family and Dependants) Act 1975 apply to an application in the county court as they do to an application under s 2 of the I(PFD)A 1975 (s 36(7)).

### [2.135.6]
### Effect

If a maintenance agreement is altered by a court on an application made under s 36 (1) of the MCA 1973, the effect on the agreement will be as if the alteration had been made immediately before the death, by agreement between the parties and for valuable consideration (s 36(4)).

### [2.136]

#### 37 Avoidance of transactions intended to prevent or reduce financial relief

(1) For the purposes of this section 'financial relief' means relief under any of the provisions of sections 22, 23, 24, [24B,] 27, 31 (except subsection (6)) and 35 above, and any reference in this section to defeating a person's claim for financial relief is a reference to preventing financial relief from being granted to that person, or to that person for the benefit of a child of the family, or reducing the amount of any financial relief which might be so granted, or frustrating or impeding the enforcement of any order which might be or has been made at his instance under any of those provisions.

(2) Where proceedings for financial relief are brought by one person against another, the court may, on the application of the first-mentioned person—

- (a) if it is satisfied that the other party to the proceedings is, with the intention of defeating the claim for financial relief, about to make any disposition or to transfer out of the jurisdiction or otherwise deal with any property, make such order as it thinks fit for restraining the other party from so doing or otherwise for protecting the claim;
- (b) if it is satisfied that the other party has, with that intention, made a reviewable disposition and that if the disposition were set aside financial relief or different financial relief would be granted to the applicant, make an order setting aside the disposition;
- (c) if it is satisfied, in a case where an order has been obtained under any of the provisions mentioned in subsection (1) above by the applicant against the other party, that the other party has, with that intention, made a reviewable disposition, make an order setting aside the disposition;

and an application for the purposes of paragraph (b) above shall be made in the proceedings for the financial relief in question.

(3) Where the court makes an order under subsection (2)(b) or (c) above setting aside a disposition it shall give such consequential directions as it thinks fit for giving effect to the order (including directions requiring the making of any payments or the disposal of any property).

(4) Any disposition made by the other party to the proceedings for financial relief in question (whether before or after the commencement of those proceedings) is a reviewable disposition for the purposes of subsection (2)(b) and (c) above unless it was made for valuable consideration (other than marriage) to a person who, at the time of the disposition, acted in relation to it in good faith and without notice of any intention on the part of the other party to defeat the applicant's claim for financial relief.

(5) Where an application is made under this section with respect to a disposition which took place less than three years before the date of the application or with respect

to a disposition or other dealing with property which is about to take place and the court is satisfied—

(a) in a case falling within subsection (2)(a) or (b) above, that the disposition or other dealing would (apart from this section) have the consequence, or

(b) in a case falling within subsection (2)(c) above, that the disposition has had the consequence,

of defeating the applicant's claim for financial relief, it shall be presumed, unless the contrary is shown, that the person who disposed of or is about to dispose of or deal with the property did so or, as the case may be, is about to do so, with the intention of defeating the applicant's claim for financial relief.

(6) In this section 'disposition' does not include any provision contained in a will or codicil but, with that exception, includes any conveyance, assurance or gift of property of any description, whether made by an instrument or otherwise.

(7) This section does not apply to a disposition made before 1st January 1968.

**Appointment**

Commencement order: SI 1973/1972.

**Amendment**

Sub-s (1): WRPA 1999, s 19, Sch 3.



## [2.136.1]
## Keypoints

- General
- Proceedings for financial relief
- Form of application
- Intention to defeat the claim for financial relief
- What is a disposition
- Reviewable dispositions
- Examples of the use of s 37
- Disposing of a tenancy
- Discretionary remedy
- Relationship with the inherent jurisdiction

## [2.136.2]
## General

Section 37 of the MCA 1973 allows the court to restrict dispositions of property which have been made or are about to be made with the intention of defeating a claim for financial relief. The section has two specific and distinct functions. First, it enables the court to make prospective orders to prevent the future transfer, disposal of or other dealing with property (s 37(2)(a)). Secondly, the court may make retrospective orders setting aside any disposition which has already been made if that would result in a different order for financial relief (s 37(2)(b)) or as a means of removing an impediment to the enforcement of an earlier order (s 37(2)(c)). The prospective powers are wider ranging than the retrospective powers since s 37(2)(a) allows the court to restrain a party not only from disposing of or transferring property but also when he is about to 'otherwise deal with' property. The retrospective powers only allow the court to set aside a disposition. The court retains an inherent jurisdiction to entertain such an application[1].

It is possible to apply for an order pursuant to s 37 of the MCA 1973 where a spouse has applied for a pension sharing order where the other spouse transfers those rights into an arrangement which is already subject to an earmarking order, and thus precludes the court from making a pension sharing order[2].

For a discussion of this topic, see generally *Rayden and Jackson on Divorce and Family Matters* (17th edn, 1997), vol 1, ch 20 and the Noter-up thereto.

1 As expressed by Lincoln J in *Shipman v Shipman* [1991] FCR 628, [1991] 1 FLR 250 following *Richards v Richards* [1984] AC 174.

2 As amended by the WRPA 1999, Sch 3, para 9.

### [2.136.3]
### Proceedings for financial relief

Proceedings for financial relief must already exist before an application can be made under s 37 of the MCA 1973. It is not possible to make either a free-standing application under s 37 or an application supported by an undertaking that substantive proceedings will be issued. Where it is not possible to commence proceedings it may be possible to obtain relief under the inherent jurisdiction of the court. The term 'financial relief' is defined in s 37(1)

### [2.136.4]
### Form of application

Rule 2.68 of the FPR 1991 provides for the form of the application for an order under s 37 of the MCA 1973. The application will usually be without notice to the other party and supported by affidavit[1].

1 Guidance as to the practice in the Family Division in ancillary relief cases is given in *W v H (ex parte injunctions)* [2000] 3 FCR 481, [2000] 2 FLR 927.

### [2.136.5]
### Intention to defeat the claim for financial relief

Before the court can make an order under s 37 of the MCA 1973 it must be satisfied that a disposal of property has been made or is about to be made and that the intention is to defeat the claim for financial relief.

Each case should be viewed subjectively and the question of whether there is such an intention is a question of fact for the judge. The intention to defeat the claim 'does not have to be the sole or even his dominant intention as long as it plays a substantial part in his intentions as a whole'[1].

The court will accept the normal inference that a man intends the consequences of his actions[2].

An intention to defeat the claim for financial relief is presumed to exist by s 37(5) if the disposition took place less than three years prior to the application and it has (or in the absence of a s37 order would have) the effect of reducing the claim for financial relief. The presumption can be rebutted.

The court can infer that a reviewable disposition is about to take place by reference to earlier dealings with the property and the conduct of the party[3].

The standard of proof required is that the judge must be 'satisfied' that the disposition was made with the intention of defeating the claim for financial relief[4].

1 Per Nourse LJ in *Kemmis v Kemmis (Welland and others intervening)* [1988] 2 FLR 223, CA.
2 See *Sherry v Sherry* [1991] 1 FLR 307, CA.
3 See *Quartermain v Quartermain* (1974) 4 Fam Law 156, FD.
4 See *K v K (Avoidance of Reviewable Disposition)* (1982) 4 FLR 31, CA per Ormrod LJ; and *Purba v Purba* [2000] 1 FCR 652, [2000] 1 FLR 444, CA.

### [2.136.6]
### What is a 'disposition'

'Disposition' is defined widely but excludes any provision made under a will (s 37(6)). Dispositions of property of any description are subject to s 37 of the MCA 1973 whether the property is real or personal and regardless of whether the property is in England and Wales[1].

To fall within the scope of s 37 there must be a positive act; refusing or omitting to deal with property (such as a refusal to sign a letter agreeing to the sale of assets) does not amount to 'dealing with' property for the purposes of s 37(2)(a)[2].

A transaction at an undervalue is likely to be a reviewable disposition[3].

The use of moneys to purchase a property or to pay off debts does amount to a disposition; there is nothing to support the proposition that a disposition can only be to a third party[4].

No order can be made under s 37 in relation to a disposition made by a company which is not an alter-ego of the party who had engineered the transaction[5].

1 See *Hamlin v Hamlin* [1986] 1 FLR 61, CA.
2 See *Crittenden v Crittenden* [1990] 2 FLR 361, CA.
3 See *Sherry v Sherry* [1991] 2 FLR 307, CA.
4 See *Shipman v Shipman* [1991] 1 FLR 250, FD.
5 See *McGladdery v McGladdery* [1999] 2 FLR 1102 at 1112F, CA per Thorpe LJ.



## [2.136.7]
## Reviewable dispositions

Where there is an intention to defeat the claim for financial relief any disposition is reviewable provided that where a disposition is made for valuable consideration to a person who acts in good faith and without notice of the intention to defeat the claim for financial relief it is not subject to review[1]. Notice of the intention can be constructive or actual[2]. In the case of *Green v Green*[3] a bank had taken a charge over land in good faith and thus was able to claim the protection of s 37(4); the judge held that the Applicant wife could not obviate s 37(4) by seeking an order that the charge be set aside as a consequential direction under s 37(3). In *Le Foe v Le Foe and Woolwich plc*[4], although it was found that the husband had mortgaged the home with the intention of defeating the wife's claim, the mortgagees had not been fixed with actual or constructive notice, and so the s 37 claim was refused. The judge found that it would be a quantum leap to conclude from constructive notice of the wife's presence that there was also constructive notice of the husband's intention to defeat her claim.

1 See the MCA 1973, s 37(4) above.
2 See *Kemmis v Kemmis (Welland and others intervening)* [1988] 2 FLR 223, CA.
3 [1981] 1 All ER 97.
4 [2001] 2 FLR 970, [2001] Fam Law 739.

## [2.136.8]
## Examples of the use of s 37

- To prevent the transfer of assets belonging to a partnership operated by the husband and his brother to a company based in the Isle of Man – *Blome v Blome*[1];
- To prevent the sale of the former matrimonial home or, if sold, the disposal of the proceeds – *Haywood v Haywood*[2];
- To restrain a husband from disposing of a lump sum payment received by way of severance pay – *Shipman v Shipman*[3];
- To set aside a mortgage between the husband and a bank which had been entered into subsequent to the wife's registration of a *lis pendens* under s 5 of the Land Charges Act 1972 – *Perez-Adamson v Perez Rivas*[4].

Section 37 cannot be used to set aside the sale of a business asset where the funds realised are paid back into the business bank account for normal business purposes[5].

It is unnecessary to make an order under s 37 to set aside a transfer of funds from a husband to his relatives. The money does not cease to be the husband's property simply because it is moved into another account where the recipient holds it as a bare trustee[6].

1 (1976) 6 Fam Law 215, FD.
2 (1977) 7 Fam Law 215, CA.
3 [1991] 1 FLR 250, FD.
4 [1987] 2 FLR 472, CA.
5 See *H v H & W and Barclays Bank Ltd* (1979) 10 Fam Law 152, FD. See also *McGladdery v McGladdery* [1999] 2 FLR 1102, CA.
6 See *Purba v Purba* [2000] 1 FCR 652, [2000] 1 FLR 444, CA.

## [2.136.9]
### Disposing of a tenancy

Serving a notice to quit a periodic tenancy can be a disposition which may be restrained under s 37(2)(a) of the MCA 1973 (under the provision that a party is dealing with the property)[1]. Once the tenancy has expired the court has no power to revive it under s 37(2)(b)[2]. Once the tenancy has come to an end there is no property to be preserved.

1 See *Bater and Bater v Greenwich London Borough Council* [1999] 3 FCR 254, [1999] 2 FLR 993, CA.
2 See *Newlon Housing Trust v Alsulaimen* [1999] 1 AC 313, HL.

## [2.136.10]
### Discretionary remedy

Once the court has found that a disposition is reviewable it may have to balance the hardship likely to be suffered by the parties when deciding whether or not to make to the order[1].

On an interim basis the question for the court is which course of action is likely to cause the least hardship should it turn out to be wrong[2].

It is essential expressly to provide for the continuation of a s 37 injunction if that is what the parties intend. The failure to make this provision cannot be remedied under the slip rule[3].

1 See *Sherry v Sherry* [1991] 1 FLR 307 at 314, CA per Butler-Sloss LJ.
2 See *Nikitenko v Leboeuf Lambe Greene & Macrae (A Firm)* (1999) The Times, 2 January, Ch D.
3 See *Langley v Langley* [1994] 1 FLR 383, CA.

## [2.136.11]
### Relationship with the inherent jurisdiction

Where the court finds that there is no intention to defeat the claim for financial relief it cannot make an injunction under s 37 of the MCA 1973. The court does retain the inherent jurisdiction 'to preserve specific assets which are the subject matter of proceedings pending the determination of the issues involved'[1]. In *Shipman v Shipman*[2] Anthony Lincoln J held that this inherent jurisdiction to restrain parties was extant.

It is also open to the parties to seek a freezing injunction (formerly *Mareva*) under CPR r 25.1. Judges of the county court have the power to grant this relief provided that they are exercising jurisdiction in family proceedings within the meaning of Pt V of the MFPA 1984[3].

The distinction between freezing injunctions and s 37 MCA orders is narrow. In most circumstances the procedure under s 37 will be preferable since the application is made supported by affidavit. In cases where there are no ongoing proceedings for financial relief or where it is impossible to prove the requisite intention the inherent jurisdiction or the powers to grant freezing injunctions may be raised.

Under s 37 there is no requirement for an undertaking that any loss suffered by the party restrained will be paid should the order turn out not to have been necessary. Schedule 2 of the draft form of freezing injunction envisages that such undertakings will be made.

For further information on freezing injunctions, search orders (formerly '*Anton Pillers*'), Writ Ne Exeat Regno and *Bayer v Winter Orders*, see *Rayden and Jackson on Divorce and Family Matters* (17th edn, 1997), Vol 1, ch 20.

1 Per Ormrod LJ in *Roche v Roche* (1981) 11 Fam Law 243.
2 [1991] 1 FLR 250, FD.
3 See the County Court Remedies Regulations 1991, SI 1991/1222. See also *Khreino v Khreino (No 2) (court's power to grant injunctions)* [2000] 1 FCR 80, [2000] Fam Law 611, CA.

[2.137]

## 38 Orders for repayment in certain cases of sums paid after cessation of order by reason of remarriage

(1) Where—

(a) a periodical payments or secured periodical payments order in favour of a party to a marriage (hereafter in this section referred to as 'a payments order') has ceased to have effect by reason of the remarriage of that party, and

(b) the person liable to make payments under the order or his or her personal representatives made payments in accordance with it in respect of a period after the date of the remarriage in the mistaken belief that the order was still subsisting,

the person so liable or his or her personal representatives shall not be entitled to bring proceedings in respect of a cause of action arising out of the circumstances mentioned in paragraphs (a) and (b) above against the person entitled to payments under the order or her or his personal representatives, but may instead make an application against that person or her or his personal representatives under this section.

(2) On an application under this section the court may order the respondent to pay to the applicant a sum equal to the amount of the payments made in respect of the period mentioned in subsection (1)(b) above or, if it appears to the court that it would be unjust to make that order, it may either order the respondent to pay to the applicant such lesser sum as it thinks fit or dismiss the application.

(3) An application under this section may be made in proceedings in the High Court or a county court for leave to enforce, or the enforcement of, payment of arrears under the order in question, but when not made in such proceedings shall be made to a county court; and accordingly references in this section to the court are references to the High Court or a county court, as the circumstances require.

(4) The jurisdiction conferred on a county court by this section shall be exercisable notwithstanding that by reason of the amount claimed in the application the jurisdiction would not but for this subsection be exercisable by a county court.

(5) An order under this section for the payment of any sum may provide for the payment of that sum by instalments of such amount as may be specified in the order.

(6) [A justices' chief executive] to whom any payments under a payments order are required to be made, and the collecting officer under an attachment of earnings order made to secure payments under a payments order, shall not be liable—

(a) in the case of [the justices' chief executive], for any act done by him in pursuance of the payments order after the date on which that order ceased to have effect by reason of the remarriage of the person entitled to payments under it, and

(b) in the case of the collecting officer, for any act done by him after that date in accordance with any enactment or rule of court specifying how payments made to him in compliance with the attachment of earnings order are to be dealt with,

if, but only if, the act was one which he would have been under a duty to do had the payments order not so ceased to have effect and the act was done before notice in writing of the fact that the person so entitled had remarried was given to him by or on behalf of that person, the person liable to make payments under the payments order or the personal representatives of either of those persons.

(7) In this section 'collecting officer', in relation to an attachment of earnings order, means the officer of the High Court, the registrar of a county court or [a justices' chief executive] to whom a person makes payments in compliance with the order.

**Appointment**

Commencement order: SI 1973/1972.

**Derivation**
This section derived from the MPPA 1970, ss 22, 34(1).

**Amendment**
Sub-ss (6), (7): AJA 1999, s 90(1), Sch 13.

### [2.137.1]
### Keypoints

- General
- Scope of section
- Application for an order
- CCR Ord 3, r 4

### [2.137.2]
### General

This section provides for the recovery of sums paid under a maintenance order after the remarriage of the recipient.

### [2.137.3]
### Scope of section

An order for periodical payments ceases to have effect upon the remarriage of the party entitled to receive the payments ordered[1].

However, there is no specific duty imposed by the MCA 1973 on the payee to notify the payer of any remarriage, nor to remit any money paid thereafter. Consequently, the payer could go on paying maintenance payments which he is under no obligation to make and which the payee is not entitled to receive.

Section 38 of the MCA 1973 applies where an order for secured or unsecured periodical payments in favour of a party to the marriage has ceased to have effect because of the remarriage of that party, and the person liable to make the payments, or his personal representatives, continues to make the payments after the remarriage in the mistaken belief that the order is still subsisting (s 38(1)).

The section only applies in the circumstances outlined in s 38(1). It has no application at all, for example, where, because of a material change in circumstances the payer would be bound to succeed on an application to reduce or discharge the amount of the order.

Note that an order for unsecured periodical payments ceases to have effect upon the death of the person ordered to make the payments, although an order for secured periodical payments may continue in force notwithstanding such death[2].

1 See the MCA 1973 s 21(1)(a) at para **[2.115]** above.
2 See the MCA 1973, s 28(1) at para **[2.126]** above.

### [2.137.4]
### Application for an order

Where s 38(1) of the MCA 1973 applies, a payer is not entitled to bring proceedings in respect of a cause of action arising from the circumstances against the person entitled to the payment, or her personal representatives, but may instead make an application under s 38 (s 38(1)).

Note that a periodical payments order, whether secured or unsecured, must come to an end on the death of the person in whose favour the order is made[1].

Where an application is made under s 38 the court may order the repayment of some or all of the overpayment. The court is not obliged to order any repayment at all. If it considers it unjust to make an order it may dismiss the application (s 38(2)).

The court may make an order by instalments (s 38(5)).

The application may be made in proceedings in the High Court or a county court for leave to enforce, or for the enforcement of, payments of arrears under the order in question, or in relation to an application to vary or discharge the order, in which case Form M11 with affidavit in support is appropriate (cf FPR 1991, r 2.52 et seq).

Where not made in such proceedings, the application must be made to a county court (s 38(3)).

This, notwithstanding the usual rules about limits to the amount of claims in the county court (s 38(4)).

Section 38(6) and (7) deal with the responsibilities of the clerk to the magistrates where an order has been registered with that court.

When the application is to the county court and is not made in proceedings for enforcement of, or leave to enforce, arrears, then it should probably be made by originating application under the provisions of CCR Ord 3, r 4.

1 See the MCA 1973, s 28(1) at para **[2.126]** above.



## [2.137.5]
## CCR Ord 3, r 4

*Originating applications*

An originating application must be in writing, and should state:

(a) the order applied for and sufficient particulars to show the grounds on which the applicant claims to be entitled to the order;
(b) the names and addresses of the persons (if any) intended to be served or that no person is intended to be served, and
(c) the applicant's address for service[1].

The applicant must file:

(a) the originating application together with as many copies as there are respondents; and
(b) a request for the issue of the originating application[2].

On the filing of the documents mentioned in paragraph (1) the proper officer shall:

(a) enter the originating application in the records of the court and fix the return day;
(b) prepare a notice to each respondent of the return day and annex to each such notice a copy of the application, and
(c) deliver a plaint note to the applicant[3].

The return day shall be a day fixed for the hearing of the originating application or, if the court so directs, a day fixed for a pre-trial review[4].

1 CCR Ord 3, r 4(2).
2 CCR Ord 3, r 4(3).
3 CCR Ord 3, r 4(4).
4 CCR Ord 3, r 4(5).

## [2.138]

### 39 Settlement, etc, made in compliance with a property adjustment order may be avoided on bankruptcy of settlor

The fact that a settlement or transfer of property had to be made in order to comply with a property adjustment order shall not prevent that settlement or transfer from being [a transaction in respect of which an order may be made under [section 339 or 340 of the Insolvency Act 1986] (transfers at an undervalue and preferences)].

**Appointment**

Commencement order: SI 1973/1972.

**Derivation**

This section derived from the MPPA 1970, s 23.

**Amendment**

First words in square brackets substituted by the IA 1985, s 235, Sch 8, para 23; words in square brackets therein substituted by the IA 1986, s 439(2), Sch 14.

## [2.138.1]
### Keypoints

- General
- Bankruptcy
- Transfers at undervalue
- Preferences

## [2.138.2]
### General

Section 39 of the MCA 1973 provides that the fact that a settlement or transfer of property is made following a property adjustment order does not prevent it from being a transfer at an undervalue or a preference, for the purposes of the Insolvency Act 1986.

## [2.138.3]
### Bankruptcy

The effect of an adjudication that a spouse is bankrupt is to vest his assets in his trustee in bankruptcy[1]. The factors set out in s 15 (which is not exclusive) of the TLATA 1996[2] gives the court some scope for change in current court practice when considering an application for sale at the request of a party, even where a Bankruptcy Order has been made against a party or indeed a creditor of a spouse.

Despite this, the court in family proceedings has jurisdiction to make an order for a lump sum or a property adjustment order against the husband whilst he remains bankrupt[3].

The property of a bankrupt vests in his trustee, however, and the court has no power under the MCA 1973, s 24 to make a property adjustment order against the trustee in bankruptcy[4].

Under r 12(3) of the Insolvency Rules 1986, SI 1986/1925 orders made in 'family proceedings' do not give rise to debts provable in the bankruptcy. The term 'family proceedings' has the same meaning as under Part V of the MFPA 1984, that is to say, proceedings assigned for the time being to the Family Division[5].

As to the apparent inconsistency between the Insolvency Act 1986, s 382 and the Insolvency Rules 1986, r 12.3 and as to the possible invalidity of r 12.3, see *Woodley v Woodley*[6].

A lump sum is not a debt provable in the bankruptcy of the spouse against whom an order for a lump sum has been made. Furthermore, neither is an order for costs made in ancillary relief proceedings[7]. However, upon discharge from bankruptcy, debts and liabilities arising under orders in 'family proceedings' are not released save in the circumstances set out in the IA 1986, s 281.

Where a person has been made bankrupt and that person has provision under a pension then on retirement that provision becomes payable to the Trustee in Bankruptcy and not to the discharged bankrupt himself[8]. Clearly this has the potential to negate the effect of an earmarking order. However, there is statutory protection on bankruptcy for pension rights in approved schemes which are excluded from the bankrupt's estate[9].

1 See the IA 1986, s 306 at para **[2.288]** below.

2 Set out at para **[2.466]** below.

3 See eg *Hellyer v Hellyer* [1997] 1 FCR 340 , [1996] 2 FLR 579, CA.

4 See *Re Holliday (a bankrupt), ex p Trustee of the Property of the Bankrupt v Bankrupt* [1981] Ch 405, [1980] 3 All ER 385, CA.

5 See the MFPA 1984, s 32.

6 [1992] 2 FLR 417 at 422G to 432B, CA.

7 See r 12.3(2) of the Insolvency Rules 1986 – debt not provable 'any obligation arising under an order made in family proceedings'. Although a court does have jurisdiction to make a bankruptcy order on the service of a petition: *Levy v Legal Services Commission* [2001] 1 All ER 895, [2001] 1 FCR 178, CA.

8 See *Re Landau (a bankrupt), Pointer v Landau* [1998] Ch 223, sub nom *Re L (a bankrupt)* [1997] 2 FLR 660; *Jones v Patel and London Borough of Brent* [1999] BPIR 509; and *Krasner v Dennison; Lesser v Lawrence* [2001] Ch 76, [2000] 3 All ER 234, CA.

9 See the WRPA 1999, s 11.

## [2.138.4]
## Transfers at undervalue

Where someone is adjudged bankrupt who has at a relevant time entered into a transaction at undervalue or given a preference, his trustee may apply to the Bankruptcy Court to restore the position which previously obtained[1].

'Transfers at undervalue' include gifts, transactions in consideration of marriage, and any transaction the value of which is significantly less (in money or money's worth) than the value of the consideration provided[2].

For transfers at undervalue, 'relevant time' means the five years leading up to the presentation of the Bankruptcy petition, unless the transaction was more than two years before the presentation and the person was then and remained solvent, notwithstanding the transaction[3].

Note that the two year provision does not apply in the case of a transfer to an 'associate', which includes a husband, wife or relative[4].

Where the court orders the transfer of property by a person against whom a bankruptcy petition has been presented, the order is a disposition by the bankrupt and consequently void[5].

On application by the husband's trustee in bankruptcy to set aside a transfer of property order in financial relief proceedings, it was held that the only consideration provided by the wife as transferee was her assumption of sole liability under the mortgage: since the value of that consideration was significantly less than that provided by the husband the transfer was at an undervalue for the purpose of s 339(2) and (3)(c) of the Insolvency Act 1986[6].

Where a consent order was made as to the proceeds of matrimonial home, and the husband, unbeknown to wife, was insolvent, it was held that the wife did give valuable consideration[7].

1 See the IA 1986, ss 339 and 340 at paras **[2.323]** and **[2.324]** below.
2 See the IA 1986, s 339(3).
3 See the IA 1986, s 341(2) at para **[2.325]** below.
4 See the IA 1986, s 435(2).
5 See the IA 1986, s 284 at para **[2.266]** below.
6 See *Re Kumar (a bankrupt), ex p Lewis v Kumar* [1993] 2 All ER 700, [1993] 1 WLR 224.
7 See *Re Abbott (a bankrupt), ex p Trustee of the Property of the Bankrupt v Abbott* [1983] Ch 45, [1982] 3 All ER 181, DC.

## [2.138.5]
## Preferences

'Preference' means favouring a given creditor, or doing or suffering to be done anything which has the effect of putting another person in a better position in relation to the bankruptcy than they would have been in if that thing had not been done[1].

If the debtor can show that he was not influenced by a desire to achieve the particular result which has given rise to the suggested preference, he may avoid his act being so held[2].

There is, however, a presumption that he was so influenced when the recipient is an 'associate'[3]. 'Associate' includes husband, wife or relative[4].

The time limit in relation to setting aside preferences is six months, or two years in the case of an associate[5]. The fact that something has been done in pursuance of a court order does not, without more, prevent it constituting a preference[6].

1 See the IA 1986, s 340(3) at para **[2.324]** below.
2 See the IA 1986, s 340(4).
3 See the IA 1986, s 340(5).
4 See the IA 1986, s 435(2).
5 See the IA 1986, s 341(1) at para **[2.325]** below.
6 See the IA 1986, s 340(6).

## [2.139]

### 40 Payments, etc, under order made in favour of person suffering from mental disorder

Where the court makes an order under this Part of this Act requiring payments (including a lump sum payment) to be made, or property to be transferred, to a party to a marriage and the court is satisfied that the person in whose favour the order is made is incapable, by reason of mental disorder within the meaning of the Mental Health Act 1959, of managing and administering his or her property and affairs then, subject to any order, direction or authority made or given in relation to that person under Part VIII of that Act, the court may order the payments to be made, or as the case may be, the property to be transferred, to such persons having charge of that person as the court may direct.

**Appointment**
Commencement order: SI 1973/1972.

**Derivation**
This section derived from the MPPA 1970, s 26.

## [2.139.1]
### Keypoints

- General
- Scope of section
- Power of the court
- Procedure

## [2.139.2]
### General

Section 40 of the MCA 1973 permits payments or property transfers under an ancillary relief order to a person incapable of managing their affairs (now) under the Mental Health Act 1983, Pt VII to be made to whoever has charge of that person.

## [2.139.3]
### Scope of section

Section 40 of the MCA 1973 applies where the court is satisfied that the person in whose favour the order is made is incapable by reason of mental disorder within the meaning of the Mental Health Act 1983, of managing and administering his or her property or affairs (s 40).

Any order made under this section is subject to any order, direction or authority made or given in relation to the person with a mental disorder under the MeHA 1983 (s 40).

The fact that one party is mentally disordered and that a receiver of his estate has been appointed does not debar the other party from claiming and obtaining orders for financial provision and property adjustment[1].

For definitions of what are now termed 'mental disorders', 'severe mental impairment', 'mental impairment' and 'psychopathic disorder', see s 1(2) of the MeHA 1983.

1 See *CL v CFW* [1928] P 223.

## [2.139.4]
### Power of the court

The power given to the court under the MCA 1973, s 40 is permissive. The court may order the payments to be made or property to be transferred to such persons having charge of the person with a disability as the court may direct (s 40).

The discretion appears wide, particularly in relation to who may be deemed 'such persons having charge'. In practice this may often be the local authority.

'Property and affairs' is restricted to property and financial affairs[1].

1 See *Re W (EEM)* [1971] Ch 123, [1970] 2 All ER 502.

## [2.139.5]
## Procedure

For the procedure to be followed generally when a party is under a disability, see Pt IX of the FPR 1991 (at para **[3.510]** et seq below).

A person under disability (ie A person who is a minor or a patient[1]) may commence and prosecute any family proceedings only by his or her next friend, and may defend such proceedings only by his guardian ad litem[2].

A patient, as defined by r 9.1 of the FPR 1991, is a person who, by reason of mental disorder within the meaning of the Mental Health Act 1983, is incapable of managing and administering his property and affairs[3].

Where the person under disability is a patient, the person (if any) authorised under the MeHA 1983, Pt VII to conduct legal proceedings on his behalf, is entitled to be next friend subject (unless he is the Official Solicitor) to lodging with the petition his written consent to act as next friend and an office copy of the order of the Court of Protection under the MeHA 1983, Pt VII[4].

Whether any person is authorised under the MeHA 1983 may be ascertained at the Court of Protection.

If no person has been so authorised then the Official Solicitor becomes guardian ad litem of the patient if he has consented to act. If the Official Solicitor does not consent to act or in any other case, then application may be made on behalf of the patient for the appointment of a guardian ad litem[5].

Where the Official Solicitor acts, or is entitled to act, application may be made for the appointment of some other person on not less than four days' notice to the Official Solicitor[6].

Such an application is by summons or, in county court proceedings, on notice to a district judge.

Where no person is authorised under the MeHA 1983, Pt VII, the proposed next friend or guardian (unless he is the Official Solicitor) must lodge his written consent to act and a certificate by the solicitor for the patient certifying:

(i) that he knows or believes the petitioner to be a patient, giving the grounds of his knowledge or belief;

(ii) that no person is authorised under the MeHA 1983, Pt VII; and

(iii) that the proposed next friend or guardian has no interest in the cause or matter adverse to that of the patient and that he is a proper person to be next friend or guardian[7].

There is no limitation on the choice of next friend except, in the case of a patient, where a person is authorised under Pt VII of the MeHA 1983. In the absence of such a person and save where the Official Solicitor has agreed to act, it is desirable, where possible, for the next friend to be a relative or friend of the person under disability.

As to the function of the Official Solicitor as children's guardian, see *Re Taylor's Application*[8].

1 See the FPR 1991, r 9.1, *Essential Family Practice*, Vol 2 – Children, Pt 3.
2 See the FPR 1991, r 9.2(1).
3 See *Re E (Mental Health Patient)* [1985] 1 All ER 609, [1985] 1 WLR 245, CA.
4 See the FPR 1991, r 9.2(3).
5 See the FPR 1991, r 9.2(4) and *Practice Note (official solicitor: declaratory proceedings: medical and welfare decisions for adults who lack capacity)* [2001] 2 FCR 569, [2001] 2 FLR 158 (set out in Vol 2 at para **[4.1062]**).
6 See the FPR 1991, r 9.2(4).
7 See the FPR 1991, r 9.2(2) and (7).
8 [1972] 2 QB 369, [1972] 2 All ER 873, CA.

PART 2
MCA 1973

**[2.139A]**

### 40A Appeals relating to pension sharing orders which have taken effect

(1) Subsections (2) and (3) below apply where an appeal against a pension sharing order is begun on or after the day on which the order takes effect.

(2) If the pension sharing order relates to a person's rights under a pension arrangement, the appeal court may not set aside or vary the order if the person responsible for the pension arrangement has acted to his detriment in reliance on the taking effect of the order.

(3) If the pension sharing order relates to a person's shareable state scheme rights, the appeal court may not set aside or vary the order if the Secretary of State has acted to his detriment in reliance on the taking effect of the order.

(4) In determining for the purposes of subsection (2) or (3) above whether a person has acted to his detriment in reliance on the taking effect of the order, the appeal court may disregard any detriment which in its opinion is insignificant.

(5) Where subsection (2) or (3) above applies, the appeal court may make such further orders (including one or more pension sharing orders) as it thinks fit for the purpose of putting the parties in the position it considers appropriate.

(6) Section 24C above only applies to a pension sharing order under this section if the decision of the appeal court can itself be the subject of an appeal.

(7) In subsection (2) above, the reference to the person responsible for the pension arrangement is to be read in accordance with section 25D(4) above.

**Amendment**

Inserted by the WRPA 1999, s 19. Date in force: 1 December 2000: see SI 2000/1116.

**[2.140]**

## PART IV
## MISCELLANEOUS AND SUPPLEMENTAL

### 52 Interpretation

(1) In this Act—

…

'child', in relation to one or both of the parties to a marriage, includes an illegitimate … child of that party or, as the case may be, of both parties;

'child of the family', in relation to the parties to a marriage, means—

(a) a child of both of those parties; and

(b) any other child, not being a child who [is placed with those parties as foster parents] by a local authority or voluntary organisation, who has been treated by both of those parties as a child of their family;

'the court' (except where the context otherwise requires) means the High Court or, where a county court has jurisdiction by virtue of [Part V of the Matrimonial and Family Proceedings Act 1984], a county court;

…

'education' includes training.

['maintenance assessment' has the same meaning as it has in the Child Support Act 1991 by virtue of section 54 of that Act as read with any regulations in force under that section.]

(2) In this Act—

(a) references to financial provision orders, periodical payments and secured periodical payments orders and orders for the payment of a lump sum, and references to property adjustment orders, shall be construed in accordance with section 21 above; and—

(i) in the case of a financial provision order or periodical payments order, as including (except where the context otherwise requires) references to an interim periodical payments order under section 22A or 23 above; and

(ii) in the case of a financial provision order or order for the payment of a lump sum, as including (except where the context otherwise requires) references to an interim order for the payment of a lump sum under section 22A or 23 above; and

(aa) references to pension sharing orders shall be construed in accordance with section 21A above; and

(b) references to orders for maintenance pending suit and to interim orders for maintenance shall be construed respectively in accordance with section 22 and section 27(5) above.

(3) For the avoidance of doubt it is hereby declared that references in this Act to remarriage include references to a marriage which is by law void or voidable.

(4) Except where the contrary intention is indicated, references in this Act to any enactment include references to that enactment as amended, extended or applied by or under any subsequent enactment, including this Act.

**Appointment**

Commencement order: SI 1973/1972.

**Derivation**

Sub-ss (1), (3), as originally enacted, derived from the MPPA 1970, s 27(1), (2); sub-s (4) derived from the MPPA 1970, s 27(3), and the MP(PM)A 1972, s 5(2).

**Amendment**

Sub-s (1): definition 'adopted' repealed and words omitted in definition 'child' repealed by the CA 1975, s 108(1)(b), Sch 4, Pt I; in definition 'child of the family' words in square brackets substituted by the ChA 1989, s 108(4), Sch 12, para 33; definition 'the court' substituted by the MFPA 1984, s 46(1), Sch 1; final definition omitted repealed by the ChA 1989, s 108(7), Sch 15, definition 'maintenance assessment' inserted by SI 1993/623, art 2, Sch 1, para 4. Sub-s (2): WRPA 1999, s 19. Date in force: 1 December 2000: see SI 2000/1116.



## [2.140.1]
## Keypoint

- Scope

## [2.140.2]
## Scope

Pension sharing orders once they have taken effect (bearing in mind the provisions provided for by the regulations) will be extremely hard to set aside or appeal. The court will have to consider whether the person responsible for the pension sharing arrangement has acted to their detriment.

A pension sharing order will only come into effect seven days after the end of a period for filing a notice of appeal against the order has elapsed, ie total time limit of 21 days. The effect of serving a notice of appeal within that time limit is to stay the order until the hearing of the appeal[1].

1 See reg 9 of the Divorce etc (Pensions) Regulations 2000, SI 2000/1123 at para **[3.650]** below.

# Inheritance (Provision for Family and Dependants) Act 1975

PART 2 I(PFD)A 1975

Contents



*An Act to make fresh provisions for empowering the court to make orders for the making out of the estate of a deceased person of provision for the spouse, former spouse, child, child of the family or dependant of that person; and for matters connected therewith*

[12th November 1975]

**[2.141]**
**Introduction**

Proceedings under the Inheritance (Provision for Family and Dependants) Act 1975

('I(PFD)A 1975') are civil proceedings. They may be heard in either the Family Division or the Chancery Division. County courts have jurisidiction to hear matters under this Act; that jurisdiction is not limited by the quantum of the claim[1].

With the coming into force of the CPR 1998 the principle guiding regulations are found in Sch 1 to those rules[2]. This applies to both proceedings in the High Court and the county court.

The proceedings are to be heard in chambers. This is a departure from the general rule expressed in CPR 1998, Pt 39.2(1) that civil proceedings are usually heard in open court. Under the first *Practice Direction* issued under this Part (PD39) I(PFD)A 1975 applications should at first be listed as private matters.

Enforcement of I(PFD)A 1975 orders (including those for a lump sum) is made as a legatee; not as a judgment debtor.

District judges (including district judges of the Principal Registry) have jurisdiction to hear any application under the I(PFD)A 1975 following the *President's Direction*[3].

The Act does not apply to Scotland.

See generally, *Rayden and Jackson on Divorce and Family Matters* (17th edn, 1997), vol 1, ch 28 and the Noter-up thereto.

1 See the CCA 1984, s 25.
2 See RSC Ord 99 set out at para **[3.551]** et seq below.
3 [1999] 2 FCR 1, [1999] 1 FLR 1295; set out at para **[4.26]** below.

## [2.142]

### 1 Application for financial provision from deceased's estate

(1) Where after the commencement of this Act a person dies domiciled in England and Wales and is survived by any of the following persons—

- (a) the wife or husband of the deceased;
- (b) a former wife or former husband of the deceased who has not remarried;
- [(ba) any person (not being a person included in paragraph (a) or (b) above) to whom subsection (1A) below applies;]
- (c) a child of the deceased;
- (d) any person (not being a child of the deceased) who, in the case of any marriage to which the deceased was at any time a party, was treated by the deceased as a child of the family in relation to that marriage;
- (e) any person (not being a person included in the foregoing paragraphs of this subsection) who immediately before the death of the deceased was being maintained, either wholly or partly, by the deceased;

that person may apply to the court for an order under section 2 of this Act on the ground that the disposition of the deceased's estate effected by his will or the law relating to intestacy, or the combination of his will and that law, is not such as to make reasonable financial provision for the applicant.

[(1A) This subsection applies to a person if the deceased died on or after 1st January 1996 and, during the whole of the period of two years ending immediately before the date when the deceased died, the person was living—

- (a) in the same household as the deceased, and
- (b) as the husband or wife of the deceased.]

(2) In this Act 'reasonable financial provision'—

- (a) in the case of an application made by virtue of subsection (1)(a) above by the husband or wife of the deceased (except where the marriage with the deceased was the subject of a decree of judicial separation and at the date of death the decree was in force and the separation was continuing), means such financial provision as it would be reasonable in all the circumstances of the case for a husband or wife to receive, whether or not that provision is required for his or her maintenance;

(b) in the case of any other application made by virtue of subsection (1) above, means such financial provision as it would be reasonable in all the circumstances of the case for the applicant to receive for his maintenance.

(3) For the purposes of subsection (1)(e) above, a person shall be treated as being maintained by the deceased, either wholly or partly, as the case may be, if the deceased, otherwise than for full valuable consideration, was making a substantial contribution in money or money's worth towards the reasonable needs of that person.

**Amendment**

Sub-s (1): para (ba) inserted by the LR(S)A 1995, s 2(2). Sub-s (1A): inserted by the LR(S)A 1995, s 2(3).



**[2.142.1]**
**Keypoints**

- General
- Wife
- Former wife
- Unmarried partners
- Child of the deceased
- Person treated as a child of the deceased
- Person who immediately before the death was being maintained
- That person may apply
- Law relating to intestacy
- Procedure
- Reasonable financial provision: the purpose of the Act
- Reasonable financial provision for the wife
- Reasonable financial provision for a former wife
- Reasonable financial provision for a child
- Reasonable financial provision for a person being maintained by deceased

**[2.142.2]**
**General**

This Act enables the courts to order financial provision for the family and dependants of a deceased person out of the estate. The jurisdiction is exercisable by the High Court (Chancery and Family Divisions) and by the county courts. The text of the Act was last amended by the Law Reform (Succession) Act 1995 so as to add s 1(1A). Prospective amendments by the FLA 1996, Sch 8 have not been brought into force at the time of going to print and are omitted from the text.

**[2.142.3]**
**Wife**

The status of wife, or husband, includes a person whose marriage was void, provided that it was not formally annulled and neither party remarried[1]. As to polygamous marriages these may also found an action but specifically see *Re Sehota, Surjit Kaur v Gian Kaur*[2].

1 See the I(PFD)A 1975, s 25(4) at para **[2.165]** below for definition.
2 [1978] 3 All ER 385, [1978] 1 WLR 1506.

**[2.142.4]**
**Former wife**

A former wife, or former husband, is one whose marriage to the deceased has been dissolved or annulled[1]. Such a person may be precluded from applying for family provision by an order of the High Court, or county court, made on or after the decree[2]. Where the death occurs within 12 months of decree absolute, without any order being made for financial provision or property adjustment, the court has a discretion to treat the parties as still married pursuant to s 14.

In *Barrass v Harding*[3] the President held that[4]:

> 'there is a two-stage process. The first stage is, did the disposition fail to make reasonable provision for the applicant? If the answer is "Yes", then the court goes on to consider what provision should have been made in the circumstances of the case. The second stage is an exercise of discretion. The first stage is an objective assessment of whether the disposition was or was not reasonable. It has been called "a value judgment" ... Where the parties had effectively settled their financial claims many years previously then no testamentary provision appeared to have been reasonable'.

1 See the I(PFD)A 1975, s 25(1) at para **[2.165]** below.
2 See the I(PFD)A 1975, ss 15 and 15A at paras **[2.156]** and **[2.157]** below.
3 [2001] 1 FCR 297, [2001] 1 FLR 138, CA.
4 [2001] 1 FCR 297 at 301.

### [2.142.5]
### Unmarried partners (Person to whom sub-s (1A) applies)

A person who was living with the deceased as man and wife for two years prior to the death and where the deceased died on or after 1 January 1996 may apply, although not maintained by the deceased. This provision was inserted by the Law Reform (Succession) Act 1995, s 2(3). A couple may be living together as husband and wife without necessarily sharing the same bedroom or having sexual relations[1].

1 See *Re John Watson's Estate* [1999] 3 FCR 595.

### [2.142.6]
### Child of the deceased

'Child' includes an illegitimate child or a child en ventre sa mere at the date of death of the deceased[1]. A child who has been adopted out of the family before the death may not apply[2].

1 See the I(PFD)A 1975, s 25(1) at para **[2.165]** below.
2 See *Re Collins* [1990] Fam 56, [1990] 2 All ER 47.

### [2.142.7]
### Person treated as child of the family

A child of the family is not excluded upon ceasing to be a minor or dependant[1]. For a case involving an adult step-child see *Re Leach, Leach v Lindeman*[2].

1 See *Re Callaghan* [1985] Fam 1, [1984] 3 All ER 790.
2 [1986] Ch 226, [1985] 2 All ER 754, CA.

### [2.142.8]
### Person who immediately before the death was being maintained

In order to qualify, the person being maintained must show that the deceased was making a substantial contribution towards his or her reasonable needs, otherwise than for full valuable consideration[1]. The court should look at all matters and it should apply a common sense approach. It should avoid fine balancing computations[2]. For reports of successful applications, see *Malone v Harrison*[3]; and *Jelley v Iliffe*[4]. As for 'immediately before the death', the court may have regard to any settled arrangement which existed prior to death and ignore variations which may happen to exist at the time of death itself[5]. Megarry V-C held that it is not sufficient that the deceased was maintaining the applicant at the date of his death; because of the provisions of the I(PFD)A 1975, s 3(4) it is essential that the deceased had actually 'assumed responsibility' for the maintenance and was maintaining him under that assumption of responsibility. Note *Kourkgy v Lusher*[6] where a claim failed because the deceased had divested himself of financial responsibility for the applicant and left her nine days before his death.

1 See the I(PFD)A 1975, s 1(3) at para **[2.142]** above.
2 See *Bishop v Plumley* [1991] 1 All ER 236, [1991] 1 WLR 562, CA (in that case the 'full valuable consideration' was discussed; it would appear to be a subjective test).
3 [1979] 1 WLR 1353.
4 [1981] Fam 128, [1981] 2 All ER 29, CA.
5 See *Re Beaumont, Martin v Midland Bank Trust Co Ltd* [1980] Ch 444, [1980] 1 All ER 266.
6 [1983] 4 FLR 65, (1983) 12 Fam Law 86.



## [2.142.9]
### That person may apply

The claim is personal to the individual concerned and does not pass on death[1]. Accordingly, if the applicant dies the action abates.

1 See *Whyte v Ticehurst* [1986] Fam 64, [1986] 2 All ER 158; *Re R, R v O* (1986) Fam Law 58 (former wife); and *Re Bramwell, Campbell v Tobin* [1988] 2 FLR 263 (widow).

## [2.142.10]
### Law relating to intestacy

See the Administration of Estates Act 1925, s 46 (as amended and as further amended by the Law Reform (Succession) Act 1995, s 1(1) and (3)).

Note that a will is revoked by the subsequent marriage of the testator (save for the circumstances set out in s18 of the Wills Act 1837; testator expecting to marry at the time and/or where it is apparent from the will that the testator expected to marry). Similarly, where the testator has died after 1 January 1996 and a decree of dissolution or annulmnet has been pronounced then the former spouse will be treated as having *predeceased* the testator[1].

1 See the WA 1837, s 18A(1) and (2).

## [2.142.11]
### Procedure

Proceedings in the High Court (Chancery or Family Division) or in the county court must be started by claim form and are governed in every case by CPR, Sch 1 – RSC Ord 99[1]. This is applied by r A1 of CPR, Sch 1 – RSC Ord 99 to the county court as well as the High Court. Applicants should use Form N208[2].

1 Set out at para **[3.522]** et seq below.
2 See CPR 1998, PD7 and *Practice Direction* (1999) 1 April, paras A.1(1) and A.3.

## [2.142.12]
### Reasonable financial provision: the purpose of the Act

The court has to decide on the evidence, without regard to any burden of proof, whether the deceased has failed to make reasonable financial provision[1]. The purpose of the Act is not to provide legacies or rewards for meritorious conduct[2]. Even where the whole estate becomes bona vacantia the question for the court is not whether it would have been reasonable to make provision but whether it was unreasonable not to have done so[3]. Where facts are in dispute the application should be heard on the merits, not struck out as not disclosing a cause of action[4].

1 See *Re Coventry* [1980] Ch 461, [1979] 3 All ER 815, CA; *Re Debenham* [1986] 1 FLR 404, [1986] Fam Law 101.
2 See *Riggs v Lloyds Bank plc* (1992) 137 Sol Jo 534, CA.
3 See *Cameron v Treasury Solicitor* [1997] 1 FCR 188, [1996] 2 FLR 716, CA.
4 See *Re Dymott, Spooner v Carroll* [1980] CA Transcript 942; and *Re Kirby, Hirons v Rolfe* (1982) 3 FLR 249, 11 Fam Law 210.

### [2.142.13]
### Reasonable financial provision for the wife

Reasonable financial provision for the wife, or husband, is defined in s 1(2)(a) and the court must have regard to the matters in s 3(1) and (2). In *Re Moody, Moody v Stevenson*[1] it was suggested that the court's starting point should be to consider what provision would have been ordered on divorce. However, such an exercise is inevitably artificial as provision needs to be made for both spouses on divorce but only one on death[2]. In *Re Besterman*[3] the court had stressed that the needs of the surviving spouse should not be a limiting, or paramount, factor; all other circumstances must be considered. In *Re Krubert (decd)*[4] the court preferred the *Besterman* approach to that taken in *Moody*.

1 [1992] Ch 486, [1992] 2 All ER 524, CA.
2 See *Re Bunning, Bunning v Salmon* [1984] 3 All ER 1 at 11.
3 [1984] Ch 458, [1984] 2 All ER 656, CA.
4 [1996] 3 FCR 281, CA.

### [2.142.14]
### Reasonable financial provision for a former wife

The court must have regard to the matters in s 3(1) and (2). It will be slow to find it reasonable to make financial provision for a former wife, or husband, where financial provision on divorce has been settled by agreement[1]. Alternatively, it may be reasonable to make provision where periodical payments cease on death or a large capital sum becomes available. (The reasonable expectations of surviving relatives need also to be weighed[2].)

1 See *Re Fullard* [1982] Fam 42, [1981] 2 All ER 796, CA; and *Brill v Proud* [1984] Fam Law 59, CA.
2 See *Talbot v Talbot* [1962] 3 All ER 174, [1962] 1 WLR 1113; *Re Harker-Thomas's Application, Harker-Thomas v Harker-Thomas* [1969] P 28, [1968] 3 All ER 17; *Re Crawford* (1983) 4 FLR 273; and *Re Farrow* [1987] 1 FLR 205, (1987) Fam Law 14.

### [2.142.15]
### Reasonable financial provision for a child

An adult child need not show any exceptional circumstance[1]. But the court must have regard to the matters in s 1(2)(b), and s 3(1) and (3) and these connote some kind of moral obligation to make financial provision for the child's maintenance[2]. Examples of successful claims include *Re Wood, Wood v Wood*[3] (mentally disabled daughter); and *Re Abram*[4].

1 See *Re Debenham* [1986] 1 FLR 404, (1986) Fam Law 101.
2 See *Re Coventry* [1980] 1 Ch 461, [1979] 3 All ER 815, CA; and *Re Jennings* [1994] Ch 286, [1994] 3 All ER 27, CA.
3 [1982] LS Gaz R 774.
4 [1996] 2 FLR 379.

### [2.142.16]
### Reasonable financial provision for a person being maintained by deceased

The court must be satisfied that the deceased was making a substantial contribution in money or money's worth, as required by s 1(3) and must have regard to the matters in s 3(1) and (4). For a successful claim by a sister who gave up her job to look after her brother in return for free board and lodging see *Re Wilkinson, Neale v Newell*[1]. Contrast with *Re Beaumont, Martin v Midland Bank Trust Co Ltd*[2].

1 [1978] Fam 22, [1978] 1 All ER 221.
2 [1980] Ch 444, [1980] 1 All ER 266.

[2.143]

## 2 Powers of court to make orders

(1) Subject to the provisions of this Act, where an application is made for an order under this section, the court may, if it is satisfied that the disposition of the deceased's estate effected by his will or the law relating to intestacy, or the combination of his will and that law, is not such as to make reasonable financial provision for the applicant, make any one or more of the following orders—

(a) an order for the making to the applicant out of the net estate of the deceased of such periodical payments and for such term as may be specified in the order;
(b) an order for the payment to the applicant out of that estate of a lump sum of such amount as may be so specified;
(c) an order for the transfer to the applicant of such property comprised in that estate as may be so specified;
(d) an order for the settlement for the benefit of the applicant of such property comprised in that estate as may be so specified;
(e) an order for the acquisition out of property comprised in that estate of such property as may be so specified and for the transfer of the property so acquired to the applicant or for the settlement thereof for his benefit;
(f) an order varying any ante-nuptial or post-nuptial settlement (including such a settlement made by will) made on the parties to a marriage to which the deceased was one of the parties, the variation being for the benefit of the surviving party to that marriage, or any child of that marriage, or any person who was treated by the deceased as a child of the family in relation to that marriage.

(2) An order under subsection (1)(a) above providing for the making out of the net estate of the deceased of periodical payments may provide for—

(a) payments of such amount as may be specified in the order,
(b) payments equal to the whole of the income of the net estate or of such portion thereof as may be so specified,
(c) payments equal to the whole of the income of such part of the net estate as the court may direct to be set aside or appropriated for the making out of the income thereof of payments under this section,

or may provide for the amount of the payments or any of them to be determined in any other way the court thinks fit.

(3) Where an order under subsection (1)(a) above provides for the making of payments of an amount specified in the order, the order may direct that such part of the net estate as may be so specified shall be set aside or appropriated for the making out of the income thereof of those payments; but no larger part of the net estate shall be so set aside or appropriated than is sufficient, at the date of the order, to produce by the income thereof the amount required for the making of those payments.

(4) An order under this section may contain such consequential and supplemental provisions as the court thinks necessary or expedient for the purpose of giving effect to the order or for the purpose of securing that the order operates fairly as between one beneficiary of the estate of the deceased and another and may, in particular, but without prejudice to the generality of this subsection—

(a) order any person who holds any property which forms part of the net estate of the deceased to make such payment or transfer such property as may be specified in the order;
(b) varying the disposition of the deceased's estate effected by the will or the law relating to intestacy, or by both the will and the law relating to intestacy, in such manner as the court thinks fair and reasonable having regard to the provisions of the order and all the circumstances of the case;
(c) confer on the trustees of any property which is the subject of an order under this section such powers as appear to the court to be necessary or expedient.

**[2.143.1]**
**Keypoints**

- Powers of the court
- Making an application
- Rectification of the will
- Definition of 'net estate' (see also s 8)
- Small estates
- Periodical payments
- Lump sum
- Orders that may be made under other sections
- Costs

**[2.143.2]**
**Powers of the court**

References in the Act to the 'court' include the High Court[1] and county courts have unlimited jurisdiction too, under the County Courts Act 1984, s 25 and the High Court and County Courts Jurisdiction Order 1991, SI 1991/724. The rights of the Crown to bona vacantia are, by s 24 of the I(PFD)A 1975, made subject to the powers of the court to order financial provision to be made out of the estate.

1 See the I(PFD)A 1975, s 25 at para **[2.165]** below.

**[2.143.3]**
**Making an application**

The procedure for making applications, whether in the High Court or county court, is by claim form in accordance with CPR, Sch 1 – RSC Ord 99, r 3[1]. This should use Form N208[2]. Note that in *Hannigan v Hannigan*[3], the failure to use the correct Form N208 was excused and CPR 1998, Pt 3.9(1) was applied. CPR 1998, Pt 3.9(1) provides, so far as material:

> 'On an application for relief from any sanction imposed for a failure to comply with any rule, practice direction or court order the court will consider all the circumstances including—
>
> (a) the interests of the administration of justice;
> (b) whether the application for relief has been made promptly;
> (c) whether the failure to comply was intentional;
> (d) whether there is a good explanation for the failure;
> (e) the extent to which the party in default had complied with other rules, practice directions and court orders and any relevant pre-action protocol;
> (f) whether the failure to comply was caused by the party or his legal representative;
> (g) whether the trial date or the likely date can still be met if relief is granted;
> (h) the effect which the failure to comply had on each party; and
> (i) the effect which the granting of relief would have on each party.'

1 See para **[3.555]** below.
2 See CPR 1998, PD7; and *Practice Direction* (1999) 1 April, paras A.1(1) and A.3.
3 [2000] 2 FCR 650, CA.

**[2.143.4]**
**Rectification of the will**

Where a will fails to give effect to the testator's intention due to a clerical error, proceedings for rectification under the Administration of Justice Act 1982, s 20(1) may be more appropriate.

**[2.143.5]**
**Definition of 'net estate' (see also s 8)**

For the meaning of 'net estate' see ss 8 and 25(1)[1]. For the treatment of joint property see s 9[2] and *Jessop v Jessop*[3]. For the purpose of determining whether there has been a failure to make reasonable provision, the estate should be valued as at the date of death; but the amount of the provision ordered should be on the basis of the value at the hearing[4].

1 See paras **[2.149]**, **[2.165]** below.
2 See para **[2.150]** below.
3 [1992] 1 FCR 253, [1992] 1 FLR 591, CA.
4 See *Lusternik v Lusternik* [1972] Fam 125, [1972] 1 All ER 592, CA.



## [2.143.6]
### Small estates

Where the estate is small and the effect of an order for provision would merely reduce the applicant's entitlement to income support, this may be grounds for not making an order[1]. Also, where the estate is small, an applicant for legal aid must so inform the Legal Services Commission[2] and every effort should be made to limit the costs falling on the estate[3]. Respondents to applications for provision out of small estates should be guided, as to whether to defend, by dicta in *Evans v Evans*[4].

1 See *Re E, E v E* [1966] 2 All ER 44, [1966] 1 WLR 709.
2 See *Brill v Proud* [1984] Fam Law 59, CA.
3 See *Re Parkinson* (1975) 125 NLJ 998.
4 [1985] 3 All ER 289, [1986] 1 WLR 101, CA.

## [2.143.7]
### Periodical payments

An order for periodical payments will usually be made from the date of the deceased's death, notwithstanding the receipt by the applicant of social security payments[1]. As to the relevance of the levels of income support in determining the amount of periodical payments, see *Shallow v Shallow*[2]. The court may set a term for the length of the order. The court may require the order to be a set income or by reference to the income from the estate or a capital part of the estate to be set aside to generate an income.

1 See *Re Goodwin, Goodwin v Goodwin* [1969] 1 Ch 283, [1968] 3 All ER 12.
2 [1979] Fam 1, [1978] 2 All ER 483, CA.

## [2.143.8]
### Lump sum

The court should take account of contingencies and inflation in assessing any lump sum[1]. Provision is made in s 5[2] for interim orders and in s 7[3] for payment by instalments. The lump sums may be payable by instalments in which event the court has power to vary the amounts due under any such instalment[4].

1 See *Re Besterman* [1984] 2 All ER 656, CA.
2 See para **[2.146]** below.
3 See para **[2.148]** below.
4 See the I(PFD)A 1975, s 7(2) at para **[2.148]** below.

## [2.143.9]
### Orders that may be made under other sections

The court also has power to deal with dispositions and contracts intended to defeat applications[1], to review and vary orders for secured periodical payments provision and maintenance agreements[2] and, in certain circumstances, to exercise powers under s 2 in applications under ss 31 and 36 of the MCA 1973[3].

1 See the I(PFD)A 1975, ss 10 and 13 at paras **[2.151]** and **[2.154]** below.
2 See the I(PFD)A 1975, ss 16 and 17 at paras **[2.158]** and **[2.159]** below.
3 See the I(PFD)A 1975, s 18 at para **[2.160]** below.

## [2.143.10]
**Costs**

It was held in *Re Bellman*[1] that a successful applicant should normally be awarded costs out of the estate on a party and party basis. But special considerations apply in the case of small estates (see above).

Also, in *Re Besterman*[2], the Court of Appeal cautioned legal representatives against excessive citation of decided cases, because particular circumstances are so many and various.

1 [1963] P 239, [1963] 1 All ER 513.
2 [1984] Ch 458, [1984] 2 All ER 656.

## [2.144]

### 3 Matters to which court is to have regard in exercising powers under section 2

(1) Where an application is made for an order under section 2 of this Act, the court shall, in determining whether the disposition of the deceased's estate effected by his will or the law relating to intestacy, or the combination of his will and that law, is such as to make reasonable financial provision for the applicant and, if the court considers that reasonable financial provision has not been made, in determining whether and in what manner it shall exercise its powers under that section, have regard to the following matters, that is to say—

(a) the financial resources and financial needs which the applicant has or is likely to have in the foreseeable future;
(b) the financial resources and financial needs which any other applicant for an order under section 2 of this Act has or is likely to have in the foreseeable future;
(c) the financial resources and financial needs which any beneficiary of the estate of the deceased has or is likely to have in the foreseeable future;
(d) any obligations and responsibilities which the deceased had towards any applicant for an order under the said section 2 or towards any beneficiary of the estate of the deceased;
(e) the size and nature of the net estate of the deceased;
(f) any physical or mental disability of any applicant for an order under the said section 2 or any beneficiary of the estate of the deceased;
(g) any other matter, including the conduct of the applicant or any other person, which in the circumstances of the case the court may consider relevant.

(2) Without prejudice to the generality of paragraph (g) of subsection (1) above, where an application for an order under section 2 of this Act is made by virtue of section 1(1)(a) or 1(1)(b) of this Act, the court shall, in addition to the matters specifically mentioned in paragraphs (a) to (f) of that subsection, have regard to—

(a) the age of the applicant and the duration of the marriage;
(b) the contribution made by the applicant to the welfare of the family of the deceased, including any contribution made by looking after the home or caring for the family;

and, in the case of an application by the wife or husband of the deceased, the court shall also, unless at the date of death a decree of judicial separation was in force and the separation was continuing, have regard to the provision which the applicant might reasonably have expected to receive if on the day on which the deceased died the marriage, instead of being terminated by death, had been terminated by a decree of divorce.

[(2A) Without prejudice to the generality of paragraph (g) of subsection (1) above, where an application for an order under section 2 of this Act is made by virtue of section 1(1)(ba) of this Act, the court shall, in addition to the matters specifically mentioned in paragraphs (a) to (f) of that subsection, have regard to—

(a) the age of the applicant and the length of the period during which the applicant lived as the husband or wife of the deceased and in the same household as the deceased;

(b) the contribution made by the applicant to the welfare of the family of the deceased, including any contribution made by looking after the home or caring for the family.]

(3) Without prejudice to the generality of paragraph (g) of subsection (1) above, where an application for an order under section 2 of this Act is made by virtue of section 1(1)(c) or 1(1)(d) of this Act, the court shall, in addition to the matters specifically mentioned in paragraphs (a) to (f) of that subsection, have regard to the manner in which the applicant was being or in which he might expect to be educated or trained, and where the application is made by virtue of section 1(1)(d) the court shall also have regard—

(a) to whether the deceased had assumed any responsibility for the applicant's maintenance and, if so, to the extent to which and the basis upon which the deceased assumed that responsibility and to the length of time for which the deceased discharged that responsibility;

(b) to whether in assuming and discharging that responsibility the deceased did so knowing that the applicant was not his own child;

(c) to the liability of any other person to maintain the applicant.

(4) Without prejudice to the generality of paragraph (g) of subsection (1) above, where an application for an order under section 2 of this Act is made by virtue of section 1(1)(e) of this Act, the court shall, in addition to the matters specifically mentioned in paragraphs (a) to (f) of that subsection, have regard to the extent to which and the basis upon which the deceased assumed responsibility for the maintenance of the applicant, and to the length of time for which the deceased discharged that responsibility.

(5) In considering the matters to which the court is required to have regard under this section, the court shall take into account the facts as known to the court at the date of the hearing.

(6) In considering the financial resources of any person for the purposes of this section the court shall take into account his earning capacity and in considering the financial needs of any person for the purposes of this section the court shall take into account his financial obligations and responsibilities.

**Amendment**

Sub-s (2A): inserted by the LR(S)A 1995, s 2(4).



## [2.144.1]
## Keypoints

- Financial resources and financial needs
- Beneficiary of the estate
- Obligations and responsibilities which the deceased had towards the applicant
- Any other matter
- Conduct of the applicant

## [2.144.2]
## Financial resources and financial needs

In *Malone v Harrison*[1], the female applicant who was in a settled relationship with the deceased was awarded a lump sum calculated by applying a life expectancy multiplier to her income needs and deducting her existing capital resources from the resulting sum. *Duxbury*-type calculations may well be appropriate, although in *Malone* Hollings J also took into account the applicant's remarriage prospects. 'Financial needs' means 'reasonable requirements'[2]. It was decided in that case that account might be taken of the applicant's standard of living during the lifetime of the deceased, the extent of his contribution and the fact that a reasonable testator would, in the circumstances, have wished her to stay on in the house. Where there are alternative ways of providing for the applicant the court is justified in taking the course which least disturbs the testator's wishes[3].

1 [1979] 1 WLR 1353.
2 See *Harrington v Gill* (1983) 4 FLR 265, CA.
3 See *Stead v Stead* [1985] FLR 16, [1985] Fam Law 154, CA.

### [2.144.3]
### Beneficiary of the estate

See the definition in s 25(1)[1].

1 See para **[2.165]** below.

### [2.144.4]
### Obligations and responsibilities which the deceased had towards the applicant

These words refer to subsisting obligations, not ones which related to the childhood of an applicant who was self-supporting at the time of the death[1]. In *Re Jennings, Harlow v National Westminster Bank* the Court of Appeal held that the 'obligations and responsibilities' referred to those immediately before the deceased's death.

1 See *Harlow v National Westminster Bank plc* (1994) 138 Sol Jo LB 31, [1994] 7 LS Gaz R 33, CA; *Re Jennings* [1994] Ch 286, [1994] 3 All ER 27, CA.

### [2.144.5]
### Any other matter

The court may receive evidence of facts from which it can infer the testator's intention[1]. Also evidence that the deceased raised expectations on which the applicant relied to her detriment may be admitted as raising an estoppel[2]. In *Re Wood, Wood v Wood*[3], the court treated as a relevant 'matter' the fact that if no provision were made under the Act for the mentally disabled daughter of the deceased, the estate would pass, under the intestacy rules, to her deceased husband's son by an earlier marriage.

1 See *Re Smallwood, Smallwood v Martins Bank Ltd* [1951] Ch 369, [1951] 1 All ER 372.
2 See *Re Basham* [1987] 1 All ER 405, [1987] 2 FLR 264.
3 [1982] LS Gaz R 774.

### [2.144.6]
### Conduct of the applicant

As a matter of public policy an applicant who intentionally kills the deceased thereby forfeits his or her rights of succession and is similarly precluded from having provision made for him or her under the Act[1]. Provision may, however, be made for the children, by virtue of the Forfeiture Act 1982, s 2(2), and for an applicant whose moral responsibility is not so great as to justify total exclusion[2]. More generally, the conduct of the applicant during the lifetime of the deceased is relevant to the same extent as under the MCA 1973, s 25[3].

1 See *Re Royse, Royse v Royse* [1985] Ch 22, [1984] 3 All ER 339, CA; and *Jones v Roberts* [1995] 2 FLR 422, [1995] Fam Law 673.
2 See *Re S (forfeiture rule)* [1996] 3 FCR 357, [1996] 1 FLR 910; and *Re K* [1985] Ch 85, [1985] 1 All ER 403.
3 See para **[2.120]** above; and *Re Snoek* (1983) 13 Fam Law 18.

### [2.145]

#### 4 Time-limit for applications

An application for an order under section 2 of this Act shall not, except with the permission of the court, be made after the end of the period of six months from the date on which representation with respect to the estate of the deceased is first taken out.

## [2.145.1]
### Keypoints

- The permission of the court
- The date on which representation is first taken out
- Date of the application
- Form of the application
- Search at the Principal Registry
- How to proceed in the absence of a grant
- Position of personal representatives

## [2.145.2]
### The permission of the court

An application for the permission of the court to start proceedings out of time should be made by application in accordance with CPR 1998, Pt 23. The application for permission may be made in the same document as the substantive application but it should be ruled on as a preliminary issue[1]. In *Re Salmon, Coard v National Westminster Bank Ltd*[2], Sir Robert Megarry V-C stressed that the onus was on the applicant to make a substantial case for proceeding out of time. He said that the court would require explanations as to:

- how the delay came about;
- whether efforts had been made to mitigate its effects;
- whether negotiations had been in progress;
- whether there had been distribution of the estate before notification of the claim; and
- whether, if leave were refused, the applicant would have a remedy against anybody else (ie usually the solicitors.)

Leave was refused in *Escritt v Escritt*[3] where the applicant was three years out of time; but it was allowed, in exceptional circumstances, in *Stock v Brown*[4], five years after the expiry of the time limit. For a late application by a minor see *Re W (a minor) (claim from deceased's estate)*[5], sub nom *Re C (leave to apply for provision)*[6].

1 See *Re Greaves, Greaves v Greaves* [1954] 2 All ER 109, [1954] 1 WLR 760.
2 [1981] Ch 167, [1980] 3 All ER 532.
3 (1981) 3 FLR 280.
4 [1994] 2 FCR 1125, [1994] 1 FLR 840.
5 [1995] 2 FCR 689.
6 [1995] 2 FLR 24.

## [2.145.3]
### The date on which representation is first taken out

The day on which representation is first taken out counts as the first day of the six month period[1]. Where a grant in common form is followed by a grant in solemn form, time runs from the date of the earlier grant[2]. Where a grant of probate is revoked and letters of administration are granted, time runs from the date of the latter[3]. Section 23[4] provides that a grant limited to settled land or to trust property should be left out of account and that a grant limited to real estate or to personal estate should also be left out of account unless a grant limited to the remainder of the estate has been previously made or is made at the same time. In *Re Johnson*[5] it was held, by analogy with s 23, that a grant to solicitors should also be left out of account where it was taken out for the limited purpose of pursuing a claim in negligence arising out of the deceased's fatal accident.

1 See *Re Kay, Kay v West* [1965] 3 All ER 724, [1965] 1 WLR 1463.
2 See *Re Miller, Miller v de Courcey* [1968] 3 All ER 844, [1969] 1 WLR 583.
3 See *Re Freeman* [1984] 3 All ER 906, [1984] 1 WLR 1419.
4 See para **[2.163]** below.
5 [1987] CLY 3882.

## [2.145.4]
### Date of the application

The application is made on the date of issue[1].

1 See *Re Chittenden, Chittenden v Doe* [1970] 3 All ER 562, [1970] 1 WLR 1618.

## [2.145.5]
### Form of the application

In *Hannigan v Hannigan*[1] a claimant widow, instructed her solicitor to institute proceedings under the I(PFD)A 1975. Counsel's advice was that the proceedings should be issued using CPR Practice Form N208 (the Pt 8 claim form). Unfortunately, on 10 June 1999 the solicitor erroneously issued the claim using CCR Form N208, which was a form of petition in use under the old County Court Rules 1984, and which had just been superseded. The claim was struck out. It was held in the Court of Appeal that the overriding objective of the new procedural code contained in the CPR 1998 was to enable the court to deal with cases justly. The factor of paramount importance was that the executors and their solicitor knew from the documents served exactly what was being claimed. Accordingly, the interests of the administration of justice required that the pleadings should stand.

Applicants should use the N208 Form as provided for in the CPR 1998.

1 [2000] 2 FCR 650, CA.

## [2.145.6]
### Search at the Principal Registry

The Record Keeper at the Principal Registry will, on payment of the appropriate fee, send to the applicant an office copy of any grant which tallies with the particulars given and which was issued within the preceding 12 months or within six months thereafter[1].

1 See *Practice Direction* [1975] 3 All ER 403, [1975] 1 WLR 1301.

## [2.145.7]
### How to proceed in the absence of a grant

It was held in *Re McBroom*[1], that no application may be made without a grant being taken out, although an application which precedes a grant is not necessarily invalid[2]. The best course, if it appears that no grant is likely to be made, is to invite the Official Solicitor at 81 Chancery Lane, London WC2A 1DD (020-7911-7127), to apply for a grant limited to accepting service of proceedings under the I(PFD)A 1975.

1 [1992] 2 FLR 49, [1992] Fam Law 376.
2 See *Re Searle, Searle v Siems* [1949] Ch 73, [1948] 2 All ER 426.

## [2.145.8]
### Position of personal representatives

Personal representatives are protected by s 20[1] from liability for any distribution under the Act so long as they do not distribute for six months from the date of the grant. If the consent is not forthcoming they may seek a court order[2].

1 See para **[2.162]** below.
2 See *Re Ralphs, Ralphs v District Bank Ltd* [1968] 3 All ER 285, [1968] 1 WLR 1522.

## [2.146]

### 5 Interim orders

(1) Where an application for an order under section 3 of this Act it appears to the court—

(a) that the applicant is in immediate need of financial assistance, but it is not yet possible to determine what order (if any) should be made under that section; and

(b) that property forming part of the net estate of the deceased is or can be made available to meet the need of the applicant;

the court may order that, subject to such conditions or restrictions, if any, as the court may impose and to any further order of the court, there shall be paid to the applicant out of the net estate of the deceased such sum or sums and (if more than one) at such intervals as the court thinks reasonable; and the court may order that, subject to the provisions of this Act, such payments are to be made until such date as the court may specify, not being later than the date on which the court either makes an order under the said section 2 or decides not to exercise its powers under that section.

(2) Subsections (2), (3) and (4) of section 2 of this Act shall apply in relation to an order under this section as they apply in relation to an order under that section.

(3) In determining what order, if any, should be made under this section the court shall, so far as the urgency of the case admits, have regard to the same matters as those to which the court is required to have regard under section 3 of this Act.

(4) An order made under section 2 of this Act may provide that any sum paid to the applicant by virtue of this section shall be treated to such an extent and in such manner as may be provided by that order as having been paid on account of any payment provided for by that order.



**[2.146.1]**
**Keypoint**

- Procedure

**[2.146.2]**
**Procedure**

An application for an interim order should be made in accordance with CPR 1998, Pt 23 supported by evidence of hardship and urgency. Any such sums may be taken into account in any final award.

Any orders under s 5 are exempt from the legal aid statutory charge pursuant to reg 94(b) of the Civil Legal Aid (General) Regulations 1989, SI 1989/339.

**[2.147]**

### 6 Variation, discharge, etc of orders for periodical payments

(1) Subject to the provisions of this Act, where the court has made an order under section 2(1)(a) of this Act (in this section referred to as 'the original order') for the making of periodical payments to any person (in this section referred to as 'the original recipient'), the court, on an application under this section, shall have power by order to vary or discharge the original order or to suspend any provision of it temporarily and to revive the operation of any provision so suspended.

(2) Without prejudice to the generality of subsection (1) above, an order made on an application for the variation of the original order may—

(a) provide for the making out of any relevant property of such periodical payments and for such term as may be specified in the order to any person who has applied, or would but for section 4 of this Act be entitled to apply, for an order under section 2 of this Act (whether or not, in the case of any application, an order was made in favour of the applicant);

(b) provide for the payment out of any relevant property of a lump sum of such amount as may be so specified to the original recipient or to any such person as is mentioned in paragraph (a) above;

(c) provide for the transfer of the relevant property, or such part thereof as may be so specified, to the original recipient or to any such person as is so mentioned.

(3) Where the original order provides that any periodical payments payable thereunder to the original recipient are to cease on the occurrence of an event specified in the order (other than the remarriage of a former wife or former husband) or on the expiration of a period so specified, then, if, before the end of the period of six months from the date of the occurrence of that event or of the expiration of that period, an application is made for an order under this section, the court shall have power to make any order which it would have had power to make if the application had been made before the date (whether in favour of the original recipient or any such person as is mentioned in subsection (2)(a) above and whether having effect from that date or from such later date as the court may specify).

(4) Any reference in this section to the original order shall include a reference to an order made under this section and any reference in this section to the original recipient shall include a reference to any person to whom periodical payments are required to be made by virtue of an order under this section.

(5) An application under this section may be made by any of the following persons, that is to say—

- (a) any person who by virtue of section 1(1) of this Act has applied, or would but for section 4 of this Act be entitled to apply, for an order under section 2 of this Act,
- (b) the personal representatives of the deceased,
- (c) the trustees of any relevant property, and
- (d) any beneficiary of the estate of the deceased.

(6) An order under this section may only affect—

- (a) property the income of which is at the date of the order applicable wholly or in part for the making of periodical payments to any person who has applied for an order under this Act, or
- (b) in the case of an application under subsection (3) above in respect of payments which have ceased to be payable on the occurrence of an event or the expiration of a period, property the income of which was so applicable immediately before the occurrence of that event or the expiration of that period, as the case may be,

and any such property as is mentioned in paragraph (a) or (b) above is in subsections (2) and (5) above referred to as 'relevant property'.

(7) In exercising the powers conferred by this section the court shall have regard to all circumstances of the case, including any change in any of the matters to which the court was required to have regard when making the order to which the application relates.

(8) Where the court makes an order under this section, it may give such consequential directions as it thinks necessary or expedient having regard to the provisions of the order.

(9) No such order as is mentioned in section 2(1)(d), (e) or (f), 9, 10 or 11 of this Act shall be made on an application under this section.

(10) For the avoidance of doubt it is hereby declared that, in relation to an order which provides for the making of periodical payments which are to cease on the occurrence of an event specified in the order (other than the remarriage of a former wife or former husband) or on the expiration of a period so specified, the power to vary an order includes power to provide for the making of periodical payments after the expiration of that period or the occurrence of that event.

**[2.147.1]**
**Keypoint**

- Circumstances justifying a variation

### [2.147.2]
### Circumstances justifying a variation

See *Re Gale, Gale v Gale*[1] for the court's approach to the exercise of its powers under this section.

1 [1966] Ch 236, [1966] 1 All ER 945, CA.

### [2.148]

## 7 Payment of lump sums by instalments

(1) An order under section 2(1)(b) or 6(2)(b) of this Act for the payment of a lump sum may provide for the payment of that sum by instalments of such amount as may be specified in the order.

(2) Where an order is made by virtue of subsection (1) above, the court shall have power, on an application made by the person to whom the lump sum is payable, by the personal representatives of the deceased or by the trustees of the property out of which the lump sum is payable, to vary that order by varying the number of instalments payable, the amount of any instalment and the date on which any instalment becomes payable.

### [2.148.1]
### Keypoint

- Lump sum

### [2.148.2]
### Lump sum

See para **[2.143.8]** above.

### [2.149]

## 8 Property treated as part of 'net estate'

(1) Where a deceased person has in accordance with the provisions of any enactment nominated any person to receive any sum of money or other property on his death and that nomination is in force at the time of his death, that sum of money, after deducting therefrom any inheritance tax payable in respect thereof, or that other property, to the extent of the value thereof at the date of the death of the deceased after deducting therefrom any inheritance tax so payable, shall be treated for the purposes of this Act as part of the net estate of the deceased; but this subsection shall not render any person liable for having paid that sum or transferred that other property to the person named in the nomination in accordance with the directions given in the nomination.

(2) Where any sum of money or other property is received by any person as a donatio mortis causa made by a deceased person, that sum of money, after deducting therefrom any inheritance tax payable thereon, or that other property, to the extent of the value thereof at the date of the death of the deceased after deducting therefrom any inheritance tax so payable, shall be treated for the purposes of this Act as part of the net estate of the deceased; but this subsection shall not render any person liable for having paid that sum or transferred that other property in order to give effect to that donatio mortis causa.

(3) The amount of inheritance tax to be deducted for the purposes of this section shall not exceed the amount of that tax which has been borne by the person nominated by the deceased or, as the case may be, the person who has received a sum of money or other property as a donatio mortis causa.

## [2.150]

**9 Property held on a joint tenancy**

(1) Where a deceased person was immediately before his death beneficially entitled to a joint tenancy of any property, then, if, before the end of the period of six months from the date on which representation with respect to the estate of the deceased was first taken out, an application is made for an order under section 2 of this Act, the court for the purpose of facilitating the making of financial provision for the applicant under this Act may order that the deceased's severable share of that property, at the value thereof immediately before his death, shall, to such extent as appears to the court to be just in all the circumstances of the case, be treated for the purposes of this Act as part of the net estate of the deceased.

(2) In determining the extent to which any severable share is to be treated as part of the net estate of the deceased by virtue of an order under subsection (1) above, the court shall have regard to any inheritance tax payable in respect of that severable share.

(3) Where an order is made under subsection (1) above, the provisions of this section shall not render any person liable for anything done by him before the order was made.

(4) For the avoidance of doubt it is hereby declared that for the purposes of this section there may be a joint tenancy of a chose in action.

## [2.150.1]
### Keypoints

- Joint tenancy of any property
- The purpose of facilitating the making of financial provision

## [2.150.2]
### Joint tenancy of any property

In *Re Crawford*[1] the deceased had paid his retirement lump sum into a bank account in the joint names of himself and his second wife. His former wife, who had a pending application for the award of a lump sum by way of financial provision, applied successfully under ss 2 and 9[2] for the deceased's share of the retirement lump sum to be treated as part of the estate and paid to her. In *Powell v Osbourne*[3] the deceased and his partner were beneficial joint tenants of a house subject to a mortgage supported by a joint policy of insurance. The court interpreted s 9(1) and (4) as enabling it to regard the joint tenancy as severed on death. This allowed the deceased's estate to benefit from the policy moneys so as to discharge his share of the mortgage and make available the value of the whole of the equity of redemption to be awarded to the applicant widow.

1 (1982) 4 FLR 273.
2 See paras **[2.143]** and **[2.150]** above.
3 [1993] 1 FCR 797, [1993] 1 FLR 1001, CA.

## [2.150.3]
### For the purpose of facilitating the making of financial provision

The phrase about facilitating the making of provision (under s 2) is not to be read as narrowing the broad discretion conferred by s 9[1]. Also note *Kourkgy v Lusher*[2] where Wood J held that the exercise of the discretion should not be postponed until the court is considering what order should be made in favour of the applicant; the discretion should also be exercised in considering the preliminary question posed by s 3, namely whether reasonable financial provision had been made for the applicant.

1 See also *Jessop v Jessop* [1992] 1 FCR 253, [1992] 1 FLR 591, CA.
2 (1981) 4 FLR 65, 12 Fam Law 86.

[2.151]

## 10 Dispositions intended to defeat applications for financial provision

(1) Where an application is made to the court for an order under section 2 of this Act, the applicant may, in the proceedings on that application, apply to the court for an order under subsection (2) below.

(2) Where on an application under subsection (1) above the court is satisfied—

(a) that, less than six years before the date of the death of the deceased, the deceased with the intention of defeating an application for financial provision under this Act made a disposition, and

(b) that full valuable consideration for that disposition was not given by the person to whom or for the benefit of whom the disposition was made (in this section referred to as 'the donee') or by any other person, and

(c) that the exercise of the powers conferred by this section would facilitate the making of financial provision for the applicant under this Act,

then, subject to the provisions of this section and of sections 12 and 13 of this Act, the court may order the donee (whether or not at the date of the order he holds any interest in the property disposed of to him or for his benefit by the deceased) to provide, for the purpose of the making of that financial provision, such sum of money or other property as may be specified in the order.

(3) Where an order is made under subsection (2) above as respects any disposition made by the deceased which consisted of the payment of money to or for the benefit of the donee, the amount of any sum of money or the value of any property ordered to be provided under that subsection shall not exceed the amount of the payment made by the deceased after deducting therefrom any inheritance tax borne by the donee in respect of that payment.

(4) Where an order is made under subsection (2) above as respects any disposition made by the deceased which consisted of the transfer of property (other than a sum of money) to or for the benefit of the donee, the amount of any sum of money or the value of any property ordered to be provided under that subsection shall not exceed the value at the date of the death of the deceased of the property disposed of by him to or for the benefit of the donee (or if that property has been disposed of by the person to whom it was transferred by the deceased, the value at the date of that disposal thereof) after deducting therefrom any inheritance tax borne by the donee in respect of the transfer of that property by the deceased.

(5) Where an application (in this subsection referred to as 'the original application') is made for an order under subsection (2) above in relation to any disposition, then, if on an application under this subsection by the donee or by any applicant for an order under section 2 of this Act the court is satisfied—

(a) that, less than six years before the date of the death of the deceased, the deceased with the intention of defeating an application for financial provision under this Act made a disposition other than the disposition which is the subject of the original application, and

(b) that full valuable consideration for that other disposition was not given by the person to whom or for the benefit of whom that other disposition was made or by any other person,

the court may exercise in relation to the person to whom or for the benefit of whom that other disposition was made the powers which the court would have had under subsection (2) above if the original application had been made in respect of that other disposition and the court had been satisfied as to the matters set out in paragraphs (a), (b) and (c) of that subsection; and where any application is made under this subsection, any reference in this section (except in subsection (2)(b)) to the donee shall include a reference to the person to whom or for the benefit of whom that other disposition was made.

(6) In determining whether and in what manner to exercise its powers under this section, the court shall have regard to the circumstances in which any disposition was made and any valuable consideration which was given therefor, the relationship, if any, of the donee to the deceased, the conduct and financial resources of the donee and all the other circumstances of the case.

(7) In this section 'disposition' does not include—

- (a) any provision in a will, any such nomination as is mentioned in section 8(1) of this Act or any donatio mortis causa, or
- (b) any appointment of property made, otherwise than by will, in the exercise of a special power of appointment,

but, subject to these exceptions, includes any payment of money (including the payment of a premium under a policy of assurance) and any conveyance, assurance, appointment or gift of property of any description, whether made by an instrument or otherwise.

(8) The provisions of this section do not apply to any disposition made before the commencement of this Act.

**[2.152]**

### 11 Contracts to leave property by will

(1) Where an application is made to a court for an order under section 2 of this Act, the applicant may, in the proceedings on that application, apply to the court for an order under this section.

(2) Where on an application under subsection (1) above the court is satisfied—

- (a) that the deceased made a contract by which he agreed to leave by his will a sum of money or other property to any person or by which he agreed that a sum of money or other property would be paid or transferred to any person out of his estate, and
- (b) that the deceased made that contract with the intention of defeating an application for financial provision under this Act, and
- (c) that when the contract was made full valuable consideration for that contract was not given or promised by the person with whom or for the benefit of whom the contract was made (in this section referred to as 'the donee') or by any other person, and
- (d) that the exercise of the powers conferred by this section would facilitate the making of financial provision for the applicant under this Act,

then, subject to the provisions of this section and of sections 12 and 13 of this Act, the court may make any one or more of the following orders, that is to say—

- (i) if any money has been paid or any other property has been transferred to or for the benefit of the donee in accordance with the contract, an order directing the donee to provide, for the purpose of the making of that financial provision, such sum of money or other property as may be specified in the order;
- (ii) if the money or all the money has not been paid or the property or all the property has not been transferred in accordance with the contract, an order directing the personal representatives not to make any payment or transfer any property, or not to make any further payment or transfer any further property, as the case may be, in accordance therewith or directing the personal representatives only to make such payment or transfer such property as may be specified in the order.

(3) Notwithstanding anything in subsection (2) above, the court may exercise its powers thereunder in relation to any contract made by the deceased only to the extent that the court considers that the amount of any sum of money paid or to be paid or the value of any property transferred or to be transferred in accordance with the contract exceeds the value of any valuable consideration given or to be given for that contract, and for this purpose the court shall have regard to the value of property at the date of the hearing.

(4) In determining whether and in what manner to exercise its powers under this section, the court shall have regard to the circumstances in which the contract was made, the relationship, if any, of the donee to the deceased, the conduct and financial resources of the donee and all the other circumstances of the case.

(5) Where an order has been made under subsection (2) above in relation to any contract the rights of any person to enforce that contract or to recover damages or to obtain other relief for the breach thereof shall be subject to any adjustment made by the court under section 12(3) of this Act and shall survive to such extent only as is consistent with giving effect to the terms of that order.

(6) The provisions of this section do not apply to a contract made before the commencement of this Act.



**[2.153]**

## 12 Provisions supplementary to ss 10 and 11

(1) Where the exercise of any of the powers conferred by section 10 or 11 of this Act is conditional on the court being satisfied that a disposition or contract was made by a deceased person with the intention of defeating an application for financial provision under this Act, that condition shall be fulfilled if the court is of the opinion that, on a balance of probabilities, the intention of the deceased (though not necessarily his sole intention) in making the disposition or contract was to prevent an order for financial provision being made under this Act or to reduce the amount of the provision which might otherwise be granted by an order thereunder.

(2) Where an application is made under section 11 of this Act with respect to any contract made by the deceased and no valuable consideration was given or promised by any person for that contract then, notwithstanding anything in subsection (1) above, it shall be presumed, unless the contrary is shown, that the deceased made that contract with the intention of defeating an application for financial provision under this Act.

(3) Where the court makes an order under section 10 or 11 of this Act it may give such consequential directions as it thinks fit (including directions requiring the making of any payment or the transfer of any property) for giving effect to the order or for securing a fair adjustment of the rights of the persons affected thereby.

(4) Any power conferred on the court by the said section 10 or 11 to order the donee, in relation to any disposition or contract, to provide any sum of money or other property shall be exercisable in like manner in relation to the personal representative of the donee, and—

- (a) any reference in section 10(4) to the disposal of property by the donee shall include a reference to disposal by the personal representative of the donee, and
- (b) any reference in section 10(5) to an application by the donee under that subsection shall include a reference to an application by the personal representative of the donee;

but the court shall not have power under the said section 10 or 11 to make an order in respect of any property forming part of the estate of the donee which has been distributed by the personal representative; and the personal representative shall not be liable for having distributed any such property before he has notice of the making of an application under the said section 10 or 11 on the ground that he ought to have taken into account the possibility that such an application would be made.

**[2.153.1]**
**Keypoint**

- Notes to ss 10, 11 and 12

## [2.153.2]
### Notes to ss 10, 11 and 12

In *Clifford v Tanner*[1], the Court of Appeal held that s 10(7) did not provide a comprehensive definition of 'disposition' but, even if it did, it would apply to the transaction then before the court. This was a deed executed by the deceased a few weeks before his death whereby he released his daughter by his first marriage from a covenant by her to allow his second wife to remain in occupation of his home until her death or re-marriage. 'Valuable consideration' does not include marriage or a promise of marriage[2].

The order may be made whether or not at the date of the order the donee retains any interest in the property which was disposed of to him or for his benefit by the deceased. For an illustration of the court's exercising its powers under s 10[3].

Section 12 makes further provision regarding the deceased's intention and how it may be proved; see also, on these aspects, *Re Kennedy, Kennedy v Official Solicitor to the Supreme Court*[4]; and *Re Dawkins, Dawkins v Judd*[5].

1 [1987] CLY 3881.
2 See the I(PFD)A 1975, s 25(1) at para **[2.165]** below.
3 See *Re Dawkins, Dawkins v Judd* [1986] 2 FLR 360, [1986] Fam Law 295.
4 [1980] CLY 2820.
5 [1986] 2 FLR 360, [1986] Fam Law 295.

## [2.154]

### 13 Provisions as to trustees in relation to ss 10 and 11

(1) Where an application is made for—

(a) an order under section 10 of this Act in respect of a disposition made by the deceased to any person as a trustee, or

(b) an order under section 11 of this Act in respect of any payment made or property transferred, in accordance with a contract made by the deceased, to any person as a trustee,

the powers of the court under the said section 10 or 11 to order that trustee to provide a sum of money or other property shall be subject to the following limitation (in addition, in a case of an application under section 10, to any provision regarding the deduction of inheritance tax) namely, that the amount of any sum of money or the value of any property ordered to be provided—

(i) in the case of an application in respect of a disposition which consisted of the payment of money or an application in respect of the payment of money in accordance with a contract, shall not exceed the aggregate of so much of that money as is at the date of the order in the hands of the trustee and the value at that date of any property which represents that money or is derived therefrom and is at that date in the hands of the trustee;

(ii) in the case of an application in respect of a disposition which consisted of the transfer of property (other than a sum of money) or an application in respect of the transfer of property (other than a sum of money) in accordance with a contract, shall not exceed the aggregate of the value at the date of the order of so much of that property as is at that date in the hands of the trustee and the value at that date of any property which represents the first mentioned property or is derived therefrom and is at that date in the hands of the trustee.

(2) Where any such application is made in respect of a disposition made to any person as a trustee or in respect of any payment made or property transferred in pursuance of a contract to any person as a trustee, the trustee shall not be liable for having distributed any money or other property on the ground that he ought to have taken into account the possibility that such an application would be made.

(3) Where any such application is made in respect of a disposition made to any person as a trustee or in respect of any payment made or property transferred in accordance with a contract to any person as a trustee, any reference in the said section

10 or 11 to the donee shall be construed as including a reference to the trustee or trustees for the time being of the trust in question and any reference in subsection (1) or (2) above to a trustee shall be construed in the same way.

**[2.155]**

### 14 Provision as to cases where no financial relief was granted in divorce proceedings, etc

(1) Where, within twelve months from the date on which a decree of divorce or nullity of marriage has been made absolute or a decree of judicial separation has been granted, a party to the marriage dies and—

(a) an application for a financial provision order under section 23 of the Matrimonial Causes Act 1973 or a property adjustment order under section 24 of that Act has not been made by the other party to that marriage, or

(b) such an application has been made but the proceedings thereon have not been determined at the time of the death of the deceased,

then, if an application for an order under section 2 of this Act is made by that other party, the court shall, notwithstanding anything in section 1 or section 3 of this Act, have power, if it thinks it just to do so, to treat that party for the purposes of that application as if the decree of divorce or nullity of marriage had not been made absolute or the decree of judicial separation had not been granted, as the case may be.

(2) This section shall not apply in relation to a decree of judicial separation unless at the date of the death of the deceased the decree was in force and the separation was continuing.

**[2.156]**

### 15 Restriction imposed in divorce proceedings, etc on application under this Act

[(1) On the grant of a decree of divorce, a decree of nullity of marriage or a decree of judicial separation or at any time thereafter the court, if it considers it just to do so, may, on the application of either party to the marriage, order that the other party to the marriage shall not on the death of the applicant be entitled to apply for an order under section 2 of this Act.

In this subsection 'the court' means the High Court or, where a county court has jurisdiction by virtue of Part V of the Matrimonial and Family Proceedings Act 1984, a county court.]

(2) In the case of a decree of divorce or nullity of marriage an order may be made under subsection (1) above before or after the decree is made absolute, but if it is made before the decree is made absolute it shall not take effect unless the decree is made absolute.

(3) Where an order made under subsection (1) above on the grant of a decree of divorce or nullity of marriage has come into force with respect to a party to a marriage, then, on the death of the other party to that marriage, the court shall not entertain any application for an order under section 2 of this Act made by the first-mentioned party.

(4) Where an order made under subsection (1) above on the grant of a decree of judicial separation has come into force with respect to any party to a marriage, then, if the other party to that marriage dies while the decree is in force and the separation is continuing, the court shall not entertain any application for an order under section 2 of this Act made by the first-mentioned party.

**Amendment**

Sub-s (1): substituted by the MFPA 1984, s 8.

[2.157]

## [15A Restriction imposed in proceedings under Matrimonial and Family Proceedings Act 1984 on application under this Act]

[(1) On making an order under section 17 of the Matrimonial and Family Proceedings Act 1984 (orders for financial provision and property adjustment following overseas divorces, etc) the court, if it considers it just to do so, may, on the application of either party to the marriage, order that the other party to the marriage shall not on the death of the applicant be entitled to apply for an order under section 2 of this Act.
In this subsection 'the court' means the High Court or, where a county court has jurisdiction by virtue of Part V of the Matrimonial and Family Proceedings Act 1984, a county court.

(2) Where an order under subsection (1) above has been made with respect to a party to a marriage which has been dissolved or annulled, then, on the death of the other party to that marriage, the court shall not entertain an application under section 2 of this Act made by the first-mentioned party.

(3) Where an order under subsection (1) above has been made with respect to a party to a marriage the parties to which have been legally separated, then, if the other party to the marriage dies while the legal separation is in force, the court shall not entertain an application under section 2 of this Act made by the first-mentioned party.]

**Amendment**
Inserted by the MFPA 1984, s 25.

[2.158]

## 16 Variation and discharge of secured periodical payments orders made under Matrimonial Causes Act 1973

(1) Where an application for an order under section 2 of this Act is made to the court by any person who was at the time of the death of the deceased entitled to payments from the deceased under a secured periodical payments order made under the Matrimonial Causes Act 1973, then, in the proceedings on that application, the court shall have power, if an application is made under this section by that person or by the personal representative of the deceased, to vary or discharge that periodical payments order or to revive the operation of any provision thereof which has been suspended under section 31 of that Act.

(2) In exercising the powers conferred by this section the court shall have regard to all the circumstances of the case, including any order which the court proposes to make under section 2 or section 5 of this Act and any change (whether resulting from the death of the deceased or otherwise) in any of the matters to which the court was required to have regard when making the secured periodical payments order.

(3) The powers exercisable by the court under this section in relation to an order shall be exercisable also in relation to any instrument executed in pursuance of the order.

[2.159]

## 17 Variation and revocation of maintenance agreements

(1) Where an application for an order under section 2 of this Act is made to the court by any person who was at the time of the death of the deceased entitled to payments from the deceased under a maintenance agreement which provided for the continuation of payments under the agreement after the death of the deceased, then, in the proceedings on that application, the court shall have power, if an application is made

under this section by that person or by the personal representative of the deceased, to vary or revoke that agreement.

(2) In exercising the powers conferred by this section the court shall have regard to all the circumstances of the case, including any order which the court proposes to make under section 2 or section 5 of this Act and any change (whether resulting from the death of the deceased or otherwise) in any of the circumstances in the light of which the agreement was made.

(3) If a maintenance agreement is varied by the court under this section the like consequences shall ensue as if the variation had been made immediately before the death of the deceased by agreement between the parties and for valuable consideration.

(4) In this section 'maintenance agreement', in relation to a deceased person, means any agreement made, whether in writing or not and whether before or after the commencement of this Act, by the deceased with any person with whom he entered into a marriage, being an agreement which contained provisions governing the rights and liabilities towards one another when living separately of the parties to that marriage (whether or not the marriage has been dissolved or annulled) in respect of the making or securing of payments or the disposition or use of any property, including such rights and liabilities with respect to the maintenance or education of any child, whether or not a child of the deceased or a person who was treated by the deceased as a child of the family in relation to that marriage.



**[2.160]**

### 18 Availability of court's powers under this Act in applications under ss 31 and 36 of the Matrimonial Causes Act 1973

(1) Where—

(a) a person against whom a secured periodical payments order was made under the Matrimonial Causes Act 1973 has died and an application is made under section 31(6) of that Act for the variation or discharge of that order or for the revival of the operation of any provision thereof which has been suspended, or

(b) a party to a maintenance agreement within the meaning of section 34 of that Act has died, the agreement being one which provides for the continuation of payments thereunder after the death of one of the parties, and an application is made under section 36(1) of that Act for the alteration of the agreement under section 35 thereof.

the court shall have power to direct that the application made under the said section 31(6) or 36(1) shall be deemed to have been accompanied by an application for an order under section 2 of this Act.

(2) Where the court gives a direction under subsection (1) above it shall have power, in the proceedings on the application under the said section 31(6) or 36(1), to make any order which the court would have had power to make under the provisions of this Act if the application under the said section 31(6) or 36(1), as the case may be, had been made jointly with an application for an order under the said section 2; and the court shall have power to give such consequential directions as may be necessary for enabling the court to exercise any of the powers available to the court under this Act in the case of an application for an order under section 2.

(3) Where an order made under section 15(1) of this Act is in force with respect to a party to a marriage, the court shall not give a direction under subsection (1) above with respect to any application made under the said section 31(6) or 36(1) by that party on the death of the other party.

**[2.160.1]**

**Keypoint**

- General

**[2.160.2]**
**General**

Section 14 sets out the circumstances in which the court may ignore a divorce which is granted less than 12 months before the death. Sections 15 and 15A empower the courts, on or after the grant of a decree, to disqualify a party from applying for provision out of the estate of the other party. Sections 16 and 17 enable the courts, in the context of an application for financial provision under s 2, to make appropriate variations to existing secured periodical payment orders and maintenance agreements. On the other hand, s 18 is the other way round: it enables the courts, in the context of applications to vary such orders and agreements, to exercise powers under s 2.

**[2.161]**

### 19 Effect, duration and form of orders

(1) Where an order is made under section 2 of this Act then for all purposes, including the purposes of the enactments relating to inheritance tax, the will or the law relating to intestacy, or both the will and the law relating to intestacy, as the case may be, shall have effect and be deemed to have had effect as from the deceased's death subject to the provisions of the order.

(2) Any order made under section 2 or 5 of this Act in favour of—

(a) an applicant who was the former husband or former wife of the deceased, or

(b) an applicant who was the husband or wife of the deceased in a case where the marriage with the deceased was the subject of a decree of judicial separation and at the date of death the decree was in force and the separation was continuing,

shall, in so far as it provides for the making of periodical payments, cease to have effect on the remarriage of the applicant, except in relation to any arrears due under the order on the date of the remarriage.

(3) A copy of every order made under this Act [other than an order made under section 15(1) of this Act] shall be sent to the principal registry of the Family Division for entry and filing, and a memorandum of the order shall be endorsed on, or permanently annexed to, the probate or letters of administration under which the estate is being administered.

**Amendment**

Sub-s (3): words in square brackets inserted by the AJA 1982, s 52.

**[2.162]**

### 20 Provisions as to personal representatives

(1) The provisions of this Act shall not render the personal representative of a deceased person liable for having distributed any part of the estate of the deceased, after the end of the period of six months from the date on which representation with respect to the estate of the deceased is first taken out, on the ground that he ought to have taken into account the possibility—

(a) that the court might permit the making of an application for an order under section 2 of this Act after the end of that period, or

(b) that, where an order has been made under the said section 2, the court might exercise in relation thereto the powers conferred on it by section 6 of this Act,

but this subsection shall not prejudice any power to recover, by reason of the making of an order under this Act, any part of the estate so distributed.

(2) Where the personal representative of a deceased person pays any sum directed by an order under section 5 of this Act to be paid out of the deceased's net estate, he shall not be under any liability by reason of that estate not being sufficient to make the

payment, unless at the time of making the payment he has reasonable cause to believe that the estate is not sufficient.

(3) Where a deceased person entered into a contract by which he agreed to leave by his will any sum of money or other property to any person or by which he agreed that a sum of money or other property would be paid or transferred to any person out of his estate, then, if the personal representative of the deceased has reason to believe that the deceased entered into the contract with the intention of defeating an application for financial provision under this Act, he may, notwithstanding anything in that contract, postpone the payment of that sum of money or the transfer of that property until the expiration of the period of six months from the date on which representation with respect to the estate of the deceased is first taken out or, if during that period an application is made for an order under section 2 of this Act, until the determination of the proceedings on that application.



**[2.163]**

### 23 Determination of date on which representation was first taken out

In considering for the purposes of this Act when representation with respect to the estate of a deceased person was first taken out, a grant limited to settled land or to trust property shall be left out of account, and a grant limited to real estate or to personal estate shall be left out of account unless a grant limited to the remainder of the estate has previously been made or is made at the same time.

**[2.164]**

### 24 Effect of this Act on s 46(1)(vi) of Administration of Estates Act 1925

Section 46(1)(vi) of the Administration of Estates Act 1925, in so far as it provides for the devolution of property on the Crown, the Duchy of Lancaster or the Duke of Cornwall as bona vacantia, shall have effect subject to the provisions of this Act.

**[2.165]**

### 25 Interpretation

(1) In this Act—

'beneficiary', in relation to the estate of a deceased person, means—

- (a) a person who under the will of the deceased or under the law relating to intestacy is beneficially interested in the estate or would be so interested if an order had not been made under this Act, and
- (b) a person who has received any sum of money or other property which by virtue of section 8(1) or 8(2) of this Act is treated as part of the net estate of the deceased or would have received that sum or other property if an order had not been made under this Act;

'child' includes an illegitimate child and a child en ventre sa mere at the death of the deceased;

'the court' [unless the context otherwise requires] means the High Court, or where a county court has jurisdiction by virtue of section 22 of this Act, a county court;

['former wife' or 'former husband' means a person whose marriage with the deceased was during the lifetime of the deceased either—

- (a) dissolved or annulled by a decree of divorce or a decree of nullity of marriage granted under the law of any part of the British Islands, or
- (b) dissolved or annulled in any country or territory outside the British Islands by a divorce or annulment which is entitled to be recognised as valid by the law of England and Wales;]

'net estate', in relation to a deceased person, means—

(a) all property of which the deceased had power to dispose by his will (otherwise than by virtue of a special power of appointment) less the amount of his funeral, testamentary and administration expenses, debts and liabilities, including any inheritance tax payable out of his estate on his death;

(b) any property in respect of which the deceased held a general power of appointment (not being a power exercisable by will) which has not been exercised;

(c) any sum of money or other property which is treated for the purposes of this Act as part of the net estate of the deceased by virtue of section 8(1) or (2) of this Act;

(d) any property which is treated for the purposes of this Act as part of the net estate of the deceased by virtue of an order made under section 9 of the Act;

(e) any sum of money or other property which is, by reason of a disposition or contract made by the deceased, ordered under section 10 or 11 of this Act to be provided for the purpose of the making of financial provision under this Act;

'property' includes any chose in action;

'reasonable financial provision' has the meaning assigned to it by section 1 of this Act;

'valuable consideration' does not include marriage or a promise of marriage;

'will' includes codicil.

(2) For the purposes of paragraph (a) of the definition of 'net estate' in sub-section (1) above a person who is not of full age and capacity shall be treated as having power to dispose by will of all property of which he would have had power to dispose by will if he had been of full age and capacity.

(3) Any reference in this Act to provision out of the net estate of a deceased person includes a reference to provision extending to the whole of that estate.

(4) For the purposes of this Act any reference to a wife or husband shall be treated as including a reference to a person who in good faith entered into a void marriage with the deceased unless either—

(a) the marriage of the deceased and that person was dissolved or annulled during the lifetime of the deceased and the dissolution or annulment is recognised by the law of England and Wales, or

(b) that person has during the lifetime of the deceased entered into a later marriage.

(5) Any reference in this Act to remarriage or to a person who has remarried includes a reference to a marriage which is by law void or voidable or to a person who has entered into such a marriage, as the case may be, and a marriage shall be treated for the purposes of this Act as a remarriage, in relation to any party thereto, notwithstanding that the previous marriage of that party was void or voidable.

(6) Any reference in this Act to an order or decree made under the Matrimonial Causes Act 1973 or under any section of that Act shall be construed as including a reference to an order or decree which is deemed to have been made under that Act or under that section thereof, as the case may be.

(7) Any reference in this Act to any enactment is a reference to that enactment as amended by or under any subsequent enactment.

**Amendment**

Sub-s (1): in definition 'the court' words in square brackets inserted by the MFPA 1984, s 8; definition 'former wife' or 'former husband' substituted by the MFPA 1984, s 25.

# Domestic Proceedings and Magistrates' Courts Act 1978

**Contents**



*An Act to make fresh provision for matrimonial proceedings in magistrates' courts; to amend enactments relating to other proceedings so as to eliminate certain differences between the law relating to those proceedings and the law relating to matrimonial proceedings in magistrates' courts; to extend section 15 of the Justices of the Peace Act 1949; to amend Part II of the Magistrates' Courts Act 1952; to amend section 2 of the Administration of Justice Act 1964; to amend the Maintenance Orders (Reciprocal Enforcement) Act 1972; to amend certain enactments relating to adoption; and for purposes connected with those matters*

[30th June 1978]

**[2.166]**

### 1 Grounds of application for financial provision

Either party to a marriage may apply to a magistrates' court for an order under section 2 of this Act on the ground that the other party to the marriage … —

(a) has failed to provide reasonable maintenance for the applicant; or
(b) has failed to provide, or to make a proper contribution towards, reasonable maintenance for any child of the family; *or*
*(c) has behaved in such a way that the applicant cannot reasonably be expected to live with the respondent; or*
*(d) has deserted the applicant.*

**Appointment**
Commencement order: SI 1980/1478.

**Amendment**
First words omitted repealed by the MFPA 1984, s 46(1), Sch 1; para (c) and the word 'or' immediately preceding it, and para (d), prospectively repealed with savings by the FLA 1996, ss 18(1), 66(3), Sch 10, as from a day to be appointed; for savings see s 66(2), Sch 9, para 5 thereof.

**Definitions**
'Child of the family' – see s 88(1) at para **[2.190]** below.
'Live with' – see s 88(2) at para **[2.190]** below.

## [2.166.1]
## Keypoints

- Scheme of the Act
- The fault-based grounds
- Procedure generally

## [2.166.2]
## Scheme of the Act

Under the Domestic Proceedings and Magistrates' Courts Act 1978 (DPMCA 1978) the Family Proceedings Court can make orders for financial provision under three different bases as set out in s 2, s 6, and s 7. The first (s 2) is fault-based[1], on any of the grounds set out in s 1. The second (s 6) is based on agreement between the parties as to the payments to be made[2]. The third (s 7) is based on the parties' living apart and some maintenance having been paid since separation[3].

On an application under s 2 (fault-based) the court can make orders for periodical payments (for spouse and/or children, subject to the Child Support Act 1991) and lump sums up to £1,000. Under s 6 (agreement) the court can make orders for periodical payments and (unlimited) lump sums in whatever amount the parties agree. Under s 7 (living apart) the court can only make orders for periodical payments.

In each case the court has power to make interim periodical payments orders for a limited period (s 19), and to vary its orders within the limitations of ss 20–25. Where an application is made under the fault-based jurisdiction (s 2, relying on grounds set out in s 1), the court has power to refuse to make an order where the court considers that the matter should be heard by the High Court[4].

Once the grounds of each application are established the law to be applied with regard to the financial provision which the court is empowered to make is, within the limits of the court's jurisdiction, very similar to that applied by the High Court and county court in relation to financial provision under the MCA 1973 (as amended). Within the limits of the jurisdiction the principles to be applied are the same as in the higher courts[5], and reference should therefore be made to the MCA 1973[6]. The notes below point up the main differences between the DPMCA 1978 and the MCA 1973.

By definition, the principle of the clean break as enshrined in the MCA 1973, s 25A and s 31(7)(a) has no place in the DPMCA 1978. Section 4 provides that spousal periodical payments orders may continue for a term or during joint lives. Although s 20(6) provides power to revive a suspended order, there is no power to revive a term order which has expired.

Where the Family Proceedings Court makes a periodical payments order against a person ordinarily resident in England and Wales ('a qualifying maintenance order' under the Magistrates' Courts Act 1980, s 59(2)), it must also specify the means of payment, which may include standing order and also an attachment of earnings order (otherwise than by consent) without the need for separate application under the AtEA 1971[7].

Lump sum orders (maximum £1,000 unless a higher amount is agreed) may be ordered to be paid by instalments[8]. If such an order is made, the court has to power to vary the number, amount, and date of the instalments[9]. Note that on an application for a variation of an order made under s 2 or s 6 the court may order a lump sum notwithstanding that it has previously ordered a lump sum[10].

Note that payments to a child may be paid to, and recovered by, the person with whom the child has his home[11] and also that, where an order has been made for periodical payments in favour of a child, the child himself may apply for a variation of that order once he is over 16 years of age[12]; or (between the ages of 16 and 18 years) for its revival if it has ceased[13].

Before the Family Proceedings Court makes a final order under s 2, s 6, or s 7, or dismisses an application for such an order, it must first decide whether or not to exercise any of its powers under the ChA 1989 with respect to any minor child of the family[14].

An order under the DPMCA 1978 does not preclude a subsequent petition for divorce[15]. Nor does a decree of divorce necessarily affect an order made under the DPMCA 1978, although note the powers of the High Court and county court under s 28[16].

See generally, *Rayden and Jackson on Divorce and Family Matters* (17th edn, 1997), vol 1, ch 49 and the Noter-up thereto.

1 See para **[2.167]** below.
2 See para **[2.171]** below.
3 See para **[2.172]** below.
4 See the DPMCA 1978, s 27 at para **[2.182]** below.
5 See *Macey v Macey* (1982) 3 FLR 7.
6 See para **[2.113]** et seq.
7 See also s 20ZA at para **[2.176]** below in relation to variation orders.
8 See the MCA 1980, s 75.
9 See the DPMCA 1978, s 22 at para **[2.178]** below.
10 See the DPMCA 1978, s 20(1), (2) and (7) at para **[2.175]** below.
11 See the MCA 1980, s 62.
12 See the DPMCA 1978, s 20(12)(b) at para **[2.175]** below.
13 See the DPMCA 1978, s 20A(1) at para **[2.177]** below.
14 See the DPMCA 1978, s 8 at para **[2.173]** below.
15 See the MCA 1973, s 4.
16 See para **[2.183]** below.

## [2.166.3]
## The fault-based grounds

Note the prospective repeal of the grounds of behaviour and desertion in s 1, if the relevant part of the FLA 1996 were to be brought into force.

For failure to maintain, and failure to make a proper contribution towards child maintenance, see the MCA 1973, s 27[1].

For behaviour and desertion (the grounds the subject of the potential prospective repeal) the grounds have the same meaning as in divorce law (subject to the same potential prospective repeal), except that the desertion need not have continued for a period of two years as required by s 1(2)(c).

Behaviour is to be judged according to the test set out (in relation to the DPMCA 1978) in *Bergin v Bergin*[2], namely 'whether any right-thinking person would come to the conclusion that this wife could not reasonably be expected to live with this husband taking in to account the whole of the circumstances and the characters and personalities of the parties'. Note the six month time limit imposed by the Magistrates' Courts Act 1980, s 127.

Desertion requires physical separation and an intention on the part of the 'deserter' to bring cohabitation permanently to an end, or conduct which (with that intention) has the effect of driving the other party out ('constructive desertion')[3].

1 See para **[2.125]** above.
2 [1983] 1 All ER 905, 4 FLR 344.
3 See *Buchler v Buchler* [1947] P 25, [1947] 1 All ER 319, CA.

## [2.166.4]
### Procedure generally

Applications under the DPMCA 1978 are governed by the Family Proceedings Courts (Matrimonial Proceedings etc) Rules 1991, SI 1991/1991 which contain detailed provisions and prescribed forms for the making of the various applications, for written statements of evidence, for directions, and as to the requirements when making a financial provision order in the absence of one of the parties. For fees payable see the Magistrates' Courts Act 1980, Sch 6. As to the requirement (under the 1991 Rules) for the court to state the reasons for its decisions see the analysis in *Hackshaw v Hackshaw*[1].

1 [1999] 3 FCR 451, [1999] 2 FLR 876.

## [2.167]

### 2 Powers of court to make orders for financial provision

(1) Where on an application for an order under this section the applicant satisfies the court of any ground mentioned in section 1 of this Act, the court may, subject to the provisions of this Part of this Act, make any one or more of the following orders, that is to say—

(a) an order that the respondent shall make to the applicant such periodical payments, and for such term, as may be specified in the order;
(b) an order that the respondent shall pay to the applicant such lump sum as may be so specified;
(c) an order that the respondent shall make to the applicant for the benefit of a child of the family to whom the application relates, or to such a child, such periodical payments, and for such term, as may be so specified;
(d) an order that the respondent shall pay to the applicant for the benefit of a child of the family to whom the application relates, or to such a child, such lump sum as may be so specified.

(2) Without prejudice to the generality of subsection (1)(b) or (d) above, an order under this section for the payment of a lump sum may be made for the purpose of enabling any liability or expenses reasonably incurred in maintaining the applicant, or any child of the family to whom the application relates, before the making of the order to be met.

(3) The amount of any lump sum required to be paid by an order under this section shall not exceed £500 or such larger amount as the [Lord Chancellor] may from time to time by order fix for the purposes of this subsection.

Any order made by the [Lord Chancellor] under this subsection shall be made by statutory instrument and shall be subject to annulment in pursuance of a resolution of either House of Parliament.

**Appointment**
Commencement order: SI 1980/1478.

**Amendment**
Sub-s (3): words in square brackets substituted by SI 1992/709, art 3(2), Sch 2.

**Definitions**
'Lump sum' – £1,000: see s 20(7) (at para **[2.175]** below), unless the respondent agrees a higher amount: see s 20(8) (at para **[2.175]** below).
'Child of the family' – see s 88(1) at para **[2.190]** below.



### [2.167.1]
### Keypoints

- Differences from the MCA 1973, s 23
- Nature of lump sum order
- Procedure

### [2.167.2]
### Differences from the MCA 1973, s 23

See 'Scheme of the Act' at para **[2.166.2]** above.

The most obvious differences from the provisions of the MCA 1973 are the absence of any provision for secured periodical payments and the limitation on the amount of the lump sum (unless the respondent agrees a higher amount[1]). Note also that the prerequisite of the applicant satisfying the court as to any of the grounds in s 1 would appear to rule out an application for financial provision orders by the applicant against himself, as in *Sherdley v Sherdley*[2]. Such an application is however covered by s 6[3].

The lump sum provision in s 2(1)(b) and (d) is singular (in contrast to that in the MCA 1973, s 23(2))[4]. However note that, in relation to spouses, there is provision for repeat lump sums on variation under s 20(7)[5]. Note also that a lump sum order under the DPMCA 1978 is specifically within the definition of 'maintenance orders' set out in the AtEA 1971, s 2 and Sch 1 and enforceable additionally by an order under that Act[6].

Before the Family Proceedings Court makes a final order or dismisses the application it must first decide whether or not to exercise any of its powers under the ChA 1989 with respect to any minor child of the family[7]. Furthermore, s 26 requires the a hearing an application under s 2 to consider the possibility of a reconciliation and gives power to adjourn the proceedings in order to facilitate this, if appropriate with the aid of a probation officer. Note that the court also has power to make a non-molestation order, even if no application for such an order has been made[8].

1 See the DPMCA 1978, s 20(8) at para **[2.175]** below.
2 [1988] AC 213.
3 See para **[2.171]** below.
4 See para **[2.117]** above.
5 See para **[2.175]** below.
6 See also the MCA 1980, s 59; and the DPMCA 1978, s 20ZA at para **[2.176]** below.
7 See the DPMCA 1978, s 8 at para **[2.173]** below.
8 See the FLA 1996, s 42(2)(b).

### [2.167.3]
### Nature of lump sum order

Lump sum orders (maximum £1,000 unless a higher amount is agreed) may be ordered to be paid by instalments[1]. If such an order is made, the court has the power to vary the number, amount, and date of the instalments[2]. Note that on an application for a variation of an order made under s 2 the court may order a lump sum notwithstanding that it has previously ordered a lump sum[3].

1 See the MCA 1980, s 75.
2 See the DPMCA 1978, s 22 at para **[2.178]** below.
3 See the DPMCA 1978, s 20(1) and (7) at para **[2.175]** below. See also para **[2.166.2]** above.

## [2.167.4]
## Procedure

See the Family Proceedings Courts (Matrimonial Proceedings etc) Rules 1991, SI 1991/1991 and para **[2.166.4]** above.

## [2.168]

### [3 Matters to which court is to have regard in exercising its powers under s 2]

[(1) Where an application is made for an order under section 2 of this Act, it shall be the duty of the court, in deciding whether to exercise its powers under that section and, if so, in what manner, to have regard to all the circumstances of the case, first consideration being given to the welfare while a minor of any child of the family who has not attained the age of eighteen.

(2) As regards the exercise of its powers under subsection (1)(a) or (b) of section 2, the court shall in particular have regard to the following matters—

(a) the income, earning capacity, property and other financial resources which each of the parties to the marriage has or is likely to have in the foreseeable future, including in the case of earning capacity any increase in that capacity which it would in the opinion of the court be reasonable to expect a party to the marriage to take steps to acquire;
(b) the financial needs, obligations and responsibilities which each of the parties to the marriage has or is likely to have in the foreseeable future;
(c) the standard of living enjoyed by the parties to the marriage before the occurrence of the conduct which is alleged as the ground of the application;
(d) the age of each party to the marriage and the duration of the marriage;
(e) any physical or mental disability of either of the parties to the marriage;
(f) the contributions which each of the parties has made or is likely in the foreseeable future to make to the welfare of the family, including any contribution by looking after the home or caring for the family;
(g) the conduct of each of the parties, if that conduct is such that it would in the opinion of the court be inequitable to disregard it.

(3) As regards the exercise of its power under subsection (1)(c) or (d) of section 2, the court shall in particular have regard to the following matters—

(a) the financial needs of the child;
(b) the income, earning capacity (if any), property and other financial resources of the child;
(c) any physical or mental disability of the child;
(d) the standard of living enjoyed by the family before the occurrence of the conduct which is alleged as the ground of the application;
(e) the manner in which the child was being and in which the parties to the marriage expected him to be educated or trained;
(f) the matters mentioned in relation to the parties to the marriage in paragraphs (a) and (b) of subsection (2) above.

(4) As regards the exercise of its power under section 2 in favour of a child of the family who is not the child of the respondent, the court shall also have regard—

(a) to whether the respondent has assumed any responsibility for the child's maintenance and, if he did, to the extent to which, and the basis on which, he assumed that responsibility and to the length of time during which he discharged that responsibility;
(b) to whether in assuming and discharging that responsibility the respondent did so knowing that the child was not his own child;
(c) to the liability of any other person to maintain the child.]

**Amendment**
Substituted by the MFPA 1984, s 9.

**Definitions**
'Child of the family' – see s 88(1) at para **[2.190]** below.



## [2.168.1]
## Keypoints
- Differences from the MCA 1973, s 25
- Proper approach

## [2.168.2]
## Differences from the MCA 1973, s 25

See 'Scheme of the Act' at para **[2.166.2]** above.

There is no significant difference between the provisions of this section and those of the MCA 1973, s 25. There is of course no equivalent in the DPMCA 1978 of the consideration of pension loss required by s 25(2)(h) of the MCA 1973, and the consideration in the DPMCA 1978, s 3(2)(c) of the standard of living enjoyed by the parties is, by definition, the standard of living before the occurrence of the conduct which is alleged as the ground of the application – not up to the breakdown of the marriage as is the consideration on divorce or nullity. Section 3(3) of the DPMCA 1978 lists the considerations relating to children in a slightly different order but the only difference of substance is the omission of the requirement to consider any physical or mental disability of either of the parties to the marriage in the MCA 1973, s 25(3)(e) incorporating, inter alia, s 25(2)(e) (as well as any such disability of the child in s 3(3)(c) of the DPMCA 1978).

## [2.168.3]
## Proper approach

Under s 3 of the DPMCA 1978 the court is required to have particular regard to the matters set out in sub-ss (2) and (3) and, in relation to a child of the family who is not a child of the respondent, also to have regard for the matters set out in sub-s (4). In *Vasey v Vasey*[1] it was held that the proper approach is for the magistrates to make findings on each of the matters in turn and then to balance those factors against one another so as to arrive at an order which is just and reasonable.

1 [1985] FLR 596.

## [2.169]

### 4 Duration of orders for financial provision for a party to a marriage

(1) The term to be specified in any order made under section 2(1)(a) of this Act shall be such term as the court thinks fit except that the term shall not begin earlier than the date of the making of the application for the order and shall not extend beyond the death of either of the parties to the marriage.

(2) Where an order is made under the said section 2(1)(a) and the marriage of the parties affected by the order is subsequently dissolved or annulled but the order continues in force, the order shall, notwithstanding anything in it, cease to have effect

on the remarriage of the party in whose favour it was made, except in relation to any arrears due under the order on the date of the remarriage.

**Appointment**
Commencement order: SI 1980/1478.

**Definitions**
'Remarriage' – see s 88(3) at para **[2.190]** below.

## [2.169.1]
## Keypoints

- Inter-relation with subsequent decree of divorce
- Term of periodical payments orders
- Effect of cohabitation

## [2.169.2]
## Inter-relation with subsequent decree of divorce

See 'Scheme of the Act' at para **[2.166.2]** above.

## [2.169.3]
## Term of periodical payments orders

Although s 20(6) provides power to revive a suspended order, there is no power to revive a term order which has expired.

## [2.169.4]
## Effect of cohabitation

Section 25 below[1] provides that in some circumstances a spousal periodical payments order continues to have effect (for a limited period of six months) notwithstanding cohabitation at the time of the order or subsequently. An order for child maintenance continues to have effect notwithstanding cohabitation by the parties, unless the court otherwise directs[2].

1 See para **[2.180]** below.
2 See the DPMCA 1978, s 25(2) at para **[2.180]** below.

## [2.170]

### 5 Age limit on making orders for financial provision for children and duration of such orders

(1) Subject to subsection (3) below, no order shall be made under section 2(1)(c) or (d) of this Act in favour of a child who has attained the age of eighteen.

(2) The term to be specified in an order made under section 2(1)(c) of this Act in favour of a child may begin with the date of the making of an application for the order in question or any later date [or a date ascertained in accordance with subsection (5) or (6) below] but—

(a) shall not in the first instance extend beyond the date of the birthday of the child next following his attaining the upper limit of the compulsory school age *(that is to say, the age that is for the time being that limit by virtue of section 35 of the Education Act 1944 together with any Order in Council made under that section)* [(construed in accordance with section 8 of the Education Act 1996)] [unless the court considers that in the circumstances of the case the welfare of the child requires that it should extend to a later date]; and

(b) shall not in any event, subject to subsection (3) below, extend beyond the date of the child's eighteenth birthday.

(3) The court—

(a) may make an order under section 2(1)(c) or (d) of this Act in favour of a child who has attained the age of eighteen, and
(b) may include in an order made under section 2(1)(c) of this Act in relation to a child who has not attained that age a provision for extending beyond the date when the child will attain that age the term for which by virtue of the order any payments are to be made to or for the benefit of that child,

if it appears to the court—

(i) that the child is, or will be, or if such an order or provision were made would be, receiving instruction at an educational establishment or undergoing training for a trade, profession or vocation, whether or not he is also, or will also be, in gainful employment; or
(ii) that there are special circumstances which justify the making of the order or provision.

(4) Any order made under section 2(1)(c) of this Act in favour of a child shall, notwithstanding anything in the order, cease to have effect on the death of the person liable to make payments under the order.

[(5) Where—

(a) a maintenance assessment ('the current assessment') is in force with respect to a child; and
(b) an application is made for an order under section 2(1)(c) of this Act—
  (i) in accordance with section 8 of the Child Support Act 1991; and
  (ii) before the end of the period of 6 months beginning with the making of the current assessment,

the term to be specified in any such order made on that application may be expressed to begin on, or at any time after, the earliest permitted date.

(6) For the purposes of subsection (5) above, 'the earliest permitted date' is whichever is the later of—

(a) the date 6 months before the application is made; or
(b) the date on which the current assessment took effect or, where successive maintenance assessments have been continuously in force with respect to a child, on which the first of those assessments took effect.

(7) Where—

(a) a maintenance assessment ceases to have effect or is cancelled by or under any provision of the Child Support Act 1991; and
(b) an application is made, before the end of the period of 6 months beginning with the relevant date, for an order under section 2(1)(c) of this Act in relation to a child with respect to whom that maintenance assessment was in force immediately before it ceased to have effect or was cancelled,

the term to be specified in any such order, or in any interim order under section 19 of this Act, made on that application, may begin with the date on which that maintenance assessment ceased to have effect or, as the case may be, the date with effect from which it was cancelled, or any later date.

(8) In subsection (7)(b) above—

(a) where the maintenance assessment ceased to have effect, the relevant date is the date on which it so ceased; and
(b) where the maintenance assessment was cancelled, the relevant date is the later of—
  (i) the date on which the person who cancelled it did so, and
  (ii) the date from which the cancellation first had effect.]

**Appointment**

Commencement order: SI 1980/1478.

**Amendment**

Sub-s (2): first words in square brackets inserted by SI 1993/623, art 2, Sch 1, para 4; words in italics prospectively repealed and subsequent words in square brackets prospectively substituted by the EA 1996, s 582(1), Sch 37, para 138, as from a day to be appointed; final words in square brackets substituted by the MFPA 1984, s 9. Sub-ss (5) to (8): inserted by SI 1993/623, art 2, Sch 1, para 5.

**Definitions**
'Child' – see s 88(1) at para **[2.190]** below.

## [2.170.1]
## Keypoint

- Differences from the MCA 1973, s 29

## [2.170.2]
## Differences from the MCA 1973, s 29

See 'Scheme of the Act' at para **[2.166.2]** above.

This section mirrors s 29 of the MCA 1973, except in so far as under the DPMCA 1978 there is neither the power to order secured provision (see above) nor the power to make a transfer of property order (whether to spouse or children). Note that under sub-s (4) a child maintenance order ceases to have effect on the death of the payer and there is no express saving (as by analogy in s 4(2) above or expressly under the MCA 1973, s 29(4)) for arrears due at the date of death.

## [2.171]

### [6 Orders for payments which have been agreed by the parties]

[(1) Either party to a marriage may apply to a magistrates' court for an order under this section on the ground that either the party making the application or the other party to the marriage has agreed to make such financial provision as may be specified in the application and, subject to subsection (3) below, the court on such an application may, if—

(a) it is satisfied that the applicant or the respondent, as the case may be, has agreed to make that provision, and
(b) it has no reason to think that it would be contrary to the interests of justice to exercise its powers hereunder,

order that the applicant or the respondent, as the case may be, shall make the financial provision specified in the application.

(2) In this section 'financial provision' means the provision mentioned in any one or more of the following paragraphs, that is to say—

(a) the making of periodical payments by one party to the other,
(b) the payment of a lump sum by one party to the other,
(c) the making of periodical payments by one party to a child of the family or to the other party for the benefit of such a child,
(d) the payment by one party of a lump sum to a child of the family or to the other party for the benefit of such a child,

and any reference in this section to the financial provision specified in an application made under subsection (1) above or specified by the court under subsection (5) below is a reference to the type of provision specified in the application or by the court, as the case may be, to the amount so specified as the amount of any payment to be made thereunder and, in the case of periodical payments, to the term so specified as the term for which the payments are to be made.

(3) Where the financial provision specified in an application under subsection (1) above includes or consists of provision in respect of a child of the family, the court shall not make an order under that subsection unless it considers that the provision which the applicant or the respondent, as the case may be, has agreed to make in respect of that child provides for, or makes a proper contribution towards, the financial needs of the child.

(4) A party to a marriage who has applied for an order under section 2 of this Act shall not be precluded at any time before the determination of that application from applying for an order under this section; but if an order is made under this section on the application of either party and either of them has also made an application for an order under section 2 of this Act, the application made for the order under section 2 shall be treated as if it had been withdrawn.

(5) Where on an application under subsection (1) above the court decides—

(a) that it would be contrary to the interests of justice to make an order for the making of the financial provision specified in the application, or

(b) that any financial provision which the applicant or the respondent, as the case may be, has agreed to make in respect of a child of the family does not provide for, or make a proper contribution towards, the financial needs of that child,

but is of the opinion—

(i) that it would not be contrary to the interests of justice to make an order for the making of some other financial provision specified by the court, and

(ii) that, in so far as that other financial provision contains any provision for a child of the family, it provides for, or makes a proper contribution towards, the financial needs of that child,

then if both the parties agree, the court may order that the applicant or the respondent, as the case may be, shall make that other financial provision.

(6) Subject to subsection (8) below, the provisions of section 4 of this Act shall apply in relation to an order under this section which requires periodical payments to be made to a party to a marriage for his own benefit as they apply in relation to an order under section 2(1)(a) of this Act.

(7) Subject to subsection (8) below, the provisions of section 5 of this Act shall apply in relation to an order under this section for the making of financial provision in respect of a child of the family as they apply in relation to an order under section 2(1)(c) or (d) of this Act.

(8) Where the court makes an order under this section which contains provision for the making of periodical payments and, by virtue of subsection (4) above, an application for an order under section 2 of this Act is treated as if it had been withdrawn, then the term which may be specified as the term for which the payments are to be made may begin with the date of the making of the application for the order under section 2 or any later date.

(9) Where the respondent is not present or represented by counsel or solicitor at the hearing of an application for an order under subsection (1) above, the court shall not make an order under this section unless there is produced to the court such evidence as may be prescribed by rules of—

(a) the consent of the respondent to the making of the order,

(b) the financial resources of the respondent, and

(c) in a case where the financial provision specified in the application includes or consists of provision in respect of a child of the family to be made by the applicant to the respondent for the benefit of the child or to the child, the financial resources of the child.]

**Amendment**

Substituted by the MFPA 1984, s 10.

**Definitions**

'Financial provision' – see s 6(2).
'Lump sum' – whatever sum the parties agree: see s 20(8) at para **[2.175]** below.
'Child'; 'Child of the family' – see s 88(1) at para **[2.190]** below.
'Evidence as may be prescribed' – see the Family Proceedings Courts (Matrimonial Proceedings etc) Rules 1991, SI 1991/1991, r 17 and Sch 1.

## [2.171.1]
### Keypoints

- Inter-relation with applications under s 2
- Nature of lump sum order
- Term of periodical payments orders
- Procedure

## [2.171.2]
### Inter-relation with applications under s 2

An application under s 2 may be supplemented with an application under s 6; but on the making of an order under s 6 the application under s 2 will be deemed withdrawn. An order under s 6 may be backdated to the date of the application under s 2[1]. Note that the order made may not be in the terms contemplated by the parties, provided that they agree with the provision which the court proposes to make (by agreement) instead[2].

1 See the DPMCA 1978, s 6(4) and (8) at para **[2.171]** above.
2 See the DPMCA 1978, s 6(5) at para **[2.171]** below.

## [2.171.3]
### Nature of lump sum order

Lump sum orders (in whatever amount is agreed, even if over £1,000 under s 6) may be ordered to be paid by instalments[1]. If such an order is made, the court has the power to vary the number, amount, and date of the instalments[2]. Note that on an application for a variation of an order made under s 6 the court may order a lump sum notwithstanding that it has previously ordered a lump sum[3].

1 See the MCA 1980, s 75.
2 See the DPMCA 1978, s 22 at para **[2.178]** below.
3 See the DPMCA 1978, s 20(2) and (7) at para **[2.175]** below. See also 'Scheme of the Act' at para **[2.166.2]** above.

## [2.171.4]
### Term of periodical payments orders

See 'Scheme of the Act' at para **[2.166.2]** above.

## [2.171.5]
### Procedure

See the Family Proceedings Courts (Matrimonial Proceedings etc) Rules 1991, SI 1991/1991; and 'Procedure generally' at para **[2.166.4]** above.

## [2.172]

### 7 Powers of court where parties are living apart by agreement

(1) Where the parties to a marriage have been living apart for a continuous period exceeding three months, *neither party having deserted the other*, and one of the parties has been making periodical payments for the benefit of the other party or of a child of the family, that other party may apply to a magistrates' court for an order under this section, and any application made under this subsection shall specify the aggregate amount of the payments so made during the period of three months immediately preceding the date of the making of the application.

(2) Where on an application for an order under this section the court is satisfied that the respondent has made the payments specified in the application, the court may, subject to the provisions of this Part of this Act, make one or both of the following orders, that is to say—

(a) an order that the respondent shall make to the applicant such periodical payments, and for such term, as may be specified in the order;

(b) an order that the respondent shall make to the applicant for the benefit of a child of the family to whom the application relates, or to such a child, such periodical payments, and for such term, as may be so specified.

(3) The court in the exercise of its powers under this section—

(a) shall not require the respondent to make payments which exceed in aggregate during any period of three months the aggregate amount paid by him for the benefit of the applicant or a child of the family during the period of three months immediately preceding the date of the making of the application;

(b) shall not require the respondent to make payments to or for the benefit of any person which exceed in amount the payments which the court considers that it would have required the respondent to make to or for the benefit of that person on an application under section 1 of this Act;

(c) shall not require payments to be made to or for the benefit of a child of the family who is not a child of the respondent unless the court considers that it would have made an order in favour of that child on an application under section 1 of this Act.

(4) Where on an application under this section the court considers that the orders which it has the power to make under this section—

(a) would not provide reasonable maintenance for the applicant, or

(b) if the application relates to a child of the family, would not provide, or make a proper contribution towards reasonable maintenance for that child,

the court shall refuse to make an order under this section, but the court may treat the application as if it were an application for an order under section 2 of this Act.

(5) The provisions of section 3 of this Act shall apply in relation to an application for an order under this section as they apply in relation to an application for an order under section 2 of this Act subject to the modification that for the reference in [subsection (2)(c)] of the said section 3 to the occurrence of the conduct which is alleged as the ground of the application there shall be substituted a reference to the living apart of the parties to the marriage.

(6) The provisions of section 4 of this Act shall apply in relation to an order under this section which requires periodical payments to be made to the applicant for his own benefit as they apply in relation to an order under section 2(1)(a) of this Act.

(7) The provisions of section 5 of this Act shall apply in relation to an order under this section for the making of periodical payments in respect of a child of the family as they apply in relation to an order under section 2(1)(c) of this Act.

**Appointment**

Commencement order: SI 1980/1478.

**Amendment**

Sub-s (1): words in italics prospectively repealed with savings by the FLA 1996, ss 18(2), 66(3), Sch 10, as from a day to be appointed; for savings see s 66(2), Sch 9, para 5 thereof. Sub-s (5): words in square brackets substituted by the MFPA 1984, s 46(1), Sch 1, para 22.

**Definitions**

'Living apart' – see para **[2.172.3]** below.
'Deserted' – see para **[2.166.3]** above.
'Child'; 'Child of the family' – see s 88(1) at para **[2.190]** below.
'Reasonable maintenance' – see (by analogy) the MCA 1973, s 27 at para **[2.125]** above.

## [2.172.1]
## Keypoints

- General
- Grounds for an application under s 7
- Periodical payments only, with court-imposed maximum/cap

- Defaulting to an application under s 2
- Term of periodical payments orders
- Procedure

### [2.172.2]
### General

This section sets out the third basis for making periodical payments orders under the Act, namely to preserve the financial status quo where the parties have been living apart for three months and some maintenance has been paid since separation.

### [2.172.3]
### Grounds for an application under s 7

The parties must have been living apart for a continuous period exceeding three months and money has been paid to a spouse or child. Note the potential prospective repeal of the requirement of absence of desertion. By analogy with the divorce legislation 'living apart' means 'not living with each other in the same household'[1].

1 See the MCA 1973, s 2(5), (6); and the DPMCA 1978, s 88(3) at para **[2.190]** below.

### [2.172.4]
### Periodical payments only, with court-imposed maximum/cap

Section 7 does not provide for the payment of a lump sum. Further, s 7(3) effectively prohibits the court from preserving a 'status quo' of financial provision in excess of that which a court would order on an application under s 2.

### [2.172.5]
### Defaulting to an application under s 2

If the financial 'status quo' is less than the court considers reasonable, it may treat the application (for a periodical payments order) as if made under s 2[1].

1 See the DPMCA 1978, s 7(4) at para **[2.172]** above.

### [2.172.6]
### Term of periodical payments orders

See 'Scheme of the Act' at para **[2.166.2]** above.

### [2.172.7]
### Procedure

See the Family Proceedings Courts (Matrimonial Proceedings etc) Rules 1991, SI 1991/1991; and see 'Procedure generally' at para **[2.166.4]** above.

### [2.173]

#### [8 Restrictions on making of orders under this Act: welfare of children]

[Where an application is made by a party to a marriage for an order under section 2, 6 or 7 of this Act, then, if there is a child of the family who is under the age of eighteen, the court shall not dismiss or make a final order on the application until it has decided whether to exercise any of its powers under the Children Act 1989 with respect to the child.]

**Amendment**
Substituted by the ChA 1989, s 108(5), Sch 13, para 36.

**Definitions**
'Child of the family' – see s 88(1) at para **[2.190]** below.

**[2.173.1]**
**Keypoint**
- Section notes

**[2.173.2]**
**Section notes**

This section requires the court, before disposing of an application for financial provision under the DPMCA 1978, to consider exercising its powers under the ChA 1989 with respect to any child of the family.



**[2.174]**

### 19 Interim orders

(1) Where an application is made for an order under section 2, 6 or 7 of this Act—

(a) the magistrates' court at any time before making a final order on, or dismissing, the application or on refusing to make an order on the application by virtue of section 27 of this Act, and

(b) the High Court on ordering the application to be reheard by a magistrates' court (either after the refusal of an order under section 27 of this Act or on an appeal under section 29 of this Act),

shall, subject to the provisions of this Part of this Act, have the … —

(i) power to make an order (in this Part of this Act referred to as an 'interim maintenance order') which requires the respondent to make to the applicant or to any child of the family who is under the age of eighteen, or to the applicant for the benefit of such a child, such periodical payments as the court thinks reasonable;

(ii) …

(2) …

(3) An interim maintenance order may provide for payments to be made from such date as the court may specify, [except that, subject to section 5(5) and (6) of this Act, the date shall not be] earlier than the date of the making of the application for an order under section 2, 6 or 7 of this Act; and where such an order made by the High Court on an appeal under section 29 of this Act provides for payments to be made from a date earlier than the date of the making of the order, the interim order may provide that payments made by the respondent under an order made by a magistrates' court shall, to such extent and in such manner as may be provided by the interim order, be treated as having been paid on account of any payment provided for by the interim order.

[(3A) Where an application is made for an order under section 6 of this Act by the party to the marriage who has agreed to make the financial provision specified in the application—

(a) subsection (1) shall apply as if the reference in paragraph (i) to the respondent were a reference to the applicant and the references to the applicant were references to the respondent; and

(b) [subsection] (3) shall apply accordingly.]

(4) …

(5) Subject to subsection (6) below, an interim order made on an application for an order under section 2, 6 or 7 of this Act shall cease to have effect on whichever of the following dates occurs first, that is to say—

(a) the date, if any, specified for the purpose in the interim order;

(b) the date of the expiration of the period of three months beginning with the date of the making of the interim order;

(c) the date on which a magistrates' court either makes a final order on or dismisses the application.

(6) Where an interim order made under subsection (1) above would, but for this subsection, cease to have effect by virtue of subsection (5)(a) or (b) above, the

magistrates' court which made the order or, in the case of an interim order made by the High Court, the magistrates' court by which the application for an order under section 2, 6 or 7 of this Act is to be reheard, shall have power by order to provide that the interim order shall continue in force for a further period, and any order continued in force under this subsection shall cease to have effect on whichever of the following dates occurs first, that is to say—

(a) the date, if any, specified for the purpose in the order made under this subsection;
(b) the date of the expiration of the period of three months beginning with the date of the making of the order under this subsection or, if more than one order has been made under this subsection with respect to the application, beginning with the date of the making of the first of those orders;
(c) the date on which the court either makes a final order on, or dismisses, the application.

(7) Not more than one interim maintenance order ... may be made with respect to any application for an order under section 2, 6 or 7 of this Act, but without prejudice to the powers of a court under this section on any further such application.

(8) No appeal shall lie from the making of or refusal to make, the variation of or refusal to vary, or the revocation of or refusal to revoke, an interim maintenance order.

**Appointment**

Commencement order: SI 1980/1478.

**Amendment**

Sub-ss (1), (4), (7), (9): words omitted repealed by the ChA 1989, s 108(7), Sch 15. Sub-s (2): words in square brackets substituted by SI 1993/623, art 2, Sch 1, para 6; words omitted repealed by the ChA 1989, s 108(7), Sch 15. Sub-s (3): words in square brackets substituted by SI 1993/623, art 2, Sch 1, para 6. Sub-s (3A): inserted by the MFPA 1984, s 46(1), Sch 1; word in paragraph (b) in square brackets substituted by the ChA 1989, s 108(5), Sch 13, para 37.

**Definitions**

'Child of the family' – see s 88(1) at para **[2.190]** below.

## [2.174.1]
## Keypoints

- No appeal
- Quantum
- Limited duration
- Procedure

## [2.174.2]
## No appeal

The decision of the Family Proceedings Court in relation to interim periodical payments is final[1].

1 See the DPMCA 1978, s 19(8) at para **[2.174]** above.

## [2.174.3]
## Quantum

If the court makes an interim order it is for 'such periodical payments as the court thinks reasonable'[1]. See the analogous provisions in relation to maintenance pending suit under s 22 of the MCA 1973[2]. The Family Proceedings Court has power to vary an interim order (although not to extend its duration)[3].

1 See the DPMCA 1978, s 19(1)(i) at para **[2.174]** above.
2 See para **[2.116]** above.
3 See the DPMCA 1978, s 20(5) at para **[2.175]** below.

### [2.174.4]
### Limited duration

Section 19(5), (6), and (7) provide that in the first instance an interim order shall last for not more than three months. This is subject to the possibility of extension(s) up to a maximum of a further three months in aggregate from the date of the first such extension. Although the court has power to vary an interim order under s 20(5) that power does not enable it to extend its duration[1]. As to the effect of cohabitation see s 25 below[2] and notes thereafter.

1 See the DPMCA 1978, s 20(5) at para **[2.175]** below.
2 See the DPMCA 1978, s 25 at para **[2.180]** below.



### [2.174.5]
### Procedure

See the Family Proceedings Courts (Matrimonial Proceedings etc) Rules 1991, SI 1991/1991; and see 'Procedure generally' at para **[2.166.4]** above.

### [2.175]

#### 20 Variation, revival and revocation of orders for periodical payments

(1) Where a magistrates' court has made an order under section 2(1)(a) or (c) of this Act for the making of periodical payments the court shall have power, on an application made under this section, to vary or revoke that order and also to make an order under section 2(1)(b) or (d) of this Act.

[(2) Where a magistrates' court has made an order under section 6 of this Act for the making of periodical payments by a party to a marriage the court shall have power, on an application made under this section, to vary or revoke that order and also to make an order for the payment of a lump sum by that party either—

(a) to the other party to the marriage, or

(b) to a child of the family or to that other party for the benefit of that child.]

(3) Where a magistrates' court has made an order under section 7 of this Act for the making of periodical payments, the court shall have power, on an application made under this section, to vary or revoke that order.

(4) …

(5) Where a magistrates' court has made an interim maintenance order under section 19 of this Act, the court, on an application made under this section, shall have power to vary or revoke that order, except that the court shall not by virtue of this subsection extend the period for which the order is in force.

(6) The power of the court under this section to vary an order for the making of periodical payments shall include power to suspend any provision thereof temporarily and to revive any provision so suspended.

(7) Where the court has power by virtue of this section to make an order for the payment of a lump sum, the amount of the lump sum shall not exceed the maximum amount that may at that time be required to be paid under section 2 (3) of this Act, but the court may make an order for the payment of a lump sum not exceeding that amount notwithstanding that the person required to pay the lump sum was required to pay a lump sum by a previous order under this Part of this Act.

(8) Where the court has power by virtue of subsection (2) above to make an order for the payment of a lump sum and the respondent [or the applicant, as the case may be,] has agreed to pay a lump sum of an amount exceeding the maximum amount that may at that time be required to be paid under section 2 (3) of this Act, the court may, notwithstanding anything in subsection (7) above, make an order for the payment of a lump sum of that amount.

(9) An order made by virtue of this section which varies an order for the making of periodical payments may, … provide that the payments as so varied shall be made from

such date as the court may specify, [except that, subject to subsections (9A) and (9B) below, the date shall not be] earlier than the date of the making of the application under this section.

[(9A) Where—

(a) there is in force an order ('the order')—

(i) under section 2(1)(c) of this Act,

(ii) under section 6(1) of this Act making provision of a kind mentioned in paragraph (c) of section 6(2) of this Act (regardless of whether it makes provision of any other kind mentioned in that paragraph),

(iii) under section 7(2)(b) of this Act, or

(iv) which is an interim maintenance order under which the payments are to be made to a child or to the applicant for the benefit of a child;

(b) the order requires payments specified in it to be made to or for the benefit of more than one child without apportioning those payments between them;

(c) a maintenance assessment ('the assessment') is made with respect to one or more, but not all, of the children with respect to whom those payments are to be made; and

(d) an application is made, before the end of the period of 6 months beginning with the date on which the assessment was made, for the variation or revocation of the order,

the court may, in exercise of its powers under this section to vary or revoke the order, direct that the variation or revocation shall take effect from the date on which the assessment took effect or any later date.

(9B) Where—

(a) an order ('the child order') of a kind prescribed for the purposes of section 10(1) of the Child Support Act 1991 is affected by a maintenance assessment;

(b) on the date on which the child order became so affected there was in force an order ('the spousal order')—

(i) under section 2(1)(a) of this Act,

(ii) under section 6(1) of this Act making provision of a kind mentioned in section 6(2)(a) of this Act (regardless of whether it makes provision of any other kind mentioned in that paragraph),

(iii) under section 7(2)(a) of this Act, or

(iv) which is an interim maintenance order under which the payments are to be made to the applicant (otherwise than for the benefit of a child); and

(c) an application is made, before the end of the period of 6 months beginning with the date on which the maintenance assessment was made, for the spousal order to be varied or revoked,

the court may, in exercise of its powers under this section to vary or revoke the spousal order, direct that the variation or revocation shall take effect from the date on which the child order became so affected or any later date.

(9C) For the purposes of subsection (9B) above, an order is affected if it ceases to have effect or is modified by or under section 10 of the Child Support Act 1991.]

(10) ...

(11) In exercising the powers conferred by this section the court shall, so far as it appears to the court just to do so, give effect to any agreement which has been reached between the parties in relation to the application and, if there is no such agreement or if the court decides not to give effect to the agreement, the court shall have regard to all the circumstances of the case, [first consideration being given to the welfare while a minor of any child of the family who has not attained the age of eighteen, and the circumstances of the case shall include any change] in any of the matters to which the court was required to have regard when making the order to which the application relates or, in the case of an application for the variation or revocation of an order made under section 6 of this Act or on an appeal under section 29 of this Act, to which the court would have been required to have regard if that order had been made under section 2 of this Act.

[(12) An application under this section may be made—

(a) where it is for the variation or revocation of an order under section 2, 6, 7 or 19 of this Act for periodical payments, by either party to the marriage in question; and

(b) where it is for the variation of an order under section 2(1)(c), 6 or 7 of this Act for periodical payments to or in respect of a child, also by the child himself, if he has attained the age of sixteen.]

(13) …

**Appointment**

Commencement order: SI 1980/1478.

**Amendment**

Sub-s (2): substituted by the MFPA 1984, s 11. Sub-s (4): repealed by the ChA 1989, s 108(7), Sch 15. Sub-s (8): words in square brackets inserted by the MFPA 1984, s 46(1), Sch 1. Sub-s (9): words omitted repealed by the ChA 1989, s 108(7), Sch 15; words in square brackets substituted by SI 1993/623, art 2, Sch 1, para 7. Sub-ss (9A) to (9C): inserted by SI 1993/623, art 2, Sch 1, para 8. Sub-ss (10), (13): repealed by the FLRA 1987, s 33(4), Sch 4. Sub-s (11): words in square brackets substituted by the MFPA 1984, s 9. Sub-s (12): substituted by the ChA 1989, s 108(5), Sch 13, para 38.

**Definitions**

'Lump sum' – maximum £1,000 or whatever higher amount the parties agree: see s 20(8) at para **[2.175]** above.
'Child'; 'Child of the family' – see s 88(1) at para **[2.190]** below.



## [2.175.1]
## Keypoints

- Differences from the MCA 1973, s 31(1) and (7)
- Proper approach on variation application

## [2.175.2]
## Differences from MCA 1973, s 31(1) and (7)

See 'Scheme of the Act' at para **[2.166.2]** above.

The basis on which the Family Proceedings Court exercises its variation jurisdiction is the same as that applied by the higher courts in ancillary relief proceedings, save that there is no provision as to clean break (nor any equivalent of capitalisation of periodical payments under the MCA 1973, s 31(7A))[1].

There are three principal differences between the two provisions. First, under the MCA 1973 the court can backdate the effect of a variation order potentially as far as the application for the original periodical payments order (usually the date of the petition)[2]. By contrast a variation under the DPMCA 1978 expressly cannot be backdated beyond the date of the application to vary[3].

The second point of difference is that the DPMCA 1978 contains detailed provisions[4] in relation to the impact of a child support assessment which overlaps with an order under the DPMCA 1978.

Thirdly, s 20(12)(b) expressly provides that a child of the age of 16 and above can apply for the variation of a periodical payments order in his or her favour[5].

1 See also the DPMCA 1978, s 20(11) at para **[2.175]** above.
2 See *Morley-Clarke v Jones (HM Inspector of Taxes)* [1986] Ch 311, [1985] FLR 242.
3 See the DPMCA 1978, s 20(9) at para **[2.175]** above.
4 See the DPMCA 1978, s 20(9A) to (9C) at para **[2.175]** above.
5 See para **[2.166.2]** above; and the DPMCA 1978, s 20A(1) at para **[2.177]** below.

## [2.175.3]
### Proper approach on variation application

Under s 20(11) of the DPMCA 1978 the court is required to have regard to any agreement reached between the parties and, in the absence of an acceptable agreement, to have regard to any change in the relevant matters set out in s 3. Note that if there is an agreement, the court should only refuse to give effect to it if the agreement would result in injustice to a party[1].

In the absence of an agreement to which the court should give effect, the court should 'consider the matter de novo looking at all the circumstances of the case'[2].

1 See *Whitton v Devizes Magistrates' Court* [1985] Fam Law 125.
2 See *Riley v Riley* [1988] 1 FLR 273 per Swinton Thomas J at 275G.

## [2.176]

### [20ZA Variation of orders for periodical payments: further provisions]

[(1) Subject to subsections (7) and (8) below, the power of the court under section 20 of this Act to vary an order for the making of periodical payments shall include power, if the court is satisfied that payment has not been made in accordance with the order, to exercise one of its powers under paragraphs (a) to (d) of section 59(3) of the Magistrates' Courts Act 1980.

(2) In any case where—

(a) a magistrates' court has made an order under this Part of this Act for the making of periodical payments, and

(b) payments under the order are required to be made by any method of payment falling within section 59(6) of the Magistrates' Courts Act 1980 (standing order, etc),

an application may be made under this subsection to the clerk to the justices for the petty sessions area for which the court is acting for the order to be varied as mentioned in subsection (3) below.

(3) Subject to subsection (5) below, where an application is made under subsection (2) above, the clerk, after giving written notice (by post or otherwise) of the application to the respondent and allowing the respondent, within the period of 14 days beginning with the date of the giving of that notice, an opportunity to make written representations, may vary the order to provide that payments under the order shall be made [to the justices' chief executive for the court].

(4) The clerk may proceed with an application under subsection (2) above notwithstanding that the respondent has not received written notice of the application.

(5) Where an application has been made under subsection (2) above, the clerk may, if he considers it inappropriate to exercise his power under subsection (3) above, refer the matter to the court which, subject to subsections (7) and (8) below, may vary the order by exercising one of its powers under paragraphs (a) to (d) of section 59(3) of the Magistrates' Courts Act 1980.

(6) Subsection (4) of section 59 of the Magistrates' Courts Act 1980 (power of court to order that account be opened) shall apply for the purposes of subsections (1) and (5) above as it applies for the purposes of that section.

(7) Before varying the order by exercising one of its powers under paragraphs (a) to (d) of section 59(3) of the Magistrates' Courts Act 1980, the court shall have regard to any representations made by the parties to the application.

(8) If the court does not propose to exercise its power [under paragraph (c), (cc) or (d)] of subsection (3) of section 59 of the Magistrates' Courts Act 1980, the court shall, unless upon representations expressly made in that behalf by the person to whom payments under the order are required to be made it is satisfied that it is undesirable to do so, exercise its power under paragraph (b) of that subsection.

(9) Subsection (12) of section 20 of this Act shall have effect for the purposes of applications under subsection (2) above as it has effect for the purposes of applications under that section.

(10) None of the powers of the court, or of the clerk to the justices, conferred by this section shall be exercisable in relation to an order under this Part of this Act for the making of periodical payments which is not a qualifying maintenance order (within the meaning of section 59 of the Magistrates' Courts Act 1980).]

**Amendment**

Inserted by the MEA 1991, s 5. Sub-s (3): AJA 1999, s 90(1), Sch 13. Sub-s (8): words in square brackets substituted by SI 1994/731, art 2.



[2.177]

### [20A Revival of orders for periodical payments]

[(1) Where an order made by a magistrates' court under this Part of this Act for the making of periodical payments to or in respect of a child (other than an interim maintenance order) ceases to have effect—

(a) on the date on which the child attains the age of sixteen, or

(b) at any time after that date but before or on the date on which he attains the age of eighteen,

the child may apply to the court which made the order for an order for its revival.

(2) If on such an application it appears to the court that—

(a) the child is, will be or (if an order were made under this subsection) would be receiving instruction at an educational establishment or undergoing training for a trade, profession or vocation, whether or not while in gainful employment, or

(b) there are special circumstances which justify the making of an order under this subsection,

the court shall have power by order to revive the order from such date as the court may specify, not being earlier than the date of the making of the application.

(3) Any order revived under this section may be varied or revoked under section 20 in the same way as it could have been varied or revoked had it continued in being.]

**Amendment**

Inserted by the FLRA 1987, s 33(1), Sch 2, para 69. Substituted by the ChA 1989, s 108(5), Sch 13, para 39.

**Definitions**

'Child' – see s 88(1) at para **[2.190]** below.

[2.178]

### 22 Variation of instalments of lump sum

Where in the exercise of its powers under [section 75 of the Magistrates' Courts Act 1980] a magistrates' court orders that a lump sum required to be paid under this Part of this Act shall be paid by instalments, the court, on an application made by either the person liable to pay or the person entitled to receive that sum, shall have power to vary that order by varying the number of instalments payable, the amount of any instalment payable and the date on which any instalment becomes payable.

**Appointment**

Commencement order: SI 1980/1478.

**Amendment**

Words in square brackets substituted by the MCA 1980, s 154, Sch 7, para 160.

**[2.179]**

### 23 Supplementary provisions with respect to variation and revocation of orders

(1) …

(2) The powers of a magistrates' court to revoke, revive or vary an order for the periodical payment of money [and the power of the clerk of a magistrates' court to vary such an order] under [section 60 of the Magistrates' Courts Act 1980] and [the power of a magistrates' court] to suspend or rescind certain other orders under [section 63 (2) of that Act] shall not apply in relation to an order made under this Part of this Act.

**Appointment**

Commencement order: SI 1980/1478.

**Amendment**

Sub-s (1): repealed by the CLSA 1990, s 125(7), Sch 20. Sub-s (2): first and third words in square brackets inserted by the MEA 1991, s 11(1), Sch 2, para 2; second and final words in square brackets substituted by the MCA 1980, s 154, Sch 7, para 161.

**[2.180]**

### 25 Effect on certain orders of parties living together

(1) Where—

(a) periodical payments are required to be made to one of the parties to a marriage (whether for his own benefit or for the benefit of a child of the family) by an order made under section 2, [or 6] of this Act or by an interim maintenance order made under section 19 of this Act (otherwise than on an application under section 7 of this Act), …

(b) …

the order shall be enforceable notwithstanding that the parties to the marriage are living with each other at the date of the making of the order or that, although they are not living with each other at that date, they subsequently resume living with each other; but the order shall cease to have effect if after that date the parties continue to live with each other, or resume living with each other, for a continuous period exceeding six months.

(2) Where any of the following orders is made under this Part of this Act, that is to say—

(a) an order under section 2, [or 6] of this Act which requires periodical payments to be made to a child of the family, [or]

(b) an interim maintenance order under section 19 of this Act (otherwise than on an application under section 7 of this Act) which requires periodical payments to be made to a child of the family,

(c), (d)…

then, unless the court otherwise directs, the order shall continue to have effect and be enforceable notwithstanding that the parties to the marriage in question are living with each other at the date of the making of the order or that, although they are not living with each other at that date, they subsequently resume living with each other.

(3) Any order made under section 7 of this Act, and any interim maintenance order made on an application for an order under that section, shall cease to have effect if the parties to the marriage resume living with each other.

(4) Where an order made under this Part of this Act ceases to have effect by virtue of subsection (1) or (3) above or by virtue of a direction given under subsection (2) above, a magistrates' court may, on an application made by either party to the marriage, make an order declaring that the first mentioned order ceased to have effect from such date as the court may specify.

**Appointment**
Commencement order: SI 1980/1478.

**Amendment**
Sub-ss (1), (2): words omitted repealed and words in square brackets substituted or inserted by the ChA 1989, s 108(5), (7), Sch 13, para 41, Sch 15.

**Definitions**
'Child'; 'Child of the family' – see s 88(1) at para **[2.190]** below.
'Living with each other' – see s 88(2) at para **[2.190]** below.



## [2.180.1]
### Keypoint

- Different treatment depending on orders

## [2.180.2]
### Different treatment depending on orders

See 'Effect of cohabitation' at para **[2.169.4]** above.

Note that an order under s 7 (living apart), and any interim order made under s 7, ceases to have effect on cohabitation[1]. In any other case spousal orders survive for six months[2]; and children's orders continue unless otherwise directed by the court[3].

1 See the DPMCA 1978, s 25(3) at para **[2.180]** above.
2 See the DPMCA 1978, s 25(1)(b) at para **[2.180]** above.
3 See the DPMCA 1978, s 25(2) at para **[2.180]** above.

## [2.181]

### 26 Reconciliation

(1) Where an application is made for an order under section 2 of this Act the court, before deciding whether to exercise its powers under that section, shall consider whether there is any possibility of reconciliation between the parties to the marriage in question; and if at any stage of the proceedings on that application it appears to the court that there is a reasonable possibility of such a reconciliation, the court may adjourn the proceedings for such period as it thinks fit to enable attempts to be made to effect a reconciliation.

(2) Where the court adjourns any proceedings under subsection (1) above, it may request [an officer of the Service (within the meaning of the Criminal Justice and Court Services Act 2000)] or any other person to attempt to effect a reconciliation between the parties to the marriage, and where any such request is made, [that officer or] other person shall report in writing to the court whether the attempt has been successful or not, but shall not include in that report any other information.

**Appointment**
Commencement order: SI 1980/1478.

**Amendment**
Sub-s (2): CJCSA 2000, s 74, Sch 7.

## [2.182]

### 27 Refusal of order in case more suitable for High Court

Where on hearing an application for an order under section 2 of this Act a magistrates' court is of the opinion that any of the matters in question between the parties would be more conveniently dealt with by the High Court, the magistrates' court shall refuse to make any order on the application, and no appeal shall lie from that refusal; but if in any proceedings in the High Court relating to or comprising the same subject matter as that application the High Court so orders, the application shall be reheard and determined by a magistrates' court acting for the same petty sessions area as the first mentioned court.

**Appointment**

Commencement order: SI 1980/1478.

**[2.182.1]**

**Keypoint**

- Concurrent jurisdiction requirement

**[2.182.2]**

**Concurrent jurisdiction requirement**

Where the High Court does not have concurrent jurisdiction (for example in cases based on desertion of under two years' duration) the Family Proceedings Court cannot refuse to hear the application. Furthermore it should not hear some points of a case and refer others if the points are inter-connected[1].

1 See *Davies v Davies* [1957] P 357, [1957] 2 All ER 444.

**[2.183]**

### 28 Powers of High Court and county court in relation to certain orders under Part I

(1) Where after the making by a magistrates' court of an order under this Part of this Act then, except in the case of an order for the payment of a lump sum, the court in which the proceedings or any application made therein are or is pending may, if it thinks fit, direct that the order made by a magistrates' court shall cease to have effect on such date as may be specified in the direction.

...

(3) Nothing in this section shall be taken as prejudicing the effect of any order made by the High Court or a county court so far as it implicitly supersedes or revokes an order or part of an order made by a magistrates' court.

**Appointment**

Commencement order: SI 1979/731.

**Amendment**

Sub-s (2): repealed by the FLA 1996, Sch 10. Date in force: 1 October 1997: see the Family Law Act 1996 (Commencement No 2) Order 1997, art 3(1)(d).

**[2.184]**

### 29 Appeals

(1) Subject to section 27 of this Act, where a magistrates' court makes or refuses to make, varies or refuses to vary, revokes or refuses to revoke an order (other than an interim maintenance order) under this Part of this Act, an appeal shall lie to the High Court.

(2) On an appeal under this section the High Court shall have power to make such orders as may be necessary to give effect to its determination of the appeal, including such incidental or consequential orders as appear to the court to be just, and, in the case of an appeal from a decision of a magistrates' court made on an application for or in respect of an order for the making of periodical payments, the High Court shall have power to order that its determination of the appeal shall have effect from such date as

the court thinks fit, not being earlier than the date of the making of the application to the magistrates' court [or, in a case where there was made to the magistrates' court an application for an order under section 2 and an application under section 6 and the term of the periodical payments was or might have been ordered to begin on the date of the making of the application for an order under section 2, the date of the making of that application].

(3) Without prejudice to the generality of subsection (2) above, where, on an appeal under this section in respect of an order of a magistrates' court requiring any person to make periodical payments, the High Court reduces the amount of those payments or discharges the order, the High Court shall have power to order the person entitled to payments under the order of the magistrates' court to pay to the person liable to make payments under that order such sum in respect of payments already made in compliance with the order as the court thinks fit and, if any arrears are due under the order of the magistrates' court, the High Court shall have power to remit the payment of those arrears or any part thereof.

(4) …

(5) Any order of the High Court made on an appeal under this section (other than an order directing that an application shall be reheard by a magistrates' court) shall for the purposes of the enforcement of the order and for the purposes of [section 20] of this Act be treated as if it were an order of the magistrates' court from which the appeal was brought and not of the High Court.



**Appointment**

Commencement orders: SI 1979/731, 1980 No 1478.

**Amendment**

Sub-s (2): words in square brackets inserted by the MFPA 1984, s 46(1), Sch 1. Sub-s (4): repealed by the ChA 1989, s 108(7), Sch 15. Sub-s (5): words in square brackets substituted by the ChA 1989, s 108(5), Sch 13, para 42.

**[2.184.1]**

**Keypoint**

- Procedure

**[2.184.2]**

**Procedure**

See the FPR 1991, SI 1991/1247, r 8.2 at para **[3.508]** below. The appeal is to the divisional court. It is not a hearing of the matter afresh[1].

This section is construed narrowly. The fact that a refusal to exercise the power to remit arrears under the Magistrates' Court Act 1980, s 95 is taken at the same time as a decision whether or not to vary a periodical payments order under the DPMCA 1978, does not render the refusal to remit the arrears a part of the variation decision, and an appeal in respect of the refusal to remit must therefore be made by way of case stated under s 111 of the Magistrates' Court Act 1980[2].

1 See *Hackshaw v Hackshaw* [1999] 2 FLR 876 per Wilson J at 879B.

2 See *Berry v Berry* [1987] Fam 1, [1987] 1 FLR 105 (considered also in *P v P (Periodical Payments: Appeals)* [1995] 2 FCR 108, [1995] 1 FLR 563).

**[2.185]**

### 30 Provisions as to jurisdiction and procedure

(1) A magistrates' court shall, subject to [section 2 of the Family Law Act 1986 and] [section 70 of the Magistrates' Courts Act 1980] and any determination of [a magistrates' courts committee] thereunder, have jurisdiction to hear an application for an order under this Part of this Act if at the date of the making of the application

either the applicant or the respondent ordinarily resides within the commission area for which the court is appointed.

(2)–(4) …

(5) It is hereby declared that any jurisdiction conferred on a magistrates' court by this Part of this Act is exercisable notwithstanding that any party to the proceedings is not domiciled in England.

**Appointment**

Commencement order: SI 1979/731.

**Amendment**

Sub-s (1): first words in square brackets inserted by the FLA 1986, s 68(1), Sch 1, para 24; second words in square brackets substituted by the MCA 1980, s 154, Sch 7, para 163; final words in square brackets substituted by the PMCA 1994, s 91, Sch 8, Part II, para 29. Sub-ss (2) to (4): repealed by the CLSA 1990, s 125(7), Sch 20.

**Definitions**

'Ordinarily resides' – see para **[2.185.2]** below.

## [2.185.1]

### Keypoint

- The meaning of 'ordinary' and 'habitual' residence

## [2.185.2]

### The meaning of 'ordinary' and 'habitual' residence

The point is a complex one on which there has been a great deal of authority. In summary the requirement that a person is ordinarily resident in England and Wales is a question of fact. It has been said that there is no distinction between 'ordinary residence' and 'habitual residence'[1] and that 'habitual residence' is to be equated with 'ordinary residence'[2] wherever it appears in family law statutes. What is required is that 'the purpose of living where one does has a sufficient degree of continuity to be properly described as settled'[3].

1 See *Shah v Barnet London Borough Council* [1983] 2 AC 309,[1983] 1 All ER 226, HL.

2 See *Ikimi v Ikimi* [2001] EWCA Civ 873, [2001] 2 FCR 385.

3 *Shah v Barnet London Borough Council* [1983] 2 AC 309 per Lord Scarman at 344D. See also *Nessa v Chief Adjudication Officer* [1999] 3 FCR 538, [1999] 2 FLR 1116, HL applying, inter alia, *Shah.*

## [2.186]

### 31 Constitution of courts

(1) Where the hearing of an application under section 1 of this Act is adjourned after the court has decided that it is satisfied of any ground mentioned in that section, the court which resumes the hearing of that application may include justices who were not sitting when the hearing began if—

(a) the parties to the proceedings agree; and

(b) at least one of the justices composing the court which resumes the hearing was sitting when the hearing of the application began.

(2) Where, by virtue of subsection (1) above, among the justices composing the court which resumes the hearing of an application under section 1 of this Act there are any justices who were not sitting when the hearing of the application began, the court which resumes the hearing shall before making any order on the application make such inquiry into the facts and circumstances of the case as will enable the justices who were not sitting when the hearing began to be fully acquainted with those facts and circumstances.

**Appointment**

Commencement order: SI 1980/1478.

[2.187]

## 32 Enforcement etc of orders for payment of money

[(1) An order for the payment of money made by a magistrates' court under this Part of this Act shall be enforceable as a magistrates' court maintenance order.]

(2) Without prejudice to [section 59 of the Magistrates' Courts Act 1980] (which relates to the power of a magistrates' court to direct periodical payments to be made through [a justices' chief executive]), a magistrates' court making an order under this Part of this Act for the making of a periodical payment by one person to another may direct that it shall be made to some third party on that other person's behalf instead of directly to that other person; and, for the purposes of any order made under this Part of this Act, [the said section 59] shall have effect as if, in [subsection (7)] thereof, for the words ['the person who applied for the maintenance order'] there were substituted the words 'the person to whom the payments under the order fall to be made'.

(3) Any person for the time being under an obligation to make payments in pursuance of any order for the payment of money made under this Part of this Act shall give notice of any change of address to such person, if any, as may be specified in the order; and any person who without reasonable excuse fails to give such a notice shall be liable on summary conviction to a fine not exceeding [level 2 on the standard scale].

(4) A person shall not be entitled to enforce through the High Court or any county court the payment of any arrears due under an order made by virtue of this Part of this Act without the leave of that court if those arrears became due more than twelve months before proceedings to enforce the payment of them are begun.

(5) The court hearing an application for the grant of leave under subsection (4) above may refuse leave, or may grant leave subject to such restrictions and conditions (including conditions as to the allowing of time for payment or the making of payment by instalments) as that court thinks proper, or may remit the payment of such arrears or any part thereof.

(6) An application for the grant of leave under subsection (4) above shall be made in such manner as may be prescribed by rules.

### Appointment

Commencement order: SI 1980/1478.

### Amendment

Sub-s (1): substituted by the FLRA 1987, s 33(1), Sch 2. Sub-s (2): MCA 1980, s 154, Sch 7; MEA 1991, s 11(1), Sch 2; AJA 1999, s 90(1), Sch 13. Sub-s (3): maximum fine converted to a level on the standard scale by the CJA 1982, ss 37, 46.

### Definitions

'An order' – includes an order of the High Court on appeal: see s 29(5) at para **[2.184]** above.

[2.188]

## 35 Orders for repayment in certain cases of sums paid after cessation of order by reason of remarriage

(1) Where—

(a) an order made under section 2(1)(a), 6 or 7 of this Act has, by virtue of section 4(2) of this Act, ceased to have effect by reason of the remarriage of the party in whose favour it was made, and

(b) the person liable to make payments under the order made payments in accordance with it in respect of a period after the date of that remarriage in the mistaken belief that the order was still subsisting, no proceedings in respect of a cause of action arising out of the circumstances mentioned in paragraphs (a) and (b) above shall be maintainable by the person so liable or his personal representatives against the person so entitled or his personal representatives, but on an application made under this section the court may exercise the powers conferred on it by subsection (2) below.

(2) The court may order the respondent to an application made under this section to pay to the applicant a sum equal to the amount of the payments made in respect of the period mentioned in subsection (1)(b) above or, if it appears to the court that it would be unjust to make that order, it may either order the respondent to pay to the applicant such lesser sum as it thinks fit or dismiss the application.

(3) An application under this section may be made by the person liable to make payments under the order made under section 2(1)(a), 6 or 7 of this Act or his personal representatives and may be made against the person entitled to payments under that order or his personal representatives.

(4) An application under this section shall be made to a county court, except that such an application may be made in proceedings in the High Court or a county court for leave to enforce, or the enforcement of, the payment of arrears under an order made under section 2(1)(a), 6 or 7 of this Act; and accordingly references in this section to the court are references to the High Court or a county court, as the circumstances require.

(5) An order under this section for the payment of any sum may provide for the payment of that sum by instalments of such amount as may be specified in the order.

(6) The jurisdiction conferred on a county court by this section shall be exercisable by a county court notwithstanding that by reason of the amount claimed in an application under this section the jurisdiction would not but for this subsection be exercisable by a county court.

(7) [A justices' chief executive] to whom any payments under an order made under section 2(1)(a), 6 or 7 of this Act are required to be made, and the collecting officer under an attachment of earnings order made to secure payments under the first mentioned order, shall not be liable—

(a) in the case of [the justices' chief executive], for any act done by him in pursuance of the first mentioned order after the date on which that order ceased to have effect by reason of the remarriage of the person entitled to payments under it, and

(b) in the case of the collecting officer, for any act done by him after that date in accordance with any enactment or rule of court specifying how payments made to him in compliance with the attachment of earnings order are to be dealt with,

if, but only if, the act was one which he would have been under a duty to do had the first mentioned order not ceased to have effect by reason of the remarriage and the act was done before notice in writing of the fact that the person so entitled had remarried was given to him by or on behalf of that person, the person liable to make payments under the first mentioned order or the personal representatives of either of those persons.

(8) In this section 'collecting officer', in relation to an attachment of earnings order, means the officer of the High Court, the officer designated by the Lord Chancellor or the [justices' chief executive] to whom a person makes payments in compliance with the order.

**Appointment**

Commencement order: SI 1980/1478.

**Amendment**

Sub-ss (7), (8): AJA 1999, s 90(1), Sch 13.

[2.189]

## 87 Expenses

There shall be defrayed out of moneys provided by Parliament any increase attributable to this Act in the sums payable out of moneys so provided under any other enactment.

**Appointment**
Commencement order: SI 1978/1489.



[2.190]

## 88 Interpretation

(1) In this Act—

…

'child', in relation to one or both of the parties to a marriage, includes [a child whose father and mother were not married to each other at the time of his birth];

'child of the family', in relation to the parties to a marriage, means—

(a) a child of both of those parties; and

(b) any other child, not being a child who is [placed with those parties as foster parents] by a local authority or voluntary organisation, who has been treated by both of those parties as a child of their family;

…

['family proceedings'] has the meaning assigned to it by [section 65 of the Magistrates' Courts Act 1980];

'local authority' means the council of a county (other than a metropolitan county), of a metropolitan district or of a London borough, or the Common Council of the City of London;

['magistrates' court maintenance order' has the same meaning as in section 150(1) of the Magistrates' Courts Act 1980;]

['maintenance assessment' has the same meaning as it has in the Child Support Act 1991 by virtue of section 54 of that Act as read with any regulations in force under that section;]

…

'rules' means rules made under [section 144 of the Magistrates' Courts Act 1980].

(2) References in this Act to the parties to a marriage living with each other shall be construed as references to their living with each other in the same household.

(3) For the avoidance of doubt it is hereby declared that references in this Act to remarriage include references to a marriage which is by law void or voidable.

(4) Anything authorised or required by this Act to be done by, to or before the magistrates' court by, to or before which any other thing was done, or is to be done, may be done by, to or before any magistrates' court acting for the same petty sessions area as that court.

(5) Any reference in this Act to an enactment shall be construed as a reference to that enactment as amended or extended by or under any subsequent enactment, including this Act.

**Appointment**
Commencement orders: SI 1978/997, 1979 No 731.

**Amendment**
Sub-s (1): definition 'actual custody' (omitted) repealed by the ChA 1989, s 108(7), Sch 15. Para (1): in definition 'child' words from 'a child' to 'time of his birth' in square brackets substituted by the ChA 1989, s 108(5), Sch 13, para 43. Para (1): in definition 'child of the family' words 'placed with those parties as foster parents' in square brackets subsituted by the ChA 1989, s 108(5), Sch 13, para 43. Sub-s (1): definition 'commission area' (omitted) repealed by the

AJA 1999, s 106, Sch 15, Pt V, Table (1). Date in force: 27 September 1999: see the AJA 1999, s 108(3)(f). Sub-s (1): in definition 'family proceedings' words 'family proceedings' in square brackets substituted by the ChA 1989, s 92, Sch 11, para 6. Sub-s (1): in definition 'family proceedings' words 'section 65 of the Magistrates' Courts Act 1980' in square brackets substituted by the MCA 1980, s 154, Sch 7, para 167. Sub-s (1): definition 'magistrates' court maintenance order' inserted by the FLRA 1987, s 33(1), Sch 2, para 71. Sub-s (1): definition 'maintenance assessment' inserted by SI 1993/623, art 2, Sch 1, para 9. Sub-s (1): definition 'petty sessions area' (omitted) repealed by the AJA 1999, s 106, Sch 15, Pt V, Table (1). Date in force: 27 September 1999: see the AJA 1999, s 108(3)(f). Sub-s (1): in definition 'rules' words 'section 144 of the Magistrates' Courts Act 1980' in square brackets substituted by the MCA 1980, s 154, Sch 7, para 167.

**[2.191]**

## 89 Transitional provisions, amendments, repeals and commencement

(1) The transitional provisions contained in Schedule 1 to this Act shall have effect.

(2) Subject to the transitional provisions contained in Schedule 1 to this Act—

(a) the enactments specified in Schedule 2 to this Act shall have effect subject to the amendments specified in that Schedule (being minor amendments and amendments consequential on the preceding provisions of this Act), and

(b) the enactments specified in Schedule 3 to this Act are hereby repealed to the extent specified in the third column of that Schedule.

(3) This Act shall come into force on such date as the Secretary of State may by order made by statutory instrument appoint and different dates may be appointed for, or for different purposes of, different provisions.

(4) Without prejudice to the transitional provisions contained in Schedule 1 to this Act, an order under subsection (3) above may make such further transitional provision as appears to the Secretary of State to be necessary or expedient in connection with the provisions thereby brought into force, including such adaptations of the provisions thereby brought into force or any provision of this Act then in force as appear to him to be necessary or expedient in consequence of the partial operation of this Act or the Children Act 1975.

(5) An order under subsection (3) above may repeal any provision of this Act which has ceased to have effect by reason of the coming into force of the Adoption Act 1976.

(6) The inclusion in this Act of any express transitional provision or amendment shall not be taken as prejudicing the general application of section 38 of the Interpretation Act 1889 with regard to the effect of repeals.

### Appointment

Commencement orders: SI 1978/997, SI 1978/1489, SI 1978/1490, SI 1980/2036.

**[2.192]**

## 90 Short title and extent

(1) This Act may be cited as the Domestic Proceedings and Magistrates' Courts Act 1978.

(2) …

(3) Except for the following provisions, that is to say—

(a) sections 54, 59, 74 (5), 88 (5), 89 (2), (3) and (4) and this section, and

(b) [paragraphs 12, 13, 14 and 33] of Schedule 2 and Schedule 3,

this Act does not extend to Northern Ireland, and in section 88 (5) of this Act any reference to an enactment includes a reference to an enactment contained in an Act of the Parliament of Northern Ireland or a Measure of the Northern Ireland Assembly.

### Appointment

Commencement order: SI 1978/997.

### Amendment

Sub-s (2): applies to Scotland only. Sub-s (3): words in square brackets substituted by the MO(RE)A 1992, s 2(1), Sch 2, para 1.

# SCHEDULE 1
## Transitional Provisions

(s 89)

**[2.193]**

**1**

This Act (including the repeals and amendments made by it) shall not have effect in relation to any application made under any enactment repealed or amended by this Act if that application is pending at the time when the provision of this Act which repeals or amends that enactment comes into force.

**2**

Any order made or other thing done under the Matrimonial Proceedings (Magistrates' Courts) Act 1960 which is in force immediately before the coming into force of Part I of this Act shall not be affected by the repeal by this Act of that Act, and the provisions of that Act shall after the coming into force of the said Part I apply in relation to such an order, and to an order made under that Act by virtue of paragraph 1 above, subject to the following modifications—

(a) on a complaint for the revocation of the order the court shall not be bound under section 8 of that Act to revoke the order by reason of an act of adultery committed by the person on whose complaint the order was made;

(b) on a complaint for the variation, revival or revocation of the order, the court, in exercising its powers under the said section 8 in relation to a provision of the order requiring the payment of money, shall have regard to any change in any of the matters to which the court would have been required to have regard when making that order if the order had been made on an application under section 2 of this Act;

[(bb) on a complaint after the coming into force of paragraph 27 of Schedule 1 to the Matrimonial and Family Proceedings Act 1984 for the variation, revival or revocation of the order, the court, in exercising its powers under the said section 8 in relation to any provision of the order requiring the payment of money, shall have power to order that payments required to be made for the maintenance of a child of the family shall be made to the child himself;]

(c) where the order contains a provision for the legal custody of a child, the court shall have power, on a complaint made by a grandparent of the child, to vary that order under the said section 8 by the addition to the order of a provision requiring access to the child to be given to that grandparent;

(d) where the court, by virtue of paragraph (c) above, varies the order by the addition of a provision requiring access to a child to be given to a grandparent, the court shall have power to vary or revoke that provision on a complaint made—

   (i) by that grandparent, or

   (ii) by either party to the marriage in question, or

   (iii) where the child is not a child of both the parties to the marriage, by any person who though not a party to the marriage is a parent of the child, or

   (iv) where under the order a child is for the time being committed to the legal custody of some person other than one of the parents or a party to the marriage, by the person to whose legal custody the child is committed by the order.

**3**

The amendment by this Act of any enactment shall not affect the operation of that enactment in relation to any order made or having effect as if made under the

Matrimonial Proceedings (Magistrates' Courts) Act 1960 (including an order made under that Act by virtue of paragraph 1 above) or in relation to any decision of a magistrates' court made on an application for such an order for the variation, revival or revocation of such an order [but as respects enactments amended by this Act in their application in relation to orders made or decisions on applications for orders or for the variation, revival or revocation of orders made or having effect as if made under other Acts those enactments shall apply as amended by this Act].

**[3A**

Any order for the payment of money in force under the Matrimonial Proceedings (Magistrates' Courts) Act 1960 (including any such order made under that Act by virtue of paragraph 1 above) shall be enforceable as a magistrates' court maintenance order.]

**4**

Any reference in paragraph 1 above to an application made under an enactment repealed by this Act shall be construed as including a reference to an application which is treated as a complaint under section 1 of the Matrimonial Proceedings (Magistrates' Courts) Act 1960 by virtue of section 27 of the Maintenance Orders (Reciprocal Enforcement) Act 1972 and any reference in [paragraph 2, 3 or 3A] above to an order made under the Matrimonial Proceedings (Magistrates' Courts) Act 1960 shall be construed as including a reference to an order which is made under that Act by virtue of section 28 of the Maintenance Orders (Reciprocal Enforcement) Act 1972.

**5–7**

…

**8**

A provision of Schedule 2 to this Act which relates to the punishment by way of fine which may be imposed for any offence shall not affect the punishment which may be imposed for an offence which is committed before the date on which that provision comes into force.

**Appointment**

Commencement order: SI 1978/997.

**Amendment**

Para 2: sub-para (bb) inserted by the MFPA 1984, s 46(1), Sch 1, para 27. Para 3: words in square brackets inserted by the MFPA 1984, s 46(1), Sch 1, para 27. Para 3A: inserted by the FLRA 1987, s 33(1), Sch 2, para 72(a). Para 4: words in square brackets substituted by the FLRA 1987, s 33(1), Sch 2, para 72(b). Para 5: spent. Paras 6, 7: repealed by the MCA 1980, s 154, Sch 9.

# Charging Orders Act 1979

**Contents**



*An Act to make provision for imposing charges to secure payment of money due, or to become due, under judgments or orders of court; to provide for restraining and prohibiting dealings with, and the making of payments in respect of, certain securities; and for connected purposes*

[6th December 1979]

**[2.194]**

### 1 Charging orders

(1) Where, under a judgment or order of the High Court or a county court, a person (the 'debtor') is required to pay a sum of money to another person (the 'creditor') then, for the purpose of enforcing that judgment or order, the appropriate court may make an order in accordance with the provisions of this Act imposing on any such property of the debtor as may be specified in the order a charge for securing the payment of any money due or to become due under the judgment or order.

(2) The appropriate court is—

(a) in a case where the property to be charged is a fund in court, the court in which that fund is lodged;

(b) in a case where paragraph (a) above does not apply and the order to be enforced is a maintenance order of the High Court, the High Court or a county court;

(c) in a case where neither paragraph (a) nor paragraph (b) above applies and the judgment or order to be enforced is a judgment or order of the High Court for a sum exceeding [the county court limit], the High Court [or a county court]; and

(d) in any other case, a county court.

In this section ['county court limit' means the county court limit for the time being specified in an Order in Council under [section 145 of the County Courts Act 1984], as the county court limit for the purposes of this section and] 'maintenance order' has the same meaning as in section 2(a) of the Attachment of Earnings Act 1971.

(3) An order under subsection (1) above is referred to in this Act as a 'charging order'.

(4) Where a person applies to the High Court for a charging order to enforce more than one judgment or order, that court shall be the appropriate court in relation to the application if it would be the appropriate court, apart from this subsection, on an application relating to one or more of the judgments or orders concerned.

(5) In deciding whether to make a charging order the court shall consider all the circumstances of the case and, in particular, any evidence before it as to—

(a) the personal circumstances of the debtor, and

(b) whether any other creditor of the debtor would be likely to be unduly prejudiced by the making of the order.

**Appointment**

Commencement order: SI 1980/627.

**Amendment**

Sub-s (2): words in square brackets in para (c) substituted or inserted and final words in square brackets substituted by the AJA 1982, ss 34, 37, Sch 3, Pt II, paras 2, 3, 6, words in square brackets therein substituted by the CCA 1984, s 148(1), Sch 2, para 71.

**Definitions**

'Debtor';'creditor' – see sub-s (1).
'The appropriate court' – see sub-s (2).
'Judgment or order' – see s 6(2) at para **[2.199]** below.
'The county court limit specified' – £5000.
'Maintenance order' – see sub-s (2) and para **[2.194.3]** below.

## [2.194.1]
## Keypoints

- Nature of a charging order
- Meaning of 'maintenance order'
- Court's discretion
- Holding the balance between the wife and the judgment creditor
- Security, not enforcement
- Procedure

## [2.194.2]
## Nature of a charging order

A charging order operates to charge an asset with payment of money. It is not in itself properly a means of direct enforcement (see below). The making of a charging order is a two-stage process: charging order nisi, followed by charging order absolute (see para **[2.194.7]** below). Each stage requires separate application of the statute.

Charging orders may only be imposed on the property listed in s 2, and then only in order to secure payment of a judgment or order of the High Court or county court made in favour of another person. The term 'judgment or order' includes a 'maintenance order', which is defined widely (see below).

A fund in court is within the list of property which may be made the subject of a charging order (provided that there has been a judgment or order made in favour of another person). However, because of the requirement that there has been a judgment or order made in favour of another person, it follows that a charging order cannot be made in order to secure an interlocutory order for the payment of money into court[1].

The 'money due or to become due' under the judgment or order must be an ascertained sum[2]. However, a charging order includes the interest due on a judgment debt, whether or not the charging order is expressed to include interest and irrespective of any period of limitation[3]. Notwithstanding the words 'due or to become due' a charging order should not be made in respect of instalments which are not yet in arrears, and in the county court this is expressly prohibited by the County Courts Act 1984, s 86[4].

Note that a liability order made by a magistrates' court for arrears of child support is recoverable by way of charging order as if it were payable under a county court order[5].

See generally, *Rayden and Jackson on Divorce and Family Matters* (17th edn, 1997), vol 1, ch 34, paras 34.39 et seq and the Noter-up thereto.

1 See (by analogy with garnishee orders) *Re Greer, Napper v Fanshawe* [1895] 2 Ch 217.
2 See *A and M Records Inc v Darakdijan* [1975] 3 All ER 983, [1975] 1 WLR 1610.
3 See *Ezekiel v Orakpo* [1997] 1 WLR 340, CA.
4 See *Woodham-Smith v Edwards* [1908] 2 KB 899, CA; and *Mercantile Credit Co Ltd v Ellis* (1987) Times, 1 April, CA.
5 See the CSA 1991, ss 33 and 36 at paras **[2.436]** and **[2.439]** below.



## [2.194.3]
## Meaning of 'maintenance order'

Maintenance orders for the purpose of this Act are defined by reference to the AtEA 1971, s 2A which in turn defines the term by reference to the AtEA 1971, Sch 1. As such a 'maintenance order' includes (inter alia) orders for the payment of money ('maintenance or other payments') under the MCA 1973, Pt II (ie including lump sums), and lump sums as well as periodical payments under the ChA 1989, Sch 1.

The term also includes an order to pay school fees direct to a school[1]; and also financial undertakings to pay, eg school fees[2].

1 See *L v L (Payment of School Fees)* [1997] 3 FCR 520, sub nom *Note: L v L (School Fees: Maintenance)* [1997] 2 FLR 252, CA.
2 See *Symmons v Symmons* [1993] 1 FLR 317.

## [2.194.4]
## Court's discretion

The court hearing an application for a charging order is obliged by s1(5) to consider all the circumstances of the case, with particular regard to evidence of:

- the personal circumstances of the debtor; and
- the position of any other creditor.

The principles upon which the court should exercise its discretion were considered in *Roberts Petroleum Ltd v Bernard Kenny Ltd*[1]. The court should exercise its discretion in the light of all relevant circumstances shown in evidence, including those occurring after charging order nisi[2]. When the court is aware 'that the debtor is, or is likely to turn out to be, insolvent' it is wrong to give one creditor an advantage over other creditors by the making of a charging order[3].

1 [1983] 2 AC 192, [1983] 1 All ER 564, HL.
2 See *Burston Finance Ltd v Godfrey* [1976] 2 All ER 976, [1976] 1 WLR 719, CA.
3 See *Rainbow v Moorgate Properties Ltd* [1975] 1 WLR 788 per Buckley LJ at 793H.

## [2.194.5]
## Holding the balance between the wife and the judgment creditor

Under s 3(5) a court which has made a charging order may 'at any time' discharge or vary the order on the application of the debtor or 'any person interested in any property to which the order relates'. A spouse of the judgment debtor is an 'interested person' if either she is a joint owner of the property charged or she is in occupation of a matrimonial home made subject to a charging order[1]. Note also, where a spouse is a joint owner of property subject to a statutory trust for sale, that RSC Ord 50, r 2(1)(d) and CCR Ord 31 make general provision for the charging order nisi to be served on such trustees as the court may direct.

The principles to be applied in weighing up the interests of the judgment creditor and the 'innocent' spouse in occupation (usually the wife) were considered in *Harman v Glencross*[2]. They are as follows:

(1) If the charging order nisi, and also the application to make the order absolute, is made before the spouse issues divorce proceedings, the charging order will be made absolute.

(2) If the spouse issues divorce proceedings after the charging order nisi but before the hearing of the application to make the order absolute, the issue becomes one of the cost of re-housing the 'innocent' spouse. The court should look first to the figures involved:

(a) If the net proceeds of sale (including any balance of the debtor's share after deduction of the judgment debt) would be 'clearly sufficient to provide adequate alternative accommodation for the wife and children'[3], the court will make the charging order absolute.

(b) Unless it is clearly proper to make the charging order absolute, the 'usual practice should be to transfer the application to the Family Division so that it may come on with the wife's application for ancillary relief'[4].

(3) Thereafter, if the issue falls for decision at the trial of the ancillary relief application (under 2(b) above) the court will look again at the cost of re-housing and re-apply the test set out in 2(a) above, 'even though that may result in the wife and children being housed at a lower standard than they might reasonably have expected had only the husband's interests been taken into account against them'[5].

(4) Failing that, the 'normal course should than be to postpone the sale of the house for such period only as may be requisite to protect the right of occupation – a *Mesher* type of order'[6]. This proposition was further considered in *Austin-Fell v Austin-Fell*[7] where Waite J upheld the appeal of a bank offering a 10 year Mesher-type order in place of the registrar's decision to set aside a charging order in its entirety, even though the wife might not be able to re-house herself at the end of the term.

(5) Finally, the court should consider whether there is any point in denying the judgment creditor his charging order if the wife's rights of occupation could in any event be defeated by the judgment creditor making the husband bankrupt.

1 See *Harman v Glencross* [1986] 2 FLR 241, CA.
2 See n 1 per Balcombe LJ at 256B.
3 See n 1 per Balcombe LJ at 256E.
4 See n 1 per Balcombe LJ at 256F.
5 See n 1 per Balcombe LJ at 256G.
6 See n 1 per Balcombe LJ at 256H.
7 [1990] FCR 743, [1989] 2 FLR 497.

**[2.194.6]**
**Security, not enforcement**

A charging order has the effect of converting a judgment creditor into a secured creditor[1]. It is not a means of enforcing the debt directly.

Once the charging order is made absolute (see procedure below) it may then be enforced by way of an application for sale of the property[2]. In both the High Court and county court an application for sale is by way of separate proceedings commenced by fresh originating summons or application in accordance with the applicable rules above. Where the land charged is held jointly with a third party, the chargee should apply for an order under the TLATA 1996, s 14. See *Lloyds Bank plc v Byrne*[3] for an equivalent case under the previous law[4]. Note that applications under the TLATA 1996 are subject to the relevant matters listed for consideration in s 15 of that Act. The court has held that the effect of s 15 of the TLATA 1996 is to change the previous law and to imbue the court with a wider discretion than under s 30 of the 1925 Act[5]. As a result authorities in relation to the old law (eg *Lloyds Bank plc v Byrne*[6]) should be regarded with caution.

On an application for sale, where there is conflict between the chargee's interest and the interest of an 'innocent' spouse, the interests of the chargee prevail except in exceptional circumstances[7]. The position of a chargee is equated with that of a trustee in bankruptcy[8]. For consideration of 'exceptional circumstances' in the context of recent bankruptcy cases, see *Claughton v Charalambous*[9], *Re Bremmer (A Bankrupt)*[10], *Judd v Brown*[11] and *Jackson v Bell*[12].

1 See *Rainbow v Moorgate Properties Ltd* [1975] 1 WLR 788; and the COA 1979, s 1(5)(b) at para **[2.194]** above.
2 See RSC Ord 88, r 5A and CCR Ord 31, r 4.
3 [1993] 2 FCR 41, [1993] 1 FLR 369, CA.
4 See the LPA 1925, s 30.
5 See *Mortgage Corpn v Shaire* [2000] 1 FLR 973, sub nom *Mortgage Corpn v Silkin* [2000] 2 FCR 222 per Neuberger J.
6 [1993] 2 FCR 41, [1993] 1 FLR 369, CA.
7 See *Barclays Bank plc v Hendricks* [1996] 1 FCR 710, [1996] 1 FLR 258 (holding that the moratorium before the grant of possession should be as short as possible, allowing only such time as was necessary to facilitate departure outside the children's school terms).
8 *Lloyds Bank plc v Byrne* [1993] 2 FCR 41, [1993] 1 FLR 369, CA. But see also now *Mortgage Corpn v Shaire* [2000] 1 FLR 973, sub nom *Mortgage Corpn v Silkin* [2000] 2 FCR 222 per Neuberger J (see above); and *Bank of Ireland Home Mortgages Ltd v Bell* [2001] 3 FCR 134.
9 [1999] 1 FLR 740, [1999] Fam Law 205.
10 [1999] 1 FLR 912, [1999] Fam Law 293.
11 [1999] 1 FLR 1191, [1999] Fam Law 523, CA.
12 [2001] EWCA Civ 387, [2001] Fam Law 879.



## [2.194.7]
### Procedure

If the order to be secured is in respect of a fund in court the application should be made to the court in which the fund is held. Otherwise, where the order to be secured is a High Court 'maintenance order' (see above), or an order (of either court) for more than the relevant county court limit (£5,000), an application for a charging order may be made in the High Court or the county court; all other applications must be made in the county court[1].

In both courts the initial application is made ex parte. If an order nisi is made, a return date is fixed for an inter partes hearing at which the court will consider whether to make the charging order absolute.

For applications in the High Court the procedure is set out in RSC Ord 50 and FPR 1991, r 7.1(1). The procedure in the county court is similar (but not identical)[2].

1 See the COA 1979, s 1(2) at para **[2.194]** above.
2 See CCR Ord 31 and FPR 1991, r 7.1(1) at paras **[3.545]** and **[3.476]** below.

## [2.195]

### 2 Property which may be charged

(1) Subject to subsection (3) below, a charge may be imposed by a charging order only on—
- (a) any interest held by the debtor beneficially—
  - (i) in any asset of a kind mentioned in subsection (2) below, or
  - (ii) under any trust; or
- (b) any interest held by a person as trustee of a trust ('the trust'), if the interest is in such an asset or is an interest under another trust and—
  - (i) the judgment or order in respect of which a charge is to be imposed was made against that person as trustee of the trust, or
  - (ii) the whole beneficial interest under the trust is held by the debtor unencumbered and for his own benefit, or
  - (iii) in a case where there are two or more debtors all of whom are liable to the creditor for the same debt, they together hold the whole beneficial interest under the trust unencumbered and for their own benefit.

(2) The assets referred to in subsection (1) above are—
- (a) land,
- (b) securities of any of the following kinds—
  - (i) government stock,

(ii) stock of any body (other than a building society) incorporated within England and Wales,

(iii) stock of any body incorporated outside England and Wales or of any state or territory outside the United Kingdom, being stock registered in a register kept at any place within England and Wales,

(iv) units of any unit trust in respect of which a register of the unit holders is kept at any place within England and Wales, or

(c) funds in court.

(3) In any case where a charge is imposed by a charging order on any interest in an asset of a kind mentioned in paragraph (b) or (c) of subsection (2) above, the court making the order may provide for the charge to extend to any interest or dividend payable in respect of the asset.

**Appointment**

Commencement order: SI 1980/627.

**Definitions**

'Debtor'; 'creditor' – see s 2(1).
'Securities' – see s 6(3) at para **[2.199]** below.
'Government stock' – see s 6(1) at para **[2.199]** below.
'Stock' – see s 6(1) at para **[2.199]** below.
'Unit trust' – see s 6(1) at para **[2.199]** below.
'Dividend' – see s 6(1) at para **[2.199]** below.

**[2.195.1]**
**Keypoint**

- Effect of section

**[2.195.2]**
**Effect of section**

This section sets out the types of property which may be made the subject of a charging order. In relation to securities this section should be read with s 5 below, Stop orders and notices.

**[2.196]**

### 3 Provisions supplementing sections 1 and 2

(1) A charging order may be made either absolutely or subject to conditions as to notifying the debtor or as to the time when the charge is to become enforceable, or as to other matters.

(2) The Land Charges Act 1972 and the Land Registration Act 1925 shall apply in relation to charging orders as they apply in relation to other orders or writs issued or made for the purpose of enforcing judgments.

(3) …

(4) Subject to the provisions of this Act, a charge imposed by a charging order shall have the like effect and shall be enforceable in the same courts and in the same manner as an equitable charge created by the debtor by writing under his hand.

(5) The court by which a charging order was made may at any time, on the application of the debtor or of any person interested in any property to which the order relates, make an order discharging or varying the charging order.

(6) Where a charging order has been protected by an entry registered under the Land Charges Act 1972 or the Land Registration Act 1925, an order under subsection (5) above discharging the charging order may direct that the entry be cancelled.

(7) The Lord Chancellor may by order made by statutory instrument amend section 2(2) of this Act by adding to, or removing from, the kinds of asset for the time

being referred to there, any asset of a kind which in his opinion ought to be so added or removed.

(8) Any order under subsection (7) above shall be subject to annulment in pursuance of a resolution of either House of Parliament.

**Appointment**

Commencement order: SI 1980/627.

**Amendment**

Sub-s (3): amends the LRA 1925, s 49.

**Definitions**

'Charging order' – see s 1 and at para **[2.194.2]** above.
'Debtor'; 'creditor' – see s 3(1).
'Person interested' – see para **[2.196.2]** below.



### [2.196.1]
### Keypoints

- Court review
- Registration provisions
- Procedure

### [2.196.2]
### Court review

Under s 3(5) a court which has made a charging order may 'at any time' discharge or vary the order on the application of the debtor or 'any person interested in any property to which the order relates'. A spouse of the judgment debtor is an 'interested person' if either she is a joint owner of the property charged or she is in occupation of a matrimonial home made subject to a charging order[1]. Note also, where a spouse is a joint owner of property subject to a statutory trust for sale, that RSC Ord 50, r 2(1)(d) and CCR Ord 31 make general provision for the charging order nisi to be served on such trustees as the court may direct. See also para **[2.194.5]** above.

1 See *Harman v Glencross* [1986] Fam 81, [1986] 2 FLR 241, CA.

### [2.196.3]
### Registration provisions

A charging order against unregistered land may be registered in the register of writs and orders affecting land in accordance with the Land Charges Act 1972, s 6. A charging order against registered land may be registered and protected in accordance with Land Registration Act 1925, ss 49(1) and 59[1]. The primary relevance of these provisions to family lawyers is in relation to the priority of interests which are registered (and thus protected) under them[2].

For the avoidance of argument a charging order is an order charging (and therefore affecting) the land, not merely the proceeds of sale of the land[3].

1 See the COA 1979, s 7(3) at para **[2.194]** below.
2 See notes under the LCA 1972 above.
3 See *Clark v Chief Land Registrar* [1994] Ch 370, [1995] 1 FLR 212, CA.

### [2.196.4]
### Procedure

An application under s 3(5) for the court to vary or discharge an order made is by interlocutory application in the normal manner, as occurred in *Harman v Glencross*[1].

As to the procedure for enforcing a charging order under s 3(4), a charging order may be enforced in the same way as an equitable charge under hand, ie by order for sale. The court may appoint a receiver. An application for sale is made in accordance with RSC Ord 88, r 5A (in the High Court) and CCR Ord 31, r 4 (in the county court). In each case this is by way of separate proceedings[2].

1 [1986] Fam 81, [1986] 2 FLR 241, CA; see also *Ahmad v Ahmad* [1999] 1 FLR 317, CA.
2 See para **[2.194.6]** above.

## [2.197]

### 4 Completion of execution

…

**Amendment**
This section amends the Bankruptcy Act 1914, s 40(2).

## [2.198]

### 5 Stop orders and notices

(1) In this section—

'stop order' means an order of the court prohibiting the taking, in respect of any of the securities specified in the order, of any of the steps mentioned in subsection (5) below;

'stop notice' means a notice requiring any person or body on whom it is duly served to refrain from taking, in respect of any of the securities specified in the notice, any of those steps without first notifying the person by whom, or on whose behalf, the notice was served; and

'prescribed securities' means securities (including funds in court) of a kind prescribed by rules of court made under this section.

(2) The power to make rules of court under section [84 of the Supreme Court Act 1981] shall include power by any such rules to make provision—

(a) for the court to make a stop order on the application of any person claiming to be entitled to an arrest in prescribed securities;
(b) for the service of a stop notice by any person claiming to be entitled to an interest in prescribed securities.

(3) The power to make rules of court under [section 75 of the County Courts Act 1984] shall include power by any such rules to make provision for the service of a stop notice by any person entitled to an interest in any securities by virtue of a charging order made by a county court.

(4) Rules of court made by virtue of subsection (2) or (3) above shall prescribe the person or body on whom a copy of any stop order or a stop notice is to be served.

(5) The steps mentioned in subsection (1) above are—

(a) the registration of any transfer of the securities;
(b) in the case of funds in court, the transfer, sale, delivery out, payment or other dealing with the funds, or of the income thereon;
(c) the making of any payment by way of dividend, interest or otherwise in respect of the securities; and
(d) in the case of a unit trust, any acquisition of or other dealing with the units by any person or body exercising functions under the trust.

(6) Any rules of court made by virtue of this section may include such incidental, supplemental and consequential provisions as the authority making them consider necessary or expedient, and may make different provision in relation to different cases or classes of case.

**Appointment**
Commencement order: SI 1980/627.

**Amendment**
Sub-s (2): words in square brackets substituted by the SCA 1981, s 152(1), Sch 5. Sub-s (3): words in square brackets substituted by the CCA 1984, s 148(1), Sch 2, para 72.

**Definitions**
'Securities' – see s 6(3) at para **[2.199]** below.
'Rules of court' – see RSC Ord 50, rr 10 to 15.
'Charging order' – see s 1 at para **[2.194]** above.
'Dividend' – see s 6(1) at para **[2.199]** below.
'Unit trust' – see s 6(1) at para **[2.199]** below.



**[2.199]**

## 6 Interpretation

(1) In this Act–

'building society' has the same meaning as in the Building Societies Act [1986];

'charging order' means an order made under section 1(1) of this Act:

'debtor' and 'creditor' have the meanings given by section 1(1) of this Act;

'dividend' includes any distribution in respect of any unit of a unit trust;

'government stock' means any stock issued by Her Majesty's government in the United Kingdom or any funds of, or annuity granted by, that government;

'stock' includes shares, debentures and any securities of the body concerned, whether or not constituting a charge on the assets of that body;

'unit trust' means any trust established for the purpose, or having the effect, of providing, for persons having funds available for investment, facilities for the participation by them, as beneficiaries under the trust, in any profits or income arising from the acquisition, holding, management or disposal of any property whatsoever.

(2) For the purposes of section 1 of this Act references to a judgment or order of the High Court or a county court shall be taken to include references to a judgment, order, decree or award (however called) of any court or arbitrator (including any foreign court or arbitrator) which is or has become enforceable (whether wholly or to a limited extent) as if it were a judgment or order of the High Court or a county court.

(3) References in section 2 of this Act to any securities include references to any such securities standing in the name of the Accountant General.

**Appointment**
Commencement order: SI 1980/627.

**Amendment**
Sub-s (1): date in square brackets substituted by the BSA 1986, s 120, Sch 18, Pt I, para 14.

**[2.200]**

## 7 Consequential amendment, repeals and transitional provisions

(1), (2) …

(3) Any order made or notice given under any enactment repealed by this Act or under any rules of court revoked by rules of court made under this Act (the 'new rules') shall, if still in force when the provisions of this Act or, as the case may be, the new rules come into force, continue to have effect as if made under this Act or, as the case may be, under the new rules.

(4) Any notice of such an order registered in the register maintained under the Land Registration Act 1925 which would have been registrable by virtue of the paragraph inserted in section 49(1) of that Act by section 3(3) of this Act, if section 3(3) had been in force when the notice was registered, shall have effect as if registered by virtue of that paragraph.

**Appointment**
Commencement order: SI 1980/627.

**Amendment**
Sub-s (1): repealed by the CCA 1984, s 148(3), Sch 4. Sub-s (2): repealed in part by the SCA 1981, s 152(4), Sch 7; remainder repealed by the CCA 1984, s 148(3), Sch 4.

**[2.201]**

### 8 Short title, commencement and extent

(1) This Act may be cited as the Charging Orders Act 1979.

(2) This Act comes into force on such day as the Lord Chancellor may appoint by order made by statutory instrument.

(3) This Act does not extend to Scotland or Northern Ireland.

**Appointment**
Commencement order: SI 1980/627.

**Notes**
The Act was brought into force on 3 June 1980 by the Charging Orders Act 1979 (Commencement) Order 1980, SI 1980/627.

# Civil Jurisdiction and Judgments Act 1982

Contents



*An Act to make further provision about the jurisdiction of courts and tribunals in the United Kingdom and certain other territories and about the recognition and enforcement of judgments given in the United Kingdom or elsewhere; to provide for the modification of certain provisions relating to legal aid; and for connected purposes*

[13th July 1982]

**[2.202]**

**1 Interpretation of references to the Conventions and Contracting States**

(1) In this Act—

'the 1968 Convention' means the Convention on jurisdiction and the enforcement of judgments in civil and commercial matters (including the Protocol annexed to that Convention), signed at Brussels on 27th September 1968;

'the 1971 Protocol' means the Protocol on the interpretation of the 1968 Convention by the European Court, signed at Luxembourg on 3rd June 1971;

'the Accession Convention' means the Convention on the accession to the 1968 Convention and the 1971 Protocol of Denmark, the Republic of Ireland and the United Kingdom, signed at Luxembourg on 9th October 1978;

['the 1982 Accession Convention' means the Convention on the accession of the Hellenic Republic to the 1968 Convention and the 1971 Protocol, with the adjustments made to them by the Accession Convention, signed at Luxembourg on 25th October 1982;]

['the 1989 Accession Convention' means the Convention on the accession of the Kingdom of Spain and the Portuguese Republic to the 1968 Convention and the 1971 Protocol, with the adjustments made to them by the Accession Convention and the 1982 Accession Convention, signed at Donostia — San Sebastián on 26th May 1989;]

['the 1996 Accession Convention' means the Convention on the accession of the Republic of Austria, the Republic of Finland and the Kingdom of Sweden to the 1968 Convention and the 1971 Protocol, with the adjustments made to them by the Accession Convention, the 1982 Accession Convention and the 1989 Accession Convention, signed at Brussels on 29th November 1996,]

[['the Brussels Conventions'] means the 1968 Convention, the 1971 Protocol, the Accession Convention, the 1982 Accession Convention *and the 1989 Accession Convention* [, the 1989 Accession Convention and the 1996 Accession Convention]]

['the Lugano Convention' means the Convention on jurisdiction and the enforcement of judgments in civil and commercial matters (including the Protocols annexed to that Convention) opened for signature at Lugano on 16th September 1988 and signed by the United Kingdom on 18th September 1989];

['the Regulation' means Council Regulation (EC) No 44/2001 of 22nd December 2000 on jurisdiction and the recognition and enforcement of judgments in civil and commercial matters].

(2) In this Act, unless the context otherwise requires—

[(a) references to, or to any provision of, the 1968 Convention or the 1971 Protocol are references to that Convention, Protocol or provision as amended by the Accession Convention, the 1982 Accession Convention *and the 1989 Accession Convention* [, the 1989 Accession Convention and the 1996 Accession Convention]; and]

[(aa) references to, or to any provision of, the Lugano Convention are references to that Convention as amended on the accession to it of Poland; and]

[(b) any reference in any provision to a numbered Article without more is a reference—

(i) to the Article so numbered of the 1968 Convention, in so far as the provision applies in relation to that Convention, and

(ii) to the Article so numbered of the Lugano Convention, in so far as the provision applies in relation to that Convention,

and any reference to a sub-division of a numbered Article shall be construed accordingly].

[(3) [In this Act—

'Contracting State', without more, in any provision means—

(a) in the application of the provision in relation to the Brussels Conventions, a Brussels Contracting State; and

(b) in the application of the provision in relation to the Lugano Convention, a Lugano Contracting State];

['Brussels Contracting State' means Denmark (which is not bound by the Regulation, but was one of the parties acceding to the 1968 Convention under the Accession Convention);]

[*'Lugano Contracting State' means one of the original parties to the Lugano Convention, that is to say—*

*Austria, Belgium, Denmark, Finland, France, the Federal Republic of Germany, the Hellenic Republic, Iceland, the Republic of Ireland, Italy, Luxembourg, the Netherlands, Norway, Portugal, Spain, Sweden, Switzerland and the United Kingdom*

['Lugano Contracting State' means—

(a) one of the original parties to the Lugano Convention, that is to say Austria, Belgium, Denmark, Finland, France, the Federal Republic of Germany, the Hellenic Republic, Iceland, the Republic of Ireland, Italy, Luxembourg, the Netherlands, Norway, Portugal, Spain, Sweden, Switzerland and the United Kingdom; or

(b) a party who has subsequently acceded to that Convention, that is to say, Poland], being a State in relation to which that Convention has taken effect in accordance with paragraph 3 or 4 of Article 61]

['Regulation State' in any provision, in the application of that provision in relation to the Regulation, has the same meaning as 'Member State' in the Regulation, that is all Members States except Denmark].]

[(4) Any question arising as to whether it is the Regulation, any of the Brussels Conventions, or the Lugano Convention which applies in the circumstances of a particular case shall be determined as follows—

(a) in accordance with Article 54B of the Lugano Convention (which determines the relationship between the Brussels Conventions and the Lugano Convention); and

(b) in accordance with Article 68 of the Regulation (which determines the relationship between the Brussels Conventions and the Regulation).]

**Appointment**

Commencement order: SI 1986/2044.

**Amendment**

Sub-s (1): definition 'the 1982 Accession Convention' inserted by SI 1989/1346, art 3; definition 'the 1989 Accession Convention' inserted by SI 1990/2591, art 3; definition 'the 1996 Accession Convention' inserted by SI 2000/1824, art 3(a). Date in force: to be appointed (date to be notified in the London, Edinburgh and Belfast Gazettes as the date on which the Convention on the accession of the Republics of Austria and Finland and the Kingdom of Sweden to the 1968 Convention and to the Protocol enters into force in respect of the United Kingdom): see SI 2000/1824, art 1(b); definition 'the Brussels Conventions' (originally enacted as 'the Conventions') substituted by SI 1990/2591, art 4; definition 'the Brussels Conventions' words 'the Brussels Conventions' in square brackets substituted by the CJJA 1991, s 2(2); in definition 'the Brussels Convention' words 'and the 1989 Accession Convention' in italics repealed and subsequent words in square brackets substituted by SI 2000/1824, art 3(b). Date in force: to be appointed (date to be notified in the London, Edinburgh and Belfast Gazettes as the date on which the Convention on the accession of the Republics of Austria and Finland and the Kingdom of Sweden to the 1968 Convention and to the Protocol enters into force in respect of the United Kingdom): see SI 2000/1824, art 1(b); definition 'the Lugano Convention' inserted by the CJJA 1991, s 2(3). Sub-s (1): definition 'the Regulation' inserted by SI 2001/3929, art 4, Sch 2. Sub-s (2): para (a) substituted by SI 1990/2591, art 5; para (a) words 'and the 1989 Accession Convention' in italics repealed and subsequent words in square brackets substituted by SI 2000/1824, art 4. Date in force: to be appointed (date to be notified in the London, Edinburgh and Belfast Gazettes as the date on which the Convention on the accession of the Republics of Austria and Finland and the Kingdom of Sweden to the 1968 Convention and to the Protocol enters into force in respect of the United Kingdom): see SI 2000/1824, art 1(b); para (aa) inserted by SI 2000/1824, art 9. Date in force: to be appointed (date to be notified in the London, Edinburgh and Belfast Gazettes as the date on which the accession of the Republic of Poland to the Lugano Convention takes effect in respect of the United Kingdom): see SI 2000/1824, art 1(a); para (b) substituted by the CJJA 1991, s 2(4). Sub-s (3): substituted by SI 1990/2591, art 6; CJJA 1991, s 2(5), (6); definition 'Brussels Contracting State' substituted by SI 2001/3929, art 4, Sch 2, Pt I. Date in force: 1 March 2002: see SI 2001/3929, art 1(b); definition 'Lugano Contracting State' inserted by the CJJA 1991, s 2(5), (6); words from 'Lugano Contracting State' to 'the United Kingdom' in italics repealed and subsequent words in square brackets substituted by SI 2000/1824, art 10. Date in force: to be appointed (date to be notified in the London, Edinburgh and Belfast Gazettes as the date on which the accession of the Republic of Poland to the Lugano Convention takes effect in respect of the United Kingdom): see SI 2000/1824, art 1(a); definition 'Regulation State' inserted by SI 2001/3929, art 4, Sch 2. Sub-s (4): inserted by SI 2001/3929, art 4, Sch 2.

**Definitions**

For definitions of terms other than those set out in this section, see s 50 of the CJJA 1982.

**[2.202.1]**

**Keypoints**

- Contracting States – Brussels
- Contracting States – Lugano

**[2.202.2]**
**Contracting States – Brussels**

As defined by s 1(3), Brussels Contracting States include:

- original parties to the 1968 Convention – Belgium, Germany, France, Italy, Luxembourg, The Netherlands;
- parties to the 1978 Accession Convention – Denmark, Eire, the United Kingdom;
- parties to the 1982 Accession Convention – Greece;
- parties to the 1989 Accession Convention – Spain, Portugal.

**[2.202.3]**
**Contracting States – Lugano**

As defined by s 1(3), Lugano Contracting States include the original parties to that convention, that is:

- Austria, Belgium, Denmark, Finland, France, Germany, Greece, Iceland, Eire, Italy, Luxembourg, the Netherlands, Norway, Portugal, Spain, Sweden, Switzerland, the United Kingdom.

**[2.203]**

### 2 The [Brussels Conventions] to have the force of law

(1) The [Brussels Conventions] shall have the force of law in the United Kingdom, and judicial notice shall be taken of them.

[(2) For convenience of reference there are set out in Schedules 1, 2, 3, 3A *and 3B* [, 3B and 3C] respectively the English texts of—

(a) the 1968 Convention as amended by Titles II and III of the Accession Convention, by Titles II and III of the 1982 Accession Convention *and* by Titles II and III of, and Annex I(d) to, the 1989 Accession Convention [and by Titles II and III of the 1996 Accession Convention];

(b) the 1971 Protocol as amended by Title IV of the Accession Convention, by Title IV of the 1982 Accession Convention *and* by Title IV of the 1989 Accession Convention [and by Title IV of the 1996 Accession Convention];

(c) Titles V and VI of the Accession Convention (transitional and final provisions) as amended by Title V of the 1989 Accession Convention;

(d) Titles V and VI of the 1982 Accession Convention (transitional and final provisions); and

(e) Titles VI and VII of the 1989 Accession Convention (transitional and final provisions),

[(f) Titles V and VI of the 1996 Accession Convention (transitional and final provisions),]

being texts prepared from the authentic English texts referred to in Articles 37 and 41 of the Accession Convention, in Article 17 of the 1982 Accession Convention *and in Article 34 of the 1989 Accession Convention* [, in Article 34 of the 1989 Accession Convention and in Article 18 of the 1996 Accession Convention].]

**Appointment**

Commencement order: SI 1986/2044.

**Amendment**

Section heading: words in square brackets substituted by the CJJA 1991, s 3, Sch 2, para 1.

Sub-s (1): words in square brackets substituted by the CJJA 1991, s 3, Sch 2, para 1.

Sub-s (2): substituted by SI 1990/2591, art 7; words 'and 3B' in italics repealed and subsequent words in square brackets substituted by SI 2000/1824, art 6(a). Date in force: to be appointed (date to be notified in the London, Edinburgh and Belfast Gazettes as the date on which the Convention on the accession of the Republics of Austria and Finland and the Kingdom of Sweden to the 1968 Convetion and to the Protocol enters into force in respect of the United Kingdom): see SI 2000/1824, art 1(b); in paras (a), (b) word 'and' in italics repealed by SI 2000/1824, art 6(b).

Date in force: to be appointed (date to be notified in the London, Edinburgh and Belfast Gazettes as the date on which the Convention on the accession of the Republics of Austria and Finland and the Kingdom of Sweden to the 1968 Convention and to the Protocol enters into force in respect of the United Kingdom): see SI 2000/1824, art 1(b); in para (a) words 'and by Titles II and III of the 1996 Accession Convention' in square brackets inserted by SI 2000/1824, art 6(c). Date in force: to be appointed (date to be notified in the London, Edinburgh and Belfast Gazettes as the date on which the Convention on the accession of the Republics of Austria and Finland and the Kingdom of Sweden to the 1968 Convention and to the Protocol enters into force in respect of the United Kingdom): see SI 2000/1824, art 1(b); in para (b) words 'and by Title IV of the 1996 Accession Convention' in square brackets inserted by SI 2000/1824, art 6(d). Date in force: to be appointed (date to be notified in the London, Edinburgh and Belfast Gazettes as the date on which the Convention on the accession of the Republics of Austria and Finland and the Kingdom of Sweden to the 1968 Convention and to the Protocol enters into force in respect of the United Kingdom): see SI 2000/1824, art 1(b); para (f) inserted by SI 2000/1824, art 6(e). Date in force: to be appointed (date to be notified in the London, Edinburgh and Belfast Gazettes as the date on which the Convention on the accession of the Republics of Austria and Finland and the Kingdom of Sweden to the 1968 Convention and to the Protocol enters into force in respect of the United Kingdom): see SI 2000/1824, art 1(b); words 'and in Article 34 of the 1989 Accession Convention' in italics repealed and subsequent words in square brackets substituted by SI 2000/1824, art 6(f). Date in force: to be appointed (date to be notified in the London, Edinburgh and Belfast Gazettes as the date on which the Convention on the accession of the Republics of Austria and Finland and the Kingdom of Sweden to the 1968 Convention and to the Protocol enters into force in respect of the United Kingdom): see SI 2000/1824, art 1(b).

**Definitions**
'the Brussels Convention' — see s 1(1) at para **[2.202]** above.



## [2.203.1]–[2.203.2]
## Keypoints

- General principles
- Brussels II
- Types of orders enforceable under the CJJA 1982
- Agreements
- Appeals
- Orders made in Contracting States
- Action for recovery of arrears
- Rules of procedure

## [2.203.3]
## General principles

Since the general principle of the Convention is that persons domiciled in a Contracting State shall be sued in the courts of that State[1], jurisdiction as regards the enforcement of maintenance orders may be founded on the residence of the payer under the order within the jurisdiction of the courts in which enforcement is sought.

However, in matters relating to maintenance a person domiciled in a contracting state may be sued in the courts of another Contracting State in which the maintenance creditor is domiciled or habitually resident[2].

The Art 5(2) provisions apply in the case of a person applying for maintenance, including a person bringing a maintenance action for the first time, and are not confined to a person who has an existing entitlement to maintenance under a court order[3].

Domicile is defined for the purposes of the Act as residence plus a substantial connection with the place of residence[4].

Where a person has been resident in the United Kingdom, or a part of it, for a period of three months or longer there is a rebuttable presumption that the nature of that person's connection is sufficiently substantial to make the United Kingdom, or the relevant part, his place of domicile[5].

Where proceedings are for enforcement, the courts of the Contracting State in which enforcement is sought will have exclusive jurisdiction regardless of domicile[6]. Accordingly, jurisdiction may also be founded on the presence of assets belonging to the payer within the jurisdiction of a Contracting State other than that in which the order was made notwithstanding that the payer himself is not residing there.

Notwithstanding the exclusive jurisdiction under Art 16, applications for protective measures alone may be made in the courts of other Contracting States contemporaneously[7].

For the *stay* of an ancillary relief application under the inherent jurisdiction and the CJJA 1982[8], *see D v P (Forum Conveniens)*[9] (stay granted under inherent jurisdiction where key issue was the importance of Italian separation agreement; the Italian court was first seised of the issue of child maintenance and the English court was obliged to decline jurisdiction under Art 21; the wife's maintenance was a related matter and the English court could stay that application under Art 22, which it did for the same reasons as granting the stay under the inherent jurisdiction), and *Krenge v Krenge*[10] (stay granted under inherent jurisdiction on terms that husband deposit sum with wife's German lawyers to cover her legal costs in Germany; fact that wife would not receive capital from the husband's inheritance was not a reason why justice would not be done in Germany. The court had a duty independently of any application to consider whether a discretionary stay should be granted). The House of Lords have now decided[11], in a case under Arts 2 to 6 of the Lugano Convention, that a person is 'sued' on the date of isue of any such proceedings, as opposed to their date of service, and the court is therefore seized at the earlier date.

See generally, *Rayden and Jackson on Divorce and Family Matters* (17th edn, 1997), vol 1, para 34.81 and the Noter-up thereto.

1 See the CJJA 1982, Sch 1, Art 2.
2 See the CJJA 1982, Sch 1, Art 5(2).
3 See *Farrell v Long (Case C–295/95)* [1997] QB 842, [1997] All ER (EC) 449, ECJ.
4 See the CJJA 1982, s 41(1) to (4).
5 See the CJJA 1982, s 41(6).
6 See the CJJA 1982, Sch 1, Art 16.
7 See the CJJA 1982, Sch 1, Art 24.
8 See the CJJA 1982, Sch 1, Arts 21 and 22.
9 [1998] 3 FCR 403, [1998] 2 FLR 25.
10 [1999] 1 FLR 969.
11 See *Canada Trust Co v Stolzenberg (No 2)* [2000] 4 All ER 481, [2000] 3 WLR 1376, HL.

## [2.203.4]
## Brussels II

On 1 March 2001 Council Regulation (EC) No 1347/2000 of 29 May 2000 on the jurisdiction and the recognition and enforcement of judgments in matrimonial matters and in matters of parental responsibility for children of both spouses[1] became directly effective in the United Kingdom and other Member States. The content of the Council Regulation is derived from the Convention on Jurisdiction and the Recognition and Enforcement of Judgments in Matrimonial Matters ('Brussels II') to which the United Kingdom became a signatory on 28 May 1998.

The detailed rules under the Council Regulation regulate the situation where there are concurrent matrimonial proceedings in courts of different Member States.

For a full commentary on the Council Regulation and of Brussels II see the Introductory Chapter 'Brussels II' at para **[1.237]** above.

1 [2000] OJ L160/19 (30 June 2000); the full text of the Council Regulation is set out at para **[3.656A]** below.

## [2.203.5]
## Types of orders enforceable under the CJJA 1982

The Convention does not apply to rights in property arising out of a matrimonial relationship[1].

In matters relating to maintenance, there is a special jurisdiction[2].

An order made in matrimonial proceedings is a maintenance order for the purposes of the Convention if it is 'designed to enable one spouse to provide for him or herself or if the needs and resources of each spouse [are] taken into consideration in the determination of its amount'.

Where an order contains provisions relating to maintenance as well as provisions arising from the matrimonial relationship (in accordance with the definitions above), then so much of the order as provides for the payment of maintenance will be enforceable under the Convention[3].

*Duxbury* orders will come within this definition, and orders should therefore specify which part of their capital provision is attributable to such a calculation.

Where the terms of an order are concerned solely with dividing property between the spouses those terms will be concerned with rights in property arising out of a matrimonial relationship and will not be enforceable under the Convention[4].

The decision of the European Court of Justice in *Van den Boogard* is of significance for practitioners in cases where there is an international element. In such cases the attention of the court should be drawn to the statement of the European Court of Justice that:

> 'Because on divorce an English Court could regulate both the matrimonial relationships of the parties and matters of maintenance, the court from which leave to enforce was sought must distinguish between those aspects of the decision which related to rights in property arising out of the matrimonial relationship and those relating to maintenance, having regard in each case to the specific aim of the decision rendered. It should be possible to deduce that aim from the reasoning of the decision in question'.



1 See the CJJA 1982, Sch 1, Art 1.
2 See the CJJA 1982, Sch 1, Art 5(2).
3 See the CJJA 1982, Sch 1, Art 42.
4 See *Van den Boogaard v Laumen* (Case C–220/95) [1997] QB 759, [1997] All ER (EC) 517, ECJ.

## [2.203.6]
## Agreements

Under Art 17 parties may 'prorogue' jurisdiction, or agree that a court of a particular Contracting State is to have exclusive jurisdiction. One party must be domiciled in a Contracting State and the agreement must be in writing for it to be considered valid. For these purposes, 'domiciled' carries the meaning found in the CJJA 1982, s 41 – that is resident in the country in question, the nature and circumstances indicating a substantial connection with that country.

Note that no such facility is open to parties under Brussels II (above), so whilst a prenuptial contract may stipulate in advance a jurisdiction for the determination of maintenance issues with which neither party has any connection other than domicile in another Contracting State, they could not so stipulate in relation to the determination of the main suit.

## [2.203.7]
## Appeals

An appeal under Art 36 or under Art 40 of the 1968 Convention shall be by way of complaint to the magistrates' court in which the order is registered, or in which the application for its registration has been refused, as the case may be[1].

For the period during which an appeal against a decision to enforce an order might be made and until any such appeal is determined, no measures, other than protective measures, may be taken to enforce the order[2].

Where the payer under the order is domiciled in the contracting state in which enforcement is sought, the time within which an appeal must be made is one month. Where the payer is not so resident the time limit is two months[3].

The party against whom enforcement is sought has no right to make representations as to whether or not an order made in a Contracting State should be registered[4].

Registration may only be refused in a limited number of circumstances:

- If such recognition is contrary to public policy in the State in which recognition is sought.
- If the defendant was not duly served in sufficient time, and recognition was given in default of appearance.
- If the judgment is irreconcilable with a judgment given in a dispute between the same parties in the State in which recognition is sought.
- Where there is a conflict of laws, in certain circumstances.
- Where there is a conflicting judgment in a non-Contracting State involving the same parties and cause of action, in certain circumstances[5].

Once a decision has been made authorizing, or refusing to authorize, enforcement of an order made in a Contracting State an appeal lies, in the first instance, to the magistrates' court within the time limits mentioned above.

The magistrates' court may stay the proceedings if an ordinary appeal has been lodged against the judgment in the state of origin[6].

Thereafter a further appeal may be made to the High Court by way of case stated[7].

Such an appeal lies only against a decision deciding the substance of an appeal against an order for the enforcement of a judgment; there is no right of appeal to the High Court against the decision to grant, or refuse, a stay of the proceedings[8].

1 See the Magistrates' Court (Civil Jurisdiction and Judgments Act 1982) Rules 1986, SI 1986/1962, r 5.
2 See the CJJA 1982, Sch 1, Art 39.
3 See the CJJA 1982, Sch 1, Art 36.
4 See the CJJA 1982, Sch 1, Art 34.
5 See the CJJA 1982, Sch 1, Art 27.
6 See the CJJA 1982, Sch 1, Art 38.
7 See the CJJA 1982, s 6(3)(a) at para **[2.208]** below; and Sch 1, Art 37.
8 See *Société d'Informatique Service Réalisation Organisation (SISRO) v Ampersand Software BV* [1996] QB 127, [1995] All ER (EC) 783, ECJ.

## [2.203.8]
## Orders made in Contracting States

Under no circumstances shall an order made in a Contracting State be reviewed by the courts of another Contracting State as to its substance[1].

Accordingly, it would seem that an English court has no power to vary or revoke an order made in another Contracting State. An application to vary or revoke a registered order should be made to the court that originally made it.

Any order made by a court in a Contracting State varying a registered order will itself be registered upon notification to the court where the original order is registered[2].

1 See the CJJA 1982, Sch 1, Art 29.
2 See the Magistrates' Courts (Civil Jurisdiction and Judgments Act 1982) Rules 1986, SI 1986 No 1962, r 7 (as amended).

## [2.203.9]
## Action for recovery of arrears

The Magistrates' Courts (Civil Jurisdiction and Judgments Act 1982) Rules 1986, SI 1986/1962, r 4 (as amended) provides for the institution of proceedings by the justices' clerk for the recovery of arrears due under an order registered under the CJJA 1982.

## [2.203.10]
## Rules of procedure

Rules of procedure (*ie service, documentary evidence, timing of proceedings, etc*) as they apply to *all* applications for the enforcement of maintenance in the magistrates' court are as set out in Sch A1 to the Magistrates' Courts (Reciprocal Enforcement of Maintenance Orders) Rules 1974, SI 1974/668.

[2.204]

### 3 Interpretation of the [Brussels Conventions]

(1) Any question as to the meaning or effect of any provision of the [Brussels Conventions] shall, if not referred to the European Court in accordance with the 1971 Protocol, be determined in accordance with the principles laid down by and any relevant decision of the European Court.

(2) Judicial notice shall be taken of any decision of, or expression of opinion by, the European Court on any such question.

(3) Without prejudice to the generality of subsection (1), the following reports (which are reproduced in the Official Journal of the Communities), namely—

(a) the reports by Mr. P. Jenard on the 1968 Convention and the 1971 Protocol; and

(b) the report by Professor Peter Schlosser on the Accession Convention [; and

(c) the report by Professor Demetrios I. Evrigenis and Professor K. D. Kerameus on the 1982 Accession Convention] [; and

(d) the report by Mr. Martinho de Almeida Cruz, Mr. Manuel Desantes Real and Mr. P. Jenard on the 1989 Accession Convention,]

may be considered in ascertaining the meaning or effect of any provision of the [Brussels Conventions] and shall be given such weight as is appropriate in the circumstances.

**Appointment**

Commencement order: SI 1986/2044.

**Amendment**

Section heading: words in square brackets substituted by the CJJA 1991, s 3, Sch 2, para 1. Sub-s 1): words in square brackets substituted by the CJJA 1991, s 3, Sch 2, para 1. Sub-s (3): para (c) inserted by SI 1989/1346, art 8; para (d) inserted by SI 1990/2591, art 8; other words in square brackets substituted by the CJJA 1991, s 3, Sch 2, para 1.

**Definitions**

'the Brussels Conventions' — see s 1(1) at para **[2.202]** above.

[2.204.1]

## Keypoints

- Principles of interpretation
- Text of 1971 Protocol
- Consideration of reports

[2.204.2]–[2.204.3]

## Principles of interpretation

Any question as to the meaning or effect of any provision of the conventions shall be determined in accordance with the principles laid down by and any relevant decision of the European Court, if not referred to that court in accordance with the 1971 Protocol.

The 1971 Protocol in included amongst the Brussels Conventions[2] and gives jurisdiction to the European Court to give rulings on the interpretation of the convention[3].

Judicial notice shall be taken of any decision of or expression of opinion by the European court on any question of interpretation of the Brussels Conventions[4].

1 See the CJJA 1982, s 3(1) at para **[2.204]** above.
2 See the CJJA 1982, s 1(1) at para **[2.202]** above.
3 See the CJJA 1982, Sch 2, Art 1.
4 See the CJJA 1982, s 3(2) at para **[2.204]** above.

**[2.204.4]**
**Consideration of reports**

By s 3(3) of the CJJA 1982, various reports reproduced in the Official Journal of the Communities may be considered in ascertaining the meaning or effect of any provision of the Brussels Conventions, and given such weight as is appropriate.

**[2.205]**

**[3A The Lugano Convention to have the force of law]**

[(1) The Lugano Convention shall have the force of law in the United Kingdom, and judicial notice shall be taken of it.

(2) For convenience of reference there is set out in Schedule 3C the English text of the Lugano Convention [as amended on the accession of Poland to that Convention].]

**Amendment**

Inserted by the CJJA 1991, s 1(1). Sub-s (2): words 'as amended on the accession of Poland to that Convention' in square brackets inserted by SI 2000/1824, art 11. Date in force: to be appointed (date to be notified in the London, Edinburgh and Belfast Gazettes as the date on which the accession of the Republic of Poland to the Lugano Convention takes effect in respect of the United Kingdom): see SI 2000/1824, art 1(a).

**Definitions**

'Lugano Convention' — see s 1(1) at para **[2.202]** above.

**[2.205.1]**
**Keypoints**

- Application
- Text of the Lugano Convention
- Purpose of the Lugano Convention

**[2.205.2]–[2.205.3]**
**Application**

This section applies the Lugano Convention to UK law. It is similar in effect to the Brussels Convention (see above), but brought a greater number of countries within the provisions of the CJJA 1982, when inserted by the CJJA 1991. The United Kingdom signed the Lugano Convention on 18 September 1989.

**[2.205.4]**
**Purpose of the Lugano Convention**

As explained in the preamble to the Convention, the Contracting States to the Lugano Convention were persuaded that the extension of the Principles of the Brussels Convention would strengthen legal and economic co-operation in Europe.

**[2.206]**

**[3B Interpretation of the Lugano Convention]**

[(1) In determining any question as to the meaning or effect of a provision of the Lugano Convention, a court in the United Kingdom shall, in accordance with Protocol No. 2 to that Convention, take account of any principles laid down in any relevant decision delivered by a court of any other Lugano Contracting State concerning provisions of the Convention.

(2) Without prejudice to any practice of the courts as to the matters which may be considered apart from this section, the report on the Lugano Convention by Mr. P. Jenard and Mr. G. Möller (which is reproduced in the Official Journal of the Communities of 28th July 1990) may be considered in ascertaining the meaning or

effect of any provision of the Convention and shall be given such weight as is appropriate in the circumstances.]

**Amendment**

Inserted by the CJJA 1991, s 1(1).

**Definitions**

'Lugano Convention' — see s 1(1) at para **[2.202]** above.



## [2.206.1]
## Keypoints

- Principles of interpretation
- Seisin

## [2.206.2]
## Principles of interpretation

Protocol No 2 to the Convention governs matters of interpretation, and in accordance with its terms, the UK court must take account of any principles found in any relevant decision of a court of any other Contracting State concerning the provisions of the Convention[1].

A report which may also be considered is specified at s 3B(2) of the CJJA 1982.

1 See the CJJA 1982, s 3B(1) at para **[2.206]** above.

## [2.206.3]
## Seisin

In *Canada Trust Co v Stolzenberg (No 2)*[1] the House of Lords decided that person was 'sued' within the meaning of Arts 2 to 6 of the Lugano Convention on the date of issue of the proceedings, rather than the date of service. Doubt was cast upon an earlier Court of Appeal decision[2] which held that seisin occurs only upon service of the writ, and not upon its issue. Consequently, the issue of a petition containing a prayer for maintenance may exclusively seize the English court of the issue of maintenance, and its service certainly will.

1 [2000] 4 All ER 481, [2000] 3 WLR 1376.
2 *Dresser UK Ltd v Falcongate Freight Management Ltd* [1992] QB 502.

## [2.207]

### 5 Recognition and enforcement of maintenance orders

(1) The function of transmitting to the appropriate court an application under Article 31 [of the 1968 Convention or of the Lugano Convention] for the recognition or enforcement in the United Kingdom of a maintenance order shall be discharged—

[(a) as respects England and Wales and Northern Ireland, by the Lord Chancellor;
(b) as respects Scotland, by the Secretary of State.]

In this subsection 'the appropriate court' means the magistrates' court or sheriff court having jurisdiction in the matter in accordance with the second paragraph of Article 32.

(2) Such an application shall be determined in the first instance by the prescribed officer of that court.

(3) Where on such an application the enforcement of the order is authorised to any extent, the order shall to that extent be registered in the prescribed manner in that court.

(4) A maintenance order registered under this section shall, for the purposes of its enforcement, be of the same force and effect, the registering court shall have in relation to its enforcement the same powers, and proceedings for or with respect to its enforcement may be taken, as if the order had been originally made by the registering court.

(5) Subsection (4) is subject to Article 39 (restriction on enforcement where appeal pending or time for appeal unexpired), to section 7 and to any provision made by rules of court as to the manner in which and conditions subject to which an order registered under this section may be enforced.

[(5A) A maintenance order which by virtue of this section is enforceable by a magistrates' court in England and Wales [shall, subject to the modifications of sections 76 and 93 of the Magistrates' Courts Act 1980 specified in subsections (5B) and (5C) below, be enforceable] in the same manner as a magistrates' court maintenance order made by that court.

In this subsection 'magistrates' court maintenance order' has the same meaning as in section 150(1) of the Magistrates' Courts Act 1980.]

[(5B) Section 76 (enforcement of sums adjudged to be paid) shall have effect as if for subsections (4) to (6) there were substituted the following subsections—

'(4) Where proceedings are brought for the enforcement of a magistrates' court maintenance order under this section, the court may vary the order by exercising one of its powers under subsection (5) below.

(5) The powers of the court are—

(a) the power to order that payments under the order be made directly to [a justices' chief executive];

(b) the power to order that payments under the order be made to [a justices' chief executive] by such method of payment falling within section 59(6) above (standing order, etc.) as may be specified;

(c) the power to make an attachment of earnings order under the Attachment of Earnings Act 1971 to secure payments under the order.

(6) In deciding which of the powers under subsection (5) above it is to exercise, the court shall have regard to any representations made by the debtor (within the meaning of section 59 above).

(7) Subsection (4) of section 59 above (power of court to require debtor to open account) shall apply for the purposes of subsection (5) above as it applies for the purposes of that section but as if for paragraph (a) there were substituted—

'(a) the court proposes to exercise its power under paragraph (b) of section 76(5) below, and,'.

(5C) In section 93 (complaint for arrears), subsection (6) (court not to impose imprisonment in certain circumstances) shall have effect as if for paragraph (b) there were substituted—

'(b) if the court is of the opinion that it is appropriate—

(i) to make an attachment of earnings order; or

(ii) to exercise its power under paragraph (b) of section 76(5) above.']

(6) A maintenance order which by virtue of this section is enforceable by a magistrates' court in … Northern Ireland [shall, subject to the modifications of Article 98 of the Magistrates' Courts (Northern Ireland) Order 1981 specified in sub-section (6A) below, be enforceable] [as an order made by that court to which that Article applies].

[(6A) Article 98 (enforcement of sums adjudged to be paid) shall have effect—

(a) as if for paragraph (7)(a) there were substituted the following paragraph—

'(a) if the court is of the opinion that it is appropriate—

(i) to make an attachment of earnings order; or

(ii) to exercise its power under paragraph (8C)(b)'; as if for paragraphs (8B) to (8D) there were substituted the following paragraphs—

'(8B) Upon the appearance of a person or proof of service of the summons on him as mentioned in paragraph (4) for the enforcement of an order to which this Article applies, the court or resident magistrate may vary the order by exercising one of the powers under paragraph (8C).

(8C) The powers mentioned in paragraph (8B) are—

(a) the power to order that payments under the order be made directly to the collecting officer;

(b) the power to order that payments under the order be made to the collecting officer by such method of payment falling within Article 85(7) (standing order, etc.) as may be specified;

(c) the power to make an attachment of earnings order under Part IX to secure payments under the order.

(8D) In deciding which of the powers under paragraph (8C) is to be exercised, the court or, as the case may be, a resident magistrate shall have regard to any representations made by the debtor (within the meaning of Article 85).

(8E) Paragraph (5) of Article 85 (power of court to require debtor to open account) shall apply for the purposes of paragraph (8C) as it applies for the purposes of that Article but as if for sub-paragraph (a) there were substituted—

'(a) the court proposes to exercise its power under sub-paragraph (b) of Article 98(8C), and.'.]

(7) The payer under a maintenance order registered under this section in a magistrates' court in England and Wales or Northern Ireland shall give notice of any change of address to the [proper officer] of that court.

A person who without reasonable excuse fails to comply with this subsection shall be guilty of an offence and liable on summary conviction to a fine not exceeding [level 2 on the standard scale].

[(8) In subsection (7) 'proper officer' means—

(a) in relation to a magistrates' court in England and Wales, the justices' chief executive for the court; and

(b) in relation to a magistrates' court in Northern Ireland, the clerk of the court.]



**Appointment**

Commencement order: SI 1986/2044.

**Modification**

Modified, in relation to the application of this section to authentic instruments and court settlements which are maintenance orders, by the Civil Jurisdiction and Judgments (Authentic Instruments and Court Settlements) Order 1993, SI 1993/604, art 3.

**Amendment**

Sub-s (1): CJJA 1991, s 3, Sch 2; SI 1992/709. Sub-s (5A): inserted by the FLRA 1987, s 33(1), Schs 2, 3. Sub-s (5A): MEA 1991, s 10, Sch 1. Sub-ss (5B), (5C): inserted by the MEA 1991, s 10, Sch 1. Sub-s (5B): AJA 1999, s 90(1), Sch 13. Sub-s (6): FLRA 1987, s 33(1), Schs 2, 3; SI 1993/1576; SI 1995/755. Sub-s (6A): inserted by SI 1993/1576. Sub-s (7): CJA 1982, ss 37, 46; AJA 1999, s 90(1), Sch 13. Sub-s (8): inserted by the AJA 1999, s 90(1), Sch 13.

**Definitions**

'maintenance order' — see s 15(1) at para **[2.213]** below.

## [2.207.1]
## Keypoints

- Appropriate court
- Effect of registration
- Powers of the court
- Magistrates' Court (Civil Jurisdiction and Judgment Act 1982) Rules 1986, SI 1986/1962

## [2.207.2]
## Appropriate court

The appropriate court will be the magistrates' court[1].

1 See the CJJA 1982, s 5(1) at para **[2.207]** above.

## [2.207.3]
### Effect of registration

Once registered, a maintenance order has the same force and effect for enforcement purposes as if the order had been originally made by the registering court[1] and is enforceable in the same manner as an order made by that court[2].

Section 5(4) of the CJJA 1982 is subject to Art 39 of Sch 3C (restriction on enforcement where appeal pending or time for appeal unexpired), and s 7 below[3] (interest on registered judgments)[4].

1 See the CJJA 1982, s 5(4) at para **[2.207]** above.
2 See the CJJA 1982, s 5(5A) at para **[2.207]** above.
3 See para **[2.209]** below.
4 See also CJJA 1982, s 5(5) at para **[2.207]** above.

## [2.207.4]
### Powers of the court

Section 5(5B) and (5C) of the CJJA 1982 makes certain changes to the Magistrates' Courts Act 1980, ss 76 and 93 for the purposes of enforcement under this Act.

The powers of the court are defined as:

- ordering payments be made directly to the clerk (either of the court concerned or of any other magistrates' court);
- ordering payments by standing order or such other method as specified in s 59(6) of the MCA 1980, to the clerk;
- making an attachment of earnings order[1].

There is consequently no power to order that the payer make payments directly to the payee under the order.

If a payer fails to give notice of a change of address, then he may be fined up to level 2 on the standard scale (£500 – Criminal Justice Act 1982, s 37(2))[2].

1 See the CJJA 1982, s 5(5B) at para **[2.207]** above, amending s 76(5) of the MCA 1980.
2 See also the CJJA 1982, s 5(7) at para **[2.207]** above.

## [2.207.5]
### Magistrates' Court (Civil Jurisdiction and Judgment Act 1982) Rules 1986, SI 1986/1962

The prescribed officer of a magistrates' court for the purposes of the Civil Jurisdiction and Judgments Act 1982 shall be the justices' clerk (r 3).

The following obligations are placed on the justices' clerk by the Magistrates' Courts (Civil Jurisdiction and Judgments Act 1982) Rules 1986, SI 1986/1962, r 4:

- to ascertain whether the payer lives in the jurisdiction;
- to register the order if he does, and if not return the documents to the Lord Chancellor with any information obtained about the payer's whereabouts;
- to notify the applicant if the application is refused;
- if the application is successful to provide notice of registration to the Lord Chancellor, the applicant and the payer;
- if appropriate to suggest registration in the High Court.

Rule 6 of the Magistrates' Courts (Civil Jurisdiction and Judgments Act 1982) Rules 1986, SI 1986/1962 provides for the duties of the justices' clerk of the registering court in relation to collection and enforcement:

- he must direct when and where payment should be made to him;
- he must post the payments to the court that made the order or otherwise as directed;
- he may, and when the arrears amount to four weeks he must, take steps for recovery of all arrears whether or not requested by the applicant, unless he consideres such action unreasonable;
- he must take reasonable steps to notify the applicant of the means of enforcement available.

Rule 6A(1) requires the clerk to record the method of payment and notify the payer accordingly.

Rule 6A(2) applies when an order for payment by standing order has been made, and requires the clerk to notify the payer of details of the account into which payments are to be made.

Rule 7 provides that the clerk must register an order varying or revoking a registered maintenance order by a minute or memorandum and give written notice to the payee and payer concerned.

Rule 8(1) provides for the transfer of registered orders between magistrates' courts where the payer is residing within the jurisdiction of another court. The clerk must then send the relevant documentation (as to which see r 8(3)) and give the appropriate notices. There should be no transfer if registration is pending in the High Court. By r 8(2), the clerk receiving the transfer repeats the procedure for registration under r 4 (above).

Rule 9 provides for the cancellation of registered orders if the payer is not within the jurisdiction of that court nor has any assets there against which the order could be enforced, and the giving of requisite notices.

Note the functions of the Secretary of State have been transferred to the Lord Chancellor, by the Transfer of Functions (Magistrates' Courts and Family Law) Order 1992, SI 1992/709, art 4.

Part III of the Magistrates' Courts (Civil Jurisdiction and Judgments Act 1982) Rules 1986, SI 1986/1962 governs applications under Art 5(2) of the Brussels Convention, and rr 10 and 11 are set out in full below:



PART III

APPLICATIONS FOR MAINTENANCE UNDER ARTICLE 5(2) OF THE 1968 CONVENTION

## 10 Complaint against person residing outside the United Kingdom

(1) This Rule applies where a complaint is made to a magistrates' court by a person who is domiciled or habitually resident in England and Wales against a person residing in a Contracting State [or a Regulation State] other than the United Kingdom, and the complaint is one in respect of which the court has jurisdiction to make a maintenance order by virtue of Article 5(2) of the 1968 Convention [or Article 5(2) of the Regulation].

(2) On the making of a complaint to which paragraph (1) of this Rule applies, the following documents, that is to say:—

- (a) notice of the institution of the proceedings, including a statement of the grounds of the complaint;
- (b) a statement signed by the [justices' chief executive], giving such information as he possesses as to the whereabouts of the defendant;
- (c) a statement giving such information as [the justices' chief executive] possesses for facilitating the identification of the defendant; and
- (d) where available, a photograph of the defendant;

shall be sent by that clerk to the Secretary of State [Lord Chancellor].

(3) The [justices' chief executive] shall give the defendant notice in writing of the date fixed for the hearing by sending the notice by post addressed to his last known or usual place of abode.

(4) Where the defendant makes any written representations or adduces any documentary evidence in advance of the hearing, a copy of the representations or evidence shall be served on the complainant by the [justices' chief executive] before the hearing.

(5) In considering whether or not to make a maintenance order pursuant to a complaint to which paragraph (1) of this Rule applies, where the defendant does not appear and is not represented at the hearing the court shall take into account any representations made and any evidence adduced by him or on his behalf under paragraph (4) above and, where the defendant does appear or is represented at the hearing, the court may take any such representations or evidence into account in addition to any oral representations made or evidence adduced at the hearing.

(6) Where a maintenance order has been made under this Rule [in respect of a complaint in relation to which the court has jurisdiction by virtue of Article 5(2) of the 1968 Convention], the [justices' chief executive] shall cause notice thereof to be given to the defendant by sending a copy of the order by post addressed to his last known or usual place of abode and, on application by the complainant, shall give to the complainant the following documents, that is to say:—

(a) a certified copy of the order;

(b) a written statement signed by the justices' clerk as to whether or not the defendant appeared in the proceedings in which the order was made, and, if he did not appear, the original or a certified copy of a document which establishes that the document mentioned in paragraph (2)(a) of this Rule had been served on the defendant;

(c) a document which establishes that notice of the order was sent to the defendant; and

(d) a written statement signed by the justices' clerk as to whether or not the complainant received legal aid in the proceedings;

with a view to an application being made by the complainant for registration and enforcement under Articles 31 and 32 of the 1968 Convention.

[(7) Where a maintenance order has been made under this Rule in respect of a complaint in relation to which the court has jurisdiction by virtue of Article 5(2) of the Regulation, the justices' chief executive shall cause notice thereof to be given to the defendant by sending a copy of the order by post addressed to his last known or usual place of abode and, on application by the complainant, shall give to the complainant the following documents—

(a) a certified copy of the order; and

(b) a completed certificate in the form of Annex V to the Regulation;

with a view to an application being made by the complainant for registration and enforcement under Articles 38 and 39 of the Regulation.]

### 11 Application for variation and revocation of a maintenance order

(1) This Rule applies where an application is made to a magistrates' court for the variation or revocation of a maintenance order where the payer under the order is residing in a Contracting State [or a Regulation State] other than the United Kingdom.

(2) Where an application to which this Rule applies is made by the payee, the following documents, that is to say:—

(a) Notice of the institution of the proceedings, including a statement of the grounds of the application;

(b) a statement signed by the [justices' chief executive], giving such information as he possesses as to the whereabouts of the [respondent];

(c) a statement giving such information as the clerk possesses for facilitating the identification of the [respondent]; and

(d) where available, a photograph of the [respondent];

shall be sent by [that justices' chief executive] to the Secretary of State [Lord Chancellor].

(3) Where an application to which this Rule applies is made by the payee:—

(a) The [justices' chief executive] shall give the [respondent] notice in writing of the date fixed for the hearing by sending the notice by post addressed to his last known or usual place of abode;

(b) where the [respondent] makes any written representations or adduces any documentary evidence in advance of the hearing, a copy of the representations or evidence shall be served on the [applicant] by the [justices' chief executive] before the hearing;

(c) the court, in considering whether to vary or revoke the order, shall, where the payer does not appear and is not represented at the hearing, take into account any representations made and any evidence adduced by or on his behalf under sub-paragraph (b) above and, where the payer does appear or is represented at the hearing, the court may take any such representations or evidence into account, in addition to any oral representations or evidence adduced at the hearing.

(4) Where an application to which this Rule applies is made by the payer, the [justices' chief executive] shall arrange for the service of the document mentioned in paragraph (2)(a) of this Rule on the payee.

(5) Where upon an application to which this Rule applies [to vary or revoke a maintenance order where the payer under the order is residing in a Contracting State] the court varies or revokes the order, the [justices' chief executive] shall cause notice thereof to be given to the [respondent] by sending a copy of the order of variation or revocation by post addressed to his last known or usual place of abode and, on application by the [applicant], shall give to the [applicant] the following documents, that is to say:—

(a) a certified copy of the order of variation or revocation;

(b) a written statement, signed by the justices' clerk as to whether or not the [respondent] appeared in the proceedings for the variation or revocation of the order and if he did not appear the original or a certified copy of a document which establishes that the notice of the institution of the proceedings had been served on the [respondent];

(c) a document which establishes that notice of the order of variation or revocation was sent to the [respondent]; and

(d) a written statement signed by the justices' clerk as to whether or not the [applicant] or the [respondent] received legal aid in the proceedings;

with a view to an application being made by the [applicant] for registration and enforcement of the order of variation or revocation under Articles 31 and 32 of the 1968 Convention.

[(6)Where upon an application to vary or revoke a maintenance order where the payer under the order is residing in a Regulation State the court varies or revokes the order, the justices' chief executive shall cause notice thereof to be given to the respondent by sending a copy of the order of variation or revocation by post addressed to his last known or usual place of abode and, on application by the applicant, shall give to the applicant the following documents—

(a) a certified copy of the order of variation or revocation; and

(b) a completed certificate in the form of Annex V to the Regulation;

with a view to an application being made by the applicant for registration and enforcement of the order of variation or revocation under Articles 38 and 39 of the Regulation.]

**[2.208]**

### 6 Appeals under Article 37, second paragraph and Article 41

(1) The single further appeal on a point of law referred to [in the 1968 Convention and the Lugano Convention] in Article 37, second paragraph and Article 41 in relation to the recognition or enforcement of a judgment other than a maintenance order lies—

(a) in England and Wales or Northern Ireland, to the Court of Appeal or to the House of Lords in accordance with Part II of the Administration of Justice Act 1969 (appeals direct from the High Court to the House of Lords);

(b) in Scotland, to the Inner House of the Court of Session.

(2) Paragraph (a) of subsection (1) has effect notwithstanding section 15(2) of the Administration of Justice Act 1969 (exclusion of direct appeal to the House of Lords in cases where no appeal to that House lies from a decision of the Court of Appeal).

(3) The single further appeal on a point of law referred to [in each of those Conventions] in Article 37, second paragraph and Article 41 in relation to the recognition or enforcement of a maintenance order lies—

(a) in England and Wales, to the High Court by way of case stated in accordance with section 111 of the Magistrates' Courts Act 1980;

(b) in Scotland, to the Inner House of the Court of Session;

(c) in Northern Ireland, to the Court of Appeal.

**Appointment**
Commencement order: SI 1986/2044.

**Amendment**
Sub-ss (1), (3): words in square brackets inserted by the CJJA Act 1991, s 3, Sch 2, para 3.

**Definitions**
'1968 Convention' — see s 1(1) at para **[2.202]** above.
'Lugano Convention' — see s 1(1) at para **[2.202]** above.
'maintenance order' — see s 15(1) at para **[2.213]** below.

## [2.208.1]
### Keypoints

- Scope of section
- Further appeal

## [2.208.2]
### Scope of section

This section provides the mechanism for appeal against a decision permitting enforcement of a maintenance order under the Conventions to the High Court.

See further, in relation to the application of this section to authentic instruments and court settlements which are not maintenance orders and to authentic instruments and court settlements which are maintenance orders: the Civil Jurisdiction and Judgments (Authentic Instruments and Court Settlements) Order 1993, SI 1993/604, arts 2, 3.

## [2.208.3]
### Further appeal

By Art 37(2), a single further appeal from the magistrates' court in relation to the recognition or enforcement of a maintenance order lies only on a point of law. Such appeal must be made to the High Court by way of case stated[1].

1 See the CJJA 1982, s 6(3) at para **[2.208]** above.

## [2.209]

**7 Interest on registered judgments**

(1) Subject to subsection (4), where in connection with an application for registration of a judgment under section 4 or 5 the applicant shows—

(a) that the judgment provides for the payment of a sum of money; and

(b) that in accordance with the law of the Contracting State in which the judgment was given interest on that sum is recoverable under the judgment from a particular date or time,

the rate of interest and the date or time from which it is so recoverable shall be registered with the judgment and, subject to any provision made under subsection (2), the debt resulting, apart from section 4(2), from the registration of the judgment shall carry interest in accordance with the registered particulars.

(2) Provision may be made by rules of court as to the manner in which and the periods by reference to which any interest payable by virtue of subsection (1) is to be calculated and paid, including provision for such interest to cease to accrue as from a prescribed date.

(3) Costs or expenses recoverable by virtue of section 4(2) shall carry interest as if they were the subject of an order for the payment of costs or expenses made by the registering court on the date of registration.

(4) Interest on arrears of sums payable under a maintenance order registered under section 5 in a magistrates' court in England and Wales or Northern Ireland shall not be recoverable in that court, but without prejudice to the operation in relation to any such

order of section 2A of the Maintenance Orders Act 1958 or section 11A of the Maintenance and Affiliation Orders Act (Northern Ireland) 1966 (which enable interest to be recovered if the order is re-registered for enforcement in the High Court).

(5) Except as mentioned in subsection (4), debts under judgments registered under section 4 or 5 shall carry interest only as provided by this section.

**Appointment**

Commencement order: SI 1986/2044.

**Definitions**

'Contracting State' — see s 1(3) at para **[2.202]** above.
'judgment' — see s 15(1) at para **[2.213]** below.
'maintenance order' — see s 15(1) at para **[2.213]** below.



## [2.209.1]
## Keypoints

- Effect of section
- Interest provisions limited

## [2.209.2]
## Effect of section

This section makes certain provisions for the enforcement of interest on registered orders.

See further, in relation to the application of this section to authentic instruments and court settlements which are not maintenance orders and to authentic instruments and court settlements which are maintenance orders: the Civil Jurisdiction and Judgments (Authentic Instruments and Court Settlements) Order 1993, SI 1993/604, arts 2, 3.

## [2.209.3]
## Interest provisions limited

Provided that:

- the original order provides for the payment of a sum of money; and
- under the law of the contracting state in which the order was made interest would be recoverable on that sum;

then the interest that is recoverable under the original order shall be registered with the order, and will carry interest from the registration[1].

However, unless the order is registered in the High Court pursuant to the provisions of the MOA 1958 the interest element of a foreign order will not be recoverable in a registering court in the United Kingdom[2].

Interest may only be enforced if the original judgment provided for the payment of interest. No more than six years' interest may be recovered[3].

1 See the CJJA 1982, s 7(1) at para **[2.209]** above.
2 See the CJJA 1982, s 7(4) at para **[2.209]** above.
3 See *Lowsley v Forbes* [1999] 1 AC 329, [1998] 3 All ER 897, HL.

## [2.210]

### 8 Currency of payment under registered maintenance orders

(1) Sums payable in the United Kingdom under a maintenance order by virtue of its registration under section 5, including any arrears so payable, shall be paid in the currency of the United Kingdom.

(2) Where the order is expressed in any other currency, the amounts shall be converted on the basis of the exchange rate prevailing on the date of registration of the order.

(3) For the purposes of this section, a written certificate purporting to be signed by an officer of any bank in the United Kingdom and stating the exchange rate prevailing

on a specified date shall be evidence, and in Scotland sufficient evidence, of the facts stated.

**Appointment**
Commencement order: SI 1986/2044.

**Definitions**
'maintenance order' — see s 15(1) at para **[2.213]** below.

**[2.210.1]**
**Keypoint**
- Provision for payment

**[2.210.2]**
**Provision for payment**

This section stipulates that payments under registered orders should be made in Sterling, and that conversion should be calculated as at the date of registration.

See further, in relation to the application of this section to authentic instruments and court settlements which maintenance orders: the Civil Jurisdiction and Judgments (Authentic Instruments and Court Settlements) Order 1993, SI 1993/604, art 3.

**[2.211]**

### 11 Proof and admissibility of certain judgments and related documents

(1) For the purposes of the 1968 Convention [and the Lugano Convention]—

(a) a document, duly authenticated, which purports to be a copy of a judgment given by a court of a Contracting State other than the United Kingdom shall without further proof be deemed to be a true copy, unless the contrary is shown; and

(b) the original or a copy of any such document as is mentioned in Article 46(2) or 47 (supporting documents to be produced by a party seeking recognition or enforcement of a judgment) shall be evidence, and in Scotland sufficient evidence, of any matter to which it relates.

(2) A document purporting to be a copy of a judgment given by any such court as is mentioned in subsection (1)(a) is duly authenticated for the purposes of this section if it purports—

(a) to bear the seal of that court; or

(b) to be certified by any person in his capacity as a judge or officer of that court to be a true copy of a judgment given by that court.

(3) Nothing in this section shall prejudice the admission in evidence of any document which is admissible apart from this section.

**Appointment**
Commencement order: SI 1986/2044.

**Amendment**
Sub-s (1): words in square brackets inserted by the CJJA Act 1991, s 3, Sch 2, para 6.

**Definitions**
'Contracting State' — see s 1(3) at para **[2.202]** above.
'1968 Convention' — see s 1(1) at para **[2.202]** above.
'Lugano Convention' — see s 1(1) at para **[2.202]** above.
'judgment' — see s 15 (1) at para **[2.213]** below.

**[2.211.1]**
**Keypoint**
- Evidence in maintenance proceedings

## [2.211.2]
## Evidence in maintenance proceedings

This is governed by Pt IV of the Magistrates' Courts (Civil Jurisdiction and Judgments Act 1982) Rules 1986, SI 1986/1962, which is set out below:

PART IV
EVIDENCE IN MAINTENANCE PROCEEDINGS

### 13 Admissibility of documents

(1) Subject to paragraph (2) of this Rule, a statement contained in—

(a) a document which purports to set out or summarise evidence given in proceedings in a court in another part of the United Kingdom or another Contracting State [or another Regulation State];

(b) a document which purports to have been received in evidence in proceedings in a court in another part of the United Kingdom or another Contracting State [or another Regulation State];

(c) a document which purports to set out or summarise evidence taken in another part of the United Kingdom or in another Contracting State [or another Regulation State] for the purpose of proceedings in a court in England and Wales under the 1982 Act [or the Regulation], whether in response to a request made by such a court or otherwise; or

(d) a document which purports to record information relating to the payments made under an order of a court in another part of the United Kingdom or another Contracting State [or another Regulation State]

shall, in any proceedings in a magistrates' court in England and Wales relating to a maintenance order to which the 1982 Act [or the Regulation] applies, be admissible as evidence of any fact stated therein to the same extent as oral evidence of that fact is admissible in those proceedings.

(2) Paragraph (1) of this Rule shall not apply unless the document concerned has been made or authenticated by the court in the other part of the United Kingdom or the other Contracting State [or the other Regulation State], as the case may be, or by a judge or official of that court, in accordance with paragraph (3), (4) or (5) of this Rule.

(3) A document purporting to set out or summarise evidence given as mentioned in paragraph (1)(a) above, or taken as mentioned in paragraph (1)(c) above, shall be deemed to be authenticated for the purposes of that paragraph if the document purports to be certified by the judge or official before whom the evidence was given or by whom it was taken, or to be the original document containing or recording or, as the case may be, summarising, the evidence or a true copy of that document.

(4) A document purporting to have been received in evidence as mentioned in paragraph (1)(b) above, or to be a copy of a document so received, shall be deemed to be authenticated for the purposes of that paragraph if the document purports to be certified by a judge or official of the court in question to be, or to be a true copy of, a document which has been so received.

(5) A document purporting to record information as mentioned in paragraph (1)(d) above shall be deemed to be authenticated for the purposes of that paragraph if the document purports to be certified by a judge or official of the court in question to be a true record of the payments made under the order concerned.

(6) It shall not be necessary in any proceedings in which evidence is to be received under this Rule to prove the signature or official position of the person appearing to have given such a certificate.

(7) Nothing in this Rule shall prejudice the admission in evidence of any document which is admissible in evidence apart from this Rule.

(8) Any request by a magistrates' court in England and Wales for the taking or providing of evidence by a court in another part of the United Kingdom or another Contracting State [or another Regulation State] for the purpose of proceedings under the 1982 Act [or the Regulation] shall be communicated in writing to the court in question.

### 14 Evidence for the purposes of proceedings outside England and Wales

(1) Subject to paragraph (2) below, where for the purposes of any proceedings in a court in another part of the United Kingdom or in a Contracting State [or in a Regulation State] other than the United Kingdom relating to a maintenance order a request is made by or on behalf of that court for the taking in England and Wales of evidence of a person residing therein relating to matters specified in the request, the following magistrates' courts shall have power to take that evidence, that is to say:—

- (a) where the maintenance order to which the proceedings in the court in the other part of the United Kingdom or Contracting State [or Regulation State] relate was made by a magistrates' court, the court which made the order;
- (b) where the maintenance order to which those proceedings relate is registered in a magistrates' court, the court in which the order is registered;
- (c) a magistrates' court which has received such a request from the Secretary of State [Lord Chancellor].

(2) The power conferred by paragraph (1) above may, with the agreement of a court having that power, be exercised by any other magistrates' court which, because the person whose evidence is to be taken resides within its jurisdiction or for any other reason, the first mentioned court considers could more conveniently take the evidence; but nothing in this paragraph shall derogate from the power of any court specified in paragraph (1) above.

(3) Before taking the evidence of a person under paragraph (1) or (2) above, a magistrates' court shall give notice of the time and place at which the evidence is to be taken to such persons and in such manner as it thinks fit.

(4) Subject to paragraph (5) below, where the evidence of a person is to be taken by a magistrates' court under the foregoing provisions of this Rule—

- (a) the evidence shall be taken in the same manner as if that person were a witness in proceedings on a complaint;
- (b) any oral evidence so taken shall be put into writing and read to the person who gave it, who shall be required to sign the document; and
- (c) the justices by whom the evidence of any person is so taken shall certify at the foot of any document setting out the evidence of, or produced in evidence by, that person that such evidence was taken, or a document received in evidence, as the case may be, by them.

(5) Where such a request as is mentioned in paragraph (1) above includes a request that the evidence be taken in a particular manner, the magistrates' court by which the evidence was taken shall, so far as circumstances permit, comply with that request.

(6) Any document such as is mentioned in paragraph (4)(c) above shall be sent to the court in the Contracting State [or the Regulation State] by or on behalf of which the request was made.

**[2.212]**

### 12 Provision for issue of copies of, and certificates in connection with, UK judgments

Rules of court may make provision for enabling any interested party wishing to secure under the 1968 Convention [or the Lugano Convention] the recognition or enforcement in another Contracting State of a judgment given by a court in the United Kingdom to obtain, subject to any conditions specified in the rules—

- (a) a copy of the judgment; and
- (b) a certificate giving particulars relating to the judgment and the proceedings in which it was given.

**Appointment**

Commencement order: SI 1986/2044.

**Amendment**

Words in square brackets inserted by the CJJA 1991, s 3, Sch 2, para 7.

**Definitions**

'Contracting State' — see s 1(3) at para **[2.202]** above.
'1968 Convention' — see s 1(1) at para **[2.202]** above.
'Lugano Convention' — see s 1(1) at para **[2.202]** above.
'judgment' — see s 15(1) at para **[2.213]** below.



### [2.212.1]
### Keypoint

- Magistrates' Courts (Civil Jurisdiction and Judgments Act 1982) Rules 1986, SI 1986/1962, r 12

### [2.212.2]
### Magistrates' Courts (Civil Jurisdiction and Judgments Act 1982) Rules 1986, SI 1986/1962, r 12

The text of r 12 is set out below:

#### 12 Copies of, and certificates in connection with, maintenance orders

(1) Without prejudice to the provisions of [Rules 10(6), 10(7), 11(5) and 11(6)] of these Rules, a person wishing to obtain for the purposes of an application for recognition or enforcement in a Contracting State [or a Regulation State] a copy of a maintenance order made by a magistrates' court in England and Wales, and a certificate giving particulars relating to the order and the proceedings in which it was made may apply in writing to the [justices' chief executive] for that court.

(2) An application under paragraph (1) above shall specify:—

(a) the names of the parties to the proceedings in the magistrates' court;

(b) the date or approximate date of the proceedings in which the maintenance order was made, and the nature of these proceedings;

(c) the Contracting State [or the Regulation State] in which the application for recognition or enforcement has been made or is to be made;

(d) the postal address of the applicant.

(3) A [justices' chief executive] who receives an application under paragraph (1) of this Rule shall send by post to the applicant at the address indicated in the application for the purposes an authenticated copy of the order concerned.

(4) For the purposes of paragraph (3) of this Rule a copy of an order shall be deemed to be authenticated if it is accompanied by a statement signed by the [justices' chief executive] that it is a true copy of the order concerned and giving particulars of the proceedings in which it was made.

(5) A person wishing to obtain for the purposes of an application made or to be made in another Contracting State [or in another Regulation State] or in another part of the United Kingdom in connection with a maintenance order which is registered in a magistrates' court in England and Wales a certificate giving particulars of any payments made and any arrears which have accrued under the order while so registered may apply in writing to the [justices' chief executive] for the registering court, and a [justices' chief executive] who receives such an application shall send by post to the applicant at the address indicated in the application for the purposes a certificate giving the information so requested.

### [2.213]–[2.216]

#### 15 Interpretation of Part I and consequential amendments

(1) In this Part, unless the context otherwise requires—

'judgment' has the meaning given by Article 25;

'maintenance order' means a maintenance judgment within the meaning of the 1968 Convention [or, as the case may be, the Lugano Convention];

'payer', in relation to a maintenance order, means the person liable to make the payments for which the order provides;

'prescribed' means prescribed by rules of court.

(2) References in this Part to a judgment registered under section 4 or 5 include, to the extent of its registration, references to a judgment so registered to a limited extent only.

(3) Anything authorised or required by the 1968 Convention [the Lugano Convention] or this Part to be done by, to or before a particular magistrates' court may be done by, to or before any magistrates' court acting for the same petty sessions area (or, in Northern Ireland, petty sessions district) as that court.

(4) The enactments specified in Part I of Schedule 12 shall have effect with the amendments specified there, being amendments consequential on this Part.

**Appointment**

Commencement order: SI 1986/2044.

**Amendment**

Sub-ss (1), (3): words in square brackets inserted by the CJJA 1991, s 3, Sch 2, para 10.

# Matrimonial and Family Proceedings Act 1984

Contents

*Section*

PART III
FINANCIAL RELIEF IN ENGLAND AND WALES AFTER OVERSEAS DIVORCE ETC



*An Act to amend the Matrimonial Causes Act 1973 so far as it restricts the time within which proceedings for divorce or nullity of marriage can be instituted; to amend that Act, the Domestic Proceedings and Magistrates' Courts Act 1978 and the Magistrates' Courts Act 1980 so far as they relate to the exercise of the jurisdiction of courts in England and Wales to make provision for financial relief or to exercise related powers in matrimonial and certain other family proceedings; to make provision for financial relief to be available where a marriage has been dissolved or annulled, or the parties to a marriage have been legally separated, in a country overseas; to make related amendments in the Maintenance Orders (Reciprocal Enforcement Act 1972 and the Inheritance (Provision for Family and Dependants) Act 1975; to make provision for the distribution and transfer between the High Court and county courts of, and the exercise in those courts of jurisdiction in, family business and family proceedings and to repeal and re-enact with amendments certain provisions conferring on designated county courts jurisdiction in matrimonial proceedings; to impose a duty to notify changes of address on persons liable to make payments under maintenance orders enforceable under Part II of the Maintenance Orders Act 1950 or Part I of the Maintenance Orders Act 1958; and for connected purposes*

[12th July 1984]

## [2.217]
### Introduction

Part III (Financial Relief in England and Wales after Overseas Divorce etc) of the Matrimonial and Family Proceedings Act 1984 (MFPA 1984) is set out below.

## [2.218]

PART III

FINANCIAL RELIEF IN ENGLAND AND WALES AFTER OVERSEAS DIVORCE ETC

### 12 Applications for financial relief after overseas divorce etc

(1) Where—

(a) a marriage has been dissolved or annulled, or the parties to a marriage have been legally separated, by means of judicial or other proceedings in an overseas country, and

(b) the divorce, annulment or legal separation is entitled to be recognised as valid in England and Wales,

either party to the marriage may apply to the court in the manner prescribed by rules of court for an order for financial relief under this Part of this Act.

(2) If after a marriage has been dissolved or annulled in an overseas country one of the parties to the marriage remarries that party shall not be entitled to make an application in relation to that marriage.

(3) For the avoidance of doubt it is hereby declared that the reference in sub-section (2) above to remarriage includes a reference to a marriage which is by law void or voidable.

(4) In this Part of this Act except sections 19, 23, and 24 'order for financial relief' means an order under section 17 or 22 below of a description referred to in that section.

**Appointment**

Commencement order: SI 1985/1316.

## [2.218.1]
### Keypoints

- Scope of section
- Application for an order
- The appropriate court
- Recognition of foreign decree necessary
- Remarriage a bar to application for any relief
- Leave required
- Part III retrospective in effect
- Limitations imposed by the Child Support Act 1991

## [2.218.2]
### Scope of section

This section (and this Part) came into force on 16 September 1985 following Law Commission Report No 117. Previously, there had been no comparable relief to that available under the MCA 1973 where a marriage had already been terminated by a foreign court[1].

1 See *Quazi v Quazi* [1980] AC 744, [1979] 3 All ER 897, HL.

## [2.218.3]
### Application for an order

Part III of the MFPA 1984 enabled the court for the first time to entertain applications for financial provision and property adjustment orders notwithstanding the existence of a prior foreign divorce.

Either party to the marriage may apply in the manner prescribed[1].

Proceedings under the MFPA 1984, Pt III are 'family proceedings' for the purposes of the CPR 1998, and so are expressly excluded from the operation of those rules.

Subject to the provisions for leave, discussed below, an application under this part is made by originating summons issued in Form M26 out of the principal registry. At the same time the applicant, unless otherwise directed, must file an affidavit in support of the summons giving full particulars of his (or more usually her) property and income[2].

The applicant must serve a sealed copy of the originating summons on the Respondent, and must annex to it a copy of the supporting affidavit, if filed, and a notice of proceedings and acknowledgment of service in Form M28[3].

If the Respondent intends to defend he must return the acknowledgment of service giving notice of that intention within 31 days from, but inclusive of, the day of service[4], applying, with amendments, r 10.8. He must then, within 28 days after the time limited for giving notice to defend, file and serve an affidavit setting out the grounds on which he relies[5].

Save that the amendments to the FPR 1991 introduced by the Family Proceedings (Amendment No 2) Rules 1999 (namely, the pilot scheme made universal) do not apply, the application is treated as far as possible as if it were a conventional application under ss 23 and 24 of the MCA 1973, and accordingly FPR 1991, r 3.18(3) provides that the following other of the rules shall apply (with necessary modifications):

- **r 2.57** – Children to be separately represented on certain applications;
- **r 2.59** – Evidence on application for property adjustment or avoidance of disposition order;
- **r 2.61** – Information on application for consent order for financial relief;
- **r 2.62(5)** – Court's power to give directions re pleadings and further conduct of proceedings;
- **r 2.62(6)** – Requirement to serve notice of application for directions;
- **r 2.63** – Request for further information;
- **r 2.66(1)** – Arrangements on referral to a judge; and
- **r 2.66(2)** – Hearing before judge in chambers, unless otherwise directed.

Similarly, by s 21 below various provisions of the MCA 1973, Pt II, are made to apply in relation to orders under ss 14 and 17 of the MFPA 1984, Pt III.

Where the application relates to land, the summons must identify whether the land is registered (with title number), and give particulars of any mortgage or other interest in the land[6]. Any mortgagee should be served, and may apply for a copy of the affidavit[7]. If the mortgagee does so, he may file an affidavit in answer in 14 days[8].

### *Exceptions*

FPR 1991, r 3.18[9], does not refer to the paragraphs in r 2.62 expressly providing for production orders to be made against non-parties[10]. Consequently, there is no jurisdiction to make production orders in proceedings for financial relief following overseas divorce. However, to achieve the same result a subpoena duces tecum can be issued under RSC Ord 32, r 7(1) out of the Principal Registry of the Family Division[11].

Where an application for variation of settlement is involved: full particulars of all settlements made on the spouses, and the funds brought in by each spouse, should be provided in the affidavit[12]. The trustees and any living settlor should be served with the summons and affidavit[13], and they may file an affidavit in answer in 14 days[14].

1 See FPR 1991, rr 3.17 to 3.19 at para **[3.469]** below.
2 See FPR 1991, r 3.18(1) at para **[3.470]** below.
3 See FPR 1991, r 3.18(2) below.
4 See FPR 1991, r 3.18(2) below.
5 See FPR 1991, r. 3.18(5) below.
6 See FPR 1991, r 2.59(2) at para **[3.439]** below.
7 See FPR 1991, r 2.59(4) below.
8 See FPR 1991, r 2.59(5) below.
9 See para **[3.470]** below.
10 See FPR 1991, r 2.62(7) to (9).

11 See *Roker International Properties Inc v Couvaras and Wolf* [2001] 1 FCR 320, [2000] 2 FLR 976.
12 See FPR 1991, r 2.59(1)(b) below.
13 See FPR 1991, r 2.59(3)(a) below.
14 See FPR 1991, r 2.59(5) below.

### [2.218.4]
### The appropriate court

The court to which all applications under the MFPA 1984, Pt III must be made is the High Court (or any county court which has jurisdiction by virtue of Pt V of the Act)[1].

Section 33(4) of the MFPA 1984 provides that the Lord Chancellor may by order designate any Divorce County Court as a court for the exercise of Pt III jurisdiction. He has not yet done so.

An application for an order for financial relief under Pt III or for an avoidance of transaction order shall be determined by a judge[2].

1 See the MFPA 1984, s 27 at para **[2.232]** below.
2 See FPR 1991, r 3.18(8) at para **[3.470]** below.

### [2.218.5]
### Recognition of foreign decree necessary

The overseas divorce, annulment or legal separation must be one which is entitled to be recognised in England and Wales. The MFPA 1984 does not apply to transnational divorces, which are not so recognised[1].

The statutory provisions governing such recognition are contained in Pt II of the FLA 1986.

In brief, recognition requires (by s 46 of the FLA 1986) either:

(1) that the divorce, annulment or legal separation was obtained by means of proceedings; that it is effective under the law of the country in which it was obtained; and that at the date of commencement of those proceedings either party was habitually resident in, domiciled in or was a national of the country in which the divorce, annulment or legal separation was obtained; or
(2) if not obtained by proceedings, then that it is effective under the law of the country in which it was obtained; that at the date on which it was obtained each party was domiciled in that country, or either was domiciled in that country and the other was domiciled in a country under whose law the divorce, annulment or legal separation was recognised as valid; and that neither party was habitually resident in the UK throughout the period of one year immediately preceding that date.

1 See *Berkovits v Grinberg (A-G intervening)* [1995] Fam 142, [1995] 2 All ER 861.

### [2.218.6]
### Remarriage a bar to application for any relief

If one of the parties to an overseas divorce or annulment has remarried, then that party is not entitled to make an application in relation to that marriage[1].

'Remarriage' includes a second marriage which is by law void or voidable[2].

1 Cf MCA 1973, s 28(3). See also the MFPA 1984, s 12(3).
2 See the MFPA 1984, s 12(4).

### [2.218.7]
### Leave required

No application for an order under Pt III of the MFPA 1984 for financial relief may be made unless the leave of the court has first been obtained, as to which, see s 13 below.

## [2.218.8]
### Part III retrospective in effect

The court may entertain an application even though the relevant divorce, annulment or legal separation took place before Pt III of the MFPA 1984 came into force[1].

1 See *Chebaro v Chebaro* [1987] Fam 127, [1987] 1 All ER 999, CA.

## [2.218.9]
### Limitations imposed by the Child Support Act 1991

The powers of the English and Welsh courts to make maintenance orders to or for the benefit of children have been severely limited by the provisions of the Child Support Act 1991, dealt with elsewhere in this work[1]. However, amongst the exceptions to the provisions of the CSA 1991 is the situation where any one (or more) of the absent parent, the person with care or the qualifying child is not habitually resident within the UK[2].

See generally, *Rayden and Jackson on Divorce and Family Matters* (17th edn, 1997), vol 1, ch 31 and the Noter-up thereto.

1 See para **[2.425]** below.
2 See the CSA 1991, s 44 at para **[2.442]** below.



## [2.219]

### 13 Leave of the court required for applications for financial relief

(1) No application for an order for financial relief shall be made under this Part of this Act unless the leave of the court has been obtained in accordance with rules of court; and the court shall not grant leave unless it considers that there is substantial ground for the making of an application for such an order.

(2) The court may grant leave under this section notwithstanding that an order has been made by a court in a country outside England and Wales requiring the other party to the marriage to make any payment or transfer any property to the applicant or a child of the family.

(3) Leave under this section may be granted subject to such conditions as the court thinks fit.

**Appointment**
Commencement order: SI 1985/1316.

## [2.219.1]
### Keypoints

- Application for leave
- Substantial grounds
- Order in foreign jurisdiction
- Conditions
- Setting aside leave

## [2.219.2]
### Application for leave

This section requires any applicant under this Part to clear a significant hurdle at the 'leave' stage. The applicant must show 'substantial' grounds before leave will be given, failing which, no application may be made.

Leave is to be obtained in accordance with rules of court[1].

The application is made ex parte by originating summons issued in Form M25, supported by an affidavit of the applicant stating the facts relied on in support of the application – particular reference is required to those matters set out in s 16(2) below[2].

*Requirements of affidavit in support*

FPR 1991, r 3.17(2) sets out in detail further matters which the affidavit is required to particularise:

- the judicial or other proceedings by means of which the marriage was dissolved or annulled (or the parties legally separated);
- the parties' names, and their date and place of marriage;
- the occupation and residence of each party;
- the full name of each living child of the family, and his date of birth unless it is stated that he is over 18;
- whether either party has remarried;
- summary estimates of the capital resources and net income of each party and of any minor child;
- the grounds on which Pt III jurisdiction is alleged.

Assistance in tracing the address of the Respondent may be obtainable, via the district judge, from a government department[3].

The application is heard by a judge in chambers, on a date notified to the applicant[4].

1 See FPR 1991, r 3.17 at para **[3.469]** below.
2 See the MFPA 1984, s 16(2) at para **[2.222]** below. See also FPR 1991, r 3.17(1) at para **[3.469]** below.
3 See *Practice Direction (Disclosure of Addresses)* [1989] 1 All ER 765, [1989] 1 WLR 219.
4 See FPR 1991, r 3.17(3) at para **[3.469]** below.

## [2.219.3]
## Substantial grounds

The court shall not grant leave unless it considers that there is substantial ground – this is a stringent test, and the burden is on the person who seeks to say that an order under Pt III of the MFPA 1984 is appropriate[1].

Whilst s 16(1) of the MFPA 1984 is to be considered on the substantive application, it must nevertheless also be taken into account in the application for leave. If the court is not satisfied that it would be appropriate (a positive onus) the court must dismiss the application as a matter of mandatory instruction[2].

Before the court may find that there is substantial ground it must find that there is some hardship or injustice suffered by the applicant[3].

In an appropriate case, delay may not be fatal to the granting of an application[4].

Note that the Court of Appeal in *Jordan v Jordan*[5] held that *N v N (Foreign Divorce: Financial Relief)*[6] went too far in requiring the applicant to prove hardship or injustice in order to obtain leave. As Thorpe LJ stated:

> '... it does not follow that hardship is a necessary prerequisite and I doubt that it was open to Cazalet J to hold that an applicant must prove some hardship or injustice in order to obtain the court's leave. Parliament might have so legislated, but it did not. The statutory criteria are fully expressed. A case in which the applicant crosses the barriers contained in ss 13 and 16 without proving some specific hardship or injustice is perfectly conceivable.'

1 See *Z v Z (Financial Provision: Overseas Divorce)* [1992] 2 FLR 291 at 297H per Ewbank J.
2 See *Holmes v Holmes* [1989] Fam 47 at 53 per Purchas LJ, [1989] 3 All ER 786.
3 See *N v N (Foreign Divorce: Financial Relief)* [1997] 2 FCR 573, [1997] 1 FLR 900 at 909 per Cazelet J.
4 See *Lamagni v Lamagni* [1996] 1 FCR 408, [1995] 2 FLR 452 (where leave was granted notwithstanding a 12 year delay).
5 [2000] 1 WLR 210, [1999] 3 FCR 481, [1999] 2 FLR 1069, CA.
6 [1997] 2 FCR 573.

## [2.219.4]
## Order in foreign jurisdiction

Section 13(2) of the MFPA 1984 provides that leave may be given notwithstanding an order in favour of the applicant or any child of the family in a foreign court, but it has been said that it was not the intention of parliament to vest in the courts powers of review or correction of competent foreign court orders after equivalent examination to that which would have taken place here[1].

Leave is unlikely to be granted where the applicant has pursued her financial rights in a competent foreign forum that dissolved the marriage including an appeal in that jurisdiction, and the English jurisdiction is being used as a second bite of the cherry[2].

Generally, refusal of leave has been confined to cases where an ancillary relief type of order has been made in a foreign court, although for a recent example of a refusal where no such order was in existence[3].

Leave was refused in *Hewitson v Hewitson*[4], though the parties had temporarily resumed cohabitation in England after a California divorce, and the applicant alleged adverse consequences as a result.

In *Jordan v Jordan*[5], Thorpe LJ said:

> 'An application for leave mounted under Part III and declared to have the sole object of enforcing a foreign order would in my opinion be unlikely to succeed unless:
>
> (a) the enforcement remedies in the foreign jurisdiction had been exhausted or the enforcement remedies were manifestly inadequate; and
>
> (b) specific enforcement remedies arising under the 1972 Act or under the common law have been exhausted or are manifestly inadequate to ensure the applicant her due.'



1 See *Holmes v Holmes* [1989] Fam 47 at 57F per Purchas LJ, [1989] 3 All ER 786.
2 See *M v M (Financial Provision after Foreign Divorce)* [1994] 2 FCR 448, [1994] 1 FLR 399.
3 See *N v N (Foreign Divorce: Financial Relief)* [1997] 1 FLR 900.
4 [1995] Fam 100, [1995] 1 FLR 241, CA (subsequent refusal of leave to appeal reported at [1995] 1 WLR 720).
5 [2000] 1 WLR 210, [1999] 3 FCR 481, [1999] 2 FLR 1069 at 1081C, CA.

## [2.219.5]
## Conditions

Leave may be granted subject to such conditions as the court thinks fit[1].

1 See the MFPA 1984, s 13(3) at para **[2.219]**.

## [2.219.6]
## Setting aside leave

It is important that the affidavit in support of the ex parte application be full and frank. If an order is made giving leave on the basis of a misleading affidavit, and a substantially different order would have been made if there had been disclosure of all relevant matters, the order will be set aside (under RSC Ord 32, r 6, and the inherent jurisdiction)[1].

An order granting ex parte leave may subsequently be set aside on an inter partes application especially if the ex parte application was tainted by partisan presentation[2].

An application for an order setting aside leave is made on summons and would normally be heard in chambers.

The practice of applying inter partes to discharge the granting of ex parte leave has been discouraged by the Court of Appeal in *Jordan v Jordan*[3]. In *Jordan* Thorpe LJ stated:

> 'It must be questioned whether the present practice in the Family Division does not lead to waste of costs. Rule 3.17 of the Family Proceedings Rules 1991 provides for the ex parte application where leave is sought under Part III. A subsequent application to set aside is not specifically provided for under the rules but in my experience such applications have been commonplace. There may be good arguments for moving at once to the inter partes hearing which would test at once whether or not leave in principle is contested and assist the court to determine its substance.'

1 See *W v W (Financial Provision)* [1989] FCR 721, [1989] 1 FLR 22.
2 See *M v M (Financial Provision after Foreign Divorce)* [1994] 2 FCR 448, [1994] 1 FLR 399.
3 [2000] 1 WLR 210, [1999] 3 FCR 481, [1999] 2 FLR 1069, CA.

## [2.220]

### 14 Interim orders for maintenance

(1) Where leave is granted under section 13 above for the making of an application for an order for financial relief and it appears to the court that the applicant or any child of the family is in immediate need of financial assistance, the court may make an interim order for maintenance, that is to say, an order requiring the other party to the marriage to make to the applicant or to the child such periodical payments, and for such term, being a term beginning not earlier than the date of the grant of leave and ending with the date of the determination of the application for an order for financial relief, as the court thinks reasonable.

(2) If it appears to the court that the court has jurisdiction to entertain the application for an order for financial relief by reason only of paragraph (c) of section 15(1) below the court shall not make an interim order under this section.

(3) An interim order under subsection (1) above may be made subject to such conditions as the court thinks fit.

**Appointment**
Commencement order: SI 1985/1316.

## [2.220.1]
### Keypoints

- Interim application
- Not if jurisdiction dependent only on s 15(1)(c)
- Conditions

## [2.220.2]
### Interim application

An application for an interim order may be made, unless the court otherwise directs, in the originating summons itself, or by summons in accordance with FPR 1991, r 10.9(1)[1].

An order may be made in favour of the applicant or any child of the family, where the recipient is found to be in immediate need of financial assistance. The term of such order may not begin earlier than the grant of leave, and may extend to the date of determination of the application for financial relief[2].

By s 21 of the MFPA 1984[3], the following provisions of the MCA 1973, Pt II apply to an interim order for maintenance under this section as they would apply to an interim order for periodical payments:

- **s 28(1)** and **(2)** – duration of continuing financial provsion orders for a party;
- **s 29** – duration of financial provision orders for children and age limit on certain orders;
- **s 31** – *(save sub-ss (2)(e) and (4))* variation;
- **s 32** – enforcement of certain arrears;
- **ss 33** and **38** – orders for repayment in certain cases;
- **s 40** – where the recipient of maintenance is suffering from a mental disorder.

1 See FPR 1991, r 3.18(4) at para **[3.470]** below.
2 See the MFPA 1984, s 14(1) at para **[2.220]** above.
3 See para **[2.227]** below.

## [2.220.3]
### Not if jurisdiction dependent only on s 15 (1)(c)

If jurisdiction is based solely on the fact that either or both parties had at the date of the application for leave a beneficial interest in a former matrimonial home within England or Wales[1], then the court shall not make an interim order[2].

1 See the MFPA 1984, s 15(1)(c) at para **[2.221]** below.
2 See the MFPA 1984, s 14(2) at para **[2.220]** above.

### [2.220.4]
### Conditions

An interim order may be made subject to such conditions as the court thinks fit[1].

1 See the MFPA 1984, s 14(3) at para **[2.220]** above.

### [2.221]

**15 Jurisdiction of the court**

(1) Subject to subsection (2) below, the court shall have jurisdiction to entertain an application for an order for financial relief if any of the following jurisdictional requirements are satisfied, that is to say—

(a) either of the parties to the marriage was domiciled in England and Wales on the date of the application for leave under section 13 above or was so domiciled on the date on which the divorce, annulment or legal separation obtained in the overseas country took effect in that country; or

(b) either of the parties to the marriage was habitually resident in England and Wales throughout the period of one year ending with the date of the application for leave or was so resident throughout the period of one year ending with the date on which the divorce, annulment or legal separation obtained in the overseas country took effect in that country; or

(c) either or both of the parties to the marriage had at the date of the application for leave a beneficial interest in possession in a dwelling-house situated in England or Wales which was at some time during the marriage a matrimonial home of the parties to the marriage.

(2) Where the jurisdiction of the court to entertain proceedings under this Part of this Act would fall to be determined by reference to the jurisdictional requirements imposed by virtue of Part I of the Civil Jurisdiction and Judgments Act 1982 (implementation of certain European conventions) [or by virtue of Council Regulation (EC) No 44/2001 of 22nd December 2000 on jurisdiction and the recognition and enforcement of judgments in civil and commercial matters or] then—

(a) satisfaction of the requirements of subsection (1) above shall not obviate the need to satisfy the requirements imposed by virtue of [that Regulation or] Part I of that Act; and

(b) satisfaction of the requirements imposed by virtue of [that Regulation or] Part I of that Act shall obviate the need to satisfy the requirements of subsection (1) above;

and the court shall entertain or not entertain the proceedings accordingly.

**Appointment**

Commencement order: SI 1985/1316.

**Amendment**

Sub-s (2): SI 2001/3929, art 5, Sch 3.

### [2.221.1]
### Keypoints

- The requirements
- Restrictions when only s 15(1)(c) applies
- Relationship with the CJJA 1982

### [2.221.2]
### The requirements

Any one of three requirements will suffice, subject to the restrictions imposed in relation to s 15(1)(c) dealt with below. These are:

- either party was **domiciled** in England and Wales – either on the date of the application for leave, or on the date when the divorce, annulment or legal separation took effect in the overseas country[1];
- either party was **habitually resident** in England and Wales for one year – either ending on the date of the application for leave, or on the date when the divorce, annulment or legal separation took effect in the overseas country[2];
- either party had a beneficial interest in possession in a dwelling-house in England and Wales which was at some time during the marriage a matrimonial home[3].

1 See the MFPA 1984, s 15(1)(a) at para **[2.221]** above.
2 See the MFPA 1984, s 15(1)(b).
3 See the MFPA 1984, s 15(1)(c).

## [2.221.3]
## Restrictions when only s 15(1)(c) applies

As discussed above, the court may not make an interim order when jurisdiction arises solely as a result of this provision[1].

Further, by s 20 of the MFPA 1984, the court is limited in relation to those orders it can make under s 17 where its jurisdiction derives solely from this subsection – in two specific ways:

- the court may not make any order for maintenance payments to the applicant[2];
- the court's power to award a lump sum is limited to the net value of the interest in the property in question[3].

1 See the MFPA 1984, s 14(2) at para **[2.220]** above.
2 See the MFPA 1984, s 20(1) at para **[2.226]**below.
3 See the MFPA 1984, s 20(2).

## [2.221.4]
## Relationship with the CJJA 1982

The CJJA 1982, Pt I gives statutory effect to the European Convention on Jurisdictions and Enforcement of Judgments of 27 September 1968, as amended by the Accession Convention of 9 October 1978 ('the Brussels Convention').

Article 21 of the Convention (set out at Sch 1 to the CJJA 1982[1]) provides:

> 'Where proceedings involving the same cause of action and between the same parties are brought in the courts of different Contracting States, any court other than the court first seized shall of its own motion decline jurisdiction in favour of that court.'

The 'Contracting States' currently include:

- Belgium; Denmark; Eire; Germany; Greece; France; Italy; Luxembourg; the Netherlands; Portugal; Spain; and the United Kingdom.

### *Exceptions*

The CJJA 1982 does not apply to rights in property 'arising out of a matrimonial relationship'[2]. A maintenance creditor may seek to sue in the country where they are domiciled or habitually resident, though the respondent is himself domiciled in a different Contracting State[3].

Where jurisdiction falls to be determined by reference to the requirements of the CJJA 1982, satisfaction of the requirements of Pt I of that Act obviates the need to satisfy the requirements of the MFPA 1984, s 15(1)[4].

By contrast, satisfaction of the requirements of s 15(1) *does not* obviate the need to satisfy the requirements of Pt I of the CJJA 1982[5]. The CJJA 1982 takes precedence.

For an example of the difficulties in interpreting the provisions of the Brussels Convention into the laws of different Contracting States, see *K v B (Brussels Convention)*[6].

Note that the House of Lords have now decided[7], in a case under Arts 2 to 6 of the Lugano Convention[8], that a person is 'sued' on the date of issue of any such proceedings, as opposed to their date of service, and the court is therefore seized from the earlier date.

1 See para **[2.214]** above.
2 See the CJJA 1982, Sch 1, Art 1(1) at para **[2.214]** above.
3 See the CJJA 1982, Sch 1, Art 5(2) at para **[2.214]** above.
4 See the MFPA 1984, s 15(2)(b) at para **[2.221]** above.
5 See the MFPA 1984, s 15(2)(a) at para **[2.221]** above.
6 *Re B (A Minor) (Brussels Convention: Jurisdiction)* [1994] 2 FCR 404, sub nom *K v B (Brussels Convention)* [1994] 1 FLR 267.
7 See *Canada Trust Co v Stolzenberg (No 2)* [2000] 4 All ER 481, [2000] 3 WLR 1376.
8 See the CJJA 1982, Sch 3C at para **[2.216]** above.



## [2.222]

### 16 Duty of the court to consider whether England and Wales is appropriate venue for application

(1) Before making an order for financial relief the court shall consider whether in all the circumstances of the case it would be appropriate for such an order to be made by a court in England and Wales, and if the court is not satisfied that it would be appropriate, the court shall dismiss the application.

(2) The court shall in particular have regard to the following matters—

(a) the connection which the parties to the marriage have with England and Wales;
(b) the connection which those parties have with the country in which the marriage was dissolved or annulled or in which they were legally separated;
(c) the connection which those parties have with any other country outside England and Wales;
(d) any financial benefit which the applicant or a child of the family has received, or is likely to receive, in consequence of the divorce, annulment or legal separation, by virtue of any agreement or the operation of the law of a country outside England and Wales;
(e) in a case where an order has been made by a court in a country outside England and Wales requiring the other party to the marriage to make any payment or transfer any property for the benefit of the applicant or a child of the family, the financial relief given by the order and the extent to which the order has been complied with or is likely to be complied with;
(f) any right which the applicant has, or has had, to apply for financial relief from the other party to the marriage under the law of any country outside England and Wales and if the applicant has omitted to exercise that right the reason for that omission;
(g) the availability in England and Wales of any property in respect of which an order under this Part of this Act in favour of the applicant could be made;
(h) the extent to which any order made under this Part of this Act is likely to be enforceable;
(i) the length of time which has elapsed since the date of the divorce, annulment or legal separation.

**Appointment**
Commencement order: SI 1985/1316.

## [2.222.1]
**Keypoints**

- Rule of comity
- Applicable at both leave stage and at hearing
- Particular matters
- Effect of delay

### [2.222.2]
### Rule of comity

It has been said that this section reflects the fundamental rule of comity as between competent courts dealing with matters of this kind[1].

Purhcas LJ stated, in *Holmes v Holmes*[2]:

> 'The purpose of the Act is generally apparent, namely, that it is there to remit hardships which have been experienced in the past in the presence of a failure in a foreign jurisdiction to afford appropriate financial relief … I do not believe that the intention of parliament in passing this Act was in any way to vest in the English Courts any powers of review or even correction of order made in a foreign forum by a competent court in which the whole matter has been examined in a way exactly equivalent to the examination which would have taken place if the application had been made in the first instance in the courts here'.

1 See *Holmes v Holmes* [1989] Fam 47, [1989] 3 All ER 786, CA. See also *M v M (financial provision after foreign divorce)* [1994] 2 FCR 448, [1994] 1 FLR 399.
2 [1989] Fam 47 at 57F per Purchas LJ.

### [2.222.3]
### Applicable at both leave stage and at hearing

Per Purchase LJ in *Holmes v Holmes*[1] – if on the application for leave it is clear that the application itself must founder at the first hurdle of s 16(1), it would clearly be wrong for the court to grant leave in the first instance. It is not possible to isolate the considerations which arise under this group of sections.

1 [1989] Fam 47 at 53.

### [2.222.4]
### Particular matters

These are set out in s 16(2) of the MFPA 1984, and broadly comprise:

- the parties' national connections;
- any financial benefit or right to claim such a benefit which the applicant or a child of the family may have or have obtained outside the jurisdiction;
- availability of assets in the jurisdiction;
- enforceability; and
- delay (as to which see below).

The mere fact the English legislation may in English eyes be better than foreign legislation, or that better relief is available here for a wife is not of itself sufficient for the English court to assume jurisdiction[1].

1 See *Holmes v Holmes* [1989] Fam 47, [1989] 3 All ER 786, CA.

### [2.222.5]
### Effect of delay

Section 16(2)(i) of the MFPA 1984 provides that the length of time which has elapsed since the date of the divorce, annulment or legal separation shall be a consideration.

There is a distinction to be drawn between those cases where wives, after obtaining orders in foreign courts which they considered unsatisfactory, then apply to the English court hoping for a more generous order, and those where the wife has, throughout, sought financial relief in the English courts, beginning in the local magistrates' court. Though a 12 year delay in the latter case might become a decisive factor in the eventual hearing, the judge was wrong to find that there was no substantial ground for making an application[1].

1 See *Lamagni v Lamagni* [1995] 2 FLR 452, [1996] 1 FCR 408, CA.

**[2.223]**

## 17 Orders for financial provision and property adjustment

(1) Subject to section 20 below, on an application by a party to a marriage for an order for financial relief under this section, the court may—

- (a) make any one or more of the orders which it could make under Part II of the 1973 Act if a decree of divorce, a decree of nullity of marriage or a decree of judicial separation in respect of the marriage had been granted in England and Wales, that is to say—
  - (i) any order mentioned in section 23(1) of the 1973 Act (financial provision orders); and
  - (ii) any order mentioned in section 24(1) of that Act (property adjustment orders); and
- (b) if the marriage has been dissolved or annulled, make one or more orders each of which would, within the meaning of that Part of that Act, be a pension sharing order in relation to the marriage.

(2) Subject to section 20 below, where the court makes a secured periodical payments order, an order for the payment of a lump sum or a property adjustment order under subsection (1) above, then, on making that order or at any time thereafter, the court may make any order mentioned in section 24A(1) of the 1973 Act (orders for sale of property) which the court would have power to make if the order under subsection (1) above had been made under Part II of the 1973 Act.

**Appointment**

Commencement order: SI 1985/1316.

**Amendment**

Sub-s (1): substituted by the WRPA 1999, s 84. Date in force: 1 December 2000: see SI 2000/1116.



**[2.223.1]**

### Keypoints

- Financial provision, property adjustment orders and pension sharing orders
- Limitation where jurisdiction only by s 15(1)(c)
- Application of powers under the MCA 1973, s 24A(1)

**[2.223.2]**

### Financial provision, property adjustment orders and pension sharing orders

Subject to the s 15(1)(c) of the MFPA 1984 exception contained in s 20 below, the court may make any of those orders that would be available to it under Pt II of the MCA 1973.

By virtue of s 21 of the MFPA 1984 below, the following provisions of the MCA 1973 apply to an order for financial provision and property adjustment under s 17 as they would to an order under Pt II of the MCA 1973:

- **s 23(3)** – provisions as to lump sums;
- **s 24A(2)** and **(4)** to **(6)** – provisions as to orders for sale;
- **s 24B** – pension sharing;
- **s 28(1)** and **(2)** – the duration of continuing financial provision orders for a party;
- **s 29** – duration of continuing financial provision orders for children, and age limit on certain orders;
- **s 31** – *(save sub-ss (2)(e) and (4))* variation;
- **s 32** – enforcement of certain arrears;
- **ss 33** and **38** – orders for repayment in certain cases;
- **s 39** – avoidance of certain settlements on bankruptcy; and
- **s 40** – where the recipient of maintenance is suffering from a mental disorder.

Subsection (1) has been substituted by the Welfare Reform and Pensions Act 1999[1].

1 See the WRPA 1999, s 84, Sch 12, paras 2 to 4.

### [2.223.3]
### Limitation where jurisdiction only by s 15(1)(c)

By s 20 of the MFPA 1984[1] the court's powers to make substantive orders under s 17(1) are curbed when jurisdiction is derived only from s 15(1)(c) above – (*either party having at the date of the application for leave a beneficial interest in possession in a former matrimonial home in England and Wales*) – in two specific ways:

- the court may not make any order for maintenance payments to the applicant[2];
- the court's power to award a lump sum is limited to the net value of the interest in the property in question[3].

1 See para **[2.226]** below.
2 See the MFPA 1984, s 20(1) at para **[2.226]** below.
3 See the MFPA 1984, s 20(2).

### [2.223.4]
### Application of powers under the MCA 1973, s 24A(1)

On making a lump sum, property adjustment or secured periodical payments order under s 17(1) of the MFPA 1984 the court may make any order for sale of property mentioned in s 24A(1) of the MCA 1973, as if the order were made under Pt II of the MCA 1973[1].

However, on an order for sale under s 20(1)(g) of the MFPA 1984 below, the amount of any lump sum which the court may order is limited to the amount of the net proceeds of sale[2].

1 See the MFPA 1984, s 17(2) at para **[2.223]** above.
2 See the MFPA 1984, s 20(2)(a) at para **[2.226]** below.

### [2.224]

**18 Matters to which the court is to have regard in exercising its powers under s 17**

(1) In deciding whether to exercise its powers under section 17 above and, if so, in what manner the court shall act in accordance with this section.

(2) The court shall have regard to all the circumstances of the case, first consideration being given to the welfare while a minor of any child of the family who has not attained the age of eighteen.

(3) As regards the exercise of those powers in relation to a party to the marriage, the court shall in particular have regard to the matters mentioned in section 25(2)(a) to (h) of the 1973 Act and shall be under duties corresponding with those imposed by section 25A(1) and (2) of the 1973 Act where it decides to exercise under section 17 above powers corresponding with the powers referred to in those subsections.

(3A) The matters to which the court is to have regard under subsection (3) above—

(a) so far as relating to paragraph (a) of section 25(2) of the 1973 Act, include any benefits under a pension arrangement which a party to the marriage has or is likely to have (whether or not in the foreseeable future), and

(b) so far as relating to paragraph (h) of that provision, include any benefits under a pension arrangement which, by reason of the dissolution or annulment of the marriage, a party to the marriage will lose the chance of acquiring.

(4) As regards the exercise of those powers in relation to a child of the family, the court shall in particular have regard to the matters mentioned in section 25(3)(a) to (e) of the 1973 Act.

(5) As regards the exercise of those powers against a party to the marriage in favour of a child of the family who is not the child of that party, the court shall also have regard to the matters mentioned in section 25(4)(a) to (c) of the 1973 Act.

(6) Where an order has been made by a court outside England and Wales for the making of payments or the transfer of property by a party to the marriage, the court in

considering in accordance with this section the financial resources of the other party to the marriage or a child of the family shall have regard to the extent to which that order has been complied with or is likely to be complied with.

(7) In this section—

(a) 'pension arrangement' has the meaning given by section 25D(3) of the 1973 Act, and

(b) references to benefits under a pension arrangement include any benefits by way of pension, whether under a pension arrangement or not.

**Appointment**

Commencement order: SI 1985/1316.

**Amendment**

Sub-ss (3A), (7): inserted by the WRPA 1999, s 22. Date in force: 1 December 2000: see SI 2000/1116.



## [2.224.1]
### Keypoints

- Court must act in accordance with section
- First consideration to minor children of the family
- Application of the MCA 1973, ss 25 and 25A
- Compliance with overseas order relevant

## [2.224.2]
### Court must act in accordance with section

Acting in accordance with the provisions of s 18(2) to (6) is made mandatory for the court by s 18(1) of the MFPA 1984. This may be compared with the language of the MCA 1973, s 25(1), where the court is under a 'duty' to have regard to all the circumstances of the case, with first consideration being given to the welfare of minor children.

*Exception*

Where the court is considering a proposed consent order[1], s 18 of the MFPA 1984 does not apply.

1 See the MFPA 1984, s 19 at para **[2.225]** below.

## [2.224.3]
### First consideration to minor children of the family

As in ancillary proceedings under the MCA 1973, s 25(1), the court must have regard to all the circumstance of the case, with first consideration being given to the welfare of any minor child of the family (under 18)[1].

1 See the MFPA 1984, s 18(2) at para **[2.224]** above.

## [2.224.4]
### Application of the MCA 1973, ss 25 and 25A

Section 18(3) of the MFPA 1984 requires regard to those matters mentioned in the MCA 1973, s 25(2)(a) to (h), that is – in brief:

(a) income, earning capacity, property and other financial resources of the parties, including any reasonable increase in earning capacity;
(b) financial needs obligations and responsibilities now or in the foreseeable future;
(c) standard of living before the breakdown of the marriage;
(d) age of the parties and duration of the marriage;
(e) any physical or mental disability of either party;
(f) past and foreseeable future contributions to the welfare of the family;
(g) conduct, if inequitable to disregard; and
(h) value of any benefit lost by reason of dissolution or annulment.

Section 18(3) of the MFPA 1984 further directs that the court shall be under corresponding duties to those imposed under the MCA 1973, s 25A(1) and (2), ie:

(1) to consider whether appropriate to so exercise its powers as to terminate the financial obligations of the parties to one another as soon as just and reasonable; and

(2) to consider whether appropriate to place only such term on any order for periodical payments as is sufficient to enable that party to adjust without undue hardship.

Section 18(4) of the MFPA 1984 requires in relation to a child of the family, regard to those matters in the MCA 1973, s 25(3)(a) to (e):

(a) financial needs of the child;
(b) income, earning capacity, property and other financial needs of the child;
(c) any physical or mental disability of the child;
(d) the manner of and expectations in relation to his education or training; and
(e) items (a), (b), (c) and (e) in relation to the parties (above).

Section 18(5) of the MFPA 1984 requires in relation to a child of the family not the child of the party in question, regard to the matters in the MCA 1973, s 25(4)(a) to (c):

(a) extent, basis and duration of any assumption of responsibility for the child;
(b) knowledge of the child's true parentage when discharging responsibility; and
(c) any other persons liability to maintain.

For a detailed consideration of these provisions, see the MCA 1973[1].

Note that sub-ss (3A) and (7) have been substituted by the Welfare Reform and Pensions Act 1999[2] with effect from 1 December 2000.

1 At para **[2.113]** above.
2 See para **[2.548]** below.

## [2.224.5]
### Compliance with overseas order relevant

The court is to have regard to the extent to which any order made by a court outside England and Wales for the making of payments or the transfer of property by one party has been complied with or is likely to be complied with, when it comes to consider the financial resources of the other party or a child of the family for the purposes of this section[1].

1 See the MFPA 1984, s 18(6) at para **[2.224]** above.

## [2.225]

### 19 Consent orders for financial provision or property adjustment

(1) Notwithstanding anything in section 18 above, on an application for a consent order for financial relief the court may, unless it has reason to think that there are other circumstances into which it ought to inquire, make an order in the terms agreed on the basis only of the prescribed information furnished with the application.

(2) Subsection (1) above applies to an application for a consent order varying or discharging an order for financial relief as it applies to an application for an order for financial relief.

(3) In this section—

'consent order', in relation to an application for an order, means an order in the terms applied for to which the respondent agrees;

'order for financial relief' means an order under section 17 above; and

'prescribed' means prescribed by rules of court.

**Appointment**

Commencement order: SI 1985/1316.

**[2.225.1]**
**Keypoints**

- Prescribed information required
- Other circumstances

**[2.225.2]**
**Prescribed information required**

Rather than go through the detail of s 18 above, the court may rely, by s 19(1) of the MFPA 1984, where the Respondent agrees to the proposed order by signed statement on the draft, on the prescribed information furnished with the application – that is, by FPR 1991, r 3.18(3), applying r 2.61(1) – a statement of information including:

- the duration of the marriage and the ages of the parties and any minor children;
- summary estimate of capital resources and net income of the parties and any minor children;
- intended accommodation arrangements for the parties and any minor children;
- details of any remarriage or intention to cohabit;
- confirmation of no objection in the event of transfer of property within 14 days of service by any mortgage;
- any other especially significant matters.

Note that r 2.61(1) also now contains provision for service of pension trustees at (dd), but ss 25B and 25C of the MCA 1973 have not yet been imported into Pt III of the MFPA 1984.

By s 19(2), s 19(1) applies also to consent orders for variation or discharge. Where the consent application is for variation only of an order for periodical payments, or in relation to an agreed interim variation, then the statement of information need only relate to net income[1].

The court retains a discretion as to what is necessary where all parties attend court[2].

1 See the FPR 1991, r 2.61(2) at para **[3.441]** below.
2 See the FPR 1991, r 2.61(3) below.

**[2.225.3]**
**Other circumstances**

The exception to the provisions of s 19(1) is where the court has 'reason to think that there are other circumstances into which it ought to inquire', but this will usually be invoked only if the limited information provided on the face of the statement suggests that an inappropriate order is proposed.

This provision is identical to the MCA 1973, s 33A, which is unsurprising given that s 33A was inserted by s 7 of the MFPA 1984.

**[2.226]**

**20 Restriction of powers of court where jurisdiction depends on matrimonial home in England or Wales**

(1) Where the court has jurisdiction to entertain an application for an order for financial relief by reason only of the situation in England or Wales of a dwelling-house which was a matrimonial home of the parties, the court may make under section 17 above any one or more of the following orders (but no other)—

(a) an order that either party to the marriage shall pay to the other such lump sum as may be specified in the order;

(b) an order that a party to the marriage shall pay to such person as may be so specified for the benefit of a child of the family, or to such a child, such lump sum as may be so specified;

(c) an order that a party to the marriage shall transfer to the other party, to any child of the family or to such person as may be so specified for the benefit of such a child, the interest of the first-mentioned party in the dwelling-house, or such part of that interest as may be so specified;

(d) an order that a settlement of the interest of a party to the marriage in the dwelling-house, or such part of that interest as may be so specified, be made to the satisfaction of the court for the benefit of the other party to the marriage and of the children of the family or either or any of them;

(e) an order varying for the benefit of the parties to the marriage and of the children of the family or either or any of them any ante-nuptial or post-nuptial settlement (including such a settlement made by will or codicil) made on the parties to the marriage so far as that settlement relates to an interest in the dwelling-house;

(f) an order extinguishing or reducing the interest of either of the parties to the marriage under any such settlement so far as that interest is an interest in the dwelling-house;

(g) an order for the sale of the interest of a party to the marriage in the dwelling-house.

(2) Where, in the circumstances mentioned in subsection (1) above, the court makes an order for the payment of a lump sum by a party to the marriage, the amount of the lump sum shall not exceed, or where more than one such order is made the total amount of the lump sums shall not exceed in aggregate, the following amount, that is to say—

(a) if the interest of that party in the dwelling-house is sold in pursuance of an order made under subsection (1)(g) above, the amount of the proceeds of the sale of that interest after deducting therefrom any costs incurred in the sale thereof;

(b) if the interest of that party is not so sold, the amount which in the opinion of the court represents the value of that interest.

(3) Where the interest of a party to the marriage in the dwelling-house is held jointly or in common with any other person or persons—

(a) the reference in subsection (1)(g) above to the interest of a party to the marriage shall be construed as including a reference to the interest of that other person, or the interest of those other persons, in the dwelling-house, and

(b) the reference in subsection (2)(a) above to the amount of the proceeds of a sale ordered under subsection (1)(g) above shall be construed as a reference to that part of those proceeds which is attributable to the interest of that party to the marriage in the dwelling-house.

**Appointment**

Commencement order: SI 1985/1316.

## [2.226.1]
### Keypoints

- Section 15(1)(c)
- The orders the court may not make
- Capital limitations

## [2.226.2]
### Section 15(1)(c)

To found jurisdiction under this subsection, either or both of the parties must have at the time of the application for leave a beneficial interest in possession in a dwelling-house in England and Wales which was at some time during the marriage a matrimonial home of the parties[1].

1 For definitions see the MFPA 1984, s 27 at para **[2.232]** below.

## [2.226.3]
## The orders the court may not make

Section 20(1) of the MFPA 1984 sets out all those orders the court **can** make, and the process of elimination leaves the following within ss 14 or 17 but excluded by this section when s 15(1)(c) only applies:

- a periodical payments order in favour of a party or a child of the family;
- a secured periodical payments order;
- an interim periodical payments order.

Where the applicant can establish neither domicile nor habitual residence for either herself or the Respondent, the court will not entertain any application for periodical payments, though there may be a former matrimonial home in the jurisdiction in respect of the Respondent's interest in which she may claim, subject to the provisions of s 20(2).

## [2.226.4]
## Capital limitations

The court will only deal under this section with the parties' interest (or interests) in any former matrimonial homes in the jurisdiction, and therefore:

- no lump sum or sums shall exceed the aggregate total of the respondent's net interest in any such properties; on sale the net value after costs of sale is taken, and if no sale a net calculation is made[1];
- where in joint ownership with a third party, the court may still exercise its power to order sale of the property under s 20(1)(g)[2] but on sale, only the amount of the net interest of the respondent is capable of being the subject of a lump sum order under s 20(1)(a) or (b)[3].

1 See the MFPA 1984, s 20(2) at para **[2.226]** above.
2 See the MFPA 1984, s 20(3)(a) above.
3 See the MFPA 1984, s 20(3)(b) above.

## [2.227]

### 21 Application to orders under ss 14 and 17 of certain provisions of Part II of Matrimonial Causes Act 1973

(1) The following provisions of Part II of the 1973 Act (financial relief for parties to marriage and children of family) shall apply in relation to an order under section 14 or 17 above as they apply in relation to a like order under that Part of that Act, that is to say—

*(a) section 23(3) (provisions as to lump sums);*
[(a) section 22A(5) (provisions about lump sums in relation to divorce or separation);
(aa) section 23(4), (5) and (6) (provisions about lump sums in relation to annulment);]
(b) section 24A(2), (4), (5) and (6) (provisions as to orders for sale);
(ba) section 24B(3) to (5) (provisions about pension sharing orders in relation to divorce and nullity);
(bb) section 24C (duty to stay pension sharing orders);
(bc) section 24D (apportionment of pension sharing charges);
(bd) section 25B(3) to (7B) (power, by financial provision order, to attach payments under a pension arrangement, or to require the exercise of a right of commutation under such an arrangement);
(be) section 25C (extension of lump sum powers in relation to death benefits under a pension arrangement);
(c) section 28(1) and (2) (duration of continuing financial provision orders in favour of party to marriage);
(d) section 29 (duration of continuing financial provision orders in favour of children, and age limit on making certain orders in their favour);

(e) section 30 (direction for settlement of instrument for securing payments or effecting property adjustment), except paragraph (b);
(f) section 31 variation, discharge etc of certain orders for financial relief), *except subsection (2)(e) and subsection (4);*
(g) section 32 (payment of certain arrears unenforceable without the leave of the court);
(h) section 33 (orders for repayment of sums paid under certain orders);
(i) section 38 (orders for repayment of sums paid after cessation of order by reason of remarriage);
(j) section 39 (settlements etc made in compliance with a property adjustment order may be avoided on bankruptcy of settlor); and
(k) section 40 (payments etc under order made in favour of person suffering from mental disorder);
(l) section 40A (appeals relating to pension sharing orders which have taken effect).

(2) Subsection (1)(bd) and (be) above shall not apply where the court has jurisdiction to entertain an application for an order for financial relief by reason only of the situation in England or Wales of a dwelling-house which was a matrimonial home of the parties.

(3) Section 25D(1) of the 1973 Act (effect of transfers on orders relating to rights under a pension arrangement) shall apply in relation to an order made under section 17 above by virtue of subsection (1)(bd) or (be) above as it applies in relation to an order made under section 23 of that Act by virtue of section 25B or 25C of the 1973 Act.

(4) The Lord Chancellor may by regulations make for the purposes of this Part of this Act provision corresponding to any provision which may be made by him under subsections (2) to (2B) of section 25D of the 1973 Act.

(5) Power to make regulations under this section shall be exercisable by statutory instrument which shall be subject to annulment in pursuance of a resolution of either House of Parliament.

**Appointment**

Commencement order: SI 1985/1316.

**Amendment**

Sub-s (1): paras (a), (aa) prospectively substituted with savings, for para (a) as originally enacted, by the FLA 1996, s 66(1), Sch 8, para 32(3), as from a day to be appointed; for savings see s 66(2), Sch 9, para 5 thereof. Sub-s (1): in para (f) words 'except subsection (2)(e) and subsection (4)' in italics prospectively repealed with savings by the FLA 1996, s 66(3), Sch 10, as from a day to be appointed; for savings see s 66(2), Sch 9, paras 5, 8–10 thereof. Sub-s (1): amended by the WRPA 1999, ss 22, 84 and 88. Date in force: 1 December 2000: see SI 2000/1116. Sub-ss (2) to (5): inserted by the WRPA 1999, s 22. Date in force (for the purpose only of the exercise of any power to make regulations): 11 November 1999: see the WRPA 1999, s 89. Date in force (for remaining purposes): 1 December 2000: see SI 2000/1116.

### [2.227.1]
### Keypoint

- Certain powers under the MCA 1973 not available

### [2.227.2]
### Certain powers under the MCA 1973 not available

Given the assimilation by the FPR 1991, r 3.18(3) of various of the rules in Pt 2 of the FPR 1991 (referred to in the note to s 12 above), the similarities in approach aimed at between the MFPA 1984, Pt III and the MCA 1973, Pt II are clear.

However, the following powers available under the MCA 1973 have not been imported into Pt III:

- the power to award interest on a lump sum[1];
- the power to direct that there be no further application for periodical or secured periodical payments orders[2];

- the power to prohibit an application to extend the maintenance term[3].

Note that sub-ss (2) to (5) have been inserted by the Welfare Reform and Pensions Act 1999[4] with effect from 1 December 2000.

1 See the MCA 1973, s 23(6) at para **[2.117]** above.
2 See the MCA 1973, s 25A(3) at para **[2.121]** above.
3 See the MCA 1973, s 28(1A) at para **[2.126]** above.
4 See para **[2.548]** below.



## [2.228]

### [22 Powers of court in relation to certain tenancies of dwelling-houses]

[(1) This section applies if—

(a) an application is made by a party to a marriage for an order for financial relief; and

(b) one of the parties is entitled, either in his own right or jointly with the other party, to occupy a dwelling-house situated in England or Wales by virtue of a tenancy which is a relevant tenancy within the meaning of Schedule 7 to the Family Law Act 1996 (certain statutory tenancies).

(2) The court may make in relation to that dwelling-house any order which it could make under Part II of that Schedule if—

(a) a divorce order,

(b) a separation order, or

(c) a decree of nullity of marriage,

had been made or granted in England and Wales in respect of the marriage.

(3) The provisions of paragraphs 10, 11 and 14(1) in Part III of that Schedule apply in relation to any order under this section as they apply to any order under Part II of that Schedule.]

**Appointment**
Commencement order: SI 1985/1316.

**Amendment**
Substituted by the FLA 1996, s 66(1), Sch 8, para 52. Date in force: 1 October 1997: see SI 1997/1892, art 3(1)(b).

## [2.228.1]
### Keypoints

- Procedural requirement
- Relevant tenancies
- Powers available
- Supplementary provisions

## [2.228.2]
### Procedural requirement

Where the originating summons contains an application for an order under s 22, the applicant must serve a copy on the landlord of the dwelling-house, and he will be entitled to be heard on the application[1].

1 See FPR 1991, r 3.18(7) at para **[3.470]** below.

## [2.228.3]
### Relevant tenancies

These are set out in the FLA 1996, Sch 7, Pt I, para 1 as follows:

(a) a protected tenancy or statutory tenancy within the meaning of the Rent Act 1977;

(b) a statutory tenancy within the meaning of the Rent (Agriculture) Act 1976;

(c) a secure tenancy within the meaning of the Housing Act 1985, s 79;
(d) an assured tenancy or assured agricultural occupancy within the meaning of the Housing Act 1988, Pt I; and
(e) an introductory tenancy within the meaning of the Housing Act 1996, Pt V, cap 1.

## [2.228.4]
### Powers available

These are set out in the FLA 1996, Sch 7, Pt II, and depend upon the type of tenancy concerned.

Where there is a protected tenancy under para **[2.228.3]**, sub-para (a) above, or those tenancies specified in (c), (d) or (e), the court may transfer a spouse's estate or interest under the lease or agreement, subject to all existing rights and covenants etc, to the other spouse[1].

Where there is a statutory tenancy under (a) above, the court may by order direct that a spouse is to cease to be entitled to occupy a dwelling-house, and that the other spouse is to be deemed to be the tenant or sole tenant under the statutory tenancy[2].

Where there is a statutory tenancy under (b) above, the court has similar powers to those where there is a statutory tenancy under (a) above[3].

1 See the FLA 1996, Sch 7, para 7, with consequential provisions.
2 See the FLA 1996, Sch 7, para 8, with consequential provisions.
3 See the FLA 1996, Sch 7, para 9.

## [2.228.5]
### Supplementary provisions

Paragraphs 10, 11 and 14(1) of Pt III of the FLA 1996, Sch 7 (applied by s 22(3)), contain provision respectively for compensation, liabilities and obligations in respect of the dwelling-house, and the making of rules of court giving the landlord the opportunity of being heard – as to which see FPR 1991, rr 3.8(12) and 3.18(7)[1].

1 See para **[3.470]** below.

## [2.229]

### 23 Avoidance of transactions intended to defeat applications for financial relief

(1) For the purposes of this section 'financial relief' means relief under section 14 or 17 above and any reference to defeating a claim by a party to a marriage for financial relief from being granted is a reference to preventing financial relief from being granted or reducing the amount of relief which might be granted, or frustrating or impeding the enforcement of any order which might be or has been made under either of those provisions at the instance of that party.

(2) Where leave is granted under section 13 above for the making by a party to a marriage of an application for an order for financial relief under section 17 above, the court may, on an application by that party—

(a) if it is satisfied that the other party to the marriage is, with the intention of defeating the claim for financial relief, about to make any disposition or to transfer out of the jurisdiction or otherwise deal with any property, make such order as it thinks fit for restraining the other party from so doing or otherwise for protecting the claim;
(b) if it is satisfied that the other party has, with that intention, made a reviewable disposition and that if the disposition were set aside financial relief or different financial relief would be granted to the applicant, make an order setting aside the disposition.

(3) Where an order for financial relief under section 14 or 17 above has been made by the court at the instance of a party to a marriage, then, on an application made by that party, the court may, if it is satisfied that the other party to the marriage has, with

the intention of defeating the claim for financial relief, made a reviewable disposition, make an order setting aside the disposition.

(4) Where the court has jurisdiction to entertain the application for an order for financial relief by reason only of paragraph (c) of section 15(1) above, it shall not make any order under subsection (2) or (3) above in respect of any property other than the dwelling-house concerned.

(5) Where the court makes an order under subsection (2)(b) or (3) above setting aside a disposition it shall give such consequential directions as it thinks fit for giving effect to the order (including directions requiring the making of any payments or the disposal of any property).

(6) Any disposition made by the other party to the marriage (whether before or after the commencement of the application) is a reviewable disposition for the purposes of subsections (2)(b) and (3) above unless it was made for valuable consideration (other than marriage) to a person who, at the time of the disposition, acted in relation to it in good faith and without notice of any intention on the part of the other party to defeat the applicant's claim for financial relief.

(7) Where an application is made under subsection (2) or (3) above with respect to a disposition which took place less than three years before the date of the application or with respect to a disposition or other dealing with property which is about to take place and the court is satisfied—

(a) in a case falling within subsection(2)(a) or (b) above, that the disposition or other dealing would (apart from this section) have the consequence, or

(b) in a case falling within subsection (3) above, that the disposition has had the consequence,

of defeating a claim by the applicant for financial relief, it shall be presumed, unless the contrary is shown, that the person who disposed of or is about to dispose of or deal with the property did so or, as the case may be, is about to do so, with the intention of defeating the applicant's claim for financial relief.

(8) In this section 'disposition' does not include any provision contained in a will or codicil but, with that exception, includes any conveyance, assurance or gift of property of any description, whether made by an instrument or otherwise.

(9) The preceding provisions of this section are without prejudice to any power of the High Court to grant injunctions under section 37 of the Supreme Court Act 1981.

**Appointment**

Commencement order: SI 1985/1316.



**[2.229.1]**
**Keypoints**

- Application
- Differences from the MCA 1973, s 37
- Limitation where jurisdiction founded only on s 15(1)(c)

**[2.229.2]**
**Application**

An application for an avoidance of transaction order under s 23 may be made, unless the court otherwise directs, in the originating summons itself or by summons in accordance with FPR 1991, r 10.9(1)[1].

An application under s 23 must be supported by an affidavit stating the facts relied on, which may be the affidavit in support of the summons filed under FPR 1991, r 3.18(1)[2].

In respect of any application under this section, the court may give such direction or make such appointment as it is empowered to do by FPR 1991, r 3.18(3) (which applies various of the rules which apply in ancillary relief claims)[3].

FPR 1991, r 2.59 (evidence on application for property adjustment or avoidance of disposition order) applies to an application for an avoidance of transaction, as it applies to an application for avoidance of disposition[4].

The affidavit in support should contain full particulars of any property to which the disposition relates, and of the person in whose favour the disposition is alleged to have been made, and where a settlement is alleged, of the trustees and beneficiaries of that settlement[5].

If the application relates to land the summons should state whether the land is registered (with title number) and particulars of any mortgage or other interest[6]. The mortgagee should be served[7].

A copy of the summons with supporting affidavit should be served on the person in whose favour the disposition is alleged to have been made[8], and that person may file an affidavit in answer in 14 days[9].

1 See FPR 1991, r 3.18(4) at para **[3.470]** below.
2 See FPR 1991, r 3.18(4) below.
3 See para **[2.218.1]** above. See also FPR 1991, r 3.18(6) at para **[3.470]** below.
4 See FPR 1991, r 3.18(6) at para **[3.470]** below.
5 See FPR 1991, r 2.59(1)(c) at para **[3.439]** below.
6 See FPR 1991, r 2.59(2) below.
7 See FPR 1991, r 2.59(4) below.
8 See FPR 1991, r 2.59(3)(b) below.
9 See FPR 1991, r 2.59(5) below.

## [2.229.3]
### Differences from the MCA 1973, s 37

Once leave under s 13 of the MFPA 1984 has been granted, this section operates in an identical way to the avoidance provisions in the MCA 1973, s 37[1], save where s 15(1)(c) only applies (see below).

Section 37 of the MCA 1973 contains no equivalent provision to s 23(9) of the MFPA 1984, in relation to s 37 of the Supreme Court Act 1981, but s 23 does not provide a date before which its provisions do not apply, as found in the MCA 1973, s 37(7).

1 See para **[2.136]** above.

## [2.229.4]
### Limitation where jurisdiction founded only on s 15(1)(c)

By s 23(4), the court may only make orders in relation to the dwelling-house concerned, and no other property, in these circumstances – note the restrictive provisions in s 20 above where s 15(1)(c) is the only basis for jurisdiction.

## [2.230]

### 24 Prevention of transactions intended to defeat prospective applications for financial relief

(1) Where, on an application by a party to a marriage, it appears to the court—

(a) that the marriage has been dissolved or annulled, or that the parties to the marriage have been legally separated, by means of judicial or other proceedings in an overseas country; and

(b) that the applicant intends to apply for leave to make an application for an order for financial relief under section 17 above as soon as he or she has been habitually resident in England and Wales for a period of one year; and

(c) that the other party to the marriage is, with the intention of defeating a claim for financial relief, about to make any disposition or to transfer out of the jurisdiction or otherwise deal with any property,

the court may make such order as it thinks fit for restraining the other party from taking such action as is mentioned in paragraph (c) above.

(2) For the purposes of an application under subsection (1) above—

(a) the reference to defeating a claim for financial relief shall be construed in accordance with subsection (1) of section 23 above (omitting the reference to any order which has been made); and

(b) subsections (7) and (8) of section 23 above shall apply for the purposes of an application under that section.

(3) The preceding provisions of this section are without prejudice to any power of the High Court to grant injunctions under section 37 of the Supreme Court Act 1981.

**Appointment**

Commencement order: SI 1985/1316.



## [2.230.1]
## Keypoints

- Application
- Requirements for jurisdiction need not be established in full
- Certain provisions of s 23 apply

## [2.230.2]
## Application

Applications under this section are made by originating summons in Form M27 out of the principal registry, supported by an affidavit of the applicant stating the facts relied on in support[1].

The applicant must serve a sealed copy of the application annexing the affidavit, and a notice of proceedings and acknowledgment of service in Form M28[2].

FPR 1991, r 10.8 (notice of intention to defend) shall apply to such an acknowledgment as if the reference at (1) to Form M6 was to Form M28, and as if the reference at (2) to seven days were 31 days[3].

The Respondent has 28 days after the time for giving notice of intention to defend to file an affidavit in answer setting out the grounds on which he relies, which he must serve on the applicant[4].

The application shall be determined by a judge[5].

FPR 1991, r 2.66 (arrangements for hearing of application by a judge) applies with necessary modifications as if the application were one for ancillary relief[6].

1 See FPR 1991, r 3.19(1) at para **[3.471]** below.
2 See FPR 1991, r 3.19(2) below.
3 See FPR 1991, r 3.19(2) below.
4 See FPR 1991, r 3.19(3) below.
5 See FPR 1991, r 3.19(4) below.
6 See FPR 1991, r 3.19(5) below.

## [2.230.3]
## Requirements for jurisdiction need not be established in full

The applicant need not have been habitually resident in England and Wales for one year prior to issuing an application under this section, but the court must be satisfied that the applicant's intention is to apply for leave as soon as that period has passed[1].

Where domicile is claimed, or if one year's habitual residence is established, then s 23 should be used, immediately upon the leave of the court being obtained under s 13.

1 See the MFPA 1984, s 24(1)(b) at para **[2.230]** above.

## [2.230.4]
## Certain provisions of s 23 apply

Section 24(2)(a) of the MFPA 1984 applies the definition of financial relief in s 23(1) above to, and by s 24(2)(b), s 23(7) (presumption of intention if disposition within three years of application) and s 23(8) (definition of disposition) apply to, an application under s 24(1).

**[2.231]**

### 25 Extension of powers under Inheritance (Provision for Family and Dependants) Act 1975 in respect of former spouses

...

**Appointment**

Commencement order: SI 1985/1316.

**Amendment**

This section amends the I(PFD)A 1975, s 25, and inserts s 15A.

**[2.232]–[2.264]**

### 27 Interpretation of Part III

In this Part of this Act—

'the 1973 Act' means the Matrimonial Causes Act 1973;

'child of the family' has the meaning as in section 52(1) of the 1973 Act;

'the court' means the High Court or, where a county court has jurisdiction by virtue of Part V of this Act, a county court;

'dwelling-house' includes any building or part thereof which is occupied as a dwelling, and any yard, garden, garage or outhouse belonging to the dwelling-house and occupied therewith;

'order for financial relief' has the meaning given by section 12(4) above;

'overseas country' means a country or territory outside the British Islands;

'possession' includes receipt of, or the right to receive, rents and profits;

*'property adjustment order' means such an order as is specified in section 24(1)(a), (b), (c) or (d) of the 1973 Act;*

['property adjustment order' and 'secured periodical payments order' mean any order which would be a property adjustment order or, as the case may be, secured periodical payments order within the meaning of Part II of the 1973 Act;]

'rent' does not include mortgage interest;

*'secured periodical payments order' means such an order as is specified in section 23(1)(b) or (e) of the 1973 Act.*

**Appointment**

Commencement order: SI 1985/1316.

**Amendment**

Definition 'property adjustment order' prospectively substituted with savings, and definition 'secured periodical payments order' prospectively repealed with savings, by the FLA 1996, s 66(1), (3), Sch 8, para 32(4), Sch 10, as from a day to be appointed; for savings see s 66(2), Sch 9, paras 5, 8–10 thereof.

# Insolvency Act 1986



## Contents



*An Act to consolidate the enactments relating to company insolvency and winding up (including the winding up of companies that are not insolvent, and of unregistered companies); enactments relating to the insolvency and bankruptcy of individuals; and other enactments bearing on those two subject matters, including the functions and qualification of insolvency practitioners, the public adminstration of insolvency, the penalisation and redress of malpractice and wrongdoing, and the avoidance of certain transactions at an undervalue*

[25th July 1986]

**[2.265]**

### 283 Definition of bankrupt's estate

(1) Subject as follows, a bankrupt's estate for the purposes of any of this Group of Parts comprises—

(a) all property belonging to or vested in the bankrupt at the commencement of the bankruptcy, and

(b) any property which by virtue of any of the following provisions of this Part is comprised in that estate or is treated as falling within the preceding paragraph.

(2) Subsection (1) does not apply to—

(a) such tools, books, vehicles and other items of equipment as are necessary to the bankrupt for use personally by him in his employment, business or vocation;

(b) such clothing, bedding, furniture, household equipment and provisions as are necessary for satisfying the basic domestic needs of the bankrupt and his family.

This subsection is subject to section 308 in Chapter IV (certain excluded property reclaimable by trustee).

(3) Subsection (1) does not apply to—

(a) property held by the bankrupt on trust for any other person, or

(b) the right of nomination to a vacant ecclesiastical benefice.

[(3A) Subject to section 308A in Chapter IV, subsection (1) does not apply to—

(a) a tenancy which is an assured tenancy or an assured agricultural occupancy, within the meaning of Part I of the Housing Act 1988, and the terms of which inhibit an assignment as mentioned in section 127(5) of the Rent Act 1977, or
(b) a protected tenancy, within the meaning of the Rent Act 1977, in respect of which, by virtue of any provision of Part IX of that Act, no premium can lawfully be required as a condition of assignment, or
(c) a tenancy of a dwelling-house by virtue of which the bankrupt is, within the meaning of the Rent (Agriculture) Act 1976, a protected occupier of the dwelling-house, and the terms of which inhibit an assignment as mentioned in section 127(5) of the Rent Act 1977, or
(d) a secure tenancy, within the meaning of Part IV of the Housing Act 1985, which is not capable of being assigned, except in the cases mentioned in section 91(3) of that Act.]

(4) References in any of this Group of Parts to property, in relation to a bankrupt, include references to any power exercisable by him over or in respect of property except in so far as the power is exercisable over or in respect of property not for the time being comprised in the bankrupt's estate and—
(a) is so exercisable at a time after either the official receiver has had his release in respect of that estate under section 299(2) in Chapter III or a meeting summoned by the trustee of that estate under section 331 in Chapter IV has been held, or
(b) cannot be so exercised for the benefit of the bankrupt;

and a power exercisable over or in respect of property is deemed for the purposes of any of this Group of Parts to vest in the person entitled to exercise it at the time of the transaction or event by virtue of which it is exercisable by that person (whether or not it becomes so exercisable at that time).

(5) For the purposes of any such provision in this Group of Parts, property comprised in a bankrupt's estate is so comprised subject to the rights of any person other than the bankrupt (whether as a secured creditor of the bankrupt or otherwise) in relation thereto, but disregarding—
(a) any rights in relation to which a statement such as is required by section 269(1)(a) was made in the petition on which the bankrupt was adjudged bankrupt, and
(b) any rights which have been otherwise given up in accordance with the rules.

(6) This section has effect subject to the provisions of any enactment not contained in this Act under which any property is to be excluded from a bankrupt's estate.

**Derivation**
This section, as originally enacted derived from the IA 1985, s 130.

**Amendment**
Sub-s (3A): inserted by the HA 1988, s 117(1).

**Notes**
See further, in relation to property comprising the bankrupt's estate: the DTA 1994, s 32.

### [2.265.1]
### Keypoints
- Property
- Transfer of property orders
- Estate

### [2.265.2]
### Property
Property does not cover future income or property accretions until such time as they are claimed for the bankrupt's estate[1].

Right to remain in a property under Pt I of the Landlord and Tenant Act 1954 is property (which trustee has power to disclaim)[2].

Retirement Annuities and Personal Pension Policies belonging to the bankrupt formed part of the estate[3].

1 See *E v G (Lump Sum Order: Bankruptcy)* [1997] 1 FCR 261, sub nom *Re G (Children Act 1989, Schedule 1)* [1996] 2 FLR 171.
2 See *Rothschild v Bell (a Bankrupt)* [2000] 1 QB 33, [1999] 2 All ER 722, CA.
3 See *Krasner v Dennison* [2001] Ch 76, [2000] 3 All ER 234, CA. Note that s 11 of the WRPA 1999 reverses this in respect of approved pension arrangements in respect to bankruptcies.



## [2.265.3]
### Transfer of property orders

On the current state of the authorities, orders under s 24(1)(a) or (b) do not take effect until the order has been put into effect[1] whereas orders under s 24(1)(c) or (d) take immediate effect[2].

1 See *Burton v Burton* [1986] 2 FLR 419; and *Beer v Higham* [1997] BPIR 349.
2 See *Burton v Burton* [1986] 2 FLR 419; and *Re Harper (a bankrupt), Harper v O'Reilly* [1998] 3 FCR 475, [1997] 2 FLR 816.

## [2.265.4]
### Estate

Estate does not include personal correspondence, even if of worth[1].

1 *Haig v Aitken* [2001] Ch 110, [2000] 3 All ER 80, [2000] 3 WLR 1117.

## [2.266]

### 284 Restrictions on dispositions of property

(1) Where a person is adjudged bankrupt, any disposition of property made by that person in the period to which this section applies is void except to the extent that it is or was made with the consent of the court, or is or was subsequently ratified by the court.

(2) Subsection (1) applies to a payment (whether in cash or otherwise) as it applies to a disposition of property and, accordingly, where any payment is void by virtue of that subsection, the person paid shall hold the sum paid for the bankrupt as part of his estate.

(3) This section applies to the period beginning with the day of the presentation of the petition for the bankruptcy order and ending with the vesting, under Chapter IV of this Part, of the bankrupt's estate in a trustee.

(4) The preceding provisions of this section do not give a remedy against any person—

(a) in respect of any property or payment which he received before the commencement of the bankruptcy in good faith, for value and without notice that the petition had been presented, or

(b) in respect of any interest in property which derives from an interest in respect of which there is, by virtue of this subsection, no remedy.

(5) Where after the commencement of his bankruptcy the bankrupt has incurred a debt to a banker or other person by reason of the making of a payment which is void under this section, that debt is deemed for the purposes of any of this Group of Parts to have been incurred before the commencement of the bankruptcy unless—

(a) that banker or person had notice of the bankruptcy before the debt was incurred, or

(b) it is not reasonably practicable for the amount of the payment to be recovered from the person to whom it was made.

(6) A disposition of property is void under this section notwithstanding that the property is not or, as the case may be, would not be comprised in the bankrupt's estate; but nothing in this section affects any disposition made by a person of property held by him on trust for any other person.

**Derivation**
This section derived from the IA 1985, s 131.

**Notes**
See further: the ChA 1989, ss 164, 175, 182(4), Sch 22, paras 7, 11.

### [2.266.1]
**Keypoints**
- Disposition
- Order under s 37(2) of the MCA 1973

### [2.266.2]
**Disposition**

Disposition pursuant to court order is still a disposition by the bankrupt[1], for orders under s 24 of the MCA 1973 see notes to s 283 above[2].

1 See *Re Flint (A Bankrupt)* [1993] Ch 319, [1993] 2 WLR 537.
2 See para **[2.265]** above.

### [2.266.3]–[2.287]
**Order under s 37(2) of the MCA 1973**

An order under s 37(2)(a) of the MCA 1973 secured property and put it beyond the reach of the debtor. As the order was made before a petition for his bankruptcy was issued the property did not form part of his estate[1].

1 See *Re Mordant, Mordant v Halls* [1997] 2 FCR 378, [1996] 1 FLR 334.

### [2.288]

**306 Vesting of bankrupt's estate in trustee**

(1) The bankrupt's estate shall vest in the trustee immediately on his appointment taking effect or, in the case of the official receiver, on his becoming trustee.
(2) Where any property which is, or is to be, comprised in the bankrupt's estate vests in the trustee (whether under this section or under any other provision of this Part), it shall so vest without any conveyance, assignment or transfer.

**Derivation**
This section derived from the IA 1985, s 153.

### [2.288.1]
**Keypoints**
- Estate
- Effect of estate vesting in trustee
- In the event of the Bankrupt's death

### [2.288.2]
**Estate**

'Estate' is defined in s 283 of the IA 1986[1], it includes contracts under a pension policy even though the payment date has not yet been reached[2] and a chose in action, including an action for damages for Personal Injuries, so far as it relates to a claim for future loss of earnings[3].

1 See para **[2.265]** above.
2 See *Re Landau (A Bankrupt)* [1998] Ch 223, [1997] 3 All ER 322.
3 See *Ord v Upton* [2000] Ch 352, [2000] 1 All ER 193, CA.

## [2.288.3]
### Effect of estate vesting in trustee

The effect of the estate vesting in the trustee is that the bankrupt can not, by law, employ those assets. Therefore a bankrupt who had failed to pay a lump sum could not be committed for failure to pay, as the trustee in bankruptcy and not he, had control over any assets that he had[1].

A property adjustment order can not be made against a bankrupt former spouse, where a property has been vested in the trustee[2], but in exceptional circumstances the court has power to order a lump sum[3].



1 See *Woodley v Woodley (No 2)* [1994] 4 All ER 1010, [1993] 2 FCR 661, CA.
2 See *Re Holliday (A Bankrupt)* [1981] Ch 405; and *McGladdery v McGladdery* [2000] 1 FCR 315, [1999] 2 FLR 1102, CA.
3 See *Hellyer v Hellyer* [1997] 1 FCR 340, CA.

## [2.288.4]–[2.292]
### In the event of the Bankrupt's death

In the event of bankrupt's death – where bankrupt is a joint beneficial owner of property, his estate will vest in the trustee in bankruptcy, if the Bankruptcy order precedes his death[1].

1 See *Re Dennis (A Bankrupt)* [1996] Ch 80, [1995] 3 All ER 171, CA.

## [2.293]

### 310 Income payments orders

(1) The court may, on the application of the trustee, make an order ('an income payments order') claiming for the bankrupt's estate so much of the income of the bankrupt during the period for which the order is in force as may be specified in the order.

(2) The court shall not make an income payments order the effect of which would be to reduce the income of the bankrupt [when taken together with any payments to which subsection (8) applies] below what appears to the court to be necessary for meeting the reasonable domestic needs of the bankrupt and his family.

(3) An income payments order shall, in respect of any payment of income to which it is to apply, either—

- (a) require the bankrupt to pay the trustee an amount equal to so much of that payment as is claimed by the order, or
- (b) require the person making the payment to pay so much of it as is so claimed to the trustee, instead of to the bankrupt.

(4) Where the court makes an income payments order it may, if it thinks fit, discharge or vary any attachment of earnings order that is for the time being in force to secure payments by the bankrupt.

(5) Sums received by the trustee under an income payments order form part of the bankrupt's estate.

(6) An income payments order shall not be made after the discharge of the bankrupt, and if made before, shall not have effect after his discharge except—

- (a) in the case of a discharge under section 279(1)(a) (order of court), by virtue of a condition imposed by the court under section 280(2)(c) (income, etc. after discharge), or

(b) in the case of a discharge under section 279(1)(b) (expiration of relevant period), by virtue of a provision of the order requiring it to continue in force for a period ending after the discharge but no later than 3 years after the making of the order.

(7) For the purposes of this section the income of the bankrupt comprises every payment in the nature of income which is from time to time made to him or to which he from time to time becomes entitled, including any payment in respect of the carrying on of any business or in respect of any office or employment and (despite anything in section 11 or 12 of the Welfare Reform and Pensions Act 1999) any payment under a pension scheme but excluding any payment to which subsection (8) applies.

(8) This subsection applies to—

(a) payments by way of guaranteed minimum pension; and

(b) payments giving effect to the bankrupt's protected rights as a member of a pension scheme.

(9) In this section, 'guaranteed minimum pension' and 'protected rights' have the same meaning as in the Pension Schemes Act 1993.

**Derivation**

This section derived from the IA 1985, s 156.

**Amendment**

Sub-s (2): PA 1995, s 122, Sch 3, para 15(a). Sub-s (7): PA 1995, s 122, Sch 3, para 15(b); WRPA 1999, s 18. Sub-ss (8), (9): inserted by the PA 1995, s 122, Sch 3, para 15(b).

**Notes**

See further, in relation to student loans for higher education: the E(SL)A 1990, Sch 2, para 5.

## [2.293.1]
### Keypoints

- Reasonable domestic needs
- Quantum of periodical payments

## [2.293.2]
### Reasonable domestic needs

Reasonable domestic needs can include school fees[1].

1 See *Re Rayatt* [1998] 2 FLR 264, [1998] Fam Law 458.

## [2.293.3]–[2.319]
### Quantum of periodical payments

In determination of the quantum of periodical payments the family court will take account of any Income Payments order made in the bankruptcy[1].

1 See *Albert v Albert (A Bankrupt)* [1998] 1 FCR 331, [1997] 2 FLR 791, CA.

## [2.320]

### 336 Rights of occupation etc of bankrupt's spouse

(1) Nothing occurring in the initial period of the bankruptcy (that is to say, the period beginning with the day of the presentation of the petition for the bankruptcy order and ending with the vesting of the bankrupt's estate in a trustee) is to be taken as having given rise to any [matrimonial home rights under Part IV of the Family Law Act 1996] in relation to a dwelling house comprised in the bankrupt's estate.

(2) Where a spouse's [matrimonial home rights under the Act of 1996] are a charge on the estate or interest of the other spouse, or of trustees for the other spouse, and the other spouse is adjudged bankrupt—

(a) the charge continues to subsist notwithstanding the bankruptcy and, subject to the provisions of that Act, binds the trustee of the bankrupt's estate and persons deriving title under that trustee, and

(b) any application for an order [under section 33 of that Act] shall be made to the court having jurisdiction in relation to the bankruptcy.

(3) …

(4) On such an application as is mentioned in subsection (2) … the court shall make such order under [section 33 of the Act of 1996] … as it thinks just and reasonable having regard to—

(a) the interests of the bankrupt's creditors,

(b) the conduct of the spouse or former spouse, so far as contributing to the bankruptcy,

(c) the needs and financial resources of the spouse or former spouse,

(d) the needs of any children, and

(e) all the circumstances of the case other than the needs of the bankrupt.

(5) Where such an application is made after the end of the period of one year beginning with the first vesting under Chapter IV of this Part of the bankrupt's estate in a trustee, the court shall assume, unless the circumstances of the case are exceptional, that the interests of the bankrupt's creditors outweigh all other considerations.



**Derivation**

This section derived from the IA 1985, s 171.

**Amendment**

Sub-s (1): words 'matrimonial home rights under Part IV of the Family Law Act 1996' in square brackets substituted by the FLA 1996, s 66(1), Sch 8, para 57(2). Date in force: 1 October 1997: see SI 1997/1892, art 3(1)(b). Sub-s (2): words 'matrimonial home rights under the Act of 1996' in square brackets substituted by the FLA 1996, s 66(1), Sch 8, para 57(3)(a). Date in force: 1 October 1997: see SI 1997/1892, art 3(1)(b). Sub-s (2): in para (b) words 'under section 33 of that Act' in square brackets substituted by the FLA 1996, s 66(1), Sch 8, para 57(3)(b). Date in force: 1 October 1997: see SI 1997/1892, art 3(1)(b). Sub-s (3): repealed by the TLATA 1996, s 25(2), Sch 4; for savings in relation to entailed interests created before the commencement of that Act, and savings consequential upon the abolition of the doctrine of conversion, see s 25(4), (5) thereof. Sub-s (4): words omitted repealed by the TLATA 1996, s 25(2), Sch 4; for savings in relation to entailed interests created before the commencement of that Act, and savings consequential upon the abolition of the doctrine of conversion, see s 25(4), (5) thereof. Sub-s (4): words 'section 33 of the Act of 1996' in square brackets substituted by the FLA 1996, s 66(1), Sch 8, para 57(4). Date in force: 1 October 1997: see SI 1997/1892, art 3(1)(b).

### [2.320.1]
### Keypoints

- Rendering homeless spouse/former spouse and children
- Beneficial joint tenants

### [2.320.2]
### Rendering homeless spouse/former spouse and children

Rendering homeless spouse/former spouse and children not per se an exceptional circumstance under the IA 1986, s 336(5)[1].

1 See *Re Citro Domenico (A Bankrupt)* [1991] Ch 142, [1990] 3 All ER 952, CA.

### [2.320.3]–[2.322]
### Beneficial joint tenants

Beneficial joint tenants owning property jointly with the bankrupt will need to establish the bankrupt's share and consider the possibility of purchasing the bankrupts share from the trustee — normal trust and equitable principles (eg equity of exoneration, credit for direct and indirect contributions) will apply[1].

1 See *Re Pittrou (A Bankrupt)* [1985] 1 All ER 285, [1985] 1 WLR 58; *Re Gorman (A Bankrupt)* [1990] 1 All ER 717, [1990] 1 WLR 616; and *Re Pavlou (A Bankrupt)* [1993] 3 All ER 955, [1993] 1 WLR 1046.

**[2.323]**

## 339 Transactions at an undervalue

(1) Subject as follows in this section and sections 341 and 342, where an individual is adjudged bankrupt and he has at a relevant time (defined in section 341) entered into a transaction with any person at an undervalue, the trustee of the bankrupt's estate may apply to the court for an order under this section.

(2) The court shall, on such an application, make such order as it thinks fit for restoring the position to what it would have been if that individual had not entered into that transaction.

(3) For the purposes of this section and sections 341 and 342, an individual enters into a transaction with a person at an undervalue if—

- (a) he makes a gift to that person or he otherwise enters into a transaction with that person on terms that provide for him to receive no consideration,
- (b) he enters into a transaction with that person in consideration of marriage, or
- (c) he enters into a transaction with that person for a consideration the value of which, in money or money's worth, is significantly less than the value, in money or money's worth, of the consideration provided by the individual.

**Derivation**

This section derived from the IA 1985, s 174(1)(in part), (2).

**Notes**

See further: the Companies Act 1989, ss 165, 182(4), Sch 22, para 8.
See further, in relation to gifts caught by the DTA 1994, s 32 of that Act.

**[2.323.1]**
### Keypoints

- 'Transaction'
- Compromise of the right to claim future relief

**[2.323.2]**
### 'Transaction'

'Transaction' includes a settlement pursuant to an Ancillary Relief order[1].

1 See *Re Abbott (A Bankrupt)* [1983] Ch 45, [1982] 3 All ER 181; and *Re O'Shea's Settlement* [1895] 1 Ch 325.

**[2.323.3]**
### Compromise of the right to claim future relief

Compromise of the right to claim future relief can be consideration for money or monies worth[1].

1 See *Re Abbot (A Bankrupt)* [1983] Ch 45, [1982] 3 All ER 181; and *Re Kumar (A Bankrupt), ex p Lewis v Kumar* [1993] 1 WLR 224, [1994] 2 FCR 373.

[3.324]

### 340 Preferences

(1) Subject as follows in this and the next two sections, where an individual is adjudged bankrupt and he has at a relevant time (defined in section 341) given a preference to any person, the trustee of the bankrupt's estate may apply to the court for an order under this section.

(2) The court shall, on such an application, make such order as it thinks fit for restoring the position to what it would have been if that individual had not given that preference.

(3) For the purposes of this and the next two sections, an individual gives a preference to a person if—

(a) that person is one of the individual's creditors or a surety or guarantor for any of his debts or other liabilities, and

(b) the individual does anything or suffers anything to be done which (in either case) has the effect of putting that person into a position which, in the event of the individual's bankruptcy, will be better than the position he would have been in if that thing had not been done.

(4) The court shall not make an order under this section in respect of a preference given to any person unless the individual who gave the preference was influenced in deciding to give it by a desire to produce in relation to that person the effect mentioned in subsection (3)(b) above.

(5) An individual who has given a preference to a person who, at the time the preference was given, was an associate of his (otherwise than by reason only of being his employee) is presumed, unless the contrary is shown, to have been influenced in deciding to give it by such a desire as is mentioned in subsection (4).

(6) The fact that something has been done in pursuance of the order of a court does not, without more, prevent the doing or suffering of that thing from constituting the giving of a preference.

**Derivation**

This section derived from the IA 1985, s 174(1) (in part), (3) to (6), (12) (in part).

**Notes**

See further: the Companies Act 1989, ss 165, 182(4), Sch 22, para 8.



[2.324.1]

**Keypoint**

- Onus of proof

[2.324.2]

**Onus of proof**

The onus of proof is upon the trustee in bankruptcy[1].

1 See *Bulteel and Colmore v Parker and Bulteel's Trustee* (1916) 32 TLR 661.

[2.325]

### 341 'Relevant time' under ss 339, 340

(1) Subject as follows, the time at which an individual enters into a transaction at an undervalue or gives a preference is a relevant time if the transaction is entered into or the preference given—

(a) in the case of a transaction at an undervalue, at a time in the period of 5 years ending with the day of the presentation of the bankruptcy petition on which the individual is adjudged bankrupt,

(b) in the case of a preference which is not a transaction at an undervalue and is given to a person who is an associate of the individual (otherwise than by reason only of being his employee), at a time in the period of 2 years ending with that day, and

(c) in any other case of a preference which is not a transaction at an undervalue, at a time in the period of 6 months ending with that day.

(2) Where an individual enters into a transaction at an undervalue or gives a preference at a time mentioned in paragraph (a), (b) or (c) of subsection (1) (not being, in the case of a transaction at an undervalue, a time less than 2 years before the end of the period mentioned in paragraph (a)), that time is not a relevant time for the purposes of sections 339 and 340 unless the individual—

(a) is insolvent at that time, or

(b) becomes insolvent in consequence of the transaction or preference;

but the requirements of this subsection are presumed to be satisfied, unless the contrary is shown, in relation to any transaction at an undervalue which is entered into by an individual with a person who is an associate of his (otherwise than by reason only of being his employee).

(3) For the purposes of subsection (2), an individual is insolvent if—

(a) he is unable to pay his debts as they fall due, or

(b) the value of his assets is less than the amount of his liabilities, taking into account his contingent and prospective liabilities.

*(4) A transaction entered into or preference given by a person who is subsequently adjudged bankrupt on a petition under section 264(1)(d) (criminal bankruptcy) is to be treated as having been entered into or given at a relevant time for the purposes of sections 339 and 340 if it was entered into or given at any time on or after the date specified for the purposes of this subsection in the criminal bankruptcy order on which the petition was based.*

*(5) No order shall be made under section 339 or 340 by virtue of subsection (4) of this section where an appeal is pending (within the meaning of section 277) against the individual's conviction of any offence by virtue of which the criminal bankruptcy order was made.*

**Derivation**

This section derived from the IA 1985, s 174(7)–(11), (12) (in part).

**Amendment**

Sub-ss (4), (5): prospectively repealed by the CJA 1988, s 170(2), Sch 16, as from a day to be appointed.

### [2.325.1]
### Keypoint

- The date of the transaction

### [2.325.2]
### The date of the transaction

The date of the transaction is clearly of major importance. Transfer of property orders pursuant to s 24(1)(a) and (b) do not take effect until the disposition is completed[1], whereas orders pursuant to s 24(1)(c) and (d) have immediate effect[2].

1 See *Burton v Burton* [1986] 2 FLR 419, [1986] Fam Law 330.

2 See *Re Harper (A Bankrupt), Harper v O'Reilly* [1998] 3 FCR 475, [1997] 2 FLR 816.

[2.326]

**342 Orders under ss 339, 340**

(1) Without prejudice to the generality of section 339(2) or 340(2), an order under either of those sections with respect to a transaction or preference entered into or given by an individual who is subsequently adjudged bankrupt may (subject as follows)—

(a) require any property transferred as part of the transaction, or in connection with the giving of the preference, to be vested in the trustee of the bankrupt's estate as part of that estate;

(b) require any property to be so vested if it represents in any person's hands the application either of the proceeds of sale of property so transferred or of money so transferred;

(c) release or discharge (in whole or in part) any security given by the individual;

(d) require any person to pay, in respect of benefits received by him from the individual, such sums to the trustee of his estate as the court may direct;

(e) provide for any surety or guarantor whose obligations to any person were released or discharged (in whole or in part) under the transaction or by the giving of the preference to be under such new or revived obligations to that person as the court thinks appropriate;

(f) provide for security to be provided for the discharge of any obligation imposed by or arising under the order, for such an obligation to be charged on any property and for the security or charge to have the same priority as a security or charge released or discharged (in whole or in part) under the transaction or by the giving of the preference; and

(g) provide for the extent to which any person whose property is vested by the order in the trustee of the bankrupt's estate, or on whom obligations are imposed by the order, is to be able to prove in the bankruptcy for debts or other liabilities which arose from, or were released or discharged (in whole or in part) under or by, the transaction or the giving of the preference.

(2) An order under section 339 or 340 may affect the property of, or impose any obligation on, any person whether or not he is the person with whom the individual in question entered into the transaction or, as the case may be, the person to whom the preference was given; but such an order—

(a) shall not prejudice any interest in property which was acquired from a person other than that individual and was acquired [in good faith and for value], or prejudice any interest deriving from such an interest, and

(b) shall not require a person who received a benefit from the transaction or preference [in good faith and for value] to pay a sum to the trustee of the bankrupt's estate, except where he was a party to the transaction or the payment is to be in respect of a preference given to that person at a time when he was a creditor of that individual.

[(2A) Where a person has acquired an interest in property from a person other than the individual in question, or has received a benefit from the transaction or preference, and at the time of that acquisition or receipt—

(a) he had notice of the relevant surrounding circumstances and of the relevant proceedings, or

(b) he was an associate of, or was connected with, either the individual in question or the person with whom that individual entered into the transaction or to whom that individual gave the preference,

then, unless the contrary is shown, it shall be presumed for the purposes of paragraph (a) or (as the case may be) paragraph (b) of subsection (2) that the interest was acquired or the benefit was received otherwise than in good faith.]

(3) Any sums required to be paid to the trustee in accordance with an order under section 339 or 340 shall be comprised in the bankrupt's estate.

[(4) For the purposes of subsection (2A)(a), the relevant surrounding circumstances are (as the case may require)—

(a) the fact that the individual in question entered into the transaction at an undervalue; or

(b) the circumstances which amounted to the giving of the preference by the individual in question.

(5) For the purposes of subsection (2A)(a), a person has notice of the relevant proceedings if he has notice—

(a) of the fact that the petition on which the individual in question is adjudged bankrupt has been presented; or

(b) of the fact that the individual in question has been adjudged bankrupt.

(6) Section 249 in Part VII of this Act shall apply for the purposes of subsection (2A)(b) as it applies for the purposes of the first Group of Parts.]

**Derivation**

This section as originally enacted derived from the IA 1985, s 175.

**Amendment**

Sub-s (2): words in square brackets substituted by the Insolvency (No 2) Act 1994, s 2(1). Sub-s (2A): inserted by the Insolvency (No 2) Act 1994, s 2(2). Sub-ss (4) to (6): substituted for sub-s (4) as originally enacted, by the Insolvency (No 2) Act 1994, s 2(3).

## [2.327]–[2.415]

### 371 Re-direction of bankrupt's letters, etc

(1) Where a bankruptcy order has been made, the court may from time to time, on the application of the official receiver or the trustee of the bankrupt's estate, order [a postal operator (within the meaning of the Postal Services Act 2000)] to re-direct and send or deliver to the official receiver or trustee or otherwise any postal packet (within the meaning of [that Act]) which would otherwise be send or delivered by [the operator concerned] to the bankrupt at such place or places as may be specified in the order.

(2) An order under this section has effect for such period, not exceeding 3 months, as may be specified in the order.

**Amendment**

Sub-s (1): Postal Services Act 2000, s 127(4), Sch 8, Pt II. Date in force: 26 March 2001: see SI 2000/2957.

# Children Act 1989

## Contents





*An Act to reform the law relating to children; to provide for local authority services for children in need and others; to amend the law with respect to children's homes, community homes, voluntary homes and voluntary organisations; to make provision with respect to fostering, child minding and day care for young children and adoption; and for connected purposes*

[16th November 1989]

**[2.416]**

### 15 Orders for financial relief with respect to children

(1) Schedule 1 (which consists primarily of the re-enactment, with consequential amendments and minor modifications, of provisions of [section 6 of the Family Law Reform Act 1969] the Guardianship of Minors Acts 1971 and 1973, the Children Act 1975 and of sections 15 and 16 of the Family Law Reform Act 1987) makes provision in relation to financial relief for children.

(2) The powers of a magistrates' court under section 60 of the Magistrates' Courts Act 1980 to revoke, revive or vary an order for the periodical payment of money [and the power of the clerk of a magistrates' court to vary such an order] shall not apply in relation to an order made under Schedule 1.

**Appointment**

Commencement order: SI 1991/828.

**Amendment**

Sub-s (1): words in square brackets inserted by the CLSA 1990, s 116, Sch 16, para 10. Sub-s (2): words in square brackets inserted by the MEA 1991, s 11(1), Sch 2, para 10.

**[2.416.1]**
**Keypoints**

- A single unified code
- Has retrospective effect
- Consider joinder with other applications between the parents
- Maintenance provisions limited by the Child Support Act 1991
- Use where the MCA 1973 not available

## [2.416.2]
## A single unified code

The provisions of s 15 of, and Sch 1 to, the ChA 1989 have, to a very large extent, replaced the previous statutory provisions that related to financial applications in respect of children (for instance, the Guardianship of Minors Act 1971, as amended, by the FLRA 1987 and the Affiliation Proceedings Act 1957). The ChA 1989 now contains a unified code for dealing with such applications. However, applications in respect of children may still be made under certain other statutes (for instance under the MCA 1973 and the DPMCA 1978).

## [2.416.3]
## Has retrospective effect

In the case of *Hager v Osborne*[1], it was held that a mother was able to apply under the provisions of s 11B of the Guardianship of Minors Act 1971 (ie the forerunner of Sch 1 to the Children Act 1991) notwithstanding that the child had been born before the Act came into force and she had been refused an order under the Affiliation Proceedings Act 1957. The same would plainly apply to an application under the 1989 Act.

1 [1992] Fam 94, [1992] 2 All ER 494, sub nom *H v O* [1992] 1 FCR 107.

## [2.416.4]
## Consider joinder with other applications between the parents

Often it will be necessary to give consideration to joining together applications that relate to the property of cohabitees (eg under the TLATA 1996) with applications for financial relief under Sch 1 to the ChA 1989. Where possible such applications should be heard together before the same court[1] (although logically, it will often be necessary to determine the trust application before the Sch 1 application in order that the court may be able to give proper consideration to the discretionary factors under Sch 1, para 4 of the ChA 1989[2]).

1 See *Hammond v Mitchell* [1991] 1 WLR 1127, sub nom *H v H* [1992] 2 FLR 229 at 1138.
2 Set out at para **[2.420]** below.

## [2.416.5]
## Maintenance provisions limited by the Child Support Act 1991

By reason of the CSA 1991 the court's powers to make maintenance orders in respect of children have been severely curtailed (eg s 8(3) of the CSA 1991). The court may still retain jurisdiction to make child maintenance orders in some limited circumstances, however, for instance under the transitional provisions of the CSA 1991, where a written agreement has been made between the parties (see the Child Maintenance (Written Agreements) Order 1993), where a parent is resident abroad or where the application relates to school fees, etc[1]. In *Phillips v Pearce*[2], Johnson J held that a lump sum order under Sch 1 to the ChA 1989 could not be used as a backdoor method of providing child maintenance.

1 See the CSA 1991, s 8(6) to (8) at para **[2.428]** below.
2 [1996] 2 FCR 237, [1996] 2 FLR 230. In the case of *V v V (child maintenance)* [2001] 2 FLR 799, Wilson J distinguished the case of *Phillips v Pearce*. In *V v V* the husband had accepted that the court should have jurisdiction to make orders for child maintenance but then refused to accept that he should pay more than he had proposed. The judge held that he could order a lump sum to raise the level of the husband's payments for the child.

## [2.416.6]
## Use where the MCA 1973 not available

In *B v B (Transfer of tenancy)*[1] the wife, who had remarried, was precluded from seeking ancillary relief due to s 28(3) of the MCA 1973; it was held that she was entitled to seek order for transfer of tenancy under Sch 1 (on the facts her claim failed).

See generally, *Rayden and Jackson on Divorce and Family Matters* (17th edn, 1997), vol 1, para 26.88 and the Noter-up thereto.

1 [1994] Fam Law 250.

SCHEDULE 1
Financial Provision for Children

(s 15(1))



**[2.417]**

*Orders for financial relief against parents*

**1**

(1) On an application made by a parent or guardian of a child, or by any person in whose favour a residence order is in force with respect to a child, the court may—

(a) in the case of an application to the High Court or a county court, make one or more of the orders mentioned in sub-paragraph (2);

(b) in the case of an application to a magistrates' court, make one or both of the orders mentioned in paragraphs (a) and (c) of that sub-paragraph.

(2) The orders referred to in sub-paragraph (1) are—

(a) an order requiring either or both parents of a child—

(i) to make to the applicant for the benefit of the child; or

(ii) to make to the child himself,

such periodical payments, for such term, as may be specified in the order;

(b) an order requiring either or both parents of a child—

(i) to secure to the applicant for the benefit of the child; or

(ii) to secure to the child himself,

such periodical payments, for such term, as may be so specified;

(c) an order requiring either or both parents of a child—

(i) to pay to the applicant for the benefit of the child; or

(ii) to pay to the child himself,

such lump sum as may be so specified;

(d) an order requiring a settlement to be made for the benefit of the child, and to the satisfaction of the court, of property—

(i) to which either parent is entitled (either in possession or in reversion); and

(ii) which is specified in the order;

(e) an order requiring either or both parents of a child—

(i) to transfer to the applicant, for the benefit of the child; or

(ii) to transfer to the child himself,

such property to which the parent is, or the parents are, entitled (either in possession or in reversion) as may be specified in the order.

(3) The powers conferred by this paragraph may be exercised at any time.

(4) An order under sub-paragraph (2)(a) or (b) may be varied or discharged by a subsequent order made on the application of any person by or to whom payments were required to be made under the previous order.

(5) Where a court makes an order under this paragraph—

(a) it may at any time make a further such order under sub-paragraph (2)(a), (b) or (c) with respect to the child concerned if he has not reached the age of eighteen;

(b) it may not make more than one order under sub-paragraph (2)(d) or (e) against the same person in respect of the same child.

(6) On making, varying or discharging a residence order the court may exercise any of its powers under this Schedule even though no application has been made to it under this Schedule.

[(7) Where a child is a ward of court, the court may exercise any of its powers under this Schedule even though no application has been made to it.]

**Appointment**

Commencement order: SI 1991/828.

**Amendment**

Para 1: sub-para (7) inserted by the CLSA 1990, s 116, Sch 16, para 10(2).

## [2.417.1]
### Keypoints

- Orders that can be made
- When Sch 1 orders can be made
- 'Parent' – defined
- 'Child' – defined
- 'Child of the family' – defined
- Respondent bankrupt
- Benefit of the child
- Orders by consent
- Appeals from Justices
- Transfer of tenancies

## [2.417.2]
### Orders that can be made

The High Court or county court may make any of the orders listed in para 1(2). A magistrates' court may only make the orders that are set out in para 1(2)(a) and (c) (that is to say the magistrates' court may only make periodical payment orders or lump sum orders)[1]. The amount of any lump sum that a magistrates' court may order may not exceed £1,000 (or such larger amount as the Secretary of State may fix)[2].

1 See the ChA 1989, Sch 1, para 1(1)(b) at para **[2.417]** above.
2 See the ChA 1989, Sch 1, para 5(2) at para **[2.421]** below.

## [2.417.3]
### When Sch 1 orders can be made

An order under Sch 1 to the ChA 1989 may be made on an application by a parent or guardian of a child or by any person in whose favour a residence order is in force with respect to a child[1]. Further, the court may make an order under Sch 1 to the ChA 1989 when it makes, varies or discharges a residence order, even though no application has been made for an order under the Schedule[2]. Similarly, where a child is a ward of court, the court may exercise any of its powers under the Schedule even though there is no application.

1 See the ChA 1989, Sch 1, para 1(1) at para **[2.417]** above.
2 See the ChA 1989, Sch 1, para 1(6) above.

## [2.417.4]
### 'Parent' – defined

The word 'parent' is defined within the Schedule as including any party to a marriage (whether or not subsisting) in relation to whom the child concerned is a child of the family[1]. However, this definition does not apply to Sch 1 to the ChA 1989.

Paragraph 2 (orders for financial provision for persons over 18) or Sch 1, para 15 (which relates to local authorities' contributions to child's maintenance). A cohabitee is not a parent for the purposes of this Schedule[2]. However, step-parents will be caught by the definition where the child concerned was a child of the family (see the definition of 'child of the family' below).

1 See the ChA 1989, Sch 1, para 16(2) at para **[2.417]** below.
2 See *J v J* [1993] 1 FCR 471, [1993] 2 FLR 56.

## [2.417.5]
### 'Child' – defined

The ChA 1989 contains a definition of 'child' within the definition section[1]:

> 'A child means a person under the age of 18, subject to Paragraph 16 of Schedule 1'.

Paragraph 16 of Sch 1 to the ChA 1989 provides that 'child' includes, in any case where an application is made under paras 2 or 6 in relation to a person who has reached the age of 18, that person.

1 See the ChA 1989, s 105.

### [2.417.6]
### 'Child of the family' – defined

Child of the family is defined in s 105 of the ChA 1989 in relation to the parties to a marriage as:

(a) a child of both of those parties;

(b) any other child, not being a child who is placed with those parties as foster parents by a local authority or voluntary organisation, who has been treated by both of those parties as a child of their family.

A child cannot be treated as a child of the family before birth[1]; the family must be in existence at the time of or following birth[2].

1 See *A v A (family: unborn child)* [1974] Fam 6, [1974] 1 All ER 755.
2 See *Re M (a minor)* (1980) 10 Fam Law 184, CA.



### [2.417.7]
### Respondent bankrupt

In *Re G (Children Act 1989, Schedule 1)*[1] it was held that an order could be made under Sch 1 to the ChA 1989 even though the father was bankrupt.

1 [1996] 2 FLR 171.

### [2.417.8]
### Benefit of the child

Orders are not limited to providing only financial benefit for the child. The phrase 'for the benefit of the child' means 'for the good of the child'[1]. Under the statutory provisions that preceded Sch 1 to the ChA 1989 (s 11B of the Guardianship of Minors Act 1971) it was decided that the court had jurisdiction to order the transfer of a council house tenancy between parents. However, in exercising the jurisdiction the court must apply the statutory check-list (then in s 12A of the 1971 Act, now in para 4 of Sch 1 to the ChA 1989)[2]. Where the settlement of a property is ordered for the benefit of the child, the order will usually provide for the property to revert to the father (ie the respondent to the application) upon the child ceasing to be a dependant[3].

1 See *Re B (Child: Property transfer)* [1999] 3 FCR 266, [1999] 2 FLR 418, CA.
2 See *K v K (Minors: Property transfer)* [1992] 2 FCR 253, [1992] 2 FLR 220, CA.
3 See *A v A* [1995] 1 FCR 309, [1994] 1 FLR 657; and *T v S* [1994] 1 FCR 743, [1994] 2 FLR 883.

### [2.417.9]
### Orders by consent

Where the court is asked to make orders by consent it should usually do so because such an order is to the benefit of the child as reflecting a consensus between the parents[1].

1 See *K v H* [1993] 1 FCR 683, [1993] 2 FLR 61, FD.

### [2.417.10]
### Appeals from Justices

Appeals from Magistrates' Schedule 1 order is under s 94 of the ChA 1989 and such an appeal may include an appeal from a refusal by the Justices to remit arrears[1].

1 See *S v S* [1993] Fam 200, [1993] 1 FLR 606, FD.

## [2.417.11]
**Transfer of tenancies**

Schedule 1 can be used in appropriate circumstances to exclude the father from the property that he and the mother rented jointly from a housing association[1].

1 See *Franklin v Pearson* [1994] 2 All ER 137, [1994] 1 WLR 370, CA; and *K v K (Minors : Property transfer)* [1992] 2 FCR 253, [1992] 2 FLR 220, CA.

## [2.418]

*Orders for financial relief for persons over eighteen*

**2**

(1) If, on an application by a person who has reached the age of eighteen, it appears to the court—

(a) that the applicant is, will be or (if an order were made under this paragraph) would be receiving instruction at an educational establishment or undergoing training for a trade, profession or vocation, whether or not while in gainful employment; or

(b) that there are special circumstances which justify the making of an order under this paragraph,

the court may make one or both of the orders mentioned in sub-paragraph (2).

(2) The orders are—

(a) an order requiring either or both of the applicant's parents to pay to the applicant such periodical payments, for such term, as may be specified in the order;

(b) an order requiring either or both of the applicant's parents to pay to the applicant such lump sum as may be so specified.

(3) An application may not be made under this paragraph by any person if, immediately before he reached the age of sixteen, a periodical payments order was in force with respect to him.

(4) No order shall be made under this paragraph at a time when the parents of the applicant are living with each other in the same household.

(5) An order under sub-paragraph (2)(a) may be varied or discharged by a subsequent order made on the application of any person by or to whom payments were required to be made under the previous order.

(6) In sub-paragraph (3) 'periodical payments order' means an order made under—

(a) this Schedule;

(b) …

(c) section 23 or 27 of the Matrimonial Causes Act 1973;

(d) Part I of the Domestic Proceedings and Magistrates' Courts Act 1978,

for the making or securing of periodical payments.

(7) The powers conferred by this paragraph shall be exercisable at any time.

(8) Where the court makes an order under this paragraph it may from time to time while that order remains in force make a further such order.

**Appointment**

Commencement order: SI 1991/828.

**Amendment**

Para 2: sub-para (6)(b) repealed by the CSA 1991, s 58(14).

## [2.418.1]
**Keypoints**

- Who may apply
- Liability to maintain students
- Disabled adult child

### [2.418.2]
### Who may apply

It would appear that the application must be made by the adult child himself and cannot be made by parent or other person for the child (unless the child is a mental patient and cannot conduct his own affairs).

### [2.418.3]
### Liability to maintain students

For a case where it was held that the father was obliged to maintain his student daughter notwithstanding the availability of a grant, see *B v B (financial provision for child)*[1].

1 [1998] 1 FCR 49, [1998] 1 FLR 373, CA.



### [2.418.4]
### Disabled adult child

For an example of a case where the parents had a continuing responsibility to maintain a disabled child, see *C v F (Disabled Child: Maintenance Orders)*[1].

1 [1999] 1 FCR 39, [1998] 2 FLR 1.

### [2.419]

*Duration of orders for financial relief*

**3**

(1) The term to be specified in an order for periodical payments made under paragraph 1(2)(a) or (b) in favour of a child may begin with the date of the making of an application for the order in question or any later date [or a date ascertained in accordance with sub-paragraph (5) or (6)] but—

(a) shall not in the first instance extend beyond the child's seventeenth birthday unless the court thinks it right in the circumstances of the case to specify a later date; and

(b) shall not in any event extend beyond the child's eighteenth birthday.

(2) Paragraph (b) of sub-paragraph (1) shall not apply in the case of a child if it appears to the court that—

(a) the child is, or will be or (if an order were made without complying with that paragraph) would be receiving instruction at an educational establishment or undergoing training for a trade, profession or vocation, whether or not while in gainful employment; or

(b) there are special circumstances which justify the making of an order without complying with that paragraph.

(3) An order for periodical payments made under paragraph 1(2)(a) or 2(2)(a) shall, notwithstanding anything in the order, cease to have effect on the death of the person liable to make payments under the order.

(4) Where an order is made under paragraph 1(2)(a) or (b) requiring periodical payments to be made or secured to the parent of a child, the order shall cease to have effect if—

(a) any parent making or securing the payments; and

(b) any parent to whom the payments are made or secured,

live together for a period of more than six months.

[(5) Where—

(a) a maintenance assessment ('the current assessment') is in force with respect to a child; and

(b) an application is made for an order under paragraph 1(2)(a) or (b) of this Schedule for periodical payments in favour of that child—

(i) in accordance with section 8 of the Child Support Act 1991; and

(ii) before the end of the period of 6 months beginning with the making of the current assessment,

the term to be specified in any such order made on that application may be expressed to begin on, or at any time after, the earliest permitted date.

(6) For the purposes of subsection (5) above, 'the earliest permitted date' is whichever is the later of—

(a) the date 6 months before the application is made; or

(b) the date on which the current assessment took effect or, where successive maintenance assessments have been continuously in force with respect to a child, on which the first of those assessments took effect.

(7) Where—

(a) a maintenance assessment ceases to have effect or is cancelled by or under any provision of the Child Support Act 1991, and

(b) an application is made, before the end of the period of 6 months beginning with the relevant date, for an order for periodical payments under paragraph 1(2)(a) or (b) in favour of a child with respect to whom that maintenance assessment was in force immediately before it ceased to have effect or was cancelled,

the term to be specified in any such order, or in any interim order under paragraph 9, made on that application may begin with the date on which that maintenance assessment ceased to have effect or, as the case may be, the date with effect from which it was cancelled, or any later date.

(8) In sub-paragraph (7)(b)—

(a) where the maintenance assessment ceased to have effect, the relevant date is the date on which it so ceased; and

(b) where the maintenance assessment was cancelled, the relevant date is the later of—

(i) the date on which the person who cancelled it did so, and

(ii) the date from which the cancellation first had effect.]

**Appointment**

Commencement order: SI 1991/828.

**Amendment**

Para 3: in sub-para (1) words in square brackets and sub-paras (5)–(8) inserted by SI 1993/623, art 2, Sch 1, paras 10, 11.

## [2.419.1]

**Keypoint**

- Similarity with s 29 of the MCA 1973

## [2.419.2]

**Similarity with s 29 of the MCA 1973**

In many respects these provisions are similar to those of s 29 of the MCA 1973 (set out at para **[2.127]** above).

## [2.420]

*Matters to which court is to have regard in making orders for financial relief*

**4**

(1) In deciding whether to exercise its powers under paragraph 1 or 2, and if so in what manner, the court shall have regard to all the circumstances including—

(a) the income, earning capacity, property and other financial resources which each person mentioned in sub-paragraph (4) has or is likely to have in the foreseeable future;

(b) the financial needs, obligations and responsibilities which each person mentioned in sub-paragraph (4) has or is likely to have in the foreseeable future;

(c) the financial needs of the child;

(d) the income, earning capacity (if any), property and other financial resources of the child;

(e) any physical or mental disability of the child;

(f) the manner in which the child was being, or was expected to be, educated or trained.

(2) In deciding whether to exercise its powers under paragraph 1 against a person who is not the mother or father of the child, and if so in what manner, the court shall in addition have regard to—

(a) whether that person has assumed responsibility for the maintenance of the child and, if so, the extent to which and basis on which he assumed that responsibility and the length of the period during which he met that responsibility;

(b) whether he did so knowing that the child was not his child;

(c) the liability of any other person to maintain the child.

(3) Where the court makes an order under paragraph 1 against a person who is not the father of the child, it shall record in the order that the order is made on the basis that the person against whom the order is made is not the child's father.

(4) The persons mentioned in sub-paragraph (1) are—

(a) in relation to a decision whether to exercise its powers under paragraph 1, any parent of the child;

(b) in relation to a decision whether to exercise its powers under paragraph 2, the mother and father of the child;

(c) the applicant for the order;

(d) any other person in whose favour the court proposes to make the order.

**Appointment**

Commencement order: SI 1991/828.



## [2.420.1]
### Keypoints

- Similarity to s 25(3) of the MCA 1973
- Welfare not paramount
- Child's needs and mother's services
- Interests of child under discretionary trust

## [2.420.2]
### Similarity to s 25(3) of the MCA 1973

These provisions are similar to those in s 25(3) of the MCA 1973.

## [2.420.3]
### Welfare not paramount

When considering an application for financial relief the welfare of the child is not the paramount consideration. However, the welfare for the child is a relevant consideration. No great significance attaches to the issue of whether a pregnancy was planned. A child is entitled to be brought up in circumstances which bear some sort of relationship with the father's current resources and the father's present standard of living; the fact that wealth was acquired after the relationship ended does not affect that entitlement. As a matter of public policy, where resources allow, the obligation towards a family should be respected in such a way as to reduce or eliminate the need for a child to be supported by public funds. Whilst a father may not be responsible for the child's half-siblings, a child may have a need to live with them and their mother[1].

1 See *J v C (Financial Provision)* [1998] 3 FCR 79, [1999] 1 FLR 152 (father won £1.4m on the lottery). See also *A v A* [1995] 1 FCR 309, [1994] 1 FLR 657 (need for child to live with half-siblings); and *R v R* [1988] FCR 307, [1988] 1 FLR 89 (parents duty to orgainse financial affairs so as to meet parental responsibility).

**[2.420.4]**
**Child's needs and mother's services**

Child's needs can include value of mother's services:

> '… The financial needs of the child. She has a financial need to be able to remunerate the full-time staff that would have to be employed to look after her, 24 hours a day. Her mother does this for nothing. It is now well established that the amount of maintenance for the child can include an allowance for the mother …'[1].

1 See *A v A* [1995] 1 FCR 309, [1994] 1 FLR 657, explaining *Haroutunian v Jennings* (1977) 1 FLR 62.

**[2.420.5]**
**Interests of child under discretionary trust**

The court should take into account a child's interest under a discretionary trust but should not assume that all of the income from that interest should be available to provide for the child's immediate maintenance[1].

1 See *J v J (C intervening)* [1989] Fam 29, [1989] 1 All ER 1121 CA.

**[2.421]**

*Provisions relating to lump sums*

**5**

(1) Without prejudice to the generality of paragraph 1, an order under that paragraph for the payment of a lump sum may be made for the purpose of enabling any liabilities or expenses—

(a) incurred in connection with the birth of the child or in maintaining the child; and

(b) reasonably incurred before the making of the order,

to be met.

(2) The amount of any lump sum required to be paid by an order made by a magistrates' court under paragraph 1 or 2 shall not exceed £1000 or such larger amount as the [Lord Chancellor] may from time to time by order fix for the purposes of this sub-paragraph.

(3) The power of the court under paragraph 1 or 2 to vary or discharge an order for the making or securing of periodical payments by a parent shall include power to make an order under that provision for the payment of a lump sum by that parent.

(4) The amount of any lump sum which a person may be required to pay by virtue of sub-paragraph (3) shall not, in the case of an order made by a magistrates' court, exceed the maximum amount that may at the time of the making of the order be required to be paid under sub-paragraph (2), but a magistrates' court may make an order for the payment of a lump sum not exceeding that amount even though the parent was required to pay a lump sum by a previous order under this Act.

(5) An order made under paragraph 1 or 2 for the payment of a lump sum may provide for the payment of that sum by instalments.

(6) Where the court provides for the payment of a lump sum by instalments the court, on an application made either by the person liable to pay or the person entitled to receive that sum, shall have power to vary that order by varying—

(a) the number of instalments payable;
(b) the amount of any instalment payable;
(c) the date on which any instalment becomes payable.

**Appointment**
Commencement order: SI 1991/828.

**Amendment**
Para 5: words in square brackets in sub-para (2) substituted by SI 1992/709, art 3(2), Sch 2.



## [2.421.1]
### Keypoint

- Lump sums and reasons

## [2.421.2]
### Lump sums and reason

Where the court is considering the making of a lump sum order, the parties should be given an opportunity to make representations on whether such an order is appropriate. The court must make findings of fact to support its conclusions[1].

1 See *Re C* [1995] 1 FLR 925, [1995] Fam Law 409.

## [2.422]

*Variation etc of orders for periodical payments*

**6**

(1) In exercising its powers under paragraph 1 or 2 to vary or discharge an order for the making or securing of periodical payments the court shall have regard to all the circumstances of the case, including any change in any of the matters to which the court was required to have regard when making the order.

(2) The power of the court under paragraph 1 or 2 to vary an order for the making or securing of periodical payments shall include power to suspend any provision of the order temporarily and to revive any provision so suspended.

(3) Where on an application under paragraph 1 or 2 for the variation or discharge of an order for the making or securing of periodical payments the court varies the payments required to be made under that order, the court may provide that the payments as so varied shall be made from such date as the court may specify, [except that, subject to sub-paragraph (9), the date shall not be] earlier than the date of the making of the application.

(4) An application for the variation of an order made under paragraph 1 for the making or securing of periodical payments to or for the benefit of a child may, if the child has reached the age of sixteen, be made by the child himself.

(5) Where an order for the making or securing of periodical payments made under paragraph 1 ceases to have effect on the date on which the child reaches the age of sixteen, or at any time after that date but before or on the date on which he reaches the age of eighteen, the child may apply to the court which made the order for an order for its revival.

(6) If on such an application it appears to the court that—

(a) the child is, will be or (if an order were made under this sub-paragraph) would be receiving instruction at an educational establishment or undergoing training for a trade, profession or vocation, whether or not while in gainful employment; or

(b) there are special circumstances which justify the making of an order under this paragraph, the court shall have power by order to revive the order from such date as the court may specify, not being earlier than the date of the making of the application.

(7) Any order which is revived by an order under sub-paragraph (5) may be varied or discharged under that provision, on the application of any person by whom or to whom payments are required to be made under the revived order.

(8) An order for the making or securing of periodical payments made under paragraph 1 may be varied or discharged, after the death of either parent, on the application of a guardian of the child concerned.

[(9) Where—

(a) an order under paragraph 1(2)(a) or (b) for the making or securing of periodical payments in favour of more than one child ('the order') is in force;

(b) the order requires payments specified in it to be made to or for the benefit of more than one child without apportioning those payments between them;

(c) a maintenance assessment ('the assessment') is made with respect to one or more, but not all, of the children with respect to whom those payments are to be made; and

(d) an application is made, before the end of the period of 6 months beginning with the date on which the assessment was made, for the variation or discharge of the order,

the court may, in exercise of its powers under paragraph 1 to vary or discharge the order, direct that the variation or discharge shall take effect from the date on which the assessment took effect or any later date.]

**Appointment**

Commencement order: SI 1991/828.

**Amendment**

Para 6: in sub-para (3) words in square brackets substituted and sub-para (9) inserted by SI 1993/623, art 2, Sch 1, paras 12, 13.

## [2.422.1]
**Keypoint**

- Variation of order made under the Guardianship of Minors Act 1971

## [2.422.2]
**Variation of order made under the Guardianship of Minors Act 1971**

The court may discharge or vary an order made under the Guardianship of Minors Act 1971, notwithstanding the repeal of that Act by the ChA 1989[1].

1 See *B v B (Minors) (periodical payments)* [1995] 1 WLR 440, [1995] 1 FCR 763.

## [2.423]

*[Variation of orders for periodical payments etc made by magistrates' courts*

**6A**

(1) Subject to sub-paragraphs (7) and (8), the power of a magistrates' court—

(a) under paragraph 1 or 2 to vary an order for the making of periodical payments, or

(b) under paragraph 5(6) to vary an order for the payment of a lump sum by instalments,

shall include power, if the court is satisfied that payment has not been made in accordance with the order, to exercise one of its powers under paragraphs (a) to (d) of section 59(3) of the Magistrates' Courts Act 1980.

(2) In any case where—

(a) a magistrates' court has made an order under this Schedule for the making of periodical payments or for the payment of a lump sum by instalments, and

(b) payments under the order are required to be made by any method of payment falling within section 59(6) of the Magistrates' Courts Act 1980 (standing order, etc),

any person entitled to make an application under this Schedule for the variation of the order (in this paragraph referred to as 'the applicant') may apply to the clerk to the justices for the petty sessions area for which the court is acting for the order to be varied as mentioned in sub-paragraph (3).

(3) Subject to sub-paragraph (5), where an application is made under sub-paragraph (2), the clerk, after giving written notice (by post or otherwise) of the application to any interested party and allowing that party, within the period of 14 days beginning with the date of the giving of that notice, an opportunity to make written representations, may vary the order to provide that payments under the order shall be made [to the justices' chief executive for the court].

(4) The clerk may proceed with an application under sub-paragraph (2) notwithstanding that any such interested party as is referred to in sub-paragraph (3) has not received written notice of the application.

(5) Where an application has been made under sub-paragraph (2), the clerk may, if he considers it inappropriate to exercise his power under sub-paragraph (3), refer the matter to the court which, subject to sub-paragraphs (7) and (8), may vary the order by exercising one of its powers under paragraphs (a) to (d) of section 59(3) of the Magistrates' Courts Act 1980.

(6) Subsection (4) of section 59 of the Magistrates' Courts Act 1980 (power of court to order that account be opened) shall apply for the purposes of sub-paragraphs (1) and (5) as it applies for the purposes of that section.

(7) Before varying the order by exercising one of its powers under paragraphs (a) to (d) of section 59(3) of the Magistrates' Courts Act 1980, the court shall have regard to any representations made by the parties to the application.

(8) If the court does not propose to exercise its power [under paragraph (c), (cc) or (d)] of subsection (3) of section 59 of the Magistrates' Courts Act 1980, the court shall, unless upon representations expressly made in that behalf by the applicant for the order it is satisfied that it is undesirable to do so, exercise its power under paragraph (b) of that subsection.

(9) None of the powers of the court, or of the clerk to the justices, conferred by this paragraph shall be exercisable in relation to an order under this Schedule for the making of periodical payments, or for the payment of a lump sum by instalments, which is not a qualifying maintenance order (within the meaning of section 59 of the Magistrates' Courts Act 1980).

(10) In sub-paragraphs (3) and (4) 'interested party', in relation to an application made by the applicant under sub-paragraph (2), means a person who would be entitled to be a party to an application for the variation of the order made by the applicant under any other provision of this Schedule if such an application were made.]

**Amendment**

Para 6A: inserted by the MEA 1991, s 6. Para 6A: SI 1994/731; AJA 1999, s 90(1), Sch 13.

### *Variation of orders for secured periodical payments after death of parent*

**7**

(1) Where the parent liable to make payments under a secured periodical payments order has died, the persons who may apply for the variation or discharge of the order shall include the personal representatives of the deceased parent.

(2) No application for the variation of the order shall, except with the permission of the court, be made after the end of the period of six months from the date on which representation in regard to the estate of that parent is first taken out.

(3) The personal representatives of a deceased person against whom a secured periodical payments order was made shall not be liable for having distributed any part of the estate of the deceased after the end of the period of six months referred to in sub-paragraph (2) on the ground that they ought to have taken into account the possibility that the court might permit an application for variation to be made after that period by the person entitled to payments under the order.

(4) Sub-paragraph (3) shall not prejudice any power to recover any part of the estate so distributed arising by virtue of the variation of an order in accordance with this paragraph.

(5) Where an application to vary a secured periodical payments order is made after the death of the parent liable to make payments under the order, the circumstances to which the court is required to have regard under paragraph 6(1) shall include the changed circumstances resulting from the death of the parent.

(6) In considering for the purposes of sub-paragraph (2) the question when representation was first taken out, a grant limited to settled land or to trust property shall be left out of account and a grant limited to real estate or to personal estate shall be left out of account unless a grant limited to the remainder of the estate has previously been made or is made at the same time.

(7) In this paragraph 'secured periodical payments order' means an order for secured periodical payments under paragraph 1(2)(b).

### *Financial relief under other enactments*

**8**

(1) This paragraph applies where a residence order is made with respect to a child at a time when there is in force an order ('the financial relief order') made under any enactment other than this Act and requiring a person to contribute to the child's maintenance.

(2) Where this paragraph applies, the court may, on the application of—

(a) any person required by the financial relief order to contribute to the child's maintenance; or

(b) any person in whose favour a residence order with respect to the child is in force,

make an order revoking the financial relief order, or varying it by altering the amount of any sum payable under the order or by substituting the applicant for the person to whom any such sum is otherwise payable under that order.

### *Interim orders*

**9**

(1) Where an application is made under paragraph 1 or 2 the court may, at any time before it disposes of the application, make an interim order—

(a) requiring either or both parents to make such periodical payments, at such times and for such term as the court thinks fit; and

(b) giving any direction which the court thinks fit.

(2) An interim order made under this paragraph may provide for payments to be made from such date as the court may specify, [except that, subject to paragraph 3(5) and (6), the date shall not be] earlier than the date of the making of the application under paragraph 1 or 2.

(3) An interim order made under this paragraph shall cease to have effect when the application is disposed of or, if earlier, on the date specified for the purposes of this paragraph in the interim order.

(4) An interim order in which a date has been specified for the purposes of sub-paragraph (3) may be varied by substituting a later date.

**Amendment**

Para 9: in sub-para (2) words in square brackets substituted by SI 1993/623, art 2, Sch 1, para 14.

*Alteration of maintenance agreements*

**10**

(1) In this paragraph and in paragraph 11 'maintenance agreement' means any agreement in writing made with respect to a child, whether before or after the commencement of this paragraph, which—

(a) is or was made between the father and mother of the child; and

(b) contains provision with respect to the making or securing of payments, or the disposition or use of any property, for the maintenance or education of the child,

and any such provisions are in this paragraph, and paragraph 11, referred to as 'financial arrangements'.

(2) Where a maintenance agreement is for the time being subsisting and each of the parties to the agreement is for the time being either domiciled or resident in England and Wales, then, either party may apply to the court for an order under this paragraph.

(3) If the court to which the application is made is satisfied either—

(a) that, by reason of a change in the circumstances in the light of which any financial arrangements contained in the agreement were made (including a change foreseen by the parties when making the agreement), the agreement should be altered so as to make different financial arrangements; or

(b) that the agreement does not contain proper financial arrangements with respect to the child,

then that court may by order make such alterations in the agreement by varying or revoking any financial arrangements contained in it as may appear to it to be just having regard to all the circumstances.

(4) If the maintenance agreement is altered by an order under this paragraph, the agreement shall have effect thereafter as if the alteration had been made by agreement between the parties and for valuable consideration.

(5) Where a court decides to make an order under this paragraph altering the maintenance agreement—

(a) by inserting provision for the making or securing by one of the parties to the agreement of periodical payments for the maintenance of the child; or

(b) by increasing the rate of periodical payments required to be made or secured by one of the parties for the maintenance of the child,

then, in deciding the term for which under the agreement as altered by the order the payments or (as the case may be) the additional payments attributable to the increase are to be made or secured for the benefit of the child, the court shall apply the provisions of sub-paragraphs (1) and (2) of paragraph 3 as if the order were an order under paragraph 1(2)(a) or (b).

(6) A magistrates' court shall not entertain an application under sub-paragraph (2) unless both the parties to the agreement are resident in England and Wales and at least one of the parties is resident in the commission area … for which the court is appointed, and shall not have power to make any order on such an application except—

(a) in a case where the agreement contains no provision for periodical payments by either of the parties, an order inserting provision for the making by one of the parties of periodical payments for the maintenance of the child;

(b) in a case where the agreement includes provision for the making by one of the parties of periodical payments, an order increasing or reducing the rate of, or terminating, any of those payments.

(7) For the avoidance of doubt it is hereby declared that nothing in this paragraph affects any power of a court before which any proceedings between the parties to a maintenance agreement are brought under any other enactment to make an order containing financial arrangements or any right of either party to apply for such an order in such proceedings.

**Amendment**

Para 10: in sub-para (6) words omitted repealed by the AJA 1999, s 106, Sch 15, Pt V, Table (1). Date in force: 27 September 1999: see the AJA 1999, s 108(3)(f).

**11**

(1) Where a maintenance agreement provides for the continuation, after the death of one of the parties, of payments for the maintenance of a child and that party dies domiciled in England and Wales, the surviving party or the personal representatives of the deceased party may apply to the High Court or a county court for an order under paragraph 10.

(2) If a maintenance agreement is altered by a court on an application under this paragraph, the agreement shall have effect thereafter as if the alteration had been made, immediately before the death, by agreement between the parties and for valuable consideration.

(3) An application under this paragraph shall not, except with leave of the High Court or a county court, be made after the end of the period of six months beginning with the day on which representation in regard to the estate of the deceased is first taken out.

(4) In considering for the purposes of sub-paragraph (3) the question when representation was first taken out, a grant limited to settled land or to trust property shall be left out of account and a grant limited to real estate or to personal estate shall be left out of account unless a grant limited to the remainder of the estate has previously been made or is made at the same time.

(5) A county court shall not entertain an application under this paragraph, or an application for leave to make an application under this paragraph, unless it would have jurisdiction to hear and determine proceedings for an order under section 2 of the Inheritance (Provision for Family and Dependants) Act 1975 in relation to the deceased's estate by virtue of section 25 of the County Courts Act 1984 (jurisdiction under the Act of 1975).

(6) The provisions of this paragraph shall not render the personal representatives of the deceased liable for having distributed any part of the estate of the deceased after the expiry of the period of six months referred to in sub-paragraph (3) on the ground that they ought to have taken into account the possibility that a court might grant leave for an application by virtue of this paragraph to be made by the surviving party after that period.

(7) Sub-paragraph (6) shall not prejudice any power to recover any part of the estate so distributed arising by virtue of the making of an order in pursuance of this paragraph.

**Appointment**
Commencement order: SI 1991/828.

**[2.423.1]**
**Keypoint**

- Introduction

**[2.423.2]**
**Introduction**

The provisions of paras 10 and 11 were originally introduced under s 15 of the FLRA 1987 and are similar to s 35 of the MCA 1973.

**[2.424]**

*Enforcement of orders for maintenance*

**12**

(1) Any person for the time being under an obligation to make payments in pursuance of any order for the payment of money made by a magistrates' court under this Act shall give notice of any change of address to such person (if any) as may be specified in the order.

(2) Any person failing without reasonable excuse to give such a notice shall be guilty of an offence and liable on summary conviction to a fine not exceeding level 2 on the standard scale.

(3) An order for the payment of money made by a magistrates' court under this Act shall be enforceable as a magistrates' court maintenance order within the meaning of section 150(1) of the Magistrates' Courts Act 1980.

*Direction for settlement of instrument by conveyancing counsel*

**13**

Where the High Court or a county court decides to make an order under this Act for the securing of periodical payments or for the transfer or settlement of property, it may direct that the matter be referred to one of the conveyancing counsel of the court to settle a proper instrument to be executed by all necessary parties.



*Financial provision for child resident in country outside England and Wales*

**14**

(1) Where one parent of a child lives in England and Wales and the child lives outside England and Wales with—

(a) another parent of his;

(b) a guardian of his; or

(c) a person in whose favour a residence order is in force with respect to the child,

the court shall have power, on an application made by any of the persons mentioned in paragraphs (a) to (c), to make one or both of the orders mentioned in paragraph 1(2)(a) and (b) against the parent living in England and Wales.

(2) Any reference in this Act to the powers of the court under paragraph 1(2) or to an order made under paragraph 1(2) shall include a reference to the powers which the court has by virtue of sub-paragraph (1) or (as the case may be) to an order made by virtue of sub-paragraph (1).

*Local authority contribution to child's maintenance*

**15**

(1) Where a child lives, or is to live, with a person as the result of a residence order, a local authority may make contributions to that person towards the cost of the accommodation and maintenance of the child.

(2) Sub-paragraph (1) does not apply where the person with whom the child lives, or is to live, is a parent of the child or the husband or wife of a parent of the child.

*Interpretation*

**16**

(1) In this Schedule 'child' includes, in any case where an application is made under paragraph 2 or 6 in relation to a person who has reached the age of eighteen, that person.

(2) In this Schedule, except paragraphs 2 and 15, 'parent' includes any party to a marriage (whether or not subsisting) in relation to whom the child concerned is a child of the family; and for this purpose any reference to either parent or both parents shall be construed as references to any parent of his and to all of his parents.

[(3) In this Schedule, 'maintenance assessment' has the same meaning as it has in the Child Support Act 1991 by virtue of section 54 of that Act as read with any regulations in force under that section.]

**Appointment**

Commencement order: SI 1991/828.

**Amendment**

Para 16: sub-para (3) inserted by SI 1993/623, art 2, Sch 1, para 15.

# Child Support Act 1991



## Contents



*An Act to make provision for the assessment, collection and enforcement of periodical maintenance payable by certain parents with respect to children of theirs who are not in their care; for the collection and enforcement of certain other kinds of maintenance; and for connected purposes*

[25th July 1991]

### [2.425A]
### Child Support, Pensions and Social Security Act 2000

The Child Support, Pensions and Social Security Act 2000 received Royal Assent on 28 July 2000. This provides for a number of significant amendments to the Child Support Act 1991 (CSA 1991). In particular:

- it simplifies the way the child support liability is calculated;
- it strengthens the sanctions to improve compliance;
- it makes alterations to the provisions relating to paternity;

- it makes alterations to the relationship between court orders and the child support system.

Further, the new Act introduces some terminological changes, for example, 'absent parents' become 'non-resident parents' and 'maintenance assessments' become 'maintenance calculations'. The strengthening of the sanctions on compliance are dealt with in the notes on ss 39A, 40 and 40B below[1]. The alteration to the provisions relating to paternity is dealt with in s 26 and the commentary thereto below[2]. It is thought that the alterations to the formula and to the relationship between court orders and the child support system will not come into force until April 2002. Taking the matter very broadly, the new formula will provide that the non-resident parent pays a percentage of his income (net of tax and payments towards pension provision) towards the maintenance of qualifying children. The percentage is 15% where there is one child, 20% where there are two children, and 25% where there are three or more absent children. The amount payable will be discounted according to how many nights the child(ren) spend with the non-resident parent: if the child(ren) spend 52–103 nights per year with the non-resident parent (an average of 1–2 nights per week – but remember holidays) the discount is 1/7, 104–105 nights per year (2–3 nights per week) the discount is 2/7, 156–174 nights per year the discount is 3/7 and over 175 nights per year the discount is 50%. Any net income in excess of £2,000 per week is ignored. Unlike under the current provisions where a court order for child maintenance will prevent the agency having jurisdiction unless the parent with care is in receipt of specified benefits, court orders for child maintenance entered into after 'the prescribed date' (a date expected to be the same as the date when the new provisions come into force) will only prevent applications to the agency for a period of one year. Court orders entered into before 'the prescribed date' will continue to prevent application to the agency under s 4[3].

1 See paras **[2.440A]**, **[2.441]** and **[2.441A]** respectively.
2 See para **[2.432]** below.
3 See s 2 of the Child Support, Pensions and Social Security Act 2000, which amends s 4 of the CSA 1991.

## [2.425]

### 3 Meaning of certain terms used in this Act

(1) A child is a 'qualifying child' if—

(a) one of his parents is, in relation to him, an absent parent; or

(b) both of his parents are, in relation to him, absent parents.

(2) The parent of any child is *an 'absent parent'* [a 'non-resident parent'], in relation to him, if—

(a) that parent is not living in the same household with the child; and

(b) the child has his home with a person who is, in relation to him, a person with care.

(3) A person is a 'person with care', in relation to any child, if he is a person—

(a) with whom the child has his home;

(b) who usually provides day to day care for the child (whether exclusively or in conjunction with any other person); and

(c) who does not fall within a prescribed category of person.

(4) The Secretary of State shall not, under subsection (3)(c), prescribe as a category—

(a) parents;

(b) guardians;

(c) persons in whose favour residence orders under section 8 of the Children Act 1989 are in force;

(d) in Scotland, persons [with whom a child is to live by virtue of a residence order under section 11 of the Children (Scotland) Act 1995.]

(5) For the purposes of this Act there may be more than one person with care in relation to the same qualifying child.

(6) Periodical payments which are required to be paid in accordance with a maintenance assessment are referred to in this Act as 'child support maintenance'.

(7) Expressions are defined in this section only for the purposes of this Act.

**Appointment**

Commencement orders: SI 1992/1431, SI 1992/2644.

**Amendment**

Sub-s (2): words in italics repealed and subsequent words in square brackets substituted by the Child Support, Pensions and Social Security Act 2000, s 26, Sch 3. Date in force (for certain purposes): 31 January 2001: see SI 2000/3354. Date in force (for remaining purposes): to be appointed. Sub-s (4): in para (d) words in square brackets substituted by the C(S)A 1995, s 105(4), Sch 4, para 52(2).

**Definitions**

See generally, ss 54 and 55 of the CSA 1991 at paras **[2.449]** and **[2.450]** below.



## [2.425.1]
### Keypoints

- Effect of section
- Persons prescribed from being a person with care

## [2.425.2]
### Effect of section

This section defines some of the main terms of the Act. The section is supplemented by ss 54 and 55[1] which further refine the definitions. In particular, the definition of 'parent' will extend to adoptive parents since, under s 54 a parent is 'any person who is in law the mother or father of the child'. Disputes about parentage are governed by ss 26 and 27 of the CSA 1991[2].

Definitions of 'home' and 'day to day care' are to be found in reg 2 of the Child Support (Maintenance Assessment and Special Cases) Regulations 1992, SI 1992/1815. The statutory framework provides no further assistance in relation to 'household'. By s 5(1) where more than one person has care of the child only those who have parental responsibility may apply for a maintenance assessment. Where people living in separate households are both entitled to apply for a maintenance assessment the case may fall to be dealt with under reg 24 of the Child Support (Maintenance Assessment and Special Cases) Regulations 1992.

The Child Support (Maintenance Assessment and Special Cases) Regulations 1992 are to be revoked and replaced by the Child Support (Maintenance Calculation and Special Cases) Regulations 2000, SI 2001/155 on a date to be appointed. The definitions are to be found at reg 1, and the provisions previously dealt with in reg 24 are to be found in the new legislation at reg 14.

1 See paras **[2.449]**, **[2.450]** below.
2 See paras **[2.432]**, **[2.433]** below.

## [2.425.3]
### Persons prescribed from being a person with care

The Child Support (Maintenance Assessment Procedure) Regulations 1992, SI 1992/1813 prescribe local authorities and foster parents (under s 22 of the ChA 1989) from being persons with care.

## [2.426]

### 4 Child support maintenance

(1) A person who is, in relation to any qualifying child or any qualifying children, either the person with care or the absent parent may apply to the Secretary of State for a

maintenance assessment to be made under this Act with respect to that child, or any of those children.

(2) Where a maintenance assessment has been made in response to an application under this section the Secretary of State may, if the person with care or absent parent with respect to whom the assessment was made applies to him under this subsection, arrange for—

(a) the collection of the child support maintenance payable in accordance with the assessment;

(b) the enforcement of the obligation to pay child support maintenance in accordance with the assessment.

(3) Where an application under subsection (2) for the enforcement of the obligation mentioned in subsection (2)(b) authorises the Secretary of State to take steps to enforce that obligation whenever he considers it necessary to do so, the Secretary of State may act accordingly.

(4) A person who applies to the Secretary of State under this section shall, so far as that person reasonably can, comply with such regulations as may be made by the Secretary of State with a view to the Secretary of State ... being provided with the information which is required to enable—

(a) the absent parent to be traced (where that is necessary);

(b) the amount of child support maintenance payable by the absent parent to be assessed; and

(c) that amount to be recovered from the absent parent.

(5) Any person who has applied to the Secretary of State under this section may at any time request him to cease acting under this section.

(6) It shall be the duty of the Secretary of State to comply with any request made under subsection (5) (but subject to any regulations made under subsection (8)).

(7) The obligation to provide information which is imposed by subsection (4)—

(a) shall not apply in such circumstances as may be prescribed; and

(b) may, in such circumstances as may be prescribed, be waived by the Secretary of State.

(8) The Secretary of State may by regulations make such incidental, supplemental or transitional provision as he thinks appropriate with respect to cases in which he is requested to cease to act under this section.

(9) No application may be made under this section if there is in force with respect to the person with care and absent parent in question a maintenance assessment made in response to an application under section 6.

[(10) No application may be made at any time under this section with respect to a qualifying child or any qualifying children if—

(a) there is in force a written maintenance agreement made before 5th April 1993, or a maintenance order, in respect of that child or those children and the person who is, at that time, the absent parent; or

(b) benefit is being paid to, or in respect of, a parent with care of that child or those children.

(11) In subsection (10) 'benefit' means any benefit which is mentioned in, or prescribed by regulations under, section 6(1).]

**Appointment**

Commencement orders: SI 1992/1431, SI 1992/2644.

**Amendment**

Sub-s (4): words omitted repealed by the SSA 1998, s 86(1), (2), Sch 7, para 19, Sch 8. Date in force: 1 June 1999: see SI 1999/1510, art 2(e)–(g). Sub-ss (10), (11): inserted by the CSA 1995, s 18(1).

**Definitions**

'qualifying child'; 'person with care'; and 'absent parent' — see s 3 at para **[2.425]** above.
'Maintenance order' – see s 8(11) at para **[2.4298]** below.
'maintenance agreement' – see s 9(1) at para **[2.429]** below.
See further s 54 (interpretation) and s 55 (meaning of 'child') at paras **[2.449]** and **[2.450]** below.

**[2.426.1]**
**Keypoints**

- Applications
- Limitations on who can apply
- Maintenance agreement or order

**[2.426.2]**
**Applications**

Applications under this section may be made by either the absent parent or the person with care. There is no obligation on either to make an application and the Secretary of State is obliged to cease making an assessment where an applicant asks him to do so. An assessment may be cancelled by the person in whose favour it was made[1].

1 See the CSA 1991, Sch 1, para 16(2).



**[2.426.3]**
**Limitations on who can apply**

Sub-s (10), as amended by the CSA 1995, establishes that where there is a maintenance agreement entered into before 5 April 1993 or a maintenance order, or the person with care is in receipt of certain prescribed benefits, there can be no application under this section. Where the person with care is in receipt of the prescribed benefits the person with care must apply under s 6[1]. Applications under s 6 are not barred by agreement or order.

Note that when the relevant provisions of the Child Support, Pensions and Social Security Act 2000 are brought into force there shall be a modification to sub-s (10) and a new sub-s (10)(aa) which together provide that maintenance orders made after a prescribed date (thought to be the date when the act comes into force) will only prevent applications to the agency for one year. It is not apparent from this subsection whether the date a maintenance order is said to be made is the date when it was first made or the date of any subsequent variation.

1 See para **[2.427]** below.

**[2.426.4]**
**Maintenance agreement or order**

A lump sum ordered in respect of child maintenance does not constitute a maintenance order, or agreement for the purposes of the Act[1].

1 See *AMS v Child Support Officer* [1998] 2 FCR 622, [1998] 1 FLR 955, CA.

**[2.427]**

**6 Applications by those receiving benefit**

(1) Where income support, [an income-based jobseeker's allowance] … or any other benefit of a prescribed kind is claimed by or in respect of, or paid to or in respect of, the parent of a qualifying child she shall, if—

(a) she is a person with care of the child; and
(b) she is required to do so by the Secretary of State,

authorise the Secretary of State to take action under this Act to recover child support maintenance from the absent parent.

(2) The Secretary of State shall not require a person ('the parent') to give him the authorisation mentioned in subsection (1) if he considers that there are reasonable grounds for believing that—

(a) if the parent were to be required to give that authorisation; or
(b) if she were to give it,

there would be a risk of her, or of any child living with her, suffering harm or undue distress as a result.

(3) Subsection (2) shall not apply if the parent requests the Secretary of State to disregard it.

(4) The authorisation mentioned in subsection (1) shall extend to all children of the absent parent in relation to whom the parent first mentioned in subsection (1) is a person with care.

(5) That authorisation shall be given, without unreasonable delay, by completing and returning to the Secretary of State an application—

(a) for the making of a maintenance assessment with respect to the qualifying child or qualifying children; and

(b) for the Secretary of State to take action under this Act to recover, on her behalf, the amount of child support maintenance so assessed.

(6) Such an application shall be made on a form ('a maintenance application form') provided by the Secretary of State.

(7) A maintenance application form shall indicate in general terms the effect of completing and returning it.

(8) Subsection (1) has effect regardless of whether any of the benefits mentioned there is payable with respect to any qualifying child.

(9) A person who is under the duty imposed by subsection (1) shall, so far as she reasonably can, comply with such regulations as may be made by the Secretary of State with a view to the Secretary of State … being provided with the information which is required to enable—

(a) the absent parent to be traced;

(b) the amount of child support maintenance payable by the absent parent to be assessed; and

(c) that amount to be recovered from the absent parent.

(10) The obligation to provide information which is imposed by subsection (9)—

(a) shall not apply in such circumstances as may be prescribed; and

(b) may, in such circumstances as may be prescribed, be waived by the Secretary of State.

(11) A person with care who has authorised the Secretary of State under subsection (1) but who subsequently ceases to fall within that subsection may request the Secretary of State to cease acting under this section.

(12) It shall be the duty of the Secretary of State to comply with any request made under subsection (11) (but subject to any regulations made under subsection (13)).

(13) The Secretary of State may by regulations make such incidental or transitional provision as he thinks appropriate with respect to cases in which he is requested under subsection (11) to cease to act under this section.

(14) The fact that a maintenance assessment is in force with respect to a person with care shall not prevent the making of a new maintenance assessment with respect to her in response to an application under this section.

**Appointment**

Commencement orders: SI 1992/1431, SI 1992/2644.

**Amendment**

Sub-s (1): words 'an income-based jobseeker's allowance' in square brackets inserted by the JA 1995, s 41(4), Sch 2, para 20(2). Words omitted repealed by the TCA 1999, s 2, Sch 2, Pt IV, para 17(a), Sch 6. Date in force: 5 October 1999: see the TCA 1999, s 20(2). Sub-s (9): words omitted repealed by the SSA 1998, s 86(1), (2), Sch 7, para 20, Sch 8. Date in force: 1 June 1999: see SI 1999/1510, art 2(e)–(g).

**Definitions**

'Person with care'; and 'absent parent' – see s 3 at para **[2.425]** above.

### [2.427.1]
### Keypoints

- Prescribed benefits
- Obligatory application
- Maintenance agreement or order no bar
- Entitlement to benefit
- Risk of harm or undue distress

### [2.427.2]
### Prescribed benefits

These are income support, income-based job-seeker's allowance, and disability working allowance. Family credit was a prescribed benefit. However, family credit has been replaced by working families' tax credit (the tax credit is not a prescribed benefit).

### [2.427.3]
### Obligatory application

The Secretary of State may require a person with care who is the parent of a qualifying child and who is in receipt of a prescribed benefit to authorise him to make an application on her behalf, save if the grounds made out in s 6(2) apply. If the person with care fails to give such authorisation they may be subject to a reduced benefit direction under s 46. If the person with care ceases to receive a prescribed benefit they may by virtue of sub-ss 11 and 12 require the Secretary of State to cease acting.

### [2.427.4]
### Maintenance agreement or order no bar

Unlike s 4 applications the existence of a maintenance agreement made before 5 April 1993 or a maintenance order is no bar to an application under s 6.

### [2.427.5]
### Entitlement to benefit

It was held in *Secretary of State for Social Security v Harmon*[1] that it was not necessary to determine whether the benefit in question was being lawfully paid, only whether it was actually being paid.

1 [1999] 1 WLR 163, [1999] 1 FCR 213, CA.

### [2.427.6]
### Risk of harm or undue distress

The Secretary of State is not obliged to consult the absent parent when considering the matters set out in s 6(2)[1]. Subsection (3) (perhaps redundantly) allows the person with care to disapply the provisions of sub-s (2).

1 See *R v Secretary of State for Social Security, ex p Lloyd* [1995] 3 FCR 97, [1995] 1 FLR 856.

### [2.428]

#### 8 Role of the courts with respect to maintenance for children

(1) This subsection applies in any case where [the Secretary of State] would have jurisdiction to make a maintenance assessment with respect to a qualifying child and an absent parent of his on an application duly made by a person entitled to apply for such an assessment with respect to that child.

(2) Subsection (1) applies even though the circumstances of the case are such that [the Secretary of State] would not make an assessment if it were applied for.

(3) In any case where subsection (1) applies, no court shall exercise any power which it would otherwise have to make, vary or revive any maintenance order in relation to the child and absent parent concerned.

[(3A) In any case in which section 4(10) or 7(10) prevents the making of an application for a maintenance assessment, and—

(a) no application has been made for a maintenance assessment under section 6, or

(b) such an application has been made but no maintenance assessment has been made in response to it,

subsection (3) shall have effect with the omission of the word 'vary'.]

(4) Subsection (3) does not prevent a court from revoking a maintenance order.

(5) The Lord Chancellor or in relation to Scotland the Lord Advocate may by order provide that, in such circumstances as may be specified by the order, this section shall not prevent a court from exercising any power which it has to make a maintenance order in relation to a child if—

(a) a written agreement (whether or not enforceable) provides for the making, or securing, by an absent parent of the child of periodical payments to or for the benefit of the child; and

(b) the maintenance order which the court makes is, in all material respects, in the same terms as that agreement.

(6) This section shall not prevent a court from exercising any power which it has to make a maintenance order in relation to a child if—

(a) a maintenance assessment is in force with respect to the child;

(b) the amount of the child support maintenance payable in accordance with the assessment was determined by reference to the alternative formula mentioned in paragraph 4(3) of Schedule 1; and

(c) the court is satisfied that the circumstances of the case make it appropriate for the absent parent to make or secure the making of periodical payments under a maintenance order in addition to the child support maintenance payable by him in accordance with the maintenance assessment.

(7) This section shall not prevent a court from exercising any power which it has to make a maintenance order in relation to a child if—

(a) the child is, will be or (if the order were to be made) would be receiving instruction at an educational establishment or undergoing training for a trade, profession or vocation (whether or not while in gainful employment); and

(b) the order is made solely for the purposes of requiring the person making or securing the making of periodical payments fixed by the order to meet some or all of the expenses incurred in connection with the provision of the instruction or training.

(8) This section shall not prevent a court from exercising any power which it has to make a maintenance order in relation to a child if—

(a) a disability living allowance is paid to or in respect of him; or

(b) no such allowance is paid but he is disabled,

and the order is made solely for the purpose of requiring the person making or securing the making of periodical payments fixed by the order to meet some or all of any expenses attributable to the child's disability.

(9) For the purposes of subsection (8), a child is disabled if he is blind, deaf or dumb or is substantially and permanently handicapped by illness, injury, mental disorder or congenital deformity or such other disability as may be prescribed.

(10) This section shall not prevent a court from exercising any power which it has to make a maintenance order in relation to a child if the order is made against a person with care of the child.

(11) In this Act 'maintenance order', in relation to any child, means an order which requires the making or securing of periodical payments to or for the benefit of the child and which is made under—

(a) Part II of the Matrimonial Causes Act 1973;

(b) the Domestic Proceedings and Magistrates' Courts Act 1978;
(c) Part III of the Matrimonial and Family Proceedings Act 1984;
(d) the Family Law (Scotland) Act 1985;
(e) Schedule 1 to the Children Act 1989; or
(f) any other prescribed enactment,

and includes any order varying or reviving such an order.

**Appointment**

Commencement orders: SI 1992/1431, SI 1992/2644.

**Amendment**

Sub-s (1): words 'the Secretary of State' in square brackets substituted by the SSA 1998, s 86(1), Sch 7, para 22. Date in force: 1 June 1999: see SI 1999/1510, art 2(e), (g). Sub-s (2): words 'the Secretary of State' in square brackets substituted by the SSA 1998, s 86(1), Sch 7, para 22. Date in force: 1 June 1999: see SI 1999/1510, art 2(e), (g). Sub-s (3A): inserted by the CSA 1995, s 18(3).

**Definitions**

'qualifying child'; 'person with care'; and 'absent parent' – see s 3 at para **[4.425]** above[1].
The 'alternative formula mentioned in paragraph 4(3) of Schedule 1' refers to the formula which applies in high income cases.

1 See further s 54 (interpretation) and s 55 (meaning of 'child') at paras **[2.449]** and **[2.450]** below.



## [2.428.1]
## Keypoints

- Effect of section
- Construction
- Power to vary
- Power to revoke
- Power to make an order where there is an agreement
- Top up orders
- School fee orders
- Orders for disabled children
- Order against person with care

## [2.428.2]
## Effect of section

This section sets out the limited circumstances in which the courts still have power to make an order for child maintenance.

## [2.428.3]
## Construction

This section needs to be read carefully. By s 8(1) to (3) the basic principle is established that where the Secretary of State has jurisdiction to make a maintenance assessment then the court shall not exercise its power to make, vary or revive a maintenance order[1]. Section 8(3A) to (10) then sets out the exceptions to the principle. Rules 10.24 and 10.25[2] of the FPR 1991 (as amended) give the court power to deal with applications for which it no longer has jurisdiction either on paper or by way of an ex parte hearing.

There is to be a new sub-s (3A) introduced by the Child Support Pensions and Social Security Act 2000 (on a date to be appointed). This introduces a modification in that where an order is made after a prescribed date (believed to be the date when the act comes into force) and there has been no subsequent maintenance calculation by the agency the court retains power to vary that order, even if the agency would also have power to make an calculation.

1 A practice has arisen of making a spousal maintenance order in ancillary relief proceedings that is automatically reduced pro tanto by any CSA assessment, thereby providing a global family budget (this type of order is often known as a Segal order). In *Dorney-Kingdom v Dorney-Kingdom* [2000] 3 FCR 20, the Court of Appeal determined that an essential prerequisite to such an order was a substantive entitlement to spousal maintenance, otherwise such an order would seem to be an attempt to circumvent the prohibitions in the CSA 1991.

2 See paras **[3.534]** and **[3.535]** below.

## [2.428.4]
### Power to vary

Section 4(10) (or s 7(10), which applies in Scotland) prohibits applications under s 4 for an assessment where there is a written maintenance agreement made before the 5 April 1993 or a court order. Where there is an extant order the court retains the power to vary it by sub-s (3A) (variation of agreements is dealt with in s 9), so long as either there has been no application under s 6 of the Act (benefit-application) or if there has been such an application there has been no assessment.

## [2.428.5]
### Power to revoke

This section does nothing to reduce the court's power to revoke maintenance orders. It has been held that the court should not revoke a maintenance order merely on the grounds that a party wishes to apply for a child support assessment[1].

1 *B v M (Child Support: Existing Child Maintenance Order)* [1994] 1 FCR 769, [1994] 1 FLR 342.

## [2.428.6]
### Power to make an order where there is an agreement

The Lord Chancellor has provided by order (the Child Maintenance (Written Agreements) Order 1993, SI 1993/620) that an order may be made in terms of a written maintenance agreement as provided for in s 8(5). The restriction on the court imposed by s 8(5)(b), that an order must reflect the terms of an agreement is nugatory because once the court has made an order it has power to vary it.

## [2.428.7]
### Top up orders

Section 8(6) allows the court to make a maintenance order to take effect in addition to a child support assessment if the amount of maintenance payable under the assessment has been determined by the alternative formula set out in para 4(3) of Sch 1. The alternative formula is used in high income cases to limit the amount payable under the child support assessment. It is commonly referred to as the maximum assessment, however, it should be remembered that it is not a fixed figure, and will depend upon the income of the person with care as well as the income of the absent parent.

Likewise, there is provision under the Child Support, Pensions and Social Security Act 2000 so that when that comes into force, if the non-resident parent's net weekly income exceeds £2,000 per week (or such other sum as is fixed by regulations as the maximum net weekly income to be taken into account in the child maintenance calculation) the court can make an order for additional child maintenance. The provision is made by a new sub-s (6)(b).

## [2.428.8]
### School fees orders

Section 8(7) allows the court to make a maintenance order to meet part or all of the expenses of providing a child with instruction or training.

## [2.428.9]
### Orders for disabled children

Section 8(8) allows the court to make a maintenance order where either disability allowance is paid to or for a child, or that child is disabled, within the meaning set out in s 8(9). In *C v F (disabled child: maintenance orders)*[1] it was held that in determining the level of maintenance to be ordered the focus should be on expenses attributable to the disability, but the focus should not be too narrow. That case is also authority for the proposition that the duration of a maintenance order made in addition to a child support assessment should be determined in accordance with the legislation under which the order is made, not the Act.

1 [1999] 1 FCR 39, [1998] 2 FLR 1.



## [2.428.10]
### Order against person with care

The child support system only provides for orders to be made against absent parents. The court retains the power to make a maintenance order against the person with care of the child.

## [2.429]

### 9 Agreements about maintenance

(1) In this section 'maintenance agreement' means any agreement for the making, or for securing the making, of periodical payments by way of maintenance, or in Scotland aliment, to or for the benefit of any child.

(2) Nothing in this Act shall be taken to prevent any person from entering into a maintenance agreement.

(3) [Subject to section 4(10)(a) and section 7(10),] the existence of a maintenance agreement shall not prevent any party to the agreement, or any other person, from applying for a maintenance assessment with respect to any child to or for whose benefit periodical payments are to be made or secured under the agreement.

(4) Where any agreement contains a provision which purports to restrict the right of any person to apply for a maintenance assessment, that provision shall be void.

(5) Where section 8 would prevent any court from making a maintenance order in relation to a child and an absent parent of his, no court shall exercise any power that it has to vary any agreement so as—

- (a) to insert a provision requiring that absent parent to make or secure the making of periodical payments by way of maintenance, or in Scotland aliment, to or for the benefit of that child; or
- (b) to increase the amount payable under such a provision.

[(6) In any case in which section 4(10) or 7(10) prevents the making of an application for a maintenance assessment, and—

- (a) no application has been made for a maintenance assessment under section 6, or
- (b) such an application has been made but no maintenance assessment has been made in response to it,

subsection (5) shall have effect with the omission of paragraph (b).]

**Appointment**
Commencement order: SI 1992/2644.

**Amendment**
Sub-s (3): words in square brackets inserted by the CSA 1995, s 18(4). Sub-s (6): inserted by the CSA 1995, s 18(4).

**Definitions**
'absent parent' – see s 3 at para **[2.425]** above.
'child' – see s 55 at para **[2.450]** below.

## [2.429.1]
### Keypoints

- Effect of section
- Effect of agreement on applications
- Jurisdiction of the court to vary agreement
- Agreement not to apply for a maintenance assessment

## [2.429.2]
### Effect of section

This section sets out the position of maintenance agreements in relation to child support, and the limited power retained by the court to vary maintenance agreements.

## [2.429.3]
### Effect of agreement on applications

Section 9(2) makes clear that people are free to enter into agreements with regard to child maintenance. However, unless the agreement is made before the 5 April 1993[1] the existence of an agreement does not prevent an application for a maintenance assessment.

1 See the CSA 1991, s 4(10)(a) at para **[2.426]** above.

## [2.429.4]
### Jurisdiction of the court to vary agreement

The combined effect of sub-ss (5) and (6) is to prevent the court varying an agreement so as to require the payment of child maintenance by way of periodical payments, or save where there is a written maintenance agreement made before 5 April 1993, increasing the amount of maintenance payable. It should be remembered however that by virtue of the Child Maintenance (Written Agreements) Order 1993, SI 1993/620 and s 8(5) the court does have the power to make a maintenance agreement into an order which it can subsequently vary.

## [2.429.5]
### Agreement not to apply for a maintenance assessment

Section 9(4) makes void any agreement not to apply for a maintenance assessment.

## [2.430]

### 10 Relationship between maintenance assessments and certain court orders and related matters

(1) Where an order of a kind prescribed for the purposes of this subsection is in force with respect to any qualifying child with respect to whom a maintenance assessment is made, the order—

(a) shall, so far as it relates to the making or securing of periodical payments, cease to have effect to such extent as may be determined in accordance with regulations made by the Secretary of State; or

(b) where the regulations so provide, shall, so far as it so relates, have effect subject to such modifications as may be so determined.

(2) Where an agreement of a kind prescribed for the purposes of this subsection is in force with respect to any qualifying child with respect to whom a maintenance assessment is made, the agreement—

(a) shall, so far as it relates to the making or securing of periodical payments, be unenforceable to such extent as may be determined in accordance with regulations made by the Secretary of State; or

(b) where the regulations so provide, shall, so far as it so relates, have effect subject to such modifications as may be so determined.

(3) Any regulations under this section may, in particular, make such provision with respect to—

(a) any case where any person with respect to whom an order or agreement of a kind prescribed for the purposes of subsection (1) or (2) has effect applies to the prescribed court, before the end of the prescribed period, for the order or agreement to be varied in the light of the maintenance assessment and of the provisions of this Act;

(b) the recovery of any arrears under the order or agreement which fell due before the coming into force of the maintenance assessment,

as the Secretary of State considers appropriate and may provide that, in prescribed circumstances, an application to any court which is made with respect to an order of a prescribed kind relating to the making or securing of periodical payments to or for the benefit of a child shall be treated by the court as an application for the order to be revoked.

(4) The Secretary of State may by regulations make provision for—

(a) notification to be given by [the Secretary of State] to the prescribed person in any case where [he] considers that the making of a maintenance assessment has affected, or is likely to affect, any order of a kind prescribed for the purposes of this subsection;

(b) notification to be given by the prescribed person to the Secretary of State in any case where a court makes an order which it considers has affected, or is likely to affect, a maintenance assessment.

(5) Rules may be made under section 144 of the Magistrates' Courts Act 1980 (rules of procedure) requiring any person who, in prescribed circumstances, makes an application to a magistrates' court for a maintenance order to furnish the court with a statement in a prescribed form, and signed by [an officer of the Secretary of State], as to whether or not, at the time when the statement is made, there is a maintenance assessment in force with respect to that person or the child concerned.

In this subsection—

'maintenance order' means an order of a prescribed kind for the making or securing of periodical payments to or for the benefit of a child; and

'prescribed' means prescribed by the rules.

**Appointment**

Commencement order: SI 1992/1431.

**Amendment**

Sub-s (4): words 'the Secretary of State' and 'he' in square brackets substituted by the SSA 1998, s 86(1), Sch 7, para 23(1). Date in force: 1 June 1999: see SI 1999/1510, art 2(e), (g). Sub-s (5): words 'an officer of the Secretary of State' in square brackets substituted by the SSA 1998, s 86(1), Sch 7, para 23(2). Date in force: 1 June 1999: see SI 1999/1510, art 2(e), (g).

**Definitions**

'qualifying child' – see s 3 at para **[2.425]** above.

'Maintenance assessment' – see s 54 at para **[2.449]** below; see also s 55 at para **[2.450]** below.

## [2.430.1]
## Keypoints

- Effect of section
- Child Support (Maintenance Arrangements and Jurisdiction) Regulations 1992
- Effective date of assessment

## [2.430.2]
## Effect of section

This section makes provision for orders to cease to have effect and agreements to be unenforceable where a maintenance assessment is made in relation to the child who is the subject of the order or agreement. The details are left to the regulations.

## [2.430.3]

### Child Support (Maintenance Arrangements and Jurisdiction) Regulations 1992

These regulations (as amended by the Child Support (Information, Evidence and Disclosure and Maintenance Arrangements and Jurisdiction) (Amendment) Regulations 2000, SI 2001/161 contain the detail for this section. They prescribe the orders and agreements (s 10(1) and (2)) and provide that the orders and agreements cease to be effective upon the making of an assessment in so far as they relate to the child who is the subject of the assessment.

## [2.430.4]

### Effective date of assessment

Where maintenance is being paid under an order or agreement there is specific provision, made in the above regulations, to determine the effective date of an assessment. This can differ from the normal effective date (the date the enquiry form is sent out) as set out in the Child Support (Maintenance Assessment Procedure) Regulations 1992, SI 1992/1813, Pt VII.

## [2.431]

### 25 Appeal from Child Support Commissioner on question of law

(1) An appeal on a question of law shall lie to the appropriate court from any decision of a Child Support Commissioner.

(2) No such appeal may be brought except—

- (a) with leave of the Child Support Commissioner who gave the decision or, where regulations made by the Lord Chancellor so provide, of a Child Support Commissioner selected in accordance with the regulations; or
- (b) if the Child Support Commissioner refuses leave, with the leave of the appropriate court.

(3) An application for leave to appeal under this section against a decision of a Child Support Commissioner ('the appeal decision') may only be made by—

- (a) a person who was a party to the proceedings in which the original decision, or appeal decision, was given;
- (b) the Secretary of State; or
- (c) any other person who is authorised to do so by regulations made by the Lord Chancellor.

[(3A) The Child Support Commissioner to whom an application for leave to appeal under this section is made shall specify as the appropriate court either the Court of Appeal or the Court of Session.

(3B) In determining the appropriate court, the Child Support Commissioner shall have regard to the circumstances of the case, and in particular the convenience of the persons who may be parties to the appeal.]

(4) In this section—

'appropriate court' [, except in subsections (3A) and (3B), means the court specified in accordance with those subsections]; and

'original decision' means the decision to which the appeal decision in question relates.

(5) The Lord Chancellor may by regulations make provision with respect to—

- (a) the manner in which and the time within which applications must be made to a Child Support Commissioner for leave under this section; and
- (b) the procedure for dealing with such applications.

(6) Before making any regulations under subsection (2), (3) or (5), the Lord Chancellor shall consult the [Secretary of State].

**Appointment**

Commencement orders: SI 1992/1431, SI 1992/2644.

**Amendment**
Sub-ss (3A), (3B): inserted by the CSA 1995, s 30(5), Sch 3, para 8(1). Sub-s (4): in definition 'appropriate court' words in square brackets substituted by the CSA 1995, s 30(5), Sch 3, para 8(2). Sub-s (6): words 'Secretary of State' in square brackets substituted by virtue of SI 1999/678, art 2(1), Schedule. Date in force: 19 May 1999: see SI 1999/678, art 1.

**Transfer of Functions**
The Secretary of State: functions of the Secretary of State under s 25(6) are transferred, in so far as they are exercisable in or as regards Scotland, to the Scottish Ministers, by the Scotland Act 1998 (Transfer of Functions to the Scottish Ministers etc) Order 1999, SI 1999/1750, art 2, Sch 1.

**Subordinate Legislation**
Child Support Commissioners (Procedure) Regulations 1999, SI 1999/1305 (made under s 25(2), (3), (5)).

**Definitions**
'Child Support Commissioners' – established by the CSA 1991, s 22.



### [2.431.1]
### Keypoints
- Effect of section
- Question of law
- Leave to appeal

### [2.431.2]
### Effect of section
The appeal route for a person dissatisfied with an assessment is to an appeal tribunal (provided for by s 20 of the CSA 1991) and then to a Child Support Commissioner (ss 22–24 of the CSA 1991). This section allows an appeal on a question of law to the Court of Appeal where leave is given.

### [2.431.3]
### Question of law
It is only possible to appeal from a Commissioner on a question of law. There is no definition within the act of a question of law. The concept is thought to be wide and in general terms covers any decision reached by 'an erroneous process of legal reasoning', see Bridge J in *Mountview Court Properties Ltd v Devlin*[1].

1 (1970) 21 P & CR 689 at 695–696.

### [2.431.4]
### Leave to appeal
Leave to appeal must be granted by the Commissioner or the Court of Appeal. The Child Support Commissioners (Procedure) Regulations 1999, SI 1999/1305 set out the procedure and timetable for applying for leave. An application must first be made to the Commissioner (within three months of the decision) and, if that fails to the Court of Appeal (within six weeks of the Commissioner's refusal). Where leave is granted rule r 3.23 of the FPR 1991 applies.

### [2.432]

## 26 Disputes about parentage

(1) Where a person who is alleged to be a parent of the child with respect to whom an application for a *maintenance assessment* [maintenance calculation] has been made [or treated as made] ('the alleged parent') denies that he is one of the child's parents, [the Secretary of State] shall not make a *maintenance assessment* [maintenance

calculation] on the assumption that the alleged parent is one of the child's parents unless the case falls within one of those set out in subsection (2).

(2) The Cases are—

[CASE A1

Where—

(a) the child is habitually resident in England and Wales;
(b) the Secretary of State is satisfied that the alleged parent was married to the child's mother at some time in the period beginning with the conception and ending with the birth of the child; and
(c) the child has not been adopted.

CASE A2

Where—

(a) the child is habitually resident in England and Wales;
(b) the alleged parent has been registered as father of the child under section 10 or 10A of the Births and Deaths Registration Act 1953, or in any register kept under section 13 (register of births and still-births) or section 44 (Register of Corrections Etc) of the Registration of Births, Deaths and Marriages (Scotland) Act 1965, or under Article 14 or 18(1)(b)(ii) of the Births and Deaths Registration (Northern Ireland) Order 1976; and
(c) the child has not subsequently been adopted.

CASE A3

Where the result of a scientific test (within the meaning of section 27A) taken by the alleged parent would be relevant to determining the child's parentage, and the alleged parent—

(a) refuses to take such a test; or
(b) has submitted to such a test, and it shows that there is no reasonable doubt that the alleged parent is a parent of the child.]

CASE A

Where the alleged parent is a parent of the child in question by virtue of having adopted him.

CASE B

Where the alleged parent is a parent of the child in question by virtue of an order under section 30 of the Human Fertilisation and Embryology Act 1990 (parental orders in favour of gamete donors).

[CASE B1

Where the Secretary of State is satisfied that the alleged parent is a parent of the child in question by virtue of section 27 or 28 of that Act (meaning of 'mother' and of 'father' respectively).]

CASE C

Where—

(a) either—

(i) a declaration that the alleged parent is a parent of the child in question (or a declaration which has that effect) is in force under section [55A or] 56 of the Family Law Act 1986 [or Article 32 of the Matrimonial and Family Proceedings (Northern Ireland) Order 1989] (declarations of parentage); or

(ii) a declarator by a court in Scotland that the alleged parent is a parent of the child in question (or a declarator which has that effect) is in force; and

(b) the child has not subsequently been adopted.

…

CASE E

Where—

(a) the child is habitually resident in Scotland;

(b) [the Secretary of State] is satisfied that one or other of the presumptions set out in section 5(1) of the Law Reform (Parent and Child) (Scotland) Act 1986 applies; and

(c) the child has not subsequently been adopted.

CASE F

Where—

(a) the alleged parent has been found, or adjudged, to be the father of the child in question—

(i) in proceedings before any court in England and Wales which are relevant proceedings for the purposes of section 12 of the Civil Evidence Act 1968 [or in proceedings before any court in Northern Ireland which are relevant proceedings for the purposes of section 8 of the Civil Evidence Act (Northern Ireland) 1971]; or

(ii) in affiliation proceedings before any court in the United Kingdom,

(whether or not he offered any defence to the allegation of paternity) and that finding or adjudication still subsists; and

(b) the child has not subsequently been adopted.

(3) In this section—

'adopted' means adopted within the meaning of Part IV of the Adoption Act 1976 or, in relation to Scotland, Part IV of the Adoption (Scotland) Act 1978; and

'affiliation proceedings', in relation to Scotland, means any action of affiliation and aliment.

**Appointment**

Commencement order: SI 1992/2644.

**Amendment**

Sub-s (1): words 'maintenance assessment' in italics in both places they occur repealed and subsequent words in square brackets substituted by the Child Support, Pensions and Social Security Act 2000, s 1(2)(a). Date in force: to be appointed: see the Child Support, Pensions and Social Security Act 2000, s 86(2). Sub-s (1): words 'or treated as made' in square brackets inserted by the Child Support, Pensions and Social Security Act 2000, s 26, Sch 3, para 11(1),(8). Date in force: to be appointed: see the Child Support, Pensions and Social Security Act 2000, s 86(2). Sub-s (1): words 'the Secretary of State' in square brackets substituted by the Social Security Act 1998, s 86(1), Sch 7, para 31(1). Date in force: 1 June 1999: see SI 1999/1510, art 2(e),(g). Sub-s (2): Cases A1–A3 inserted by the Child Support, Pensions and Social Security Act 2000, s 15(1). Date in force: 31 January 2001: see SI 2000/3354, art 2(1)(a). Sub-s (2): Case B1 inserted by the Child Support, Pensions and Social Security Act 2000, s 15(2). Date in force: 31 January 2001: see SI 2000/3354, art 2(1)(a). Sub-s (2): in Case C words '55A or' in square brackets inserted by the Child Support, Pensions and Social Security Act 2000, s 83(5), Sch 8, paras 11, 12. Date in force: 1 April 2001: see SI 2001/774, art 2(c). Sub-s (2): in Case C words 'or Article 32 of the Matrimonial and Family Proceedings (Northern Ireland) Order 1989' in square brackets inserted by SI 1995/756, art 13. Sub-s (2): Case D repealed by the Child Support, Pensions and Social Security Act 2000, s 85, Sch 9, Pt IX. Date in force: 1 April 2001: see SI 2001/774, art 2(d). Sub-s (2): in Case E words 'the Secretary of State' in square brackets substituted by the Social Security Act 1998, s 86(1), Sch 7, para 31(2). Date in force: 1 June 1999: see SI 1999/1510, art 2(e), (g). Sub-s (2): in Case F words 'or in proceedings before any court in Northern Ireland which are relevant proceedings for the purposes of section 8 of the Civil Evidence Act (Northern Ireland) 1971' in square brackets inserted by SI 1995/756, art 13.

**[2.432.1]**
**Keypoints**

- Effect of section
- Adoption and the HFEA 1990
- Relevant findings

**[2.432.2]**
**Effect of section**

This section provides that where parentage of a child is in dispute an assessment shall not be made unless the case falls into one of the categories A1–F listed above.

**[2.432.3]**
**Adoption and the HFEA 1990**

Where there has been a relevant order for adoption or an order under s 30 of the HFEA 1990 any denial of parenthood is ignored for the purposes of this section (Case B).

**[2.432.4]**
**Relevant findings**

Where there has been a finding of paternity in affiliation proceedings or in proceedings prescribed by s 12 of the Civil Evidence Act 1968, most pertinently proceedings under the ChA 1989, any denial of parenthood is ignored for the purposes of this section[1]. Notably proceedings under the MCA 1973 are not included by s 12 of the Civil Evidence Act 1968 (Case F).

1 In *R v Secretary of State for Social Security, ex p W* [1999] 3 FCR 693 it was held that a parental responsibility order could only be made in favour of someone who satisfied the court that he was a parent of the child, and that therefore the making of a parental responsibility order fell within Category F.

**[2.433]**

**27 [Applications for declaration of parentage under Family Law Act 1986]**

[(1) This section applies where—

(a) an application for a maintenance calculation has been made (or is treated as having been made), or a maintenance calculation is in force, with respect to a person ('the alleged parent') who denies that he is a parent of a child with respect to whom the application or calculation was made or treated as made;

(b) the Secretary of State is not satisfied that the case falls within one of those set out in section 26(2); and

(c) the Secretary of State or the person with care makes an application for a declaration under section 55A of the Family Law Act 1986 as to whether or not the alleged parent is one of the child's parents.

(2) Where this section applies—

(a) if it is the person with care who makes the application, she shall be treated as having a sufficient personal interest for the purposes of subsection (3) of that section; and

(b) if it is the Secretary of State who makes the application, that subsection shall not apply.

(3) This section does not apply to Scotland.]

**Appointment**

1 April 2001 (except in relation to proceedings pursuant to an application under this section which are pending immediately before that date): see the Child Support, Pensions and Social Security Act 2000, s 83 and SI 2001/774.

**Amendment**

Substituted by the Child Support, Pensions and Social Security Act 2000, s 83, Sch 8.



## [2.433.1]
## Keypoints

- Effect of section
- Who may apply
- Which court
- Scientific tests
- Refusing tests
- Appeal

## [2.433.2]
## Effect of section

This section gives the Secretary of State and the person with care power to apply to the courts to determine parentage.

With effect from 1 April 2001 the old s 27 has been replaced by the section set out above and a new s 55A of the FLA 1986 has been introduced. Section 27, coupled with s 55A, allows for the determination of parentage by the Secretary of State, if he is not satisfied that the non-resident parent falls into one of the categories set out in s 27, or the person with care. Further amendments have been made to the FLRA 1969 and the FLA 1986 by the Child Support, Pensions and Social Security Act 2000 to deal with some of the problems arising under the previous state of the legislation. There is by amendment to s 21 of the FLRA 1969 power given to the court to allow testing of the child if the person with care and control of the child does not consent and s 60(5) of the FLA 1986 allows a right to appeal from the magistrates' court to the High Court.

See further, in relation to the application of the Family Proceedings Courts (Matrimonial Proceedings etc) Rules 1991, SI 1991/1991 to applications under this section: the Family Proceedings Courts (Child Support Act 1991) Rules 1993, SI 1993/627, r 4.

## [2.433.3]
## Who may apply

The Secretary of State or the person with care of the child may apply where either an application has been made, or an assessment has been made and the absent parent denies parentage so long as the case does not fall within one of the categories set out in s 26(2).

## [2.433.4]
## Which court

By virtue of the Children (Allocation of Proceedings) Order 1991, SI 1991/1677, art 3(1)(s) (as amended) applications are made to the magistrates' court in the first instance.

### [2.433.5]
**Scientific tests**

Proceedings under this section are civil proceedings for the purposes of s 20 of the FLRA 1969. The court therefore should give a direction for the use of scientific tests to ascertain whether such tests show that a party to the proceedings is or is not the father or mother of the child unless satisfied that it would be against the child's interest to do so[1].

1 See the FLRA 1969, s 20(1); *W v Official Solicitor (or W)* [1972] AC 24, [1970] 3 All ER 107, HL; and *Re E (Child Support: Blood Tests)* [1995] 1 FCR 245, [1994] 2 FLR 548.

### [2.433.6]
**Refusing tests**

If a putative parent chooses to exercise his right not to submit to tests an inference of paternity is virtually inescapable[1]. This maybe so even if such an inference requires rebutting the presumption of legitimacy[2].

1 See *R v Secretary of State for Social Security, ex p G* [1997] 3 FCR 728; *Re G (a minor) (paternity: blood tests)* [1997] 2 FCR 325, CA; and *Re GW (blood tests)* [1994] 2 FCR 908, CA.
2 See *F v Child Support Agency* [1999] 2 FCR 385, [1999] 2 FLR 244.

### [2.433.7]
**Appeal**

It was a peculiarity of the legislation that where a declaration of parentage is made by the magistrates it was not possible to appeal. This problem does not arise if the matter has been transferred to either the county court or the High Court[1]. In the peculiar circumstances of *T v Child Support Agency* a subsequent (and contrary) declaration was made by the High Court pursuant to RSC Ord 15, r 16. This problem no longer arises as there is a statutory right of appeal from the magistrates' court to the High Court by virtue of s 60(5) of the FLA 1986.

1 See *T v Child Support Agency* [1997] 4 All ER 27, [1998] 1 FCR 62.

### [2.434]

**[27A Recovery of fees for scientific tests]**

[(1) This section applies in any case where—
- (a) an application for a maintenance assessment has been made or a maintenance assessment is in force;
- (b) scientific tests have been carried out (otherwise than under a direction or in response to a request) in relation to bodily samples obtained from a person who is alleged to be a parent of a child with respect to whom the application or assessment is made;
- (c) the results of the tests do not exclude the alleged parent from being one of the child's parents; and
- (d) one of the conditions set out in subsection (2) is satisfied.

(2) The conditions are that—
- (a) the alleged parent does not deny that he is one of the child's parents;
- (b) in proceedings under [section 55A of the Family Law Act 1986], a court has made a declaration that the alleged parent is a parent of the child in question; or
- (c) in an action under section 7 of the Law Reform (Parent and Child) (Scotland) Act 1986, brought by the Secretary of State by virtue of section 28, a court has granted a decree of declarator of parentage to the effect that the alleged parent is a parent of the child in question.

(3) In any case to which this section applies, any fee paid by the Secretary of State in connection with scientific tests may be recovered by him from the alleged parent as a debt due to the Crown.

(4) In this section—

'bodily sample' means a sample of bodily fluid or bodily tissue taken for the purpose of scientific tests;

'direction' means a direction given by a court under section 20 of the Family Law Reform Act 1969 (tests to determine paternity);

'request' means a request made by a court under section 70 of the Law Reform (Miscellaneous Provisions) (Scotland) Act 1990 (blood and other samples in civil proceedings); and

'scientific tests' means scientific tests made with the object of ascertaining the inheritable characteristics of bodily fluids or bodily tissue.

(5) Any sum recovered by the Secretary of State under this section shall be paid by him into the Consolidated Fund.]

**Amendment**

Inserted by the CSA 1995, s 21. Sub-s (2): Child Support, Pensions and Social Security Act 2000, s 83, Sch 8.

**Definitions**

'Child' – see s 55 at para **[2.450]** below.
'parent' – see s 54 at para **[2.449]** below.



## [2.434.1]
### Keypoint

- Scope of section

## [2.434.2]
### Scope of section

By virtue of this section the Secretary of State can recover the costs of scientific tests to determine parentage.

## [2.435]

### 32 Regulations about deduction from earnings orders

(1)–(4) [*Omitted.*]

(5) The regulations may include a provision that a liable person may appeal to a magistrates' court (or in Scotland to the sheriff) if he is aggrieved by the making of a deduction from earnings order against him, or by the terms of any such order, or there is a dispute as to whether payments constitute earnings or as to any other prescribed matter relating to the order.

(6) On an appeal under subsection (5) the court or (as the case may be) the sheriff shall not question the maintenance assessment by reference to which the deduction from earnings order was made.

(7) Regulations made by virtue of subsection (5) may include provision as to the powers of a magistrates' court, or in Scotland of the sheriff, in relation to an appeal (which may include provision as to the quashing of a deduction from earnings order or the variation of the terms of such an order).

(8) If any person fails to comply with the requirements of a deduction from earnings order, or with any regulation under this section which is designated for the purposes of this subsection, he shall be guilty of an offence.

(9) In subsection (8) 'designated' means designated by the regulations.

(10) It shall be a defence for a person charged with an offence under subsection (8) to prove that he took all reasonable steps to comply with the requirements in question.

(11) Any person guilty of an offence under subsection (8) shall be liable on summary conviction to a fine not exceeding level two on the standard scale.

**Appointment**
Commencement orders: SI 1992/1431, SI 1992/2644.

**Definitions**
'Earnings'; 'employer'; and 'employment' – see the Child Support (Collection and Enforcement) Regulations 1992, SI 1992/1989.

## [2.435.1]
### Keypoints
- Effect of section
- Regulations
- Appeals

## [2.435.2]
### Effect of section
Section 31 of the CSA 1991 makes provision for deduction from earnings orders to be made by the Secretary of State without reference to the courts. This section provides for regulations to be made governing deduction from earnings orders and an appeal to the magistrates' court following such an order in limited circumstances.

## [2.435.3]
### Regulations
The relevant regulations are the Child Support (Collection and Enforcement) Regulations 1992, SI 1992/1989, as amended by the Child Support (Collection and Enforcement and Miscellaneous Amendments) Regulations 2000, SI 2001/162.

## [2.435.4]
### Appeals
Regulation 22 of the Child Support (Collection and Enforcement) Regulations 1992, SI 1992/1989 provides that there are only two grounds for appeal: that the deduction of earnings order is defective, or that the payments in question do not constitute earnings. It is not open to the court to question the assessment or whether an order will effect the welfare of the child[1].

1 See *Secretary of State for Social Security v Shotton* [1996] 3 FCR 346, [1996] 2 FLR 241; and *R v Secretary of State for Social Security, ex p Biggin* [1995] 2 FCR 595, sub nom *B v Secretary of State for Social Security* [1995] 1 FLR 851.

## [2.436]

### 33 Liability orders

(1) This section applies where—
 (a) a person who is liable to make payments of child support maintenance ('the liable person') fails to make one or more of those payments; and
 (b) it appears to the Secretary of State that—
  (i) it is inappropriate to make a deduction from earnings order against him (because, for example, he is not employed); or
  (ii) although such an order has been made against him, it has proved ineffective as a means of securing that payments are made in accordance with the maintenance assessment in question.

(2) The Secretary of State may apply to a magistrates' court or, in Scotland, to the sheriff for an order ('a liability order') against the liable person.

(3) Where the Secretary of State applies for a liability order, the magistrates' court or (as the case may be) sheriff shall make the order if satisfied that the payments in question have become payable by the liable person and have not been paid.

(4) On an application under subsection (2), the court or (as the case may be) the sheriff shall not question the maintenance assessment under which the payments of child support maintenance fell to be made.

[(5) If the Secretary of State designates a liability order for the purposes of this subsection it shall be treated as a judgment entered in a county court for the purposes of section 73 of the County Courts Act 1984 (register of judgments and orders).]

[(6) Where regulations have been made under section 29(3)(a)—

(a) the liable person fails to make a payment (for the purposes of subsection (1)(a) of this section); and

(b) a payment is not paid (for the purposes of subsection (3)),

unless the payment is made to, or through, the person specified in or by virtue of those regulations for the case of the liable person in question.]



**Appointment**

Commencement order: SI 1992/2644.

**Amendment**

Sub-s (5): inserted by the CSA 1995, s 30(5), Sch 3, para 10. Sub-s (6): inserted by the Child Support, Pensions and Social Security Act 2000, s 26, Sch 3.

**Definitions**

'Child support maintenance' – see s 3(6) at para **[2.425]** above.
'deduction from earnings orders' – see CSA 1991, s 31(2).

### [2.436.1]
### Keypoints

- Effect of section
- Courts' function
- Freezing injunctions

### [2.436.2]
### Effect of section

Where a maintenance assessment cannot be enforced by a deduction from earnings order a liability order can be obtained under this section which allows arrears to be enforced by distress, as a county court debt, or by way of committal.

### [2.436.3]
### Courts' function

Application is made by the Secretary of State to the magistrates' court. The only question for the magistrates is set out in s 33(3): '*have the assessed payments become payable?*'

### [2.436.4]
### Freezing injunctions

It is not open to the Secretary of State to seek an injunction preventing an absent parent from dealing with his assets[1].

1 See *Department of Social Security v Butler* [1995] 4 All ER 193, [1996] 1 FCR 63.

### [2.437]

**34 Regulations about liability orders**

(1) The Secretary of State may make regulations in relation to England and Wales

(a) prescribing the procedure to be followed in dealing with an application by the Secretary of State for a liability order;

(b) prescribing the form and contents of a liability order; and

(c) providing that where a magistrates' court has made a liability order, the person against whom it is made shall, during such time as the amount in respect of which the order was made remains wholly or partly unpaid, be under a duty to supply relevant information to the Secretary of State.

(2) In subsection (1) 'relevant information' means any information of a prescribed description which is in the possession of the liable person and which the Secretary of State has asked him to supply.

**Appointment**

Commencement order: SI 1992/1431.

**Definitions**

'liability order' – see s 33(2) at para **[2.436]** above.

**[2.437.1]**

**Keypoint**

- Child Support (Collection and Enforcement) Regulations 1992, SI 1992/1989

**[2.437.2]**

**Child Support (Collection and Enforcement) Regulations 1992, SI 1992/1989**

The relevant regulations are made in Pt IV of the Child Support (Collection and Enforcement) Regulations 1992, SI 1992/1989, as amended by the Child Support (Collection and Enforcement and Miscellaneous Amendments) Regulations 2000, SI 2001/162. An application for a liability order is made by way of complaint to the magistrates' court having jurisdiction in the area in which the liable person resides[1]. Applications can be brought up to six years after payment was due[2].

1 See the Child Support (Collection and Enforcement) Regulations 1992, SI 1992/1989, reg 28(1).
2 See SI 1992/1989, reg 28(2).

**[2.438]**

## 35 Enforcement of liability orders by distress

(1) Where a liability order has been made against a person ('the liable person'), the Secretary of State may levy the appropriate amount by distress and sale of the liable person's goods.

(2) In subsection (1), 'the appropriate amount' means the aggregate of—

(a) the amount in respect of which the order was made, to the extent that it remains unpaid; and

(b) an amount, determined in such manner as may be prescribed, in respect of the charges connected with the distress.

(3) The Secretary of State may, in exercising his powers under subsection (1) against the liable person's goods, seize—

(a) any of the liable person's goods except—

(i) such tools, books, vehicles and other items of equipment as are necessary to him for use personally by him in his employment, business or vocation;

(ii) such clothing, bedding, furniture, household equipment and provisions as are necessary for satisfying his basic domestic needs; and

(b) any money, banknotes, bills of exchange, promissory notes, bonds, specialties or securities for money belonging to the liable person.

(4) For the purposes of subsection (3), the liable person's domestic needs shall be taken to include those of any member of his family with whom he resides.

(5) No person levying a distress under this section shall be taken to be a trespasser—

(a) on that account; or

(b) from the beginning, on account of any subsequent irregularity in levying the distress.

(6) A person sustaining special damage by reason of any irregularity in levying a distress under this section may recover full satisfaction for the damage (and no more) by proceedings in trespass or otherwise.

(7) The Secretary of State may make regulations supplementing the provisions of this section.

(8) The regulations may, in particular—

(a) provide that a distress under this section may be levied anywhere in England and Wales;

(b) provide that such a distress shall not be deemed unlawful on account of any defect or want of form in the liability order;

(c) provide for an appeal to a magistrates' court by any person aggrieved by the levying of, or an attempt to levy, a distress under this section;

(d) make provision as to the powers of the court on an appeal (which may include provision as to the discharge of goods distrained or the payment of compensation in respect of goods distrained and sold).

**Appointment**

Commencement orders: SI 1992/1431, SI 1992/2644.

**Definitions**

'liability order' – see s 33(2) at para **[2.436]** above.



**[2.438.1]**

**Keypoint**

- Powers of the court

**[2.438.2]**

**Powers of the court**

Distress can be levied once a liability order has been made without further reference to the court. However, by virtue of reg 31 of the Child Support (Collection and Enforcement) Regulations 1992, SI 1992/1989 a person aggrieved by a levy can appeal to the magistrates' court. The magistrates can order that goods be returned or that there be compensation by way of special damages.

**[2.439]**

## 36 Enforcement in county courts

(1) Where a liability order has been made against a person, the amount in respect of which the order was made, to the extent that it remains unpaid, shall, if a county court so orders, be recoverable by means of garnishee proceedings or a charging order, as if it were payable under a county court order.

(2) In subsection (1) 'charging order' has the same meaning as in section 1 of the Charging Orders Act 1979.

**Appointment**

Commencement order: SI 1992/2644.

**Definitions**

'liability order' – see s 33(2) at para **[2.436]** above.

**[2.439.1]**

**Keypoints**

- Who may apply
- Role of the court

## [2.439.2]
### Who may apply

This section enables arrears that have become subject to a liability order to be enforced by way of a charging order or garnishee proceedings in the county court. It appears, by virtue of the omission of any restriction to the contrary, that whereas only the Secretary of State can apply for a liability order, once that order has been obtained it is open to the person with care to apply for a garnishee order or charging order.

## [2.439.3]
### Role of the court

The county court appears from the wording of s 36(1) ('if a county court so orders') to retain its normal discretion as to whether or not to make a charging order or a garnishee order.

## [2.440]

### 39 Liability orders: enforcement throughout United Kingdom

(1) The Secretary of State may by regulations provide for—

(a) any liability order made by a court in England and Wales; or

(b) any corresponding order made by a court in Northern Ireland,

to be enforced in Scotland as if it had been made by the sheriff.

(2) The power conferred on the Court of Session by section 32 of the Sheriff Courts (Scotland) Act 1971 (power of Court of Session to regulate civil procedure in the sheriff court) shall extend to making provision for the registration in the sheriff court for enforcement of any such order as is referred to in subsection (1).

(3) The Secretary of State may by regulations make provision for, or in connection with, the enforcement in England and Wales of—

(a) any liability order made by the sheriff in Scotland; or

(b) any corresponding order made by a court in Northern Ireland,

as if it had been made by a magistrates' court in England and Wales.

(4) Regulations under subsection (3) may, in particular, make provision for the registration of any such order as is referred to in that subsection in connection with its enforcement in England and Wales.

**Appointment**

Commencement order: SI 1992/1431.

**Definitions**

'liability order' – see s 33(2) at para **[2.436]** above.

## [2.440A]

### [39A Commitment to prison and disqualification from driving]

[(1) Where the Secretary of State has sought—

(a) in England and Wales to levy an amount by distress under this Act; or

(b) to recover an amount by virtue of section 36 or 38,

and that amount, or any portion of it, remains unpaid he may apply to the court under this section.

(2) An application under this section is for whichever the court considers appropriate in all the circumstances of—

(a) the issue of a warrant committing the liable person to prison; or

(b) an order for him to be disqualified from holding or obtaining a driving licence.

(3) On any such application the court shall (in the presence of the liable person) inquire as to—

(a) whether he needs a driving licence to earn his living;

(b) his means; and
(c) whether there has been wilful refusal or culpable neglect on his part.

(4) The Secretary of State may make representations to the court as to whether he thinks it more appropriate to commit the liable person to prison or to disqualify him from holding or obtaining a driving licence; and the liable person may reply to those representations.

(5) In this section and section 40B, 'driving licence' means a licence to drive a motor vehicle granted under Part III of the Road Traffic Act 1988.

(6) In this section 'the court' means—
(a) in England and Wales, a magistrates' court;
(b) in Scotland, the sheriff.]

**Appointment**
2 April 2001: see SI 2000/3354.

**Amendment**
Inserted by the Child Support, Pensions and Social Security Act 2000, s 16(1). Date in force: 2 April 2001: see SI 2000/3354.



**[2.440A.1]**
**Keypoint**
- General

**[2.440A.2]**
**General**
See commentary to s 40 at para **[2.441.1]** et seq below.

**[2.441]**

### 40 Commitment to prison

(1) …
(2) …
(3) If, but only if, the court is of the opinion that there has been wilful refusal or culpable neglect on the part of the liable person it may—
(a) issue a warrant of commitment against him; or
(b) fix a term of imprisonment and postpone the issue of the warrant until such time and on such conditions (if any) as it thinks just.

(4) Any such warrant—
(a) shall be made in respect of an amount equal to the aggregate of—
(i) the amount mentioned in section 35(1) or so much of it as remains outstanding; and
(ii) an amount (determined in accordance with regulations made by the Secretary of State) in respect of the costs of commitment; and
(b) shall state that amount.

(5) No warrant may be issued under this section against a person who is under the age of 18.

(6) A warrant issued under this section shall order the liable person—
(a) to be imprisoned for a specified period; but
(b) to be released (unless he is in custody for some other reason) on payment of the amount stated in the warrant.

(7) The maximum period of imprisonment which may be imposed by virtue of subsection (6) shall be calculated in accordance with Schedule 4 to the Magistrates' Courts Act 1980 (maximum periods of imprisonment in default of payment) but shall not exceed six weeks.

(8) The Secretary of State may by regulations make provision for the period of imprisonment specified in any warrant issued under this section to be reduced where there is part payment of the amount in respect of which the warrant was issued.

(9) A warrant issued under this section may be directed to such person or persons as the court issuing it thinks fit.

(10) Section 80 of the Magistrates' Courts Act 1980 (application of money found on defaulter) shall apply in relation to a warrant issued under this section against a liable person as it applies in relation to the enforcement of a sum mentioned in subsection (1) of that section.

(11) The Secretary of State may by regulations make provision—

(a) as to the form of any warrant issued under this section;

(b) allowing an application under this section to be renewed where no warrant is issued or term of imprisonment is fixed;

(c) that a statement in writing to the effect that wages of any amount have been paid to the liable person during any period, purporting to be signed by or on behalf of his employer, shall be evidence of the facts stated;

(d) that, for the purposes of enabling an inquiry to be made as to the liable person's conduct and means, a justice of the peace may issue a summons to him to appear before a magistrates' court and (if he does not obey) may issue a warrant for his arrest;

(e) that for the purpose of enabling such an inquiry, a justice of the peace may issue a warrant for the liable person's arrest without issuing a summons;

(f) as to the execution of a warrant for arrest.

[(12) This section does not apply to Scotland.]

**Appointment**

Commencement orders: SI 1992/1431, SI 1992/2644.

**Amendment**

Sub-ss (1), (2): repealed by the Child Support, Pensions and Social Security Act 2000, s 16. Date in force: 2 April 2001: see SI 2000/3354. Sub-s (12): substituted, for sub-ss (12) to (14) as originally enacted, by the Child Support, Pensions and Social Security Act 2000, s 17.

**[2.441.1]**
**Keypoints**

- Regulations
- Application
- Wilful refusal or culpable neglect
- Suspension
- Part payment

**[2.441.2]**
**Regulations**

The relevant regulations are regs 33 and 34 of the Child Support (Collection and Enforcement) Regulations 1992, SI 1992/1989, as amended by the Child Support (Collection and Enforcement and Miscellaneous Amendments) Regulations 2000, SI 2001/162.

**[2.441.3]**
**Application**

Only the Secretary of State may apply for committal (or commitment) and then only where he has sought to recover arrears by way of distress or through the county court first. Rule 97 of the Magistrates' Courts Rules 1981, SI 1981/552 sets out the procedure to be followed in the application, and the appropriate form is found in Sch 3 to the Child Support (Collection and Enforcement) Regulations 1992, SI 1992/1989. The procedure governing a commitment application and, perhaps, the new power to disqualify a person from driving, is likely to be reconsidered following the introduction of the Human Rights Act 1998. The

**ratio** of *Murbarak v Murbarak*[1], a case dealing with Judgment Summons applications in the High Court would appear to apply.

1 [2001] 1 FCR 193, [2001] 1 FLR 698, CA.

### [2.441.4]
### Wilful refusal or culpable neglect

When committing a person to prison the magistrates have to consider not only whether there are arrears but whether there has been a wilful refusal or culpable neglect to meet the arrears. Further, even if there is such refusal or neglect, committal remains a discretionary remedy. Consideration is given to these points in a similar matrimonial case[1].

1 See *R v Slough Magistrates' Court, ex p Lindsay* [1997] 2 FCR 636, [1997] 1 FLR 695.



### [2.441.5]
### Suspension

Section 40(3)(b) allows the magistrates to suspend a committal order on terms. Such terms might be the regular payment of arrears.

### [2.441.6]
### Part payment

Regulations have been made pursuant to s 40(8), namely, reg 34(5) of the Child Support (Collection and Enforcement) Regulations 1992, SI 1992/1989. This provides that where there is part payment of arrears there is a proportional diminution of the sentence.

### [2.441A]

#### 40B Disqualification from driving: further provision

[(1) If, but only if, the court is of the opinion that there has been wilful refusal or culpable neglect on the part of the liable person, it may—

- (a) order him to be disqualified, for such period specified in the order but not exceeding two years as it thinks fit, from holding or obtaining a driving licence (a 'disqualification order'); or
- (b) make a disqualification order but suspend its operation until such time and on such conditions (if any) as it thinks just.

(2) The court may not take action under both section 40 and this section.

(3) A disqualification order must state the amount in respect of which it is made, which is to be the aggregate of—

- (a) the amount mentioned in section 35(1), or so much of it as remains outstanding; and
- (b) an amount (determined in accordance with regulations made by the Secretary of State) in respect of the costs of the application under section 39A.

(4) A court which makes a disqualification order shall require the person to whom it relates to produce any driving licence held by him, and its counterpart (within the meaning of section 108(1) of the Road Traffic Act 1988).

(5) On an application by the Secretary of State or the liable person, the court—

- (a) may make an order substituting a shorter period of disqualification, or make an order revoking the disqualification order, if part of the amount referred to in subsection (3) (the 'amount due') is paid to any person authorised to receive it; and
- (b) must make an order revoking the disqualification order if all of the amount due is so paid.

(6) The Secretary of State may make representations to the court as to the amount which should be paid before it would be appropriate to make an order revoking the disqualification order under subsection (5)(a), and the person liable may reply to those representations.

(7) The Secretary of State may make a further application under section 39A if the amount due has not been paid in full when the period of disqualification specified in the disqualification order expires.

(8) Where a court—

(a) makes a disqualification order;

(b) makes an order under subsection (5); or

(c) allows an appeal against a disqualification order,

it shall send notice of that fact to the Secretary of State; and the notice shall contain such particulars and be sent in such manner and to such address as the Secretary of State may determine.

(9) Where a court makes a disqualification order, it shall also send the driving licence and its counterpart, on their being produced to the court, to the Secretary of State at such address as he may determine.

(10) Section 80 of the Magistrates' Courts Act 1980 (application of money found on defaulter) shall apply in relation to a disqualification order under this section in relation to a liable person as it applies in relation to the enforcement of a sum mentioned in subsection (1) of that section.

(11) The Secretary of State may by regulations make provision in relation to disqualification orders corresponding to the provision he may make under section 40(11).

(12) In the application to Scotland of this section—

(a) in subsection (2) for 'section 40' substitute 'section 40A';

(b) in subsection (3) for paragraph (a) substitute—

'(a) the appropriate amount under section 38;';

(c) subsection (10) is omitted; and

(d) for subsection (11) substitute—

'(11) The power of the Court of Session by Act of Sederunt to regulate the procedure and practice in civil proceedings in the sheriff court shall include power to make, in relation to disqualification orders, provision corresponding to that which may be made by virtue of section 40A(8).'.]

**Appointment**

2 April 2001: see SI 2000/3354.

**Amendment**

Inserted by the Child Support, Pensions and Social Security Act 2000, s 16. Date in force: 2 April 2001: see SI 2000/3354.

**[2.441A.1]**
**Keypoint**

- General

**[2.441A.2]**
**General**

See commentary to s 40 at para **[2.441.1]** et seq above. The governing regulation is reg 35 of the Child Support (Collection and Enforcement) Regulations, as amended by the Child Support (Collection and Enforcement and Miscellaneous Amendments) Regulations 2000, SI 2001/162.

**[2.442]**

### 44 Jurisdiction

(1) [The Secretary of State] shall have jurisdiction to make a *maintenance assessment* [maintenance calculation] with respect to a person who is—

(a) a person with care;

(b) *an absent parent* [a non-resident parent]; or
(c) a qualifying child,

only if that person is habitually resident in the United Kingdom [, except in the case of a non-resident parent who falls within subsection (2A)].

(2) Where the person with care is not an individual, subsection (1) shall have effect as if paragraph (a) were omitted.

[(2A) A non-resident parent falls within this subsection if he is not habitually resident in the United Kingdom, but is—

(a) employed in the civil service of the Crown, including Her Majesty's Diplomatic Service and Her Majesty's Overseas Civil Service;
(b) a member of the naval, military or air forces of the Crown, including any person employed by an association established for the purposes of Part XI of the Reserve Forces Act 1996;
(c) employed by a company of a prescribed description registered under the Companies Act 1985 in England and Wales or in Scotland, or under the Companies (Northern Ireland) Order 1986; or
(d) employed by a body of a prescribed description.]

*(3) The Secretary of State may by regulations make provision for the cancellation of any maintenance assessment [maintenance calculation] where—*

*(a) the person with care, absent parent [non-resident parent] or qualifying child with respect to whom it was made ceases to be habitually resident in the United Kingdom;*
*(b) in a case falling within subsection (2), the absent parent [non-resident parent] or qualifying child with respect to whom it was made ceases to be habitually resident in the United Kingdom; or*
*(c) in such circumstances as may be prescribed, a maintenance order of a prescribed kind is made with respect to any qualifying child with respect to whom the maintenance assessment [maintenance calculation] was made.*



**Appointment**

Commencement orders: SI 1992/1431, SI 1992/2644.

**Amendment**

Sub-s (1): words 'The Secretary of State' in square brackets substituted by the Social Security Act 1998, s 86(1), Sch 7, para 41. Date in force: 1 June 1999: see SI 1999/1510, art 2(e), (g). Sub-s (1): words 'maintenance assessment' in italics repealed and subsequent words in square brackets substituted by the Child Support, Pensions and Social Security Act 2000, s 1(2)(a). Date in force: to be appointed: see the Child Support, Pensions and Social Security Act 2000, s 86(2). Sub-s (1): in para (b) words 'an absent parent' in italics repealed and subsequent words in square brackets substituted by the Child Support, Pensions and Social Security Act 2000, s 26, Sch 3, para 11(1), (2). Date in force: to be appointed: see the Child Support, Pensions and Social Security Act 2000, s 86(2). Sub-s (1): words ', except in the case of a non-resident parent who falls within subsection (2A)' in square brackets inserted by the Child Support, Pensions and Social Security Act 2000, s 22(1), (2). Date in force: 31 January 2001: see SI 2000/3354, art 2(1)(a). Sub-s (2A): inserted by the Child Support, Pensions and Social Security Act 2000, s 22(1),(3). Date in force (for certain purposes): 10 November 2000: see SI 2000/2994, art 2(1), Schedule, Pt I. Date in force (for remaining purposes): 31 January 2001: see SI 2000/3354, art 2(1)(a). Sub-s (3): repealed by the Child Support, Pensions and Social Security Act 2000, ss 22(1), (4), 85, Sch 9, Pt I. Date in force: to be appointed: see the Child Support, Pensions and Social Security Act 2000, s 86(2). Sub-s (3): words 'maintenance assessment' repealed and subsequent words in square brackets substituted by the Child Support, Pensions and Social Security Act 2000, s 1(2)(a). Date in force: to be appointed: see the Child Support, Pensions and Social Security Act 2000, s 86(2). Sub-s (3): in para (a) words 'absent parent' repealed and subsequent words in square brackets substituted by the Child Support, Pensions and Social Security Act 2000, s 26, Sch 3, para 11(1), (2). Date in force: to be appointed: see the Child Support, Pensions and Social Security Act 2000, s 86(2). Sub-s (3): in para (b) words 'absent parent' repealed and subsequent words in square brackets substituted by the Child Support, Pensions and Social Security Act 2000, s 26, Sch 3, para 11(1), (2). Date in force: to be appointed: see the Child Support, Pensions and Social Security Act 2000, s 86(2). Sub-s (3): in para (c) words 'maintenance assessment' repealed and subsequent words in square brackets substituted by the Child Support, Pensions and Social Security Act 2000, s 1(2)(a). Date in force: to be appointed: see the Child Support, Pensions and Social Security Act 2000, s 86(2).

## [2.442.1]
### Keypoints
- Habitual Residence
- Cancellation of assessments

## [2.442.2]
### Habitual Residence

Habitual residence is not defined within the CSA 1991. Reference should be made to the speech of Lord Brandon in *Re J (A Minor) (Abduction)*[1]. There, in the context of the CACA 1985, where similarly no definition was offered by the Act, it was held that the words were to be given their ordinary and natural meaning. So whether or not a person was habitually resident in a specified country was a question of fact to be decided by reference to all the circumstances of a particular case. See also the decision of the House of Lords in *Nessa v Chief Adjudication Officer*[2] where habitual residence is dealt with in the context of Income Support. In general it was held residence for an appreciable period was necessary before it became habitual . There were however exceptions, such as resuming a previous habitual residence.

Amendments to this section by the Child Support, Pensions and Social Security Act 2000, to be introduced on a date to be appointed, provide that even when the non-resident parent is living abroad the CSA will have jurisdiction in the case set out in sub-s (2A).

1 [1990] 2 AC 562 at 578, [1991] FCR 129, sub nom *C v S (A Minor) (Abduction: Illegitimate Child)* [1990] 2 FLR 442.
2 [1999] 4 All ER 677, [1999] 1 WLR 1937, HL.

## [2.442.3]
### Cancellation of assessments

Regulation 7 of the Child Support (Maintenance Arrangements and Jurisdiction) Regulations 1992, SI 1992/2645 makes provision for an assessment to be cancelled when one of the three relevant parties ceases to be habitually resident in the UK.

Subsection (3) is to be deleted under the provisions of the new Act. Cancellations in these circumstances are subsumed into supersession decisions provided for in the amended s 17.

## [2.443]

### 45 Jurisdiction of courts in certain proceedings under this Act

(1) The Lord Chancellor or, in relation to Scotland, the [Secretary of State] may by order make such provision as he considers necessary to secure that appeals, or such class of appeals as may be specified in the order—

(a) shall be made to a court instead of being made to [an appeal tribunal]; or

(b) shall be so made in such circumstances as may be so specified.

(2) In subsection (1), 'court' means

(a) in relation to England and Wales and subject to any provision made under Schedule 11 to the Children Act 1989 (jurisdiction of courts with respect to certain proceedings relating to children) the High Court, a county court or a magistrates' court; and

(b) in relation to Scotland, the Court of Session or the sheriff.

(3) Schedule 11 to the Act of 1989 shall be amended in accordance with subsections (4) and (5).

(4), (5) …

(6) Where the effect of any order under subsection (1) is that there are no longer any appeals which fall to be dealt with by [appeal tribunals], the Lord Chancellor after consultation with the [Secretary of State] may by order provide for the abolition of those tribunals.

(7) Any order under subsection (1) or (6) may make—

(a) such modifications of any provision of this Act or of any other enactment; and
(b) such transitional provision,

as the Minister making the order considers appropriate in consequence of any provision made by the order.

**Appointment**

Commencement order: SI 1992/1431.

**Amendment**

Sub-s (1): words 'Secretary of State' in square brackets substituted by virtue of SI 1999/678, art 2(1), Schedule. Date in force: 19 May 1999: see SI 1999/678, art 1. In para (a) words 'an appeal tribunal' in square brackets substituted by the SSA 1998, s 86(1), Sch 7, para 42(1). Date in force: 1 June 1999: see SI 1999/1510, art 2(e), (g). Sub-s (4): inserts the ChA 1989, Sch 11, Part I, para 1(2A). Sub-s (5): amends the ChA 1989, Sch 11, Part I, paras 1(3), 2(3). Sub-s (6): words 'appeal tribunals' in square brackets substituted by the SSA 1998, s 86(1), Sch 7, para 42(2). Date in force: 1 June 1999: see SI 1999/1510, art 2(e), (g). Words 'Secretary of State' in square brackets substituted by virtue of SI 1999/678, art 2(1), Schedule. Date in force: 19 May 1999: see SI 1999/678, art 1.



**[2.443.1]**
**Keypoint**

- Parentage

**[2.443.2]**
**Parentage**

By virtue of arts 3 and 4 of the Child Support Appeals (Jurisdiction of Courts) Order 1993, SI 1993/961 appeals concerning parentage are made to the magistrates' court.

**[2.444]–[2.447]**

### [46A Finality of decisions]

[(1) Subject to the provisions of this Act, any decision of the Secretary of State or an appeal tribunal made in accordance with the foregoing provisions of this Act shall be final.

(2) If and to the extent that regulations so provide, any finding of fact or other determination embodied in or necessary to such a decision, or on which such a decision is based, shall be conclusive for the purposes of—

(a) further such decisions;
(b) decisions made in accordance with sections 8 to 16 of the Social Security Act 1998, or with regulations under section 11 of that Act; and
(c) decisions made under the Vaccine Damage Payments Act 1979.]

**Amendment**

Inserted by the SSA 1998, s 86(1), Sch 7, para 44. Date in force (sub-s (2), to the extent the making of regulations is authorised): 4 March 1999: see SI 1999/528, art 2(a), Schedule. Date in force (sub-s (2), for remaining purposes): 1 June 1999: see SI 1999/1510, art 2(e), (g). Date in force (remainder): 1 June 1999: see SI 1999/1510, art 2(e), (g).

**[2.448]**

### 48 Right of audience

(1) Any [officer of the Secretary of State who is authorised] by the Secretary of State for the purposes of this section shall have, in relation to any proceedings under this Act before a magistrates' court, a right of audience and the right to conduct litigation.

(2) In this section 'right of audience' and 'right to conduct litigation' have the same meaning as in section 119 of the Courts and Legal Services Act 1990.

**Appointment**
Commencement order: SI 1992/2644.

**Amendment**
Sub-s (1): words in square brackets substituted by the CSA 1995, s 30(5), Sch 3, para 14.

## [2.448.1]
### Keypoint

- Scope of section

## [2.448.2]
### Scope of section

This section gives the Secretary of State the power to authorise a member of his staff to address the court and to conduct litigation.

## [2.449]

### 54 Interpretation

In this Act—

'absent parent', has the meaning given in section 3(2);

*'adjudication officer' has the same meaning as in the benefit Acts;*

['appeal tribunal' means an appeal tribunal constituted under Chapter I of Part I of the Social Security Act 1998;]

['application for a departure direction' means an application under section 28A;]

'assessable income' has the meaning given in paragraph 5 of Schedule 1;

'benefit Acts' means the [Social Security Contributions and Benefits Act 1992 and the Social Security Administration Act 1992];

*'Chief Adjudication Officer' has the same meaning as in the benefit Acts;*

...

'child benefit' has the same meaning as in the Child Benefit Act 1975;

...

'child support maintenance' has the meaning given in section 3(6);

...

['current assessment', in relation to an application for a departure direction, means (subject to any regulations made under paragraph 10 of Schedule 4A) the maintenance assessment with respect to which the application is made;]

'deduction from earnings order' has the meaning given in section 31(2);

['departure direction' has the meaning given in section 28A; and]

'disability living allowance' has the same meaning as in the [benefit Acts];

'[working families' tax credit]' has the same meaning as in the benefit Acts;

'general qualification' shall be construed in accordance with section 71 of the Courts and Legal Services Act 1990 (qualification for judicial appointments);

'income support' has the same meaning as in the benefit Acts;

['income-based jobseeker's allowance' has the same meaning as in the Jobseekers Act 1995;]

'interim maintenance assessment' has the meaning given in section 12;

'liability order' has the meaning given in section 33(2);

'maintenance agreement' has the meaning given in section 9(1);

'maintenance assessment' means an assessment of maintenance made under this Act and, except in prescribed circumstances, includes an interim maintenance assessment;

'maintenance order' has the meaning given in section 8(11);

'maintenance requirement' means the amount calculated in accordance with paragraph 1 of Schedule 1;

'parent', in relation to any child, means any person who is in law the mother or father of the child;

['parental responsibility', in the application of this Act—

(a) to England and Wales, has the same meaning as in the Children Act 1989; and

(b) to Scotland, shall be construed as a reference to 'parental responsibilities' within the meaning given by section 1(3) of the Children (Scotland) Act 1995;]

...

['parent with care' means a person who is, in relation to a child, both a parent and a person with care]

'person with care' has the meaning given in section 3(3);

'prescribed' means prescribed by regulations made by the Secretary of State;

'qualifying child' has the meaning given in section 3(1).



**Appointment**

Commencement order: SI 1992/1431.

**Amendment**

Definitions 'adjudication officer' and 'Chief Adjudication Officer' in italics, and definitions 'Chief Child Support Officer', 'child support appeal tribunal' and 'child support officer' omitted, repealed by the SSA 1998, s 86(1), (2), Sch 7, para 47(b), Sch 8. Date in force (insofar as this repeal relates to the definitions 'Chief Child Support Officer', 'child support appeal tribunal' and 'child support officer'): 1 June 1999: see SI 1999/1510, art 2(e)–(g). Definition 'appeal tribunal' inserted by the SSA 1998, s 86(1), Sch 7, para 47(a). Date in force: 1 June 1999: see SI 1999/1510, art 2(e), (g). Definition 'application for a departure direction' inserted by the CSA 1995, s 30(5), Sch 3, para 16. In definition 'benefit Acts' words 'Social Security Contributions and Benefits Act 1992 and the Social Security Administration Act 1992' in square brackets substituted by the SS(CP)A 1992, s 4, Sch 2, para 114. Definition 'current assessment' inserted by the CSA 1995, s 30(5), Sch 3, para 16. Definition 'departure direction' inserted by the CSA 1995, s 30(5), Sch 3, para 16. In definition 'disability living allowance' words 'benefit Acts' in square brackets substituted by the SS(CP)A 1992, s 4, Sch 2, para 114. In definition 'working families' tax credit' words 'working families' tax credit' in square brackets substituted by the TCA 1999, s 1(2), Sch 1, paras 1(a), 6(f)(ii). Date in force: 5 October 1999: see the TCA 1999, s 20(2). Definition 'income-based jobseeker's allowance' inserted by the JA 1995, s 41(4), Sch 2, para 20(6). Definition 'parental responsibility' substituted by the C(S)A 1995, s 105(4), Sch 4, para 52(4). Definition omitted repealed by the C(S)A 1995, s 105(4), (5), Sch 4, para 52(4), Sch 5. Definition 'parent with care' inserted by the CSA 1995, s 30(5), Sch 3, para 16.

**Definitions**

See generally s 3 (at para **[2.425]** above) and s 55 (at para **[2.450]** below).

**[2.450]**

## 55 Meaning of 'child'

(1) For the purposes of this Act a person is a child if—

(a) he is under the age of 16;

(b) he is under the age of 19 and receiving full-time education (which is not advanced education)—

(i) by attendance at a recognised educational establishment; or

(ii) elsewhere, if the education is recognised by the Secretary of State; or

(c) he does not fall within paragraph (a) or (b) but—

(i) he is under the age of 18, and

(ii) prescribed conditions are satisfied with respect to him.

(2) A person is not a child for the purposes of this Act if he—

(a) is or has been married;

(b) has celebrated a marriage which is void; or

(c) has celebrated a marriage in respect of which a decree of nullity has been granted.

(3) In this section—

'advanced education' means education of a prescribed description; and

'recognised educational establishment' means an establishment recognised by the Secretary of State for the purposes of this section as being, or as comparable to, a university, college or school.

(4) Where a person has reached the age of 16, the Secretary of State may recognise education provided for him otherwise than at a recognised educational establishment only if the Secretary of State is satisfied that education was being so provided for him immediately before he reached the age of 16.

(5) The Secretary of State may provide that in prescribed circumstances education is or is not to be treated for the purposes of this section as being full-time.

(6) In determining whether a person falls within subsection (1)(b), no account shall be taken of such interruptions in his education as may be prescribed.

(7) The Secretary of State may by regulations provide that a person who ceases to fall within subsection (1) shall be treated as continuing to fall within that subsection for a prescribed period.

(8) No person shall be treated as continuing to fall within subsection (1) by virtue of regulations made under subsection (7) after the end of the week in which he reaches the age of 19.

**Appointment**

Commencement order: SI 1992/1431.

**[2.450.1]**
**Keypoint**

- Regulations

**[2.450.2]**
**Regulations**

The Child Support (Maintenance Assessment Procedure) Regulations 1992, SI 1992/1813, Sch 1 contains the prescriptions for s 55(1)(c) (child is in youth training or not in remunerative employment), s 55(3) (advanced education is degree level, or of a standard above that of a national diploma), s 55(5) (full-time is 12 hours or more a week), s 55(6) (interruptions can be up to six months where reasonable) and s 55(7) (usually shortly after the cessation of full-time education but see para 5 of Sch 1 to SI 1992/1813).

The Child Support (Maintenance Assessment Procedure) Regulations 1992 are to be replaced on a date to be appointed by the Child Support (Maintenance Calculation Procedure) Regulations 2000.

# Maintenance Enforcement Act 1991

PART 2
MEA 1991

## Contents



*An Act to make provision as to the methods of payment, and the variation of the methods of payment, under maintenance orders made by the High Court and county courts; to re-enact with modifications certain provisions relating to the making and variation of orders requiring money to be paid periodically; to make further provision as to the making, variation and enforcement by magistrates' courts of maintenance orders; to make further provision about proceedings by clerks of magistrates' courts in relation to arrears under certain orders requiring money to be paid periodically; to make further provision as to maintenance orders registered in, or confirmed by, magistrates' courts or registered in the High Court; to extend the power to make attachment of earnings orders in the case of maintenance orders; to amend section 10 of the Courts and Legal Services Act 1990; and for connected purposes*

[27th June 1991]

**[2.450A]**

### 1 Maintenance orders in the High Court and county courts: means of payment, attachment of earnings and revocation, variation etc

(1) Where the High Court or a county court makes a qualifying periodical maintenance order, it may at the same time exercise either of its powers under subsection (4) below in relation to the order, whether of its own motion or on an application made under this subsection by an interested party.

(2) For the purposes of this section, a periodical maintenance order is an order—

(a) which requires money to be paid periodically by one person ('the debtor') to another ('the creditor'); and
(b) which is a maintenance order;

and such an order is a 'qualifying periodical maintenance order' if, at the time it is made, the debtor is ordinarily resident in England and Wales.

(3) Where the High Court or a county court has made a qualifying periodical maintenance order, it may at any later time—

(a) on an application made under this subsection by an interested party, or
(b) of its own motion, in the course of any proceedings concerning the order,

exercise either of its powers under subsection (4) below in relation to the order.

(4) The powers mentioned in subsections (1) and (3) above are—

(a) the power to order that payments required to be made by the debtor to the creditor under the qualifying periodical maintenance order in question shall be so made by such a method of payment falling within subsection (5) below as the court may specify in the particular case; or
(b) the power, by virtue of this section, to make an attachment of earnings order under the Attachment of Earnings Act 1971 to secure payments under the qualifying periodical maintenance order in question.

(5) The methods of payment mentioned in subsection (4)(a) above are—

(a) payment by standing order; or
(b) payment by any other method which requires the debtor to give his authority for payments of a specific amount to be made from an account of his to an account of the creditor's on specific dates during the period for which the authority is in force and without the need for any further authority from the debtor.

(6) In any case where—

(a) the court proposes to exercise its power under paragraph (a) of subsection (4) above, and
(b) having given the debtor an opportunity of opening an account from which payments under the order may be made in accordance with the method of payment proposed to be ordered under that paragraph, the court is satisfied that the debtor has failed, without reasonable excuse, to open such an account,

the court in exercising its power under that paragraph may order that the debtor open such an account.

(7) Where in the exercise of its powers under subsection (1) or (3) above, the High Court or a county court has made in relation to a qualifying periodical maintenance order such an order as is mentioned in subsection (4)(a) above (a 'means of payment order'), it may at any later time—

(a) on an application made under this subsection by an interested party, or
(b) of its own motion, in the course of any proceedings concerning the qualifying periodical maintenance order,

revoke, suspend, revive or vary the means of payment order.

(8) In deciding whether to exercise any of its powers under this section the court in question having (if practicable) given every interested party an opportunity to make representations shall have regard to any representations made by any such party.

(9) Nothing in this section shall be taken to prejudice—

(a) any power under the Attachment of Earnings Act 1971 which would, apart from this section, be exercisable by the High Court or a county court; or
(b) any right of any person to make any application under that Act;

and subsection (7) above is without prejudice to any other power of the High Court or a county court to revoke, suspend, revive or vary an order.

(10) For the purposes of this section—

'debtor' and 'creditor' shall be construed in accordance with subsection (2) above;

'interested party' means any of the following, that is to say—

(a) the debtor;
(b) the creditor; and

(c) in a case where the person who applied for the qualifying periodical maintenance order in question is a person other than the creditor, that other person;

'maintenance order' means any order specified in Schedule 8 to the Administration of Justice Act 1970 and includes any such order which has been discharged, if any arrears are recoverable under it;

'qualifying periodical maintenance order' shall be construed in accordance with subsection (2) above, and the references to such an order in subsections (3) and (7) above are references to any such order, whether made before or after the coming into force of this section;

and the reference in subsection (2) above to an order requiring money to be paid periodically by one person to another includes a reference to an order requiring a lump sum to be paid by instalments by one person to another.

**Appointment**

Commencement order: SI 1992/455.

**Definitions**

'Qualifying periodical maintenance order' – see s 1(2) and (10) and para **[2.450A.1]** et seq below.
'Interested party' – see s 1(10).
'Debtor'; 'creditor' – s 1(2).
'Ordinarily resident' – see para **[2.450A.1]** et seq below.
'Means of payment order' – see s 1(7) and para **[2.450A.1]** et seq below.



## [2.450A.1]
## Keypoints

- Means of payment orders
- 'Qualifying periodical maintenance orders'
- Payer must be 'ordinarily resident' in England and Wales
- Court can act of its own motion
- Procedure

## [2.450A.2]
## Means of payment orders

The MEA 1991 introduced two types of power, both in relation to the High Court and county courts (by s 1) and in relation to the magistrates' courts (by the Magistrates' Courts Act 1980, s 59 in the form substituted by the MEA 1991, s 2[1]).

The two new types of power are, firstly, the power to make an attachment of earnings order (otherwise than by consent) without the need for separate application under the AtEA 1971 and, secondly, the power to order payments by standing order (or equivalent). It is the latter power, to order payments by standing order or equivalent, which results in what are referred to in the MEA 1991 and elsewhere as 'means of payment orders'. There is ancillary power, in s 1(6), to require the payer to open an account in order to make payments by standing order (or equivalent).

Prior to the MEA 1991, although the magistrates' court could direct that maintenance payments be made through the clerk, the High Court and county court could only order that payments be made direct to the payee (enforced if necessary, where there was already default, by means of separate attachment of earnings). The new provisions were brought into force on 1 April 1992 by virtue of the Maintenance Enforcement Act 1991 (Commencement No 2) Order 1992 SI 1992/455 made under s 12(2) below[2].

Note that the means of payment contemplated by s 1(5) do not include payments by direct debit: the payment must be by a method which requires the payer to give his authority for payments of a specific amount to be made on specific dates.

1 See para **[2.450B]** below.
2 See para **[2.450K]** below.

## [2.450A.3]
### 'Qualifying periodical maintenance orders'

In accordance with s 1(10) the term 'maintenance order' means any order specified in Administration of Justice Act 1970, Sch 8. Schedule 8 to the Administration of Justice Act 1970 refers to orders 'for periodical or other payments' and thus includes orders for lump sums. However, the MEA 1991 only applies the power to make means of payment and attachment of earnings orders to 'periodical maintenance orders'[1], and then only if the periodical maintenance order also qualifies under s 1(2).

A 'periodical maintenance order' is defined restrictively under s 1(2) and it is only a 'qualifying periodical maintenance order' if the payer ('the debtor') is ordinarily resident in England and Wales[2].

It is suggested that the term 'periodical maintenance order', being periodic and a maintenance order, includes an order to pay school fees direct to a school[3]; and also financial undertakings to pay eg school fees[4]. However, this would require (in each case) that the amount and regularity of payments should be fixed (in accordance with s 1(5)(b)) and it may be therefore that such an application would be rare in practice.

1 See the MEA 1991, s 1(2) at para **[2.450A]** above.
2 See the MEA 1991, s 1(2) at para **[2.450A]** above. For the wider application of attachment of earnings orders under the AtEA 1971, to include attachments in relation to lump sums and other 'maintenance orders', see the AtEA 1971, s 2, Sch 1 at para **[2.83]** above.
3 See *L v L (Payment of School Fees)* [1997] 3 FCR 520, CA, sub nom *L v L (School Fees: Maintenance)* [1997] 2 FLR 252.
4 See *Symmons v Symmons* [1993] 1 FLR 317.

## [2.450A.4]
### Payer must be 'ordinarily resident' in England and Wales

The requirement that the payer ('the debtor') is ordinarily resident in England and Wales[1] is a question of fact. It has been said that there is no distinction between 'ordinary residence' and 'habitual residence'[2], and that 'habitual residence' is to be equated with 'ordinary residence'[3] wherever it appears in family law statutes. What is required is that 'the purpose of living where one does has a sufficient degree of continuity to be properly described as settled'[4]. See also *Nessa v Chief Adjudication Officer*[5] applying, inter alia, *Shah*.

1 See the MEA 1991, s 1(2) at para **[2.450A]** above.
2 See *Shah v Barnet London Borough Council* [1983] 2 AC 309, HL.
3 See *Ikimi v Ikimi* [2001] EWCA Civ 873, [2001] 2 FCR 385 at 395(g) para [31] per Thorpe LJ, CA.
4 See *Shah v Barnet London Borough Council* [1983] 2 AC 309 per Lord Scarman at 344D, HL.
5 [1999] 3 FCR 538, [1999] 2 FLR 1116, HL.

## [2.450A.5]
### Court can act of its own motion

As stated in s 1(1) of the MEA 1991 the court can act of its own motion, in the course of any proceedings concerning the order, or on application. By s 1(3) where the court has previously made a qualifying periodical maintenance order (see above) it may 'at any later time' add a means of payment order (see above). Equally, where the court has previously made a means of payment order, it may 'at any later time' revoke, suspend, revive or vary the means of payment order. In both cases, just as with the original means of payment order, the court can act of its own motion, in the course of any proceedings concerning the order, or on application.

In relation to attachments of earnings to enforce maintenance orders there is no longer any requirement of previous default[1]. But note that the power to make an attachment of earnings order imports also the power to order the payer to give a statement of his earnings, anticipated earnings, needs and resources (under the AtEA 1971, s 14(1)(a)); and/or to order any employer of the payer to give details of the payer's earnings and anticipated earnings (under the AtEA 1971, s 14(1)(b)).

1 See the AtEA 1971, s 3(3A) at para **[2.58]** above (which was inserted into that Act by the MEA 1991, s 11(1), Sch 2, para 1).

### [2.450A.6]
**Procedure**

Where the court acts of its own motion no application is necessary, save on occasion an oral request to exercise the power. If formal application is made, whether under s 1(1), (3) or (7) of the MEA 1991, it should be by summons or notice of application as appropriate to the court level. If a separate application for an attachment of earnings order is made, not under the MEA 1991, it should be made in accordance with FPR 1991, r 7.1(4) and CCR Ord 27 (CPR 1998, Sch 1).



### [2.450B]

**2 Orders for periodical payment in magistrates' courts: means of payment**

…

**Appointment**
Commencement order: SI 1992/455.

**Amendment**
This section substitutes the MCA 1980, s 59.

### [2.450C]

**3 Orders for periodical payment in magistrates' courts: proceedings by clerk and penalty for breach**

…

**Appointment**
Commencement order: SI 1992/455.

**Amendment**
This section inserts the MCA 1980, ss 59A, 59B.

### [2.450D]

**4 Revocation, variation, etc. of orders for periodical payment in magistrates' courts: general**

…

**Appointment**
Commencement order: SI 1992/455.

**Amendment**
This section substitutes the MCA 1980, s 60.

### [2.450E]

**5 Variation of orders for periodical payment made under Part I of the Domestic Proceedings and Magistrates' Courts Act 1978**

…

**Appointment**
Commencement order: SI 1992/455.

**Amendment**
This section inserts the DPMCA 1978, s 20ZA.

[2.450F]

### 6 Variation of orders for periodical payment made in magistrates' courts under Schedule 1 to the Children Act 1989

...

**Appointment**
Commencement order: SI 1992/455.

**Amendment**
This section inserts the ChA 1989, Sch 1, para 6A.

[2.450G]

### 7 Maintenance orders in magistrates' courts: enforcement

...

**Appointment**
Commencement order: SI 1992/455.

**Amendment**
This section inserts the MCA 1980, s 76(4) to (6).

[2.450H]

### 8 Interest on arrears

...

**Appointment**
Commencement order: SI 1992/455.

**Amendment**
This section inserts the MCA 1980, s 94A.

[2.450I]

### 10 Amendment of certain enactments relating to registered or confirmed maintenance orders

Schedule 1 to this Act, which by amending certain enactments applies some of the preceding provisions of this Act with modifications to maintenance orders registered in or confirmed by magistrates' courts or registered in the High Court, shall have effect.

**Appointment**
Commencement order: SI 1992/455.

[2.450J]

### 11 Minor and consequential amendments and repeals

(1) Schedule 2 to this Act, which contains minor amendments and amendments consequential on the provisions of this Act, shall have effect.

(2) The enactments specified in Schedule 3 to this Act are hereby repealed to the extent specified in the third column of that Schedule.

**Appointment**
Commencement orders: SI 1991/2042, SI 1992/455.

[2.450K]–[2.450N]

**12 Short title, commencement, application and extent**

(1) This Act may be cited as the Maintenance Enforcement Act 1991.

(2) The provisions of this Act, other than this section (which comes into force on the passing of this Act), shall come into force on such day as the Secretary of State may by order made by statutory instrument appoint, and different days may be so appointed for different provisions or for different purposes of the same provision.

(3) In the application of any amendment made by this Act which has effect in relation to orders made, confirmed or registered by a court, it is immaterial whether the making, confirmation or registration occurred before or after the coming into force of the amendment.

(4) Except for paragraphs 3 to 6 of Schedule 1, section 10 (in so far as it relates to those paragraphs) and this section, which extend to Scotland and Northern Ireland, this Act extends to England and Wales only.

# Trusts of Land and Appointment of Trustees Act 1996

PART 2
TLATA 1996

## Contents

*Section*

PART I
TRUSTS OF LAND



PART II
APPOINTMENT AND RETIREMENT OF TRUSTEES



PART III
SUPPLEMENTARY

# Trusts of Land and Appointment of Trustees Act 1996

*An Act to make new provision about trusts of land including provision phasing out the Settled Land Act 1925, abolishing the doctrine of conversion and otherwise amending the law about trusts for sale of land; to amend the law about the appointment and retirement of trustees of any trust; and for connected purposes*

[24th July 1996]

**[2.451]**
**RSC Ord 31 / CPR 1998, Pt 40**

RSC Ord 31 remains of application in family proceedings by operation of FPR 1991, r 2.64(3) (set out at para **[3.449]** below). However, it has been superseded by CPR 1998, Pt 40 in respect of TLATA 1996 matters and applications under s 17 of the MWPA 1882. The old RSC Ord 31 is set out at para **[3.543]** below and is followed by the relevant text of the new CPR 1998, Pt 40. Note that CPR 1998, Pt 40 is accompanied by a *Practice Direction*. The relevant text of the *Practice Direction* is set out at para **[4.37]** below.

**[2.452]**

PART I
TRUSTS OF LAND

**1 Meaning of 'trust of land'**

(1) In this Act—

(a) 'trust of land' means (subject to subsection (3)) any trust of property which consists of or includes land, and

(b) 'trustees of land' means trustees of a trust of land.

(2) The reference in subsection (1)(a) to a trust—

(a) is to any description of trust (whether express, implied, resulting or constructive), including a trust for sale and a bare trust, and

(b) includes a trust created, or arising, before the commencement of this Act.

(3) The reference to land in subsection (1)(a) does not include land which (despite section 2) is settled land or which is land to which the Universities and College Estates Act 1925 applies.

**[2.452.1]**
**Keypoints**

- General
- Coming into force
- Trusts of Land
- Trusts for sale and strict settlements
- Alternative remedies

**[2.452.2]**
**General**

The court only has power to state what the parties' rights are; its jurisdiction is procedural and declaratory only. It has no jurisdiction akin to the MCA 1973 to transfer one party's rights to the other.

**[2.452.3]**
**Coming into force**

The Act came into force on 1 January 1997. Any proceedings under the old Law of Propery Act 1925, s 30 will automatically be converted into being applications under the TLATA 1996.

District Judges (including District Judges of the Principal Registry) have jurisdiction to hear any application under s 14 of the TLATA 1996 following the *President's Direction*[1].

1 [1999] 2 FCR 1, [1999] 1 FLR 1295.

## [2.452.4]
## Trusts of Land

Where there was formerly a statutory trust for sale, it was held on the basis that there was a duty to sell. However where a joint tenant of property wished to sell that property and realise his share, it was necessary for both the joint tenants to concur in the sale. In the absence of that agreement an application would be made to the court to enforce the duty to sell. The general rule was that a sale would be ordered unless all the trustees agreed otherwise. The power to retain required unanimity. In order to mitigate the effect of this general rule, the exception developed that a sale would not be ordered where there existed a collateral purpose to the trust, for example, to provide a family home[1] or to run a business at particular premises[2]. However, under the TLATA 1996, there is no duty to sell and the court is, therefore, able to adopt a more flexible approach. The basis of that approach is the s 15 exercise.

1 See *Jones v Challenger* [1961] 1 QB 176, [1960] 1 All ER 785, CA.
2 See *Bedson v Bedson* [1965] 2 QB 666, [1965] 3 All ER 307, CA.



## [2.452.5]
## Trusts for sale and strict settlements

Both trusts for sale and strict settlements are replaced by the new trusts of land.

## [2.452.6]
## Alternative remedies

If the court can use its wider powers under the MCA 1973, s 24[1], it should do so[2]. However, these powers are only available where there is a petition for divorce, nullity or judicial separation. In other circumstances, proceedings under the MWPA 1882, s 17[3] or under the TLATA 1996, s 14[4] (or under both sections) are likely to be the only remedies available. Where the parties have not been married, proceedings under the TLATA 1996, s 14 is likely to be the only remedy available[5].

1 See para **[2.118]** above.
2 See *Browne v Pritchard* [1975] 3 All ER 721, [1975] 1 WLR 1366, CA; *Williams v Williams* [1976] Ch 278, [1977] 1 All ER 28, CA; and *Fielding v Fielding* [1978] 1 All ER 267, [1977] 1 WLR 1146n, CA.
3 See para **[2.11]** above.
4 See para **[2.465]** below.
5 Where the parties have been married but there is no petition for divorce, nullity or judicial separation proceedings under the MWPA 1882, s 17 should also be considered see para **[2.11]** above. See generally *Rayden and Jackson on Divorce and Family Matters* (17th edn, 1997), vol 1, para 30.14 and the Noter-up thereto.

## [2.453]

### 2 Trusts in place of settlements

(1) No settlement created after the commencement of this Act is a settlement for the purposes of the Settled Land Act 1925; and no settlement shall be deemed to be made under that Act after that commencement.

(2) Subsection (1) does not apply to a settlement created on the occasion of an alteration in any interest in, or of a person becoming entitled under, a settlement which—

(a) is in existence at the commencement of this Act, or
(b) derives from a settlement within paragraph (a) or this paragraph.

(3) But a settlement created as mentioned in subsection (2) is not a settlement for the purposes of the Settled Land Act 1925 if provision to the effect that it is not is made in the instrument, or any of the instruments, by which it is created.

(4) Where at any time after the commencement of this Act there is in the case of any settlement which is a settlement for the purposes of the Settled Land Act 1925 no relevant property which is, or is deemed to be, subject to the settlement, the settlement permanently ceases at that time to be a settlement for the purposes of that Act.
In this subsection 'relevant property' means land and personal chattels to which section 67(1) of the Settled Land Act 1925 (heirlooms) applies.

(5) No land held on charitable, ecclesiastical or public trusts shall be or be deemed to be settled land after the commencement of this Act, even if it was or was deemed to be settled land before that commencement.

(6) Schedule 1 has effect to make provision consequential on this section (including provision to impose a trust in circumstances in which, apart from this section, there would be a settlement for the purposes of the Settled Land Act 1925 (and there would not otherwise be a trust)).

**Note**

Settled land is abolished by this section.

**[2.454]**

### 3 Abolition of doctrine of conversion

(1) Where land is held by trustees subject to a trust for sale, the land is not to be regarded as personal property; and where personal property is subject to a trust for sale in order that the trustees may acquire land, the personal property is not to be regarded as land.

(2) Subsection (1) does not apply to a trust created by a will if the testator died before the commencement of this Act.

(3) Subject to that, subsection (1) applies to a trust whether it is created, or arises, before or after that commencement.

**Note**

No longer is a beneficiary's interest an interest in money (as it was under a trust for sale). This section also applies to declarations made under the MWPA 1882.

**[2.455]**

### 4 Express trusts for sale as trusts of land

(1) In the case of every trust for sale of land created by a disposition there is to be implied, despite any provision to the contrary made by the disposition, a power for the trustees to postpone sale of the land; and the trustees are not liable in any way for postponing sale of the land, in the exercise of their discretion, for an indefinite period.

(2) Subsection (1) applies to a trust whether it is created, or arises, before or after the commencement of this Act.

(3) Subsection (1) does not affect any liability incurred by trustees before that commencement.

**[2.456]**

### 5 Implied trusts for sale as trusts of land

(1) Schedule 2 has effect in relation to statutory provisions which impose a trust for sale of land in certain circumstances so that in those circumstances there is instead a trust of the land (without a duty to sell).

(2) Section 1 of the Settled Land Act 1925 does not apply to land held on any trust arising by virtue of that Schedule (so that any such land is subject to a trust of land).

[2.457]

## 6 General powers of trustees

(1) For the purpose of exercising their functions as trustees, the trustees of land have in relation to the land subject to the trust all the powers of an absolute owner.

(2) Where in the case of any land subject to a trust of land each of the beneficiaries interested in the land is a person of full age and capacity who is absolutely entitled to the land, the powers conferred on the trustees by subsection (1) include the power to convey the land to the beneficiaries even though they have not required the trustees to do so; and where land is conveyed by virtue of this subsection—

(a) the beneficiaries shall do whatever is necessary to secure that it vests in them, and

(b) if they fail to do so, the court may make an order requiring them to do so.

(3) The trustees of land have power to [acquire land under the power conferred by section 8 of the Trustee Act 2000.]

(4) …

(5) In exercising the powers conferred by this section trustees shall have regard to the rights of the beneficiaries.

(6) The powers conferred by this section shall not be exercised in contravention of, or of any order made in pursuance of, any other enactment or any rule of law or equity.

(7) The reference in subsection (6) to an order includes an order of any court or of the Charity Commissioners.

(8) Where any enactment other than this section confers on trustees authority to act subject to any restriction, limitation or condition, trustees of land may not exercise the powers conferred by this section to do any act which they are prevented from doing under the other enactment by reason of the restriction, limitation or condition.

[(9) The duty of care under section 1 of the Trustee Act 2000 applies to trustees of land when exercising the powers conferred by this section.]

**Amendment**

Sub-s (3): TrA 2000, s 40(1), Sch 2. Sub-s (4): repealed by the TrA 2000, s 40, Schs 2, 4. Sub-s (9): inserted by the TrA 2000, s 40, Sch 2.

[2.458]

## 7 Partition by trustees

(1) The trustees of land may, where beneficiaries of full age are absolutely entitled in undivided shares to land subject to the trust, partition the land, or any part of it, and provide (by way of mortgage or otherwise) for the payment of any equality money.

(2) The trustees shall give effect to any such partition by conveying the partitioned land in severalty (whether or not subject to any legal mortgage created for raising equality money), either absolutely or in trust, in accordance with the rights of those beneficiaries.

(3) Before exercising their powers under subsection (2) the trustees shall obtain the consent of each of those beneficiaries.

(4) Where a share in the land is affected by an incumbrance, the trustees may either give effect to it or provide for its discharge from the property allotted to that share as they think fit.

(5) If a share in the land is absolutely vested in a minor, subsections (1) to (4) apply as if he were of full age, except that the trustees may act on his behalf and retain land or other property representing his share in trust for him.

**[2.459]**

### 8 Exclusion and restriction of powers

(1) Sections 6 and 7 do not apply in the case of a trust of land created by a disposition in so far as provision to the effect that they do not apply is made by the disposition.

(2) If the disposition creating such a trust makes provision requiring any consent to be obtained to the exercise of any power conferred by section 6 or 7, the power may not be exercised without that consent.

(3) Subsection (1) does not apply in the case of charitable, ecclesiastical or public trusts.

(4) Subsections (1) and (2) have effect subject to any enactment which prohibits or restricts the effect of provision of the description mentioned in them.

**[2.460]**

### 9 Delegation by trustees

(1) The trustees of land may, by power of attorney, delegate to any beneficiary or beneficiaries of full age and beneficially entitled to an interest in possession in land subject to the trust any of their functions as trustees which relate to the land.

(2) Where trustees purport to delegate to a person by a power of attorney under subsection (1) functions relating to any land and another person in good faith deals with him in relation to the land, he shall be presumed in favour of that other person to have been a person to whom the functions could be delegated unless that other person has knowledge at the time of the transaction that he was not such a person.

And it shall be conclusively presumed in favour of any purchaser whose interest depends on the validity of that transaction that that other person dealt in good faith and did not have such knowledge if that other person makes a statutory declaration to that effect before or within three months after the completion of the purchase.

(3) A power of attorney under subsection (1) shall be given by all the trustees jointly and (unless expressed to be irrevocable and to be given by way of security) may be revoked by any one or more of them; and such a power is revoked by the appointment as a trustee of a person other than those by whom it is given (though not by any of those persons dying or otherwise ceasing to be a trustee).

(4) Where a beneficiary to whom functions are delegated by a power of attorney under subsection (1) ceases to be a person beneficially entitled to an interest in possession in land subject to the trust—

- (a) if the functions are delegated to him alone, the power is revoked,
- (b) if the functions are delegated to him and to other beneficiaries to be exercised by them jointly (but not separately), the power is revoked if each of the other beneficiaries ceases to be so entitled (but otherwise functions exercisable in accordance with the power are so exercisable by the remaining beneficiary or beneficiaries), and
- (c) if the functions are delegated to him and to other beneficiaries to be exercised by them separately (or either separately or jointly), the power is revoked in so far as it relates to him.

(5) A delegation under subsection (1) may be for any period or indefinite.

(6) A power of attorney under subsection (1) cannot be an enduring power within the meaning of the Enduring Powers of Attorney Act 1985.

(7) Beneficiaries to whom functions have been delegated under subsection (1) are, in relation to the exercise of the functions, in the same position as trustees (with the same duties and liabilities); but such beneficiaries shall not be regarded as trustees for any other purposes (including, in particular, the purposes of any enactment permitting the delegation of functions by trustees or imposing requirements relating to the payment of capital money).

(8) …

(9) Neither this section nor the repeal by this Act of section 29 of the Law of Property Act 1925 (which is superseded by this section) affects the operation after the commencement of this Act of any delegation effected before that commencement.

**Amendment**

Sub-s (8): repealed by the TrA 2000, s 40, Schs 2, 4.



**[2.460A]**

### [9A Duties of trustees in connection with delegation etc]

[(1) The duty of care under section 1 of the Trustee Act 2000 applies to trustees of land in deciding whether to delegate any of their functions under section 9.

(2) Subsection (3) applies if the trustees of land—

(a) delegate any of their functions under section 9, and

(b) the delegation is not irrevocable.

(3) While the delegation continues, the trustees—

(a) must keep the delegation under review,

(b) if circumstances make it appropriate to do so, must consider whether there is a need to exercise any power of intervention that they have, and

(c) if they consider that there is a need to exercise such a power, must do so.

(4) 'Power of intervention' includes—

(a) a power to give directions to the beneficiary;

(b) a power to revoke the delegation.

(5) The duty of care under section 1 of the 2000 Act applies to trustees in carrying out any duty under subsection (3).

(6) A trustee of land is not liable for any act or default of the beneficiary, or beneficiaries, unless the trustee fails to comply with the duty of care in deciding to delegate any of the trustees' functions under section 9 or in carrying out any duty under subsection (3).

(7) Neither this section nor the repeal of section 9(8) by the Trustee Act 2000 affects the operation after the commencement of this section of any delegation effected before that commencement.]

**Amendment**

Inserted by the TrA 2000, s 40, Sch 2.

**[2.461]**

### 10 Consents

(1) If a disposition creating a trust of land requires the consent of more than two persons to the exercise by the trustees of any function relating to the land, the consent of any two of them to the exercise of the function is sufficient in favour of a purchaser.

(2) Subsection (1) does not apply to the exercise of a function by trustees of land held on charitable, ecclesiastical or public trusts.

(3) Where at any time a person whose consent is expressed by a disposition creating a trust of land to be required to the exercise by the trustees of any function relating to the land is not of full age—

(a) his consent is not, in favour of a purchaser, required to the exercise of the function, but

(b) the trustees shall obtain the consent of a parent who has parental responsibility for him (within the meaning of the Children Act 1989) or of a guardian of his.

**[2.462]**

### 11 Consultation with beneficiaries

(1) The trustees of land shall in the exercise of any function relating to land subject to the trust—

(a) so far as practicable, consult the beneficiaries of full age and beneficially entitled to an interest in possession in the land, and

(b) so far as consistent with the general interest of the trust, give effect to the wishes of those beneficiaries, or (in case of dispute) of the majority (according to the value of their combined interests).

(2) Subsection (1) does not apply—

(a) in relation to a trust created by a disposition in so far as provision that it does not apply is made by the disposition,

(b) in relation to a trust created or arising under a will made before the commencement of this Act, or

(c) in relation to the exercise of the power mentioned in section 6(2).

(3) Subsection (1) does not apply to a trust created before the commencement of this Act by a disposition, or a trust created after that commencement by reference to such a trust, unless provision to the effect that it is to apply is made by a deed executed—

(a) in a case in which the trust was created by one person and he is of full capacity, by that person, or

(b) in a case in which the trust was created by more than one person, by such of the persons who created the trust as are alive and of full capacity.

(4) A deed executed for the purposes of subsection (3) is irrevocable.

**[2.463]**

### 12 The right to occupy

(1) A beneficiary who is beneficially entitled to an interest in possession in land subject to a trust of land is entitled by reason of his interest to occupy the land at any time if at that time—

(a) the purposes of the trust include making the land available for his occupation (or for the occupation of beneficiaries of a class of which he is a member or of beneficiaries in general), or

(b) the land is held by the trustees so as to be so available.

(2) Subsection (1) does not confer on a beneficiary a right to occupy land if it is either unavailable or unsuitable for occupation by him.

(3) This section is subject to section 13.

**[2.464]**

### 13 Exclusion and restriction of right to occupy

(1) Where two or more beneficiaries are (or apart from this subsection would be) entitled under section 12 to occupy land, the trustees of land may exclude or restrict the entitlement of any one or more (but not all) of them.

(2) Trustees may not under subsection (1)—

(a) unreasonably exclude any beneficiary's entitlement to occupy land, or

(b) restrict any such entitlement to an unreasonable extent.

(3) The trustees of land may from time to time impose reasonable conditions on any beneficiary in relation to his occupation of land by reason of his entitlement under section 12.

(4) The matters to which trustees are to have regard in exercising the powers conferred by this section include—

(a) the intentions of the person or persons (if any) who created the trust,

(b) the purposes for which the land is held, and

(c) the circumstances and wishes of each of the beneficiaries who is (or apart from any previous exercise by the trustees of those powers would be) entitled to occupy the land under section 12.

(5) The conditions which may be imposed on a beneficiary under subsection (3) include, in particular, conditions requiring him—

(a) to pay any outgoings or expenses in respect of the land, or

(b) to assume any other obligation in relation to the land or to any activity which is or is proposed to be conducted there.

(6) Where the entitlement of any beneficiary to occupy land under section 12 has been excluded or restricted, the conditions which may be imposed on any other beneficiary under subsection (3) include, in particular, conditions requiring him to—

(a) make payments by way of compensation to the beneficiary whose entitlement has been excluded or restricted, or

(b) forgo any payment or other benefit to which he would otherwise be entitled under the trust so as to benefit that beneficiary.

(7) The powers conferred on trustees by this section may not be exercised—

(a) so as prevent any person who is in occupation of land (whether or not by reason of an entitlement under section 12) from continuing to occupy the land, or

(b) in a manner likely to result in any such person ceasing to occupy the land,

unless he consents or the court has given approval.

(8) The matters to which the court is to have regard in determining whether to give approval under subsection (7) include the matters mentioned in subsection (4)(a) to (c).

**Note**

This section together with the preceding section will give a right to occupy a property which may be protected in, inter alia, proceedings under Pt IV of the FLA 1996. For a definition of 'beneficiary' see s 22 at para **[2.472]** below.

**[2.465]**

## 14 Applications for order

(1) Any person who is a trustee of land or has an interest in a property subject to a trust of land may make an application to the court for an order under this section.

(2) On an application for an order under this section the court may make any such order—

(a) relating to the exercise by the trustees of any of their functions (including an order relieving them of any obligation to obtain the consent of, or to consult, any person in connection with the exercise of any of their functions), or

(b) declaring the nature or extent of a person's interest in property subject to the trust,

as the court thinks fit.

(3) The court may not under this section make any order as to the appointment or removal of trustees.

(4) The powers conferred on the court by this section are exercisable on an application whether it is made before or after the commencement of this Act.

**[2.465.1]**
**Keypoints**

- Beneficial interests where there is an express declaration in the conveyance (or deed of trust)
- Where the parties hold the land as beneficial joint tenants
- Express intention
- Resulting trusts

- Presumption of advancement
- Contributions from joint money and from mortgage money
- Constructive trusts
- Establishing the extent of the parties' shares
- Proprietary estoppel
- Width of the court's discretion

### [2.465.2]
### Beneficial interests where there is an express declaration in the conveyance (or deed of trust)

If the conveyance expressly states the parties' beneficial interests, this is conclusive in the absence of fraud or mistake[1].

Practitioners should apply in every case for:

(1) a copy of any Transfer;
(2) a copy of the TR 1 (if this has been used instead of a Transfer simpliciter);
(3) a copy of the AP 5 (or its predecessor);
(4) enquire of the original conveyancing file as to whether there has been express declaration of trust or discussions to the effect.

Any of these may result in an express declaration of trust.

This may include the *Re Gorman* situation where the land is to be held beneficially by just the parties and the survivor of one may give good receipt for capital monies following the death of the other (in which case the parties hold the land as beneficial joint tenants).

1 *Goodman v Gallant* [1986] Fam 106, [1986] 1 All ER 311, CA.

### [2.465.3]
### Where the parties hold the land as beneficial joint tenants

If the home is conveyed to both parties as joint tenants on trust for sale for themselves as joint tenants in equity, this will give them an equitable joint tenancy and, if this is severed, they will become equitable tenants in common in equal shares. If a transfer of registered land declares that the transferees *are entitled to the land for their own benefit* and that the survivor can give a valid receipt for capital money arising on the disposition of the land, this must give them a joint equitable interest because otherwise the survivor would not take the whole interest on the other's death[1]. But this inference may not be capable of being drawn in the absence of the words italicised above because the remainder would be equally consistent with the parties' holding as trustees for a third person[2].

However, doubt surrounds *Huntingford v Hobbs*[3], which relied on the parole rule (now comprehensively abandoned following the House of Lords decision in *Investors Compensation Scheme Ltd v West Bromwich Building Society*[4] and *Harwood v Harwood*[5] (which was manifestly in per curiam).

1 See *Re Gorman* [1990] 1 All ER 717, [1990] 1 WLR 616.
2 See *Harwood v Harwood* [1991] 2 FLR 274, CA; and *Huntingford v Hobbs* [1993] 1 FLR 736, CA.
3 [1993] 1 FLR 736, CA.
4 [1998] 1 WLR 896.
5 [1991] 2 FLR 274, CA.

### [2.465.4]
### Express intention

If the conveyance does not spell out the parties' beneficial interests but they agree when the property is purchased what share each is to take, this will be conclusive of their intention in the absence of fraud or mistake. However, such an agreement is only enforceable where the property is in one of the parties' names where the document is either:

(a) in the prescribed form set out in the Law Reform (Miscellaneous Provisions) Act 1989 (Declarations of trust have to be in writing: see s 53(1)(b) of the Law of Property Act 1925);

(b) the claimant provided valuable consideration (and so can enforce the agreement as a contract to create a trust);
(c) the claimant can establish a constructive trust (see below);
(d) the claimant can rely on a proprietary estoppel (see below).



## [2.465.5]
## Resulting trusts

If a husband purchases the home with his wife's money, he will presumptively hold the property on trust for her. The money should 'result' to her[1].

1 See *Mercier v Mercier* [1903] 2 Ch 98, CA.

## [2.465.6]
## Presumption of advancement

If a husband purchases a property with his own money and has it conveyed into his wife's name, equity presumes that the husband intention is to fulfil his duty to maintain her and to make a gift of the property to her. This is known as the presumption of advancement. Its importance is that it rebuts the presumption of a resulting trust. However, it too can easily be rebutted by evidence of a contrary express intention.

## [2.465.7]
## Contributions from joint money and from mortgage money

If part of the purchase money is derived from joint funds that part will presumptively be regarded as contributed by the parties in equal shares. Likewise if the purchase money is provided by a joint loan or a joint mortgage[1]. If one party alone pays off the mortgage or loan, in the absence of other evidence this will be regarded as his or her sole contribution. But if the parties agree on the extent to which each is to be responsible for payment, it will be presumed that their shares in the property will be in the same proportion, even though in the event the loan is repaid in a different way from that contemplated[2].

1 See *Re Gorman* [1990] 1 All ER 717.
2 See *Huntingford v Hobbs* [1993] 1 FLR 736, CA.

## [2.465.8]
## Constructive trusts

If (a) the parties have a common intention that one of them should take a beneficial interest in property acquired by the other; and (b) the other party has acted to his or her detriment on the basis of, or in reliance on, that intention, then equity will compel the first party to give effect to that intention. Equity will 'construe' a trust whereby the first party hold the land on trust for the second party.

(a) The common intention may have been made by express agreement or it may be inferred from what was said and done at the time. But the conduct relied on must clearly indicate that the claimant is to take an interest in the property. It is not sufficient that the property is acquired as the parties' home or as a joint venture. A *direct* contribution to the purchase of the home, whether to the deposit, legal charges or mortgage repayments, will readily justify the inference necessary to give rise to a constructive trust[1].
(b) The party claiming the benefit of a constructive trust must show that she has acted to her detriment AND also that she did so on the basis of, or in reliance on, their common intention. In the absence of evidence, 'the law is not so cynical as to infer that a woman will only go to live with a man to whom she is not married if she understands that she is to have an interest in the house[2]. Thus the detriment need not be financial[3].

1 See *Lloyds Bank plc v Rosset* [1991] 1 AC 107, [1990] 1 All ER 1111, HL.
2 Per Nourse LJ in *Grant v Edwards* [1986] Ch 638 at 648, CA.
3 See *Cooke v Head* [1972] 2 All ER 38, CA; and *Eves v Eves* [1975] 3 All ER 768 (the famous sledge-hammer wielding case).

## [2.465.9]
### Establishing the extent of the parties' shares

The size of shares based on a constructive trust must reflect the parties' common intention when the property was acquired. Usually a resulting trust will reflect the proportion of capital originally invested which is now to result to the settlor. It may be very difficult to determine the size of the contributions; the court retains a wide judicial discretion, thus in *Stokes v Anderson*[1] the defendant had contributed less than 15% of the price but the court took 'the fair view' that she was entitled to a quarter. In *Midland Bank v Cooke*[2] the Court of Appeal took the view that the duty of the judge is to 'undertake a survey of the whole course of dealing between the parties relevant to their ownership and occupation of the property and their sharing of its burdens and advantages. That scrutiny will … take into consideration all conduct which throws light on the question what shares were intended'. This approach does not sit well with Lord Bridge's attempt to bring certainty to this area of law as expressed in *Lloyds Bank v Rosset*[3].

1 [1991] FCR 539, CA.
2 [1995] 4 All ER 562, CA.
3 [1991] 1 AC 107, HL.

## [2.465.10]
### Proprietary estoppel

'If [a person], by his words or conduct, so behaves as to lead another to believe that he will not insist on his strict legal rights – knowing or intending that the other will act on that belief – and he does so act, that … will raise an equity in favour of the other; and it is for a court of equity to say in what way the equity may be satisfied'[1].

1 Per Lord Denning in *Crabb v Arun District Council* [1976] Ch 179 at 188, CA.

## [2.465.11]
### Width of the court's discretion

In *Mortgage Corpn v Silkin*[1] in which it was held that under s 15 of the TLATA 1996 the court has a greater flexibility than before in deciding how to exercise its jurisdiction on an application for an order for sale at the suit of a chargee. Once the relevant factors set out in s 15(1) to be taken into account have been identified, it is a matter for the court as to what weight to give each factor in a particular case. In enacting s 15 of the TLATA 1996, it is not unlikely that the legislature intends to relax the fetters on the way in which the court exercises its discretion so as to tip the balance somewhat more in favour of families and against banks and other chargees.

1 [2000] 2 FCR 222.

## [2.466]

### 15 Matters relevant in determining applications

(1) The matters to which the court is to have regard in determining an application for an order under section 14 include—

- (a) the intentions of the person or persons (if any) who created the trust,
- (b) the purposes for which the property subject to the trust is held,
- (c) the welfare of any minor who occupies or might reasonably be expected to occupy any land subject to the trust as his home, and
- (d) the interests of any secured creditor of any beneficiary.

(2) In the case of an application relating to the exercise in relation to any land of the powers conferred on the trustees by section 13, the matters to which the court is to have regard also include the circumstances and wishes of each of the beneficiaries who is (or apart from any previous exercise by the trustees of those powers would be) entitled to occupy the land under section 12.

(3) In the case of any other application, other than one relating to the exercise of the power mentioned in section 6(2), the matters to which the court is to have regard also include the circumstances and wishes of any beneficiaries of full age and entitled to an interest in possession in property subject to the trust or (in case of dispute) of the majority (according to the value of their combined interests).

(4) This section does not apply to an application if section 335A of the Insolvency Act 1986 (which is inserted by Schedule 3 and relates to applications by a trustee of a bankrupt) applies to it.

**Definitions**

'Beneficiaries' — see s 22 at para **[2.472]** below.



### [2.466.1]
### Keypoints

- General
- Beneficiaries

### [2.466.2]
### General

See the commentary set out under s 14 at para **[2.465.1]** et seq above.

### [2.466.3]
### Beneficiaries

For a definition of beneficiary see s 22 at para **[2.472]** below.

### [2.467]

### 17 Application of provisions to trusts of proceeds of sale

(1) …

(2) Section 14 applies in relation to a trust of proceeds of sale of land and trustees of such a trust as in relation to a trust of land and trustees of land.

(3) In this section 'trust of proceeds of sale of land' means (subject to subsection (5)) any trust of property (other than a trust of land) which consists of or includes—

(a) any proceeds of a disposition of land held in trust (including settled land), or

(b) any property representing any such proceeds.

(4) The references in subsection (3) to a trust—

(a) are to any description of trust (whether express, implied, resulting or constructive), including a trust for sale and a bare trust, and

(b) include a trust created, or arising, before the commencement of this Act.

(5) A trust which (despite section 2) is a settlement for the purposes of the Settled Land Act 1925 cannot be a trust of proceeds of sale of land.

(6) In subsection (3)—

(a) 'disposition' includes any disposition made, or coming into operation, before the commencement of this Act, and

(b) the reference to settled land includes personal chattels to which section 67(1) of the Settled Land Act 1925 (heirlooms) applies.

**Amendment**

Sub-s (1): repealed by the TrA 2000, s 40, Schs 2, 4.

**Note**

This section extends s 14 so as to include by s 17(2) any net proceeds of sale of land. Thus an application can be brought some time after the property has been disposed of. If there has been a distribution of that money then the agreement which led to this may be treated as varying the original common intention where a constructive trust is relied upon. Where no constructive, implied or resulting trust is relied upon the new agreement will have to have been in writing and the formal requirements of s 2 of the LP(MP)A 1989 complied with[1].

1 Note *United Bank of Kuwait plc v Sahib* [1997] Ch 107, [1996] 3 All ER 215, CA; *all* dispositions of interests in land and all previous legislation and case law is subject to s 2 of the LP(MP)A 1989.

**[2.468]**

### 18 Application of Part to personal representatives

(1) The provisions of this Part relating to trustees, other than sections 10, 11 and 14, apply to personal representatives, but with appropriate modifications and without prejudice to the functions of personal representatives for the purposes of administration.

(2) The appropriate modifications include—

(a) the substitution of references to persons interested in the due administration of the estate for references to beneficiaries, and

(b) the substitution of references to the will for references to the disposition creating the trust.

(3) Section 3(1) does not apply to personal representatives if the death occurs before the commencement of this Act.

**[2.469]**

## PART II
## APPOINTMENT AND RETIREMENT OF TRUSTEES

### 19 Appointment and retirement of trustee at instance of beneficiaries

(1) This section applies in the case of a trust where—

(a) there is no person nominated for the purpose of appointing new trustees by the instrument, if any, creating the trust, and

(b) the beneficiaries under the trust are of full age and capacity and (taken together) are absolutely entitled to the property subject to the trust.

(2) The beneficiaries may give a direction or directions of either or both of the following descriptions—

(a) a written direction to a trustee or trustees to retire from the trust, and

(b) a written direction to the trustees or trustee for the time being (or, if there are none, to the personal representative of the last person who was a trustee) to appoint by writing to be a trustee or trustees the person or persons specified in the direction.

(3) Where—

(a) a trustee has been given a direction under subsection (2)(a),

(b) reasonable arrangements have been made for the protection of any rights of his in connection with the trust,

(c) after he has retired there will be either a trust corporation or at least two persons to act as trustees to perform the trust, and

(d) either another person is to be appointed to be a new trustee on his retirement (whether in compliance with a direction under subsection (2)(b) or otherwise) or the continuing trustees by deed consent to his retirement,

he shall make a deed declaring his retirement and shall be deemed to have retired and be discharged from the trust.

(4) Where a trustee retires under subsection (3) he and the continuing trustees (together with any new trustee) shall (subject to any arrangements for the protection of his rights) do anything necessary to vest the trust property in the continuing trustees (or the continuing and new trustees).

(5) This section has effect subject to the restrictions imposed by the Trustee Act 1925 on the number of trustees.

**Note**

This section may assist an applicant for financial provision under the I(PFD)A 1975; enforcement under that Act is as legatee not as judgment creditor.



## [2.470]

### 20 Appointment of substitute for incapable trustee

(1) This section applies where—

(a) a trustee is incapable by reason of mental disorder of exercising his functions as trustee,

(b) there is no person who is both entitled and willing and able to appoint a trustee in place of him under section 36(1) of the Trustee Act 1925, and

(c) the beneficiaries under the trust are of full age and capacity and (taken together) are absolutely entitled to the property subject to the trust.

(2) The beneficiaries may give to—

(a) a receiver of the trustee,

(b) an attorney acting for him under the authority of a power of attorney created by an instrument which is registered under section 6 of the Enduring Powers of Attorney Act 1985, or

(c) a person authorised for the purpose by the authority having jurisdiction under Part VII of the Mental Health Act 1983,

a written direction to appoint by writing the person or persons specified in the direction to be a trustee or trustees in place of the incapable trustee.

## [2.471]

### 21 Supplementary

(1) For the purposes of section 19 or 20 a direction is given by beneficiaries if—

(a) a single direction is jointly given by all of them, or

(b) (subject to subsection (2)) a direction is given by each of them (whether solely or jointly with one or more, but not all, of the others),

and none of them by writing withdraws the direction given by him before it has been complied with.

(2) Where more than one direction is given each must specify for appointment or retirement the same person or persons.

(3) Subsection (7) of section 36 of the Trustee Act 1925 (powers of trustees appointed under that section) applies to a trustee appointed under section 19 or 20 as if he were appointed under that section.

(4) A direction under section 19 or 20 must not specify a person or persons for appointment if the appointment of that person or those persons would be in contravention of section 35(1) of the Trustee Act 1925 or section 24(1) of the Law of Property Act 1925 (requirements as to identity of trustees).

(5) Sections 19 and 20 do not apply in relation to a trust created by a disposition in so far as provision that they do not apply is made by the disposition.

(6) Sections 19 and 20 do not apply in relation to a trust created before the commencement of this Act by a disposition in so far as provision to the effect that they do not apply is made by a deed executed—

(a) in a case in which the trust was created by one person and he is of full capacity, by that person, or
(b) in a case in which the trust was created by more than one person, by such of the persons who created the trust as are alive and of full capacity.

(7) A deed executed for the purposes of subsection (6) is irrevocable.

(8) Where a deed is executed for the purposes of subsection (6)—
(a) it does not affect anything done before its execution to comply with a direction under section 19 or 20, but
(b) a direction under section 19 or 20 which has been given but not complied with before its execution shall cease to have effect.

**[2.472]**

## PART III
## SUPPLEMENTARY

### 22 Meaning of 'beneficiary'

(1) In this Act 'beneficiary', in relation to a trust, means any person who under the trust has an interest in property subject to the trust (including a person who has such an interest as a trustee or a personal representative).

(2) In this Act references to a beneficiary who is beneficially entitled do not include a beneficiary who has an interest in property subject to the trust only by reason of being a trustee or personal representative.

(3) For the purposes of this Act a person who is a beneficiary only by reason of being an annuitant is not to be regarded as entitled to an interest in possession in land subject to the trust.

**[2.473]**

### 23 Other interpretation provisions

(1) In this Act 'purchaser' has the same meaning as in Part I of the Law of Property Act 1925.

(2) Subject to that, where an expression used in this Act is given a meaning by the Law of Property Act 1925 it has the same meaning as in that Act unless the context otherwise requires.

(3) In this Act 'the court' means—
(a) the High Court, or
(b) a county court.

**[2.474]**

### 24 Application to Crown

(1) Subject to subsection (2), this Act binds the Crown.

(2) This Act (except so far as it relates to undivided shares and joint ownership) does not affect or alter the descent, devolution or nature of the estates and interests of or in—
(a) land for the time being vested in Her Majesty in right of the Crown or of the Duchy of Lancaster, or
(b) land for the time being belonging to the Duchy of Cornwall and held in right or respect of the Duchy.

**[2.474A]**

### 25 Amendments, repeals etc

(1) The enactments mentioned in Schedule 3 have effect subject to the amendments specified in that Schedule (which are minor or consequential on other provisions of this Act).

(2) The enactments mentioned in Schedule 4 are repealed to the extent specified in the third column of that Schedule.

(3) Neither section 2(5) nor the repeal by this Act of section 29 of the Settled Land Act 1925 applies in relation to the deed of settlement set out in the Schedule to the Chequers Estate Act 1917 or the trust instrument set out in the Schedule to the Chevening Estate Act 1959.

(4) The amendments and repeals made by this Act do not affect any entailed interest created before the commencement of this Act.

(5) The amendments and repeals made by this Act in consequence of section 3—

(a) do not affect a trust created by a will if the testator died before the commencement of this Act, and

(b) do not affect personal representatives of a person who died before that commencement;

and the repeal of section 22 of the Partnership Act 1890 does not apply in any circumstances involving the personal representatives of a partner who died before that commencement.

**[2.474B]**

### 26 Power to make consequential provision

(1) The Lord Chancellor may by order made by statutory instrument make any such supplementary, transitional or incidental provision as appears to him to be appropriate for any of the purposes of this Act or in consequence of any of the provisions of this Act.

(2) An order under subsection (1) may, in particular, include provision modifying any enactment contained in a public general or local Act which is passed before, or in the same Session as, this Act.

(3) A statutory instrument made in the exercise of the power conferred by this section is subject to annulment in pursuance of a resolution of either House of Parliament.

**[2.474C]**

### 27 Short title, commencement and extent

(1) This Act may be cited as the Trusts of Land and Appointment of Trustees Act 1996.

(2) This Act comes into force on such day as the Lord Chancellor appoints by order made by statutory instrument.

(3) Subject to subsection (4), the provisions of this Act extend only to England and Wales.

(4) The repeal in section 30(2) of the Agriculture Act 1970 extends only to Northern Ireland.

## SCHEDULE 1
Provisions consequential on section 2

(s 2)

**[2.475]**

*Minors*

**1**

(1) Where after the commencement of this Act a person purports to convey a legal estate in land to a minor, or two or more minors, alone, the conveyance—

(a) is not effective to pass the legal estate, but

(b) operates as a declaration that the land is held in trust for the minor or minors (or if he purports to convey it to the minor or minors in trust for any persons, for those persons).

(2) Where after the commencement of this Act a person purports to convey a legal estate in land to—

(a) a minor or two or more minors, and

(b) another person who is, or other persons who are, of full age,

the conveyance operates to vest the land in the other person or persons in trust for the minor or minors and the other person or persons (or if he purports to convey it to them in trust for any persons, for those persons).

(3) Where immediately before the commencement of this Act a conveyance is operating (by virtue of section 27 of the Settled Land Act 1925) as an agreement to execute a settlement in favour of a minor or minors—

(a) the agreement ceases to have effect on the commencement of this Act, and

(b) the conveyance subsequently operates instead as a declaration that the land is held in trust for the minor or minors.

**2**

Where after the commencement of this Act a legal estate in land would, by reason of intestacy or in any other circumstances not dealt with in paragraph 1, vest in a person who is a minor if he were a person of full age, the land is held in trust for the minor.

*Family charges*

**3**

Where, by virtue of an instrument coming into operation after the commencement of this Act, land becomes charged voluntarily (or in consideration of marriage) or by way of family arrangement, whether immediately or after an interval, with the payment of—

(a) a rentcharge for the life of a person or a shorter period, or

(b) capital, annual or periodical sums for the benefit of a person,

the instrument operates as a declaration that the land is held in trust for giving effect to the charge.

*Charitable, ecclesiastical and public trusts*

**4**

(1) This paragraph applies in the case of land held on charitable, ecclesiastical or public trusts (other than land to which the Universities and College Estates Act 1925 applies).

(2) Where there is a conveyance of such land—

(a) if neither section 37(1) nor section 39(1) of the Charities Act 1993 applies to the conveyance, it shall state that the land is held on such trusts, and

(b) if neither section 37(2) nor section 39(2) of that Act has been complied with in relation to the conveyance and a purchaser has notice that the land is held on such trusts, he must see that any consents or orders necessary to authorise the transaction have been obtained.

(3) Where any trustees or the majority of any set of trustees have power to transfer or create any legal estate in the land, the estate shall be transferred or created by them in the names and on behalf of the persons in whom it is vested.

### *Entailed interests*

**5**

(1) Where a person purports by an instrument coming into operation after the commencement of this Act to grant to another person an entailed interest in real or personal property, the instrument—

(a) is not effective to grant an entailed interest, but

(b) operates instead as a declaration that the property is held in trust absolutely for the person to whom an entailed interest in the property was purportedly granted.

(2) Where a person purports by an instrument coming into operation after the commencement of this Act to declare himself a tenant in tail of real or personal property, the instrument is not effective to create an entailed interest.

### *Property held on settlement ceasing to exist*

**6**

Where a settlement ceases to be a settlement for the purposes of the Settled Land Act 1925 because no relevant property (within the meaning of section 2(4)) is, or is deemed to be, subject to the settlement, any property which is or later becomes subject to the settlement is held in trust for the persons interested under the settlement.

# Family Law Act 1996

Contents





*An Act to make provision with respect to: divorce and separation; legal aid in connection with mediation in disputes relating to family matters; proceedings in cases where marriages have broken down; rights of occupation of certain domestic premises; prevention of molestation; the inclusion in certain orders under the Children Act 1989 of provisions about the occupation of a dwelling-house; the transfer of tenancies between spouses and persons who have lived together as husband and wife; and for connected purposes*

[4th July 1996]

**[2.476]**

### 53 Transfer of certain tenancies

Schedule 7 makes provision in relation to the transfer of certain tenancies on divorce etc or on separation of cohabitants.

**Appointment**
Appointment: 1 October 1997: see SI 1997/1892, art 3(1)(a).

**Definitions**
'cohabitants' – by s 62(1)(a) of the FLA 1996, 'cohabitants' are a man and a woman who, though not married to each other, are living together as husband and wife.

**Notes**
This section re-enacts s 7 of, and Sch 1 to the Matrimonial Homes Act 1983, enabling former spouses to apply for a transfer of tenancy. It extends the jurisdiction to cohabitants, and allows the court to direct a payment to the transferor, where appropriate.

## SCHEDULE 7
Transfer of Certain Tenancies on Divorce etc or on Separation of Cohabitants

(s 53)

**[2.477]**

PART I
GENERAL

*Interpretation*

**1**

In this Schedule—

'cohabitant', except in paragraph 3, includes (where the context requires) former cohabitant;

'the court' does not include a magistrates' court,

'landlord' includes—

(a) any person from time to time deriving title under the original landlord; and

(b) in relation to any dwelling-house, any person other than the tenant who is, or (but for Part VII of the Rent Act 1977 or Part II of the Rent (Agriculture) Act 1976) would be, entitled to possession of the dwelling-house;

'Part II order' means an order under Part II of this Schedule;

'a relevant tenancy' means—

(a) a protected tenancy or statutory tenancy within the meaning of the Rent Act 1977;

(b) a statutory tenancy within the meaning of the Rent (Agriculture) Act 1976;

(c) a secure tenancy within the meaning of section 79 of the Housing Act 1985; …

(d) an assured tenancy or assured agricultural occupancy within the meaning of Part I of the Housing Act 1988; [or

(e) an introductory tenancy within the meaning of Chapter I of Part V of the Housing Act 1996;]

'spouse', except in paragraph 2, includes (where the context requires) former spouse; and

'tenancy' includes sub-tenancy.

**Amendment**

Para 1: in definition 'a relevant tenancy' word omitted revoked, and sub-para (e) added, by SI 1997/74, art 2, Schedule, para 10(b)(i).

**Definitions**

'cohabitants' – by s 62(1)(a) of the FLA 1996, 'cohabitants' are a man and a woman who, though not married to each other, are living together as husband and wife.

**[2.478]**

*Cases in which the court may make an order*

**2**

(1) This paragraph applies if one spouse is entitled, either in his own right or jointly with the other spouse, to occupy a dwelling-house by virtue of a relevant tenancy.

(2) At any time when it has power to make a property adjustment order under section 23A (divorce or separation) or 24 (nullity) of the Matrimonial Causes Act 1973 with respect to the marriage, the court may make a Part II order.

**Definitions**

'Part II order' – see para **[2.477]** above.

'a relevant tenancy'; 'tenancy' – see para **[2.477]** above.

'the court' – see para **[2.477]** above.

'dwelling-house' – by s 63(1), (4) of the FLA 1996 'dwelling-house' includes any building or part of a building which is occupied as a dwelling, and any yard, garden, garage or outhouse belonging to it and occupied with it. It does not include a caravan, house-boat etc.

'spouse' – see para **[2.477]** above.

**Notes**

This paragraph permits the court to make an order under Pt II of this Schedule (see below) where the parties are married, and at least one is entitled to occupy a dwelling-house under a relevant tenancy, if it has power under the MCA 1973, ss 23A, 24. Note that in this paragraph, 'spouse' does not include former spouse (see Sch 7, para 1 above).

## [2.479]

**3**

(1) This paragraph applies if one cohabitant is entitled, either in his own right or jointly with the other cohabitant, to occupy a dwelling-house by virtue of a relevant tenancy.

(2) If the cohabitants cease to live together as husband and wife, the court may make a Part II order.

**Definitions**
'cohabitants' – see para **[2.476]** above.
'Part II order' – see para **[2.477]** above.
'dwelling-house' – see para **[2.477]** above.
'relevant tenancy'; 'tenancy' – see para **[2.477]** above.
'the court' – see para **[2.477]** above.

## [2.480]

**4**

The court shall not make a Part II order unless the dwelling-house is or was—

(a) in the case of spouses, a matrimonial home; or
(b) in the case of cohabitants, a home in which they lived together as husband and wife.

**Definitions**
'Part II order' – see para **[2.477]** above.
'the court' – see para **[2.477]** above.
'dwelling-house' – see para **[2.477]** above.
'spouse' – see para **[2.477]** above.
'cohabitants' – see paras **[2.477]** and **[2.476]** above.

## [2.481]

*Matters to which the court must have regard*

**5**

In determining whether to exercise its powers under Part II of this Schedule and, if so, in what manner, the court shall have regard to all the circumstances of the case including—

(a) the circumstances in which the tenancy was granted to either or both of the spouses or cohabitants or, as the case requires, the circumstances in which either or both of them became tenant under the tenancy;
(b) the matters mentioned in section 33(6)(a), (b) and (c) and, where the parties are cohabitants and only one of them is entitled to occupy the dwelling-house by virtue of the relevant tenancy, the further matters mentioned in section 36(6)(e), (f), (g) and (h); and
(c) the suitability of the parties as tenants.

**Definitions**
'the court' – see para **[2.477]** above.
'tenancy'; 'relevant tenancy' – see para **[2.477]** above.
'cohabitants' – see paras **[2.477]** and **[2.476]** above.
'spouse' – see para **[2.477]** above.
'dwelling-house' – see para **[2.478]** above.

## [2.481.1]
### Keypoints

- Scheme of Pt 1
- Application for an order
- Matters for the court

## [2.481.2]
### Scheme of Pt 1

Before the enactment of Pt IV of the FLA 1996 the childless cohabiting couple had no recourse to the courts to obtain the long-term solution to their housing problems if they shared rented accommodation. If the tenancy was in the sole name of one, there was no power to transfer it to the other.

Part I of Sch 7 to the FLA 1996 defines the terms used, the circumstances in which the court now has power, and the matters to be considered in the exercise of that power, in relation to the transfer of those tenancies listed in para 1, both in relation to married and cohabiting couples.

The orders that may be made in each case are set out in Pt II (see below).

## [2.481.3]
### Application for an order

There is no prescribed form of application for transfer of tenancy. Application should therefore be made to a district judge, by summons in the High Court and notice in county courts in accordance with FPR 1991, r 10.9.

Notice of the application for transfer of tenancy must be served by the applicant on the other cohabitant or spouse and on the landlord (as defined in para 1 above[1]), and any person so served shall be entitled to be heard on the application[2].

The following apply, with necessary modifications, to an application for a transfer of tenancy:

- FPR 1991, rr 2.62(4), (5), (6) and 2.63 *(investigation, requests for further information)*, as they apply to an application for ancillary relief[3].
- FPR 1991 r 3.6(7), (8), (9) *(MWPA 1882)*, as it applies to an application under r.3.6[4].

The applicant must file a statement in form FL415 *(statement of service)* after he has served the application[5].

1 See para **[2.477]** above.
2 See FPR 1991, r 3.8(12).
3 See FPR 1991, r 3.8(13)(b).
4 See FPR 1991, r 3.8(14).
5 See FPR 1991, r 3.8(15).

## [2.481.4]
### Matters for the court

In addition to all the circumstances of the case, para 5 makes specific reference to certain matters to be considered by the court in the exercise of its powers. These include the circumstances in which the tenancy was granted or otherwise acquired (see para 5(a)), and the suitability of the parties as tenants (see para 5(c)).

By para 5(b), matters mentioned elsewhere in the FLA 1996 are included for consideration. These are:

(1) under s 33(6) —

- the housing needs and housing resources of each of the parties and of any relevant child;
- the financial resources of each of the parties; and
- the likely effect of any order, or of any decision by the court not to exercise its powers, on the health, safety or well-being of the parties and of any relevant child.

(2) under s 36(6), where the parties are cohabitants, and only one of them is entitled to occupy under a relevant tenancy —
- the nature of the parties' relationship;
- the length of time during which they have lived together as husband and wife;
- whether there are or have been any children who are children of both parties or for whom both parties have or have had parental responsibility; and
- the length of time that has elapsed since the parties ceased to live together.

For a decision on para 3 of Sch 7 to the FLA 1996, see *Gay v Sheeran*[1], where the court held that there is no power to order the transfer of a secure tenancy of a dwelling-house under Sch 7 to the FLA 1996 to a cohabitant who is not a tenant where the other cohabitant, being the tenant, is no longer entitled to occupy the property by virtue of the secure tenancy as a result of having ceased occupation. An order for transfer may only be made if the other cohabitant is entitled to occupy by virtue of a relevant tenancy at the relevant time and for that purpose the relevant time is either the time of the application or the time of the making of the order (it was not necessary in this case to decide which of those two dates should be adopted, but Peter Gibson LJ was 'inclined to the view' that the latter was to be preferred and he rejected in any event the contention that the relevant time was the cessation of cohabitation). Moreover, where, as here, the interest in respect of which a transfer is sought is that of a cohabitant who is a joint tenant with a third party, the court has no jurisdiction to order the transfer of that interest to the other cohabitant; the effect of para 3 of Sch 7 to the FLA 1996 is that the power to order a transfer between cohabitants may only be exercised where the estate or interest in question arises by virtue of a tenancy vested in one of them as sole tenant or in both of them as joint tenants together.

1 [1999] 3 All ER 795, [2000] 1 WLR 673, CA.



**[2.482]**

PART II
ORDERS THAT MAY BE MADE

*References to entitlement to occupy*

**6**

References in this Part of this Schedule to a spouse or a cohabitant being entitled to occupy a dwelling-house by virtue of a relevant tenancy apply whether that entitlement is in his own right or jointly with the other spouse or cohabitant.

**Definitions**
'cohabitant' – see paras **[2.477]** and **[2.476]** above.
'dwelling-house' – see para **[2.478]** above.
'spouse' – see para **[2.477]** above.
'tenancy'; 'relevant tenancy' – see para **[2.477]** above.

**[2.483]**

*Protected, secure or assured tenancy or assured agricultural occupancy*

**7**

(1) If a spouse or cohabitant is entitled to occupy the dwelling-house by virtue of a protected tenancy within the meaning of the Rent Act 1977, a secure tenancy within the meaning of the Housing Act 1985[, an assured tenancy] or assured agricultural occupancy within the meaning of Part I of the Housing Act 1988 [or an introductory tenancy within the meaning of Chapter I of Part V of the Housing Act 1996], the court may by order direct that, as from such date as may be specified in the order, there shall, by virtue of the order and without further assurance, be transferred to, and vested in, the other spouse or cohabitant—

(a) the estate or interest which the spouse or cohabitant so entitled had in the dwelling-house immediately before that date by virtue of the lease or agreement creating the tenancy and any assignment of that lease or agreement, with all rights, privileges and appurtenances attaching to that estate or interest but subject to all covenants, obligations, liabilities and incumbrances to which it is subject; and

(b) where the spouse or cohabitant so entitled is an assignee of such lease or agreement, the liability of that spouse or cohabitant under any covenant of indemnity by the assignee express or implied in the assignment of the lease or agreement to that spouse or cohabitant.

(2) If an order is made under this paragraph, any liability or obligation to which the spouse or cohabitant so entitled is subject under any covenant having reference to the dwelling-house in the lease or agreement, being a liability or obligation falling due to be discharged or performed on or after the date so specified, shall not be enforceable against that spouse or cohabitant.

(3) If the spouse so entitled is a successor within the meaning of Part IV of the Housing Act 1985, his former spouse or former cohabitant (or, if a separation order is in force, his spouse) shall be deemed also to be a successor within the meaning of that Part.

[(3A) If the Spouse or cohabitant so entitled is a successor within the meaning of section 132 of the Housing Act 1996, his former spouse or former cohabitant (or, if a separation order is in force, his spouse) shall be deemed also to be a successor within the meaning of that section.]

(4) If the spouse or cohabitant so entitled is for the purpose of section 17 of the Housing Act 1988 a successor in relation to the tenancy or occupancy, his former spouse or former cohabitant (or, if a separation order is in force, his spouse) is to be deemed to be a successor in relation to the tenancy or occupancy for the purposes of that section.

(5) If the transfer under sub-paragraph (1) is of an assured agricultural occupancy, then, for the purposes of Chapter III of Part I of the Housing Act 1988—

(a) the agricultural worker condition is fulfilled with respect to the dwelling-house while the spouse or cohabitant to whom the assured agricultural occupancy is transferred continues to be the occupier under that occupancy, and

(b) that condition is to be treated as so fulfilled by virtue of the same paragraph of Schedule 3 to the Housing Act 1988 as was applicable before the transfer.

(6) In this paragraph, references to a separation order being in force include references to there being a judicial separation in force.

**Amendment**

Para 7: in sub-para (1) first words in square brackets substituted and second words in square brackets added, and sub-para (3A) added, by SI 1997/74, art 2, Schedule, para 10(b)(ii), (iii).

**Modification**

Modification: para 7(3), (4), (6) temporarily modified by the Family Law Act 1996 (Commencement No 2) Order 1997, SI 1997 No 1892, art 4(b), (c), until such time as Pt II of this Act is brought into force.

**Definitions**

'cohabitant' – see paras **[2.477]** and **[2.476]** above.
'dwelling-house' – see para **[2.478]** above.
'spouse' – see para **[2.477]** above.
'tenancy' – see para **[2.477]** above.

**[2.483.1]**
**Keypoints**

- Relevant tenancies

- Such date as may be specified
- Advantages over application under the MCA 1973
- Domestic violence as a ground for possession

### [2.483.2]
### Relevant tenancies

The tenancies to which this paragraph applies are set out in para 7(1) and are:

- a protected tenancy under the Rent Act 1977;
- a secure tenancy under the Housing Act 1985;
- an assured tenancy under the Housing Act 1988, Pt I;
- an assured agricultural occupancy under the Housing Act 1988, Pt I;
- an introductory tenancy under the Housing Act 1996, Pt V.



### [2.483.3]
### Such date as may be specified

Under para 7(1), the court may by order direct a transfer of one of the above tenancies 'as from such date as may be specified in the order'.

In the case of nullity the order cannot take effect before the date of decree absolute[1].

In the case of divorce and separation proceedings, the order cannot presently take effect until the date of decree absolute[2].

An order between former cohabitants may take effect at any time on or after the making of the order.

1 See the FLA 1996, Sch 7, Pt III, para 12(1) at para **[2.488]** below.
2 See the FLA 1996, Sch 7, Pt III, para 12(1) at para **[2.488]** below as amended by SI 1997/1892, until the coming into force of Pt II of the FLA 1996.

### [2.483.4]
### Advantages over application under the MCA 1973

By para 7(1), the court may direct transfer 'by virtue of this order and without further assurance', obviating the need to apply to the court at a later stage for the district judge to execute the transfer on behalf of the transferor.

By para 7(1)(a), the interest vested is that which the spouse or cohabitant had immediately before the date specified in the order, which may avoid any breach by virtue of the order of covenants against assignment contained in the tenancy agreement itself.

Neither of these powers are available under the MCA 1973, s 24, which section furthermore only applies to married couples, and not to cohabitants or former cohabitants.

The ChA 1989, s 15, Sch 1, provides that a parent or a person with a residence order in respect of a child may apply for financial provision against a parent of that child, including a transfer of property order to the applicant for the benefit of the child[1]. 'Property' includes a tenancy[2].

See further *Kingston upon Thames Royal London Borough v Prince*[3] (held that a minor could succeed to a secure tenancy within the meaning of the Housing Act 1985; declaration that the minor was a secure tenant in equity until she reached her majority and the legal estate would be held by her mother as her guardian ad litem until that time).

See also *Newlon Housing Trust v Alsulaimen*[4]. Note that a periodic tenancy is 'property' within the MCA 1973, s 24 (at para **[2.118]** above).

1 See the ChA 1989, Sch 1, para 1(2)(e) at para **[2.417]** above.
2 See *K v K* [1992] 2 All ER 727.
3 [1999] 1 FLR 593, CA.
4 [1997] 2 FCR 33, [1997] 1 FLR 914, CA, reversed for other reasons [1999] 1 AC 313, [1998] 4 All ER 1, HL.

### [2.483.5]
### Domestic Violence as a ground for possession

The Housing Acts 1985 and 1988 have been amended with effect from February 1997 by the Housing Act 1996, Pt V, Cap II, in relation to secure and assured tenancies respectively. The landlord may now recover possession on the grounds that the dwelling-house was occupied (whether alone or with others) by a married couple or a couple living together as husband and wife and:

- one or both of the partners is a tenant of the dwelling-house;
- one partner has left because of violence or threats of violence by the other towards that partner or a member of the family of that partner who was residing with that partner immediately before the partner left; and
- the court is satisfied that the partner who has left is unlikely to return.

### [2.484]

*Statutory tenancy within the meaning of the Rent Act 1977*

**8**

(1) This paragraph applies if the spouse or cohabitant is entitled to occupy the dwelling-house by virtue of a statutory tenancy within the meaning of the Rent Act 1977.

(2) The court may by order direct that, as from the date specified in the order—

(a) that spouse or cohabitant is to cease to be entitled to occupy the dwelling-house; and

(b) the other spouse or cohabitant is to be deemed to be the tenant or, as the case may be, the sole tenant under that statutory tenancy.

(3) The question whether the provisions of paragraphs 1 to 3, or (as the case may be) paragraphs 5 to 7 of Schedule 1 to the Rent Act 1977, as to the succession by the surviving spouse of a deceased tenant, or by a member of the deceased tenant's family, to the right to retain possession are capable of having effect in the event of the death of the person deemed by an order under this paragraph to be the tenant or sole tenant under the statutory tenancy is to be determined according as those provisions have or have not already had effect in relation to the statutory tenancy.

**Definitions**

'tenancy' – see para **[2.477]** above.
'cohabitant' – see paras **[2.477]** and **[2.476]** above.
'spouse' – see para **[2.477]** above.
'dwelling-house' – see para **[2.478]** above.

### [2.484.1]
### Keypoints

- Differences where there is a statutory tenancy
- Authority relating to statutory tenancy

### [2.484.2]
### Differences where there is a statutory tenancy

The powers granted to the court under para 8(2) in respect of statutory tenancies under the Rent Act 1977 are identical to those in respect of statutory tenancies under the Rent (Agriculture) Act 1976 under para 9(2) below.

By virtue of the different nature and characteristics of such tenancies (outside the scope of this work) the powers under these paragraphs contain significant simplifications to those in para 7 above.

### [2.484.3]
### Authority relating to statutory tenancy

A statutory tenancy must be in existence at the date of the application for its transfer[1].

The ability to make an order that a party is to cease to be entitled to occupy does not of itself enable the court to order that that party leave the dwelling-house[2].

1 See *Lewis v Lewis* [1985] AC 828, [1985] 2 All ER 449, HL.
2 See *Maynard v Maynard* [1969] P 88, [1969] 1 All ER 1.

### [2.485]

*Statutory tenancy within the meaning of the Rent (Agriculture) Act 1976*

**9**

(1) This paragraph applies if the spouse or cohabitant is entitled to occupy the dwelling-house by virtue of a statutory tenancy within the meaning of the Rent (Agriculture) Act 1976.

(2) The court may by order direct that, as from such date as may be specified in the order—

(a) that spouse or cohabitant is to cease to be entitled to occupy the dwelling-house; and

(b) the other spouse or cohabitant is to be deemed to be the tenant or, as the case may be, the sole tenant under that statutory tenancy.

(3) A spouse or cohabitant who is deemed under this paragraph to be the tenant under a statutory tenancy is (within the meaning of that Act) a statutory tenant in his own right, or a statutory tenant by succession, according as the other spouse or cohabitant was a statutory tenant in his own right or a statutory tenant by succession.

**Definitions**
'cohabitant' – see paras **[2.477]** and **[2.476]** above.
'dwelling-house' – see para **[2.478]** above.
'tenancy' – see para **[2.477]** above.
'spouse' – see para **[2.477]** above.

### [2.486]

PART III
SUPPLEMENTARY PROVISIONS

*Compensation*

**10**

(1) If the court makes a Part II order, it may by the order direct the making of a payment by the spouse or cohabitant to whom the tenancy is transferred ('the transferee') to the other spouse or cohabitant ('the transferor').

(2) Without prejudice to that, the court may, on making an order by virtue of sub-paragraph (1) for the payment of a sum—

(a) direct that payment of that sum or any part of it is to be deferred until a specified date or until the occurrence of a specified event, or

(b) direct that that sum or any part of it is to be paid by instalments.

(3) Where an order has been made by virtue of sub-paragraph (1), the court may, on the application of the transferee or the transferor—

(a) exercise its powers under sub-paragraph (2), or

(b) vary any direction previously given under that sub-paragraph,

at any time before the sum whose payment is required by the order is paid in full.

(4) In deciding whether to exercise its powers under this paragraph and, if so, in what manner, the court shall have regard to all the circumstances including—

- (a) the financial loss that would otherwise be suffered by the transferor as a result of the order;
- (b) the financial needs and financial resources of the parties; and
- (c) the financial obligations which the parties have, or are likely to have in the foreseeable future, including financial obligations to each other and to any relevant child.

(5) The court shall not give any direction under sub-paragraph (2) unless it appears to it that immediate payment of the sum required by the order would cause the transferee financial hardship which is greater than any financial hardship that would be caused to the transferor if the direction were given.

**Definitions**

'Part II order' – see para **[2.477]** above.
'the court' – see para **[2.477]** above.
'cohabitant' – see paras **[2.477]** and **[2.476]** above.
'spouse' – see para **[2.477]** above.

## [2.486.1]
### Keypoints

- Structure of the paragraph
- Matters for the court

## [2.486.2]
### Structure of the paragraph

Paragraph 10(1) for the first time enables the court to direct payment by the recipient spouse or cohabitant to the transferor of the tenancy, as compensation for their loss of rights in the tenancy so transferred.

Paragraph 10(2) enables the court to direct that such sum as has been ordered under para 10(1) may be paid by installments (para 10(2)(b)) or may be deferred in whole or in part to a specific date or happening (para 10(2)(a)).

Paragraph 10(3) permits the court, at the application of either party, and at any time before payment in full of a sum ordered under para 10(1), to vary any direction already given under para 10(2) (para 10(3)(b)) or exercise its powers under para 10(2) afresh by directing deferment (or payment in installments) of a sum already ordered but not yet paid in full (para 10(3)(a)).

Paragraph 10(5) prevents the court from exercising its powers under para 10(2) unless it is satisfied that immediate payment of the sum would cause financial hardship to the recipient greater than any such hardship caused to the transferor if a direction under para 10(2) were given.

## [2.486.3]
### Matters for the court

Paragraph 10(4) sets out that the court should have regard to all the circumstances in deciding whether to exercise its powers under para 10, and if so, how. Expressly, those circumstances include:

- such financial loss as would otherwise be suffered by the transferor as a result of the Pt II order;
- the financial needs and resources of the parties; and
- the financial obligations of the parties, including to each other and to any relevant child, which they have or are likely to have in the foreseeable future.

[2.487]

*Liabilities and obligations in respect of the dwelling-house*

**11**

(1) If the court makes a Part II order, it may by the order direct that both spouses or cohabitants are to be jointly and severally liable to discharge or perform any or all of the liabilities and obligations in respect of the dwelling-house (whether arising under the tenancy or otherwise) which—

(a) have at the date of the order fallen due to be discharged or performed by one only of them; or

(b) but for the direction, would before the date specified as the date on which the order is to take effect fall due to be discharged or performed by one only of them.

(2) If the court gives such a direction, it may further direct that either spouse or cohabitant is to be liable to indemnify the other in whole or in part against any payment made or expenses incurred by the other in discharging or performing any such liability or obligation.

**Definitions**

'the court' – see para **[2.477]** above.
'Part II order' – see para **[2.477]** above.
'cohabitant' – see paras **[2.477]** and **[2.476]** above.
'spouse' – see para **[2.477]** above.
'dwelling-house' – see para **[2.478]** above.
'tenancy' – see para **[2.477]** above.

[2.488]

*Date when order made between spouses is to take effect*

**12**

(1) In the case of a decree of [divorce or] nullity of marriage, the date specified in a Part II order as the date on which the order is to take effect must not be earlier than the date on which the decree is made absolute.

(2) In the case of divorce proceedings or separation proceedings, the date specified in a Part II order as the date on which the order is to take effect is to be determined as if the court were making a property adjustment order under section 23A of the Matrimonial Causes Act 1973 (regard being had to the restrictions imposed by section 23B of that Act).

**Definitions**

'Part II order' – see para **[2.477]** above.

[2.489]

*Remarriage of either spouse*

**13**

(1) If after the making of a divorce order or the grant of a decree annulling a marriage either spouse remarries, that spouse is not entitled to apply, by reference to the making of that order or the grant of that decree, for a Part II order.

(2) For the avoidance of doubt it is hereby declared that the reference in sub-paragraph (1) to remarriage includes a reference to a marriage which is by law void or voidable.

**Definitions**

'Part II order' – see para **[2.477]** above.

**[2.490]**

*Rules of court*

**14**

(1) Rules of court shall be made requiring the court, before it makes an order under this Schedule, to give the landlord of the dwelling-house to which the order will relate an opportunity of being heard.

(2) Rules of court may provide that an application for a Part II order by reference to an order or decree may not, without the leave of the court by which that order was made or decree was granted, be made after the expiration of such period from the order or grant as may be prescribed by the rules.

**Definitions**

'landlord' – see para **[2.477]** above.
'dwelling-house' – see para **[2.478]** above.
'Part II order' – see para **[2.477]** above.

**[2.491]**

*Saving for other provisions of Act*

**15**

(1) If a spouse is entitled to occupy a dwelling-house by virtue of a tenancy, this Schedule does not affect the operation of sections 30 and 31 in relation to the other spouse's matrimonial home rights.

(2) If a spouse or cohabitant is entitled to occupy a dwelling-house by virtue of a tenancy, the court's powers to make orders under this Schedule are additional to those conferred by sections 33, 35 and 36.

**Definitions**

'spouse' – see para **[2.477]** above.
'dwelling-house' – see para **[2.478]** above.
'tenancy' – see para **[2.477]** above.
'cohabitant' – see paras **[2.477]** and **[2.476]** above.

# Access to Justice Act 1999

## Contents

*Section*

PART I
LEGAL SERVICES COMMISSION



PART II
OTHER FUNDING OF LEGAL SERVICES



PART III
PROVISION OF LEGAL SERVICES

PART IV
APPEALS, COURTS, JUDGES AND COURT PROCEEDINGS



PART VII
SUPPLEMENTARY



---

*An Act to establish the Legal Services Commission, the Community Legal Service and the Criminal Defence Service; to amend the law of legal aid in Scotland; to make further provision about legal services; to make provision about appeals, courts, judges and court proceedings; to amend the law about magistrates and magistrates' courts; and to make provision about immunity from action and costs and indemnities for certain officials exercising judicial functions*

[27th July 1999]

**[2.491A]**

PART I
LEGAL SERVICES COMMISSION

**1 Legal Services Commission**

(1) There shall be a body known as the Legal Services Commission (in this Part referred to as 'the Commission').

(2) The Commission shall have the functions relating to—

(a) the Community Legal Service, and

(b) the Criminal Defence Service,

which are conferred or imposed on it by the provisions of this Act or any other enactment.

(3) The Commission shall consist of—

(a) not fewer than seven members, and

(b) not more than twelve members;

but the Lord Chancellor may by order substitute for either or both of the numbers for the time being specified in paragraphs (a) and (b) such other number or numbers as he thinks appropriate.

(4) The members of the Commission shall be appointed by the Lord Chancellor; and the Lord Chancellor shall appoint one of the members to chair the Commission.

(5) In appointing persons to be members of the Commission the Lord Chancellor shall have regard to the desirability of securing that the Commission includes members who (between them) have experience in or knowledge of—

(a) the provision of services which the Commission can fund as part of the Community Legal Service or Criminal Defence Service,

(b) the work of the courts,

(c) consumer affairs,

(d) social conditions, and

(e) management.

(6) Schedule 1 (which makes further provision about the Commission) has effect.

**Appointment**

1 April 2000: SI 2000/774, art 2.



**[2.492]**

### 2 Power to replace Commission with two bodies

(1) The Lord Chancellor may by order establish in place of the Commission two bodies—

(a) one to have functions relating to the Community Legal Service, and

(b) the other to have functions relating to the Criminal Defence Service.

(2) The order may make any consequential, incidental, supplementary or transitional provisions, and any savings, which appear to the Lord Chancellor to be appropriate.

(3) The order shall include amendments of—

(a) any provisions of, or amended by, this Part which refer to the Commission, and

(b) any other enactments which so refer,

to replace references to the Commission with references to either or both of the bodies established by the order.

**Appointment**

1 April 2000: SI 2000/774, art 2.

**[2.493]**

### 3 Powers of Commission

(1) Subject to the provisions of this Part, the Commission may do anything which it considers—

(a) is necessary or appropriate for, or for facilitating, the discharge of its functions, or

(b) is incidental or conducive to the discharge of its functions.

(2) In particular, the Commission shall have power—

(a) to enter into any contract,

(b) to make grants (with or without conditions),

(c) to make loans,

(d) to invest money,
(e) to promote or assist in the promotion of publicity relating to its functions,
(f) to undertake any inquiry or investigation which it may consider appropriate in relation to the discharge of any of its functions, and
(g) to give the Lord Chancellor any advice which it may consider appropriate in relation to matters concerning any of its functions.

(3) Subsections (1) and (2) do not confer on the Commission power to borrow money.

(4) The Commission may make such arrangements as it considers appropriate for the discharge of its functions, including the delegation of any of its functions.

(5) The Lord Chancellor may by order require the Commission—
(a) to delegate any function specified in the order or to delegate any function so specified to a person (or person of a description) so specified,
(b) not to delegate any function so specified or not to delegate any function so specified to a person (or person of a description) so specified, or
(c) to make arrangements such as are specified in the order in relation to the delegation of any function so specified.

**Appointment**
1 April 2000: SI 2000/774, art 2.

**[2.494]**

### 4 Community Legal Service

(1) The Commission shall establish, maintain and develop a service known as the Community Legal Service for the purpose of promoting the availability to individuals of services of the descriptions specified in subsection (2) and, in particular, for securing (within the resources made available, and priorities set, in accordance with this Part) that individuals have access to services that effectively meet their needs.

(2) The descriptions of services referred to in subsection (1) are—
(a) the provision of general information about the law and legal system and the availability of legal services,
(b) the provision of help by the giving of advice as to how the law applies in particular circumstances,
(c) the provision of help in preventing, or settling or otherwise resolving, disputes about legal rights and duties,
(d) the provision of help in enforcing decisions by which such disputes are resolved, and
(e) the provision of help in relation to legal proceedings not relating to disputes.

(3) Services which the Commission is required to fund as part of the Criminal Defence Service do not fall within subsection (2).

(4) Every person who exercises any function relating to the Community Legal Service shall have regard to the desirability of exercising it, so far as is reasonably practicable, so as to—
(a) promote improvements in the range and quality of services provided as part of the Community Legal Service and in the ways in which they are made accessible to those who need them,
(b) secure that the services provided in relation to any matter are appropriate having regard to its nature and importance, and
(c) achieve the swift and fair resolution of disputes without unnecessary or unduly protracted proceedings in court.

(5) The Commission shall fund services of the descriptions specified in subsection (2) as part of the Community Legal Service in accordance with the following sections.

(6) The Commission shall also inform itself about the need for, and the provision of, services of the descriptions specified in subsection (2) and about the quality of the services provided and, in co-operation with such authorities and other bodies and persons as it considers appropriate—

(a) plan what can be done towards meeting that need by the performance by the Commission of its functions, and

(b) facilitate the planning by other authorities, bodies and persons of what can be done by them to meet that need by the use of any resources available to them;

and the Commission shall notify the Lord Chancellor of what it has done under this subsection.

(7) The Commission may set and monitor standards in relation to services of the descriptions specified in subsection (2).

(8) In particular, the Commission may accredit, or authorise others to accredit, persons or bodies providing services of the descriptions specified in subsection (2); and any system of accreditation shall include provision for the monitoring of the services provided by accredited persons and bodies and for the withdrawal of accreditation from any providing services of unsatisfactory quality.

(9) The Commission may charge—

(a) for accreditation,

(b) for monitoring the services provided by accredited persons and bodies, and

(c) for authorising accreditation by others;

and persons or bodies authorised to accredit may charge for accreditation, and for such monitoring, in accordance with the terms of their authorisation.

(10) The Lord Chancellor may by order require the Commission to discharge the functions in subsections (6) to (9) in accordance with the order.

**Appointment**
1 April 2000: SI 2000/774, art 2.



**[2.495]**

### 5 Funding of services

(1) The Commission shall establish and maintain a fund known as the Community Legal Service Fund from which it shall fund services as part of the Community Legal Service.

(2) The Lord Chancellor—

(a) shall pay to the Commission the sums which he determines are appropriate for the funding of services by the Commission as part of the Community Legal Service, and

(b) may determine the manner in which and times at which the sums are to be paid to the Commission and may impose conditions on the payment of the sums.

(3) In making any determination under subsection (2) the Lord Chancellor shall take into account (in addition to such other factors as he considers relevant) the need for services of the descriptions specified in subsection (2) of section 4 as notified to him by the Commission under subsection (6) of that section.

(4) The Lord Chancellor shall lay before each House of Parliament a copy of every determination under subsection (2)(a).

(5) The Commission shall pay into the Community Legal Service Fund—

(a) sums received from the Lord Chancellor under subsection (2), and

(b) sums received by the Commission by virtue of regulations under section 10 or 11.

(6) The Lord Chancellor may by direction impose requirements on the Commission as to the descriptions of services to be funded from any specified amount paid into the Community Legal Service Fund.

(7) In funding services as part of the Community Legal Service the Commission shall aim to obtain the best possible value for money.

**Appointment**
1 April 2000: SI 2000/774, art 2.

**[2.496]**

## 6 Services which may be funded

(1) The Commission shall set priorities in its funding of services as part of the Community Legal Service and the priorities shall be set—

- (a) in accordance with any directions given by the Lord Chancellor, and
- (b) after taking into account the need for services of the descriptions specified in section 4(2).

(2) Subject to that (and to subsection (6)), the services which the Commission may fund as part of the Community Legal Service are those which the Commission considers appropriate.

(3) The Commission may fund services as part of the Community Legal Service by—

- (a) entering into contracts with persons or bodies for the provision of services by them,
- (b) making payments to persons or bodies in respect of the provision of services by them,
- (c) making grants or loans to persons or bodies to enable them to provide, or facilitate the provision of, services,
- (d) establishing and maintaining bodies to provide, or facilitate the provision of, services,
- (e) making grants or loans to individuals to enable them to obtain services,
- (f) itself providing services, or
- (g) doing anything else which it considers appropriate for funding services.

(4) The Lord Chancellor may by order require the Commission to discharge the function in subsection (3) in accordance with the order.

(5) The Commission may fund as part of the Community Legal Service different descriptions of services or services provided by different means—

- (a) in relation to different areas or communities in England and Wales, and
- (b) in relation to descriptions of cases.

(6) The Commission may not fund as part of the Community Legal Service any of the services specified in Schedule 2.

(7) Regulations may amend that Schedule by adding new services or omitting or varying any services.

(8) The Lord Chancellor—

- (a) may by direction require the Commission to fund the provision of any of the services specified in Schedule 2 in circumstances specified in the direction, and
- (b) may authorise the Commission to fund the provision of any of those services in specified circumstances or, if the Commission request him to do so, in an individual case.

(9) The Lord Chancellor shall either—

- (a) publish, or
- (b) require the Commission to publish,

any authorisation under subsection (8)(b) unless it relates to an individual case (in which case he or the Commission may publish it if appropriate).

**Appointment**
1 April 2000: SI 2000/774, art 2.

**[2.497]**

## 7 Individuals for whom services may be funded

(1) The Commission may only fund services for an individual as part of the Community Legal Service if his financial resources are such that, under regulations, he is an individual for whom they may be so funded.

(2) Regulations may provide that, in prescribed circumstances and subject to any prescribed conditions, services of a prescribed description may be so funded for individuals without reference to their financial resources.

(3) Regulations under this section may include provision requiring the furnishing of information.

**Appointment**
1 April 2000: SI 2000/774, art 2.

**[2.498]**

## 8 Code about provision of funded services

(1) The Commission shall prepare a code setting out the criteria according to which it is to decide whether to fund (or continue to fund) services as part of the Community Legal Service for an individual for whom they may be so funded and, if so, what services are to be funded for him.

(2) In settling the criteria to be set out in the code the Commission shall consider the extent to which they ought to reflect the following factors—

- (a) the likely cost of funding the services and the benefit which may be obtained by their being provided,
- (b) the availability of sums in the Community Legal Service Fund for funding the services and (having regard to present and likely future demands on that Fund) the appropriateness of applying them to fund the services,
- (c) the importance of the matters in relation to which the services would be provided for the individual,
- (d) the availability to the individual of services not funded by the Commission and the likelihood of his being able to avail himself of them,
- (e) if the services are sought by the individual in relation to a dispute, the prospects of his success in the dispute,
- (f) the conduct of the individual in connection with services funded as part of the Community Legal Service (or an application for funding) or in, or in connection with, any proceedings,
- (g) the public interest, and
- (h) such other factors as the Lord Chancellor may by order require the Commission to consider.

(3) The criteria set out in the code shall reflect the principle that in many family disputes mediation will be more appropriate than court proceedings.

(4) The code shall seek to secure that, where more than one description of service is available, the service funded is that which (in all the circumstances) is the most appropriate having regard to the criteria set out in the code.

(5) The code shall also specify procedures for the making of decisions about the funding of services by the Commission as part of the Community Legal Service, including—

- (a) provision about the form and content of applications for funding,
- (b) provision imposing conditions which must be satisfied by an individual applying for funding,
- (c) provision requiring applicants to be informed of the reasons for any decision to refuse an application,

(d) provision for the giving of information to individuals whose applications are refused about alternative ways of obtaining or funding services, and
(e) provision establishing procedures for appeals against decisions about funding and for the giving of information about those procedures.

(6) The code may make different provision for different purposes.

(7) The Commission may from time to time prepare a revised version of the code.

(8) Before preparing the code the Commission shall undertake such consultation as appears to it to be appropriate; and before revising the code the Commission shall undertake such consultation as appears to it to be appropriate unless it considers that it is desirable for the revised version to come into force without delay.

(9) The Lord Chancellor may by order require the Commission to discharge its functions relating to the code in accordance with the order.

**Appointment**
1 April 2000: SI 2000/774, art 2.

**[2.499]**

### 9 Procedure relating to funding code

(1) After preparing the code or a revised version of the code the Commission shall send a copy to the Lord Chancellor.

(2) If he approves it he shall lay it before each House of Parliament.

(3) The Commission shall publish—
(a) the code as first approved by the Lord Chancellor, and
(b) where he approves a revised version, either the revisions or the revised code as appropriate.

(4) The code as first approved by the Lord Chancellor shall not come into force until it has been approved by a resolution of each House of Parliament.

(5) A revised version of the code which does not contain changes in the criteria set out in the code shall not come into force until it has been laid before each House of Parliament.

(6) Subject as follows, a revised version of the code which does contain such changes shall not come into force until it has been approved by a resolution of each House of Parliament.

(7) Where the Lord Chancellor considers that it is desirable for a revised version of the code containing such changes to come into force without delay, he may (when laying the revised version before Parliament) also lay before each House a statement of his reasons for so considering.

(8) In that event the revised version of the code—
(a) shall not come into force until it has been laid before each House of Parliament, and
(b) shall cease to have effect at the end of the period of 120 days beginning with the day on which it comes into force unless a resolution approving it has been made by each House (but without that affecting anything previously done in accordance with it).

**Appointment**
1 April 2000: SI 2000/774, art 2.

**[2.500]**

### 10 Terms of provision of funded services

(1) An individual for whom services are funded by the Commission as part of the Community Legal Service shall not be required to make any payment in respect of the services except where regulations otherwise provide.

(2) Regulations may provide that, in prescribed circumstances, an individual for whom services are so funded shall—

(a) pay a fee of such amount as is fixed by or determined under the regulations,

(b) if his financial resources are, or relevant conduct is, such as to make him liable to do so under the regulations, pay the cost of the services or make a contribution in respect of the cost of the services of such amount as is so fixed or determined, or

(c) if the services relate to a dispute and he has agreed to make a payment (which may exceed the cost of the services) only in specified circumstances, make in those circumstances a payment of the amount agreed, or determined in the manner agreed, by him;

and in paragraph (b) 'relevant conduct' means conduct in connection with the services (or any application for their funding) or in, or in connection with, any proceedings in relation to which they are provided.

(3) The regulations may include provision for any amount payable in accordance with the regulations to be payable by periodical payments or one or more capital sums, or both.

(4) The regulations may also include provision for the payment by an individual of interest (on such terms as may be prescribed) in respect of—

(a) any loan made to him by the Commission as part of the Community Legal Service,

(b) any payment in respect of the cost of services required by the regulations to be made by him later than the time when the services are provided, or

(c) so much of any payment required by the regulations to be made by him which remains unpaid after the time when it is required to be paid.

(5) The regulations shall include provision for the repayment to an individual of any payment made by him in excess of his liability under the regulations.

(6) The regulations may—

(a) include provision requiring the furnishing of information, and

(b) make provision for the determination of the cost of services for the purposes of the regulations.

(7) Except so far as regulations otherwise provide, where services have been funded by the Commission for an individual as part of the Community Legal Service—

(a) sums expended by the Commission in funding the services (except to the extent that they are recovered under section 11), and

(b) other sums payable by the individual by virtue of regulations under this section,

shall constitute a first charge on any property recovered or preserved by him (whether for himself or any other person) in any proceedings or in any compromise or settlement of any dispute in connection with which the services were provided.

(8) Regulations may make provision about the charge, including—

(a) provision as to whether it is in favour of the Commission or the body or person by whom the services were provided, and

(b) provision about its enforcement.

**Appointment**

1 April 2000: SI 2000/774, art 2.



**[2.501]**

### 11 Costs in funded cases

(1) Except in prescribed circumstances, costs ordered against an individual in relation to any proceedings or part of proceedings funded for him shall not exceed the amount (if any) which is a reasonable one for him to pay having regard to all the circumstances including—

(a) the financial resources of all the parties to the proceedings, and
(b) their conduct in connection with the dispute to which the proceedings relate;

and for this purpose proceedings, or a part of proceedings, are funded for an individual if services relating to the proceedings or part are funded for him by the Commission as part of the Community Legal Service.

(2) In assessing for the purposes of subsection (1) the financial resources of an individual for whom services are funded by the Commission as part of the Community Legal Service, his clothes and household furniture and the tools and implements of his trade shall not be taken into account, except so far as may be prescribed.

(3) Subject to subsections (1) and (2), regulations may make provision about costs in relation to proceedings in which services are funded by the Commission for any of the parties as part of the Community Legal Service.

(4) The regulations may, in particular, make provision—

(a) specifying the principles to be applied in determining the amount of any costs which may be awarded against a party for whom services are funded by the Commission as part of the Community Legal Service,
(b) limiting the circumstances in which, or extent to which, an order for costs may be enforced against such a party,
(c) as to the cases in which, and extent to which, such a party may be required to give security for costs and the manner in which it is to be given,
(d) requiring the payment by the Commission of the whole or part of any costs incurred by a party for whom services are not funded by the Commission as part of the Community Legal Service,
(e) specifying the principles to be applied in determining the amount of any costs which may be awarded to a party for whom services are so funded,
(f) requiring the payment to the Commission, or the person or body by which the services were provided, of the whole or part of any sum awarded by way of costs to such a party, and
(g) as to the court, tribunal or other person or body by whom the amount of any costs is to be determined and the extent to which any determination of that amount is to be final.

**Appointment**
1 April 2000: SI 2000/774, art 2.

**[2.502]**

## 19 Foreign law

(1) The Commission may not fund as part of the Community Legal Service or Criminal Defence Service services relating to any law other than that of England and Wales, unless any such law is relevant for determining any issue relating to the law of England and Wales.

(2) But the Lord Chancellor may, if it appears to him necessary to do so for the purpose of fulfilling any obligation imposed on the United Kingdom by any international agreement, by order specify that there may be funded as part of the Community Legal Service or Criminal Defence Service (or both) services relating to the application of such other law as may be specified in the order.

**Appointment**
1 April 2000: SI 2000/774, art 2.

**[2.503]**

## 20 Restriction of disclosure of information

(1) Subject to the following provisions of this section, information which is furnished—

(a) to the Commission or any court, tribunal or other person or body on whom functions are imposed or conferred by or under this Part, and
(b) in connection with the case of an individual seeking or receiving services funded by the Commission as part of the Community Legal Service or Criminal Defence Service,

shall not be disclosed except as permitted by subsection (2).

(2) Such information may be disclosed—

(a) for the purpose of enabling or assisting the Commission to discharge any functions imposed or conferred on it by or under this Part,
(b) for the purpose of enabling or assisting the Lord Chancellor to discharge any functions imposed or conferred on him by or under this Part,
(c) for the purpose of enabling or assisting any court, tribunal or other person or body to discharge any functions imposed or conferred on it by or under this Part,
(d) except where regulations otherwise provide, for the purpose of the investigation or prosecution of any offence (or suspected offence) under the law of England and Wales or any other jurisdiction,
(e) in connection with any proceedings relating to the Community Legal Service or Criminal Defence Service, or
(f) for the purpose of facilitating the proper performance by any tribunal of disciplinary functions.

(3) Subsection (1) does not limit the disclosure of—

(a) information in the form of a summary or collection of information so framed as not to enable information relating to any individual to be ascertained from it, or
(b) information about the amount of any grant, loan or other payment made to any person or body by the Commission.

(4) Subsection (1) does not prevent the disclosure of information for any purpose with the consent of the individual in connection with whose case it was furnished and, where he did not furnish it himself, with that of the person or body who did.

(5) A person who discloses any information in contravention of this section shall be guilty of an offence and liable on summary conviction to a fine not exceeding level 4 on the standard scale.

(6) Proceedings for an offence under this section shall not be brought without the consent of the Director of Public Prosecutions.

(7) Nothing in this section applies to information furnished to a person providing services funded as part of the Community Legal Service or the Criminal Defence Service by or on behalf of an individual seeking or receiving such services.

**Appointment**
1 April 2000: SI 2000/774, art 2.



**[2.504]**

## 21 Misrepresentation etc

(1) Any person who—

(a) intentionally fails to comply with any requirement imposed by virtue of this Part as to the information to be furnished by him, or
(b) in furnishing any information required by virtue of this Part makes any statement or representation which he knows or believes to be false,

shall be guilty of an offence.

(2) A person guilty of an offence under subsection (1) is liable on summary conviction to—

(a) a fine not exceeding level 4 on the standard scale, or
(b) imprisonment for a term not exceeding three months,

or to both.

(3) Proceedings in respect of an offence under subsection (1) may (despite anything in the Magistrates' Courts Act 1980) be brought at any time within the period of six months beginning with the date on which evidence sufficient in the opinion of the prosecutor to justify a prosecution comes to his knowledge.

(4) But subsection (3) does not authorise the commencement of proceedings for an offence at a time more than two years after the date on which the offence was committed.

(5) A county court shall have jurisdiction to hear and determine any action brought by the Commission to recover loss sustained by reason of—

(a) the failure of any person to comply with any requirement imposed by virtue of this Part as to the information to be furnished by him, or
(b) a false statement or false representation made by any person in furnishing any information required by virtue of this Part.

**Appointment**

1 April 2000: SI 2000/774, art 2.

**[2.505]**

### 22 Position of service providers and other parties etc

(1) Except as expressly provided by regulations, the fact that services provided for an individual are or could be funded by the Commission as part of the Community Legal Service or Criminal Defence Service shall not affect—

(a) the relationship between that individual and the person by whom they are provided or any privilege arising out of that relationship, or
(b) any right which that individual may have to be indemnified in respect of expenses incurred by him by any other person.

(2) A person who provides services funded by the Commission as part of the Community Legal Service or Criminal Defence Service shall not take any payment in respect of the services apart from—

(a) that made by way of that funding, and
(b) any authorised by the Commission to be taken.

(3) The withdrawal of a right to representation previously granted to an individual shall not affect the right of any person who has provided to him services funded by the Commission as part of the Criminal Defence Service to remuneration for work done before the date of the withdrawal.

(4) Except as expressly provided by regulations, any rights conferred by or by virtue of this Part on an individual for whom services are funded by the Commission as part of the Community Legal Service or Criminal Defence Service in relation to any proceedings shall not affect—

(a) the rights or liabilities of other parties to the proceedings, or
(b) the principles on which the discretion of any court or tribunal is normally exercised.

(5) Regulations may make provision about the procedure of any court or tribunal in relation to services funded by the Commission as part of the Community Legal Service or Criminal Defence Service.

(6) Regulations made under subsection (5) may in particular authorise the exercise of the functions of any court or tribunal by any member or officer of that or any other court or tribunal.

**Appointment**

1 April 2000: SI 2000/774, art 2.

[2.506]

### 23 Guidance

(1) The Lord Chancellor may give guidance to the Commission as to the manner in which he considers it should discharge its functions.

(2) The Commission shall take into account any such guidance when considering the manner in which it is to discharge its functions.

(3) Guidance may not be given under this section in relation to individual cases.

(4) The Lord Chancellor shall either—

(a) publish, or

(b) require the Commission to publish,

any guidance given under this section.

**Appointment**

1 April 2000: SI 2000/774, art 2.



[2.507]

### 24 Consequential amendments

Schedule 4 (which makes amendments consequential on this Part) has effect.

**Appointment**

1 April 2000: SI 2000/774, art 2.

[2.508]

### 25 Orders, regulations and directions

(1) Any power of the Lord Chancellor under this Part to make an order or regulations is exercisable by statutory instrument.

(2) Before making any remuneration order relating to the payment of remuneration to barristers or solicitors the Lord Chancellor shall consult the General Council of the Bar and the Law Society.

(3) When making any remuneration order the Lord Chancellor shall have regard to—

(a) the need to secure the provision of services of the description to which the order relates by a sufficient number of competent persons and bodies,

(b) the cost to public funds, and

(c) the need to secure value for money.

(4) In subsections (2) and (3) 'remuneration order' means an order under section 6(4), 13(3) or 14(3) which relates to the payment by the Commission of remuneration—

(a) for the provision of services by persons or bodies in individual cases, or

(b) by reference to the provision of services by persons or bodies in specified numbers of cases.

(5) No directions may be given by the Lord Chancellor to the Commission under this Part in relation to individual cases.

(6) Any directions given by the Lord Chancellor to the Commission under this Part may be varied or revoked.

(7) The Lord Chancellor shall either—

(a) publish, or

(b) require the Commission to publish,

any directions given by him under this Part.

(8) Orders, regulations and directions of the Lord Chancellor under this Part may make different provision for different purposes (including different areas).

(9) No order shall be made under section 2 or 8 or paragraph 5(3) of Schedule 3, and no regulations shall be made under section 6(7), 11(1) or (4)(b) or (d) or 15(2)(a) or (5) or paragraph 4 of Schedule 3, unless a draft of the order or regulations has been laid before, and approved by a resolution of, each House of Parliament.

(10) A statutory instrument containing any other order or regulations under this Part shall be subject to annulment in pursuance of a resolution of either House of Parliament.

**Appointment**

1 April 2000: see SI 2000/774, arts 2, 5.

**[2.509]**

### 26 Interpretation

In this Part—

'the Commission' means the Legal Services Commission,

'the Community Legal Service Fund' has the meaning given by section 5(1),

'criminal proceedings' has the meaning given in section 12(2),

'prescribed' means prescribed by regulations and 'prescribe' shall be construed accordingly,

'regulations' means regulations made by the Lord Chancellor, and

'representation' means representation for the purposes of proceedings and includes the assistance which is usually given by a representative in the steps preliminary or incidental to any proceedings and, subject to any time limits which may be prescribed, advice and assistance as to any appeal.

**Appointment**

1 April 2000: see SI 2000/774, arts 2, 5.

**[2.510]**

## PART II
## OTHER FUNDING OF LEGAL SERVICES

### 27 Conditional fee agreements

(1) For section 58 of the Courts and Legal Services Act 1990 substitute—

### '58 Conditional fee agreements

(1) A conditional fee agreement which satisfies all of the conditions applicable to it by virtue of this section shall not be unenforceable by reason only of its being a conditional fee agreement; but (subject to subsection (5)) any other conditional fee agreement shall be unenforceable.

(2) For the purposes of this section and section 58A—

(a) a conditional fee agreement is an agreement with a person providing advocacy or litigation services which provides for his fees and expenses, or any part of them, to be payable only in specified circumstances; and

(b) a conditional fee agreement provides for a success fee if it provides for the amount of any fees to which it applies to be increased, in specified circumstances, above the amount which would be payable if it were not payable only in specified circumstances.

(3) The following conditions are applicable to every conditional fee agreement—

(a) it must be in writing;

(b) it must not relate to proceedings which cannot be the subject of an enforceable conditional fee agreement; and

(c) it must comply with such requirements (if any) as may be prescribed by the Lord Chancellor.

(4) The following further conditions are applicable to a conditional fee agreement which provides for a success fee—

(a) it must relate to proceedings of a description specified by order made by the Lord Chancellor;

(b) it must state the percentage by which the amount of the fees which would be payable if it were not a conditional fee agreement is to be increased; and

(c) that percentage must not exceed the percentage specified in relation to the description of proceedings to which the agreement relates by order made by the Lord Chancellor.

(5) If a conditional fee agreement is an agreement to which section 57 of the Solicitors Act 1974 (non-contentious business agreements between solicitor and client) applies, subsection (1) shall not make it unenforceable.



### 58A Conditional fee agreements: supplementary

(1) The proceedings which cannot be the subject of an enforceable conditional fee agreement are—

(a) criminal proceedings, apart from proceedings under section 82 of the Environmental Protection Act 1990; and

(b) family proceedings.

(2) In subsection (1) 'family proceedings' means proceedings under any one or more of the following—

(a) the Matrimonial Causes Act 1973;

(b) the Adoption Act 1976;

(c) the Domestic Proceedings and Magistrates' Courts Act 1978;

(d) Part III of the Matrimonial and Family Proceedings Act 1984;

(e) Parts I, II and IV of the Children Act 1989;

(f) Part IV of the Family Law Act 1996; and

(g) the inherent jurisdiction of the High Court in relation to children.

(3) The requirements which the Lord Chancellor may prescribe under section 58(3)(c)—

(a) include requirements for the person providing advocacy or litigation services to have provided prescribed information before the agreement is made; and

(b) may be different for different descriptions of conditional fee agreements (and, in particular, may be different for those which provide for a success fee and those which do not).

(4) In section 58 and this section (and in the definitions of 'advocacy services' and 'litigation services' as they apply for their purposes) 'proceedings' includes any sort of proceedings for resolving disputes (and not just proceedings in a court), whether commenced or contemplated.

(5) Before making an order under section 58(4), the Lord Chancellor shall consult—

(a) the designated judges;

(b) the General Council of the Bar;

(c) the Law Society; and

(d) such other bodies as he considers appropriate.

(6) A costs order made in any proceedings may, subject in the case of court proceedings to rules of court, include provision requiring the payment of any fees payable under a conditional fee agreement which provides for a success fee.

(7) Rules of court may make provision with respect to the assessment of any costs which include fees payable under a conditional fee agreement (including one which provides for a success fee).'

(2) In section 120(4) of the Courts and Legal Services Act 1990 (orders and regulations subject to affirmative procedure), for '58,' substitute '58(4),'.

**Appointment**

1 April 2000: SI 2000/774, art 2.

[2.511]

### 28 Litigation funding agreements

In the Courts and Legal Services Act 1990, after section 58A (inserted by section 27 above) insert—

### '58B Litigation funding agreements

(1) A litigation funding agreement which satisfies all of the conditions applicable to it by virtue of this section shall not be unenforceable by reason only of its being a litigation funding agreement.

(2) For the purposes of this section a litigation funding agreement is an agreement under which—

- (a) a person ('the funder') agrees to fund (in whole or in part) the provision of advocacy or litigation services (by someone other than the funder) to another person ('the litigant'); and
- (b) the litigant agrees to pay a sum to the funder in specified circumstances.

(3) The following conditions are applicable to a litigation funding agreement—

- (a) the funder must be a person, or person of a description, prescribed by the Lord Chancellor;
- (b) the agreement must be in writing;
- (c) the agreement must not relate to proceedings which by virtue of section 58A(1) and (2) cannot be the subject of an enforceable conditional fee agreement or to proceedings of any such description as may be prescribed by the Lord Chancellor;
- (d) the agreement must comply with such requirements (if any) as may be so prescribed;
- (e) the sum to be paid by the litigant must consist of any costs payable to him in respect of the proceedings to which the agreement relates together with an amount calculated by reference to the funder's anticipated expenditure in funding the provision of the services; and
- (f) that amount must not exceed such percentage of that anticipated expenditure as may be prescribed by the Lord Chancellor in relation to proceedings of the description to which the agreement relates.

(4) Regulations under subsection (3)(a) may require a person to be approved by the Lord Chancellor or by a prescribed person.

(5) The requirements which the Lord Chancellor may prescribe under subsection (3)(d)—

- (a) include requirements for the funder to have provided prescribed information to the litigant before the agreement is made; and
- (b) may be different for different descriptions of litigation funding agreements.

(6) In this section (and in the definitions of 'advocacy services' and 'litigation services' as they apply for its purposes) 'proceedings' includes any sort of proceedings for resolving disputes (and not just proceedings in a court), whether commenced or contemplated.

(7) Before making regulations under this section, the Lord Chancellor shall consult—

- (a) the designated judges;
- (b) the General Council of the Bar;
- (c) the Law Society; and
- (d) such other bodies as he considers appropriate.

(8) A costs order made in any proceedings may, subject in the case of court proceedings to rules of court, include provision requiring the payment of any amount payable under a litigation funding agreement.

(9) Rules of court may make provision with respect to the assessment of any costs which include fees payable under a litigation funding agreement.'

**Initial Commencement**

To be appointed: see s 108(1) at para **[2.539]** below.



**[2.512]**

### 29 Recovery of insurance premiums by way of costs

Where in any proceedings a costs order is made in favour of any party who has taken out an insurance policy against the risk of incurring a liability in those proceedings, the costs payable to him may, subject in the case of court proceedings to rules of court, include costs in respect of the premium of the policy.

**Appointment**

1 April 2000: SI 2000/774.

**[2.513]**

### 30 Recovery where body undertakes to meet costs liabilities

(1) This section applies where a body of a prescribed description undertakes to meet (in accordance with arrangements satisfying prescribed conditions) liabilities which members of the body or other persons who are parties to proceedings may incur to pay the costs of other parties to the proceedings.

(2) If in any of the proceedings a costs order is made in favour of any of the members or other persons, the costs payable to him may, subject to subsection (3) and (in the case of court proceedings) to rules of court, include an additional amount in respect of any provision made by or on behalf of the body in connection with the proceedings against the risk of having to meet such liabilities.

(3) But the additional amount shall not exceed a sum determined in a prescribed manner; and there may, in particular, be prescribed as a manner of determination one which takes into account the likely cost to the member or other person of the premium of an insurance policy against the risk of incurring a liability to pay the costs of other parties to the proceedings.

(4) In this section 'prescribed' means prescribed by regulations made by the Lord Chancellor by statutory instrument; and a statutory instrument containing such regulations shall be subject to annulment in pursuance of a resolution of either House of Parliament.

(5) Regulations under subsection (1) may, in particular, prescribe as a description of body one which is for the time being approved by the Lord Chancellor or by a prescribed person.

**Appointment**

1 April 2000: SI 2000/774.

**[2.514]**

### 31 Rules as to costs

In section 51 of the Supreme Court Act 1981 (costs), in subsection (2) (rules regulating matters relating to costs), insert at the end 'or for securing that the amount awarded to a party in respect of the costs to be paid by him to such representatives is not limited to what would have been payable by him to them if he had not been awarded costs.'

**Initial Commencement**

To be appointed: see s 108(1) at para **[2.539]** below.

**[2.515]**

PART III
PROVISION OF LEGAL SERVICES

### 35 Replacement of ACLEC by Consultative Panel

(1) The Lord Chancellor's Advisory Committee on Legal Education and Conduct is abolished.

(2) In the Courts and Legal Services Act 1990, after section 18 insert—

*'The Legal Services Consultative Panel*

### 18A The Consultative Panel

(1) The Lord Chancellor shall appoint persons to form a panel to be known as the Legal Services Consultative Panel.

(2) In appointing persons to the Consultative Panel the Lord Chancellor shall have regard to the desirability of securing that the Consultative Panel includes persons who (between them) have experience in or knowledge of—

(a) the provision of legal services;
(b) the lay advice sector;
(c) civil or criminal proceedings and the working of the courts;
(d) legal education and training;
(e) the maintenance of the professional standards of persons who provide legal services;
(f) the maintenance of standards in professions other than the legal profession;
(g) consumer affairs;
(h) commercial affairs; and
(i) social conditions.

(3) The Consultative Panel shall have—

(a) the duty of assisting in the maintenance and development of standards in the education, training and conduct of persons offering legal services by considering relevant issues in accordance with a programme of work approved by the Lord Chancellor and, where the Consultative Panel considers it appropriate to do so, making recommendations to him;
(b) the duty of providing to the Lord Chancellor, at his request, advice about particular matters relating to any aspect of the provision of legal services (including the education, training and conduct of persons offering legal services); and
(c) the functions conferred or imposed on it by other provisions of this Act or any other enactment.

(4) The Consultative Panel may, in performance of the duty in subsection (3)(a), seek information from or give advice to any body or person.

(5) The Lord Chancellor shall publish—

(a) any recommendations made to him by the Consultative Panel in performance of the duty in paragraph (a) of subsection (3); and
(b) any advice provided to him by the Consultative Panel in performance of the duty in paragraph (b) of that subsection.

(6) The Lord Chancellor shall consider any recommendations made to him by the Consultative Panel in performance of the duty in subsection (3)(a).

(7) The Lord Chancellor—

(a) shall make available to the Consultative Panel appropriate administrative support; and
(b) may pay to any of the persons forming it any such allowances, and make any such reimbursement of expenses, as he considers appropriate.

(8) For the purposes of the law of defamation the publication of any advice by the Consultative Panel in the exercise of any of its functions shall be absolutely privileged.'

(3) In section 119(1) of that Act (interpretation), after the definition of 'authorised practitioner' insert—

'"Consultative Panel" means the Legal Services Consultative Panel;'.

(4) In Schedule 9 to that Act (exemption from prohibition on preparation of probate papers: approval)—

(a) for 'Advisory Committee'(in each place) substitute 'Consultative Panel',
(b) in paragraph 2(1), for 'Advisory Committee's' substitute 'Consultative Panel's', and
(c) in paragraphs 2(3) and 8(3), for 'Committee'(in each place) substitute 'Consultative Panel'.

(5) In the First Schedule to the Public Records Act 1958 (definition of public records), in Part II of the Table set out at the end of paragraph 3, insert at the appropriate place—

'The Legal Services Consultative Panel.'



**Appointment**
1 January 2000: see SI 1999/3344.

**[2.516]**

## 36 Barristers and solicitors

For sections 31 to 33 of the Courts and Legal Services Act 1990 (deemed rights of barristers and solicitors) substitute—

### '31 Barristers and solicitors

(1) Every barrister shall be deemed to have been granted by the General Council of the Bar a right of audience before every court in relation to all proceedings (exercisable in accordance with the qualification regulations and rules of conduct of the General Council of the Bar approved for the purposes of section 27 in relation to the right).

(2) Every solicitor shall be deemed to have been granted by the Law Society—

(a) a right of audience before every court in relation to all proceedings (exercisable in accordance with the qualification regulations and rules of conduct of the Law Society approved for the purposes of section 27 in relation to the right); and
(b) a right to conduct litigation in relation to every court and all proceedings (exercisable in accordance with the qualification regulations and rules of conduct of the Law Society approved for the purposes of section 28 in relation to the right).

(3) A person shall not have a right of audience by virtue of subsection (1) if—

(a) he has not been called to the Bar by an Inn of Court; or
(b) he has been disbarred, or is temporarily suspended from practice, by order of an Inn of Court.'

**Appointment**
27 September 1999: see SI 1999/2657.

**[2.517]**

## 37 Rights of audience: employed advocates

In the Courts and Legal Services Act 1990, after section 31 (as substituted by section 36 above) insert—

### '31A Employed advocates

(1) Where a person who has a right of audience granted by an authorised body is employed as a Crown Prosecutor or in any other description of employment, any qualification regulations or rules of conduct of the body relating to that right which fall within subsection (2) shall not have effect in relation to him.

(2) Qualification regulations or rules of conduct relating to a right granted by a body fall within this subsection if—

- (a) they limit the courts before which, or proceedings in which, that right may be exercised by members of the body who are employed or limit the circumstances in which that right may be exercised by them by requiring them to be accompanied by some other person when exercising it; and
- (b) they do not impose the same limitation on members of the body who have the right but are not employed.'

**Appointment**

31 July 2000: see SI 2000/1920.

**[2.518]**

## 38 Employees of Legal Services Commission

In the Courts and Legal Services Act 1990, after section 31A (inserted by section 37 above) insert—

### '31B Advocates and litigators employed by Legal Services Commission

(1) Where a person who has a right of audience or right to conduct litigation granted by an authorised body is employed by the Legal Services Commission, or by any body established and maintained by the Legal Services Commission, any rules of the authorised body which fall within subsection (2) shall not have effect in relation to him.

(2) Rules of a body fall within this subsection if they are—

- (a) rules of conduct prohibiting or limiting the exercise of the right on behalf of members of the public by members of the body who are employees; or
- (b) rules of any other description prohibiting or limiting the provision of legal services to members of the public by such members of the body,

and either of the conditions specified in subsection (3) is satisfied.

(3) Those conditions are—

- (a) that the prohibition or limitation is on the exercise of the right, or the provision of the services, otherwise than on the instructions of solicitors (or other persons acting for the members of the public); and
- (b) that the rules do not impose the same prohibition or limitation on members of the body who have the right but are not employees.'

**Appointment**

31 July 2000: see SI 2000/1920.

**[2.519]**

## 39 Rights of audience: change of authorised body

In the Courts and Legal Services Act 1990, after section 31B (inserted by section 38 above) insert—

### '31C Change of authorised body

(1) Where a person—

(a) has at any time had, and been entitled to exercise, a right of audience before a court in relation to proceedings of any description granted by one authorised body; and
(b) becomes a member of another authorised body and has a right of audience before that court in relation to that description of proceedings granted by that body,

any qualification regulations of that body relating to that right shall not have effect in relation to him.

(2) Subsection (1) does not apply in relation to any qualification regulations to the extent that they impose requirements relating to continuing education or training which have effect in relation to the exercise of the right by all members of the body who have the right.

(3) Subsection (1) does not apply to a person if he has been banned from exercising the right of audience by the body mentioned in paragraph (a) of that subsection as a result of disciplinary proceedings and that body has not lifted the ban.'



**Appointment**

31 July 2000: see SI 2000/1920.

**[2.520]**

### 40 Rights to conduct litigation: barristers and legal executives

(1) Section 28 of the Courts and Legal Services Act 1990 (rights to conduct litigation) is amended as follows.

(2) In the definition of 'authorised body' in subsection (5), after paragraph (a) (which specifies the Law Society), insert—

'(aa) the General Council of the Bar;
(ab) the Institute of Legal Executives; and'.

(3) After that subsection insert—

'(5A) Nothing in this section shall be taken to require the General Council of the Bar or the Institute of Legal Executives to grant a right to conduct litigation.'

**Appointment**

27 September 1999: see SI 1999/2657.

**[2.521]**

### 41 Authorised bodies: designation and regulations and rules

Schedule 5 (which substitutes new provisions for sections 29 and 30 of, and Schedule 4 to, the Courts and Legal Services Act 1990) has effect.

**Appointment**

1 January 2000: see SI 1999/3344.

**[2.522]**

### 42 Overriding duties of advocates and litigators

(1) In section 27 of the Courts and Legal Services Act 1990 (rights of audience), after subsection (2) insert—

'(2A) Every person who exercises before any court a right of audience granted by an authorised body has—

(a) a duty to the court to act with independence in the interests of justice; and
(b) a duty to comply with rules of conduct of the body relating to the right and approved for the purposes of this section;

and those duties shall override any obligation which the person may have (otherwise than under the criminal law) if it is inconsistent with them.'

(2) In section 28 of that Act (rights to conduct litigation), after subsection (2) insert—

'(2A) Every person who exercises in relation to proceedings in any court a right to conduct litigation granted by an authorised body has—

(a) a duty to the court to act with independence in the interests of justice; and

(b) a duty to comply with rules of conduct of the body relating to the right and approved for the purposes of this section;

and those duties shall override any obligation which the person may have (otherwise than under the criminal law) if it is inconsistent with them.'

**Appointment**

27 September 1999: see SI 1999/2657.

**[2.523]**

### 43 Minor and consequential amendments

Schedule 6 (which makes minor and consequential amendments relating to rights of audience and rights to conduct litigation) has effect.

**Appointment**

27 September 1999 / 1 January 2000: see SI 1999/2657 and SI 1999/3344.

**[2.524]**

## PART IV
## APPEALS, COURTS, JUDGES AND COURT PROCEEDINGS

### 54 Permission to appeal

(1) Rules of court may provide that any right of appeal to—

(a) a county court,

(b) the High Court, or

(c) the Court of Appeal,

may be exercised only with permission.

(2) This section does not apply to a right of appeal in a criminal cause or matter.

(3) For the purposes of subsection (1) rules of court may make provision as to—

(a) the classes of case in which a right of appeal may be exercised only with permission,

(b) the court or courts which may give permission for the purposes of this section,

(c) any considerations to be taken into account in deciding whether permission should be given, and

(d) any requirements to be satisfied before permission may be given,

and may make different provision for different circumstances.

(4) No appeal may be made against a decision of a court under this section to give or refuse permission (but this subsection does not affect any right under rules of court to make a further application for permission to the same or another court).

(5) For the purposes of this section a right to make an application to have a case stated for the opinion of the High Court constitutes a right of appeal.

(6) For the purposes of this section a right of appeal to the Court of Appeal includes—

(a) the right to make an application for a new trial, and

(b) the right to make an application to set aside a verdict, finding or judgment in any cause or matter in the High Court which has been tried, or in which any issue has been tried, by a jury.

**Initial Commencement**

Specified date: 27 September 1999: see s 108(3)(b) at para **[2.539]** below.

[2.525]

### 55 Second appeals

(1) Where an appeal is made to a county court or the High Court in relation to any matter, and on hearing the appeal the court makes a decision in relation to that matter, no appeal may be made to the Court of Appeal from that decision unless the Court of Appeal considers that—

(a) the appeal would raise an important point of principle or practice, or
(b) there is some other compelling reason for the Court of Appeal to hear it.

(2) This section does not apply in relation to an appeal in a criminal cause or matter.

**Initial Commencement**
Specified date: 27 September 1999: see s 108(3)(b) at para **[2.539]** below.

[2.526]

### 56 Power to prescribe alternative destination of appeals

(1) The Lord Chancellor may by order provide that appeals which would otherwise lie to—

(a) a county court,
(b) the High Court, or
(c) the Court of Appeal,

shall lie instead to another of those courts, as specified in the order.

(2) This section does not apply to an appeal in a criminal cause or matter.

(3) An order under subsection (1)—

(a) may make different provision for different classes of proceedings or appeals, and
(b) may contain consequential amendments or repeals of enactments.

(4) Before making an order under subsection (1) the Lord Chancellor shall consult—

(a) the Lord Chief Justice,
(b) the Master of the Rolls,
(c) the President of the Family Division, and
(d) the Vice-Chancellor.

(5) An order under subsection (1) shall be made by statutory instrument.

(6) No such order may be made unless a draft of it has been laid before and approved by resolution of each House of Parliament.

(7) For the purposes of this section an application to have a case stated for the opinion of the High Court constitutes an appeal.

**Initial Commencement**
Specified date: 27 September 1999: see s 108(3)(b) at para **[2.539]** below.

[2.527]

### 57 Assignment of appeals to Court of Appeal

(1) Where in any proceedings in a county court or the High Court a person appeals, or seeks permission to appeal, to a court other than the Court of Appeal or the House of Lords—

(a) the Master of the Rolls, or
(b) the court from which or to which the appeal is made, or from which permission to appeal is sought,

may direct that the appeal shall be heard instead by the Court of Appeal.

(2) The power conferred by subsection (1)(b) shall be subject to rules of court.

**Initial Commencement**
Specified date: 27 September 1999: see s 108(3)(b) at para **[2.539]** below.

**[2.528]**

### 58 Criminal appeals: minor amendments

(1) …

(2) In section 8(1B)(b) of the Criminal Appeal Act 1968 (power of Court to direct entry of judgment and verdict of acquittal on applications relating to order for retrial), after 'to' insert 'set aside the order for retrial and'.

(3) In section 9(2) of that Act (right of appeal against sentence for summary offence), insert at the end 'or sub-paragraph (4) of that paragraph.'

(4) Section 10 of that Act (appeal to Court of Appeal by person dealt with by Crown Court for offence of which he was not convicted on indictment) is amended in accordance with subsections (5) to (7).

(5) In subsection (2) (proceedings from which an appeal lies), insert at the end—

'; or

(c) having been released under Part II of the Criminal Justice Act 1991 after serving part of a sentence of imprisonment or detention imposed for the offence, is ordered by the Crown Court to be returned to prison or detention.'

(6) …

(7) In subsection (4) (calculation of length of term of imprisonment), after 'imprisonment' insert 'or detention'.

**Initial Commencement**

Specified date: 27 September 1999: see s 108(3)(b) at para **[2.539]** below.

**Amendment**

Sub-ss (1), (6): repealed by the PCC(S)A 2000, s 165. Date in force: 25 August 2000: see the PCC(S)A 2000, s 168.

**[2.529]**

### 59 Composition

In section 54 of the Supreme Court Act 1981 (composition of court of civil division of Court of Appeal), for subsections (2) to (4) (number of judges) substitute—

'(2) Subject as follows, a court shall be duly constituted for the purpose of exercising any of its jurisdiction if it consists of one or more judges.

(3) The Master of the Rolls may, with the concurrence of the Lord Chancellor, give (or vary or revoke) directions about the minimum number of judges of which a court must consist if it is to be duly constituted for the purpose of any description of proceedings.

(4) The Master of the Rolls, or any Lord Justice of Appeal designated by him, may (subject to any directions under subsection (3)) determine the number of judges of which a court is to consist for the purpose of any particular proceedings.

(4A) The Master of the Rolls may give directions as to what is to happen in any particular case where one or more members of a court which has partly heard proceedings are unable to continue.'

**Initial Commencement**

Specified date: 27 September 1999: see s 108(3)(b) at para **[2.539]** below.

**[2.530]**

### 60 Calling into question of incidental decisions

For section 58 of the Supreme Court Act 1981 (exercise of incidental jurisdiction in civil division of Court of Appeal) substitute—

### '58 Calling into question of incidental decisions in civil division

(1) Rules of court may provide that decisions of the Court of Appeal which—

(a) are taken by a single judge or any officer or member of staff of that court in proceedings incidental to any cause or matter pending before the civil division of that court; and

(b) do not involve the determination of an appeal or of an application for permission to appeal,

may be called into question in such manner as may be prescribed.

(2) No appeal shall lie to the House of Lords from a decision which may be called into question pursuant to rules under subsection (1).'

**Initial Commencement**

Specified date: 27 September 1999: see s 108(3)(b) at para **[2.539]** below.



## [2.531]

### 61 Cases stated by Crown Court

For section 28A of the Supreme Court Act 1981 (proceedings on case stated by magistrates' court) substitute—

### '28A Proceedings on case stated by magistrates' court or Crown Court

(1) This section applies where a case is stated for the opinion of the High Court—

(a) by a magistrates' court under section 111 of the Magistrates' Courts Act 1980; or

(b) by the Crown Court under section 28(1) of this Act.

(2) The High Court may, if it thinks fit, cause the case to be sent back for amendment and, where it does so, the case shall be amended accordingly.

(3) The High Court shall hear and determine the question arising on the case (or the case as amended) and shall—

(a) reverse, affirm or amend the determination in respect of which the case has been stated; or

(b) remit the matter to the magistrates' court, or the Crown Court, with the opinion of the High Court,

and may make such other order in relation to the matter (including as to costs) as it thinks fit.

(4) Except as provided by the Administration of Justice Act 1960 (right of appeal to House of Lords in criminal cases), a decision of the High Court under this section is final.'

**Initial Commencement**

Specified date: 27 September 1999: see s 108(3)(b) at para **[2.539]** below.

## [2.532]

### 62 Power to vary committal in default

In the Supreme Court Act 1981, after section 43 insert—

### '43ZA Power of High Court to vary committal in default

(1) Where the High Court quashes the committal of a person to prison or detention by a magistrates' court or the Crown Court for—

(a) a default in paying a sum adjudged to be paid by a conviction; or

(b) want of sufficient distress to satisfy such a sum,

the High Court may deal with the person for the default or want of sufficient distress in any way in which the magistrates' court or Crown Court would have power to deal with him if it were dealing with him at the time when the committal is quashed.

(2) If the High Court commits him to prison or detention, the period of imprisonment or detention shall, unless the High Court otherwise directs, be treated as having begun when the person was committed by the magistrates' court or the Crown Court (except that any time during which he was released on bail shall not be counted as part of the period).'

**Initial Commencement**

Specified date: 27 September 1999: see s 108(3)(b) at para **[2.539]** below.

**[2.533]**

### 63 Criminal causes and matters

(1) In section 1(1)(a) of the Administration of Justice Act 1960 (appeal to House of Lords from decision of Divisional Court of the Queen's Bench Division in a criminal cause or matter), for 'a Divisional Court of the Queen's Bench Division' substitute 'the High Court'.

(2) In sections 4(2) and (3) and 9(2) of that Act (bail pending appeal), for 'a Divisional Court' substitute 'the High Court'.

**Initial Commencement**

Specified date: 27 September 1999: see s 108(3)(b) at para **[2.539]** below.

**[2.534]**

### 64 Contempt of court

(1) Section 13(2) of the Administration of Justice Act 1960 (appeals in cases of contempt of court) is amended as follows.

(2) In paragraph (a) (appeal from inferior courts from which appeal does not lie to Court of Appeal to lie to a Divisional Court of the High Court), omit 'a Divisional Court of'.

(3) In paragraph (b) (appeal to Court of Appeal from county court or single judge of High Court), for 'decision, of a single' substitute 'decision (other than a decision on an appeal under this section) of a single'.

(4) In paragraph (c) (appeal from Divisional Court or Court of Appeal to House of Lords), insert at the beginning 'from a decision of a single judge of the High Court on an appeal under this section,'.

**Initial Commencement**

Specified date: 27 September 1999: see s 108(3)(b) at para **[2.539]** below.

**[2.535]**

### 65 Habeas corpus

(1) In the Administration of Justice Act 1960, omit—

- (a) section 14(1) (order for release on criminal application for habeas corpus to be refused only by Divisional Court of Queen's Bench Division), and
- (b) section 15(2) (no appeal to House of Lords from order made by single judge on criminal application for habeas corpus).

(2) In section 15 of that Act (appeals in habeas corpus cases)—

- (a) in subsection (3) (no restriction on grant of leave to appeal to House of Lords against decision of Divisional Court on a criminal application for habeas corpus), and

(b) in subsection (4) (exceptions to right to be discharged in case of appeal to House of Lords against order of Divisional Court on such an application),

for 'a Divisional Court' substitute 'the High Court'.

**Initial Commencement**

Specified date: 27 September 1999: see s 108(3)(b) at para **[2.539]** below.



**[2.536]**

PART VII

SUPPLEMENTARY

### 105 Transitional provisions and savings

Schedule 14 (transitional provisions and savings) has effect.

**Appointment**

27 September 1999: see SI 1999/2657.

**[2.537]**

### 106 Repeals and revocations

Schedule 15 (repeals and revocations) has effect.

**Appointment**

27 September 1999 – 19 February 2001.

**[2.538]**

### 107 Crown application

This Act binds the Crown.

**Initial Commencement**

Specified date: 27 September 1999: see s 108(3)(g) at para **[2.539]** below.

**[2.539]**

### 108 Commencement

(1) Subject to subsections (2) and (3), the preceding provisions of this Act shall come into force on such day as the Lord Chancellor may by order made by statutory instrument appoint; and different days may be appointed for different purposes and, in the case of section 67(2), for different areas.

(2) Section 45 shall come into force on the day on which this Act is passed.

(3) The following provisions shall come into force at the end of the period of two months beginning with the day on which this Act is passed—

(a) in Part II, sections 32 to 34,

(b) Part IV, apart from section 66 and Schedule 9 and sections 67(2) and 71,

(c) in Part V, sections 74 to 76, 81, 82, 84, 86 and 87 and Schedule 10,

(d) in Part VI, section 104,

(e) Schedule 14,

(f) in Schedule 15, Part III and Part V(1) and (5), apart from the provisions specified in subsection (4), and

(g) section 107.

(4) The provisions excepted from subsection (3)(f) are the repeal of section 67(8) of the Magistrates' Courts Act 1980 (and that in Schedule 11 to the Children Act 1989) contained in Part V(1) of Schedule 15.

**Initial Commencement**
Royal Assent: 27 July 1999: (no specific commencement provision).

**[2.540]**

### 109 Extent

(1) Sections 32 to 34 and 73(2) extend to Scotland.
(2) Sections 98(2) and (3) and 104(2) extend to Northern Ireland.
(3) Sections 68, 101, 102 and 103 extend to England and Wales, Scotland and Northern Ireland.
(4) The other provisions of this Act which make amendments or repeals or revocations in other enactments also have the same extent as the enactments which they amend or repeal or revoke.
(5) Subject to subsection (4), the provisions of this Part (including paragraph 1, but not the rest, of Schedule 14) extend to England and Wales, Scotland and Northern Ireland.
(6) Subject to the preceding provisions, this Act extends to England and Wales.
(7) For the purposes of the Scotland Act 1998 this Act, so far as it extends to Scotland, shall be taken to be a pre-commencement enactment within the meaning of that Act.

**Initial Commencement**
Royal Assent: 27 July 1999: (no specific commencement provision).

**[2.541]**

### 110 Short title

This Act may be cited as the Access to Justice Act 1999.

**Initial Commencement**
Royal Assent: 27 July 1999: (no specific commencement provision).

## SCHEDULE 1
## Legal Services Commission

(s 1)

**[2.542]**

*Incorporation and status*

**1**

The Commission shall be a body corporate.

**2**

The Commission shall not be regarded—
(a) as the servant or agent of the Crown, or
(b) as enjoying any status, immunity or privilege of the Crown;
and the Commission's property shall not be regarded as property of, or held on behalf of, the Crown.

*Tenure of members*

**3**

(1) Subject to paragraphs 4 and 5, any member of the Commission shall hold and vacate office in accordance with the terms of his appointment.

(2) But a person shall not be appointed a member of the Commission for a period of more than five years.

**4**

(1) A member of the Commission, or the person appointed to chair it, may resign office by giving notice in writing to the Lord Chancellor.

(2) If the person appointed to chair the Commission ceases to be a member of it, he shall cease to chair it.

(3) A person who ceases to be a member of the Commission, or to chair it, shall be eligible for reappointment.

**5**

The Lord Chancellor may terminate the appointment of a member of the Commission if satisfied that—

(a) he has become bankrupt or made an arrangement with his creditors,

(b) he is unable to carry out his duties as a member of the Commission by reason of illness,

(c) he has been absent from meetings of the Commission for a period longer than six consecutive months without the permission of the Commission, or

(d) he is otherwise unable or unfit to discharge the functions of a member of the Commission.

*Members' interests*

**6**

(1) Before appointing a person to be a member of the Commission, the Lord Chancellor shall satisfy himself that that person will have no such financial or other interest as is likely to affect prejudicially the exercise or performance by him of his functions as a member of the Commission.

(2) The Lord Chancellor shall from time to time satisfy himself with respect to every member of the Commission that he has no such interest as is referred to in sub-paragraph (1).

(3) Any person whom the Lord Chancellor proposes to appoint as, and who has consented to be, a member of the Commission, and any member of the Commission, shall (whenever requested by the Lord Chancellor to do so) supply him with such information as the Lord Chancellor considers necessary for the performance by the Lord Chancellor of his duties under this paragraph.

**7**

(1) A member of the Commission who is in any way directly or indirectly interested in an individual contract entered into or proposed to be entered into, or an individual grant, loan or other payment made or proposed to be made, by the Commission shall disclose the nature of his interest at a meeting of the Commission; and—

(a) the disclosure shall be recorded in the minutes of the Commission, and

(b) the member shall not take any part in any deliberation or decision of the Commission with respect to that contract or grant, loan or other payment.

(2) For the purposes of sub-paragraph (1), a general notice given at a meeting of the Commission by a member of the Commission to the effect—

(a) that he is a person with whom a contract may be entered into, or to whom a grant, loan or other payment may be made, by the Commission, or

(b) that he is a member of a specified body with which a contract may be entered into, or to which a grant, loan or other payment may be made, by the Commission,

shall be regarded as a sufficient disclosure of his interest in relation to any contract subsequently entered into with, or grant, loan or other payment made to, him or the body.

(3) A member of the Commission need not attend in person at a meeting of the Commission in order to make any disclosure which he is required to make under this paragraph if he takes reasonable steps to secure that the disclosure is made by a notice which is brought up and read out at the meeting.

### *Remuneration of members*

**8**

(1) The Commission may—

(a) pay to its members such remuneration, and

(b) make provision for the payment of such pensions, allowances or gratuities to or in respect of its members,

as the Lord Chancellor may determine.

(2) Where a person ceases to be a member of the Commission otherwise than on the expiry of his term of office, and it appears to the Lord Chancellor that there are special circumstances which make it right for that person to receive compensation, the Lord Chancellor may require the Commission to make that person a payment of such amount as the Lord Chancellor may determine.

### *Staff*

**9**

(1) The Commission shall appoint a person to be the chief executive of the Commission who shall be responsible to the Commission for the exercise of its functions.

(2) The Commission may appoint such other employees as it thinks fit.

(3) The Commission may only appoint a person to be—

(a) its chief executive, or

(b) the holder of any other employment of a description specified by the Lord Chancellor by direction given to the Commission,

after consultation with, and subject to the approval of, the Lord Chancellor.

(4) An appointment under this paragraph may be made on such terms and conditions as the Commission, with the approval of the Lord Chancellor, may determine.

**10**

(1) The Commission shall make, in respect of such of its employees as, with the approval of the Lord Chancellor, it may determine such arrangements for providing pensions, allowances or gratuities, including pensions, allowances or gratuities by way of compensation for loss of employment, as it may determine.

(2) Arrangements under sub-paragraph (1) may include the establishment and administration, by the Commission or otherwise, of one or more pension schemes.

(3) If an employee of the Commission—

(a) becomes a member of the Commission, and

(b) was by reference to his employment by the Commission a participant in a pension scheme established and administered by it for the benefit of its employees,

the Commission may determine that his service as a member shall be treated for the purposes of the scheme as service as an employee of the Commission whether or not any benefits are to be payable to or in respect of him by virtue of paragraph 8.

(4) Where the Commission exercises the power conferred by sub-paragraph (3), any discretion as to the benefits payable to or in respect of the member concerned which the scheme confers on the Commission shall be exercised only with the approval of the Lord Chancellor.

*Funding of costs relating to administration etc*

**11**

(1) The Lord Chancellor shall pay to the Commission such sums as he may determine as appropriate for—

(a) the exercise by the Commission of functions in relation to the Community Legal Service other than the funding of services, and
(b) the administrative costs of the Commission.

(2) The Lord Chancellor may—

(a) determine the manner in which and times at which the sums mentioned in sub-paragraph (1) are to be paid to the Commission, and
(b) impose conditions on the payment of those sums.



*Proceedings*

**12**

(1) Subject to anything in any instrument made under this Part, the Commission may regulate its own proceedings.

(2) Committees—

(a) may be appointed, and may be dissolved, by the Commission, and
(b) may include, or consist entirely of, persons who are not members of the Commission,

but the Lord Chancellor may by direction require the Commission to make such provision relating to committees as is specified in the direction.

(3) A committee shall act in accordance with such instructions as the Commission may from time to time give; and the Commission may provide for anything done by a committee to have effect as if it had been done by the Commission.

(4) The Commission may pay to the members of any committee such fees and allowances as the Lord Chancellor may determine.

(5) The validity of any proceedings of the Commission or of any committee appointed by the Commission shall not be affected by any vacancy among its members or by any defect in the appointment of any member.

*Provision of information*

**13**

(1) The Commission shall provide the Lord Chancellor with such information as he may require relating to its property and to the discharge or proposed discharge of its functions.

(2) The Commission shall—

(a) permit any person authorised by the Lord Chancellor to inspect and make copies of any accounts or documents of the Commission, and
(b) provide such explanation of them as any such person, or the Lord Chancellor, may require.

*Annual report*

**14**

(1) The Commission shall provide to the Lord Chancellor, as soon as possible after the end of each financial year, a report on how it has during that year—

(a) funded services from the Community Legal Service Fund,

(b) funded services as part of the Criminal Defence Service, and
(c) exercised its other functions.

(2) The Lord Chancellor may by direction require the Commission to deal with the matters specified in the direction in reports, or a particular report, under this paragraph.

(3) The Lord Chancellor shall lay before each House of Parliament a copy of each report provided to him under this paragraph and the Commission shall publish a report once it has been so laid.

(4) In this paragraph and paragraphs 15 and 16 'financial year' means—
(a) the period beginning with the day on which the Commission is established and ending with the next 31st March, and
(b) each subsequent period of twelve months ending with 31st March.

### *Annual plan*

**15**

(1) The Commission shall, before the beginning of each financial year (other than that specified in paragraph 14(4)(a)), prepare a plan setting out how it intends in that year—
(a) to fund services from the Community Legal Service Fund,
(b) to fund services as part of the Criminal Defence Service, and
(c) to exercise its other functions,
and the plan shall include a summary of what the Commission has ascertained in the exercise of its functions under section 4(6).

(2) The Lord Chancellor may by direction require the Commission to deal with the matters specified in the direction in plans, or a particular plan, under sub-paragraph (1).

(3) The Commission shall send a copy of each plan prepared under sub-paragraph (1) to the Lord Chancellor.

(4) If the Lord Chancellor approves it, he shall lay a copy before each House of Parliament and the Commission shall publish the plan once it has been so laid.

(5) If he does not approve it, he shall by direction require the Commission to revise it in accordance with the direction; and the direction shall include the Lord Chancellor's reasons for not approving the plan.

(6) When the Commission has revised the plan it shall send the Lord Chancellor a copy of the revised plan and he shall lay a copy before each House of Parliament and the Commission shall publish the revised plan once it has been so laid.

### *Accounts and audit*

**16**

(1) The Commission shall keep accounts and shall prepare in respect of each financial year a statement of accounts.

(2) The accounts shall be kept, and the statement of accounts shall be prepared, in such form as the Lord Chancellor may, with the approval of the Treasury, specify by direction given to the Commission.

(3) The Commission shall send a copy of the statement of accounts in respect of each financial year to the Lord Chancellor and to the Comptroller and Auditor General within such period after the end of the financial year to which it relates as the Lord Chancellor may specify by direction given to the Commission.

(4) The Comptroller and Auditor General shall—
(a) examine, certify and report on each statement of accounts received by him under sub-paragraph (3), and
(b) lay a copy of each such statement of accounts, and his report on it, before each House of Parliament.

*Instruments*

**17**

(1) The fixing of the seal of the Commission shall be authenticated by a member of the Commission or by some other person authorised either generally or specially by the Commission to act for that purpose.

(2) A document purporting to be duly executed under the seal of the Commission or to be signed on the Commission's behalf—

(a) shall be received in evidence, and

(b) unless the contrary is proved, shall be deemed to be so executed or signed.

**Appointment**

1 April 2000: see SI 2000/774.



## SCHEDULE 2
## Community Legal Service: Excluded Services

(s 6)

**[2.543]**

The services which may not be funded as part of the Community Legal Service are as follows.

**1**

Services consisting of the provision of help (beyond the provision of general information about the law and the legal system and the availability of legal services) in relation to—

(a) allegations of negligently caused injury, death or damage to property, apart from allegations relating to clinical negligence,

(b) conveyancing,

(c) boundary disputes,

(d) the making of wills,

(e) matters of trust law,

(f) defamation or malicious falsehood,

(g) matters of company or partnership law, or

(h) other matters arising out of the carrying on of a business.

**2**

Advocacy in any proceedings except—

(1) proceedings in—

(a) the House of Lords in its judicial capacity,

(b) the Judicial Committee of the Privy Council in the exercise of its jurisdiction under the Government of Wales Act 1998, the Scotland Act 1998 or the Northern Ireland Act 1998,

(c) the Court of Appeal,

(d) the High Court,

(e) any county court,

(f) the Employment Appeal Tribunal, or

(g) any Mental Health Review Tribunal,

(h) the Immigration Appeal Tribunal or before an adjudicator,

(2) proceedings in the Crown Court—

(a) for the variation or discharge of an order under section 5 of the Protection from Harassment Act 1997,

(b) which relate to an order under section … 10 of the Crime and Disorder Act 1998, or

(c) … [or

(d) which relate to an order under paragraph 6 of Schedule 1 to the Anti-terrorism, Crime and Security Act 2001,]

(3) proceedings in a magistrates' court—

(a) under section 43 or 47 of the National Assistance Act 1948, section 22 of the Maintenance Orders Act 1950, section 4 of the Maintenance Orders Act 1958 or section 106 of the Social Security Administration Act 1992,

(b) under Part I of the Maintenance Orders (Reciprocal Enforcement) Act 1972 relating to a maintenance order made by a court of a country outside the United Kingdom,

(c) in relation to an application for leave of the court to remove a child from a person's custody under section 27 or 28 of the Adoption Act 1976 or in which the making of an order under Part II or section 29 or 55 of that Act is opposed by any party to the proceedings,

(d) for or in relation to an order under Part I of the Domestic Proceedings and Magistrates' Courts Act 1978,

[(da) under section 55A of the Family Law Act 1986 (declarations of parentage),]

(e) under the Children Act 1989,

(f) under section 30 of the Human Fertilisation and Embryology Act 1990,

(g) under section 20 of the Child Support Act 1991,

(h) under Part IV of the Family Law Act 1996,

(i) for the variation or discharge of an order under section 5 of the Protection from Harassment Act 1997, or

(j) under section 8 or 11 of the Crime and Disorder Act 1998, [or

(k) for an order or direction under paragraph 3, 5, 6, 9 or 10 of Schedule 1 to the Anti-terrorism, Crime and Security Act 2001,] and

(4) proceedings before any person to whom a case is referred (in whole or in part) in any proceedings within paragraphs (1) to (3).

**Initial Commencement**

To be appointed: see s 108(1) at para **[2.539]** above.

**Amendment**

Para 2: SI 2000/822. Date in force: 1 April 2000; Child Support, Pensions and Social Security Act 2000, ss 83, 85, Schs 8, 9. Date in force: 1 April 2001. Anti-terrorism, Crime and Security Act 2001, ss 2, 125, Sch 8.

## SCHEDULE 3
## Criminal Defence Service: Right to Representation

(s 14)

**[2.544]**

### *Individuals to whom right may be granted*

**1**

(1) A right to representation for the purposes of any kind of criminal proceedings before a court may be granted to an individual such as is mentioned in relation to that kind of proceedings in section 12(2).

(2) A right to representation for the purposes of criminal proceedings may also be granted to an individual to enable him to resist an appeal to the Crown Court otherwise than in an official capacity.

(3) In this Schedule 'court' includes any body before which criminal proceedings take place.

### *Grant of right by court*

**2**

(1) A court before which any criminal proceedings take place, or are to take place, has power to grant a right to representation in respect of those proceedings except in such circumstances as may be prescribed.

(2) Where a right to representation is granted for the purposes of criminal proceedings it includes the right to representation for the purposes of any related bail proceedings and any preliminary or incidental proceedings; and regulations may make provision specifying whether any proceedings are or are not to be regarded as preliminary or incidental.

(3) A court also has power to grant a right to representation for the purposes of criminal proceedings before another court in such circumstances as may be prescribed.

(4) The form of the application for a grant of a right to representation under this paragraph, and the form of the grant of such a right, shall be such as may be prescribed.

(5) A right to representation in respect of proceedings may be withdrawn by any court before which the proceedings take place; and a court must consider whether to withdraw a right to representation in such circumstances as may be prescribed.

(6) The powers of a magistrates' court for any area under this paragraph may be exercised by a single justice of the peace for the area.

(7) Any rules under section 144 of the Magistrates' Courts Act 1980 which provide for the functions of a single justice under sub-paragraph (6) to be exercised by a justices' clerk may make different provision for different areas.

### *Grant of right by commission*

**3**

(1) Regulations may provide that the Commission shall have power to grant rights to representation in respect of any one or more of the descriptions of proceedings prescribed under section 12(2)(g), and to withdraw any rights to representation granted by it.

(2) The form of any application for a grant of a right to representation under this paragraph, and the form of the grant of such a right, shall be such as may be prescribed.

(3) Regulations under sub-paragraph (1) may make such transitional provisions as the Lord Chancellor may consider appropriate.

### *Appeals*

**4**

Except where regulations otherwise provide, an appeal shall lie to such court or other person or body as may be prescribed against a decision to refuse to grant a right to representation or to withdraw a right to representation.

### *Criteria for grant of right*

**5**

(1) Any question as to whether a right to representation should be granted shall be determined according to the interests of justice.

(2) In deciding what the interests of justice consist of in relation to any individual, the following factors must be taken into account—

(a) whether the individual would, if any matter arising in the proceedings is decided against him, be likely to lose his liberty or livelihood or suffer serious damage to his reputation,

(b) whether the determination of any matter arising in the proceedings may involve consideration of a substantial question of law,

(c) whether the individual may be unable to understand the proceedings or to state his own case,

(d) whether the proceedings may involve the tracing, interviewing or expert cross-examination of witnesses on behalf of the individual, and

(e) whether it is in the interests of another person that the individual be represented.

(3) The Lord Chancellor may by order amend sub-paragraph (2) by adding new factors or varying any factor.

(4) A right to representation shall always be granted in such circumstances as may be prescribed.

**Initial Commencement**

To be appointed: see s 108(1) at para **[2.539]** above.

## SCHEDULE 6
## Rights of Audience and Rights to Conduct Litigation

(s 43)

**[2.545]**

### *The Solicitors Act 1974 (c 47)*

**1**

The Solicitors Act 1974 has effect subject to the following amendments.

**2**

In section 2(4) (Lord Chief Justice or Master of the Rolls deemed to concur in making of regulations approved by him under Schedule 4 to the Courts and Legal Services Act 1990), for the words from 'the Lord Chief Justice' to the end substitute 'approves any regulation such as is mentioned in subsection (1), the requirement of the concurrence of the Lord Chief Justice and the Master of the Rolls imposed by that subsection shall not apply.'

**3**

In section 31(3) (Master of the Rolls deemed to concur in making of rules approved by him under Schedule 4 to the Courts and Legal Services Act 1990), for the words from 'Master of the Rolls' to the end substitute 'Lord Chancellor approves any rule such as is mentioned in subsection (1), the requirement of the concurrence of the Master of the Rolls imposed by that subsection shall not apply.'

### *The Courts and Legal Services Act 1990 (c 41)*

**4**

The Courts and Legal Services Act 1990 has effect subject to the following amendments.

**5**

(1) Section 18 (duty to exercise functions as soon as reasonably practicable and in accordance with that section) is amended as follows.

(2) In subsection (1) (matters to which duty relates), in paragraph (c) (approval of qualification regulations or rules of conduct), after 'approval' insert 'or alteration'.

(3) After that subsection insert—

'(1A) Where any person other than the Lord Chancellor is called upon to exercise any such functions, the Lord Chancellor may require him to do so within such time as the Lord Chancellor may reasonably specify.'

**6**

(1) Section 27 (rights of audience) is amended as follows.

(2) In subsection (2)(a)(ii) (approval of qualification regulations and rules of conduct in relation to granting of right), omit 'the granting of'.

(3) After subsection (8) insert—

'(8A) But a court may not limit the right to appear before the court in any proceedings to only some of those who have the right by virtue of the provisions of this section.'

(4) In subsection (9)—

(a) in the definition of 'qualification regulations', after 'entitled to' insert or ', to exercise,', and

(b) in the definition of 'qualified litigator', for '('practising' having the same meaning as in section 19(8)(b))' substitute '(that is, one who has a practising certificate in force or is employed wholly or mainly for the purpose of providing legal services to his employer)'.

**7**

(1) Section 28 (rights to conduct litigation) is amended as follows.

(2) In subsection (2)(a)(ii) (approval of qualification regulations and rules of conduct in relation to granting of right), omit 'the granting of'.

(3) After subsection (4) insert—

'(4A) A court may not limit the right to conduct litigation in relation to proceedings before the court to only some of those who have the right by virtue of the provisions of this section.'

(4) In subsection (5), in the definition of 'qualification regulations', after 'entitled to' insert ', or to exercise,'.

**8**

In section 53(6)(a) (Council for Licensed Conveyancers), for 'section 29' substitute 'Schedule 4'.

**9**

In section 71 (qualification for judicial appointments), for subsection (6) substitute—

'(6) Any period during which a person had a right of audience but was, as a result of disciplinary proceedings, prevented by the authorised body concerned from exercising it shall not count towards the period mentioned in subsection (5)(b).'

**10**

(1) Section 119(1) (interpretation) is amended as follows.

(2) In the definition of 'right of audience', for 'exercise any of the functions of appearing before and addressing a court including the calling and examining of' substitute 'appear before and address a court including the right to call and examine'.

(3) In the definition of 'right to conduct litigation', for 'exercise all or any of the functions of issuing a writ or otherwise commencing' substitute 'issue'.

**11**

(1) Section 120 (subordinate legislation) is amended as follows.

(2) In subsection (4) (orders and regulations subject to affirmative procedure), for 'or paragraph 4' substitute ', paragraph 24 of Schedule 4, paragraph 4'.

(3) In subsection (5) (Orders in Council subject to affirmative procedure), for 'section 29(2) or 30(1)' substitute 'Part I or Part IV of Schedule 4'.

**Appointment**

Paras 1–5, 8, 11: 1 January 2000: see SI 1999/3344. Paras 6, 7, 9, 10: 27 September 1999: see SI 1999/2657.

## SCHEDULE 7
## Powers of Law Society

(s 48)

[2.546]

*Monitoring of compliance with rules*

**1**

In section 31(1) of the Solicitors Act 1974 (power of Council of the Law Society to make rules about professional practice, conduct and discipline), insert at the end 'and for empowering the Society to take such action as may be appropriate to enable the Society to ascertain whether or not the provisions of rules made, or of any code or guidance issued, by the Council are being complied with.'

*Bank and building society accounts*

**2**

In—

(a) section 32(4) of that Act (power of Council of the Law Society to disclose report or information about solicitor's accounts to Director of Public Prosecutions for investigation and prosecution of offences), and

(b) paragraph 3 of Schedule 2 to the Administration of Justice Act 1985 (corresponding provision in relation to accounts of incorporated practices),

omit 'to the Director of Public Prosecutions' and ', if the Director thinks fit,'.

**3**

In the Solicitors Act 1974, after section 33 insert—

**'33A Inspection of practice bank accounts etc**

(1) The Council may make rules, with the concurrence of the Master of the Rolls, empowering the Council to require a solicitor to produce documents relating to any account kept by him at a bank or with a building society—

(a) in connection with his practice; or

(b) in connection with any trust of which he is or formerly was a trustee,

for inspection by a person appointed by the Council pursuant to the rules.

(2) The Council shall be at liberty to disclose information obtained in exercise of the powers conferred by rules made under subsection (1) for use in investigating the possible commission of an offence by the solicitor and for use in connection with any prosecution of the solicitor consequent on the investigation.'

**4**

In section 87(1) of that Act (interpretation), in the definition of 'building society', omit '; and a reference to an account with a building society is a reference to a deposit account'.

**5**

In Schedule 2 to the Administration of Justice Act 1985, after paragraph 4 insert—

*'Inspection of bank accounts*

**4A**

Where rules made under section 33A(1) of the 1974 Act are applied to recognised bodies in accordance with section 9(2)(f) of this Act, the Council shall be at liberty to disclose information about a recognised body's accounts obtained in pursuance of the rules for use in investigating the possible commission of an offence by that body and for use in connection with any prosecution of that body consequent on the investigation.'

### *Intervention for breach of rules on practice, conduct and discipline*

**6**

In Schedule 1 to the Solicitors Act 1974 (intervention in solicitor's practice), in paragraph 1(1) (circumstances in which Law Society may intervene), in paragraph (c) (failure to comply with rules made by virtue of section 32 or 37(2)(c)), after 'section' insert '31,'.

### *Solicitors' employees and consultants*

**7**

(1) Section 43 of that Act (control of employment of clerks) is amended as follows.

(2) In subsection (1) (power of Law Society to apply to Solicitors Disciplinary Tribunal for order in the case of clerk guilty of an offence of dishonesty or other act which makes it undesirable for him to be employed by solicitor)—

(a) for 'a clerk to a solicitor' substitute 'employed or remunerated by a solicitor in connection with his practice',

(b) after 'employed' (in both places) insert 'or remunerated',

(c) for 'to whom he is or was clerk' substitute 'by whom he is or was employed or remunerated', and

(d) for the words from 'an application' to the end substitute 'the Society may either make, or make an application to the Tribunal for it to make, an order under subsection (2) with respect to him.'

(3) After that subsection insert—

'(1A) Where the Society investigates whether there are grounds for making, or making an application to the Tribunal for it to make, an order under subsection (2) with respect to a person, the Council may direct him to pay to the Council an amount which—

(a) is calculated by the Council as the cost to the Society of investigating the matter; or

(b) in the opinion of the Council represents a reasonable contribution towards that cost.'

(4) In subsection (2) (order of Tribunal barring solicitor from employing the clerk)—

(a) for the words from the beginning to 'an order' substitute 'An order under this subsection made by the Society or the Tribunal shall state', and

(b) for 'application is' substitute 'order is'.

(5) For subsection (3) (revocation by Tribunal) substitute—

'(3) Where an order has been made under subsection (2) with respect to a person by the Society or the Tribunal—

(a) that person or the Society may make an application to the Tribunal for it to be reviewed, and

(b) whichever of the Society and the Tribunal made it may at any time revoke it.

(3A) On the review of an order under subsection (3) the Tribunal may order—

(a) the quashing of the order;

(b) the variation of the order; or

(c) the confirmation of the order;

and where in the opinion of the Tribunal no prima facie case for quashing or varying the order is shown, the Tribunal may order its confirmation without hearing the applicant.'

(6) In subsection (5) (inspection of orders), for 'this section and filed with the Society' substitute 'subsection (2) by the Society, or made, varied or confirmed under this section by the Tribunal and filed with the Society,'.

(7) In the sidenote, for 'employment of certain clerks' substitute 'solicitors' employees and consultants'.

**8**

In section 44(2) of that Act (breach of order by solicitor), for the words from 'an order' to the end of paragraph (b) substitute 'an order under section 43(2) is in force in respect of a person'.

**9**

(1) Section 49 of that Act (appeals from Tribunal) is amended as follows.

(2) In subsection (3) (who can appeal)—

- (a) for '43(2)' substitute '43(3A)', and
- (b) for 'application' substitute 'order'.

(3) In subsection (6) (finality of appeal), for '43(2)' substitute '43(3A)'.

**10**

In paragraph 11(1) of Schedule 2 to the Administration of Justice Act 1985 (control of employment of employees of recognised bodies)—

- (a) after 'employed' (in each place) insert 'or remunerated', and
- (b) for the words from 'an application' to the end substitute 'the Society may either make, or make an application to the Tribunal for it to make, an order under subsection (2) of section 43 of the 1974 Act with respect to him.'

### *Power to examine files*

**11**

(1) Section 44B of the Solicitors Act 1974 (power of Law Society to examine files of solicitor or his firm in connection with complaints) is amended as follows.

(2) In subsection (1), for the words from 'investigating' to the end of paragraph (b) substitute—

'investigating—

- (a) whether there has been professional misconduct by a solicitor;
- (b) whether a solicitor has failed to comply with any requirement imposed by or by virtue of this Act or any rules made by the Council;
- (c) whether any professional services provided by a solicitor were not of the quality which it is reasonable to expect of him as a solicitor; or
- (d) whether there are grounds for making, or making an application to the Tribunal for it to make, an order under section 43(2) with respect to a person who is or was employed or remunerated by a solicitor in connection with his practice,';

and for the words from 'all documents' to the end substitute 'all relevant documents in the possession of the solicitor or his firm.'

(3) For the sidenote substitute 'Examination of files.'

**12**

In paragraph 14(1) of Schedule 2 to the Administration of Justice Act 1985 (power of Law Society to examine files of recognised body in connection with complaints), for paragraphs (a) and (b) substitute—

- '(a) whether a recognised body has failed to comply with any requirement imposed by or by virtue of this Act or any rules made by the Council and applicable to it by virtue of section 9 of this Act;
- (b) whether any professional services provided by a recognised body were not of the quality which it is reasonable to expect of it as a recognised body; or

(c) whether there are grounds for making, or making an application to the Tribunal for it to make, an order under section 43(2) with respect to a person who is or was employed or remunerated by a recognised body in connection with its business,';

and for the words from 'all documents' to the end substitute 'all relevant documents in the body's possession.'

*Payment of costs by solicitor under investigation*

**13**

In the Solicitors Act 1974, after section 44B insert—

*'Costs of investigations*

**44C Payment of costs of investigations**

Where the Society investigates possible professional misconduct by a solicitor, or a failure or apprehended failure by a solicitor to comply with any requirement imposed by or by virtue of this Act or any rules made by the Council, the Council may direct him to pay to the Council an amount which—

(a) is calculated by the Council as the cost to the Society of investigating and dealing with the matter; or

(b) in the opinion of the Council represents a reasonable contribution towards that cost.'

**14**

In Schedule 2 to the Administration of Justice Act 1985, after paragraph 14 insert—

*'Payment of costs of investigations*

**14A**

Where the Society investigates a failure or apprehended failure by a recognised body to comply with any requirement imposed by or by virtue of this Act or any rules applicable to it by virtue of section 9 of this Act, the Council may direct the body to pay to the Council an amount which—

(a) is calculated by the Council as the cost to the Society of the investigation; or

(b) in the opinion of the Council represents a reasonable contribution towards that cost.'

*Registered foreign lawyers*

**15**

Subsections (5) to (7) of section 89 of the Courts and Legal Services Act 1990 (power to apply existing provisions to registered foreign lawyers with or without modifications and power to modify existing provisions in their application to recognised bodies whose officers include registered foreign lawyers) apply in relation to the provisions contained in this Schedule as if they were contained in an Act passed before the commencement of that section.

**Appointment**

27 September 1999: see SI 1999/2657.

## SCHEDULE 8
## Legal Services Complaints Commissioner

(s 51)

**[2.547]**

*Provision for discharge of functions*

**1**

(1) The Lord Chancellor may give general directions concerning the discharge of the functions of the Legal Services Complaints Commissioner.

(2) Any such directions shall be published by the Lord Chancellor in such manner as appears to him to be appropriate.

(3) Subject to any such direction and to the provisions of this Act, the Commissioner may make such provision as he considers appropriate for the discharge of his functions.

*Delegation of functions*

**2**

(1) The Commissioner may delegate any of his functions to such members of his staff as he thinks fit.

(2) All reports prepared by or on behalf of the Commissioner must be signed by him.

*Remuneration*

**3**

(1) The Lord Chancellor shall pay to, or in respect of, the Commissioner such amounts—

(a) by way of remuneration, pensions, allowances or gratuities, or

(b) by way of provision for any such benefits, as he may determine.

(2) If—

(a) the Commissioner ceases to hold office, and

(b) it appears to the Lord Chancellor that there are special circumstances which make it right that he should receive compensation,

the Lord Chancellor may pay to him such sum as the Lord Chancellor may determine.

*Staff*

**4**

(1) The Commissioner may appoint such staff as he thinks necessary for the discharge of his functions.

(2) Appointments shall be made by the Commissioner on such terms and conditions (including terms as to pensions, allowances and gratuities) as he may, with the approval of the Lord Chancellor, determine.

(3) The reference in sub-paragraph (2) to pensions, allowances or gratuities includes a reference to pensions, allowances or gratuities by way of compensation to or in respect of any of the Commissioner's staff who suffer loss of employment or loss or diminution of emoluments.

*Annual and other reports*

**5**

(1) The Commissioner shall make an annual report to the Lord Chancellor on the discharge of his functions during the year to which the report relates.

(2) The Commissioner may, in addition, report to the Lord Chancellor at any time on any matter relating to the discharge of the Commissioner's functions.

(3) The Commissioner shall provide the Lord Chancellor with such information relating to the discharge of his functions as the Lord Chancellor may see fit to require.

(4) The Lord Chancellor shall lay before each House of Parliament a copy of any annual report made to him under sub-paragraph (1).

*Accounts and audit*

**6**

(1) The Commissioner shall keep accounts with respect to his receipts and expenditure and shall prepare a statement of accounts with respect to each financial year.

(2) The accounts shall be kept, and the statement of accounts prepared, in such form as the Lord Chancellor may, with the approval of the Treasury, direct.

(3) The accounts shall be audited by persons appointed by the Lord Chancellor in respect of each financial year.

(4) The auditors shall send to the Lord Chancellor a copy of the statement of accounts and of their report.

(5) The Lord Chancellor shall lay before each House of Parliament a copy of every statement of accounts and auditors' report sent to him under this paragraph.

*Financial provisions*

**7**

(1) The Lord Chancellor may require any professional body in relation to which a direction under section 52 of this Act has been given (and not revoked) to make payments of such amounts as the Lord Chancellor considers appropriate to the Commissioner towards meeting the expenditure incurred (or to be incurred) by him in the discharge of his functions.

(2) To the extent that that expenditure is not met by payments under sub-paragraph (1), it shall be met by the Lord Chancellor out of money provided by Parliament.

(3) The Commissioner may, with the approval of the Lord Chancellor, pay fees or allowances to any person who, in the Commissioner's opinion, is qualified to assist him in the discharge of his functions and who so assists him.

*Parliamentary disqualification*

**8**

In Part III of Schedule 1 to—

(a) the House of Commons Disqualification Act 1975, and

(b) the Northern Ireland Assembly Disqualification Act 1975,

(disqualifying offices), insert (at the appropriate place in alphabetical order)—

'The Legal Services Complaints Commissioner.'

*Parliamentary Commissioner*

**9**

In Schedule 2 to the Parliamentary Commissioner Act 1967 (which lists the bodies subject to the jurisdiction of the Parliamentary Commissioner), insert (at the appropriate place in alphabetical order)—

'The Legal Services Complaints Commissioner.'

*Acting Commissioner*

**10**

(1) The Lord Chancellor may appoint a person to exercise the functions of the Commissioner where—

(a) the Commissioner's office becomes vacant, or

(b) the Commissioner is incapable of exercising his functions or considers that it would be inappropriate for him to exercise any of his functions in connection with a particular matter (because of a possible conflict of interests or for any other reason).

(2) A person so appointed shall have the powers of the Commissioner but shall act only in accordance with the terms on which he is appointed.

(3) The Lord Chancellor may pay to any person so appointed such remuneration as he may determine.

**Initial Commencement**

To be appointed: see s 108(1) at para **[2.539]** above.

# Welfare Reform and Pensions Act 1999



## Contents

*Section*

PART IV
PENSION SHARING



**[2.548]**
**Introductory Chapter – Pensions**

The provisions of the Welfare Reform and Pensions Act 1999 (WRPA 1999) are considered in detail in the Introductory Chapter on 'Pensions' at para **[1.90]** above.

## [2.549]

PART IV
PENSION SHARING

CHAPTER I
SHARING OF RIGHTS UNDER PENSION ARRANGEMENTS

*Pension sharing mechanism*

### 27 Scope of mechanism

(1) Pension sharing is available under this Chapter in relation to a person's shareable rights under any pension arrangement other than an excepted public service pension scheme.

(2) For the purposes of this Chapter, a person's shareable rights under a pension arrangement are any rights of his under the arrangement, other than rights of a description specified by regulations made by the Secretary of State.

(3) For the purposes of subsection (1), a public service pension scheme is excepted if it is specified by order made by such Minister of the Crown or government department as may be designated by the Treasury as having responsibility for the scheme.

**Appointment**
1 December 2000: see SI 2000/1047, art 2(2)(d), Schedule, Pt IV.

## [2.549.1]
**Keypoint**
- Regulations

## [2.549.2]
**Regulations**

See reg 2 of the Pension Sharing (Valuation) Regulations 2000, SI 2000/1052[1] for the rights under a pension arrangement that are not shareable.

See also the Introductory Chapter on 'Pensions' at paras **[1.162]** and **[1.170]** above.

1 See para **[3.583]** below.

## [2.550]

### 28 Activation of pension sharing

(1) Section 29 applies on the taking effect of any of the following relating to a person's shareable rights under a pension arrangement—

(a) a pension sharing order under the Matrimonial Causes Act 1973,

(b) provision which corresponds to the provision which may be made by such an order and which—

(i) is contained in a qualifying agreement between the parties to a marriage, and

(ii) takes effect on the dissolution of the marriage under the Family Law Act 1996,

(c) provision which corresponds to the provision which may be made by such an order and which—

(i) is contained in a qualifying agreement between the parties to a marriage or former marriage, and

(ii) takes effect after the dissolution of the marriage under the Family Law Act 1996,

(d) an order under Part III of the Matrimonial and Family Proceedings Act 1984 (financial relief in England and Wales in relation to overseas divorce etc) corresponding to such an order as is mentioned in paragraph (a),

(e) a pension sharing order under the Family Law (Scotland) Act 1985,

(f) provision which corresponds to the provision which may be made by such an order and which—

(i) is contained in a qualifying agreement between the parties to a marriage,

(ii) is in such form as the Secretary of State may prescribe by regulations, and

(iii) takes effect on the grant, in relation to the marriage, of decree of divorce under the Divorce (Scotland) Act 1976 or of declarator of nullity,

(g) an order under Part IV of the Matrimonial and Family Proceedings Act 1984 (financial relief in Scotland in relation to overseas divorce etc) corresponding to such an order as is mentioned in paragraph (e),

(h) a pension sharing order under Northern Ireland legislation, and

(i) an order under Part IV of the Matrimonial and Family Proceedings (Northern Ireland) Order 1989 (financial relief in Northern Ireland in relation to overseas divorce etc) corresponding to such an order as is mentioned in paragraph (h).



(2) For the purposes of subsection (1)(b) and (c), a qualifying agreement is one which—

(a) has been entered into in such circumstances as the Lord Chancellor may prescribe by regulations, and

(b) satisfies such requirements as the Lord Chancellor may so prescribe.

(3) For the purposes of subsection (1)(f), a qualifying agreement is one which—

(a) has been entered into in such circumstances as the Secretary of State may prescribe by regulations, and

(b) is registered in the Books of Council and Session.

(4) Subsection (1)(b) does not apply if—

(a) the pension arrangement to which the provision relates is the subject of a pension sharing order under the Matrimonial Causes Act 1973 in relation to the marriage, or

(b) there is in force a requirement imposed by virtue of section 25B or 25C of that Act (powers to include in financial provision orders requirements relating to benefits under pension arrangements) which relates to benefits or future benefits to which the party who is the transferor is entitled under the pension arrangement to which the provision relates.

(5) Subsection (1)(c) does not apply if—

(a) the marriage was dissolved by an order under section 3 of the Family Law Act 1996 (divorce not preceded by separation) and the satisfaction of the requirements of section 9(2) of that Act (settlement of future financial arrangements) was a precondition to the making of the order,

(b) the pension arrangement to which the provision relates—

(i) is the subject of a pension sharing order under the Matrimonial Causes Act 1973 in relation to the marriage, or

(ii) has already been the subject of pension sharing between the parties, or

(c) there is in force a requirement imposed by virtue of section 25B or 25C of that Act which relates to benefits or future benefits to which the party who is the transferor is entitled under the pension arrangement to which the provision relates.

(6) Subsection (1)(f) does not apply if there is in force an order under section 12A(2) or (3) of the Family Law (Scotland) Act 1985 which relates to benefits or future benefits to which the party who is the transferor is entitled under the pension arrangement to which the provision relates.

(7) For the purposes of this section, an order or provision falling within subsection (1)(e), (f) or (g) shall be deemed never to have taken effect if the person responsible for the arrangement to which the order or provision relates does not receive before the end of the period of 2 months beginning with the relevant date—

(a) copies of the relevant matrimonial documents, and
(b) such information relating to the transferor and transferee as the Secretary of State may prescribe by regulations under section 34(1)(b)(ii).

(8) The relevant date for the purposes of subsection (7) is—
(a) in the case of an order or provision falling within subsection (1)(e) or (f), the date of the extract of the decree or declarator responsible for the divorce or annulment to which the order or provision relates, and
(b) in the case of an order falling within subsection (1)(g), the date of disposal of the application under section 28 of the Matrimonial and Family Proceedings Act 1984.

(9) The reference in subsection (7)(a) to the relevant matrimonial documents is—
(a) in the case of an order falling within subsection (1)(e) or (g), to copies of the order and the order, decree or declarator responsible for the divorce or annulment to which it relates, and
(b) in the case of provision falling within subsection (1)(f), to—
(i) copies of the provision and the order, decree or declarator responsible for the divorce or annulment to which it relates, and
(ii) documentary evidence that the agreement containing the provision is one to which subsection (3)(a) applies.

(10) The sheriff may, on the application of any person having an interest, make an order—
(a) extending the period of 2 months referred to in subsection (7), and
(b) if that period has already expired, providing that, if the person responsible for the arrangement receives the documents and information concerned before the end of the period specified in the order, subsection (7) is to be treated as never having applied.

(11) In subsections (4)(b), (5)(c) and (6), the reference to the party who is the transferor is to the party to whose rights the provision relates.

**Appointment**
1 December 2000: see SI 2000/1047, art 2(2)(d), Schedule, Pt IV.

**[2.550.1]**
**Keypoint**
- General

**[2.550.2]**
**General**

Sub-ss (1)(b)(c), (2) and (5)(a) are dependent on the FLA 1996. Now it is clear that the FLA 1996 is not to be implemented, they are irrelevant.

Sub-ss (1)(e), (f) and (g), (3) and (6) to (10) apply only to Scotland.

Sub-s (1)(h) and (i) apply only to Northern Ireland.

**[2.551]**

### 29 Creation of pension debits and credits

(1) On the application of this section—
(a) the transferor's shareable rights under the relevant arrangement become subject to a debit of the appropriate amount, and
(b) the transferee becomes entitled to a credit of that amount as against the person responsible for that arrangement.

(2) Where the relevant order or provision specifies a percentage value to be transferred, the appropriate amount for the purposes of subsection (1) is the specified percentage of the cash equivalent of the relevant benefits on the valuation day.

(3) Where the relevant order or provision specifies an amount to be transferred, the appropriate amount for the purposes of subsection (1) is the lesser of—

(a) the specified amount, and
(b) the cash equivalent of the relevant benefits on the valuation day.

(4) Where the relevant arrangement is an occupational pension scheme and the transferor is in pensionable service under the scheme on the transfer day, the relevant benefits for the purposes of subsections (2) and (3) are the benefits or future benefits to which he would be entitled under the scheme by virtue of his shareable rights under it had his pensionable service terminated immediately before that day.

(5) Otherwise, the relevant benefits for the purposes of subsections (2) and (3) are the benefits or future benefits to which, immediately before the transfer day, the transferor is entitled under the terms of the relevant arrangement by virtue of his shareable rights under it.

(6) The Secretary of State may by regulations provide for any description of benefit to be disregarded for the purposes of subsection (4) or (5).

(7) For the purposes of this section, the valuation day is such day within the implementation period for the credit under subsection (1)(b) as the person responsible for the relevant arrangement may specify by notice in writing to the transferor and transferee.

(8) In this section—

'relevant arrangement' means the arrangement to which the relevant order or provision relates;
'relevant order or provision' means the order or provision by virtue of which this section applies;
'transfer day' means the day on which the relevant order or provision takes effect;
'transferor' means the person to whose rights the relevant order or provision relates;
'transferee' means the person for whose benefit the relevant order or provision is made.

**Appointment**
1 December 2000: see SI 2000/1047, art 2(2)(d), Schedule, Pt IV.



**[2.551.1]**
**Keypoint**
- General

**[2.551.2]**
**General**
See the Introductory Chapter on 'Pensions' at paras **[1.162]**, **[1.169]** and **[1.188A]** above. Sub-ss (3) and (6) apply only to Scotland.

**[2.552]**

### 30 Cash equivalents

(1) The Secretary of State may by regulations make provision about the calculation and verification of cash equivalents for the purposes of section 29.

(2) The power conferred by subsection (1) includes power to provide for calculation or verification—

(a) in such manner as may, in the particular case, be approved by a person prescribed by the regulations, or
(b) in accordance with guidance from time to time prepared by a person so prescribed.

**Appointment**
1 December 2000: see SI 2000/1047, art 2(2)(d), Schedule, Pt IV.

**[2.552.1]**
**Keypoint**
- Regulations

**[2.552.2]**
**Regulations**

The relevant regulations under s 30(1) of the WRPA 1999 are the Pension Sharing (Valuation) Regulations 2000, SI 2000/1052[1].

1 See para **[3.582]** below.

**[2.553]**

*Pension debits*

**31 Reduction of benefit**

(1) Subject to subsection (2), where a person's shareable rights under a pension arrangement are subject to a pension debit, each benefit or future benefit—

(a) to which he is entitled under the arrangement by virtue of those rights, and

(b) which is a qualifying benefit,

is reduced by the appropriate percentage.

(2) Where a pension debit relates to the shareable rights under an occupational pension scheme of a person who is in pensionable service under the scheme on the transfer day, each benefit or future benefit—

(a) to which the person is entitled under the scheme by virtue of those rights, and

(b) which corresponds to a qualifying benefit,

is reduced by an amount equal to the appropriate percentage of the corresponding qualifying benefit.

(3) A benefit is a qualifying benefit for the purposes of subsections (1) and (2) if the cash equivalent by reference to which the amount of the pension debit is determined includes an amount in respect of it.

(4) The provisions of this section override any provision of a pension arrangement to which they apply to the extent that the provision conflicts with them.

(5) In this section—

'appropriate percentage', in relation to a pension debit, means—

(a) if the relevant order or provision specifies the percentage value to be transferred, that percentage;

(b) if the relevant order or provision specifies an amount to be transferred, the percentage which the appropriate amount for the purposes of subsection (1) of section 29 represents of the amount mentioned in subsection (3)(b) of that section;

'relevant order or provision', in relation to a pension debit, means the pension sharing order or provision on which the debit depends;

'transfer day', in relation to a pension debit, means the day on which the relevant order or provision takes effect.

**Appointment**

1 December 2000: see SI 2000/1047, art 2(2)(d), Schedule, Pt IV.

**[2.553.1]**
**Keypoint**
- General

**[2.553.2]**
**General**

See the Introductory Chapter on 'Pensions' at para **[1.173]** above.
Sub-s (5)(b) applies only to Scotland.

**[2.554]**

### 32 Effect on contracted-out rights

(1) The Pension Schemes Act 1993 shall be amended as follows.

(2) In section 10 (protected rights), in subsection (1), for 'subsections (2) and (3)' there shall be substituted 'the following provisions of this section', and at the end there shall be added—

'(4) Where, in the case of a scheme which makes such provision as is mentioned in subsection (2) or (3), a member's rights under the scheme become subject to a pension debit, his protected rights shall exclude the appropriate percentage of the rights which were his protected rights immediately before the day on which the pension debit arose.

(5) For the purposes of subsection (4), the appropriate percentage is—

(a) if the order or provision on which the pension debit depends specifies the percentage value to be transferred, that percentage;

(b) if the order or provision on which the pension debit depends specifies an amount to be transferred, the percentage which the appropriate amount for the purposes of subsection (1) of section 29 of the Welfare Reform and Pensions Act 1999 (lesser of specified amount and cash equivalent of transferor's benefits) represents of the amount mentioned in sub-section (3)(b) of that section (cash equivalent of transferor's benefits).'

(3) After section 15 there shall be inserted—

#### '15A Reduction of guaranteed minimum in consequence of pension debit

(1) Where—

(a) an earner has a guaranteed minimum in relation to the pension provided by a scheme, and

(b) his right to the pension becomes subject to a pension debit,

his guaranteed minimum in relation to the scheme is, subject to subsection (2), reduced by the appropriate percentage.

(2) Where the earner is in pensionable service under the scheme on the day on which the order or provision on which the pension debit depends takes effect, his guaranteed minimum in relation to the scheme is reduced by an amount equal to the appropriate percentage of the corresponding qualifying benefit.

(3) For the purposes of subsection (2), the corresponding qualifying benefit is the guaranteed minimum taken for the purpose of calculating the cash equivalent by reference to which the amount of the pension debit is determined.

(4) For the purposes of this section the appropriate percentage is—

(a) if the order or provision on which the pension debit depends specifies the percentage value to be transferred, that percentage;

(b) if the order or provision on which the pension debit depends specifies an amount to be transferred, the percentage which the appropriate amount for the purposes of subsection (1) of section 29 of the Welfare Reform and Pensions Act 1999 (lesser of specified amount and cash equivalent of transferor's benefits) represents of the amount mentioned in sub-section (3)(b) of that section (cash equivalent of transferor's benefits).'

(4) In section 47 (entitlement to guaranteed minimum pensions for the purposes of the relationship with social security benefits), at the end there shall be added—

'(6) For the purposes of section 46, a person shall be treated as entitled to any guaranteed minimum pension to which he would have been entitled but for any reduction under section 15A.'

(5) In section 181(1), there shall be inserted at the appropriate place—

''pension debit' means a debit under section 29(1)(a) of the Welfare Reform and Pensions Act 1999;'.

**Appointment**

1 December 2000: see SI 2000/1047, art 2(2)(d), Schedule, Pt IV.

**[2.554.1]**

- General

**[2.554.2]**

**General**

Note that the amended ss 10(5)(b) and 15A(4)(b) of the Pension Schemes Act 1993 apply only to Scotland.

**[2.555]**

*Pension credits*

### 33 Time for discharge of liability

(1) A person subject to liability in respect of a pension credit shall discharge his liability before the end of the implementation period for the credit.

(2) Where the trustees or managers of an occupational pension scheme have not done what is required to discharge their liability in respect of a pension credit before the end of the implementation period for the credit—

(a) they shall, except in such cases as the Secretary of State may prescribe by regulations, notify the Regulatory Authority of that fact within such period as the Secretary of State may so prescribe, and

(b) section 10 of the Pensions Act 1995 (power of the Regulatory Authority to impose civil penalties) shall apply to any trustee or manager who has failed to take all such steps as are reasonable to ensure that liability in respect of the credit was discharged before the end of the implementation period for it.

(3) If trustees or managers to whom subsection (2)(a) applies fail to perform the obligation imposed by that provision, section 10 of the Pensions Act 1995 shall apply to any trustee or manager who has failed to take all reasonable steps to ensure that the obligation was performed.

(4) On the application of the trustees or managers of an occupational pension scheme who are subject to liability in respect of a pension credit, the Regulatory Authority may extend the implementation period for the credit for the purposes of this section if it is satisfied that the application is made in such circumstances as the Secretary of State may prescribe by regulations.

(5) In this section 'the Regulatory Authority' means the Occupational Pensions Regulatory Authority.

**Appointment**

1 December 2000: see SI 2000/1047, art 2(2)(d), Schedule, Pt IV.

**[2.555.1]**

**Keypoints**

- Regulations
- 'Implementation period'

## [2.555.2]
### Regulations

The time prescribed under s 33(2)(a) of the WRPA 1999 is 21 days beginning with the day immediately following the end of the implementation period[1].

1 See reg 2 of the Pension Sharing (Implementation and Discharge of Liability) Regulations 2000, SI 2000/1053 at para **[3.590]** below.

## [2.555.3]
### 'Implementation period'

This is defined by s 34 below.

## [2.556]

### 34 'Implementation period'

(1) For the purposes of this Chapter, the implementation period for a pension credit is the period of 4 months beginning with the later of—

- (a) the day on which the relevant order or provision takes effect, and
- (b) the first day on which the person responsible for the pension arrangement to which the relevant order or provision relates is in receipt of—
  - (i) the relevant matrimonial documents, and
  - (ii) such information relating to the transferor and transferee as the Secretary of State may prescribe by regulations.

(2) The reference in subsection (1)(b)(i) to the relevant matrimonial documents is to copies of—

- (a) the relevant order or provision, and
- (b) the order, decree or declarator responsible for the divorce or annulment to which it relates,

and, if the pension credit depends on provision falling within subsection (1)(f) of section 28, to documentary evidence that the agreement containing the provision is one to which subsection (3)(a) of that section applies.

(3) Subsection (1) is subject to any provision made by regulations under section 41(2)(a).

(4) The Secretary of State may by regulations—

- (a) make provision requiring a person subject to liability in respect of a pension credit to notify the transferor and transferee of the day on which the implementation period for the credit begins;
- (b) provide for this section to have effect with modifications where the pension arrangement to which the relevant order or provision relates is being wound up;
- (c) provide for this section to have effect with modifications where the pension credit depends on a pension sharing order and the order is the subject of an application for leave to appeal out of time.

(5) In this section—

'relevant order or provision', in relation to a pension credit, means the pension sharing order or provision on which the pension credit depends;

'transferor' means the person to whose rights the relevant order or provision relates;

'transferee' means the person for whose benefit the relevant order or provision is made.

**Appointment**

(For the purpose only of the exercise of any power to make regulations): 11 November 1999: see s 89(5)(a).

**[2.556.1]**
**Keypoint**
- Regulations
- Cross-reference

**[2.556.2]**
**Regulations**

Regulation 5 of the Pensions on Divorce etc (Provision of Information) Regulations 2000, SI 2000/1048[1] specifies the information that must be supplied to the pension arranger under s 34(1)(b)(ii). Regulation 4 of the Pension Sharing (Implementation and Discharge of Liability) Regulations 2000, SI 2000/1053[2] relates to s 34(4) of the WRPA 1999.

1 See para **[3.566]** below.
2 See para **[3.592]** below.

**[2.556.3]**
**Cross-reference**

See the Introductory Chapter on 'Pensions' at para **[1.188A]** above.

**[2.557]**

**35 Mode of discharge of liability**

(1) Schedule 5 (which makes provision about how liability in respect of a pension credit may be discharged) shall have effect.

(2) Where the person entitled to a pension credit dies before liability in respect of the credit has been discharged—

(a) Schedule 5 shall cease to have effect in relation to the discharge of liability in respect of the credit, and

(b) liability in respect of the credit shall be discharged in accordance with regulations made by the Secretary of State.

**Appointment**

1 December 2000: see SI 2000/1047, art 2(2)(d), Schedule, Pt IV.

**[2.557.1]**
**Keypoint**
- Regulations
- Cross-reference

**[2.557.2]**
**Regulations**

See the Pension Sharing (Implementation and Discharge of Liability) Regulations 2000, SI 2000/1053[1] for the Regulations under this section.

1 See para **[3.589]** below.

**[2.557.3]**
**Cross-reference**

See the Introductory Chapter on 'Pensions' at para **[1.187]** above.

**[2.558]**

*Treatment of pension credit rights under schemes*

**36 Safeguarded rights**

After section 68 of the Pension Schemes Act 1993 there shall be inserted—

'PART IIIA
SAFEGUARDED RIGHTS

### 68A Safeguarded rights

(1) Subject to subsection (2), the safeguarded rights of a member of an occupational pension scheme or a personal pension scheme are such of his rights to future benefits under the scheme as are attributable (directly or indirectly) to a pension credit in respect of which the reference rights are, or include, contracted-out rights or safeguarded rights.

(2) If the rules of an occupational pension scheme or a personal pension scheme so provide, a member's safeguarded rights are such of his rights falling within subsection (1) as—

(a) in the case of rights directly attributable to a pension credit, represent the safeguarded percentage of the rights acquired by virtue of the credit, and

(b) in the case of rights directly attributable to a transfer payment, represent the safeguarded percentage of the rights acquired by virtue of the payment.

(3) For the purposes of subsection (2)(a), the safeguarded percentage is the percentage of the rights by reference to which the amount of the credit is determined which are contracted-out rights or safeguarded rights.

(4) For the purposes of subsection (2)(b), the safeguarded percentage is the percentage of the rights in respect of which the transfer payment is made which are contracted-out rights or safeguarded rights.

(5) In this section—

'contracted-out rights' means such rights under, or derived from—

(a) an occupational pension scheme contracted-out by virtue of section 9(2) or (3), or

(b) an appropriate personal pension scheme,

as may be prescribed;

'reference rights', in relation to a pension credit, means the rights by reference to which the amount of the credit is determined.

### 68B Requirements relating to safeguarded rights

Regulations may prescribe requirements to be met in relation to safeguarded rights by an occupational pension scheme or a personal pension scheme.

### 68C Reserve powers in relation to non-complying schemes

(1) This section applies to—

(a) any occupational pension scheme, other than a public service pension scheme, and

(b) any personal pension scheme.

(2) If any scheme to which this section applies does not comply with a requirement prescribed under section 68B and there are any persons who—

(a) have safeguarded rights under the scheme, or

(b) are entitled to any benefit giving effect to such rights under the scheme,

the Inland Revenue may direct the trustees or managers of the scheme to take or refrain from taking such steps as they may specify in writing for the purpose of safeguarding the rights of persons falling within paragraph (a) or (b).

(3) A direction under subsection (2) shall be final and binding on the trustees or managers to whom the direction is given and any person claiming under them.

(4) An appeal on a point of law shall lie to the High Court or, in Scotland, the Court of Session from a direction under subsection (2) at the instance of the trustees or managers, or any person claiming under them.

(5) A direction under subsection (2) shall be enforceable—

(a) in England and Wales, in a county court, as if it were an order of that court, and

(b) in Scotland, by the sheriff, as if it were an order of the sheriff and whether or not the sheriff could himself have given such an order.

### 68D Power to control transfer or discharge of liability

Regulations may prohibit or restrict the transfer or discharge of any liability under an occupational pension scheme or a personal pension scheme in respect of safeguarded rights except in prescribed circumstances or on prescribed conditions.'

**Appointment**

1 December 2000: see SI 2000/1047, art 2(2)(d), Schedule, Pt IV.

**[2.558.1]**

**Keypoint**

- Regulations

**[2.558.2]**

**Regulations**

See the Pension Sharing (Safeguarding Rights) Regulations 2000, SI 2000/1055[1] for Regulations under this section.

1 See para **[3.641A]** below.

**[2.559]**

### 37 Requirements relating to pension credit benefit

After section 101 of the Pension Schemes Act 1993 there shall be inserted—

'PART IVA

REQUIREMENTS RELATING TO PENSION CREDIT BENEFIT

CHAPTER I

PENSION CREDIT BENEFIT UNDER OCCUPATIONAL SCHEMES

### 101A Scope of Chapter I

(1) This Chapter applies to any occupational pension scheme whose resources are derived in whole or part from—

(a) payments to which subsection (2) applies made or to be made by one or more employers of earners to whom the scheme applies, or

(b) such other payments by the earner or his employer, or both, as may be prescribed for different categories of scheme.

(2) This subsection applies to payments—

(a) under an actual or contingent legal obligation, or

(b) in the exercise of a power conferred, or the discharge of a duty imposed, on a Minister of the Crown, government department or any other person, being a power or duty which extends to the disbursement or allocation of public money.

### 101B Interpretation

In this Chapter—

'scheme' means an occupational pension scheme to which this Chapter applies;

'pension credit rights' means rights to future benefits under a scheme which are attributable (directly or indirectly) to a pension credit;

'pension credit benefit', in relation to a scheme, means the benefits payable under the scheme to or in respect of a person by virtue of rights under the scheme attributable (directly or indirectly) to a pension credit;

'normal benefit age', in relation to a scheme, means the earliest age at which a person who has pension credit rights under the scheme is entitled to receive a pension by virtue of those rights (disregarding any scheme rule making special provision as to early payment of pension on grounds of ill-health or otherwise).

### 101C Basic principle as to pension credit benefit

(1) Normal benefit age under a scheme must be between 60 and 65.

(2) A scheme must not provide for payment of pension credit benefit in the form of a lump sum at any time before normal benefit age, except in such circumstances as may be prescribed.

### 101D Form of pension credit benefit and its alternatives

(1) Subject to subsection (2) and section 101E, a person's pension credit benefit under a scheme must be—

(a) payable directly out of the resources of the scheme, or

(b) assured to him by such means as may be prescribed.

(2) Subject to subsections (3) and (4), a scheme may, instead of providing a person's pension credit benefit, provide—

(a) for his pension credit rights under the scheme to be transferred to another occupational pension scheme or a personal pension scheme with a view to acquiring rights for him under the rules of the scheme, or

(b) for such alternatives to pension credit benefit as may be prescribed.

(3) The option conferred by subsection (2)(a) is additional to any obligation imposed by Chapter II of this Part.

(4) The alternatives specified in subsection (2)(a) and (b) may only be by way of complete or partial substitute for pension credit benefit—

(a) if the person entitled to the benefit consents, or

(b) in such other cases as may be prescribed.

### 101E Discharge of liability where pension credit or alternative benefits secured by insurance policies or annuity contracts

(1) A transaction to which section 19 applies discharges the trustees or managers of a scheme from their liability to provide pension credit benefit or any alternative to pension credit benefit for or in respect of a member of the scheme if and to the extent that—

(a) it results in pension credit benefit, or any alternative to pension credit benefit, for or in respect of the member being appropriately secured (within the meaning of that section),

(b) the transaction is entered into with the consent of the member or, if the member has died, of the member's widow or widower, and

(c) such requirements as may be prescribed are met.

(2) Regulations may provide that subsection (1)(b) shall not apply in prescribed circumstances.

CHAPTER II

TRANSFER VALUES

### 101F Power to give transfer notice

(1) An eligible member of a qualifying scheme may by notice in writing require the trustees or managers of the scheme to use an amount equal to the cash equivalent of his pension credit benefit for such one or more of the authorised purposes as he may specify in the notice.

(2) In the case of a member of an occupational pension scheme, the authorised purposes are—

- (a) to acquire rights allowed under the rules of an occupational pension scheme, or personal pension scheme, which is an eligible scheme,
- (b) to purchase from one or more insurance companies such as are mentioned in section 19(4)(a), chosen by the member and willing to accept payment on account of the member from the trustees or managers, one or more annuities which satisfy the prescribed requirements, and
- (c) in such circumstances as may be prescribed, to subscribe to other pension arrangements which satisfy prescribed requirements.

(3) In the case of a member of a personal pension scheme, the authorised purposes are—

- (a) to acquire rights allowed under the rules of an occupational pension scheme, or personal pension scheme, which is an eligible scheme, and
- (b) in such circumstances as may be prescribed, to subscribe to other pension arrangements which satisfy prescribed requirements.

(4) The cash equivalent for the purposes of subsection (1) shall—

- (a) in the case of a salary related occupational pension scheme, be taken to be the amount shown in the relevant statement under section 101H, and
- (b) in any other case, be determined by reference to the date the notice under that subsection is given.

(5) The requirements which may be prescribed under subsection (2) or (3) include, in particular, requirements of the Inland Revenue.

(6) In subsections (2) and (3), references to an eligible scheme are to a scheme—

- (a) the trustees or managers of which are able and willing to accept payment in respect of the member's pension credit rights, and
- (b) which satisfies the prescribed requirements.

(7) In this Chapter, 'transfer notice' means a notice under subsection (1).

### 101G Restrictions on power to give transfer notice

(1) In the case of a salary related occupational pension scheme, the power to give a transfer notice may only be exercised if—

- (a) the member has been provided with a statement under section 101H, and
- (b) not more than 3 months have passed since the date by reference to which the amount shown in the statement is determined.

(2) The power to give a transfer notice may not be exercised in the case of an occupational pension scheme if—

- (a) there is less than a year to go until the member reaches normal benefit age, or
- (b) the pension to which the member is entitled by virtue of his pension credit rights, or benefit in lieu of that pension, or any part of it has become payable.

(3) Where an eligible member of a qualifying scheme—

- (a) is entitled to make an application under section 95 to the trustees or managers of the scheme, or

(b) would be entitled to do so, but for the fact that he has not received a statement under section 93A in respect of which the guarantee date is sufficiently recent,

he may not, if the scheme so provides, exercise the power to give them a transfer notice unless he also makes an application to them under section 95.

(4) The power to give a transfer notice may not be exercised if a previous transfer notice given by the member to the trustees or managers of the scheme is outstanding.



### 101H Salary related schemes: statements of entitlement

(1) The trustees or managers of a qualifying scheme which is a salary related occupational pension scheme shall, on the application of an eligible member, provide him with a written statement of the amount of the cash equivalent of his pension credit benefit under the scheme.

(2) For the purposes of subsection (1), the amount of the cash equivalent shall be determined by reference to a date falling within—

(a) the prescribed period beginning with the date of the application, and

(b) the prescribed period ending with the date on which the statement under that subsection is provided to the applicant.

(3) Regulations may make provision in relation to applications under subsection (1) and may, in particular, restrict the making of successive applications.

(4) If trustees or managers to whom subsection (1) applies fail to perform an obligation under that subsection, section 10 of the Pensions Act 1995 (power of the Regulatory Authority to impose civil penalties) shall apply to any trustee or manager who has failed to take all such steps as are reasonable to secure that the obligation was performed.

### 101I Calculation of cash equivalents

Cash equivalents for the purposes of this Chapter shall be calculated and verified in the prescribed manner.

### 101J Time for compliance with transfer notice

(1) Trustees or managers of a qualifying scheme who receive a transfer notice shall comply with the notice—

(a) in the case of an occupational pension scheme, within 6 months of the valuation date or, if earlier, by the date on which the member to whom the notice relates reaches normal benefit age, and

(b) in the case of a personal pension scheme, within 6 months of the date on which they receive the notice.

(2) The Regulatory Authority may, in prescribed circumstances, extend the period for complying with the notice.

(3) If the Regulatory Authority are satisfied—

(a) that there has been a relevant change of circumstances since they granted an extension under subsection (2), or

(b) that they granted an extension under that subsection in ignorance of a material fact or on the basis of a mistake as to a material fact,

they may revoke or reduce the extension.

(4) Where the trustees or managers of an occupational pension scheme have failed to comply with a transfer notice before the end of the period for compliance—

(a) they shall, except in prescribed cases, notify the Regulatory Authority of that fact within the prescribed period, and

(b) section 10 of the Pensions Act 1995 (power of the Regulatory Authority to impose civil penalties) shall apply to any trustee or manager who has failed to take all such steps as are reasonable to ensure that the notice was complied with before the end of the period for compliance.

(5) If trustees or managers to whom subsection (4)(a) applies fail to perform the obligation imposed by that provision, section 10 of the Pensions Act 1995 shall apply to any trustee or manager who has failed to take all such steps as are reasonable to ensure that the obligation was performed.

(6) Regulations may—

(a) make provision in relation to applications under subsection (2), and

(b) provide that subsection (4) shall not apply in prescribed circumstances.

(7) In this section, 'valuation date', in relation to a transfer notice given to the trustees or managers of an occupational pension scheme, means—

(a) in the case of a salary related scheme, the date by reference to which the amount shown in the relevant statement under section 101H is determined, and

(b) in the case of any other scheme, the date the notice is given.

### 101K Withdrawal of transfer notice

(1) Subject to subsections (2) and (3), a person who has given a transfer notice may withdraw it by giving the trustees or managers to whom it was given notice in writing that he no longer requires them to comply with it.

(2) A transfer notice may not be withdrawn if the trustees or managers have already entered into an agreement with a third party to use the whole or part of the amount they are required to use in accordance with the notice.

(3) If the giving of a transfer notice depended on the making of an application under section 95, the notice may only be withdrawn if the application is also withdrawn.

### 101L Variation of the amount required to be used

(1) Regulations may make provision for the amount required to be used under section 101F(1) to be increased or reduced in prescribed circumstances.

(2) Without prejudice to the generality of subsection (1), the circumstances which may be prescribed include—

(a) failure by the trustees or managers of a qualifying scheme to comply with a notice under section 101F(1) within 6 months of the date by reference to which the amount of the cash equivalent falls to be determined, and

(b) the state of funding of a qualifying scheme.

(3) Regulations under subsection (1) may have the effect of extinguishing an obligation under section 101F(1).

### 101M Effect of transfer on trustees' duties

Compliance with a transfer notice shall have effect to discharge the trustees or managers of a qualifying scheme from any obligation to provide the pension credit benefit of the eligible member who gave the notice.

### 101N Matters to be disregarded in calculations

In making any calculation for the purposes of this Chapter—

(a) any charge or lien on, and

(b) any set-off against,

the whole or part of a pension shall be disregarded.

### 101O Service of notices

A notice under section 101F(1) or 101K(1) shall be taken to have been given if it is delivered to the trustees or managers personally or sent by post in a registered letter or by recorded delivery service.

### 101P Interpretation of Chapter II

(1) In this Chapter—

'eligible member', in relation to a qualifying scheme, means a member who has pension credit rights under the scheme;

'normal benefit age', in relation to an eligible member of a qualifying scheme, means the earliest age at which the member is entitled to receive a pension by virtue of his pension credit rights under the scheme (disregarding any scheme rule making special provision as to early payment of pension on grounds of ill-health or otherwise);

'pension credit benefit', in relation to an eligible member of a qualifying scheme, means the benefits payable under the scheme to or in respect of the member by virtue of rights under the scheme attributable (directly or indirectly) to a pension credit;

'pension credit rights', in relation to a qualifying scheme, means rights to future benefits under the scheme which are attributable (directly or indirectly) to a pension credit;

'qualifying scheme' means a funded occupational pension scheme and a personal pension scheme;

'transfer notice' has the meaning given by section 101F(7).

(2) For the purposes of this Chapter, an occupational pension scheme is salary related if—

(a) it is not a money purchase scheme, and

(b) it does not fall within a prescribed class.

(3) In this Chapter, references to the relevant statement under section 101H, in relation to a transfer notice given to the trustees or managers of a salary related occupational pension scheme, are to the statement under that section on which the giving of the notice depended.

(4) For the purposes of this section, an occupational pension scheme is funded if it meets its liabilities out of a fund accumulated for the purpose during the life of the scheme.

### 101Q Power to modify Chapter II in relation to hybrid schemes

Regulations may apply this Chapter with prescribed modifications to occupational pension schemes—

(a) which are not money purchase schemes, but

(b) where some of the benefits that may be provided are money purchase benefits.'

**Appointment**

1 December 2000: see SI 2000/1047, art 2(2)(d), Schedule, Pt IV.

## [2.559.1]
## Keypoint

- Regulations
- Cross-reference

## [2.559.2]
## Regulations

See the Pension Sharing (Pension Credit Benefit) Regulations 2000, SI 2000/1054[1] for Regulations under this section.

1 See para **[3.607]** below.

## [2.559.3]
## Cross-reference

See the Introductory Chapter on 'Pensions' at para **[1.172]** above.

[2.560]

## 38 Treatment in winding up

(1) In section 73 of the Pensions Act 1995 (treatment of rights on winding up of an occupational pension scheme to which section 56 of that Act (minimum funding requirement) applies), in subsection (3) (classification of liabilities), in paragraph (c) (accrued rights), at the end of sub-paragraph (i) there shall be inserted—

'(ia) future pensions, or other future benefits, attributable (directly or indirectly) to pension credits (but excluding increases to pensions),'.

(2) In the case of an occupational pension scheme which is not a scheme to which section 56 of the Pensions Act 1995 applies, rights attributable (directly or indirectly) to a pension credit are to be accorded in a winding up the same treatment—

(a) if they have come into payment, as the rights of a pensioner member, and
(b) if they have not come into payment, as the rights of a deferred member.

(3) Subsection (2) overrides the provisions of a scheme to the extent that it conflicts with them, and the scheme has effect with such modifications as may be required in consequence.

(4) In subsection (2)—

(a) 'deferred member' and 'pensioner member' have the same meanings as in Part I of the Pensions Act 1995,
(b) 'pension credit' includes a credit under Northern Ireland legislation corresponding to section 29(1)(b), and
(c) references to rights attributable to a pension credit having come into payment are to the person to whom the rights belong having become entitled by virtue of the rights to the present payment of pension or other benefits.

**Appointment**

1 December 2000: see SI 2000/1047, art 2(2)(d), Schedule, Pt IV.

[2.561]

*Indexation*

## 39 Public service pension schemes

(1) The Pensions (Increase) Act 1971 shall be amended as follows.

(2) In section 3 (qualifying conditions), after subsection (2) there shall be inserted—

'(2A) A pension attributable to the pensioner having become entitled to a pension credit shall not be increased unless the pensioner has attained the age of fifty-five years.'

(3) In section 8, in subsection (1) (definition of 'pension'), in paragraph (a), the words from '(either' to 'person)' shall be omitted.

(4) In that section, in subsection (2) (when pension deemed for purposes of the Act to begin), after 'pension', in the first place, there shall be inserted 'which is not attributable to a pension credit', and after that subsection there shall be inserted—

'(2A) A pension which is attributable to a pension credit shall be deemed for purposes of this Act to begin on the day on which the order or provision on which the credit depends takes effect.'

(5) In section 17(1) (interpretation)—

(a) for the definitions of 'derivative pension' and 'principal pension' there shall be substituted—

''derivative pension' means a pension which—

(a) is not payable in respect of the pensioner's own services, and
(b) is not attributable to the pensioner having become entitled to a pension credit;',

(b) after the definition of 'pension' there shall be inserted—
''pension credit' means a credit under section 29(1)(b) of the Welfare Reform and Pensions Act 1999 or under corresponding Northern Ireland legislation;
'principal pension' means a pension which—
(a) is payable in respect of the pensioner's own services, or
(b) is attributable to the pensioner having become entitled to a pension credit;', and

(c) for the definition of 'widow's pension' there shall be substituted—
''widow's pension' means a pension payable—
(a) in respect of the services of the pensioner's deceased husband, or
(b) by virtue of the pensioner's deceased husband having become entitled to a pension credit.'

**Appointment**
1 December 2000: see SI 2000/1047, art 2(2)(d), Schedule, Pt IV.



### [2.562]

#### 40 Other pension schemes

(1) The Secretary of State may by regulations make provision for a pension to which subsection (2) applies to be increased, as a minimum, by reference to increases in the retail prices index, so far as not exceeding 5% per annum.

(2) This subsection applies to—
(a) a pension provided to give effect to eligible pension credit rights of a member under a qualifying occupational pension scheme, and
(b) a pension provided to give effect to safeguarded rights of a member under a personal pension scheme.

(3) In this section—
'eligible', in relation to pension credit rights, means of a description prescribed by regulations made by the Secretary of State;
'pension credit rights', in relation to an occupational pension scheme, means rights to future benefits under the scheme which are attributable (directly or indirectly) to a credit under section 29(1)(b) or under corresponding Northern Ireland legislation;
'qualifying occupational pension scheme' means an occupational pension scheme which is not a public service pension scheme;
'safeguarded rights' has the meaning given in section 68A of the Pension Schemes Act 1993.

**Appointment**
1 December 2000: see SI 2000/1047, art 2(2)(d), Schedule, Pt IV.

### [2.562.1]
### Keypoint
- Regulations

### [2.562.2]
### Regulations
See the Pension Sharing (Pension Credit Benefit) Regulations 2000, SI 2000/1054[1] for Regulations under this section.

1 See para **[3.607]** below.

**[2.563]**

*Charges by pension arrangements*

## 41 Charges in respect of pension sharing costs

(1) The Secretary of State may by regulations make provision for the purpose of enabling the person responsible for a pension arrangement involved in pension sharing to recover from the parties to pension sharing prescribed charges in respect of prescribed descriptions of pension sharing activity.

(2) Regulations under subsection (1) may include—

(a) provision for the start of the implementation period for a pension credit to be postponed in prescribed circumstances;

(b) provision, in relation to payments in respect of charges recoverable under the regulations, for reimbursement as between the parties to pension sharing;

(c) provision, in relation to the recovery of charges by deduction from a pension credit, for the modification of Schedule 5;

(d) provision for the recovery in prescribed circumstances of such additional amounts as may be determined in accordance with the regulations.

(3) For the purposes of regulations under subsection (1), the question of how much of a charge recoverable under the regulations is attributable to a party to pension sharing is to be determined as follows—

(a) where the relevant order or provision includes provision about the apportionment of charges under this section, there is attributable to the party so much of the charge as is apportioned to him by that provision;

(b) where the relevant order or provision does not include such provision, the charge is attributable to the transferor.

(4) For the purposes of subsection (1), a pension arrangement is involved in pension sharing if section 29 applies by virtue of an order or provision which relates to the arrangement.

(5) In that subsection, the reference to pension sharing activity is to activity attributable (directly or indirectly) to the involvement in pension sharing.

(6) In subsection (3)—

(a) the reference to the relevant order or provision is to the order or provision which gives rise to the pension sharing, and

(b) the reference to the transferor is to the person to whose rights that order or provision relates.

(7) In this section 'prescribed' means prescribed in regulations under subsection (1).

**Appointment**

1 December 2000: see SI 2000/1047, art 2(2)(d), Schedule, Pt IV.

**[2.563.1]**
**Keypoint**

- Regulations

**[2.563.2]**
**Regulations**

See the Pensions on Divorce etc (Charging) Regulations 2000, SI 2000/1049[1] for Regulations under this section.

1 See para **[3.572]** below.

[2.564]

*Adaptation of statutory schemes*

## 42 Extension of scheme-making powers

(1) Power under an Act to establish a pension scheme shall include power to make provision for the provision, by reference to pension credits which derive from rights under—

(a) the scheme, or

(b) a scheme in relation to which the scheme is specified as an alternative for the purposes of paragraph 2 of Schedule 5,

of benefits to or in respect of those entitled to the credits.

(2) Subsection (1) is without prejudice to any other power.

(3) Subsection (1) shall apply in relation to Acts whenever passed.

(4) No obligation to consult shall apply in relation to the making, in exercise of a power under an Act to establish a pension scheme, of provision of a kind authorised by subsection (1).

(5) Any provision of, or under, an Act which makes benefits under a pension scheme established under an Act a charge on, or payable out of—

(a) the Consolidated Fund,

(b) the Scottish Consolidated Fund, or

(c) the Consolidated Fund of Northern Ireland,

shall be treated as including any benefits under the scheme which are attributable (directly or indirectly) to a pension credit which derives from rights to benefits charged on, or payable out of, that fund.

(6) In this section—

'pension credit' includes a credit under Northern Ireland legislation corresponding to section 29(1)(b);

'pension scheme' means a scheme or arrangement providing benefits, in the form of pensions or otherwise, payable on termination of service, or on death or retirement, to or in respect of persons to whom the 'scheme or arrangement applies.

**Appointment**

1 December 2000: see SI 2000/1047, art 2(2)(d), Schedule, Pt IV.

[2.565]

## 43 Power to extend judicial pension schemes

(1) The appropriate minister may by regulations amend the Sheriffs' Pensions (Scotland) Act 1961, the Judicial Pensions Act 1981 or the Judicial Pensions and Retirement Act 1993 for the purpose of—

(a) extending a pension scheme under the Act to include the provision, by reference to pension credits which derive from rights under—

(i) the scheme, or

(ii) a scheme in relation to which the scheme is specified as an alternative for the purposes of paragraph 2 of Schedule 5,

of benefits to or in respect of those entitled to the credits, or

(b) restricting the power of the appropriate minister to accept payments into a pension scheme under the Act, where the payments represent the cash equivalent of rights under another pension scheme which are attributable (directly or indirectly) to a pension credit.

(2) Regulations under subsection (1)—

(a) may make benefits provided by virtue of paragraph (a) of that subsection a charge on, and payable out of, the Consolidated Fund;

(b) may confer power to make subordinate legislation, including subordinate legislation which provides for calculation of the value of rights in accordance with guidance from time to time prepared by a person specified in the subordinate legislation.

(3) The appropriate minister for the purposes of subsection (1) is—

(a) in relation to a pension scheme whose ordinary members are limited to those who hold judicial office whose jurisdiction is exercised exclusively in relation to Scotland, the Secretary of State, and

(b) in relation to any other pension scheme, the Lord Chancellor.

(4) In this section—

'pension credit' includes a credit under Northern Ireland legislation corresponding to section 29(1)(b);

'pension scheme' means a scheme or arrangement providing benefits, in the form of pensions or otherwise, payable on termination of service, or on death or retirement, to or in respect of persons to whom the scheme or arrangement applies.

**Appointment**

1 December 2000: see SI 2000/1047, art 2(2)(d), Schedule, Pt IV.

**[2.566]**

*Supplementary*

### 44 Disapplication of restrictions on alienation

(1) Nothing in any of the following provisions (restrictions on alienation of pension rights) applies in relation to any order or provision falling within section 28(1)—

(a) section 203(1) and (2) of the Army Act 1955, section 203(1) and (2) of the Air Force Act 1955, section 128G(1) and (2) of the Naval Discipline Act 1957 and section 159(4) and (4A) of the Pension Schemes Act 1993,

(b) section 91 of the Pensions Act 1995,

(c) any provision of any enactment (whether passed or made before or after this Act is passed) corresponding to any of the enactments mentioned in paragraphs (a) and (b), and

(d) any provision of a pension arrangement corresponding to any of those enactments.

(2) In this section, 'enactment' includes an enactment comprised in subordinate legislation (within the meaning of the Interpretation Act 1978).

**Appointment**

1 December 2000: see SI 2000/1047, art 2(2)(d), Schedule, Pt IV.

**[2.566.1]**
**Keypoint**

- Service pensions

**[2.566.2]**
**Service pensions**

As a result of this section service pensions are not protected from pension sharing orders. There is a line of authority that suggested that service pensions were protected from financial provision orders under the statutory provisions that applied prior to the implementation of the Pensions Act 1995 and the WRPA 1999[1].

1 See eg, *Cotgrave v Cotgrave* [1992] Fam 33, [1991] FCR 838, CA; *Happé v Happé* [1991] FCR 23, [1990] 2 FLR 212; and *Legrove v Legrove* [1995] 1 FCR 102, [1994] 2 FLR 119, CA.

**[2.567]**

### 45 Information

(1) The Secretary of State may by regulations require the person responsible for a pension arrangement involved in pension sharing to supply to such persons as he may specify in the regulations such information relating to anything which follows from the application of section 29 as he may so specify.

(2) Section 168 of the Pension Schemes Act 1993 (breach of regulations) shall apply as if this section were contained in that Act (otherwise than in Chapter II of Part VII).

(3) For the purposes of this section, a pension arrangement is involved pension sharing if section 29 applies by virtue of an order or provision which relates to the arrangement.

**Appointment**

1 December 2000: see SI 2000/1047, art 2(2)(d), Schedule, Pt IV.



**[2.567.1]**

**Keypoint**

- Regulations

**[2.567.2]**

**Regulations**

See the Pensions on Divorce etc (Provision of Information) Regulations 2000, SI 2000/1048[1] for Regulations under this section.

1 See para **[3.562]** below.

**[2.568]**

### 46 Interpretation of Chapter I

(1) In this Chapter—

'implementation period', in relation to a pension credit, has the meaning given by section 34;

'occupational pension scheme' has the meaning given by section 1 of the Pension Schemes Act 1993;

'pension arrangement' means—

(a) an occupational pension scheme,

(b) a personal pension scheme,

(c) a retirement annuity contract,

(d) an annuity or insurance policy purchased, or transferred, for the purpose of giving effect to rights under an occupational pension scheme or a personal pension scheme, and

(e) an annuity purchased, or entered into, for the purpose of discharging liability in respect of a credit under section 29(1)(b) or under corresponding Northern Ireland legislation;

'pension credit' means a credit under section 29(1)(b);

'pension debit' means a debit under section 29(1)(a);

'pensionable service', in relation to a member of an occupational pension scheme, means service in any description or category of employment to which the scheme relates which qualifies the member (on the assumption that it continues for the appropriate period) for pension or other benefits under the scheme;

'personal pension scheme' has the meaning given by section 1 of the Pension Schemes Act 1993;

'retirement annuity contract' means a contract or scheme approved under Chapter III of Part XIV of the Income and Corporation Taxes Act 1988;

'shareable rights' has the meaning given by section 27(2);

'trustees or managers', in relation to an occupational pension scheme or a personal pension scheme means—

(a) in the case of a scheme established under a trust, the trustees of the scheme, and

(b) in any other case, the managers of the scheme.

(2) In this Chapter, references to the person responsible for a pension arrangement are—

(a) in the case of an occupational pension scheme or a personal pension scheme, to the trustees or managers of the scheme,

(b) in the case of a retirement annuity contract or an annuity falling within paragraph (d) or (e) of the definition of 'pension arrangement' in subsection (1), to the provider of the annuity, and

(c) in the case of an insurance policy falling within paragraph (d) of the definition of that expression, to the insurer.

(3) In determining what is 'pensionable service' for the purposes of this Chapter—

(a) service notionally attributable for any purpose of the scheme is to be disregarded, and

(b) no account is to be taken of any rules of the scheme by which a period of service can be treated for any purpose as being longer or shorter than it actually is.

**Appointment**

1 December 2000: see SI 2000/1047, art 2(2)(d), Schedule, Pt IV.

**[2.569]**

CHAPTER II

SHARING OF STATE SCHEME RIGHTS

### 47 Shareable state scheme rights

(1) Pension sharing is available under this Chapter in relation to a person's shareable state scheme rights.

(2) For the purposes of this Chapter, a person's shareable state scheme rights are—

(a) his entitlement, or prospective entitlement, to a Category A retirement pension by virtue of section 44(3)(b) of the Contributions and Benefits Act (earnings-related additional pension), and

(b) his entitlement, or prospective entitlement, to a pension under section 55A of that Act (shared additional pension).

**Appointment**

1 December 2000: see SI 2000/1047, art 2(2)(d), Schedule, Pt IV.

**[2.569.1]**

**Keypoint**

- Cross-reference

**[2.569.2]**

**Cross-reference**

See the Introductory Chapter on 'Pensions' at paras **[1.162]** and **[1.170]** above.

**[2.570]**

### 48 Activation of benefit sharing

(1) Section 49 applies on the taking effect of any of the following relating to a person's shareable state scheme rights—

(a) a pension sharing order under the Matrimonial Causes Act 1973,
(b) provision which corresponds to the provision which may be made by such an order and which—
  (i) is contained in a qualifying agreement between the parties to a marriage, and
  (ii) takes effect on the dissolution of the marriage under the Family Law Act 1996,
(c) provision which corresponds to the provision which may be made by such an order and which—
  (i) is contained in a qualifying agreement between the parties to a marriage or former marriage, and
  (ii) takes effect after the dissolution of the marriage under the Family Law Act 1996,
(d) an order under Part III of the Matrimonial and Family Proceedings Act 1984 (financial relief in England and Wales in relation to overseas divorce etc) corresponding to such an order as is mentioned in paragraph (a),
(e) a pension sharing order under the Family Law (Scotland) Act 1985,
(f) provision which corresponds to the provision which may be made by such an order and which—
  (i) is contained in a qualifying agreement between the parties to a marriage,
  (ii) is in such form as the Secretary of State may prescribe by regulations, and
  (iii) takes effect on the grant, in relation to the marriage, of decree of divorce under the Divorce (Scotland) Act 1976 or of declarator of nullity,
(g) an order under Part IV of the Matrimonial and Family Proceedings Act 1984 (financial relief in Scotland in relation to overseas divorce etc) corresponding to such an order as is mentioned in paragraph (e),
(h) a pension sharing order under Northern Ireland legislation, and
(i) an order under Part IV of the Matrimonial and Family Proceedings (Northern Ireland) Order 1989 (financial relief in Northern Ireland in relation to overseas divorce etc) corresponding to such an order as is mentioned in paragraph (h).

(2) For the purposes of subsection (1)(b) and (c), a qualifying agreement is one which—
(a) has been entered into in such circumstances as the Lord Chancellor may prescribe by regulations, and
(b) satisfies such requirements as the Lord Chancellor may so prescribe.

(3) For the purposes of subsection (1)(f), a qualifying agreement is one which—
(a) has been entered into in such circumstances as the Secretary of State may prescribe by regulations, and
(b) is registered in the Books of Council and Session.

(4) Subsection (1)(b) does not apply if the provision relates to rights which are the subject of a pension sharing order under the Matrimonial Causes Act 1973 in relation to the marriage.

(5) Subsection (1)(c) does not apply if—
(a) the marriage was dissolved by an order under section 3 of the Family Law Act 1996 (divorce not preceded by separation) and the satisfaction of the requirements of section 9(2) of that Act (settlement of future financial arrangements) was a precondition to the making of the order,
(b) the provision relates to rights which are the subject of a pension sharing order under the Matrimonial Causes Act 1973 in relation to the marriage, or
(c) shareable state scheme rights have already been the subject of pension sharing between the parties.

(6) For the purposes of this section, an order or provision falling within subsection (1)(e), (f) or (g) shall be deemed never to have taken effect if the Secretary of State does not receive before the end of the period of 2 months beginning with the relevant date—

(a) copies of the relevant matrimonial documents, and

(b) such information relating to the transferor and transferee as the Secretary of State may prescribe by regulations under section 34(1)(b)(ii).

(7) The relevant date for the purposes of subsection (6) is—

(a) in the case of an order or provision falling within subsection (1)(e) or (f), the date of the extract of the decree or declarator responsible for the divorce or annulment to which the order or provision relates, and

(b) in the case of an order falling within subsection (1)(g), the date of disposal of the application under section 28 of the Matrimonial and Family Proceedings Act 1984.

(8) The reference in subsection (6)(a) to the relevant matrimonial documents is—

(a) in the case of an order falling within subsection (1)(e) or (g), to copies of the order and the order, decree or declarator responsible for the divorce or annulment to which it relates, and

(b) in the case of provision falling within subsection (1)(f), to—

(i) copies of the provision and the order, decree or declarator responsible for the divorce or annulment to which it relates, and

(ii) documentary evidence that the agreement containing the provision is one to which subsection (3)(a) applies.

(9) The sheriff may, on the application of any person having an interest, make an order—

(a) extending the period of 2 months referred to in subsection (6), and

(b) if that period has already expired, providing that, if the Secretary of State receives the documents and information concerned before the end of the period specified in the order, subsection (6) is to be treated as never having applied.

**Appointment**

1 December 2000: see SI 2000/1047, art 2(2)(d), Schedule, Pt IV.

**[2.570.1]**

**Keypoint**

- General

**[2.570.2]**

**General**

Sub-ss (1)(b) and (c), (2) and (5)(a) are dependent on the FLA 1996. Now it is clear that the FLA 1996 is not to be implemented they are irrelevant.

Sub-ss (1)(e), (f), (g), (3) and (6) to (9) apply only to Scotland.

Sub-s (1)(h) and (i) apply only to Northern Ireland.

**[2.571]**

### 49 Creation of state scheme pension debits and credits

(1) On the application of this section—

(a) the transferor becomes subject, for the purposes of Part II of the Contributions and Benefits Act (contributory benefits), to a debit of the appropriate amount, and

(b) the transferee becomes entitled, for those purposes, to a credit of that amount.

(2) Where the relevant order or provision specifies a percentage value to be transferred, the appropriate amount for the purposes of subsection (1) is the specified percentage of the cash equivalent on the transfer day of the transferor's shareable state scheme rights immediately before that day.

(3) Where the relevant order or provision specifies an amount to be transferred, the appropriate amount for the purposes of subsection (1) is the lesser of—

(a) the specified amount, and
(b) the cash equivalent on the transfer day of the transferor's relevant state scheme rights immediately before that day.

[(4) The Secretary of State may by regulations make provision about the calculation and verification of cash equivalents for the purposes of this section.

(4A) The power conferred by subsection (4) above includes power to provide—
(a) for calculation or verification in such manner as may be approved by or on behalf of the Government Actuary, and
(b) for things done under the regulations to be required to be done in accordance with guidance from time to time prepared by a person prescribed by the regulations.]

(5) In determining prospective entitlement to a Category A retirement pension for the purposes of this section, only tax years before that in which the transfer day falls shall be taken into account.

(6) In this section—

'relevant order or provision' means the order or provision by virtue of which this section applies;

'transfer day' means the day on which the relevant order or provision takes effect;

'transferor' means the person to whose rights the relevant order or provision relates;

'transferee' means the person for whose benefit the relevant order or provision is made.

**Appointment**

1 December 2000: see SI 2000/1047, art 2(2)(d), Schedule, Pt IV.

**Amendment**

Sub-ss (4), (4A): substituted, for sub-s (4) as originally enacted, by the Child Support, Pensions and Social Security Act 2000, s 41.

**[2.571.1]**

**Keypoint**

- General

**[2.571.2]**

**General**

Sub-s (3) applies only to Scotland.

**[2.572]**

### 50 Effect of state scheme pension debits and credits

(1) Schedule 6 (which amends the Contributions and Benefits Act for the purpose of giving effect to debits and credits under section 49(1)) shall have effect.

(2) Section 55C of that Act (which is inserted by that Schedule) shall have effect, in relation to incremental periods (within the meaning of that section) beginning on or after 6th April 2010, with the following amendments—
(a) in subsection (3), for 'period of enhancement' there is substituted 'period of deferment',
(b) in subsection (4), for '1/7th per cent' there is substituted '1/5th per cent',
(c) in subsection (7), for 'period of enhancement', in both places, there is substituted 'period of deferment', and
(d) in subsection (9), the definition of 'period of enhancement' (and the preceding 'and') are omitted.

**Appointment**

1 December 2000: see SI 2000/1047, art 2(2)(d), Schedule, Pt IV.

[2.573]

## 51 Interpretation of Chapter II

In this Chapter—

'shareable state scheme rights' has the meaning given by section 47(2); and

'tax year' has the meaning given by section 122(1) of the Contributions and Benefits Act.

**Appointment**

1 December 2000: see SI 2000/1047, art 2(2)(d), Schedule, Pt IV.

## SCHEDULE 5
## Pension Credits: Mode of Discharge

(s 35)

[2.574]

*Funded pension schemes*

**1**

(1) This paragraph applies to a pension credit which derives from—
- (a) a funded occupational pension scheme, or
- (b) a personal pension scheme.

(2) The trustees or managers of the scheme from which a pension credit to which this paragraph applies derives may discharge their liability in respect of the credit by conferring appropriate rights under that scheme on the person entitled to the credit—
- (a) with his consent, or
- (b) in accordance with regulations made by the Secretary of State.

(3) The trustees or managers of the scheme from which a pension credit to which this paragraph applies derives may discharge their liability in respect of the credit by paying the amount of the credit to the person responsible for a qualifying arrangement with a view to acquiring rights under that arrangement for the person entitled to the credit if—
- (a) the qualifying arrangement is not disqualified as a destination for the credit,
- (b) the person responsible for that arrangement is able and willing to accept payment in respect of the credit, and
- (c) payment is made with the consent of the person entitled to the credit, or in accordance with regulations made by the Secretary of State.

(4) For the purposes of sub-paragraph (2), no account is to be taken of consent of the person entitled to the pension credit unless—
- (a) it is given after receipt of notice in writing of an offer to discharge liability in respect of the credit by making a payment under sub-paragraph (3), or
- (b) it is not withdrawn within 7 days of receipt of such notice.

*Unfunded public service pension schemes*

**2**

(1) This paragraph applies to a pension credit which derives from an occupational pension scheme which is—
- (a) not funded, and
- (b) a public service pension scheme.

(2) The trustees or managers of the scheme from which a pension credit to which this paragraph applies derives may discharge their liability in respect of the credit by conferring appropriate rights under that scheme on the person entitled to the credit.

(3) If such a scheme as is mentioned in sub-paragraph (1) is closed to new members, the appropriate authority in relation to that scheme may by regulations specify another public service pension scheme as an alternative to it for the purposes of this paragraph.

(4) Where the trustees or managers of a scheme in relation to which an alternative is specified under sub-paragraph (3) are subject to liability in respect of a pension credit, they may—

(a) discharge their liability in respect of the credit by securing that appropriate rights are conferred on the person entitled to the credit by the trustees or managers of the alternative scheme, and

(b) for the purpose of so discharging their liability, require the trustees or managers of the alternative scheme to take such steps as may be required.

(5) In sub-paragraph (3), 'the appropriate authority', in relation to a public service pension scheme, means such Minister of the Crown or government department as may be designated by the Treasury as having responsibility for the scheme.



### *Other unfunded occupational pension schemes*

**3**

(1) This paragraph applies to a pension credit which derives from an occupational pension scheme which is—

(a) not funded, and

(b) not a public service pension scheme.

(2) The trustees or managers of the scheme from which a pension credit to which this paragraph applies derives may discharge their liability in respect of the credit by conferring appropriate rights under that scheme on the person entitled to the credit.

(3) The trustees or managers of the scheme from which a pension credit to which this paragraph applies derives may discharge their liability in respect of the credit by paying the amount of the credit to the person responsible for a qualifying arrangement with a view to acquiring rights under that arrangement for the person entitled to the credit if—

(a) the qualifying arrangement is not disqualified as a destination for the credit,

(b) the person responsible for that arrangement is able and willing to accept payment in respect of the credit, and

(c) payment is made with the consent of the person entitled to the credit, or in accordance with regulations made by the Secretary of State.

### *Other pension arrangements*

**4**

(1) This paragraph applies to a pension credit which derives from—

(a) a retirement annuity contract,

(b) an annuity or insurance policy purchased or transferred for the purpose of giving effect to rights under an occupational pension scheme or a personal pension scheme, or

(c) an annuity purchased, or entered into, for the purpose of discharging liability in respect of a pension credit.

(2) The person responsible for the pension arrangement from which a pension credit to which this paragraph applies derives may discharge his liability in respect of the credit by paying the amount of the credit to the person responsible for a qualifying arrangement with a view to acquiring rights under that arrangement for the person entitled to the credit if—

(a) the qualifying arrangement is not disqualified as a destination for the credit,

(b) the person responsible for that arrangement is able and willing to accept payment in respect of the credit, and

(c) payment is made with the consent of the person entitled to the credit, or in accordance with regulations made by the Secretary of State.

(3) The person responsible for the pension arrangement from which a pension credit to which this paragraph applies derives may discharge his liability in respect of the credit by entering into an annuity contract with the person entitled to the credit if the contract is not disqualified as a destination for the credit.

(4) The person responsible for the pension arrangement from which a pension credit to which this paragraph applies derives may, in such circumstances as the Secretary of State may prescribe by regulations, discharge his liability in respect of the credit by assuming an obligation to provide an annuity for the person entitled to the credit.

(5) In sub-paragraph (1)(c), 'pension credit' includes a credit under Northern Ireland legislation corresponding to section 29(1)(b).

### *Appropriate rights*

**5**

For the purposes of this Schedule, rights conferred on the person entitled to a pension credit are appropriate if—

(a) they are conferred with effect from, and including, the day on which the order, or provision, under which the credit arises takes effect, and

(b) their value, when calculated in accordance with regulations made by the Secretary of State, equals the amount of the credit.

### *Qualifying arrangements*

**6**

(1) The following are qualifying arrangements for the purposes of this Schedule—

(a) an occupational pension scheme,

(b) a personal pension scheme,

(c) an appropriate annuity contract,

(d) an appropriate policy of insurance, and

(e) an overseas arrangement within the meaning of the Contracting-out (Transfer and Transfer Payment) Regulations 1996.

(2) An annuity contract or policy of insurance is appropriate for the purposes of sub-paragraph (1) if, at the time it is entered into or taken out, the [insurer] with which it is entered into or taken out—

(a) is carrying on … long-term insurance business in the United Kingdom or any other member State, and

(b) satisfies such requirements as the Secretary of State may prescribe by regulations.

[(3) 'Insurer' and 'long-term insurance business' have the meaning given in section 180A of the Pension Schemes Act 1993.]

### *Disqualification as destination for pension credit*

**7**

(1) If a pension credit derives from a pension arrangement which is approved for the purposes of Part XIV of the Income and Corporation Taxes Act 1988, an arrangement is disqualified as a destination for the credit unless—

(a) it is also approved for those purposes, or

(b) it satisfies such requirements as the Secretary of State may prescribe by regulations.

(2) If the rights by reference to which the amount of a pension credit is determined are or include contracted-out rights or safeguarded rights, an arrangement is disqualified as a destination for the credit unless—

(a) it is of a description prescribed by the Secretary of State by regulations, and

(b) it satisfies such requirements as he may so prescribe.

(3) An occupational pension scheme is disqualified as a destination for a pension credit unless the rights to be acquired under the arrangement by the person entitled to the credit are rights whose value, when calculated in accordance with regulations made by the Secretary of State, equals the credit.

(4) An annuity contract or insurance policy is disqualified as a destination for a pension credit in such circumstances as the Secretary of State may prescribe by regulations.

(5) The requirements which may be prescribed under sub-paragraph (1)(b) include, in particular, requirements of the Inland Revenue.

(6) In sub-paragraph (2)—

'contracted-out rights' means such rights under, or derived from—

(a) an occupational pension scheme contracted-out by virtue of section 9(2) or (3) of the Pension Schemes Act 1993, or

(b) a personal pension scheme which is an appropriate scheme for the purposes of that Act,

as the Secretary of State may prescribe by regulations;

'safeguarded rights' has the meaning given by section 68A of the Pension Schemes Act 1993.



### *Adjustments to amount of pension credit*

**8**

(1) If—

(a) a pension credit derives from an occupational pension scheme,

(b) the scheme is one to which section 56 of the Pensions Act 1995 (minimum funding requirement for funded salary related schemes) applies,

(c) the scheme is underfunded on the valuation day, and

(d) such circumstances as the Secretary of State may prescribe by regulations apply,

paragraph 1(3) shall have effect in relation to the credit as if the reference to the amount of the credit were to such lesser amount as may be determined in accordance with regulations made by the Secretary of State.

(2) Whether a scheme is underfunded for the purposes of sub-paragraph (1)(c) shall be determined in accordance with regulations made by the Secretary of State.

(3) For the purposes of that provision, the valuation day is the day by reference to which the cash equivalent on which the amount of the pension credit depends falls to be calculated.

**9**

If—

(a) a person's shareable rights under a pension arrangement have become subject to a pension debit, and

(b) the person responsible for the arrangement makes a payment which is referable to those rights without knowing of the pension debit,

this Schedule shall have effect as if the amount of the corresponding pension credit were such lesser amount as may be determined in accordance with regulations made by the Secretary of State.

**10**

The Secretary of State may by regulations make provision for paragraph 1(3), 3(3) or 4(2) to have effect, where payment is made after the end of the implementation period for the pension credit, as if the reference to the amount of the credit were to such larger amount as may be determined in accordance with the regulations.

*General*

**11**

Liability in respect of a pension credit shall be treated as discharged if the effect of paragraph 8(1) or 9 is to reduce it to zero.

**12**

Liability in respect of a pension credit may not be discharged otherwise than in accordance with this Schedule.

**13**

Regulations under paragraph 5(b) or 7(3) may provide for calculation of the value of rights in accordance with guidance from time to time prepared by a person specified in the regulations.

**14**

In this Schedule—

'funded', in relation to an occupational pension scheme, means that the scheme meets its liabilities out of a fund accumulated for the purpose during the life of the scheme;

'public service pension scheme' has the same meaning as in the Pension Schemes Act 1993.

**Appointment**

1 December 2000: see SI 2000/1047, art 2(2)(d), Schedule, Pt IV.

**Amendment**

Para 6: SI 2001/3649, art 159.

### [2.574.1]
### Keypoint

- Cross-references

### [2.574.2]
### Cross-references

- **Sch 5, para 1** – See the Introductory Chapter on 'Pensions' at para **[1.166]** above.
- **Sch 5, para 2** – See the Introductory Chapter on 'Pensions' at para **[1.167]** above.
- **Sch 5, para 3** – See the Introductory Chapter on 'Pensions' at para **[1.166]** above.
- **Sch 5, para 4** – See the Introductory Chapter on 'Pensions' at para **[1.166]** above.

## SCHEDULE 6
## Effect of State Scheme Pension Debits and Credits

(s 50)

### [2.575]

**1**

The Contributions and Benefits Act is amended as follows.

2
After section 45A there is inserted—

### '45B Reduction of additional pension in Category A retirement pension: pension sharing

(1) The weekly rate of the additional pension in a Category A retirement pension shall be reduced as follows in any case where—

(a) the pensioner has become subject to a state scheme pension debit, and

(b) the debit is to any extent referable to the additional pension.

(2) If the pensioner became subject to the debit in or after the final relevant year, the weekly rate of the additional pension shall be reduced by the appropriate weekly amount.

(3) If the pensioner became subject to the debit before the final relevant year, the weekly rate of the additional pension shall be reduced by the appropriate weekly amount multiplied by the relevant revaluation percentage.

(4) The appropriate weekly amount for the purposes of subsections (2) and (3) above is the weekly rate, expressed in terms of the valuation day, at which the cash equivalent, on that day, of the pension mentioned in subsection (5) below is equal to so much of the debit as is referable to the additional pension.

(5) The pension referred to above is a notional pension for the pensioner by virtue of section 44(3)(b) above which becomes payable on the later of—

(a) his attaining pensionable age, and

(b) the valuation day.

(6) For the purposes of subsection (3) above, the relevant revaluation percentage is the percentage specified, in relation to earnings factors for the tax year in which the pensioner became subject to the debit, by the last order under section 148 of the Administration Act to come into force before the end of the final relevant year.

(7) Cash equivalents for the purposes of this section shall be calculated in accordance with regulations.

(8) In this section—

'final relevant year' means the tax year immediately preceding that in which the pensioner attains pensionable age;

'state scheme pension debit' means a debit under section 49(1)(a) of the Welfare Reform and Pensions Act 1999 (debit for the purposes of this Part of this Act);

'valuation day' means the day on which the pensioner became subject to the state scheme pension debit.'

3
After section 55 there is inserted—

*'Shared additional pension*

### 55A Shared additional pension

(1) A person shall be entitled to a shared additional pension if he is—

(a) over pensionable age, and

(b) entitled to a state scheme pension credit.

(2) A person's entitlement to a shared additional pension shall continue throughout his life.

(3) The weekly rate of a shared additional pension shall be the appropriate weekly amount, unless the pensioner's entitlement to the state scheme pension credit arose before the final relevant year, in which case it shall be that amount multiplied by the relevant revaluation percentage.

(4) The appropriate weekly amount for the purposes of subsection (3) above is the weekly rate, expressed in terms of the valuation day, at which the cash equivalent, on that day, of the pensioner's entitlement, or prospective entitlement, to the shared additional pension is equal to the state scheme pension credit.

(5) The relevant revaluation percentage for the purposes of that subsection is the percentage specified, in relation to earnings factors for the tax year in which the entitlement to the state scheme pension credit arose, by the last order under section 148 of the Administration Act to come into force before the end of the final relevant year.

(6) Cash equivalents for the purposes of this section shall be calculated in accordance with regulations.

(7) In this section—

'final relevant year' means the tax year immediately preceding that in which the pensioner attains pensionable age;

'state scheme pension credit' means a credit under section 49(1)(b) of the Welfare Reform and Pensions Act 1999 (credit for the purposes of this Part of this Act);

'valuation day' means the day on which the pensioner becomes entitled to the state scheme pension credit.

### 55B Reduction of shared additional pension: pension sharing

(1) The weekly rate of a shared additional pension shall be reduced as follows in any case where—

(a) the pensioner has become subject to a state scheme pension debit, and

(b) the debit is to any extent referable to the pension.

(2) If the pensioner became subject to the debit in or after the final relevant year, the weekly rate of the pension shall be reduced by the appropriate weekly amount.

(3) If the pensioner became subject to the debit before the final relevant year, the weekly rate of the additional pension shall be reduced by the appropriate weekly amount multiplied by the relevant revaluation percentage.

(4) The appropriate weekly amount for the purposes of subsections (2) and (3) above is the weekly rate, expressed in terms of the valuation day, at which the cash equivalent, on that day, of the pension mentioned in subsection (5) below is equal to so much of the debit as is referable to the shared additional pension.

(5) The pension referred to above is a notional pension for the pensioner by virtue of section 55A above which becomes payable on the later of—

(a) his attaining pensionable age, and

(b) the valuation day.

(6) For the purposes of subsection (3) above, the relevant revaluation percentage is the percentage specified, in relation to earnings factors for the tax year in which the pensioner became subject to the debit, by the last order under section 148 of the Administration Act to come into force before the end of the final relevant year.

(7) Cash equivalents for the purposes of this section shall be calculated in accordance with regulations.

(8) In this section—

'final relevant year' means the tax year immediately preceding that in which the pensioner attains pensionable age;

'state scheme pension debit', means a debit under section 49(1)(a) of the Welfare Reform and Pensions Act 1999 (debit for the purposes of this Part of this Act);

'valuation day' means the day on which the pensioner became subject to the state scheme pension debit.

### 55C Increase of shared additional pension where entitlement is deferred

(1) For the purposes of this section, a person's entitlement to a shared additional pension is deferred—

(a) where he would be entitled to a Category A or Category B retirement pension but for the fact that his entitlement to such a pension is deferred, if and so long as his entitlement to such a pension is deferred, and

(b) otherwise, if and so long as he does not become entitled to the shared additional pension by reason only of not satisfying the conditions of section 1 of the Administration Act (entitlement to benefit dependent on claim),

and, in relation to a shared additional pension, 'period of deferment' shall be construed accordingly.

(2) Where a person's entitlement to a shared additional pension is deferred, the rate of his shared additional pension shall be increased by an amount equal to the aggregate of the increments to which he is entitled under subsection (3) below, but only if that amount is enough to increase the rate of the pension by at least 1 per cent.

(3) A person is entitled to an increment under this subsection for each complete incremental period in his period of enhancement.

(4) The amount of the increment for an incremental period shall be 1/7th per cent of the weekly rate of the shared additional pension to which the person would have been entitled for the period if his entitlement had not been deferred.

(5) Amounts under subsection (4) above shall be rounded to the nearest penny, taking any 1/2p as nearest to the next whole penny.

(6) Where an amount under subsection (4) above would, apart from this subsection, be a sum less than 1/2p, the amount shall be taken to be zero, notwithstanding any other provision of this Act, the Pensions Act 1995 or the Administration Act.

(7) Where one or more orders have come into force under section 150 of the Administration Act during the period of enhancement, the rate for any incremental period shall be determined as if the order or orders had come into force before the beginning of the period of enhancement.

(8) The sums which are the increases in the rates of shared additional pensions under this section are subject to alteration by order made by the Secretary of State under section 150 of the Administration Act.

(9) In this section—

'incremental period' means any period of six days which are treated by regulations as days of increment for the purposes of this section in relation to the person and pension in question; and

'period of enhancement', in relation to that person and that pension, means the period which—

(a) begins on the same day as the period of deferment in question, and

(b) ends on the same day as that period or, if earlier, on the day before the 5th anniversary of the beginning of that period.'

**Appointment**

1 December 2000: see SI 2000/1047, art 2(2)(d), Schedule, Pt IV.



## [2.575.1]
### Keypoint

- Cross-reference

## [2.575.2]
### Cross-reference

See the Introductory Chapter on 'Pensions' at para **[1.168]** above.

# PART 3

# Subordinate Legislation

## Family Proceedings Rules 1991

**SI 1991 No 1247**



**Contents**

*Rule*

PART I
PRELIMINARY



PART II
MATRIMONIAL CAUSES

*Decrees and orders*



*Ancillary relief*

## PART III
### OTHER MATRIMONIAL ETC PROCEEDINGS



## PART IV
### PROCEEDINGS UNDER THE CHILDREN ACT 1989



## PART VII
### ENFORCEMENT OF ORDERS

#### CHAPTER 1
#### GENERAL

CHAPTER 2
JUDGMENT SUMMONSES



CHAPTER 4
ENFORCEMENT OF MAINTENANCE ORDERS



*Proceedings under Part II of Act of 1950*



*Registration etc of certain orders under the Act of 1958*



*Proceedings under Act of 1972*



CHAPTER 5
REGISTRATION AND ENFORCEMENT UNDER THE COUNCIL REGULATION

PART VIII
APPEALS



PART X
PROCEDURE (GENERAL)

[3.1]–[3.401]

## 1.1 Citation and commencement

These rules may be cited as the Family Proceedings Rules 1991 and shall come into force on 14th October 1991.

[3.402]

## 1.2 Interpretation

(1) In these rules, unless the context otherwise requires—

'the Act of 1973' means the Matrimonial Causes Act 1973;

'the Act of 1984' means the Matrimonial and Family Proceedings Act 1984;

'the Act of 1986' means the Family Law Act 1986;

'the Act of 1989' means the Children Act 1989;

['the Act of 1991' means the Child Support Act 1991;]

'ancillary relief' means—

(a) an avoidance of disposition order,
(b) a financial provision order,
(c) an order for maintenance pending suit,
(d) a property adjustment order,
(e) a variation order; or
(f) a pension sharing order.

'avoidance of disposition order' means an order under section 37(2)(b) or (c) of the Act of 1973;

'business day' has the meaning assigned to it by rule 1.5(6);

'cause' means a matrimonial cause as defined by section 32 of the Act of 1984 or proceedings under section 19 of the Act of 1973 (presumption of death and dissolution of marriage);

'child' and 'child of the family' have, except in Part IV, the meanings respectively assigned to them by section 52(1) of the Act of 1973;

'consent order' means an order under section 33A of the Act of 1973;

'Contracting State' means—

(a) one of the original parties to the Council Regulation, that is to say Belgium, Germany, Greece, Spain, France, Ireland, Italy, Luxembourg, the Netherlands, Austria, Portugal, Finland, Sweden and the United Kingdom, and
(b) a party which has subsequently adopted the Council Regulation;

'the Council Regulation' means Council Regulation (EC) No 1347/2000 of 29th May 2000 on jurisdiction and the recognition and enforcement of judgments in matrimonial matters and in matters of parental responsibility for children of both spouses;

'court' means a judge or the district judge;

'court of trial' means a divorce county court designated by the Lord Chancellor as a court of trial pursuant to section 33(1) of the Act of 1984 and, in relation to matrimonial proceedings pending in a divorce county court, the principal registry shall be treated as a court of trial having its place of sitting at the Royal Courts of Justice;

'defended cause' means a cause not being an undefended cause;

'district judge', in relation to proceedings in the principal registry, a district registry or a county court, means the district judge or one of the district judges of that registry or county court, as the case may be;

'district registry'[, except in rule 4.22(2A),] means any district registry having a divorce county court within its district;

'divorce county court' means a county court so designated by the Lord Chancellor pursuant to section 33(1) of the Act of 1984;

'divorce town', in relation to any matrimonial proceedings, means a place at which sittings of the High Court are authorised to be held outside the Royal Courts of Justice for the hearing of such proceedings or proceedings of the class to which they belong;

'document exchange' means any document exchange for the time being approved by the Lord Chancellor;

'family proceedings' has the meaning assigned to it by section 32 of the Act of 1984;

'financial provision order' means any of the orders mentioned in section 21(1) of the Act of 1973 except an order under section 27(6) of that Act;

'financial relief' has the same meaning as in section 37 of the Act of 1973;

'judge' does not include a district judge;

'notice of intention to defend' has the meaning assigned to it by rule 10.8;

'officer of the service' has the same meaning as in the Criminal Justice and Court Services Act 2000;

'order for maintenance pending suit' means an order under section 22 of the Act of 1973;

'person named' includes a person described as 'passing under the name of AB';

'the President' means the President of the Family Division or, in the case of his absence or incapacity through illness or otherwise or of a vacancy in the office of President, the senior puisne judge of that Division;

'principal registry' means the Principal Registry of the Family Division;

'proper officer' means—

(a) in relation to the principal registry, the [family proceedings department manager], and

(b) in relation to any other court or registry, the [court manager],

or other officer of the court or registry acting on his behalf in accordance with directions given by the Lord Chancellor;

'property adjustment order' means any of the orders mentioned in section 21(2) of the Act of 1973;

'registry for the divorce town' shall be construed in accordance with rule 2.32(6);

'Royal Courts of Justice', in relation to matrimonial proceedings pending in a divorce county court, means such place, being the Royal Courts of Justice or elsewhere, as may be specified in directions given by the Lord Chancellor pursuant to section 42(2)(a) of the Act of 1984;

'senior district judge' means the senior district judge of the Family Division or, in his absence from the principal registry, the senior of the district judges in attendance at the registry;

'special procedure list' has the meaning assigned to it by rule 2.24(3);

'undefended cause' means—

(i) a cause in which no answer has been filed or any answer filed has been struck out, or

(ii) a cause which is proceeding only on the respondent's answer and in which no reply or answer to the respondent's answer has been filed or any such reply or answer has been struck out, or

(iii) a cause to which rule 2.12(4) applies and in which no notice has been given under that rule or any notice so given has been withdrawn, or

(iv) a cause in which an answer has been filed claiming relief but in which no pleading has been filed opposing the grant of a decree on the petition or answer or any pleading or part of a pleading opposing the grant of such relief has been struck out, or

(v) any cause not within (i) to (iv) above in which a decree has been pronounced;

'variation order' means an order under section 31 of the Act of 1973.

(2) Unless the context otherwise requires, a cause begun by petition shall be treated as pending for the purposes of these rules notwithstanding that a final decree or order has been made on the petition.

(3) Unless the context otherwise requires, a rule or Part referred to by number means the rule or Part so numbered in these rules.

(4) In these rules a form referred to by number means the form so numbered in Appendix 1 [or 1A] to these rules with such variation as the circumstances of the particular case may require.

(5) In these rules any reference to an Order and rule is—

(a) if prefixed by the letters 'CCR', a reference to that Order and rule in the County Court Rules 1981, and

(b) if prefixed by the letters 'RSC', a reference to that Order and rule in the Rules of the Supreme Court 1965.

[(5A) In these rules a reference to a Part or rule, if prefixed by the letters 'CPR', is a reference to that Part or rule in the Civil Procedure Rules 1998.]

(6) References in these rules to a county court shall, in relation to matrimonial proceedings, be construed as references to a divorce county court.

(7) In this rule and in rule 1.4, 'matrimonial proceedings' means proceedings of a kind with respect to which divorce county courts have jurisdiction by or under section 33, 34 or 35 of the Act of 1984.

**Amendment**

Para (1): definition 'the Act of 1991' inserted by SI 1993/295, r 3. Para (1): definition 'ancillary relief' amended by SI 2000/2267. Date in force: 2 October 2000. Para (1): in definition 'district registry' words ', except in rule 4.22(2A),' in square brackets inserted by SI 1992/2067, r 3. Para (1): in definition 'proper office' in para (a) words 'family proceedings department manager' in square brackets substituted by SI 1997/1056, r 6. Para (1): in definition 'proper office' in para (b) words 'court manager' in square brackets substituted by SI 1997/1056, r 6. Para (1): SI 2001/821. Para (4): words 'or 1A' in square brackets inserted by SI 1999/3491, rr 2, 4(1). Date in force: 5 June 2000 (in relation to proceedings commenced by Form A or B on or after that date and, where the court considers it just and so directs, proceedings commenced before that date): see SI 1999/3491, r 1. Para (5A): inserted by SI 1999/3491, rr 2, 4(2). Date in force: 5 June 2000 (in relation to proceedings commenced by Form A or B on or after that date and, where the court considers it just and so directs, proceedings commenced before that date): see SI 1999/3491, r 1.



**[3.403]**

## 1.3 Application of other rules

(1) Subject to the provisions of these rules and of any enactment the County Court Rules 1981 and the Rules of the Supreme Court 1965 shall [continue to] apply, with the necessary modifications, to family proceedings in a county court and the High Court respectively.

(2) For the purposes of paragraph (1) any provision of these rules authorising or requiring anything to be done in family proceedings shall be treated as if it were, in the case of proceedings pending in a county court, a provision of the County Court Rules 1981 and, in the case of proceedings pending in the High Court, a provision of the Rules of the Supreme Court 1965.

**Amendment**

Para (1): words 'continue to' in square brackets inserted by SI 1999/1012, rr 2, 3(2). Date in force: 26 April 1999: see SI 1999/1012, r 1.

**[3.404]**

## 1.4 County court proceedings in principal registry

(1) Subject to the provisions of these rules, matrimonial proceedings pending at any time in the principal registry which, if they had been begun in a divorce county court,

would be pending at that time in such a court, shall be treated, for the purposes of these rules and of any provision of the County Court Rules 1981 and the County Courts Act 1984, as pending in a divorce county court and not in the High Court.

(2) Unless the context otherwise requires, any reference to a divorce county court in any provision of these rules which relates to the commencement or prosecution of proceedings in a divorce county court, or the transfer of proceedings to or from such a court, includes a reference to the principal registry.

**[3.405]**

### 1.5 Computation of time

(1) Any period of time fixed by these rules, or by any rules applied by these rules, or by any decree, judgment, order or direction for doing any act shall be reckoned in accordance with the following provisions of this rule.

(2) Where the act is required to be done not less than a specified period before a specified date, the period starts immediately after the date on which the act is done and ends immediately before the specified date.

(3) Where the act is required to be done within a specified period after or from a specified date, the period starts immediately after that date.

(4) Where, apart from this paragraph, the period in question, being a period of seven days or less, would include a day which is not a business day, that day shall be excluded.

(5) Where the time so fixed for doing an act in the court office expires on a day on which the office is closed, and for that reason the act cannot be done on that day, the act shall be in time if done on the next day on which the office is open.

(6) In these rules 'business day' means any day other than—

- (a) a Saturday, Sunday, Christmas Day or Good Friday; or
- (b) a bank holiday under the Banking and Financial Dealings Act 1971, in England and Wales.

**[3.406]**

## Part II
## Matrimonial Causes

### *Decrees and orders*

### 2.45 Application under section 10(2) of Act of 1973

(1) An application by a respondent to a petition for divorce for the court to consider the financial position of the respondent after the divorce shall be made by notice in [Form B].

(2) …

(3) …

(4) The powers of the court on hearing the application may be exercised by the district judge.

(5) Where the petitioner has relied on the fact of two or five years' separation and the court has granted a decree nisi without making any finding as to any other fact mentioned in section 1(2) of the Act of 1973, … [rules 2.51B to 2.70] and 10.10 shall apply as if the application were an application for ancillary relief [and, unless the context otherwise requires, those rules shall be read as if all references to Form A were references to Form B].

(6) A statement of any of the matters mentioned in section 10(3) of the Act of 1973 with respect to which the court is satisfied, or, where the court has proceeded under section 10(4), a statement that the conditions for which that subsection provides have been fulfilled, shall be entered in the records of the court.

**Amendment**

SI 1999/3491.

**[3.407]**

## FAMILY PROCEEDINGS RULES 1991

### Introduction

The Family Proceedings (Amendment No 2) Rules 1999, SI 1999/3491 came into force on 5 June 2000, amending the FPR 1991.

These amended rules have many features which will be familiar to those who have gained experience since 1996 of the Ancillary Relief 'Pilot Scheme' and since 1999 of the Civil Procedure Rules 1998.

The purpose of this section is not to give a comprehensive lesson in the conduct of Ancillary Relief litigation, but rather to provide practitioners with an easy means of ensuring that they are fully aware of, and complying with, all the requirements of the rules.

*Practice Directions* issued by the President during 2000 have added to the procedural requirements specified in the rules. They are set out in full in **Part 4 – Practice Directions** and are as follows:

- ***Practice Direction (family proceedings: ancillary relief)* [2000] 1 FLR 997**
  Set out at para **[4.28]** below. Annexed to the *Practice Direction* is the ancillary relief pre-action protocol.
- ***Practice Direction (Costs: Civil Procedure Rules 1998)* [2000] 2 FCR 767, [2000] 2 FLR 428**
  Set out at para **[4.29]** below. By this latest edition to the *Practice Directions* about costs (that supplement Pts 43 to 48 of the CPR 1998) apply to family proceedings and to proceedings in the Family Division.
- ***Practice Direction (Human Rights Act 1998: citation of authorities)* [2000] 2 FCR 768, [2000] 2 FLR 429**
  Set out at para **[4.30]** below. This *Practice Direction* specifies the manner in which authorities under s 2 of the Human Rights Act 1998 should be produced to the court and also provides for the level of judge that should hear issues under the HRA 1998.



#### *Inter-relation of the Civil Procedure Rules 1998 and the Family Proceedings Rules 1991*

By r 2.51B[1] the objectives of the CPR 1998 are applied to the FPR 1991. That being said, the process is somewhat circular owing to the debt owed by the former to the latter, the CPR incorporating so much of the requirements, spirit and good practice of what was formerly the Ancillary Relief 'Pilot Scheme'. Indeed, little change was noticed in the management of cases in the former Pilot Scheme Courts when the CPR 1998 was introduced.

#### *Case management*

If a case is dealt with according to the requirements of rr 2.61A to 2.61E[2] that will satisfy the overriding objective in its various aspects as far as the management of the case is concerned. Having said this the apparent dichotomy between the flexibility of approach required by r 2.51B and the strict procedural requirements of rr 2.61A to 2.61E is yet to be resolved, especially in cases where the assets are of low value.

#### *Costs*

In relation to costs, the more stringent approach to costs introduced by the CPR 1998 and adopted in the new rr 2.69A to 2.69E[3] (and the associated *Practice Direction* cited above) does profoundly impact upon matrimonial finance matters. They must be read together with r 2.51B and 2.61F[4].

1 Set out at para **[3.434]** below.
2 Set out at paras **[3.442]** to **[3.446]** below.
3 Set out at paras **[3.455]** to **[3.459]** below.
4 Set out at paras **[3.434]** and **[3.447]** below.

## [3.408]–[3.432]
## The decision-making framework

The Rules provide that all procedural decisions in the course of Ancillary Relief litigation made by the court must be made with reference to the 'overriding objective'[1]. The 'overriding objective' is '*enabling the court to deal with cases justly*'.

Rule 2.51B(2) goes on to define some of the elements of the above phrase. Dealing with a case *justly* includes, so far as it is practicable:

- ensuring that the parties are on an equal footing;
- saving expense;
- dealing with cases in ways which are proportionate–
  - to the amount of money involved;
  - to the importance of the case;
  - to the complexity of the issues;
  - to the financial position of each party.
- ensuring that it is dealt with expeditiously and fairly;
- allotting to it an appropriate share of the court's resources, while taking into account the need to allot resources to other cases.

Furthermore, r 2.51B(5) and (6) requires the court to 'actively manage' the case by doing the following to further the overriding objective:

- encouraging the parties to co-operate with each other in the conduct of the proceedings;
- encouraging the parties to settle their disputes through mediation, where appropriate;
- identifying the issues at an early date;
- regulating the extent of disclosure of documents and expert evidence so that they are proportionate to the issues in question;
- helping the parties to settle the whole or part of the case;
- fixing timetables or otherwise controlling the progress of the case;
- making use of technology;
- giving directions to ensure that the trial of a case proceeds quickly and efficiently.

It is not possible to give a great deal of informed advice on the implications of each part of this structure. Suffice to say that the above provides the best of frameworks for oral and written submissions. Even if no application is to be made imminently, the practitioner should find some place at an early stage to consider the case within this framework, not least to ensure that unnecessary costs and attendant criticism are not incurred.

1 See r 2.51B(1) at para **[3.434]** below.

## [3.433]

*Ancillary relief*

### [2.51A Application of ancillary relief rules]

[(1) The procedures set out in rules 2.51B to 2.70 ('the ancillary relief rules') apply to any ancillary relief application and to any application under section 10(2) of the Act of 1973.

(2) In the ancillary relief rules, unless the context otherwise requires:

'applicant' means the party applying for ancillary relief;

'respondent' means the respondent to the application for ancillary relief;

'FDR appointment' means a Financial Dispute Resolution appointment in accordance with rule 2.61E.]

**Amendment**

Inserted by SI 1999/3491. Date in force: 5 June 2000 (in relation to proceedings commenced by Form A or B on or after that date and, where the court considers it just and so directs, proceedings commenced before that date).

[3.434]

### [2.51B The overriding objective]

[(1) The ancillary relief rules are a procedural code with the overriding objective of enabling the court to deal with cases justly.

(2) Dealing with a case justly includes, so far as is practicable—

(a) ensuring that the parties are on an equal footing;

(b) saving expense;

(c) dealing with the case in ways which are proportionate—

(i) to the amount of money involved;

(ii) to the importance of the case;

(iii) to the complexity of the issues; and

(iv) to the financial position of each party;

(d) ensuring that it is dealt with expeditiously and fairly; and

(e) allotting to it an appropriate share of the court's resources, while taking into account the need to allot resources to other cases.

(3) The court must seek to give effect to the overriding objective when it—

(a) exercises any power given to it by the ancillary relief rules; or

(b) interprets any rule.

(4) The parties are required to help the court to further the overriding objective.

(5) The court must further the overriding objective by actively managing cases.

(6) Active case management includes—

(a) encouraging the parties to co-operate with each other in the conduct of the proceedings;

(b) encouraging the parties to settle their disputes through mediation, where appropriate;

(c) identifying the issues at an early date;

(d) regulating the extent of disclosure of documents and expert evidence so that they are proportionate to the issues in question;

(e) helping the parties to settle the whole or part of the case;

(f) fixing timetables or otherwise controlling the progress of the case;

(g) making use of technology; and

(h) giving directions to ensure that the trial of a case proceeds quickly and efficiently.]

**Amendment**

Inserted by SI 1999/3491. Date in force: 5 June 2000 (in relation to proceedings commenced by Form A or B on or after that date and, where the court considers it just and so directs, proceedings commenced before that date).

[3.435]

### [2.52 Right to be heard on ancillary questions]

A respondent may be heard on any question of ancillary relief without filing an answer and whether or not he has returned to the court office an acknowledgment of service stating his wish to be heard on that question.

**Amendment**

Provision heading: substituted by SI 1999/3491, rr 2, 3. Date in force: 5 June 2000 (in relation to proceedings commenced by Form A or B on or after that date and, where the court considers it just and so directs, proceedings commenced before that date): see SI 1999/3491, r 1.

[3.435.1]

**Keypoint**

- Need for application

### [3.435.2]
### Need for application

This rule does not remove the requirement that a respondent must apply for an ancillary relief order if he seeks such relief[1]; this is of particular importance in the light of s 28(3) of the MCA 1973 whereby an application for ancillary relief cannot be made after remarriage.

1 See *Robin v Robin* (1983) 4 FLR 632, CA.

### [3.436]

### [2.53 Application by petitioner or respondent for ancillary relief]

(1) Any application by a petitioner, or by a respondent who files an answer claiming relief, for—

- (a) an order for maintenance pending suit,
- (b) a financial provision order,
- (c) a property adjustment order,
- [(d) a pension sharing order,]

shall be made in the petition or answer, as the case may be.

(2) Notwithstanding anything in paragraph (1), an application for ancillary relief which should have been made in the petition or answer may be made subsequently—

- (a) by leave of the court, either by notice in [Form A] or at the trial, or
- (b) where the parties are agreed upon the terms of the proposed order, without leave by notice in [Form A].

(3) An application by a petitioner or respondent for ancillary relief, not being an application which is required to be made in the petition or answer, shall be made by notice in [Form A].

**Amendment**
SI 1999/3491; SI 2000/2267.

### [3.436.1]
### Keypoints

- Application for ancillary relief
- Effect of remarriage
- Indication of intention insufficient
- Leave to apply
- Limitation Period
- Applications against oneself
- Applications under s 37(2)(b) and (c) of the MCA 1973

### [3.436.2]
### Application for ancillary relief

A party must make an application if he seeks an ancillary relief order in his favour[1]. This is important due to the provisions of s 28(3) of the MCA 1973[2] which prevents an application being presented after remarriage. An application made within the petition is sufficient to prevent the bar in s 28(3) of the MCA 1973 applying[3].

1 See *Robin v Robin* (1983) 4 FLR 632, CA.
2 Set out at para **[2.126]** above.
3 See *Jackson v Jackson* [1973] Fam 99, [1973] 2 All ER 395.

### [3.436.3]
### Effect of remarriage

An application seeking maintenance made prior to remarriage does not permit an application to be made for a lump sum after remarriage[1]. Similarly an application for child periodical payments made before remarriage does not permit a subsequent lump sum application to be made[2]. However, it has been held that an application for a property transfer order does not prevent a party from amending the application after remarriage to include an application for a lump sum[3].

1 See *Wilson v Wilson* [1976] Fam 142, [1975] 3 All ER 464, CA.
2 See *Nixon v Fox* [1978] Fam 173, [1978] 3 All ER 995.
3 See *Doherty v Doherty* [1976] Fam 71, [1975] 2 All ER 635, CA.

## [3.436.4]
### Indication of intention insufficient

An indication, given prior to remarriage, in the acknowledgement of service of the petition, of a party's intention to make an application for ancillary relief is insufficient[1].

1 See *Hargood v Jenkins* [1978] Fam 148, sub nom *Jenkins v Hargood* [1978] 3 All ER 1001.

## [3.436.5]
### Leave to apply

Where an applicant requires leave of the court to apply for ancillary relief, the test to be applied is: 'Does the applicant have or appear to have reasonable prospects of obtaining the relief claimed?'[1]. Regard will be had to 'the way in which the parties have conducted themselves and their affairs up to the time of the application'[2].

1 See *Chaterjee v Chaterjee* [1976] Fam 199, [1976] 1 All ER 719, CA.
2 See *Chaterjee v Chaterjee* [1976] Fam 199 at 208 per Ormrod LJ.



## [3.436.6]
### Limitation Period

Ancillary relief proceedings are not subject to a limitation period[1]. Delay will not prevent a party from applying for an order. However, it may be taken into account when considering the merits of the application[2].

1 See *Twiname v Twiname* [1992] 1 FCR 185, [1992] 1 FLR 29, CA.
2 See *D v W (Application for Financial Provision: Effect of Delay)* [1984] 14 Fam Law 152; and *Chaterjee v Chaterjee* [1976] Fam 199, [1976] 1 All ER 719, CA.

## [3.436.7]
### Applications against oneself

A party may apply for an order for ancillary relief against himself[1].

1 See *Simister v Simister* [1987] 1 All ER 233, [1987] 1 FLR 189. See also *Sherdley v Sherdley* [1997] 1 FCR 242, [1987] 2 FLR 242; *Peacock v Peacock* [1984] 1 All ER 1069, [1984] FLR 263; and *Dart v Dart* [1997] 1 FCR 21, [1996] 2 FLR 286, CA.

## [3.436.8]
### Applications under s 37(2)(b) and (c) of the MCA 1973

Rule 1.2 specifies that applications under s 37(2)(b) and (c) of the MCA 1973[1] are applications for ancillary relief. Accordingly, applications should be made by notice in Form A.

1 Set out at para **[2.136]** above.

## [3.437]

### [2.54 Application by parent, guardian etc for ancillary relief in respect of children]

(1) Any of the following persons, namely—

(a) a parent or guardian of any child of the family,

(b) any person in whose favour a residence order has been made with respect to a child of the family, and any applicant for such an order,

(c) any other person who is entitled to apply for a residence order with respect to a child,

(d) a local authority, where an order has been made under section 30(1)(a) of the Act of 1989 placing a child in its care,

(e) the Official Solicitor, if appointed the guardian ad litem of a child of the family under rule 9.5, and

(f) a child of the family who has been given leave to intervene in the cause for the purpose of applying for ancillary relief,

may apply for an order for ancillary relief as respects that child by notice in [Form A].

(2) In this rule 'residence' order has the meaning assigned to it by section 8(1) of the Act of 1989.

**Amendment**
SI 1999/3491.

## [3.437.1]
### Keypoints

- FPR 1991, rr 2.55 and 2.56
- Children
- Children over 18 years of age

## [3.437.2]
### FPR 1991, rr 2.55 and 2.56

Former rr 2.55 and 2.56 have been omitted: there are now no provisions so numbered.

## [3.437.3]
### Children

Children should generally not be included as parties to the proceedings. Where an order is sought in relation to a child, the custodial parent will, in most cases, pursue the application on the child's behalf. Where a child is to be a party to the proceedings, he should be represented by a guardian ad litem or a next friend[1].

1 See FPR 1991, r 9.5.

## [3.437.4]
### Children over 18 years of age

Where the child is over 18 years of age he may apply for leave to intervene in the proceedings. The court has jurisdiction to hear this application[1]. For a case where a father unsuccessfully sought to argue that maintenance for his daughter should end when she became a grant-aided student see *B v B (Financial Provision for child)*[2].

1 See *Downing v Downing* [1976] Fam 288, [1976] 3 All ER 474.
2 [1998] 1 FCR 49, [1998] 1 FLR 373, CA.

[3.438]

### [2.57 Children to be separately represented on certain applications]

(1) Where an application is made to the High Court or a divorce county court for an order for a variation of settlement, the court shall, unless it is satisfied that the proposed variation does not adversely affect the rights or interests of any children concerned, direct that the children be separately represented on the application, either by a solicitor or by a solicitor and counsel, and may appoint the Official Solicitor or other fit person to be guardian ad litem of the children for the purpose of the application.

(2) On any other application for ancillary relief the court may give such a direction or make such appointment as it is empowered to give or make by paragraph (1).

(3) Before a person other than the Official Solicitor is appointed guardian ad litem under this rule there shall be filed a certificate by the solicitor acting for the children that the person proposed as guardian has no interest in the matter adverse to that of the children and that he is a proper person to be such guardian.

**Amendment**
SI 1999/3491.



[3.438.1]
**Keypoints**
- FPR 1991, rr 2.58 and 2.59(1)
- Effect of rule

[3.438.2]
**FPR 1991, rr 2.58 and 2.59(1)**

Former rr 2.58 and 2.59(1) have been omitted: there are now no provisions so numbered.

[3.438.3]
**Effect of rule**

Under this rule, the court has a duty to order that a child becomes a party to the proceedings where his financial interests are directly affected.

[3.439]

### [2.59 Evidence on application for property adjustment or avoidance of disposition order]

(1) …

(2) Where an application for a property adjustment order or an avoidance of disposition order relates to land, the notice in [Form A] shall identify the land and—

(a) state whether the title to the land is registered or unregistered and, if registered, the Land Registry title number; and

(b) give particulars, so far as known to the applicant, of any mortgage of the land or any interest therein.

(3) [Copies of Form A and of Form E completed by the applicant], shall be served on the following persons as well as on the respondent to the application, that is to say—

(a) in the case of an application for an order for a variation of settlement … , the trustees of the settlement and the settlor if living;

(b) in the case of an application for an avoidance of disposition order, the person in whose favour the disposition is alleged to have been made;

and such other persons, if any, as the district judge may direct.

(4) In the case of an application to which paragraph [(2)] refers, a copy of [Form A], shall be served on any mortgagee of whom particulars are given pursuant to that

paragraph; any person so served may apply to the court in writing, within 14 days after service, for a copy of the applicant's [Form E].

(5) Any person who—

(a) is served with [copies of Forms A and E] pursuant to paragraph (3), or

(b) receives [a copy of Form E] following an application made in accordance with paragraph (4),

may, within 14 days after service or receipt, as the case may be, [file a statement] in answer.

[(6) A statement filed under paragraph (5) shall be sworn to be true.]

**Amendment**

SI 1992/456; SI 1999/3491.

## [3.439.1]
### Keypoints

- Full disclosure
- Third party interests

## [3.439.2]
### Full disclosure

Full particulars must be given of any property or trusts involved in the application.

## [3.439.3]
### Third party interests

Details of third party interests in any property must be given. Service on a third party will not necessarily result in that party being joined[1]. Trustees may be joined where there is a discretionary trust and where the control of the trust is in issue[2]. This will not always be the case, however[3]. Upon intervention by the third party, the court may determine that party's rights[4].

1 See *T v T (Financial Provision)* [1990] FCR 169, sub nom *Re T* [1990] 1 FLR 1.
2 See *T v T (Joinder of Third Parties)* [1997] 1 FCR 98, [1996] 2 FLR 357.
3 See *Browne v Browne* [1989] 1 FLR 291, CA.
4 See *Tebbutt v Haynes* [1981] 2 All ER 238; and *Harwood v Harwood* [1992] 1 FCR 1, [1991] 2 FLR 274, CA.

## [3.440]

### [2.60 Service of statement in answer]

[(1) Where a form or other document filed with the court contains an allegation of adultery or of an improper association with a named person ('the named person'), the court may direct that the party who filed the relevant form or document serve a copy of all or part of that form or document on the named person, together with Form F.

(2) If the court makes a direction under paragraph (1), the named person may file a statement in answer to the allegations.

(3) A statement under paragraph (2) shall be sworn to be true.

(4) Rule 2.37(3) shall apply to a person served under paragraph (1) as it applies to a co-respondent.]

**Amendment**

Substituted by SI 1999/3491.

## [3.440.1]
### Keypoints

- Effect of rule
- Liability for costs

## [3.440.2]
### Effect of rule

Where a third party is served with a form or document he may file an answer if the court so directs.

## [3.440.3]
### Liability for costs

Under r 2.37(3) a third party may be made liable for costs if he is either a party to the proceedings or has notice of the intention to apply for an order relating to costs.

## [3.441]

### [2.61 Information on application for consent order for financial relief]

(1) Subject to paragraphs (2) and (3), there shall be lodged with every application for a consent order under any of sections 23, 24 or 24A of the Act of 1973 two copies of a draft of the order in the terms sought, one of which shall be indorsed with a statement signed by the respondent to the application signifying his agreement, and a statement of information (which may be made in more than one document) which shall include—

(a) the duration of the marriage, the age of each party and of any minor or dependent child of the family;

(b) an estimate in summary form of the approximate amount or value of the capital resources and net income of each party and of any minor child of the family;

(c) what arrangements are intended for the accommodation of each of the parties and any minor child of the family;

(d) whether either party has remarried or has any present intention to marry or to cohabit with another person;

[(dd) where the order [includes provision to be made under section 24B,] 25B or 25C of the Act of 1973, a statement confirming that [the person responsible for the pension arrangement in question has been served with the documents required by rule 2.70(11)] and that no objection to such an order has been made by [that person] within 14 days from such service;]

(e) where the terms of the order provide for a transfer of property, a statement confirming that any mortgagee of that property has been served with notice of the application and that no objection to such a transfer has been made by the mortgagee within 14 days from such service; and

(f) any other especially significant matters.

(2) Where an application is made for a consent order varying an order for periodical payments paragraph (1) shall be sufficiently complied with if the statement of information required to be lodged with the application includes only the information in respect of net income mentioned in paragraph (1)(b) [(and, where appropriate, a statement under paragraph (1)(dd))], and an application for a consent order for interim periodical payments pending the determination of an application for ancillary relief may be made in like manner.

(3) Where all or any of the parties attend the hearing of an application for financial relief the court may dispense with the lodging of a statement of information in accordance with paragraph (1) and give directions for the information which would otherwise be required to be given in such a statement to be given in such a manner as it sees fit.

**Amendment**

SI 1996/1674; SI 1999/3491; SI 2000/2267.

## [3.441.1]
### Keypoints

- Time
- Investigation by the district judge

## [2.441.2]
### Time

According to ss 23 and 24 of the MCA 1973, an order may only be made on the granting of the decree nisi or anytime after that. An order made prior to that date is a nullity[1]. However, an order made before that date will be treated as valid until it is set aside, provided that it was made by a court of appropriate jurisdiction. An invalid order will not become valid by subsequently changing its date[2]. However, a draft consent order may be approved by the district judge prior to the granting of the decree nisi, provided that the judge directs that the order should take effect from a date subsequent to the decree nisi[3]. In addition, where a clerical error results in the order being dated before the making of the decree nisi, the order may be amended[4].

1 See *Munks v Munks* [1985] FLR 576, [1985] Fam Law 131, CA.
2 See *Munks v Munks* [1985] FLR 576, [1985] Fam Law 131, CA. See also *Keystone Knitting Mills' Trade Mark* [1929] 1 Ch 92, CA and *Board v Checkland* [1987] 2 FLR 257.
3 See *Pounds v Pounds* [1994] 4 All ER 777, [1994] 1 WLR 1535, CA.
4 See n 3 above.

## [3.441.3]
### Investigation by the district judge

The district judge should carry out a 'broad appraisal of the parties' financial circumstances … without the descent into the valley of detail'[1].

1 See *Pounds v Pounds* [1994] 4 All ER 777, [1994] 1 WLR 1535, CA per Waite LJ.

## [3.442]

### [2.61A Application for ancillary relief]

[(1) A notice of intention to proceed with an application for ancillary relief made in the petition or answer or an application for ancillary relief must be made by notice in Form A.

(2) The notice must be filed:
- (a) if the case is pending in a divorce county court, in that court; or
- (b) if the case is pending in the High Court, in the registry in which it is proceeding.

(3) Where the applicant requests an order for ancillary relief that includes provision to be made by virtue of section [24B,] 25B or 25C of the Act of 1973 the terms of the order requested must be specified in the notice in Form A.

(4) Upon the filing of Form A the court must:
- (a) fix a first appointment not less than 12 weeks and not more than 16 weeks after the date of the filing of the notice and give notice of that date;
- (b) serve a copy on the respondent within 4 days of the date of the filing of the notice.

(5) The date fixed under paragraph (4) for the first appointment, or for any subsequent appointment, must not be cancelled except with the court's permission and, if cancelled, the court must immediately fix a new date.]

**Amendment**
Inserted by SI 1999/3491. Para (3): SI 2000/2267.

## [3.442.1]
### Keypoint

- Overview

## [3.442.2]
## Overview

The following is a 'checklist' of the steps the practitioner must follow at each stage of the proceedings:

| | |
|---|---|
| **Rule** | 2.61A(1) |
| **Step** | **Application** |
| **Timing** | Any time after a petition is issued |
| **Procedure** | In Form A or B (serve also in accordance with r 2.59(3) and (4) and r 2.70) |
| **Comment** | See r 2.61A for choice of court. Note the standard Form A does not provide for pension provision (and therefore such claims must be added). The application must contain full details of all relief sought: *Sandford v Sandford* [1985] FLR 1056 |

| | |
|---|---|
| **Rule** | 2.61A(4)(a) |
| **Step** | **Listing date of First Appointment** |
| **Timing** | Listed by the court 12 to 14 weeks after first application |
| **Procedure** | Will be notified by Form C |
| **Comment** | Should be done within four days of Application. Can only be cancelled with permission of the court and refixed immediately: r 2.61A(3) |

| | |
|---|---|
| **Rule** | 2.61B(1) and (2) |
| **Step** | **Form E** |
| **Timing** | No later than 35 days before First Appointment |
| **Procedure** | Form E with required documents attached, see r 2.61B(3) (serve also in accordance with r 2.59(3)) |
| **Comment** | See r 2.61B(1) – exchange and filing should be simultaneous. NB *Livesey (formerly Jenkins) v Jenkins* [1985] AC 424, [1985] FLR 813 – full disclosure must be made of the property and income of the party (see also *Evans v Evans* [1990] FCR 498, [1990] 1 FLR 319) |

| | |
|---|---|
| **Rule** | 2.61B(7) |
| **Step** | **Concise statement of issues, chronology** |
| **Timing** | No later than 14 days before First Appointment |
| **Procedure** | May be in form of a 'Case Outline' / Scott Schedule |

| | |
|---|---|
| **Rule** | 2.61B(7) |
| **Step** | **Requests for documents / Questionnaire** |
| **Timing** | No later than 14 days before First Appointment |
| **Procedure** | Now must be done with reference to the statement of issues No prescribed form |
| **Comment** | Note the seven areas of disclosure now required with Form E |

| | |
|---|---|
| **Rule** | 2.61B(7) |
| **Step** | **Alternatively a statement that no further information is required** |
| **Timing** | No later than 14 days before First Appointment |
| **Procedure** | No prescribed form |

| | |
|---|---|
| **Rule** | 2.61B(7) |
| **Step** | **Statement of whether First Appointment can be used as FDR** |
| **Timing** | No later than 14 days before First Appointment |
| **Procedure** | Form G |
| **Comment** | The statement may be subject to caveats |

| | |
|---|---|
| **Rule** | 2.61B(7) |
| **Step** | **Statement of costs under CPR 1998, Pt 44** |
| **Timing** | 24 hours before First Appointment |
| **Procedure** | CPR 1998, Appendix 3 |
| **Comment** | If an application for costs and summary assessment is to be made |

| | |
|---|---|
| **Rule** | 2.61F(1) |
| **Step** | **Statement of costs** |
| **Timing** | At First Appointment |
| **Procedure** | Form H |
| **Comment** | The statement should include all costs since issue |

| | |
|---|---|
| **Rule** | 2.61E |
| **Step** | **Notice of FDR** |
| **Timing** | Served by court. No time prescribed |
| **Procedure** | Form D |

| | |
|---|---|
| **Rule** | 2.61E / 2.69 |
| **Step** | **Filing of offers** |
| **Timing** | No later than 14 days before the FDR |
| **Procedure** | No prescribed form |
| **Comment** | Must include all without prejudice 'offers and proposals' |

| | |
|---|---|
| **Rule** | 2.61E / 2.69 |
| **Step** | **Statement of costs under CPR 1998, Pt 44** |
| **Timing** | 24 hours before FDR |
| **Procedure** | CPR 1998, Appendix 3 |
| **Comment** | If an application for costs and summary assessment is to be made |

| | |
|---|---|
| **Rule** | 2.61F |
| **Step** | **Statement of costs** |
| **Timing** | At FDR |
| **Procedure** | Form H |
| **Comment** | The statement should include all costs since issue |

| | |
|---|---|
| **Rule** | 2.69E(1) |
| **Step** | **Applicant's statement of open proposals** |
| **Timing** | 14 days before final hearing |

| | |
|---|---|
| **Rule** | 2.69E(2) |
| **Step** | **Respondent's statement of open proposals** |
| **Timing** | Seven days before final hearing |

| | |
|---|---|
| **Rule** | 2.61F |
| **Step** | **Statement of costs under CPR 1998, Pt 44** |
| **Timing** | 24 hours before final hearing |
| **Procedure** | CPR 1998, Appendix 3 |
| **Comment** | If application for summary assessment |

| | |
|---|---|
| **Rule** | 2.61F |
| **Step** | **Statement of costs** |
| **Timing** | At final hearing |
| **Procedure** | Include all costs since issue |

**[3.443]**

### [2.61B Procedure before the first appointment]

[(1) Both parties must, at the same time, exchange with each other, and each file with the court, a statement in Form E, which—

(a) is signed by the party who made the statement;

(b) is sworn to be true, and

(c) contains the information and has attached to it the documents required by that Form.

(2) Form E must be exchanged and filed not less than 35 days before the date of the first appointment.

(3) Form E must have attached to it:

(a) any documents required by Form E; …

(b) any other documents necessary to explain or clarify any of the information contained in Form E[; and

(c) any documents furnished to the party producing the form by a person responsible for a pension arrangement, either following a request under rule 2.70(2) or as part of a 'relevant valuation' as defined in rule 2.70(4)].

(4) Form E must have no documents attached to it other than the documents referred to in paragraph (3).

(5) Where a party was unavoidably prevented from sending any document required by Form E, that party must at the earliest opportunity:

(a) serve copies of that document on the other party; and

(b) file a copy of that document with the court, together with a statement explaining the failure to send it with Form E.

(6) No disclosure or inspection of documents may be requested or given between the filing of the application for ancillary relief and the first appointment, except—

(a) copies sent with Form E, or in accordance with paragraph (5); or

(b) in accordance with paragraph (7).

(7) At least 14 days before the hearing of the first appointment, each party must file with the court and serve on the other party—

(a) a concise statement of the issues between the parties;

(b) a chronology;

(c) a questionnaire setting out by reference to the concise statement of issues any further information and documents requested from the other party or a statement that no information and documents are required;

(d) a notice in Form G stating whether that party will be in a position at the first appointment to proceed on that occasion to a FDR appointment.

(8) …

(9) At least 14 days before the hearing of the first appointment, the applicant must file with the court and serve on the respondent, confirmation of the names of all persons served in accordance with rule 2.59(3) and (4), and that there are no other persons who must be served in accordance with those paragraphs.]

**Amendment**

Inserted by SI 1999/3491, rr 2, 3, 11. Paras (3), (8): SI 2000/2267.

## [3.443.1]
**Keypoint**

- Overview
- Disclosure of Documents

## [3.443.2]
**Overview**

See Table set out at para **[3.442.2]** above.

## [3.443.3]
**Disclosure of Documents**

Disclosure of the following documents should be provided with the Form E:

- a valuation of the former matrimonial home if one has been obtained in the last six months;
- a valuation of any other properties, land and buildings;
- account statements for the last 12 months;
- any surrender value quotations;
- the last two years' accounts of any relevant business or partnership and other relevant documentation;
- evidence of income (pay slips/P60 etc);
- valuations of pension rights.

There can then be no further disclosure of documentary evidence until is ordered at the First Appointment[1], although this does not prohibit voluntary disclosure.

The parties may then make their requests for other documentation at the First Appointment (see above).

After the Form E and First Appointment there are only two further routes to obtaining further disclosure of documents:

- r 2.61B(5) provides that: 'Where a party was unavoidably prevented from sending any document required by Form E, that party must at the earliest opportunity–
  (a) serve copies of that document on the other party; and
  (b) file a copy of that document with the court together with a statement explaining the failure to send it with the Form E';
- r 2.61D(3) provides that after the first appointment (and the disclosure there ordered): 'a party is not entitled to production of any further documents except … with the permission of the court'.

It naturally follows that practitioners must not expect the serial requests for documentation that some have become used to in the past and must be clear from an early stage exactly what disclosure is required.

1 See r 2.61B(6) above.

## [3.444]

**[2.61C Expert evidence]**

[CPR rules 35.1 to 35.14 relating to expert evidence (with appropriate modifications), except CPR rules 35.5(2) and 35.8(4)(b) apply to all ancillary relief proceedings.]

**Amendment**

Inserted by SI 1999/3491.

[3.444.1]
**Keypoint**
- Experts

[3.444.2]
**Experts**

The amended Rules adopt the provisions of the CPR 1998, Pt 35.1 to 35.14, **except** Pt 35.5(2) and 35.8(4)(b) with regard to expert evidence. There is not yet, of course, a body of authorities applying the provisions precisely to ancillary relief matters, thus the best guidance on this area is, for now, to be found in works dealing with civil procedure. *Practice Direction (Ancillary relief procedure)*[1] provides some amplification.

1 Set out at para **[4.28]** below.

[3.445]

**[2.61D The first appointment]**

[(1) The first appointment must be conducted with the objective of defining the issues and saving costs.

(2) At the first appointment the district judge—

(a) must determine—

(i) the extent to which any questions seeking information under rule 2.61B must be answered; and

(ii) what documents requested under rule 2.61B must be produced,

and give directions for the production of such further documents as may be necessary;

(b) must give directions about—

(i) the valuation of assets (including, where appropriate, the joint instruction of joint experts);

(ii) obtaining and exchanging expert evidence, if required; and

(iii) evidence to be adduced by each party and, where appropriate, about further chronologies or schedules to be filed by each party;

(c) must, unless he decides that a referral is not appropriate in the circumstances, direct that the case be referred to a FDR appointment;

(d) must, where he decides that a referral to a FDR appointment is not appropriate, direct one of the following:

(i) that a further directions appointment be fixed;

(ii) that an appointment be fixed for the making of an interim order;

(iii) that the case be fixed for final hearing and, where that direction is given, the district judge must determine the judicial level at which the case should be heard; or

(iv) that the case be adjourned for out-of-court mediation or private negotiation or, in exceptional circumstances, generally;

(e) must consider whether, having regard to all the circumstances (including the extent to which each party has complied with this Part, and in particular the requirement to send documents with Form E), to make an order about the costs of the hearing; and

(f) may—

(i) make an interim order where an application for it has been made in accordance with rule 2.69F returnable at the first appointment;

(ii) having regard to the contents of Form G filed by the parties, treat the appointment (or part of it) as a FDR appointment to which rule 2.61E applies;

(iii) in a case where an order for ancillary relief is requested that includes provision to be made under section 25B or 25C of the Act of 1973, require any party to request a valuation under regulation 4 of the Divorce etc (Pensions) Regulations 1996 from the trustees or managers of any pension scheme under which the party has, or is likely to have, any benefits.

(3) After the first appointment, a party is not entitled to production of any further documents except in accordance with directions given under paragraph (2)(a) above or with the permission of the court.

(4) At any stage:

(a) a party may apply for further directions or a FDR appointment;

(b) the court may give further directions or direct that the parties attend a FDR appointment.

(5) Both parties must personally attend the first appointment unless the court orders otherwise.]

**Amendment**

Inserted by SI 1999/3491.

## [3.446]

### [2.61E The FDR appointment]

[(1) The FDR appointment must be treated as a meeting held for the purposes of discussion and negotiation and paragraphs (2) to (9) apply.

(2) The district judge or judge hearing the FDR appointment must have no further involvement with the application, other than to conduct any further FDR appointment or to make a consent order or a further directions order.

(3) Not later than 7 days before the FDR appointment, the applicant must file with the court details of all offers and proposals, and responses to them.

(4) Paragraph (3) includes any offers, proposals or responses made wholly or partly without prejudice, but paragraph (3) does not make any material admissible as evidence if, but for that paragraph, it would not be admissible.

(5) At the conclusion of the FDR appointment, any documents filed under paragraph (3), and any filed documents referring to them, must, at the request of the party who filed them, be returned to him and not retained on the court file.

(6) Parties attending the FDR appointment must use their best endeavours to reach agreement on the matters in issue between them.

(7) The FDR appointment may be adjourned from time to time.

(8) At the conclusion of the FDR appointment, the court may make an appropriate consent order, but otherwise must give directions for the future course of the proceedings, including, where appropriate, the filing of evidence and fixing a final hearing date.

(9) Both parties must personally attend the FDR appointment unless the court orders otherwise.]

**Amendment**

Inserted by SI 1999/3491.

## [3.446.1]
### Keypoints

- Overview
- The First and the Financial Dispute Resolution Appointments

## [3.446.2]
### Overview

See Table set out at para **[3.442.2]** above.

## [3.446.3]
## The First and the Financial Dispute Resolution Appointments

*The First Appointment*

The state purpose of the First Appointment is 'the defining of issues and saving costs'. Therefore it must be remembered that the requirements of the 'overriding objective' and 'active case management' apply throughout Ancillary Relief proceedings and many First Appointments will be treated in all, or in part, as FDR's. The court only has to 'have regard to the contents of Form G filed by the parties' in deciding whether to use the appointment as an FDR and so may of its own volition do so.

Accordingly, whoever has conduct of the First Appointment must be fully informed for the purposes of the hearing.

The practitioner with conduct of a hearing being used as a First Appointment will have to consider what directions/orders they intend to obtain in relation to the following[1]:

- the extent to which Questionnaires should be answered;
- what requested documents must be produced;
- the valuation of assets (including, where appropriate, the joint instruction of joint experts);
- the obtaining and exchanging of expert evidence;
- evidence to be adduced by each party;
- further chronologies or schedules to be filed;
- a valuation under reg 4 of the Divorce etc (Pensions) Regulations 1996 (SI 1996/1676) if there is an appropriate application;
- an interim order where there is an appropriate application returnable at the appointment;
- costs.

The practitioner with conduct of the hearing will have to consider which of the following 'next steps' they hope to be the outcome of the First Appointment[2]:

- an FDR appointment;
- a further directions appointment;
- an appointment for the making of an interim order;
- an appointment for a final hearing;
- an adjournment for out-of-court mediation;
- an adjournment for private negotiation;
- an adjournment generally (in exceptional circumstances).

*The Financial Dispute Resolution Appointment*

The FDR is stated to be for the purposes of discussion and negotiation[3], and the parties must use their best endeavours to reach agreement on the matters in issue[4]. The President of the Family Division has expanded on this in *Practice Direction (Ancillary relief procedure)*[5]. The *Practice Direction* says:

> 'In order for the FDR appointment to be effective, parties must approach the occasion openly and without reserve ... Courts therefore expect parties to make offers and proposals; recipients of offers and proposals to given them proper consideration; that parties whether separately or together, will not seek to exclude from consideration at the appointment any such offer or proposal.'

It is therefore incumbent on every practitioner to have done everything necessary to present their client's case simply, fully and in the best possible light.

It is the intention of the Rules that the FDR can be adjourned from time-to-time to allow the parties to negotiate further in the light of the judge's assistance. In practice, the demands on the court's time often do not facilitate this and it cannot be relied upon. Thus it is even more incumbent upon the practitioner to use what time is available usefully.

It is the normal rule that because of the judge's involvement with without prejudice discussions the judge with conduct of the FDR should have no further involvement with the case save to make a consent order at a later directions appointment or conduct an FDR[6]. The without prejudice nature of the hearing is affirmed and expanded upon in *Re D (Minors) (Conciliation: Privilege)*[7].

All documents filed for the purposes of the FDR outlining offers and proposals must be retrieved from the court file at the conclusion of the FDR in order not to disqualify a future tribunal[8]. It is the advocates' responsibility to request this. In addition, it is prudent to mark all such documents very clearly:

> 'For the purposes of the Financial Dispute Resolution Appointment / First Appointment only'.

A feature of the 'Pilot Scheme' that has continued into the new Rules is that there is still no provision that discussion and judicial indications at an FDR can be referred to on the issue of costs after a final hearing. It might be thought that such an approach would encourage parties to approach the FDR in the manner which the Rules envisage.

Further, FDR's can be listed on the application of a party or the direction of the court[9].

1 See r 2.61D(2)(a), (b), (e) and (f).
2 See r 2.61D(2)(d).
3 See r 2.61E(1).
4 See r 2.61E(6).
5 25 May 2000, see para **[4.28]** below.
6 See r 2.61E(2).
7 [1993] Fam 231, 1993] 1 FLR 932, CA.
8 See r 2.61E.
9 See r 2.61D(4).

## [3.447]

### [2.61F Costs]

[(1) At every court hearing or appointment each party must produce to the court an estimate in Form H of the costs incurred by him up to the date of that hearing or appointment.

(2) The parties' obligation under paragraph (1) is without prejudice to their obligations under paragraphs 4.1 to 4.11 of the Practice Direction relating to CPR Part 44.]

**Amendment**

Inserted by SI 1999/3491.

## [3.447.1]

**Keypoint**

- Forms

## [3.447.2]

**Forms**

This rule could be read so as to require the filing of both Form H under the FPR 1991 and Form I under the CPR 1998. The latter is in a specified form and, provided all matters required by it are covered in the completion of Form H or are available in addition, that should suffice.

## [3.448]

### [2.62 Investigation by district judge of application for ancillary relief]

(1) ...

(2) An application for an avoidance of disposition order shall, if practicable, be heard at the same time as any related application for financial relief.

(3) ...

(4) At the hearing of an application for ancillary relief the district judge shall, subject to rules 2.64, 2.65 and 10.10 investigate the allegations made in support of and in answer to the application, and may take evidence orally and may at any stage of the proceedings, whether before or during the hearing, order the attendance of any person for the purpose of being examined or cross-examined and order the [disclosure and inspection] of any document or require further [statements].

[(4A) A statement filed under paragraph (4) shall be sworn to be true.]

(5) …

(6) …

(7) Any party may apply to the court for an order that any person do attend an appointment [(an 'inspection appointment')] before the court and produce any documents to be specified or described in the order, the [inspection] of which appears to the court to be necessary for disposing fairly of the application for ancillary relief or for saving costs.

(8) No person shall be compelled by an order under paragraph (7) to produce any document at [an inspection] appointment which he could not be compelled to produce at the hearing of the application for ancillary relief.

(9) The court shall permit any person attending [an inspection] appointment pursuant to an order under paragraph (7) above to be represented at the appointment.

**Amendment**
SI 1999/3491.



## [3.448.1]
### Keypoints

- FPR 1991, rr 2.62 and 2.63
- Practice Direction 1995
- Evidence
- Guidance for time estimates
- Transfers between courts
- Inspection Appointments
- Use of a witness summons

## [3.448.2]
### FPR 1991, rr 2.62 and 2.63

Former rr 2.62(1), (3), (5) and 2.63 have been omitted: there are now no provisions so numbered.

## [3.448.3]
### Practice Direction 1995

The *Practice Direction* [1995] 2 FCR 340, [1995] 1 FLR 456, issued by the President of the Family Division shows a further move towards greater control over cases by the court:

'(1) The importance of reducing the cost and delay of civil litigation makes it necessary for the court to assert greater control over the preparation for and conduct of hearings than has hitherto been customary. Failure by practitioners to conduct cases economically will be visited by appropriate orders for costs, including wasted costs orders.

(2) The court will accordingly exercise its discretion to limit:

(a) discovery;
(b) the length of opening and closing oral submissions;
(c) the time allowed for the examination and cross-examination of witnesses;
(d) the issues on which it wishes to be addressed;
(e) reading aloud from documents and authorities.

(3) Unless otherwise ordered, every witness statement or affidavit shall stand as the evidence-in-chief of the witness concerned. The substance of the evidence which a party intends to adduce at the hearing must be sufficiently detailed, but without

prolixity; it must be confined to material matters of fact, not (except in the case of the evidence of professional witnesses) of opinion; and if hearsay evidence is to be adduced, the source of the information must be declared or good reason given for not doing so.

(4) It is a duty owed to the court both by the parties and by their legal representatives to give full and frank disclosure in ancillary relief applications and also in all matters in respect of children. The parties and their advisers must also use their best endeavours:

- (a) to confine the issues and the evidence called to what is reasonably considered to be essential for the proper presentation of their case;
- (b) to reduce or eliminate issues for expert evidence;
- (c) in advance of the hearing to agree which are the issues or the main issues.

(5) Unless the nature of the hearing makes it unnecessary and in the absence of specific directions, bundles should be agreed and prepared for use by the court, the parties and the witnesses and shall be in A4 format where possible, suitably secured. The bundles for use by the court shall be lodged with the court (the Clerk of the Rules in matters in the Royal Courts of Justice, London) at least 2 clear days before the hearing. Each bundle should be paginated, indexed, wholly legible, and arranged chronologically. Where documents are copied unnecessarily or bundled incompetently the cost will be disallowed.

(6) In cases estimated to last for 5 days or more and in which no pre-trial review has been ordered, application should be made for a pre-trial review. It should, when practicable, be listed at least 3 weeks before the hearing and be conducted by the judge or district judge before whom the case is to be heard and should be attended by the advocates who are to represent the parties at the hearing. Whenever possible, all statements of evidence and all reports should be filed before the date of the review and in good time for them to have been considered by all parties.

(7) Whenever practicable and in any matter estimated to last 5 days or more, each party should, not less than 2 clear days before the hearing, lodge with the court, or the Clerk of the Rules in matters in the Royal Courts of Justice, in London, and deliver to other parties, a chronology and a skeleton argument concisely summarising that party's submissions in relation to each of the issues, and citing the main authorities relied upon. It is important that skeleton arguments should be brief.

(8) In advance of the hearing upon request, and otherwise in the course of their opening, parties should be prepared to furnish the court, if there is no core bundle, with a list of documents essential for a proper understanding of the case.

(9) The opening speech should be succinct. At its conclusion, other parties may be invited briefly to amplify their skeleton arguments. In a heavy case the court may in conjunction with final speeches require written submissions, including the findings of fact for which each party contends.

(10) This Practice Direction which follows the directions handed down by the Lord Chief Justice and the Vice-Chancellor to apply in the Queen's Bench and Chancery Divisions, shall apply to all family proceedings in the High Court and in all care centres, family hearing centres and divorce county courts.

(11) Issued with the concurrence of the Lord Chancellor.'

## [3.448.4]
## Evidence

Despite the abolition of affidavits in favour of the Form E[1] the affidavit (sworn statement) is not entirely dead. Increasingly, sworn statement evidence is being used confined to providing evidence in relation to a particular issue, for example the respective contributions of parties[2].

1 See FPR 1991, r 2.61B(1) at para **[3.443]** above.
2 See *W v W* (1981) 2 FLR 291.

## [3.448.5]
### Guidance for time estimates

*Re MD and TD (Minors) (Time Estimates)*[1] gives guidance regarding the preparation of time estimates for cases falling under the ChA 1989. This advice may be considered applicable to cases involving ancillary relief.

1 [1994] 2 FCR 94, [1994] 2 FLR 336.

## [3.448.6]
### Transfers between courts

Assistance regarding transfers can be found in *Practice Direction (Family Division: Distribution of Business)* [1992] 3 All ER 151, [1992] 2 FLR 87.

## [3.448.7]
### Inspection Appointments

The old r 2.62(7) is considered in the case of *Frary v Frary*[1] which remains good law. If the applicant can show that it is necessary and relevant for a third party to attend a production appointment, the court will order such attendance[2]. The application should be made inter partes, unless there is a reasonable concern that notice would lead to the destruction of the document.

1 [1994] 1 FCR 595, [1993] 2 FLR 696, CA.
2 See *D v D (Production Appointment)* [1995] 3 FCR 183, [1995] 2 FLR 497.



## [3.448.8]
### Use of a witness summons

Under the Matrimonial Causes Rules 1977 the court does not have the power to order a third party to produce documents or file an affidavit. However, a witness summons or subpoena may be used to secure the attendance of that third party[1]. A subpoena may be set aside by the court[2], and if it is considered to be oppressive and wrong to order a subpoena or witness summons, the court will not order it[3].

1 See *Wynne v Wynne* [1980] 3 All ER 659, [1981] 1 WLR 69; and *W v W* (1981) 2 FLR 291.
2 See *H v H (Disclosure by third parties)* (1981) 2 FLR 303.
3 See *Morgan v Morgan* [1977] Fam 122, [1977] 2 All ER 515.

## [3.449]

**[2.64 Order on application for ancillary relief]**

(1) Subject to rule 2.65 the district judge shall, after completing his investigation under rule 2.62, make such order as he thinks just.

(2) Pending the final determination of the application, [and subject to rule 2.69F,] the district judge may make an interim order upon such terms as he thinks just.

(3) RSC Order 31, rule 1 (power to order sale of land) shall apply to applications for ancillary relief as it applies to causes and matters in the Chancery Division.

**Amendment**
SI 1999/3491.

## [3.449.1]
### Keypoints

- Drafting an order
- Enforcement of undertakings
- Enforcement of preamble
- Interim orders

## [3.449.2]
### Drafting an order

Care must be taken when drafting an order[1]. The order must precisely define how the parties intend to dispose of the petitioner's claim for ancillary relief.

1 See *Dinch v Dinch* [1987] 1 All ER 818, [1987] 1 WLR 252, HL.

## [3.449.3]
### Enforcement of undertakings

In many cases an appropriately worded undertaking may be enforced as if it were an order[1]. It must be shown that the undertaking is capable of being enforced based upon its wording. An undertaking will not be varied by the court. However, in some circumstances the party giving the undertaking may be relieved from it[2].

1 See *Symmons v Symmons* [1993] 1 FLR 317. See also *Gandolfo v Gandolfo* [1981] QB 359, [1980] 1 All ER 833, CA; *Buckley v Crawford* [1893] 1 QB 105; and *Livesey v Jenkins* [1985] AC 424, [1985] FLR 813, HL.

2 See *Cutler v Wandsworth Stadium Ltd* [1945] 1 All ER 103, CA.

## [3.449.4]
### Enforcement of preamble

Agreements contained within the preamble to an order may be enforced[1].

1 See *Horsman v Horsman* [1993] 2 FCR 357, sub nom *H v H (financial provision)* [1993] 2 FLR 35.

## [3.449.5]
### Interim orders

The court is not permitted to make an interim order for a lump sum nor an order akin to an administration order[1].

1 See *Wicks v Wicks* [1999] Fam 65, [1998] 1 FLR 470 overruling *Barry v Barry* [1992] Fam 140, [1992] 2 FLR 233; *Green v Green* [1993] 1 FLR 326; and *F v F (Ancillary Relief: Substantial Assets)* [1996] 2 FCR 397, [1995] 2 FLR 45.

## [3.450]

### [2.65 Reference of application to judge]

The district judge may at any time refer an application for ancillary relief, or any question arising thereon, to a judge for his decision.

**Amendment**
SI 1999/3491.

## [3.451]

### [2.66 Arrangements for hearing of application etc by judge]

(1) Where an application for ancillary relief or any question arising thereon has been referred or adjourned to a judge, the proper officer shall fix a date, time and place for the hearing of the application or the consideration of the question and give notice thereof to all parties.

(2) The hearing or consideration shall, unless the court otherwise directs, take place in chambers.

(3) Where the application is proceeding in a divorce county court which is not a court of trial or is pending in the High Court and proceeding in a district registry which is not in a divorce town, the hearing or consideration shall take place at such court of

trial or divorce town as in the opinion of the district judge is the nearest or most convenient.

For the purposes of this paragraph the Royal Courts of Justice shall be treated as a divorce town.

(4) In respect of any application referred to him under this rule, a judge shall have the same powers [to make directions as a district judge has under these rules].

**Amendment**

SI 1999/3491.

## [3.452]

### [2.67 Request for periodical payments order at same rate as order for maintenance pending suit]

(1) Where at or after the date of a decree nisi of divorce or nullity of marriage an order for maintenance pending suit is in force, the party in whose favour the order was made may, if he has made an application for an order for periodical payments for himself in his petition or answer, as the case may be, request the district judge in writing to make such an order (in this rule referred to as a 'corresponding order') providing for payments at the same rate as those provided for by the order for maintenance pending suit.

(2) Where such a request is made, the proper officer shall serve on the other spouse a notice in [Form I] requiring him, if he objects to the making of a corresponding order, to give notice to that effect to the court and to the applicant within 14 days after service of the notice on [Form I].

(3) If the other spouse does not give notice of objection within the time aforesaid, the district judge may make a corresponding order without further notice to that spouse and without requiring the attendance of the applicant or his solicitor, and shall in that case serve a copy of the order on the applicant as well as on the other spouse.

**Amendment**

SI 1999/3491.



## [3.453]

### [2.68 Application for order under section 37(2)(a) of Act of 1973]

(1) An application under section 37(2)(a) of the Act of 1973 for an order restraining any person from attempting to defeat a claim for financial provision or otherwise for protecting the claim may be made to the district judge.

(2) Rules 2.65 and 2.66 shall apply, with the necessary modifications, to the application as if it were an application for ancillary relief.

**Amendment**

SI 1999/3491.

## [3.453.1]
### Keypoints

- When to apply
- Applications under s 37(2)(b) and (c) of the MCA 1973
- Jurisdiction of the court to preserve assets

## [3.453.2]
### When to apply

An application for an order relating to ancillary relief must be filed before an application under s 37(2)(a) of the MCA 1973 can be made[1]. There must also be a petition.

1 Set out at para **[2.136]** above.

### [3.453.3]
### Applications under s 37(2)(b) and (c) of the MCA 1973

The applicant should apply by notice in Form A[1].

1 See FPR 1991, r 2.53(3) (as amended) at para **[3.436]** above.

### [3.453.4]
### Jurisdiction of the court to preserve assets

The High Court has an inherent jurisdiction to preserve assets pending determination of ancillary relief proceedings[1]. The county court has jurisdiction conferred on it by statutory provision under reg 3(3)(b) of the County Court Remedies Regulations 1991, SI 1991/1222:

> '(2) In these Regulations, "prescribed relief" means relief of any of the following kinds—
>
> (a) an order requiring a party to admit any other party to premises for the purpose of inspecting or removing documents or articles which may provide evidence in any proceedings, whether or not the proceedings have been commenced;
>
> (b) an interlocutory injunction—
>
> (i) restraining a party from removing from the jurisdiction of the High Court assets located within that jurisdiction; or
>
> (ii) restraining a party from dealing with assets whether located within the jurisdiction of the High Court or not.
>
> (3) … (3) A county court may grant relief of a kind referred to in regulation 2(b)—
>
> …
>
> (b) for the purpose of making an order for the preservation, custody or detention of property which forms or may form the subject matter of proceedings.'

1 See *Shipman v Shipman* [1991] FCR 628, [1991] 1 FLR 250.

### [3.454]

**[2.69 Offers to settle]**

[(1) Either party to the application may at any time make a written offer to the other party which is expressed to be 'without prejudice except as to costs' and which relates to any issue in the proceedings relating to the application.

(2) Where an offer is made under paragraph (1), the fact that such an offer has been made shall not be communicated to the court, except in accordance with rule 2.61E(3), until the question of costs falls to be decided.]

**Amendment**

Inserted by SI 1992/2067. Substituted, together with rr 2.69A to 2.69F, for 2.69 as originally enacted, by SI 1999/3491.

### [3.454.1]
### Keypoints

- *Calderbank* offers
- Part 36 offers
- Effective *Calderbank* offer
- Effect of *Calderbank* offers on costs

### [3.454.2]

### *Calderbank* offers

As named after *Calderbank v Calderbank*[1].

1 [1976] Fam 93, [1975] 3 All ER 333, CA.

### [3.454.3]
### Part 36 offers

The principle of the *Calderbank* offer is now reflected in the provisions of Pt 36 of the CPR 1998 and FPR 1991, r 2.69.

### [3.454.4]
### Effective *Calderbank* offer

A *Calderbank* offer must be supported by disclosure of relevant information, so that the other party is placed in a position to consider it[1]. The offer should be made sufficiently early so that savings in relation to costs are possible[2].

1 See *Gojkovic v Gojkovic (No 2)* [1992] Fam 40, [1991] 2 FLR 233, CA.
2 See *Sharp v Sharp* [1984] FLR 752, CA.

### [3.454.5]
### Effect of *Calderbank* offers on costs

The court in exercising its discretion in relation to costs may be influenced but not persuaded by the *Calderbank* offer[1]. If, following a *Calderbank* offer, the applicant received less than or equal to the amount offered, she may be at risk of paying her costs and those of the other party's from a date after the communication of the offer[2]. If an order was made which resulted in the applicant getting more than had been offered, she would, prima facie, be entitled to her costs[3].

1 See *A v A (costs appeal)* [1996] 1 FCR 186, [1996] 1 FLR 14.
2 See *Thompson v Thompson* [1994] 1 FCR 97, [1993] 2 FLR 464.
3 See *Gojkovic v Gojkovic (No 2)* [1992] Fam 40, [1991] 2 FLR 233.



### [3.455]

#### [2.69A Interpretation of rules 2.69B to 2.69D]

[In rules 2.69B to 2.69D, 'base rate' has the same meaning as in the Civil Procedure Rules 1998.]

**Amendment**
Substituted, together with rr 2.69, 2.69B to 2.69F, for r 2.69 as originally enacted, by SI 1999/3491.

### [3.456]

#### [2.69B Judgment or order more advantageous than an offer made by the other party]

[(1) This rule applies where the judgment or order in favour of the applicant or respondent is more advantageous to him than an offer made under rule 2.69(1) by the other party.

(2) The court must, unless it considers it unjust to do so, order that other party to pay any costs incurred after the date beginning 28 days after the offer was made.]

**Amendment**
Substituted, together with rr 2.69, 2.69A, 2.69C to 2.69F, for r 2.69 as originally enacted, by SI 1999/3491.

## [3.457]

### [2.69C Judgment or order more advantageous than offers made by both parties]

[[(1) This rule applies where

(a) both the applicant and the respondent have made offers under rule 2.69(1); and

(b) the judgment or order in favour of the applicant or the respondent, as the case may be, is more advantageous to him than both of the offers referred to in paragraph (a).

(2) The court may, where it considers it just, order interest in accordance with paragraph (3) on the whole or part of any sum of money (excluding interest and periodical payments) to be awarded to the applicant or respondent, as the case may be.

(3) Interest under paragraph (2) may be at a rate not exceeding 10 per cent above base rate for some or all of the period beginning 28 days after the offer was made.

(4) The court may also order that the applicant or respondent, as the case may be, is entitled to:

(a) his costs on the indemnity basis beginning 28 days after the offer was made; and

(b) interest on those costs at a rate not exceeding 10 per cent above base rate.]

(5) The court's powers under this rule are in addition to its powers under rule 2.69B.]

**Amendment**

Substituted, together with rr 2.69, 2.69A, 2.69B, 2.69D to 2.69F, for r 2.69 as originally enacted, by SI 1999/3491.

## [3.458]

### [2.69D Factors for court's consideration under rules 2.69B and 2.69C]

[(1) In considering whether it would be unjust, or whether it would be just, to make the orders referred to in rules 2.69B and 2.69C, the court must take into account all the circumstances of the case, including—

(a) the terms of any offers made under rule 2.69(1);

(b) the stage in the proceedings when any offer was made;

(c) the information available to the parties at the time when the offer was made;

(d) the conduct of the parties with regard to the giving or refusing to give information for the purposes of enabling the offer to be made or evaluated; and

(e) the respective means of the parties.

(2) The power of the court to award interest under rule 2.69C(2) and (4)(b) is in addition to any other power it may have to award interest.]

**Amendment**

Substituted, together with rr 2.69, 2.69A to 2.69C, 2.69E, 2.69F, for r 2.69 as originally enacted, by SI 1999/3491.

## [3.458.1]
**Keypoint**

- Costs

## [3.458.2]
**Costs**

The guiding principle for every practitioner remains the statement of Butler-Sloss LJ in *Gojkovic v Gojkovic (No 2)*[1]:

'It is incumbent on both parties to negotiate if possible and at least to make the attempt to settle the case'.

The danger of an award of costs against a party who in any way hinders this process and the smooth progression of a case according to the Rules is an ever present one. Having outlined this general principle, however, the Rules on costs are in fact specific in their stipulations regarding costs after final judgment or order, although less specific in their out-working.

Either party can, at any stage of the proceedings make an offer to settle all or part of the case expressed to be 'without prejudice except as to costs'[2]. The offer, however, initially made must be reduced to writing. Two scenarios now fall to be considered.

### *Where the judgment or order in favour of the applicant or respondent is more advantageous than an offer made by the other party*

If the order made is 'more advantageous' to the other party than the offer made the court *must* order the offering party to pay the costs incurred by the other side from 28 days after the date of the offer unless the court considers it unjust to do so. The question of whether it is 'just' so to do is considered below.

A number of issues arise from this provision:

- If an offer is likely to be exceeded in the view of the practitioner involved (but is nonetheless the best that can be made on the client's instructions), it would appear prudent, when considering the rule in isolation, to make the offer as late as possible in order to start the period for which costs are to be made as late as possible. On a strict construction of the rule it could, theoretically, be advantageous not to make an offer at all under r 2.69(1) albeit making an open offer under r 2.61E(3) and (4) / r 2.69E then the rule does not appear to apply.
- The arrangement is not reciprocal. In other words if the order party is less advantageous to the party receiving the offer than the offer there is no stipulation that the offering party should receive their costs on the same basis. This is a most extraordinary situation.
- The proper conclusion is probably that the courts will continue to exercise the wide discretion available to them in relation to costs and as exemplified in *Gojkovic* but the wise practitioner will nonetheless retain these arguments in their armour.

PART 3 FPR 1991

### *Where both parties have made offers and the judgment or order is more advantageous than the offers made by both parties*

This situation arises where a party exceeds both their own offer and that of the other party. In such an instance it is provided that the court may do all or some of the following[3]:

- Order costs (r 2.69C(5));
- Order costs on an indemnity basis from 28 days after the offer was made (r 2.69C(4)(a));
- Order interest on indemnity costs at a rate not exceeding 10% above base rate (r 2.69C(b));
- Order, where it considers just, interest at a rate not exceeding 10% above base rate for some or all of the period beginning 28 days after the offer was made on the whole or part of any sum of money (excluding interest and periodical payments) to be awarded to the successful party (r 2.69C(2)).

The powers under r 2.69C are in addition to those under r 2.69B and again only apply once offers are made under r 2.69. Thus the same observations as made at point 1 of the list under: *Where the judgment or order in favour of the applicant or respondent is more advantageous than an offer made by the other party* above, apply but with an additional consideration. If a party reserves its position under r 2.69(1) as outlined above in order to prevent rr 2.69B and 2.69C applying, the party also loses the possibility of receiving any of the additional benefits of r 2.69C.

*Justice in costs*

As referred to above there is a presumption under r 2.61B(2) that the court will order costs against a party whose offer under r 2.69(1) is exceeded by the decision of the court unless it would be unjust to do so. Likewise the discretion to award interest under r 2.69C(2) is to be exercised 'where the court considers it just'. The matters which the court have to consider in deciding this question of 'justice' are set out in r 2.69D and are as follows:

- All the circumstances of the case;
- The terms of any offers under r 2.69(1);
- The information available to the parties at the time when the offer was made;
- The conduct of the parties with regard to the giving of or refusing to give information for the purposes of enabling the offer to be made or evaluated;
- The respective means of the parties.

Amidst all this the guiding principle of *Gojkovic* remains.

1 [1991] 2 FLR 233 at 238.
2 See r 2.69(1).
3 See r 2.69C.

## [3.459]

### [2.69E Open proposals]

[(1) Not less than 14 days before the date fixed for the final hearing of an application for ancillary relief, the applicant must (unless the court directs otherwise) file with the court and serve on the respondent an open statement which sets out concise details, including the amounts involved, of the orders which he proposes to ask the court to make.

(2) Not more than 7 days after service of a statement under paragraph (1), the respondent must file with the court and serve on the applicant an open statement which sets out concise details, including the amounts involved, of the orders which he proposes to ask the court to make.]

**Amendment**

Substituted, together with rr 2.69, 2.69A to 2.69D, 2.69F, for r 2.69 as originally enacted, by SI 1999/3491, rr 2, 3, 17.

## [3.459.1]
### Keypoints

- Overview
- 'Generous' without prejudice / conservative 'open' offers

## [3.459.2]
### Overview

See Table set out at para **[3.442.2]** above.

## [3.459.3]
### 'Generous' without prejudice / conservative 'open' offers

This rule allows the practitioner to make a 'generous' without prejudice offer under r 2.69(1) and a conservative 'open' offer under r 2.69E.

## [3.460]

### [2.69F Application for interim orders]

[(1) A party may apply at any stage of the proceedings for an order for maintenance pending suit, interim periodical payments or an interim variation order.

(2) An application for such an order must be made by notice of application and the date fixed for the hearing of the application must be not less than 14 days after the date the notice of application is issued.

(3) The applicant shall forthwith serve the respondent with a copy of the notice of application.

(4) Where an application is made before a party has filed Form E, that party must file with the application and serve on the other party, a draft of the order requested and a short sworn statement explaining why the order is necessary and giving the necessary information about his means.

(5) Not less than 7 days before the date fixed for the hearing, the respondent must file with the court and serve on the other party, a short sworn statement about his means, unless he has already filed Form E.

(6) A party may apply for any other form of interim order at any stage of the proceedings with or without notice.

(7) Where an application referred to in paragraph (6) is made with notice, the provisions of paragraphs (1) to (5) apply to it.

(8) Where an application referred to in paragraph (6) is made without notice, the provisions of paragraph (1) apply to it.]

**Amendment**

Substituted, together with rr 2.69, 2.69A to 2.69E, for r 2.69 as originally enacted, by SI 1999/3491.



## [3.460.1]
## Keypoint

- Applications for interim orders

## [3.460.2]
## Applications for interim orders

An application for an interim order can be made by either party at any stage of the proceedings. The application must be made by notice of application (in Form A or B). It must be fixed for a hearing which cannot be earlier than 14 days after the date on which notice of application is issued[1].

Once issued the applicant must forthwith serve the respondent with a copy of the notice of application.

The application can be for[2]:

- Maintenance pending suit;
- Interim periodical payments; or
- An interim variation order.

A problem that arises as a result of this is the position of the applicant in desperate need of interim *capital* provision[3]. An example would be where an applicant needs to buy a car because the respondent has removed the family vehicle, availability of which was a prerequisite for the applicant continuing in employment or is essential because the applicant is totally reliant on a vehicle through disability or living in a remote area. The Rules do not provide for the making of such orders and whilst it may be possible to persuade a court to 'disguise' capital provision as an income order, for example by ordering interim periodical payments at a level which would allow the applicant to meet the monthly repayments under a loan taken out to buy a car, this is by no means a certain or desirable approach.

Clearly, because an application for an interim order can be heard as early as two weeks after the launch of the ancillary relief proceedings, many occasions will arise where the parties are yet to file their Form E's[4]. This eventuality is provided for in r 2.69F(4) and (5), by which the procedure is that the applicant must file with the application and serve on the respondent:

- a draft of the order sought;
- a short sworn statement explaining why the order is necessary and giving the necessary information about the respondent's means.

The respondent must reply not less than seven days before the hearing date by filling and serving a short sworn statement of the respondent's means.

Once one application has been made for interim provision further application for any other form of order may be made at any time[5]. If the application is with notice the full procedure set out above must be complied with[6]. Normally it will be practical to comply with the full procedure in order that the respondent and court are fully aware of the issues involved in good time.

1 See r 2.69F(1) and (2).
2 See r 2.69F(2).
3 See also *Wicks v Wicks* [1999] Fam 65, [1998] 1 FLR 470, CA.
4 Note r 2.61D(2)(f)(i) – the application may be heard at the First Appointment.
5 See r 2.69F(7).
6 See r 2.69F(8).

## [3.461]

### [2.70 Pensions]

[(1) This rule applies where an application for ancillary relief has been made, or notice of intention to proceed with the application has been given, in Form A, or an application has been made in Form B, and the applicant or respondent has or is likely to have any benefits under a pension arrangement.

(2) When the court fixes a first appointment as required by rule 2.61A(4)(a), the party with pension rights shall, within seven days after receiving notification of the date of that appointment, request the person responsible for each pension arrangement under which he has or is likely to have benefits to furnish the information referred to in regulation 2(2) and (3)(b) to (f) of the Pensions on Divorce etc (Provision of Information) Regulations 2000.

(3) Within seven days of receiving information under paragraph (2) the party with pension rights shall send a copy of it to the other party, together with the name and address of the person responsible for each pension arrangement.

(4) A request under paragraph (2) above need not be made where the party with pension rights is in possession of, or has requested, a relevant valuation of the pension rights or benefits accrued under the pension arrangement in question.

(5) In this rule, a relevant valuation means a valuation of pension rights or benefits as at a date not more than twelve months earlier than the date fixed for the first appointment which has been furnished or requested for the purposes of any of the following provisions—

(a) the Pensions on Divorce etc (Provision of Information) Regulations 2000;
(b) regulation 5 of and Schedule 2 to the Occupational Pension Schemes (Disclosure of Information) Regulations 1996 and regulation 11 of and Schedule 1 to the Occupational Pension Schemes (Transfer Value) Regulations 1996;
(c) section 93A or 94(1)(a) or (aa) of the Pension Schemes Act 1993;
(d) section 94(1)(b) of the Pension Schemes Act 1993 or paragraph 2(a) (or, where applicable, 2(b)) of Schedule 2 to the Personal Pension Schemes (Disclosure of Information) Regulations 1987.

(6) Upon making or giving notice of intention to proceed with an application for ancillary relief including provision to be made under section 24B (pension sharing) of the Act of 1973, or upon adding a request for such provision to an existing application for ancillary relief, the applicant shall send to the person responsible for the pension arrangement concerned a copy of Form A.

(7) Upon making or giving notice of intention to proceed with an application for ancillary relief including provision to be made under section 25B or 25C (pension attachment) of the Act of 1973, or upon adding a request for such provision to an

existing application for ancillary relief, the applicant shall send to the person responsible for the pension arrangement concerned—

(a) a copy of Form A;

(b) an address to which any notice which the person responsible is required to serve on the applicant under the Divorce etc (Pensions) Regulations 2000 is to be sent;

(c) an address to which any payment which the person responsible is required to make to the applicant is to be sent; and

(d) where the address in sub-paragraph (c) is that of a bank, a building society or the Department of National Savings, sufficient details to enable payment to be made into the account of the applicant.

(8) A person responsible for a pension arrangement on whom a copy of a notice under paragraph (7) is served may, within 21 days after service, require the applicant to provide him with a copy of section 2.16 of the statement in Form E supporting his application; and the applicant must then provide that person with the copy of that section of the statement within the time limited for filing it by rule 2.61B(2), or 21 days after being required to do so, whichever is the later.

(9) A person responsible for a pension arrangement who receives a copy of section 2.16 of Form E as required pursuant to paragraph (8) may within 21 days after receipt send to the court, the applicant and the respondent a statement in answer.

(10) A person responsible for a pension arrangement who files a statement in answer pursuant to paragraph (9) shall be entitled to be represented at the first appointment, and the court must within 4 days of the date of filing of the statement in answer give the person notice of the date of the first appointment.

(11) Where the parties have agreed on the terms of an order including provision under section 25B or 25C (pension attachment) of the Act of 1973, then unless service has already been effected under paragraph (7), they shall serve on the person responsible for the pension arrangement concerned—

(a) the notice of application for a consent order under rule 2.61(1);

(b) a draft of the proposed order under rule 2.61(1), complying with paragraph (13) below; and

(c) the particulars set out in sub-paragraphs (b), (c) and (d) of paragraph (7) above.

(12) No consent order under paragraph (11) shall be made unless either—

(a) the person responsible has not made any objection within 21 days after the service on him of such notice; or

(b) the court has considered any such objection

and for the purpose of considering any objection the court may make such direction as it sees fit for the person responsible to attend before it or to furnish written details of his objection.

(13) An order for ancillary relief, whether by consent or not, including provision under section 24B (pension sharing), 25B or 25C (pension attachment) of the Act of 1973, shall—

(a) in the body of the order, state that there is to be provision by way of pension sharing or pension attachment in accordance with the annex or annexes to the order; and

(b) be accompanied by an annex containing the information set out in paragraph (14) or paragraph (15) as the case may require; and if provision is made in relation to more than one pension arrangement there shall be one annex for each pension arrangement.

(14) Where provision is made under section 24B (pension sharing) of the Act of 1973, the annex shall state—

(a) the name of the court making the order, together with the case number and the title of the proceedings;

(b) that it is a pension sharing order made under Part IV of the Welfare Reform and Pensions Act 1999;

(c) the names of the transferor and the transferee;
(d) the national insurance number of the transferor;
(e) sufficient details to identify the pension arrangement concerned and the transferor's rights or benefits from it (for example a policy reference number);
(f) the specified percentage, or where appropriate the specified amount, required in order to calculate the appropriate amount for the purposes of section 29(1) of the Welfare Reform and Pensions Act 1999 (creation of pension debits and credits);
(g) how the pension sharing charges are to be apportioned between the parties or alternatively that they are to be paid in full by the transferor;
(h) that the person responsible for the pension arrangement has furnished the information required by regulation 4 of the Pensions on Divorce etc (Provision of Information) Regulations 2000 and that it appears from that information that there is power to make an order including provision under section 24B (pension sharing) of the Act of 1973;
(i) the day on which the order or provision takes effect; and
(j) that the person responsible for the pension arrangement concerned must discharge his liability in respect of the pension credit within a period of 4 months beginning with the day on which the order or provision takes effect or, if later, with the first day on which the person responsible for the pension arrangement concerned is in receipt of—
    (i) the order for ancillary relief, including the annex;
    (ii) the decree of divorce or nullity of marriage; and
    (iii) the information prescribed by regulation 5 of the Pensions on Divorce etc (Provision of Information) Regulations 2000;

provided that if the court knows that the implementation period is different from that stated in sub-paragraph (j) by reason of regulations under section 34(4) or 41(2)(a) of the Welfare Reform and Pensions Act 1999, the annex shall contain details of the implementation period as determined by those regulations instead of the statement in sub-paragraph (j).

(15) Where provision is made under section 25B or 25C (pension attachment) of the Act of 1973, the annex shall state—

(a) the name of the court making the order, together with the case number and the title of the proceedings;
(b) that it is an order making provision under section 25B or 25C, as the case may be, of the Act of 1973;
(c) the names of the party with pension rights and the other party;
(d) the national insurance number of the party with pension rights;
(e) sufficient details to identify the pension arrangement concerned and the rights or benefits from it to which the party with pension rights is or may become entitled (for example a policy reference number);
(f) in the case of an order including provision under section 25B(4) of the Act of 1973, what percentage of any payment due to the party with pension rights is to be paid for the benefit of the other party;
(g) in the case of an order including any other provision under section 25B or 25C of the Act of 1973, what the person responsible for the pension arrangement is required to do;
(h) the address to which any notice which the person responsible for the pension arrangement is required to serve on the other party under the Divorce etc (Pensions) Regulations 2000 is to be sent, if not notified under paragraph (7)(b);
(i) an address to which any payment which the person responsible for the pension arrangement is required to make to the other party is to be sent, if not notified under paragraph (7)(c);

(j) where the address in sub-paragraph (i) is that of a bank, a building society or the Department of National Savings, sufficient details to enable payment to be made into the account of the other party, if not notified under paragraph (7)(d); and

(k) where the order is made by consent, that no objection has been made by the person responsible for the pension arrangement, or that an objection has been received and considered by the court, as the case may be.

(16) A court which makes, varies or discharges an order including provision under section 24B (pension sharing), 25B or 25C (pension attachment) of the Act of 1973, shall send to the person responsible for the pension arrangement concerned—

(a) a copy of the decree of divorce, nullity of marriage or judicial separation;

(b) in the case of divorce or nullity of marriage, a copy of the certificate under rule 2.51 that the decree has been made absolute; and

(c) a copy of that order, or as the case may be of the order varying or discharging that order, including any annex to that order relating to that pension arrangement but no other annex to that order.

(17) The documents referred to in paragraph (16) shall be sent within 7 days after the making of the relevant order, or within 7 days after the decree absolute of divorce or nullity or decree of judicial separation, whichever is the later.

(18) In this rule—

(a) all words and phrases defined in sections 25D(3) and (4) of the Act of 1973 have the meanings assigned by those subsections;

(b) all words and phrases defined in section 46 of the Welfare Reform and Pensions Act 1999 have the meanings assigned by that section.]

**Amendment**

Inserted by SI 1996/1674, r 5, with effect from 1 July 1996. Substituted by SI 2000/2267, r 9. Amended by SI 2001/821.



**[3.461.1]**
**Keypoints**

- FPR 1991, r 2.70
- Pre-Application Protocol

**[3.461.2]**
**FPR 1991, r 2.70**

Former rr 2.70(1) and 2.70(3)(b) have been omitted: there are now no provisions so numbered.

**[3.461.3]**
**Pre-Application Protocol**

The *Practice Direction (family proceedings: ancillary relief procedure)* issued by the President of the Family Division on 25 May 2000 requires compliance with the Pre-Application Protocol annexed to the *Direction* The protocol applies to all claims for ancillary relief and is reproduced in full at para **[4.28]** below. The protocol sets out a number of specific principles for those with conduct of such claims to follow which can be said to be subject to seven general principles:

- The aim of all pre-application steps must be to assist the parties to resolve their differences speedily and fairly or at least to narrow the issues for themselves and/or the court;
- It should be ensured that proper pre-application disclosure and negotiation takes place, in appropriate cases, in a cost-effective manner;
- All parties must always bear in mind the overriding objective of the Rules;
- Compliance with the protocol is the normal reasonable approach to pre-application conduct;

- Attempts should be made to place the parties in a position to settle the case fairly and early and without litigation;
- The issue of an application should not be seen as a hostile act but rather the commencement of the court's active case management, although an application should not be issued where a settlement is in prospect;
- There is a need to balance the advantages of pre-application disclosure and negotiation with the advantages of court management of the case;
- Whether at any stage it would be appropriate to suggest mediation to the parties.

The specific principles can be summarised as follows:

*Disclosure*

- The parties must seek to clarify and identify the issues in the case as soon as possible. To that end open, accurate, full, frank and clear disclosure of facts, information and documents material to proper negotiations must take place.
- If pre-application disclosure is made Form E should be used as a guide to the format of disclosure and documents only disclosed to the extent that they are required by Form E.
- Any 'first letter' requesting information must focus on the clarification of claims and identification of issues and the impact of any correspondence on the reader must be considered.

*Experts*

- Experts should only be used for valuations when the parties do not have the information or cannot agree.
- The parties should seek to instruct a joint expert by providing lists of experts to the other side and attempting to reach agreement. A joint letter of instruction should be agreed.
- If agreement cannot be reached, parties should think carefully before instructing their own expert prior to an application because of the cost implications and because the issue may be better managed by the court within the context of an application.
- Whatever the basis of the instruction, the expert should be prepared to answer reasonable questions raised by either party.
- Any expert instructed must consider themselves bound by Pt 35 of the CPR 1998.
- Prior to a joint instruction the parties must disclose if they have already consulted an expert.
- If there are separately instructed experts the parties should be encouraged to agree in advance that the reports will be disclosed.

*Costs*

- Proportionality between the value of the claim and the costs of the litigation must be maintained.
- The court's costs direction extends to pre-application offers to settle and the conduct of disclosure[1].

1 See CPR 1998, Pt 44.3, para 1.

**[3.462]**

PART III

OTHER MATRIMONIAL ETC PROCEEDINGS

### 3.1 Application in case of failure to provide reasonable maintenance

(1) Every application under section 27 of the Act of 1973 shall be made by originating application in Form M19.

(2) The application may be made to any divorce county court and there shall be filed with the application an affidavit by the applicant and also a copy of the application and of the affidavit for service on the respondent.

(3) The affidavit shall state—

(a) the same particulars regarding the marriage, the court's jurisdiction, the children and the previous proceedings as are required in the case of a petition by sub-paragraphs (a), (c), (d), (f) and (i) of paragraph 1 of Appendix 2;

(b) particulars of the respondent's failure to provide reasonable maintenance for the applicant, or, as the case may be, of the respondent's failure to provide, or to make a proper contribution towards, reasonable maintenance for the children of the family; and

(c) full particulars of the applicant's property and income and of the respondent's property and income, so far as may be known to the applicant.

(4) A copy of the application and of the affidavit referred to in paragraph (2) shall be served on the respondent, together with a notice in Form M20 with Form M6.

(5) Subject to paragraph (6), the respondent shall, within 14 days after the time allowed for sending the acknowledgment of service, file an affidavit stating—

(a) whether the alleged failure to provide, or to make proper contribution towards, reasonable maintenance is admitted or denied, and, if denied, the grounds on which he relies;

(b) any allegation which he wishes to make against the applicant; and

(c) full particulars of his property and income, unless otherwise directed.

(6) Where the respondent challenges the jurisdiction of the court to hear the application he shall, within 14 days after the time allowed for sending the acknowledgment of service, file an affidavit setting out the grounds of the challenge; and the obligation to file an affidavit under paragraph (5) shall not arise until 14 days after the question of jurisdiction has been determined and the court has decided that the necessary jurisdiction exists.

(7) Where the respondent's affidavit contains an allegation of adultery or of an improper association with a person named, the provisions of rule 2.60 (which deal with service on, and [filing of a statement in answer by], a named person) shall apply.

(8) If the respondent does not file an affidavit in accordance with paragraph (5), the court may order him to file an affidavit containing full particulars of his property and income, and in that case the respondent shall serve a copy of any such affidavit on the applicant.

(9) Within 14 days after being served with a copy of any affidavit filed by the respondent, the applicant may file a further affidavit as to means and as to any fact in the respondent's affidavit which is disputed, and in that case the applicant shall serve a copy on the respondent.

No further affidavit shall be filed without leave.

(10) Rules 2.61 to 2.66 and rule 10.10 shall apply, with such modifications as may be appropriate, to an application for an order under section 27 of the Act of 1973 as if the application were an application for ancillary relief.

**Amendment**

Para (7): words in square brackets substituted by SI 1999/3491, rr 2, 21.



**[3.463]**

### 3.2 Application for alteration of maintenance agreement during lifetime of parties

(1) An application under section 35 of the Act of 1973 for the alteration of a maintenance agreement shall be made by originating application containing, unless otherwise directed, the information required by Form M21.

(2) The application may be made to any divorce county court and may be heard and determined by the district judge.

(3) There shall be filed with the application an affidavit by the applicant exhibiting a copy of the agreement and verifying the statements in the application and also a copy of the application and of the affidavit for service on the respondent.

(4) A copy of the application and of the affidavit referred to in paragraph (3) shall be served on the respondent, together with a notice in Form M20 with Form M6 attached.

(5) The respondent shall, within 14 days after the time limited for giving notice of intention to defend, file an affidavit in answer to the application containing full particulars of his property and income and, if he does not do so, the court may order him to file an affidavit containing such particulars.

(6) A respondent who files an affidavit under paragraph (5) shall at the same time file a copy which the proper officer shall serve on the applicant.

**[3.464]**

## 3.3 Application for alteration of maintenance agreement after death of one party

(1) An application under section 36 of the Act of 1973 for the alteration of a maintenance agreement after the death of one of the parties shall be made—

(a) in the High Court, by originating summons out of the principal registry or any district registry, or

(b) in a county court, by originating application,

in Form M22.

(2) There shall be filed in support of the application an affidavit by the applicant exhibiting a copy of the agreement and an official copy of the grant of representation to the deceased's estate and of every testamentary document admitted to proof and stating—

(a) whether the deceased died domiciled in England and Wales;

(b) the place and date of the marriage between the parties to the agreement and the name and status of the wife before the marriage;

(c) the name of every child of the family and of any other child for whom the agreement makes financial arrangements, and

(i) the date of birth of each such child who is still living (or, if it be the case, that he has attained 18) and the place where and the person with whom any such minor child is residing,

(ii) the date of death of any such child who has died since the agreement was made;

(d) whether there have been in any court any, and if so what, previous proceedings with reference to the agreement or to the marriage or to the children of the family or any other children for whom the agreement makes financial arrangements, and the date and effect of any order or decree made in such proceedings;

(e) whether there have been in any court any proceedings by the applicant against the deceased's estate under the Inheritance (Provision for Family and Dependants) Act 1975 or any Act repealed by that Act and the date and effect of any order made in such proceedings;

(f) in the case of an application by the surviving party, the applicant's means;

(g) in the case of an application by the personal representatives of the deceased, the surviving party's means, so far as they are known to the applicant, and the information mentioned in sub-paragraphs (a), (b) and (c) of rule 3.4(4);

(h) the facts alleged by the applicant as justifying an alteration in the agreement and the nature of the alteration sought;

(i) if the application is made after the end of the period of six months from the date on which representation in regard to the deceased's estate was first taken out, the grounds on which the court's permission to entertain the application is sought.

(3) CCR Order 48, rules 3(1), 7 and 9 shall apply to an originating application under the said section 36 as they apply to an application under section 1 of the Inheritance (Provision for Family and Dependants) Act 1975.

(4) In this rule and the next following rule 'the deceased' means the deceased party to the agreement to which the application relates.

**[3.465]**

### 3.4 Further proceedings on application under rule 3.3

(1) Without prejudice to his powers under RSC Order 15 (which deals with parties and other matters), the district judge may at any stage of the proceedings direct that any person be added as a respondent to an application under rule 3.3.

(2) RSC Order 15, rule 13 (which enables the court to make representation orders in certain cases) shall apply to the proceedings as if they were mentioned in paragraph (1) of the said rule 13.

(3) Where the application is in a county court, the references in paragraphs (1) and (2) to RSC Order 15 and Order 15, rule 13 shall be construed as references to CCR Order 5 and Order 5, rule 6 respectively.

(4) A respondent who is a personal representative of the deceased shall, within 14 days after the time limited for giving notice of intention to defend, file an affidavit in answer to the application stating—

- (a) full particulars of the value of the deceased's estate for probate, after providing for the discharge of the funeral, testamentary and administration expenses, debts and liabilities payable thereout, including the amount of the [inheritance tax or any other tax replaced by that tax] and interest thereon;
- (b) the person or classes of persons beneficially interested in the estate (giving the names and addresses of all living beneficiaries) and the value of their interests so far as ascertained, and
- (c) if such be the case, that any living beneficiary (naming him) is a minor or a patient within the meaning of rule 9.1.

(5) If a respondent who is a personal representative of the deceased does not file an affidavit stating the matters mentioned in paragraph (4) the district judge may order him to do so.

(6) A respondent who is not a personal representative of the deceased may, within 14 days after the time limited for giving notice of intention to defend, file an affidavit in answer to the application.

(7) Every respondent who files an affidavit in answer to the application shall at the same time lodge a copy, which the proper officer shall serve on the applicant.

**Amendment**

Para (4): in sub-para (a) words 'inheritance tax or any other tax replaced by that tax' substituted by SI 1991/2113, r 4.

**[3.466]**

### 3.5 Application of other rules to proceedings under section 35 or 36 of Act of 1973

(1) The following rules shall apply, with the necessary modifications, to an application under section 35 or 36 of the Act of 1973, as if it were an application for ancillary relief—

- (a) in the case of an application under either section, rules 2.60, 2.62(4) to (6), 2.63, 2.64, 2.65 and 10.10;
- (b) in the case of an application under section 35, rule 2.66;
- (c) in the case of an application under section 36, rule 2.66(1) and (2).

(2) Subject to paragraph (1) and to the provisions of rules 3.2 to 3.4, these rules shall, so far as applicable, apply with the necessary modifications to an application under section 35 or section 36 (as the case may be) of the Act of 1973, as if the application were a cause, the originating application or summons a petition, and the applicant the petitioner.

**[3.467]**

### 3.6 Married Women's Property Act 1882

(1) Subject to paragraph (2) below, an application under section 17 of the Married Women's Property Act 1882 (in this and the next following rule referred to as 'section 17') shall be made—

- (a) in the High Court, by originating summons, which may be issued out of the principal registry or any district registry, or
- (b) in a county court, by originating application,

in Form M23 and shall be supported by affidavit.

(2) An order under section 17 may be made in any ancillary relief proceedings upon the application of any party thereto in Form M11 by notice of application or summons.

(3) An application under section 17 to a county court shall be filed—

- (a) subject to sub-paragraph (b), in the court for the district in which the applicant or respondent resides, or
- (b) in the divorce county court in which any pending matrimonial cause has been commenced by or on behalf of either the applicant or the respondent, or in which any matrimonial cause is intended to be commenced by the applicant.

(4) Where the application concerns the title to or possession of land, the originating summons or application shall—

- (a) state whether the title to the land is registered or unregistered and, if registered, the Land Registry title number; and
- (b) give particulars, so far as known to the applicant, of any mortgage of the land or any interest therein.

(5) The application shall be served on the respondent, together with a copy of the affidavit in support and an acknowledgment of service in Form M6.

(6) Where particulars of a mortgage are given pursuant to paragraph (4), the applicant shall file a copy of the originating summons or application, which shall be served on the mortgagee; and any person so served may apply to the court in writing, within 14 days after service, for a copy of the affidavit in support; and within 14 days of receiving such affidavit may file an affidavit in answer and shall be entitled to be heard on the application.

(7) If the respondent intends to contest the application, he shall, within 14 days after the time allowed for sending the acknowledgment of service, file an affidavit in answer to the application setting out the grounds on which he relies, and lodge in the court office a copy of the affidavit for service on the applicant.

(8) If the respondent fails to comply with paragraph (7), the applicant may apply for directions; and the district judge may give such directions as he thinks fit, including a direction that the respondent shall be debarred from defending the application unless an affidavit is filed within such time as the district judge may specify.

(9) A district judge may grant an injunction in proceedings under section 17 if, but only so far as, the injunction is ancillary or incidental to any relief sought in those proceedings.

(10) Rules 2.62(4) to (6) and 2.63 to 2.66 shall apply, with the necessary modifications, to an application under section 17 as they apply to an application for ancillary relief.

(11) Subject to the provisions of this rule, these rules shall apply, with the necessary modifications, to an application under section 17 as if the application were a cause, the originating summons or application a petition, and the applicant a petitioner.

### [3.467.1]
**Keypoints**

- Discovery
- Ex parte

### [3.467.2]
**Discovery**

Rule 3.6(10), by applying rr 2.62(4) to (6) and 2.63 to 2.66, enables a party to an application under s 17 to require, by letter, the other party to provide further information regarding matters contained in the filed affidavits, or to provide a list of documents, or to permit inspection of such documents. If the other party fails to comply, an application may be made to the district judge for directions. In complex cases discovery needs to be controlled[1].

1 See *Hammond v Mitchell* [1992] 2 All ER 109, [1991] 1 WLR 1127.

### [3.467.3]
**Ex parte**

An application under s 17 may be made ex parte. If the case is one of particular urgency, the judge may grant an injunction before an originating summons has been issued[1].

1 See the SCA 1981, s 33. See also *Re N (infants)* [1967] Ch 512, [1967] 1 All ER 161; and *Re Ferrar's Application* [1966] P 126, [1966] 3 All ER 78, CA.



### [3.468]

**3.7 Exercise in principal registry of county court jurisdiction under section 17 of Married Women's Property Act 1882**

(1) Where any proceedings for divorce, nullity or judicial separation which are either pending in the principal registry, or are intended to be commenced there by the applicant, are or will be treated as pending in a divorce county court, an application under section 17 by one of the parties to the marriage may be made to the principal registry as if it were a county court.

(2) In relation to proceedings commenced or intended to be commenced in the principal registry under paragraph (1) of this rule or transferred from the High Court to the principal registry by an order made under section 38 of the Act of 1984—

(a) section 42 of the Act of 1984 and the rules made thereunder shall have effect, with the necessary modifications, as they have effect in relation to proceedings commenced in or transferred to the principal registry under that section; and

(b) CCR Order 4, rule 8 and rule 3.6(3) (which relate to venue) shall not apply.

(3) Rule 1.4(1) shall apply, with the necessary modifications, to proceedings in, or intended to be commenced in, the principal registry under paragraph (1) of this rule as it applies to matrimonial proceedings.

### [3.469]

**3.17 Application for leave under section 13 of Act of 1984**

(1) An application for leave to apply for an order for financial relief under Part III of the Act of 1984 shall be made ex parte by originating summons issued in Form M25 out of the principal registry and shall be supported by an affidavit by the applicant stating the facts relied on in support of the application with particular reference to the matters set out in section 16(2) of that Act.

(2) The affidavit in support shall give particulars of the judicial or other proceedings by means of which the marriage to which the application relates was dissolved or annulled or by which the parties to the marriage were legally separated and shall state, so far as is known to the applicant:

(a) the names of the parties to the marriage and the date and place of the marriage;
(b) the occupation and residence of each of the parties to the marriage;
(c) whether there are any living children of the family and, if so, the number of such children and the full names (including surname) of each and his date of birth or, if it be the case, that he is over 18;
(d) whether either party to the marriage has remarried;
(e) an estimate in summary form of the appropriate amount or value of the capital resources and net income of each party and of any minor child of the family;
(f) the grounds on which it is alleged that the court has jurisdiction to entertain an application for an order for financial relief under Part III of the Act of 1984.

(3) The proper officer shall fix a date, time and place for the hearing of the application by a judge in chambers and give notice thereof to the applicant.

### [3.469.1]
### Keypoints

- All material facts disclosed
- 'Substantial ground'
- Burden on applicant
- Setting aside

### [3.469.2]
### All material facts disclosed

A judge must be made aware of all material facts known to the applicant. Failure on the part of the applicant to make full disclosure of all relevant facts known to him may result in the leave granted being set aside[1].

1 See *W v W (financial provision)* [1989] FCR 721, [1989] 1 FLR 22.

### [3.469.3]
### 'Substantial ground'

Under s 13(1) the applicant must show that there is 'substantial ground for the making of an application for such an order.' The court must be persuaded that there is a substantial ground on which it could exercise its powers under s 12 of the Act of 1984[1]. The court will have considerable regard to the likely outcome of the application[2].

1 See *Holmes v Holmes* [1989] Fam 47, [1989] 3 All ER 786, CA.
2 See *Hewitson v Hewitson* [1995] Fam 100, [1995] 1 All ER 472, CA.

### [3.469.4]
### Burden on applicant

The applicant has to satisfy the court that it is appropriate for an English court to make the order[1]. An applicant should not be allowed to litigate a point in the United Kingdom, having raised the matter fully in another country[2]. Butler-Sloss LJ described this as having 'two bites at the one cherry'[3].

1 See *Z v Z (Financial Provision after Foreign Divorce)* [1992] 2 FCR 152, [1992] 2 FLR 291.
2 See *M v M (Financial Provision after Foreign Divorce)* [1994] 2 FCR 448, [1994] 1 FLR 399.
3 See *Lamagni v Lamagni* [1996] 1 FCR 408, [1995] 2 FLR 452, CA.

### [3.469.5]
### Setting aside

An application may be made by the respondent to a High Court judge to set aside the leave granted under s 13.

[3.470]

### 3.18 Application for order for financial relief or avoidance of transaction order under Part III of Act of 1984

(1) An application for an order for financial relief under Part III of the Act of 1984 shall be made by originating summons issued in Form M26 out of the principal registry and at the same time the applicant, unless otherwise directed, shall file an affidavit in support of the summons giving full particulars of his property and income.

(2) The applicant shall serve a sealed copy of the originating summons on the respondent and shall annex thereto a copy of the affidavit in support, if one has been filed, and a notice of proceedings and acknowledgment of service in Form M28, and rule 10.8 shall apply to such an acknowledgment of service as if the references in paragraph (1) of that rule to Form M6 and in paragraph (2) of that rule to seven days were, respectively, references to Form M28 and 31 days.

(3) Rules 2.57, 2.59, 2.61, 2.62(5) and (6), 2.63 and 2.66(1) and (2) shall apply, with the necessary modifications, to an application for an order for financial relief under this rule as they apply to an application for ancillary relief made by notice in Form M11 and the court may order the attendance of any person for the purpose of being examined or cross-examined and the discovery and production of any document.

(4) An application for an interim order for maintenance under section 14 or an avoidance of transaction order under section 23 of the Act of 1984 may be made, unless the court otherwise directs, in the originating summons under paragraph (1) or by summons in accordance with rule 10.9(1) and an application for an order under section 23 shall be supported by an affidavit, which may be the affidavit filed under paragraph (1), stating the facts relied on.

(5) If the respondent intends to contest the application he shall, within 28 days after the time limited for giving notice to defend, file an affidavit in answer to the application setting out the grounds on which he relies and shall serve a copy on the applicant.

(6) In respect of any application for an avoidance of transaction order the court may give such a direction or make such appointment as it is empowered to give or make by paragraph (3), and rule 2.59 shall apply, with the necessary modifications, to an application for an avoidance of transaction order as it applies to an application for an avoidance of disposition order.

(7) Where the originating summons contains an application for an order under section 22 of the Act of 1984 the applicant shall serve a copy on the landlord of the dwelling house and he shall be entitled to be heard on the application.

(8) An application for an order for financial relief under Part III of the Act of 1984 or for an avoidance of transaction order shall be determined by a judge.



[3.471]

### 3.19 Application for order under section 24 of Act of 1984 preventing transaction

(1) An application under section 24 of the Act of 1984 for an order preventing a transaction shall be made by originating summons issued in Form M27 out of the principal registry and shall be supported by an affidavit by the applicant stating the facts relied on in support of the application.

(2) The applicant shall serve a sealed copy of the originating summons on the respondent and shall annex thereto a copy of the affidavit in support and a notice of proceedings and acknowledgment of service in Form M28 and rule 10.8 shall apply to such an acknowledgment of service as if the references in paragraph (1) of that rule to Form M6 and in paragraph (2) of that rule to seven days were, respectively, references to Form M28 and 31 days.

(3) If the respondent intends to contest the application he shall, within 28 days after the time limited for giving notice of intention to defend, file an affidavit in answer to the application setting out the grounds on which he relies and shall serve a copy on the applicant.

(4) The application shall be determined by a judge.

(5) Rule 2.66 (except paragraph (3)) shall apply, with the necessary modifications, to the application as if it were an application for ancillary relief.

**[3.472]**

### [3.21 Application under section 27 of the Act of 1991 for declaration of parentage]

[(1) Rule 4.6 shall apply to an application under section 55A of the Act of 1986 (declarations of parentage) as it applies to an application under the Act of 1989.

(2) Where an application under section 55A of the Act of 1986 has been transferred to the High Court or a county court the court shall, as soon as practicable after a transfer has occurred, consider what directions to give for the conduct of the proceedings.

(3) Without prejudice to the generality of paragraph (2), the court may, in particular, direct that—

- (a) the proceedings shall proceed as if they had been commenced by originating summons or originating application;
- (b) any document served or other thing done while the proceedings were pending in another court, including a magistrates' court, shall be treated for such purposes as may be specified in the direction as if it had been such document or other thing, being a document or other thing provided for by the rules of court applicable in the court to which the proceedings have been transferred, as may be specified in the direction and had been served or done pursuant to any such rule;
- (c) a pre-trial hearing shall be held to determine what further directions, if any, should be given.

(4) The application may be heard and determined by a district judge.]

**Amendment**

Inserted by SI 1993/295, r 4. Amended by SI 2001/821.

**[3.473]**

### [3.22 Appeal under section 20 of the Act of 1991]

[(1) Rule 4.6 shall apply to an appeal under section 20 of the Act of 1991 (appeals to appeal tribunals) as it applies to an application under the Act of 1989.

(2) Where an appeal under section 20 of the Act of 1991 is transferred to the High Court or a county court, Rule 3.21(2) and (3) shall apply to the appeal as it applies to an application under section 55A of the Act of 1986.]

**Amendment**

Inserted by SI 1993/295, r 4. Amended by SI 2001/821.

**[3.474]**

### [3.23 Appeal from Child Support Commissioner]

[(1) This rule shall apply to any appeal to the Court of Appeal under section 25 of the Act of 1991 (appeal from Child Support Commissioner on question of law).

(2) Where leave to appeal is granted by the Commissioner, the notice of appeal must be served within 6 weeks from the date on which notice of the grant was given in writing to the appellant.

(3) Where leave to appeal is granted by the Court of Appeal upon an application made within 6 weeks of the date on which notice of the Commissioner's refusal of leave to appeal was given in writing to the appellant, the notice of appeal must be served—

(a) before the end of the said period of 6 weeks; or

(b) within 7 days after the date on which leave is granted,

whichever is the later, or within such other period as the Court of Appeal may direct.]

**Amendment**

Inserted by SI 1993/295, r 4.

**[3.475]**

PART IV

PROCEEDINGS UNDER THE CHILDREN ACT 1989

### 4.4 Application

(1) Subject to paragraph (4), an applicant shall—

[(a) file the documents referred to in paragraph (1A) below (which documents shall together be called the 'application') together with sufficient copies for one to be served on each respondent, and]

(b) serve a copy of the application [together with Form C6 and such (if any) of Forms C7 and C10A as are given to him by the proper officer under paragraph (2)(b)] on each respondent such number of days prior to the date fixed under paragraph (2)(a) as is specified for that application in column (ii) of Appendix 3 to these rules.

[(1A) The documents to be filed under paragraph (1)(a) above are—

(a)

(i) whichever is appropriate of Forms C1 to C4 or C51, and

(ii) such of the supplemental Forms C10 or C11 to C20 as may be appropriate, or

(b) where there is no appropriate form a statement in writing of the order sought, and where the application is made in respect of more than one child, all the children shall be included in one application.]

(2) On receipt of the documents filed under paragraph (1)(a) the proper officer shall—

(a) fix the date for a hearing or a directions appointment, allowing sufficient time for the applicant to comply with paragraph (1)(b),

(b) endorse the date so fixed upon [Form C6 and, where appropriate, Form C6A], and

[(c) return forthwith to the applicant the copies of the application and Form C10A if filed with it, together with Form C6 and such of Forms C6A and C7 as are appropriate].

[(3) The applicant shall, at the same time as complying with paragraph (1)(b), serve Form C6A on the persons set out for the relevant class of proceedings in column (iv) of Appendix 3 to these rules.]

(4) An application for—

(a) a [section 8 order],

(b) an emergency protection order,

(c) a warrant under section 48(9), …

(d) a recovery order,[or

(e) a warrant under section 102(1),]

may be made ex parte in which case the applicant shall—

PART 3 FPR 1991

(i) file the application … in the appropriate form in Appendix 1 to these rules—
(a) where the application is made by telephone, within 24 hours after the making of the application, or
(b) in any other case, at the time when the application is made, and
(ii) in the case of an application for a [section 8 order] or an emergency protection order, serve a copy of the application on each respondent within 48 hours after the making of the order.

(5) Where the court refuses to make an order on an ex parte application it may direct that the application be made inter partes.

(6) In the case of proceedings under Schedule 1, the application under paragraph (1) shall be accompanied by a statement [in Form C10A] setting out the financial details which the applicant believes to be relevant to the application …, together with sufficient copies for one to be served on each respondent.

**Amendment**
SI 1994/3155.

**[3.476]**

PART VII
ENFORCEMENT OF ORDERS

CHAPTER 1
GENERAL

### 7.1 Enforcement of order for payment of money, etc

(1) Before any process is issued for the enforcement of an order made in family proceedings for the payment of money to any person, an affidavit shall be filed verifying the amount due under the order and showing how that amount is arrived at.

In a case to which CCR Order 25 rule 11 (which deals with the enforcement of a High Court judgment in the county court) applies, the information required to be given in an affidavit under this paragraph may be given in the affidavit filed pursuant to that rule.

(2) Except with the leave of the district judge, no writ of fieri facias or warrant of execution shall be issued to enforce payment of any sum due under an order for ancillary relief or an order made under the provisions of section 27 of the Act of 1973 where an application for a variation order is pending.

(3) Where a warrant of execution has been issued to enforce an order made in family proceedings pending in the principal registry which are treated as pending in a divorce county court, the goods and chattels against which the warrant has been issued shall, wherever they are situate, be treated for the purposes of section 103 of the County Courts Act 1984 as being out of the jurisdiction of the principal registry.

(4) The Attachment of Earnings Act 1971 and CCR Order 27 (which deals with attachment of earnings) shall apply to the enforcement of an order made in family proceedings in the principal registry which are treated as pending in a divorce county court as if the order were an order made by such a court.

(5) Where an application under CCR Order 25, rule 3 (which deals with the oral examination of a judgment debtor) relates to an order made by a divorce county court—
(a) the application shall be made to such divorce county court as in the opinion of the applicant is nearest to the place where the debtor resides or carries on business, and
(b) there shall be filed with the application the affidavit required by paragraph (1) of this rule and, except where the application is made to the court in which the order sought to be enforced was made, a copy of the order shall be exhibited to the affidavit;

and accordingly paragraph (2) of the said rule 3 shall not apply.

**[3.477]**

## 7.2 Committal and injunction

(1) Subject to RSC Order 52, rule 6 (which, except in certain cases, requires an application for an order of committal to be heard in open court) an application for an order of committal in family proceedings pending in the High Court shall be made by summons.

(2) Where no judge is conveniently available to hear the application, then, without prejudice to CCR Order 29, rule 3(2) (which in certain circumstances gives jurisdiction to a district judge) an application for—

(a) the discharge of any person committed, or

(b) the discharge by consent of an injunction granted by a judge,

may be made to the district judge who may, if satisfied of the urgency of the matter and that it is expedient to do so, make any order on the application which a judge could have made.

(3) Where an order or warrant for the committal of any person to prison has been made or issued in family proceedings pending in the principal registry which are treated as pending in a divorce county court [or a county court], that person shall, wherever he may be, be treated for the purposes of section 122 of the County Courts Act 1984 as being out of the jurisdiction of the principal registry; but if the committal is for failure to comply with the terms of an injunction, the order or warrant may, if [the court] so directs, be executed by the tipstaff within any county court district.

[(3A) Where an order or warrant for the arrest or committal of any person has been made or issued in proceedings under Part IV of the Family Law Act 1996 pending in the principal registry which are treated as pending in a county court, the order or warrant may, if the court so directs, be executed by the tipstaff within any county court district.]

(4) For the purposes of section 118 of the County Courts Act 1984 in its application to the hearing of family proceedings at the Royal Courts of Justice [or the principal registry], the tipstaff shall be deemed to be an officer of the court.

**Amendment**

SI 1997/1893.



**[3.478]**

## 7.3 Transfer of county court order to High Court

(1) Any person who desires the transfer to the High Court of any order made by a divorce county court in family proceedings except an order for periodical payments or for the recovery of arrears of periodical payments shall apply to the court ex parte by affidavit stating the amount which remains due under the order, and on the filing of the application the transfer shall have effect.

(2) Where an order is so transferred, it shall have the same force and effect and the same proceedings may be taken on it as if it were an order of the High Court.

**[3.479]**

CHAPTER 2

JUDGMENT SUMMONSES

## 7.4 General provisions

(1) In this chapter, unless the context otherwise requires—

'order' means an order made in family proceedings for the payment of money;

'judgment creditor' means a person entitled to enforce an order under section 5 of the Debtors Act 1869;

'debtor' means a person liable under an order;

'judgment summons' means a summons under the said section 5 requiring a debtor to appear and be examined on oath as to his means.

(2) An application for the issue of a judgment summons may be made—

(a) in the case of an order of the High Court, to the principal registry, a district registry or a divorce county court, whichever in the opinion of the judgment creditor is most convenient,

(b) in the case of an order of a divorce county court, to whichever divorce county court is in the opinion of the judgment creditor most convenient,

having regard (in either case) to the place where the debtor resides or carries on business and irrespective of the court or registry in which the order was made.

(3) The application shall be made by filing a request in Form M16 together with the affidavit required by rule 7.1(1) and, except where the application is made to the registry or divorce county court in which the order was made, a copy of the order shall be exhibited to the affidavit.

(4) A judgment summons shall not be issued without the leave of a judge if the debtor is in default under an order of commitment made on a previous judgment summons in respect of the same order.

(5) Every judgment summons shall be in Form M17 and shall be served on the debtor personally not less than 10 days before the hearing and at the time of service there shall be paid or tendered to the debtor a sum reasonably sufficient to cover his expenses in travelling to and from the court at which he is summoned to appear.

(6) CCR Order 28, rule 3 (which deals among other things with the issue of successive judgment summonses) shall apply to a judgment summons, whether issued in the High Court or a divorce county court, but as if the said rule 3 did not apply CCR Order 7, rule 19(2).

(7) Successive judgment summonses may be issued notwithstanding that the judgment debtor has ceased to reside or carry on business at the address stated in Form M16 since the issue of the original judgment summons.

(8) Where an applicant has obtained one or more orders in the same application but for the benefit of different persons—

(a) he shall be entitled to issue a judgment summons in respect of those orders on behalf of any judgment creditor without (where the judgment creditor is a child) seeking leave to act as his next friend; and

(b) only one judgment summons need be issued in respect of those orders.

(9) On the hearing of the judgment summons the judge may—

(a) where the order is for lump sum provision or costs, or

(b) where the order is for maintenance pending suit or other periodical payments and it appears to him that the order would have been varied or suspended if the debtor had made an application for that purpose,

make a new order for payment of the amount due under the original order, together with the costs of the judgment summons, either at a specified time or by instalments.

(10) If the judge makes an order of committal, he may direct its execution to be suspended on terms that the debtor pays to the judgment creditor the amount due, together with the costs of the judgment summons, either at a specified time or by instalments, in addition to any sums accruing due under the original order.

(11) All payments under a new order or an order of committal shall be made to the judgment creditor unless the judge otherwise directs.

(12) Where an order of committal is suspended on such terms as are mentioned in paragraph (10)—

(a) all payments thereafter made under the said order shall be deemed to be made, first, in or towards the discharge of any sums from time to time accruing due under the original order and, secondly, in or towards the discharge of a debt in respect of which the judgment summons was issued and the costs of the summons;

(b) CCR Order 28, rule 7(4) and (5) (which deal with an application for a further suspension) shall apply to the said order, whether it was made in the High Court or a divorce county court; and

(c) the said order shall not be issued until the judgment creditor has filed an affidavit of default on the part of the debtor.

### [3.479.1]

**Keypoint**

- Rule alone not HRA 1998 compliant

### [3.479.2]

**Rule alone not HRA 1998 compliant**

Note the impact of the HRA 1998 on the judgment summons procedure and the criticism of FPR 1991, r 7.4 and the Form M17 in the case of *Murbarak v Murbarak*[1], as followed in *Quinn v Cuff*[2]. See also *Practice Direction: Committal Applications*[3], which, as Thorpe LJ observed in *Murbarak*:

> 'should be sufficient to make the procedures under the Family Proceedings rule 7.4 compliant with the convention.'

1 [2001] 1 FCR 193, [2001] All ER (D) 2302, CA, also reported as *Mubarak* at [2001] 1 FLR 673, 698.
2 [2001] EWCA Civ 36, [2001] All ER (D) 29.
3 [2001] 1 FCR 767, [2001] 1 FLR 949. Set out at para **[4.30A]** below.



### [3.480]

**7.5 Special provisions as to judgment summonses in the High Court**

(1) RSC Order 38, rule 2(3) (which enables evidence to be given by affidavit in certain cases) shall apply to a judgment summons issued in the High Court as if it were an originating summons.

(2) Witnesses may be summoned to prove the means of the debtor in the same manner as witnesses are summoned to give evidence on the hearing of a cause, and writs of subpoena may for that purpose be issued out of the registry in which the judgment summons is issued.

(3) Where the debtor appears at the hearing, the travelling expenses paid to him, if the judge so directs, be allowed as expenses of a witness, but if the debtor appears at the hearing and no order of committal is made, the judge may allow to the debtor, by way of set-off or otherwise, his proper costs, including compensation for loss of time, as upon an attendance by a defendant at a trial in court.

(4) Where a new order or an order of committal is made, the proper officer of the registry in which the judgment summons was issued shall send notice of the order to the debtor and, if the original order was made in another registry, to the proper officer of that registry.

(5) An order of commitment shall be directed to the tipstaff, for execution by him, or to the proper officer of the county court within the district of which the debtor is to be found, for execution by a deputy tipstaff.

(6) Unless the judge otherwise directs, the judgment creditor's costs of and incidental to the judgment summons shall be fixed and allowed without taxation in accordance with RSC Order 62, rule 7(4).

(7) Where the judge directs that the judgment creditor's costs of and incidental to a judgment summons are to be taxed, RSC Order 62 shall have effect in relation to those costs with such modifications as may be necessary.

**[3.481]**

### 7.6 Special provisions as to judgment summonses in divorce county courts

(1) CCR Order 25, rules 3, 4 and 11 (which deal with the oral examination of debtors and the execution of High Court orders in county courts) and Order 28, rules 1, 2, 3(2), 7(3) and 9(2) (which deal with the issue of a judgment summons in a county court and the subsequent procedure) shall not apply to a judgment summons issued in a divorce county court.

(2) CCR Order 28, rule 9(1) (which relates to a judgment summons heard in a county court on a judgment or order of the High Court) shall apply to such a summons as if for the words 'the High Court' there were substituted the words 'any other court' where they first appear and 'that other court' where they next appear.

(3) CCR Order 28, rule 7(1) and (2) (which relates to the suspension of a committal order) shall apply to such a summons subject to rule 7.4(10) and (11) of these Rules.

**[3.482]**

## CHAPTER 4
## ENFORCEMENT OF MAINTENANCE ORDERS

### 7.16 Interpretation

In this chapter—

'the Act of 1920' means the Maintenance Orders (Facilities for Enforcement) Act 1920;

'the Act of 1950' means the Maintenance Orders Act 1950;

'the Act of 1958' means the Maintenance Orders Act 1958;

'the Act of 1965' means the Matrimonial Causes Act 1965;

'the Act of 1971' means the Attachment of Earnings Act 1971;

'the Act of 1972' means the Maintenance Orders (Reciprocal Enforcement) Act 1972;

'English maintenance order' means a maintenance order made in the High Court.

**[3.483]**

### 7.17 Registration etc of orders under Act of 1920

(1) The prescribed officer for the purposes of section 1(1) of the Act of 1920 shall be the senior district judge, and on receiving from the Secretary of State a copy of a maintenance order made by a court in any part of Her Majesty's dominions outside the United Kingdom to which the Act of 1920 extends he shall cause the order to be registered in the register kept for the purpose of that Act (in this rule referred to as 'the register').

The copy of the order received from the Secretary of State shall be filed in the principal registry.

(2) An application for the transmission of an English maintenance order under section 2 of the Act of 1920 shall be made to the district judge by lodging in the principal registry a certified copy of the order and an affidavit stating the applicant's reasons for believing that the person liable to make payments under the order is resident in some part of Her Majesty's dominions outside the United Kingdom to which the Act of 1920 extends, together with full particulars, so far as known to the applicant, of that person's address and occupation and any other information which may be required by the law of that part of Her Majesty's dominions for the purpose of the enforcement of the order.

(3) If it appears to the district judge mentioned in paragraph (2) that the person liable to make payments under the English maintenance order is resident in some part of Her Majesty's dominions outside the United Kingdom to which the Act of 1920 extends, he shall send the certified copy of the order to the Secretary of State for transmission to the Governor of that part of Her Majesty's dominions.

Particulars of any English maintenance order sent to the Secretary of State under the said section 2 shall be entered in the register and the fact that this has been done shall be noted in the records of the court.

(4) Where an English maintenance order has been made in a cause or matter proceeding in a district registry, an application for the transmission of the order under the said section 2 may be made to the district judge of that registry and paragraphs (2) and (3) of this rule shall have effect as if for reference to the principal registry there were substituted references to the district registry.

The proper officer shall send to the principal registry for entry in the register particulars of any order sent by him to the Secretary of State.

(5) Any person who satisfies a district judge that he is entitled to or liable to make payments under an English maintenance order or a maintenance order made by a court in any part of Her Majesty's dominions outside the United Kingdom to which the Act of 1920 extends or a solicitor acting on behalf of any such person or, with the leave of a district judge, any other person may inspect the register and bespeak copies of any order which has been registered and of any document filed therewith.



**[3.484]**

*Proceedings under Part II of Act of 1950*

### 7.18 Interpretation of rules 7.18 to 7.21

In this rule and rules 7.19 to 7.21—

'the clerk of the Court of Session' means the deputy principal clerk in charge of the petition department of the Court of Session;

'maintenance order' means a maintenance order to which section 16 of the Act of 1950 applies;

'Northern Irish order' means a maintenance order made by the Supreme Court of Northern Ireland;

'register' means the register kept for the purposes of the Act of 1950;

'the registrar in Northern Ireland' means the chief registrar of the Queen's Bench Division (Matrimonial) of the High Court of Justice in Northern Ireland;

'registration' means registration under Part II of the Act of 1950 and 'registered' shall be construed accordingly;

'Scottish order' means a maintenance order made by the Court of Session.

**[3.485]**

### 7.19 Registration etc of English order

(1) An application for the registration of an English maintenance order may be made by lodging with the proper officer a certified copy of the order, together with an affidavit by the applicant (and a copy thereof) stating—

(a) the address in the United Kingdom, and the occupation, of the person liable to make payments under the order;

(b) the date of service of the order on the person liable to make payments thereunder or, if the order has not been served, the reason why service has not been effected;

(c) the reason why it is convenient that the order should be enforceable in Scotland or Northern Ireland, as the case may be;

(d) the amount of any arrears due to the applicant under the order; and
(e) that the order is not already registered.

(2) If it appears to the district judge that the person liable to make payments under the order resides in Scotland or Northern Ireland and that it is convenient that the order should be enforceable there, the proper officer shall (subject to paragraph (6) below) send a certified copy of the order and the applicant's affidavit to the clerk of the Court of Session or to the registrar in Northern Ireland, as the case may be.

(3) On receipt of notice of the registration of an English maintenance order in the Court of Session or the Supreme Court of Northern Ireland, the proper officer shall—
(a) cause particulars of the notice to be entered in the register;
(b) note the fact of registration in the records of the court; and
(c) send particulars of the notice to the principal registry.

(4) Where an English order registered in the Court of Session or the Supreme Court of Northern Ireland is discharged or varied the proper officer of the court ordering the discharge or variation shall give notice thereof to the clerk of the Court of Session or to the registrar in Northern Ireland, as the case may be, by sending him a certified copy of the order discharging or varying the maintenance order.

(5) Where the registration of an English maintenance order registered in the Court of Session or the Supreme Court of Northern Ireland is cancelled under section 24(1) of the Act of 1950, notice of the cancellation shall be sent (as required by section 24(3)(a) of that Act) to the proper officer; and on receipt of such notice he shall cause particulars of it to be entered in Part I of the register.

(6) Where the order sought to be registered was made in a county court, this rule shall apply as though references to the Court of Session, the clerk of the Court of Session, the Supreme Court of Northern Ireland and the registrar of Northern Ireland were references to the sheriff court, the sheriff-clerk of the sheriff court, the court of summary jurisdiction and the clerk of the court of summary jurisdiction respectively.

**[3.486]**

### 7.20 Registration etc of Scottish and Northern Irish orders

(1) In relation to a Scottish or Northern Irish order the prescribed officer for the purposes of section 17(2) of the Act of 1950 shall be the proper officer of the principal registry.

(2) On receipt of a certified copy of a Scottish or Northern Irish order for registration, the proper officer shall—
(a) cause the order to be registered in Part II of the register and notify the clerk of the Court of Session or the registrar in Northern Ireland, as the case may be, that this has been done; and
(b) file the certified copy and any statutory declaration or affidavit as to the amount of any arrears due under the order.

(3) An application [under section 21(2)] of the Act of 1950 by a person liable to make payments under a Scottish order registered in the High Court to adduce before that court such evidence as is mentioned in that section shall be made by lodging a request for an appointment before a district judge of the principal registry; and notice of the date, time and place fixed for the hearing shall be sent by post to the applicant and to the person entitled to payments under the order.

(4) The prescribed officer to whom notice of the discharge or variation of a Scottish or Northern Irish order registered in the High Court is to be given under section 23(1)(a) of the Act of 1950 shall be the proper officer, and on receipt of the notice he shall cause particulars of it to be registered in Part II of the register.

(5) An application under section 24(1) of the Act of 1950 for the cancellation of the registration of a Scottish or Northern Irish order shall be made ex parte by affidavit to district judge of the principal registry who, if he cancels the registration, shall note the cancellation in Part II of the register, whereupon the proper officer shall send notice of

the cancellation to the clerk of the Court of Session or the registrar in Northern Ireland, as the case may be, and also to the clerk of any magistrates' court in which the order has been registered in accordance with section 2(5) of the Act of 1958.

(6) A person entitled to payments under a Scottish or Northern Irish order registered in the High Court who wishes to take proceedings for or with respect to the enforcement of the order in a district registry may apply by letter to the senior district judge of the principal registry who may, if satisfied that the order ought to be enforceable in the district registry, make an order accordingly on such terms, if any, as may be just.

**Amendment**

Para (3): SI 1997/1893.

**[3.487]**

## 7.21 Inspection of register

Any person who satisfies a district judge of the principal registry that he is entitled to or liable to make payments under a maintenance order of a superior court or a solicitor acting on behalf of any such person or, with the leave of the district judge, any other person may inspect the register and bespeak copies of any such order which is registered in the High Court under Part II of the Act of 1950 and of any statutory declaration or affidavit filed therewith.



**[3.488]**

*Registration etc of certain orders under the Act of 1958*

## 7.22 Application and interpretation of rules 7.22 to 7.29

Section 21 of the Act of 1958 shall apply to the interpretation of this rule and rules 7.23 to 7.29 as it applies to the interpretation of that Act; and in those rules—

'cause book' includes cause card; and

'the register' means any register kept for the purposes of the Act of 1958.

**[3.489]**

## 7.23 Application for registration

(1) An application under section 2(1) of the Act of 1958 for the registration in a magistrates' court of a maintenance order shall be made by lodging with the proper officer—

(i) a certified copy of the maintenance order, and

(ii) two copies of the application in Form [M33].

(2) The period required to be prescribed by rules of court for the purpose of section 2(2) of the Act of 1958 shall be 14 days.

(3) The proper officer shall cause the certified copy of an order required by the said section 2(2) to be sent to the justices' chief executive for a magistrates' court to be endorsed with a note that the application for registration of the order has been granted and to be accompanied by a copy of the application lodged under paragraph (1).

(4) On receipt of notice that a maintenance order has been registered in a magistrates' court in accordance with section 2(5) of the Act of 1958, the proper officer shall enter particulars of the registration in the records of the court.

**Amendment**

Para (1): SI 1992/2067. Para (3): SI 2001/821.

[3.490]

### 7.24 Registration in a magistrates' court of an order registered in the High Court

On receipt of notice that a maintenance order registered in the High Court in accordance with section 17(4) of the Act of 1950 has been registered in a magistrates' court in accordance with section 2(5) of the Act of 1958, the proper officer shall cause particulars of the registration to be entered in Part II of the register.

[3.491]

### 7.25 Registration of magistrates' court order

On receipt of a certified copy of a magistrates' court order sent to him pursuant to section 2(4)(c) of the Act of 1958, the proper officer shall cause the order to be registered in the High Court by filing the copy and making an entry in the register where the copy order is received in a district registry, in the cause book and shall send notice to the justices' chief executive for the magistrates' court that the order has been duly registered.

[3.492]

### 7.26 Registration in the High Court of an order registered in a magistrates' court

(1) This rule applies where a sheriff court in Scotland or a magistrates' court in Northern Ireland has made an order for the registration in the High Court of an order previously registered in a magistrates' court in England and Wales in accordance with section 17(4) of the Act of 1950, and has sent a certified copy of the maintenance order to the proper officer of the High Court, pursuant to section 2(4)(c) of the Act of 1958.

(2) On receipt of the certified copy, the proper officer shall cause the order to be registered in the High Court by filing the copy and making an entry in the register, and shall send notice of the registration to the clerk of the original court and also to the justices' chief executive for the magistrates' court in which the order was registered in accordance with section 17(4) of the Act of 1950.

**Amendment**
SI 2001/821.

[3.493]

### 7.27 Variation or discharge of registered order

(1) Where the court makes an order varying or discharging an order registered in a magistrates' court under Part I of the Act of 1958, the proper officer shall send a certified copy of the first-mentioned order to the justices' chief executive for the magistrates' court.

(2) Where a certified copy of an order varying an order registered in a magistrates' court under Part I of the Act of 1958 is received from the justices' chief executive for the magistrates' court, the proper officer shall file the copy and enter particulars of the variation on the same documents or in the same records as particulars of registration are required by rule 7.23(4) to be entered.

(3) Where a certified copy of an order varying or discharging an order made by a magistrates' court and registered in the High Court under Part I of the Act of 1958 is received from the justices' chief executive for the magistrates' court, the proper officer shall—

(a) file the copy,
(b) enter particulars of the variation or discharge in the register or, where the copy order is received in a district registry, in the cause book, and
(c) send notice of the variation or discharge to any proper officer of a county court—
  (i) who has given notice to the proper officer of proceedings taken in that court for the enforcement of the registered order, or
  (ii) to whom any payment is to be made under an attachment of earnings order made by the High Court for the enforcement of the registered order.

**Amendment**
SI 2001/821.

**[3.493.1]**
**Keypoint**
- Procedure

**[3.493.2]**
**Procedure**
This paragraph sets out the procedure for variation and discharge of registered orders. The subject has been considered recently in *K v M, M and L (Financial Relief: Foreign Orders)*[1] and *Hackshaw v Hackshaw*[2].

1 [1998] 2 FLR 59, [1998] Fam Law 396.
2 [1999] 3 FCR 451, [1999] 2 FLR 876.



**[3.494]**

### 7.28 Appeal from variation etc of order by magistrates' court

An appeal to the High Court under section 4(7) of the Act of 1958 shall be heard and determined by a Divisional Court of the Family Division, and rule 8.2 shall apply as it applies in relation to an appeal from a magistrates' court under the Domestic Proceedings and Magistrates' Courts Act 1978.

**[3.494.1]**
**Keypoint**
- Nature of appeal

**[3.494.2]**
**Nature of appeal**
See *Hackshaw v Hackshaw*[1]: the appeal itself is not a hearing of the matter afresh.

1 [1999] 3 FCR 451, [1999] 2 FLR 876.

**[3.495]**

### 7.29 Cancellation of registration

(1) A notice under section 5 of the Act of 1958 by a person entitled to receive payments under an order registered in the High Court must be given to the proper officer.

(2) Where the High Court gives notice under the said section 5, the proper officer shall endorse the notice on the certified copy mentioned in rule 7.27(1).

(3) Where notice under the said section 5 is given in respect of an order registered in the High Court, the proper officer on being satisfied by an affidavit by the person

entitled to receive payments under the order that no process for the enforcement of the order issued before the giving of the notice remains in force, shall—

(a) cancel the registration by entering particulars of the notice in the register or cause book, as the case may be, and

(b) send notice of the cancellation to the justices' chief executive for the court by which the order was made and, where applicable, to the justices' chief executive for the magistrates' court in which the order was registered in accordance with section 17(4) of the Act of 1950 stating, if such be the case, that the cancellation is in consequence of a notice given under subsection (1) of the said section 5.

(4) On receipt of notice from the justices' chief executive for a magistrates' court that the registration in that court under the Act of 1958 of an order made by the High Court or a county court has been cancelled, the proper officer shall enter particulars of the cancellation on the same documents or in the same records as particulars of registration are required by rule 7.23(4) to be entered.

(5) On receipt of notice from the justices' chief executive for a magistrates' court that the registration in that court under the Act of 1958 of an order registered in the High Court in accordance with section 17(4) of the Act of 1950 has been cancelled, the proper officer shall note the cancellation in Part II of the register.

**Amendment**
SI 2001/821.

**[3.496]**

*Proceedings under Act of 1972*

### 7.30 Interpretation of rules 7.31 to 7.39

[(1)] Expressions used in rules 7.31 to [7.39] which are used in the Act of 1972 have the same meanings as in that Act.

[(2) The references in the Act of 1972 to the prescribed officer shall be construed as references to the proper officer within the meaning of rule 1.2(1).

(3) The reference in section 21 of the Act of 1972 to the proper officer shall be the proper officer within the meaning of rule 1.2(1).]

**Amendment**
SI 1996/816.

**[3.497]**

### 7.31 Application for transmission of maintenance order to reciprocating country

An application for a maintenance order to be sent to a reciprocating country under section 2 of the Act of 1972 shall be made by lodging with the court—

(a) an affidavit by the applicant stating—

  (i) the applicant's reason for believing that the payer under the maintenance order is residing in that country, and

  (ii) the amount of any arrears due to the applicant under the order, the date to which those arrears have been calculated and the date on which the next payment under the order falls due;

(b) a certified copy of the maintenance order;

(c) a statement giving such information as the applicant possesses as to the whereabouts of the payer;

(d) a statement giving such information as the applicant possesses for facilitating the identification of the payer (including, if known to the applicant, the name and address of any employer of the payer, his occupation and the date and place of issue of any passport of the payer) and

(e) if available to the applicant, a photograph of the payer.

**[3.498]**

### 7.32 Certification of evidence given on provisional order

Where the court makes a provisional order under section 5 of the Act of 1972, the document required by subsection (4) of that section to set out or summarise the evidence given in the proceedings shall be authenticated by a certificate signed by the district judge.

**[3.499]**

### 7.33 Confirmation of provisional order

(1) On receipt of a certified copy of a provisional order made in a reciprocating country, together with the document mentioned in section 5(5) of the Act of 1972, the proper officer shall fix a date, time and place for the court to consider whether or not the provisional order should be confirmed, and shall send to the payee under the maintenance order notice of the date, time and place so fixed together with a copy of the provisional order and that document.

(2) The proper officer shall send to the court which made the provisional order a certified copy of any order confirming or refusing to confirm that order.



**[3.500]**

### 7.34 Taking of evidence for court in reciprocating country

(1) The High Court shall be the prescribed court for the purposes of taking evidence pursuant to a request by a court in a reciprocating country under section 14 of the Act of 1972 where—

(a) the request for evidence relates to a maintenance order made by a superior court in the United Kingdom, and

(b) the witness resides in England and Wales.

(2) The evidence may be taken before a judge or officer of the High Court as the court thinks fit, and the provisions of RSC Order 39 shall apply with the necessary modifications as if the evidence were required to be taken pursuant to an order made under rule 1 of that Order.

(3) The county court shall be the prescribed court for the purposes of taking evidence pursuant to a request by a court in a reciprocating country pursuant to section 14 of the Act of 1972 where the request for evidence relates to a maintenance order made by a county court which has not been registered in a magistrates' court under the Act of 1958.

(4) Paragraph (2) shall apply to the taking of such evidence as though references therein to the High Court and RSC Order 39 were to the county court and CCR Order 20, rule 13 respectively.

**[3.501]**

### 7.35 Notification of variation or revocation

Where the court makes an order (other than a provisional order) varying or revoking a maintenance order a copy of which has been sent to a reciprocating country in pursuance of section 2 of the Act of 1972, the proper officer shall send a certified copy of the order to the court in the reciprocating country.

**[3.502]**

### 7.36 Transmission of documents

Any document required to be sent to a court in a reciprocating country under section 5(4) or section 14(1) of the Act of 1972 or by rule 7.33(2) or 7.36 shall be sent to the Secretary of State for transmission to that court unless the district judge is satisfied that, in accordance with the law of that country, the document may properly be sent by him direct to that court.

**[3.503]**

### 7.37 Application of rules 7.30 to 7.36 to Republic of Ireland

(1) In relation to the Republic of Ireland rules 7.30 to 7.36 shall have effect subject to the provisions of this rule.

[(1A) A reference to the Act of 1972 in this rule, and in any rule which has effect in relation to the Republic of Ireland by virtue of this rule, shall be a reference to the said Act as modified by Schedule 2 to the Reciprocal Enforcement of Maintenance Orders (Republic of Ireland) Order 1993.]

(2) The following paragraphs shall be added to rule 7.31—

'(f) a statement as to whether or not the payer appeared in the proceedings in which the maintenance order was made and, if he did not, the original or a copy certified by the applicant or his solicitor to be a true copy of a document which establishes that notice of the institution of the proceedings was served on the payer;

(g) a document which establishes that notice of the order was sent to the payer; and;

(h) if the payer received legal aid in the proceedings in which the order was made, a copy certified by the applicant or his solicitor to be a true copy of the legal aid certificate.'.

(3) For rule 7.32 there shall be substituted the following rule—

### '7.32 Certification of evidence given on application for variation or revocation

(1) Where an application is made to the court for the variation or revocation of an order to which section 5 of the Act of 1972 applies, the certified copy of the application and the documents required by [subsection (3)] of that section to set out or summarise the evidence in support of the application shall be authenticated by a certificate signed by the district judge.'.

(4) Rule 7.33 shall not apply.

(5) For rule 7.35 there shall be substituted the following rule—

### '7.35 Notification of variation or revocation

Where the High Court makes an order varying or revoking a maintenance order to which section 5 of the Act of 1972 applies, the proper officer shall send a certified copy of the order and a statement as to the service on the payer of the documents mentioned in [subsection (3)] of that section to the court in the Republic of Ireland by which the maintenance order is being enforced.'.

(6) Rule 7.36 shall not apply.

**Amendment**

SI 1996/816.

[3.504]

### 7.38 Application of rules 7.30 to 7.36 to the Hague Convention countries

(1) In relation to the Hague Convention countries, rules 7.30, 7.31, 7.34, 7.35 and 7.36 shall have effect subject to the provisions of this rule, but rules 7.32 and 7.33 shall not apply.

[(1A) A reference to the Act of 1972 in this rule, and in any rule which has effect in relation to the Hague Convention countries by virtue of this rule, shall be a reference to the said Act as modified by Schedule 3 to the Reciprocal Enforcement of Maintenance Orders (Hague Convention Countries) Order 1993.]

(2) A reference in rules 7.31 and 7.34 to a reciprocating country shall be construed as a reference to a Hague Convention country.

(3) The following words shall be inserted after paragraph (a)(ii) of rule 7.31—

'and (iii) whether the time for appealing against the order has expired and whether an appeal is pending;'.

(4) The following paragraphs shall be inserted after paragraph (e) of rule 7.31—

'(f) a statement as to whether or not the payer appeared in the proceedings in which the maintenance order was made, and, if he did not, the original or a copy certified by the applicant or his solicitor to be a true copy of a document which establishes that notice of the institution of proceedings, including notice of the substance of the claim, was served on the payer;

(g) a document which establishes that notice of the order was sent to the payer;

(h) a written statement as to whether or not the payee received legal aid in the proceedings in which the order was made, or in connection with the application under section 2 of the Act of 1972 and, if he did, a copy certified by the applicant or his solicitor to be a true copy of the legal aid certificate.'.

(5) In relation to the Hague Convention countries the following rules shall apply in place of rules 7.35 and 7.36—

### '7.35 Notification of variation or revocation

(1) Where the court makes an order varying or revoking a maintenance order to which section 5 of the Act of 1972, as modified, applies, and the time for appealing has expired without an appeal having been entered, the proper officer shall send to the Secretary of State such documents as are required by [subsection (8)] of that section, as it applies to Hague Convention countries, including a certificate signed by the district judge that the order of variation or revocation is enforceable and that it is no longer subject to the ordinary forms of review.

(2) Where either party enters an appeal against the order of variation or revocation he shall, at the same time, inform the proper officer thereof by a notice in writing.

### 7.36 Transmission of documents

Any document required to be sent to a court in a Hague Convention country shall be sent to the Secretary of State for transmission to the court.'.

**Amendment**

SI 1996/816.

[3.505]

### [7.39 Application of rules 7.30 to 7.36 to a Specified State of the United States of America]

(1) In this rule unless the context otherwise requires—

'specified State' means a State of the United States of America specified in Schedule 1 to the Reciprocal Enforcement of Maintenance Orders (United States of America) Order 1995.

(2) In relation to a specified State, rules 7.30, 7.31, 7.34, 7.35 and 7.36 shall have effect subject to the provisions of this rule, but rules 7.32 and 7.33 shall not apply.

(3) A reference to the Act of 1972 in this rule, and in any rule which has effect in relation to a specified State by virtue of this rule, shall be a reference to the said Act as modified by Schedule 3 to the Reciprocal Enforcement of Maintenance Orders (United States of America) Order 1995.

(4) A reference in rules 7.31 and 7.34 to a reciprocating country shall be construed as a reference to a specified State.

(5) Paragraph (c) of rule 7.31 shall not apply to a specified State.

(6) The following paragraphs shall be inserted after paragraph (a)(ii) of rule 7.31—

'(iii) the address of the payee;

(iv) such information as is known as to the whereabouts of the payer; and

(v) a description, so far as is known, of the nature and location of any assets of the payer available for execution.'.

(7) A reference in paragraph (b) of rule 7.31 to a certified copy shall be construed as a reference to 3 certified copies.

(8) In relation to a specified State the following rules shall apply in place of rules 7.35 and 7.36—

### '7.35 Notification of variation of revocation

Where the court makes an order varying or revoking a maintenance order to which section 5 of the Act of 1972, as modified, applies, the proper officer shall send to the Secretary of State such documents as are required by subsection (7) of that section, as it applies to specified States.

### 7.36 Transmission of documents

Any document required to be sent to a court in a specified State shall be sent to the Secretary of State for transmission to the court.'.'

**Amendment**

Inserted by SI 1996/816, r 8.

## [3.505A]

CHAPTER 5

REGISTRATION AND ENFORCEMENT UNDER THE COUNCIL REGULATION

### 7.40 Interpretation

In this chapter 'judgment' is to be construed in accordance with the definition in Article 13 of the Council Regulation.

**Amendment**

Inserted by SI 2001/821.

## [3.505A.1]
**Keypoint**

- Council Regulation

## [3.505A.2]
**Council Regulation**

Council Regulation (EC) No 1347/2000 of 29 May 2000 ('Brussels II') is set out at para **[3.656A]** below.

[3.505B]

### 7.41 Filing of applications

Every application to the High Court under the Council Regulation, other than an application under rule 7.49 for a certified copy of a judgment, shall be filed with the principal registry.

**Amendment**
Inserted by SI 2001/821.

[3.505B.1]
**Keypoint**
- Council Regulation

[3.505B.2]
**Council Regulation**
Council Regulation (EC) No 1347/2000 of 29 May 2000 ('Brussels II') is set out at para **[3.656A]** below.



[3.505C]

### 7.42 Application for registration

An application for registration of a judgment under Article 21(2) of the Council Regulation shall be made without notice being served on any other party.

**Amendment**
Inserted by SI 2001/821.

[3.505C.1]
**Keypoint**
- Council Regulation

[3.505C.2]
**Council Regulation**
Council Regulation (EC) No 1347/2000 of 29 May 2000 ('Brussels II') is set out at para **[3.656A]** below.

[3.505D]

### 7.43 Evidence in support of application

(1) An application for registration under Article 21(2) of the Council Regulation must be supported by a statement that is sworn to be true or an affidavit—
- (a) exhibiting—
  - (i) the judgment or a verified or certified or otherwise duly authenticated copy thereof together with such other document or documents as may be requisite to show that, according to the law of the Contracting State in which it has been given, the judgment is enforceable and has been served;
  - (ii) in the case of a judgment given in default, the original or a certified true copy of the document which establishes that the party in default was served with the document instituting the proceedings or with an equivalent document;
  - (iii) where it is the case, a document showing that the party making the application is in receipt of legal aid in the Contracting State in which the judgment was given;

(iv) where the judgment or document is not in the English language, a translation thereof into English certified by a notary public or a person qualified for the purpose in one of the Contracting States or authenticated by witness statement or affidavit;

(v) the certificate, in the form set out in Annex IV or Annex V of the Council Regulation, issued by the Contracting State in which judgment was given;

(b) stating—

(i) whether the judgment provides for the payment of a sum or sums of money;

(ii) whether interest is recoverable on the judgment or part thereof in accordance with the law of the State in which the judgment was given, and if such be the case, the rate of interest, the date from which interest is recoverable, and the date on which interest ceases to accrue;

(c) giving an address within the jurisdiction of the court for service of process on the party making the application and stating, so far as is known to the witness, the name and the usual or last known address or place of business of the person against whom judgment was given; and

(d) stating to the best of the information or belief of the witness—

(i) the grounds on which the right to enforce the judgment is vested in the party making the application;

(ii) as the case may require, either that at that date of the application the judgment has not been satisfied, or the part or amount in respect of which it remains unsatisfied.

(2) Where the party making the application does not produce the documents referred to in paragraphs 1(a)(ii) and (iii) of this rule, the court may—

(a) fix a time within which the documents are to be produced;

(b) accept equivalent documents; or

(c) dispense with production of the documents.

**Amendment**

Inserted by SI 2001/821.

**[3.505D.1]**

**Keypoint**

- Council Regulation

**[3.505D.2]**

**Council Regulation**

Council Regulation (EC) No 1347/2000 of 29 May 2000 ('Brussels II') is set out at para **[3.656A]** below.

**[3.505E]**

### 7.44 Order for registration

(1) An order giving permission to register a judgment under Article 21(2) of the Council Regulation must be drawn up by the court.

(2) Every such order shall state the period within which an appeal may be made against the order for registration and shall contain a notification that the court will not enforce the judgment until after the expiration of that period.

(3) The notification referred to in paragraph (2) shall not prevent any application for protective measures under Article 12 of the Council Regulation pending final determination of any issue relating to enforcement of the judgment.

**Amendment**

Inserted by SI 2001/821.

**[3.505E.1]**
**Keypoint**
- Council Regulation

**[3.505E.2]**
**Council Regulation**

Council Regulation (EC) No 1347/2000 of 29 May 2000 ('Brussels II') is set out at para **[3.656A]** below.

**[3.505F]**

### 7.45 Register of judgments

There shall be kept in the principal registry by the proper officer a register of the judgments ordered to be registered under Article 21(2) of the Council Regulation.

**Amendment**
Inserted by SI 2001/821.

**[3.505F.1]**
**Keypoint**
- Council Regulation

**[3.505F.2]**
**Council Regulation**

Council Regulation (EC) No 1347/2000 of 29 May 2000 ('Brussels II') is set out at para **[3.656A]** below.

**[3.505G]**

### 7.46 Notice of registration

(1) Notice of the registration of a judgment under Article 21(2) of the Council Regulation must be served on the person against whom judgment was given by delivering it to him personally or by sending it to him at his usual or last known address or place of business or in such other manner as the court may direct.

(2) Permission is not required to serve such a notice out of the jurisdiction and rule 10.6 shall apply in relation to such a notice.

(3) The notice of the registration must state—

(a) full particulars of the judgment registered and the order for registration;

(b) the name of the party making the application and his address for service within the jurisdiction;

(c) the right of the person against whom judgment was given to appeal against the order for registration; and

(d) the period within which an appeal against the order for registration may be made.

**Amendment**
Inserted by SI 2001/821.

**[3.505G.1]**
**Keypoint**
- Council Regulation

**[3.505G.2]**
**Council Regulation**

Council Regulation (EC) No 1347/2000 of 29 May 2000 ('Brussels II') is set out at para **[3.656A]** below.

**[3.505H]**

### 7.47 Enforcement of judgment

(1) A judgment registered under Article 21(2) of the Council Regulation shall not be enforced until after the expiration of the period specified in accordance with rule 7.44(2) or, if that period has been extended by the Court, until after the expiration of the period so extended.

(2) Any party wishing to apply for the enforcement of a judgment registered under Article 21(2) of the Council Regulation must produce to the proper officer a witness statement or affidavit of service of the notice of registration of the judgment and of any order made by the court in relation to the judgment.

(3) Nothing in this rule shall prevent the court from granting protective measures under Article 12 of the Council Regulation pending final determination of any issue relating to enforcement of the judgment.

**Amendment**
Inserted by SI 2001/821.

**[3.505H.1]**
**Keypoint**

- Council Regulation

**[3.505H.2]**
**Council Regulation**

Council Regulation (EC) No 1347/2000 of 29 May 2000 ('Brussels II') is set out at para **[3.656A]** below.

**[3.505I]**

### 7.48 Application for recognition

(1) Registration of the judgment under these rules shall serve for the purposes of Article 14(3) of the Council Regulation as a decision that the judgment is recognised.

(2) Where it is sought to apply for recognition of a judgment, the rules of this chapter shall apply to such application as they apply to an application for registration under Article 21(2) of the Council Regulation, with the exception that the applicant shall not be required to produce—

(a) a document or documents which establish that according to the law of the Contracting State in which it has been given the judgment is enforceable and has been served, or

(b) the document referred to in rule 7.43(1)(a)(iii).

**Amendment**
Inserted by SI 2001/821.

**[3.505I.1]**
**Keypoint**

- Council Regulation

**[3.505I.2]**
**Council Regulation**
Council Regulation (EC) No 1347/2000 of 29 May 2000 ('Brussels II') is set out at para **[3.656A]** below.

**[3.505J]**

### 7.49 Enforcement of judgments in other Contracting States

(1) Subject to rules 10.16(2) and 10.20, an application for a certified copy of a judgment referred to in Article 32(1) of the Council Regulation must be made to the court which made the order on a witness statement or affidavit without notice being served on any other party.

(2) A witness statement or affidavit by which such an application is made must—

(a) give particulars of the proceedings in which the judgment was obtained;

(b) have annexed to it a copy of the petition or application by which the proceedings were begun, the evidence of service thereof on the respondent, copies of the pleadings and particulars, if any, and a statement of the grounds on which the judgment was based together, where appropriate, with any document showing that the applicant is entitled to legal aid or assistance by way of representation for the purposes of the proceedings;

(c) state whether the respondent did or did not object to the jurisdiction, and, if so, on what grounds;

(d) show that the judgment has been served in accordance with rules 4.8, 10.2, 10.3, 10.4, 10.5, 10.6, 10.16 or 10.17 and is not subject to any order for the stay of proceedings;

(e) state that the time for appealing has expired, or, as the case may be, the date on which it will expire and in either case whether notice of appeal against the judgment has been given; and

(f) state—

(i) whether the judgment provides for the payment of a sum of money;

(ii) whether interest is recoverable on the judgment or part thereof and if so, the rate of interest, the date from which interest is recoverable, and the date on which interest ceases to accrue.

(3) The certified copy of the judgment shall be an office copy sealed with the seal of the court and signed by the district judge and there shall be issued with the copy of the judgment a certified copy of any order which was varied any of the terms of the original order.

**Amendment**
Inserted by SI 2001/821.



**[3.505J.1]**
**Keypoint**
- Council Regulation

**[3.505J.2]**
**Council Regulation**
Council Regulation (EC) No 1347/2000 of 29 May 2000 ('Brussels II') is set out at para **[3.656A]** below.

**[3.505K]**

### 7.50 Authentic instruments and court settlements

Rules 7.40 to 7.49 (except rule 7.43(1)(a)(ii)) shall apply to an authentic instrument and a settlement to which Article 13(3) of the Council Regulation applies, as they apply to a judgment subject to any necessary modifications.

**Amendment**
Inserted by SI 2001/821.

**[3.505K.1]**
**Keypoint**
- Council Regulation

**[3.505K.2]**
**Council Regulation**
Council Regulation (EC) No 1347/2000 of 29 May 2000 ('Brussels II') is set out at para **[3.656A]** below.

**[3.506]**

## PART VIII
## APPEALS

### 8.1 Appeals from district judges

(1) Except where paragraph (2) applies, any party may appeal from an order or decision made or given by the district judge in family proceedings in a county court to a judge on notice; and in such a case—

(a) CCR Order 13, rule 1(10) (which enables the judge to vary or rescind an order made by the district judge in the course of proceedings), and

(b) CCR Order 37, rule 6 (which gives a right of appeal to the judge from a judgment or final decision of the district judge),

shall not apply to the order or decision.

(2) Any order or decision granting or varying an order (or refusing to do so)—

(a) on an application for ancillary relief, or

(b) in proceedings to which rules 3.1, 3.2, 3.3 [or 3.6] apply,

shall be treated as a final order for the purposes of CCR Order 37, rule 6.

(3) On hearing an appeal to which paragraph (2) above applies, the judge may exercise his own discretion in substitution for that of the district judge.

(4) Unless the court otherwise orders, any notice under this rule must be issued within 14 days of the order or decision appealed against and served not less than 14 days before the day fixed for the hearing of the appeal.

(5) Appeals under this rule shall be heard in chambers unless the judge otherwise directs.

(6) Unless the court otherwise orders, an appeal under this rule shall not operate as a stay of proceedings on the order or decision appealed against.

**Amendment**
SI 1997/1893.

**[3.507]**

### [8.1A Appeals from orders made under Part IV of the Family Law Act 1996]

[(1) This rule applies to all appeals from orders made under Part IV of the Family Law Act 1996 and on such an appeal—

(a) paragraphs (2), (3), (4), (5), (7) and (8) of rule 4.22,
(b) paragraphs (5) and (6) of rule 8.1, and
(c) paragraphs (4)(e) and (6) of rule 8.2,

shall apply subject to the following provisions of this rule and with the necessary modifications.

(2) The justices' chief executive for the magistrates' court from which an appeal is brought shall be served with the documents mentioned in rule 4.22(2).

(3) Where an appeal lies to the High Court, the documents required to be filed by rule 4.22(2) shall be filed in the registry of the High Court which is nearest to the magistrates' court from which the appeal is brought.

(4) Where the appeal is brought against the making of a hospital order or a guardianship order under the Mental Health Act 1983, a copy of any written evidence considered by the magistrates' court under section 37(1)(a) of the 1983 Act shall be sent by the justices' chief executive to the registry of the High Court in which the documents relating to the appeal are filed in accordance with paragraph (3).

(5) A district judge may dismiss an appeal to which this rule applies for want of prosecution and may deal with any question of costs arising out of the dismissal or withdrawal of an appeal.

(6) Any order or decision granting or varying an order (or refusing to do so) in proceedings in which an application is made in accordance with rule 3.8 for—

(a) an occupation order as described in section 33(4) of the Family Law Act 1996,
(b) an occupation order containing any of the provisions specified in section 33(3) where the applicant or the respondent has matrimonial home rights, or
(c) a transfer of tenancy,

shall be treated as a final order for the purposes of CCR Order 37, rule 6 and, on an appeal from such an order, the judge may exercise his own discretion in substitution for that of the district judge and the provisions of CCR Order 37, rule 6 shall apply.]

**Amendment**

Inserted, in relation to proceedings commenced after 1 October 1997, by SI 1997/1893, rr 7, 9. Amended by SI 2001/821.



**[3.508]**

### 8.2 Appeals under Domestic Proceedings and Magistrates Courts' Act 1978

(1) Subject to paragraph (9) below, every appeal to the High Court under the Domestic Proceedings and Magistrates' Courts Act 1978 shall be heard by a Divisional Court of the Family Division and shall be entered by lodging three copies of the notice of motion in the principal registry.

(2) The notice must be served, and the appeal entered, within 6 weeks after the date of the order appealed against.

(3) Notice of the motion may be served in accordance with RSC Order 65, rule 5.

(4) On entering the appeal, or as soon as practicable thereafter, the appellant shall, unless otherwise directed, lodge in the principal registry—

(a) three certified copies of the summons and of the order appealed against, and of any order staying its execution,
(b) three copies of the clerk's notes of the evidence,
(c) three copies of the justices' reasons for their decision,
(d) a certificate that notice of the motion has been duly served on the clerk and on every party affected by the appeal, and
(e) where the notice of the motion includes an application to extend the time for bringing the appeal, a certificate (and a copy thereof by the appellant's solicitor, or the appellant if he is acting in person, setting out the reasons for the delay and the relevant dates.

(5) If the clerk's notes of the evidence are not produced, the court may hear and determine the appeal on any other evidence or statement of what occurred in the proceedings before the magistrates' court as appears to the court to be sufficient.

(6) The court shall not be bound to allow the appeal on the ground merely of misdirection or improper reception or rejection of evidence unless, in the opinion of the court, substantial wrong or miscarriage of justice has been thereby occasioned.

(7) A district judge may dismiss an appeal to which this rule applies for want of prosecution or, with the consent of the parties, may dismiss the appeal or give leave for it to be withdrawn, and may deal with any question of costs arising out of the dismissal or withdrawal.

(8) Any interlocutory application in connection with or for the purpose of any appeal to which this rule applies may be heard and disposed of before a single judge.

(9) Where an appeal to which this rule applies relates only to the amount of any periodical or lump sum payment ordered to be made, it shall, unless the President otherwise directs, be heard and determined by a single judge, and in that case—

- (a) for the references in paragraphs (1) and (4)(a), (b) and (c) to three copies of the documents therein mentioned there shall be substituted references to one copy;
- (b) the parties may agree in writing or the President may direct that the appeal be heard and determined at a divorce town.

**[3.509]**

### [8.3 Appeals under section 13 of the Administration of Justice Act 1960]

[Proceedings within paragraph 3(d) of Schedule 1 to the Supreme Court Act 1981 shall be heard and determined by a Divisional Court of the Family Division and rule 8.2(4) shall apply, with the necessary modifications, to such proceedings.]

**Amendment**

Inserted by SI 1991/2113, r 15.

**[3.510]**

## PART X
## PROCEDURE (GENERAL)

### 10.1 Application

The provisions of this Part apply to all family proceedings, but have effect subject to the provisions of any other Part of these rules.

**[3.511]**

### 10.2 Service on solicitors

(1) Where a document is required by these rules to be sent to any person who is acting by a solicitor, service shall, subject to any other direction or order, be effected—

- (a) by sending the document by first class post to the solicitor's address for service; or
- (b) where that address includes a numbered box at a document exchange, at that document exchange or at a document exchange which transmits documents every business day to that document exchange; or
- (c) by FAX (as defined by RSC Order 1, rule 4(1)) in accordance with the provisions of RSC Order 65, rule 5(2B).

(2) Any document which is left at a document exchange in accordance with paragraph (1)(b) shall, unless the contrary is proved, be deemed to have been served on the second day after the day on which it is left.

(3) Where no other mode of service is prescribed, directed or ordered, service may additionally be effected by leaving the document at the solicitor's address.

**[3.512]**

### 10.3 Service on person acting in person

(1) Subject to paragraph (3) and to any other direction or order, where a document is required by these rules to be sent to any person who is acting in person, service shall be effected by sending the document by first class post to the address given by him or, if he has not given an address for service, to his last known address.

(2) Subject to paragraph (3), where no other mode of service is prescribed, directed or ordered, service may additionally be effected by delivering the document to him or by leaving it at the address specified in paragraph (1).

(3) Where it appears to the district judge that it is impracticable to deliver the document to the person to be served and that, if the document were left at, or sent by post to, the address specified in paragraph (1) it would be unlikely to reach him, the district judge may dispense with service of the document.



**[3.513]**

### 10.4 Service by bailiff in proceedings in principal registry

Where, in any proceedings pending in the principal registry which are treated as pending in a divorce county court, a document is to be served by bailiff, it shall be sent for service to the proper officer of the county court within the district of which the document is to be served.

**[3.514]**

### 10.5 Proof of service by officer of court etc

(1) Where a petition is sent to any person by an officer of the court, he shall note the date of posting in the records of the court.

(2) Without prejudice to section 133 of the County Courts Act 1984 (proof of service of summonses etc) a record made pursuant to paragraph (1) shall be evidence of the facts stated therein.

(3) Where the court has authorised notice by advertisement to be substituted for service and the advertisement has been inserted by some person other than the proper officer, that person shall file copies of the newspapers containing the advertisement.

**[3.515]**

### 10.6 Service out of England and Wales

(1) Any document in family proceedings may be served out of England and Wales without leave either in the manner prescribed by these rules or—

- (a) where the proceedings are pending in the High Court, in accordance with RSC Order 11, rules 5 and 6 (which relate to the service of a writ abroad); or
- (b) where the proceedings are pending in a divorce county court, in accordance with CCR Order 8, rules 8 to 10 (which relate to the service of process abroad).

(2) Where the document is served in accordance with RSC Order 11, rules 5 and 6, those rules and rule 8 of the said Order 11 (which deals with expenses incurred by the

Secretary of State) shall have effect in relation to service of the document as they have effect in relation to service of notice of a writ, except that the official certificate of service referred to in paragraph (5) of the said rule 5 shall, if the document was served personally, show the server's means of knowledge of the identity of the person served.

(3) Where the document is served in accordance with CCR Order 8, rules 8 to 10, those rules shall have effect subject to the following modifications—

(a) the document need not be served personally on the person required to be served so long as it is served in accordance with the law of the country in which service is effected;

(b) the official certificate or declaration with regard to service referred to in paragraph (6) of the said rule 10 shall, if the document was served personally, show the server's means of knowledge of the identity of the person served; and

(c) in paragraph (7) of the said rule 10 the words or in the manner in which default summonses are required to be served shall be omitted.

(4) Where a petition is to be served on a person out of England and Wales, then—

(a) the time within which that person must give notice of intention to defend shall be determined having regard to the practice adopted under RSC Order 11, rule 4(4) (which requires an order for leave to serve a writ out of the jurisdiction to limit the time for appearance) and the notice in Form M5 shall be amended accordingly;

(b) if the petition is to be served otherwise than in accordance with RSC Order 11, rules 5 and 6, or CCR Order 8, rules 8 to 10, and there is reasonable ground for believing that the person to be served does not understand English, the petition shall be accompanied by a translation, approved by the district judge, of the notice in Form M5, in the official language of the country in which service is to be effected or, if there is more than one official language of that country, in any one of those languages which is appropriate to the place where service is to be effected; but this sub-paragraph shall not apply in relation to a document which is to be served in a country in which the official language, or one of the official languages, is English.

(5) Where a document specifying the date of hearing of any proceedings is to be served out of England and Wales, the date shall be fixed having regard to the time which would be limited under paragraph (4)(a) for giving notice of intention to defend if the document were a petition.

**[3.515.1]**
**Keypoint**

- Petitions

**[3.515.2]**
**Petitions**

See 'Postal Service of a Petition', extracted from *Court Business* at [2001] Fam Law 718.

**[3.516]**

### 10.7 Mode of giving notice

Unless otherwise directed, any notice which is required by these rules to be given to any person shall be in writing and, may be given in any manner in which service may be effected under RSC Order 65, rule 5.

[3.517]

### 10.8 Notice of intention to defend

(1) In these rules any reference to a notice of intention to defend is a reference to an acknowledgment of service in Form M6 containing a statement to the effect that the person by whom or on whose behalf it is signed intends to defend the proceedings to which the acknowledgment relates, and any reference to giving notice of intention to defend is a reference to returning such a notice to the court office.

(2) In relation to any person on whom there is served a document requiring or authorising an acknowledgment of service to be returned to the court office, references in these rules to the time limited for giving notice of intention to defend are references—

(a) to seven days after service of the document, in the case of notice of intention to defend a petition under Part II of these rules, and

(b) in any other case, to 14 days or such other time as may be fixed.

(3) Subject to paragraph (2) a person may give notice of intention to defend notwithstanding that he has already returned to the court office an acknowledgment of service not constituting such a notice.

**Note – Form M6**

Note that Form M6 has been amended in accordance with r 36 of the Family Proceedings (Amendment) Rules 2001, SI 2001/821 with effect from 3 September 2001 to take account of the jurisdictional requirements of Brussels II and the European Communities (Matrimonial Jurisdiction and Judgments) Regulations 2001, SI 2001/310.



[3.518]

### 10.9 Mode of making applications

Except where these rules, or any rules applied by these rules, otherwise provide, every application in family proceedings—

(a) shall be made to a district judge;

(b) shall, if the proceedings are pending in the High Court, be made by summons or, if the proceedings are pending in a divorce county court, be made in accordance with CCR Order 13, rule 1 (which deals with applications in the course of proceedings).

[3.519]

### 10.10 Orders for transfer of family proceedings

(1) Where a cause is pending in the High Court, the district judge of the registry in which the cause is pending or a judge may order that the cause be transferred to another registry.

(2) Where a cause is pending in a divorce county court, the court may order that the cause be transferred to another divorce county court.

(3) Paragraphs (1) and (2) shall apply to applications in causes as they apply to causes; but before making an order for transfer of an application the court shall consider whether it would be more convenient to transfer the cause under paragraph (1) or (2), as the case may be.

(4) The court shall not, either of its own motion or on the application of any party, make an order under paragraph (1), (2) or (3) unless the parties have either—

(a) had an opportunity of being heard on the question, or

(b) consented to such an order.

(5) Where the parties, or any of them, desire to be heard on the question of a transfer, the court shall give the parties notice of a date, time and place at which the question will be considered.

(6) Paragraphs (4) and (5) shall apply with the necessary modifications to an order for the transfer of family proceedings under section 38 or 39 of the Act of 1984 as they apply to an order under paragraph (1) or (2) of this rule.

(7) Paragraphs (4) and (5) shall not apply where the court makes an order for transfer under paragraphs (1), (2) or (3) in compliance with the provisions of any Order made under Part I of Schedule 11 to the Children Act 1989.

**[3.520]**

### 10.11 Procedure on transfer of cause or application

(1) Where any cause or application is ordered to be transferred from one court or registry to another, the proper officer of the first-mentioned court or registry shall, unless otherwise directed, give notice of the transfer to the parties.

(2) Any provision in these rules, or in any order made or notice given pursuant to these rules, for the transfer of proceedings between a divorce county court and the High Court shall, in relation to proceedings which, after the transfer, are to continue in the principal registry, be construed—

(a) in the case of a transfer from the High Court to a divorce county court, as a provision for the proceedings to be treated as pending in a divorce county court, and

(b) in the case of a transfer from a divorce county court to the High Court, as a provision for the proceedings no longer to be treated as pending in a divorce county court.

(3) Proceedings transferred from a divorce county court to the High Court pursuant to any provision in these rules shall, unless the order for transfer otherwise directs, proceed in the registry nearest to the divorce county court from which they are transferred, but nothing in this paragraph shall prejudice any power under these rules to order the transfer of the proceedings to a different registry.

**[3.521]**

### 10.12 Evidence by affidavit

On any application made—

(a) in a county court, by originating application or in accordance with CCR Order 13, rule 1 (which deals with applications in the course of proceedings), or

(b) in the High Court, by originating summons, notice or motion,

evidence may be given by affidavit unless these rules otherwise provide or the court otherwise directs, but the court may, on the application of any party, order the attendance for cross-examination of the person making any such affidavit; and where, after such an order has been made, that person does not attend, his affidavit shall not be used as evidence without the leave of the court.

**[3.522]**

### 10.13 Taking of affidavit in county court proceedings

In relation to family proceedings pending or treated as pending in a divorce county court, section 58(1) of the County Courts Act 1984 shall have effect as if after paragraph (c) there were inserted the following words—

'or

(d) a district judge of the principal registry; or

(e) any officer of the principal registry authorised by the President under section 2 of the Commissioners for Oaths Act 1889; or

(f) any clerk in the Central Office of the Royal Courts of Justice authorised to take affidavits for the purposes of proceedings in the Supreme Court.'.

**[3.523]**

### 10.14 Evidence of marriage outside England and Wales

(1) The celebration of a marriage outside England and Wales and its validity under the law of the country where it was celebrated may, in any family proceedings in which the existence and validity of the marriage is not disputed, be proved by the evidence of one of the parties to the marriage and the production of a document purporting to be—

(a) a marriage certificate or similar document issued under the law in force in that country; or

(b) a certified copy of an entry in a register of marriages kept under the law in force in that country.

(2) Where a document produced by virtue of paragraph (1) is not in English it shall, unless otherwise directed, be accompanied by a translation certified by a notary public or authenticated by affidavit.

(3) This rule shall not be construed as precluding the proof of marriage in accordance with the Evidence (Foreign, Dominion and Colonial Documents) Act 1933 or in any other manner authorised apart from this rule.



**[3.523A]**

### 10.14A Power of court to limit cross-examination

The court may limit the issues on which an officer of the service may be cross-examined.

**Amendment**

Inserted by SI 2001/821.

**[3.524]**

### 10.15 Official shorthand note etc of proceedings

(1) Unless the judge otherwise directs, an official shorthand note shall be taken of the proceedings at the trial in open court of every cause pending in the High Court.

(2) An official shorthand note may be taken of any other proceedings before a judge or district judge if directions for the taking of such a note are given by the Lord Chancellor.

(3) The shorthand writer shall sign the note and certify it to be a correct shorthand note of the proceedings and shall retain the note unless he is directed by the district judge to forward it to the court.

(4) On being so directed the shorthand writer shall furnish the court with a transcript of the whole or such part as may be directed of the shorthand note.

(5) Any party, any person who has intervened in a cause, the Queen's Proctor or, where a declaration of parentage has been made under section 55A of the Act of 1986, the Registrar General shall be entitled to require from the shorthand writer a transcript of the shorthand note, and the shorthand writer shall, at the request of any person so entitled, supply that person with a transcript of the whole or any part of the note on payment of the shorthand writer's charges authorised by any scheme in force providing for the taking of official shorthand notes of legal proceedings.

(6) Except as aforesaid, the shorthand writer shall not, without the permission of the court, furnish the shorthand note or a transcript of the whole or any part thereof to anyone.

(7) In these Rules references to a shorthand note include references to a record of the proceedings made by mechanical means and in relation to such a record references to the shorthand writer shall have effect as if they were references to the person responsible for transcribing the record.

**Amendment**

SI 2001/821.

**[3.525]**

### 10.16 Copies of decrees and orders

(1) A copy of every decree shall be sent by the proper officer to every party to the cause.

(2) A sealed or other copy of a decree or order made in open court shall be issued to any person requiring it on payment of the prescribed fee.

**[3.526]**

### 10.17 Service of order

(1) Where an order made in family proceedings has been drawn up, the proper officer of the court where the order is made shall, unless otherwise directed, send a copy of the order to every party affected by it.

(2) Where a party against whom the order is made is acting by a solicitor, a copy may, if the district judge thinks fit, be sent to that party as if he were acting in person, as well as to his solicitor.

(3) It shall not be necessary for the person in whose favour the order was made to prove that a copy of the order has reached any other party to whom it is required to be sent.

(4) This rule is without prejudice to RSC Order 45, rule 7 (which deals with the service of an order to do or abstain from doing an act), CCR Order 29, rule 1 (which deals with orders enforceable by committal) and any other rule or enactment for the purposes of which an order is required to be served in a particular way.

**[3.527]**

### 10.18 No notice of intention to proceed after year's delay

RSC Order 3, rule 6 (which requires a party to give notice of intention to proceed after a year's delay) shall not apply to any proceedings pending in the High Court.

**[3.528]**

### 10.19 Filing of documents at place of hearing etc

Where the file of any family proceedings has been sent from one divorce county court or registry to another for the purpose of a hearing or for some other purpose, any document needed for that purpose and required to be filed shall be filed in the other court or registry.

**[3.529]**

### 10.20 Inspection etc of documents retained in court

(1) Subject to rule 10.21, a party to any family proceedings or his solicitor or the Queen's Proctor or a person appointed under rule 2.57 or 9.5 to be the guardian ad litem of a child in any family proceedings may have a search made for, and may inspect and bespeak a copy of, any document filed or lodged in the court office in those proceedings.

(2) Any person not entitled to a copy of a document under paragraph (1) above who intends to make an application under the Hague Convention (as defined in section 1(1) of the Child Abduction and Custody Act 1985) in a Contracting State (as defined in section 2 of that Act) other than the United Kingdom shall, if he satisfies the [court] that he intends to make such an application, be entitled to obtain a copy bearing the seal of the court of any order relating to the custody of the child in respect of whom the application is to be made.

(3) Except as provided by rules 2.36(4) and 3.16(10) and paragraphs (1) and (2) of this rule, no document filed or lodged in the court office other than a decree or order made in open court shall be open to inspection by any person without the leave of the district judge, and no copy of any such document, or of an extract from any such document, shall be taken by, or issued to, any person without such leave.

**Amendment**
Para (2): SI 1992/2067.



**[3.529.1]**
**Keypoint**
- Disclosure

**[3.529.2]**
**Disclosure**

This paragraph, which provides for very limited disclosure of documents retained in court, should be read in the light of the two different results reported in *S v S (disclosure to revenue)*[1] and *R v R (Disclosure to Revenue)*[2] and referred to in the recent case of *Nayler v Beard*[3]. See also Introductory Chapter on 'Confidentiality, disclosure and publicity' in EFP, vol 2 at para **[1.1028]**. In relation to confidentiality and publicity see now also *Clibbery v Allan*[4] which was subject to appeal and affirmed at [2002] NLJR 222, 146 Sol Jo LB 38, CA.

See also *A v A; B v B*[5] in which Charles J conducted a detailed and critical review of both the practice and the principles to be applied with regard to the English court's powers of disclosure of case papers to public authorities (including, as Charles J ordered in this case, to the Isle of Man court). On the basis of this authority the prevailing wind is now firmly in the direction of such disclosure being initiated by the court in an appropriate case. In relation to disclosure see also the discussion in 'The Privilege against Self-Incrimination in Ancillary Relief Proceedings' by Brent Molyneux at [2001] Fam Law 603.

1 [1997] 3 FCR 1, [1997] 2 FLR 774 per Wilson J.
2 [1998] 1 FCR 597, [1998] 1 FLR 922 per Wilson J.
3 [2001] EWCA Civ 1201, [2001] 3 FCR 61.
4 [2001] 2 FCR 577, [2001] Fam Law 654.
5 [2000] 1 FCR 577, [2000] 1 FLR 701.

**[3.530]**

### 10.21 Disclosure of addresses

(1) [Subject to rule 2.3,] nothing in these rules shall be construed as requiring any party to reveal the address of their private residence (or that of any child) save by order of the court.

(2) Where a party declines to reveal an address in reliance upon paragraph (1) above, he shall give notice of that address to the court in Form [C8] and that address shall not be revealed to any person save by order of the court.

**Amendment**
Para (1): SI 1991/2113. Para (2): SI 1994/3155.

**[3.531]**

### [10.21A Disclosure of information under the Act of 1991]

[Where the Secretary of State requires a person mentioned in regulation 2(2) or (3)(a) of the Child Support (Information, Evidence and Disclosure) Regulations 1992 to furnish information or evidence for a purpose mentioned in regulation 3(1) of those Regulations, nothing in rules 4.23 (confidentiality of documents), 10.20 (inspection etc of documents in court) or 10.21 (disclosure of addresses) shall prevent that person from furnishing the information or evidence sought or require him to seek leave of the court before doing so.]

**Amendment**
Inserted by SI 1993/295, r 5.

**[3.532]**

### 10.22 Practice to be observed in district registries and divorce county courts

(1) The President and the senior district judge may, with the concurrence of the Lord Chancellor, issue directions for the purpose of securing in the district registries and the divorce county courts due observance of statutory requirements and uniformity of practice in family proceedings.

(2) RSC Order 63, rule 11 (which requires the practice of the Central Office to be followed in the district registries) shall not apply to family proceedings.

**[3.533]**

### 10.23 Transitional Provisions

(1) Subject to paragraph (2) below, these rules shall apply, so far as practicable, to any proceedings pending on the day on which they come into force.

(2) Rule 8.1 shall not apply to an appeal from an order or decision made or given by a district judge in matrimonial proceedings in a divorce county court where notice of appeal has been filed before the day on which these rules come into force.

(3) Where, by reason of paragraph (1) above, these rules do not apply to particular proceedings pending on the day on which they come into force, the rules in force immediately before that day shall continue to apply to those proceedings.

(4) Nothing in this rule shall be taken as prejudicing the operation of the provisions of the Interpretation Act 1978 as regards the effect of repeals.

(5) Without prejudice to the generality of paragraph (1) above (and for the avoidance of doubt) rule 2.39 shall not apply to any proceedings which are pending within the meaning of paragraph 1(1) of Schedule 14 to the Children Act 1989.

**[3.534]**

### [10.24 Applications for relief which is precluded by the Act of 1991]

[(1) Where an application is made for an order which, in the opinion of the district judge, the court would be prevented from making by section 8 or 9 of the Act of 1991, the proper officer may send a notice in Form M34 to the applicant.

(2) In the first instance, the district judge shall consider the matter under paragraph (1) himself, without holding a hearing.

(3) Where a notice is sent under paragraph (1), no requirement of these rules, except for those of this rule, as to the service of the application by the proper officer or as to any other procedural step to follow the making of an application of the type in question, shall apply unless and until the court directs that they shall apply or that they shall apply to such extent and subject to such modifications as may be specified in the direction.

(4) Where an applicant who has been sent a notice under paragraph (1) informs the proper officer in writing, within 14 days of the date of the notice, that he wishes to persist with his application, the proper officer shall refer the matter to the district judge for action in accordance with paragraph (5).

(5) Where the district judge acts in accordance with this paragraph, he shall give such directions as he considers appropriate for the matter to be heard and determined by the court and, without prejudice to the generality of the foregoing, such directions may provide for the hearing to be ex parte.

(6) Where directions are given under paragraph (5), the proper officer shall inform the applicant of the directions and, in relation to the other parties,—

- (a) send them a copy of the application;
- (b) where the hearing is to be ex parte, inform them briefly—
  - (i) of the nature and effect of the notice under this rule,
  - (ii) that the matter is being resolved ex parte, and
  - (iii) that they will be informed of the result in due course; and
- (c) where the hearing is to be inter partes, inform them of—
  - (i) the circumstances which led to the directions being given, and
  - (ii) the directions.

(7) Where a notice has been sent under paragraph (1) and the proper officer is not informed under paragraph (4), the application shall be treated as having been withdrawn.

(8) Where the matter is heard pursuant to directions under paragraph (5) and the court determines that it would be prevented by section 8 or 9 of the Act of 1991 from making the order sought by the application, it shall dismiss the application.

(9) Where the court dismisses an application under this rule it shall give its reasons in writing, copies of which shall be sent to the parties by the proper officer.

(10) In this rule, 'the matter' means the question whether the making of an order in the terms sought by the application would be prevented by section 8 or 9 of the Act of 1991.]

**Amendment**

Inserted by SI 1993/295, r 6.



## [3.535]

### [10.25 Modification of rule 10.24 in relation to non-free-standing applications]

[Where a notice is sent under rule 10.24(1) in respect of an application which is contained in a petition or other document ('the document') which contains material extrinsic to the application—

- (a) the document shall, until the contrary is directed under sub-paragraph (c) of this rule, be treated as if it did not contain the application in respect of which the notice was served;
- (b) the proper officer shall, when he sends copies of the document to the respondents under any provision of these rules, attach a copy of the notice under rule 10.24(1) and a notice informing the respondents of the effect of sub-paragraph (a) of this paragraph; and

(c) if it is determined, under rule 10.24, that the court would not be prevented, by section 8 or 9 of the Act of 1991, from making the order sought by the application, the court shall direct that the document shall be treated as if it contained the application, and it may give such directions as it considers appropriate for the conduct of the proceedings in consequence of that direction.]

**Amendment**

Inserted by SI 1993/295, r 6.

## [3.535A]

### [10.26 Human Rights Act 1998]

[(1) In this rule—

'originating document' means a petition, application, originating application, originating summons or other originating process;

'answer' means an answer or other document filed or served by a party in reply to an originating document (but not an acknowledgement of service);

'Convention right' has the same meaning as in the Human Rights Act 1998;

'declaration of incompatibility' means a declaration of incompatibility under section 4 of the Human Rights Act 1998.

(2) A party who seeks to rely on any provision of or right arising under the Human Rights Act 1998 or seeks a remedy available under that Act—

(a) shall state that fact in his originating document or (as the case may be) answer; and

(b) shall in his originating document or (as the case may be) answer—

(i) give precise details of the Convention right which it is alleged has been infringed and details of the alleged infringement;

(ii) specify the relief sought;

(iii) state if the relief sought includes a declaration of incompatibility.

(3) A party who seeks to amend his originating document or (as the case may be) answer to include the matters referred to in paragraph (2) shall, unless the court orders otherwise, do so as soon as possible and in any event not less than 28 days before the hearing.

(4) The court shall not make a declaration of incompatibility unless 21 days' notice, or such other period of notice as the court directs, has been given to the Crown.

(5) Where notice has been given to the Crown a Minister, or other person permitted by the Human Rights Act 1998, shall be joined as a party on giving notice to the court.

(6) Where a party has included in his originating document or (as the case may be) answer:

(a) a claim for a declaration of incompatibility, or

(b) an issue for the court to decide which may lead to the court considering making a declaration of incompatibility,

then the court may at any time consider whether notice should be given to the Crown as required by the Human Rights Act 1998 and give directions for the content and service of the notice.

(7) In the case of an appeal for which permission to appeal is required, the court shall, unless it decides that it is appropriate to do so at another stage in the proceedings, consider the issues and give the directions referred to in paragraph (6) when deciding whether to give such permission.

(8) If paragraph (7) does not apply, and a hearing for directions would, but for this rule, be held, the court shall, unless it decides that it is appropriate to do so at another stage in the proceedings, consider the issues and give the directions referred to in paragraph (6) at the hearing for directions.

(9) If neither paragraph (7) nor paragraph (8) applies, the court shall consider the issues and give the directions referred to in paragraph (6) when it considers it appropriate to do so, and may fix a hearing for this purpose.

(10) Where a party amends his originating document or (as the case may be) answer to include any matter referred to in paragraph (6)(a), then the court will consider whether notice should be given to the Crown and give directions for the content and service of the notice.

(11) In paragraphs (12) to (16), 'notice' means the notice given under paragraph (4).

(12) The notice shall be served on the person named in the list published under section 17 of the Crown Proceedings Act 1947.

(13) The notice shall be in the form directed by the court.

(14) Unless the court orders otherwise, the notice shall be accompanied by the directions given by the court and the originating document and any answers in the proceedings.

(15) Copies of the notice shall be served on all the parties.

(16) The court may require the parties to assist in the preparation of the notice.

(17) Unless the court orders otherwise, the Minister or other person permitted by the Human Rights Act 1998 to be joined as a party shall, if he wishes to be joined, give notice of his intention to be joined as a party to the court and every other party, and where the Minister has nominated a person to be joined as a party the notice must be accompanied by the written nomination.

(18) Where a claim is made under section 7(1) of the Human Rights Act 1998 in respect of a judicial act the procedure in paragraphs (6) to (17) shall also apply, but the notice to be given to the Crown:

(a) shall be given to the Lord Chancellor and shall be served on the Treasury Solicitor on his behalf; and

(b) shall also give details of the judicial act which is the subject of the claim and of the court that made it.

(19) Where in any appeal a claim is made under section 7(1) of that Act and section 9(3) and (4) applies—

(a) that claim must be set out in the notice of appeal; and

(b) notice must be given to the Crown in accordance with paragraph (18).

(20) The appellant must in a notice of appeal to which paragraph (19)(a) applies—

(a) state that a claim is being made under section 7(1) of the Human Rights Act 1998 in respect of a judicial act and section 9(3) applies; and

(b) give details of—

(i) the Convention right which it is alleged has been infringed;

(ii) the infringement;

(iii) the judicial act complained of; and

(iv) the court which made it.

(21) Where paragraph (19) applies and the appropriate person (as defined in section 9(5) of the Human Rights Act 1998) has not applied within 21 days, or such other period as the court directs, after the notice is served to be joined as a party, the court may join the appropriate person as a party.

(22) On any application or appeal concerning—

(a) a committal order;

(b) a refusal to grant habeas corpus; or

(c) a secure accommodation order made under section 25 of the Act of 1989,

if the court ordering the release of the person concludes that his Convention rights have been infringed by the making of the order to which the application or appeal relates, the judgment or order should so state, but if the court does not do so, that failure will not prevent another court from deciding the matter.]

**Amendment**

Inserted by SI 2000/2267, rr 4, 10. Amended by SI 2001/821.

# The Civil Procedure Rules 1998 and Family Proceedings

Contents





## The Civil Procedure Rules 1998

**[3.536]**

The Civil Procedure Rules 1998[1] came into force on 26 April 1999 and the Rules of the Supreme Court 1965 and the County Court Rules 1981 cease to have effect, except as specifically preserved, as from that date. The Civil Procedure Rules 1998 ('CPR 1998') apply to all proceedings in the High Court, the county court and the Civil Division of the Court of Appeal, but do not apply to family proceedings[2] (for which rules are made under the MFPA 1984, s 40[3]), or to adoption proceedings (for which rules are made under the AA 1976, s 66[4]) or to certain other types of proceedings specifically excluded, except to the extent that they are applied by another enactment[5]. Accordingly, the CPR do apply to proceedings in the Family Division which are not family proceedings (eg proceedings under the I(PFD)A 1975 or the TLATA 1996).

In relation to proceedings to which the CPR 1998 apply, the new rules replace the Rules of the Supreme Court 1965 (RSC) and the County Court Rules 1981 (CCR), although many of their provisions are re-enacted, with some modifications, in CPR 1998, Schs 1 and 2 respectively[6].

1 SI 1998/3132 amended with effect from 26 April 1999 by the Civil Procedure (Amendment) Rules 1999, SI 1999/1008. The CPR 1998 have been further amended by the following orders:
- (a) The Civil Procedure (Amendment) Rules 2000, SI 2000/221, the principal effects of which were–
  - (i) to insert, with effect from 28 February 2000, Pt 53 relating to defamation claims;
  - (ii) to amend or add, with effect from 2 May 2000, rules relating to service out of the jurisdiction (Pt 6), parties and group litigation (Pt 19), security for costs (Pt 25) and certain other matters; and
  - (iii) to amend the rules relating to appeals by inserting, with effect from 2 May 2000, Pt 52, which establishes a procedural code governing appeals to the Civil Division of the Court of Appeal, the High Court and the county court: the provisions of Pt 52 (as amended by SI 2000/2092 from 2 October 2000) apply to all appeals in the Civil Division of the Court of Appeal and to appeals in the High Court and county court in proceedings to which the CPR 1998 apply (except appeals from an authorised court officer in detailed assessment proceedings); CPR 1998, Sch 1 – RSC Ords 55, 56, 58 and 59 and Sch 2 – CCR Ords 3,

13 and 37, r 6 are revoked as from 2 May 2000. The new rules do not apply to any appeal in relation to which a notice of appeal or an application for permission to appeal was filed before 2 May 2000 and the rules in force immediately before that date shall continue to apply thereto (Civil Procedure (Amendment) Rules 2000, SI 2000/221, r 39 (as amended by SI 2000/940)). Note that since the CPR 1998 do not apply to family proceedings (except in relation to costs and certain other specified matters) appeals to the High Court and county court in such proceedings continue to be governed by the provisions of the RSC, CCR and FPR 1991 as appropriate.

(b) The Civil Procedure (Amendment No 2) Rules 2000, SI 2000/940 which, amended the transitional provisions relating to appeals (as noted above) and amended the provisions of Pt 47 relating to appeals in proceedings for the detailed assessment of costs; CPR 1998, rr 47.20 to 47.23 are amended with effect from 2 May 2000 to apply only to appeals from authorised court officers in detailed assessment proceedings and rr 47.24 to 47.26 are deleted; as from 2 May 2000, an appeal from the decision of a costs judge or district judge on a detailed assessment in proceedings to which the CPR 1998 apply is governed by the provisions of CPR 1998, Pt 52; however, while CPR 1998, Pts 43, 44, 47 and 48 apply to family proceedings, Pt 52 has not been specifically applied to such proceedings and there is some doubt as to the procedural basis for an appeal from the decision of a costs judge or district judge on a detailed assessment in family proceedings. As to the procedure on an appeal in detailed assessment proceedings, see *Rayden and Jackson on Divorce and Family Matters* (17th ed, 1997), Noter-up to Vol 1, para 54.1; and as to appeals generally, Noter-up to Vol 1, Chap 50.

(c) The Civil Procedure (Amendment No 3) Rules 2000, SI 2000/1317 which, as from 3 July 2000–
 (i) made amendments to the costs provisions of the CPR 1998 (Pts 43 to 48) consequent on the changes to the funding of legal services in civil matters introduced by the AJA 1999 (as to which see generally, *Rayden and Jackson on Divorce and Family Matters* (17th ed, 1997), Noter-up to Vol 1, para 52.1); the amendments include changes in terminology to reflect the replacement of the Legal Aid Board by the Legal Services Commission and of the Legal Aid Fund by the Community Legal Service Fund, provisions in relation to conditional fee agreements and other funding arrangements and a new procedure for costs-only proceedings (r 44.12A);
 (ii) revoked CPR 1998, r 48.7(3), which was held in *General Mediterranean Holdings SA v Patel* [1999] 3 All ER 673 to be ultra vires;
 (iii) made a number of minor amendments to other Parts of the CPR 1998.

(d) The Civil Procedure (Amendment No 4) Rules 2000, SI 2000/2092 which have effect from 2 October 2000 and which include–
 (i) amendments to Pts 7, 19 and 33 in relation to the procedure for certain claims under the HRA 1998 or where an issue arises under the HRA 1998; as to which see para 3;
 (ii) the amendment of CPR 1998, r 36.21(6) to provide that where the court awards interest under Pt 36 and also awards interest on the same sum for the same period under any other power, the total rate of interest may not exceed 10% above base rate;
 (iii) the amendment of Pt 27 and of CPR 1998, Pt 52.1(2) to apply Pt 52 to appeals in small claims;
 (iv) the addition of Pt 54, which (together with the *Practice Direction* supplementing Pt 54) governs the practice and procedure relating to judicial review; CPR 1998, Sch 1 – RSC Ord 53 is revoked as from 2 October 2000, but continues to apply to any application for permission to apply for judicial review filed before that date and to the application for judicial review to which that application relates; CPR 1998, Sch 1 – RSC Ord 57 is also revoked. A Pre-Action Protocol for Judicial Review was introduced on 4 March 2002.

(e) The Civil Procedure (Amendment) Rules 2001, SI 2001/256 which–
 (i) insert Pt 55 (Possession claims) and Pt 56 (Landlord and tenant claims and miscellaneous provisions about land), with effect from 26 March 2001;
 (ii) inserts from 26 March 2001 a new r 19.8A providing a power to make a judgment binding on a non-party in a claim in the High Court relating to the estate of a deceased person or to property subject to a trust;
 (iii) makes certain other minor amendments, including amendments to Sch 1 – RSC Ord 112 and Sch 2 – CCR Ord 47 consequent on the implementation of s 23 of the FLRA 1987 relating to the use of scientific tests in determining parentage.

(f) The Civil Procedure (Amendment No 2) Rules 2001, SI 2001/1388 which–
 (i) introduce with effect from 31 May 2001 provision for service of a claim form and other documents in accordance with Council Regulation (EC) No 1348/2000 of 29 May 2000 on the service in the Member States of judicial and extrajudicial documents in civil and commercial matters (the Service Regulation): CPR 1998, r 6.26A;

(ii) insert with effect from 15 October 2001 Pt 57 relating to probate claims (excluding non-contentious or common form probate business) and claims for the rectification of wills and for the substitution and removal of personal representatives; these provisions do not apply to proceedings issued before 15 October 2001; and
(iii) make certain other amendments, including provisions relating to claims under the Race Relations Act 1976 and to the enforcement of traffic offences.

(g) The Civil Procedure (Amendment No 3) Rules 2001, SI 2001/1769, which, as from 31 May 2001, amend the CPR 1998, r 22.1 (documents to be verified by a statement of truth), inter alia, to require an acknowledgement of service to a claim brought under the Pt 8 procedure to be so verified (with effect from 31 May 2001).

(h) The Civil Procedure (Amendment No 4) Rules 2001, SI 2001/2792, which–
(i) insert, with effect from 25 March 2002, Pts 70 to 73 relating to enforcement; Pt 70 contains general rules about the enforcement of judgments and orders; Pt 71 provides for orders to obtain information from judgment debtors (formerly oral examination); Pt 72 deals with Third Party Debt orders (formerly garnishee orders); and Pt 73 relates to Charging orders and Stop orders; the relevant provisions of the CPR 1998, Sch 1 – RSC and Sch 2 – CCR are revoked as from 25 March 2002, but will continue to apply to enforcement proceedings issued before that date; the new provisions do not apply to the enforcement of orders made in family proceedings, which will continue to be governed by the FPR 1991, together with the RSC and CCR; and
(ii) make certain other amendments, with effect from 15 October 2001, including, in Sch 2: CCR Ord 49, provisions relating to arrest and remand under the Housing Act 1996 and a new r 51.2 providing that any provision of the rules may be modified or disapplied during the operation of pilot schemes for assessing new practices and procedures.

(j) The Civil Procedure (Amendment No 5) Rules 2001, SI 2001/4015, the principal purpose of which is to insert, from 25 March 2002, the following further Parts: Pt 58 (Commercial Court); Pt 59 (Mercantile Courts); Pt 60 (Technology and Construction Court claims); Pt 61 (Admiralty claims); and Pt 62 (Arbitration claims); other amendments include:
(i) an addition to CPR 1998, r 31.14 to allow a party to seek inspection of any document mentioned in an expert's report subject to the limitation in r 35.10(4) on disclosure of instructions) and changes to rr 35.12 and 35.14 relating to directions to, or sought by, an expert (with effect from 25 March 2002);
(ii) a new table of fixed enforcement costs (r 45.6) for applications under Pts 70 to 73 (with effect from 25 March 2002); and
(iii) amendments to Pts 6, 12 and 25, Sch 1 – RSC Ord 71 and Sch 2 – CCR Ord 35 (all with effect from 1 March 2002) consequent on the implementation of Council Regulation (EC) No 44/2001 of 22 December 2000 on jurisdiction and the recognition and enforcement of judgments in civil and commercial matters.

(k) The Civil Procedure (Amendment No 6) Rules 2001, SI 2001/4016 which amend CPR 1998, Sch 1 – RSC Ord 115 (restraint orders under the Terrorism Act 2000, Sch 4) in the light of the Anti-terrorism, Crime and Security Act 2001.

2 As defined in the MFPA 1984, s 32.
3 See above.
4 Set out in Vol 2, Pt 2, para **[2.1082]**.
5 CPR 1998, Pt 2.1, as amended by SI 1999/1008 with effect from 26 April 1999; the other proceedings to which the CPR do not apply are:
(i) insolvency proceedings;
(ii) non-contentious or common form probate proceedings;
(iii) proceedings in the High Court when acting as a Prize Court; and
(iv) proceedings before the judge within the meaning of Pt VII of the MeHA 1983.
6 CPR 1998, Pt 50.



## The effect on family proceedings

### [3.537]

In relation to family proceedings the FPR 1991 have been amended with effect from 26 April 1999[1] to provide that the RSC 1965 and the CCR 1981 in force immediately before 26 April shall continue to apply to family proceedings and that references in the FPR 1991 to the provisions of the RSC and the CCR are to be read accordingly. A similar provision has been made in relation to proceedings under the Adoption Act 1976[2].

In relation to costs, however, the provisions of the CPR 1998 are specifically applied to family proceedings and proceedings in the Family Division and to adoption proceedings. With effect from 26 April 1999, CCR Ord 38 and RSC Ord 62 no longer apply to the assessment of costs in such proceedings and the provisions of CPR 1998, Pts 43, 44 (except CPR 1998, Pt 44.9 to 44.12), 47 and 48 apply, with certain modifications, in their place[3]. The Family Proceedings (Costs) Rules 1991 are revoked with effect from the same date[4].

The general effect of the above provisions is that in family proceedings or adoption proceedings where no specific provision is made in the FPR 1991 or the Adoption Rules 1984, for example in relation to committals or the enforcement of orders, recourse should be had to the RSC and CCR in force immediately before 26 April 1999, except in relation to costs. In all other proceedings (apart from those specifically excluded) and in appeals to the Court of Appeal, Civil Division, the procedure is governed by the CPR 1998 and the Schedules thereto and the *Practice Directions* supplementing the CPR 1998. A table showing the rules applicable to particular kinds of proceedings is set out below[5].

1 Family Proceedings (Miscellaneous Amendments) Rules 1999, SI 1999/1012, r 3.
2 Adoption Rules 1984, r 3(2), as substituted by the Adoption (Amendment) Rules 1999, SI 1999/1477, with effect from 16 June 1999.
3 Family Proceedings (Miscellaneous Amendments) Rules 1999, SI 1999/1012, r 4(1), and in relation to adoption proceedings, the Adoption Rules 1984, r 51(2), inserted by SI 1999/1477 with effect from 16 June 1999. For the application of the *Practice Direction about Costs* supplementing CPR 1998, Pts 43 to 48 to family proceedings and proceedings in the Family Division, see *President's Direction (Civil Procedure Rules: allocation of cases: costs)* [1999] 2 FCR 1, [1999] 1 FLR 1295 also reported as *Practice Direction (Family Division: allocation of cases: costs)* [1999] 3 All ER 192 and as *Practice Direction (Family Proceedings: Allocation and Costs)* [1999] 1 WLR 1128; see also *Rayden and Jackson on Divorce and Family Matters* (17th edn, 1997).
The *Practice Direction about Costs* supplementing Pts 43 to 48 has been revised and restructured with effect from 3 July 2000 in the light of the changes to the funding of legal services in civil matters introduced by the AJA 1999 and to incorporate other changes; the President has directed that the new edition (and all subsequent editions) of the *Practice Direction* shall extend to family proceedings and proceedings in the Family Division in the same manner and to the same extent as the previous *Practice Direction*: see *Practice Direction (Family Proceedings: Costs)* [2000] 1 WLR 1781, also reported as *Practice Direction (Costs: Civil Procedure Rules 1998)* [2000] 4 All ER 1072; set out at para **[4.29]** below.
4 SI 1999/1012, r 4(1).
5 See para **[3.542]** below.

## Ancillary relief proceedings

### [3.538]

The FPR 1991 are further amended with effect from 5 June 2000 to establish a new procedural code for ancillary relief applications in the High Court and in all county courts (including the Principal Registry)[1]. The amended ancillary relief rules (which are modelled on the pilot scheme operated in some courts since 1 October 1996) incorporate some of the concepts introduced by the CPR 1998. In particular:

(i) FPR 1991, r 2.51B sets out the overriding objective of the code, namely that of enabling the court to deal with cases justly, and explains how and when the overriding objective is to be applied; the rule follows closely the provisions of CPR 1998, Pt 1;
(ii) in relation to expert evidence, FPR 1991, r 2.61C specifically applies CPR 1998, Pt 35.1 to 35.14[2] (except Pt 35.5(2) and 35.8(4)(b)) to all ancillary relief proceedings;
(iii) the new code substitutes for the existing FPR 1991, r 2.69 a new rule relating to offers to settle, supplemented by rr 2.69A to 2.69D which provide for the effect of such offers on the exercise of the court's discretion as to costs in terms similar to the provisions of CPR 1998, Pt 36.20 and 36.21.

1 Family Proceedings (Amendment No 2) Rules 1999, SI 1999/3491; for further details of the amended ancillary relief rules see para **[3.432.1]** above and *Rayden and Jackson on Divorce and Family Matters* (17th edn, 1997).

2 CPR 1998, r 35.12 has been amended to clarify the purpose of discussions between experts on the direction of the court and r 35.14 amended to require an expert who wishes to seek directions to give notice to the party instructing him and to the other parties: SI 2001/4015 with effect from 25 March 2002. From the same date CPR 1998, Pt 31.14 is amended to allow a party to seek inspection of any document mentioned in an expert's report (subject to the limitation in Pt 35.10(4) on disclosure of instructions); note, however, that Pt 31 does not apply to family proceedings.

## Inheritance (Provision for Family and Dependants) Act 1975 and Trusts of Land and Appointment of Trustees Act 1996

### [3.539]

As noted above, proceedings under the I(PFD)A 1975 and under the TLATA 1996, s 14 (whether proceeding in the Chancery Division or the Family Division of the High Court or in the county court) are governed by the provisions of the CPR 1998. In both cases, a claim is commenced in accordance with the provisions of Pt 8 (Alternative Procedure for Claims)[1], subject, in the case of applications under the 1975 Act, to the procedure set out in CPR 1998, Sch 1 – RSC Ord 99[2].

1 *Practice Direction 8B* supplementing CPR 1998, Pt 8. In the Family Division, proceedings under the I(PFD)A 1975 and under the TLATA 1996, s 14 may be heard and disposed of by a district judge (including a district judge of the Principal Registry): *President's Direction (Civil Procedure Rules: allocation of cases - costs)* [1999] 2 FCR 1, [1999] 1 FLR 1295 also reported as *Practice Direction (Family Division: allocation of cases: costs)* [1999] 3 All ER 192 and as *Practice Direction (Family Proceedings: Allocation and Costs)* [1999] 1 WLR 1128 (see *Rayden and Jackson on Divorce and Family Matters* (17th edn, 1997), Noter-up para 55.73C); for the jurisdiction of masters and district judges generally to hear and determine such proceedings see *Practice Direction 2B* supplementing CPR 1998, Pt 2. Note also the power of the High Court to make a judgment binding on a non-party in a claim relating to the estate of a deceased person or to property subject to a trust: CPR 1998, Pt 19.8A inserted with effect from 26 March 2001 by SI 2001/256.

2 For the procedure on applications under the I(PFD)A 1975, see *Rayden and Jackson on Divorce and Family Matters* (17th edn, 1997), Noter-up para 28.41; for applications under the TLATA 1996, s 14, see *Rayden and Jackson on Divorce and Family Matters* (17th edn, 1997), vol 1, para 30.30 and Noter-up thereto.



## Committal applications

### [3.539A]

The *Practice Direction on Committal Applications* supplementing CPR 1998, Sch 1 – RSC Ord 52 and Sch 2 – CCR Ord 29 applies to family proceedings in the same manner and to the same extent as it applies to proceedings governed by the CPR 1998 (the *Direction* is set out at para **[4.39]** below). A *Practice Direction* issued by the President of the Family Division on 16 March 2001[1] provides that, as from that date, the CPR *Direction* shall apply to applications in family proceedings for an order of committal, subject to the provisions of the FPR 1991 and appropriate procedural modifications. In any other family proceedings in which a committal order may be made, including proceedings for the enforcement of an existing order by way of judgment summons, full effect is to be given to the Human Rights Act 1998 and to the rights afforded under that Act[2]; the *Direction* emphasises that Art 6 of the ECHR is fully applicable to such proceedings and those involved must ensure that in the conduct of the proceedings there is due observance of the 1998 Act in the same manner as if the CPR *Direction* applied.

1 *Practice Direction (family proceedings: committal applications)* [2001] 2 All ER 704, [2001] 1 FCR 767: set out at para **[4.32]** below; the *Direction* was issued in the light of the decision of the Court of Appeal in *Mubarak v Mubarak* [2001] 1 FCR 193, [2001] 1 FLR 698, concerning the application of Art 6 of the ECHR to judgment summonses and other proceedings where a committal

order may be made. *Mubarak* was followed in *Quinn v Cuff* [2001] All ER (D) 49 (Jan), CA, where the Court of Appeal stated that it was now settled law that proceedings under the Debtors Act 1869 were criminal proceedings for the purpose of the ECHR and that the change in the conduct of judgment summonses had to be understood rapidly by practitioners in the field of ancillary relief.

2 *Practice Direction (family proceedings: committal applications)* [2001] 2 All ER 704, [2001] 1 FCR 767, para 2: set out at para **[4.32]** below.

## Transitional provisions

### [3.540]

Transitional provisions are made by the *Practice Direction* issued pursuant to CPR 1998, Pt 51[1]. Where an initiating step has been taken in a case before 26 April 1999 the case is to proceed in the first instance under the previous rules and any response must be in accordance with the previous rules. However, CPR 1998, Pt 1 (overriding objective) applies to all existing proceedings governed by the CPR 1998 from 26 April 1999 and where any new step is to be taken in existing proceedings on or after that date, it is to be taken under the CPR 1998. In particular, any application made in existing proceedings must be made in accordance with CPR 1998, Pt 23 and any other relevant CPR 1998 will apply to the substance of the application, unless otherwise provided by the *Practice Direction*. Any assessment of costs that takes place on or after 26 April 1999 will take place in accordance with the CPR 1998, but no costs for work undertaken before that date are to be disallowed if those costs would have been allowed on a taxation before that date[2]. With limited exceptions, any existing proceedings to which the CPR 1998 apply which have not come before a judge, at a hearing or on paper, between 26 April 1999 and 25 April 2000 are stayed[3].

1 See *Rayden and Jackson on Divorce and Family Matters* (17th edn, 1997), Service, Division B, para 652 et seq.

2 See para 18 of the *Practice Direction* supplementing CPR 1998, Pt 51, Family Proceedings (Miscellaneous Amendments) Rules 1999, r 4; and Adoption (Amendment) Rules 1999, r 4(2). The *Practice Direction about Costs* supplementing CPR 1998, Pts 43 to 48 contains further transitional provisions in relation to costs.

3 See para 19 of the *Practice Direction* supplementing CPR 1998, Pt 51. The mere writing of a letter to the court by one of the parties, even if brought to the judge's attention and responded to, does not mean that the case has come before a judge on paper for the purpose of this provision, unless it has resulted in an exercise of the court's case management powers under CPR 1998, Pt 3.3: *Reliance National Insurance Co (Europe) Ltd v Ropner Insurance Services Ltd* [2001] 1 Lloyd's Rep 477, CA. Proceedings are no longer 'existing proceedings' for the purposes of this paragraph once final judgment has been given: para 19(4).

## The CPR 1998 and the Human Rights Act 1998

### [3.540A]

The CPR 1998 have been amended with effect from 2 October 2000[1] to provide for the practice and procedure to be followed where an issue under the Human Rights Act 1998 arises in proceedings governed by those rules, including appeals governed by CPR 1998, Pt 52. The principal relevance of these provisions for family practitioners will be in relation to appeals to the Court of Appeal from orders or decisions in family proceedings[2].

1 SI 2000/2092; and see para **[3.536]** above.

2 In relation to the equivalent procedure in family proceedings in the High Court and county court, see FPR 1991, r 10.26, inserted by SI 2000/2267 with effect from 2 October 2000; see also *Practice Direction (Family Proceedings: Human Rights)* [2000] 4 All ER 288, [2000] 1 WLR 1782, reported as *Practice Direction (Human Rights Act 1998: citation of authorities)* [2000] 2 FCR 768 and as *Practice Direction (Human Rights Act 1998)* [2000] 2 FLR 429; set out at para **[4.30]** below.

## [3.540B]
### Procedure generally

A party who seeks to rely on any provision of or right arising under the HRA 1998 or seeks a remedy available under that Act must state that fact in his statement of case[1] or, in the case of an appeal, in his appellant's or respondent's notice[2] and must:

- give precise details of the convention right which it is alleged has been infringed and details of the alleged infringement;
- specify the relief sought;
- state if the relief sought includes a declaration of incompatibility in accordance with s 4 of the HRA 1998 or damages in respect of a judicial act to which s 9(3) of the HRA 1998 applies;
- where the relief sought includes a declaration of incompatibility, give precise details of the legislative provision alleged to be incompatible and details of the alleged incompatibility;
- where the claim is founded on a finding of unlawfulness by another court or tribunal, give details of the finding;
- where the claim is founded on a judicial act which is alleged to have infringed a convention right, give details of the judicial act complained of and the court or tribunal which is alleged to have made it.

A party who seeks to amend his statement of case to include any of the above matters must, unless the court orders otherwise, do so as soon as possible[3].

1 See *Practice Direction* supplementing CPR 1998, Pt 16, para 16.1.
2 See *Practice Direction* supplementing CPR 1998, Pt 16, para 16.1, as applied to appeals by the *Practice Direction* supplementing CPR 1998, Pt 52, paras 5.1A (appellant's notice) and 7.3A (respondent's notice).
3 See *Practice Direction* supplementing CPR 1998, Pt 16, para 16.2, applied to appeals by the *Practice Direction* supplementing CPR 1998, Pt 52, para 5.1A.

PART 3 CPR 1998

## [3.540C]
### Notice of proceedings

A court may not make a declaration of incompatibility under s 4 of the HRA 1998 unless 21 days notice has been given to the Crown and where such notice is given, a Minister or other permitted person shall be joined as a party on giving notice to the court[1].

Where a claim is made for damages under s 9 of the HRA 1998 in respect of a judicial act, the claim must be set out in the statement of case or appeal notice and notice must be given to the Crown[2].

Further provision as to the giving of notice and as to joinder in each of these cases is made by paras 6.1 to 6.6 of the *Practice Direction* supplementing CPR 1998, Pt 19.

1 CPR 1998, Pt 19.4A(1), (2). The formal notice which is required to be given to the Crown under the HRA 1998, s 5 and the CPR 1998, Pt 19.4A where the court is considering whether to make a declaration of incompatibility should always be given by the court which will hear the proceedings. Where a party seeks such a declaration or acknowledges that such a declaration might be made, he should give the Crown as much informal notice as practicable of the proceedings and the issues involved and should send a copy of the notice to the court and to the other parties. Both the formal and informal notice should be addressed to the person named in the list published under the Crown Proceedings Act 1947, s 17: *Poplar Housing and Regeneration Community Association Ltd v Donoghue* [2001] EWCA Civ 595, [2002] QB 48, [2001] 3 FCR 74.
2 CPR 1998, Pt 19.4A(3).

## [3.540D]
### Citation of authority

Where it is necessary for a party to give evidence at a hearing of an authority referred to in s 2 of the HRA 1998:

(i) the authority to be cited should be an authoritative and complete report; and
(ii) the party must give to the court and any other party a list of the authorities he intends to cite and copies of the reports not less than three days before the hearing.

Copies of the complete original texts issued by the European Court and Commission either paper-based or from the European Court's judgment database (HUDOC), which is available on the Internet, may be used[1].

1 Paragraph 8.1 of the first *Practice Direction* supplementing CPR 1998, Pt 39; as to the citation of such authority in family proceedings, see *Practice Direction (Family Proceedings: Human Rights)* [2000] 4 All ER 288, [2000] 1 WLR 1782, also reported as *Practice Direction (Human Rights Act 1998: citation of authorities)* [2000] 2 FCR 768 and as *Practice Direction (Human Rights Act 1998)* [2000] 2 FLR 429; set out at para **[4.30]** below.

### [3.540E]
### Allocation to judges

A claim under s 7(1)(a) of the HRA 1998 (proceedings against a public authority claiming that the authority has acted, or proposes to act, in a way which is incompatible with a convention right) in respect of a judicial act may be brought only in the High Court[1]. Any other claim under s 7(1)(a) of the HRA 1998 may be brought in any court[2].

Further provision as to allocation is made in *Practice Direction 2B* supplementing CPR 1998, Pt 2.

In the High Court a deputy High Court Judge, a Master or District Judge may not try a case in a claim made in respect of a judicial act under the Human Rights Act 1998 or a claim for a declaration of incompatibility in accordance with s 4 of the HRA 1998[3]. Since such a claim cannot be brought in a county court, the provision originally made for allocation in the county court has now been deleted[4].

1 CPR 1998, Pt 7.11(1).
2 CPR 1998, Pt 7.11(2).
3 See *Practice Direction* 2B, para 7A.
4 See *Practice Direction* 2B, para 15, deleted with effect from 12 February 2001 by the 21st supplement to the CPR 1998 (January 2001).

## The structure of the CPR 1998

### [3.541]

The Rules (as amended) are arranged in 66 Parts (Pts 63 to 69 have yet to be allocated) and two Schedules, Schedules 1 and 2 containing the re-enacted and modified Rules of the Supreme Court and County Court Rules respectively. The Rules are supplemented by a number of *Practice Directions*[1].

1 The *Practice Directions* supplementing the CPR 1998 were made on 23 April 1999, pursuant to the CPA 1997, s 5: *Practice Direction (Civil litigation: procedure)* [1999] 3 All ER 380, [1999] 1 WLR 1124. Section 5 does not give rise to a separate category of *Practice Directions* derived from any new power; the civil procedure *Practice Directions* are made for the county court under the County Courts Act 1984, s 74A, inserted by s 5(2) of the 1997 Act, and for the High Court under the inherent power of the Heads of Division; neither the County Courts Act 1984 nor the Civil Procedure Act 1997 confers any power on those making the *Practice Directions* to revoke or amend rules or regulations made by statutory instrument: see *Re C (Legal Aid: Preparation of Bill of Costs)* [2001] 1 FLR 602, CA.

## Table of Applicable Rules

### [3.542]

| Type of proceedings | Applicable rules |
|---|---|
| Adoption | Adoption Rules 1984 and RSC/CCR |
| Child Abduction and Custody Act 1985 | FPR 1991 and RSC |
| Child Support Act 1991 | FPR 1991 and RSC |

| Type of proceedings | Applicable rules |
|---|---|
| Children Act 1989 | FPR 1991 and RSC/CCR |
| Family Law Act 1986 | FPR 1991 and RSC |
| Family Law Act 1996, Pt IV | FPR 1991 and RSC/CCR |
| Human Fertilisation and Embryology Act 1990, s 30 | FPR 1991 and RSC |
| Inherent Jurisdiction with respect to minors | FPR 1991 and RSC |
| Inheritance (Provision for Family and Dependants) Act 1975 | CPR 1998, Sch 1 – RSC Ord 99 (applies in High Court and county court) and CPR 1998 generally |
| Judicial review<br>(i) where application for permission to apply filed before 2 October 2000<br>(ii) where application for permission to apply filed on or after 2 October 2000 | <br>(i) CPR 1998, Sch 1 – RSC Ord 53<br>(ii) CPR 1998, Pt 54 and the supplementary *Practice Direction* |
| Legitimacy | FPR 1991 and RSC |
| Married Women's Property Act 1882 | FPR 1991 and RSC/CCR |
| Matrimonial causes and matters | FPR 1991 and RSC/CCR |
| Matrimonial and Family Proceedings Act 1984, Pt III | FPR 1991 and RSC |
| Trusts of Land and Appointment of Trustees Act 1996 and other non-matrimonial property disputes | CPR 1998, Sch 1 – RSC, Sch 2 – CCR and CPR 1998 generally |

| Costs, enforcement and appeals | Applicable rules |
|---|---|
| Orders for and assessment of costs in family proceedings and proceedings in the Family Division | CPR 1998, Pts 43, 44, 47 and 48 and *Practice Direction* supplementing those Parts |
| Enforcement of orders in family proceedings | FPR 1991 and RSC/CCR |
| Enforcement of orders in proceedings to which the CPR 1998 apply | CPR 1998, Sch 1 – RSC and Sch 2 – CCR |
| Appeals from District Judge to High Court Judge/Circuit Judge in family proceedings | FPR 1991, RSC Ord 58 and CCR Ord 37 |
| Appeals from District Judge to High Court Judge/Circuit Judge in proceedings to which the CPR 1998 apply, where:<br>(i) the appeal or application for permission to appeal was filed before 2 May 2000<br>(ii) the appeal or application for permission to appeal is filed on or after 2 May 2000 | <br>(i) CPR 1998, Sch 1 – RSC Ord 58 and Sch 2 – CCR Ord 37<br>(ii) CPR 1998, Pt 52 (see also the supplementary *Practice Direction* |

PART 3
CPR 1998

| Type of proceedings | Applicable rules |
|---|---|
| Appeals to the High Court from the Magistrates' Court/Family Proceedings Court (Children Act 1989, Domestic Proceedings and Magistrates' Courts Act 1978, Family Law Act 1996, Pt IV and orders under the Magistrates' Courts Act 1980, s 63(3)) | FPR 1991 and RSC Ord 55 |
| Appeals to the High Court from the Magistrates' Court/Family Proceedings Court by case stated where:<br>(i) the appeal was filed before 2 May 2000<br>(ii) the appeal is filed on or after 2 May 2000 | <br><br>(i) CPR 1998, Sch 1 – RSC Ord 56<br>(ii) CPR 1998, Pt 52 (see also the supplementary *Practice Direction*) |
| Appeals and applications to the Court of Appeal, Civil Division where:<br>(i) the appeal or application for permission to appeal was filed before 2 May 2000<br>(ii) the appeal or application for permission to appeal is filed on or after 2 May 2000 | <br><br>(i) CPR 1998, Sch 1 – RSC Ord 59<br>(ii) CPR 1998, Pt 52 (see also the supplementary *Practice Direction*) |

# RSC ORDER 31
# Sales, etc of Land by Order of Court: Conveyancing Counsel of the Court

# CIVIL PROCEDURE RULES 1998
# Pt 40

Contents



**[3.543]**
**RSC Ord 31 / CPR 1998, Pt 40**

RSC Ord 31 remains of application in family proceedings by operation of FPR 1991, r 2.64(3). However, it has been superseded by CPR 1998, Pt 40 in respect of TLATA 1996[1] matters and applications under s 17 of the MWPA 1882[2]. The old RSC Ord 31 is set out below and is followed by the relevant part of CPR 1998, Pt 40. The new CPR 1998, Pt 40 is accompanied by a *Practice Direction*, the relevant text of which is set out below at para **[4.37]**.

The following text should be read with the TLATA 1996 and the commentary thereto[3].

1 See para **[2.452]** above.
2 See para **[2.11]** above.
3 See para **[2.452]** above.

## RSC ORDER 31

**[3.544]**

### Ord 31, r A1 Order to apply to High Court and County Court

This Order applies to proceedings both in the High Court and the county court.

**[3.544.1]**
**Keypoint**

- Family Division
- General

**[3.544.2]**
**Family Division**

The operation of this rule is extended to the Family Division by FPR 1991, r 2.64(3).

**[3.544.3]**
**General**

All applications will now be governed by the provisions of Pt I of RSC Ord 31. Proceedings under the TLATA 1996 are subject to the CPR 1998.

**[3.545]**

## I SALES, ETC OF LAND BY ORDER OF COURT

### Ord 31, r 1 Power to order sale of land

Where in any proceedings relating to any land it appears necessary or expedient for the purposes of the proceedings that the land or any part thereof should be sold, the Court may order that land or part to be sold, and any party bound by the order and in possession of that land or part, or in receipt of the rents and profits thereof, may be compelled to deliver up such possession or receipt to the purchaser or to such other person as the Court may direct.

In this Order 'land' includes any interest in, or right over, land.

**[3.545.1]**
**Keypoint**

- General

**[3.545.2]**
**General**

The court will usually give detailed directions for sale under r 2. Where the circumstances are appropriate, the court may merely make an order for sale leaving the parties to agree the manner and mode of sale, adjourning the determination of directions for sale to be dealt with on a future application in the event the parties are unable to agree.

The operation of this rule is extended to the Family Division by FPR 1991, r 2.64(3). It extends to the enforcement of the TLATA 1996 and the MWPA 1882. The old RSC Ord 31, r 1 (which applies in ancillary relief is repeated in the new RSC Ord 31, r 1). For civil proceedings the new CPR 1998, Pt 40 should be used for orders for sale.

**[3.546]**

### Ord 31, r 2 Manner of carrying out sale

(1) Where an order is made directing any land to be sold, the Court may permit the party or person having the conduct of the sale to sell the land in such manner as he

thinks fit, or may direct that the land be sold in such manner as the Court may either by the order or subsequently direct for the best price that can be obtained, and all proper parties shall join in the sale and conveyance as the Court shall direct.

(2) The Court may give such directions as it thinks fit for the purpose of effecting the sale, including, without prejudice to the generality of the foregoing words, directions—

(a) appointing the party or person who is to have the conduct of the sale;
(b) fixing the manner of sale, whether by contract conditional on the approval of the Court, private treaty, public auction, tender or some other manner;
(c) fixing a reserve or minimum price;
(d) requiring payment of the purchase money into Court or to trustees or other persons;
(e) for settling the particulars and conditions of sale;
(f) for obtaining evidence of the value of the property;
(g) fixing the security (if any) to be given by the auctioneer, if the sale is to be by public auction, and the remuneration to be allowed him;
(h) requiring an abstract of the title to be referred to conveyancing counsel of the Court or some other conveyancing counsel for his opinion thereon and to settle the particulars and conditions of sale.



**[3.546.1]**
**Keypoint**

- General

**[3.546.2]**
**General**

The court will generally make an order:

- directing that the conduct of the sale should be entrusted to the party who has obtained the order;
- directing how the sale should be conducted, eg by private treaty or by auction;
- fixing a minimum price with permission to apply if necessary to the court for a variation;
- making any necessary vesting order under s 47 of the Trustee Act 1925 or appointing a person to convey under s 50 of that Act to enable the sale to be completed.

**[3.547]**

### II Conveyancing Counsel of the Court

### Ord 31, r 5 Reference of matters to conveyancing counsel of Court

The Court may refer to the conveyancing counsel of the Court—

(a) any matter relating to the investigation of the title to any property with a view to an investment of money in the purchase or on mortgage thereof, or with a view to the sale thereof;
(b) any matter relating to the settlement of a draft of a conveyance, mortgage, settlement or other instrument; and
(c) any other matter it thinks fit,

and may act upon his opinion in the matter referred.

**[3.548]**

### Ord 31, r 6 Objection to conveyancing counsel's opinion

Any party may object to the opinion given by an conveyancing counsel on a reference under rule 5, and if he does so the point in dispute shall be determined by the Judge.

**[3.549]**

### Ord 31, r 8 Obtaining counsel's opinion on reference

The order referring any matter to conveyancing counsel of the Court shall be recorded in the books of the Court and a copy of such order shall be sent by the Court to counsel and shall constitute sufficient authority for him to proceed with the reference.

## CPR 1998, PT 40

**[3.550]**

II SALE OF LAND ETC AND CONVEYANCING COUNSEL

### 40.15 Scope of this Section

(1) This Section—

(a) deals with the court's power to order the sale, mortgage, partition or exchange of land; and

(b) contains provisions about conveyancing counsel.

(Section 131 of the Supreme Court Act 1981 provides for the appointment of the conveyancing counsel of the Supreme Court)

(2) In this Section 'land' includes any interest in, or right over, land.

**Amendment**

Inserted by SI 2000/221, r 18(4), Sch 4, Pt II. Date in force: 2 May 2000: see SI 2000/221, r 1(b).

**[3.550A]**

### 40.16 Power to order sale etc

In any proceedings relating to land, the court may order the land, or part of it, to be—

(a) sold;

(b) mortgaged;

(c) exchanged; or

(d) partitioned.

**Amendment**

Inserted by SI 2000/221, r 18(4), Sch 4, Pt II. Date in force: 2 May 2000: see SI 2000/221, r 1(b).

**[3.550B]**

### 40.17 Power to order delivery up of possession etc

Where the court has made an order under rule 40.16, it may order any party to deliver up to the purchaser or any other person—

(a) possession of the land;

(b) receipt of rents or profits relating to it; or

(c) both.

**Amendment**

Inserted by SI 2000/221, r 18(4), Sch 4, Pt II. Date in force: 2 May 2000: see SI 2000/221, r 1(b).

**[3.550C]**

### 40.18 Reference to conveyancing counsel

(1) The court may direct conveyancing counsel to investigate and prepare a report on the title of any land or to draft any document.

(2) The court may take the report on title into account when it decides the issue in question.

(Provisions dealing with the fees payable to conveyancing counsel are set out in the practice direction relating to Part 44)

**Amendment**

Inserted by SI 2000/221, r 18(4), Sch 4, Pt II. Date in force: 2 May 2000: see SI 2000/221, r 1(b).

## [3.550D]

### 40.19 Party may object to report

(1) Any party to the proceedings may object to the report on title prepared by conveyancing counsel.

(2) Where there is an objection, the issue will be referred to a judge for determination.

(Part 23 contains general rules about making an application)

**Amendment**

Inserted by SI 2000/221, r 18(4), Sch 4, Pt II. Date in force: 2 May 2000: see SI 2000/221, r 1(b).

# RSC ORDER 99
# Inheritance (Provision for Family and Dependants) Act 1975

Contents





**[3.551]**
**CPR 1998, Sch 1 (RSC Ord 99)**

The following text should be read with the Inheritance (Provision for Family and Dependants) Act 1975 and commentary thereto[1].

1 See para **[2.142]** et seq above.

**[3.552]**

**Ord 99, r A1 Order to apply to High Court and County Court**

This Order applies to proceedings both in the High Court and the county court.

**[3.552.1]**
**Keypoint**

- General

**[3.552.2]**
**General**

The former CCR Ord 48 (family provision) which regulated procedure in the county court in relation to applications for family provision is not a Schedule rule for the purpose of CPR 1998, Pt 50. Accordingly all applications will now be regulated by this Order. The county court has unlimited jurisdiction in relation to applications.

[3.553]

### Ord 99, r 1 Interpretation

In this Order 'the Act' means the Inheritance (Provision for Family and Dependants) Act 1975 and a section referred to by number means the section so numbered in that Act.

[3.554]

### Ord 99, r 2 Assignment to Chancery or Family Division if proceedings in High Court

Proceedings in the High Court under the Act may be assigned to the Chancery Division or to the Family Division.

[3.555]

### Ord 99, r 3 Application for financial provision

(1) An application under section 1 is made by the issue of a claim form.

(3) There shall be filed with the Court a witness statement or affidavit by the applicant in support of the claim, exhibiting an official copy of the grant of representation to the deceased's estate and of every testamentary document admitted to proof, and a copy of the witness statement or affidavit shall be served on every defendant with the claim form.

[3.555.1]

**Keypoint**

- Procedure

[3.555.2]

**Procedure**

Use Form N208, see above.

[3.556]

### Ord 99, r 4 Powers of Court as to parties

(1) The Court may at any stage of proceedings under the Act direct that any person be added as a party to the proceedings or that notice of the proceedings be served on any person.

(2) [CPR rule 19.7], shall apply to proceedings under the Act as it applies to the proceedings mentioned in paragraph (1) of that rule.

**Amendment**

SI 2000/221.

[3.557]

### Ord 99, r 5 Witness statement or affidavit in answer

(1) A defendant to an application under section 1 who is a personal representative of the deceased shall and any other defendant may, within 21 days after service of the claim form on him, inclusive of the day of service, file with the Court a witness statement or affidavit in answer to the application.

(2) The witness statement or affidavit filed by a personal representative pursuant to paragraph (1) shall state to the best of the witness's ability—

(a) full particulars of the value of the deceased's net estate, as defined by section 25(1);

(b) the person or classes of persons beneficially interested in the estate, giving the names and (in the case of those who are not already parties) the addresses of all living beneficiaries, and the value of their interests so far as ascertained;

(c) if such be the case, that any living beneficiary (naming him) is a child or patient within the meaning of CPR rule 21.1(2); and

(d) any facts known to the witness which might affect the exercise of the Court's powers under the Act.

(3) Every defendant who lodges a witness statement or affidavit shall at the same time serve a copy on the claimant and on every other defendant who is not represented by the same solicitor.

**[3.557.1]**
**Keypoints**

- Procedure
- Parties
- Witness statements and affidavits
- Leave of the court where application is more than six months after grant



**[3.557.2]**
**Procedure**

Proceedings may be begun in the Chancery Division or in the Family Division (r 2). The former r 3(1) which provided that proceedings could be begun in any district registry does not appear in the Order with the result that proceedings in the Chancery Division will have to be begun either in the High Court or in a Chancery district registry. Any difficulties with this can be avoided by either bringing the claim in the Family Division or the county court.

The former RSC Ord 99, r 3(1) and (2) (which is repealed) provided that the proceedings should be begun by originating summons and specifically in the expedited form. Proceedings should now be commenced in accordance with CPR 1998, Pt 8 but a hearing date (for directions) may be sought (pursuant to the CPR 1998, Pt 8 – *Practice Direction 8A*, para 4.1 at the time the claim form is issued. See CPR 1998, Pt 8 – *Practice Direction 8B*, Section A).

**[3.557.3]**
**Parties**

The claimant is the applicant in the proceedings (which should be entitled 'In the estate of A B deceased'); the personal representatives and all beneficiaries who may be affected by the order of the court are defendants. The court may at any stage direct that any person be added as a party or that notice of the proceedings be served on any person (r 4(1)). If there are any beneficiaries with the same interest a representation order under CPR 1998, Sch 1 – RSC Ord 15, r 13(2)(c) should be made (r 4(2)).

**[3.557.4]**
**Witness statements and affidavits**

On issuing the claim form the applicant must lodge a witness statement or an affidavit exhibiting an official copy of the grant of representation and will and a copy of the witness statement or affidavit must be served with the claim form on every defendant (r 3(3)). The rule does not prescribe the contents of the evidence but it is important to set out particulars of any known previous proceedings relevant to the application and the means of the applicant. A defendant who is a personal representative must, and any other defendant may, within 21 days after service of the claim for file evidence in answer (r 5(1)). The evidence filed by the personal representative must include the matters set out in r 5(2). A defendant other than a personal representative who does not file evidence in particular (if relevant) of his or her means may be at a disadvantage. The defendant's evidence must be served on the claimant and any other defendant (r 5(3)).

### [3.557.5]
### Leave of the court where application is more than six months after grant

An application under the I(PFD)A 1975 cannot without the permission of the court be made after six months from the date of the grant of representation (s 4)[1]. If such permission is required, it should be sought in a separate paragraph in the claim form. The Act gives the court an unfettered discretion to extend the time. Applications for permission are usually heard prior to the substantive hearing, the evidence being limited to that which is required for the application.

1 For s 4 of the I(PFD)A 1975, see para **[2.145]** above.

### [3.558]

**Ord 99, r 6 Separate representation**

Where an application under section 1 is made jointly by two or more applicants and the claim form is accordingly issued by one solicitor on behalf of all of them, they may, if they have conflicting interests, appear on any hearing of the claim by separate solicitors or counsel or in person, and where at any stage of the proceedings it appears to the Court that one of the applicants is not but ought to be separately represented, the Court may adjourn the proceedings until he is.

### [3.558.1]
### Keypoint

- Conflicting interests

### [3.558.2]
### Conflicting interests

Where there are two or more claimants whose interests conflict all should be made claimants and the claim form should be issued by one firm of solicitors.

Rule 6 provides that notwithstanding the general rule claimants with conflicting interests can nevertheless appear at the hearing by separate solicitors or counsel or in person.

### [3.559]

**Ord 99, r 7 Endorsement of memorandum on grant**

On the hearing of an application under section 1 the personal representative shall produce to the Court the grant of representation to the deceased's estate and, if an order is made under the Act, the grant shall remain in the custody of the Court until a memorandum of the order has been endorsed on or permanently annexed to the grant in accordance with section 19(3).

### [3.559.1]
### Keypoint

- Grant of representation

**[3.559.2]**
**Grant of representation**

Rule 7 provides that the personal representatives must produce the grant of representation at the hearing. If an order is made, the grant is kept by the court for the purpose of transmitting it to the Principal Registry of the Family Division where a memorandum is endorsed in accordance with s 19(3) of the I(PFD)A 1975[1].

1 See para **[2.161]** above.

**[3.560]**

**Ord 99, r 9 Subsequent applications in proceedings under section 1**

Where an order has been made on an application under section 1, any subsequent application under the Act, whether made by a party to the proceedings or by any other person, shall be made by the issue of an application notice in accordance with CPR Part 23.

**[3.561]**

**Ord 99, r 10 Drawing up and service of orders**

The provisions of the Family Proceedings Rules relating to the drawing up and service of orders shall apply to proceedings in the Family Division under this Order as if they were proceedings under those Rules. In this rule 'Family Proceedings Rules' means rules made under section 40 of the Matrimonial and Family Proceedings Act 1984.



**[3.561.1]**
**Keypoint**

- Consent orders under the I(PFD)A 1975

**[3.561.2]**
**Consent orders under the I(PFD)A 1975**

Every final order embodying terms of compromise made in proceedings in the Chancery Division under the I(PFD)A 1975 shall contain a direction that a memorandum of the order shall be endorsed on, or permanently annexed to, the probate or letters of administration and a copy of the order shall be sent to the Principal Registry of the Family Division with the relevant grant of probate or letters of administration for endorsement, notwithstanding that any particular order may not, strictly speaking, be an order under the I(PFD)A 1975.

# Community Legal Service (Costs) Regulations 2000

## SI 2000 No 441

Contents

*Regulation*

## [3.561A]

PART I
GENERAL

### 1 Citation and commencement

These Regulations may be cited as the Community Legal Service (Costs) Regulations 2000 and shall come into force on 1st April 2000.

**Initial Commencement**
Specified date: 1 April 2000.

## [3.561B]

### 2 Interpretation

In these Regulations:

'the Act' means the Access to Justice Act 1999;

'certificate' means a certificate issued under the Funding Code certifying a decision to fund services for the client;

'client' means an individual who receives funded services;

'Commission' means the Legal Services Commission established under section 1 of the Act;

'costs judge' has the same meaning as in the CPR;

'costs order' means an order that a party pay all or part of the costs of proceedings;

'costs order against the Commission' means an order, made under regulation 5 of the Community Legal Service (Cost Protection) Regulations 2000 (but not one under regulation 6 of those Regulations), that the Commission pay all or part of the costs of a party to proceedings who has not received funded services in relation to those proceedings under a certificate, other than a certificate which has been revoked;

'cost protection' means the limit on costs awarded against a client set out in section 11(1) of the Act;

'court' includes any tribunal having the power to award costs in favour of, or against, a party;

'CPR' means the Civil Procedure Rules 1998, and a reference to a Part or rule, prefixed by 'CPR', means the Part or rule so numbered in the CPR;

'Financial Regulations' means the Community Legal Service (Financial) Regulations 2000;

'Funding Code' means the code approved under section 9 of the Act;

'full costs' means, where a section 11(1) costs order is made against a client, the amount of costs which that client would, but for section 11(1) of the Act, have been ordered to pay;

'funded services' means services which are provided directly for a client and funded for that client by the Commission as part of the Community Legal Service under sections 4 to 11 of the Act;

'partner', in relation to a party to proceedings, means a person with whom that party lives as a couple, and includes a person with whom the party is not currently living but from whom he is not living separate and apart;

'proceedings' include proceedings in any tribunal which is a court, as defined, in this paragraph;

'receiving party' means a party in favour of whom a costs order is made;

'Regional Director' means any Regional Director appointed by the Commission in accordance with the Funding Code and any other person authorised to act on his behalf, except a supplier;

'rules of court', in relation to a tribunal, means rules or regulations made by the authority having power to make rules or regulations regulating the practice and procedure of that tribunal and, in relation to any court, includes practice directions;

'section 11(1) costs order' means a costs order against a client where cost protection applies;

'solicitor' means solicitor or other person who is an authorised litigator within the meaning of section 119(1) of the Courts and Legal Services Act 1990;

'statement of resources' means:

(a) a statement, verified by a statement of truth, made by a party to proceedings setting out:

(i) his income and capital and financial commitments during the previous year and, if applicable, those of his partner;

(ii) his estimated future financial resources and expectations and, if applicable, those of his partner; and

(iii) a declaration that he and, if applicable, his partner, has not deliberately foregone or deprived himself of any resources or expectations, particulars of any application for funding made by him in connection with the proceedings, and any other facts relevant to the determination of his resources; or

(b) a statement, verified by a statement of truth, made by a client receiving funded services, setting out the information provided by the client under regulation 6 of the Financial Regulations, and stating that there has been no significant change in the client's financial circumstances since the date on which the information was provided or, as the case may be, details of any such change;

'statement of truth' has the same meaning as in CPR Part 22;

'supplier' means any person or body providing funded services to the client, including any authorised advocate (within the meaning of section 119(1) of the Courts and Legal Services Act 1990) engaged by the client's solicitor to act in proceedings.

**Initial Commencement**

Specified date: 1 April 2000.



**[3.561C]**

### 3 Effect of these Regulations

Nothing in these Regulations shall be construed, in relation to proceedings where one or more parties are receiving, or have received, funded services, as:

(a) requiring a court to make a costs order where it would not otherwise have made a costs order; or

(b) affecting the court's power to make a wasted costs order against a legal representative.

**Initial Commencement**

Specified date: 1 April 2000.

**[3.561D]**

### 4 Termination of retainer where funding is withdrawn

(1) The following paragraphs of this regulation apply where funding is withdrawn by revoking or discharging the client's certificate.

(2) Subject to paragraphs (3) and (4), on the revocation or discharge of the client's certificate, the retainer of any supplier acting under that certificate shall terminate immediately.

(3) Termination of retainers under paragraph (2) shall not take effect unless and until any procedures under the Funding Code for review of the decision to withdraw the client's funding are concluded, and confirm the decision to withdraw funding.

(4) The solicitor's retainer shall not terminate until he has complied with any procedures under the Funding Code that require him to send or serve notices.

**Initial Commencement**

Specified date: 1 April 2000.

**[3.561E]**

PART II

COSTS ORDERS AGAINST CLIENT AND AGAINST COMMISSION

## 5 Application of regulations 6 to 13

Regulations 6 to 13 apply only where cost protection applies.

**Initial Commencement**

Specified date: 1 April 2000.

**[3.561F]**

## 6 Security for costs

Where in any proceedings a client is required to give security for costs, the amount of that security shall not exceed the amount (if any) which is a reasonable one having regard to all the circumstances, including the client's financial resources and his conduct in relation to the dispute to which the proceedings relate.

**Initial Commencement**

Specified date: 1 April 2000.

**[3.561G]**

## 7 Assessment of resources

(1) The first £100,000 of the value of the client's interest in the main or only dwelling in which he resides shall not be taken into account in having regard to the client's resources for the purposes of section 11(1) of the Act.

(2) Where, but only to the extent that, the court considers that the circumstances are exceptional, having regard in particular to the quantity or value of the items concerned, the court may take into account the value of the client's clothes and household furniture, or the tools and implements of his trade, in having regard to the client's resources for the purposes of section 11(1) of the Act.

(3) Subject to paragraph (4), in having regard to the resources of a party for the purposes of section 11(1) of the Act, the resources of his partner shall be treated as his resources.

(4) The resources of a party's partner shall not be treated as that party's resources if the partner has a contrary interest in the dispute in respect of which the funded services are provided.

(5) Where a party is acting in a representative, fiduciary or official capacity, the court shall not take the personal resources of the party into account for the purposes of section 11(1) of the Act, but shall have regard to the value of any property or estate, or the amount of any fund out of which he is entitled to be indemnified, and may also have regard to the resources of the persons, if any, including that party where appropriate, who are beneficially interested in that property, estate or fund.

**Initial Commencement**

Specified date: 1 April 2000.

[3.561H]

## 8 Statements of resources

(1) Any person who is a party to proceedings in which another party is a client may make a statement of resources, and file it with the court.

(2) A person making and filing a statement of resources under paragraph (1) shall serve a copy of it on the client.

(3) Where a copy of a statement of resources has been served under paragraph (2) not less than seven days before the date fixed for a hearing at which the amount to be paid under a section 11(1) costs order falls, or may fall, to be decided, the client shall also make a statement of resources, and shall produce it at that hearing.

**Initial Commencement**

Specified date: 1 April 2000.

[3.561I]

## 9 Procedures for ordering costs against client and Commission

(1) [Where the court is considering whether to make] a section 11(1) costs order, it shall consider whether, but for cost protection, it would have made a costs order against the client and, if so, whether it would, on making the costs order, have specified the amount to be paid under that order.

(2) If the court considers that it would have made a costs order against the client, but that it would not have specified the amount to be paid under it, the court shall, when making the section 11(1) costs order:

- (a) specify the amount (if any) that the client is to pay under that order if, but only if:
  - (i) it considers that it has sufficient information before it to decide what amount is, in that case, a reasonable amount for the client to pay, in accordance with section 11(1) of the Act; and
  - (ii) it is satisfied that, if it were to determine the full costs at that time, they would exceed the amount referred to in sub-paragraph (i);
- (b) otherwise, it shall not specify the amount the client is to pay under the … costs order.

(3) If the court considers that it would have made a costs order against the client, and that it would have specified the amount to be paid under it, the court shall, when making the section 11(1) costs order:

- (a) specify the amount (if any) that the client is to pay under that order if, but only if, it considers that it has sufficient information before it to decide what amount is, in that case, a reasonable amount for the client to pay, in accordance with section 11(1) of the Act;
- (b) otherwise, it shall not specify the amount the client is to pay under the … costs order.

(4) Any order made under paragraph (3) shall state the amount of the full costs.

(5) The amount (if any) to be paid by the client under an order made under paragraph (2)(b) or paragraph (3)(b), and any application for a costs order against the Commission, shall be determined in accordance with regulation 10, and at any such determination following an order made under paragraph (2)(b), the amount of the full costs shall also be assessed.

(6) Where the court makes a section 11(1) costs order that does not specify the amount which the client is to pay under it, it may also make findings of fact, as to the parties' conduct in the proceedings or otherwise, relevant to the determination of that amount, and those findings shall be taken into consideration in that determination.

**Initial Commencement**
Specified date: 1 April 2000.

**Amendment**
SI 2001/822.

## [3.561J]

**10**

(1) The following paragraphs of this regulation apply where the amount to be paid under a section 11(1) costs order, or an application for a costs order against the Commission, is to be determined under this regulation, by virtue of regulation 9(5).

(2) The receiving party may, within three months after a section 11(1) costs order is made, request a hearing to determine the costs payable to him.

(3) A request under paragraph (2) shall be accompanied by:

- (a) if the section 11(1) costs order does not state the full costs, the receiving party's bill of costs, which shall comply with any requirements of relevant rules of court relating to the form and content of a bill of costs where the court is assessing a party's costs;
- (b) a statement of resources; and
- (c) if the receiving party is seeking, or, subject to the determination of the amount to be paid under the section 11(1) costs order, may seek, a costs order against the Commission, written notice to that effect.

(4) The receiving party shall file the documents referred to in paragraph (3) with the court and at the same time serve copies of them:

- (a) on the client, if a determination of costs payable under section 11(1) of the Act is sought; and
- (b) on the Regional Director, if notice has been given under paragraph (3)(c).

(5) Where documents are served on the client under paragraph (4)(a), the client shall make a statement of resources.

(6) The client shall file the statement of resources made under paragraph (5) with the court, and serve copies of it on the receiving party and, if notice has been given under paragraph (3)(c), on the Regional Director, not more than 21 days after the client receives a copy of the receiving party's statement of resources.

(7) The client may, at the same time as filing and serving a statement of resources under paragraph (6), file, and serve on the same persons, a statement setting out any points of dispute in relation to the bill of costs referred to in paragraph (3)(a).

(8) If the client, without good reason, fails to file a statement of resources in accordance with paragraph (6), the court shall determine the amount which the client shall be required to pay under the section 11(1) costs order (and, if relevant, the full costs), having regard to the statement made by the receiving party, and the court need not hold an oral hearing for such determination.

(9) If the client files a statement of resources in accordance with paragraph (6), or the period for filing such notice expires, or if the costs payable by the client have already been determined, the court shall set a date for the hearing and, at least 14 days before that date, serve notice of it on:

- (a) the receiving party;
- (b) the client (unless the costs payable by the client have already been determined); and
- (c) if a costs order against the Commission is or may be sought, the Regional Director.

(10) The court's functions under this regulation may be exercised:

- (a) in relation to proceedings in the House of Lords, by the Clerk to the Parliaments;
- (b) in relation to proceedings in the Court of Appeal, High Court or a county court, a costs judge or a district judge;

(c) in relation to proceedings in a magistrates' court, by a single justice or by the justices' clerk;

(d) in relation to proceedings in the Employment Appeal Tribunal, by the Registrar of that Tribunal.

(11) The amount of costs to be determined under this regulation may include the costs incurred in relation to a request made under this regulation.

**Initial Commencement**

Specified date: 1 April 2000.

## [3.561JA]

### 10A

(1) Subject to paragraph (2), where the court makes a section 11(1) costs order but does not specify the amount which the client is to pay under it, the court may order the client to pay an amount on account of the costs which are the subject of the order.

(2) The court may order a client to make a payment on account of costs under this regulation only if it has sufficient information before it to decide the minimum amount which the client is likely to be ordered to pay on a determination under regulation 10.

(3) The amount of the payment on account of costs shall not exceed the minimum amount which the court decides that the client is likely to be ordered to pay on such a determination.

(4) Where the court orders a client to make a payment on account of costs—

(a) it shall order the client to make the payment into court; and

(b) the payment shall remain in court unless and until the court—

(i) makes a determination under regulation 10 of the amount which the client should pay to the receiving party under the section 11(1) costs order, and orders the payment on account or part of it to be paid to the receiving party in satisfaction or part satisfaction of the client's liability under that order; or

(ii) makes an order under paragraph (5)(b) or (5)(c) of this regulation that the payment on account or part of it be repaid to the client.

(5) Where a client has made a payment on account of costs pursuant to an order under paragraph (1) of this regulation—

(a) the receiving party shall request a hearing under regulation 10 to determine the amount of costs payable to him;

(b) if the receiving party fails to request such a hearing within the time permitted by regulation 10(2), the payment on account shall be repaid to the client;

(c) if upon the hearing under regulation 10 the amount of costs which it is determined that the client should pay is less than the amount of the payment on account, the difference shall be repaid to the client.]

**Appointment**

2 April 2001: see SI 2001/822.

**Amendment**

Inserted by SI 2001/822, reg 4.

## [3.561K]

### 11 Appeals, etc

(1) Subject to the following paragraphs of this regulation, and to regulation 12, any determination made under regulation 9 or regulation 10 shall be final.

(2) Any party with a financial interest in an assessment of the full costs may appeal against that assessment, if and to the extent that that party would, but for these

Regulations, be entitled to appeal against an assessment of costs by the court in which the relevant proceedings are taking place.

(3) Where, under regulation 9(2)(a), the court has specified the amount which a client is required to pay under a section 11(1) costs order, the client may apply to the court for a determination of the full costs and if, on that determination, the amount of the full costs is less than the amount which the court previously specified under regulation 9(2)(a), the client shall instead be required to pay the amount of the full costs.

(4) The receiving party or the Commission may appeal, on a point of law, against the making of a costs order against the Commission (including the amount of costs which the Commission is required to pay under the order), or against the court's refusal to make such an order.

**Initial Commencement**

Specified date: 1 April 2000.

**[3.561L]**

## 12 Variation and late determination of amount of costs

(1) The following paragraphs of this regulation apply where the court makes a section 11(1) costs order.

(2) Where the amount (if any) which the client is required to pay under the section 11(1) costs order, together with the amount which the Commission is required to pay under any costs order against the Commission, is less than the full costs, the receiving party may, on the ground set out in paragraph (4)(a), apply to the court for an order varying the amount which the client is required to pay under the section 11(1) costs order.

(3) Where the court has not specified the amount to be paid under the section 11(1) costs order, and the receiving party has not, within the time limit in regulation 10(2), applied to have that amount determined in accordance with regulation 10, the receiving party may, on any of the grounds set out in paragraph (4), apply for a determination of the amount that the client is required to pay.

(4) The grounds referred to in paragraphs (2) and (3) are the grounds that:

- (a) there has been a significant change in the client's circumstances since the date of the order;
- (b) material additional information as to the client's financial resources is available, and that information could not with reasonable diligence have been obtained by the receiving party in time to make an application in accordance with regulation 10; or
- (c) there were other good reasons justifying the receiving party's failure to make an application within the time limit in regulation 10(2).

(5) Any application under paragraph (2) or (3) shall be made by the receiving party within six years from the date on which the section 11(1) costs order is first made.

(6) On any application under paragraph (2), the order may be varied as the court thinks fit, but the amount of costs ordered (excluding any costs ordered to be paid under paragraph (9)) shall not exceed the amount of the full costs as stated in any previous order of the court.

(7) When the amount which the client is required to pay under the section 11(1) costs order has been determined under regulation 9(2)(a), and the receiving party applies under paragraph (2) for an order varying that amount:

- (a) the receiving party shall file with the application under paragraph (2) his bill of costs, which shall comply with any requirements of relevant rules of court relating to the form and content of a bill of costs where the court is assessing a party's costs; and
- (b) the court shall, when determining the application, assess the full costs.

(8) Where the receiving party has received funded services in relation to the proceedings, the Commission may make an application under paragraph (2) or paragraph (3), and:

(a) when making the application the Commission shall file with the court a statement of the receiving party's costs or, if those costs have not been assessed, the receiving party's bill of costs; and

(b) paragraphs (4) to (6) shall apply to that application as if 'the Commission' were substituted for 'the receiving party' in those paragraphs.

(9) The amount of costs to be determined under this regulation may include the costs incurred in relation to an application made under this regulation.

**Initial Commencement**

Specified date: 1 April 2000.

**[3.561M]**

### 13 Rights to appear

(1) The Regional Director may appear at:

(a) any hearing in relation to which notice has been given under regulation 10(3)(c);

(b) the hearing of any appeal under regulation 11(4); or

(c) the hearing of any application under regulation 12(8).

(2) The Regional Director may, instead of appearing under paragraph (1), give evidence in the form of a written statement to the court, verified by a statement of truth.

(3) The Regional Director shall file with the court any statement under paragraph (2), and serve a copy on the receiving party, not less than seven days before the hearing to which it relates.

**Initial Commencement**

Specified date: 1 April 2000.



**[3.561N]**

## PART III
## PROPERTY AND COSTS RECOVERED FOR A FUNDED CLIENT

### 14 Application of this Part

(1) In this Part:

'the awarded sum' means the amount of costs to be paid in accordance with a client's costs order or a client's costs agreement;

'client's costs order' and 'client's costs agreement' mean, respectively, an order and an agreement that another party to proceedings or prospective proceedings pay all or part of the costs of a client;

'Fund' means the Community Legal Service Fund established under section 5 of the Act;

'the funded sum' means the amount of remuneration payable by the Commission to a supplier for the relevant work under a contract or any other arrangements that determine that supplier's remuneration, including those that apply by virtue of article 4 of the Community Legal Service (Funding) Order 2000; and, where funding is provided by the Commission under a contract which does not differentiate between the remuneration for the client's case and remuneration for other cases, means such part of the remuneration payable under the contract as may be specified in writing by the Commission as being the funded sum;

'relevant work' means the funded services provided in relation to the dispute or proceedings to which the client's costs order or client's costs agreement relates;

'remuneration' includes fees and disbursements and value added tax on fees and disbursements;

'statutory charge' means the charge created by section 10(7) of the Act.

**Initial Commencement**

Specified date: 1 April 2000.

**[3.561O]**

### 15 Amount of costs under client's costs order or client's costs agreement

(1) Subject to the following paragraphs of this regulation, the amount of the costs to be paid under a client's costs order or client's costs agreement shall, subject to regulation 16, be determined on the same basis as it would be if the costs were to be paid to a person who had not received funded services.

(2) Subject to paragraph (3), the amount of the awarded sum shall not be limited to the amount of the funded sum by any rule of law which limits the costs recoverable by a party to proceedings to the amount he is liable to pay to his legal representatives.

(3) Paragraph (2) applies only to the extent that the Commission has authorised the supplier under section 22(2)(b) of the Act to take payment for the relevant work other than that funded by the Commission.

**Initial Commencement**

Specified date: 1 April 2000.

**[3.561P]**

### 16 Costs of serving notices and other documents

The amount of costs to be paid under a client's costs order or client's costs agreement may include costs incurred in filing with the court, or serving on any other party to proceedings, notices or any other documents in accordance with these Regulations, the Financial Regulations or the Funding Code.

**Initial Commencement**

Specified date: 1 April 2000.

**[3.561Q]**

### 17 Application of regulations 18 to 24

(1) Regulations 18 to 24 apply only where funded services have been provided under a certificate.

(2) If the client is no longer being represented by a solicitor, all money to which regulation 18(1) applies shall be paid (or repaid) to the Commission, and all references in regulations 18(1) and 19 to the client's solicitor shall be construed as references to the Commission.

**Initial Commencement**

Specified date: 1 April 2000.

**[3.561R]**

### 18 Money recovered to be paid to solicitor

(1) Subject to the following paragraphs of this regulation, and to regulation 17(2), all money payable to or recovered by a client in connection with a dispute by way of

damages, costs or otherwise, whether or not proceedings were begun, and whether under an order of the court or an agreement or otherwise, shall be paid to the client's solicitor, and only the client's solicitor shall be capable of giving a good discharge for that money.

(2) Paragraph (1) shall not apply to:

(a) any periodical payment of maintenance; or

(b) any money recovered or preserved by a client in any proceedings which:

(i) has been paid into, or remains in, court, and is invested for the client's benefit; and

(ii) under regulation 50 of the Financial Regulations, is not subject to the statutory charge.

(3) Where the client's solicitor has reason to believe that an attempt may be made to circumvent the provisions of paragraph (1), he shall inform the Commission immediately.

**Initial Commencement**

Specified date: 1 April 2000.



**[3.561S]**

### 19 Notice to third parties

(1) Where money is payable under regulation 18, and that money is payable by a trustee in bankruptcy, a trustee or assignee of a deed of arrangement, a liquidator of a company in liquidation, a trustee of a pension fund or any other third party ('the third party') the client's solicitor shall send to the third party notice that funded services have been funded for the client by the Commission.

(2) Notice under paragraph (1) shall operate as a request by the client that money payable under regulation 18 be paid to his solicitor, and shall be a sufficient authority for that purpose.

**Initial Commencement**

Specified date: 1 April 2000.

**[3.561T]**

### 20 Solicitor to pay money recovered to Commission

(1) The client's solicitor shall forthwith:

(a) inform the Regional Director of any money or other property recovered or preserved, and send him a copy of the order or agreement by virtue of which the property was recovered or preserved;

(b) subject to the following paragraphs of this regulation, pay to the Commission all money or other property received by him under regulation 18.

(2) Paragraph (1)(b) shall not apply to any money or other property to which the statutory charge does not apply, by virtue of the Financial Regulations.

(3) Where he considers it essential to protect the client's interests or welfare, the Regional Director shall pay, or direct the client's solicitor to pay, to the client any money received by way of any interim payment made in accordance with an order made under CPR rule 25.6, or in accordance with an agreement having the same effect as such an order.

(4) The Regional Director may direct the client's solicitor to:

(a) pay to the Commission under paragraph (1)(b) only such sums as, in the Regional Director's opinion, should be retained by the Commission in order to safeguard its interests; and

(b) pay any other money to the client.

(5) Where the solicitor pays money to the Commission in accordance with this regulation, he shall identify what sums relate respectively to:

(a) costs;

(b) damages;

(c) interest on costs; and

(d) interest on damages.

**Initial Commencement**

Specified date: 1 April 2000.

## [3.561U]

### 21 Postponement of statutory charge

(1) In this regulation:

'conveyancer' means a solicitor or any other person who lawfully provides conveyancing services;

'family proceedings' means proceedings which arise out of family relationships, including proceedings in which the welfare of children is determined. Family proceedings also include all proceedings under any one or more of the following:

(a) the Matrimonial Causes Act 1973;

(b) the Inheritance (Provision for Family and Dependants) Act 1975;

(c) the Adoption Act 1976;

(d) the Domestic Proceedings and Magistrates' Courts Act 1978;

(e) Part III of the Matrimonial and Family Proceedings Act 1984;

(f) Parts I, II and IV of the Children Act 1989;

(g) Part IV of the Family Law Act 1996; and

(h) the inherent jurisdiction of the High Court in relation to children;

'purchase money' means money recovered or preserved by the client in family proceedings which, by virtue of an order of the court or an agreement, is to be used to purchase a home to be used by the client or the client's dependants, and 'the purchased property' means the property purchased or to be purchased with that money.

(2) The following paragraphs of this regulation apply, and (subject to paragraph (6)) regulation 20(1)(b) does not apply, where the Commission decides to postpone enforcement of the statutory charge under regulation 52 of the Financial Regulations.

(3) The solicitor may release the purchase money to the seller or the seller's representative on completion of the purchase of the purchased property; and shall as soon as practicable provide the Commission with sufficient information to enable it to protect its interest in accordance with regulation 52(1)(c) of the Financial Regulations.

(4) The client's solicitor may release the purchase money to a conveyancer acting for the client in the purchase of the purchased property, if he is satisfied that adequate steps have been, or will be, taken to protect the interests of the Commission.

(5) The steps referred to in paragraph (4) shall include, but are not limited to, the securing of an undertaking from the conveyancer referred to in that paragraph to:

(a) provide the information referred to in paragraph (3); and

(b) repay the purchase money under paragraph (6).

(6) Where the purchase of the purchased property has not been completed within 12 months after the date of the Commission's decision referred to in paragraph (2), or such longer period as the Commission considers reasonable, regulation 20(1)(b) shall apply and the purchase money shall accordingly be repaid to the Commission.

**Initial Commencement**

Specified date: 1 April 2000.

[3.561V]

## 22 Retention and payment out of money by the Commission

(1) The Commission shall deal with the money paid to it under this Part in accordance with this regulation.

(2) The Commission shall retain:

(a) an amount equal to the costs incurred in taking steps under regulation 23;

(b) an amount equal to that part of the funded sum already paid to the supplier in respect of the relevant work; and

(c) where costs are paid to the Commission together with interest, an amount equal to that interest, less the amount of any interest payable to the supplier under paragraph (3)(b)(ii).

(3) The Commission shall pay to the supplier:

(a) any outstanding amount of the funded sum payable to him in respect of the relevant work;

(b) where costs are ordered or agreed to be paid to the client, and those costs are received by the Commission, and those costs (less any amount retained under paragraph (2)(a) or payable under paragraph (5)) exceed the funded sum:

(i) an amount equal to the amount of the excess; and

(ii) where those costs are paid to the Commission together with interest, an amount equal to the interest attributable to the excess referred to in sub-paragraph (i).

(4) Paragraph (5) applies where a solicitor has acted on behalf of the client in proceedings before that client receives funded services in respect of the same proceedings, or has a lien on any documents necessary to proceedings to which a client is a party, and has handed them over subject to the lien, but applies only so far as is consistent with the express terms of any contract between the Commission and the solicitor.

(5) Where the solicitor referred to in paragraph (4) gives the Commission written notice that this paragraph applies, the Commission shall pay to that solicitor the costs to which that solicitor would have been entitled if those costs had been assessed on an indemnity basis.

(6) Where the amount of costs payable under paragraph (5) have not been assessed by the court, they may instead be assessed by the Commission.

(7) Where the amount received by the Commission, less any amount retained under paragraph (2)(a), is insufficient to meet the funded sum and any sum payable under paragraph (5), the Commission shall apportion the amount received proportionately between the two.

(8) The Commission shall pay all the money paid to it under this Part, which is not paid or retained under paragraphs (2) to (5), to the client.

**Initial Commencement**

Specified date: 1 April 2000.

[3.561W]

## 23 Enforcement of order etc in favour of client

(1) Where, in relation to any dispute to which a client is a party, whether or not proceedings are begun:

(a) an order or agreement is made providing for the recovery or preservation of property by the client (whether for himself or any other person); or

(b) there is a client's costs order or client's costs agreement

the Commission may take any steps, including proceedings in its own name, as may be necessary to enforce or give effect to that order or agreement.

(2) A client may, with the consent of the Regional Director, take proceedings to give effect to an order or agreement under which he is entitled to recover or preserve money or other property.

(3) Subject to paragraph (4), the client's solicitor may take proceedings for the recovery of costs where a client's costs order or a client's costs agreement has been made.

(4) Where the client's costs order or client's costs agreement relates wholly or partly to costs incurred in carrying out work which is remunerated, or to be remunerated, in the funded sum, but those costs have not been reimbursed by payment from any other party in favour of the client, the solicitor shall require the consent of the Regional Director before taking proceedings to which paragraph (3) refers.

(5) Where the Commission takes proceedings, it may authorise any person to make a statement, file a proof or take any other step in the proceedings in its name.

(6) The costs incurred by the Commission in taking any step to enforce an order or agreement where paragraph (1) applies shall be a first charge on any property or sum so recovered.

**Initial Commencement**

Specified date: 1 April 2000.

**[3.561X]**

## 24 Interest on damages

(1) Where the Commission receives damages paid in favour of a client it shall, subject to the following paragraphs, pay to the client a sum representing gross interest earned while the damages are being held by the Commission.

(2) Without prejudice to its other powers to invest money, the Commission shall maintain and may deposit damages to which this regulation refers in one general account at a bank or building society.

(3) The rate of interest payable to the client under this regulation shall be 0.5% per annum less than the rate payable on damages deposited in the general account.

(4) The Commission shall not be required to pay interest where the damages received do not exceed £500 or where the period during which they are held by the Commission is less than 28 days.

(5) Interest shall be payable for the period beginning on the third business day after the date on which damages are received by the Commission to and including the date on which the Commission determines the amount to be paid under regulation 22(8).

(6) In this regulation:

'bank' means the Bank of England, or the branch, situated in England or Wales, of any institution authorised under the Banking Act 1987;

'building society' means the branch, situated in England or Wales, of a building society within the meaning of the Building Societies Act 1986;

'business day' means a day other than a Saturday, a Sunday, Christmas Day, Good Friday or a bank holiday under the Banking and Financial Dealings Act 1971;

'general account' means an interest bearing account opened in the name of the Commission, the title of which does not identify any client.

**Initial Commencement**

Specified date: 1 April 2000.

# Community Legal Service (Financial) Regulations 2000

## SI 2000 No 516

Contents

*Regulation*

PART III
THE STATUTORY CHARGE





**[3.561Y]**

PART III
THE STATUTORY CHARGE

### 42 Calculation of the statutory charge

In regulations 43 to 53:

'relevant dispute' means the dispute in connection with which funded services are provided;

'relevant proceedings' means proceedings in connection with which funded services are provided;

'recovered', in relation to property or money, means property or money recovered or preserved by a client, whether for himself or for any other person;

'statutory charge' means the charge created by section 10(7) of the Act in respect of the amount defined in regulation 43; and

'success fee' is defined in accordance with section 58 of the Courts and Legal Services Act 1990.

**Initial Commencement**

1 April 2000.

**[3.561Y.1]**

**Keypoint**

- Recovered

## [3.561Y.2]
### Recovered

'Recovered' includes property preserved – preservation may occur when a party retains the right to occupy a property even if her interest in the property is not an issue[1].

1 See *Curling v Law Society* [1985] 1 All ER 705, [1985] 1 WLR 470; and *Parkes v Legal Aid Board* [1997] 1 FCR 430, [1997] 1 FLR 77, CA.

## [3.561Z]

**43**

(1) Subject to paragraphs (3) and (4), where any money or property is recovered for a client in a relevant dispute or proceedings, the amount of the statutory charge shall be the aggregate of the sums referred to in section 10(7)(a) and (b) of the Act.

(2) For the purposes of this regulation:

- (a) the sum referred to in section 10(7)(a) shall be defined in accordance with regulation 40(2) to (4), less any contribution paid by the client;
- (b) the sum referred to in section 10(7)(b) shall include:
  - (i) any interest payable under regulation 52; and
  - (ii) any sum which the client has agreed to pay only in specific circumstances under section 10(2)(c) of the Act, including that proportion of any success fee payable by a client in receipt of Litigation Support which he has agreed should be payable to the Commission under the terms of a conditional fee agreement.

(3) Subject to paragraph (4), the amount of the charge created by section 10(7) of the Act shall not include sums expended by the Commission in funding any of the following services:

- (a) Legal Help;
- (b) Help at Court;
- (c) Family Mediation; or
- (d) Help with Mediation.

(4) Paragraph (3)(a) and (b) does not apply where the funded services are given in relation to family, clinical negligence or personal injury proceedings or a dispute which may give rise to such proceedings.

**Initial Commencement**

1 April 2000.

## [3.561Z.1]
### Keypoint

- The amount of the statutory charge

## [3.561Z.2]
### The amount of the statutory charge

The amount of the statutory charge is calculated in accordance with the provisions of the AJA 1999, s 10(7) which provides as follows:

> '(7) Except so far as regulations otherwise provide, where services have been funded by the Commission for an individual as part of the Community Legal Service–
>
> (a) sums expended by the Commission in funding the services (except to the extent that they are recovered under section 11), and
>
> (b) other sums payable by the individual by virtue of regulations under this section,
>
> shall constitute a first charge on any property recovered or preserved by him (whether for himself or any other person) in any proceedings or in any compromise or settlement of any dispute in connection with which the services were provided.'

[3.561AA]

### 44 Exemptions from the statutory charge

(1) The charge created by section 10(7) of the Act shall not apply to any of the following:

(a) any periodical payment of maintenance;

(b) other than in circumstances which are exceptional having regard in particular to the quantity or value of the items concerned, the client's clothes or household furniture or the tools or implements of his trade;

(c) any sum or sums ordered to be paid under section 5 of the Inheritance (Provision for Family and Dependants) Act 1975 or Part IV of the Family Law Act 1996;

[(d) other than for the purposes of registration under regulation 52(1)(c), the first £3,000 of any money or the value of any property recovered by virtue of an order made or deemed to be made under any of the enactments specified in paragraph (2), or an agreement which has the same effect as such an order, but where the enforcement of the charge is postponed under regulation 52 this exemption will apply when the amount of the charge is paid;]

(e) one-half of any redundancy payment within the meaning of Part XI of the Employment Rights Act 1996 recovered by the client;

(f) any payment of money made in accordance with an order made by the Employment Appeal Tribunal (excluding an order for costs);

(g) where the statutory charge is in favour of the supplier, the client's main or only dwelling; or

(h) any sum, payment or benefit which, by virtue of any provision of or made under an Act of Parliament, cannot be assigned or charged.

(2) The enactments referred to in paragraph (1)(d) are:

(a) section 23(1)(c) or (f), 23(2), 24, 27(6)(c) or (f), 31(7A) or (7B), or 35 of the Matrimonial Causes Act 1973;

(b) section 2 or 6 of the Inheritance (Provision for Family and Dependants) Act 1975;

(c) section 17 of the Married Women's Property Act 1882;

(d) section 2(1)(b) or (d), 6(1) or (5), or 20(2) of the Domestic Proceedings and Magistrates' Courts Act 1978; and

(e) Schedule 1 to the Children Act 1989.

(4) In paragraph (1)(a), 'maintenance' means money or money's worth paid towards the support of a former partner, child or any other person for whose support the payer has previously been responsible or has made payments.

**Initial Commencement**

1 April 2000.

**Amendment**

Para (1): sub-para (d) substituted, in relation to all cases to which the statutory charge applies, by SI 2001/3663, regs 3, 20.

[3.561AA.1]

### Keypoints

- Arrears of periodical payments
- Succession of applications
- Variation

[3.561AA.2]

### Arrears of periodical payments

Arrears of periodical payments will be exempt from the charge. However, a lump sum that 'capitalises' maintenance will not[1].

1 See *Stewart v Law Society* [1987] 1 FLR 223, [1987] Fam Law 52; and *Manley v Law Society* [1981] 1 All ER 401, [1981] 1 WLR 335, CA.

PART 3 CLS (Financial) Regs 2000

### [3.561AA.3]
### Succession of applications

Where there is a succession of applications that are governed by the same certificate (eg residence, then contact, then money) the charge will attach for the costs of all of the proceedings. Therefore legal advisers should consider discharging the certificate after an application has been resolved and then applying for a fresh certificate to deal with the further proceedings.

### [3.561AA.4]
### Variation

Variation under s 31(7A) of the MCA 1973 resulting in an order under s 31(7B) would attract the statutory charge.

### [3.561BB]

**45**

(1) Subject to paragraph (2), the statutory charge shall be in favour of the Commission.

(2) Subject to paragraph (3), where it relates to the cost of Legal Help or Help at Court, the statutory charge shall be in favour of thc supplier.

(3) Where Legal Help or Help at Court has been provided, the statutory charge shall be in favour of the Commission if it attaches to money or property recovered after a certificate has been granted in relation to the same matter.

**Initial Commencement**

1 April 2000.

### [3.561CC]

**46 Supplier's authority to waive statutory charge**

(1) This regulation applies only where the statutory charge is in favour of the supplier.

(2) The Commission may grant a supplier authority, either in respect of individual cases or generally, to waive either all or part of the amount of the statutory charge where its enforcement would cause grave hardship or distress to the client or would be unreasonably difficult because of the nature of the property.

**Initial Commencement**

1 April 2000.

### [3.561DD]

**47 Waiver of charge in case of wider public interest**

(1) …

(2) Paragraph (3) applies where:

(a) the Commission funds Legal Representation or Support Funding in proceedings which it considers have a significant wider public interest; and

(b) the Commission considers it cost-effective to fund those services for a specified claimant or claimants, but not for other claimants or potential claimants who might benefit from the litigation.

(3) Where this paragraph applies, the Commission may, if it considers it equitable to do so, waive some or all of the amount of the statutory charge.

**Initial Commencement**

1 April 2000.

**Amendment**

Para (1): revoked by SI 2001/3663, reg 21.

[3.561EE]

### 48 Application of regulations 49 to 53

Regulations 49 to 53 apply only in relation to a statutory charge in favour of the Commission.

**Initial Commencement**
1 April 2000.

[3.561FF]

### 49 Operation of statutory charge where certificate revoked or discharged

(1) Where a certificate has been revoked or discharged, section 10(7) of the Act shall apply to any money or property recovered as a result of the client continuing to pursue the relevant dispute or take, defend or be a party to the relevant proceedings.

(2) In paragraph (1), 'client' means the person whose certificate has been revoked or discharged, or, as the case may be, his personal representatives, trustee in bankruptcy or the Official Receiver.

**Initial Commencement**
1 April 2000.



[3.561GG]

### 50 Operation of statutory charge on money in court

(1) Paragraph (2) applies where any money recovered by a client in any proceedings is ordered to be paid into or remain in court and invested for the benefit of the client.

(2) Where this paragraph applies, the statutory charge shall attach only to such part of the money as, in the opinion of the Commission, will be sufficient to safeguard the interests of the Commission, and the Commission shall notify the court in writing of the amount so attached.

**Initial Commencement**
1 April 2000.

[3.561HH]

### 51 Enforcement of statutory charge

Subject to regulation 52, the Commission may enforce the statutory charge in any manner which would be available to a chargee in respect of a charge given between parties.

**Initial Commencement**
1 April 2000.

[3.561II]

### 52

(1) The Commission may postpone the enforcement of the statutory charge where (but only where):

(a) by order of the court or agreement it relates to property to be used as a home by the client or his dependants, or, where the relevant proceedings were family proceedings, to money to pay for such a home;

(b) the Commission is satisfied that the property in question will provide such security for the statutory charge as it considers appropriate; and

(c) as soon as it is possible to do so, the Commission registers a charge under the Land Registration Act 1925 to secure the amount in regulation 43 or, as appropriate, takes equivalent steps (whether in England and Wales or in any other jurisdiction) to protect its interest in the property.

(2) Where the client wishes to purchase a property in substitution for the property over which a charge is registered under paragraph (1)(c), the Commission may release the charge if the conditions in paragraph (1)(b) and (c) are satisfied.

(3) Where the enforcement of the statutory charge is postponed, interest shall accrue for the benefit of the Commission in accordance with regulation 53.

(4) Without prejudice to the provisions of the Land Registration Act 1925 and the Land Charges Act 1972, all conveyances and acts done to defeat, or operating to defeat, any charge shall, except in the case of a bona fide purchaser for value without notice, be void as against the Commission.

**Initial Commencement**

1 April 2000.

### [3.561II.1]
### Keypoints

- Lump sum not increased due to charge
- Discretion

### [3.561II.2]
### Lump sum not increased due to charge

A lump sum order should not be increased due to the incidence of the charge[1].

1 See *Collins v Collins* [1987] 1 FLR 226, [1987] Fam Law 54, CA. For a discussion of the operation of the statutory charge and the power to postpone, see generally *Rayden and Jackson on Divorce and Family Matters* (17th edn, 1997), vol 1, paras 52.26 to 52.28.

### [3.561II.3]
### Discretion

The Legal Services Commission retains a discretion as to whether it will postpone the charge[1].

1 See *Scallon v Scallon* [1990] FCR 911, [1990] 1 FLR 194, CA.

### [3.561JJ]

#### 53 Payment and recovery of interest

(1) Where interest is payable by the client under regulation 52, that interest shall continue to accrue until the amount of the statutory charge is paid.

(2) The client may make interim payments of interest or capital in respect of the outstanding amount of the statutory charge, but no interim payment shall be used to reduce the capital outstanding while any interest remains outstanding.

[(3) Where interest is payable by the client under regulation 52:

(a) it shall run from the date when the charge is first registered;

(b) the applicable rate shall be:

(i) 8% per annum until 31st March 2002;

(ii) thereafter, 1 percentage point above the Bank of England base rate current on 1st April 2002;

(c) subject to sub-paragraph (d), the applicable rate shall be varied on 1st April of each subsequent year so that it remains at the rate of 1 percentage point above the Bank of England base rate then current;

(d) the variation set out in sub-paragraph (c) shall take place only if the application of the new base rate has the effect of varying the base rate previously applicable by 1 percentage point or more; and

(e) the capital on which it is calculated shall be the lesser of:

(i) the amount of the statutory charge outstanding from time to time, less any interest accrued by virtue of regulation 52(3), or

(ii) the value of the property recovered at the time of such recovery, less the amount of any exemption under regulation 44(1)(d) which would apply were the amount of the charge to be paid.]

**Initial Commencement**

1 April 2000.

**Amendment**

Para (3): substituted, in relation to all cases to which the statutory charge applies, by SI 2001/3663, regs 3, 22.

# Pensions on Divorce etc (Provision of Information) Regulations 2000

**SI 2000 No 1048**

**Contents**

*Regulation*





**[3.562]**

### 1 Citation, commencement and interpretation

(1) These Regulations may be cited as the Pensions on Divorce etc (Provision of Information) Regulations 2000 and shall come into force on 1st December 2000.

(2) In these Regulations—

'the 1993 Act' means the Pension Schemes Act 1993;

'the 1995 Act' means the Pensions Act 1995;

'the 1999 Act' means the Welfare Reform and Pensions Act 1999;

'the Charging Regulations' means the Pensions on Divorce etc (Charging) Regulations 2000;

'the Implementation and Discharge of Liability Regulations' means the Pension Sharing (Implementation and Discharge of Liability) Regulations 2000;

'the Valuation Regulations' means the Pension Sharing (Valuation) Regulations 2000;

'active member' has the meaning given by section 124(1) of the 1995 Act;

'day' means any day other than—

(a) Christmas Day or Good Friday; or

(b) a bank holiday, that is to say, a day which is, or is to be observed as, a bank holiday or a holiday under Schedule 1 to the Banking and Financial Dealings Act 1971;

'deferred member' has the meaning given by section 124(1) of the 1995 Act;

'implementation period' has the meaning given by section 34(1) of the 1999 Act;
'member' means a person who has rights to future benefits, or has rights to benefits payable, under a pension arrangement;
'money purchase benefits' has the meaning given by section 181(1) of the 1993 Act;
'normal benefit age' has the meaning given by section 101B of the 1993 Act;
'notice of discharge of liability' means a notice issued to the member and his former spouse by the person responsible for a pension arrangement when that person has discharged his liability in respect of a pension credit in accordance with Schedule 5 to the 1999 Act;
'notice of implementation' means a notice issued by the person responsible for a pension arrangement to the member and his former spouse at the beginning of the implementation period notifying them of the day on which the implementation period for the pension credit begins;
'occupational pension scheme' has the meaning given by section 1 of the 1993 Act;
'the party with pension rights' and 'the other party' have the meanings given by section 25D(3) of the Matrimonial Causes Act 1997;
'pension arrangement' has the meaning given in section 46(1) of the 1999 Act;
'pension credit' means a credit under section 29(1)(b) of the 1999 Act;
'pension credit benefit' means the benefits payable under a pension arrangement or a qualifying arrangement to or in respect of a person by virtue of rights under the arrangement in question which are attributable (directly or indirectly) to a pension credit;
'pension credit rights' means rights to future benefits under a pension arrangement or a qualifying arrangement which are attributable (directly or indirectly) to a pension credit;
'pension sharing order or provision' means an order or provision which is mentioned in section 28(1) of the 1999 Act;
'pensionable service' has the meaning given by section 124(1) of the 1995 Act;
'person responsible for a pension arrangement' has the meaning given by section 46(2) of the 1999 Act;
'personal pension scheme' has the meaning given by section 1 of the 1993 Act;
'qualifying arrangement' has the meaning given by paragraph 6 of Schedule 5 to the 1999 Act;
. . .
'retirement annuity contract' means a contract or scheme approved under Chapter III of Part XIV of the Income and Corporation Taxes Act 1988;
'salary related occupational pension scheme' has the meaning given by regulation 1A of the Occupational Pension Schemes (Transfer Values) Regulations 1996;
'the Regulatory Authority' means the Occupational Pensions Regulatory Authority;
'transfer day' has the meaning given by section 29(8) of the 1999 Act;
'transferee' has the meaning given by section 29(8) of the 1999 Act;
'transferor' has the meaning given by section 29(8) of the 1999 Act;
'trustees or managers' has the meaning given by section 46(1) of the 1999 Act.

**Initial Commencement**

1 December 2000.

**Amendment**

SI 2000/2691.

**[3.563]**

## 2 Basic information about pensions and divorce

(1) The requirements imposed on a person responsible for a pension arrangement for the purposes of section 23(1)(a) of the 1999 Act (supply of pension information in connection with divorce etc) are that he shall furnish—

(a) on request from a member, the information referred to in paragraphs (2) and (3)(b) to (f);

(b) on request from the spouse of a member, the information referred to in paragraph (3); or

(c) pursuant to an order of the court, the information referred to in paragraph (2), (3) or (4),

to the member, the spouse of the member, or, as the case may be, to the court.

(2) The information in this paragraph is a valuation of pension rights or benefits accrued under that member's pension arrangement.

(3) The information in this paragraph is—

(a) a statement that on request from the member, or pursuant to an order of the court, a valuation of pension rights or benefits accrued under that member's pension arrangement, will be provided to the member, or, as the case may be, to the court;

(b) a statement summarising the way in which the valuation referred to in paragraph (2) and sub-paragraph (a) is calculated;

(c) the pension benefits which are included in a valuation referred to in paragraph (2) and sub-paragraph (a);

(d) whether the person responsible for the pension arrangement offers membership to a person entitled to a pension credit, and if so, the types of benefits available to pension credit members under that arrangement;

(e) whether the person responsible for the pension arrangements intends to discharge his liability for a pension credit other than by offering membership to a person entitled to a pension credit; and

(f) the schedule of charges which the person responsible for the pension arrangement will levy in accordance with regulation 2(2) of the Charging Regulations (general requirements as to charges).

(4) The information in this paragraph is any other information relevant to any power with respect to the matters specified in section 23(1)(a) of the 1999 Act and which is not specified in Schedule 1 or 2 to the Occupational Pension Schemes (Disclosure of Information) Regulations 1996 (basic information about the scheme and information to be made available to individuals), or in Schedule 1 or 2 to the Personal Pension Schemes (Disclosure of Information) Regulations 1987 (basic information about the scheme and information to be made available to individuals), in a case where either of those Regulations applies.

(5) Where the member's request for, or the court order for the provision of, information includes a request for, or an order for the provision of, a valuation under paragraph (2), the person responsible for the pension arrangement shall furnish all the information requested, or ordered, to the member—

(a) within 3 months beginning with the date the person responsible for the pension arrangement receives that request or order for the provision of the information;

(b) within 6 weeks beginning with the date the person responsible for the pension arrangement receives the request, or order, for the provision of the information, if the member has notified that person on the date of the request or order that the information is needed in connection with proceedings commenced under any of the provisions referred to in section 23(1)(a) of the 1999 Act; or

(c) within such shorter period specified by the court in an order requiring the person responsible for the pension arrangement to provide a valuation in accordance with paragraph (2).

(6) Where—

(a) the member's request for, or the court order for the provision of, information does not include a request or an order for a valuation under paragraph (2); or

(b) the member's spouse requests the information specified in paragraph (3),

the person responsible for the pension arrangement shall furnish that information to the member, his spouse, or the court, as the case may be, within one month beginning with the date that person responsible for the pension arrangement receives the request for, or the court order for the provision of, the information.

(7) At the same time as furnishing the information referred to in paragraph (1), the person responsible for a pension arrangement may furnish the information specified in regulation 4(2) (provision of information in response to a notification that a pension sharing order or provision may be made).

**Initial Commencement**

1 December 2000.

**[3.564]**

### 3 Information about pensions and divorce: valuation of pension benefits

(1) Where an application for financial relief under any of the provisions referred to in section 23(1)(a)(i) or (iii) of the 1999 Act (supply of pension information in connection with domestic and overseas divorce etc in England and Wales and corresponding Northern Ireland powers) has been made or is in contemplation, the valuation of benefits under a pension arrangement shall be calculated and verified for the purposes of regulation 2 of these Regulations in accordance with—

(a) paragraph (3), if the person with pension rights is a deferred member of an occupational pension scheme;

(b) paragraph (4), if the person with pension rights is an active member of an occupational pension scheme;

(c) paragraphs (5) and (6), if—

(i) the person with pension rights is a member of a personal pension scheme; or

(ii) those pension rights are contained in a retirement annuity contract; or

(d) paragraphs (7) to (9), if—

(i) the pension of the person with pension rights is in payment;

(ii) the rights of the person with pension rights are contained in an annuity contract other than a retirement annuity contract; or

(iii) the rights of the person with pension rights are contained in a deferred annuity contract other than a retirement annuity contract.

(2) Where an application for financial provision under any of the provisions referred to in section 23(1)(a)(ii) of the 1999 Act (corresponding Scottish powers) has been made, or is in contemplation, the valuation of benefits under a pension arrangement shall be calculated and verified for the purposes of regulation 2 of these Regulations in accordance with regulation 3 of the Divorce etc (Pensions) (Scotland) Regulations 2000 (valuation).

(3) Where the person with pension rights is a deferred member of an occupational pension scheme, the value of the benefits which he has under that scheme shall be taken to be—

(a) in the case of an occupational pension scheme other than a salary related scheme, the cash equivalent to which he acquired a right under section 94(1)(a) of the 1993 Act (right to cash equivalent) on the termination of his pensionable service, calculated on the assumption that he has made an application under section 95 of that Act (ways of taking right to cash equivalent) on the date on which the request for the valuation was received; or

(b) in the case of a salary related occupational pension scheme, the guaranteed cash equivalent to which he would have acquired a right under section 94(1)(aa) of the 1993 Act if he had made an application under section 95(1) of that Act, calculated on the assumption that he has made such an application on the date on which the request for the valuation was received.

(4) Where the person with pension rights is an active member of an occupational pension scheme, the valuation of the benefits which he has accrued under that scheme shall be calculated and verified—

(a) on the assumption that the member had made a request for an estimate of the cash equivalent that would be available to him were his pensionable service to terminate on the date on which the request for the valuation was received; and

(b) in accordance with regulation 11 of and Schedule 1 to the Occupational Pension Schemes (Transfer Values) Regulations 1996 (disclosure).

(5) Where the person with pension rights is a member of a personal pension scheme, or those rights are contained in a retirement annuity contract, the value of the benefits which he has under that scheme or contract shall be taken to be the cash equivalent to which he would have acquired a right under section 94(1)(b) of the 1993 Act, if he had made an application under section 95(1) of that Act on the date on which the request for the valuation was received.

(6) In relation to a personal pension scheme which is comprised in a retirement annuity contract made before 4th January 1988, paragraph (5) shall apply as if such a scheme were not excluded from the scope of Chapter IV of Part IV of the 1993 Act by section 93(1)(b) of that Act (scope of Chapter IV).

(7) Except in a case to which, or to the extent to which, paragraph (9) applies, the cash equivalent of benefits in respect of a person referred to in paragraph (1)(d) shall be calculated and verified in such manner as may be approved in a particular case by—

(a) a Fellow of the Institute of Actuaries;

(b) a Fellow of the Faculty of Actuaries; or

(c) a person with other actuarial qualifications who is approved by the Secretary of State, at the request of the person responsible for the pension arrangement in question, as being a proper person to act for the purposes of this regulation in connection with that arrangement.

(8) Except in a case to which paragraph (9) applies, cash equivalents are to be calculated and verified by adopting methods and making assumptions which—

(a) if not determined by the person responsible for the pension arrangement in question, are notified to him by an actuary referred to in paragraph (7); and

(b) are certified by the actuary to the person responsible for the pension arrangement in question as being consistent with 'Retirement Benefit Schemes—Transfer Values (GN 11)' published by the Institute of Actuaries and the Faculty of Actuaries and current at the date on which the request for the valuation is received.

(9) Where the cash equivalent, or any portion of it represents rights to money purchase benefits under the pension arrangement in question of the person with pension rights, and those rights do not fall, either wholly or in part, to be valued in a manner which involves making estimates of the value of benefits, then that cash equivalent, or that portion of it, shall be calculated and verified in such manner as may be approved in a particular case by the person responsible for the pension arrangement in question, and by adopting methods consistent with the requirements of Chapter IV of Part IV of the 1993 Act (protection for early leavers—transfer values).

(10) Where paragraph (3), (4) or (9) has effect by reference to provisions of Chapter IV of Part IV of the 1993 Act, section 93(1)(a)(i) of that Act (scope of Chapter IV) shall apply to those provisions as if the words 'at least one year' had been omitted from section 93(1)(a)(i).

**Initial Commencement**

1 December 2000.

**[3.565]**

### 4 Provision of information in response to a notification that a pension sharing order or provision may be made

(1) A person responsible for a pension arrangement shall furnish the information specified in paragraph (2) to the member or to the court, as the case may be—

- (a) within 21 days beginning with the date that the person responsible for the pension arrangement received the notification that a pension sharing order or provision may be made; or
- (b) if the court has specified a date which is outside the 21 days referred to in sub-paragraph (a), by that date.

(2) The information referred to in paragraph (1) is—

- (a) the full name of the pension arrangement and address to which any order or provision referred to in section 28(1) of the 1999 Act (activation of pension sharing) should be sent;
- (b) in the case of an occupational pension scheme, whether the scheme is winding up, and, if so,—
  - (i) the date on which the winding up commenced; and
  - (ii) the name and address of the trustees who are dealing with the winding up;
- (c) in the case of an occupational pension scheme, whether a cash equivalent of the member's pension rights, if calculated on the date the notification referred to in paragraph (1)(a) was received by the trustees or managers of that scheme, would be reduced in accordance with the provisions of regulation 8(4), (6) or (12) of the Occupational Pension Schemes (Transfer Values) Regulations 1996 (further provisions as to reductions of cash equivalents);
- (d) whether the person responsible for the pension arrangement is aware that the member's rights under the pension arrangement are subject to any, and if so, to specify which, of the following—
  - (i) any order or provision specified in section 28(1) of the 1999 Act;
  - (ii) an order under section 23 of the Matrimonial Causes Act 1973 (financial provision orders in connection with divorce etc), so far as it includes provision made by virtue of section 25B or 25C of that Act (powers to include provisions about pensions);
  - (iii) an order under section 12A(2) or (3) of the Family Law (Scotland) Act 1985 (powers in relation to pensions lump sums when making a capital sum order) which relates to benefits or future benefits to which the member is entitled under the pension arrangement;
  - (iv) an order under Article 25 of the Matrimonial Causes (Northern Ireland) Order 1978, so far as it includes provision made by virtue of Article 27B or 27C of that Order (Northern Ireland powers corresponding to those mentioned in paragraph (2)(d)(ii));
  - (v) a forfeiture order;
  - (vi) a bankruptcy order;
  - (vii) an award of sequestration on a member's estate or the making of the appointment on his estate of a judicial factor under section 41 of the Solicitors (Scotland) Act 1980 (appointment of judicial factor);
- (e) whether the member's rights under the pension arrangement include rights specified in regulation 2 of the Valuation Regulations (rights under a pension arrangement which are not shareable);
- (f) if the person responsible for the pension arrangement has not at an earlier stage provided the following information, whether that person requires the charges specified in regulation 3 (charges recoverable in respect of the provision of basic information), 5 (charges in respect of pension sharing activity), or 6 (additional amounts recoverable in respect of pension sharing activity) of the Charging Regulations to be paid before the commencement of the implementation period, and if so,—

(i) whether that person requires those charges to be paid in full; or
(ii) the proportion of those charges which he requires to be paid;

(g) whether the person responsible for the pension arrangement may levy additional charges specified in regulation 6 of the Charging Regulations, and if so, the scale of the additional charges which are likely to be made;
(h) whether the member is a trustee of the pension arrangement;
(i) whether the person responsible for the pension arrangement may request information about the member's state of health from the member if a pension sharing order or provision were to be made;
(j) …
(k) whether the person responsible for the pension arrangement requires information additional to that specified in regulation 5 (information required by the person responsible for the pension arrangement before the implementation period may begin) in order to implement the pension sharing order or provision.

**Initial Commencement**
1 December 2000.

**Amendment**
SI 2000/2691.



**[3.566]**

### 5 Information required by the person responsible for the pension arrangement before the implementation period may begin

The information prescribed for the purposes of section 34(1)(b) of the 1999 Act (information relating to the transferor and the transferee which the person responsible for the pension arrangement must receive) is—

(a) in relation to the transferor—
(i) all names by which the transferor has been known;
(ii) date of birth;
(iii) address;
(iv) National Insurance number;
(v) the name of the pension arrangement to which the pension sharing order or provision relates; and
(vi) the transferor's membership or policy number in that pension arrangement;

(b) in relation to the transferee—
(i) all names by which the transferee has been known;
(ii) date of birth;
(iii) address;
(iv) National Insurance number; and
(v) if the transferee is a member of the pension arrangement from which the pension credit is derived, his membership or policy number in that pension arrangement;

(c) where the transferee has given his consent in accordance with paragraph 1(3)(c), 3(3)(c) or 4(2)(c) of Schedule 5 to the 1999 Act (mode of discharge of liability for a pension credit) to the payment of the pension credit to the person responsible for a qualifying arrangement—
(i) the full name of that qualifying arrangement;
(ii) its address;
(iii) if known, the transferee's membership number or policy number in that arrangement; and

(iv) the name or title, business address, business telephone number, and, where available, the business facsimile number and electronic mail address of a person who may be contacted in respect of the discharge of liability for the pension credit;

(d) where the rights from which the pension credit is derived are held in an occupational pension scheme which is being wound up, whether the transferee has given an indication whether he wishes to transfer his pension credit rights which may have been reduced in accordance with the provisions of regulation 16(1) of the Implementation and Discharge of Liability Regulations (adjustments to the amount of the pension credit—occupational pension schemes which are underfunded on the valuation day) to a qualifying arrangement; and

(e) any information requested by the person responsible for the pension arrangement in accordance with regulation 4(2)(i) or (k).

**Initial Commencement**

1 December 2000.

**[3.567]**

## 6 Provision of information after the death of the person entitled to the pension credit before liability in respect of the pension credit has been discharged

[(1) Where the person entitled to the pension credit dies before the person responsible for the pension arrangement has discharged his liability in respect of the pension credit, the person responsible for the pension arrangement shall, within 21 days of the date of receipt of the notification of the death of the person entitled to the pension credit, notify in writing any person whom the person responsible for the pension arrangement considers should be notified of the matters specified in paragraph (2).]

(2) The matters specified in this paragraph are—

(a) how the person responsible for the pension arrangement intends to discharge his liability in respect of the pension credit;

(b) whether the person responsible for the pension arrangement intends to recover charges from the person nominated to receive pension credit benefits, in accordance with regulations 2 to 9 of the Charging Regulations, and if so, a copy of the schedule of charges issued to the parties to pension sharing in accordance with regulation 2(2)(b) of the Charging Regulations (general requirements as to charges); and

(c) a list of any further information which the person responsible for the pension arrangement requires in order to discharge his liability in respect of the pension credit.

**Initial Commencement**

1 December 2000.

**Amendment**

SI 2000/2691.

**[3.568]**

## 7 Provision of information after receiving a pension sharing order or provision

(1) A person responsible for a pension arrangement who is in receipt of a pension sharing order or provision relating to that arrangement shall provide in writing to the transferor and transferee, or, where regulation 6(1) applies, to the person other than the

person entitled to the pension credit referred to in regulation 6 of the Implementation and Discharge of Liability Regulations (discharge of liability in respect of a pension credit following the death of the person entitled to the pension credit), as the case may be,—

- (a) a notice in accordance with the provisions of regulation 7(1) of the Charging Regulations (charges in respect of pension sharing activity—postponement of implementation period);
- (b) a list of information relating to the transferor or the transferee, or, where regulation 6(1) applies, the person other than the person entitled to the pension credit referred to in regulation 6 of the Implementation and Discharge of Liability Regulations, as the case may be, which—
  - (i) has been requested in accordance with regulation 4(2)(i) and (k), or, where appropriate, 6(2)(c), or should have been provided in accordance with regulation 5;
  - (ii) the person responsible for the pension arrangement considers he needs in order to begin to implement the pension sharing order or provision; and
  - (iii) remains outstanding;
- (c) a notice of implementation; or
- (d) a statement by the person responsible for the pension arrangement explaining why he is unable to implement the pension sharing order or agreement.

(2) The information specified in paragraph (1) shall be furnished in accordance with that paragraph within 21 days beginning with—

- (a) in the case of sub-paragraph (a), (b) or (d) of that paragraph, the day on which the person responsible for the pension arrangement receives the pension sharing order or provision; or
- (b) in the case of sub-paragraph (c) of that paragraph, the later of the days specified in section 34(1)(a) and (b) of the 1999 Act (implementation period).

**Initial Commencement**

1 December 2000.



**[3.569]**

## 8 Provision of information after the implementation of a pension sharing order or provision

(1) The person responsible for the pension arrangement shall issue a notice of discharge of liability to the transferor and the transferee, or, as the case may be, the person entitled to the pension credit by virtue of regulation 6 of the Implementation and Discharge of Liability Regulations no later than the end of the period of 21 days beginning with the day on which the discharge of liability in respect of the pension credit is completed.

(2) In the case of a transferor whose pension is not in payment, the notice of discharge of liability shall include the following details—

- (a) the value of the transferor's accrued rights as determined by reference to the cash equivalent value of those rights calculated and verified in accordance with regulation 3 of the Valuation Regulations (calculation and verification of cash equivalents for the purposes of the creation of pension debits and credits);
- (b) the value of the pension debit;
- (c) any amount deducted from the value of the pension rights in accordance with regulation 9(2)(c) of the Charging Regulations (charges in respect of pension sharing activity—method of recovery);
- (d) the value of the transferor's rights after the amounts referred to in sub-paragraphs (b) and (c) have been deducted; and
- (e) the transfer day.

(3) in the case of a transferor whose pension is in payment, the notice of discharge of liability shall include the following details—

(a) the value of the transferor's benefits under the pension arrangement as determined by reference to the cash equivalent value of those rights calculated and verified in accordance with regulation 3 of the Valuation Regulations;

(b) the value of the pension debit;

(c) the amount of the pension which was in payment before liability in respect of the pension credit was discharged;

(d) the amount of pension which is payable following the deduction of the pension debit from the transferor's pension benefits;

(e) the transfer day;

(f) if the person responsible for the pension arrangement intends to recover charges, the amount of any unpaid charges—

(i) not prohibited by regulation 2 of the Charging Regulations (general requirements as to charges); and

(ii) specified in regulations 3 and 6 of those Regulations;

(g) how the person responsible for the pension arrangement will recover the charges referred to in sub-paragraph (f), including—

(i) whether the method of recovery specified in regulation 9(2)(d) of the Charging Regulations will be used;

(ii) the date when payment of those charges in whole or in part is required; and

(iii) the sum which will be payable by the transferor, or which will be deducted from his pension benefits, on that date.

(4) In the case of a transferee—

(a) whose pension is not in payment; and

(b) who will become a member of the pension arrangement from which the pension credit rights were derived,

the notice of discharge of liability to the transferee shall include the following details—

(i) the value of the pension credit;

(ii) any amount deducted from the value of the pension credit in accordance with regulation 9(2)(b) of the Charging Regulations;

(iii) the value of the pension credit after the amount referred to in sub-paragraph (b)(ii) has been deducted;

(iv) the transfer day;

(v) any periodical charges the person responsible for the pension arrangement intends to make, including how and when those charges will be recovered from the transferee; and

(vi) information concerning membership of the pension arrangement which is relevant to the transferee as a pension credit member.

(5) In the case of a transferee who is transferring his pension credit rights out of the pension arrangement from which those rights were derived, the notice of discharge of liability to the transferee shall include the following details—

(a) the value of the pension credit;

(b) any amount deducted from the value of the pension credit in accordance with regulation 9(2)(b) of the Charging Regulations;

(c) the value of the pension credit after the amount referred to in sub-paragraph (b) has been deducted;

(d) the transfer day; and

(e) details of the pension arrangement, including its name, address, reference number, telephone number, and, where available, the business facsimile number and electronic mail address, to which the pension credit has been transferred.

(6) In the case of a transferee, who has reached normal benefit age on the transfer day, and in respect of whose pension credit liability has been discharged in accordance with paragraph 1(2), 2(2), 3(2) or 4(4) of Schedule 5 to the 1999 Act (pension credits:

mode of discharge— funded pension schemes, unfunded public service pension schemes, other unfunded pension schemes, or other pension arrangements), the notice of discharge of liability to the transferee shall include the following details—

(a) the amount of pension credit benefit which is to be paid to the transferee;
(b) the date when the pension credit benefit is to be paid to the transferee;
(c) the transfer day;
(d) if the person responsible for the pension arrangement intends to recover charges, the amount of any unpaid charges—
    (i) not prohibited by regulation 2 of the Charging Regulations; and
    (ii) specified in regulations 3 and 6 of those Regulations; and
(e) how the person responsible for the pension arrangement will recover the charges referred to in sub-paragraph (d), including—
    (i) whether the method of recovery specified in regulation 9(2)(e) of the Charging Regulations will be used;
    (ii) the date when payment of those charges in whole or in part is required; and
    (iii) the sum which will be payable by the transferee, or which will be deducted from his pension credit benefits, on that date.

(7) In the case of a person entitled to the pension credit by virtue of regulation 6 of the Implementation and Discharge of Liability Regulations, the notice of discharge of liability shall include the following details—

(a) the value of the pension credit rights as determined in accordance with regulation 10 of the Implementation and Discharge of Liability Regulations (calculation of the value of appropriate rights);
(b) any amount deducted from the value of the pension credit in accordance with regulation 9(2)(b) of the Charging Regulations;
(c) the value of the pension credit;
(d) the transfer day; and
(e) any periodical charges the person responsible for the pension arrangement intends to make, including how and when those charges will be recovered from the payments made to the person entitled to the pension credit by virtue of regulation 6 of the Implementation and Discharge of Liability Regulations.

**Initial Commencement**
1 December 2000.

**[3.570]**

### 9 Penalties

Where any trustee or manager of an occupational pension scheme fails, without reasonable excuse, to comply with any requirement imposed under regulation 6, 7 or 8, the Regulatory Authority may require that trustee or manager to pay within 28 days from the date of its imposition, a penalty which shall not exceed—

(a) £200 in the case of an individual, and
(b) £1,000 in any other case.

**Initial Commencement**
1 December 2000.

**[3.571]**

### 10 Provision of information after receipt of an earmarking order

(1) The person responsible for the pension arrangement shall, within 21 days beginning with the day that he receives—

(a) an order under section 23 of the Matrimonial Causes Act 1973, so far as it includes provision made by virtue of section 25B or 25C of that Act (powers to include provision about pensions);
(b) an order under section 12A(2) or (3) of the Family Law (Scotland) Act 1985; or
(c) an order under Article 25 of the Matrimonial Causes (Northern Ireland) Order 1978, so far as it includes provision made by virtue of Article 27B or 27C of that Order (Northern Ireland powers corresponding to those mentioned in sub-paragraph (a)),

issue to the party with pension rights and the other party a notice which includes the information specified in paragraphs (2) and (5), or (3), (4) and (5), as the case may be.

(2) Where an order referred to in paragraph (1)(a), (b) or (c) is made in respect of the pension rights or benefits of a party with pension rights whose pension is not in payment, the notice issued by the person responsible for a pension arrangement to the party with pension rights and the other party shall include a list of the circumstances in respect of any changes of which the party with pension rights or the other party must notify the person responsible for the pension arrangement.

(3) Where an order referred to in paragraph (1)(a) or (c) is made in respect of the pension rights or benefits of a party with pension rights whose pension is in payment, the notice issued by the person responsible for a pension arrangement to the party with pension rights and the other party shall include—

(a) the value of the pension rights or benefits of the party with pension rights;
(b) the amount of the pension of the party with pension rights after the order has been implemented;
(c) the first date when a payment pursuant to the order is to be made; and
(d) a list of the circumstances, in respect of any changes of which the party with pension rights or the other party must notify the person responsible for the pension arrangement.

(4) Where an order referred to in paragraph (1)(a) or (c) is made in respect of the pension rights of a party with pension rights whose pension is in payment, the notice issued by the person responsible for a pension arrangement to the party with pension rights shall, in addition to the items specified in paragraph (3), include—

(a) the amount of the pension of the party with pension rights which is currently in payment; and
(b) the amount of pension which will be payable to the party with pension rights after the order has been implemented.

(5) Where an order referred to in paragraph (1)(a), (b) or (c) is made the notice issued by the person responsible for a pension arrangement to the party with pension rights and the other party shall include—

(a) the amount of any charges which remain unpaid by—
    (i) the party with pension rights; or
    (ii) the other party,

    in respect of the provision by the person responsible for the pension arrangement of information about pensions and divorce pursuant to regulation 3 of the Charging Regulations, and in respect of complying with an order referred to in paragraph (1)(a), (b) or (c); and
(b) information as to the manner in which the person responsible for the pension arrangement will recover the charges referred to in sub-paragraph (a), including—
    (i) the date when payment of those charges in whole or in part is required;
    (ii) the sum which will be payable by the party with pension rights or the other party, as the case may be; and
    (iii) whether the sum will be deducted from payments of pension to the party with pension rights, or, as the case may be, from payments to be made to the other party pursuant to an order referred to in paragraph (1)(a), (b) or (c).

**Initial Commencement**

1 December 2000.

# Pensions on Divorce etc (Charging) Regulations 2000

## SI 2000 No 1049

Contents

*Regulation*



**[3.572]**

### 1 Citation, commencement and interpretation

(1) These Regulations may be cited as the Pensions on Divorce etc (Charging) Regulations 2000 and shall come into force on 1st December 2000.

(2) In these Regulations, unless the context otherwise requires—

'the 1999 Act' means the Welfare Reform and Pensions Act 1999;

'the Provision of Information Regulations' means the Pensions on Divorce etc (Provision of Information) Regulations 2000;

'day' means any day other than—

(a) Christmas Day or Good Friday; or

(b) a bank holiday, that is to say, a day which is, or is to be observed as, a bank holiday or a holiday under Schedule 1 to the Banking and Financial Dealings Act 1971;

'implementation period' has the meaning given by section 34(1) of the 1999 Act;

'normal pension age' has the meaning given by section 180 of the Pension Schemes Act 1993;]

'notice of implementation' has the meaning given by regulation 1(2) of the Provision of Information Regulations;

'pension arrangement' has the meaning given to that expression in section 46(1) of the 1999 Act;

'pension credit' means a credit under section 29(1)(b) of the 1999 Act;

'pension credit benefit' has the meaning given by section 101B of the Pensions Schemes Act 1993;

'pension credit rights' has the meaning given by section 101B of the Pension Schemes Act 1993;

'pension sharing activity' has the meaning given by section 41(5) of the 1999 Act;

'pension sharing order or provision' means an order or provision which is mentioned in section 28(1) of the 1999 Act;

'person responsible for a pension arrangement' has the meaning given to that expression in section 46(2) of the 1999 Act;

'the Regulatory Authority' means the Occupational Pensions Regulatory Authority;

'the relevant date' has the meaning given by section 10(3) of the Family Law (Scotland) Act 1985;

'trustees or managers' has the meaning given by section 46(1) of the 1999 Act.

**Initial Commencement**

1 December 2000.

**Amendment**

SI 2000/2691.

**[3.573]**

## 2 General requirements as to charges

(1) Subject to paragraph (8), a person responsible for a pension arrangement shall not recover any charges incurred in connection with—

- (a) the provision of information under—
  - (i) regulation 2 of the Provision of Information Regulations (basic information about pensions and divorce);
  - (ii) regulation 4 of those Regulations (provision of information in response to a notification that a pension sharing order or provision may be made); or
  - (iii) regulation 10 of those Regulations (provision of information after receipt of an earmarking order);
- (b) complying with any order specified in section 24 of the 1999 Act (charges by pension arrangements in relation to earmarking orders); or
- (c) any description of pension sharing activity specified in regulation 5 of these Regulations,

unless he has complied with the requirements of paragraphs (2) to (5).

(2) The requirements mentioned in paragraph (1) are that the person responsible for a pension arrangement shall, before a pension sharing order or provision is made—

- (a) inform the member or his spouse, as the case may be, in writing of his intention to recover costs incurred in connection with any of the matters specified in sub-paragraph (a), (b) or (c) of paragraph (1); and
- (b) provide the member or his spouse, as the case may be, with a written schedule of charges in accordance with paragraphs (3) and (4) in respect of those matters specified in sub-paragraph (a) or (c) of paragraph (1) for which a charge may be recoverable.

(3) No charge shall be recoverable in respect of any of the items mentioned in paragraph (4) unless the person responsible for a pension arrangement has specified in the written schedule of charges mentioned in paragraph (2)(b) that a charge may be recoverable in respect of that item.

(4) The items referred to in paragraph (3) are—

- (a) the provision of a cash equivalent other than one which is provided in accordance with the provisions of—
  - (i) section 93A or 94 of the 1993 Act (salary related schemes: right to statement of entitlement, and right to cash equivalent);

(ii) regulation 11(1) of the Occupational Pension Schemes (Transfer Values) Regulations 1996 (disclosure); or

(iii) regulation 5 (information to be made available to individuals) of, and paragraph 2(b) of Schedule 2 (provision of cash equivalent) to the Personal Pension Schemes (Disclosure of Information) Regulations 1987;

(b) subject to regulation 3(2)(b) or (c), as the case may be, the provision of a valuation in accordance with regulation 2(2) of the Provision of Information Regulations;

(c) whether a person responsible for a pension arrangement intends to recover the cost of providing membership of the pension arrangement to the person entitled to a pension credit, before or after the pension sharing order is implemented;

(d) whether the person responsible for a pension arrangement intends to recover additional charges in the circumstances prescribed in regulation 6 of these Regulations in respect of pension sharing activity described in regulation 5 of these Regulations;

(e) whether the charges are inclusive or exclusive of value added tax, where the person responsible for a pension arrangement is required to charge value added tax in accordance with the provisions of the Value Added Tax Act 1994;

(f) periodical charges in respect of pension sharing activity which the person responsible for a pension arrangement may make when a person entitled to a pension credit becomes a member of the pension arrangement from which the pension credit is derived;

(g) whether the person responsible for a pension arrangement intends to recover charges specified in regulation 10 of these Regulations.

(5) In the case of the cost referred to in paragraph (4)(c) or the charges to be imposed in respect of pension sharing activity described in regulation 5 of these Regulations, the person responsible for a pension arrangement shall provide—

(a) a single estimate of the overall cost of the pension sharing activity;

(b) a range of estimates of the overall cost of the pension sharing activity which is dependent upon the complexity of an individual case; or

(c) a breakdown of the cost of each element of pension sharing activity for which a charge shall be made.

(6) Subject to regulation 9(3) and (4), a person responsible for a pension arrangement shall recover only those sums which represent the reasonable administrative expenses which he has incurred or is likely to incur in connection with any of the activities mentioned in paragraph (1), or in relation to a pension sharing order having been made the subject of an application for leave to appeal out of time.

(7) The requirements of paragraph (2) do not apply in connection with the recovery by a person responsible for a pension arrangement of costs incurred in relation to a pension sharing order having been made the subject of an application for leave to appeal out of time.

[(8) The information specified in regulation 2(2) and (3) of the Provision of Information Regulations shall be provided to the member or his spouse without charge unless—

(a) the person responsible for the pension arrangement has furnished the information to the member, his spouse or the court within a period of 12 months immediately prior to the date of the request or the court order for the provision of that information;

(b) the member has reached normal pension age on or before the date of the request or the court order for the provision of the information;

(c) the request or the court order for the provision of the information is made within 12 months prior to the member reaching normal pension age; or

(d) the circumstances referred to in regulation 3(2)(b)(i) apply.]

**Initial Commencement**
1 December 2000.

**Amendment**
SI 2000/2691.

**[3.574]**

### 3 Charges recoverable in respect of the provision of basic information

(1) Subject to paragraph (2), the charges prescribed for the purposes of section 23(1)(d) of the 1999 Act (charges which a person responsible for a pension arrangement may recover in respect of supplying pension information in connection with divorce etc) are any charges incurred by the person responsible for the pension arrangement in connection with the provision of any of the information set out in—

(a) regulation 2 of the Provision of Information Regulations which may be recovered in accordance with regulation 2(8) of these Regulations;

(b) regulation 4 of those Regulations; or

(c) regulation 10 of those Regulations.

(2) The charges mentioned in paragraph (1) shall not include any costs incurred by a person responsible for a pension arrangement in respect of the matters specified in sub-paragraphs (a) to (f)—

(a) any costs incurred by the person responsible for a pension arrangement which are directly related to the fulfilment of his obligations under regulation 2(3) of the Provision of Information Regulations, other than charges which may be recovered in the circumstances described in regulation 2(8) of these Regulations;

(b) any costs incurred by the person responsible for the pension arrangement as a result of complying with a request for, or an order of the court requiring, a valuation under regulation 2(2) of the Provision of Information Regulations, unless—

(i) he is required by a member or a court to provide that valuation in less than 3 months beginning with the date the person responsible for the pension arrangement receives that request or order for the valuation;

(ii) the valuation is requested by a member who is not entitled to a cash equivalent under any of the provisions referred to in regulation 2(4)(a);

(iii) a member has requested a cash equivalent in accordance with any of those provisions within 12 months immediately prior to the date of the request for a valuation under regulation 2(2) of the Provision of Information Regulations;

(c) any costs incurred by the person responsible for the pension arrangement as a result of providing a valuation of benefits calculated and verified in accordance with regulation 3 of the Divorce etc (Pensions) (Scotland) Regulations 2000 (valuation), unless—

(i) he is required by the court to provide that valuation in less than 3 months beginning with the date the person responsible for the pension arrangement receives that order;

(ii) the valuation is requested by a member who is not entitled to a cash equivalent under any of the provisions referred to in regulation 2(4)(a);

(iii) a member has requested a cash equivalent in accordance with any of those provisions within 12 months immediately prior to the date of the request for a valuation under regulation 2(2) of the Provision of Information Regulations; or

(iv) the relevant date is more than 12 months immediately prior to the date the person responsible for the pension arrangement receives the request for the valuation;

(d) any costs incurred by the trustees or managers of—

(i) an occupational pension scheme in connection with the provision of information under regulation 4 of the Occupational Pension Schemes (Disclosure of Information) Regulations 1996 (basic information about the scheme); or

(ii) a personal pension scheme in connection with the provision of information under regulation 4 of the Personal Pension Schemes (Disclosure of Information) Regulations 1987 (basic information about the scheme),

which the trustees or managers shall provide to the member free of charge under those Regulations;

(e) any costs incurred by the trustees or managers of an occupational pension scheme, or a personal pension scheme, as the case may be, in connection with the provision of a transfer value in accordance with the provisions of—

(i) section 93A or 94 of the 1993 Act;

(ii) regulation 11(1) of the Occupational Pension Schemes (Transfer Values) Regulations 1996; or

(iii) regulation 5 of, and paragraph 2(b) of Schedule 2 to, the Personal Pension Schemes (Disclosure of Information) Regulations 1987; or

(f) any costs not specified by the person responsible for a pension arrangement in the information on charges provided to the member pursuant to regulation 2 of the Provision of Information Regulations with the exception of any additional amounts under regulation 6(1)(a) of these Regulations.

**Initial Commencement**

1 December 2000.



**[3.575]**

## 4 Charges in respect of the provision of information — method of recovery

(1) A person responsible for a pension arrangement may recover the charges specified in regulation 3(1) by using either of the methods described in sub-paragraph (a) or (b)—

(a) requiring payment of charges at any specified time between the request for basic information and the completion of the implementation of a pension sharing order or provision, or the compliance with an order specified in section 24 of the 1999 Act, as the case may be; or

(b) subject to paragraph (2), requiring as a condition of providing information in accordance with—

(i) regulation 2 of the Provision of Information Regulations; or

(ii) regulation 10 of those Regulations,

that payment of the charges to which regulation 3(1) refers shall be made in full by the member before the person responsible for the pension arrangement becomes obliged to provide the information.

(2) Paragraph (1)(b) shall not apply—

(a) where a court has ordered a member to obtain the information specified in regulation 2 of the Provision of Information Regulations;

(b) where, in accordance with regulation 2(8) of these Regulations, the person responsible for the pension arrangement shall provide that information without charge; or

(c) where the person responsible for the pension arrangement is required to supply that information by virtue of regulation 4 of the Provision of Information Regulations.

**Initial Commencement**

1 December 2000.

**[3.576]**

### 5 Charges in respect of pension sharing activity

(1) The charges prescribed in respect of prescribed descriptions of pension sharing activity for the purposes of section 41(1) of the 1999 Act (charges in respect of pension sharing costs) are any costs reasonably incurred by the person responsible for the pension arrangement in connection with pension sharing activity other than those costs specified in paragraph (3).

(2) The descriptions of pension sharing activity prescribed for the purposes of section 41(1) of the 1999 Act are any type of activity which fulfils the requirements of section 41(5) of the 1999 Act.

(3) The costs specified in this paragraph are any costs which are not directly related to the costs which arise in relation to an individual case.

**Initial Commencement**
1 December 2000.

**[3.577]**

### 6 Additional amounts recoverable in respect of pension sharing activity

(1) The circumstances in which a person responsible for a pension arrangement may recover additional amounts are—

- (a) where a period of more than 12 months has elapsed between the person responsible for the pension arrangement supplying information in accordance with regulation 2 of the Provision of Information Regulations and the taking effect of an order or provision specified in subsection (1) of section 28 of the 1999 Act (activation of pension sharing); or
- (b) in the case of an occupational pension scheme, where the trustees or managers of that scheme undertake activity from time to time associated with pension credit rights or pension credit benefit in that scheme which belong to a member.

(2) For the purposes of section 41(2)(d) of the 1999 Act, the additional amounts are—

- (a) in the circumstances described in paragraph (1)(a), interest calculated at a rate not exceeding increases in the retail prices index on the amounts of any charges not yet due, or of any charges requested but yet to be recovered, which are specified in the schedule of charges issued to the member in accordance with regulation 2(2)(b) of these Regulations; and
- (b) in the circumstances described in paragraph (1)(b), an amount not exceeding an increase calculated by reference to increases in the retail prices index on the amounts which relate to the costs referred to in regulation 2(4)(d) and which are specified in the schedule of charges provided to the member and his spouse in accordance with regulation 2(2)(b).

(3) Where a person responsible for a pension arrangement intends to recover an additional amount specified in paragraph (2)(a) in the circumstances described in paragraph (1)(a), he shall set out this intention, the rate of interest to be used, and the total costs recoverable in the notice of implementation and final costs issued in accordance with regulation 7 of the Provision of Information Regulations (provision of information after receiving a pension sharing order or provision).

(4) Where the trustees or managers of an occupational pension scheme intend to recover an additional amount specified in paragraph (2)(b) in the circumstances described in paragraph (1)(b), they shall inform the parties involved in pension sharing in writing of this intention in the schedule of charges issued in accordance with regulation 2(2)(b) of these Regulations.

**Initial Commencement**
1 December 2000.

[3.578]

### 7 Charges in respect of pension sharing activity — postponement of implementation period

(1) The circumstances when the start of the implementation period may be postponed are when a person responsible for a pension arrangement—

(a) issues a notice to the member and the person entitled to the pension credit no later than 21 days after the day on which the person responsible for the pension arrangement receives the pension sharing order or provision; and

(b) in that notice, requires the charges specified in regulation 3, 5 or 6 to be paid before the implementation of the pension sharing order or provision is commenced.

(2) Paragraph (1) shall apply only if the person responsible for the pension arrangement has specified at a stage no later than in his response to the notification that a pension sharing order or provision may be made, issued in accordance with regulation 4 of the Provision of Information Regulations

(a) that he requires the charges mentioned in paragraph (1) to be paid before the implementation period is commenced; and either

(b) whether he requires those charges to be paid in full; or

(c) the proportion of those charges which he requires to be paid as full settlement of those charges.

(3) Once payment of the charges mentioned in paragraph (1) has been made in accordance with the requirements of the person responsible for the pension arrangement—

(a) that person shall

(i) issue the notice of implementation in accordance with regulation 7(1)(c) of the Provision of Information Regulations, and

(ii) begin the implementation period for the pension credit,

within 21 days from the date the charges are paid, provided that the person responsible for the pension arrangement would otherwise be able to begin to implement the pension sharing order or provision, and

(b) subject to paragraph (4), that person shall not be entitled to recover any further charges in respect of the pension sharing order or provision in question.

(4) Paragraph (3)(b) shall not apply—

(a) in relation to the recovery of charges referred to in regulations 2(4)(d) and 6(2)(b); or

(b) where the pension credit depends on a pension sharing order and the order is the subject of an application for leave to appeal out of time.

**Initial Commencement**

1 December 2000.



[3.579]

### 8 Charges in respect of pension sharing activity — reimbursement as between the parties to pension sharing

A payment in respect of charges recoverable under regulation 3, 5 or 6 made by one party to pension sharing on behalf of the other party to pension sharing, shall be recoverable by the party who made the payment from that other party as a debt.

**Initial Commencement**

1 December 2000.

**[3.580]**

### 9 Charges in respect of pension sharing activity — method of recovery

(1) Subject to paragraphs (7) and (8), a person responsible for a pension arrangement may recover the charges specified in regulations 3, 5 and 6 by using any of the methods described in paragraph (2).

(2) The methods of recovery described in this paragraph are—

(a) subject to regulation 7 requiring the charges referred to in paragraph (1) to be paid before the implementation period for the pension sharing order or provision is commenced;

(b) deduction from a pension credit;

(c) deduction from the accrued rights of the member;

(d) where a pension sharing order or provision is made in respect of a pension which is in payment, deduction from the member's pension benefits;

(e) where liability in respect of a pension credit is discharged by the person responsible for the pension arrangement in accordance with paragraph 1(2), 2(2), or 3(2) of Schedule 5 to the 1999 Act (mode of discharge of liability for pension credits), deduction from payments of pension credit benefit; or

(f) deduction from the amount of a transfer value which is calculated in accordance with—

(i) regulation 7 of the Occupational Pension Schemes (Transfer Values) Regulations 1996 (manner of calculation and verification of cash equivalents); or

(ii) regulation 3 of the Personal Pension Schemes (Transfer Values) Regulations 1987 (manner of calculation and verification of cash equivalents).

(3) A person responsible for a pension arrangement shall not recover charges referred to in paragraph (1) by using any of the methods described in paragraph (2)(b), (c), (d), (e) or (f) unless—

(a) a pension sharing order or provision corresponding to any order or provision specified in subsection (1) of section 28 of the 1999 Act has been made;

(b) the implementation period has commenced;

(c) where a pension sharing order has been made, the person responsible for a pension arrangement is not aware of an appeal against the order having begun on or after the day on which the order takes effect;

(d) there are charges which are unpaid and for which the party, to whom paragraph (2)(b), (c), (d), (e) or (f) applies, is liable;

(e) the person responsible for the pension arrangement has issued a notice of implementation in accordance with regulation 7 of the Provision of Information Regulations;

(f) the person responsible for a pension arrangement specifies in the notice of implementation that recovery of the charges may be made by using any of those methods; and

(g) 21 days have elapsed since the notice of implementation was issued to the parties to pension sharing in accordance with the requirements of regulation 7 of the Provision of Information Regulations.

(4) If a pension sharing order or provision includes provision about the apportionment between the parties to pension sharing of any charge under section 41 of the 1999 Act or under corresponding Northern Ireland legislation, by virtue of section 24D of the Matrimonial Causes Act 1973 (pension sharing orders: apportionment of charges) or section 8A of the Family Law (Scotland) Act 1985 (pension sharing orders: apportionment of charges), the recovery of charges using any of the methods described in paragraph (2) by the person responsible for the pension arrangement shall comply with the terms of the order or provision.

(5) A person responsible for a pension arrangement shall not recover charges referred to in paragraph (1) by using any of the methods described in paragraph (2), from a party to pension sharing, if that party has paid in full the proportion of the charges for which he is liable.

(6) A person responsible for a pension arrangement may recover charges by using any of the methods described in paragraph (2)(b), (c) or (d)—

(a) at any time within the implementation period prescribed by section 34 of the 1999 Act ('implementation period');

(b) following an application by the trustees or managers of an occupational pension scheme, such longer period as the Regulatory Authority may allow in accordance with section 33(4) of the 1999 Act (extension of time for discharge of liability); or

(c) within 21 days after the end of the period referred to in sub-paragraph (a) or (b).

(7) Where the commencement of the implementation period is postponed, or its operation ceases in accordance with regulation 4 of the Pension Sharing (Implementation and Discharge of Liability) Regulations 2000 (postponement or cessation of implementation period where an application is made for leave to appeal out of time) a person responsible for a pension arrangement may require any outstanding charges referred to in paragraph (1) to be paid immediately, in respect of—

(a) all costs which have been incurred prior to the date of postponement or cessation; or

(b) any reasonable costs related to—

(i) the application for leave to appeal out of time; or

(ii) the appeal out of time itself.

(8) Paragraph (7) applies even if, prior to receiving the notification of the application for leave to appeal out of time, a person responsible for a pension arrangement has indicated to the parties to pension sharing that he will not be using the method of recovery specified in paragraph (2)(a).

**Initial Commencement**

1 December 2000.



**[3.581]**

## 10 Charges in relation to earmarking orders

The prescribed charges which a person responsible for a pension arrangement may recover in respect of complying with an order specified in section 24 of the 1999 Act are those charges which represent the reasonable administrative expenses which he has incurred or is likely to incur by reason of the order.

**Initial Commencement**

1 December 2000.

# Pension Sharing (Valuation) Regulations 2000

## SI 2000 No 1052

Contents

*Regulation*





**[3.582]**

### 1 Citation, commencement and interpretation

(1) These Regulations may be cited as the Pension Sharing (Valuation) Regulations 2000 and shall come into force on 1st December 2000.

(2) In these Regulations—

'the 1993 Act' means the Pension Schemes Act 1993;
'the 1995 Act' means the Pensions Act 1995;
'the 1999 Act' means the Welfare Reform and Pensions Act 1999;
'employer' has the meaning given by section 181(1) of the 1993 Act;
'occupational pension scheme' has the meaning given by section 1 of the 1993 Act;
'pension arrangement' has the meaning given by section 46(1) of the 1999 Act;
'relevant arrangement' has the meaning given by section 29(8) of the 1999 Act;
'relevant benefits' has the meaning given by section 612 of the Income and Corporation Taxes Act 1988;
'scheme' means an occupational pension scheme;
'scheme actuary', in relation to a scheme to which section 47(1)(b) of the 1995 Act applies, means the actuary mentioned in section 47(1)(b) of that Act;
'transfer credits' has the meaning given by section 181(1) of the 1993 Act;
['transfer day' has the meaning given by section 29(8) of the 1999 Act;]
'transferor' has the meaning given by section 29(8) of the 1999 Act;
'trustees or managers' has the meaning given by section 46(1) of the 1999 Act;
'valuation day' has the meaning given by section 29(7) of the 1999 Act.

**Initial Commencement**
1 December 2000.

**Amendment**
SI 2000/2691.

[3.583]

### 2 Rights under a pension arrangement which are not shareable

(1) Rights under a pension arrangement which are not shareable are—

(a) subject to paragraph (2), any rights accrued between 1961 and 1975 which relate to contracted-out equivalent pension benefit within the meaning of section 57 of the National Insurance Act 1965 (equivalent pension benefits, etc);

(b) any rights in respect of which a person is in receipt of—

(i) a pension;

(ii) an annuity;

(iii) payments under an interim arrangement within the meaning of section 28(1A) of the 1993 Act (ways of giving effect to protected rights); or

(iv) income withdrawal within the meaning of section 630(1) of the Income and Corporation Taxes Act 1988 (interpretation),

by virtue of being the widow, widower or other dependant of a deceased person with pension rights under a pension arrangement; and

(c) any rights which do not result in the payment of relevant benefits.

(2) Paragraph (1)(a) applies only when those rights are the only rights held by a person under a pension arrangement.

**Initial Commencement**

1 December 2000.

[3.584]

### 3 Calculation and verification of cash equivalents for the purposes of the creation of pension debits and credits

For the purposes of section 29 of the 1999 Act (creation of pension debits and credits), cash equivalents may be calculated and verified—

(a) where the relevant arrangement is an occupational pension scheme in accordance with regulations 4 and 5; or

(b) in any other case, in accordance with regulations 6 and 7.

**Initial Commencement**

1 December 2000.

[3.585]

### 4 Occupational pension schemes: manner of calculation and verification of cash equivalents

(1) In a case to which, or to the extent to which, paragraph (2) or (5) does not apply, cash equivalents are to be calculated and verified in such manner as may be approved in a particular case by the scheme actuary or, in relation to a scheme to which section 47(1)(b) of the 1995 Act (professional advisers) does not apply, by—

(a) a Fellow of the Institute of Actuaries;

(b) a Fellow of the Faculty of Actuaries; or

(c) a person with other actuarial qualifications who is approved by the Secretary of State, at the request of the trustees or managers of the scheme in question, as being a proper person to act for the purposes of these Regulations in connection with that scheme

and, subject to paragraph (2), in the following paragraphs of this regulation and in regulation 5 'actuary' means the scheme actuary or, in relation to a scheme to which section 47(1)(b) of the 1995 Act does not apply, the actuary referred to in sub-paragraph (a), (b) or (c) of this paragraph.

(2) Where the transferor in respect of whose rights a cash equivalent is to be calculated and verified, is a member of a scheme having particulars from time to time set out in regulations made under section 7 of the Superannuation Act 1972 (superannuation of persons employed in local government service, etc), that cash equivalent shall be calculated and verified in such manner as may be approved by the Government Actuary or by an actuary authorised by the Government Actuary to act on his behalf for that purpose and in such a case 'actuary' in this regulation and in regulation 5 means the Government Actuary or the actuary so authorised.

[(2A) Where the person with pension rights is a deferred member of an occupational pension scheme on the transfer day, the value of the benefits which he has accrued under that scheme shall be taken to be—

- (a) in the case of an occupational pension scheme other than a salary related scheme, the cash equivalent to which he acquired a right under section 94(1)(a) of the 1993 Act (right to cash equivalent) on the termination of his pensionable service, calculated on the assumption that he has made an application under section 95(1) of that Act (ways of taking right to cash equivalent); or
- (b) in the case of a salary related occupational pension scheme, the guaranteed cash equivalent to which he would have acquired a right under section 94(1)(aa) of the 1993 Act if he had made an application under section 95(1) of that Act.

(2B) Where the person with pension rights is an active member of an occupational pension scheme on the transfer day, the value of the benefits which he has accrued under that scheme shall be calculated and verified—

- (a) on the assumption that the member had made a request for an estimate of the cash equivalent that would be available to him were his pensionable service to terminate on the transfer day; and
- (b) in accordance with regulation 11 of, and Schedule 1 to, the Occupational Pension Schemes (Transfer Values) Regulations 1996 (disclosure).]

(3) Except in a case to which paragraph (5) applies, cash equivalents are to be calculated and verified by adopting methods and making assumptions which—

- (a) if not determined by the trustees or managers of the scheme in question, are notified to them by the actuary; and
- (b) are certified by the actuary to the trustees or managers of the scheme—
  - (i) as being consistent with 'Retirement Benefit Schemes—Transfer Values (GN11)' published by the Institute of Actuaries and the Faculty of Actuaries and current on the valuation day;
  - (ii) as being consistent with the methods adopted and assumptions made, at the time when the certificate is issued, in calculating the benefits to which entitlement arises under the rules of the scheme in question for a person who is acquiring transfer credits under those rules; and
  - (iii) in the case of a scheme to which section 56 of the 1995 Act (minimum funding requirement) applies as providing as a minimum an amount, consistent with the methods adopted and assumptions made in calculating, for the purposes of section 57 of that Act (valuation and certification of assets and liabilities), the liabilities mentioned in section 73(3)(a), (aa), (b), (c)(i) and (d) of that Act (preferential liabilities on winding up), subject, in any case where the cash equivalent calculation is made on an individual and not a collective basis, to any adjustments which are appropriate to take account of that fact.

(4) If, by virtue of Schedule 5 to the Occupational Pension Schemes (Minimum Funding Requirement and Actuarial Valuations) Regulations 1996 (modifications), section 56 of the 1995 Act applies to a section of a scheme as if that section were a separate scheme, paragraph (3)(b)(iii) shall apply as if that section were a separate

scheme and if the reference therein to a scheme were accordingly a reference to that section.

(5) Where a cash equivalent or any portion of a cash equivalent relates to money purchase benefits which do not fall to be valued in a manner which involves making estimates of the value of benefits, then that cash equivalent or that portion shall be calculated and verified in such manner as may be approved in particular cases by the trustees or managers of the scheme[, and by adopting methods consistent with the requirements of Chapter IV of Part IV of the 1993 Act (protection for early leavers — transfer values)].

**Initial Commencement**

1 December 2000.

**Amendment**

SI 2000/2691.

**[3.586]**

## 5 Occupational pension schemes: further provisions as to the calculation of cash equivalents and increases and reductions of cash equivalents

(1) Where it is the established custom for additional benefits to be awarded from the scheme at the discretion of the trustees or managers or the employer, the cash equivalent shall, unless the trustees or managers have given a direction that cash equivalents shall not take account of such benefits, take account of any such additional benefits as will accrue to the transferor if the custom continues unaltered.

(2) The trustees or managers shall not make a direction such as is mentioned in paragraph (1) unless, within 3 months before making the direction, they have consulted the actuary and have obtained the actuary's written report on the implications for the state of funding of the scheme of making such a direction, including the actuary's advice as to whether or not in the actuary's opinion there would be any adverse implications for the funding of the scheme should the trustees or managers not make such a direction.

(3) Subject to paragraph (6), in the case of a scheme to which section 56 of the 1995 Act applies, each respective part of the cash equivalent which relates to liabilities referred to in section 73(3)(a), (aa), (b), (c)(i) or (d) of the 1995 Act may be reduced by the percentage which is the difference between—

- (a) 100 per cent; and
- (b) the percentage of the liabilities mentioned in the relevant paragraph of section 73(3) which the actuarial valuation shows the scheme assets as being sufficient to satisfy

where the actuarial valuation is the latest actuarial valuation obtained in accordance with section 57 of the 1995 Act before the valuation day.

(4) If, by virtue of Schedule 5 to the Occupational Pension Schemes (Minimum Funding Requirement and Actuarial Valuations) Regulations 1996, section 56 of the 1995 Act applies to a section of a scheme as if that section were a separate scheme, paragraph (3) shall apply as if that section were a separate scheme, and as if the reference therein to a scheme were accordingly a reference to that section.

[(5) The reduction referred to in paragraph (3) shall not apply to a case where liability in respect of a pension credit is to be discharged in accordance with—

- (a) paragraph 1(2) of Schedule 5 to the 1999 Act (pension credits: mode of discharge—funded pension schemes); or
- (b) paragraph 1(3) of that Schedule, in a case where regulation 7(2) of the Pension Sharing (Implementation and Discharge of Liability) Regulations 2000 applies.]

(6) Where a scheme has begun to be wound up, a cash equivalent may be reduced to the extent necessary for the scheme to comply with sections 73 and 74 of the 1995 Act (discharge of liabilities by insurance, etc), and the Occupational Pension Schemes (Winding Up) Regulations 1996.

(7) If, by virtue of the Occupational Pension Schemes (Winding Up) Regulations 1996, section 73 of the 1995 Act applies to a section of a scheme as if that section were a separate scheme, paragraph (6) shall apply as if that section were a separate scheme and as if the references therein to a scheme were accordingly references to that section.

(8) Where all or any of the benefits to which a cash equivalent relates have been surrendered, commuted or forfeited before the date on which the trustees or managers discharge their liability in respect of the pension credit in accordance with the provisions of Schedule 5 to the 1999 Act, the cash equivalent of the benefits so surrendered, commuted or forfeited shall be reduced to nil.

(9) In a case where two or more of the paragraphs of this regulation fall to be applied to a calculation, they shall be applied in the order in which they occur in this regulation.

**Initial Commencement**
1 December 2000.

**Amendment**
SI 2000/2691.



**[3.587]**

### 6 Other relevant arrangements: manner of calculation and verification of cash equivalents

(1) Except in a case to which paragraph (3) applies, cash equivalents are to be calculated and verified in such manner as may be approved in a particular case by—

(a) a Fellow of the Institute of Actuaries;
(b) a Fellow of the Faculty of Actuaries; or
(c) a person with other actuarial qualifications who is approved by the Secretary of State, at the request of the person responsible for the relevant arrangement, as being a proper person to act for the purposes of this regulation and regulation 7 in connection with that arrangement,

and in paragraph (2) 'actuary' means any person such as is referred to in sub-paragraph (a), (b) or (c) of this paragraph.

[(1A) Where the person with pension rights is a member of a personal pension scheme, or those rights are contained in a retirement annuity contract, the value of the benefits which he has accrued under that scheme or contract on the transfer day shall be taken to be the cash equivalent to which he would have acquired a right under section 94(1)(b) of the 1993 Act, if he had made an application under section 95(1) of that Act on the date on which the request for the valuation was received.

(1B) In relation to a personal pension scheme which is comprised in a retirement annuity contract made before 4th January 1988, paragraph (2) shall apply as if such a scheme were not excluded from the scope of Chapter IV of Part IV of the 1993 Act by section 93(1)(b) of that Act (scope of Chapter IV).]

(2) Except in a case to which paragraph (3) applies, cash equivalents are to be calculated and verified by adopting methods and making assumptions which—

(a) if not determined by the person responsible for the relevant arrangement, are notified to them by an actuary; and
(b) are certified by an actuary to the person responsible for the relevant arrangement as being consistent with 'Retirement Benefit Schemes—Transfer Values (GN11)', published by the Institute of Actuaries and the Faculty of Actuaries and current on the valuation day.

(3) Where a transferor's cash equivalent, or any portion of it—

(a) represents his rights to money purchase benefits under the relevant arrangement; and
(b) those rights do not fall, either wholly or in part, to be valued in a manner which involves making estimates of the value of benefits,

then that cash equivalent, or that portion of it, shall be calculated and verified in such manner as may be approved in a particular case by the person responsible for the relevant arrangement [, and by adopting methods consistent with the requirements of Chapter IV of Part IV of the 1993 Act].

(4) This regulation and regulation 7 apply to a relevant arrangement other than an occupational pension scheme.

**Initial Commencement**
1 December 2000.

**Amendment**
SI 2000/2691.

**[3.588]**

## 7 Other relevant arrangements: reduction of cash equivalents

Where all or any of the benefits to which a cash equivalent relates have been surrendered, commuted or forfeited before the date on which the person responsible for the relevant arrangement discharges his liability for the pension credit in accordance with the provisions of Schedule 5 to the 1999 Act, the cash equivalent of the benefits so surrendered, commuted or forfeited shall be reduced in proportion to the reduction in the total value of the benefits.

**Initial Commencement**
1 December 2000.

# Pension Sharing (Implementation and Discharge of Liability) Regulations 2000

**SI 2000 No 1053**

---

**Contents**

*Regulation*

PART I
GENERAL



PART II
EXTENSION, POSTPONEMENT OR CESSATION OF IMPLEMENTATION PERIOD



PART III
DEATH OF PERSON ENTITLED TO A PENSION CREDIT BEFORE LIABILITY IN RESPECT OF THE PENSION CREDIT IS DISCHARGED



PART IV
DISCHARGE OF LIABILITY IN RESPECT OF A PENSION CREDIT

---

**[3.589]**

## PART I
## GENERAL

### 1 Citation, commencement and interpretation

(1) These Regulations may be cited as the Pension Sharing (Implementation and Discharge of Liability) Regulations 2000 and shall come into force on 1 December 2000.

(2) In these Regulations—

'the 1993 Act' means the Pension Schemes Act 1993;

'the 1995 Act' means the Pensions Act 1995;

'the 1999 Act' means the Welfare Reform and Pensions Act 1999;

'base rate' means the base rate for the time being quoted by the reference banks or, where there is for the time being more than one such base rate, the base rate which, when the base rate quoted by each bank is ranked in a descending sequence of seven, is fourth in the sequence;

. . .

'the implementation period' has the meaning given by section 34 of the 1999 Act;

['the Inland Revenue' means the Commissioners of Inland Revenue;]

'normal benefit age' has the meaning given by section 101B of the 1993 Act;

'occupational pension scheme' has the meaning given by section 1 of the 1993 Act;

'pension arrangement' has the meaning given by section 46(1) of the 1999 Act;

'pension credit' means a credit under section 29(1)(b) of the 1999 Act;

['pension sharing order' means an order which is mentioned in section 28(l) of the 1999 Act;]

'personal pension scheme' has the meaning given by section 1 of the 1993 Act;

'person responsible for a pension arrangement' has the meaning given to that expression in section 46(2) of the 1999 Act;

. . .

'the reference banks' means the seven largest institutions for the time being which—

[(a) are authorised by the Financial Services Authority under the Banking Act 1987;]

(b) are incorporated in and carrying on within the United Kingdom a deposit-taking business (as defined in section 6, but subject to any order under section 7 of that Act); and

(c) quote a base rate in sterling;

and for the purpose of this definition the size of an institution at any time is to be determined by reference to the gross assets denominated in sterling of that institution, together with any subsidiary (as defined in section 736 of the Companies Act 1985), as shown in the audited end of year accounts last published before that time;

'the Regulatory Authority' means the Occupational Pensions Regulatory Authority;

'safeguarded rights' has the meaning given in section 68A(1) of the 1993 Act;

'scheme actuary', in relation to a scheme to which section 47(1)(b) of the 1995 Act applies, means the actuary mentioned in section 47(1)(b) of that Act;

'section 9(2B) rights' has the meaning given in regulation 1(2) of the Occupational Pension Schemes (Contracting-out) Regulations 1996;
'transferee' has the meaning given by section 34(5) of the 1999 Act;
'transferor' has the meaning given by section 34(5) of the 1999 Act;
'trustees or managers', in relation to an occupational pension scheme or a personal pension scheme means—
(a) in the case of a scheme established under a trust, the trustees of the scheme, and
(b) in any other case, the managers of the scheme;
'the valuation day' has the meaning given in section 29(7) of the 1999 Act.

**Initial Commencement**
1 December 2000.

**Amendment**
SI 2000/2691.



**[3.590]**

PART II
EXTENSION, POSTPONEMENT OR CESSATION OF IMPLEMENTATION PERIOD

### 2 Time period for notification to the Regulatory Authority of failure by the trustees or managers of an occupational pension scheme to discharge their liability in respect of a pension credit

The period prescribed for the purposes of section 33(2)(a) of the 1999 Act (period within which notice must be given of non-discharge of pension credit liability) is the period of 21 days beginning with the day immediately following the end of the implementation period.

**Initial Commencement**
1 December 2000.

**[3.591]**

### 3 Circumstances in which an application for an extension of the implementation period may be made

The circumstances in which an application may be made for the purposes of section 33(4) of the 1999 Act (application for extension of period within which pension credit liability is to be discharged) are that the application is made to the Regulatory Authority before the end of the implementation period; and—
(a) the Regulatory Authority is satisfied that—
(i) the scheme is being wound up or is about to be wound up;
(ii) the scheme is ceasing to be a contracted-out scheme;
(iii) the financial interests of the members of the scheme generally will be prejudiced if the trustees or managers do what is needed to discharge their liability for the pension credit within that period;
(iv) the transferor or the transferee has not taken such steps as the trustees or managers can reasonably expect in order to satisfy them of any matter which falls to be established before they can properly discharge their liability for the pension credit;
(v) the trustees or managers have not been provided with such information as they reasonably require properly to discharge their liability for the pension credit within the implementation period;

(vi) the transferor or the transferee has disputed the amount of the cash equivalent calculated and verified for the purposes of section 29 of the 1999 Act (creation of pension debits and credits);

(b) the provisions of section 53 of the 1993 Act (supervision: former contracted-out schemes) apply; or

(c) the application has been made on one or more of the grounds specified in paragraph (a) or (b), and the Regulatory Authority's consideration of the application cannot be completed before the end of the implementation period.

**Initial Commencement**
1 December 2000.

**[3.592]**

## 4 Postponement or cessation of implementation period when an application is made for leave to appeal out of time

(1) The modifications to the operation of section 34 of the 1999 Act ('implementation period') where the pension credit depends on a pension sharing order and the order is the subject of an application for leave to appeal out of time are—

(a) where the implementation period has not commenced, its commencement shall be postponed; or

(b) where the implementation period has commenced, its operation shall cease and it shall not commence afresh until the person responsible for the pension arrangement has received the documents referred to in paragraph (2).

(2) The postponement or cessation referred to in paragraph (1)(a) or (b) shall continue until the person responsible for the pension arrangement is in receipt of—

(a) confirmation from the court that the order which was the subject of the application for leave to appeal out of time has not been varied or discharged; or

(b) a copy of the varied pension sharing order.

(3) Where the person responsible for the pension arrangement has discharged his liability in respect of the pension credit which depends on a pension sharing order and that person subsequently receives notification of an application for leave to appeal out of time in respect of that order, he shall inform the court within 21 days from the date on which he received the notification that liability in respect of that pension credit has been discharged.

**Initial Commencement**
1 December 2000.

**[3.593]**

## 5 Civil penalties

For the purpose of section 33(2)(b) or (3) of the 1999 Act, the maximum amount of the penalty which may be imposed by the Regulatory Authority under section 10(2)(b) of the 1995 Act is—

(a) £1,000 in the case of an individual, and

(b) £10,000 in any other case.

**Initial Commencement**
1 December 2000.

**[3.594]**

## PART III
## DEATH OF PERSON ENTITLED TO A PENSION CREDIT BEFORE LIABILITY IN RESPECT OF THE PENSION CREDIT IS DISCHARGED

### 6 Discharge of liability in respect of a pension credit following the death of the person entitled to the pension credit

[(1) The person responsible for the pension arrangement shall following the death of the person entitled to the pension credit discharge his liability in respect of a pension credit in accordance with this regulation.

(2) Where the rules or provisions of a pension arrangement so provide and provided that any requirements of the Inland Revenue under Part XIV of the Income and Corporation Taxes Act 1988 are satisfied, the person responsible for the pension arrangement shall discharge his liability in respect of a pension credit by undertaking to—

(a) make—
   (i) a payment of a lump sum; or
   (ii) payments of a pension; or
   (iii) payments of both a lump sum and a pension,

   to one or more persons; or

(b) enter into an annuity contract or take out a policy of insurance with an insurance company for the benefit of one or more persons; or

(c) make a payment or, as the case may be, payments under sub-paragraph (a) and enter into an annuity contract or take out an insurance policy under sub-paragraph (b).

(3) Where paragraph (2)(b) or (c) applies, the annuity contract entered into or insurance policy taken out must satisfy the requirements of paragraph 6(2) of Schedule 5 to the 1999 Act (qualifying arrangements) and regulation 11 of these Regulations.

(4) Where the provisions of paragraph (2) do not apply, liability in respect of a pension credit shall be discharged by retaining the value of the pension credit in the pension arrangement from which that pension credit was derived.

(5) Where—

(a) liability in respect of a pension credit has been discharged in accordance with paragraph (2); and

(b) the value of the payment or payments made, the annuity contract entered into or the insurance policy taken out, as the case may be, is less than the value of the pension credit,

the value of an amount equal to the difference between the value of the pension credit and the value of that payment or those payments, that contract or policy, as the case may be, shall be retained in the pension arrangement from which that pension credit was derived.]

**Initial Commencement**

1 December 2000.

**Amendment**

Substituted by SI 2000/2691, reg 11(1), (3). Date in force: 1 December 2000: see SI 2000/2691, reg 1(1).

**[3.595]**

## PART IV
## DISCHARGE OF LIABILITY IN RESPECT OF A PENSION CREDIT

### 7 Funded pension schemes

(1) The circumstances in which the trustees or managers of a scheme, to which paragraph 1 of Schedule 5 to the 1999 Act applies, may discharge their liability in

respect of a pension credit in accordance with sub-paragraph (2)(b) of that paragraph are where—

(a) the person entitled to the credit has failed to provide his consent in accordance with paragraph 1(2)(a) and (4) of that Schedule; and

(b) the circumstances set out in paragraph 1(3) of that Schedule do not apply.

(2) The circumstances in which the trustees or managers of a scheme, to which paragraph 1 of Schedule 5 to the 1999 Act applies, may discharge their liability in respect of a pension credit in accordance with sub-paragraph (3)(c) of that paragraph are where—

(a) the person entitled to the credit has failed to provide his consent in accordance with [paragraph 1(3)(c)] of that Schedule; and

[(b) either—

(i) the person entitled to the pension credit has failed to provide his consent in accordance with paragraph 1(2)(a) and (4) of that Schedule; or

(ii) the trustees or managers of the scheme have not discharged their liability in accordance with paragraph (1) above].

**Initial Commencement**

1 December 2000.

**Amendment**

SI 2000/2691.

**[3.596]**

## 8 Unfunded occupational pension schemes other than public service pension schemes

(1) The circumstances in which the trustees or managers of a scheme, to which paragraph 3 of Schedule 5 to the 1999 Act applies, may discharge their liability in respect of a pension credit in accordance with sub-paragraph (3)(c) of that paragraph are those specified in—

(a) sub-paragraphs (a) and (b) of paragraph (2), in the case of an approved scheme; and

(b) sub-paragraphs (a), (b) and (c) of paragraph (2), in the case of an unapproved scheme.

(2) The circumstances specified in this paragraph are—

(a) the liability of the trustees or managers has not been discharged in accordance with the provisions of paragraph 3(2) of that Schedule;

(b) the person entitled to the pension credit has not consented to the discharge of liability in accordance with paragraph 3(3) of that Schedule; and

(c) the employer who is associated with the scheme from which the pension credit derives—

(i) consents to the trustees or managers discharging their liability for the credit in accordance with paragraph 3(3) of that Schedule; and

(ii) agrees to compensate the person entitled to the credit fully for any tax liability which he may incur as a result of the trustees or managers of the scheme discharging their liability for the credit in accordance with paragraph 3(3) of that Schedule.

(3) In this regulation 'approved scheme' means an occupational pension scheme which is approved for the purposes of Part XIV of the Income and Corporation Taxes Act 1988 and an 'unapproved scheme' means an occupational pension scheme which is not approved for those purposes.

**Initial Commencement**

1 December 2000.

[3.597]

## 9 Other pension arrangements

(1) The circumstances in which the person responsible for a pension arrangement, to which paragraph 4 of Schedule 5 to the 1999 Act applies, may discharge his liability in respect of a pension credit in accordance with sub-paragraph (2)(c) of that paragraph are where his liability has not been discharged in accordance with the provisions of paragraph 4(3) or (4) of that Schedule.

(2) The circumstances in which the person responsible for the pension arrangement may discharge his liability in respect of the pension credit under paragraph 4(4) of Schedule 5 to the 1999 Act are where the person responsible for the pension arrangement has not discharged his liability in accordance with the provisions of—

- (a) paragraph (1) above;
- (b) paragraph 4(2) of that Schedule; or
- (c) paragraph 4(3) of that Schedule.

**Initial Commencement**

1 December 2000.



[3.598]

## 10 Calculation of the value of appropriate rights

(1) Except in a case to which paragraph (4) applies, the value of the rights conferred on a person entitled to a pension credit shall be calculated by adopting methods and making assumptions which the scheme actuary or, in relation to a scheme to which section 47(1)(b) of the 1995 Act (professional advisers) does not apply, by a person referred to in paragraph (2), has certified to the person responsible for the pension arrangement as being consistent with—

- (a) the methods adopted and assumptions made when transfers of other pension rights are received by the person responsible for the pension arrangement; and
- (b) the Guidance Note 11 'Retirement Benefit Schemes—Transfer Values' published by the Institute of Actuaries and the Faculty of Actuaries and which is current on the valuation day.

(2) A person referred to in this paragraph is—

- (a) a Fellow of the Institute of Actuaries;
- (b) a Fellow of the Faculty of Actuaries; or
- (c) a person with other actuarial qualifications who is approved by the Secretary of State, at the request of the person responsible for the pension arrangement in question, as being a proper person to act for the purposes of these Regulations in connection with that scheme.

(3) Where the person entitled to a pension credit in respect of whom a cash equivalent is to be calculated and verified is a member of a scheme having particulars from time to time set out in regulations made under section 7 of the Superannuation Act 1972 (superannuation of persons employed in local government service, etc), that cash equivalent shall be calculated and verified in such manner as may be approved by the Government Actuary or by an actuary authorised by the Government Actuary to act on his behalf for that purpose.

(4) Where the rights conferred on a person entitled to a pension credit are derived from money purchase rights in whole or in part, the value of those rights shall be calculated by the person responsible for the pension arrangement in a manner consistent with the methods adopted and assumptions made when transfers of other pension rights are received by the person responsible for the pension arrangement [, and by adopting methods consistent with the requirements of Chapter IV of Part IV of the 1993 Act (protection for early leavers — transfer values)].

**Initial Commencement**
1 December 2000.

**Amendment**
SI 2000/2691.

## [3.599]

### 11 Qualifying arrangements

(1) The requirements referred to in paragraph 6(2)(b) of Schedule 5 to the 1999 Act (requirements applying to annuity contracts or policies of insurance for the purpose of sub-paragraph (1) of that paragraph) are that the annuity contract is entered into or the insurance policy is taken out with an insurance company which is—

- (a) authorised under section 3 or 4 of the Insurance Companies Act 1982 (authorisation of insurance business) to carry on long term business (within the meaning of section 1 of that Act (classification));
- (b) in the case of a friendly society authorised under section 32 of the Friendly Societies Act 1992 (grant of authorisation by Commission: general) to carry out long term business under any of the Classes specified in Head A of Schedule 2 to that Act (the activities of a friendly society: long term business); or
- (c) an EC company as defined in section 2 of the Insurance Companies Act 1982 (restriction on carrying on insurance business), and which falls within paragraph (2).

(2) An EC company falls within this paragraph if it—

- (a) carries on ordinary long-term insurance business (within the meaning of section 96(1) of the Insurance Companies Act 1982) in the United Kingdom through a branch in respect of which such of the requirements of Part I of Schedule 2F to that Act (recognition in the United Kingdom of EC and EFTA companies: EC companies carrying on business etc in the United Kingdom) as are applicable have been complied with; or
- (b) provides ordinary long term insurance in the United Kingdom and such of the requirements of Part I of Schedule 2F to that Act as are applicable have been complied with in respect of insurance.

**Initial Commencement**
1 December 2000.

## [3.600]

### 12 Disqualification as a destination for pension credit—general

The requirements referred to in paragraph 7(1)(b) of Schedule 5 to the 1999 Act (requirements to be satisfied to qualify pension arrangements as destinations for pension credits) are that the pension arrangement—

- (a) is an arrangement which carries on pension business as defined by section 431B of the Income and Corporation Taxes Act 1988 (meaning of 'pension business');
- (b) is an overseas arrangement within the meaning given by regulation 1(2) of the Contracting-out (Transfer and Transfer Payment) Regulations 1996 (citation, commencement and interpretation); [or]
- (c) is an overseas scheme within the meaning given by regulation 1(2) of the Contracting-out (Transfer and Transfer Payment) Regulations 1996.

**Initial Commencement**
1 December 2000.

**Amendment**
SI 2000/2691.

**[3.601]**

## 13 Disqualification as a destination for pension credit—contracted-out or safeguarded rights

(1) The descriptions of pension arrangements referred to in paragraph 7(2)(a) of Schedule 5 to the 1999 Act (pension arrangements which qualify as destinations for pension credits, where the rights by reference to which the amount of the credits are determined are or include contracted-out rights or safeguarded rights) are—

(a) a contracted-out salary related occupational pension scheme which satisfies the requirements of section 9(2) of the 1993 Act (requirements for certification of occupational salary related schemes);

(b) a contracted-out money purchase occupational pension scheme which satisfies the requirements of section 9(3) of the 1993 Act (requirements for certification of occupational money purchase schemes);

(bb) a contracted-out occupational pension scheme to which section 149 of the 1995 Act (hybrid occupational pension schemes) applies;

(c) an appropriate personal pension scheme within the meaning of section 7(4) of the 1993 Act (issue of appropriate scheme certificates);

(d) an annuity contract or an insurance policy which satisfies the requirements of paragraph 6 of Schedule 5 to the 1999 Act (qualifying arrangements);

(e) an overseas arrangement within the meaning given by regulation 1(2) of the Contracting-out (Transfer and Transfer Payment) Regulations 1996; or

(f) an overseas scheme within the meaning given by regulation 1(2) of the Contracting-out (Transfer and Transfer Payment) Regulations 1996.

(2) The requirements referred to in paragraph 7(2)(b) of Schedule 5 to the 1999 Act (requirements to be satisfied by a pension arrangement which qualifies as a destination for a pension credit, where the rights by reference to which the amount of the credit are determined are or include contracted-out rights or safeguarded rights) are—

(a) in relation to the descriptions of pension arrangement referred to in paragraph (1)(a) to (d), the requirements specified in the Pension Sharing (Safeguarded Rights) Regulations 2000 to be met by an occupational pension scheme or a personal pension scheme;

(b) in relation to the descriptions of pension arrangement referred to in paragraph (1)(e), the requirements specified in regulation 15 (disqualification as a destination for pension credit—annuity contracts and insurance policies) and regulation 7(3) and (4) of the Pension Sharing (Safeguarded Rights) Regulations 2000 (the pension and annuity requirements—money purchase schemes);

(c) in relation to the descriptions of pension arrangement referred to in paragraph (1)(f) and (g), the requirements specified in regulation 11 of the Contracting-out (Transfer and Transfer Payment) Regulations 1996 (transfer payments to overseas schemes or arrangements in respect of section 9(2B) rights), as if the references in that regulation to—

(i) 'earner' were to 'the person entitled to a pension credit'; and

(ii) 'accrued section 9(2B) rights' were to 'safeguarded rights'.

(3) The rights for the purposes of paragraph 7(6) of Schedule 5 to the 1999 Act (meaning of 'contracted-out' rights under or derived from an occupational pension scheme or a personal pension scheme) are those which fall within the categories specified in regulation 2 of the Pension Sharing (Safeguarded Rights) Regulations 2000 (definition of contracted-out rights).

**Initial Commencement**

1 December 2000.

**Amendment**

Para (1): amended by SI 2000/2691, reg 11.

PART 3
Pension Sharing etc Regs 2000

[3.602]

### 14 Disqualification as a destination for pension credit—occupational pension schemes

The calculation of the value of the rights of the person entitled to the pension credit for the purposes of paragraph 7(3) of Schedule 5 to the 1999 Act shall be made in accordance with the methods adopted and assumptions made by the scheme which are consistent with the methods adopted and assumptions made by that scheme when transfers of other pension rights are received by the scheme.

**Initial Commencement**
1 December 2000.

[3.603]

### 15 Disqualification as a destination for pension credit—annuity contracts and insurance policies

(1) The circumstances referred to in paragraph 7(4) of Schedule 5 to the 1999 Act (circumstances in which an annuity contract or insurance policy is disqualified as a destination for a pension credit) are where the requirements specified in paragraphs (2) to (7) are not satisfied.

(2) The annuity contract or insurance policy must provide that that contract or policy, as the case may be, may not be assigned or surrendered unless—

- (a) the person entitled to the pension credit; or
- (b) if the person entitled to the pension credit has died, his widow or widower,

has consented to the assignment or surrender.

(3) The benefits previously secured by the annuity contract or insurance policy become secured, or are replaced by benefits which are secured by another qualifying arrangement.

(4) The annuity contract or insurance policy, as the case may be, must provide that the benefits secured by that contract or policy may be commuted if either—

- (a) the conditions set out in paragraph (5) are satisfied; or
- (b) the conditions set out in paragraph (6) are satisfied.

(5) The conditions referred to in paragraph (4)(a) are—

- (a) the benefits secured by the annuity contract or insurance policy have become payable, and the aggregate of those benefits does not exceed £260 per annum;
- (b) an actuary certifies that the methods and assumptions to be used to calculate any benefit in a lump sum form will result in the benefit being broadly equivalent to the annual amount of benefits which would have been payable in pension benefits; and
- (c) all of the interest of the person entitled to the pension credit under the annuity contract or insurance policy is discharged upon payment of a lump sum.

(6) The conditions referred to in paragraph (4)(b) are—

- (a) the benefits secured by the annuity contract or insurance policy have become payable and the person entitled to the pension credit requests or consents to the commutation;
- (b) the person entitled to the pension credit is suffering from serious ill health prior to normal benefit age; and
- (c) the insurance company with which the annuity contract is entered into, or with which the insurance policy is taken out, assumes an obligation to pay the benefits secured by the annuity contract or insurance policy to—
  - (i) the person entitled to the pension credit;
  - (ii) the trustees of a trust for the benefit of the person entitled to the pension credit; or

(iii) the trustees of a trust for the benefit of the dependants of the person entitled to the pension credit.

(7) The annuity contract or insurance policy must contain, or be endorsed with, terms so as to provide for any increase in accordance with regulation 32 of the Pension Sharing (Pension Credit Benefit) Regulations 2000 (increase of relevant pension) which would have been applied to the benefits which have become secured or been replaced by the annuity contract or insurance policy had the discharge of liability not taken place.

(8) In this regulation—

'serious ill health' means ill health which is such as to give rise to a life expectancy of less than one year from the date on which commutation of the benefits secured by the annuity contract or insurance policy is applied for.

**Initial Commencement**

1 December 2000.

**[3.604]**

### 16 Adjustments to the amount of the pension credit—occupational pension schemes which are underfunded on the valuation day

(1) The circumstances referred to in paragraph 8(1)(d) of Schedule 5 to the 1999 Act (adjustments to amount of pension credit) are—

(a) the discharge of liability in respect of the pension credit in accordance with paragraph 1(3) of Schedule 5 to the 1999 Act is at the request, or with the consent, of the person entitled to the pension credit;

(b) the person entitled to the pension credit has refused an offer by the trustees or managers of the occupational pension scheme from which the pension credit is derived to discharge their liability in respect of the pension credit, without any reduction in the amount of the credit, in accordance with the provisions of paragraph 1(2) of Schedule 5 to the 1999 Act (conferring appropriate rights in that scheme on the person entitled to the pension credit); and

(c) prior to making his request or giving his consent in accordance with sub-paragraph (a) the person entitled to the pension credit has received from the trustees or managers of the occupational pension scheme from which the pension credit is derived, a written statement which provides the following information—

(i) the reasons why the amount of the pension credit has been reduced;

(ii) the amount by which the pension credit has been reduced; and

(iii) where possible, an estimate of the date by which it will be possible to pay the full, unadjusted amount of the pension credit.

(2) The lesser amount referred to in paragraph 8(1) of Schedule 5 to the 1999 Act may be determined for the purposes of that paragraph by reducing the amount of the pension credit which relates to liabilities referred to in section 73(3)(a), (aa), (b), (c)(i) or (d) of the 1995 Act (preferential liabilities on winding-up) by the percentage which is the difference between—

(a) 100 per cent; and

(b) the percentage of the pension credit which the actuarial valuation shows the scheme assets as being sufficient to satisfy,

where the actuarial valuation is the latest actuarial valuation obtained in accordance with section 57 of the 1995 Act (valuation and certification of assets and liabilities) before the valuation day.

(3) If, by virtue of Schedule 5 to the Occupational Pension Schemes (Minimum Funding Requirement and Actuarial Valuations) Regulations 1996, section 56 of the 1995 Act (minimum funding requirement) applies to a section of a scheme as if that section were a separate scheme, paragraph (2) shall apply as if that section were a

separate scheme, and as if the reference therein to a scheme were accordingly a reference to that section.

**Initial Commencement**
1 December 2000.

**[3.605]**

### 17 Adjustments to the amount of the pension credit—payments made without knowledge of the pension debit

For the purposes of paragraph 9 of Schedule 5 to the 1999 Act (adjustments to amount of pension credit), where the cash equivalent of the member's shareable rights after deduction of the payment referred to in sub-paragraph (b) of that paragraph, is less than the amount of the pension debit, the pension credit shall be reduced to that lesser amount.

**Initial Commencement**
1 December 2000.

**[3.606]**

### 18 Adjustments to the amount of the pension credit—increasing the amount of the pension credit

(1) For the purposes of paragraph 10 of Schedule 5 to the 1999 Act (adjustments to amount of pension credit) the trustees or managers of an occupational pension scheme to which paragraph 1(3) or 3(3) of Schedule 5 to the 1999 Act applies shall increase the amount of the pension credit by—

- (a) the amount, if any, by which the amount of that pension credit falls short of what it would have been if the valuation day had been the day on which the trustees or managers make the payment; or
- (b) if it is greater, interest on the amount of that pension credit calculated on a daily basis over the period from the valuation day to the day on which the trustees or managers make the payment, at an annual rate of one per cent above the base rate.

(2) For the purposes of paragraph 10 of Schedule 5 to the 1999 Act the trustees or managers of a personal pension scheme to which paragraph 1(3) of Schedule 5 to the 1999 Act applies, or a person responsible for a pension arrangement to which paragraph 4(2) of Schedule 5 to the 1999 Act applies, shall increase the amount of the pension credit by—

- (a) the interest on the amount of that pension credit, calculated on daily basis over the period from the valuation day to the day on which the trustees or managers or the person responsible for the pension arrangement make the payment, at the same rate as that payable for the time being on judgment debts by virtue of section 17 of the Judgments Act 1838; or
- (b) if it is greater, the amount, if any, by which the amount of that pension credit falls short of what it would have been if the valuation day had been the day on which the trustees or managers or the person responsible for the pension arrangement make the payment.

**Initial Commencement**
1 December 2000.

# Pension Sharing (Pension Credit Benefit) Regulations 2000

## SI 2000 No 1054

Contents

*Regulation*

PART I
GENERAL



PART II
PENSION CREDIT BENEFIT UNDER OCCUPATIONAL PENSION SCHEMES



PART III
TRANSFER VALUES

---

**[3.607]**

PART I
GENERAL

### 1 Citation, commencement and interpretation

(1) These Regulations may be cited as the Pension Sharing (Pension Credit Benefit) Regulations 2000 and shall come into force on 1st December 2000.

(2) In these Regulations—

'the 1993 Act' means the Pension Schemes Act 1993;

'the 1995 Act' means the Pensions Act 1995;

'the 1999 Act' means the Welfare Reform and Pensions Act 1999;

'the Taxes Act' means the Income and Corporation Taxes Act 1988;

'active member', in relation to an occupational pension scheme, means a person who is in pensionable service under the scheme;

'appropriate scheme' shall be construed in accordance with section 9(5) of the 1993 Act;

'base rate' means the base rate for the time being quoted by the reference banks or, where there is for the time being more than one such base rate, the base rate which, when the base rate quoted by each bank is ranked in a descending sequence of seven, is fourth in the sequence;

'contracted-out rights' has the meaning given by section 68A(5) of the 1993 Act;

'eligible member' has the meaning given by section 101P(1) of the 1993 Act;

'employer' has the meaning given by section 181(1) of the 1993 Act;

'incapacity' means physical or mental deterioration which is sufficiently serious to prevent a person from following his normal employment or which seriously impairs his earning capacity;

'the Inland Revenue' means the Commissioners of Inland Revenue;

'member' means a member of an occupational pension scheme or a personal pension scheme and includes an eligible member;

'money purchase benefits' has the meaning given by section 181(1) of the 1993 Act;
'money purchase contracted-out scheme' has the meaning given by section 8(1)(a)(ii) of the 1993 Act;
'money purchase scheme' has the meaning given by section 181(1) of the 1993 Act;
'normal benefit age' has the meaning given by section 101B of the 1993 Act;
'occupational pension scheme' has the meaning given by section 1 of the 1993 Act;
'overseas arrangement' has the meaning given by regulation 1(2) of the Contracting-out (Transfer and Transfer Payment) Regulations 1996;
'overseas scheme' has the meaning given by regulation 1(2) of the Contracting-out (Transfer and Transfer Payment) Regulations 1996;
'pension credit benefit' has the meaning given by—
(a) section 101B of the 1993 Act insofar as that expression is used in Part II of these Regulations; and
(b) section 101P of the 1993 Act insofar as that expression is used in Part III of these Regulations;
'pension credit rights' has the meaning given by—
(a) section 101B of the 1993 Act insofar as that expression is used in Part II of these Regulations; and
(b) section 101P of the 1993 Act insofar as that expression is used in Part III of these Regulations;
'pensionable service' has the meaning given by section 124(1) of the Pensions Act 1995;
'personal pension scheme' has the meaning given by section 1 of the 1993 Act;
'principal appointed day' has the meaning given by section 7(2B) of the 1993 Act;
'qualifying occupational pension scheme' has the meaning given by section 40(3) of the 1999 Act;
'qualifying scheme' has the meaning given by section 101P(1) of the 1993 Act;
'the reference banks' means the seven largest institutions for the time being which—
[(a) are authorised by the Financial Services Authority under the Banking Act 1987;]
(b) are incorporated in and carrying on within the United Kingdom a deposit-taking business (as defined in section 6, but subject to any order under section 7 of that Act); and
(c) quote a base rate in sterling;

and for the purpose of this definition the size of an institution at any time is to be determined by reference to the gross assets denominated in sterling of that institution, together with any subsidiary (as defined in section 736 of the Companies Act 1985), as shown in the audited end of year accounts last published before that time;
'Regulatory Authority' means the Occupational Pensions Regulatory Authority;
'relevant pension' means a pension to which section 40(2) of the 1999 Act applies;
'safeguarded rights' has the meaning given by section 68A of the 1993 Act;
'salary related contracted-out scheme' has the meaning given by section 8(1)(a)(i) of the 1993 Act;
'scheme' has the meaning given by section 101B of the 1993 Act;
'statement of entitlement' means the statement of the amount of the cash equivalent of an eligible member's pension credit benefit under a qualifying scheme referred to in section 101H(1) of the 1993 Act;
'transfer credits' means rights allowed to a person under the rules of an occupational or personal pension scheme by reference to a transfer to that scheme of his accrued rights from another scheme (including any transfer credits allowed by that scheme);

'transfer notice' has the meaning given by section 101F(7) of the 1993 Act;
'trustees or managers' has the meaning given by section 46(1) of the 1999 Act;
'valuation date' has the meaning given by section 101J(7) of the 1993 Act.

**Initial Commencement**
1 December 2000.

**Amendment**
SI 2000/2691.

**[3.608]**

### 2 Salary related schemes

For the purposes of Chapter II of Part IVA of the 1993 Act (requirements relating to pension credit benefit—transfer values) and these Regulations, an occupational pension scheme is salary related if it is not a money purchase scheme and it is not a scheme—

(a) the only benefit provided by which (other than money purchase benefits) are death benefits; and

(b) under the provisions of which no member has accrued rights (other than rights to money purchase benefits).

**Initial Commencement**
1 December 2000.

**[3.609]**

## PART II
## PENSION CREDIT BENEFIT UNDER OCCUPATIONAL PENSION SCHEMES

### 3 Commutation of the whole of pension credit benefit

(1) Subject to paragraphs (3) and (4) and regulation 9 of the Pension Sharing (Safeguarded Rights) Regulations 2000 (ways of giving effect to safeguarded rights—salary related schemes), the circumstances in which the whole of the pension credit benefit may be commuted for the purposes of section 101C(2) of the 1993 Act (payment of pension credit benefit in the form of a lump sum before normal benefit age) are those described in paragraph (2).

(2) The circumstances described in this paragraph are that—

(a) the person entitled to the pension credit benefit is suffering from serious ill health prior to normal benefit age; or

(b) the aggregate of total benefits payable to the person under an occupational pension scheme, including any pension credit benefit, does not exceed £260 per annum.

(3) This regulation does not apply to an occupational pension scheme which is approved under section 590 of the Taxes Act (mandatory approval).

(4) In this regulation, 'serious ill health' means ill health which is such as to give rise to a life expectancy of less than one year from the date on which commutation of the pension credit benefit is applied for.

**Initial Commencement**
1 December 2000.

**[3.610]**

### 4 Commutation of part of pension credit benefit

(1) Subject to paragraphs (2) and (3) and regulation 9 of the Pension Sharing (Safeguarded Rights) Regulations 2000, the circumstances in which part of the pension

credit benefit may be commuted for the purposes of section 101C(2) of the 1993 Act (payment of pension credit benefit in the form of a lump sum before normal benefit age) are—

(a) that the person entitled to the pension credit benefit—

(i) subject to paragraph (2), is suffering from an incapacity prior to normal benefit age; or

(ii) has reached the age of 50; and

(b) that the commutation would not prevent approval or continuing approval of the scheme under section 591 of the Taxes Act (discretionary approval).

(2) Paragraph (1)(a)(i) applies where the person entitled to the pension credit benefit—

(a) is an active member of the occupational pension scheme in which his pension credit rights are held; and

(b) has become entitled to the early payment of benefits derived from his accrued rights, other than his pension credit rights, in that scheme as a result of his incapacity prior to normal benefit age.

(3) Safeguarded rights which are held in a money purchase contracted-out scheme shall not be commuted where the circumstances specified in paragraph (1)(a) apply.

(4) This regulation does not apply to an occupational pension scheme which is approved under section 590 of the Taxes Act.

**Initial Commencement**
1 December 2000.



**[3.611]**

## 5 Means of assuring pension credit benefit

(1) The prescribed means by which a person's pension credit benefit under a scheme must be assured for the purposes of section 101D(1)(b) of the 1993 Act (form of pension credit benefit and its alternatives) is by means of a transaction to which section 19 of the 1993 Act (discharge of liability where guaranteed minimum pensions are secured by insurance policies or annuity contracts) applies.

(2) A transaction referred to in paragraph (1) must satisfy the requirements of regulation 12, 13 or 14 (discharge of liability where pension credit benefit or alternative benefits are secured by insurance policies or annuity contracts, conditions on which insurance policies and annuity contracts may be commuted, or other requirements applying to insurance policies and annuity contracts).

(3) Where a transaction referred to in paragraph (1) applies, the insurance policy must be taken out, or the annuity contract must be entered into, with an insurance company which is—

(a) authorised under section 3 or 4 of the Insurance Companies Act 1982 (authorisation of insurance business) to carry on long term business (within the meaning of section 1 of that Act (classification));

(b) in the case of a friendly society, authorised under section 32 of the Friendly Societies Act 1992 (grant of authorisation by Commission: general) to carry out long term business under any of the Classes specified in Head A of Schedule 2 to that Act (the activities of a friendly society: long term business); or

(c) an EC company as defined in section 2(6) of the Insurance Companies Act 1982 (restriction on carrying on insurance business), and which falls within paragraph (4).

(4) An EC company falls within this paragraph if it—

(a) carries on ordinary long-term insurance business (within the meaning of section 96(1) of the Insurance Companies Act 1982) in the United Kingdom through a branch in respect of which such of the requirements of Part I of Schedule 2F to that Act (recognition in the United Kingdom of EC and EFTA companies: EC companies carrying on business etc in the United Kingdom) as are applicable have been complied with; or

(b) provides ordinary long term insurance in the United Kingdom and such of the requirements of Part I of Schedule 2F to that Act as are applicable have been complied with in respect of insurance.

**Initial Commencement**

1 December 2000.

**[3.612]**

### 6 Alternatives to pension credit benefit

(1) The prescribed alternatives to pension credit benefit which a scheme may provide for the purposes of section 101D(2) of the 1993 Act are described in regulations 7 to 9.

(2) For the purposes of section 101D(4)(b) of the 1993 Act, the cases in which the alternatives described in regulations 7 to 9 may be provided without the consent of the person entitled to the benefit are described in regulations 7(4) and 8(4).

**Initial Commencement**

1 December 2000.

**[3.613]**

### 7 Early retirement or deferred retirement

(1) Subject to paragraph (2), the scheme may provide benefits which are different from those required to constitute pension credit benefit in respect of the—

(a) amount;

(b) recipient; and

(c) time at which the benefits are payable.

(2) The benefits referred to in paragraph (1) must include a benefit that is payable to the person entitled to the pension credit benefit.

(3) The benefit of the person entitled to the benefit must not be payable before normal benefit age except in the circumstances referred to in regulation 3 or 4 (commutation of the whole of pension credit benefit, or commutation of part of pension credit benefit).

(4) Benefits consisting of, or including, a benefit that becomes payable to the person entitled to the benefit before normal benefit age may be provided without that person's consent where—

(a) that person's earning capacity is destroyed or seriously impaired by incapacity or serious ill heath; and

(b) in the opinion of the trustees or managers of the scheme, the person entitled to the benefit is incapable of deciding whether it is in his interests to consent.

(5) Any scheme rule that allows the alternative described in this regulation must require the trustees or managers of the scheme to be reasonably satisfied that, when the benefit of the person entitled to the benefit becomes payable, the total value of the benefits to be provided under this regulation is at least equal to the amount described in regulation 11 (value of alternatives to pension credit benefit).

(6) In this regulation, 'serious ill health' means ill health which is such as to give rise to a life expectancy of less than one year from the date on which the benefit of the person entitled to the pension credit becomes payable.

**Initial Commencement**

1 December 2000.

[3.614]

## 8 Bought out benefits

(1) The scheme may provide for benefits different from those required to constitute pension credit benefit to be appropriately secured by a transaction to which section 19 of the 1993 Act applies (discharge of liability where guaranteed minimum pensions are secured by insurance policies or annuity contracts).

(2) Any scheme rule that allows the alternative described in this regulation must require the trustees or managers of the scheme to be reasonably satisfied that, except where paragraph (3) applies, the payment made to the insurance company is at least equal to the amount described in regulation 11.

(3) The exception to paragraph (2) is where the person entitled to the benefit is requiring the trustees or managers to provide the alternative by exercising his right to give a transfer notice under section 101F of the 1993 Act (power to give transfer notice).

(4) A scheme may allow the alternative described in this regulation to be provided without the consent of the person entitled to the pension credit where—

(a) the person entitled to the pension credit will be able to assign or surrender the insurance policy or annuity contract on the conditions set out in regulation 3 of the Occupational Pension Schemes (Discharge of Liability) Regulations 1997 (conditions on which policies of insurance and annuity contracts may be assigned or surrendered); and

(b) the requirements of paragraph (5) are satisfied.

(5) The requirements of this paragraph are that—

(a) the scheme is being wound up; or

(b) the trustees or managers of the scheme consider that, in the circumstances, it is reasonable for the scheme to provide the alternative without the consent of the person entitled to the benefit and the requirements of paragraph (6) are satisfied.

(6) The requirements of this paragraph are that all the conditions set out in sub-paragraphs (a) and (b) are satisfied, namely—

(a) the trustees or managers of the scheme give the person entitled to the benefit at least 30 days' written notice of their intention to take out the insurance policy or enter into the annuity contract unless the person entitled to the benefit exercises a right to give a transfer notice under section 101F of the 1993 Act (the first mentioned notice being sent to that person at his last known address or delivered to that person personally); and

(b) when the trustees or managers of the scheme agree with the insurance company to take out the insurance policy or enter into the annuity contract, there is no outstanding transfer notice by the person entitled to the benefit under section 101F of the 1993 Act.

(7) For the purposes of this regulation 'appropriately secured' means secured by an insurance policy or annuity contract to which regulation 5 applies.

**Initial Commencement**

1 December 2000.

[3.615]

## 9 Money purchase benefits

(1) The scheme may, with the consent of the person entitled to the benefit, provide money purchase benefits instead of all or any of the benefits that constitute pension credit benefit.

(2) Any scheme rule which allows this alternative must require the trustees or managers of the scheme to be reasonably satisfied that the amount allocated to provide

money purchase benefits in respect of the person entitled to the benefit is at least equal to the amount described in regulation 11.

**Initial Commencement**
1 December 2000.

**[3.616]**

### 10 Transfer of a person's pension credit rights without consent

(1) For the purposes of section 101D(4) of the 1993 Act (form of pension credit benefit and its alternatives), the trustees or managers of an occupational pension scheme may provide for a person's pension credit rights under that scheme to be transferred to another occupational pension scheme without that person's consent where the conditions set out in paragraphs (2) and either (3) or (7), as the case may be, are satisfied.

(2) The condition set out in this paragraph is that the trustees or managers of the transferring scheme consider that, in the circumstances, it is reasonable for the transfer to be made without the person's consent and the requirements of paragraph (5) are satisfied.

(3) The condition set out in this paragraph is that, subject to [paragraph (6), a] relevant actuary certifies to the trustees or managers of the transferring scheme that—

- (a) the transfer credits to be acquired for each person with pension credit rights under the receiving scheme are, broadly, no less favourable than the rights to be transferred; and
- (b) where it is the established custom for discretionary benefits or increases in benefits to be awarded under the transferring scheme, there is good cause to believe that the award of discretionary benefits or increases in benefits under the receiving scheme will (making allowance for any amount by which transfer credits under the receiving scheme are more favourable than the rights to be transferred) be broadly no less favourable.

(4) For the purpose of paragraph (3)(b), the relevant actuary shall, in considering whether there is good cause, have regard to all the circumstances of the case and in particular—

- (a) to any established custom of the receiving scheme with regard to the provision of discretionary benefits or increases in benefits; and
- (b) to any announcements made with regard to the provision of such benefits under the receiving scheme.

(5) The requirements of this paragraph are that all the conditions set out in sub-paragraphs (a) and (b) are satisfied, namely—

- (a) the trustees or managers of the scheme give the person with pension credit rights at least 30 days' written notice of their intention to transfer those rights to another occupational pension scheme unless the person with those rights exercises a right to give a transfer notice under section 101F of the 1993 Act (the first mentioned notice being sent to that person at his last known address or delivered to that person personally); and
- (b) when the trustees or managers of the scheme agree with the trustees or managers of the receiving scheme to transfer those rights, there is no outstanding transfer notice by the person with pension credit rights under section 101F of the 1993 Act.

(6) Paragraph (3) does not apply where the whole of the pension credit rights to be transferred are derived from rights accrued in a money purchase scheme.

(7) The condition set out in this paragraph is that any scheme rule which allows the transfer of a person's pension credit rights derived from rights accrued in a money purchase scheme without the consent of the person with those rights must require the trustees or managers of the scheme to be reasonably satisfied that the amount transferred is at least equal to the amount described in regulation 11.

(8) In this regulation—

'relevant actuary' means—

(a) where the transferring scheme is a scheme for which an actuary is required under section 47 of the 1995 Act (professional advisers) to be appointed, the individual for the time being appointed in accordance with subsection (1) of that section as actuary for that scheme;

(b) in any other case, a Fellow of the Institute of Actuaries, a Fellow of the Faculty of Actuaries, or a person with other actuarial qualifications who is approved by the Secretary of State, at the request of the trustees or managers of the scheme, as being a proper person to act for the purposes of this regulation in connection with the scheme.

(9) Where the pension credit rights which are to be transferred in accordance with this regulation are or include safeguarded rights, the pension credit rights must be transferred to either a salary related contracted-out scheme or a money purchase contracted-out scheme.]

**Initial Commencement**

1 December 2000.

**Amendment**

SI 2000/2691.



**[3.617]**

### 11 Value of alternatives to pension credit benefit

The amount referred to in regulations 7, 8 and 9 is an amount equal to the value of the benefits (or, where the alternative is provided by way of partial substitute for pension credit benefit, the relevant part of the benefits) that have accrued to or in respect of the person entitled to the benefit.

**Initial Commencement**

1 December 2000.

**[3.618]**

### 12 Discharge of liability where pension credit benefit or alternative benefits are secured by insurance policies or annuity contracts

The requirements which must be met for the purposes of section 101E(1)(c) of the 1993 Act (discharge of liability where pension credit or alternative benefits are secured by insurance policies or annuity contracts) are those described in regulations 13 and 14.

**Initial Commencement**

1 December 2000.

**[3.619]**

### 13 Conditions on which pension credit benefit secured by insurance policies and annuity contracts may be commuted

Pension credit benefit secured by an insurance policy or an annuity contract may be commuted if it satisfies the requirements of regulation 3 or 4 (commutation of the whole of pension credit benefit, or commutation of part of pension credit benefit).

**Initial Commencement**

1 December 2000.

**[3.620]**

### 14 Other requirements applying to insurance policies and annuity contracts

The requirements described in this regulation are—

(a) that the insurance company with which the insurance policy is taken out or the annuity contract is entered into assumes an obligation to the person entitled to the benefit or to the trustees of a trust for the benefit of the person entitled to the benefit and, if appropriate, dependants of his, to pay the benefits secured by that policy or contract to him or, as the case may be, to dependants of his, or to the trustees of such a trust; and

(b) that the insurance policy or annuity contract contains, or is endorsed with, terms so as to provide for any increase, which would have been applicable as a consequence of section 40 of the 1999 Act (indexation: other pension schemes) had the discharge of liability of the pension credit benefit, or its alternative, not taken place, to apply to the benefits which have become secured or been replaced by that policy or contract.

**Initial Commencement**

1 December 2000.

**[3.621]**

### 15 Further conditions on which liability may be discharged

(1) Subsection (1)(b) of section 101E of the 1993 Act (transactions with the consent of the person entitled to the benefit which discharge liability where pension credit or alternative benefits secured by insurance policies or annuity contracts) shall not apply in the circumstances described in paragraph (2), (3), (4) or (5).

(2) The circumstances described in this paragraph are that—

(a) the person entitled to the benefit is dead and the benefit is payable to a person other than his widow or widower; and

(b) the arrangement for securing the pension credit benefit or its alternative was made at the request of the person entitled to it.

(3) The circumstances described in this paragraph are that the benefit is provided as an alternative to pension credit benefit by virtue of regulation 8(4) (bought out benefits without consent).

(4) The circumstances described in this paragraph are that—

(a) the scheme is being wound up;

(b) sections 73 and 74 of the 1995 Act (preferential liabilities on winding up, and discharge of liabilities by insurance, etc) and the Occupational Pension Schemes (Winding Up) Regulations 1996 do not apply;

(c) the person entitled to the benefit is able to assign or surrender the insurance policy or the annuity contract; and

(d) the condition set out in section 101E(1)(a) of the 1993 Act is satisfied.

(5) The circumstances described in this paragraph are that—

(a) the trustees or managers of the scheme consider that, in the circumstances, it is reasonable for the scheme to provide the alternative without the consent of the person entitled to the benefit;

(b) the trustees or managers of the scheme give the person entitled to the benefit at least 30 days' written notice of their intention to take out the insurance policy or enter into the annuity contract, unless the person entitled to the benefit exercises a right to give a transfer notice under section 101F of the 1993 Act (power to give transfer notice) (the first mentioned notice being sent to that person at his last known address or delivered to that person personally); and

(c) when the trustees or managers of the scheme agree with the insurance company to take out the insurance policy or enter into the annuity contract, there is no outstanding transfer notice given by the person entitled to the benefit under section 101F of the 1993 Act.

(6) The payment made to the insurance company in the circumstances described in paragraph (5) must be at least an amount equal to the value of the pension credit benefit which has accrued to the person entitled to the benefit at the date the payment is made.

**Initial Commencement**
1 December 2000.

**[3.622]**

PART III
TRANSFER VALUES

### 16 Transfer payments in respect of safeguarded rights—general

(1) A transfer of liability from—

(a) a salary related contracted-out scheme (or a scheme which has ceased to be a salary related contracted-out scheme); or

(b) a money purchase contracted-out scheme or an appropriate scheme (or a scheme which has ceased to be a money purchase contracted-out scheme or an appropriate scheme),

may give effect to the safeguarded rights of a person entitled to a pension credit by the making of a transfer payment to a scheme referred to in paragraph (2).

(2) A transfer payment in respect of safeguarded rights may be made to—

(a) an appropriate scheme;

(b) a money purchase contracted-out scheme;

(c) a salary related contracted-out scheme;

(d) a personal pension scheme which has ceased to be an appropriate scheme; or

(e) an occupational pension scheme which has ceased to be contracted-out,

in accordance with regulations 17 to 19 and no such transfer may be made otherwise.

(3) In this regulation and in regulations 17 to 19 a 'transfer payment' means a transfer payment such as is described in this regulation.

**Initial Commencement**
1 December 2000.



**[3.623]**

### 17 Transfer payments to money purchase contracted-out schemes and appropriate schemes

A transfer of any liability in respect of safeguarded rights may be made to a money purchase contracted-out scheme or an appropriate scheme if—

(a) the person with pension credit rights consents;

(b) the transfer payment (or, if it forms part of a larger payment giving effect to both safeguarded and other rights, that part of it which gives effect to safeguarded rights) is of an amount at least equal to the cash equivalent of the safeguarded rights to which effect is being given, as calculated and verified in a manner consistent with regulations 3 to 7 of the Pension Sharing (Valuation) Regulations 2000 (calculation, verification and reduction of cash equivalents);

(c) in the case of a transfer payment to a money purchase contracted-out scheme, the person with pension credit rights is employed by an employer who is a contributor to the receiving scheme; and

(d) the transfer payment is applied so as to provide money purchase benefits under the receiving scheme for or in respect of the person with pension credit rights in respect of safeguarded rights.

**Initial Commencement**
1 December 2000.

**[3.624]**

## 18 Transfer payments to salary related contracted-out schemes

A transfer of any liability in respect of safeguarded rights may be made to a salary related contracted-out scheme if—

(a) the person with pension credit rights consents;
(b) the transfer payment (or, if it forms part of a larger payment giving effect to both safeguarded and other rights, that part of it which gives effect to safeguarded rights) is of an amount at least equal to the cash equivalent of the safeguarded rights to which effect is being given, as calculated and verified in a manner consistent with regulations 3 to 7 of the Pension Sharing (Valuation) Regulations 2000;
(c) the person with pension credit rights is employed by an employer who is a contributor to the receiving scheme; and
(d) the transfer payment is applied to provide rights for the person with pension credit rights which, had they accrued in the receiving scheme, would be provided in accordance with the rules of the receiving scheme relating to earners who are in employment which is contracted-out in relation to the receiving scheme or have been in employment which was so contracted-out on or after the principal appointed day.

**Initial Commencement**
1 December 2000.

**[3.625]**

## 19 Transfer payments to overseas schemes or overseas arrangements

A transfer of any liability in respect of safeguarded rights may be made to an overseas scheme or an overseas arrangement if—

(a) the person with pension credit rights consents;
(b) the trustees or managers of the transferring scheme have taken reasonable steps to satisfy themselves that the person with pension credit rights has emigrated on a permanent basis and, where the receiving scheme is an occupational pension scheme, that he has entered employment to which the receiving scheme applies;
(c) the transfer payment (or, if it forms part of a larger payment giving effect to both safeguarded and other rights, that part which gives effect to safeguarded rights) is of an amount at least equal to the cash equivalent of the safeguarded rights to which effect is being given, as calculated and verified in a manner consistent with regulations 3 to 7 of the Pension Sharing (Valuation) Regulations 2000;
(d) the person with pension credit rights has acknowledged that he accepts that the scheme or arrangement to which the transfer payment is to be made may not be regulated in any way by the law of the United Kingdom and that as a consequence there may be no obligation under that law on the receiving scheme or arrangement or its trustees or managers to provide any particular value or benefit in return for the transfer payment; and

(e) the trustees or managers of the transferring scheme have taken reasonable steps to satisfy themselves that the person with pension credit rights has received a statement from the receiving scheme or arrangement showing the benefits to be awarded in respect of the transfer payment and the conditions (if any) on which these could be forfeited or withheld.

**Initial Commencement**

1 December 2000.

**[3.626]**

### 20 Requirements to be met by annuities

Subject to regulation 19, the prescribed requirements referred to in section 101F(2)(b) of the 1993 Act (cash equivalent to be used for purchasing annuities) are those specified in regulation 15(2) to (7) of the Pension Sharing (Implementation and Discharge of Liability) Regulations 2000 (disqualification as a destination for pension credit—annuity contracts and insurance policies).

**Initial Commencement**

1 December 2000.



**[3.627]**

### 21 Requirements of other pension arrangements

(1) The prescribed requirements referred to in section 101F(2)(c) and (3)(b) of the 1993 Act (cash equivalent of pension credit benefit to be used to subscribe to other pension arrangements which satisfy prescribed requirements) are that the pension arrangement to which it is proposed to subscribe—

(a) is an overseas arrangement;

(b) if it is an overseas arrangement and the cash equivalent is or includes the cash equivalent of safeguarded rights, the arrangement is one to which a transfer payment in respect of such rights may be made in accordance with regulation 6 or 9 of the Pension Sharing (Safeguarded Rights) Regulations 2000 (ways of giving effect to safeguarded rights—money purchase schemes, and ways of giving effect to safeguarded rights—salary related schemes); or

(c) if the scheme from which rights are transferred is of a kind described in any of sub-paragraphs (a) to (e) of paragraph (2), satisfies the requirements of the Inland Revenue.

(2) The kinds of scheme mentioned in paragraph (1)(c) are—

(a) a scheme which is approved by the Inland Revenue for the purposes of Chapter I of Part XIV of the Taxes Act (pension schemes, social security benefits, life annuities etc: retirement benefit schemes);

(b) a scheme which is being considered for approval by the Inland Revenue for the purposes of Chapter I of Part XIV of the Taxes Act;

(c) a relevant statutory scheme as defined in section 611A(1) (definition of relevant statutory scheme) of the Taxes Act;

(d) a fund to which section 608 of the Taxes Act (superannuation funds approved before 6th April 1980) applies; and

(e) a scheme which is approved by the Inland Revenue under Chapter IV of Part XIV of the Taxes Act.

(3) The prescribed circumstances referred to in section 101F(2)(c) and (3)(b) of the 1993 Act are those referred to in paragraph (1)(b) and (c).

**Initial Commencement**

1 December 2000.

**[3.628]**

## 22 Requirements to be met by an eligible scheme

(1) The prescribed requirements referred to in section 101F(6)(b) of the 1993 Act (references to an eligible scheme which satisfies the prescribed requirements) are that—

- (a) if the eligible member's cash equivalent (or any portion of it to be used under section 101F(2) or (3) of the 1993 Act) is or includes the cash equivalent of safeguarded rights, then the eligible scheme under whose rules rights are acquired is one—
  - (i) to which those safeguarded rights may be transferred; or
  - (ii) to which a transfer payment in respect of those safeguarded rights may be made, in accordance with regulations 16 to 19 of these Regulations (transfers of safeguarded rights) and [regulation 9(5)(c)] of the Pension Sharing (Safeguarded Rights) Regulations 2000; and
- (b) if the scheme from which pension credit rights are transferred or from which a transfer payment of such rights is made is of a kind described in any of sub-paragraphs (a) to (e) of paragraph (2) of regulation 21, the eligible scheme to which pension credit rights are transferred or to which a transfer payment in respect of those rights is made is of a kind described in paragraph (2)(a), (c) or (e) of regulation 21.

(2) In this regulation 'eligible scheme' means a scheme described in section 101F(6) of the 1993 Act.

**Initial Commencement**

1 December 2000.

**Amendment**

SI 2000/2691.

**[3.629]**

## 23 Statements of entitlement

(1) Subject to paragraph (2), for the purposes of subsection (2)(a) of section 101H of the 1993 Act (salary related schemes: statements of entitlement), the prescribed period beginning with the date of the eligible member's application under that section for a statement of entitlement is a period of 3 months.

(2) Where the trustees or managers of the scheme are for reasons beyond their control unable within the period referred to in paragraph (1) to obtain the information required to calculate the cash equivalent, the prescribed period is such longer period as they may reasonably require as a result of that inability, provided that such longer period does not exceed 6 months beginning with the date of the eligible member's application.

(3) For the purposes of subsection (2)(b) of section 101H of the 1993 Act, the prescribed period is the period of 10 days (excluding Saturdays, Sundays, Christmas Day, New Year's Day and Good Friday) ending with the date on which the statement of entitlement is provided to the eligible member.

(4) For the purposes of subsection (3) of section 101H of the 1993 Act, an eligible member who has made an application under section 101H(1) of the 1993 Act for a statement of entitlement may not, within a period of 12 months beginning on the date of that application, make any further such application unless the rules of the scheme provide otherwise or the trustees or managers allow him to do so.

**Initial Commencement**

1 December 2000.

[3.630]

## 24 Manner of calculation and verification of cash equivalents

(1) Except in a case to which, or to the extent to which, paragraph (2) or (5) applies, cash equivalents are to be calculated and verified in such manner as may be approved in particular cases by the scheme actuary or, in relation to a scheme to which section 47(1)(b) of the 1995 Act does not apply, by—

(a) a Fellow of the Institute of Actuaries;
(b) a Fellow of the Faculty of Actuaries; or
(c) a person with other actuarial qualifications who is approved by the Secretary of State, at the request of the trustees or managers of the scheme in question, as being a proper person to act for the purposes of these Regulations in connection with that scheme,

and, subject to paragraph (2), in this regulation, 'actuary' means the scheme actuary or, in relation to a scheme to which section 47(1)(b) of the 1995 Act does not apply, the actuary referred to in sub-paragraph (a), (b) or (c) of this paragraph.

(2) Where the eligible member in respect of whom a cash equivalent is to be calculated and verified is an eligible member of an occupational pension scheme having particulars from time to time set out in regulations made under section 7 of the Superannuation Act 1972 (superannuation of persons employed in local government service, etc), that cash equivalent shall be calculated and verified in such manner as may be approved by the Government Actuary or by an actuary authorised by the Government Actuary to act on his behalf for that purpose and in such a case 'actuary' in this regulation means the Government Actuary or the actuary so authorised.

(3) Except in a case to which paragraph (5) applies, cash equivalents are to be calculated and verified by adopting methods and making assumptions which—

(a) if not determined by the trustees or managers of the scheme in question, are notified to them by the actuary; and
(b) are certified by the actuary to the trustees or managers of the scheme—
    (i) as being consistent with the requirements of Chapter II of Part IVA of the 1993 Act;
    (ii) as being consistent with 'Retirement Benefit Schemes—Transfer Values (GN11)' published by the Institute of Actuaries and the Faculty of Actuaries and current on the valuation date;
    (iii) as being consistent with the methods adopted and assumptions made, on the valuation date, in calculating the benefits to which entitlement arises under the rules of the scheme in question for a person who is acquiring transfer credits including transfer credits in respect of pension credit rights under those rules; and
    (iv) in the case of a scheme to which section 56 of the 1995 Act (minimum funding requirement) applies, as providing as a minimum an amount consistent with the methods and assumptions adopted in calculating, for the purposes of section 57 of that Act (valuation and certification of assets and liabilities), the liabilities mentioned in paragraphs (a), (c)(i) and (d) of section 73(3) of that Act, subject, in any case where the cash equivalent calculation is made on an individual and not a collective basis, to any adjustments which are appropriate to take account of that fact.

(4) If, by virtue of Schedule 5 of the Occupational Pension Schemes (Minimum Funding Requirement and Actuarial Valuations) Regulations 1996 (modifications), section 56 of the 1995 Act applies to a section of a scheme as if that section were a separate scheme, paragraph (3)(b)(iv) shall apply as if that section were a separate scheme and as if the reference therein to a scheme were accordingly a reference to that section.

(5) Where a cash equivalent or any portion of a cash equivalent relates to money purchase benefits which do not fall to be valued in a manner which involves making

estimates of the value of benefits, then that cash equivalent or that portion shall be calculated and verified in such manner as may be approved in a particular case by the trustees or managers of the scheme and in accordance with methods consistent with the requirements of [Chapter IV of Part IV of the 1993 Act (protection for early leavers — transfer values) and] Chapter II of Part IVA of the 1993 Act.

**Initial Commencement**
1 December 2000.

**Amendment**
SI 2000/2691.

**[3.631]**

### 25 Time period for notification to the Regulatory Authority of failure by the trustees or managers of an occupational pension scheme to comply with a transfer notice

The period prescribed for the purpose of section 101J(4)(a) of the 1993 Act (time for compliance with transfer notice) is the period of 21 days beginning with the day immediately following the end of the period for compliance specified in section 101J(1) of that Act.

**Initial Commencement**
1 December 2000.

**[3.632]**

### 26 Extension of time limits for payment of cash equivalents

The Regulatory Authority may grant an extension of the period mentioned in section 101J(1)(a) of the 1993 Act to the trustees or managers of an occupational pension scheme if the trustees or managers have within that period applied to the Regulatory Authority for an extension and—

(a) the Regulatory Authority is satisfied that—
   (i) the scheme is being wound up or is about to be wound up;
   (ii) the scheme is ceasing to be a contracted-out scheme;
   (iii) the interests of the members of the scheme generally will be prejudiced if the trustees or managers do what is needed to carry out what is required within that period;
   (iv) the eligible member has not taken all such steps as the trustees or managers can reasonably expect in order to satisfy them of any matter which falls to be established before they can properly carry out what the eligible member requires;
   (v) the trustees or managers have not been provided with such information as they reasonably require properly to carry out what the eligible member requires; or
   (vi) the eligible member's statement of entitlement has been reduced or increased under regulation 27 or 28 or the eligible member has disputed the amount of the cash equivalent;
(b) the provisions of section 53 of the 1993 Act (supervision: former contracted-out schemes) apply; or
(c) an application has been made for an extension on one or more of the grounds specified in paragraph (a) or (b) and the Regulatory Authority's consideration of the application cannot be completed before the end of the period mentioned in section 101J(1)(a) of the 1993 Act.

**Initial Commencement**
1 December 2000.

[3.633]

## 27 Increases and reductions of cash equivalents before a statement of entitlement has been sent to the eligible member

(1) A cash equivalent referred to in section 101H of the 1993 Act shall not be reduced under this regulation once [a statement of the value of] that cash equivalent has been sent to the eligible member and a direction referred to in paragraph (2) shall not affect such a cash equivalent unless that direction is made before that cash equivalent.

(2) Where it is the established custom for additional benefits to be awarded from the scheme at the discretion of the trustees or managers or the employer, the cash equivalent shall, unless the trustees or managers have given a direction that cash equivalents shall not take account of such benefits, take account of any such additional benefits as will accrue to the eligible member in question if the custom continues unaltered.

(3) The trustees or managers shall not make a direction such as is mentioned in paragraph (2) unless, within 3 months before making the direction, they have consulted the actuary and have obtained the actuary's written report on the implications for the state of funding of the scheme of making such a direction, including the actuary's advice as to whether or not in the actuary's opinion there would be any adverse implications for the funding of the scheme should the trustees or managers not make such a direction.

(4) In the case of a scheme to which section 56 of the 1995 Act applies, each respective part of the cash equivalent which relates to liabilities referred to in paragraph (a), (c)(i) or (d) of section 73(3) of the 1995 Act may be reduced by the percentage which is the difference between—

- (a) 100 per cent; and
- (b) the percentage of the liabilities mentioned in the relevant paragraph of section 73(3) which the actuarial valuation shows the scheme assets as being sufficient to satisfy,

where the actuarial valuation is the latest actuarial valuation obtained in accordance with section 57 of the 1995 Act prior to the date by reference to which the cash equivalent is determined under section 101F(4) of the 1993 Act (power to give transfer notice).

(5) If, by virtue of Schedule 5 to the Occupational Pension Schemes (Minimum Funding Requirement and Actuarial Valuations) Regulations 1996, section 56 of the 1995 Act applies to a section of a scheme as if that section were a separate scheme, paragraph (4) shall apply as if that section were a separate scheme and as if the reference therein to a scheme were accordingly a reference to that section.

(6) Where an eligible member's cash equivalent is to be used for acquiring transfer credits under the rules of another scheme or for acquiring rights under the rules of a personal pension scheme and the receiving scheme has undertaken to provide benefits at least equal in value to the benefits represented by that cash equivalent on payment of a lesser sum, including nil, then that cash equivalent shall be reduced to that lesser sum.

(7) Where all or any of an eligible member's benefits have been appropriately secured by a transaction to which section 19 of the 1993 Act (discharge of liability of guaranteed minimum pensions secured by insurance policies or annuity contracts) applies, the cash equivalent in respect of those benefits shall be reduced to nil.

(8) For the purposes of paragraph (7), 'appropriately secured' means the same as in section 19 of the 1993 Act except that an insurance policy or annuity contract which is taken out or entered into with an authorised friendly society (referred to in regulation 5(3)(b) of these Regulations), but which otherwise satisfies the conditions for being appropriate for the purposes of section 19, is to be treated as if it were appropriate for the purposes of that section provided the terms of such policy or contract are not capable of being amended, revoked or rescinded.

(9) Where a scheme has (in the case of a cash equivalent mentioned in section 101H of the 1993 Act, before the valuation date) begun to be wound up, a cash equivalent may be reduced to the extent necessary for the scheme to comply with section 73 of the 1995 Act and the Occupational Pension Schemes (Winding Up) Regulations 1996.

(10) If, by virtue of regulations made under section 73 of the 1995 Act, section 73 of that Act applies to a section of a scheme as if that section were a separate scheme, paragraph (9) shall apply as if that section were a separate scheme and as if the references therein to a scheme were accordingly references to that section.

(11) Where all or any of the benefits to which a cash equivalent relates have been surrendered, commuted or forfeited before the date on which the trustees or managers do what is needed to carry out what the eligible member requires, the cash equivalent of the benefits so surrendered, commuted or forfeited shall be reduced to nil.

(12) In a case where two or more of the paragraphs of this regulation fall to be applied to a calculation, they shall be applied in the order in which they occur in this regulation.

(13) In this regulation 'actuary' has the meaning given by regulation 24.

**Initial Commencement**
1 December 2000.

**Amendment**
SI 2000/2691.

**[3.634]**

## 28 Increases and reductions of cash equivalents once the statement of entitlement has been sent to the eligible member

(1) This regulation applies to a cash equivalent when a statement of entitlement has been sent to an eligible member of a salary related scheme by the trustees or managers of that scheme.

(2) Where all or any of the benefits to which the cash equivalent relates have been surrendered, commuted or forfeited before the date on which the trustees or managers do what is needed to carry out what the eligible member requires, that part of the cash equivalent which relates to the benefits so surrendered, commuted or forfeited shall be reduced to nil.

(3) Where a scheme has on or after the valuation date begun to be wound up, a cash equivalent may be reduced to the extent necessary for the scheme to comply with sections 73 and 74 of the 1995 Act and the Occupational Pension Schemes (Winding Up) Regulations 1996.

(4) If, by virtue of the Occupational Pension Schemes (Winding Up) Regulations 1996, section 73 of the 1995 Act applies to a section of a scheme as if that section were a separate scheme, paragraph (3) shall apply as if that section were a separate scheme and as if the references therein to a scheme were accordingly references to that section.

(5) If an eligible member's cash equivalent falls short of or exceeds the amount which it would have been had it been calculated in accordance with Chapter II of Part IVA of the 1993 Act and these Regulations it shall be increased or reduced to that amount.

(6) In a case where two or more of the paragraphs of this regulation fall to be applied to a calculation, they shall be applied in the order in which they occur in this regulation except that where paragraph (5) falls to be applied it shall be applied as at the date on which it is established that the cash equivalent falls short of or exceeds the proper amount.

**Initial Commencement**
1 December 2000.

[3.635]

## 29 Increases of cash equivalents on late payment

(1) Subject to paragraph (2), if the trustees or managers of a scheme, having received an application under section 101F(1) of the 1993 Act (power to give transfer notice), fail to comply with the transfer notice within 6 months of the valuation date, the eligible member's cash equivalent, as calculated in accordance with regulations 24, 27 and 28, shall be increased by the amount, if any, by which that cash equivalent falls short of what it would have been if the valuation date had been the date on which the trustees or managers carry out what the eligible member requires.

(2) If the trustees or managers of a scheme, having received an application under section 101H of the 1993 Act, fail without reasonable excuse to do what is needed to carry out what the eligible member requires within 6 months of the valuation date, the eligible member's cash equivalent, as calculated in accordance with regulations 24, 27 and 28, shall be increased by—

(a) the interest on that cash equivalent calculated on a daily basis over the period from the valuation date to the date on which the trustees or managers carry out what the eligible member requires, at an annual rate of one per cent above base rate; or, if it is greater,

(b) the amount, if any, by which that cash equivalent falls short of what it would have been if the valuation date had been the date on which the trustees or managers carry out what the eligible member requires.

**Initial Commencement**

1 December 2000.



[3.636]

## 30 Personal pension schemes: increases and reductions of cash equivalents

(1) If the whole or any part of the cash equivalent of the pension credit benefit under section 101F of the 1993 Act has been surrendered, commuted or forfeited before the date on which the trustees or managers comply with the transfer notice, the cash equivalent shall be reduced in proportion to the reduction in the total value of the benefits.

(2) If the trustees or managers of a personal pension scheme, having received a transfer notice under section 101F(1) of the 1993 Act, fail without reasonable excuse to comply with the transfer notice within 6 months of the valuation date, the eligible member's cash equivalent shall be increased by—

(a) the interest on that cash equivalent, calculated on a daily basis over the period from the date the notice is given until the date on which the trustees or managers carry out what the eligible member requires, at the same rate as that payable for the time being on judgment debts by virtue of section 17 of the Judgments Act 1838; or, if it is greater,

(b) the amount, if any, by which that cash equivalent falls short of what it would have been if the date on which the transfer notice is given had been the date on which the trustees or managers comply with it.

**Initial Commencement**

1 December 2000.

[3.637]

### 31 Civil Penalties

Where section 10 of the 1995 Act (civil penalties) applies by virtue of section 101H(4) or section 101J(4)(b) of the 1993 Act, the maximum amount for the purposes of section 10(1) of the 1995 Act shall be £1,000 in the case of an individual, and £10,000 in any other case.

**Initial Commencement**
1 December 2000.

[3.638]

## PART IV
## INDEXATION

### 32 Increase of relevant pension

(1) Subject to regulations 33 and 34, a relevant pension shall be increased each year by whichever is the lesser of—

(a) either—

(i) the appropriate percentage; or

(ii) where the rules of an occupational pension scheme require the relevant pension to be increased at intervals of not more than 12 months, the relevant percentage; or

(b) 5 per cent.

(2) In this regulation—

'appropriate percentage' means the revaluation percentage for the latest revaluation period specified in the order under paragraph 2 of Schedule 3 to the 1993 Act (revaluation of accrued pension benefits) which is in force at the time of the increase (expressions used in this definition having the same meaning as in that paragraph);

'relevant percentage' means the lesser of—

(a) the percentage increase in the retail prices index for the reference period, being a period determined, in relation to each periodic increase, under the rules of the scheme; or

(b) the percentage for that period which corresponds to 5 per cent per annum.

**Initial Commencement**
1 December 2000.

[3.639]

### 33 Annual increase in rate of pension: qualifying occupational and personal pension schemes

(1) The first increase required by regulation 32 in the rate of a relevant pension must take effect not later than the first anniversary of the date on which the pension is first paid; and subsequent increases must take effect at intervals of not more than 12 months.

(2) Where the first such increase takes effect on a date when the pension has been in payment for a period of less than 12 months, the increase must be of an amount at least equal to one twelfth of the amount of the increase so required (apart from this paragraph) for each complete month in that period.

**Initial Commencement**
1 December 2000.

[3.640]

### 34 Effect of increase above the statutory requirement: qualifying occupational pension schemes

(1) Where in any tax year the trustees or managers of a qualifying occupational pension scheme make an increase in a member's pension which is a relevant pension, not being an increase required by regulation 32, they may deduct the amount of the increase from any increase which but for this paragraph, they would be required to make under that regulation in the next tax year.

(2) Where in any tax year the trustees or managers of such a scheme make an increase in a member's pension which is a relevant pension, and part of the increase is not required by regulation 32, they may deduct that part of the increase from any increase which, but for this paragraph, they would be required to make under that regulation in the next tax year.

(3) Where by virtue of paragraph (1) or (2) any such pension is not required to be increased in pursuance of regulation 32, or not by the full amount that it otherwise would be, its amount shall be calculated for any purposes as if it had been increased in pursuance of regulation 32 or, as the case may be, by that full amount.

**Initial Commencement**
1 December 2000.

[3.641]

### 35 Definition of eligible pension credit rights

For the purposes of section 40(3) of the 1999 Act, pension credit rights are eligible if they fall within the descriptions in paragraph (a) or (b)—

(a) rights which are derived from—

(i) rights attributable to pensionable service on or after 6th April 1997 (excluding rights derived from additional voluntary contributions); or

(ii) in the case of money purchase benefits, rights attributable to payments in respect of employment on or after 6th April 1997 (excluding rights derived from additional voluntary contributions),

of the member whose pension rights were the subject of a pension sharing order or provision; or

(b) safeguarded rights.

**Initial Commencement**
1 December 2000.

# Pension Sharing (Safeguarded Rights) Regulations 2000

## SI 2000 No 1055

### Contents

*Regulation*





**[3.641A]**

### 1 Citation, commencement and interpretation

(1) These Regulations may be cited as the Pension Sharing (Safeguarded Rights) Regulations 2000 and shall come into force on 1st December 2000.

(2) In these Regulations—

'the 1993 Act' means the Pension Schemes Act 1993;

'the 1999 Act' means the Welfare Reform and Pensions Act 1999;

'the Pension Credit Benefit Regulations' means the Pension Sharing (Pension Credit Benefit) Regulations 2000;

'appropriate scheme' and 'appropriate personal pension scheme' shall be construed in accordance with section 9(5) of the 1993 Act;

'guaranteed minimum pension' has the meaning given by section 8(2) of the 1993 Act;

'the Inland Revenue' means the Commissioners of Inland Revenue;

'interim arrangement' means an interim arrangement which complies with section 28A of the 1993 Act, and satisfies the conditions specified in regulation 6 of the Personal and Occupational Pension Schemes (Protected Rights) Regulations 1996;

'member' means member of an occupational pension scheme or a personal pension scheme;

'money purchase contracted-out scheme' has the meaning given by section 8(1)(a)(ii) of the 1993 Act;

'normal benefit age' has the meaning given by section 101B of the 1993 Act;
'occupational pension scheme' has the meaning given by section 1 of the 1993 Act;
'personal pension scheme' has the meaning given by section 1 of the 1993 Act;
'pension credit' means a credit under section 29(1)(b) of the 1999 Act;
'pension credit benefit' has the meaning given by section 101P(1) of the 1993 Act;
'protected rights' has the meaning given by section 10 of the 1993 Act;
'salary related contracted-out scheme' has the meaning given by section 8(1)(a)(i) of the 1993 Act;
'section 9(2B) rights' has the same meaning as in regulation 1(2) of the Occupational Pension Schemes (Contracting-out) Regulations 1996;
'trustees or managers' has the meaning given by section 46(1) of the 1999 Act.

**Initial Commencement**

1 December 2000: see para (1) above.

**[3.641B]**

### 2 Definition of contracted-out rights

For the purposes of section 68A(5) of the 1993 Act (safeguarded rights) 'contracted-out rights' are such rights, under or derived from an occupational pension scheme, or an appropriate personal pension scheme, as fall within the following categories—

(a) entitlement to payment of, or accrued rights to, guaranteed minimum pensions;
(b) protected rights;
(c) section 9(2B) rights; or
(d) any of the rights in sub-paragraph (a), (b) or (c) above which themselves derive from any of those rights which have been the subject of a transfer payment.

**Initial Commencement**

1 December 2000: see reg 1(1).

**[3.641C]**

### 3 Requirements for schemes holding safeguarded rights

(1) The trustees or managers of a money purchase contracted-out scheme, a salary related contracted-out scheme, or an appropriate scheme may hold safeguarded rights under the scheme, if the scheme has satisfied the requirements—

(a) in these Regulations for the preservation of safeguarded rights under the scheme; or
(b) in regulations 16 to 19 of the Pension Credit Benefit Regulations (transfers of safeguarded rights), for the transfer of safeguarded rights under the scheme.

(2) The trustees or managers of an occupational pension scheme which has ceased to contract out or a personal pension scheme which has ceased to be an appropriate scheme may hold safeguarded rights under the scheme if the Inland Revenue has approved the arrangements made, or to be made, in relation to the scheme, or for the scheme's purposes, for the preservation or transfer of safeguarded rights under the scheme.

(3) The arrangements referred to in paragraph (2) in respect of an occupational pension scheme shall not be approved by the Inland Revenue unless the conditions specified in paragraph (4) or (5) are satisfied.

(4) To the extent that the arrangements concern the transfer or discharge of safeguarded rights, the Inland Revenue must be satisfied that such arrangements will be

completed within 2 years of the date of cessation or such later date as the Inland Revenue may specify in relation to a particular case or class of case.

(5) To the extent that the arrangements concern the preservation of safeguarded rights within the scheme, the scheme must comply with the requirements of sub-paragraph (a) or (b), as the case may be—

(a) in the case of a salary related contracted-out scheme, the scheme must continue to satisfy the requirements of section 9(2) of the 1993 Act and any regulations which would apply to that scheme by reason of it being a scheme to which section 9(2) of that Act relates, other than section 9(2B)(a) of that Act (requirement to comply with section 12A of that Act) and any regulations which relate to compliance with that section, and the scheme must contain a protection rule within the meaning given to that expression in regulation 45(3A) of the Occupational Pension Schemes (Contracting-out) Regulations 1996 (approval of arrangements for schemes ceasing to be contracted-out);

(b) in the case of a money purchase contracted-out scheme, the scheme must continue to satisfy the requirements of section 9(3) of that Act and any regulations which apply to the scheme by reason of it being a scheme to which section 9(3) of that Act relates.

**Initial Commencement**

1 December 2000: see reg 1(1).



**[3.641D]**

## 4 Identification of safeguarded rights

Where the rules of an occupational pension scheme or appropriate scheme make such provision as is mentioned in section 68A(2) of the 1993 Act (safeguarded rights), the rules must require the trustees or managers to make provision for the identification of safeguarded rights.

**Initial Commencement**

1 December 2000: see reg 1(1).

**[3.641E]**

## 5 Valuation of safeguarded rights in money purchase schemes

Where the rules of a money purchase contracted-out scheme, an appropriate scheme or a scheme which has ceased to be a contracted-out scheme or an appropriate scheme make such provision as is mentioned in section 68A(2) of the 1993 Act, the value of the safeguarded rights must be calculated in a manner no less favourable than that in which the value of—

(a) any other rights which the member with safeguarded rights has under that scheme or, as the case may be, has accrued under that scheme up to the date that the scheme ceased to be a contracted-out scheme or an appropriate scheme; and

(b) any protected rights under the scheme from which the member's safeguarded rights are derived[,

are calculated].

**Initial Commencement**

1 December 2000: see reg 1(1).

**Amendment**

Words ', are calculated' in square brackets inserted by SI 2000/2691, reg 13(1), (2). Date in force: 1 December 2000: see SI 2000/2691, reg 1(1).

**[3.641F]**

## 6 Ways of giving effect to safeguarded rights—money purchase schemes

(1) The rules of a scheme must provide for effect to be given to the safeguarded rights of a member [either]—

(a) … by the provision of a pension or the purchase of an annuity which satisfies the requirements specified in—

(i) paragraph (4) or (5), as the case may be; and

(ii) regulation 7 (the pension and annuity requirements—money purchase schemes); or

(b) in any other case, in such of the ways provided for by the following paragraphs as the rules may specify.

(2) Where the scheme provides for the member to elect to receive payments in accordance with this paragraph, and the member so elects, effect shall be given to his safeguarded rights during the interim period by the making of payments under an interim arrangement which—

(a) complies with the requirements of section 28A(1), (3), (4) and (5) and 28B of the 1993 Act (requirements for interim arrangements and information about interim arrangements), except insofar as those provisions concern payments to be made to the member's widow or widower; and

(b) satisfies the conditions prescribed in regulations 6 and 7 of the Personal and Occupational Pension Schemes (Protected Rights) Regulations 1996 (interim arrangements and payments made under interim arrangements), except insofar as those provisions concern payments to be made to the member's widow, widower, a person in accordance with directions given by the member, or to the member's estate, in the event of the death of the member,

as if references in those provisions to protected rights were to safeguarded rights.

(3) Where paragraph (2) applies, paragraphs (4) to (7), and regulations 7 and 8 (the pension and annuity requirements—money purchase schemes, and insurance companies that may provide safeguarded rights by way of annuities) apply in order to give effect to the member's safeguarded rights from the end of the period referred to in paragraph (2).

(4) Effect may be given to safeguarded rights by the provision by the scheme of a pension, or, subject to paragraph (5), an annuity, which complies with the requirements of regulations 7 and 8 of these Regulations and regulations 32 and 33 of the Pension Credit Benefit Regulations (increase of relevant pension and annual increase in rate of pension: qualifying occupational and personal pension schemes), provided that—

(a) the pension or annuity gives effect to all the safeguarded rights of the member, and the terms on which the pension is provided, or the terms of the purchase of the annuity—

(i) satisfy the requirements of sub-paragraphs (b) to (d);

(ii) make no provision other than such as is necessary to establish what the initial rate and the method of payment of the pension or annuity are to be, and that it shall continue to be paid throughout the lifetime of the member; and

(iii) make no provision other than such as is necessary to satisfy the requirements of sub-paragraphs (b) to (d);

(b) the rate of the pension or annuity is determined without regard to the sex of the member;

(c) except with the consent of the member, the pension or annuity, if paid in arrears, is paid no less frequently than by monthly instalments; and

(d) the pension or annuity is paid no less frequently than by annual instalments.

(5) Where paragraph (4) applies, an annuity may be provided if—

(a) the rules of the scheme do not provide for a pension; or

(b) the member so elects.

(6) Effect may be given to safeguarded rights by the making of a transfer payment in such circumstances and subject to such conditions as are prescribed in regulations 16 to 19 and regulation 24 of the Pension Credit Benefit Regulations (manner of calculation and verification of cash equivalents) in the case of a money purchase contracted-out scheme, an appropriate scheme, or a scheme which has ceased to be a contracted-out scheme or an appropriate scheme—

- (a) to another money purchase contracted-out scheme or to a salary related contracted-out scheme, if the person with safeguarded rights is an active member of such a scheme; or
- (b) to an appropriate scheme,

where the scheme to which the payment is made satisfies the requirements prescribed in regulation 22 of the Pension Credit Benefit Regulations (requirements to be met by an eligible scheme).

(7) Effect may be given to safeguarded rights by the provision of a lump sum in accordance with the provisions of regulation 3 or 4 of the Pension Credit Benefit Regulations (commutation of the whole or part of pension credit benefit).

(8) If the member has died—

- (a) after having elected to receive payments in accordance with paragraph (2); or
- (b) without effect being given to safeguarded rights under paragraph (3), (4), (5), (6) or (7),

effect may be given to those rights by the payment, as soon as [practicable, of a lump sum or a pension or annuity, or both a lump sum and a pension or annuity in accordance with the provisions of regulation 6 of the Pension Sharing (Implementation and Discharge of Liability) Regulations 2000 (discharge of liability in respect of a pension credit following the death of the person entitled to the pension credit)].

(9) The rules of a scheme may provide for effect to be given to the safeguarded rights of a member by making payments to—

- (a) the widow or widower of the member;
- (b) another person in accordance with a direction given by the member; or
- (c) in any other case, to the member's estate,

if the member dies after he has become entitled to the payment of benefit derived from his safeguarded rights.

(10) In this regulation—

'the interim period' means the period beginning with the starting date in relation to the member in question and ending with the termination date;

'scheme' means a money purchase contracted-out scheme or an appropriate scheme;

'the starting date' means the date, which must not be earlier than the member's 60th birthday, by reference to which the member elects to begin to receive payments under the interim arrangement;

'the termination date' means the date by reference to which the member elects to terminate the interim arrangement, and that date must not be later than the member's 75th birthday.

PART 3 Pens Sharing (SR) Regs 2000

**Initial Commencement**

1 December 2000: see reg 1(1).

**Amendment**

Para (1): word 'either' in square brackets inserted by SI 2000/2691, reg 13(1), (3)(a)(i). Date in force: 1 December 2000: see SI 2000/2691, reg 1(1). Sub-para (a) word omitted revoked by SI 2000/2691, reg 13(1), (3)(a)(ii). Date in force: 1 December 2000: see SI 2000/2691, reg 1(1). Para (8): words from 'practicable, of a lump sum' to 'the pension credit)' in square brackets substituted by SI 2000/2691, reg 13(1), (3)(b). Date in force: 1 December 2000: see SI 2000/2691, reg 1(1).

**[3.641G]**

## 7 The pension and annuity requirements—money purchase schemes

(1) For the purposes of regulation 6(4) (ways of giving effect to safeguarded rights—money purchase schemes) the pension requirements are those specified in paragraph (2), and the annuity requirements are those specified in paragraphs (3) and (5).

(2) A pension complies with the pension requirements if in the case of a money purchase contracted-out scheme or an appropriate scheme it commences on a date not earlier than the member's 60th birthday, and not later than his 65th birthday, or on such later date as has been agreed by him, and continues until the date of his death.

(3) An annuity complies with the annuity requirements if—

- (a) it commences on a date not earlier than the member's 60th birthday, and not later than his 65th birthday, or on such later date as has been agreed by him, and continues until the date of his death; and
- (b) it is provided by an insurance company which—
  - (i) satisfies the conditions specified in regulation 8 (insurance companies that may provide safeguarded rights by way of annuities); and
  - (ii) subject to paragraphs (5) and (6), has been chosen by the member.

(4) Where the member has elected under regulation 6(2) to receive payments under an interim arrangement—

- (a) in the case of a money purchase contracted-out scheme, a pension or annuity; or
- (b) in the case of an appropriate scheme, an annuity,

must commence on the termination date and must continue until the date of the member's death.

(5) A member is only to be taken to have chosen an insurance company if he gives notice of his choice to the trustees or managers of the scheme—

- (a) within a period of 5 months (or such longer period as the rules of the scheme may allow) beginning on the date which is 6 months earlier than that on which he will attain the age referred to in the following provisions of this sub-paragraph, as the case may be, where the trustees or managers of the scheme know of no reason to suppose that the pension or annuity will not commence on the date on which the member will attain—
  - (i) in the case of a money purchase contracted-out scheme the normal benefit age if that age is not less than 60 years; or
  - (ii) in the case of an appropriate scheme, the agreed age at which he is entitled to receive benefits under the scheme if that age is not less than 60 years; and
- (b) in any other case—
  - (i) if the date of the agreement in respect of when the pension or annuity is to commence ('the date of agreement') is more than one month before the agreed date for commencement of payment ('the agreed date'), within a period beginning on the date of agreement and ending one month before the agreed date; and
  - (ii) on the date of agreement if that date is not more than one month before the agreed date,

or such longer period as the rules of the scheme may allow.

(6) If a member fails to give notice of his choice of insurance company in accordance with paragraph (5), the trustees or managers of the scheme may choose the insurance company instead.

[(7) In this regulation 'the termination date' has the meaning given by regulation 6(10).]

**Initial Commencement**

1 December 2000: see reg 1(1).

**Amendment**

Para (7): inserted by SI 2000/2691, reg 13(1), (4). Date in force: 1 December 2000: see SI 2000/2691, reg 1(1).

[3.641H]

## 8 Insurance companies that may provide safeguarded rights by way of annuities

(1) A money purchase contracted-out scheme or an appropriate scheme may only discharge its liability in respect of safeguarded rights in accordance with regulation 6(4) above if the annuity is provided by an insurance company which satisfies the conditions set out in paragraphs (2) to (4) below.

(2) The insurance company must be—

(a) authorised under section 3 or 4 of the Insurance Companies Act 1982 (authorisation of insurance business) to carry on long term business (within the meaning of section 1 of that Act (classification)); or

(b) in the case of a friendly society, authorised under section 32 of the Friendly Societies Act 1992 (grant of authorisation by Commission: general) to carry out long term business under any of the Classes specified in Head A of Schedule 2 to that Act (the activities of a friendly society: long term business); or

(c) an EC company as defined in section 2(6) of the Insurance Companies Act 1982 (restriction on carrying on insurance business), and which falls within this sub-paragraph if it—

(i) carries on ordinary long-term insurance business (within the meaning of section 96(1) of that Act) in the United Kingdom through a branch in respect of which such of the requirements of Part I of Schedule 2F to that Act (recognition in the United Kingdom of EC and EFTA companies: EC companies carrying on business etc in the United Kingdom) as are applicable have been complied with; or

(ii) provides ordinary long term insurance in the United Kingdom and such of the requirements of Part I of Schedule 2F to that Act as are applicable have been complied with in respect of insurance.

(3) The insurance company must offer annuities with a view to purchase of those annuities by money purchase contracted-out schemes or appropriate schemes in order to give effect to the safeguarded rights of their members, without having regard to the sex of the members either in making the offers or in determining the rates at which the annuities are paid.

(4) Where the annuities are issued by a friendly society as described in paragraph (2)(b), the insurance company must provide that the terms of the annuities are not capable of being amended, revoked or rescinded.

**Initial Commencement**

1 December 2000: see reg 1(1).



[3.641I]

## 9 Ways of giving effect to safeguarded rights—salary related schemes

(1) The rules of a salary related contracted-out scheme which satisfy the requirements of section 9(2B) of the 1993 Act must provide for effect to be given to the safeguarded rights of a member by the provision of a pension for life except where the circumstances specified in paragraph (2), (3) or (4) apply.

(2) The circumstances specified in this paragraph are that the member consents to a transaction by which the trustees or managers of the scheme are to discharge their liability in respect of safeguarded rights and the transaction to discharge the liability satisfies all the conditions specified in paragraphs (6) and (7).

(3) The circumstances specified in this paragraph are that a transfer payment may be made in such circumstances and subject to such conditions as are prescribed in

regulations 16 to 19 and regulation 24 of the Pension Credit Benefit Regulations in the case of a salary related contracted-out scheme—

(a) to another salary related contracted-out scheme or to a money purchase contracted-out scheme, if the person with safeguarded rights is an active member of such a scheme; or

(b) to an appropriate scheme,

where the scheme to which the payment is made satisfies the requirements prescribed in regulation 22 of the Pension Credit Benefit Regulations.

[(4) The circumstances specified in this paragraph are that effect may be given to safeguarded rights by the provision of—

(a) a lump sum in accordance with the provisions of regulation 3 or 4 of the Pension Credit Benefit Regulations; or

(b) a lump sum or a pension or annuity, or both a lump sum and a pension or annuity, in accordance with the provisions of regulation 6 of the Pension Sharing (Implementation and Discharge of Liability) Regulations 2000.]

(5) For the purposes of paragraph (2) 'transaction' means—

(a) the taking out of an insurance policy or a number of such policies;

(b) the entry into an annuity contract or a number of such contracts; or

(c) the transfer of pensions and accrued rights to such a policy or policies or such a contract or contracts.

(6) The insurance policy or annuity contract must be taken out or entered into with an insurance company such as is described in regulation 8(2).

(7) The insurance policy or annuity contract must contain provision to the effect, or must be endorsed so as to provide that—

(a) the benefits secured under the policy or contract shall become payable with the beneficiary's consent, and the beneficiary—

(i) has reached normal benefit age; or

(ii) is suffering from an incapacity or serious ill health prior to normal benefit age;

(b) any rights of a beneficiary to a payment under the policy or contract which derive from a pension or accrued rights under the salary related contracted-out scheme shall be treated as if this regulation were applicable to them; and

(c) any increase in accordance with regulation 32 of the Pension Credit Benefit Regulations (increase of relevant pension) which would have been applied to the benefits derived from safeguarded rights which have become secured or been replaced by the annuity contract or insurance policy, is applied to them.

(8) The rules of a salary related contracted-out scheme may provide for effect to be given to the safeguarded rights of a member by making payments to—

(a) the widow or widower of the member;

(b) another person in accordance with a direction given by the member; or

(c) in any other case, to the member's estate,

if the member dies after he has become entitled to the payment of benefit derived from his safeguarded rights.

(9) For the purposes of paragraph (7)—

'beneficiary' means a member of a salary related contracted-out scheme, in respect of whose safeguarded rights the trustees or managers of that scheme have discharged their liability by entering into an insurance policy or an annuity contract;

'incapacity' means physical or mental deterioration which is sufficiently serious to prevent a person from following his normal employment or which seriously impairs his earning capacity;

'serious ill health' has the same meaning as in [regulation 3(4)] of the Pension Credit Benefit Regulations.

**Initial Commencement**

1 December 2000: see reg 1(1).

**Amendment**

Para (4): substituted by SI 2000/2691, reg 13(1), (5)(a). Date in force: 1 December 2000: see SI 2000/2691, reg 1(1). Para (9): in definition 'serious ill health' words 'regulation 3(4)' in square brackets substituted by SI 2000/2691, reg 13(1), (5)(b). Date in force: 1 December 2000: see SI 2000/2691, reg 1(1).

**[3.641J]**

### 10 Payable age in salary related contracted-out schemes

In respect of pension credit benefit arising out of safeguarded rights, schemes must provide for pension credit benefit to be paid by reference to an age which is equal for men and women and which—

(a) in the case of a scheme which is exempt approved within the meaning of section 592(1) of the Income and Corporation Taxes Act 1988 (tax reliefs: exempt approved schemes) or a scheme which has applied for such approval which has not yet been determined, is permitted under the rules of that scheme in accordance with that approval; or

(b) in the case of a relevant statutory scheme within the meaning of section 611A of the Income and Corporation Taxes Act 1988 (definition of relevant statutory scheme), is permitted under the regulations or rules governing the scheme as a relevant statutory scheme.

**Initial Commencement**

1 December 2000: see reg 1(1).

**[3.641K]**

### 11 Investment and resources of safeguarded rights

All payments made in respect of safeguarded rights which are paid to a money purchase contracted-out scheme in respect of one of its members must be applied so as to provide money purchase benefits for or in respect of that member except so far as they are used—

(a) to defray the administrative expenses of the scheme, including the administration costs incurred by the scheme in respect of which the scheme may levy a charge in accordance with the Pensions on Divorce etc (Charging) Regulations 2000, insofar as those costs relate to pension sharing in that member's case; or

(b) to pay commission.

**Initial Commencement**

1 December 2000: see reg 1(1).

**[3.641L]**

### 12 Suspension and forfeiture of safeguarded rights

(1) Except in the circumstances referred to in paragraphs (2) and (3), the rules of an occupational or personal pension scheme must not permit the suspension or forfeiture of a member's safeguarded rights or of payments giving effect to them.

(2) The circumstances in which the rules of an occupational or personal pension scheme may provide for payments giving effect to a member's safeguarded rights to be suspended are those described in paragraph (1) of regulation 9 of the Personal and Occupational Pension Schemes (Protected Rights) Regulations 1996 (suspension of payments giving effect to protected rights), as if in that regulation—

(a) the reference to section 32 of the 1993 Act (suspension or forfeiture) was to this regulation; and

(b) the references to protected rights were to safeguarded rights.

(3) The circumstances in which the rules of an occupational or personal pension scheme may provide for payments giving effect to a member's safeguarded rights to be forfeited are those described in paragraph (2) of regulation 9 of the Personal and Occupational Pension Schemes (Protected Rights) Regulations 1996 (forfeiture of payments giving effect to protected rights), as if in that regulation—

(a) the reference to section 32 of the 1993 Act was to this regulation; and

(b) the references to protected rights were to safeguarded rights.

**Initial Commencement**

1 December 2000: see reg 1(1).

# Divorce etc (Pensions) Regulations 2000

## SI 2000 No 1123

Contents





**[3.642]**

### 1 Citation, commencement and transitional provisions

(1) These Regulations may be cited as the Divorce etc (Pensions) Regulations 2000 and shall come into force on 1st December 2000.

(2) These Regulations shall apply to any proceedings for divorce, judicial separation or nullity of marriage commenced on or after 1st December 2000, and any such proceedings commenced before that date shall be treated as if these Regulations had not come into force.

**Initial Commencement**

1 December 2000.

**[3.643]**

### 2 Interpretation

In these Regulations:

(a) a reference to a section by number alone means the section so numbered in the Matrimonial Causes Act 1973;

(b) 'the 1984 Act' means the Matrimonial and Family Proceedings Act 1984;

(c) expressions defined in sections 21A and 25D(3) have the meanings assigned by those sections;

(d) every reference to a rule by number alone means the rule so numbered in the Family Proceedings Rules 1991.

**Initial Commencement**

1 December 2000.

**[3.644]**

### 3 Valuation

(1) For the purposes of the court's functions in connection with the exercise of any

of its powers under Part II of the Matrimonial Causes Act 1973, benefits under a pension arrangement shall be calculated and verified in the manner set out in regulation 3 of the Pensions on Divorce etc (Provision of Information) Regulations 2000, and—

(a) the benefits shall be valued as at a date to be specified by the court (being not earlier than one year before the date of the petition and not later than the date on which the court is exercising its power);

(b) in determining that value the court may have regard to information furnished by the person responsible for the pension arrangement pursuant to any of the provisions set out in paragraph (2); and

(c) in specifying a date under sub-paragraph (a) above the court may have regard to the date specified in any information furnished as mentioned in sub-paragraph (b) above.

(2) The relevant provisions for the purposes of paragraph (1)(b) above are:

(a) the Pensions on Divorce etc (Provision of Information) Regulations 2000;

(b) regulation 5 of and Schedule 2 to the Occupational Pension Schemes (Disclosure of Information) Regulations 1996 and regulation 11 of and Schedule 1 to the Occupational Pension Schemes (Transfer Value) Regulations 1996;

(c) section 93A or 94(1)(a) or (aa) of the Pension Schemes Act 1993;

(d) section 94(1)(b) of the Pension Schemes Act 1993 or paragraph 2(a) (or, where applicable, 2(b)) of Schedule 2 to the Personal Pension Schemes (Disclosure of Information) Regulations 1987.

**Initial Commencement**

1 December 2000.

**[3.645]**

### 4 Pension attachment: notices

(1) This regulation applies in the circumstances set out in section 25D(1)(a) (transfers of pension rights).

(2) Where this regulation applies, the person responsible for the first arrangement shall give notice in accordance with the following paragraphs of this regulation to—

(a) the person responsible for the new arrangement, and

(b) the other party.

(3) The notice to the person responsible for the new arrangement shall include copies of the following documents—

(a) every order made under section 23 imposing any requirement on the person responsible for the first arrangement in relation to the rights transferred;

(b) any order varying such an order;

(c) all information or particulars which the other party has been required to supply under any provision of rule 2.70 for the purpose of enabling the person responsible for the first arrangement—

(i) to provide information, documents or representations to the court to enable it to decide what if any requirement should be imposed on that person; or

(ii) to comply with any order imposing such a requirement;

(d) any notice given by the other party to the person responsible for the first arrangement under regulation 6;

(e) where the pension rights under the first arrangement were derived wholly or partly from rights held under a previous pension arrangement, any notice given to the person responsible for the previous arrangement under paragraph (2) of this regulation on the occasion of that acquisition of rights.

(4) The notice to the other party shall contain the following particulars—

(a) the fact that the pension rights have been transferred;
(b) the date on which the transfer takes effect;
(c) the name and address of the person responsible for the new arrangement;
(d) the fact that the order made under section 23 is to have effect as if it had been made in respect of the person responsible for the new arrangement.

(5) Both notices shall be given—
(a) within the period provided by section 99 of the Pension Schemes Act 1993 for the person responsible for the first arrangement to carry out what the member requires; and
(b) before the expiry of 21 days after the person responsible for the first arrangement has made all required payments to the person responsible for the new arrangement.

**Initial Commencement**
1 December 2000.

**[3.646]**

## 5 Pension attachment: reduction in benefits

(1) This regulation applies where—
(a) an order under section 23 or under section 17 of the 1984 Act has been made by virtue of section 25B or 25C imposing any requirement on the person responsible for a pension arrangement;
(b) an event has occurred which is likely to result in a significant reduction in the benefits payable under the arrangement, other than:
(i) the transfer from the arrangement of all the rights of the party with pension rights in the circumstances set out in section 25D(1)(a), or
(ii) a reduction in the value of assets held for the purposes of the arrangement by reason of a change in interest rates or other market conditions.

(2) Where this regulation applies, the person responsible for the arrangement shall, within 14 days of the occurrence of the event mentioned in paragraph (1)(b), give notice to the other party of—
(a) that event;
(b) the likely extent of the reduction in the benefits payable under the arrangement.

(3) Where the event mentioned in paragraph (1)(b) consists of a transfer of some but not all of the rights of the party with pension rights from the arrangement, the person responsible for the first arrangement shall, within 14 days of the transfer, give notice to the other party of the name and address of the person responsible for any pension arrangement under which the party with pension rights has acquired rights as a result of that event.

**Initial Commencement**
1 December 2000.

**[3.647]**

## 6 Pension attachment: change of circumstances

(1) This regulation applies where—
(a) an order under section 23 or under section 17 of the 1984 Act has been made by virtue of section 25B or 25C imposing any requirement on the person responsible for a pension arrangement; and
(b) any of the events set out in paragraph (2) has occurred.

(2) Those events are—

(a) any of the particulars supplied by the other party under rule 2.70 for any purpose mentioned in regulation 4(3)(c) has ceased to be accurate; or
(b) by reason of the remarriage of the other party or otherwise, the order has ceased to have effect.

(3) Where this regulation applies, the other party shall, within 14 days of the event, give notice of it to the person responsible for the pension arrangement.

(4) Where, because of the inaccuracy of the particulars supplied by the other party under rule 2.70 or because the other party has failed to give notice of their having ceased to be accurate, it is not reasonably practicable for the person responsible for the pension arrangement to make a payment to the other party as required by the order—

(a) it may instead make that payment to the party with pension rights, and
(b) it shall then be discharged of liability to the other party to the extent of that payment.

(5) Where an event set out in paragraph (2)(b) has occurred and, because the other party has failed to give notice in accordance with paragraph (3), the person responsible for the pension arrangement makes a payment to the other party as required by the order—

(a) its liability to the party with pension rights shall be discharged to the extent of that payment, and
(b) the other party shall, within 14 days of the payment being made, make a payment to the party with pension rights to the extent of that payment.

**Initial Commencement**
1 December 2000.

**[3.648]**

## 7 Pension attachment: transfer of rights

(1) This regulation applies where—

(a) a transfer of rights has taken place in the circumstances set out in section 25D(1)(a);
(b) notice has been given in accordance with regulation 4(2)(a) and (b);
(c) any of the events set out in regulation 6(2) has occurred; and
(d) the other party has not, before receiving notice under regulation 4(2)(b), given notice of that event to the person responsible for the first arrangement under regulation 6(3).

(2) Where this regulation applies, the other party shall, within 14 days of the event, give notice of it to the person responsible for the new arrangement.

(3) Where, because of the inaccuracy of the particulars supplied by the other party under rule 2.70 for any purpose mentioned in regulation 4(3)(c) or because the other party has failed to give notice of their having ceased to be accurate, it is not reasonably practicable for the person responsible for the new arrangement to make a payment to the other party as required by the order—

(a) it may instead make that payment to the party with pension rights, and
(b) it shall then be discharged of liability to the other party to the extent of that payment.

(4) Subject to paragraph (5), where this regulation applies and the other party, within one year from the transfer, gives to the person responsible for the first arrangement notice of the event set out in regulation 6(2) in purported compliance with regulation 7(2), the person responsible for the first arrangement shall—

(a) send that notice to the person responsible for the new arrangement, and
(b) give the other party a second notice under regulation 4(2)(b);

and the other party shall be deemed to have given notice under regulation 7(2) to the person responsible for the new arrangement.

(5) Upon complying with paragraph (4) above, the person responsible for the first arrangement shall be discharged from any further obligation under regulation 4 or 7(4), whether in relation to the event in question or any further event set out in regulation 6(2) which may be notified to it by the other party.

**Initial Commencement**
1 December 2000.

**[3.649]**

## 8 Service

A notice under regulation 4, 5, 6 or 7 may be sent by fax or by ordinary first class post to the last known address of the intended recipient and shall be deemed to have been received on the seventh day after the day on which it was sent.

**Initial Commencement**
1 December 2000.

**[3.650]**

## 9 Pension sharing order not to take effect pending appeal

(1) No pension sharing order under section 24B or variation of a pension sharing order under section 31 shall take effect earlier than 7 days after the end of the period for filing notice of appeal against the order.

(2) The filing of a notice of appeal within the time allowed for doing so prevents the order taking effect before the appeal has been dealt with.

**Initial Commencement**
1 December 2000.

**[3.651]**

## 10 Revocation

The Divorce etc (Pensions) Regulations 1996 and the Divorce etc (Pensions) (Amendment) Regulations 1997 are revoked.

**Initial Commencement**
1 December 2000.

# Family Proceedings (Amendment) Rules 2000

## SI 2000 No 2267

Contents

*Rule*





**[3.652]**

### 1 Citation and commencement

(1) These rules may be cited as the Family Proceedings (Amendment) Rules 2000.

(2) Rules 3, 4 and 10 and this rule shall come into force on 2nd October 2000, and the remainder of these Rules shall come into force on 1st December 2000.

**Initial Commencement**
1 December 2000.

**[3.653]**

### 2 Transitional provisions

(1) Subject to paragraphs (2) and (3), the Family Proceedings Rules 1991, as amended by these rules, shall apply to all proceedings for divorce, nullity of marriage or judicial separation, whether commenced before, on or after 1st December 2000.

(2) This paragraph applies where before 1st December 2000—

(a) an application for ancillary relief has been made, or notice of intention to proceed with the application has been given, in Form A; and

(b) that application or notice specified that the relief sought includes provision to be made under section 25B or 25C of the Matrimonial Causes Act 1973, or a request for such provision has been added to the application.

(3) Where paragraph (2) applies—

(a) the Family Proceedings Rules 1991 shall have effect as if rules 4(a), 5 to 9 and 11 of these Rules had not come into force; but

(b) in rule 2.70(5) and (6), any reference to an affidavit in support of an application shall be construed as referring to paragraph 2.16 of the statement in Form E, and any reference to an affidavit in reply shall be construed as meaning a statement in reply.

**Initial Commencement**
1 December 2000.

**[3.654]**

### 3 Interpretation

A reference to a rule by number alone refers to the rule so numbered in the Family Proceedings Rules 1991, and a reference to a Form by letter refers to the Form identified by that letter in Appendix 1A to those Rules.

**Initial Commencement**
1 December 2000.

**[3.655]**

### 4 Amendments to the Family Proceedings Rules 1991

*[Omitted]*

**[3.656]**
**Amendments to the Family Proceedings Rules 1991**

Please note that the amendments to the FPR 1991 listed in r 4 of SI 2000/2267 have been incorporated into the text of the rules set out in **Part 3 – Subordinate Legislation** at para **[3.401]** et seq.

# COUNCIL REGULATION (EC) No 1347/2000 of 29 May 2000 on the jurisdiction and the recognition and enforcement of judgments in matrimonial matters and in matters of parental responsibility for children of both spouses



**[3.656A]**

THE COUNCIL OF THE EUROPEAN UNION

Having regard to the Treaty establishing the European Community, and in particular Article 61(c) and Article 67(1) thereof,

Having regard to the proposal from the Commission,

Having regard to the opinion of the European Parliament,

Having regard to the opinion of the Economic and Social Committee,

Whereas:

(1) The Member States have set themselves the objective of maintaining and developing the Union as an area of freedom, security and justice, in which the free movement of persons is assured. To establish such an area, the Community is to adopt, among others, the measures in the field of judicial cooperation in civil matters needed for the proper functioning of the internal market.

(2) The proper functioning of the internal market entails the need to improve and simplify the free movement of judgments in civil matters.

(3) This is a subject now falling within the ambit of Article 65 of the Treaty.

(4) Differences between certain national rules governing jurisdiction and enforcement hamper the free movement of persons and the sound operation of the internal market. There are accordingly grounds for enacting provisions to unify the rules of conflict of jurisdiction in matrimonial matters and in matters of parental responsibility so as to simplify the formalities for rapid and automatic recognition and enforcement of judgments.

(5) In accordance with the principles of subsidiarity and proportionality as set out in Article 5 of the Treaty, the objectives of this Regulation cannot be sufficiently achieved by the Member States and can therefore be better achieved by the Community. This Regulation does not go beyond what is necessary to achieve those objectives.

(6) The Council, by an Act dated 28 May 1998, drew up a Convention on jurisdiction and the recognition and enforcement of judgments in matrimonial matters and recommended it for adoption by the Member States in accordance with their respective constitutional rules. Continuity in the results of the negotiations for conclusion of the Convention should be ensured. The content of this Regulation is substantially taken over from the Convention, but this Regulation contains a number of new provisions not in the Convention in order to secure consistency with certain provisions of the proposed regulation on jurisdiction and the recognition and enforcement of judgments in civil and commercial matters.

(7) In order to attain the objective of free movement of judgments in matrimonial matters and in matters of parental responsibility within the Community, it is necessary and appropriate that the cross-border recognition of jurisdiction and judgments in relation to the dissolution of matrimonial ties and to parental responsibility for the children of both spouses be governed by a mandatory, and directly applicable, Community legal instrument.

(8) The measures laid down in this Regulation should be consistent and uniform, to enable people to move as widely as possible. Accordingly, it should also apply to nationals of non-member States whose links with the territory of a Member State are sufficiently close, in keeping with the grounds of jurisdiction laid down in the Regulation.

(9) The scope of this Regulation should cover civil proceedings and non-judicial proceedings in matrimonial matters in certain States, and exclude purely religious procedures. It should therefore be provided that the reference to 'courts' includes all the authorities, judicial or otherwise, with jurisdiction in matrimonial matters.

(10) This Regulation should be confined to proceedings relating to divorce, legal separation or marriage annulment. The recognition of divorce and annulment rulings affects only the dissolution of matrimonial ties; despite the fact that they may be interrelated, the Regulation does not affect issues such as the fault of the spouses, property consequences of the marriage, the maintenance obligation or any other ancillary measures.

(11) This Regulation covers parental responsibility for children of both spouses on issues that are closely linked to proceedings for divorce, legal separation or marriage annulment.

(12) The grounds of jurisdiction accepted in this Regulation are based on the rule that there must be a real link between the party concerned and the Member State exercising jurisdiction; the decision to include certain grounds corresponds to the fact that they exist in different national legal systems and are accepted by the other Member States.

(13) One of the risks to be considered in relation to the protection of the children of both spouses in a marital crisis is that one of the parents will take the child to another country. The fundamental interests of the children must therefore be protected, in accordance with, in particular, the Hague Convention of 25 October 1980 on the Civil Aspects of the International Abduction of Children. The lawful habitual residence is accordingly maintained as the grounds of jurisdiction in cases where, because the child has been moved or has not been returned without lawful reason, there has been a de facto change in the habitual residence.

(14) This Regulation does not prevent the courts of a Member State from taking provisional, including protective, measures, in urgent cases, with regard to persons or property situated in that State.

(15) The word 'judgment' refers only to decisions that lead to divorce, legal separation or marriage annulment. Those documents which have been formally drawn up or registered as authentic instruments and are enforceable in one Member State are treated as equivalent to such 'judgments'.

(16) The recognition and enforcement of judgments given in a Member State are based on the principle of mutual trust. The grounds for non-recognition are kept to the minimum required. Those proceedings should incorporate provisions to ensure observance of public policy in the State addressed and to safeguard the rights of the defence and those of the parties, including the individual rights of any child involved, and so as to withhold recognition of irreconcilable judgments.

(17) The State addressed should review neither the jurisdiction of the State of origin nor the findings of fact.

(18) No procedures may be required for the updating of civil-status documents in one Member State on the basis of a final judgment given in another Member State.

(19) The Convention concluded by the Nordic States in 1931 should be capable of application within the limits set by this Regulation.

(20) Spain, Italy and Portugal had concluded Concordats before the matters covered by this Regulation were brought within the ambit of the Treaty: It is necessary to ensure that these States do not breach their international commitments in relation to the Holy See.

(21) The Member States should remain free to agree among themselves on practical measures for the application of the Regulation as long as no Community measures have been taken to that end.

(22) Annexes I to III relating to the courts and redress procedures should be amended by the Commission on the basis of amendments transmitted by the Member State concerned. Amendments to Annexes IV and V should be adopted in accordance with Council Decision 1999/468/EC of 28 June 1999 laying down the procedures for the exercise of implementing powers conferred on the Commission.

(23) No later than five years after the date of the entry into force of this Regulation, the Commission is to review its application and propose such amendments as may appear necessary.

(24) The United Kingdom and Ireland, in accordance with Article 3 of the Protocol on the position of the United Kingdom and Ireland annexed to the Treaty on European Union and the Treaty establishing the European Community, have given notice of their wish to take part in the adoption and application of this Regulation.

(25) Denmark, in accordance with Articles 1 and 2 of the Protocol on the position of Denmark annexed to the Treaty on European Union and the Treaty establishing the European Community, is not participating in the adoption of this Regulation, and is therefore not bound by it nor subject to its application,

HAS ADOPTED THIS REGULATION:



## CHAPTER I
## SCOPE

### *Article 1*

1. This Regulation shall apply to:
   (a) civil proceedings relating to divorce, legal separation or marriage annulment;
   (b) civil proceedings relating to parental responsibility for the children of both spouses on the occasion of the matrimonial proceedings referred to in (a).

2. Other proceedings officially recognised in a Member State shall be regarded as equivalent to judicial proceedings. The term 'court' shall cover all the authorities with jurisdiction in these matters in the Member States.

3. In this Regulation, the term 'Member State' shall mean all Member States with the exception of Denmark.

## CHAPTER II
## JURISDICTION

### SECTION 1
### GENERAL PROVISIONS

### *Article 2*
### *Divorce, legal separation and marriage annulment*

1. In matters relating to divorce, legal separation or marriage annulment, jurisdiction shall lie with the courts of the Member State:
   (a) in whose territory:
      – the spouses are habitually resident, or
      – the spouses were last habitually resident, in so far as one of them still resides there, or
      – the respondent is habitually resident, or
      – in the event of a joint application, either of the spouses is habitually resident, or
      – the applicant is habitually resident if he or she resided there for at least a year immediately before the application was made, or

– the applicant is habitually resident if he or she resided there for at least six months immediately before the application was made and is either a national of the Member State in question or, in the case of the United Kingdom and Ireland, has his 'domicile' there;

(b) of the nationality of both spouses or, in the case of the United Kingdom and Ireland, of the 'domicile' of both spouses.

2. For the purpose of this Regulation, 'domicile' shall have the same meaning as it has under the legal systems of the United Kingdom and Ireland.

### *Article 3*
### *Parental responsibility*

1. The Courts of a Member State exercising jurisdiction by virtue of Article 2 on an application for divorce, legal separation or marriage annulment shall have jurisdiction in a matter relating to parental responsibility over a child of both spouses where the child is habitually resident in that Member State.

2. Where the child is not habitually resident in the Member State referred to in paragraph 1, the courts of that State shall have jurisdiction in such a matter if the child is habitually resident in one of the Member States and:

(a) at least one of the spouses has parental responsibility in relation to the child; and

(b) the jurisdiction of the courts has been accepted by the spouses and is in the best interests of the child.

3. The jurisdiction conferred by paragraphs 1 and 2 shall cease as soon as:

(a) the judgment allowing or refusing the application for divorce, legal separation or marriage annulment has become final;

or

(b) in those cases where proceedings in relation to parental responsibility are still pending on the date referred to in (a), a judgment in these proceedings has become final;

or

(c) the proceedings referred to in (a) and (b) have come to an end for another reason.

### *Article 4*
### *Child abduction*

The courts with jurisdiction within the meaning of Article 3 shall exercise their jurisdiction in conformity with the Hague Convention of 25 October 1980 on the Civil Aspects of International Child Abduction, and in particular Articles 3 and 16 thereof.

### *Article 5*
### *Counterclaim*

The court in which proceedings are pending on the basis of Articles 2 to 4 shall also have jurisdiction to examine a counterclaim, in so far as the latter comes within the scope of this Regulation.

### *Article 6*
### *Conversion of legal separation into divorce*

Without prejudice to Article 2, a court of a Member State which has given a judgment on a legal separation shall also have jurisdiction for converting that judgment into a divorce, if the law of that Member State so provides.

### *Article 7*
### *Exclusive nature of jurisdiction under Articles 2 to 6*

A spouse who:

(a) is habitually resident in the territory of a Member State;
or

(b) is a national of a Member State, or, in the case of the United Kingdom and Ireland, has his or her 'domicile' in the territory of one of the latter Member States,

may be sued in another Member State only in accordance with Articles 2 to 6.

### *Article 8*
### *Residual jurisdiction*

1. Where no court of a Member State has jurisdiction pursuant to Articles 2 to 6, jurisdiction shall be determined, in each Member State, by the laws of that State.

2. As against a respondent who is not habitually resident and is not either a national of a Member State or, in the case of the United Kingdom and Ireland, does not have his 'domicile' within the territory of one of the latter Member States, any national of a Member State who is habitually resident within the territory of another Member State may, like the nationals of that State, avail himself of the rules of jurisdiction applicable in that State.



## SECTION 2
## EXAMINATION AS TO JURISDICTION AND ADMISSIBILITY

### *Article 9*
### *Examination as to jurisdiction*

Where a court of a Member State is seised of a case over which it has no jurisdiction under this Regulation and over which a court of another Member State has jurisdiction by virtue of this Regulation, it shall declare of its own motion that it has no jurisdiction.

### *Article 10*
### *Examination as to admissibility*

1. Where a respondent habitually resident in a State other than the Member State where the action was brought does not enter an appearance, the court with jurisdiction shall stay the proceedings so long as it is not shown that the respondent has been able to receive the document instituting the proceedings or an equivalent document in sufficient time to enable him to arrange for his defence, or that all necessary steps have been taken to this end.

2. Article 19 of Council Regulation (EC) No 1348/2000 of 29 May 2000 on the service in the Member States of judicial and extrajudicial documents in civil or commercial matters, shall apply instead of the provisions of paragraph 1 of this Article if the document instituting the proceedings or an equivalent document had to be transmitted from one Member State to another pursuant to that Regulation.

3. Where the provisions of Council Regulation (EC) No 1348/2000 are not applicable, Article 15 of the Hague Convention of 15 November 1965 on the service abroad of judicial and extrajudicial documents in civil or commercial matters shall apply if the document instituting the proceedings or an equivalent document had to be transmitted abroad pursuant to that Convention.

SECTION 3

LIS PENDENS AND DEPENDENT ACTIONS

*Article 11*

1. Where proceedings involving the same cause of action and between the same parties are brought before courts of different Member States, the court second seised shall of its own motion stay its proceedings until such time as the jurisdiction of the court first seised is established.

2. Where proceedings for divorce, legal separation or marriage annulment not involving the same cause of action and between the same parties are brought before courts of different Member States, the court second seised shall of its own motion stay its proceedings until such time as the jurisdiction of the court first seised is established.

3. Where the jurisdiction of the court first seised is established, the court second seised shall decline jurisdiction in favour of that court.

In that case, the party who brought the relevant action before the court second seised may bring that action before the court first seised.

4. For the purposes of this Article, a court shall be deemed to be seised:

(a) at the time when the document instituting the proceedings or an equivalent document is lodged with the court, provided that the applicant has not subsequently failed to take the steps he was required to take to have service effected on the respondent;

or

(b) if the document has to be served before being lodged with the court, at the time when it is received by the authority responsible for service, provided that the applicant has not subsequently failed to take the steps he was required to take to have the document lodged with the court.

SECTION 4

PROVISIONAL, INCLUDING PROTECTIVE, MEASURES

*Article 12*

In urgent cases, the provisions of this Regulation shall not prevent the courts of a Member State from taking such provisional, including protective, measures in respect of persons or assets in that State as may be available under the law of that Member State, even if, under this Regulation, the court of another Member State has jurisdiction as to the substance of the matter.

CHAPTER III

RECOGNITION AND ENFORCEMENT

*Article 13*

*Meaning of 'judgment'*

1. For the purposes of this Regulation, 'judgment' means a divorce, legal separation or marriage annulment pronounced by a court of a Member State, as well as a judgment relating to the parental responsibility of the spouses given on the occasion of such matrimonial proceedings, whatever the judgment may be called, including a decree, order or decision.

2. The provisions of this chapter shall also apply to the determination of the amount of costs and expenses of proceedings under this Regulation and to the enforcement of any order concerning such costs and expenses.

3. For the purposes of implementing this Regulation, documents which have been formally drawn up or registered as authentic instruments and are enforceable in one Member State and also settlements which have been approved by a court in the course

of proceedings and are enforceable in the Member State in which they were concluded shall be recognised and declared enforceable under the same conditions as the judgments referred to in paragraph 1.

### SECTION 1
### RECOGNITION

### *Article 14*
### *Recognition of a judgment*

1. A judgment given in a Member State shall be recognised in the other Member States without any special procedure being required.

2. In particular, and without prejudice to paragraph 3, no special procedure shall be required for up-dating the civil-status records of a Member State on the basis of a judgment relating to divorce, legal separation or marriage annulment given in another member State, and against which no further appeal lies under the law of that Member State.

3. Any interested party may, in accordance with the procedures provided for in Sections 2 and 3 of this Chapter, apply for a decision that the judgment be or not be recognised.

4. Where the recognition of a judgment is raised as an incidental question in a court of a Member State, that court may determine that issue.

### *Article 15*
### *Grounds of non-recognition*

1. A judgment relating to a divorce, legal separation or marriage annulment shall not be recognised:

(a) if such recognition is manifestly contrary to the public policy of the Member State in which recognition is sought;

(b) where it was given in default of appearance, if the respondent was not served with the document which instituted the proceedings or with an equivalent document in sufficient time and in such a way as to enable the respondent to arrange for his or her defence unless it is determined that the respondent has accepted the judgment unequivocally;

(c) if it is irreconcilable with a judgment given in proceedings between the same parties in the Member State in which recognition is sought;
or

(d) if it is irreconcilable with an earlier judgment given in another Member State or in a non-member State between the same parties, provided that the earlier judgment fulfils the conditions necessary for its recognition in the Member State in which recognition is sought.

2. A judgment relating to the parental responsibility of the spouses given on the occasion of matrimonial proceedings as referred to in Article 13 shall not be recognised:

(a) if such recognition is manifestly contrary to the public policy of the Member State in which recognition is sought taking into account the best interests of the child;

(b) if it was given, except in case of urgency, without the child having been given an opportunity to be heard, in violation of fundamental principles of procedure of the Member State in which recognition is sought;

(c) where it was given in default of appearance if the person in default was not served with the document which instituted the proceedings or with an equivalent document in sufficient time and in such a way as to enable that person to arrange for his or her defence unless it is determined that such person has accepted the judgment unequivocally;

(d) on the request of any person claiming that the judgment infringes his or her parental responsibility, if it was given without such person having been given an opportunity to be heard;

(e) if it is irreconcilable with a later judgment relating to parental responsibility given in the Member State in which recognition is sought;

or

(f) if it is irreconcilable with a later judgment relating to parental responsibility given in another Member State or in the non-member State of the habitual residence of the child provided that the later judgment fulfils the conditions necessary for its recognition in the Member State in which recognition is sought.

### *Article 16*
### *Agreement with third States*

A court of a Member State may, on the basis of an agreement on the recognition and enforcement of judgments, not recognise a judgment given in another Member State where, in cases provided for in Article 8, the judgment could only be founded on grounds of jurisdiction other than those specified in Articles 2 to 7.

### *Article 17*
### *Prohibition of review of jurisdiction of court of origin*

The jurisdiction of the court of the Member State of origin may not be reviewed. The test of public policy referred to in Article 15(1)(a) and (2)(a) may not be applied to the rules relating to jurisdiction set out in Articles 2 to 8.

### *Article 18*
### *Differences in applicable law*

The recognition of a judgment relating to a divorce, legal separation or a marriage annulment may not be refused because the law of the Member State in which such recognition is sought would not allow divorce, legal separation or marriage annulment on the same facts.

### *Article 19*
### *Non-review as to substance*

Under no circumstances may a judgment be reviewed as to its substance.

### *Article 20*
### *Stay of proceedings*

1. A court of a Member State in which recognition is sought of a judgment given in another Member State may stay the proceedings if an ordinary appeal against the judgment has been lodged.

2. A court of a Member State in which recognition is sought of a judgment given in Ireland or the United Kingdom may stay the proceedings if enforcement is suspended in the Member State of origin by reason of an appeal.

SECTION 2
ENFORCEMENT

## *Article 21*
## *Enforceable judgments*

1. A judgment on the exercise of parental responsibility in respect of a child of both parties given in a Member State which is enforceable in that Member State and has been served shall be enforced in another Member State when, on the application of any interested party, it has been declared enforceable there.

2. However, in the United Kingdom, such a judgment shall be enforced in England and Wales, in Scotland or in Northern Ireland when, on the application of any interested party, it has been registered for enforcement in that part of the United Kingdom.

## *Article 22*
## *Jurisdiction of local courts*

1. An application for a declaration of enforceability shall be submitted to the court appearing in the list in Annex I.

2. The local jurisdiction shall be determined by reference to the place of the habitual residence of the person against whom enforcement is sought or by reference to the habitual residence of any child to whom the application relates.

Where neither of the places referred to in the first subparagraph can be found in the Member State where enforcement is sought, the local jurisdiction shall be determined by reference to the place of enforcement.

3. In relation to procedures referred to in Article 14(3), the local jurisdiction shall be determined by the internal law of the Member State in which proceedings for recognition or non-recognition are brought.

## *Article 23*
## *Procedure for enforcement*

1. The procedure for making the application shall be governed by the law of the Member State in which enforcement is sought.

2. The applicant must give an address for service within the area of jurisdiction of the court applied to. However, if the law of the Member State in which enforcement is sought does not provide for the furnishing of such an address, the applicant shall appoint a representative ad litem.

3. The documents referred to in Articles 32 and 33 shall be attached to the application.

## *Article 24*
## *Decision of the court*

1. The court applied to shall give its decision without delay. The person against whom enforcement is sought shall not at this stage of the proceedings be entitled to make any submissions on the application.

2. The application may be refused only for one of the reasons specified in Articles 15, 16 and 17.

3. Under no circumstances may a judgment be reviewed as to its substance.

## *Article 25*
## *Notice of the decision*

The appropriate officer of the court shall without delay bring to the notice of the applicant the decision given on the application in accordance with the procedure laid down by the law of the Member State in which enforcement is sought.

### *Article 26*
### *Appeal against the enforcement decision*

1. The decision on the application for a declaration of enforceability may be appealed against by either party.
2. The appeal shall be lodged with the court appearing in the list in Annex II.
3. The appeal shall be dealt with in accordance with the rules governing procedure in contradictory matters.
4. If the appeal is brought by the applicant for a declaration of enforceability, the party against whom enforcement is sought shall be summoned to appear before the appellate court. If such person fails to appear, the provisions of Article 10 shall apply.
5. An appeal against a declaration of enforceability must be lodged within one month of service thereof. If the party against whom enforcement is sought is habitually resident in a Member State other than that in which the declaration of enforceability was given, the time for appealing shall be two months and shall run from the date of service, either on him or at his residence. No extension of time may be granted on account of distance.

### *Article 27*
### *Courts of appeal and means of contest*

The judgment given on appeal may be contested only by the proceedings referred to in Annex III.

### *Article 28*
### *Stay of proceedings*

1. The court with which the appeal is lodged under Articles 26 or 27 may, on the application of the party against whom enforcement is sought, stay the proceedings if an ordinary appeal has been lodged in the Member State of origin or if the time for such appeal has not yet expired. In the latter case, the court may specify the time within which an appeal is to be lodged.
2. Where the judgment was given in Ireland or the United Kingdom, any form of appeal available in the Member State of origin shall be treated as an ordinary appeal for the purposes of paragraph 1.

### *Article 29*
### *Partial enforcement*

1. Where a judgment has been given in respect of several matters and enforcement cannot be authorised for all of them, the court shall authorise enforcement for one or more of them.
2. An applicant may request partial enforcement of a judgment.

### *Article 30*
### *Legal aid*

An applicant who, in the Member State of origin, has benefited from complete or partial legal aid or exemption from costs or expenses shall be entitled, in the procedures provided for in Articles 22 to 25, to benefit from the most favourable legal aid or the most extensive exemption from costs and expenses provided for by the law of the Member State addressed.

### *Article 31*
### *Security, bond or deposit*

No security, bond or deposit, however described, shall be required of a party who in one Member State applies for enforcement of a judgment given in another Member State on the following grounds:

(a) that he or she is not habitually resident in the Member State in which enforcement is sought;

or

(b) that he or she is either a foreign national or, where enforcement is sought in either the United Kingdom or Ireland, does not have his or her "domicile" in either of those Member States.

## SECTION 3
## COMMON PROVISIONS

### *Article 32*
### *Documents*

1. A party seeking or contesting recognition or applying for a declaration of enforceability shall produce:

(a) a copy of the judgment which satisfies the conditions necessary to establish its authenticity;

and

(b) a certificate referred to in Article 33.

2. In addition, in the case of a judgment given in default, the party seeking recognition or applying for a declaration of enforceability shall produce:

(a) the original or certified true copy of the document which establishes that the defaulting party was served with the document instituting the proceedings or with an equivalent document;

or

(b) any document indicating that the defendant has accepted the judgment unequivocally.

### *Article 33*
### *Other documents*

The competent court or authority of a Member State where a judgment was given shall issue, at the request of any interested party, a certificate using the standard form in Annex IV (judgments in matrimonial matters) or Annex V (judgments on parental responsibility).

### *Article 34*
### *Absence of documents*

1. If the documents specified in Article 32(1)(b) or (2) are not produced, the court may specify a time for their production, accept equivalent documents or, if it considers that it has sufficient information before it, dispense with their production.

2. If the Court so requires, a translation of such documents shall be furnished. The translation shall be certified by a person qualified to do so in one of the Member States.

### *Article 35*
### *Legalisation or other similar formality*

No legalisation or other similar formality shall be required in respect of the documents referred to in Articles 32, 33 and 34(2) or in respect of a document appointing a representative ad litem.

## CHAPTER IV
## GENERAL PROVISIONS

### *Article 36*
### *Relation with other instruments*

1. Subject to the provisions of Articles 38, 42 and paragraph 2 of this Article, this Regulation shall, for the Member States, supersede conventions existing at the time of entry into force of this Regulation which have been concluded between two or more Member States and relate to matters governed by this Regulation.

(2)

(a) Finland and Sweden shall have the option of declaring that the Convention of 6 February 1931 between Denmark, Finland, Iceland, Norway and Sweden comprising international private law provisions on marriage, adoption and guardianship, together with the Final Protocol thereto, will apply, in whole or in part, in their mutual relations, in place of the rules of this Regulation. Such declarations shall be annexed to this Regulation and published in the Official Journal of the European Communities. They may be withdrawn, in whole or in part, at any moment by the said Member States.

(b) The principle of non-discrimination on the grounds of nationality between citizens of the Union shall be respected.

(c) The rules of jurisdiction in any future agreement to be concluded between the Member States referred to in subparagraph (a) which relate to matters governed by this Regulation shall be in line with those laid down in this Regulation.

(d) Judgments handed down in any of the Nordic States which have made the declaration provided for in subparagraph (a) under a forum of jurisdiction corresponding to one of those laid down in Chapter II, shall be recognised and enforced in the other Member States under the rules laid down in Chapter III.

3. Member States shall send to the Commission:

(a) a copy of the agreements and uniform laws implementing these agreements referred to in paragraphs 2(a) and (c);

(b) any denunciations of, or amendments to, those agreements or uniform laws.

### *Article 37*
### *Relations with certain multilateral conventions*

In relations between Member States, this Regulation shall take precedence over the following Conventions in so far as they concern matters governed by this Regulation:

- the Hague Convention of 5 October 1961 concerning the Powers of Authorities and the Law Applicable in respect of the Protection of Minors,
- the Luxembourg Convention of 8 September 1967 on the Recognition of Decisions Relating to the Validity of Marriages,
- the Hague Convention of 1 June 1970 on the Recognition of Divorces and Legal Separations,
- the European Convention of 20 May 1980 on Recognition and Enforcement of Decisions concerning Custody of Children and on Restoration of Custody of Children,
- the Hague Convention of 19 October 1996 on Jurisdiction, Applicable law, Recognition, Enforcement and Cooperation in Respect of Parental Responsibility and Measures for the Protection of Children, provided that the child concerned is habitually resident in a Member State.

*Article 38*
*Extent of effects*

1. The agreements and conventions referred to in Articles 36(1) and 37 shall continue to have effect in relation to matters to which this Regulation does not apply.

2. They shall continue to have effect in respect of judgments given and documents formally drawn up or registered as authentic before the entry into force of this Regulation.

*Article 39*
*Agreements between Member States*

1. Two or more Member States may conclude agreements or arrangements to amplify this Regulation or to facilitate its application.

Member States shall send to the Commission:

(a) a copy of the draft agreements;
and

(b) any denunciations of, or amendments to, these agreements.

2. In no circumstances may the agreements or arrangements derogate from Chapters II or III.

*Article 40*
*Treaties with the Holy See*

1. This Regulation shall apply without prejudice to the International Treaty (Concordat) between the Holy See and Portugal, signed at the Vatican City on 7 May 1940.

2. Any decision as to the invalidity of a marriage taken under the Treaty referred to in paragraph 1 shall be recognised in the Member States on the conditions laid down in Chapter III.

3. The provisions laid down in paragraphs 1 and 2 shall also apply to the following international treaties (Concordats) with the Holy See:

(a) Concordato lateranense of 11 February 1929 between Italy and the Holy See, modified by the agreement, with additional Protocol signed in Rome on 18 February 1984;

(b) Agreement between the Holy See and Spain on legal affairs of 3 January 1979.

4. Recognition of the decisions provided for in paragraph 2 may, in Italy or in Spain, be subject to the same procedures and the same checks as are applicable to decisions of the ecclesiastical courts handed down in accordance with the international treaties concluded with the Holy See referred to in paragraph 3.

5. Member States shall send to the Commission:

(a) a copy of the Treaties referred to in paragraphs 1 and 3;

(b) any denunciations of or amendments to those Treaties.

*Article 41*
*Member States with two or more legal systems*

With regard to a Member State in which two or more systems of law or sets of rules concerning matters governed by this Regulation apply in different territorial units:

(a) any reference to habitual residence in that Member State shall refer to habitual residence in a territorial unit;

(b) any reference to nationality, or in the case of the United Kingdom 'domicile', shall refer to the territorial unit designated by the law of that State;

(c) any reference to the authority of a Member State having received an application for divorce or legal separation or for marriage annulment shall refer to the authority of a territorial unit which has received such an application;

(d) any reference to the rules of the requested Member State shall refer to the rules of the territorial unit in which jurisdiction, recognition or enforcement is invoked.

## CHAPTER V
## TRANSITIONAL PROVISIONS

### *Article 42*

1. The provisions of this Regulation shall apply only to legal proceedings instituted, to documents formally drawn up or registered as authentic instruments and to settlements which have been approved by a court in the course of proceedings after its entry into force.

2. Judgments given after the date of entry into force of this Regulation in proceedings instituted before that date shall be recognised and enforced in accordance with the provisions of Chapter III if jurisdiction was founded on rules which accorded with those provided for either in Chapter II of this Regulation or in a convention concluded between the Member State of origin and the Member State addressed which was in force when the proceedings were instituted.

## CHAPTER VI
## FINAL PROVISIONS

### *Article 43*
### *Review*

No later than 1 March 2006, and every five years thereafter, the Commission shall present to the European Parliament, the Council and the Economic and Social Committee a report on the application of this Regulation, and in particular Articles 36, 39 and 40(2) thereof. The report shall be accompanied if need be by proposals for adaptations.

### *Article 44*
### *Amendment to lists of courts and redress procedures*

1. Member States shall notify the Commission of the texts amending the lists of courts and redress procedures set out in Annexes I to III. The Commission shall adapt the Annexes concerned accordingly.

2. The updating or making of technical amendments to the standard forms set out in Annexes IV and V shall be adopted in accordance with the advisory procedure set out in Article 45(2).

### *Article 45*

1. The Commission shall be assisted by a committee.

2. Where reference is made to this paragraph, Articles 3 and 7 of Decision 1999/468 EC shall apply.

3. The committee shall adopt its rules of procedure.

### *Article 46*
### *Entry into force*

This Regulation shall enter into force on 1 March 2001

This Regulation shall be binding in its entirety and directly applicable in the Member States in accordance with the Treaty establishing the European Community.

Done at Brussels, 29 May 2000.

## ANNEX I

The applications provided for by Article 22 shall be submitted to the following courts:

- in Belgium, the 'tribunal de première instance'/'rechtbank van eerste aanleg'/'erstinstanzliches Gericht',
- in Germany:
  - in the district of the 'Kammergericht' (Berlin), the 'Familiengericht Pankow/Weissensee',
  - in the districts of the remaining 'Oberlandesgerichte' to the 'Familiengericht' located at the seat of the respective 'Oberlandesgericht'
- in Greece, the 'ÌïíïìåëÝò Ðñùôïäéêåßï',
- in Spain, the 'Juzgado de Primera Instancia',
- in France, the presiding Judge of the 'tribunal de grande instance',
- in Ireland, the High Court,
- in Italy, the 'Corte d'apello',
- in Luxembourg, the presiding Judge of the 'Tribunal d'arrondissement',
- in the Netherlands, the presiding Judge of the 'arrondissementsrechtbank',
- in Austria, the 'Bezirksgericht',
- in Portugal, the 'Tribunal de Comarca' or 'Tribunal de Familia',
- in Finland, the 'käräjäoikeus'/'tingsrätt',
- in Sweden, the 'Svea hovrätt',
- in the United Kingdom:
  (a) in England and Wales, the High Court of Justice;
  (b) in Scotland, the Court of Session;
  (c) in Northern Ireland, the High Court of Justice;
  (d) in Gibraltar, the Supreme Court.

## ANNEX II

The appeal provided for by Article 26 shall be lodged with the courts listed below:

- in Belgium:
  (a) a person applying for a declaration of enforceability may lodge an appeal with the 'cour d'appel' or the 'hof van beroep';
  (b) the person against whom enforcement is sought may lodge opposition with the 'tribunal de première instance'/'rechtbank van eerste aanleg'/'erstinstanzliches Gericht',
- in Germany, the 'Oberlandesgericht',
- in Greece, the 'Åöåôåßï',
- in Spain, the 'Audiencia Provincial',
- in France, the 'Cour d'appel',
- in Ireland, the High Court,
- in Italy, the 'Corte d'appello',
- Luxembourg, the 'Cour d'appel',
- in the Netherlands:
  (a) if the applicant or the respondent who has appeared lodges the appeal: with the 'gerechtshof';

(b) if the respondent who has been granted leave not to appear lodges the appeal: with the 'arrondissementsrechtbank',
- in Austria, the 'Bezirksgericht',
- in Portugal, the 'Tribunal da Relação',
- in Finland, the 'hovioikeus'/'hovrätt',
- in Sweden, the 'Svea hovrätt',
- in the United Kingdom:
  (a) in England and Wales, the High Court of Justice;
  (b) in Scotland, the Court of Session;
  (c) in Northern Ireland, the High Court of Justice;
  (d) in Gibraltar, the Court of Appeal.

## ANNEX III

The appeals provided for by Article 27 may be brought only:
- in Belgium, Greece, Spain, France, Italy, Luxembourg and in the Netherlands, by an appeal in cassation,
- in Germany, by a 'Rechtsbeschwerde',
- in Ireland, by an appeal on a point of law to the Supreme Court,
- in Austria, by a 'Revisionsrekurs',
- in Portugal, by a 'recurso restrito à matéria de direito',
- in Finland, by an appeal to 'korkein oikeus'/'högsta domstolen',
- in Sweden, by an appeal to the 'Högsta domstolen',
- in the United Kingdom, by a single further appeal on a point of law.

## ANNEX IV

Certificate referred to in Article 33 concerning judgments in matrimonial matters

1. Country of origin: ..............................................................................
2. Court or authority issuing the certificate:..........................................
   2.1. Name ...............................................................................
   2.2. Address:...........................................................................
   2.3. Tel/fax/E-mail: ..................................................................
3. Marriage
   3.1. Wife
      3.1.1. Full name: ....................................................................
      3.1.2. Country and place of birth: ...........................................
      3.1.3. Date of birth:................................................................
   3.2. Husband
      3.2.1. Full name: ....................................................................
      3.2.2. Country and place of birth: ...........................................
      3.2.3. Date of birth:................................................................
   3.3. Country, place (where available) and date of marriage
      3.3.1. Country of marriage:.....................................................
      3.3.2. Place of marriage (where available):..............................
      3.3.3. Date of marriage ..........................................................
4. Court which delivered the judgment
   4.1. Name of Court:..................................................................
   4.2. Place of Court:..................................................................
5. Judgment
   5.1. Date:..................................................................................
   5.2. Reference number: .............................................................
   5.3. Type of judgment
      5.3.1. Divorce ☐
      5.3.2. Marriage annulment ☐
      5.3.3. Legal separation ☐

5.4. Was the judgment given in default of appearance?
  5.4.1. No ☐
  5.4.2. Yes[1] ☐
6. Names of parties to whom legal aid has been granted: ....................
7. Is the judgment subject to further appeal under the law of the Member State of origin?
  7.1. ☐
  7.2. ☐
8. Date of legal effect in the Member State where the judgment was given
  8.1. Divorce: ....................
  8.2. Legal separation: ....................

Done at: .................... Date: .................... Signature and/or stamp

1 Documents referred to in Article 32(2) must be attached.

## ANNEX V

Certificate referred to in Article 33 concerning judgments on parental responsibility

1. Country of origin: ....................
2. Court or authority issuing the certificate ....................
  2.1. Name: ....................
  2.2. Address: ....................
  2.3. Tel/Fax/E-mail: ....................
3. Parents
  3.1. Mother
    3.1.1. Full name: ....................
    3.1.2. Date and place of birth: ....................
  3.2. Father
    3.2.1. Full name: ....................
    3.2.2. Date and place of birth: ....................
4. Court which delivered the judgment
  4.1. Name of Court: ....................
  4.2. Place of Court: ....................
5. Judgment
  5.1. Date: ....................
  5.2. Reference number: ....................
  5.3. Was the judgment given in default of appearance?
    5.3.1. No ☐
    5.3.2. Yes[1] ☐
6. Children who are covered by the judgment[2]
  6.1. Full name and date of birth: ....................
  6.2. Full name and date of birth: ....................
  6.3. Full name and date of birth: ....................
  6.4. Full name and date of birth: ....................
7. Names of parties to whom legal aid has been granted: ....................
8. Attestation of enforceability and service
  8.1. Is the judgment enforceable according to the law of the Member State of origin?
    8.1.1. Yes ☐
    8.1.2. No ☐
  8.2. Has the judgment been served on the party against whom enforcement is sought?
    8.2.1. Yes ☐
      8.2.1.1. Full name of the party: ....................
      8.2.1.2. Date of service: ....................
    8.2.2. No ☐

Done at: .................... Date: .................... Signature and/or stamp

1 Documents referred to in Article 32(2) must be attached.
2 If more than four children are covered, use a second form.

# Family Proceedings (Amendment) Rules 2001

**SI 2001 No 821**

Contents





[3.657]

### 1 Citation, commencement and interpretation

These Rules may be cited as the Family Proceedings (Amendment) Rules 2001 and shall come into force—

(a) as to rules 35, 36 and 42 and paragraphs (a) and (b) of rule 43 on 3rd September 2001; and

(b) as to the remainder of these Rules on 1st April 2001.

**Initial Commencement**
1 April 2001.

[3.658]

### 2

In the following Rules—

(a) a reference to a rule, chapter, Part or Appendix by number alone means the rule, chapter, Part or Appendix so numbered in the Family Proceedings Rules 1991; and

(b) a reference to a Form by letter means the Form so identified by that letter in Appendix 1 or (as the case may be) 1A to those Rules.

**Initial Commencement**
1 April 2001.

[3.659]

### 3 Transitional provisions

(1) Where—

(a) before the coming into force of these Rules a person, other than the Official Solicitor, has been appointed as guardian ad litem under section 41 of the Children Act 1989; and

(b) the proceedings in which he was appointed are still continuing, that person shall, for the purposes of the Family Proceedings Rules 1991, be treated as if he had been appointed—

(i) children's guardian; or

(ii) parental order reporter,

as the case may be.

(2) Where—

(a) before the coming into force of these Rules the Official Solicitor had been appointed as guardian ad litem under section 41 of the Children Act 1989; and

(b) the proceedings in which he was appointed are still continuing,

the person in the office of the Official Solicitor who had day to day conduct of the proceedings shall, for the purposes of the Family Proceedings Rules 1991, be treated as if he had been appointed:

(i) children's guardian; or

(ii) parental order reporter,

as the case may be.

**Initial Commencement**

1 April 2001.

**[3.660]**

**4**

Where—

(a) before the coming into force of these Rules a person had been requested to prepare a welfare report in accordance with section 7(1)(a) of the Children Act 1989; and

(b) the proceedings in which the report was requested are still continuing,

that person shall, for the purposes of the Family Proceedings Rules 1991, be treated as the children and family reporter in those proceedings.

**Initial Commencement**

1 April 2001.

**[3.661]**

**5**

The amendments to the Family Proceedings Rules 1991 made by rules 11 and 37 below shall not apply in respect of proceedings commenced before 1st April 2001.

**Initial Commencement**

1 April 2001.

**[3.662]**

**6**

The amendments to the Family Proceedings Rules 1991 made by rules 9 and 29 below shall not apply in respect of proceedings commenced before 1st March 2001.

**Initial Commencement**

1 April 2001.

**[3.663]**

**Amendments to the FPR 1991**

Please note that the amendments to the FPR 1991 listed in rr 7 to 43 of SI 2001/821 have been incorporated into the text of the rules set out at para **[3.401]** et seq above.

# PART 4

# Practice Directions

Contents

---

**[4.1]**

# 22 December 1972
# [1973] 1 All ER 192, [1973] 1 WLR 72

## Family Division

## *Ancillary relief—Affidavit of means*

The [district judges] of the [Principal] Registry (in consultation with the Law Society and other interested bodies) have prepared a suggested form of affidavit of means including a questionnaire designed to provide the information which seems likely to be required on the hearing of most applications for ancillary relief. The form is appended. Clearly such a questionnaire cannot include every relevant question in every case without being unduly long, and it may require alterations and additions in particular cases. Nevertheless, it is thought that there are advantages both to practitioners and to the court in a uniform presentation of the facts in ordinary cases and that the questionnaire may be useful as an aide-memoire so that necessary information will not be omitted through mere inadvertence. It is hoped, therefore, that practitioners will find it convenient to use the form in most cases, modifying it and adding to it as may be necessary. In particular, there will be cases in which an applicant desires to proceed in default of evidence from a respondent, where an additional section may have to be added giving evidence of the respondent's means including a statement of the source of knowledge, and other cases where the respondent wishes to allege misconduct by the applicant material to the application.

Where, instead of using the suggested form, an affidavit is drawn in the conventional narrative style, it will be convenient if information is presented in the order in which the questions appear in the form.

Issued with the concurrence of the Lord Chancellor.

**[4.2]**

## 10 February 1976

## Family Division

## *Tracing payers overseas*

Difficulties can arise where a person in this country wishes to take proceedings under the Maintenance Orders (Facilities for Enforcement) Act 1920 or Part I of the Maintenance Orders (Reciprocal Enforcement) Act 1972 to obtain or enforce a maintenance order against a payer living overseas whose address is unknown to the applicant.

To mitigate these difficulties, arrangements have now been made with the appropriate authorities in Australia, Canada, New Zealand and South Africa, whereby the court may on request ask the authorities in those countries to make enquiries with a view to tracing the whereabouts of the payer. The following procedure should be followed.

On or before an application is made for a provisional maintenance order, or for transmission of an absolute maintenance order under the above Acts by an applicant who does not know the payer's actual address in either Australia, Canada, New Zealand or South Africa, there should be completed and lodged with the [district judge] a questionnaire, in duplicate, ([Principal] Registry Form D312 or county court Form D85 as appropriate) obtainable from the registry or court office, together with a written undertaking from the solicitor (or from the applicant if acting in person) that any address of the payer received in response to the enquiries will not be disclosed or used except for the purpose of the proceedings.

**[4.3]**

## 4 March 1976

## Family Division

## *Ancillary relief—Appointment for hearing of application*

Recent experience has shown that, notwithstanding the advice contained in the Practice Note of 28 December 1973 (published in [1974] 124 NLJ 29, 118 Sol Jo 40) about the fixing of appointments before the [district judges] in the [Principal] Registry in London for the hearing of applications for ancillary relief, the estimated length of the hearing given by the applicant's solicitor often proves totally inaccurate, with the result that the [district judges'] lists become congested or the court's time is wasted.

In an attempt to remedy this situation, the [district judges] have decided that where a hearing is likely to be lengthy (ie a half-day's duration or longer) then, before an appointment for the hearing is given by the [district judge's] clerk, a certificate will be required signed by counsel for all parties to the application or, where the application is not to be attended by counsel, signed by the parties' solicitors, to the effect that the application is ready for hearing and that its estimated length has been agreed. This certificate may be endorsed on Form D270 (form of application for appointment, obtainable from the [Principal] Registry) or given separately. If, after an appointment has been fixed, an agreed estimate is substantially revised or a settlement in respect of the application is reached, it is essential that the [district judge's] clerk should be informed immediately by telephone.

This procedure applies only to applications proceeding in the [Principal] Registry.

**[4.4]**

## 26 March 1976
## [1976] 2 All ER 447, [1976] 1 WLR 418

## *Family provision*

1. The Inheritance (Provision for Family and Dependants) Act 1975 comes into force on 1st April 1976. In respect of deaths occurring on or after that date the Act repeals and replaces and enlarges the scope of the existing legislation relating to family provision as contained in the Inheritance (Family Provision) Act 1938 (as amended) and applications for maintenance out of the estate of a deceased former spouse under s 26 of the Matrimonial Causes Act 1965 (as amended).

### Assignment and commencement of proceedings

2. The new RSC Ord 99, introduced by the Rules of the Supreme Court 1976, assigns applications in the High Court under the Act to the Chancery Division or the Family Division and provides a code of procedure common to both Divisions. Application is to be made by general form of originating summons (Form No 10 in RSC Appendix A which has been slightly amended) and may be commenced either in London (in the Central Office or the Principal Registry of the Family Division) or any district registry of the High Court. The applicant must lodge with the court an affidavit in support of the originating summons and serve a copy with the summons.

3. Where an applicant wishes the court to exercise its discretion under s 4 of the 1975 Act by extending the time for making an application for an order, such relief should be expressly asked for in the originating summons and the grounds on which the court's leave to entertain the application is sought should be included in the supporting affidavit.

4. Although new RSC Ord 99 does not prescribe the contents of the applicant's affidavit in support, the attention of practitioners is drawn to the importance of setting out in it particulars of any known previous proceedings relevant to the application. Such proceedings will often be material to the question whether the application ought to be transferred from the Family Division to the Chancery Division or vice versa under RSC Ord 4, r 3. Transfer of the proceedings might also be appropriate in other instances, for example, on sufficient grounds being shown by the parties or where the application involves the taking of complicated accounts, for which special facilities exist in the Chancery Division.

5. RSC Ord 99, r 5(2)(d), makes it clear that it is only facts known to the deponent which have to be stated in the affidavit of a personal representative. He is obviously not obliged to make enquiries and investigations in order to ascertain or confirm other matters within the 21 days after service of the summons. Nor is he required to set out facts (possibly distasteful) which are not necessarily relevant at that stage; if they become relevant later he may lodge a further affidavit.

### Jurisdiction

6. Under new RSC Ord 99, r 8, masters, [district judges] of the Principal Registry of the Family Division and district [judges of the district registries] may hear applications and make final orders disposing of proceedings under the Act, subject to the directions of the judges. Whilst at the present time it is not proposed to make any formal directions under RSC Ord 32, r 14(1), and masters, [district judges] of the Family Division and district [judges of the district registries] may therefore deal with either contested or uncontested applications, it is envisaged that they will exercise their discretion so as to refer to a judge any case which is likely to involve a long or complex issue of fact or law or a question of jurisdiction, unless the amount of the estate in the case is small.

**[4.5]**

## 5 April 1978
## [1978] 2 All ER 167, [1978] 1 WLR 585

## Chancery Division

### *Family provision—Appeal from master's decision*

1. Applications under the Inheritance (Provision for Family and Dependants) Act 1975 are now frequently heard and disposed of by masters. The question arises how the case is to proceed if a party is dissatisfied with the master's decision.

2. It is open to the master, with the consent of the parties, to try the case in court under RSC Ord 36, r 9, and if he does so an appeal lies to the Court of Appeal under RSC Ord 58, r 3.

3. If, however, the case is heard in chambers a dissatisfied party must apply for an adjournment to the judge, in which case there must be a rehearing, normally in court.

4. Though the judge or the parties may require any cross-examination on affidavits or other oral evidence to be heard again in full, in most cases this should not be necessary if a full note or a transcript of the evidence before the master has been made.

5. A master hearing a case in chambers should therefore ensure, if possible, that the proceedings before him are recorded by a shorthand writer or a recording instrument. If he is unable to arrange this he should take as full a note as practicable of the oral evidence given before him. On the adjournment to the judge there should be sent to the judge, with the affidavits, a transcript or copy of the master's note of the oral evidence and a transcript or copy of the master's judgment.

6. No provision should be made for the attendance of witnesses at the rehearing before the judge unless a judge so directs. A party requiring such a direction should apply to the master to adjourn that question to a judge in chambers as a preliminary point.

By the direction of the Vice-Chancellor.

**[4.6]**

## 22 May 1978
## [1978] 2 All ER 432, [1978] 1 WLR 797

## Family Division

### *Matrimonial order—Appeal against periodical or lump sum payments*

Unless the President otherwise directs, an appeal under the Matrimonial Proceedings (Magistrates' Courts) Act 1960 to the Family Division of the High Court may be determined by a single judge, instead of by a Divisional Court, in cases where the appeal relates only to the amount of any [periodical or lump sum] payment ordered to be made. The President may also direct that such an appeal be heard and determined by a single judge at 'a divorce town' within the meaning of the [FPR 1991 r 8.2(9)(a) stipulates] the number of copy documents required to be lodged where the appeal is to quantum only.

The practice to be followed in respect of any such appeal to a single judge of the Family Division will be that contained in the *Practice Direction* dated 11 May 1977[1] subject to the following modifications: (i) one copy only of the various documents in support of the appeal need be lodged, unless the President directs that an appeal which has been listed before a single judge shall instead be heard by a Divisional Court when the Clerk of the Rules will notify the appellant's solicitor (or the appellant if acting in person) and request that he do lodge the additional copies required by [FPR 1991, r 8.2(4)] and the *Practice Direction* dated 11 May 1977[1] prior to the date fixed for the hearing; (ii) any request to fix an appeal for hearing by a single judge at a place other than at the Royal Courts of Justice should be made in writing to the Clerk of the Rules; (iii) where the President directs that the appeal be heard at a divorce town as defined by the [FPR 1991], the Clerk of the Rules will inform the appellant of the relevant town and will refer the papers to the listing officer of the appropriate Circuit Office for a date of hearing to be fixed and notified to the appellant.

The *Registrar's Direction* dated 16 December 1971 (Divisional Court appeal: date of hearing) is hereby cancelled.

1 [1977] 2 All ER 543, [1977] 1 WLR 609.

**[4.7]**

## 8 November 1978
## [1978] 3 All ER 1032, [1979] 1 WLR 1

## Chancery Division

## *Family provision—Endorsement—Consent order*

1. In June 1953 Vaisey J directed that a consent order made in proceedings under the Inheritance (Family Provision) Act 1938, all parties being sui juris, was not an order under that Act and accordingly that no memorandum of the order should be endorsed on the probate or letters of administration, but that it was otherwise if a compromise was approved by the court on behalf of a party not sui juris. This ruling is equally applicable to consent orders in proceedings in the Chancery Division under the Inheritance (Provision for Family and Dependants) Act 1975.

2. In the Family Division memoranda of all consent orders in proceedings under the 1975 Act are endorsed on the probate or letters of administration, whether or not the parties are all sui juris.

3. To avoid any divergence of practice between two divisions having concurrent jurisdiction, the direction of Vaisey J is now withdrawn. In future, every final order embodying terms of compromise made in proceedings in the Chancery Division under the 1975 Act shall contain a direction that a memorandum thereof shall be endorsed on or permanently annexed to the probate or letters of administration and a copy thereof shall be sent to the Principal Registry of the Family Division with the relevant grant of probate or letters of administration for endorsement, notwithstanding that any particular order may not, strictly speaking, be an order under the 1975 Act.

By the direction of the Vice-Chancellor.



**[4.8]**

## 5 March 1979
## [1979] 1 All ER 831, [1979] 1 WLR 290

## Family Division

## *Consent applications—Periodical payments direct to child*

Where a consent summons or notice of application seeks an order which includes agreed terms for periodical payments direct to a child in excess of the amounts qualifying for the time being as 'small maintenance payments' under s 65 of the Income and Corporation

Taxes Act 1970, it is no longer necessary for the solicitor to certify whether the child is or is not living with the party who will be making the payments under the proposed terms.

Paragraph 2 of the *Registrar's Direction* of 22 December 1975[1] is accordingly hereby cancelled.

1 [1976] 1 All ER 272, [1976] 1 WLR 74.

### [4.9]

## 10 March 1980
## [1980] 1 All ER 1007, [1980] 1 WLR 354

## Family Division

## *Maintenance – Registration in magistrates' court*

### (a) Children's orders

[Section 62 of the Magistrates' Court Act 1980] makes provision, inter alia, for a magistrates' clerk to transmit payments under a maintenance order registered in his court, which provides for payment directly to a child, either directly to that child or to the person with whom the child has his home. It also provides that that person may proceed in his own name for variation, revival or revocation of the order and may enforce non-payment either in his own name or by requesting the magistrates to do so.

It is therefore no longer necessary for the High Court or the divorce county court when granting an application for registration to place on the order the wording required by the *Practice Direction* of 2 November 1977[1] and that direction is hereby cancelled.

The registration in a magistrates' court of an order made direct to a child entails a considerable amount of work. Accordingly, when the court is considering the form of an order where there are children, care should be taken not to make orders for payment direct where such orders would be of no benefit to the parties or where the parties would derive no immediate tax advantage.

### (b) Nominal orders for spouses

Applications for leave to register orders for nominal amounts in favour of spouses only should not be allowed and, except in special circumstances, leave to register should not be granted in respect of orders for maintenance pending suit and interim orders.

Issued with the concurrence of the Lord Chancellor.

1 [1977] 3 All ER 942, [1977] 1 WLR 1222.

### [4.10]

## 4 February 1981
## [1981] 1 All ER 627, [1981] 1 WLR 274

## Family Division

## *Failure to maintain – Application for hearing date*

As from 1 February 1981 s 27 of the Matrimonial Causes Act 1973 is amended by the Domestic Proceedings and Magistrates' Court Act 1978 so as to provide that either party to a marriage may apply to the court for an order under that section that the other party has failed to provide reasonable maintenance for the applicant or has failed to provide, or to make a proper contribution towards, reasonable maintenance for any child of the family. The revised jurisdiction does not require that the failure should be wilful.

[FPR 1991, r 3.1(10) provides] inter alia, that these applications may be dealt with by a [district judge].

In the [Principal] Registry it will not be the practice to allocate a hearing date on the notice of the application which is served on the respondent. Application for a hearing date should be made by lodging form D270 as in any other application for financial provision in a matrimonial cause proceeding in this registry.

**[4.11]**

## 16 April 1981

## Family Division

### *Ex parte injunctions granted by district judge*

Where a [district judge] of the Principal Registry of the Family Division grants an application for an interim injunction under s 37(2)(a) of the Matrimonial Causes Act 1973 or under s 17 of the Married Women's Property Act 1882, the respondent should be given an indication that he may apply to have the injunction lifted.

Accordingly the wording of the injunction should be framed to make it interim until the final determination of the substantive application or unless the respondent, on two clear days' notice, applies for the injunction to be lifted.

Where the respondent so applies, his application should be heard by the [district judge] for the day so that it may be disposed of as speedily as possible.



**[4.12]**

## 4 June 1981
## [1981] 2 All ER 642, [1981] 1 WLR 1010

## Family Division

### *Ancillary relief—procedure*

The experiment in operation from 1 April 1980 to secure the settlement of financial applications at a pre-trial review has resulted in a success rate so low as not to justify its continuance. Consequently pre-trial reviews on such applications will not take place as from 1 July next.

Nevertheless the following procedures laid down by the *Registrar's Direction* of 12 February 1980 ([1980] 1 All ER 592, [1980] 1 WLR 245), are still useful and should be continued.

(a) After affidavits have been filed mutual discovery should take place without order 14 days from the last affidavit, unless some other period is agreed, with inspection 7 days thereafter.

(b) Where a dispute arises as to the value of any property, a valuation should be made without order by an agreed valuer, or in default of agreement, by an independent valuer chosen by the President of the Institution of Chartered Surveyors. The valuation should be produced to the [district judge] at the hearing.

(c) If a dispute arises as to the extent of discovery or as to answers in a questionnaire, an appointment for directions should be taken out. Where the [district judge] considers that to answer any question would entail considerable expense and that there is doubt whether the answer would provide any information of value, he may make the order for the question to be answered at the questioner's risk as to costs. The [district judge] may refuse to order an answer to a question if he considers that its value would be small in relation to the property or income of the party to whom the question is addressed.

(d) Where an issue of conduct is raised on the affidavits, an appointment for directions should be taken out at which the [district judge] will enquire whether the issue is being pursued and, if so, will order particulars to be given of the precise allegations relied on.

The *Registrar's Direction* of 12 February 1980 is hereby cancelled.

**[4.13]**

## 16 June 1983
## [1983] 2 All ER 679, [1983] 1 WLR 800

## Family Division

## *Ancillary relief—Payment of school fees—Tax*

Maintenance orders which contain an element in respect of school fees frequently have to be varied when the school fees increase. This requirement could be avoided if the relevant part of the maintenance order were to be automatically adjusted when the school fees go up.

The Inland Revenue have agreed to this principle. A form of order which they would find acceptable is as follows:

'It is ordered that the [petitioner] [respondent] do pay or cause to be paid to the child AB as from the day of 19 until [he] [she] shall attain the age of 17 years [or until [he] [she] shall cease to receive full-time education (whichever is the [later] [earlier])] or further order periodical payments for [himself] [herself]–

(a) of an amount equivalent to such sum as after deduction of income tax at the basic rate equals the school fees [but not the extras in the school bill] [including specified extras] at the school the said child attends for each financial year [by way of three payments on and and ] [payable monthly]; together with

(b) the sum of £ per annum less tax payable monthly in respect of general maintenance of the said child'.

It should be noted that, even if the amount referred to in part (b) is within the current limits of small maintenance payments, it should still be expressed as 'less tax' because the relevant figure for the maintenance order will be the combined total of the two parts.

In such cases the Revenue will require to be satisfied that the payer under the order has no contractual liability for payment of the school fees.

If an order expressed as payable to the child, whether made in this form, or in a form which includes an element in respect of school fees for a specific amount, also provides that payment of the element representing school fees should be paid direct to the school (because, for example, it is feared that the other spouse might dissipate it) the Revenue have agreed subject to the condition hereafter set out, that tax relief will be given on that element. The wording of the order should be:

'And it is further ordered that that part of the order which reflects the school fees shall be paid to the [Headmaster] [Bursar] [School Secretary] as agent for the said child and the receipt of that payee shall be sufficient discharge.'

The school fees should be paid *in full* and should be paid out of the net amount under the maintenance order after deduction of tax. Certificates for the full tax deduction should continue to be provided [to] the other spouse (or other person referred to in [para 1 of Sch 1 to the Children Act 1989]) in the normal way.

It is a condition of such an order being acceptable for tax purposes that the contract for the child's education (which should preferably be in writing) should be between the child (whose income is being used) and the school and that the fees are received by the officer of the school as the appointed agent for the child.

A form of contract which is acceptable to the Inland Revenue is as follows:

'THIS AGREEMENT is made between THE GOVERNORS OF ........................ by their duly authorised officer ........................ (hereinafter called "the School") of the first part; ........................ and the [Headmaster] [Bursar] [School Secretary] of the second part, and ........................ (hereinafter called "the Child") of the third part.

WHEREAS [it is proposed to ask the ........................ Court to make an order] [the ........................ Court has made an order] in cause number ......... that the Father of the Child do make periodical payments to the child at the rate of £......... per annum less tax until the Child completes full-time education (or as the case may be) and that that part of the order which reflects the school fees shall be paid to the [Headmaster] [Bursar] [School Secretary] as agent for the Child and the receipt of that agent shall be a sufficient discharge.

1. The Child hereby constitutes the [Headmaster] [Bursar] [School Secretary] to be his agent for the purpose of receiving the said fees and the Child agrees to pay the said fees to the said School in consideration of being educated there.
2. In consideration of the said covenant the [Headmaster] [Bursar] [School Secretary] agrees to accept the said payments by the Father as payments on behalf of the Child and the School agrees to educate the Child during such time as the said school fees are paid.

Dated the..................day of...................19.........

This Direction supersedes the Registrar's Direction of November 10, 1980 which is hereby cancelled.

**Note** This Direction has been amended by *Registrar's Direction* of 10 July 1987.

**[4.14]**

## 7 February 1984
## [1984] 1 All ER 684, [1984] 1 WLR 306

## Family Division

## ***Husband and wife—Principal Registry—Fixed date of hearing—Filing affidavits and documents***

1. Where in any cause or matter proceeding in the Principal Registry, a party wishes to file an affidavit or other document in connection with an application for which a hearing date has been fixed, the affidavit or other document must be lodged in the Principal Registry *not less than 14 clear days* before the appointed hearing date.

2. Where insufficient time remains before the hearing date to lodge the affidavit or other document as required by 1 above, it should, in case of an application before the judge, be lodged in Room [W5] (Summons Clerk, Clerk of the Rules [Branch]) at the Royal Courts of Justice as soon as possible *before* the hearing: where the application is before the [district judge], it should be handed to the clerk to that [district judge] immediately before the hearing. Service should be effected upon the opposing party in the normal way.

3. The *Registrar's Direction* of 12 January 1981, [1981] 1 All ER 323, [1981] 1 WLR 106, except paragraph 3, is cancelled.

**[4.15]**

## 17 February 1986
## [1986] 1 All ER 704, [1986] 1 WLR 381

## Family Division

### *Consent orders for financial relief*

This Direction is issued with the concurrence of the Lord Chancellor.

(1) [*deleted*]

(2) [FPR 1991, r 2.61] requires an application for a consent order under any of ss 23, 24, 24A or 27 of the Matrimonial Causes Act 1973 to be accompanied by minutes of the order in the terms sought indorsed with a statement signed by the respondent to the application signifying his agreement, together with a statement containing the information as required by the rules.

(3) It is considered that the rule is properly complied with if the statement indorsed on the minutes is signed by solicitors on record as acting for the respondent.

(4) A suggested form of accompanying statement of information is [now prescribed as Form M1 in the FPR 1991].

(5) Although the rule does not require the statement of information to be signed by either party, practitioners may consider it appropriate for the form to be signed by or on behalf of other parties as a means of establishing the accuracy of the information relating to their respective clients.

**[4.16]**

## 10 July 1987
## [1987] 2 All ER 1084, [1987] 1 WLR 1165

## Family Division

### *Children—Periodical payments*

Orders for periodical payments in respect of a child have been frequently expressed as lasting until the child attains the age of 17 years or ceases full time education or further order. It has recently been learned that the Inland Revenue treat such orders as ceasing when the first event occurs. They would of course accept orders as lasting beyond the child's 17th birthday if the order contained wording such as 'until the child attains the age of 17 years or ceases full time education (whichever is the later) or further order'.

Orders which are intended to run until a date determined by such alternatives should clearly indicate whether the order is to cease on the happening of the earlier or later event. The words 'or until further order' do not have to be qualified in this way, because such further order will only be made where the current order has not yet ceased and will immediately supersede the provisions of that current order. Where the court has made an order in the terms of the *Registrar's Direction* of 16 June 1983 (Payment of School Fees) [1983] 2 All ER 679, [1983] 1 WLR 800, with the intention that the order should continue until the occurrence of the later of the two events, the reaching of a specified age or cessation of full-time education, the Revenue has indicated that they will recognise for tax purposes the correction of the order by the Court, inserting the words 'whichever is the later'.

At county court level, the corrected order should be noted 'Corrected under CCR Ord 15 r 5'. At High Court level, unless formal application is made under RSC Ord 20 r 11, the corrected order should be noted 'Corrected under the Court's inherent jurisdiction'. In either case, a copy of the corrected order should be supplied to the petitioner and respondent by the

Court in the usual way. Where the order is currently registered in a magistrates' court, a certified copy of the corrected order, for which no fee is chargeable, should also be sent to that court.

It will normally be sufficient if the application for correction of the order is made by consent on notice or summons, without the need for attendance, subject to the Court's discretion to require otherwise. No fee is chargeable on the consent application.

**[4.17]**

## 28 March 1988
## [1988] 2 All ER 63, [1988] 1 WLR 561

## Family Division

## *Ancillary relief—Costs estimates*

The costs of applications for ancillary relief relating to capital assets (applications for property adjustment and lump sum orders) are, in a great number of cases, so high in relation to the value of the assets involved that a Judge or [District Judge] will be unable to make a realistic determination without an approximate indication of the anticipated costs of each side. It is, moreover, in the interests of the parties themselves that each should be aware, as early as possible before the hearing, of their potential liability for costs.

Estimates of costs on each side should therefore be prepared for submission to the Court at the commencement of the hearing and at any pre-trial review of the application. The estimates should be available by the time that the case is fixed for hearing and should differentiate between costs already incurred and the expected costs of the hearing, so far as the latter can be ascertained.

This Direction supersedes the *Registrar's Direction* of 13 July 1982 (Estimate of Costs on lump sum applications) [1982] 2 All ER 800, [1982] 1 WLR 1082.



**[4.18]**

## August 1989
## [1989] Fam Law 294

## CF Turner, Senior Registrar, Family Division

## *The Finance Act 1988 and maintenance orders—Questions posed by the Senior Registrar of the Family Division to the Inland Revenue*

Questions have been put to me by members of the Family Law Bar Association about which I have consulted the Inland Revenue. The questions and answers are set out below in the hope that they will be of use.

The Inland Revenue, in answering or assisting in answering the questions, has stated that it hopes that practitioners will bear in mind that the reason for last year's tax changes was to simplify the tax system and make it fairer between individuals. The Chancellor of the Exchequer allowed people who had maintenance arrangements before the 1988 Budget a whole year in which to re-arrange their affairs if they wished, without losing tax relief. The answers which follow assume that they are concerned with genuine arrangements by people who have the means to carry them out, and fully intend to do so. If more artificial arrangements were attempted in order to get round the legislation by trying to establish an unrealistic base figure of tax relief for 1988–89 in order to take advantage of higher tax relief in later years, the Revenue would need to consider the facts of the individual case.

***QUESTION 1: Is it agreed that, if an upwards variation order was made before 5 April 1989 and was backdated to 6 April 1988, the payer was entitled to get tax relief on the increase for the whole year (and for this and subsequent years, pursuant to the pegging provision) provided that he paid the arrears created by the backdating on a date after the variation order was made?***

Yes, provided that the payments satisfied the conditions for tax relief in s 38, and the terms of the court order are such that payments became due on the date the order was made (*Morley-Clarke v Jones* [1986] Ch 311, [1985] 1 All ER 31; revsd [1986] Ch 311, [1985] 3 All ER 193, CA), or between the date of the order and 5 April 1989. If the arrears are paid in the current year, they will still fall within the phrase in s 38(3): 'the aggregate amount of the payments made by him which fall due in that year'.

***QUESTION 2: In the above circumstances, is it agreed that, in respect of such a backdated order, the payer is not entitled to tax relief on the increase by claiming credits for sums previously paid?***

Yes – there can be no tax relief in respect of sums paid voluntarily in these circumstances and increases paid prior to the order, even if subsequently required to be paid by a later order, are caught by this principle.

***QUESTION 3: Is the position that, for the purpose of the pegging provision, the Revenue will look not only at what was due for the fiscal year 1988–89 but also at what was paid in that fiscal year pursuant to such obligation?***

The ceiling for relief in 1989–90 and later years is the amount of the payments due and paid for 1988–89, since this was the amount for which the payer will be 'entitled to make a deduction' for 1988–89 (s 38(3)). This means that where payments were in arrears at the end of 1988–89, the arrears will neither qualify for relief for 1988–89 nor count towards the pegged limit for later years, until such time as they are actually paid. Once they have been paid, they will count towards the limit for the year for which they were due.

***QUESTION 4: As obligations increase beyond their 1988–89 levels, many orders are going to become partly subject to tax relief (and to payment of tax in the hands of the payee) and partly not. It will obviously become very confusing for everybody. Has the Inland Revenue given any indication as to how long the Government is minded to continue to give tax relief on old orders, as pegged?***

The legislation does not set any time limit. Any question of introducing one is a matter for Treasury Ministers. However, s 39 of the Finance Act 1988 allows the payer to elect to switch to the new regime. That will often be simpler, but, of course, it will give less relief in some cases – eg payments to children would get no relief.

***QUESTION 5: The effect of the requirement to pay maintenance without deduction of income tax commencing in the year 1989–90 is unclear with regard to orders for school fees under the Practice Direction of 16 June 1983 ([1983] 2 All ER 679, [1983] 1 WLR 800), which require payments of 'an amount equivalent to such sum as after deduction of income tax at the basic rate equals the school fees'.***

There are two possible interpretations applicable from April 1989. Either: (a) the obligation becomes one to pay the net amount of school fees, or (b) the obligation is to pay the grossed-up sum to the child – by paying the school fees to the school and the balance to the child. The latter may be considered to be the more natural reading of the order; it being a formula to calculate the gross amount of maintenance due. The Inland Revenue does not consider that it is for it to give a definitive ruling on the amount such an order requires to be paid. The Inland Revenue will interpret the order in whichever way the parties agree. For example, if the order is agreed from 1989–90 to require payment of the grossed-up sum, the payer will get tax relief accordingly, and the payee will be assessed on that sum. It is assumed that the terms of the original order will either have been agreed or have been decided by the court. In both cases, the object will have been clear. Account may have been taken of the effect of reimbursement of part of the tax on the school fees on the amount specified in the order for general maintenance. It should be possible in most cases for parties to agree which interpretation produces the figures closest to the net sums which were anticipated to flow from the original order. It is not possible to state by Practice Direction which interpretation is correct; only a judicial decision can decide the point.

***QUESTION 6: How often will a payee be expected to remit the tax due on the orders to the Inland Revenue, eg monthly, quarterly or annually? How will the payee's tax coding be calculated to ensure that there will be no overpayments? Will there be a system of repayments as in the past?***

Maintenance paid under arrangements to which the new rules apply is not liable to tax. Taxation of recipients of maintenance payments to which the old rules apply for 1989–90 onwards will depend on the personal tax situation of the individual. If he or she is in employment, any taxable maintenance might be taken into account in the PAYE coding, so that the tax due is recovered from earnings each week or month. Alternatively, an assessment might be made on which the tax will be payable in one sum each year.

***QUESTION 7: Can the total amount of tax relief due under the 'pegging' provisions be swapped between payees? For example: in 1988–89 a husband/father is ordered to pay a wife and three children each £5,000 pa, so that he would be entitled to the full tax relief on a total of £20,000 in this year and subsequent years. When the children cease to be entitled to maintenance, assume that the wife's order is increased to £20,000 pa. Will the husband still receive tax relief on the full amount of the order even though the wife's entitlement in 1988–89 was only £5,000 pa?***

Yes, but new recipients cannot be added – see s 36(5).

***QUESTION 8: Assume that a deed was registered with the Inland Revenue before 30 June 1988 setting out a husband's obligation to pay maintenance to a wife (tax efficient under the old law) and direct to the children (not tax deductible under the old law). Will the husband be entitled to tax relief on subsequent court orders made payable to the children (subject to the pegging provisions) although the deed itself would not have created a tax efficient method of payment?***

Yes, provided the order was made before 6 April 1989 and it can be shown that it effectively replaced a pre-existing agreement (s 36(4)(d)). Only payments made under the court order, and not payments under the prior agreement, will qualify for tax relief and count towards the payer's pegged limit. If the order is made after 5 April 1989, payments 'to' a child will not qualify for tax relief since the agreement in force for 1988–89 meant payments to a child did not qualify.



## School Fees Orders

The views of the registrars of the Principal Registry of the Family Division on the subject of school fees orders (both 'new' and 'old') are as follows.

(1) The *Practice Direction* of 16 June 1983 (above) (amended by the Direction dated 10 July 1987 ([1987] 2 All ER 1084, [1987] 1 WLR 1165)), set out a form of order which included provision for the payment of a child's school fees by way of maintenance. The right of the payer to income tax relief in respect of the payment of school fees, where these were to be paid direct to the school, was conditional upon his payments being in discharge of the child's own liability for the fees and not in discharge of the payer's liability therefor. To establish the child's liability, a contract between the child and the school was necessary. The form of order was designed to provide that any increase in the school fees should be payable without the necessity of variation of the order. The formula designed to achieve this was to order the payer to pay to the child 'an amount equivalent to such sum as after deduction of income tax at the basic rate equalled the school fees' (ie the grossed-up amount) in each financial year.

(2) The Finance Act 1988 provides that, in respect of new orders, income tax relief for the payer in respect of sums payable under an order (but excluding sums payable direct to a child) would be limited to a maximum of the difference between the single person's and the married person's relief, and that sums payable under an order would be payable without deduction of income tax. The payee would receive payments without deduction and the payments would not be taxable in his hands. 'New' orders in this context mean orders made on or after 15 March 1988, with the exception of those made before the end of June 1988 on

an application which was made on or before 15 March 1988. The expression does not include existing orders in respect of which payers received in 1988–89 full income tax relief on the sums payable (referred to as 'old' orders) or orders which vary, supplement or replace such orders.

(3) New orders for maintenance, including school fees and their increases, should omit all reference to the grossed-up sum of the fees. The appropriate form of new order should direct payment to the child (or to the custodial parent) of an amount equivalent to the school fees (excluding extras or including specified extras in the school bills) at the school the child attends for each financial year by three payments on specified dates (or payable monthly). It should be noted that if the order directs payment to the child, the limited income tax relief for the payer will not be claimable in respect of such payments. In cases where it is desired that payments should be made direct to the school (because, for example, it is feared that the other party might dissipate them), the order may direct that payment to the appropriate official of the school should be a sufficient discharge of the payer's liability under the order for school fees. Any sum which is to be paid in addition to the school fees for the general maintenance of the child should be specified in the order. No contract between the school and the child will be required.

(4) By s 38 of the Finance Act 1988, orders which vary, replace or supplement old orders must be paid without deduction of income tax in 1989–90 and in succeeding years. Accordingly, orders varying, supplementing or replacing old school fees orders should state that the school fees should be paid to the child without making any reference to income tax.

Provisions for the school fees to be paid direct to the school (in the circumstances mentioned above) may be included, but for the payer to receive income tax relief in respect of those payments (subject to the limitations in s 38 of the Finance Act 1988) there will continue to be a need for a contract between the school and the child.

(5) The limitations on a payer's income tax relief and on a payee's liability for income tax for 1989–90 and succeeding years are set out in s 38(3) and (4) of the Finance Act 1988.

**[4.19]**

## 27 April 1990
## [1990] 2 All ER 147, [1990] 1 WLR 575

## Practice Note – *Evans v Evans*

## Family Division

### *Divorce—Ancillary proceedings—Guidelines to ensure that unnecessary costs not incurred*

**26 January 1990**

Booth J read the following judgment. This is a wife's application for ancillary relief following upon a divorce. She seeks for herself a clean financial break from the husband and for the two minor children of the family who live with her she seeks periodical payments. The case has caused me anxiety because of the enormity of the costs which have been incurred in comparison with the assets which are available to meet the needs of the parties. On the husband's side the costs amount in all to £35,000 and on the wife's side they are estimated at £25,000. The available assets consist broadly of two properties both subject to mortgages which are the homes of the respective parties and the husband's shareholding in a small company which provides his livelihood and that of the children and which will not be sold in the foreseeable future. The wife is legally aided and has no independent means. It will thus be seen that the costs are out of all proportion to the assets.

This is by no means an isolated case in this respect. The situation recurs again and again when the court finds itself unable to make appropriate provision for the parties and their children because of their liability for legal costs and it is a matter of the gravest concern to all judges. With the concurrence of the President of the Family Division I shall commence my judgment with some general guidelines to be followed by the practitioner in the preparation of a substantial ancillary relief case.

1. Affidavit evidence should be confined to relevant facts and should not be proflix or diffuse. Each party should normally file one substantive affidavit dealing with the matters to which the court should have regard under s 25 of the Matrimonial Causes Act 1973, as substituted by s 3 of the Matrimonial and Family Proceedings Act 1984, and matters which are material to the application. If any further affidavit is necessary it should be confined to such matters as answering any serious allegation made by the other party, dealing with any serious issue raised or setting out any material change of circumstances.

2. Inquiries made under [FPR 1991, r 2.62] should, as far as possible, be contained in one comprehensive questionnaire and should not be made piecemeal at different times.

3. Wherever possible valuations of properties should be obtained from a valuer jointly instructed by both parties. Where each party instructs a valuer then reports should be exchanged and the valuers should meet in an attempt to resolve any differences between them or otherwise to narrow the issues.

4. While it may be necessary to obtain a broad assessment of the value of a shareholding in a private company it is inappropriate to undertake an expensive and meaningless exercise to achieve a precise valuation of a private company which will not be sold: see *P v P* [1989] 2 FLR 241.

5. All professional witnesses should be careful to avoid a partisan approach and should maintain proper professional standards.

6. Care should be taken in deciding what evidence, other than professional evidence, should be adduced and emotive issues which are not material to the case should be avoided. Where affidavit evidence is filed the deponents must be available for cross-examination on notice from the other side.

7. Solicitors on both sides should together prepare bundles of documents for use at the hearing and should reach agreement as to what should be included and what excluded: duplication of documents should always be avoided.

8. A chronology of material facts should be agreed and made available to the court.

9. In a substantial case it may be desirable to have a pre-trial review to explore the possibility of settlement and to define the issues and to ensure readiness for hearing if a settlement cannot be reached.

10. Solicitors and counsel should keep their clients informed of the costs at all stages of the proceedings and, where appropriate, should ensure that they understand the implications of the legal aid charge: the court will require an estimate of the approximate amount of the costs on each side before it can make a lump sum award: see [*Practice Direction (Ancillary Relief: costs estimates)*].

11. The desirability of reaching a settlement should be borne in mind throughout the proceedings. While it is necessary for the legal advisers to have sufficient knowledge of the financial situation of both parties before advising their client on a proposed settlement, the necessity to make further inquiries must always be balanced by a consideration of what they are realistically likely to achieve and the increased costs which are likely to be incurred by making them.



**[4.20]**

## 19 August 1991
## [1991] 3 All ER 896, [1991] 1 WLR 955

## Family Division

## *Legal aid—Statutory charge*

Regulation 90(3) of the Civil Legal Aid (General) Regulations 1989[1] directs that where, in proceedings under the Married Women's Property Act 1882, the Matrimonial Causes Act

1973, the Inheritance (Provision for Family and Dependants) Act 1975 [or Schedule 1 to the Children Act 1989] property is recovered or preserved for an assisted person, which by order of the court is to be used as a home or a sum of money is to be used to purchase a home for the assisted person or his dependants, the assisted person's solicitor shall inform the Area Director.

In such a case, by virtue of regulations 96 and 97, the Legal Aid Board may, subject to conditions, agree to defer enforcing the statutory charge on the property recovered or preserved imposed by s 16(6) of the Legal Aid Act 1988.

To avoid any doubt whether the order of the court must expressly state that the property is to be used as a home or to purchase a home, the Legal Aid Board has agreed that a certificate incorporated in the body of the order in the following form will be regarded as a sufficient compliance with the Regulations:

> 'And it is certified for the purpose of the Civil Legal Aid (General) Regulations 1989 [that the lump sum of £ x has been ordered to be paid to enable the Petitioner/ Respondent to purchase a home for himself/ herself (or his/her dependants)] [that the property (*address*) has been preserved/recovered for the Petitioner/Respondent for use as a home for himself/herself (or his/her dependants)]'.

Issued with the concurrence of the Lord Chancellor.

1 As amended.

**[4.21]**

## 22 November 1993
## [1994] 1 All ER 155, [1994] 1 WLR 16

## Family Division

# *Children Act 1989—Hearing before High Court judge—Time estimates*

1. As from the date of this direction, parties to proceedings under the Children Act 1989 or under the inherent jurisdiction of the High Court relating to children, which are pending in the High Court in London and in other centres and which are to be heard by a judge, will be required to provide an estimate of length of the hearing (a 'time estimate') in accordance with the procedure set out in the following paragraphs. This procedure is intended to enable the court and the parties to be kept fully informed of any changes in time estimates so as to facilitate the listing and disposal of cases in the most effective manner.

2. When any hearing which is expected to last *one day or more* is fixed, whether upon application or at a directions hearing or on any other occasion, the party applying for the hearing ('the applicant') and such other parties as may then be before the court, shall give a time estimate. Unless otherwise directed, this shall be in writing and shall be signed by the solicitor and by counsel, if instructed. A suitable form will be available from the court.

3. If any party to the proceedings is not before the court when the hearing is fixed, the applicant shall serve that party forthwith with a copy of the time estimate.

4. Any party served with a time estimate shall acknowledge receipt and shall inform the applicant and the court forthwith whether they agree or disagree with the estimate and, in the latter case, shall also give their own time estimate.

5. If, at any time after a time estimate has been given, any party considers that the time estimate should be revised, that party shall forthwith provide the court with a further time estimate and shall serve a copy on the other parties. It is the duty of solicitors to keep counsel informed of the time estimates given in the case and it is the duty of both solicitors and counsel to keep the length of the hearing under review and to inform the court promptly of any change in the time estimate.

6. In cases where a hearing has been fixed for *less than a day*, if any party considers that it is likely to last for one day or more, then a time estimate shall be given by that party to the court and served on the other parties. If an additional application or cross-application is issued returnable on the same date, a further time estimate will only be required if the latest time estimate is affected.

7. A party shall provide a time estimate if so required by the court.

8. If, in the light of the information provided, the court considers that further directions are necessary or if any of the parties fail to provide the requisite information, a directions hearing will be fixed and notice of the appointment given to all parties by the court. In the event of a party failing to provide information when requested or if default is otherwise made in the provision of time estimates, liability for any wasted costs may arise for consideration.

9. This direction does not apply to parties in person. Where the applicant is a party in person, the other parties to the proceedings, if represented by a solicitor, must provide a time estimate to the court immediately upon being notified of the hearing.

10. This direction is not to be read as affecting the right of any party to apply to the court for directions at any time in relation to the listing of any application or for any other purpose.

11. *Practice Direction (Family Division: Hearing Duration)*, [1984] 1 All ER 783, [1984] 1 WLR 475 dated 1 March 1984 shall continue to apply to proceedings other than proceedings under the Children Act 1989 or the inherent jurisdiction of the court relating to children.

12. Issued with the concurrence of the Lord Chancellor.

**[4.22]**

## 31 January 1995
## [1995] 1 All ER 586, [1995] 1 FLR 456

## Case Management

### *Greater court control over preparation for, and conduct of, hearings—Cost consequences of cases not being conducted economically*



#### DIRECTION

(1) The importance of reducing the cost and delay of civil litigation makes it necessary for the court to assert greater control over the preparation for and conduct of hearings than has hitherto been customary. Failure by practitioners to conduct cases economically will be visited by appropriate order for costs, including wasted costs orders.

(2) The court will accordingly exercise its discretion to limit:

(a) discovery;
(b) the length of opening and closing oral submissions;
(c) the time allowed for the examination and cross-examination of witnesses;
(d) the issues on which it wishes to be addressed;
(e) reading aloud from documents and authorities.

(3) Unless otherwise ordered, every witness statement or affidavit shall stand as the evidence-in-chief of the witness concerned. The substance of the evidence which a party intends to adduce at the hearing must be sufficiently detailed, but without prolixity; it must be confined to material matters of fact, not (except in the case of the evidence of professional witnesses) of opinion; and if hearsay evidence is to be adduced, the source of the information must be declared or good reason given for not doing so.

(4) It is a duty owed to the court both by the parties and by their legal representatives to give full and frank disclosure in ancillary relief applications and also in all matters in respect of children. The parties and their advisers must also use their best endeavours:

(a) to confine the issues and the evidence called to what is reasonably considered to be essential for the proper presentation of their case;
(b) to reduce or eliminate issues for expert evidence;
(c) in advance of the hearing to agree which are the issues or the main issues.

*(5) Unless the nature of the hearing makes it unnecessary and in the absence of specific directions, bundles should be agreed and prepared for use by the court, the parties and the witnesses and shall be in A4 format where possible, suitably secured. The bundles for use by the court shall be lodged with the court (the Clerk of the Rules in matters in the Royal Courts of Justice, London) at least two clear days before the hearing. Each bundle should be paginated, indexed, wholly legible, and arranged chronologically. Where documents are copied unnecessarily or bundled incompetently the cost will be disallowed*[1].

(6) In cases estimated to last for five days or more and in which no pre-trial review has been ordered, application should be made for a pre-trial review. It should, when practicable, be listed at least three weeks before the hearing and be conducted by the judge or district judge before whom the case is to be heard and should be attended by the advocates who are to represent the parties at the hearing. Whenever possible, all statements of evidence and all reports should be filed before the date of the review and in good time for them to have been considered by all parties.

(7) Whenever practicable and in any matter estimated to last five days or more, each party should, not less than two clear days before the hearing, lodge with the court, or the Clerk of the Rules in matters in the Royal Courts of Justice, in London, and deliver to other parties, a chronology and a skeleton argument concisely summarising that party's submissions in relation to each of the issues, and citing the main authorities relied upon. It is important that skeleton arguments should be brief.

*(8) In advance of the hearing upon request, and otherwise in the course of their opening, parties should be prepared to furnish the court, if there is no core bundle, with a list of documents essential for a proper understanding of the case.*

(9) The opening speech should be succinct. At its conclusion, other parties may be invited briefly to amplify their skeleton arguments. In a heavy case the court may in conjunction with final speeches require written submissions, including the findings of fact for which each party contends.

(10) This *Practice Direction* which follows the directions handed down by the Lord Chief Justice and the Vice-Chancellor to apply in the Queen's Bench and Chancery Divisions, shall apply to all family proceedings in the High Court and in all care centres, family hearing centres and divorce county courts.

(11) Issued with concurrence of the Lord Chancellor.

**Note:** Note that para (5) is replaced from 2 May 2000 by *President's Direction: Court Bundles* of 10 March 2000, which is set out below at para **[4.27]** below.
**Note:** Note that para (8) is replaced from 2 May 2000 by *President's Direction: Court Bundles* of 10 March 2000, which is set out below at para **[4.27]** below.

**[4.23]**

22 April 1998
[1998] 2 FCR 1

## Queen's Bench Division: Practice Statement (Supreme Court judgments)

## *Practice—Delivery of judgments in all divisions of High Court and in Court of Appeal*

### (1) Introduction

I am making this statement with the agreement of the Master of the Rolls, the Vice-Chancellor and the President of the Family Division. It applies to judgments delivered in all divisions of the High Court and the Court of Appeal.

In recent years a practice has developed for the written judgment of the court to be handed down without, as in the past, being read aloud. In this way much time is saved for the court, for practitioners and for litigants. The development of this practice, coupled with the increasing use of information technology, has, however, also led to the development of problems which have hindered the efficient administration of justice.

One of these problems is associated with the delays that have often been experienced before the approved judgment of the court can be made available from an official source. A second problem has arisen as a direct consequence of the first: because of these delays, there has been widespread dissemination of many unapproved judgments of the court, which often omit significant last minute changes to the text, sometimes without any clear warning about their unapproved status. A third problem has been that the judgments delivered in courts not staffed by official shorthand writers have lacked a common format, and inconsistent practices have developed in the way they are distributed. There is also a contemporary need for the courts to facilitate the speedy publication of their approved judgments by electronic means, including the Internet's Worldwide Web.

The Vice-Chancellor and Brooke LJ were invited to study these problems last autumn and to make recommendations as to how they might be resolved. Although they consulted quite widely, they are conscious that they have not consulted everyone who might have an interest in these matters. The arrangements I am announcing today should be regarded as experimental. Although they will take immediate effect, they will be kept under review, and if they meet with general approval they will be formalised in a practice direction in due course.

## (2) Availability of handed down judgments in advance of the hearing: new arrangements

Unless the court otherwise orders – for example, if a judgment contains price-sensitive information – copies of the written judgment will now be made available in these cases to the parties' legal advisers at about 4pm on the second working day before judgment is due to be pronounced on condition that the contents are not communicated to the parties themselves until one hour before the listed time for pronouncement of judgment. Delivery to legal advisers is made primarily to enable them to consider the judgment and decide what consequential orders they should seek. The condition is imposed to prevent the outcome of the case being publicly reported before judgment is given, since the judgment is confidential until then. Some judges may decide to allow the parties' legal advisers to communicate the contents of the judgment to their clients two hours before the listed time, in order that they may be able to submit minutes of the proposed order, agreed by their clients, to the judge before the judge comes into court, and it will be open to judges to permit more information about the result of a case to be communicated on a confidential basis to the client at an earlier stage if good reason is shown for making such a direction.

If, for any reason, a party's legal advisers have special grounds for seeking a relaxation of the usual condition restricting disclosure to the party itself, a request for relaxation of the condition may be made informally through the judge's clerk (or through the associate, if the judge has no clerk).

A copy of the written judgment will be made available to any party who is not legally represented at the same time as to legal advisers. It must be treated as confidential until judgment is given.

Every page of every judgment which is made available in this way will be marked 'Unapproved judgment: No permission is granted to copy or use in court'. These words will carry the authority of the judge, and will mean what they say.

The time at which copies of the judgment are being made available to the parties' legal advisers is being brought forward 24 hours in order to enable them to submit any written suggestions to the judge about typing errors, wrong references and other minor corrections of that kind in good time, so that, if the judge thinks fit, the judgment can be corrected before it is handed down formally in court. The parties' legal advisers are therefore being requested to submit a written list of corrections of this kind to the judge's clerk(or to the associate, if the judge has no clerk) by 3pm on the day before judgment is handed down. In divisions of the court which have two or more judges, the list should be submitted in each case to the judge who is to deliver the judgment in question. Lawyers are not being asked to carry out proofreading for the judiciary, but a significant cause of the present delays is the fact that minor corrections of this type are being mentioned to the judge for the first time in court, when there is no time to make any necessary corrections to the text.

## (3) Availability of approved versions of handed down judgments: new arrangements

This course will make it very much easier for the judge to make any necessary corrections and to hand down the judgment formally as the approved judgment of the court without any need for the delay involved in requiring the court shorthand writer, in courts which have an official shorthand writer, to resubmit the judgment to the judge for approval. It will always be open to the judge to direct the shorthand writer at the time of the hearing in court to include in the text of the judgment any last minute corrections which are mentioned for the first time in court, or which it has proved impractical to incorporate in the judgments handed down. In such an event the judge will make it clear whether the shorthand writer can publish the judgment, as corrected, as the approved judgment of the court without any further reference to the judge, or whether it should be resubmitted to the judge for approval. It will be open to judges, if they wish, to decline to approve their judgments at the time they are delivered, in which case the existing practice of submitting the judgment for their approval will continue.

## (4) Handing down judgment in court: availability of uncorrected copies

When the court hands down its written judgment, it will pronounce judgment in open court. Copies of the written judgment will then be made available to accredited representatives of the media, and to accredited law reporters who are willing to comply with the restrictions on copying, who identify themselves as such. In cases of particular interest to the media, it is helpful if requests for copies can be intimated to the judge's clerk, or the presiding lord justice's clerk, in advance of judgment, so that the likely demand for copies can be accurately estimated. Because there will usually be insufficient time for the judge's clerk to prepare the necessary number of copies of the corrected judgment in advance, in most cases these uncorrected copies will similarly bear the warning 'Unapproved Judgment: No permission is granted to copy or use in court'. The purpose of these arrangements is to place no barrier in the way of accredited representatives of the media who wish to report the judgments of the court immediately in the usual way, or to accredited law reporters who wish to prepare a summary or digest of the judgment or to read it for the purpose of deciding whether to obtain an approved version for reporting purposes. Its purpose is to put a stop to the dissemination of unapproved, uncorrected, judgments for other purposes, while seeking to ensure that everyone who is interested in the judgment (other than the immediate parties) may be able to buy a copy of the approved judgment in most cases much more quickly than is possible at present.

If any member of the public (other than a party to the case) or any law reporter who is not willing to comply with the restrictions on copying, wishes to read the written judgment of the court on the occasion when it is handed down, a copy will be made available for him or her to read and note in court on request made to the associate or to the clerk to the judge or the presiding lord justice. The copy must not be removed from the court and must be handed back after reading. The object is to ensure that such a person is in no worse a position than if the judgment had been read aloud in full.

## (5) Availability of approved judgments

In courts without an official shorthand writer, the approved judgment should contain on its frontispiece the rubric 'This is the official judgment of the court and I direct that no further note or transcript be made'. (This will cover the requirements of RSC Ord 68, r 1, in the cases to which that rule applies, and will provide for certainty in all other cases.) In future, all judgments delivered at the Royal Courts of Justice will be published in a common format.

For cases decided in the two divisions of the Court of Appeal and in the Crown Office List, copies of the approved judgment can be ordered from the official shorthand writers, on payment of the appropriate fee. In the other courts in the Royal Courts of Justice, copies of the approved judgment can be ordered from the Mechanical Recording Department, on payment of the fee prescribed for copy documents. Disks containing the judgment will also be available from the official shorthand writers, and the Mechanical Recording Department, where relevant, on payment of an appropriate charge. It is hoped that in most cases copies of the approved judgment will be available from these sources on the same day as the judgment is handed down: they should no longer be sought from judges' clerks.

## (6) Restrictions on disclosure or reporting

Anyone who is supplied with a copy of the handed down judgment, or who reads it in court, will be bound by any direction which the court may have given in a child case under s 39 of the Children and Young Persons Act 1933, or any other form of restriction on disclosure, or reporting, of information in the judgment.

## (7) Availability of approved versions of ex tempore judgments

Delays have also been experienced in the publication of approved versions of ex tempore judgments, whether they are produced by the official shorthand writers or by contractors transcribing the tapes which have been mechanically recorded.

Sometimes the delay is caused in courts without an official shorthand writer because a transcript is bespoken by one of the parties a long time after the judgment was delivered. If a transcribed copy of such a judgment is to be required, in connection with an appeal, for example, it should be ordered as soon as practicable after judgment was delivered.

Delays are also sometimes caused in these cases because judgments are delivered to a judge for approval without supplying the judge with copies of the material quoted in the judgment In future no judge should be invited to approve any such transcript unless the transcriber has been provided by the party ordering the transcript with copies of all the material from which the judge has quoted. If the transcript is ordered by a person who is not a party to the case (such as a law reporter), that person should make arrangements with one of the parties to ensure that the transcriber (and the judge) will have access to all the material quoted in the judgment.

From time to time delays are also caused because judges have been slow in returning approved transcripts to the transcribers. I and the other Heads of Division have recently asked judges, as a general rule, that they should endeavour to return approved transcripts to the transcribers within two weeks of their being delivered to them for approval. If anyone encounters serious delay on this account, the relevant Head of Division should be informed.

## (8) Citation of authorities in court

For citation of authorities in court, the practice set out in the *Practice Notes* [1995] 3 All ER 256, [1995] 1 WLR 1096 and [1996] 3 All ER 382, [1996] 1 WLR 854 on Citation of Authorities (Court of Appeal (Civil Division)) are now to be followed in all courts to which this practice statement applies. For convenience of reference, the relevant parts of these practice notes read:

'When authority is cited, whether in written or oral submissions, the following practice should in general be followed. If a case is reported in the official Law Reports published by the Incorporated Council of Law Reporting for England and Wales, that report should be cited. These are the most authoritative reports; they contain a summary of argument; and they are the most readily available. If a case is not (or not yet) reported in the official Law Reports, but is reported in the Weekly Law Reports or the All England Law Reports, that report should be cited. If a case is not reported in any of these series of reports, a report in any of the authoritative specialist series of reports may be cited. Such reports may not be readily available: photostat copies of the leading authorities or the relevant parts of such authorities should be annexed to written submissions; and it is helpful if photostat copies of the less frequently used series are made available in court. It is recognised that occasions arise when one report is fuller than another, or when there are discrepancies between reports. On such occasions, the practice outlined above need not be followed. It is always helpful if alternative references are given. Where a reserved written judgment has not been reported reference should be made to the official transcript (if this is available) and not to the handed down text of the judgment...Leave to cite unreported cases will not usually be granted unless counsel are able to assure the court that the transcript in question contains a relevant statement of legal principle not found in reported authority and that the authority is not cited because of the phraseology used or as an illustration of the application of an established legal principle.'

### (9) Conclusion

The purpose of these changes, which are being made on an experimental basis after full consultation with the Court Service, is to improve the quality of service rendered by the judges to those who use the courts. Any comments on these changes, or suggestions about further improvements in relation to the matters set out in this statement, should be addressed to Brooke LJ at the Royal Courts of Justice. They will be taken fully into account when the time comes to decide whether these arrangements should be formalised, with or without amendment, in a practice direction.

**[4.24]**

## 4 December 1998
## [1999] 1 FCR 1

## Official Solicitor

## *The Official Solicitor—Appointment in Family Proceedings*

1. This note supersedes the previous practice notes published at [1993] 2 FLR 641 and [1996] 1 FCR 78. Its purpose is to provide fresh guidance on the appointment of the Official Solicitor.

### APPOINTMENT AS GUARDIAN AD LITEM OF CHILD SUBJECT TO PROCEEDINGS

#### *Private law proceedings*

2. In non-specified (private law) proceedings under the Children Act 1989, and in proceedings under the inherent jurisdiction of the High Court, the Official Solicitor may act either in the High Court or in a county court (but not in a family proceedings court), under r 9.5 of the Family Proceedings Rules 1991, SI 1991/1247. It is only where, in accordance

with r 9.5, it appears to the court that the child ought to have party status and be separately represented that the question of the appointment of the Official Solicitor may arise.

3. In most private law cases a child's interests will be sufficiently safeguarded by a court welfare officer's report. Care should be taken to avoid duplication by the Official Solicitor of the inquiries already conducted by the welfare officer: *Re S (a minor) (care proceedings: reports)* [1992] 2 FCR 554. Reference to the Official Solicitor is likely to be warranted in cases where: (1) there is a significant foreign element such as a challenge to the English court's jurisdiction or a need for inquiries to be conducted abroad; (2) there is conflicting or controversial medical evidence, and the court considers that it would be appropriate to give leave for further medical evidence to be adduced; (3) there is a need for expert evidence which cannot be obtained by the parties jointly instructing an appropriate expert in accordance with *Re K (contact: psychiatric report)* [1996] 1 FCR 474 and *The Handbook of Best Practice in Children Act Cases 1997*, para 64 in the following circumstances: (a) a child is ignorant of the truth as to its parentage; (b) a psychiatric assessment is required in relation to a child who is refusing contact with a parent; (4) an application is made for leave to seek contact with an adopted child (the procedure is set out in *Re S (adopted child: contact)* [1993] 2 FCR 234); (5) the Official Solicitor is acting or is likely to be required to act for the child in other proceedings, for instance, proceedings arising from the death of a parent, or where there are children from different families who fall to be represented in linked proceedings, such as paedophile ring cases; (6) there are exceptionally difficult, unusual or sensitive issues; such cases will be likely to be High Court matters.

4. The Official Solicitor will almost invariably accept appointment in cases where judicial guidance has been given about his appointment, that is to say: (1) where a child wants to instruct a solicitor direct but the court does not consider he is competent (see *Re T (a minor) (independent representation)* [1993] 2 FCR 445, [1994] Fam 49 – see also para 8 below). If a child has been granted leave pursuant to the Family Proceedings Rules 1991, r 9.2A to instruct a solicitor but the court needs the assistance of the Official Solicitor as guardian ad litem then he will normally be prepared to act (r 9.2A(6A)); (2) in 'special category' medical treatment cases, such as sterilisation and vegetative state cases, and cases involving children actually or potentially refusing medical treatment. Applications in such cases should be made under the inherent jurisdiction of the High Court.

## *Public law proceedings*

5. The Official Solicitor may only be appointed in the High Court, an in accordance with a Direction of the Lord Chancellor dated 7 October 1991 and reported at [1991] 2 FLR 471, where the court considers that the circumstances are that: (1) the child does not have a guardian ad litem in the proceedings; and (2) there are exceptional circumstances which make it desirable in the interests of the welfare of the child concerned that the Official Solicitor, rather than a panel guardian should be appointed, having regard to– (a) any foreign element in the case which is likely to require inquiries, or other action, to be pursued outside England and Wales; (b) the burden of having to represent several children; (c) other High Court proceedings in which the Official Solicitor is representing the child; (d) any other circumstances which the court considers relevant.

6. The Official Solicitor, in accordance with the direction, may also give informal advice and other assistance as he considers appropriate to any guardian ad litem in specified proceedings in the High Court. The court will be very slow to remove a panel guardian ad litem already substantially involved in the case. It is open to the court to retain the panel guardian and invite the Official Solicitor to act as amicus curiae to conduct particular legal inquiries or carry out other duties which the panel guardian and solicitor cannot be expected to undertake.

## *Adoption*

7. Provision for the appointment of the Official Solicitor as the child's guardian ad litem in adoption and freeing for adoption proceedings in the High Court is to be found at rr 6(4)

and 18(4) of the Adoption Rules 1984, SI 1984/265. As a general rule, the Official Solicitor can be expected to accept the appointment as the child's guardian ad litem in contested applications under the Adoption Act 1976, although where the adoption or freeing proceedings follow on from former public law proceedings, the likelihood is that the child's former guardian ad litem will be a more appropriate candidate. With certain exceptions, which are noted in the *Practice Direction* dated 25 June 1986 ([1986] 2 All ER 832, [1986] 1 WLR 933), the Official Solicitor is unlikely to accept appointment as the child's guardian ad litem in adoption or freeing for adoption applications which are expected to proceed with the agreement of the birth parent.

## APPOINTMENT AS NEXT FRIEND AND FOR CHILD NOT SUBJECT OF PROCEEDINGS

8. Subject to his being satisfied that the proposed proceedings would benefit the child, the Official Solicitor may also act as next friend of a child seeking leave to make an application (typically for sibling contact) under s 10(8) of the Children Act 1989. The Official Solicitor may also accept appointment under r 9.2(1) in respect of any minor who is a party to family proceedings, such as a minor mother of a child who is the subject of the proceedings. Minor parents, as well as children who are the subject of the proceedings, may invoke r 9.2A if they wish to instruct a solicitor directly.

## APPOINTMENT AS GUARDIAN AD LITEM OF AN ADULT PARTY UNDER DISABILITY

9. In the absence of any other suitable and willing person, the Official Solicitor is available to be appointed, in the High Court or in a county court pursuant to Family Proceedings Rules 1991, r 9.2(1) as the guardian ad litem or next friend of an adult party to family proceedings who is a patient. The term 'patient' means someone who is incapable by reason of mental disorder within the meaning of s 1 of the Mental Health Act 1983 of managing and administering his property and affairs. Medical evidence will usually be required before the Official Solicitor can act and his staff can provide a standard form of medical certificate. Where there are practical difficulties in obtaining such medical evidence, the Official Solicitor should be consulted.

## TERMS OF APPOINTMENT

10. Orders appointing the Official Solicitor should be expressed as being made subject to his consent. Save in the most urgent of cases, a substantive hearing date less than three months ahead should not be fixed without consulting his office. It is often helpful to discuss the question of appointment with the Official Solicitor or one of his staff by telephoning: 020 7911 7127.

11. The following documents should be forwarded to the Official Solicitor without delay: (1) a copy of the order appointing him (subject to his consent and a note of the reasons approved by the judge); (2) the court file; (3) wherever practicable, a chronology and a statement of issues.

**THE OFFICIAL SOLICITOR CANNOT DECIDE WHETHER TO ACCEPT APPOINTMENT UNTIL HE HAS RECEIVED THESE DOCUMENTS.**

The Official Solicitor's address is:

81 Chancery Lane,
London,
WC2A 1DD
DX 0012 London/Chancery Lane
Fax: 020 7911 7105

**[4.25]**

## 12 January 1999
## [1999] 1 FCR 481

## Family Division

### *Names of deceased—death certificates*

In order to facilitate the operation of standing searches and caveats and to ensure the accuracy of probate records, it is directed that in all instances where the deceased died in the United Kingdom and the death has been recorded in the Register of Deaths: (a) the name and dates of birth and death of the deceased as recorded in the register shall be included in the oath lodged in support of an application made through a solicitor or probate practitioner for a grant of representation; (b) the name and date of death of the deceased as recorded in the register shall be included in the notice lodged for a standing search or caveat; and (c) in any case where the name of the deceased or by which the deceased was known differs from that recorded in the register, that name shall also be included in the oath or the notice, as the case may be.

**[4.26]**

## 22 April 1999
## [1999] 2 FCR 1

## Family Division

### *Civil Procedure Rules 1998—Allocation of cases—Costs*

It is directed that upon the coming into force on 26 April 1999 of the Civil Procedure Rules 1998, SI 1998/3132 (the 1998 Rules) and the Family Proceedings (Miscellaneous Amendments) Rules 1999, SI 1999/1012:

(a) Paragraph 3.2 of the (Civil Procedure) Practice Direction 'Allocation of Cases to Levels of Judiciary' shall apply to the Family Division. District Judges (including District Judges of the Principal Registry) shall have jurisdiction to hear and dispose of proceedings under the Inheritance (Provision for Family and Dependants) Act 1975 and under s 14 of the Trusts of Land and Appointment of Trustees Act 1996.

(b) The (Civil Procedure) Practice Direction about Costs 'Supplementing Parts 43 to 48 of the Civil Procedure Rules' (the costs direction) shall apply to family proceedings to which the Family Proceedings Rules 1991, SI 1991/1247 apply and to proceedings in the Family Division. References in the costs direction to 'claimant' and 'defendant' are to be read as references to the equivalent terms used in family proceedings and other terms and expressions used in the costs direction shall be similarly treated. References to procedural steps and other parts of the 1998 Rules which have not yet been applied to family proceedings are to be read as referring to equivalent or similar procedures under the rules applicable to family proceedings, as the context may permit. The previous practice in relation to 'costs reserved' will no longer be followed and such an order will have the effect specified in the costs direction. It should also be noted that the period for commencing detailed assessment proceedings will be as specified in Pt 47.7 (three months) in substitution for the period of six months previously applicable.

Issued with the approval and concurrence of the Lord Chancellor.

[4.27]

10 March 2000
[2000] 1 FCR 521, [2000] 2 All ER 287

Family Division

## ***President's Direction—Court Bundles***

1. The following practice applies to all hearings in family proceedings in the High Court, to all hearings of family proceedings in the Royal Courts of Justice and to hearings with a time estimate of ½ day or more in all care centres, family hearing centres and divorce county courts (including the Principal Registry of the Family Division when so treated), except as specified in paragraph 2.3 below, and subject to specific directions given in any particular case. 'Hearing' extends to all hearings before judges and district judges and includes the hearing of any application.

2.1. A bundle for the use of the court at the hearing shall be provided by the party in the position of applicant at the hearing or by any other party who agrees to do so. It shall contain copies of all documents relevant to the hearing in chronological order, paginated and indexed and divided into separate sections, as follows: (a) applications and orders; (b) statements and affidavits; (c) experts' reports and other reports including those of a guardian ad litem, and (d) other documents, divided into further sections as may be appropriate.

2.2. Where the nature of the hearing is such that a complete bundle of all documents is unnecessary, the bundle may comprise only those documents necessary for the hearing but the summary (paragraph 3.1(a) below) must commence with a statement that the bundle is limited or incomplete. The summary should be limited to those matters which the court needs to know for the purpose of the hearing and for management of the case.

2.3. The requirement to provide a bundle shall not apply to the hearing of any urgent application where the circumstances are such that it is not reasonably practicable for a bundle to be provided.

3.1. At the commencement of the bundle there shall be:

(a) A summary of the background to the hearing limited, if practicable, to one A4 page;
(b) A statement of the issue or issues to be determined;
(c) A summary of the order or directions sought by each party;
(d) A chronology if it is a final hearing or if the summary under (a) is insufficient;
(e) Skeleton arguments as may be appropriate, with copies of all authorities relied on.

3.2. If possible the bundle shall be agreed. In all cases, the party preparing the bundle shall paginate it and provide an index to all other parties prior to the hearing.

3.3. The bundle should normally be contained in a ring binder or lever arch file (limited to 350 pages in each file). Where there is more than one bundle, each should be clearly distinguishable. Bundles shall be lodged, if practicable, 2 clear days prior to the hearing. For hearings in the Royal Courts of Justice bundles shall be lodged with the Clerk of the Rules. All bundles shall have clearly marked on the outside, the title and number of the case, the hearing date and time and, if known, the name of the Judge hearing the case.

4. After each hearing which is not a final hearing, the party responsible for the bundle shall retrieve it from the court. The bundle with any additional documents shall be re-lodged for further hearings in accordance with the above provisions.

5. This direction replaces paragraphs 5 and 8 of the direction 'Case Management' dated 31 January 1995 and shall have effect from the 2 May 2000.

6. Issued with the approval and concurrence of the Lord Chancellor.

**[4.28]**

## 25 May 2000
## [2000] 2 FCR 216, [2000] 1 FLR 997

## Family Division

# *Ancillary relief procedure—Pre-application protocol—Financial dispute resolution appointment*

### (1) Introduction

1.1 The Family Proceedings (Amendment No 2) Rules 1999 (SI 1999/3491) make important amendments to the Family Proceedings Rules 1991 (SI 1991/1247) ('FPR 1991'), as from 5 June 2000. The existing 'pilot scheme' rules in relation to ancillary relief which have applied since 1996 but only in specified courts will become, with significant revisions, of general application. In the same way as the pilot scheme, the new procedure is intended to reduce delay, facilitate settlements, limit costs incurred by parties and provide the court with greater and more effective control over the conduct of the proceedings.

### (2) 'Pre-application protocol'

2.1 The 'Pre-application protocol' annexed to this Direction outlines the steps parties should take to seek and provide information from and to each other prior to the commencement of any ancillary relief application. The court will expect the parties to comply with the terms of the protocol.

### (3) Financial dispute resolution ('FDR') appointment

3.1 A key element in the new procedure is the Financial Dispute Resolution ('FDR') appointment. Rule 2.61E provides that the FDR appointment is to be treated as a meeting held for the purposes of discussion and negotiation. Such meetings which were previously described as meetings held for the purposes of conciliation have been developed as a means of reducing the tension which inevitably arises in matrimonial and family disputes and facilitating settlement of those disputes.

3.2 In order for the FDR appointment to be effective, parties must approach the occasion openly and without reserve. Non-disclosure of the content of such meetings is accordingly vital and is an essential prerequisite for fruitful discussion directed to the settlement of the dispute between the parties. The FDR appointment is an important part of the settlement process. As a consequence of *Re D (Minors) (Conciliation: Disclosure of Information)* [1993] 1 FCR 877, [1993] Fam 231, sub nom *Re D (Minors) (Conciliation: Privilege)* [1993] 1 FLR 932, evidence of anything said or of any admission made in the course of an FDR appointment will not be admissible in evidence, except at the trial of a person for an offence committed at the appointment or in the very exceptional circumstances indicated in *Re D*.

3.3 Courts will therefore expect:

- parties to make offers and proposals;
- recipients of offers and proposals to give them proper consideration;
- that parties, whether separately or together, will not seek to exclude from consideration at the appointment any such offer or proposal.

3.4 In order to make the most effective use of the first appointment and the FDR appointment, the legal representatives attending those appointments will be expected to have full knowledge of the case.

## (4) Single joint expert

4.1 The introduction of expert evidence in proceedings is likely to increase costs substantially and consequently the court will use its powers to restrict the unnecessary use of experts. Accordingly, where expert evidence is sought to be relied upon, parties should if possible agree upon a single expert whom they can jointly instruct. Where parties are unable to agree upon the expert to be instructed, the court will consider using its powers under Pt 35 of the Civil Procedure Rules 1998 (SI 1998/3132) to direct that evidence be given by one expert only. In such cases parties must be in a position at the first appointment or when the matter comes to be considered by the court to provide the court with a list of suitable experts or to make submissions as to the method by which the expert is to be selected.

5 This Direction shall have effect as from 5 June 2000 and replaces *Practice Direction: Ancillary Relief Procedure: Pilot Scheme* (16 June 1997) [1997] 2 FLR 304.

6 Issued with the approval and concurrence of the Lord Chancellor.

# PRE-APPLICATION PROTOCOL

## (1) Introduction

1.1

1.1.1 Lord Woolf in his final *Access to Justice* Report of July 1996 recommended the development of pre-application protocols:

> 'to build on and increase the benefits of early but well informed settlement which genuinely satisfy both parties to dispute'.

1.1.2 Subsequently, in April 2000 the Lord Chancellor's Ancillary Relief Advisory Committee agreed this Pre-application protocol.

1.2 The aim of the pre-application protocol is to ensure that:

- (a) pre-application disclosure and negotiation takes place in appropriate cases;
- (b) where there is pre-application disclosure and negotiation, it is dealt with:
  - (i) cost-effectively;
  - (ii) in line with the overriding objectives of the Family Proceedings (Amendment) Rules 1999;
- (c) the parties are in a position to settle the case fairly and early without litigation.

1.3 The court will be able to treat the standard set in the pre-application protocol as the normal reasonable approach to pre-application conduct. If proceedings are subsequently issued, the court will be entitled to decide whether there has been non-compliance with the protocol and, if so, whether non-compliance merits consequences.

## (2) Notes of guidance

### *Scope of the protocol*

2.1 This protocol is intended to apply to all claims for ancillary relief as defined by FPR 1991, r 1(2). It is designed to cover all classes of case, ranging from a simple application for periodical payments to an application for a substantial lump sum and property adjustment order. The protocol is designed to facilitate the operation of what was called the pilot scheme and is from 5 June 2000 the standard procedure for ancillary relief applications.

2.2 In considering the option of pre-application disclosure and negotiation, solicitors should bear in mind the advantage of having a court timetable and court-managed process. There is sometimes an advantage in preparing disclosure before proceedings are commenced. However, solicitors should bear in mind the objective of controlling costs and in particular the costs of discovery and that the option of pre-application disclosure and negotiation has risks of excessive and uncontrolled expenditure and delay. This option should only be encouraged where both parties agree to follow this route and disclosure is not likely to be an issue or has been adequately dealt with in mediation or otherwise.

2.3 Solicitors should consider at an early stage and keep under review whether it would be appropriate to suggest mediation to the clients as an alternative to solicitor negotiation or court-based litigation.

2.4 Making an application to the court should not be regarded as a hostile step or a last resort, rather as a way of starting the court timetable, controlling disclosure and endeavouring to avoid the costly final hearing and the preparation for it.

### *First letter*

2.5 The circumstances of parties to an application for ancillary relief are so various that it would be difficult to prepare a specimen first letter. The request for information will be different in every case. However, the tone of the initial letter is important and the guidelines in para 3.7 should be followed. It should be approved in advance by the client. Solicitors writing to an unrepresented party should always recommend that he seeks independent legal advice and enclose a second copy of the letter to be passed to any solicitor instructed. A reasonable time-limit for a response may be 14 days.

### *Negotiation and settlement*

2.6 In the event of pre-application disclosure and negotiation, as envisaged in para 2.2 an application should not be issued when a settlement is a reasonable prospect.

### *Disclosure*

2.7 The protocol underlines the obligation of parties to make full and frank disclosure of all material facts, documents and other information relevant to the issues. Solicitors owe their clients a duty to tell them in clear terms of this duty and of the possible consequences of breach of the duty. This duty of disclosure is an ongoing obligation and includes the duty to disclose any material changes after initial disclosure has been given. Solicitors are referred to the *Good Practice Guide for Disclosure* produced by the Solicitors Family Law Association (obtainable from the Administrative Director, 366A Crofton Road, Orpington, Kent BR2 8NN).



## (3) The protocol

### *General principles*

3.1 All parties must always bear in mind the overriding objective set out at FPR 1991, r 2.51B and try to ensure that all claims should be resolved and a just outcome achieved as speedily as possible without costs being unreasonably incurred. The needs of any children should be addressed and safeguarded. The procedures which it is appropriate to follow should be conducted with minimum distress to the parties and in a manner designed to promote as good a continuing relationship between the parties and any children affected as is possible in the circumstances.

3.2 The principle of proportionality must be borne in mind at all times. It is unacceptable for the costs of any case to be disproportionate to the financial value of the subject matter of the dispute.

3.3 Parties should be informed that where a court exercises a discretion as to whether costs are payable by one party to another, this discretion extends to pre-application offers to settle and conduct of disclosure (r 44.3, para 1 of the Civil Procedure Rules 1998).

### *Identifying the issues*

3.4 Parties must seek to clarify their claims and identify the issues between them as soon as possible. So that this can be achieved they must provide full, frank and clear disclosure of facts, information and documents which are material and sufficiently accurate to enable proper negotiations to take place to settle their differences. Openness in all dealings is essential.

### *Disclosure*

3.5 If parties carry out voluntary disclosure before the issue of proceedings the parties should exchange schedules of assets, income, liabilities and other material facts, using Form E as a guide to the format of the disclosure. Documents should only be disclosed to the extent that they are required by Form E. Excessive or disproportionate costs should not be incurred.

### *Correspondence*

3.6 Any first letter and subsequent correspondence must focus on the clarification of claims and identification of issues and their resolution. Protracted and unnecessary correspondence and 'trial by correspondence' must be avoided.

3.7 The impact of any correspondence upon the reader and in particular the parties must always be considered. Any correspondence which raises irrelevant issues or which might cause the other party to adopt an entrenched, polarised or hostile position is to be discouraged.

### *Experts*

3.8 Expert valuation evidence is only necessary where the parties cannot agree or do not know the value of some significant asset. The cost of a valuation should be proportionate to the sums in dispute. Wherever possible, valuations of properties, shares, etc should be obtained from a single valuer instructed by both parties. To that end, a party wishing to instruct an expert (the first party) should first give the other party a list of the names of one or more experts in the relevant speciality whom he considers are suitable to instruct. Within 14 days the other party may indicate an objection to one or more of the named experts and, if so, should supply the names of one or more experts whom he considers suitable.

3.9 Where the identity of the expert is agreed, the parties should agree the terms of a joint letter of instructions.

3.10 Where no agreement is reached as to the identity of the expert, each party should think carefully before instructing his own expert because of the costs implications. Disagreements about disclosure such as the use and identity of an expert may be better managed by the court within the context of an application for ancillary relief.

3.11 Whether a joint report is commissioned or the parties have chosen to instruct separate experts, it is important that the expert is prepared to answer reasonable questions raised by either party.

3.12 When experts' reports are commissioned pre-application, it should be made clear to the expert that they may in due course be reporting to the court and that they should therefore consider themselves bound by the guidance as to expert witnesses in Part 35 of the Civil Procedure Rules 1998.

3.13 Where the parties propose to instruct a joint expert, there is a duty on both parties to disclose whether they have already consulted that expert about the assets in issue.

3.14 If the parties agree to instruct separate experts the parties should be encouraged to agree in advance that the reports will be disclosed.

### *Summary*

3.15 The aim of all pre-application proceedings steps must be to assist the parties to resolve their differences speedily and fairly or at least narrow the issues and, should that not be possible, to assist the court to do so.

## [4.29]

## 24 July 2000
## [2000] 2 FCR 767, [2000] 2 FLR 428

## Family Division

## *Costs—Civil Procedure Rules 1998*

The *President's Direction: Civil Procedure Rules 1998: Allocation of Cases: Costs* (22 April 1999) [1999] 2 FCR 1 applied the (Civil Procedure) *Practice Direction* about Costs *Supplementing Parts 43 to 48 of the Civil Procedure Rules* ('the costs direction') to family proceedings (within the Family Proceedings Rules 1991 (SI 1991/1247)) and to proceedings in the Family Division. A further edition of the costs direction (effective from 3 July 2000) has been published and it is hereby directed that the further edition (and all subsequent editions as and when they are published and come into effect) shall extend to family proceedings and to proceedings in the Family Division in the same way as did the costs direction and to the extent applicable to such proceedings.

The further edition of the costs direction includes provisions applicable to proceedings following changes in the manner in which legal services are funded pursuant to the Access to Justice Act 1999. It should be noted that although the cost of the premium in respect of legal costs insurance (s 29) or the cost of funding by a prescribed membership organisation (s 30) may be recoverable, family proceedings (within s 58A(2) of the Courts and Legal Services Act 1990) cannot be the subject of an enforceable conditional fee agreement.

Issued with the approval of the Lord Chancellor.

## [4.30]

## 24 July 2000
## [2000] 2 FCR 768, [2000] 2 FLR 429

## Family Division

## *Human Rights Act 1998: citation of authorities*



1 It is directed that the following practice shall apply as from 2 October 2000 in all family proceedings:

### Citation of authorities

2 When an authority referred to in s 2 of the Human Rights Act 1998 ('the Act') is to be cited at a hearing:

(a) the authority to be cited shall be an authoritative and complete report;
(b) the court must be provided with a list of authorities it is intended to cite and copies of the reports:
  (i) in cases to which *Practice Direction (family proceedings: court bundles)* [2000] 1 FCR 521, [2000] 2 All ER 287 dated 10 March 2000 applies, as part of the bundle;
  (ii) otherwise, not less than two clear days before the hearing; and

(c) copies of the complete original texts issued by the European Court and Commission, either paper based or from the Court's judgment database (HUDOC) which is available on the internet, may be used.

## Allocation to judges

3(1) The hearing and determination of the following will be confined to a High Court judge:

(a) a claim for a declaration of incompatibility under s 4 of the Act; or

(b) an issue which may lead to the court considering making such a declaration.

3(2) The hearing and determination of a claim made under the Act in respect of a judicial act shall be confined in the High Court to a High Court judge and in county courts to a circuit judge.

Issued with the concurrence and approval of the Lord Chancellor.

**[4.31]**

## 11 January 2001
## [2001] 1 FCR 286

## Court of Appeal

## *Practice—Preparation of judgments—Numbering of approved judgments—Paragraph numbering—Neutral citation*

LORD WOOLF CJ gave the following direction at the sitting of the court.

This practice direction is made with the concurrence of the Master of the Rolls, the Vice-Chancellor and the President of the Family Division. It represents the next stage in the process of modernising the arrangements for the preparation, distribution and citation of judgments given in every division of the High Court, whether in London or in courts outside London.

## Form of judgments

1.1 With effect from 11 January 2001, all judgments in every division of the High Court and the Court of Appeal will be prepared for delivery, or issued as approved judgments, with single spacing, paragraph numbering (in the margins) but no page numbers. In courts with more than one judge, the paragraph numbering will continue sequentially through each judgment, and will not start again at the beginning of the second judgment. Indented paragraphs will not be given a number.

1.2 The main reason for these changes is to facilitate the publication of judgments on the World Wide Web and their subsequent use by the increasing numbers of those who have access to the Web. The changes should also assist those who use and wish to search judgments stored on electronic databases.

1.3 It is desirable in the interests of consistency that all judgments prepared for delivery, (or issued as approved judgments) in county courts, should also contain paragraph numbering (in the margins).

## Neutral citation of judgments

2.1 With effect from 11 January 2001 a form of neutral citation will be introduced in both divisions of the Court of Appeal and in the Administrative Court. A unique number will be given by the official shorthand writers to each approved judgment issued out of these courts. The judgments will be numbered in the following way:

| | |
|---|---|
| Court of Appeal (Civil Division) | [2000] EWCA Civ 1, 2, 3 etc |
| Court of Appeal (Criminal Division) | [2000] EWCA Crim 1, 2, 3 etc |
| High Court (Administrative Court) | [2000] EWHC Admin 1, 2, 3 etc |

2.2 Under these new arrangements, para 59 in *Smith v Jones*, the tenth numbered judgment of the year in the Civil Division of the Court of Appeal, would b cited: *Smith v Jones* [2001] EWCA Civ 10 at [59].

2.3 The neutral citation will be the official number attributed to the judgment by the court and must always be used on at least one occasion when the judgment is cited in a later judgment. Once the judgment is reported, the neutral citation will appear in front of the familiar citation from the law report series. Thus: *Smith v Jones* [2001] EWCA Civ 10 at [30], [2001] QB 124, [2001] 2 All ER 364, etc. The paragraph number must be the number allotted by the court in all future versions of the judgment.

2.4 If a judgment is cited on more than one occasion in a later judgment, it will be of the greatest assistance if only one abbreviation (if desired) is used. Thus *Smith v Jones* [2001] EWCA Civ 10 could be abbreviated on subsequent occasions to *Smith v Jones*, or *Smith*'s case, but preferably not both (in the same judgment).

2.5 If it is desired to cite more than one paragraph of a judgment each numbered paragraph should be enclosed with a square bracket. Thus: *Smith v Jones* [2001] EWCA Civ 10 at [30]–[35], or *Smith v Jones* [2001] EWCA Civ 10 at [30], [35], and [40]–[43].

2.6 The neutral citation arrangements will be extended to include other parts of the High Court as soon as the necessary administrative arrangements can be made.

2.7 The Administrative Court citation will be given to all judgments in the Administrative Court, whether they are delivered by a Divisional Court or by a single judge.

## Citation of judgments in court

3.1 For the avoidance of doubt, it should be emphasised that both the High Court and the Court of Appeal require that where a case has been reported in the official law reports published by the Incorporated Council of Law Reporting for England and Wales it must be cited from that source. Other series of reports may only be used when a case is not reported in the law reports.

3.2 It will in future be permissible to cite a judgment reported in a series of reports, including those of the Incorporated Council of Law Reporting, by means of a copy of a reproduction of the judgment in electronic form that has been authorised by the publisher of the relevant series, provided that (1) the report is presented to the court in an easily legible form (a 12-point font is preferred but a 10 or 11-point font is acceptable) and (2) the advocate presenting the report is satisfied that it has not been reproduced in a garbled form from the data source. In any case of doubt the court will rely on the printed text of the report (unless the editor of the report has certified that an electronic version is more accurate because it corrects an error contained in an earlier printed text of the report).



## Concluding comments

4.1 The changes described in this Practice Direction follow what is becoming accepted international practice. They are intended to make it easier to distribute, store and search judgments, and less expensive and time-consuming to reproduce them for use in court. Brooke LJ is still responsible for advising the Judges' Council on these matters, and any comments on these new arrangements, or suggestions about ways in which they could be improved still further, should be addressed to him at the Royal Courts of Justice, WC2A 2LL.

Kate O'Hanlon
Barrister

**[4.32]**

## 16 March 2001
## [2001] 1 FLR 949

## Family Division

## *Practice—Committal applications—Proceedings in which committal order might be made*

1. As for the date of this direction, the Civil Procedure Practice Direction supplemental to RSC Order 52 (Sch 1 to the CPR) and CCR Ord 29 (Sch 2 to the CPR) [set out at para **[4.39]** below], ('The CPR Direction') shall apply to all applications in family proceedings for an order of committal in the same manner and to the same extent as it applies to proceedings governed by the Civil Procedure Rules ('the CPR') but subject to: (a) the provisions of the Family Proceedings Rules 1991 (SI 1991/1247) ('the FPR') and the rules applied by those rules namely, the Rules of the Supreme Court (RSC) and the County Court Rules (CCR) in force immediately before 26 April 1999, and (b) the appropriate modifications consequent upon the limited application of the CPR to family proceedings.

1.1 In particular, the following modifications apply: (a) where the alleged contempt is in connection with existing proceedings (other than contempt in the face of the court) or with an order made or an undertaking given in existing proceedings, the committal application shall be made in those proceedings; (b) as required by FPR r 7.2, committal applications in the High Court are to be made by summons. In county court proceedings applications are to be made in the manner prescribed by CCR Ord 29. References in the CPR direction to 'claim form' and 'application notice' are to be read accordingly; (c) In instances where the CPR direction requires more information to be provided than is required to be provided under the RSC and the CCR, the court will expect the former to be observed; (d) Having regard to the periods specified in RSC Ord 52, r 3, Ord 32, r 3(2)(a) and CCR Ord 13, r 1(2), the time specified in para 4.2 of the CPR direction shall not apply. Nevertheless, the court will ensure that adequate time is afforded to the respondent for the preparation of his defence; (e) Paragraph 9 of the CPR direction is to be read with para 3 of each of the directions issued on 17 December 1997, entitled 'Children Act 1989—Exclusion requirement' and 'Family Law Act 1996—Pt IV'.

2. In any family proceedings (not falling within 1 above), in which a committal order may be made, including proceedings for the enforcement of an existing order by way of judgment summons or other process, full effect will be given to the Human Rights Act 1998 and to the rights afforded under that Act. In particular, Art 6 of the Convention (as set out in Sch 1 to the Human Rights Act 1998) is fully applicable to such proceedings. Those involved must ensure that in the conduct of the proceedings there is due observance of the Human Rights Act 1998 in the same manner as if the proceedings fell within the CPR direction.

3. As with all family proceedings, the CPR costs provisions apply to all committal proceedings.

4. Issued with the approval and concurrence of the Lord Chancellor.

Dame Elizabeth Butler-Sloss
President

**[4.33]**

## 2 April 2001
## [2001] 2 FCR 566

## Official Solicitor

## *Practice directions and notes—Official Solicitor—Appointment as guardian ad litem—Appointment as next friend—Terms of appointment*

**[1]** This Practice Note supersedes the Practice Note dated 4 December 1998 issued by the Official Solicitor in relation to his appointment in family proceedings (see *Practice Note (The Official Solicitor: appointment in family proceedings)* [1999] 1 FCR 1, [1999] 1 FLR 310). It is issued in conjunction with a Practice Note dealing with the appointment of Officers of CAFCASS Legal Services and Special Casework in family proceedings (see *CAFCASS Practice Note (officers of CAFCASS legal services and special casework: appointment in family proceedings)* [2001] 2 FCR 562, [2001] 2 FLR 151. This Practice Note is intended to be helpful guidance, but always subject to Practice Directions, decisions of the court and other legal guidance.

**[2]** The Children and Family Court Advisory and Support Service (CAFCASS) has responsibilities in relation to children in family proceedings in which their welfare is or may be in question (Criminal Justice and Court Services Act 2000, s 12). From 1 April 2001 the Official Solicitor will no longer represent children who are the subject of family proceedings (other than in very exceptional circumstances and after liaison with CAFCASS).

**[3]** This Practice Note summarises the continuing role of the Official Solicitor in family proceedings. Since there are no provisions for parties under disability in the Family Proceedings Courts (Children Act 1989) Rules 1991, the Official Solicitor can only act in the High Court or in a county court, pursuant to Pt IX of Family Proceedings Rules 1991. The Official Solicitor will shortly issue an updated Practice Note about his role for adults under disability who are the subject of declaratory proceedings in relation to their medical treatment or welfare.



### Adults under disability

**[4]** The Official Solicitor will, in the absence of any other willing and suitable person, act as next friend or guardian ad litem of an adult party under disability, a 'patient'. 'Patient' means someone who is incapable by reason of mental disorder of managing and administering his property and affairs (Family Proceedings Rules 1991, r 9.1). Medical evidence will usually be required before the Official Solicitor can consent to act and his staff can provide a standard form of medical certificate. Where there are practical difficulties in obtaining such medical evidence, the Official Solicitor should be consulted.

### Non-subject children

**[5]** Again in the absence of any other willing and suitable person, the Official Solicitor will act as next friend or guardian ad litem of a child party whose own welfare is not the subject of family proceedings (Family Proceedings Rules 1991, r 2.57, r 9.2 and r 9.5). The most common examples will be: (a) a child who is also the parent of a child, and who is a respondent to a Children Act or Adoption Act application. If a child respondent is already represented by a CAFCASS officer in pending proceedings of which he or she is the subject, then the Official Solicitor will liaise with CAFCASS to agree the most appropriate arrangements; (b) a child who wishes to make an application for a Children Act order naming another child (typically a contact order naming a sibling). The Official Solicitor will need to satisfy himself that the proposed proceedings would benefit the child applicant before proceeding; (c) a child witness to some disputed factual issue in a children case and who may require intervener status. In such circumstances the need for party status and legal representation should be weighed in the light of *Re H (care proceedings: intervener)* [2000] 2 FCR 53, [2000] 1 FLR 775; (d) a child party to a petition for a declaration of status under Pt III of the Family Law Act 1986; (e) a child intervener in divorce or ancillary relief proceedings (r 2.57 or r 9.5); (f) a child applicant for, or respondent to, an application for an order under Pt IV of the Family Law Act 1996. In the case of a child applicant, the Official Solicitor will need to satisfy himself that the proposed proceedings would benefit the child before pursuing them, with leave under Family Law Act 1996, s 43 if required.

**[6]** Any children who are parties to Children Act or inherent jurisdiction proceedings may rely on the provisions of Family Proceedings Rules 1991, r 9.2A if they wish to instruct a solicitor without the intervention of a next friend or guardian ad litem. Rule 9.2A does not apply to Adoption Act 1976, Family Law Act 1996 or Matrimonial Causes Act 1973 proceedings.

## Older children who are also patients

**[7]** Officers of CAFCASS will not be able to represent anyone who is over the age of 18. The Official Solicitor may therefore be the more appropriate next friend or guardian ad litem of a child who is also a patient and whose disability will persist beyond his or her 18th birthday, especially in non-emergency cases where the substantive hearing is unlikely to take place before the child's 18th birthday. The Official Solicitor may also be the more appropriate next friend or guardian ad litem in medical treatment cases such as sterilisation or vegetative state cases, in which his staff have particular expertise deriving from their continuing role for adult patients.

## Advising the court

**[8]** The Official Solicitor may be invited to act or instruct counsel as a friend of the court (amicus) if it appears to the court that such an invitation is more appropriately addressed to him rather than (or in addition to) CAFCASS Legal Services and Special Casework.

## Liaison with CAFCASS

**[9]** In cases of doubt or difficulty, staff of the Official Solicitor's office will liaise with staff of CAFCASS Legal Services and Special Casework to avoid duplication and ensure the most suitable arrangements are made.

## Invitations to act in new cases

**[10]** Solicitors who have been consulted by a child or an adult under disability (or by someone acting on their behalf, or concerned about their interests) should write to the Official Solicitor setting out the background to the proposed case and explaining why there is no other willing and suitable person to act as next friend or guardian ad litem. Where the person concerned is an adult, medical evidence in the standard form of the Official Solicitor's medical certificate should be provided.

## Invitations to act in pending proceedings

**[11]** Where a case is already before the court, an order appointing the Official Solicitor should be expressed as being made subject to his consent. The Official Solicitor aims to provide a response to any invitation within 10 working days. He will be unable to consent to act for an adult until satisfied that the party is a 'patient'. A further directions appointment after 28 days may therefore be helpful. If he accepts appointment the Official Solicitor will need time to prepare the case on behalf of the child or patient and may wish to make submissions about any substantive hearing date. The following documents should be forwarded to the Official Solicitor without delay: (a) a copy of the order inviting him to act (with a note of the reasons approved by the judge if appropriate); (b) the court file, (c) if available, a bundle with summary, statement of issues and chronology (as required by President's Direction of 10 March 2000).

### Contacting the Official Solicitor

**[12]** It is often helpful to discuss the question of appointment with the Official Solicitor or one of his staff by telephoning 020 7911 7127. Inquiries about family proceedings should be addressed to the Team Manager, Family Litigation.

The Official Solicitor's address is:

81 Chancery Lane,
London WC2A 1DD.
DX 0012 London Chancery Lane
Tel: 020 7911 7127
Fax: 020 7911 7105
Email: enquiries@offsol.gsi.gov.uk

Laurence Oates
Official Solicitor

## CIVIL PROCEDURE RULES 1998

**[4.34]**

## CPR 1998, PT 25
## PD25A – INTERIM INJUNCTIONS

CPR PD25A
THIS PRACTICE DIRECTION SUPPLEMENTS CPR 1998, PART 25

### JURISDICTION

1.1 High Court Judges and any other Judge duly authorised may grant 'search orders' and 'freezing injunctions'.

1.2 In a case in the High Court, Masters and district judges have the power to grant injunctions:

(1) by consent,
(2) in connection with charging orders and appointments of receivers,
(3) in aid of execution of judgments.

1.3 In any other case any judge who has jurisdiction to conduct the trial of the action has the power to grant an injunction in that action.

1.4 A Master or district judge has the power to vary or discharge an injunction granted by any Judge with the consent of all the parties.

### MAKING AN APPLICATION

2.1 The application notice must state:

(1) the order sought, and
(2) the date, time and place of the hearing.

2.2 The application notice and evidence in support must be served as soon as practicable after issue and in any event not less than 3 days before the court is due to hear the application[3].

2.3 Where the court is to serve, sufficient copies of the application notice and evidence in support for the court and for each respondent should be filed for issue and service.

2.4 Whenever possible a draft of the order sought should be filed with the application notice and a disk containing the draft should also be available to the court [in a format compatible with the word processing software used by the court]. This will enable the court officer to arrange for any amendments to be incorporated and for the speedy preparation and sealing of the order. *The current word processing system to be used is WordPerfect 5.1.*

## EVIDENCE

3.1 Applications for search orders and freezing injunctions must be supported by affidavit evidence.

3.2 Applications for other interim injunctions must be supported by evidence set out in either:

(1) a witness statement, or
(2) a statement of case provided that it is verified by a statement of truth,[4] or
(3) the application provided that it is verified by a statement of truth,

unless the court, an Act, a rule or a practice direction requires evidence by affidavit.

3.3 The evidence must set out the facts on which the applicant relies for the claim being made against the respondent, including all material facts of which the court should be made aware.

3.4 Where an application is made without notice to the respondent, the evidence must also set out why notice was not given.

(See Part 32 and the practice direction that supplements it for information about evidence.)

## URGENT APPLICATIONS AND APPLICATIONS WITHOUT NOTICE

4.1 These fall into two categories:

(1) applications where a claim form has already been issued, and
(2) applications where a claim form has not yet been issued,

and, in both cases, where notice of the application has not been given to the respondent.

4.2 These applications are normally dealt with at a court hearing but cases of extreme urgency may be dealt with by telephone.

4.3 Applications dealt with at a court hearing after issue of a claim form:

(1) the application notice, evidence in support and a draft order (as in 2.4 above) should be filed with the court two hours before the hearing wherever possible,
(2) if an application is made before the application notice has been issued, a draft order (as in 2.4 above) should be provided at the hearing, and the application notice and evidence in support must be filed with the court on the same or next working day or as ordered by the court, and
(3) except in cases where secrecy is essential, the applicant should take steps to notify the respondent informally of the application.

4.4 Applications made before the issue of a claim form:

(1) in addition to the provisions set out at 4.3 above, unless the court orders otherwise, either the applicant must undertake to the court to issue a claim form immediately or the court will give directions for the commencement of the claim[5],
(2) where possible the claim form should be served with the order for the injunction,
(3) an order made before the issue of a claim form should state in the title after the names of the applicant and respondent 'the Claimant and Defendant in an Intended Action'.

4.5 Applications made by telephone:

(1) where it is not possible to arrange a hearing, application can be made between 10.00 a.m. and 5.00 p.m. weekdays by telephoning the Royal Courts of Justice on 020 7936 6000 and asking to be put in contact with a High Court Judge of the appropriate Division available to deal with an emergency application in a High Court matter. The appropriate district registry may also be contacted by telephone. In county court proceedings, the appropriate county court should be contacted,

(2) where an application is made outside those hours the applicant should either

(a) telephone the Royal Courts of Justice on 020 7936 6000 where he will be put in contact with the clerk to the appropriate duty judge in the High Court (or the appropriate area Circuit Judge where known), or

(b) the Urgent Court Business Officer of the appropriate Circuit who will contact the local duty judge.

(3) where the facility is available it is likely that the judge will require a draft order to be faxed to him,

(4) the application notice and evidence in support must be filed with the court on the same or next working day or as ordered, together with two copies of the order for sealing,

(5) injunctions will be heard by telephone only where the applicant is acting by counsel or solicitors.

## Orders for injunctions

5.1 Any order for an injunction, unless the court orders otherwise, must contain:

(1) an undertaking by the applicant to the court to pay any damages which the respondent(s) (or any other party served with or notified of the order) sustain which the court considers the applicant should pay,

(2) if made without notice to any other party, an undertaking by the applicant to the court to serve on the respondent the application notice, evidence in support and any order made as soon as practicable,

(3) if made without notice to any other party, a return date for a further hearing at which the other party can be present,

(4) if made before filing the application notice, an undertaking to file and pay the appropriate fee on the same or next working day, and

(5) if made before issue of a claim form—

(a) an undertaking to issue and pay the appropriate fee on the same or next working day, or

(b) directions for the commencement of the claim.

5.2 An order for an injunction made in the presence of all parties to be bound by it or made at a hearing of which they have had notice, may state that it is effective until trial or further order.

5.3 Any order for an injunction must set out clearly what the respondent must do or not do.

## FREEZING INJUNCTIONS

### *Orders to restrain disposal of assets worldwide and within England and Wales*

6 Examples of Freezing Injunctions are annexed to this practice direction.

## SEARCH ORDERS

### *Orders for the preservation of evidence and property*

7.1 The following provisions apply to search orders in addition to those listed above.

### *The Supervising Solicitor*

7.2 The Supervising solicitor must be experienced in the operation of search orders. A Supervising solicitor may be contacted either through the Law Society or, for the London area, through the London Solicitors Litigation Association.

7.3 Evidence:

(1) the affidavit must state the name, firm and its address, and experience of the Supervising Solicitor, also the address of the premises and whether it is a private or business address, and

(2) the affidavit must disclose very fully the reason the order is sought, including the probability that relevant material would disappear if the order were not made.

7.4 Service:

(1) the order must be served personally by the Supervising Solicitor, unless the court otherwise orders, and must be accompanied by the evidence in support and any documents capable of being copied,

(2) confidential exhibits need not be served but they must be made available for inspection by the respondent in the presence of the applicant's solicitors while the order is carried out and afterwards be retained by the respondent's solicitors on their undertaking not to permit the respondent–

(a) to see them or copies of them except in their presence, and

(b) to make or take away any note or record of them,

(3) the Supervising Solicitor may be accompanied only by the persons mentioned in the order,

(4) the Supervising Solicitor must explain the terms and effect of the order to the respondent in every day language and advise him of his right to–

(a) legal advice, and

(b) apply to vary or discharge the order,

(5) where the Supervising Solicitor is a man and the respondent is likely to be an unaccompanied woman, at least one other person named in the order must be a woman and must accompany the Supervising Solicitor, and

(6) the order may only be served between 9.30 a.m. and 5.30 p.m. Monday to Friday unless the court otherwise orders.

7.5 Search and custody of materials:

(1) no material shall be removed unless clearly covered by the terms of the order,

(2) the premises must not be searched and no items shall be removed from them except in the presence of the respondent or a person who appears to be a responsible employee of the respondent,

(3) where copies of documents are sought, the documents should be retained for no more than 2 days before return to the owner,

(4) where material in dispute is removed pending trial, the applicant's solicitors should place it in the custody of the respondent's solicitors on their undertaking to retain it in safekeeping and to produce it to the court when required.

(5) in appropriate cases the applicant should insure the material retained in the respondent's solicitors' custody,

(6) the Supervising Solicitor must make a list of all material removed from the premises and supply a copy of the list to the respondent,

(7) no material shall be removed from the premises until the respondent has had reasonable time to check the list,

(8) if any of the listed items exists only in computer readable form, the respondent must immediately give the applicant's solicitors effective access to the computers, with all necessary passwords, to enable them to be searched, and cause the listed items to be printed out,

(9) the applicant must take all reasonable steps to ensure that no damage is done to any computer or data,

(10) the applicant and his representatives may not themselves search the respondent's computers unless they have sufficient expertise to do so without damaging the respondent's system,

(11) the Supervising Solicitor shall provide a report on the carrying out of the order to the applicant's solicitors,

(12) as soon as the report is received the applicant's solicitors shall

(a) serve a copy of it on the respondent, and

(b) file a copy of it with the court, and

(13) where the Supervising Solicitor is satisfied that full compliance with paragraph 7.5(7) and (8) above is impracticable, he may permit the search to proceed and items to be removed without compliance with the impracticable requirements.

## GENERAL

8.1 The Supervising Solicitor must not be an employee or member of the applicant's firm of solicitors.

8.2 If the court orders that the order need not be served by the Supervising Solicitor, the reason for so ordering must be set out in the order.

8.3 The search order must not be carried out at the same time as a police search warrant.

8.4 There is no privilege against self incrimination in Intellectual Property cases (see the Supreme Court Act 1981, section 72) therefore in those cases, paragraph (4) of the Respondent's Entitlements and any other references to incrimination in the Search Order, should be removed.

8.5 Applications in intellectual property cases should be made in the Chancery Division.

8.6 An example of a Search Order is annexed to this Practice Direction.

## ANNEX

| | |
|---|---|
| **Freezing Injunction** | **IN THE [HIGH COURT OF JUSTICE]** |
| **Order to restrain assets in** | **[CHANCERY DIVISION]** |
| **England and Wales** | **[Strand, London WC2A 2LL]** |
| **Before The Honourable Mr Justice** | **[ ]** |
| | **Claim No.** |
| | **Dated** |
| **Applicant** | **Seal** |
| **Respondent** | |

Name, address and reference of Respondent

## PENAL NOTICE

**IF YOU THE WITHIN NAMED [ ] DISOBEY THIS ORDER YOU MAY BE HELD IN CONTEMPT OF COURT AND LIABLE TO IMPRISONMENT OR FINED OR YOUR ASSETS SEIZED**

**IMPORTANT**

**NOTICE TO THE RESPONDENT**

**You should read the terms of the Order and the Guidance Notes very carefully. You are advised to consult a Solicitor as soon as possible.**

This Order prohibits you, the Respondent, from dealing with your assets up to the amount stated in the Order, but subject to any exceptions set out at the end of the Order. You have a right to ask the Court to vary or discharge this Order.

If you disobey this Order you may be found guilty of Contempt of Court and may be sent to prison or fined. In the case of a Corporate Respondent, it may be fined, its Directors may be sent to prison or fined or its assets may be seized.

**THE ORDER**

An application was made today (*date*) by [Counsel][Solicitors] (or *as may be*) for the Applicant to Mr Justice ................................ who heard the application. The Judge read the affidavits listed in Schedule A and accepted the undertakings set out in Schedule B at the end of this Order. As a result of the application IT IS ORDERED that until ................................... ('the return date') [or further Order of the Court]:

1 The Respondent must not remove from England and Wales or in any way dispose of or deal with or diminish the value of any of his assets which are in England and Wales whether in his own name or not and whether solely or jointly owned up to the value of £......

This prohibition includes the following assets in particular:—

(a) the property known as (*title/address*) or the net sale money after payment of any mortgages if it has been sold;

(b) the property and assets of the Respondent's business known as [or carried on at (*address*)] or the sale money if any of them have been sold; and

(c) any money in the account numbered (*a/c number*) at (*title/address*).

2 If the total unencumbered value of the Respondent's assets in England and Wales exceeds £...... the Respondent may remove any of those assets from England and Wales or may dispose of or deal with them so long as the total unencumbered value of his assets still in England and Wales remains above £...... .

3 Exceptions to this Order:

(1) This Order does not prohibit the Respondent from spending £...... a week towards his ordinary living expenses [and £...... a week towards his ordinary and proper business expenses] and also £...... a week [*or* a reasonable sum] on legal advice and representation. But before spending any money the Respondent must tell the Applicant's legal representatives where the money is to come from.

[(2) This Order does not prohibit the Respondent from dealing with or disposing of any of his assets in the ordinary and proper course of business.]

(3) The Respondent may agree with the Applicant's legal representatives that the above spending limits should be increased or that this Order should be varied in any other respect, but any agreement must be in writing.

(4) The Respondent may cause this Order to cease to have effect if the Respondent provides security by paying the sum of £ into Court or makes provision for security in that sum by another method agreed with the Applicant's legal representatives.

4 The Respondent must:

(1) Inform the Applicant in writing at once of all his assets in England and Wales and whether in his own name or not and whether solely or jointly owned, giving the value, location and details of all such assets.

[The Respondent may be entitled to refuse to provide some or all of this information on the grounds that it may incriminate him. (*This sentence may be inserted in cases not covered by the Theft Act 1968 s31.*)]

(2) Confirm the information in an affidavit which must be served on the Applicant's legal representatives within ... days after this Order has been served on the Respondent.

[5 *Where an Order for service by an alternative means or service out of the jurisdiction has been made*

(1) The Applicant may issue and serve a Claim Form on the Respondent at (*address*) by (*method of service*).

(2) If the Respondent wishes to defend the Claim where the Claim Form states that Particulars of Claim are to follow he must complete and return the Acknowledgement of Service within ... days of being served with the Claim Form. Where the Particulars of Claim are served with the Claim Form, and the Respondent wishes to defend part or all of the Claim he must complete and return an Acknowledgement of Service within ... days of being served with the Claim Form or a Defence within ... days.]

## GUIDANCE NOTES

### EFFECT OF THIS ORDER

(1) A respondent who is an individual who is ordered not to do something must not do it himself or in any other way. He must not do it through others acting on his behalf or on his instructions or with his encouragement.

(2) A respondent which is a corporation and which is ordered not to do something must not do it itself or by its directors, officers, employees or agents or in any other way.



### VARIATION OR DISCHARGE OF THIS ORDER

The Respondent (or anyone notified of this Order) may apply to the court at any time to vary or discharge this Order (or so much of it as affects that person), but anyone wishing to do so must first inform the Applicant's legal representatives.

### PARTIES OTHER THAN THE APPLICANT AND RESPONDENT

#### *(1) Effect of this Order:*

It is a Contempt of Court for any person notified of this Order knowingly to assist in or permit a breach of this Order. Any person doing so may be sent to prison, fined or have his assets seized.

#### *(2) Set off by banks:*

This injunction does not prevent any bank from exercising any right of set off it may have in respect of any facility which it gave to the respondent before it was notified of this Order.

### (3) *Withdrawals by the Respondent:*

No bank need enquire as to the application or proposed application of any money withdrawn by the Respondent if the withdrawal appears to be permitted by this Order.

## INTERPRETATION OF THIS ORDER

(1) In this Order, where there is more than one Respondent, (unless otherwise stated), references to 'the Respondent' means both or all of them.

(2) A requirement to serve on the Respondent means on each of them. However, the Order is effective against any Respondent on whom it is served.

(3) An Order requiring 'the Respondent' to do or not to do anything applies to all Respondents.

## COMMUNICATIONS WITH THE COURT

All communications to the Court about this Order should be sent, where the Order is made in the Chancery Division, to [Room TM 510], Royal Courts of Justice, Strand, London WC2A 2LL quoting the case number The telephone number is 020 7936 [6827]; and where the order is made in the Queen's Bench Division, to Room W11 (020 7936 6009). The offices are open between 10 a.m. and 4.30 p.m. Monday to Friday.

## **SCHEDULE A**

## AFFIDAVITS

The Applicant relied on the following affidavits:

| (*name*) | (*number of affidavit*) | (*date sworn*) | [*filed on behalf of*] |
|---|---|---|---|
| (1) | | | |
| (2) | | | |

## **SCHEDULE B**

## UNDERTAKINGS GIVEN TO THE COURT BY THE APPLICANT

(1) If the Court later finds that this Order has caused loss to the Respondent, and decides that the Respondent should be compensated for that loss, the Applicant will comply with any Order the Court may make.

(2) The Applicant will on or before (*date*) cause a written guarantee in the sum of £...... to be issued from a bank having a place of business within England or Wales, such guarantee being in respect of any Order the Court may make pursuant to paragraph (1) above. The Applicant will further, forthwith upon issue of the guarantee, cause a copy of it to be served on the Respondent.

(3) As soon as practicable the Applicant will [issue and serve on the Respondent a Claim Form in the form of the draft produced to the Court] [serve on the Respondent the Claim Form] claiming the appropriate relief, together with this Order.

(4) The Applicant will cause an affidavit to be sworn and filed [substantially in the terms of the draft affidavit produced to the Court] [confirming the substance of what was said to the Court by the Applicant's Counsel/Solicitors].

[(5) (*Where a return date has been given.)* As soon as practicable the Applicant will serve on the Respondent an Application for the return date together with a copy of the affidavits and exhibits containing the evidence relied on by the Applicant.]

(6) Anyone notified of this Order will be given a copy of it by the Applicant's legal representatives.

(7) The Applicant will pay the reasonable costs of anyone other than the Respondent which have been incurred as a result of this Order including the costs of ascertaining whether that person holds any of the Respondent's assets and if the Court later finds that this Order has caused such person loss, and decides that such person should be compensated for that loss, the Applicant will comply with any Order the Court may make.

(8) If for any reason this Order ceases to have effect (including in particular where the Respondent provides security as provided for above or the Applicant does not provide a bank guarantee as provided for above), the Applicant will forthwith take all reasonable steps to inform, in writing, any person or company to whom he has given notice of this Order, or who he has reasonable grounds for supposing may act upon this Order, that it has ceased to have effect.

## NAME AND ADDRESS OF APPLICANT'S LEGAL REPRESENTATIVES

The Applicant's Legal Representatives are:
[Name, address, reference, fax and telephone numbers both in and out of office hours.]

| | |
|---|---|
| **Freezing Injunction** | **IN THE [HIGH COURT OF JUSTICE]** |
| **Order to restrain assets worldwide** | **[CHANCERY DIVISION]** |
| | **[Strand, London WC2A 2LL]** |
| **Before The Honourable Mr Justice** | **[ ]** |
| | **Claim No.** |
| | **Dated** |
| **Applicant** | **Seal** |
| **Respondent** | |

Name, address and reference of Respondent

**PENAL NOTICE**

**IF YOU THE WITHIN NAMED [.......................................................] DISOBEY THIS ORDER YOU MAY BE HELD TO BE IN CONTEMPT OF COURT AND LIABLE TO IMPRISONMENT OR FINED OR YOUR ASSETS SEIZED**

**IMPORTANT**

**NOTICE TO THE RESPONDENT**

**You should read the terms of the Order and the Guidance Notes very carefully. You are advised to consult a Solicitor as soon as possible.**

This Order prohibits you, the Respondent, from dealing with your assets up to the amount stated in the Order, but subject to any exceptions set out at the end of the Order. You have a right to ask the Court to vary or discharge this Order.

If you disobey this Order you may be found guilty of Contempt of Court and may be sent to prison or fined. In the case of a Corporate Respondent, it may be fined, its Directors may be sent to prison or fined or its assets may be seized.

**THE ORDER**

An application was made today (*date*) by [Counsel][Solicitors](or *as may be*) for the Applicant to Mr Justice .......................... who heard the application. The Judge read the affidavits listed in Schedule A and accepted the undertakings set out in Schedule B at the end of this Order. As a result of the application IT IS ORDERED that until .................. ('the return date')] [further Order of the Court]:

1 The Respondent must not:

(1) remove from England and Wales or in any way dispose of or deal with or diminish the value of any of his assets which are in England and Wales whether in his own name or not and whether solely or jointly owned up to the value of £...... ,or

(2) in any way dispose of or deal with or diminish the value of any of his assets whether they are in or outside England or Wales whether in his own name or not and whether solely or jointly owned up to the same value. This prohibition includes the following assets in particular:

(a) the property known as (*title/address*) or the net sale money after payment of any mortgages if it has been sold;

(b) the property and assets of the Respondent's business known as [or carried on at (*address*)] or the sale money if any of them have been sold; and

(c) any money in the account numbered (*a/c number*) at (*title/address*).

2

(1) If the total unencumbered value of the Respondent's assets in England and Wales exceeds £...... , the Respondent may remove any of those assets from England and Wales or may dispose of or deal with them so long as the total unencumbered value of his assets still in England and Wales remains above £...... .

(2) If the total unencumbered value of the Respondent's assets in England and Wales does not exceed £...... , the Respondent must not remove any of those assets from England and Wales and must not dispose of or deal with any of them, but if he has other assets outside England and Wales the Respondent may dispose of or deal with those assets so long as the total unencumbered value of all his assets whether in or outside England and Wales remains above £...... .

3 Exceptions to this Order:

(1) This Order does not prohibit the Respondent from spending £...... a week towards his ordinary living expenses [and £...... a week towards his ordinary and proper business expenses] and also £...... a week [*or* a reasonable sum] on legal advice and representation. But before spending any money the Respondent must tell the Applicant's legal representatives where the money is to come from.

(2) This Order does not prohibit the Respondent from dealing with or disposing of any of his assets in the ordinary and proper course of business.

(3) The Respondent may agree with the Applicant's legal representatives that the above spending limits should be increased or that this Order should be varied in any other respect, but any agreement must be in writing.

(4) The Respondent may cause this Order to cease to have effect if the Respondent provides security by paying the sum of £...... into Court or makes provision for security in that sum by another method agreed with the Applicant's legal representatives.

4 The Respondent must:

(1) Inform the Applicant in writing at once of all his assets whether in or outside England and Wales and whether in his own name or not and whether solely or jointly owned, giving the value, location and details of all such assets.

[The Respondent may be entitled to refuse to provide some or all of this information on the grounds that it may incriminate him. *This sentence may be inserted in cases not covered by the Theft Act 1968 s 31.*]

(2) Confirm the information in an affidavit which must be served on the Applicant's legal representatives within ... days after this Order has been served on the Respondent.

[5 Where an Order for service by an alternative means or service out of the jurisdiction has been made]

(1) The Applicant may issue and serve a Claim Form on the Respondent at (*address*) by (*method of service*)

(2) If the Respondent wishes to defend the Claim he must complete and return the Notice of Intention to Defend within ... days of being served with the Claim Form.]

## GUIDANCE NOTES

### EFFECT OF THIS ORDER

(1) A Respondent who is an individual who is ordered not to do something must not do it himself or in any other way. He must not do it through others acting on his behalf or on his instructions or with his encouragement.

(2) A Respondent which is a corporation and which is ordered not to do something must not do it itself or by its directors, officers, employees or agents or in any other way.

### VARIATION OR DISCHARGE OF THIS ORDER

The Respondent (or anyone notified of this Order) may apply to the Court at any time to vary or discharge this Order (or so much of it as affects that person), but anyone wishing to do so must first inform the Applicant's legal representatives.

### PARTIES OTHER THAN THE APPLICANT AND RESPONDENT

#### *(1) Effect of this Order:*

It is a Contempt of Court for any person notified of this Order knowingly to assist in or permit a breach of this Order. Any person doing so may be sent to prison, fined or have his assets seized.

(2) Effect of this Order outside England and Wales: The terms of this Order do not affect or concern anyone outside the jurisdiction of this Court until it is declared enforceable by or is enforced by a Court in the relevant country and then they are to affect him only to the extent they have been declared enforceable or have been enforced UNLESS the person is:

(i) a person to whom this Order is addressed or an officer or an agent appointed by power of attorney of that person; or

(ii) a person who is subject to the jurisdiction of this Court and (a) has been given written notice of this Order at his residence or place of business within the jurisdiction of this Court and (b) is able to prevent acts or omissions outside the jurisdiction of this Court which constitute or assist in a breach of the terms of this Order.

### *(3) Set off by Banks:*

This injunction does not prevent any bank from exercising any right of set off it may have in respect of any facility which it gave to the Respondent before it was notified of this Order.

(4) Withdrawals by the Respondent: No bank need enquire as to the application or proposed application of any money withdrawn by the Respondent if the withdrawal appears to be permitted by this Order.

## INTERPRETATION OF THIS ORDER

(1) In this Order, where there is more than one Respondent, (unless otherwise stated) references to 'the Respondent' means both or all of them.

(2) A requirement to serve on 'the Respondent' means on each of them. However, the Order is effective against any Respondent on whom it is served.

(3) An Order requiring 'the Respondent' to do or not to do anything applies to all Respondents.

## COMMUNICATIONS WITH THE COURT

All communications to the Court about this Order should be sent, where the Order is made in the Chancery Division, to [Room TM 510], Royal Courts of Justice, Strand, London WC2A 2LL quoting the case number. The telephone number is 020 7936 [6827]; and where the order is made in the Queen's Bench Division, to Room W11 (020 7936 6009). The offices are open between 10 a.m. and 4.30 p.m. Monday to Friday.

## SCHEDULE A

## AFFIDAVITS

The Applicant relied on the following affidavits:

| (*name*) | (*number of affidavit*) | (*date sworn*) | [*filed on behalf of*] |
|---|---|---|---|
| (1) | | | |
| (2) | | | |

## SCHEDULE B

## Undertakings Given to the Court by the Applicant

(1) If the Court later finds that this Order has caused loss to the Respondent, and decides that the Respondent should be compensated for that loss, the Applicant will comply with any Order the Court may make.

(2) The Applicant will on or before (*date*) cause a written guarantee in the sum of £...... to be issued from a bank having a place of business within England or Wales, such guarantee being in respect of any Order the Court may make pursuant to paragraph (1) above. The Applicant will further, forthwith upon issue of the guarantee, cause a copy of it to be served on the Respondent.

[(3) As soon as practicable the Applicant will [issue and serve on the Respondent a Claim Form in the form of the draft produced to the Court] [serve on the Respondent the Claim Form] claiming the appropriate relief, together with this Order.]

(4) The Applicant will cause an affidavit to be sworn and filed [substantially in the terms of the draft affidavit produced to the Court] [confirming the substance of what was said to the Court by the Applicant's Counsel/Solicitors].

[(5) *Where a return date has been given*—As soon as practicable the Applicant will serve on the Respondent an application for the return date together with a copy of the affidavits and exhibits containing the evidence relied on by the Applicant.]

(6) Anyone notified of this Order will be given a copy of it by the Applicant's legal representatives.

(7) The Applicant will pay the reasonable costs of anyone other than the Respondent which have been incurred as a result of this Order including the costs of ascertaining whether that person holds any of the Respondent's assets and if the Court later finds that this Order has caused such person loss, and decides that such person should be compensated for that loss, the Applicant will comply with any Order the Court may make.

(8) If for any reason this Order ceases to have effect (including in particular where the Respondent provides security as provided for above or the Applicant does not provide a bank guarantee as provided for above), the Applicant will forthwith take all reasonable steps to inform, in writing, any person or company to whom he has given notice of this Order, or who he has reasonable grounds for supposing may act upon this Order, that it has ceased to have effect.

[(9) The Applicant will not without the leave of the Court begin proceedings against the Respondent in any other jurisdiction or use information obtained as a result of an Order of the Court in this jurisdiction for the purpose of civil or criminal proceedings in any other jurisdiction.]

[(10) The Applicant will not without the leave of the Court seek to enforce this Order in any country outside England and Wales [or seek an Order of a similar nature including Orders conferring a charge or other security against the Respondent or the Respondent's assets].]

## Name and Address of Applicant's Legal Representatives

The Applicant's Legal Representatives are:
[Name, address, reference, fax and telephone numbers both in and out of office hours.]

| | |
|---|---|
| **Search Order** | **IN THE [HIGH COURT OF JUSTICE]** |
| **Order to preserve evidence** | **[CHANCERY DIVISION]** |
| **and property** | **[Strand, London WC2A 2LL]** |
| **Before The Honourable Mr Justice** | **[ ]** |

**Claim No.**

**Dated**

**Applicant**

**Seal**

**Respondent**

Name, address and reference of Respondent

**PENAL NOTICE**

**IF YOU THE WITHIN NAMED [.........] DISOBEY THIS ORDER YOU MAY BE HELD TO BE IN CONTEMPT OF COURT AND LIABLE TO IMPRISONMENT OR FINED OR YOUR ASSETS SEIZED**

**SEIZED**

**IMPORTANT**

**NOTICE TO THE RESPONDENT**

**You should read the terms of the Order and the Guidance Notes very carefully. You are advised to consult a Solicitor as soon as possible.**

This Order orders you, the Respondent, to allow the persons mentioned in the Order to enter the premises described in the Order and to search for, examine and remove or copy the articles specified in the Order. The persons so named will have no right to enter the premises or, having entered, to remain at the premises, unless you give your consent to their doing so. If, however, you withhold your consent you will be in breach of this Order and may be held to be in Contempt of Court.

The Order also requires you to hand over any of such articles which are under your control and to provide information to the Applicant's Solicitors, and prohibits you from doing certain acts.

If you, the Respondent, disobey this Order you may be found guilty of contempt of Court and may be sent to prison or fined. In the case of a Corporate Respondent, it may be fined, its Directors may be sent to prison or fined or its assets may be seized.

**THE ORDER**

AN APPLICATION was made today (*date*) by [Counsel] [Solicitors] for the Applicant to Mr Justice ..................................... who heard the application. The Judge read the affidavits listed in Schedule F at the end of this Order and accepted the undertakings by the Applicant, the Applicant's Solicitors and the Supervising Solicitor set forth in the Schedules at the end of this Order. As a result of the application IT IS ORDERED that until .......................... ('the return date' )] [or further Order of the Court]:

1

(1) The Respondent must allow Mr/Mrs/Miss ......... ('the Supervising Solicitor'), together with Mr ......... a Solicitor of the Supreme Court, and a partner in the firm of ......... the Applicant's Solicitors and up to ... other persons being *(their capacity)* accompanying them, to enter the premises mentioned in Schedule A to this Order and any other premises of the Respondent disclosed under paragraph 4(1) below and any vehicles under the Respondent's control on or around the premises so that they can search for, inspect, photograph or photocopy, and deliver into the safekeeping of the Applicant's Solicitors all the documents and articles which are listed in Schedule B to this Order ('the listed items') or which Mr ......... believes to be listed items.

(2) The Respondent must allow those persons to remain on the premises until the search is complete, and to re-enter the premises on the same or the following nay in order to complete the search.

2

(1) No item may be removed from the premises until a list of the items to be removed has been prepared, and a copy of the list has been supplied to the person served with the Order, and he has been given a reasonable opportunity to check the list.

(2) The premises must not be searched, and items must not be removed from them, except in the presence of the Respondent or a person appearing to be a responsible employee of the Respondent or in control of the premises.

(3) If the Supervising Solicitor is satisfied that full compliance with paragraph 2(1) or (2) above is impracticable, he may permit the search to proceed and items to be removed without compliance with the impracticable requirements.

3

(1) The Respondent must immediately hand over to the Applicant's Solicitors any of the listed items which are in his possession or under his control save for any computer or hard disk integral to any computer.

(2) If any of the listed items exists only in computer readable form, the Respondent must immediately give the Applicant's Solicitors effective access to the computers, with all necessary passwords, to enable them to be searched, and cause the listed items to be printed out. A print-out of the items must be given to the Applicant's Solicitors or displayed on the computer screen so that they can be read and copied. All reasonable steps shall be taken by the Applicant to ensure that no damage is done to any computer or data. The Applicant and his representatives may not themselves search the Respondent's computers unless they have sufficient expertise to do so without damaging the Respondent's system.

4

(1) The Respondent must immediately inform the Applicant's Solicitors:—

(a) where all the listed items are; and

(b) so far as he is aware—

(i) the name and address of everyone who has supplied him, or offered to supply him, with listed items,

(ii) the name and address of everyone to whom he has supplied, or offered to supply, listed items, and

(iii) full details of the dates and quantities of every such supply and offer.

(2) Within ... days after being served with this Order the Respondent must swear an affidavit setting out the above information.

5

(1) Except for the purpose of obtaining legal advice, the Respondent or anyone else with knowledge of this Order must not directly or indirectly inform anyone of these proceedings or of the contents of this Order, or warn anyone that proceedings have been or may be brought against him by the Applicant until ......... 19/20... (the return date)[or further Order of the Court].

(2) The Respondent must not destroy, tamper with, cancel or part with possession, power, custody or control of the listed items otherwise than in accordance with the terms of this Order.

(3) (*Insert any negative injunctions.*)

(6 *Insert any further order.*)

## GUIDANCE NOTES

## EFFECT OF THIS ORDER

(1) A Respondent who is an individual who is ordered not to do something must not do it himself or in any other way. He must not do it through others acting on his behalf or on his instructions or with his encouragement.

(2) A Respondent which is a corporation and which is ordered not to do something must not do it itself or by its directors officers employees or agents or in any other way.

(3) This Order must be complied with either by the Respondent himself or by an employee of the Respondent or other person appearing to be in control of the premises and having authority to permit the premises to be entered and the search to proceed.

(4) This Order requires the Respondent or his employee or other person appearing to be in control of the premises and having that authority to permit entry to the premises immediately the Order is served upon him, except as stated in paragraph 6 below.

## RESPONDENT'S ENTITLEMENTS

(1) Before you the Respondent or the person appearing to be in control of the premises allow anybody onto the premises to carry out this Order you are entitled to have the solicitor who serves you with this Order explain to you what it means in everyday language.

(2) You are entitled to insist that there is nobody [or nobody except Mr ......... ] present who could gain commercially from anything he might read or see on your premises.

(3) You are entitled to refuse to permit entry before 9:30 a.m. or after 5:30 p.m. or at all on Saturday and Sunday unless the Court has ordered otherwise.

(4) Except in certain cases, you may be entitled to refuse to permit disclosure of any documents which may incriminate you ('incriminating documents') or to answer any questions if to do so may incriminate you. It may be prudent to take advice, because if you so refuse, your refusal may be taken into account by the Court at a later stage.

(5) You are entitled to refuse to permit disclosure of any documents passing between you and your Solicitors or Patent or Trade Mark Agents for the purpose of obtaining advice ('privileged documents').

(6) You are entitled to seek legal advice, and to ask the Court to vary or discharge this Order, provided you do so at once, and provided you do not disturb or move anything in the interim and that meanwhile you permit the Supervising Solicitor (who is a Solicitor acting independently of the Applicant) to enter, but not start to search.

(7) Before permitting entry to the premises by any person other than the Supervising Solicitor, you (or any other person appearing to be in control of the premises) may gather together any documents you believe may be [incriminating or] privileged and hand them to the Supervising Solicitor for the Supervising Solicitor to assess whether they are [incriminating or] privileged as claimed. If the Supervising Solicitor concludes that any of the documents may be [incriminating or] privileged documents or if there is any doubt as to their status the Supervising Solicitor shall exclude them from the search and shall retain the documents of doubtful status in his possession pending further order of the Court. While this is being done, you may refuse entry to the premises by any other person, and may refuse to permit the search to begin, for a short time (not to exceed two hours, unless the Supervising Solicitor agrees to a longer period). If you wish to take legal advice and gather documents as permitted, you must first inform the Supervising Solicitor and keep him informed of the steps being taken.

## RESTRICTIONS ON SERVICE

Paragraph 1 of the Order is subject to the following restrictions:—

(1) This Order may only be served between 9:30 a.m. and 5:30 p.m. on a weekday unless the Court has ordered otherwise.

(2) This Order may not be carried out at the same time as a police search warrant.

(3) This Order must be served by the Supervising Solicitor, and paragraph 1 of the Order must be carried out in his presence and under his supervision. Where the premises are likely to be occupied by an unaccompanied woman and the Supervising Solicitor is a man, at least one of the persons accompanying him as provided by paragraph 1 of the Order shall be a woman.

(4) This Order does not require the person served with the Order to allow anyonc [or anyone cxcept Mr ......... ] to enter the premises who in the view of the Supervising Solicitor could gain commercially from anything he might read or see on the premises if the person served with the Order objects.

## VARIATION OR DISCHARGE OF THIS ORDER

The Respondent (or anyone notified of this Order) may apply to the Court at any time to vary or discharge this Order (or so much of it as affects that person), but anyone wishing to do so must first inform the Applicant's Solicitors.

## INTERPRETATION OF THIS ORDER

(1) In this Order, where there is more than one Respondent, references to 'the Respondent' means both or all of them.
(2) A requirement to serve on the 'Respondent' means on each of them. However, the Order is effective against any Respondent on whom it is served.
(3) An Order requiring 'the Respondent' to do or not to do anything applies to all Respondents.
(4) Any other requirement that something shall be done to or in the presence of 'the Respondent' means to or in the presence of any one of them or in the case of a firm or company a director or a person appearing to the Supervising Solicitor to be a responsible employee.

## COMMUNICATIONS WITH THE COURT

All communications to the Court about this Order should be sent, where the Order is made in the Chancery Division, to [Room TM 510], Royal Courts of Justice, Strand, London, WC2A 2LL quoting the case number. The telephone number is 020 7936 [6827]; and where the order is made in the Queen's Bench Division, to Room W11 (020 7936 6009). The offices are open between 10 a.m. and 4.30 p.m. Monday to Friday.



## SCHEDULE A

The premises

## SCHEDULE B

The listed items

## SCHEDULE C

## UNDERTAKINGS GIVEN TO THE COURT BY THE APPLICANT

(1) If the Court later finds that this Order or carrying it out has caused loss to the Respondent, and decides that the Respondent should be compensated for that loss, the Applicant will comply with any Order the Court may make. Further, if the carrying out of this Order has been in breach of the terms of this Order or otherwise in a manner inconsistent with the Applicant's Solicitors' duties as Officers of the Court the Applicant will comply with any order for damages the Court may make.
[(2) As soon as practicable to issue a Claim Form [in the form of the draft produced to the Court] [claiming appropriate relief.].]

[(3) To [swear and file an affidavit] [cause an affidavit to be sworn and filed] [substantially in the terms of the draft produced to the Court] [confirming the substance of what was said to the Court by the Applicant's Counsel/Solicitors].]

(4) To serve on the Respondent at the same time as this Order is served upon him:

(i) the Claim Form, or if not issued, the draft produced to the Court,

(ii) an Application for hearing on *(date)*,

(iii) copies of the affidavits [or draft affidavits] and exhibits capable of being copied containing the evidence relied on by the Applicant [Copies of the confidential exhibits need not be served, but they must be made available for inspection by or on behalf of the Respondent in the presence of the Applicant's Solicitors while the Order is carried out. Afterwards they must be provided to a Solicitor representing the Respondent who gives a written undertaking not to permit the Respondent to see them or copies of them except in his presence and not to permit the Respondent to make or take away any note or record of the exhibits.], and

(iv) a note of any allegation of fact made orally to the Judge where such allegation is not contained in the affidavits or draft affidavits read by the Judge.

(5) To serve on the Respondent a copy of the Supervising Solicitor's report on the carrying out of this Order as soon as it is received.

(6) Not, without the leave of the Court, to use any information or documents obtained as a result of carrying out this Order nor to inform anyone else of these proceedings (including adding further Respondents) or commencing civil proceedings in relation to the same or related subject matter to these proceedings until after the return date.

[(7) To maintain pending further order the sum of £...... in an account controlled by the Applicant's Solicitors.]

[(8) To insure the items removed from the premises.]

## SCHEDULE D

## UNDERTAKINGS GIVEN BY THE APPLICANT'S SOLICITORS

(1) To answer at once to the best of their ability any question whether a particular item is a listed item.

(2) To return the originals of all documents obtained as a result of this Order (except original documents which belong to the Applicant) as soon as possible and in any event within two working days of their removal.

(3) While ownership of any item obtained as a result of this Order is in dispute, to deliver the article into the keeping of Solicitors acting for the Respondent within two working days from receiving a written undertaking by them to retain the article in safe keeping and to produce it to the Court when required.

(4) To retain in their own safe keeping all other items obtained as a result of this Order until the Court directs otherwise.

## SCHEDULE E

## UNDERTAKINGS GIVEN BY THE SUPERVISING SOLICITOR

(1) To offer to explain to the person served with the Order its meaning and effect fairly and in everyday language, and to inform him of his right to seek legal advice (such advice to include an explanation that the Respondent may be entitled to avail himself of [the privilege against self-incrimination or] [legal professional privilege]) and apply to vary or discharge the Order as mentioned in the Respondent's Entitlements above.

(2) To make and provide to the Applicant's Solicitors and to the Judge who made this Order (for the purposes of the Court file) a written report on the carrying out of the Order.

## SCHEDULE F

AFFIDAVITS

The Applicant relied on the following affidavits:

| *(name)* | *(number of affidavit)* | *(date sworn)* | *[filed on behalf of]* |
|---|---|---|---|

NAME AND ADDRESS OF APPLICANT'S SOLICITORS

The Applicant's Solicitors are:
(Name, address, reference, fax and telephone numbers both in and out of office hours.)

**[4.35]**

# CPR 1998, PT 25
# PD25B – Interim Payments

**CPR PD25B**
**THIS PRACTICE DIRECTION SUPPLEMENTS CPR 1998, PART 25**

## GENERAL

1.1 Rule 25.7 sets out the conditions to be satisfied and matters to be taken into account before the court will make an order for an interim payment.

1.2 The permission of the court must be obtained before making a voluntary interim payment in respect of a claim by a child or patient.



## EVIDENCE

2.1 An application for an interim payment of damages must be supported by evidence dealing with the following:

(1) the sum of money sought by way of an interim payment,
(2) the items or matters in respect of which the interim payment is sought,
(3) the sum of money for which final judgment is likely to be given,
(4) the reasons for believing that the conditions set out in rule 25.7 are satisfied,
(5) any other relevant matters,
(6) in claims for personal injuries, details of special damages and past and future loss, and
(7) in a claim under the Fatal Accidents Act 1976, details of the person(s) on whose behalf the claim is made and the nature of the claim.

2.2 Any documents in support of the application should be exhibited, including, in personal injuries claims, the medical report(s).

2.3 If a respondent to an application for an interim payment wishes to rely on written evidence at the hearing he must comply with the provisions of rule 25.6(4).

2.4 If the applicant wishes to rely on written evidence in reply he must comply with the provisions of rule 25.6(5).

## INTERIM PAYMENT WHERE ACCOUNT TO BE TAKEN

2A.1 This section of this practice direction applies if a party seeks an interim payment under rule 25.7(b) where the court has ordered an account to be taken.

2A.2 If the evidence on the application for interim payment shows that the account is bound to result in a payment to the applicant the court will, before making an order for interim payment, order that the liable party pay to the applicant 'the amount shown by the account to be due'.

## INSTALMENTS

3 Where an interim payment is to be paid in instalments the order should set out:
(1) the total amount of the payment,
(2) the amount of each instalment,
(3) the number of instalments and the date on which each is to be paid, and
(4) to whom the payment should be made.

## COMPENSATION RECOVERY PAYMENTS

4.1 Where in a claim for personal injuries there is an application for an interim payment of damages:
(1) which is other than by consent,
(2) which falls under the heads of damage set out in column 1 of Schedule 2 of the Social Security (Recovery of Benefits) Act 1997 in respect of recoverable benefits received by the claimant set out in column 2 of that Schedule, and
(3) where the defendant is liable to pay recoverable benefits to the Secretary of State,

the defendant should obtain from the Secretary of State a certificate of recoverable benefits.

4.2 A copy of the certificate should be filed at the hearing of the application for an interim payment.

4.3 The order will set out the amount by which the payment to be made to the claimant has been reduced according to the Act and the Social Security (Recovery of Benefits) Regulations 1997.

4.4 The payment made to the claimant will be the net amount but the interim payment for the purposes of paragraph 5 below will be the gross amount.

## ADJUSTMENT OF FINAL JUDGMENT FIGURE

5.1 In this paragraph 'judgment' means:
(1) any order to pay a sum of money,
(2) a final award of damages,
(3) an assessment of damages.

5.2 In a final judgment where an interim payment has previously been made which is less than the total amount awarded by the judge, the order should set out in a preamble:
(1) the total amount awarded by the judge, and
(2) the amounts and dates of the interim payment(s).

5.3 The total amount awarded by the judge should then be reduced by the total amount of any interim payments, and an order made for entry of judgment and payment of the balance.

5.4 In a final judgment where an interim payment has previously been made which is more than the total amount awarded by the judge, the order should set out in a preamble:
(1) the total amount awarded by the judge, and
(2) the amounts and dates of the interim payment(s).

5.5 An order should then be made for repayment, reimbursement, variation or discharge under rule 25.8(2) and for interest on an overpayment under rule 25.8(5).

5.6 A practice direction supplementing Part 40 provides further information concerning adjustment of the final judgment sum.

**[4.36]**

# CPR 1998, PT 25
# PD25C – Accounts and Inquiries

**CPR PD 25C**

**THIS PRACTICE DIRECTION SUPPLEMENTS CPR PART 25**

An application for an order for accounts and inquiries may also be made under Part 24 (summary judgment). Reference should be made to paragraph 6 of the practice direction that supplements that Part.

1. The remedies that the court may grant under Part 25 include orders directing accounts to be taken and inquiries to be made.

2. The court may, on application or on its own initiative, at any stage in the proceedings, whether before or after judgment, make an order directing any necessary accounts to be taken or inquiries to be made.

3. Every direction for an account to be taken or an inquiry to be made shall be numbered in the order so that, as far as possible, each distinct account and inquiry is given its own number.

(This practice direction replaces RSC Ord 43 r 2 and applies to county court proceedings as well as to High Court proceedings.)

(The accounts and inquiries practice direction supplementing Part 40 contains provisions regarding the taking of an account or conduct of an inquiry after the order for the account or inquiry has been made.)

**[4.37]**

# CPR 1998, PT 40
# PD40D

**CPR PD40D**

**THIS PRACTICE DIRECTION SUPPLEMENTS CPR 1998, PART 40**

## PART 1
## COURT'S POWERS IN RELATION TO LAND

### APPLICATION TO THE COURT WHERE LAND SUBJECT TO AN INCUMBRANCE

1.1 In this paragraph 'incumbrance' has the same meaning as it has in section 205(1) of the Law of Property Act 1925.

1.2 Where land subject to any incumbrance is sold or exchanged any party to the sale or exchange may apply to the court for a direction under section 50 of the Law of Property Act 1925 (discharge of incumbrances by the court on sales or exchanges).

1.3 The directions a court may give on such an application include a direction for the payment into court of a sum of money that the court considers sufficient to meet-

1. the value of the incumbrance; and
2. further costs, expenses and interest that may become due on or in respect of the incumbrance.

(Section 50(1) of the Law of Property Act 1925 contains provisions relating to the calculation of these amounts)

1.4 Where a payment into court has been made in accordance with a direction under section 50(1) the court may–

1. declare the land to be freed from the incumbrance; and
2. make any order it considers appropriate for giving effect to an order made under rule 40.16 or relating to the money in court and the income thereof.

1.5 An application under section 50 should

1. if made in existing proceedings, be made in accordance with CPR Part 23;
2. otherwise, be made by claim form under CPR Part 8.

## DIRECTIONS ABOUT THE SALE ETC

2 Where the court has made an order under rule 40.16 it may give any other directions it considers appropriate for giving effect to the order. In particular the court may give directions–

1. appointing a party or other person to conduct the sale;
2. for obtaining evidence of the value of the land;
3. as to the manner of sale;
4. settling the particulars and conditions of the sale;
5. fixing a minimum or reserve price;
6. as to the fees and expenses to be allowed to an auctioneer or estate agent;
7. for the purchase money to be paid
   (a) into court;
   (b) to trustees; or
   (c) to any other person;
8. for the result of a sale to be certified;
9. under rule 40.18.

## APPLICATION FOR PERMISSION TO BID

3.1 Where–

1. the court has made an order under rule 40.16 for land to be sold; and
2. a party wishes to bid for the land, he should apply to the court for permission to do so.

3.2 An application for permission to bid must be made before the sale takes place.

3.3 If the court gives permission to all the parties to bid, it may appoint an independent person to conduct the sale.

3.4 'Bid' in this paragraph includes submitting a tender or other offer to buy.

## CERTIFYING SALE RESULT

4.1 If–

1. the court has directed the purchase money to be paid into court; or
2. the court has directed that the result of the sale be certified

the result of the sale must be certified by the person having conduct of the sale.

4.2 Unless the court directs otherwise, the certificate must give details of

1. the amount of the purchase price;
2. the amount of the fees and expenses payable to any auctioneer or estate agent;
3. the amount of any other expenses of the sale;
4. the net amount received in respect of the sale;

and must be verified by a statement of truth.

(Part 22 sets out requirements about statements of truth)

4.3 The certificate must be filed

1. if the proceedings are being dealt with in the Royal Courts of Justice, in Chancery Chambers;
2. if the proceedings are being dealt with anywhere else, in the court where the proceedings are being dealt with.

## FEES AND EXPENSES OF AUCTIONEERS AND ESTATE AGENTS

5.1

1. Where the court has ordered the sale of land under rule 40.16, auctioneer's and estate agent's charges may, unless the court orders otherwise, include
   (a) commission;
   (b) fees for valuation of the land;

(c) charges for advertising the land;
(d) other expenses and disbursements but not charges for surveys.
2. The court's authorisation is required for charges relating to surveys.

5.2 If the total amount of the auctioneer's and estate agent's charges authorised under paragraph 5.1(1)

1. does not exceed 2.5% of the sale price; and
2. does not exceed the rate of commission that that agent would normally charge on a sole agency basis

the charges may, unless the court orders otherwise and subject to paragraph 5.3(3) and (4), be met by deduction of the amount of the charges from the proceeds of sale without the need for any further authorisation from the court.

5.3 If–

1. a charge made by an auctioneer or estate agent (whether in respect of fees or expenses or both) is not authorised under paragraph 5.1(1);
2. the total amount of the charges so authorised exceeds the limits set out in paragraph 5.2;
3. the land is sold in lots or by valuation; or
4. the sale is of investment property, business property or farm property

an application must be made to the court for approval of the fees and expenses to be allowed.

5.4 An application under paragraph 5.3 may be made by any party or, if he is not a party, by the person having conduct of the sale, and may be made either before or after the sale has taken place.

## PART 2
## CONVEYANCING COUNSEL OF THE COURT

### REFERENCE TO CONVEYANCING COUNSEL

6.1 When the court refers a matter under rule 40.18, the court may specify a particular conveyancing counsel.

6.2 If the court does not specify a particular conveyancing counsel, references will be distributed among conveyancing counsel in accordance with arrangements made by the Chief Chancery Master.

6.3 Notice of every reference under rule 40.18 must be given to the Chief Chancery Master.

6.4 The court will send a copy of the order, together with all other necessary documents, to conveyancing counsel.

6.5 A court order sent to conveyancing counsel under paragraph 6.4 will be sufficient authority for him to prepare his report or draft the document.

6.6

1. An objection under rule 40.19 to a report on title prepared by conveyancing counsel must be made by application notice.
2. The application notice must state–
   (a) the matters the applicant objects to; and
   (b) the reason for the objection.



**[4.38]**

# CPR 1998, Pt 52
# PD52 – Appeals

**CPR 1998, PD52**
**THIS PRACTICE DIRECTION SUPPLEMENTS CPR 1998, PART 52**

CONTENTS OF THIS PRACTICE DIRECTION

1.1 This practice direction is divided into three sections:

Section I – General provisions about appeals
Section II – General provisions about statutory appeals and appeals by way of case stated
Section III – Provisions about specific appeals

## SECTION I
## GENERAL PROVISIONS ABOUT APPEALS

2.1 This practice direction applies to all appeals to which Part 52 applies except where specific provision is made for appeals to the Court of Appeal.

2.2 For the purpose only of appeals to the Court of Appeal from cases in family proceedings this Practice Direction will apply with such modifications as may be required.

## ROUTES OF APPEAL

2A.1 Subject to paragraph 2A.2, the following table sets out to which court or judge an appeal is to be made (subject to obtaining any necessary permission):

| **Decision of:** | **Appeal made to:** |
|---|---|
| District judge of a county court | Circuit judge |
| Master or district judge of the High Court | High Court judge |
| Circuit judge | High Court judge |
| High Court judge | Court of Appeal |

2A.2 Where the decision to be appealed is a final decision–
- (a) in a claim allocated to the multi-track under rules 12.7, 14.8 or 26.5; or
- (b) made in specialist proceedings (to which rule 49(2) refers) the appeal is to be made to the Court of Appeal (subject to obtaining any necessary permission).

2A.3 A 'final decision' is a decision of a court that would finally determine (subject to any possible appeal or detailed assessment of costs) the entire proceedings whichever way the court decided the issues before it.

2A.4 A decision of a court is to be treated as a final decision for routes of appeal purposes where it:
- (a) is made at the conclusion of part of a hearing or trial which has been split into parts; and
- (b) would, if it had been made at the conclusion of that hearing or trial, have been a final decision.

2A.5 An order made:
- (a) on a summary or detailed assessment of costs; or
- (b) is not a 'final decision' and any appeal from such an order will follow the appeal routes set out in the table in paragraph 2A.1.

Section 16(1) of the Supreme Court Act 1981 (as amended); section 77(1) of the County Courts Act 1984 (as amended); and the Access to Justice Act 1999 (Destination of Appeals) Order 2000 set out the provisions governing routes of appeal)

2A.6 (a) Where the decision to be appealed is a final decision in a Part 8 claim treated as allocated to the multi-track under rule 8.9(c) the court to which the permission application is made should, if permission is given, and unless the appeal would lie to the Court of Appeal in any event, consider whether to order the appeal to be transferred to the Court of Appeal under rule 52.14.

(b) An appeal against a final decision on a point of law in a case which did not involve any substantial dispute of fact would normally be a suitable appeal to be so transferred.

(see also paragraph 10.1)

## GROUNDS FOR APPEAL

3.1 Rule 52.11(3) (a) and (b) sets out the circumstances in which the appeal court will allow an appeal.

3.2 The grounds of appeal should set out clearly the reasons why rule 52.11(3)(a) or (b) is said to apply.

## PERMISSION TO APPEAL

4.1 Rule 52.3 sets out the circumstances when permission to appeal is required.

4.2 The permission of-

(a) the Court of Appeal; or

(b) where the lower court's rules allow, the lower court

is required for all appeals to the Court of Appeal except as provided for by statute or rule 52.3

(The requirement of permission to appeal may be imposed by a practice direction – see rule 52.3(b))

4.3 Where the rules of the lower court or any other enactment do not provide for the giving of permission to appeal, the lower court may give an indication of its opinion as to whether permission should be given.

### Appeals from case management decisions

4.4 Case management decisions include decisions made under rule 3.1(2) and decisions about:

(1) disclosure

(2) filing of witness statements or experts reports

(3) directions about the timetable of the claim

(4) adding a party to a claim

(5) security for costs

4.5 Where the application is for permission to appeal from a case management decision , the court dealing with the application may take into account whether:

(1) the issue is of sufficient significance to justify the costs of an appeal;

(2) the procedural consequences of an appeal (eg loss of trial date) outweigh the significance of the case management decision ;

(3) it would be more convenient to determine the issue at or after trial.



### Court to which permission to appeal application should be made

4.6 An application for permission should be made orally at the hearing at which the decision to be appealed against is made.

4.7 Where:

(a) no application for permission to appeal is made at the hearing; or

(b) the lower court refuses permission to appeal,

an application for permission to appeal may be made to the appeal court in accordance with rules 52.3(2) and (3).

4.8 There is no appeal from a decision of the appeal court, made at an oral hearing, to allow or refuse permission to appeal to that court. See section 54(4) of the Access to Justice Act 1999 and rule 52.3(3) and (4).

### Second appeals

4.9 An application for permission to appeal from a decision of the High Court or a county court which was itself made on appeal must be made to the Court of Appeal.

4.10 If permission to appeal is granted the appeal will be heard by the Court of Appeal.

## Consideration of Permission without a hearing

4.11 Applications for permission to appeal may be considered by the appeal court without a hearing.

4.12 If permission is granted without a hearing the parties will be notified of that decision and the procedure in paragraphs 6.1 to 6.7 [*6.6*] will then apply.

4.13 If permission is refused without a hearing the parties will be notified of that decision with the reasons for it. The decision is subject to the appellant's right to have it reconsidered at an oral hearing. This may be before the same judge.

4.14 A request for the decision to be reconsidered at an oral hearing must be filed at the appeal court within 7 days after service of the notice that permission has been refused. A copy of the request must be served by the appellant on the respondent at the same time. If no request is made for the decision to be reconsidered, it will become final after the time limit for making the request has expired.

## Permission hearing

4.15 Notice of the hearing need not be given to the respondent unless the court so directs. The appeal court will usually so direct if the appellant is asking for a remedy against the respondent pending the appeal.

4.16 If notice of the hearing is to be given to the respondent, the appellant must supply the respondent with a copy of the bundle (see paragraph 5.6) within 7 days of being notified, or such other period as the court may direct. The costs of providing that bundle shall be borne by the appellant initially, but will form part of the costs of the permission application.

## Appellants in receipt of services funded by the Legal Services Commission applying for permission to appeal

4.17 Where the appellant is in receipt of services funded by the Legal Services Commission (or legally aided) and permission to appeal has been refused without a hearing, the appellant must send a copy of the reasons the appeal court gave for refusing permission to the relevant office of the Legal Services Commission as soon as it has been received from the court. The court will require confirmation that this has been done if a hearing is requested to re-consider the question of permission.

## Limited permission

4.18 Where a court, under rule 52.3(7) confines its permission to some issues only, it should expressly refuse permission on any remaining issues. Those other issues may only be raised at the hearing of the appeal with the appeal court's permission. The court and the respondent should be informed of any intention to raise such an issue as soon as practicable after notification of the court's order.

4.19 An application to raise a remaining issue will normally be dealt with at the outset of the appeal unless the court otherwise directs.

## Appellant's Notice

5.1 An appellant's notice (N161) must be filed and served in all cases. Where an application for permission to appeal is made to the appeal court it must be applied for in the appellant's notice.

## Human Rights

5.1A Where the appellant is seeking to rely on any issue under the Human Rights Act 1998, or seeks a remedy available under that Act, for the first time in an appeal he must include in his appeal notice the information required by paragraph 16.1 of the practice direction to CPR Part 16. Paragraph 16.2 of that practice direction also applies as if references to statement of case were to appeal notice.

5.1B CPR rule 19.4A and the practice direction supplementing it shall apply as if references to the case management conference were to the application for permission to appeal. (The practice direction to Part 19 provides for notice to be given and parties joined in certain circumstances to which this paragraph applies)

## Extension of time for filing appellant's notice

5.2 If an appellant requires an extension of time for filing his notice the application must be made in the appellant's notice. The notice should state the reason for the delay and the steps taken prior to the application being made.

5.3 Where the appellant's notice includes an application for an extension of time and permission to appeal has been given or is not required the respondent has the right to be heard on that application. He must be served with a copy of the appellant's bundle. However, a respondent who unreasonably opposes an extension of time runs the risk of being ordered to pay the appellant's costs of that application.

5.4 If an extension of time is given following such an application the procedure at paragraphs 6.1 to 6.6 applies.

## Applications

5.5 Notice of an application to be made to the appeal court for a remedy incidental to the appeal (e.g. an interim remedy under rule 25.1 or an order for security for costs) may be included in the appeal notice or in a Part 23 application notice.

(Rule 25.15 deals with security for costs of an appeal)

(Paragraph 10 *[11]* of this practice direction contains other provisions relating to applications)

## Documents

5.6 The appellant must lodge the following documents with his appellant's notice in every case except where the appellant's notice relates to a refusal of permission to apply for judicial review (see paragraph 15.3 below):

(1) one additional copy of the appellant's notice for the appeal court; and
(2) one copy of the appellant's notice for each of the respondents ;
(3) one copy of any skeleton argument (see paragraph 5.9)
(4) a sealed copy of the order being appealed;
(5) any order giving or refusing permission to appeal, together with a copy of the reasons for that decision;
(6) any witness statements or affidavits in support of any application included in the appellant's notice; and
(7) a bundle of documents in support of the appeal– this should include copies of the documents referred to in paragraphs (1) to (6) and any other documents which the appellant reasonably considers necessary to enable the appeal court to reach its decision on the hearing of the application or appeal. Documents which are extraneous to the issues to be considered should be excluded. The other documents will, subject to paragraph 5.7, include:

(a) any affidavit or witness statement filed in support of the application for permission to appeal or the appeal,

(b) a suitable record of the reasons for judgment of the lower court (see paragraph 5.12);
(c) where permission to appeal has been given or permission is not required; any relevant transcript or note of evidence (see paragraph 5.15 below)
(d) statements of case,
(e) any application notice (or case management documentation) relevant to the subject of the appeal,
(f) in cases where the decision appealed was itself made on appeal, the first order, the reasons given and the appellant's notice of appeal from that order,
(g) in cases where the appeal is from a Tribunal, a copy of the Tribunal's reasons for the decision, a copy of the decision reviewed by the Tribunal and the reasons for the original decision
(h) in the case of judicial review or a statutory appeal, the original decision which was the subject of the application to the lower court
(i) relevant affidavits, witness statements, summaries, experts' reports and exhibits;
(j) any skeleton arguments relied on in the lower court; and
(k) such other documents as the court may direct.

5.7 Where it is not possible to file all the above documents, the appellant must indicate which documents have not yet been filed and the reasons why they are not currently available.

5.8 Where bundles comprise more than 150 pages excluding transcripts of judgment and other transcripts of the proceedings in the lower court only those documents which the court may reasonably be expected to pre-read should be included. A full set of documents should then be brought to the hearing for reference.

## Small Claims

5.8A Where the appeal relates to a claim allocated to the small claims track, the appellant must file the following documents with his appellant's notice–

(1) a sealed copy of the order being appealed;
(2) any order giving or refusing permission to appeal, together with a copy of the reasons for that decision; and
(3) a suitable record of the reasons for judgment of the lower court (see paragraph 5.12 below).

5.8B The appellant may file any other document listed in paragraph 5.6 in addition to the documents referred to in paragraph 5.8A.

## Skeleton arguments

5.9

(1) The appellant's notice must, subject to (2) and (3) below, be accompanied by a skeleton argument. Alternatively the skeleton argument may be included in the appellant's notice. Where the skeleton argument is so included it will not form part of the notice for the purposes of rule 52.8.

(2) Where it is impracticable for the appellant's skeleton argument to accompany the appellant's notice it must be lodged and served on all respondents within 14 days of filing the notice.

(3) An appellant who is not represented need not lodge a skeleton argument but is encouraged to do so since this will be helpful to the court.

## Content of skeleton arguments

5.10 Skeleton arguments for the appeal court should contain a numbered list of points stated in no more than a few sentences which should both define and confine the areas of controversy. Each point should be followed by references to any documentation on which the appellant proposes to rely.

5.11 The appellant should consider what other information the appeal court will need. This may include a list of persons who feature in the case or glossaries of technical terms. A chronology of relevant events will be necessary in most appeals. In the case of points of law, authorities relied on should be cited with reference to the particular pages where the principle concerned is set out.

## Suitable record of the judgment

5.12 Where the judgment to be appealed has been officially recorded by the court, an approved transcript of that record should accompany the appellant's notice. Photocopies will not be accepted for this purpose. However, where there is no officially recorded judgment, the following documents will be acceptable:

## Written judgments

(1) Where the judgment was made in writing a copy of that judgment endorsed with the judge's signature.

## Note of judgment

(2) When judgment was not officially recorded or made in writing a note of the judgment (agreed between the appellant's and respondent's advocates) should be submitted for approval to the judge whose decision is being appealed. If the parties cannot agree on a single note of the judgment, both versions should be provided to that judge with an explanatory letter. For the purpose of an application for permission to appeal the note need not be approved by the respondent or the lower court judge.

## Advocates' notes of judgments where the appellant is unrepresented

(3) When the appellant was unrepresented in the lower court it is the duty of any advocate for the respondent to make his/her note of judgment promptly available, free of charge to the appellant where there is no officially recorded judgment or if the court so directs. Where the appellant was represented in the lower court it is the duty of his/her own former advocate to make his/her note available in these circumstances. The appellant should submit the note of judgment to the appeal court.



## Reasons for Judgment in Tribunal cases

(4) A sealed copy of the Tribunal's reasons for the decision.

5.13 An appellant may not be able to obtain an official transcript or other suitable record of the lower court's decision within the time within which the appellant's notice must be filed. In such cases the appellant's notice must still be completed to the best of the appellant's ability on the basis of the documentation available. However it may be amended subsequently with the permission of the appeal court.

## Advocate's notes of judgments

5.14 Advocates' brief (or, where appropriate, refresher) fee includes:

(1) remuneration for taking a note of the judgment of the court;
(2) having the note transcribed accurately;
(3) attempting to agree the note with the other side if represented;
(4) submitting the note to the judge for approval where appropriate;
(5) revising it if so requested by the judge, and
(6) providing any copies required for the appeal court, instructing solicitors and lay client; and
(7) providing a copy of his note to an unrepresented appellant.

## Transcripts or Notes of Evidence

5.15 When the evidence is relevant to the appeal an official transcript of the relevant evidence must be obtained. Transcripts or notes of evidence are generally not needed for the purpose of determining an application for permission to appeal.

## Notes of evidence

5.16 If evidence relevant to the appeal was not officially recorded, a typed version of the judge's notes of evidence must be obtained.

## Transcripts at public expense

5.17 Where the lower court or the appeal court is satisfied that an unrepresented appellant is in such poor financial circumstances that the cost of a transcript would be an excessive burden the court may certify that the cost of obtaining one official transcript should be borne at public expense.

5.18 In the case of a request for an official transcript of evidence or proceedings to be paid for at public expense, the court must also be satisfied that there are reasonable grounds for appeal. Whenever possible a request for a transcript at public expense should be made to the lower court when asking for permission to appeal.

## Filing and service of appellant's notice

5.19 Rule 52.4 sets out the procedure and time limits for filing and serving an appellant's notice. The appellant must file the appellant's notice at the appeal court within such period as may be directed by the lower court which should not normally exceed 28 days or, where the lower court directs no such period, within 14 days of the date of the decision that the appellant wishes to appeal.

Skeleton arguments must be filed with the appellant's notice whether they are included within the notice or accompany it except as provided by paragraph 5.9(2),

The fee must be paid at the time the notice is presented for filing

5.20 Where the lower court judge announces his decision and reserves the reasons for his judgment or order until a later date, he should, in the exercise of powers under rule 52.4(2)(a), fix a period for filing the appellant's notice at the appeal court that takes this into account.

5.21 Except where the appeal court orders otherwise a sealed copy of the appellant's notice, including any skeleton arguments must be served on all respondents to the appeal in accordance with the timetable prescribed by rule 52.4(3) except where this requirement is modified by paragraph 5.9(2) in which case the skeleton argument should be served as soon as it is lodged.

5.22 Unless the court otherwise directs a respondent need not take any action when served with an appellant's notice until such time as notification is given to him that permission to appeal has been given.

5.23 The court may dispense with the requirement for service of the notice on a respondent. Any application notice seeking an order under rule 6.9 to dispense with service should set out the reasons relied on and be verified by a statement of truth.

5.24 Where the appellant is applying for permission to appeal in his appellant's notice, there is no requirement at this stage for copies of the documents referred to at paragraph 5.6 to be served on the respondents. However, if permission has been given by the lower court or permission is not required, copies of all the documents must be served on the respondents with the appellant's notice.

(Paragraph 5.6 provides for certain documents to be filed with an appellant's notice.)

## Amendment of Appeal Notice

5.25 An appeal notice may be amended with permission. Such an application to amend and any application in opposition will normally be dealt with at the hearing unless that course would cause unnecessary expense or delay in which case a request should be made for the application to amend to be heard in advance.

## Procedure after Permission is Obtained

6.1 This paragraph sets out the procedure where:
- (1) permission to appeal is given by the appeal court; or
- (2) the appellant's notice is filed in the appeal court and–
  - (a) permission was given by the lower court; or
  - (b) permission is not required.

6.2 If the appeal court gives permission to appeal, copies of all the documents referred to at paragraph 5.6 must be served on the respondents within 7 days of receiving the order giving permission to appeal.

(Part 6 (service of documents) provides rules on service.)

6.3 The appeal court will send the parties-
- (1) notification of–
  - (a) the date of the hearing or the period of time (the 'listing window') during which the appeal is likely to be heard; and
  - (b) in the Court of Appeal, the date by which the appeal will be heard (the 'hear by date');
- (2) where permission is granted by the appeal court a copy of the order giving permission to appeal; and
- (3) any other directions given by the court.

## Appeal Questionnaire in the Court of Appeal

6.4 The Court of Appeal will send an Appeal Questionnaire to the appellant when it notifies him of the matters referred to in paragraph 6.3.

6.5 The appellant must complete and lodge the Appeal Questionnaire within 14 days of the date of the letter of notification of the matters in paragraph 6.3. The Listing Questionaire must contain:
- (1) if the appellant is legally represented, the advocate's time estimate for the hearing of the appeal;
- (2) where a transcript of evidence is relevant to the appeal, confirmation that a transcript of evidence has been ordered where this is not already in the bundle of documents;
- (3) confirmation that copies of the appeal bundle are being prepared and will be held ready for the use of the Court of Appeal and an undertaking that they will be supplied to the court on request. For the purpose of these bundles photocopies of the transcripts will be accepted;
- (4) confirmation that copies of the Appeal Questionnaire and the appeal bundle have been served on the respondents and the date of that service.

## Time estimates

6.6 The time estimate included in an Appeal Questionnaire must be that of the advocate who will argue the appeal. It should exclude the time required by the court to give judgment. If the respondent disagrees with the time estimate, the respondent must inform the court within 7 days of receipt of the Appeal Questionnaire . In the absence of such notification the respondent will be deemed to have accepted the estimate proposed on behalf of the appellant.

## RESPONDENT

7.1 A respondent who wishes to ask the appeal court to vary the order of the lower court in any way must appeal and permission will be required on the same basis as for an appellant.

7.2 A respondent who wishes only to request that the appeal court upholds the judgment or order of the lower court whether for the reasons given in the lower court or otherwise does not make an appeal and does not therefore require permission to appeal in accordance with rule 52.3(1).

7.3 A respondent who wishes to appeal or who wishes to ask the appeal court to uphold the order of the lower court for reasons different from or additional to those given by the lower court must file a respondent's notice.

7.3A Paragraphs 5.1A and 5.1B of this practice direction also apply to a respondent and a respondent's notice.

### Time limits

7.4 The time limits for filing a respondent's notice are set out in rule 52.5 (4) and (5).

7.5 Where an extension of time is required the extension must be requested in the respondent's notice and the reasons why the respondent failed to act within the specified time must be included.

### Respondent's skeleton argument

7.6 The respondent must provide a skeleton argument for the court in all cases where he proposes to address arguments to the court. The respondent's skeleton argument may be included within a respondent's notice. Where a skeleton argument is included within a respondent's notice it will not form part of the notice for the purposes of rule 52.8.

7.7 Where the skeleton argument is not included within a respondent's notice it should be lodged and served no later than 21 days after the respondent receives the appellant's skeleton argument.

(Rule 52.5(4) sets out the period for filing and serving a respondent's notice)

### Content of skeleton arguments

7.8 A respondent's skeleton argument must conform to the directions at paragraphs 5.10 and 5.11 above with any necessary modifications. It should, where appropriate, answer the arguments set out in the appellant's skeleton argument.

### Applications within respondent's notices

7.9 A respondent may include an application within a respondent's notice in accordance with paragraph 5.5 above.

### Filing respondent's notices and skeleton arguments

7.10 The respondent must lodge the following documents with his respondent's notice in every case:

(1) two additional copies of the respondent's notice for the appeal court

(2) one copy each for the appellant and any other respondents; and

(3) two copies of any skeleton arguments.

7.11 If the respondent does not file a respondent's notice, he will not be entitled, except with the permission of the court, to rely on any ground not relied on in the lower court.

7.12 If the respondent wishes to rely on any documents in addition to those filed by the appellant he must prepare a supplemental bundle and lodge it at the appeal court with his respondent's notice. He must serve a copy of the supplemental bundle at the same time as serving the respondent's notice on the persons required to be served in accordance with rule 52.5(6).

7.13 The respondent's notice and any skeleton argument must be served in accordance with the time limits set out in rule 52.5(6) except [where] this requirement is modified by paragraph 7.7.

## Appeals to the High Court

8.1 This paragraph applies where an appeal lies to a High Court judge from the decision of a county court or a district judge of the High Court.

8.2 The following table sets out the following venues for each Circuit–

(a) Appeal centres – court centres where appeals to which this paragraph applies may be managed and heard.

(b) Hearing only centres – court centres where appeals to which this paragraph applies may be heard by order made at an appeal centre (see paragraph 8.5).

| Circuit | Appeal Centres | Hearing Only Centres |
|---|---|---|
| Midland and Oxford Circuit | Birmingham<br>Nottingham | Oxford<br>Lincoln<br>Leicester<br>Northampton<br>Stafford |
| North Eastern Circuit | Leeds<br>Newcastle<br>Sheffield | Teeside |
| Northern Circuit | Manchester<br>Liverpool<br>Preston | Carlisle |
| Wales and Chester Circuit | Cardiff<br>Swansea<br>Chester | |
| Western Circuit | Bristol<br>Exeter<br>Winchester | Truro<br>Plymouth |
| South Eastern Circuit | Central London:<br>Royal Courts of Justice<br>Provincial:<br>Lewes<br>Luton<br>Norwich<br>Reading | <br><br><br>Chelmsford<br>St Albans<br>Maidstone |

8.3 The appellant's notice must be filed in the District Registry at an appeal centre on the Circuit in which the lower court is situated. Unless the appeal court otherwise orders the appeal will be managed and heard at that appeal centre.

8.4 The appeal court may transfer an appeal to another appeal centre (whether or not on the same circuit). In deciding whether to do so the court will have regard to the criteria in rule 30.3 (criteria for a transfer order). The appeal court may do so either on application by a party or of its own initiative. Where an appeal is transferred under this paragraph, notice of transfer must be served on every person on whom the appellant's notice has been served. An appeal may not be transferred to an appeal centre on another circuit, either for management or hearing, unless the consent of a Presiding Judge of that circuit has been obtained.

8.5 Directions may be given for–

(a) an appeal to be heard at a hearing only centre; or

(b) an application in an appeal to be heard at any other venue

instead of at the appeal centre managing the appeal.

8.6 Unless a direction has been made under 8.5, any application in the appeal must be made at the appeal centre where the appeal is being managed.

8.7 A respondent's notice must be filed at the appeal centre where the appellant's notice was filed unless the appeal has been transferred to another appeal centre, in which case it must be filed at that appeal centre.

8.8 The appeal court may adopt all or any part of the procedure set out in paragraphs 6.4 to 6.6.

8.9

(1) Appeals and applications for permission to appeal will be heard by a High Court Judge or by a person authorised under paragraphs (1), (2) or (4) of the Table in section 9 (1) of the Supreme Court Act 1981 to act as a judge of the High Court;

(2) Other applications in the appeal may be heard and directions in the appeal may be given either by a High Court Judge or by any person authorised under section 9 (1) of the Supreme Court Act 1981 to act as a judge of the High Court.

## APPEALS TO A JUDGE OF A COUNTY COURT FROM A DISTRICT JUDGE

8A.1 The Designated Civil Judge in Consultation with his Presiding Judges has responsibility for allocating appeals from decisions of district judges to circuit judges

## Re-hearings

9.1 The hearing of an appeal will be a re-hearing (as opposed to a review of the decision of the lower court) if the appeal is from the decision of a minister, person or other body and the minister, person or other body–

(a) did not hold a hearing to come to that decision; or

(b) held a hearing to come to that decision, but the procedure adopted did not provide for the consideration of evidence.

## Appeals Transferred to the Court of Appeal

10.1 Where an appeal is transferred to the Court of Appeal under rule 52.14 the Court of Appeal may give such additional directions as are considered appropriate.

## Applications

11.1 Where a party to an appeal makes an application whether in an appeal notice or by Part 23 application notice, the provisions of Part 23 will apply.

11.2 The applicant must file the following documents with the notice–

(1) one additional copy of the application notice for the appeal court and one copy for each of the respondents;

(2) where applicable a sealed copy of the order which is the subject of the main appeal;

(3) a bundle of documents in support which should include:

(a) the Part 23 application notice

(b) any witness statements and affidavits filed in support of the application notice

(c) the documents specified in paragraph 5.6 (6) [*5.6 (7)*]above in so far as they have not already been filed with the appellant's notice.

## DISPOSING OF APPLICATIONS OR APPEALS BY CONSENT

### Dismissal of applications or appeals by consent

12.1 These paragraphs do not apply where any party to the proceedings is a child or patient.

12.2 Where an appellant does not wish to pursue an application or an appeal, he may request the appeal court for an order that his application or appeal be dismissed. Such a request must contain a statement that the appellant is not a child or patient. If such a request is granted it will usually be on the basis that the appellant pays the costs of the application or appeal.

12.3 If the appellant wishes to have the application or appeal dismissed without costs, his request must be accompanied by a consent signed by the respondent or his legal representative stating that the respondent is not a child or patient and consents to the dismissal of the application or appeal without costs.

12.4 Where a settlement has been reached disposing of the application or appeal, the parties may make a joint request to the court stating that none of them is a child or patient, and asking that the application or appeal be dismissed by consent. If the request is granted the application or appeal will be dismissed.

### Allowing Unopposed Appeals or Applications on Paper

13.1 The appeal court will not make an order allowing an application or appeal unless satisfied that the decision of the lower court was wrong. Where the appeal court is requested by all parties to allow an application or an appeal the court may consider the request on the papers. The request should state that none of the parties is a child or patient and set out the relevant history of the proceedings and the matters relied on as justifying the proposed order and be accompanied by a copy of the proposed order.

### Procedure for Structured settlements and consent orders involving a child or patient

13.2 Settlements relating to appeals and applications where one of the parties is a child or a patient; and structured settlements which are agreed upon at the appeal stage require the court's approval.

### Child

13.3 In cases involving a child a copy of the proposed order signed by the parties' solicitors should be sent to the appeal court, together with an opinion from the advocate acting on behalf of the child.

### Patient

13.4 Where a party is a patient the same procedure will be adopted, but the documents filed should also include any relevant reports prepared for the Court of Protection and a document evidencing formal approval by that court where required.

### Structured settlements

13.5 Where a structured settlement has been negotiated in a case which is under appeal the documents filed should include those which would be required in the case of a structured settlement dealt with at first instance. Details can be found in the Practice Direction which supplements CPR Part 40.

## SUMMARY ASSESSMENT OF COSTS

14.1 Costs are likely to be assessed by way of summary assessment at the following hearings:

(1) contested directions hearings;
(2) applications for permission to appeal at which the respondent is present;
(3) dismissal list hearings in the Court of Appeal at which the respondent is present;
(4) appeals from case management decisions; and
(5) appeals listed for less than one day.

14.2 Parties attending any of the hearings referred to in paragraph 13.1 should be prepared to deal with the summary assessment.

## OTHER SPECIAL PROVISIONS REGARDING THE COURT OF APPEAL

### Filing of Documents

15.1

(1) The documents relevant to proceedings in the Court of Appeal, Civil Division must be filed in the Civil Appeals Office Registry, Room E307, Royal Courts of Justice, Strand, London, WC2A 2LL
(2) The Civil Appeals Office will not serve documents and where service is required by the CPR or this practice direction it must be effected by the parties.

### Master in the Court of Appeal, Civil Division

15.2 When the Head of the Civil Appeals Office acts in a judicial capacity pursuant to rule 52.16, he shall be known as Master. Other eligible officers may also be designated by the Master of the Rolls to exercise judicial authority under rule 52.16 and shall then be known as Deputy Masters.

### Judicial Review Appeals

15.3 Where the Court of appeal gives permission to apply for judicial review under rule 52.15(3) the court may, hear the application for judicial review. This will be rare, but may be appropriate where, for example, the High Court is bound by authority or for some other reason, an appeal to the Court of Appeal will be inevitable.

15.4 Paragraphs 5.6 and 5.19 above do not apply to cases where the appeal notice seeks permission to appeal a refusal to give permission to apply for judicial review. In such cases the following documents must be filed with the appellant's notice:

(1) one additional copy of the appellant's notice for the Court of Appeal
(2) one copy of the appellant's notice for each of the respondents to be sealed and returned
(3) the order refusing permission to apply for judicial review
(4) Form 86A;
(5) a copy of the original decision which is the subject of the application to the High Court
(6) any witness statements or affidavits in support of any application included in the appellant's notice;
(7) a copy of the bundle of documents used in the High Court
(8) the skeleton argument relied on in the High Court; and
(9) a transcript of the judgment.

15.5 The time for filing an appellant's notice in these circumstances is set out in rule 52.15(1). The arrangements for service on the respondent in paragraph 5.24 apply.

15.6 Where it is not possible to file all these documents, the appellant must indicate which documents have not yet been filed and the reasons why they are not currently available.

## Listing and hear-by dates

15.7 The management of the list will be dealt with by the listing officer under the direction of the Master.

15.8 The Civil Appeals List of the Court of Appeal is divided as follows:

- *The applications list* – applications for permission to appeal and other applications.
- *The appeals list* – appeals where permission to appeal has been given or where an appeal lies without permission being required.
- *The expedited list* – appeals or applications where the Court of Appeal has directed an expedited hearing. The current practice of the Court of Appeal is summarised in *Unilever plc v Chefaro Proprietaries Ltd (Practice Note)* [1995] 1 WLR 243.
- *The stand-out list* – appeals or applications which, for good reason, are not at present ready to proceed and have been stood out by judicial direction.
- *The fixtures list* – where a hearing date for the appeal is fixed in advance.
- *The second fixtures list* – if an appeal is designated as a 'second fixture' it means that a hearing date is arranged in advance on the express basis that the list is fully booked for the period in question and therefore the case will be heard only if a suitable gap occurs in the list.
- *The short-warned list* – appeals which the court considers may be prepared for the hearing by an advocate other than the one originally instructed with a half day's notice, or, if the court so directs, 48 hours notice.

15.9 Once an appeal is listed for hearing from the short warned list it becomes the immediate professional duty of the advocate instructed in the appeal, if he is unable to appear at the hearing, to take all practicable measures to ensure that his lay client is represented at the hearing by an advocate who is fully instructed and able to argue the appeal.

## Requests for directions

15.10 To ensure that all requests for directions are centrally monitored and correctly allocated, all requests for directions or rulings (whether relating to listing or any other matters) should be made to the Civil Appeals Office. Those seeking directions or rulings must not approach the supervising Lord Justice either directly, or via his or her clerk.



## Lists of authorities

15.11 Once the parties have been notified of the date fixed for hearing the appellant's advocate shall file, after consulting his opponent, for the purpose of pre-reading by the court, one bundle containing photocopies of the principal authorities upon which each side will rely at the hearing, with the relevant passages marked. There will in general be no need to include authorities for propositions not in dispute. This bundle should be made available 28 days before the hearing, unless the period of notice of the hearing is less than 28 days in which case the bundle should be filed immediately. Such bundles should not normally contain more than 10 authorities. If any party intends, during the hearing to refer to other authorities these may be included in a second agreed bundle to be filed by the parties at the hearing. Alternatively, and in place of the second bundle only, a list of authorities and text may be delivered to the office of the Head Usher of the Court of Appeal no later than 5.30pm on the last working day before the hearing is to commence.

## Reserved judgments of the Court of Appeal

15.12 Unless the court orders otherwise, copies of a written judgment will be made available to the parties' legal advisers by 4pm on the second working day before judgment is due to be pronounced on the condition that the contents are not communicated to the parties themselves until one hour before the listed time for pronouncement of judgment.

15.13 The judgment is made available to legal advisers primarily to enable them to consider the judgment and decide what consequential orders they should seek. The condition is imposed to prevent the outcome of the case being publicly reported before judgment is given, since the judgment is confidential until then. Every page of the judgment will be marked 'Unapproved judgment: No permission is given to copy or use in court'. These words carry the authority of the court.

15.14 Where a party is not legally represented a copy of the judgment will be made available to him at the same time as to legal advisers. It must be treated as confidential until pronouncement of judgment.

## SECTION II
## GENERAL PROVISIONS ABOUT STATUTORY APPEALS AND APPEALS BY WAY OF CASE STATED

16.1 This section of this practice direction contains general provisions about statutory appeals (paragraphs 17.1–17.6) and appeals by way of case stated (paragraphs 18.1–18.20).

16.2 Where any of the provisions in this section provide for documents to be filed at the appeal court, these documents are in addition to any documents required under Part 52 or section I of this practice direction.

## STATUTORY APPEALS

17.1 This part of this section–

(1) applies where under any enactment an appeal (other than by way of case stated) lies to the court from a Minister of State, government department, tribunal or other person ('statutory appeals'); and

(2) is subject to any provision about a specific category of appeal in any enactment or Section III of this practice direction.

### Part 52

17.2 Part 52 applies to statutory appeals with the following amendments:

### Filing of appellant's notice

17.3 The appellant must file the appellant's notice at the appeal court within 28 days after the date of the decision of the lower court he wishes to appeal.

17.4 Where a statement of the reasons for a decision is given later than the notice of that decision, the period for filing the appellant's notice is calculated from the date on which the statement is received by the appellant.

### Service of appellant's notice

17.5 In addition to the respondents to the appeal, the appellant must serve the appellant's notice in accordance with rule 52.4(3) on the chairman of the tribunal, Minister of State, government department or other person from whose decision the appeal is brought.

### Right of Minister etc to be heard on the appeal

17.6 Where the appeal is from an order or decision of a Minister of State or government department, the Minister or department, as the case may be, is entitled to attend the hearing and to make representations to the court.

## APPEALS BY WAY OF CASE STATED

18.1 This part of this section–

(1) applies where under any enactment-

(a) an appeal lies to the court by way of case stated; or

(b) a question of law may be referred to the court by way of case stated; and

(2) is subject to any provision about [*to*] a specific category of appeal in any enactment or Section III of this practice direction.

### Part 52

18.2 Part 52 applies to appeals by way of case stated subject to the following amendments.

### Case stated by Crown Court or Magistrates' Court

#### *Application to state a case*

18.3 The procedure for applying to the Crown Court or a Magistrates' Court to have a case stated for the opinion of the High Court is set out in the Crown Court Rules 1982 and the Magistrates' Courts Rules 1981 respectively.

#### *Filing of appellant's notice*

18.4 The appellant must file the appellant's notice at the appeal court within 10 days after he receives the stated case.



#### *Documents to be lodged*

18.5 The appellant must lodge the following documents with his appellant's notice:

(1) the stated case;

(2) a copy of the judgment, order or decision in respect of which the case has been stated; and

(3) where the judgment, order or decision in respect of which the case has been stated was itself given or made on appeal, a copy of the judgment, order or decision appealed from.

#### *Service of appellant's notice*

18.6 The appellant must serve the appellant's notice and accompanying documents on all respondents within 4 days after they are filed or lodged at the appeal court.

### Case stated by Minister, government department, tribunal or other person

#### *Application to state a case*

18.7 The procedure for applying to a Minister, government department, tribunal or other person ('Minister or tribunal etc.') to have a case stated for the opinion of the court may be set out in–

(1) the enactment which provides for the right of appeal; or

(2) any rules of procedure relating to the Minister or tribunal etc.

### *Signing of stated case by Minister or tribunal etc*

18.8 A case stated by a tribunal must be signed by the chairman or president of the tribunal. A case stated by any other person must be signed by that person or by a person authorised to do so.

### *Service of stated case by Minister or tribunal etc*

18.9 The Minister or tribunal etc. must serve the stated case on–

(1) the party who requests the case to be stated; or

(2) the party as a result of whose application to the court, the case was stated.

18.10 Where an enactment provides that a Minister or tribunal etc. may state a case or refer a question of law to the court by way of case stated without a request being made, the Minister or tribunal etc must–

(1) serve the stated case on those parties that the Minister or tribunal etc. considers appropriate; and

(2) give notice to every other party to the proceedings that the stated case has been served on the party named and on the date specified in the notice.

### *Filing and service of appellant's notice*

18.11 The party on whom the stated case was served must file the appellant's notice and the stated case at the appeal court and serve copies of the notice and stated case on–

(1) the Minister or tribunal etc. who stated the case; and

(2) every party to the proceedings to which the stated case relates,

within 14 days after the stated case was served on him.

18.12 Where paragraph 18.10 applies the Minister or tribunal etc. must–

(1) file an appellant's notice and the stated case at the appeal court; and

(2) serve copies of those documents on the persons served under paragraph 18.10

within 14 days after stating the case.

18.13 Where–

(1) a stated case has been served by the Minister or Tribunal etc in accordance with paragraph 18.9; and

(2) the party on whom the stated case was served does not file an appellant's notice in accordance with paragraph 18.11,

any other party may file an appellant's notice with the stated case at the appeal court and serve a copy of the notice and the case on the persons listed in paragraph 18.11 within the period of time set out in paragraph 18.14.

18.14 The period of time referred to in paragraph 18.13 is 14 days from the last day on which the party on whom the stated case was served may file an appellant's notice in accordance with paragraph 18.11.

### *Amendment of stated case*

18.15 The court may amend the stated case or order it to be returned to the Minister or tribunal etc. for amendment and may draw inferences of fact from the facts stated in the case.

### *Right of Minister etc to be heard on the appeal*

18.16 Where the case is stated by a Minister or government department, that Minister or department, as the case may be, is entitled to appear on the appeal and to make representations to the court.

### *Application for order to state a case*

18.17 An application to the court for an order requiring a minister or tribunal etc. to state a case for the decision of the court, or to refer a question of law to the court by way of case stated must be made to the court which would be the appeal court if the case were stated.

18.18 An application to the court for an order directing a Minister or tribunal etc. to–
(1) state a case for determination by the court; or
(2) refer a question of law to the court by way of case stated,
must be made in accordance with CPR Part 23.
18.19 The application notice must contain-
(1) the grounds of the application;
(2) the question of law on which it is sought to have the case stated; and
(3) any reasons given by the minister or tribunal etc for his or its refusal to state a case.
18.20 The application notice must be filed at the appeal court and served on–
(1) the minister, department, secretary of the tribunal or other person as the case may be; and
(2) every party to the proceedings to which the application relates,
within 14 after the appellant receives notice of the refusal of his request to state a case.

## EXTRADITION

19.1 Paragraphs 18.3 to 18.6 apply to appeals by case stated under-
(1) section 7 of the Criminal Justice Act 1988; and
(2) section 7A of the Fugitive Offenders Act 1967,
and references in those paragraphs to appellant and respondent shall be construed as references to the requesting state and the person whose surrender is sought respectively.

19.2 An application for an order under either of the sections mentioned in paragraph 19.1 or under section 2A of the Backing of Warrants (Republic of Ireland) Act 1965 requiring a court to state a case must be made in accordance with paragraphs 18.17 to 18.20 and the references in those paragraphs to a tribunal and the secretary of a tribunal shall be construed as references to the court and the clerk of the court respectively.

## SECTION III
## PROVISIONS ABOUT SPECIFIC APPEALS

20.1 This section of this Practice Direction provides special provisions about the appeals to which the following table refers. This Section is not exhaustive and does not create, amend or remove any right of appeal.

20.2 Part 52 applies to all appeals to which this section applies subject to any special provisions set out in this section.

20.3 Where any of the provisions in this section provide for documents to be filed at the appeal court, these documents are in addition to any documents required under Part 52 or sections I or II of this practice direction.

| APPEALS TO THE COURT OF APPEAL | Paragraph |
|---|---|
| Competition Commission Appeal Tribunals | 21.10 |
| Contempt of Court | 21.4 |
| Decree nisi of divorce | 21.1 |
| Immigration Appeal Tribunal | 21.7 |
| Lands Tribunal | 21.9 |
| Nullity of marriage | 21.1 |
| Patents Court on appeal from Comptroller | 21.3 |
| Revocation of patent | 21.2 |
| Social Security Commissioners | 21.5 |
| Special Commissioner (where the appeal is direct to the Court of Appeal) | 21.8 |
| Value Added Tax and Duties Tribunals (where the appeal is direct to the Court of Appeal) | 21.6 |

| APPEALS TO THE HIGH COURT | Paragraph |
|---|---|
| Agriculture Land Tribunal | 22.7 |
| Architects Act 1997, s 22 | 22.3 |
| Clergy Pensions Measure Act 1961, s 38(3) | 23.2 |
| Commons Registration Act 1965 | 23.9 |
| Consumer Credit Act 1974 | 22.4 |
| Friendly Societies Act 1974 | 23.7 |
| Friendly Societies Act 1992 | 23.7 |
| Industrial and Provident Societies Act 1965 | 23.2, 23.7 |
| Industrial Assurance Act 1923 | 23.2, 23.7 |
| Industrial Assurance Act 1923, s 17 | 23.6 |
| Inheritance Tax Act 1984, s 222 | 23.3 |
| Inheritance Tax Act 1984, s 225 | 23.5 |
| Inheritance Tax Act 1984, ss 249(3) and 251 | 23.4 |
| Land Registration Act 1925 | 23.2 |
| Law of Property Act 1922, para 16 of Sched 15 | 23.2 |
| Medicines Act 1968, ss 82(3) and 83(2) | 22.3 |
| Mental Health Review Tribunal | 22.9 |
| Merchant Shipping Act 1995 | 22.2 |
| Nurses, Midwives and Health Visitors Act 1977, s 12 | 22.3 |
| Pensions Act 1995, s 97 | 23.2 |
| Pensions Schemes Act 1993, ss 151 and 173 | 23.2 |
| Pensions Appeal Tribunal Act 1943 | 22.5 |
| Pharmacy Act 1954 | 22.3 |
| Social Security Administration Act 1992 | 22.6 |
| Stamp Duty Reserve Tax Regulations 1986, reg 10 | 23.5 |
| Taxes Management Act 1970, ss 53 and 100C(4) | 23.4 |
| Taxes Management Act 1970, s 56A | 23.5 |
| Value Added Tax and Duties Tribunal | 22.8, 23.8 |
| Water Resources Act 1991, s 205(4) | 23.2 |

| APPEALS TO COUNTY COURT | Paragraph |
|---|---|
| Local Government (Miscellaneous) Provisions Act 1976 | 24.1 |

## APPEALS TO THE COURT OF APPEAL

### Appeal against decree nisi of divorce or nullity of marriage

21.1 (1) The appellant must file the appellant's notice at the Court of Appeal within 28 days after the date on which the decree was pronounced.

(2) The appellant must file the following documents with the appellant's notice–

(a) the decree; and

(b) a certificate of service of the appellant's notice.

(3) The appellant's notice must be served on the appropriate district judge (see sub-paragraph (6)) in addition to the persons to be served under rule 52.4(3) and in accordance with that rule.

(4) The lower court may not alter the time limits for filing of the appeal notices.

(5) Where an appellant intends to apply to the Court of Appeal for an extension of time for serving or filing the appellant's notice he must give notice of that intention to the appropriate district judge (see sub-paragraph 6) before the application is made.

(6) In this paragraph 'the appropriate district judge' means, where the lower court is–

(a) a county court, the district judge of that court;

(b) a district registry, the district judge of that registry;
(c) the Principal Registry of the Family Division, the senior district judge of that division.

## Appeal against order for revocation of patent

21.2
(1) This paragraph applies where an appeal lies to the Court of Appeal from an order for the revocation of a patent.
(2) The appellant must serve the appellant's notice on the Comptroller-General of Patents, Designs and Trade Marks (the 'Comptroller') in addition to the persons to be served under rule 52.4(3) and in accordance with that rule.
(3) Where, before the appeal hearing, the respondent decides not to oppose the appeal or not to attend the appeal hearing, he must immediately serve notice of that decision on–
  (a) the Comptroller; and
  (b) the appellant
(4) Where the respondent serves a notice in accordance with paragraph (2), he must also serve copies of the following documents on the Comptroller with that notice–
  (a) the petition;
  (b) any statements of claim;
  (c) any written evidence filed in the claim.
(5) Within 14 days after receiving the notice in accordance with paragraph (2), the Comptroller must serve on the appellant a notice stating whether or not he intends to attend the appeal hearing.
(6) The Comptroller may attend the appeal hearing and oppose the appeal–
  (a) in any case where he has given notice under paragraph (4) of his intention to attend; and
  (b) in any other case (including, in particular, a case where the respondent withdraws his opposition to the appeal during the hearing) if the Court of Appeal so directs or permits.



## Appeal from Patents Court on appeal from Comptroller

21.3 Where the appeal is from a decision of the Patents Court which was itself made on an appeal from a decision of the Comptroller-General of Patents, Designs and Trade Marks, the appellant must serve the appellant's notice on the Comptroller in addition to the persons to be served under rule 52.4(3) and in accordance with that rule.

## Appeals in cases of contempt of court

21.4 In an appeal under section 13 of the Administration of Justice Act 1960 (appeals in cases of contempt of court), the appellant must serve the appellant's notice on the court from whose order or decision the appeal is brought in addition to the persons to be served under rule 52.4(3) and in accordance with that rule.

**[NOTE: The remainder of this *Practice Direction* (paras 21.5 to 24.1) has been omitted]**

**[4.39]**

# Practice Direction on committal applications, supplemental to CPR Sch 1 – RSC Ord 52 and Sch 2 – CCR Ord 29

**Note** – The practice set out in this Direction is to be followed in all cases of civil contempt, including judgment summonses and contempt in family proceedings: *Mubarak v Mubarak* [2001] 1 FCR 193.

## GENERAL

1.1 Part I of this practice direction applies to any application for an order for committal of a person to prison for contempt of court (a 'committal application'). Part II makes additional provision where the committal application relates to a contempt in the face of the court.

1.2 Where the alleged contempt of court consists of or is based upon disobedience to an order made in a county court or breach of an undertaking given to a county court or consists of an act done in the course of proceedings in a county court, or where in any other way the alleged contempt is a contempt which the county court has power to punish, the committal application may be made in the county court in question.

1.3 In every other case (other than one within Part II of this practice direction), a committal application must be made in the High Court.

1.4 In all cases the Convention rights of those involved should particularly be borne in mind. It should be noted that the burden of proof, having regard to the possibility that a person may be sent to prison, is that the allegation be proved beyond reasonable doubt. (Section 1 of the Human Rights Act defines 'the Convention rights')

## PART I
## COMMENCEMENT OF COMMITTAL PROCEEDINGS

2.1 A committal application must, subject to paragraph 2.2, be commenced by the issue of a Part 8 claim form (see paragraph 2.5).

2.2

(1) If the committal application is made in existing proceedings it may be commenced by the filing of an application notice in those proceedings.

(2) An application to commit for breach of an undertaking or order may be commenced by the filing of an application notice in the proceedings in which the undertaking was given or the order was made.

(3) The application notice must state that the application is made in the proceedings in question and its title and reference number must correspond with the title and reference number of those proceedings.

2.3 If the committal application is one which cannot be made without permission, the claim form or application notice, as the case may be, may not be issued or filed until the requisite permission has been granted.

2.4 If the permission of the court is needed in order to make a committal application:

(i) the permission must be applied for by filing an application notice (see rule 23.2(4));

(ii) the application notice need not be served on the respondent;

(iii) the date on which and the name of the judge by whom the requisite permission was granted must be stated on the claim form or application notice by which the committal application is commenced;

(iv) the permission may only be granted by a judge who, under paragraph 11, would have power to hear the committal application if permission were granted; and

(v) CPR rules 23.9 and 23.10 do not apply.

2.5 If the committal application is commenced by the issue of a claim form, Part 8 of these Rules shall, subject to the provisions of this practice direction, apply as though references to 'claimant' were references to the person making the committal application and references to 'defendant' were references to the person against whom the committal application is made (in this practice direction referred to as 'the respondent') but:

- (i) the claim form together with copies of all written evidence in support must, unless the court otherwise directs, be served personally on the respondent;
- (ii) the claim form must set out in full the grounds on which the committal application is made and should identify, separately and numerically, each alleged act of contempt;
- (iii) an amendment to the claim form can be made with the permission of the court but not otherwise;
- (iv) CPR rule 8.4 does not apply. and
- (v) the claim form must contain a prominent notice stating the possible consequences of the court making a committal order and of the respondent not attending the hearing. A form of notice, which may be used, is annexed to this practice direction.

2.6 If a committal application is commenced by the filing of an application notice, Part 23 of these Rules shall, subject to the provisions of this practice direction, apply but

- (i) the application notice together with copies of all written evidence in support must, unless the court otherwise directs, be served personally on the respondent;
- (ii) the application notice must set out in full the grounds on which the committal application is made and should identify, separately and numerically, each alleged act of contempt;
- (iii) an amendment to the application notice can be made with the permission of the court but not otherwise; and
- (iv) the court may not dispose of the committal application without a hearing.
- (v) the application notice must contain a prominent notice stating the possible consequences of the court making a committal order and of the respondent not attending the hearing. A form of notice, which may be used, is annexed to this practice direction.

## WRITTEN EVIDENCE

3.1 Written evidence in support of or in opposition to a committal application must be given by affidavit.

3.2 Written evidence served in support of or in opposition to a committal application must, unless the court otherwise directs, be filed

3.3 A respondent, notwithstanding that he has not filed or served any written evidence, may give oral evidence at the hearing if he expresses a wish to do so. If he does so, he may be cross-examined.

3.4 A respondent may, with the permission of the court, call a witness to give oral evidence at the hearing notwithstanding that the witness has not sworn an affidavit.

## CASE MANAGEMENT AND DATE OF HEARING

4.1 The applicant for the committal order must, when lodging the claim form or application notice with the court for issuing or filing, as the case may be, obtain from the court a date for the hearing of the committal application.

4.2 Unless the court otherwise directs, the hearing date of a committal application shall be not less than 14 clear days after service of the claim form or of the application notice, as the case may be, on the respondent. The hearing date must be specified in the claim form or application notice or in a Notice of Hearing or Application attached to and served with the claim form or application notice.

4.3 The court may, however, at any time give case management directions, including directions for the service of written evidence by the respondent and written evidence in reply by the applicant, or may convene and hold a directions hearing.

4.4 The court may on the hearing date:

(i) give case management directions with a view to a hearing of the committal application on a future date, or

(ii) if the committal application is ready to be heard, proceed forthwith to hear it.

4.5 In dealing with any committal application, the court will have regard to the need for the respondent to have details of the alleged acts of contempt and the opportunity to respond to the committal application.

4.6 The court should also have regard to the need for the respondent to be:

(i) allowed a reasonable time for responding to the committal application including, if necessary, preparing a defence;

(ii) made aware of the availability of assistance from the Community Legal Service and how to contact the Service;

(iii) given the opportunity, if unrepresented, to obtain legal advice; and

(iv) if unable to understand English, allowed to make arrangements, seeking the assistance of the court if necessary, for an interpreter to attend the hearing.

## STRIKING OUT

5. The court may, on application by the respondent or on its own initiative, strike out a committal application if it appears to the court:

(a) that the committal application and the evidence served in support of it disclose no reasonable ground for alleging that the respondent is guilty of a contempt of court;

(b) that the committal application is an abuse of the court's process or, if made in existing proceedings, is otherwise likely to obstruct the just disposal of those proceedings; or

(c) that there has been a failure to comply with a rule, practice direction or court order.

(CPR Part 3 contains general powers for management by the court).

## MISCELLANEOUS

6. CPR Rules 35.7 (Court's power to direct that evidence is to be given by a single joint expert), 35.8 (Instructions to single joint expert) and 35.9 (Power of court to direct a party to provide information) do not apply to committal applications.

7. An order under CPR rule 18.1 (Order for a party to give additional information) may not be made against a respondent to a committal application.

8. A committal application may not be discontinued without the permission of the court.

9. A committal application should normally be heard in public (see CPR rule 39.2), but if it is heard in private and the court finds the respondent guilty of contempt of court, the judge shall, when sitting next in public, state:

(i) the name of the respondent;

(ii) in general terms the nature of the contempt or contempts found proved; and

(iii) the penalty (if any) imposed.

10. The court may waive any procedural defect in the commencement or conduct of a committal application if satisfied that no injustice has been caused to the respondent by the defect.

11. Except where under an enactment a master or district judge has power to make a committal order, a committal order can only be made:

(i) in High Court proceedings, by a High Court judge or a person authorised to act as such;

(ii) in County Court proceedings by a circuit judge or a person authorised to act or capable by virtue of his office of acting as such.

## PART II

12. Where the committal application relates to a contempt in the face of the court the following matters should be given particular attention. Normally, it will be appropriate to defer consideration of the behaviour to allow the respondent time to reflect on what has occurred. The time needed for the following procedures should allow such a period of reflection.

13. A Part 8 claim form and an application notice are not required for Part II, but other provisions of this practice direction should be applied, as necessary, or adapted to the circumstances. In addition the judge should:

- (i) tell the respondent of the possible penalty he faces;
- (ii) inform the respondent in detail, and preferably in writing, of the actions and behaviour of the respondent which have given rise to the committal application;
- (iii) if he considers that an apology would remove the need for the committal application, tell the respondent;
- (iv) have regard to the need for the respondent to be:
  - (a) allowed a reasonable time for responding to the committal application, including, if necessary, preparing a defence;
  - (b) made aware of the availability of assistance from the Community Legal Service and how to contact the Service;
  - (c) given the opportunity, if unrepresented, to obtain legal advice;
  - (d) if unable to understand English, allowed to make arrangements, seeking the court's assistance if necessary, for an interpreter to attend the hearing; and
  - (e) brought back before the court for the committal application to be heard within a reasonable time.
- (v) allow the respondent an opportunity to:
  - (a) apologise to the court;
  - (b) explain his actions and behaviour; and,
  - (c) if the contempt is proved, to address the court on the penalty to be imposed on him;
- (vi) if there is a risk of the appearance of bias, ask another judge to hear the committal application.
- (vii) where appropriate, nominate a suitable person to give the respondent the information.

(It is likely to be appropriate to nominate a person where the effective communication of information by the judge to the respondent was not possible when the incident occurred.)

14. Where the committal application is to be heard by another judge, a written statement by the judge before whom the actions and behaviour of the respondent which have given rise to the committal application took place may be submitted as evidence of those actions and behaviour.

## ANNEX

### IMPORTANT NOTICE

The Court has power to send you to prison and to fine you if it finds that any of the allegations made against you are true and amount to a contempt of court.

**You must attend court** on the date shown on the front of this form. It is in your own interest to do so. You should bring with you any witnesses and documents which you think will help you put your side of the case.

If you consider the allegations are not true you must tell the court why. If it is established that they are true, you must tell the court of any good reason why they do not amount to a contempt of court, or, if they do, why you should not be punished.

If you need advice you should show this document at once to your solicitor or go to a Citizens' Advice Bureau.

4086–5000

# PART 5

# Precedents

## Contents

**Orders**



**Pension Orders**



---

## Notice of application to a divorce county court

**[5.1]**

| IN THE | COUNTY COURT | No of Matter |
|---|---|---|
| Between | AB | Petitioner |
| | and | |
| | BB | Respondent |

TAKE NOTICE that the Petitioner [Respondent] intends to apply to the Judge [District Judge] of this court [in Chambers] at [*state address where hearing will take place*] on [Mon]day the day of 20 at o'clock for [*state concisely the relief claimed eg* an order that the Petitioner be at liberty to amend the petition herein in accordance with the copy served herewith]

[The estimated length of the hearing is ...........]
[Counsel will [not] be attending]
Dated this day of 20
Solicitors for the Petitioner [Respondent] of (*address*)
To the [District] Judge
and to the Respondent [Petitioner]

1 Adapted from Form D11 used in divorce county courts: see FPR 1991, r 10.9(b) applying CCR Ord 13, r 1.

## Notice of application to the Principal Registry in a cause treated as pending in a divorce county court[1]

### [5.2]

| IN THE | HIGH COURT OF JUSTICE | No | of 20 |
|---|---|---|---|
| Between | AB | | Petitioner |
| | and | | |
| | BB | | Respondent |

TAKE NOTICE that the Petitioner [Respondent] intends to apply to a [Judge in chambers/court at the Royal Courts of Justice, Strand London at or after 10.30 am[2]] [District Judge at the Principal Registry of the Family Division, First Avenue House, 42–49 High Holborn, London WC1V 6NP] on [Mon]day the day of 20 [at o'clock for [*state concisely the relief required*]

Dated this day of 20
The estimated duration of this application is
Counsel will [not] be appearing on behalf of the applicant
Solicitors for the Petitioner [Respondent] of (*address*)
To the [District] Judge
and to the Petitioner [Respondent]

1 Adapted from Form D261. See FPR 1991, rr 1.4, 10.9 applying CCR Ord 13, r 1.
2 In the case of judge's summonses the number of the court and a better estimate of the time when the summons will be heard can be found in the Daily Cause List published on the morning of the hearing date, a draft of which is available in the office of the Clerk of the Rules at the Royal Courts of Justice.

## Summons to a High Court District Judge[1]

### [5.3]

| IN THE | HIGH COURT OF JUSTICE<br>FAMILY DIVISION | No | of 20 [2] |
|---|---|---|---|
| | [DISTRICT REGISTRY] | | |
| Between | AB | | Petitioner |
| | and | | |
| | BB | | Respondent |
| | and | | |
| | XY | | Co-Respondent |

LET the Petitioner [Respondent] [All Parties] attend [one of the District Judges of this Division at First Avenue House, 42–49 High Holborn, London WC1V 6NP] [the District Judge in Chambers at the District Registry of the High Court of Justice at [*address*] on [Mon]day the day of 20 at o'clock on the hearing of an application by the Respondent [Petitioner] for [*state concisely the relief required*]

The estimated duration of this summons is
Counsel will [not] be appearing on behalf of the applicant
To the Respondent [Petitioner] and to EF & Co his [her] Solicitors
To the Co-Respondent and GH & Co his [her] Solicitors
Dated this day of 20
This summons was issued by LM & Co of (*address*), [Agents for (*name and address*)]
Solicitors for the Respondent [Petitioner]

1 Adapted from Form D262: see FPR 1991, r 10.9(b).
2 In a District Registry 'No of Matter'.

## Summons to a High Court Judge[1]

**[5.4]**

| IN THE | HIGH COURT OF JUSTICE<br>FAMILY DIVISION<br>[DISTRICT REGISTRY] | No 20 [2] |
|---|---|---|
| Between | AB | Petitioner |
| | and | |
| | BB | Respondent |
| | and | |
| | XY | Co-Respondent |

LET the Respondent [Petitioner] [All Parties] attend the Judge in Chambers [court] at the Royal Courts of Justice, Strand, London, WC2A 2LL on [Mon]day the day of 20 at o'clock on the hearing of an application by the Respondent [Petitioner] for (*state concisely the relief required*)

Dated this day of 20
The estimated duration of this summons is [3]
Counsel will [not] be appearing for the applicant
To the Respondent [Petitioner] and to EF & Co his [her] Solicitors
To the Co-Respondent and GH & Co his [her] Solicitors
This summons was issued by LM & Co of (*address*) [Agents for (*name and address*)]
Solicitors for the Petitioner [Respondent]

1 Adapted from Form D262: see FPR 1991, r 10.9(b).
2 In a District Registry 'No of Matter'.
3 If the estimated length of hearing is more than a day the prescribed form of notice of estimate (D208), which can be obtained from the Clerk of the Rules Dept at the RCJ or from Somerset House, must be lodged with the Clerk of the Rules: *Practice Direction* [1984] 1 All ER 783, [1984] 1 WLR 475. As to hearings pursuant to the Children Act 1989 see *Practice Direction* [1994] 1 All ER 155, [1994] 1 WLR 16.

## High Court order: general form: Principal Registry[1]

**[5.5]**

IN THE HIGH COURT OF JUSTICE No of 20
FAMILY DIVISION
PRINCIPAL REGISTRY

Before [the Honourable Mr Justice sitting at the Royal Courts of Justice, Strand, London *or* in Chambers] [District Judge in Chambers]

| Between | AB | Petitioner |
|---|---|---|
| | and | |
| | BB | Respondent |
| | and | |
| | XY | Co-Respondent |

[*If made in court* On the day of 20 ]
UPON HEARING Counsel [the Solicitors] for the parties
AND UPON reading the affidavit of RS sworn on 20
IT IS ORDERED (*set out the order made*)
[*If made in Chambers:* DATED this day of 20 ]

1 Adapted from Form D210 (which is used in open court and has the date after the heading) and Form D264 (which is used in chambers and has the date at the foot of the order. Orders are drawn up by the court: see FPR 1991, r 2.43.

## High Court order: general form: District Registry[1]

**[5.6]**

IN THE HIGH COURT OF JUSTICE No of Matter
FAMILY DIVISION
[DISTRICT REGISTRY]
[Before The Honourable Mr Justice ]

| Between | AB | Petitioner |
|---|---|---|
| | and | |
| | BB | Respondent |
| | and | |
| | XY | Co-Respondent |

UPON HEARING Counsel [the Solicitors] for the parties
AND UPON reading the affidavit of RS sworn on 20
IT IS ORDERED [*set out the order made*]
DATED this day of 20

1 Orders are drawn up by the courts. See FPR 1991, r 2.43.

## Answer under section 5[1]

### [5.7]

The Respondent CB, in ANSWER to the Petition filed in this suit, says that:

1. [There is no other living child born to her during the said marriage.]
2. (*In a case where the petition is based on five years' separation*) There is no agreement or arrangement made or proposed to be made between the Petitioner and the Respondent for the support of the Petitioner [and the said children].
3. She denies that the parties have lived apart for a continuous period of at least five years immediately preceding the presentation of the Petition herein. The parties have cohabited together at (*give full particulars of periods spent living together during the five years, such periods to exceed six months in all*).
4. [In the alternative, if which is denied, the parties have lived apart for the said five-year period,] the Respondent will, by reason of the dissolution of the said marriage suffer grave financial or other hardships, and it would in all the circumstances be wrong to dissolve the said marriage. The Respondent relies on the matters hereinafter alleged.

**Financial hardship**

5. If a dissolution is granted the Respondent will lose pension rights under (*give details of scheme*) and there would be a substantial financial difference between the benefits which she would be entitled to receive from the Department of Social Security (*give full particulars*) (*or as the case may be*). The Respondent would further lose the right to occupy the Petitioner's ancestral home in which she has resided for 35 years.

**Other hardship, eg religious objections**

6. By virtue of her religious beliefs and because of the society in which she lives, the Respondent would be a social outcast, and she would be deprived as a married woman which would be anathema to her on religious and moral grounds (*give full pariticulars*).

THE RESPONDENT THEREFORE PRAYS:

[*Set out prayer and conclude as appropriate*]

1 See the MCA 1973, s 5.

## Married Women's Property Act 1882: originating summons (High Court) or originating application (county court)[1]

### [5.8]

[IN THE HIGH COURT OF JUSTICE] No 20
[FAMILY DIVISION]
( District Registry)
(In the County Court)

In the Matter of an application by under s 17 of the Married Women's Property Act 1882 and s 37 of the Matrimonial Proceedings and Property Act 1970.

| Between | AB | Applicant |
|---|---|---|
| | and | |
| | BB | Respondent |

LET [*name*] of [*address*] attend before District Judge in chambers at [the Principal Registry, First Avenue House, 42–49 High Holborn, London WC1V 6NP[2]] on day the day of 20 at o'clock in the fore/afternoon on the hearing of an application by the Applicant for an order in the following terms:

[*Set out order sought—the following are examples*]

1. A declaration that the property [*address*] the title to which property is not registered (or the title to which property is registered in HM Land Registry at [*place*] under Title Number )[3] and in respect of which property there is a mortgage in favour of the Building Society of [*address of Head Office*][4] is owned by the Applicant and the Respondent jointly.
2. An order that the said property be sold with vacant possession and the nett proceeds of sale be divided between the applicant and respondent equally or in such other shares as may be just.
3. A declaration that the chattels mentioned in the Schedule hereto are the property of the Applicant and an order (if and so far as is necessary) that they do vest in her/him absolutely.
4. An order that the Respondent do pay the costs of and incidental to this application

[*Schedule before referred to*]

DATED this day of 20

This summons [application] was taken out by [*name*] [Solicitor for] the above-named Applicant whose address for service is [*address*]

To: the Respondent

TAKE NOTICE THAT:

1. A copy of the affidavit used in support of the application is delivered herewith.
2. You must complete the accompanying acknowledgment of service[5] and send it so as to reach the court within eight days after you receive this summons [application].
3. If you wish to dispute the claim made by the Applicant you must file an affidavit in answer within 14 days after the time allowed for sending the acknowledgment of service.
4. If you intend to instruct a solicitor to act for you you should at once give him all the documents served on you so that he may take the necessary steps on your behalf.

1 FPR 1991, Form M23 is a prescribed form. This precedent is based on that form.
2 Or the full address of the district registry or county court as the case may be.
3 FPR 1991, r 3.6(4)(a).
4 FPR 1991, r 3.6(4)(b). This information is required in the Originating Summons. It is good practice to refer to it both in here and in the affidavit in support.
5 Ie Form M16, FPR 1991, r 3.6(5).

## Summons for injunction under Married Women's Property Act 1882 (High Court)

### [5.9]

[*Heading as appropriate*]

LET the Respondent attend the District Judge in Chambers at [address] on day the day of 20 at o'clock in the fore/afternoon on the hearing of an application by the Applicant herein for an injunction restraining the Respondent from selling disposing of or otherwise dealing with the property [address] the subject matter of the originating summons herein until the hearing of the said originating summons or until further order.

DATED this day of 20 .

This summons was issued by [*Solicitor's name*] of [*address*] solicitors for the applicant.

To: The Respondent and to his solicitors [*name*] of [*address*].

## Summons for injunction under Married Women's Property Act 1882 (county court)

### [5.10]

[*Heading as appropriate*]

TAKE NOTICE that the above named applicant intends to apply to the District Judge sitting in Chambers at [give address of court] on day the day of 20 at o'clock for the following orders:

[*set out orders sought*]

## Injunction in Married Women's Property Act 1882 proceedings

### [5.11]

[*Heading as appropriate*]

BEFORE DISTRICT JUDGE in Chambers[1]

UPON HEARING Counsel [the Solicitor] for the Applicant and Counsel [the Solicitor] for the Respondent

AND UPON READING the affidavit of the applicant filed the day of 20 [and the affidavit of the Respondent filed the day of 20 ]

AND UPON HEARING the evidence of the Applicant and the Respondent[2]

THE Applicant undertaking by her Counsel [or Solicitor] to abide by any order this court may make for the payment of damages in case this court shall hereafter find that the Respondent has sustained any loss or damage by reason of this order.

IT IS ORDERED that the Respondent by himself his servants or agents or otherwise be strictly enjoined and restrained and an injunction is hereby granted restraining him from selling, disposing of or otherwise dealing with the property [*here describe the property*][3] until the final hearing of the originating application [or summons as the case may be] or until further order [OR] until the day of 20 at [*time*] at [*address of court*] when the court will consider whether this injunction should be further continued.

Liberty to either party to apply.

Costs in cause[4].

DATED

District Judge

To the Respondent:

TAKE NOTICE that unless you obey the directions contained in this order you will be guilty of contempt of court and will be liable to be committed to prison[5].

1 If the injunction is heard by a judge this heading should be amended accordingly.
2 The first three paragraphs should recite who attended, what affidavits were read and who gave oral evidence.
3 The form of the injunction should describe the property mentioned in the summons and should be adapted to cover the relief claimed. If a mandatory injunction is applied for and granted it should be ordered in a separate paragraph.
4 Or such other order for costs as is sought including legal aid costs if appropriate.
5 In the High Court the party to whom the injunction is granted should endorse the penal notice.

## Notice of severance of a jointly held property

### [5.12]

Dear Sir/Madam,

The property [*address*] is held by us as joint tenants in law in trust for ourselves.

I hereby give you notice that as from the date of this letter the joint tenancy in equity is hereby severed and henceforth the property is held by us in trust for ourselves as tenants in common in equal shares.

Yours faithfully,

[*Signature*]

## PROCEDURAL FORMS

### [5.13]
### Introduction

There are now many standard forms that must be used in relation to claims for ancillary relief. Copies of these standard forms are set out in the paragraphs that follow. A description of the forms is set out below.

### [5.14]
### Form A[1]

This is the form by which the procedure is commenced. The application for ancillary relief should have been made in the petition (or, if an answer was filed, in that pleading)[2]. If the application was omitted from the petition or answer an application may be made by leave of the court, either in Form A or at trial (or, where the parties are agreed to the terms of a proposed order, without leave in Form A)[3]. Where an application for ancillary relief has been made in the petition or answer Form A serves as the notice of intention to proceed with the claim for ancillary relief; where a Respondent who has not filed an answer seeking relief wishes to make an application for ancillary relief, the application is made in Form A[4]. The application should specify the orders that are being sought by the Applicant, including any orders for pension attachment or pension sharing[5]. The application may be made at any time after the filing of the petition.

1 Form A is set out at para **[5.23]** below.

2 FPR 1991, r 2.53 (set out at para **[3.436]**). It is essential that a properly constituted application should be made before a party remarries in the light of s 28(3) of the MCA 1973: *Robin v Robin* (1983) 4 FLR 632. It is essential that, if a party seeks any orders in his favour, he files his own application for ancillary relief. Where only a partial application has been made before remarriage, the following authorities may be considered upon the issue of whether a broader application may be pursued after remarriage: *Wilson v Wilson* [1976] Fam 142 (application for periodical payments before remarriage insufficient to permit an application for a lump sum after remarriage); *Nixon v Fox* [1978] Fam 173 (application for child periodical payments does not permit post-remarriage application for lump sum); *Doherty v Doherty* [1976] Fam 71 (application for property adjustment order permits post-remarriage amendment to seek lump sum); and *Hargood v Jenkins* [1978] Fam 148 (indication in acknowledgement of service of petition insufficient to permit post-remarriage application).

3 FPR 1991, r 2.53(2) (set out at para **[3.436]**). For the principles that a court applies to an application for leave, see *Chaterjee v Chaterjee* [1976] Fam 199, [1976] 1 All ER 719, [1976] 2 WLR 397, CA.

4 See r 2.61A of the FPR 1991 (set out at para **[3.442]**).

5 See r 2.70 of the FPR 1991 (set out at para **[3.461]**).

## [5.15]
### Form B

This is the form by which an application is made under s 10(2) of the MCA 1973[1] by a Respondent to a petition for divorce, where the petition has been filed under s 1(2)(d) (two years living apart and consent) or s 1(2)(e) (five years living apart) of the MCA 1973. By such an application the Respondent seeks to delay the making of the decree absolute until the court has considered the financial position of the respondent after the divorce[2].

1 Set out at para **[2.114]** above.
2 See r 2.45 of the FPR 1991 (set out at para **[3.406]**).

## [5.16]
### Form C[1]

This the Form by which the court fixes the date of the first appointment. Upon the filing of Form A the court must:

- fix a first appointment not less than 12 weeks and not more than 16 weeks after the date of the filing of the notice and give notice of that date;
- serve a copy on the Respondent within four days of the date of the filing of the notice.

The date fixed under para (4) for the first appointment, or for any subsequent appointment, must not be cancelled except with the court's permission and, if cancelled, the court must immediately fix a new date[2].

1 Form C is set out at para **[5.24]** below.
2 See r 2.61A(4) of the FPR 1991 (set out at para **[3.442]**).

## [5.17]
### Form D

This is the Form used by the court at the first appointment either to give directions for the case to be referred to an FDR appointment or, where it decides not to direct an FDR, to give directions[1].

1 See r 2.61D(2)(c) and (d) of the FPR 1991 (set out at para **[3.445]**).

## [5.18]
### Form E[1]

This is the Form that must be sworn by both parties in order to give details of their financial and other relevant circumstances. The parties must both file and exchange it simultaneously at least 35 days before the first appointment. The parties must exhibit to the Form the documents that are specified within it (ie recent valuations, property valuations, the most recent mortgage statements, the last 12 months' bank statements, surrender values of insurance policies, business accounts for the last two years and recent pension information)[2].

1 Form E is set out at para **[5.25]** below.
2 See r 2.61B(1) and (2) of the FPR 1991 (set out at para **[3.443]**).

## [5.19]
### Form F[1]

Where a form or other document filed with the court contains an allegation of adultery or of an improper association with a named person ('the named person'), the court may direct that the party who filed the relevant form or document serve a copy of all or part of that form or document on the named person, together with Form F. Form F notifies the named person of the allegations that have been made and what that person should do if he wishes to intervene or seek directions. Where the court directs that such notice is given to a named person, the named person may file a statement in answer to the allegations; the named person must swear that the statement is true[2].

1 Form F is set out at para **[5.26]** below.
2 See r 2.60 of the FPR 1991 (set out at para **[3.440]**).

## [5.20]
## Form G[1]

This is the Form by which the parties give notice about whether they consider that the first appointment can be treated as an FDR (thereby reducing the number of court hearings and the costs of the proceedings). It must be filed at least 14 days before the hearing of the first appointment[2].

1 Form G is set out at para **[5.27]** below.
2 See r 2.61B(7)(d) of the FPR 1991 (set out at para **[3.443]**).

## [5.21]
## Form H[1]

This is the Form by which the parties give estimates of their costs. Such estimates must be produced to the court at every court hearing or appointment. If a party is to seek a summary assessment of costs at a hearing, a full schedule of costs must be prepared in accordance with Pt 44 of the CPR 1998 at least 24 hours before the hearing[2].

1 Form H is set out at para **[5.28]** below.
2 See r 2.61F of the FPR 1991 (set out at para **[3.447]**).

## [5.22]
## Form I[1]

This is the Form by which a party in receipt of maintenance pending suit may apply for the order to continue as a periodical payments order after decree absolute[2].

1 Form I is set out at para **[5.29]** below.
2 Ie under r 2.67 of the FPR 1991 (set out at para **[3.452]**).

## Form A—Notice of Intention to proceed with an Application for Ancillary Relief

[5.23]

### Notice of [intention to proceed with] an Application for Ancillary Relief

| In the | |
|---|---|
| | *[County Court]<br>*[Principal Registry of the Family Division] |
| Case No.<br>*Always quote this* | |
| Applicant's solicitor's reference | |
| Respondents Solicitor's reference | |

(*delete as appropriate)

**Respondents (Solicitor(s)) name and address**

Postcode

**The marriage of** **and**

**Take Notice that**

the Applicant intends; ***to apply** to the Court for

*delete as appropriate

***to proceed** with the application in the [petition][answer] for

***to apply to vary**:

- ☐ an order for maintenance pending suit
- ☐ a secured provision order
- ☐ a property adjustment order *(please provide address)*
- ☐ a periodical payments order
- ☐ a lump sum order
- ☐ an order under Section 24B, 25B or 25C of the Act of 1973

**If an application is made for any** periodical payments or secured periodical payments for children:

- and there is a written agreement made before 5 April 1993 about maintenance for the benefit of children, **tick this box** ☐
- and there is a written agreement made on or after 5 April 1993 about maintenance for the benefit of children, **tick this box** ☐
- but there is no agreement, tick any of the boxes below to show if you are applying for payment:

- ☐ for a stepchild or stepchildren
- ☐ in addition to child support maintenance already paid under a Child Support Agency assessment
- ☐ to meet expenses arising from a child's disability
- ☐ to meet expenses incurred by a child in being educated or training for work
- ☐ when either the child **or** the person with care of the child **or** the absent parent of the child is not habitually resident in the United Kingdom
- ☐ Other *(please state)*

Signed: Dated:

[Applicant/Solicitor for the Applicant]

The court office at

is open between 10 am and 4 pm (4.30pm at the Principal Registry of the Family Division) Monday to Friday. When corresponding with the court, please address forms or letters to the Court Manager and quote the case number. If you do not do so, your correspondence may be returned.

**Form A** Notice of [Intention to proceed with] an Application for Ancillary Relief (12.00) *Printed on behalf of The Court Service*

## Form C—Notice of a First Appointment

[5.24]

# Notice of a First Appointment

| In the *[County Court] *[Principal Registry of the Family Division] | |
|---|---|
| Case No *Always quote this* | |
| Applicant's solicitor's reference | |
| Respondents Solicitor's reference | |

*(*delete as appropriate)*

**The marriage of** **and**

**Take Notice that**

**By [ ]** you must file with the Court a statement which gives full details of your property and income. You must sign and swear the Statement. At the same time each party must exchange a copy of the statement with the [legal representative of the] other party. You must use the standard form of statement (Form E) which you may obtain from the Court office.

**By [ ]** you must file with the Court and the [legal representative of the] other party:

- a concise statement of the apparent issues between yourself and the other party:
- a chronology:
- a questionaire setting out the further information and documents you require from the other party, or a statement that no information or documents are required;
- a Notice in Form G.

The First Appointment will be heard by

(the District Judge in chaambers) at

on 20

at [a.m.][p.m.]

The probable length of the hearing is

**You and your legal representative, if you have one, must attend the appointment. At the appointment you must provide the Court with a written estimate (in Form H) of any legal costs which you have incurred. Non-compliance may render you liable to cost penalties**

**Dated:**

The court office at

is open between 10am and 4 pm (4.30pm at the Principal Registry of the Family Division) Monday to Friday. When corresponding with the court, please address forms or letters to the Court Manager and quote the case number. If you do not do so, your crrespondence may be returned.

**Form C Notice of a First Appointment**

## Form E—Financial Statement

**[5.25]**

# FINANCIAL STATEMENT

***Applicant/*Respondent**

| **In the** | |
|---|---|
| ***[County Court]** ***[Principal Registry of the Family Division]** | |
| **Case No** *Always quote this* | |

**(delete as appropriate)*

| Between | Applicant<br><br>Solicitor's Ref: | and | Respondent<br><br>Solicitor's Ref: |
|---|---|---|---|

Please fill in this form fully and accurately. Where any box is not applicable write "N/A". You have a duty to the court to give a full, frank and clear disclosure of all your financial and other relevant circumstances.

A failure to give full and accurate disclosure may result in any order the court makes being set aside.

If you are found to have been deliberately untruthful, criminal proceedings for perjury may be taken against you.

You must attach documents to the form where they are specifically sought and you may attach other documents where it is necessary to explain or clarify any of the information that you give.

**Essential documents,** which **must** accompany this Statement, are detailed at questions 2.1, 2.2, 2.3, 2.5, 2.14, 2.18 and 2.20.

If there is not enough room on the form for any particular piece of information, you may continue on an attached sheet of paper.

This statement must be sworn before an Officer of the Court
[a solicitor] or a Commissioner for Oaths
before it is filed with the Court
or sent to the other party
(see page 20).

Form E Financial Statement

## Part 1 General Information

**1.1 Full Name**

**1.2 Date of Birth**

| Date | Month | Year |
|---|---|---|
| | | |

**1.3 Date of Marriage**

| Date | Month | Year |
|---|---|---|
| | | |

**1.4 Occupation**

**1.5 Date of the separation**

| Date | Month | Year | |
|---|---|---|---|
| | | | Tick here ☐ if not applicable |

**1.6 Date of the:**

| Petition | | | Decree Nisi/Decree of Judicial Separation | | | Decree Absolute | | |
|---|---|---|---|---|---|---|---|---|
| Date | Month | Year | Date | Month | Year | Date | Month | Year |
| | | | | | | | | |

**1.7 If you have remarried, or will remarry, state the date**

| Date | Month | Year |
|---|---|---|
| | | |

**1.8 Do you live with another person?** ☐ Yes ☐ No

**1.9 Do you intend to live with someone within the next six months?** ☐ Yes ☐ No

**1.10 Details of any children of the family**

| Full names | Date of Birth | | | With whom does the child live? |
|---|---|---|---|---|
| | Date | Month | Year | |
| | | | | |

**1.11 Give details of the state of health of yourself and the children**

| Yourself | Children |
|---|---|
| | |

PART 5 Precedents

**1.12 Give details of the present and proposed future educational arrangements for the children.**

| Present arrangements | Future arrangements |
|---|---|
| | |

**1.13 Give details on any Child Support Maintenance Assessments or Child Maintenance Orders made between the parties. If no assessment or agreement has been made, give an estimate of the liability of the non-residential parent under the Child Support Act 1991, in respect of the children of the family**

**1.14 If this application is to vary an order, give details of the order that is to be varied and attach a copy of the order. Give the reasons for asking for the order to be varied.**

**1.15 Give details of any other court cases between you and your husband/wife, whether in relation to money, property, children or anything else.**

| Case No | Court |
|---|---|
| | |

**1.16 Specify your present residence and the occupants of it and on what terms you occupy** it (e.g. tenant, owner-occupier).

| Address | Occupants | Terms of occupation |
|---|---|---|
| | | |

## Part 2 Financial Details *Capital: Realisable Assets*

**If you have obtained a valuation within the last six months attach a copy. If not, give your own estimate of the property value. A copy of your most recent mortgage statement is also required.*

### 2.1 Give details of your interest in the matrimonial home.

| Property name and address | Land Registry Title No | Nature and extent of your interest | *Property value |
|---|---|---|---|
| | | | |

| Mortgagee's Name and address | Type of mortgage | Balance outstanding on any mortgage | Total current value of your interest |
|---|---|---|---|
| 1st | | | |
| 2nd | | | |
| Other | | | |
| **NET value of your interest in the matrimonial home (A)** | | | £ |

### 2.2 Give details of all other properties, land, and buildings in which you have an interest

| Property name(s) and address(es) | Land Registry Title No | Nature and extent of your interest | *Property value |
|---|---|---|---|
| 1. | | | |
| 2. | | | |
| 3. | | | |

| Mortgagee's Name(s) and address(es) | Type of mortgage | Balance outstanding on any mortgage | Total current value of your interest |
|---|---|---|---|
| 1. | | | |
| 2. | | | |
| 3. | | | |
| **TOTAL value of the above** (not including the matrimonial home) | | | (B1) £ |

**2.3 Give details of all bank, building society, and National savings accounts, in credit, which you hold or have an interest in. Include all PEPs, TESSAs and ISAs. For joint accounts, give your interest and the name of the account holder.** If the account is overdrawn, include in Liabilities section at 2.12

*You must attach your bank statements covering the last 12 months for each account listed*

| Name of bank or building society including Branch name | Type of account (e.g. current) | Account number | Name of other acccount holder *(if applicable)* | Balance at the date of this Statement | Total current value of your interest |
|---|---|---|---|---|---|
| 1. | | | | | |
| 2. | | | | | |
| 3. | | | | | |
| 4. | | | | | |
| 5. | | | | | |
| | | | | **TOTAL value of your interest in ALL accounts** | (B2) £ |

**2.4 Give details of all stocks, gilts and other quoted securities which you hold or have an interest in.** Do not include dividend income as this will be dealt with separately later on.

| Name | Type | Size | Current value | Total current value of your interest |
|---|---|---|---|---|
| | | | | |
| | | | **TOTAL value of your interest in ALL holdings** | (B3) £ |

**2.5 Give details of all life insurance policies which you hold or in which you have an interest, including those that do not have a surrender value, for each policy.**

| Policy details including name of company, policy type and number | If policy is charged, state in whose favour and amount of charge | Maturity date | | | Surrender Value | Total current value of your interest |
|---|---|---|---|---|---|---|
| | | Date | Month | Year | | |
| | | | | | | |
| *You must attach any surrender value quotations* | **TOTAL value of your interest in ALL policies** | | | | | (B4) £ |

**2.6 Give details of all issues of National Savings Certificates which you hold or have an interest in.**

| Name of issue | Nominal amount | Current value | Total current value of your interest |
|---|---|---|---|
| | | | |

**TOTAL value of ALL your certificates** (B5) £

**2.7 Give details of all of National Savings Bonds (including Premium bonds) and other bonds which you hold or have an interest in.**

| Name of Bond | Bond holder's number | Current value | Total current value of your interest |
|---|---|---|---|
| | | | |

**TOTAL value of ALL your bonds** (B6) £

**2.8 Give details of all monies which are OWED TO YOU. Include sums owed in director's or partnership accounts**

| Brief description of debt | Balance outstanding | Total current value of your interest |
|---|---|---|
| | | |

**TOTAL value of your interest in ALL debts owed to you** (B7) £

**2.9 Give details of all of cash savings held in excess of £300. You must state where it is held and the currency it is held in.**

| Where held | Amount | Currency | Total current value of your interest |
|---|---|---|---|
| | | | |

**TOTAL value of ALL your cash** (B8) £

**2.10 Give details of personal belongings individually worth more than £500.**
Include cars (gross value), collections, pictures, jewellery, furniture, and household belongings (this list is not exhaustive).

| Item | Sale value | Total estimated current value of your interest |
|---|---|---|
| | | |

**TOTAL value of your interest in ALL personal belongings** (B9) £

**2.11 Give details of any other realisable assets not yet mentioned, for example, unit trusts, investment trusts, commodities, business expansion schemes and futures (this list is not exhaustive).** This is where you must mention any other realisable assets.

| Type | Current value | Total current value of your interest |
|---|---|---|
| | | |

**TOTAL value of your interest in ALL other realisable assets** (B10) £

Now add together all the figures in the previous total boxes (B1 to B10) to give the TOTAL current value of ALL your interest in realisable assets. (B) £

## Part 2 Financial Details *Capital: Liabilities*

**2.12 Give details of any liabilities you have. Exclude** mortgages on property dealt with above. **Include** money owed on credit cards and store cards, bank loans, hire purchase agreements and any overdrawn bank or building society accounts.

| Liability (i.e. total amount owed, current monthly payments and term of loan/debt) | Current amount | Total current value of your share of the liability |
|---|---|---|
| | | |
| | **TOTAL value of ALL your liabilities** | (C1) £ |

## Part 2 Financial Details *Capital: Capital Gains Tax*

**2.13 If any Capital Gains Tax would be payable on the disposal now of any of your realisable assets, give your estimate of the tax.**

| Asset | Capital Gains Tax | Total current value of your liability |
|---|---|---|
| | | |
| | **TOTAL value of ALL your Capital Gains Tax liabilities** | (C2) £ |

Now add together C1 + C2 to give:-
TOTAL net value of your liabilities **(C)** £

Now take the liabilities total from the realisable assets total (A+B-C), to give:-
TOTAL net value of your personal assets **(D)** £

## Part 2 Financial Details *Capital: Business Assets*

**2.14 Give details of all your business interests.** *You must attach a copy of the last 2 years accounts and any other document on which you base your valuation*

| Name and nature of your business | Your ESTIMATE of the current value of your interest | Your ESTIMATE of any possible Capital Gains Tax payable on disposal | Basis of valuation *(No formal valuation is required at this time)* | What is the extent of your interest? | Total net current value of your interest |
|---|---|---|---|---|---|
| | | | | | |

**TOTAL current value of your interest in business assets (E)** £

**2.15 List any directorships you hold or held in the last 12 months**

## Part 2 Financial Details *Capital: Pensions (including SERPS but excluding Basic State Pensions)*

**2.16 Give details of your pension interests.**

If you have been provided with a valuation of your pension rights by the trustees or managers of the pension scheme you must attach it. Where the information is not available, give the estimated date when it will be available and attach the letter to the pension company or administrators from whom the information was sought. If you have more than one pension plan or scheme, you must provide the information in respect of each one, continuing, if necessary, on a separate piece of paper. If you have made Additional Voluntary Contributions or any Free Standing Additional Voluntary Contributions to any plan or scheme, you must give the information separately if the benefits referable to such contributions are separately recorded or paid. If you have more than one pension scheme you should reproduce the information for each scheme. Please include any SERPS.

Information about the Scheme(s)

| | |
|---|---|
| Name and address of scheme, plan or policy | |
| [Your national insurance number] | |
| Number of scheme, plan or policy | |
| Type of scheme, plan or policy *(e.g. final salary, money purchase or other)* | |

CETV - Cash Equivalent Transfer Value

| | |
|---|---|
| CETV Value | |
| The lump sum payable on death in service before retirement | |
| The lump sum payable on death in deferment before retirement | |
| The lump sum payable on death after retirement | |

Retirement Benefits

| | |
|---|---|
| Earliest date when benefit can be paid | |
| The estimated lump sum and monthly pension payable on retirement, assuming you take the maximum lump sum. | |
| The estimated monthly pension without taking any lump sum | |

Spouse's Benefit

| | |
|---|---|
| On death in service | |
| On death in deferment | |
| On death in retirement | |

Dependants's Benefit

| | |
|---|---|
| On death in service | |
| On death in deferment | |
| On death in retirement | |

**TOTAL value of your pension assests** **(F)** £

PART 5 Precedents

## Part 2 Financial Details *Capital: Other Assets*

**2.17 Give details of any other assets not listed above.**
Include the following: (this list is not exhaustive)

- **Unrealisable assets**
- **Share option scheme,** stating the estimated net sale proceeds of the shares if the options were capable of exercise now, and whether Capital Gains Tax or Income Tax would be payable.
- **Trust interests,** (including interests under a discretionary trust), stating your estimate of the value of the interest and when it is likely to become realisable. If you say it will never be realisable, or has no value, give your reasons.
- Specify also any asset that is likely to be received in the forseeable future, any assets held on your behalf by a third party and any assets not mentioned elsewhere in this form held outside England and Wales.

| Type of Asset | Value | Total net value of your interest |
|---|---|---|
| | | |

| | | |
|---|---|---|
| **Total value of your other assets** | **(G)** | £ |
| **Total value of your net assets (excluding pensions) (D+E+G)** | **(H)** | £ |
| **Total value of your net assets (including pension) (H+F)** | **(I)** | £ |

**Part 2 Financial Details** ***Income***

*You must attach your last three payslips and your P60 for the most recently completed financial year*

**2.18 Earned Income: Give details of your gross and net income in the last financial year, and in the current financial year.**

| Nature of income (e.g. salary, bonus) | Last financial year | | Current financial year *(estimated for the whole year)* | |
|---|---|---|---|---|
| | Gross | Net | Gross | Net |
| | | | | |

**2.19 Additional Income: benefits etc. Give details and the value of all benefits in kind, perks, or other remuneration not disclosed elsewhere, received in the last financial year and current financial year.**

| Nature of income | Last financial year | Current financial year *(estimated for the whole year)* |
|---|---|---|
| | | |

## *Income continued*

**2.20 Self employed or partnership income:** Give details of annual net profit or loss for the last two accounting years, your share of this figure and tax payable to date of the last accounts and the estimate of income since that date. State the date on which your accounting year begins. Year 2 should be the most recent year, Year 1 the previous year. Please state the "from" and "to" dates for the years concerned.

| Nature of income and date your accounting year begins | Details of the last two accounting periods | | | | | |
|---|---|---|---|---|---|---|
| | Net profit/loss | | Your share of profit/loss | | Tax payable by you | |
| | Year 1 | Year 2 | Year 1 | Year 2 | Year 1 | Year 2 |
| | | | | | | |
| | Net Income | Estimate | *You must attach the accounts for the last two completed accounting years* | | | |
| Net income SINCE date of last accounts and estimate for the whole year | | | | | | |

**2.21 Investment income (e.g. dividends, interest)** Give details of net income received in the last financial year, and in the current financial year and state whether it was paid gross or net of income tax. You are not required to calculate any tax payable that may arise.

| Nature of income and the asset from which it derived | Paid gross or net *(delete that which is not applicable)* | Last financial year | Current financial year |
|---|---|---|---|
| | Gross / Net | | |

**2.22 State benefits (including state pension)** Give details of all state benefits received in the last 52 weeks

| Nature of income | Total Income received in the last 52 weeks |
|---|---|
| | |

**2.23 Any other income** Give details of any other income recieved in the last 52 weeks

| Nature of income | Total Income for the last 52 weeks |
|---|---|
| | |

## Part 2 Financial Details *Summaries*

### 2.24 Summary of your income

| Your estimate of your current annual net income from all sources (2.18 -2.23) | Your estimate of your net income from all sources for the next 52 weeks |
|---|---|
| £ | £<br>**(J)** |

| | Reference of the section on this statement | Value |
|---|---|---|
| Net value of your interest in the matrimonial home | **A** | |
| Total current value of all your interests in the other realisable assets | **B** | |
| Total net value of your liabilities | **C** | |
| Total net value of your personal assets | **D** | |
| Total current value of your interest in business assets | **E** | |
| Total current value of your pension or transfer values | **F** | |
| Total value of your other assets | **G** | |
| Total value of your net assets *(excluding pension)* | **H** | |
| Total value of your net assets *(including pesion)* | **I** | |
| Your estimated net income for the next 52 weeks | **J** | |

**Part 3 Requirements** *Income Needs*

**3.1 Give the reasonable future income needs of yourself (e.g. housing, car etc) and of any children living with you, or provided for by you.** This may be expressed as annual, monthly or weekly figures (state which), but you should not use a combination of any of these periods

| Item | *Income needs of yourself* | Amount |
|---|---|---|
| | | |
| | sub-total | |

| Item | *Income needs of child(ren) living with you, or provided for by you.* | Amount |
|---|---|---|
| | | |
| | sub-total | |
| | **Total income needs** | £ |

## Part 3 Requirements *Capital Needs*

**3.2 Give the reasonable future capital needs of yourself and of any children living with you, or provided for by you.**

| Item | *Capital needs of yourself* | Cost |
|---|---|---|
| | | |
| | sub-total | |

| Item | *Capital needs of child(ren) living with you, or provided for by you* | Cost |
|---|---|---|
| | | |
| | sub-total | |
| | **Total capital needs** | £ |

## Part 4 Other Information

**4.1 State whether there has been any significant change in your net assets during the last 12 months,** including any assets held outside England and Wales (e.g. closure of any bank or building society accounts).

**4.2 Give brief details of the standard of living enjoyed by you and your spouse during the marriage.**

**4.3 Are there any particular contributions to the family property and assets or outgoings, or to family life, that have been made by you, your partner or anyone else that you think should be taken into account? If so, give a brief description of the contribution, the amount, when it was made, and by whom.**

**4.4 Bad behaviour or conduct by the other party will only be taken into account in very exceptional circumstances when deciding how the assets should be divided after divorce. If you feel it should be taken into account in your case identify the nature of the behaviour or conduct.**

## Part 4 Other Information *continued*

**4.5 Give details of any other circumstances which you consider could significantly affect the extent of the financial provision to be made by or for you or for any child of the family e.g. earning capacity, disability, inheritance prospects or redundancy, remarriage and cohabitation plans, any contingent liabilities.** (This list is not exhaustive).

**4.6 If you have remarried (or intend to) or are living with another person (or intend to), give brief details, so far as they are known to you, of his or here income and assets.**

| Annual Income | | Assets | |
|---|---|---|---|
| Nature of income | Value (state whether gross or net, if known) | Item | Value (if known) |
| | | | |
| **Total:** | | **Total:** | |

## Part 5 Order Sought

**5.1 If you are able to at this stage, specify what kind of orders you are asking the court to make, and state whether at this stage you see the case being appropriate for a "clean break".** (A "clean break" means a settlement or order which provides, amongst other things, that neither you nor your spouse will have any further claim against the income or capital of the other party. A clean break does not terminate the responsibility of a parent of a child).

**5.2 **If you are seeking a transfer or settlement of any property or other asset, you must identity the asset in question.**

**5.3 **If you are seeking a variation of a pre-nuptial or post-nuptial settlement, you must identify the settlement, by whom it was made, its trustees and beneficiaries, and state why you allege it is a nuptial settlement.**

** **Important Note:** Where 5.2, 5.3 (above) or 5,4 (overleaf) apply, you should seek legal advice before completing the section.

## Part 5 Order Sought *continued*

**5.4 **If you are seeking an avoidance of disposition order, you must identify the property to which the disposition relates and the person or body in whose favour the disposition is alleged to have been made**

# Sworn confirmation of the information

I ____________ *(the above-named Applicant/Respondent)*

of ____________

make oath and confirm that the information given above is a full, frank, clear and accurate disclosure of my financial and other relevant circumstances

Signed ____________ Dated ____________

Sworn by the above named [Applicant] [Respondent] at

on

before me

A [solicitor] [Commissioner for Oaths] [Officer of a Court, appointed by the Judge to take Affidavits]

Address all communications to the Court Manager of the Court and quote the case number from page 1. If you do not quote this number, your correspondence may be returned.

The court office at

is open from 10 a.m. to 4 p.m. (4.30 p.m. at the Principal Registry of the Family Division) on Monday to Friday only.

## Form F—Notice of allegation in proceedings for ancillary relief

[5.26]

# Notice of Allegation in Proceedings for Ancillary Relief

| In the *[County Court] *[Principal Registry of the Family Division] | |
|---|---|
| Case No *Always quote this* | |
| Applicant's solicitor's reference | |
| Respondents Solicitors reference | |

*(*delete as appropriate)*

**The marriage of** **and**

**Take Notice that**

The following statement has been filed in proceedings for ancillary relief:

Signed Dated
[Applicant / Respondent/Solicitor for the Applicant / Respondent]

**If you wish to be heard on any matter affecting you in these proceedings** you may intervene by applying to the Court directions regarding:

- the filing and service of pleadings
- the conduct of further proceedings

You must apply for directions **within seven days** after you receive this Notice. The period of seven days includes the day you receive it.

The court office at

is open between 10am and 4 pm (4.30pm at the Principal Registry of the Family Division) Monday to Friday.When corresponding with the court, please address forms or letters to the Court Manager and quote the case number. If you do not do so, your crrespondence may be returned.

**Form F Notice of allegation in proceedings for ancillary relief**

## Form G—Notice of response to First Appointment

[5.27]

# Notice of response to First Appointment

| In the *[County Court] *[Principal Registry of the Family Division] | |
|---|---|
| **Case No** *Always quote this* | |
| Applicant's solicitor's reference | |
| Respondents Solicitor's reference | |

*(*delete as appropriate)*

**The marriage of** **and**

**Take Notice that**

At the First Appointment which will be heard on 20

at [am][pm]

the [Applicant] [Respondent] [will][will not] be in a position to proceed on that occasion with a Financial Dispute Resolution appointment for the following reasons:-

**Dated:**

The court office at

is open between 10am and 4 pm (4.30pm at the Principal Registry of the Family Division) Monday to Friday.When corresponding with the court, please address forms or letters to the Court Manager and quote the case number. If you do not do so, your crrespondence may be returned.

**Form G Notice of response to First Appointment**

## Form H—Costs Estimate

[5.28]

# Anclliary Relief Costs Estimate of *[Applicant] *[Respondent]

| In the | |
|---|---|
| *[County Court]<br>*[Principal Registry of the Family Division] | |
| Case No<br>*Always quote this* | |
| Applicant's Solicitor's reference | |
| Respondents Solicitor's reference | |

*(*delete as appropriate)*

**PART 1** **The marriage of** **and**

| | Prescribed rates for publicly funded services £ | Indemnity Rate £ |
|---|---|---|
| 1. Ancillary relief solicitor's costs *(including VAT)* including costs of the current hearing, and any previous solicitor's costs. | | |
| 2. Disbursements *(include VAT, if appropriate, and any incurred by previous solicitors)* | | |
| 3. All Counsel's fees *(including VAT)* | | |
| **TOTAL** | | |

**PART 2**

| | | |
|---|---|---|
| 4. Add any private client costs previously incurred *(In publicly funded cases only)* | | |
| 5. **GRAND TOTAL** | | |

**PART 3**

| | | |
|---|---|---|
| 6. State what has been paid towards the total at 5 above | | |
| 7. Amount of any contributions paid by the funded client towards their publicly funded services. | | |

**NB. If you are publicly funded and might be seeking an order for costs against the other party complete both rates**

Dated

The court office at

is open between 10 am and 4 pm (4.30pm at the Principal registry of the Family Division) Monday to Friday. When corresponding with the court, please address forms or letters to the Court Manager and quote the case number. If you do not do so, your correspondance may be returned.

**Form H** Costs Estimate (12 00) *Printed on behalf of The Court Service*

## Form I—Notice of Request for Periodical Payments Order at same rate as Order for Maintenance Pending Suit

[5.29]

# Notice of Request for Periodical Payments Order at same rate as Order for Maintenance Pending Suit

| In the<br>*[County Court]<br>*[Principal Registry of the Family Division] | |
|---|---|
| Case No<br>*Always quote this* | |
| Applicant's solicitor's reference | |
| Respondents Solicitor's reference | |

*(*delete as appropriate)*

**The marriage of** **and**

**Take Notice that**

**On 1999 [20 ] the Applicant obtained an Order for you to pay maintenance pending suit at the rate of £**

**The Applicant having applied in his/her petition (answer) for a Periodical Payments Order for himself/herself has requested the Court to make such an Order at the same rate as above.**

**Signed (District Judge)** **Dated**

**What to do if you object to this Order being made.**

**If you object in the making of such a Periodical Payments Order, you must notify the District Judge and the Applicant/Respondent of your objections within 14 days of this notice being served on you. If you do not do so, the District Judge may make am Order without notifying you further**

The court office at

is open between 10am and 4 pm (4.30pm at the Principal Registry of the Family Division) Monday to Friday.When corresponding with the court, please address forms or letters to the Court Manager and quote the case number. If you do not do so, your crrespondence may be returned.

**Form 1 Notice of Request for Periodical Payments Order at same rate as Order for Maintenance Pending Suit**

## APPLICATIONS WITHIN ANCILLARY RELIEF PROCEEDINGS

### A letter written under the principles of *Calderbank v Calderbank*

### [5.30]

Without prejudice—*Calderbank* and Part 36 offer.

Dear Sir,

Re: v

We send this letter in order to set out our clients offer to settle the financial issues between the parties. We propose as follows:

[*Set out proposed terms*]

Although this letter is headed 'without prejudice' we reserve the right to refer the contents of this letter to the judge upon the issue of costs, in accordance with the principles stated in *Calderbank v Calderbank* [1976] Fam 93. Further, this letter stands as our offer under Part 36 of the Civil Procedure Rules 1998.

## APPLICATIONS UNDER THE MATRIMONIAL CAUSES ACT 1973, s 37

### Application to restrain disposal of assets

### [5.31]

[*Heading as appropriate*]

TAKE NOTICE etc [*as appropriate*] for an order that the Respondent by himself or by his servants or agents or howsoever be restrained from:

(1) selling or charging or leasing or disposing of or otherwise dealing with the property known as [*address or description*] or any part thereof,
(2) selling or charging or disposing of or otherwise dealing with his shares in BB & Co PLC,
(3) withdrawing or spending or disposing of or otherwise using or dealing with the monies standing to his credit [in account number ] at TU Bank PLC [RS Building Society],
(4) spending or transferring or disposing of or otherwise using or dealing with the monies recovered by him as damages in his action [in the county court] against XY,

until the determination of the Petitioner's application for ancillary relief or until further order of the court.

[*Conclude as appropriate*]

### Injunction to restrain disposal of assets

### [5.32]

[*Heading as appropriate*]

BEFORE DISTRICT JUDGE in Chambers.

UPON HEARING [Counsel] [the Solicitor] for the Petitioner [ex parte] [and [Counsel] [the Solicitor] for the Respondent].

AND UPON HEARING the affidavit of the Petitioner sworn on 20 .

AND UPON HEARING the Petitioner [and Respondent] on oath.

*AND UPON the Petitioner undertaking by her Counsel [Solicitor] to abide by any order this court may make for the payment of damages in case this court shall hereafter find that the Respondent has sustained any loss or damage by reason of this order*[1].

IT IS ORDERED that the Respondent by himself or by his servants or agents or otherwise be strictly enjoined and restrained and an injunction is hereby granted restraining him from selling, charging, leasing, disposing of, or otherwise dealing with the property [*address or description*] and from withdrawing, spending, disposing of, or otherwise using or dealing with the monies standing to his credit with TU Bank PLC [RS Building Society] and from spending, transferring or disposing of money recovered by him in damages in his action in the County Court against XY.

UNTIL the final determination of the Petitioner's application for ancillary relief or until further order.

PROVIDED THAT [*state any savings for the Respondent for example*] the Respondent shall be entitled to permit the said Bank to meet all the exising standing orders and direct debits as are on the date of this order addressed to the said account and in addition to draw from the said account the weekly sum of £ for his own purposes.

*or*

PROVIDED THAT upon the Respondent undertaking through his Counsel that the proceeds of sale of the paddock forming part of the property known as [*address or description*] shall be placed in a joint client deposit account in the names of the Petitioner's Solicitors and Respondent's Solicitors pending agreement as to their distribution or further order of the court the Respondent shall be at liberty to complete the sale of the said paddock in pursuance of the contract for sale dated 20 .

Liberty to either party to apply [*or in the case of an ex parte order*:

Liberty to the Respondent to apply on 24 hours' notice].

[Costs reserved] [Costs in ancillary cause] [Respondent to pay the Petitioner's costs of and incidental to this application in any event].

DATED this day of 20 .

DISTRICT JUDGE

1 In family proceedings an undertaking as to damages will not be included in an order unless specifically required by the court and expressly offered: see *Practice Direction (undertaking as to damages)* [1974] 1 WLR 576; and *W v H (Family Division: Without Notice Orders)* [2001] 1 All ER 300, sub nom *W v H (Ex Part Injunctions)* [2000] 3 FCR 481, [2000] 2 FLR 927.



## Application for an avoidance of disposition order

### [5.33]

(Rule 1.2 of the FPR 1991 provides that applications under s 37(2)(b) and (c) of the MCA 1973 are applications for 'ancillary relief'. Accordingly, applications should be made by notice in Form A.)

## ORDERS

### Order for maintenance pending suit

**[5.34]**

The Respondent do pay or cause to be paid to the Petitioner maintenance pending suit [continuing after decree absolute as interim periodical payments] at the rate of £ a month payable monthly as from the day of during their joint lives or until she shall remarry or until determination of the application for ancillary relief (whichever is the earlier) or further order.

### Order for periodical payments at the same rate as maintenance pending suit

**[5.35]**

As from the day of the Respondent do make periodical payments to the Petitioner during their joint lives or until she shall remarry or until further order at the same rate as that provided by the order for maintenance pending suit dated , being £ per annum, payable monthly[1].

1 See the FPR 1991, r 2.67 for the rules relating to an application for such an order.

### Order for periodical payments

**[5.36]**

The Respondent do make or cause to be made periodical payments to the Petitioner during their joint lives or until she shall remarry or further order at the rate of £ a month, payable monthly in arrears/advance, the first such payment to be made on . Payments to be made by standing order into such bank account as the Petitioner shall notify to the Respondent in writing.

### Order dismissing periodical payments and preventing further applications

**[5.37]**

The Petitioner's claims for periodical payments and secured provision are hereby dismissed and it is directed that she shall not be entitled hereafter to make any further application in relation to this marriage for orders under sections 23(1)(a) or (b) of the Matrimonial Causes Act 1973.

### Order for deferred clean break—including s 28(1A) direction

**[5.38]**

The Respondent do make or cause to be made periodical payments to the Petitioner at the rate of £ payable monthly in [advance *or arrears*] as from the day of until whichever shall first occur of the following:

(a) the remarriage of the Petitioner;
(b) the death of either party;
(c) the day of .
(d) further order of the court,

whereupon this order shall be discharged and all claims by the Petitioner for periodical payments and secured provision shall stand dismissed and it is directed pursuant to section 28(1A) of the Matrimonial Causes Act 1973 that the Petitioner shall not be entitled to apply under section 31 of that Act for the extension of the term of this order.

## Order for deferred clean break—extendable on application[1]

### [5.39]

The Respondent do make or cause to be made periodical payments to the Petitioner at the rate of £ payable monthly in [advance *or arrears*] as from the day of until whichever shall first occur of the following:

(a) the remarriage of the Petioner;
(b) the death of either party;
(c) the day of ;
(d) further order of the court,

whereupon this order shall be discharged and any outstanding claims by the Petitioner for periodical payments or secured provision shall stand dismissed.

1 See *Jones v Jones* [2000] 2 FCR 201, [2000] 2 FLR 307, CA. The application to extend must be made before the term of the order expires. It is not necessary for the application to vary to be heard during the currency of the term (disapproving *G v G* [1997] 1 FCR 441, [1997] 1 FLR 368).

## Secured periodical payments order

### [5.40]

The Respondent do secure to the Petitioner periodical payments at the rate of £ per annum payable monthly as from the day of until her death or remarriage or further order of the court upon the following securities:

.

## Maintenance order to increase by Retail Price Index

### [5.41]

The rate of periodical payments shall be increased automatically with effect from the payment due on the day of 20 and thereafter on the anniversary of that date by the percentage by which the retail price index shall have increased between the date 15 months prior to the variation and the date 3 months prior thereto.

## Discharge of magistrates court order made under the Domestic Proceedings and Magistrates' Courts Act 1978

### [5.42]

Pursuant to section 28 of the Domestic Proceedings and Magistrates' Courts Act 1978, the order of the Justices, dated is hereby discharged [and all arrears thereunder are remitted].

## Leave to enforce arrears[1]

### [5.43]

Pursuant to section 32 of the Matrimonial Causes Act 1973 the Petitioner is hereby given leave to enforce the arrears under the order dated day of .

1 For the need to obtain leave to enforce arrears which are more than 12 months old, see the MCA 1973, s 32.

## Child periodical payments

### [5.44]

The Respondent do make or cause to be made child periodical payments to the Petitioner for the benefit of the children at the rate of £ a month, payable monthly in arrears/advance, for each child until they respectively attain the age of 17 or cease full-time secondary/tertiary education (whichever shall be the later) or further order. The first such payment to be made on the day of with the payments to be made thereafter by standing order into such bank account as the Petitioner shall notify to the Respondent in writing.

## School fees order

### [5.45]

The Respondent do make or cause to be made to the Petitioner for the benefit of the child such child periodical payments as shall be equal to the school fees [including or excluding extras] for such school as the child shall attend from time to time until he shall cease full-time secondary education or further order of the court. Such payments to be made as required by the school and the receipt by the headmaster of the amounts provided by this order shall be sufficient discharge by the Respondent of his obligations hereunder.

## Order for the payment of a lump sum

### [5.46]

The Respondent do pay pay or cause to be paid to the Petitioner on or before the day of a lump sum of £ .

## Order for the payment of lump sum by instalments with interest being paid until payment made[1]

### [5.47]

The Respondent do pay or cause to be paid to the Petitioner a lump sum of £ payable in the following instalments:

(i) £ (being the first instalment) to be paid on or before the day of .
(ii) £ (being the second instalment) to be paid on or before the day of .

Pending payment of each of the above instalments, the Respondent do pay interest on each instalment from the date of this order until the date that each instalment is due in accordance with the above order, at the rate of % pa.

1 Interest may be ordered under the MCA 1973, s 23(6) from the date of the order until the date that payment is due. Interest will accrue at the judgment rate under the Judgments Act 1838, s 17 from the date when payment is due, unless the order is made in the county court and the sum is less than £5,000—County Courts (Interest on Judgment Debts) Order 1991, SI 1991/1184.

## Property transfer order

### [5.48]

On or before the day of the Respondent do transfer to the Petitioner:

(i) all his estate and interest in the property known as 'Pottage Cottage', Plain Lane, etc subject to the existing mortgage thereon in favour of the building society;
(ii) all his interest in the chattels within the above property, Pottage Cottage;
(iii)all his interest in the endowment policy number with the insurance company.

(*and, in the event that the Respondent shall fail to execute any documents necessary to give effect to this order within 14 days of a written request by the Petitioner that he do so, a District Judge of this court shall have the power to execute the same on his behalf*[1]).

1 The power of the district judge to execute documents appears to be derived from the County Courts Act 1984, s 37.



## Order for sale of property

### [5.49]

The property at be sold forthwith with vacant possession by way of private treaty *or* by public auction and:

(a) the [Petitioner *or* Respondent]'s solicitors do have conduct of the sale;
(b) the property be sold at a price to be agreed between the parties, or in default of agreement, to be fixed by court;
(c) the proceeds of sale of the property be applied as follows:
  (i) to the legal costs and estate agents fees of sale;
  (ii) to the redemption of the mortgage in favour of (*name of lender*); and
  (iii) the payment of the balance as to % to the Petitioner and % to the Respondent.

## Deferred sale—*Mesher* order[1]

### [5.50]

As from the date of this order, the property ('the Property') be held by the Petitioner and the Respondent on trust as to % of the beneficial interest to the Petitioner and % of that interest to the Respondent and upon the following terms:

(a) The Petitioner shall have the sole right to occupy the Property to the exclusion of the Respondent;

(b) The Property shall not be sold until the happening of the first of the following events:
  (i) the death or remarriage of the Petitioner;
  (ii) the cohabitation of the Petitioner for a period in excess of 6 months;
  (iii) the Petitioner choosing to sell the Property or vacating it for more than 3 months;
  (iv) the youngest child attaining the age of 18 years or ceasing full-time secondary education (whichever shall be the later);
  (v) further order of the court.

(c) On the occurrence of the first of the above events, the Property shall be sold and the proceeds of sale of the property be applied as follows:
  (i) to the legal costs and estate agents fees of sale;
  (ii) to the redemption of the sum then outstanding on the mortgage in favour of (*name of lender*); and
  (iii) the payment of the balance to the parties in accordance with their beneficial interests therein.

(d) The cost of any necessary repairs to the Property prior to sale shall be borne by the parties [*specify the proportions in which they will bear those costs*], provided that, in the event of disagreement between the parties as to the necessity or cost of any repairs there shall be liberty to either party to apply to the court in respect thereof.

(e) The [Petitioner *or* Respondent] shall with effect from the date of this order be responsible for all monthly payments of capital and interest on the mortgage in respect of the Property and shall have credit in respect of [one half of] the element of repayment of capital comprised in such payments made by that party to the date of sale.

(f) At any time on or before the date on which the sale is carried into effect the Petitioner may elect to purchase the interest of the Respondent by paying to him the value of that interest (on the basis of the Property having a gross value agreed between the parties or, in default, specified by the court and the notional costs and fees of sale being % of that gross value).

1 So named after *Mesher v Mesher and Hall* [1980] 1 All ER 126, CA.

## Deferred sale—*Martin* order[1]

### [5.51]

As from the date of this order, the property ('the Property') be held by the Petitioner and the Respondent on trust as to % of the beneficial interest to the Petitioner and % of that interest to the Respondent and upon the following terms:

(a) The Petitioner shall have the sole right to occupy the Property to the exclusion of the Respondent;

(b) The Property shall not be sold until the happening of the first of the following events:
  (i) the death or remarriage of the Petitioner;
  (ii) the cohabitation of the Petitioner for a period in excess of 6 months;
  (iii) the Petitioner choosing to sell the Property or vacating it for more than 3 months;
  (iv) further order of the court.

(c) On the occurrence of the first of the above events, the Property shall be sold and the proceeds of sale of the property be applied as follows:
  (i) to the legal costs and estate agents fees of sale;
  (ii) to the redemption of the sum then outstanding on the mortgage in favour of (*name of lender*); and
  (iii) the payment of the balance to the parties in accordance with their beneficial interests therein.

(d) The cost of any necessary repairs to the Property prior to sale shall be borne by the parties [*specify the proportions in which they will bear those costs*], provided that, in the event of disagreement between the parties as to the necessity or cost of any repairs there shall be liberty to either party to apply to the court in respect thereof.

(e) The [Petitioner *or* Respondent] shall with effect from the date of this order be responsible for all payments of capital and interest on the mortgage in respect of the Property and shall have credit in respect of [one half of] the element of repayment of capital comprised in such payments made by that party to the date of sale.

(f) At any time on or before the date on which the sale is carried into effect the Petitioner may elect to purchase the interest of the Respondent by paying to him the value of that interest (on the basis of the Property having a gross value agreed between the parties or, in default, specified by the court and the notional costs and fees of sale being % of that gross value).

1 Named after *Martin v Martin* [1977] 3 All ER 762, CA.

## Property adjustment order subject to a charge-back

### [5.52]

(a) The Respondent do transfer to the Petitioner on or before the day of all his estate and interest in the property ('the Property') subject to:
  (i) the mortgage secured on the Property in favour of the (*name of lender*); and
  (ii) the charge specified in paragraph (b) below in favour of the Respondent.

(b) The charge referred to in paragraph (a)(ii) above shall be for % of the net proceeds of sale of the Property as defined below and shall not be enforceable until the happening of the first of the following:
  (i) the death or remarriage of the Petitioner;
  (ii) the cohabitation of the Petitioner for a period of more than 6 months;
  (iii) the Petitioner vacating the Property for more than 3 months;
  (iv) the Petitioner selling the Property;
  (v) the youngest child of the family attaining the age of (*specify*) or ceasing full-time secondary *or tertiary* education (whichever shall last occur); or
  (vi) further order of the court.

For the purposes of the above provision the net proceeds of sale of the Property shall mean the gross proceeds of sale less the estate agents' fees and legal costs of sale and the sum due under the mortgage with the (*name of lender*) [as at the date of this order *or* as at the date of the sale or realisation of the charge].



## Property adjustment order subject to a transferable charge-back

### [5.53]

(a) The Respondent do transfer to the Petitioner on or before the day of all estate and interest in the property ('the Property') subject to:
  (i) the mortgage secured on the Property in favour of (*name of lender*); and
  (ii) the charge specified in paragraph (b) below in favour of the Respondent.

(b) The charge referred to in paragraph (a)(ii) above shall be for % of the net proceeds of sale of the Property as defined below and shall not be enforceable until the happening of the first of the following:
 (i) the death or remarriage of the Petitioner;
 (ii) the cohabitation of the Petitioner for a period of more than 6 months;
 (iii) the Petitioner vacating the Property for more than 3 months;
 (iv) the Petitioner selling the Property, unless at least (*specify*) days prior to the sale of the Property the Petitioner *or* Respondent shall have served notice in writing on the Respondent of her election for the charge to be transferred to a substitute property to be purchased in her sole name in accordance with paragraph (c) below;
 (v) the youngest child of the family attaining the age of (*specify*) or ceasing full-time secondary *or tertiary* education (whichever shall last occur); or
 (vi) further order of the court.

For the purposes of the above provision the net proceeds of sale of the Property shall mean the gross proceeds of sale less the estate agents' fees and legal costs of sale and the sum due under the mortgage with the (*name of lender*) [as at the date of this order *or* as at the date of the sale or realisation of the charge].

(c) In the event of the Petitioner exercising the election referred to in paragraph (b)(iv) above prior to the happening of any of the events in paragraph (b)(i), (ii), (iii), (v), (vi) above, she shall be entitled to apply the net proceeds of sale of the Property to the purchase of a substitute property to be agreed by the parties or, in default of agreement, to be specified by the court, upon the following terms:
 (i) upon sale of the Property, any of the net proceeds of sale thereof which are not used for the purchase of the substitute property shall be divided between the parties in the following proportions (*specify proportions*);
 (ii) the substitute property shall be bought in the sole name of the Petitioner subject to the charge specified in paragraph (c)(iii) below in favour of the Respondent;
 (iii) the charge referred to in paragraph (c)(ii) above shall be:
  (a) for such proportion of the gross value of the purchase price of the substitute property as is represented by the outstanding amount due under the charge in favour of the Respondent as at the time of the sale of the Property [save that in calculating the amount under that charge, the costs and fees of sale of the Property shall be ignored on the basis that they shall be born solely by the [Petitioner *or* Respondent]]; and
  (b) enforceable on the happening of the first of the events in paragraph (b)(i), (ii), (iii), (v), and (vi) above or upon sale of the substitute property.

## Immediate clean break order (dismissing both parties' claims)

### [5.54]

Save as aforesaid, all claims by either party for financial provision, pension sharing orders and property adjustment orders under the Matrimonial Causes Act 1973 do stand dismissed. In particular the parties' respective claims for periodical payments and secured provision are hereby dismissed with a direction that neither party shall be entitled to make any further application in relation to this marriage for orders under section 23(1)(a) or (b) of the said Act.

## Prohibition of future claims under the Inheritance (Provision for Family and Dependants) Act 1975

### [5.55]

The court considering it just so to order, neither party shall be entitled to claim against the others' estate upon the death of the other under the Inheritance (Provision for Family and Dependants) Act 1975.

## Postponement of public funding statutory charge

### [5.56]

It is certified for the purpose of regulation 52 of the Community Legal Service (Financial) Regulations 2000 [that the lump sum of £X has been ordered to be paid to enable the Petitioner/Respondent to purchase a home for himself/herself (or his/her dependants)] [that the property (*address*) has been preserved/recovered for the Petitioner/Respondent for use as a home for himself/herself (or his/her dependants).

## PENSION ORDERS

### [5.57]
### Introduction

There is now a full array of orders that may be made in relation to pensions. In appropriate circumstances the court may:

- refuse to make a decree nisi under s 1(2)(e) of the MCA 1973 where a defence is filed under s 5 of that Act (by that defence the Respondent contends that the grant of a decree would cause her grave financial or other hardship);
- refuse to make a decree absolute of divorce under ss 1(2)(d) or (e) of the MCA 1973 until the Petitioner has made reasonable financial provision for the Respondent[1];
- afford to one party greater financial provision than it otherwise would order as a result of the other party having a pension (ie 'off-set');
- make a pension attachment order (previously referred to as a pension earmarking order[2];
- make a pension sharing order[3].

Orders for pension attachment and pension sharing must now contain prescribed information and must be annexed to the order[4].

1 Under s 10(2) of the MCA 1973 (set out at para **[2.114]**).
2 Ie under ss 25B to 25C of the MCA 1973 (set out at para **[2.122]** et seq).
3 Ie under s 24B of the MCA 1973 (set out at para **[2.119A]**).
4 See r 2.70(13) to (17) of the FPR 1991 (set out at para **[3.461]**).

### [5.58]
### Pensions attachment / sharing order

The Pensions attachment / sharing order set out below do take effect[1]. [*Provided the Applicant remains alive [and has not remarried] at the time of implementation.*]

1 Orders for pension attachment and pension sharing must now contain prescribed information and must be annexed to the order – see r 2.70(13) to (17) of the FPR 1991 (set out at para **[3.461]**).

## [5.59]

### Pension Sharing Annex under Section 24B of the Matrimonial Causes Act 1973 (Rule 2.70 (14) FPR 1991)

| **In the** <br> ***[County Court]** <br> ***[Principal Registry of the Family Division]** | |
|---|---|
| **Case No.** <br> *Always quote this* | |
| Applicant's Solicitor's reference | |
| Respondent's Solicitor's reference | |

**The marriage of** **and**

**Take Notice that:**

On ____________________ the court

- made a pension sharing order under Part IV of the Welfare Reform and Pensions Act 1999.
- [varied] [discharged] an order which included provision for pension sharing made under Part IV of the Welfare Reform and Pensions Act 1999 and dated ____________________.

This annex to the order provides the person responsible for the pension arrangement with the information required by virtue of The Family Proceedings Rules 1991 as amended.

1. Name of the Transferor:

____________________ ____________________

2. Name of the Transferee:

____________________ ____________________

3. The Transferor's National Insurance Number:

____________________ ____________________

4. Details of the Pension Arrangement and Policy Reference Number:
   *(or such other details to enable the pension arrangement to be identified).*

____________________ ____________________

5. The specified percentage value of the pension arrangement to be transferred:
   *(The specified amount required in order to create a pension credit and debit should only be inserted where specifically ordered by the court).*

____________________

   In accordance with The Divorce etc. (Pensions) Regulations 2000 the court has specified that the benefits shall be valued as at the following date:

____________________ ____________________

**Form P1** Pension Sharing Annex under Section 24B of the Matrimonial Causes Act 1973 (Rule 2.70 (14) FPR 1991) (12.00)
*Printed on behalf of The Court Service*

6. Pension Sharing Charges:
   *(*Delete as appropriate)*

It is directed that:

*The pension sharing charges be apportioned between the parties as follows:

______________________________ ______________________________

*The pension sharing charges be paid in full by the transferor.

______________________________ ______________________________

The court is satisfied that the person responsible for the pension arrangement has furnished the information required by Regulation 4 of the Pensions on Divorce etc. (Provision of Information) Regulations 2000 and, that it appears from the information that there is power to make an order including provision under section 24B (pension sharing) of the Act of 1973.

THIS [ORDER] [PROVISION] TAKES EFFECT FROM ______________________________

To the person responsible for the pension arrangement:
*(*Delete as appropriate)*

1. *Take notice that you must discharge your liability within the period of 4 months beginning with the later of:

   - the day on which this order or provision takes effect; or,

   - the first day on which you are in receipt of –
     a. this [order] [provision] for ancillary relief, including the annex;
     b. the decree of divorce or nullity of marriage; and
     c. the information prescribed by Regulation 5 of the Pensions on Divorce etc. (Provision of Information) Regulations 2000.

2. *The court directs that the implementation period for discharging your liability should be determined by regulations made under section 34(4) or 41(2)(a) of the Welfare Reform and Pensions Act 1999, in that:

## [5.60]

### Pension Attachment Annex under Section 25B or 25C of the Matrimonial Causes Act 1973 (Rule 2.70 (15) FPR 1991)

| **In the** *[County Court] *[Principal Registry of the Family Division] | |
|---|---|
| **Case No.** *Always quote this* | |
| Applicant's Solicitor's reference | |
| Respondent's Solicitor's reference | |

**The marriage of** **and**

**Take Notice that:**

On ____________________ the court

- made an order including provision under section [25B] [25C]* of the Matrimonial Causes Act 1973.
- [varied] [discharged] an order which included provision under section [25B] [25C]* of the Matrimonial Causes Act 1973 and dated ________________

(*delete as appropriate)

This annex to the order provides the person responsible for the pension arrangement with the information required by virtue of The Family Proceedings Rules 1991 as amended.

1. Name of the party with the pension rights:

______________________________ ______________________________

2. Name of the other party:

______________________________ ______________________________

3. The National Insurance Number of the party with pension rights:

______________________________ ______________________________

4. Details of the Pension Arrangement and Policy Reference Number:
*(or such other details to enable the pension arrangement to be identified).*

______________________________ ______________________________

5. *The specified percentage of any payment due to the party with pension rights that is to be paid for the benefit of the other party:

______________________________

*The person responsible for the pension arrangement is required to:

(*delete as appropriate)

______________________________

In accordance with The Divorce etc. (Pensions) Regulations 2000 the court has specified that the benefits shall be valued as at the following date:

______________________________

**Form P2** Pension Attachment Annex under Section 25B or 25C of the Matrimonial Causes Act 1973 (Rule 2.70 (15) FPR 1991) (12.00)
*Printed on behalf of The Court Service*

To the person responsible for the pension arrangement:
*(*Delete if this information has already been provided to the person responsible for the pension arrangement with Form A or pursuant to FPR 2.70(11))*

1. *You are required to serve any notice under the Divorce etc. (Pensions) Regulations 2000 on the other party at the following address:

2. *You are required to to make any payments due under the pension arrangement to the other party at the following address:

3. *If the address at 2. above is that of a bank, building society or the Department of National Savings the following details will enable you to make payment into the account of the other party (e.g. Account Name, Number, Bank/Building Society/etc. Sort code):

Note: Where the order to which this annex applies was made by consent the following section should also be completed.

The court also confirms:
(*Delete as appropriate)

- *That notice under Rule 2.70(11) of the Family Proceedings Rules 1991 has been served on the person responsible for the pension arrangement and that no objection has been received under Rule 2.70(12).
- *That notice under Rule 2.70(11) of the Family Proceedings Rules 1991 has been served on the person responsible for the pension arrangement and that the court has considered any objection received under Rule 2.70(12)(b).

5052–6000

# INDEX

6050